T0212053

Lecture Notes in Computer Science 11210

Commenced Publication in 1973
Founding and Former Series Editors:
Gerhard Goos, Juris Hartmanis, and Jan van Leeuwen

More information about this series at http://www.springer.com/series/7412

Vittorio Ferrari · Martial Hebert
Cristian Sminchisescu · Yair Weiss (Eds.)

Computer Vision – ECCV 2018

15th European Conference
Munich, Germany, September 8–14, 2018
Proceedings, Part VI

 Springer

Editors
Vittorio Ferrari
Google Research
Zurich
Switzerland

Martial Hebert
Carnegie Mellon University
Pittsburgh, PA
USA

Cristian Sminchisescu
Google Research
Zurich
Switzerland

Yair Weiss
Hebrew University of Jerusalem
Jerusalem
Israel

ISSN 0302-9743 ISSN 1611-3349 (electronic)
Lecture Notes in Computer Science
ISBN 978-3-030-01230-4 ISBN 978-3-030-01231-1 (eBook)
https://doi.org/10.1007/978-3-030-01231-1

Library of Congress Control Number: 2018955489

LNCS Sublibrary: SL6 – Image Processing, Computer Vision, Pattern Recognition, and Graphics

This Springer imprint is published by the registered company Springer Nature Switzerland AG
The registered company address is: Gewerbestrasse 11, 6330 Cham, Switzerland

Foreword

It was our great pleasure to host the European Conference on Computer Vision 2018 in Munich, Germany. This constituted by far the largest ECCV event ever. With close to 2,900 registered participants and another 600 on the waiting list one month before the conference, participation more than doubled since the last ECCV in Amsterdam. We believe that this is due to a dramatic growth of the computer vision community combined with the popularity of Munich as a major European hub of culture, science, and industry. The conference took place in the heart of Munich in the concert hall Gasteig with workshops and tutorials held at the downtown campus of the Technical University of Munich.

One of the major innovations for ECCV 2018 was the free perpetual availability of all conference and workshop papers, which is often referred to as open access. We note that this is not precisely the same use of the term as in the Budapest declaration. Since 2013, CVPR and ICCV have had their papers hosted by the Computer Vision Foundation (CVF), in parallel with the IEEE Xplore version. This has proved highly beneficial to the computer vision community.

We are delighted to announce that for ECCV 2018 a very similar arrangement was put in place with the cooperation of Springer. In particular, the author's final version will be freely available in perpetuity on a CVF page, while SpringerLink will continue to host a version with further improvements, such as activating reference links and including video. We believe that this will give readers the best of both worlds; researchers who are focused on the technical content will have a freely available version in an easily accessible place, while subscribers to SpringerLink will continue to have the additional benefits that this provides. We thank Alfred Hofmann from Springer for helping to negotiate this agreement, which we expect will continue for future versions of ECCV.

September 2018

Horst Bischof
Daniel Cremers
Bernt Schiele
Ramin Zabih

Preface

Welcome to the proceedings of the 2018 European Conference on Computer Vision (ECCV 2018) held in Munich, Germany. We are delighted to present this volume reflecting a strong and exciting program, the result of an extensive review process. In total, we received 2,439 valid paper submissions. Of these, 776 were accepted (31.8%): 717 as posters (29.4%) and 59 as oral presentations (2.4%). All oral presentations were presented as posters as well. The program selection process was complicated this year by the large increase in the number of submitted papers, +65% over ECCV 2016, and the use of CMT3 for the first time for a computer vision conference. The program selection process was supported by four program co-chairs (PCs), 126 area chairs (ACs), and 1,199 reviewers with reviews assigned.

We were primarily responsible for the design and execution of the review process. Beyond administrative rejections, we were involved in acceptance decisions only in the very few cases where the ACs were not able to agree on a decision. As PCs, and as is customary in the field, we were not allowed to co-author a submission. General co-chairs and other co-organizers who played no role in the review process were permitted to submit papers, and were treated as any other author is.

Acceptance decisions were made by two independent ACs. The ACs also made a joint recommendation for promoting papers to oral status. We decided on the final selection of oral presentations based on the ACs' recommendations. There were 126 ACs, selected according to their technical expertise, experience, and geographical diversity (63 from European, nine from Asian/Australian, and 54 from North American institutions). Indeed, 126 ACs is a substantial increase in the number of ACs due to the natural increase in the number of papers and to our desire to maintain the number of papers assigned to each AC to a manageable number so as to ensure quality. The ACs were aided by the 1,199 reviewers to whom papers were assigned for reviewing. The Program Committee was selected from committees of previous ECCV, ICCV, and CVPR conferences and was extended on the basis of suggestions from the ACs. Having a large pool of Program Committee members for reviewing allowed us to match expertise while reducing reviewer loads. No more than eight papers were assigned to a reviewer, maintaining the reviewers' load at the same level as ECCV 2016 despite the increase in the number of submitted papers.

Conflicts of interest between ACs, Program Committee members, and papers were identified based on the home institutions, and on previous collaborations of all researchers involved. To find institutional conflicts, all authors, Program Committee members, and ACs were asked to list the Internet domains of their current institutions. We assigned on average approximately 18 papers to each AC. The papers were assigned using the affinity scores from the Toronto Paper Matching System (TPMS) and additional data from the OpenReview system, managed by a UMass group. OpenReview used additional information from ACs' and authors' records to identify collaborations and to generate matches. OpenReview was invaluable in refining conflict definitions and in generating quality matches. The only glitch is that, once the matches were generated, a small percentage of papers were unassigned because of discrepancies between the OpenReview conflicts and the conflicts entered in CMT3. We manually assigned these papers. This glitch is revealing of the challenge of using multiple systems at once (CMT3 and OpenReview in this case), which needs to be addressed in future.

After assignment of papers to ACs, the ACs suggested seven reviewers per paper from the Program Committee pool. The selection and rank ordering were facilitated by the TPMS affinity scores visible to the ACs for each paper/reviewer pair. The final assignment of papers to reviewers was generated again through OpenReview in order to account for refined conflict definitions. This required new features in the OpenReview matching system to accommodate the ECCV workflow, in particular to incorporate selection ranking, and maximum reviewer load. Very few papers received fewer than three reviewers after matching and were handled through manual assignment. Reviewers were then asked to comment on the merit of each paper and to make an initial recommendation ranging from definitely reject to definitely accept, including a borderline rating. The reviewers were also asked to suggest explicit questions they wanted to see answered in the authors' rebuttal. The initial review period was five weeks. Because of the delay in getting all the reviews in, we had to delay the final release of the reviews by four days. However, because of the slack included at the tail end of the schedule, we were able to maintain the decision target date with sufficient time for all the phases. We reassigned over 100 reviews from 40 reviewers during the review period. Unfortunately, the main reason for these reassignments was reviewers declining to review, after having accepted to do so. Other reasons included technical relevance and occasional unidentified conflicts. We express our thanks to the emergency reviewers who generously accepted to perform these reviews under short notice. In addition, a substantial number of manual corrections had to do with reviewers using a different email address than the one that was used at the time of the reviewer invitation. This is revealing of a broader issue with identifying users by email addresses that change frequently enough to cause significant problems during the timespan of the conference process.

The authors were then given the opportunity to rebut the reviews, to identify factual errors, and to address the specific questions raised by the reviewers over a seven-day rebuttal period. The exact format of the rebuttal was the object of considerable debate among the organizers, as well as with prior organizers. At issue is to balance giving the author the opportunity to respond completely and precisely to the reviewers, e.g., by including graphs of experiments, while avoiding requests for completely new material or experimental results not included in the original paper. In the end, we decided on the two-page PDF document in conference format. Following this rebuttal period, reviewers and ACs discussed papers at length, after which reviewers finalized their evaluation and gave a final recommendation to the ACs. A significant percentage of the reviewers did enter their final recommendation if it did not differ from their initial recommendation. Given the tight schedule, we did not wait until all were entered.

After this discussion period, each paper was assigned to a second AC. The AC/paper matching was again run through OpenReview. Again, the OpenReview team worked quickly to implement the features specific to this process, in this case accounting for the existing AC assignment, as well as minimizing the fragmentation across ACs, so that each AC had on average only 5.5 buddy ACs to communicate with. The largest number was 11. Given the complexity of the conflicts, this was a very efficient set of assignments from OpenReview. Each paper was then evaluated by its assigned pair of ACs. For each paper, we required each of the two ACs assigned to certify both the final recommendation and the metareview (aka consolidation report). In all cases, after extensive discussions, the two ACs arrived at a common acceptance decision. We maintained these decisions, with the caveat that we did evaluate, sometimes going back to the ACs, a few papers for which the final acceptance decision substantially deviated from the consensus from the reviewers, amending three decisions in the process.

We want to thank everyone involved in making ECCV 2018 possible. The success of ECCV 2018 depended on the quality of papers submitted by the authors, and on the very hard work of the ACs and the Program Committee members. We are particularly grateful to the OpenReview team (Melisa Bok, Ari Kobren, Andrew McCallum, Michael Spector) for their support, in particular their willingness to implement new features, often on a tight schedule, to Laurent Charlin for the use of the Toronto Paper Matching System, to the CMT3 team, in particular in dealing with all the issues that arise when using a new system, to Friedrich Fraundorfer and Quirin Lohr for maintaining the online version of the program, and to the CMU staff (Keyla Cook, Lynnetta Miller, Ashley Song, Nora Kazour) for assisting with data entry/editing in CMT3. Finally, the preparation of these proceedings would not have been possible without the diligent effort of the publication chairs, Albert Ali Salah and Hamdi Dibeklioğlu, and of Anna Kramer and Alfred Hofmann from Springer.

September 2018

Vittorio Ferrari
Martial Hebert
Cristian Sminchisescu
Yair Weiss

Organization

General Chairs

Horst Bischof   Graz University of Technology, Austria
Daniel Cremers   Technical University of Munich, Germany
Bernt Schiele   Saarland University, Max Planck Institute for Informatics, Germany
Ramin Zabih   CornellNYCTech, USA

Program Committee Co-chairs

Vittorio Ferrari   University of Edinburgh, UK
Martial Hebert   Carnegie Mellon University, USA
Cristian Sminchisescu   Lund University, Sweden
Yair Weiss   Hebrew University, Israel

Local Arrangements Chairs

Björn Menze   Technical University of Munich, Germany
Matthias Niessner   Technical University of Munich, Germany

Workshop Chairs

Stefan Roth   TU Darmstadt, Germany
Laura Leal-Taixé   Technical University of Munich, Germany

Tutorial Chairs

Michael Bronstein   Università della Svizzera Italiana, Switzerland
Laura Leal-Taixé   Technical University of Munich, Germany

Website Chair

Friedrich Fraundorfer   Graz University of Technology, Austria

Demo Chairs

Federico Tombari   Technical University of Munich, Germany
Joerg Stueckler   Technical University of Munich, Germany

Publicity Chair

Giovanni Maria   University of Catania, Italy
  Farinella

Industrial Liaison Chairs

Florent Perronnin   Naver Labs, France
Yunchao Gong   Snap, USA
Helmut Grabner   Logitech, Switzerland

Finance Chair

Gerard Medioni   Amazon, University of Southern California, USA

Publication Chairs

Albert Ali Salah   Boğaziçi University, Turkey
Hamdi Dibeklioğlu   Bilkent University, Turkey

Area Chairs

Kalle Åström   Lund University, Sweden
Zeynep Akata   University of Amsterdam, The Netherlands
Joao Barreto   University of Coimbra, Portugal
Ronen Basri   Weizmann Institute of Science, Israel
Dhruv Batra   Georgia Tech and Facebook AI Research, USA
Serge Belongie   Cornell University, USA
Rodrigo Benenson   Google, Switzerland
Hakan Bilen   University of Edinburgh, UK
Matthew Blaschko   KU Leuven, Belgium
Edmond Boyer   Inria, France
Gabriel Brostow   University College London, UK
Thomas Brox   University of Freiburg, Germany
Marcus Brubaker   York University, Canada
Barbara Caputo   Politecnico di Torino and the Italian Institute
                        of Technology, Italy
Tim Cootes   University of Manchester, UK
Trevor Darrell   University of California, Berkeley, USA
Larry Davis   University of Maryland at College Park, USA
Andrew Davison   Imperial College London, UK
Fernando de la Torre Carnegie Mellon University, USA
Irfan Essa   GeorgiaTech, USA
Ali Farhadi   University of Washington, USA
Paolo Favaro   University of Bern, Switzerland
Michael Felsberg   Linköping University, Sweden

Sanja Fidler	University of Toronto, Canada
Andrew Fitzgibbon	Microsoft, Cambridge, UK
David Forsyth	University of Illinois at Urbana-Champaign, USA
Charless Fowlkes	University of California, Irvine, USA
Bill Freeman	MIT, USA
Mario Fritz	MPII, Germany
Jürgen Gall	University of Bonn, Germany
Dariu Gavrila	TU Delft, The Netherlands
Andreas Geiger	MPI-IS and University of Tübingen, Germany
Theo Gevers	University of Amsterdam, The Netherlands
Ross Girshick	Facebook AI Research, USA
Kristen Grauman	Facebook AI Research and UT Austin, USA
Abhinav Gupta	Carnegie Mellon University, USA
Kaiming He	Facebook AI Research, USA
Martial Hebert	Carnegie Mellon University, USA
Anders Heyden	Lund University, Sweden
Timothy Hospedales	University of Edinburgh, UK
Michal Irani	Weizmann Institute of Science, Israel
Phillip Isola	University of California, Berkeley, USA
Hervé Jégou	Facebook AI Research, France
David Jacobs	University of Maryland, College Park, USA
Allan Jepson	University of Toronto, Canada
Jiaya Jia	Chinese University of Hong Kong, SAR China
Fredrik Kahl	Chalmers University, USA
Hedvig Kjellström	KTH Royal Institute of Technology, Sweden
Iasonas Kokkinos	University College London and Facebook, UK
Vladlen Koltun	Intel Labs, USA
Philipp Krähenbühl	UT Austin, USA
M. Pawan Kumar	University of Oxford, UK
Kyros Kutulakos	University of Toronto, Canada
In Kweon	KAIST, South Korea
Ivan Laptev	Inria, France
Svetlana Lazebnik	University of Illinois at Urbana-Champaign, USA
Laura Leal-Taixé	Technical University of Munich, Germany
Erik Learned-Miller	University of Massachusetts, Amherst, USA
Kyoung Mu Lee	Seoul National University, South Korea
Bastian Leibe	RWTH Aachen University, Germany
Aleš Leonardis	University of Birmingham, UK
Vincent Lepetit	University of Bordeaux, France and Graz University of Technology, Austria
Fuxin Li	Oregon State University, USA
Dahua Lin	Chinese University of Hong Kong, SAR China
Jim Little	University of British Columbia, Canada
Ce Liu	Google, USA
Chen Change Loy	Nanyang Technological University, Singapore
Jiri Matas	Czech Technical University in Prague, Czechia

Tinne Tuytelaars	KU Leuven, Belgium
Jasper Uijlings	Google, Switzerland
Joost van de Weijer	Computer Vision Center, Spain
Nuno Vasconcelos	University of California, San Diego, USA
Andrea Vedaldi	University of Oxford, UK
Olga Veksler	University of Western Ontario, Canada
Jakob Verbeek	Inria, France
Rene Vidal	Johns Hopkins University, USA
Daphna Weinshall	Hebrew University, Israel
Chris Williams	University of Edinburgh, UK
Lior Wolf	Tel Aviv University, Israel
Ming-Hsuan Yang	University of California at Merced, USA
Todd Zickler	Harvard University, USA
Andrew Zisserman	University of Oxford, UK

Technical Program Committee

Hassan Abu Alhaija	Peter Anderson	Arunava Banerjee
Radhakrishna Achanta	Juan Andrade-Cetto	Atsuhiko Banno
Hanno Ackermann	Mykhaylo Andriluka	Aayush Bansal
Ehsan Adeli	Anelia Angelova	Yingze Bao
Lourdes Agapito	Michel Antunes	Md Jawadul Bappy
Aishwarya Agrawal	Pablo Arbelaez	Pierre Baqué
Antonio Agudo	Vasileios Argyriou	Dániel Baráth
Eirikur Agustsson	Chetan Arora	Adrian Barbu
Karim Ahmed	Federica Arrigoni	Kobus Barnard
Byeongjoo Ahn	Vassilis Athitsos	Nick Barnes
Unaiza Ahsan	Mathieu Aubry	Francisco Barranco
Emre Akbaş	Shai Avidan	Adrien Bartoli
Eren Aksoy	Yannis Avrithis	E. Bayro-Corrochano
Yağız Aksoy	Samaneh Azadi	Paul Beardlsey
Alexandre Alahi	Hossein Azizpour	Vasileios Belagiannis
Jean-Baptiste Alayrac	Artem Babenko	Sean Bell
Samuel Albanie	Timur Bagautdinov	Ismail Ben
Cenek Albl	Andrew Bagdanov	Boulbaba Ben Amor
Saad Ali	Hessam Bagherinezhad	Gil Ben-Artzi
Rahaf Aljundi	Yuval Bahat	Ohad Ben-Shahar
Jose M. Alvarez	Min Bai	Abhijit Bendale
Humam Alwassel	Qinxun Bai	Rodrigo Benenson
Toshiyuki Amano	Song Bai	Fabian Benitez-Quiroz
Mitsuru Ambai	Xiang Bai	Fethallah Benmansour
Mohamed Amer	Peter Bajcsy	Ryad Benosman
Senjian An	Amr Bakry	Filippo Bergamasco
Cosmin Ancuti	Kavita Bala	David Bermudez

Jesus Bermudez-Cameo
Leonard Berrada
Gedas Bertasius
Ross Beveridge
Lucas Beyer
Bir Bhanu
S. Bhattacharya
Binod Bhattarai
Arnav Bhavsar
Simone Bianco
Adel Bibi
Pia Bideau
Josef Bigun
Arijit Biswas
Soma Biswas
Marten Bjoerkman
Volker Blanz
Vishnu Boddeti
Piotr Bojanowski
Terrance Boult
Yuri Boykov
Hakan Boyraz
Eric Brachmann
Samarth Brahmbhatt
Mathieu Bredif
Francois Bremond
Michael Brown
Luc Brun
Shyamal Buch
Pradeep Buddharaju
Aurelie Bugeau
Rudy Bunel
Xavier Burgos Artizzu
Darius Burschka
Andrei Bursuc
Zoya Bylinskii
Fabian Caba
Daniel Cabrini Hauagge
Cesar Cadena Lerma
Holger Caesar
Jianfei Cai
Junjie Cai
Zhaowei Cai
Simone Calderara
Neill Campbell
Octavia Camps

Xun Cao
Yanshuai Cao
Joao Carreira
Dan Casas
Daniel Castro
Jan Cech
M. Emre Celebi
Duygu Ceylan
Menglei Chai
Ayan Chakrabarti
Rudrasis Chakraborty
Shayok Chakraborty
Tat-Jen Cham
Antonin Chambolle
Antoni Chan
Sharat Chandran
Hyun Sung Chang
Ju Yong Chang
Xiaojun Chang
Soravit Changpinyo
Wei-Lun Chao
Yu-Wei Chao
Visesh Chari
Rizwan Chaudhry
Siddhartha Chaudhuri
Rama Chellappa
Chao Chen
Chen Chen
Cheng Chen
Chu-Song Chen
Guang Chen
Hsin-I Chen
Hwann-Tzong Chen
Kai Chen
Kan Chen
Kevin Chen
Liang-Chieh Chen
Lin Chen
Qifeng Chen
Ting Chen
Wei Chen
Xi Chen
Xilin Chen
Xinlei Chen
Yingcong Chen
Yixin Chen

Erkang Cheng
Jingchun Cheng
Ming-Ming Cheng
Wen-Huang Cheng
Yuan Cheng
Anoop Cherian
Liang-Tien Chia
Naoki Chiba
Shao-Yi Chien
Han-Pang Chiu
Wei-Chen Chiu
Nam Ik Cho
Sunghyun Cho
TaeEun Choe
Jongmoo Choi
Christopher Choy
Wen-Sheng Chu
Yung-Yu Chuang
Ondrej Chum
Joon Son Chung
Gökberk Cinbis
James Clark
Andrea Cohen
Forrester Cole
Toby Collins
John Collomosse
Camille Couprie
David Crandall
Marco Cristani
Canton Cristian
James Crowley
Yin Cui
Zhaopeng Cui
Bo Dai
Jifeng Dai
Qieyun Dai
Shengyang Dai
Yuchao Dai
Carlo Dal Mutto
Dima Damen
Zachary Daniels
Kostas Daniilidis
Donald Dansereau
Mohamed Daoudi
Abhishek Das
Samyak Datta

Achal Dave
Shalini De Mello
Teofilo deCampos
Joseph DeGol
Koichiro Deguchi
Alessio Del Bue
Stefanie Demirci
Jia Deng
Zhiwei Deng
Joachim Denzler
Konstantinos Derpanis
Aditya Deshpande
Alban Desmaison
Frédéric Devernay
Abhinav Dhall
Michel Dhome
Hamdi Dibeklioğlu
Mert Dikmen
Cosimo Distante
Ajay Divakaran
Mandar Dixit
Carl Doersch
Piotr Dollar
Bo Dong
Chao Dong
Huang Dong
Jian Dong
Jiangxin Dong
Weisheng Dong
Simon Donné
Gianfranco Doretto
Alexey Dosovitskiy
Matthijs Douze
Bruce Draper
Bertram Drost
Liang Du
Shichuan Du
Gregory Dudek
Zoran Duric
Pınar Duygulu
Hazım Ekenel
Tarek El-Gaaly
Ehsan Elhamifar
Mohamed Elhoseiny
Sabu Emmanuel
Ian Endres

Aykut Erdem
Erkut Erdem
Hugo Jair Escalante
Sergio Escalera
Victor Escorcia
Francisco Estrada
Davide Eynard
Bin Fan
Jialue Fan
Quanfu Fan
Chen Fang
Tian Fang
Yi Fang
Hany Farid
Giovanni Farinella
Ryan Farrell
Alireza Fathi
Christoph Feichtenhofer
Wenxin Feng
Martin Fergie
Cornelia Fermuller
Basura Fernando
Michael Firman
Bob Fisher
John Fisher
Mathew Fisher
Boris Flach
Matt Flagg
Francois Fleuret
David Fofi
Ruth Fong
Gian Luca Foresti
Per-Erik Forssén
David Fouhey
Katerina Fragkiadaki
Victor Fragoso
Jan-Michael Frahm
Jean-Sebastien Franco
Ohad Fried
Simone Frintrop
Huazhu Fu
Yun Fu
Olac Fuentes
Christopher Funk
Thomas Funkhouser
Brian Funt

Ryo Furukawa
Yasutaka Furukawa
Andrea Fusiello
Fatma Güney
Raghudeep Gadde
Silvano Galliani
Orazio Gallo
Chuang Gan
Bin-Bin Gao
Jin Gao
Junbin Gao
Ruohan Gao
Shenghua Gao
Animesh Garg
Ravi Garg
Erik Gartner
Simone Gasparin
Jochen Gast
Leon A. Gatys
Stratis Gavves
Liuhao Ge
Timnit Gebru
James Gee
Peter Gehler
Xin Geng
Guido Gerig
David Geronimo
Bernard Ghanem
Michael Gharbi
Golnaz Ghiasi
Spyros Gidaris
Andrew Gilbert
Rohit Girdhar
Ioannis Gkioulekas
Georgia Gkioxari
Guy Godin
Roland Goecke
Michael Goesele
Nuno Goncalves
Boqing Gong
Minglun Gong
Yunchao Gong
Abel Gonzalez-Garcia
Daniel Gordon
Paulo Gotardo
Stephen Gould

Venu Govindu
Helmut Grabner
Petr Gronat
Steve Gu
Josechu Guerrero
Anupam Guha
Jean-Yves Guillemaut
Alp Güler
Erhan Gündoğdu
Guodong Guo
Xinqing Guo
Ankush Gupta
Mohit Gupta
Saurabh Gupta
Tanmay Gupta
Abner Guzman Rivera
Timo Hackel
Sunil Hadap
Christian Haene
Ralf Haeusler
Levente Hajder
David Hall
Peter Hall
Stefan Haller
Ghassan Hamarneh
Fred Hamprecht
Onur Hamsici
Bohyung Han
Junwei Han
Xufeng Han
Yahong Han
Ankur Handa
Albert Haque
Tatsuya Harada
Mehrtash Harandi
Bharath Hariharan
Mahmudul Hasan
Tal Hassner
Kenji Hata
Soren Hauberg
Michal Havlena
Zeeshan Hayder
Junfeng He
Lei He
Varsha Hedau
Felix Heide

Wolfgang Heidrich
Janne Heikkila
Jared Heinly
Mattias Heinrich
Lisa Anne Hendricks
Dan Hendrycks
Stephane Herbin
Alexander Hermans
Luis Herranz
Aaron Hertzmann
Adrian Hilton
Michael Hirsch
Steven Hoi
Seunghoon Hong
Wei Hong
Anthony Hoogs
Radu Horaud
Yedid Hoshen
Omid Hosseini Jafari
Kuang-Jui Hsu
Winston Hsu
Yinlin Hu
Zhe Hu
Gang Hua
Chen Huang
De-An Huang
Dong Huang
Gary Huang
Heng Huang
Jia-Bin Huang
Qixing Huang
Rui Huang
Sheng Huang
Weilin Huang
Xiaolei Huang
Xinyu Huang
Zhiwu Huang
Tak-Wai Hui
Wei-Chih Hung
Junhwa Hur
Mohamed Hussein
Wonjun Hwang
Anders Hyden
Satoshi Ikehata
Nazlı Ikizler-Cinbis
Viorela Ila

Evren Imre
Eldar Insafutdinov
Go Irie
Hossam Isack
Ahmet Işcen
Daisuke Iwai
Hamid Izadinia
Nathan Jacobs
Suyog Jain
Varun Jampani
C. V. Jawahar
Dinesh Jayaraman
Sadeep Jayasumana
Laszlo Jeni
Hueihan Jhuang
Dinghuang Ji
Hui Ji
Qiang Ji
Fan Jia
Kui Jia
Xu Jia
Huaizu Jiang
Jiayan Jiang
Nianjuan Jiang
Tingting Jiang
Xiaoyi Jiang
Yu-Gang Jiang
Long Jin
Suo Jinli
Justin Johnson
Nebojsa Jojic
Michael Jones
Hanbyul Joo
Jungseock Joo
Ajjen Joshi
Amin Jourabloo
Frederic Jurie
Achuta Kadambi
Samuel Kadoury
Ioannis Kakadiaris
Zdenek Kalal
Yannis Kalantidis
Sinan Kalkan
Vicky Kalogeiton
Sunkavalli Kalyan
J.-K. Kamarainen

Shih-Yao Lin
Tsung-Yi Lin
Weiyao Lin
Yen-Yu Lin
Haibin Ling
Or Litany
Roee Litman
Anan Liu
Changsong Liu
Chen Liu
Ding Liu
Dong Liu
Feng Liu
Guangcan Liu
Luoqi Liu
Miaomiao Liu
Nian Liu
Risheng Liu
Shu Liu
Shuaicheng Liu
Sifei Liu
Tyng-Luh Liu
Wanquan Liu
Weiwei Liu
Xialei Liu
Xiaoming Liu
Yebin Liu
Yiming Liu
Ziwei Liu
Zongyi Liu
Liliana Lo Presti
Edgar Lobaton
Chengjiang Long
Mingsheng Long
Roberto Lopez-Sastre
Amy Loufti
Brian Lovell
Canyi Lu
Cewu Lu
Feng Lu
Huchuan Lu
Jiajun Lu
Jiasen Lu
Jiwen Lu
Yang Lu
Yujuan Lu

Simon Lucey
Jian-Hao Luo
Jiebo Luo
Pablo Márquez-Neila
Matthias Müller
Chao Ma
Chih-Yao Ma
Lin Ma
Shugao Ma
Wei-Chiu Ma
Zhanyu Ma
Oisin Mac Aodha
Will Maddern
Ludovic Magerand
Marcus Magnor
Vijay Mahadevan
Mohammad Mahoor
Michael Maire
Subhransu Maji
Ameesh Makadia
Atsuto Maki
Yasushi Makihara
Mateusz Malinowski
Tomasz Malisiewicz
Arun Mallya
Roberto Manduchi
Junhua Mao
Dmitrii Marin
Joe Marino
Kenneth Marino
Elisabeta Marinoiu
Ricardo Martin
Aleix Martinez
Julieta Martinez
Aaron Maschinot
Jonathan Masci
Bogdan Matei
Diana Mateus
Stefan Mathe
Kevin Matzen
Bruce Maxwell
Steve Maybank
Walterio Mayol-Cuevas
Mason McGill
Stephen Mckenna
Roey Mechrez

Christopher Mei
Heydi Mendez-Vazquez
Deyu Meng
Thomas Mensink
Bjoern Menze
Domingo Mery
Qiguang Miao
Tomer Michaeli
Antoine Miech
Ondrej Miksik
Anton Milan
Gregor Miller
Cai Minjie
Majid Mirmehdi
Ishan Misra
Niloy Mitra
Anurag Mittal
Nirbhay Modhe
Davide Modolo
Pritish Mohapatra
Pascal Monasse
Mathew Monfort
Taesup Moon
Sandino Morales
Vlad Morariu
Philippos Mordohai
Francesc Moreno
Henrique Morimitsu
Yael Moses
Ben-Ezra Moshe
Roozbeh Mottaghi
Yadong Mu
Lopamudra Mukherjee
Mario Munich
Ana Murillo
Damien Muselet
Armin Mustafa
Siva Karthik Mustikovela
Moin Nabi
Sobhan Naderi
Hajime Nagahara
Varun Nagaraja
Tushar Nagarajan
Arsha Nagrani
Nikhil Naik
Atsushi Nakazawa

P. J. Narayanan
Charlie Nash
Lakshmanan Nataraj
Fabian Nater
Lukáš Neumann
Natalia Neverova
Alejandro Newell
Phuc Nguyen
Xiaohan Nie
David Nilsson
Ko Nishino
Zhenxing Niu
Shohei Nobuhara
Klas Nordberg
Mohammed Norouzi
David Novotny
Ifeoma Nwogu
Matthew O'Toole
Guillaume Obozinski
Jean-Marc Odobez
Eyal Ofek
Ferda Ofli
Tae-Hyun Oh
Iason Oikonomidis
Takeshi Oishi
Takahiro Okabe
Takayuki Okatani
Vlad Olaru
Michael Opitz
Jose Oramas
Vicente Ordonez
Ivan Oseledets
Aljosa Osep
Magnus Oskarsson
Martin R. Oswald
Wanli Ouyang
Andrew Owens
Mustafa Özuysal
Jinshan Pan
Xingang Pan
Rameswar Panda
Sharath Pankanti
Julien Pansiot
Nicolas Papadakis
George Papandreou
N. Papanikolopoulos

Hyun Soo Park
In Kyu Park
Jaesik Park
Omkar Parkhi
Alvaro Parra Bustos
C. Alejandro Parraga
Vishal Patel
Deepak Pathak
Ioannis Patras
Viorica Patraucean
Genevieve Patterson
Kim Pedersen
Robert Peharz
Selen Pehlivan
Xi Peng
Bojan Pepik
Talita Perciano
Federico Pernici
Adrian Peter
Stavros Petridis
Vladimir Petrovic
Henning Petzka
Tomas Pfister
Trung Pham
Justus Piater
Massimo Piccardi
Sudeep Pillai
Pedro Pinheiro
Lerrel Pinto
Bernardo Pires
Aleksis Pirinen
Fiora Pirri
Leonid Pischulin
Tobias Ploetz
Bryan Plummer
Yair Poleg
Jean Ponce
Gerard Pons-Moll
Jordi Pont-Tuset
Alin Popa
Fatih Porikli
Horst Possegger
Viraj Prabhu
Andrea Prati
Maria Priisalu
Véronique Prinet

Victor Prisacariu
Jan Prokaj
Nicolas Pugeault
Luis Puig
Ali Punjani
Senthil Purushwalkam
Guido Pusiol
Guo-Jun Qi
Xiaojuan Qi
Hongwei Qin
Shi Qiu
Faisal Qureshi
Matthias Rüther
Petia Radeva
Umer Rafi
Rahul Raguram
Swaminathan Rahul
Varun Ramakrishna
Kandan Ramakrishnan
Ravi Ramamoorthi
Vignesh Ramanathan
Vasili Ramanishka
R. Ramasamy Selvaraju
Rene Ranftl
Carolina Raposo
Nikhil Rasiwasia
Nalini Ratha
Sai Ravela
Avinash Ravichandran
Ramin Raziperchikolaei
Sylvestre-Alvise Rebuffi
Adria Recasens
Joe Redmon
Timo Rehfeld
Michal Reinstein
Konstantinos Rematas
Haibing Ren
Shaoqing Ren
Wenqi Ren
Zhile Ren
Hamid Rezatofighi
Nicholas Rhinehart
Helge Rhodin
Elisa Ricci
Eitan Richardson
Stephan Richter

Zhaowen Wang
Zhe Wang
Anne Wannenwetsch
Simon Warfield
Scott Wehrwein
Donglai Wei
Ping Wei
Shih-En Wei
Xiu-Shen Wei
Yichen Wei
Xie Weidi
Philippe Weinzaepfel
Longyin Wen
Eric Wengrowski
Tomas Werner
Michael Wilber
Rick Wildes
Olivia Wiles
Kyle Wilson
David Wipf
Kwan-Yee Wong
Daniel Worrall
John Wright
Baoyuan Wu
Chao-Yuan Wu
Jiajun Wu
Jianxin Wu
Tianfu Wu
Xiaodong Wu
Xiaohe Wu
Xinxiao Wu
Yang Wu
Yi Wu
Ying Wu
Yuxin Wu
Zheng Wu
Stefanie Wuhrer
Yin Xia
Tao Xiang
Yu Xiang
Lei Xiao
Tong Xiao
Yang Xiao
Cihang Xie
Dan Xie
Jianwen Xie

Jin Xie
Lingxi Xie
Pengtao Xie
Saining Xie
Wenxuan Xie
Yuchen Xie
Bo Xin
Junliang Xing
Peng Xingchao
Bo Xiong
Fei Xiong
Xuehan Xiong
Yuanjun Xiong
Chenliang Xu
Danfei Xu
Huijuan Xu
Jia Xu
Weipeng Xu
Xiangyu Xu
Yan Xu
Yuanlu Xu
Jia Xue
Tianfan Xue
Erdem Yörük
Abhay Yadav
Deshraj Yadav
Payman Yadollahpour
Yasushi Yagi
Toshihiko Yamasaki
Fei Yan
Hang Yan
Junchi Yan
Junjie Yan
Sijie Yan
Keiji Yanai
Bin Yang
Chih-Yuan Yang
Dong Yang
Herb Yang
Jianchao Yang
Jianwei Yang
Jiaolong Yang
Jie Yang
Jimei Yang
Jufeng Yang
Linjie Yang

Michael Ying Yang
Ming Yang
Ruiduo Yang
Ruigang Yang
Shuo Yang
Wei Yang
Xiaodong Yang
Yanchao Yang
Yi Yang
Angela Yao
Bangpeng Yao
Cong Yao
Jian Yao
Ting Yao
Julian Yarkony
Mark Yatskar
Jinwei Ye
Mao Ye
Mei-Chen Yeh
Raymond Yeh
Serena Yeung
Kwang Moo Yi
Shuai Yi
Alper Yılmaz
Lijun Yin
Xi Yin
Zhaozheng Yin
Xianghua Ying
Ryo Yonetani
Donghyun Yoo
Ju Hong Yoon
Kuk-Jin Yoon
Chong You
Shaodi You
Aron Yu
Fisher Yu
Gang Yu
Jingyi Yu
Ke Yu
Licheng Yu
Pei Yu
Qian Yu
Rong Yu
Shoou-I Yu
Stella Yu
Xiang Yu

Yang Yu
Zhiding Yu
Ganzhao Yuan
Jing Yuan
Junsong Yuan
Lu Yuan
Stefanos Zafeiriou
Sergey Zagoruyko
Amir Zamir
K. Zampogiannis
Andrei Zanfir
Mihai Zanfir
Pablo Zegers
Eyasu Zemene
Andy Zeng
Xingyu Zeng
Yun Zeng
De-Chuan Zhan
Cheng Zhang
Dong Zhang
Guofeng Zhang
Han Zhang
Hang Zhang
Hanwang Zhang
Jian Zhang
Jianguo Zhang
Jianming Zhang
Jiawei Zhang
Junping Zhang
Lei Zhang
Linguang Zhang
Ning Zhang
Qing Zhang

Quanshi Zhang
Richard Zhang
Runze Zhang
Shanshan Zhang
Shiliang Zhang
Shu Zhang
Ting Zhang
Xiangyu Zhang
Xiaofan Zhang
Xu Zhang
Yimin Zhang
Yinda Zhang
Yongqiang Zhang
Yuting Zhang
Zhanpeng Zhang
Ziyu Zhang
Bin Zhao
Chen Zhao
Hang Zhao
Hengshuang Zhao
Qijun Zhao
Rui Zhao
Yue Zhao
Enliang Zheng
Liang Zheng
Stephan Zheng
Wei-Shi Zheng
Wenming Zheng
Yin Zheng
Yinqiang Zheng
Yuanjie Zheng
Guangyu Zhong
Bolei Zhou

Guang-Tong Zhou
Huiyu Zhou
Jiahuan Zhou
S. Kevin Zhou
Tinghui Zhou
Wengang Zhou
Xiaowei Zhou
Xingyi Zhou
Yin Zhou
Zihan Zhou
Fan Zhu
Guangming Zhu
Ji Zhu
Jiejie Zhu
Jun-Yan Zhu
Shizhan Zhu
Siyu Zhu
Xiangxin Zhu
Xiatian Zhu
Yan Zhu
Yingying Zhu
Yixin Zhu
Yuke Zhu
Zhenyao Zhu
Liansheng Zhuang
Zeeshan Zia
Karel Zimmermann
Daniel Zoran
Danping Zou
Qi Zou
Silvia Zuffi
Wangmeng Zuo
Xinxin Zuo

Contents – Part VI

Human Sensing

Poster Session

Learning Visual Question Answering
by Bootstrapping Hard Attention

Mateusz Malinowski[✉], Carl Doersch, Adam Santoro, and Peter Battaglia

DeepMind, London, UK
mateuszm@google.com

Abstract. Attention mechanisms in biological perception are thought to select subsets of perceptual information for more sophisticated processing which would be prohibitive to perform on all sensory inputs. In computer vision, however, there has been relatively little exploration of *hard* attention, where some information is selectively ignored, in spite of the success of *soft* attention, where information is re-weighted and aggregated, but never filtered out. Here, we introduce a new approach for hard attention and find it achieves very competitive performance on a recently-released visual question answering datasets, equalling and in some cases surpassing similar soft attention architectures while entirely ignoring some features. Even though the hard attention mechanism is thought to be non-differentiable, we found that the feature magnitudes correlate with semantic relevance, and provide a useful signal for our mechanism's attentional selection criterion. Because hard attention selects important features of the input information, it can also be more efficient than analogous soft attention mechanisms. This is especially important for recent approaches that use *non-local pairwise* operations, whereby computational and memory costs are quadratic in the size of the set of features.

Keywords: Visual question answering · Visual Turing Test · Attention

1 Introduction

Visual attention is instrumental to many aspects of complex visual reasoning in humans [1,2]. For example, when asked to identify a dog's owner among a group of people, the human visual system adaptively allocates greater computational resources to processing visual information associated with the dog and potential owners, versus other aspects of the scene. The perceptual effects can be so dramatic that prominent entities may not even rise to the level of awareness when the viewer is attending to other things in the scene [3–5]. Yet attention has not been a transformative force in computer vision, possibly because many standard computer vision tasks like detection, segmentation, and classification do not involve the sort of complex reasoning which attention is thought to facilitate.

Electronic supplementary material The online version of this chapter (https://doi.org/10.1007/978-3-030-01231-1_1) contains supplementary material, which is available to authorized users.

V. Ferrari et al. (Eds.): ECCV 2018, LNCS 11210, pp. 3–20, 2018.
https://doi.org/10.1007/978-3-030-01231-1_1

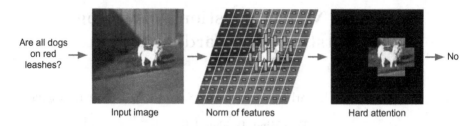

Input image   Norm of features   Hard attention

Fig. 1. Given a natural image and a textual question as input, our visual QA architecture outputs an answer. It uses a hard attention mechanism that selects only the important visual features for the task for further processing. We base our architecture on the premise that the norm of the visual features correlates with their relevance, and that those feature vectors with high magnitudes correspond to image regions which contain important semantic content.

Answering detailed questions about an image is a type of task which requires more sophisticated patterns of reasoning, and there has been a rapid recent proliferation of computer vision approaches for tackling the *visual question answering* (visual QA) task [6,7]. Successful visual QA architectures must be able to handle many objects and their complex relations while also integrating rich background knowledge, and attention has emerged as a promising strategy for achieving good performance [7–14].

We recognize a broad distinction between types of attention in computer vision and machine learning – *soft* versus *hard* attention. Existing attention models [7–10] are predominantly based on soft attention, in which all information is adaptively re-weighted before being aggregated. This can improve accuracy by isolating important information and avoiding interference from unimportant information. Learning becomes more data efficient as the complexity of the interactions among different pieces of information reduces; this, loosely speaking, allows for more unambiguous credit assignment.

By contrast, hard attention, in which only a subset of information is selected for further processing, is much less widely used. Like soft attention, it has the potential to improve accuracy and learning efficiency by focusing computation on the important parts of an image. But beyond this, it offers better computational efficiency because it only fully processes the information deemed most relevant. However, there is a key downside of hard attention within a gradient-based learning framework, such as deep learning: because the choice of which information to process is discrete and thus non-differentiable, gradients cannot be backpropagated into the selection mechanism to support gradient-based optimization. There have been various efforts to address this shortcoming in visual attention [15], attention to text [16], and more general machine learning domains [17–19], but this is still a very active area of research.

Here we explore a simple approach to hard attention that bootstraps on an interesting phenomenon [20] in the feature representations of convolutional neural networks (CNNs): learned features often carry an easily accessible signal for hard attentional selection. In particular, selecting those feature vectors with the greatest $L2$-norm values proves to be a heuristic that can facilitate hard attention – and provide the performance and efficiency benefits associated with – without requiring specialized learning procedures (see Fig. 1). This attentional signal results indirectly from a standard supervised task loss, and does not require explicit supervision to incentivize norms to be proportional to object presence, salience, or other potentially meaningful measures [20,21].

We rely on a canonical visual QA pipeline [7,9,22–25] augmented with a hard attention mechanism that uses the $L2$-norms of the feature vectors to select subsets of the information for further processing. The first version, called the Hard Attention Network (HAN), selects a fixed number of feature vectors by choosing those with the top norms. The second version, called the Adaptive Hard Attention Network (AdaHAN), selects a variable number of feature vectors that depends on the input. Our results show that our algorithm can actually outperform comparable soft attention architectures on a challenging visual QA task. This approach also produces interpretable hard attention masks, where the image regions which correspond to the selected features often contain semantically meaningful information, such as coherent objects. We also show strong performance when combined with a form of non-local pairwise model [25–28]. This algorithm computes features over pairs of input features and thus scale quadratically with number of vectors in the feature map, highlighting the importance of feature selection.

2 Related Work

Visual question answering, or more broadly the Visual Turing Test, asks "Can machines understand a visual scene only from answering questions?" [6,23,29–32]. Creating a good visual QA dataset has proved non-trivial: biases in the early datasets [6,22,23,33] rewarded algorithms for exploiting spurious correlations, rather than tackling the reasoning problem head-on [7,34,35]. Thus, we focus on the recently-introduced VQA-CP [7] and CLEVR [34] datasets, which aim to reduce the dataset biases, providing a more difficult challenge for rich visual reasoning.

One of the core challenges of visual QA is the problem of *grounding language*: that is, associating the meaning of a language term with a specific perceptual input [36]. Many works have tackled this problem [37–40], enforcing that language terms be grounded in the image. In contrast, our algorithm does not directly use correspondence between modalities to enforce such grounding but instead relies on learning to find a discrete representation that captures the required information from the raw visual input, and question-answer pairs.

The most successful visual QA architectures build multimodal representations with a combined CNN+LSTM architecture [22,33,41], and recently have begun including attention mechanisms inspired by soft and hard attention for image captioning [42]. However, only soft attention is used in the majority of visual QA works [7–12,43–52]. In these architectures, a full-frame CNN representation is used to compute a spatial weighting (attention) over the CNN grid cells. The visual representation is then the weighted-sum of the input tensor across space.

The alternative is to select CNN grid cells in a discrete way, but due to many challenges in training non-differentiable architectures, such hard attention alternatives are severely under-explored. Notable exceptions include [6,13,14,53–55], but these run state-of-the-art object detectors or proposals to compute the hard attention maps. We argue that relying on such external tools is fundamentally limited: it requires costly annotations, and cannot easily adapt to new visual concepts that aren't previously labeled. Outside visual QA and captioning, some prior work in vision has explored limited forms of hard attention. One line of work on discriminative patches builds a representation by selecting some patches and ignoring others, which has proved useful for object detection and classification [56–58], and especially visualization [59]. However, such methods have recently been largely supplanted by end-to-end feature learning for practical vision problems. In deep learning, spatial transformers [60] are one method for selecting an image regions while ignoring the rest, although these have proved challenging to train in practice. Recent work on compressing neural networks (e.g. [61]) uses magnitudes to remove weights of neural networks. However it prunes permanently based on weight magnitudes, not dynamically based on activation norms, and has no direct connection to hard-attention or visual QA.

Attention has also been studied outside of vision. While the focus on soft attention predominates these works as well, there are a few examples of hard attention mechanisms and other forms of discrete gating [15–19]. In such works the decision of *where to look* is seen as a discrete variable that had been optimized either by reinforce loss or various other approximations (e.g. straight-through). However, due to the high variance of these gradients, learning can be inefficient, and soft attention mechanisms usually perform better.

3   Method

Answering questions about images is often formulated in terms of predictive models [24]. These architectures maximize a conditional distribution over answers a, given questions q and images x:

$$\hat{a} = \arg\max_{a \in \mathcal{A}} p(a|x, q) \tag{1}$$

where $\mathcal{A}$ is a countable set of all possible answers. As is common in question answering [7,9,22–24], the question is a sequence of words $q = [q_1, ..., q_n]$, while the output is reduced to a classification problem between a set of common answers (this is limited compared to approaches that generate answers [41], but works better in practice). Our architecture for learning a mapping from image and question, to answer, is shown in Figure 2. We encode the image with a CNN [62] (in our case, a pre-trained ResNet-101 [63], or a small CNN trained from scratch), and encode the question to a fixed-length vector representation

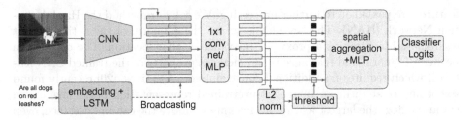

Fig. 2. Our hard attention replaces commonly used soft attention mechanism. Otherwise, we follow the canonical visual QA pipeline [7,9,22–25]. Questions and images are encoded into their vector representations. Next, the spatial encoding of the visual features is unraveled, and the question embedding is broadcasted and concatenated (or added) accordingly to form a multimodal representation of the inputs. Our attention mechanism selectively chooses a subset of the multimodal vectors that are next aggregated and processed by the answering module.

with an LSTM [64]. We compute a combined representation by copying the question representation to every spatial location in the CNN, and concatenating it with (or simply adding it to) the visual features, like previous work [7,9,22–25]. After a few layers of combined processing, we apply attention over spatial locations, following previous works which often apply soft attention mechanisms [7–10] at this point in the architecture. Finally, we aggregate features, using either sum-pooling, or relational [25,27] modules. We train the whole network end-to-end with a standard logistic regression loss over answer categories.

3.1   Attention Mechanisms

Here, we describe prior work on soft attention, and our approach to hard attention.

Soft Attention. In most prior work, soft attention is implemented as a weighted mask over the spatial cells of the CNN representation. Let $x := CNN(x), q := LSTM(q)$ for image x and question q. We compute a weight w_{ij} for every x_{ij} (where i and j index spatial locations), using a neural network that takes x_{ij} and q as input. Intuitively, weight w_{ij} measures the "relevance" of the cell to the input question. w is nonnegative and normalized to sum to 1 across the image (generally with softmax). Thus, w is applied to the visual input via $\hat{h}_{ij} := w_{ij}x_{ij}$ to build the multi-modal representation. This approach has some advantages, including conceptual simplicity and differentiability. The disadvantage is that the weights, in practice, are never 0. Irrelevant background can affect the output, no features can be dropped from potential further processing, and credit assignment is still challenging.

Hard Attention. Our main contribution is a new mechanism for hard attention. It produces a binary mask over spatial locations, which determines which features are passed on to further processing. We call our method the Hard Attention Network (HAN). The key idea is to use the $L2$-norm of the activations at each spatial location as a proxy for relevance at that location. The correlation between $L2$-norm and relevance is an emergent property of the trained CNN features, which requires no additional constraints or objectives. [20] recently found something related: in an ImageNet-pretrained representation of an image of a cat and a dog, the largest feature norms appear above the cat and dog face, even though the representation was trained purely for classification. Our architecture bootstraps on this phenomenon without explicitly training the network to have it.

As above, let x_{ij} and q be a CNN cell at the spatial position i,j, and a question representation respectively. We first embed $q \in \mathbb{R}^q$ and $x \in \mathbb{R}^x$ into two feature spaces that share the same dimensionality d, i.e.,

$$\hat{x} := CNN^{1\times1}(x;\theta_x) \in \mathbb{R}^{w\times h\times d} \tag{2}$$

$$\hat{q} := MLP(q;\theta_q) \in \mathbb{R}^d \tag{3}$$

where $CNN^{1\times1}$ stands for a 1×1 convolutional network and MLP stands for a multilayer perceptron. We then combine both the convolutional image features with the question features into a shared *multimodal* embedding by first broadcasting the question features to match the $w \times d$ shape of the image feature map, and then performing element-wise addition (1×1 conv net/MLP in Fig. 2):

$$m_{ij} := \hat{x}_{ij} \oplus \hat{q} \text{ where } m := [m_{ij}]_{ij} \in \mathbb{R}^{w\times h\times d} \tag{4}$$

Element-wise addition keeps the dimensionality of each input, as opposed to concatenation, yet is still effective [12,24]. Next, we compute the *presence vector*, $p := [p_{ij}]_{ij} \in \mathbb{R}^{w\times h}$ which measures the relevance of entities given the question:

$$p_{ij} := ||m_{ij}||_2 \in \mathbb{R} \tag{5}$$

where $||\cdot||_2$ denotes $L2$-norm. To select k entities from m for further processing, the indices of the top k entries in p, denoted $l = [l_1, \ldots, l_k]$ are used to form $\hat{m}^k = [m_{l_1}, \ldots, m_{l_k}] \in \mathbb{R}^{k\times d}$.

This set of features is passed to the decoder module and gradients will flow back to the weights of the CNN/MLP through the selected features. Our assumption is that important outputs of the CNN/MLP will tend to grow in norm, and therefore are likely to be selected. Intuitively if non-useful features are selected, the gradients will push the norm of these features down, making them less likely to be selected again. But there is nothing in our framework which explicitly incorporates this behavior into a loss. Despite its simplicity, our experiments (Sect. 4) show the HAN is very competitive with canonical soft attention [9] while also offering interpretability and efficiency.

Thus far, we have assumed that we can fix the number of features k that are passed through the attention mechanism. However, it is likely that different questions require different spatial support within the image. Thus, we also introduce a second approach which adaptively chooses the number of entities to attend to (termed Adaptive-HAN, or AdaHAN) as a function of the inputs, rather than using a fixed k. The key idea is to make the presence vector $\boldsymbol{p}$ (the norm of the embedding at each spatial location) "compete" against a threshold τ. However, since the norm is unbounded from above, to avoid trivial solutions in which the network sets the presence vector very high and selects all entities, we apply a softmax operator to $\boldsymbol{p}$. We put both parts into the competition by only selecting those elements of $\boldsymbol{m}$ whose presence values exceed the threshold,

$$\hat{m}^k = [\boldsymbol{m}_{l_1}, ..., \boldsymbol{m}_{l_k}] \in \mathbb{R}^{k \times d} \text{ where } \{l_i : \text{softmax}(\boldsymbol{p}_{l_i}) > \tau\} \tag{6}$$

Note that due to the properties of softmax, the competition is encouraged not only between both sides of the inequality, but also between the spatially distributed elements of the presence vector $\boldsymbol{p}$. Although τ could be chosen through the hyper-parameter selection, we decide to use $\tau := \frac{1}{w \cdot h}$ where w and h are spatial dimensions of the input vector x_{ij}. Such value for τ has an interesting interpretation. If each spatial location of the input were equally important, we would sample the locations from a uniform probability distribution $p(\cdot) := \tau = \frac{1}{w \cdot h}$. This is equivalent to a probability distribution induced by the presence vector of a neural network with uniformly distributed spatial representation, i.e. $\tau = \text{softmax}(\boldsymbol{p}_{\text{uniform}})$, and hence the trained network with the presence vector $\boldsymbol{p}$ has to "win" against the $\boldsymbol{p}_{\text{uniform}}$ of the random network in order to select right input features by shifting the probability mass accordingly. It also naturally encourages higher selectivity as the increase in the probability mass at one location would result in decrease in another location.

In contrast to the commonly used soft-attention mechanism, our approaches do not require extra learnable parameters. HAN requires a single extra but interpretable hyper-parameter: a fraction of input cells to use, which trades off speed for accuracy. AdaHAN requires no extra hyper-parameters.

3.2 Feature Aggregation

Sum Pooling. A simple way to reduce the set of feature vectors after attention is to sum pool them into a constant length vector. In the case of a soft attention module with an attention weight vector w, it is straightforward to compute a pooled vector as $\sum_{ij} w_{ij} x_{ij}$. Given features selected with hard attention, an analogous pooling can be written as $\sum_{\kappa=1}^{k} \boldsymbol{m}_{l_\kappa}$.

Non-local Pairwise Operator. To improve on sum pooling, we explore an approach which performs reasoning through non-local and pairwise computations, one of a family of similar architectures which has shown promising results for question-answering and video understanding [25–27]. An important aspect of these non-local pairwise methods is that the computation is quadratic in the number of features, and thus hard attention can provide significant computational savings. Given some set of embedding vectors (such as the spatial cells of the output of a convolutional layer) x_{ij}, one can use three simple linear projections to produce a matrix of queries, $\boldsymbol{q}_{ij} := \boldsymbol{W}_q x_{ij}$, keys, $\boldsymbol{k}_{ij} := \boldsymbol{W}_k x_{ij}$, and values, $v_{ij} = W_v x_{ij}$ at each spatial location. Then, for each spatial location i, j, we compare the query q_{ij} with the keys at all other locations, and sum the values v weighted by the similarity. Mathematically, we compute

$$\tilde{x}_{lk} = \sum_{ij} \text{softmax}\left(q_{lk}^T k_{ij}\right) v_{ij} \qquad (7)$$

Here, the softmax operates over all i, j locations. The final representation of the input is computed by summarizing all $\tilde{x}_{lk}$ representations, e.g. we use sum-pooling to achieve this goal. Thus, the mechanism computes non-local [26] pairwise relations between embeddings, independent of spatial or temporal proximity. The separation between keys, queries, and values allows semantic information about each object to remain separated from the information that binds objects together across space. The result is an effective, if somewhat expensive, spatial reasoning mechanism. Although expensive, similar mechanism has been shown useful in various tasks, from synthetic visual question [25], to machine translation [27], to video recognition [26]. Hard attention can help to reduce the set of comparisons that must be considered, and thus we aim to test whether the features selected by hard attention are compatible with this operator.

4 Results

To show the importance of hard attention for visual QA, we first compare HAN to existing soft-attention (SAN) architectures on VQA-CP v2, and exploring the effect of varying degrees of hard attention by directly controlling the number of attended spatial cells in the convolutional map. We then examine AdaHAN, which adaptively chooses the number of attended cells, and briefly investigate the effect of network depth and pretraining. Finally, we present qualitative results, and also provide results on CLEVR to show the method's generality.

4.1 Datasets

VQA-CP v2. This dataset [7] consists of about 121K (98K) images, 438K (220K) questions, and 4.4M (2.2M) answers in the train (test) set; and it is created so that the distribution of the answers between train and test splits differ, and hence the models cannot excessively rely on the language prior [7]. As expected, [7] show that performance of all visual QA approaches they tested drops significantly between train to test sets. The dataset provides a standard train-test split, and also breaks questions into different question types: those where the answer is yes/no, those where the answer is a number, and those where the answer is something else. Thus, we report accuracy on each question type as well as the overall accuracy for each network architecture.

CLEVR. This synthetic dataset [34] consists of 100K images of 3D rendered objects like spheres and cylinders, and roughly 1 m questions that were automatically generated with a procedural engine. While the visual task is relatively simple, solving this dataset requires reasoning over complex relationships between many objects.

4.2 Effect of Hard Attention

We begin with the most basic hard attention architecture, which applies hard attention and then does sum pooling over the attended cells, followed by a small MLP. For each experiment, we take the top k cells, out of 100, according to our $L2$-norm criterion, where k ranges from 16 to 100 (with 100, there is no attention, and the whole image is summed). Results are shown in the top of Table 1. Considering that the hard attention selects only a subset of the input cells, we might expect that the algorithm would lose important information and be unable to recover. In fact, however, the performance is almost the same with less than half of the units attended. Even with just 16 units, the performance loss is less than 1%, suggesting that hard attention is quite capable of capturing the important parts of the image.

Table 1. Comparison between different number of attended cells (percentage of the whole input), and aggregation operation. We consider a simple summation, and non-local pairwise computations as the aggregation tool.

	Percentage of cells	Overall	Yes/No	Number	Other
HAN+sum	16%	26.99	40.53	11.38	24.15
HAN+sum	32%	27.43	41.05	11.38	24.68
HAN+sum	48%	27.94	41.35	11.93	25.27
HAN+sum	64%	27.80	40.74	11.29	25.52
sum	100%	27.96	43.23	12.09	24.29
HAN+pairwise	16%	26.81	41.24	10.87	23.61
HAN+pairwise	32%	27.45	40.91	11.48	24.75
HAN+pairwise	48%	28.23	41.23	11.40	25.98
Pairwise	100%	28.06	44.10	13.20	23.71
SAN [7,9]	-	24.96	38.35	11.14	21.74
SAN (ours)	-	26.60	39.69	11.25	23.92
SAN+pos (ours)	-	27.77	40.73	11.31	25.47
GVQA [7]	-	31.30	57.99	13.68	22.14

The fact that hard attention can work is interesting itself, but it should be especially useful for models that devote significant processing to each attended cell. We therefore repeat the above experiment with the non-local pairwise aggregation mechanism described in Sect. 3, which computes activations for every pair of attended cells, and therefore scales quadratically with the number of attended cells. These results are shown in the middle of Table 1, where we can see that hard attention (48 entitties) actually boosts performance over an analogous model without hard attention.

Finally, we compare standard soft attention baselines in the bottom of Table 1. In particular, we include previous results using a basic soft attention network [7,9], as well as our own re-implementation of the soft attention pooling algorithm presented in [7,9] with the same features used in other experiments. Surprisingly, soft attention does not outperform basic sum pooling, even with careful implementation that outperforms the previously reported results with the same method on this dataset; in fact, it performs slightly worse. The non-local pairwise aggregation performs better than SAN on its own, although the best result includes hard attention. Our results overall are somewhat worse than the state-of-the-art [7], but this is likely due to several architectural decisions not included here, such as a split pathway for different kinds of questions, special question embeddings, and the use of the question extractor.

Table 2. Comparison between different adaptive hard-attention techniques with average number of attended parts, and aggregation operation. We consider a simple summation, and the non-local pairwise aggregation. Since AdaHAN adaptively selects relevant features, based on the fixed threshold $\frac{1}{w*h}$, we report here the average number of attended parts.

	Percentage of cells	Overall	Yes/No	Number	Other
AdaHAN+sum	25.66%	27.40	40.70	11.13	24.86
AdaHAN+pairwise	32.63%	28.65	52.25	13.79	20.33
HAN+sum	32%	27.43	41.05	11.38	24.68
HAN+sum	48%	27.94	41.35	11.93	25.27
HAN+pairwise	32%	27.45	40.91	11.48	24.75
HAN+pairwise	48%	28.23	41.23	11.40	25.98

4.3   Adaptive Hard Attention

Thus far, our experiments have dealt with networks that have a fixed threshold for all images. However, some images and questions may require reasoning about more entities than others. Therefore, we explore a simple adaptive method, where the network chooses how many cells to attend to for each image. Table 2 shows results, where AdaHAN refers to our adaptive mechanism. We can see that on average, the adaptive mechanism uses surprisingly few cells: 25.66 out of 100 when sum pooling is used, and 32.63 whenever the non-local pairwise aggregation mechanism is used. For sum pooling, this is on-par with a non-adaptive network that uses more cells on average (HAN+sum 32); for the non-local pairwise aggregation mechanism, just 32.63 cells are enough to outperform our best

Table 3. Comparison between different number of the attended cells as the percentage of the whole input. The results are reported on VQA-CP v2. The second column denotes the percentage of the attended input. The third column denotes number of layers of the MLP (Eqs. 2 and 3).

	Percentage of cells	Number of layers	Overall	Yes/No	Number	Other
HAN+sum	25%	0	26.38	43.21	13.12	21.17
HAN+sum	50%	0	26.75	41.42	10.94	23.38
HAN+sum	75%	0	26.82	41.30	11.48	23.42
HAN+sum	25%	2	26.99	40.53	11.38	24.15
HAN+sum	50%	2	27.43	41.05	11.38	24.68
HAN+sum	75%	2	27.94	41.35	11.93	25.27

non-adaptive model, which uses roughly 50% more cells. This shows that even very simple methods of adapting hard attention to the image and the question can lead to both computation and performance gains, suggesting that more sophisticated methods will be an important direction for future work.

4.4 Effects of Network Depth

In this section, we briefly analyze an important architectural choice: the number of layers used on top of the pretrained embeddings. That is, before the question and image representations are combined, we perform a small amount of processing to "align" the information, so that the embedding can easily tell the relevance of the visual information to the question. Table 3 shows the results of removing the two layers which perform this function. We consistently see a drop of about 1% without the layers, suggesting that deciding which cells to attend to requires different information than the classification-tuned ResNet is designed to provide.

4.5 Implementation Details

All our models use the same LSTM size 512 for questions embeddings, and the last convolutional layer of the ImageNet pre-trained ResNet-101 [63] (yielding 10-by-10 spatial representation, each with 2048 dimensional cells) for image embedding. We also use MLP with 3 layers of sizes: $1024, 2048, 1000$, as a classification module. We use ADAM for optimization [65]. We use a distributed setting with two workers computing a gradient over a batch of 128 elements each. We normalize images by dividing them by their norm. We do not perform a hyperparameter search as there is no separated validation set available. Instead, we rather choose default hyper-parameters based on our prior experience on visual QA datasets. We trained our models until we notice a saturation on the training set. Then we evaluate these models on the test set. Our tables show the performance of all the methods wrt. the second digits precision obtained by rounding.

Table 1 shows SAN's [9] results reported by [7] together with our in-house implementation (denoted as "ours"). Our implementation has 2 attention hops, 1024 dimensional multimodal embedding size, a fixed learning rate 0.0001, and ResNet-101. In these experiments we pool the attended representations by weighted average with the attention weights. Our in-house implementation of the non-local pairwise mechanism strongly resembles implementations of [26], and [27]. We use 2 heads, with embedding size 512. In Eqs. 2 and 3, we use $d := 2048$ (the same as dimensionality as the image encoding) and two linear layers with RELU that follows up each layer.

4.6   Qualitative Results

One advantage of our formulation is that it is straightforward to visualize the masks of attended cells given questions and images (which we defer to Figs. 1 and 2 in the supplementary material due to space constraints). In general, relevant objects are usually attended, and that significant portions of the irrelevant background is suppressed. Although some background might be kept, we hypothesize the context matters in answering some questions. These masks are occasionally useful for diagnosing behavior: for example, AdaHAN with sum pooling (row 2 in Fig. 1) attends incorrectly to the bridge but not the train in the second column, and therefore answers incorrectly. In the tennis court, however, the same method attends incorrectly, but still answers correctly by chance.

We can also see broad differences between the network architectures. For instance, the sum pooling method (row 2) is much more spatially constrained than the pairwise pooling version (row 1), even though the adaptive attention can select an arbitrarily large region. This suggests that sum pooling struggles to integrate across complex scenes. The support is also not always contiguous: non-adaptive hard attention with 16 entities (row 4) in particular distributes its attention widely.

4.7   End-to-End Training

Since our network is not fully differentiable, one might suspect that it will become more difficult to train the lower-level features, or worse, that untrained features might prevent us from bootstrapping the attention mechanism. Therefore, we also trained HAN+sum (with 16% of the input cells) end-to-end together with a relatively small convolutional neural network initialized from scratch. We compare our method against our implementation of the SAN method trained using the same simple convolutional neural network. We call the models: simple-SAN, and simple-HAN.

Analysis. In our experiments, simple-SAN achieves about 21% performance on the test set. Surprisingly, simple-HAN+sum achieves about 24% performance on the same split, on-par with the performance of normal SAN that uses more complex and deeper visual architecture [66]; the results are reported by [7]. This result shows that the hard attention mechanism can indeed be tightly coupled within the training process, and that the whole procedure does not rely heavily on the properties of the ImageNet pre-trained networks. In a sense, we see that a discrete notion of entities also "emerges" through the learning process, leading to efficient training.

Implementation Details. In our experiments we use a simple CNN built of: 1 layer with 64 filters and 7-by-7 filter size followed up by 2 layers with 256 filters and 2 layers with 512 filters, all with 3-by-3 filter size. We use strides 2 for all the layers.

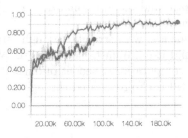
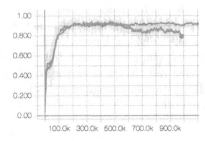

(a) HAN+RN (purple), RN (green)   (b) HAN+RN (orange), ST+RN (blue)

Fig. 3. Validation accuracy plots on CLEVR of the methods under the same hyper-parameters setting [25]. (a) HAN+RN (0.25 of the input cells) and standard RN (all input cells) trained for 12 h to measure the efficiency of the methods. (b) Our approaches to hard attention: the proposed one (orange), and the straight-through estimator (blue). (Color figure online)

4.8 CLEVR

To demonstrate the generality of our hard attention method, particularly in domains that are visually different from the VQA images, we experiment with a synthetic visual QA dataset termed CLEVR [34], using a setup similar to the one used for VQA-CP and [25]. Due to the visual simplicity of CLEVR, we follow up the work of [25], and instead of relying on the ImageNet pre-trained features, we train our HAN+sum and HAN+RN (hard attention with relation network) architectures end-to-end together with a relatively small CNN (following [25]).

Analysis. As reported in prior work [25,34], the soft attention mechanism used in SAN does not perform well on the CLEVR dataset, and achieves only 68.5% [34] (or 76.6% [25]) performance. In contrast, relation network, which also realizes a non-local and pairwise computational model, essentially solves this task, achieving 95.5% performance on the test set. Surprisingly, our HAN+sum achieves 89.7% performance even without a relation network, and HAN+RN (i.e., relation network is used as an aggregation mechanism) achieves 93.9% on the test set. These results show the mechanism can readily be used with other architectures on another dataset with different visuals. Training with HAN requires far less computation than the original relation network [25], although performance is slightly below relation network's 95.5%. Figure 3a compares computation time: HAN+RN and relation network are trained for 12 h under the same hyper-parameter set-up. Here, HAN+RN achieves around 90% validation accuracy, whereas RN only 70%. Notably, owing to hard-attention, we are able to train larger models, and achieve 94.7% and 98.8% for HAN+sum and HAN+RN respectively (more details are found in the supplementary material). Although others report slightly better results on CLEVR [49,50], these are not evaluated on real-world datasets such as VQA-CP, or use higher image resolution. We also found the performance to be sensitive to depth, and batch normalization [67], which we present in more detail is the supplementary material.

As an additional baseline, we have experimented with straight-through estimator [17] (supplementary), but we have found it quite unstable (Fig. 3b). We also point out that it lacks the training-time computational benefit of our approach: in straight-though, the gradients are still back-propagated through non-selected cells.

5   Summary

We have introduced a new approach for hard attention in computer vision that selects a subset of the feature vectors for further processing based on the their magnitudes. We explored two models, one which selects subsets with a pre-specified number of vectors (HAN), and the other one that adaptively chooses the subset size as a function of the inputs (AdaHAN). Hard attention is often avoided in the literature because it poses a challenge for gradient-based methods due to non-differentiability. However, since we found our feature vectors' magnitudes correlate with relevant information, our hard attention mechanism exploits this property to perform the selection. Our results showed our HAN and AdaHAN gave competitive performance on challenging visual QA datasets. Our approaches seem to be at least as good as a more commonly used soft attention mechanism while providing additional computational efficiency benefits. This is especially important for the increasingly popular class of non-local approaches, which often require computations and memory which are quadratic in the number of the input vectors. Finally, our approach also provides interpretable representations, as the spatial locations of the selected features correspond most strongly to those parts of the image which contributed most strongly.

Acknowledgments. We would like to thank Aishwarya Agrawal, Relja Arandjelovic, David G.T. Barrett, Joao Carreira, Timothy Lillicrap, Razvan Pascanu, David Raposo, and many others on the DeepMind team for critical feedback and discussions.

References

1. Çukur, T., Nishimoto, S., Huth, A.G., Gallant, J.L.: Attention during natural vision warps semantic representation across the human brain. Nat. Neurosci. **16**(6), 763 (2013)
2. Sheinberg, D.L., Logothetis, N.K.: Noticing familiar objects in real world scenes: the role of temporal cortical neurons in natural vision. J. Neurosci. **21**(4), 1340–1350 (2001)
3. Simons, D.J., Rensink, R.A.: Change blindness: past, present, and future. Trends in Cogn. Sci. **9**(1), 16–20 (2005)
4. Mack, A., Rock, I.: Inattentional Blindness, vol. 33. MIT Press, Cambridge (1998)
5. Simons, D.J., Chabris, C.F.: Gorillas in our midst: sustained inattentional blindness for dynamic events. Perception **28**(9), 1059–1074 (1999)
6. Malinowski, M., Fritz, M.: A multi-world approach to question answering about real-world scenes based on uncertain input. In: Advances in Neural Information Processing Systems (NIPS) (2014)
7. Agrawal, A., Batra, D., Parikh, D., Kembhavi, A.: Don't just assume; look and answer: overcoming priors for visual question answering. arXiv preprint arXiv:1712.00377 (2017)
8. Xu, H., Saenko, K.: Ask, attend and answer: exploring question-guided spatial attention for visual question answering. arXiv:1511.05234 (2015)
9. Yang, Z., He, X., Gao, J., Deng, L., Smola, A.: Stacked attention networks for image question answering. In: Proceedings of the IEEE Conference on Computer Vision and Pattern Recognition (CVPR) (2016)
10. Fukui, A., Park, D.H., Yang, D., Rohrbach, A., Darrell, T., Rohrbach, M.: Multimodal compact bilinear pooling for visual question answering and visual grounding. In: Proceedings of the Conference on Empirical Methods in Natural Language Processing (EMNLP) (2016)
11. Perez, E., Strub, F., De Vries, H., Dumoulin, V., Courville, A.: FiLM: visual reasoning with a general conditioning layer. In: Proceedings of the Conference on Artificial Intelligence (AAAI) (2018)
12. Kazemi, V., Elqursh, A.: Show, ask, attend, and answer: a strong baseline for visual question answering. arXiv preprint arXiv:1704.03162 (2017)
13. Teney, D., Anderson, P., He, X., van der Hengel, A.: Tips and tricks for visual question answering: learnings from the 2017 challenge. arXiv preprint arXiv:1708.02711 (2017)
14. Ilievski, I., Yan, S., Feng, J.: A focused dynamic attention model for visual question answering. arXiv:1604.01485 (2016)
15. Mnih, V., Heess, N., Graves, A., et al.: Recurrent models of visual attention. In: Advances in Neural Information Processing Systems, pp. 2204–2212 (2014)
16. Gulcehre, C., Chandar, S., Cho, K., Bengio, Y.: Dynamic neural turing machine with soft and hard addressing schemes. arXiv preprint arXiv:1607.00036 (2016)
17. Bengio, Y., Léonard, N., Courville, A.: Estimating or propagating gradients through stochastic neurons for conditional computation. arXiv preprint arXiv:1308.3432 (2013)
18. Jang, E., Gu, S., Poole, B.: Categorical reparameterization with Gumbel-softmax. arXiv preprint arXiv:1611.01144 (2016)
19. Maddison, C.J., Mnih, A., Teh, Y.W.: The concrete distribution: a continuous relaxation of discrete random variables. arXiv preprint arXiv:1611.00712 (2016)
20. Olah, C., et al.: The building blocks of interpretability. Distill (2018)

21. Oliva, A., Torralba, A., Castelhano, M.S., Henderson, J.M.: Top-down control of visual attention in object detection. In: Proceedings of 2003 International Conference on Image Processing, ICIP 2003, vol. 1, p. I-253. IEEE (2003)
22. Ren, M., Kiros, R., Zemel, R.: Image question answering: a visual semantic embedding model and a new dataset. In: Advances in Neural Information Processing Systems (NIPS) (2015)
23. Antol, S., et al.: VQA: visual question answering. In: Proceedings of the IEEE International Conference on Computer Vision (ICCV) (2015)
24. Malinowski, M., Rohrbach, M., Fritz, M.: Ask your neurons: a deep learning approach to visual question answering. Int. J. Comput. Vis. (IJCV) **125**(1–3), 110–135 (2017)
25. Santoro, A., et al.: A simple neural network module for relational reasoning. In: Advances in Neural Information Processing Systems (NIPS), pp. 4974–4983 (2017)
26. Wang, X., Girshick, R., Gupta, A., He, K.: Non-local neural networks. arXiv preprint arXiv:1711.07971 (2017)
27. Vaswani, A., et al.: Attention is all you need. In: Advances in Neural Information Processing Systems, pp. 6000–6010 (2017)
28. Shaw, P., Uszkoreit, J., Vaswani, A.: Self-attention with relative position representations. arXiv preprint arXiv:1803.02155 (2018)
29. Malinowski, M., Fritz, M.: Towards a visual turing challenge. In: Learning Semantics (NIPS Workshop) (2014)
30. Malinowski, M., Fritz, M.: Hard to cheat: a turing test based on answering questions about images. In: AAAI Workshop: Beyond the Turing Test (2015)
31. Malinowski, M.: Towards holistic machines: from visual recognition to question answering about real-world images. Ph.D. thesis (2017)
32. Geman, D., Geman, S., Hallonquist, N., Younes, L.: Visual turing test for computer vision systems. In: Proceedings of the National Academy of Sciences. National Academy of Sciences (2015)
33. Gao, H., Mao, J., Zhou, J., Huang, Z., Wang, L., Xu, W.: Are you talking to a machine? dataset and methods for multilingual image question answering. In: Advances in Neural Information Processing Systems (NIPS) (2015)
34. Johnson, J., Hariharan, B., van der Maaten, L., Fei-Fei, L., Zitnick, C.L., Girshick, R.: CLEVR: a diagnostic dataset for compositional language and elementary visual reasoning. In: 2017 IEEE Conference on Computer Vision and Pattern Recognition (CVPR), pp. 1988–1997. IEEE (2017)
35. Goyal, Y., Khot, T., Summers-Stay, D., Batra, D., Parikh, D.: Making the V in VQA matter: elevating the role of image understanding in visual question answering. In: Proceedings of the IEEE Conference on Computer Vision and Pattern Recognition (CVPR) (2017)
36. Harnad, S.: The symbol grounding problem. Phys. D: Nonlinear Phenom. **42**(1), 335–346 (1990)
37. Guadarrama, S., et al.: Grounding spatial relations for human-robot interaction. In: IROS (2013)
38. Kong, C., Lin, D., Bansal, M., Urtasun, R., Fidler, S.: What are you talking about? Text-to-image coreference. In: Proceedings of the IEEE Conference on Computer Vision and Pattern Recognition (CVPR) (2014)
39. Karpathy, A., Fei-Fei, L.: Deep visual-semantic alignments for generating image descriptions. In: Proceedings of the IEEE Conference on Computer Vision and Pattern Recognition (CVPR) (2015)

40. Rohrbach, A., Rohrbach, M., Hu, R., Darrell, T., Schiele, B.: Grounding of textual phrases in images by reconstruction. In: Leibe, B., Matas, J., Sebe, N., Welling, M. (eds.) ECCV 2016 Part I. LNCS, vol. 9905, pp. 817–834. Springer, Cham (2016). https://doi.org/10.1007/978-3-319-46448-0_49

41. Malinowski, M., Rohrbach, M., Fritz, M.: Ask your neurons: a neural-based approach to answering questions about images. In: Proceedings of the IEEE International Conference on Computer Vision (ICCV), pp. 1–9 (2015)

42. Xu, K., et al.: Show, attend and tell: neural image caption generation with visual attention. In: Proceedings of the International Conference on Machine Learning (ICML) (2015)

43. Xiong, C., Merity, S., Socher, R.: Dynamic memory networks for visual and textual question answering. arXiv preprint arXiv:1603.01417 (2016)

44. De Vries, H., Strub, F., Mary, J., Larochelle, H., Pietquin, O., Courville, A.C.: Modulating early visual processing by language. In: Advances in Neural Information Processing Systems, pp. 6597–6607 (2017)

45. Zhu, Y., Groth, O., Bernstein, M., Fei-Fei, L.: Visual7W: grounded question answering in images. In: Proceedings of the IEEE Conference on Computer Vision and Pattern Recognition (CVPR) (2016)

46. Chen, K., Wang, J., Chen, L.C., Gao, H., Xu, W., Nevatia, R.: ABC-CNN: an attention based convolutional neural network for visual question answering. arXiv:1511.05960 (2015)

47. Shih, K.J., Singh, S., Hoiem, D.: Where to look: focus regions for visual question answering. In: Proceedings of the IEEE Conference on Computer Vision and Pattern Recognition (CVPR) (2016)

48. Gulcehre, C., et al.: Hyperbolic attention networks. arXiv preprint arXiv:1805.09786 (2018)

49. Hudson, D.A., Manning, C.D.: Compositional attention networks for machine reasoning. arXiv preprint arXiv:1803.03067 (2018)

50. Mascharka, D., Tran, P., Soklaski, R., Majumdar, A.: Transparency by design: closing the gap between performance and interpretability in visual reasoning. In: Proceedings of the IEEE Conference on Computer Vision and Pattern Recognition (CVPR), pp. 4942–4950 (2018)

51. Kim, Y., Denton, C., Hoang, L., Rush, A.M.: Structured attention networks. arXiv preprint arXiv:1702.00887 (2017)

52. Hu, R., Andreas, J., Darrell, T., Saenko, K.: Explainable neural computation via stack neural module networks. In: Proceedings of the European Conference on Computer Vision (ECCV) (2018)

53. Mokarian, A., Malinowski, M., Fritz, M.: Mean box pooling: a rich image representation and output embedding for the visual madlibs task. In: Proceedings of the British Machine Vision Conference (BMVC) (2016)

54. Tommasi, T., Mallya, A., Plummer, B., Lazebnik, S., Berg, A.C., Berg, T.L.: Solving visual madlibs with multiple cues. In: Proceedings of the British Machine Vision Conference (BMVC) (2016)

55. Desta, M.T., Chen, L., Kornuta, T.: Object-based reasoning in VQA. arXiv preprint arXiv:1801.09718 (2018)

56. Singh, S., Gupta, A., Efros, A.A.: Unsupervised discovery of mid-level discriminative patches. In: Fitzgibbon, A., Lazebnik, S., Perona, P., Sato, Y., Schmid, C. (eds.) ECCV 2012 Part II. LNCS, pp. 73–86. Springer, Heidelberg (2012). https://doi.org/10.1007/978-3-642-33709-3_6

57. Doersch, C., Gupta, A., Efros, A.A.: Mid-level visual element discovery as discriminative mode seeking. In: Advances in Neural Information Processing Systems (NIPS), pp. 494–502 (2013)
58. Juneja, M., Vedaldi, A., Jawahar, C., Zisserman, A.: Blocks that shout: distinctive parts for scene classification. In: Proceedings of the IEEE Conference on Computer Vision and Pattern Recognition (CVPR), pp. 923–930. IEEE (2013)
59. Doersch, C., Singh, S., Gupta, A., Sivic, J., Efros, A.: What makes Paris look like Paris? In: SIGGRAPH (2012)
60. Jaderberg, M., Simonyan, K., Zisserman, A., et al.: Spatial transformer networks. In: Advances in Neural Information Processing Systems (NIPS), pp. 2017–2025 (2015)
61. Mallya, A., Lazebnik, S.: PackNet: adding multiple tasks to a single network by iterative pruning. In: Proceedings of the IEEE Conference on Computer Vision and Pattern Recognition (CVPR). IEEE (2018)
62. Krizhevsky, A., Sutskever, I., Hinton, G.E.: Imagenet classification with deep convolutional neural networks. In: Advances in Neural Information Processing Systems (NIPS) (2012)
63. He, K., Zhang, X., Ren, S., Sun, J.: Deep residual learning for image recognition. arXiv:1512.03385 (2015)
64. Hochreiter, S., Schmidhuber, J.: Long short-term memory. Neural Comput. **9**, 1735–1780 (1997)
65. Kingma, D., Ba, J.: Adam: a method for stochastic optimization. arXiv:1412.6980 (2014)
66. Simonyan, K., Zisserman, A.: Very deep convolutional networks for large-scale image recognition. arXiv:1409.1556 (2014)
67. Ioffe, S., Szegedy, C.: Batch normalization: accelerating deep network training by reducing internal covariate shift. arXiv preprint arXiv:1502.03167 (2015)

Multi-modal Cycle-Consistent Generalized Zero-Shot Learning

Rafael Felix[✉], B. G. Vijay Kumar[✉], Ian Reid[✉], and Gustavo Carneiro[✉]

Australian Institute for Machine Learning, University of Adelaide, Adelaide, Australia
{rafael.felixalves,vijay.kumar,ian.reid,gustavo.carneiro}@adelaide.edu.au

Abstract. In generalized zero shot learning (GZSL), the set of classes are split into seen and unseen classes, where training relies on the semantic features of the seen and unseen classes and the visual representations of only the seen classes, while testing uses the visual representations of the seen and unseen classes. Current methods address GZSL by learning a transformation from the visual to the semantic space, exploring the assumption that the distribution of classes in the semantic and visual spaces is relatively similar. Such methods tend to transform unseen testing visual representations into one of the seen classes' semantic features instead of the semantic features of the correct unseen class, resulting in low accuracy GZSL classification. Recently, generative adversarial networks (GAN) have been explored to synthesize visual representations of the unseen classes from their semantic features - the synthesized representations of the seen and unseen classes are then used to train the GZSL classifier. This approach has been shown to boost GZSL classification accuracy, but there is one important missing constraint: there is no guarantee that synthetic visual representations can generate back their semantic feature in a multi-modal cycle-consistent manner. This missing constraint can result in synthetic visual representations that do not represent well their semantic features, which means that the use of this constraint can improve GAN-based approaches. In this paper, we propose the use of such constraint based on a new regularization for the GAN training that forces the generated visual features to reconstruct their original semantic features. Once our model is trained with this multi-modal cycle-consistent semantic compatibility, we can then synthesize more representative visual representations for the seen and, more importantly, for the unseen classes. Our proposed approach shows the best GZSL classification results in the field in several publicly available datasets.

Keywords: Generalized zero-shot learning
Generative adversarial networks · Cycle consistency loss

All authors gratefully acknowledge the support of the Australian Research Council through the Centre of Excellence for Robotic Vision (project number CE140100016), Laureate Fellowship FL130100102 to IR and Discover Project DP180103232 to GC.

ⓒ Springer Nature Switzerland AG 2018
V. Ferrari et al. (Eds.): ECCV 2018, LNCS 11210, pp. 21–37, 2018.
https://doi.org/10.1007/978-3-030-01231-1_2

1   Introduction

Generalized Zero-shot Learning (GZSL) separates the classes of interest into a sub-set of seen classes and another sub-set of unseen classes. The training process uses the semantic features of both sub-sets and the visual representations of only the seen classes; while the testing process aims to classify the visual representations of both sub-sets [2,3]. The semantic features available for both the training and testing classes are typically acquired from other domains, such as visual features [4], text [3,5,6], or learned classifiers [7]. The traditional approach to address this challenge [2] involves the learning of a transformation from the visual to the semantic space of the seen classes. Testing is then performed by transforming the visual representation of the seen and unseen classes into this semantic space, where classification is typically achieved with a nearest neighbor classifier that selects the closest class in the semantic space. In contrast to Zero-shot Learning (ZSL), which uses only the unseen domain for testing, GZSL approaches tend to be biased towards the seen classes, producing poor classification results, particularly for the unseen testing classes [1].

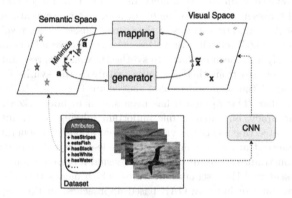

Fig. 1. Overview of the proposed multi-modal cycle-consistent GZSL approach. Our approach extends the idea of synthesizing visual representations of seen and unseen classes in order to train a classifier for the GZSL problem [1]. The main contribution of the paper is the use of a new multi-modal cycle consistency loss in the training of the visual feature generator that minimizes the reconstruction error between the semantic feature $\mathbf{a}$, which was used to synthesize the visual feature $\tilde{\mathbf{x}}$, and the reconstructed semantic feature $\tilde{\mathbf{a}}$ mapped from $\tilde{\mathbf{x}}$. This loss is shown to constrain the optimization problem more effectively in order to produce useful synthesized visual features for training the GZSL classifier.

These traditional approaches rely on the assumption that the distributions observed in the semantic and visual spaces are relatively similar. Recently, this assumption has been relaxed to allow the semantic space to be optimized together with the transformation from the visual to the semantic space [8] - this alleviates the classification bias mentioned above to a certain degree. More recent approaches consist of building a generative adversarial network (GAN) that synthesizes visual representations of the seen and unseen classes directly from their semantic representation [8,9]. These synthesized features are then used to train a multi-class classifier of seen and unseen classes. This approach has been shown to improve the GZSL classification accuracy, but an obvious weakness is that the unconstrained nature of the generation process may let the approach generate unrepresentative synthetic visual representations, particularly of the unseen classes (i.e., representations that are far from possible visual representations of the test classes).

The **main contribution** of this paper is a **new regularization of the generation of synthetic visual representations in the training of GAN-based methods that address the GZSL classification problem**. This regularization is **based on a multi-modal cycle consistency loss term that enforces good reconstruction from the synthetic visual representations back to their original semantic features** (see Fig. 1). This regularization is motivated by the cycle consistency loss applied in training GANs [10] that forces the generative training approach to produce more constrained visual representations. We argue that this constraint preserves the semantic compatibility between visual features and semantic features. Once our model is trained with this multi-modal cycle consistency loss term, we can then synthesize visual representations for unseen classes in order to train a GZSL classifier [1,11].

Using the experimental setup described by Xian et al. [1], we show that our proposed regularization provides significant improvements not only in terms of GZSL classification accuracy, but also ZSL on the following datasets: Caltech-UCSD-Birds 200-2011 (CUB) [2,12], Oxford-Flowers (FLO) [13], Scene Categorization Benchmark (SUN) [2,14], Animals with features (AWA) [2,4], and *ImageNet* [15]. In fact, the experiments show that our proposed approach holds the current best ZSL and GZSL classification results in the field for these datasets.

2   Literature Review

The starting point for our literature review is the work by Xian et al. [1,2], who proposed new benchmarks using commonly accepted evaluation protocols on publicly available datasets. These benchmarks allow a fair comparison among recently proposed ZSL and GZSL approaches, and for this reason we explore those benchmarks to compare our results with the ones obtained from the current state of the art in the field. We provide a general summary of the methods presented in [2], and encourage the reader to study that paper in order to obtain more details on previous works. The majority of the ZSL and GZSL methods tend to compensate the lack of visual representation of the unseen classes with the learning of a mapping between visual and semantic spaces [16,17]. For instance, a fairly successful approach is based on a bi-linear compatibility function that associates visual representation and semantic features. Examples of such approaches are ALE [18], DEVISE [19], SJE [20], ESZSL [21], and SAE [22]. Despite their simplicity, these methods tend to produce the current state-of-the-art results on benchmark datasets [2]. A straightforward extension of the methods above is the exploration of a non-linear compatibility function between visual and semantic spaces. These approaches, exemplified by LATEM [23] and CMT [6], tend not to be as competitive as their bi-linear counterpart, probably because the more complex models need larger training sets to generalize more effectively. Seminal ZSL and GZSL methods were based on models relying on learning intermediate feature classifiers, which are combined to predict image classes (e.g., DAP and IAP) [4] – these models tend to present relatively poor classification results. Finally, hybrid models, such as SSE [3], CONSE [24], SYNC [25], rely on a mixture model of seen classes to represent images and semantic embeddings. These methods tend to be competitive for classifying the seen classes, but not for the unseen classes.

The main disadvantage of the methods above is that the lack of visual training data for the unseen classes biases the mapping between visual and semantic spaces towards the semantic features of seen classes, particularly for unseen test images. This is an issue for GZSL because it has a negative effect in the classification accuracy of the unseen classes. Recent research address this issue using GAN models that are trained to synthesize visual representations for the seen and unseen classes, which can then be used to train a classifier for both the seen and unseen classes [8,9]. However, the unconstrained generation of synthetic visual representations for the unseen classes allows the production of synthetic samples that may be too far from the actual distribution of visual representations, particularly for the unseen classes. In GAN literature, this problem is known as unpaired training [10], where not all source samples (e.g., semantic features) have corresponding target samples (e.g., visual features) for training. This creates a highly unconstrained optimization problem that has been solved by Zhu et al. [10] with a cycle consistency loss to push the representation from the target domain back to the source domain, which helped constraining the optimization problem. In this paper, we explore this idea for GZSL, which is a novelty compared to previous GAN-based methods proposed in GZSL and ZSL.

3   Multi-modal Cycle-Consistent Generalized Zero Shot Learning

In GZSL and ZSL [2], the dataset is denoted by $\mathcal{D} = \{(\mathbf{x}, \mathbf{a}, y)_i\}_{i=1}^{|\mathcal{D}|}$ with $\mathbf{x} \in \mathcal{X} \subseteq \mathbb{R}^K$ representing visual representation (e.g., image features from deep residual nets [26]), $\mathbf{a} \in \mathcal{A} \subseteq \mathbb{R}^L$ denoting L-dimensional semantic feature (e.g., set of binary attributes [4] or a dense *word2vec* representation [27]), $y \in \mathcal{Y} = \{1, ..., C\}$ denoting the image class, and $|.|$ representing set cardinality. The set $\mathcal{Y}$ is split into seen and unseen subsets, where the seen subset is denoted by $\mathcal{Y}_S$ and the unseen subset by $\mathcal{Y}_U$, with $\mathcal{Y} = \mathcal{Y}_S \cup \mathcal{Y}_U$ and $\mathcal{Y}_S \cap \mathcal{Y}_U = \emptyset$. The dataset $\mathcal{D}$ is also divided into mutually exclusive training and testing subsets: $\mathcal{D}^{Tr}$ and $\mathcal{D}^{Te}$, respectively. Furthermore, the training and testing sets can also be divided in terms of the seen and unseen classes, so this means that $\mathcal{D}_S^{Tr}$ denotes the training samples of the seen classes, while $\mathcal{D}_U^{Tr}$ represents the training samples of the unseen classes (similarly for $\mathcal{D}_S^{Te}$ and $\mathcal{D}_U^{Te}$ for the testing set). During training, samples in $\mathcal{D}_S^{Tr}$ contain the visual representation $\mathbf{x}_i$, semantic feature $\mathbf{a}_i$ and class label y_i; while the samples in $\mathcal{D}_U^{Tr}$ comprise only the semantic feature and class label. During ZSL testing, only the samples from $\mathcal{D}_U^{Te}$ are used; while in GZSL testing, all samples from $\mathcal{D}^{Te}$ are used. Note that for ZSL and GZSL problems, only the visual representation of the testing samples is used to predict the class label.

Below, we first explain the f-CLSWGAN model [1], which is the baseline for the implementation of the main contribution of this paper: the multi-modal cycle consistency loss used in the training for the feature generator in GZSL models based on GANs. The loss, feature generator, learning and testing procedures are explained subsequently.

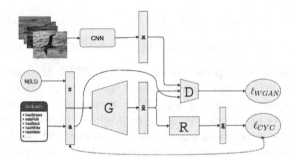

Fig. 2. Overview of the multi-modal cycle-consistent GZSL model. The visual features, represented by $\mathbf{x}$, are extracted from a state-of-art CNN model, and the semantic features, represented by $\mathbf{a}$, are available from the training set. The generator $G(.)$ synthesizes new visual features $\tilde{\mathbf{x}}$ using the semantic feature and a randomly sampled noise vector $\mathbf{z} \sim \mathcal{N}(\mathbf{0}, \mathbf{I})$, and the discriminator $D(.)$ tries to distinguish between real and synthesized visual features. Our main contribution is focused on the integration of a multi-modal cycle consistency loss (at the bottom) that minimizes the error between the original semantic feature $\mathbf{a}$ and its reconstruction $\tilde{\mathbf{a}}$, produced by the regressor $R(.)$.

3.1   f-CLSWGAN

Our approach is an extension of the feature generation method proposed by Xian et al. [1], which consists of a classification regularized generative adversarial network (f-CLSWGAN). This network is composed of a generative model $G :$ $\mathcal{A} \times \mathcal{Z} \to \mathcal{X}$ (parameterized by θ_G) that produces a visual representation $\tilde{\mathbf{x}}$ given its semantic feature $\mathbf{a}$ and a noise vector $\mathbf{z} \sim \mathcal{N}(\mathbf{0}, \mathbf{I})$ sampled from a multi-dimensional centered Gaussian, and a discriminative model $D : \mathcal{X} \times \mathcal{A} \to [0, 1]$ (parameterized by θ_D) that tries to distinguish whether the input $\mathbf{x}$ and its semantic representation $\mathbf{a}$ represent a true or generated visual representation and respective semantic feature. Note that while the method developed by Yan et al. [28] concerns the generation of realistic images, our proposed approach, similarly to [1,8,9], aims to generate visual representations, such as the features from a deep residual network [26] - the strategy based on visual representation has shown to produce more accurate GZSL classification results compared to the use of realistic images. The training algorithm for estimating θ_G and θ_D follows a minimax game, where $G(.)$ generates synthetic visual representations that are supposed to fool the discriminator, which in turn tries to distinguish the real from the synthetic visual representations. We rely on one of the most stable training methods for GANs, called Wasserstein GAN, which uses the following loss function [29]:

$$\theta_G^*, \theta_D^* = \arg \min_{\theta_G} \max_{\theta_D} \ell_{WGAN}(\theta_G, \theta_D), \tag{1}$$

with

$$\ell_{WGAN}(\theta_G, \theta_D) = \mathbb{E}_{(\mathbf{x},\mathbf{a})\sim\mathbb{P}^{x,a}_S}[D(\mathbf{x}, \mathbf{a}; \theta_D)] - \mathbb{E}_{(\widetilde{\mathbf{x}},\mathbf{a})\sim\mathbb{P}^{x,a}_G}[D(\widetilde{\mathbf{x}}, \mathbf{a}; \theta_D)]$$
$$- \lambda \mathbb{E}_{(\hat{\mathbf{x}},\mathbf{a})\sim\mathbb{P}^{x,a}_\alpha}[(\|\nabla_{\hat{\mathbf{x}}} D(\hat{\mathbf{x}}, \mathbf{a}; \theta_D)\|_2 - 1)^2], \tag{2}$$

where $\mathbb{E}[.]$ represents the expected value operator, $\mathbb{P}^{x,a}_S$ is the joint distribution of visual and semantic features from the seen classes (in practice, samples from that distribution are the ones in $\mathcal{D}^{Tr}_S$), $\mathbb{P}^{x,a}_G$ represents the joint distribution of semantic features and the visual features produced by the generative model $G(.)$, λ denotes the penalty coefficient, and $\mathbb{P}^{x,a}_\alpha$ is the joint distribution of the semantic features and the visual features produced by $\hat{\mathbf{x}} \sim \alpha\mathbf{x} + (1 - \alpha)\widetilde{\mathbf{x}}$ with $\alpha \sim \mathcal{U}(0, 1)$ (i.e., uniform distribution).

Finally, the f-CLSWGAN is trained with the following objective function:

$$\theta_G^*, \theta_C^*, \theta_D^* = \arg \min_{\theta_G, \theta_C} \max_{\theta_D} \ell_{WGAN}(\theta_G, \theta_D) + \beta \ell_{CLS}(\theta_C, \theta_G), \tag{3}$$

where $\ell_{CLS}(\theta_C, \theta_G) = -\mathbb{E}_{(\widetilde{\mathbf{x}},y)\sim\mathbb{P}^{x,y}_G}[\log P(y|\widetilde{\mathbf{x}}, \theta_C)]$, with

$$P(y|\widetilde{\mathbf{x}}, \theta_C) = \frac{\exp((\theta_C(y))^T\widetilde{\mathbf{x}})}{\sum_{c\in\mathcal{Y}} \exp((\theta_C(c))^T\widetilde{\mathbf{x}})} \tag{4}$$

representing the probability that the sample $\widetilde{\mathbf{x}}$ has been predicted with its true label y, and β is a hyper-parameter that weights the contribution of the loss function. This regularization with the classification loss was found by Xian et al. [1] to enforce $G(.)$ to generate discriminative visual representations. The model obtained from the optimization in (3) is referred to as **baseline** in the experiments.

3.2   Multi-modal Cycle Consistency Loss

The main issue present in previously proposed GZSL approaches based on generative models [1,8,9] is that the unconstrained nature of the generation process (from semantic to visual features) may produce image representations that are too far from the real distribution present in the training set, resulting in an ineffective multi-class classifier training, particularly for the unseen classes. The approach we propose to alleviate this problem consists of constraining the synthetic visual representations to generate back their original semantic features - this regularization has been inspired by the cycle consistency loss [10]. Figure 2 shows an overview of our proposal. This approach, representing the main contribution of this paper, is represented by the following loss:

$$\ell_{CYC}(\theta_R, \theta_G) = \mathbb{E}_{\mathbf{a} \sim \mathbb{P}_S^a, \mathbf{z} \sim \mathcal{N}(\mathbf{0}, \mathbf{I})} \left[\|\mathbf{a} - R(G(\mathbf{a}, \mathbf{z}; \theta_G); \theta_R)\|_2^2 \right]$$
$$+ \mathbb{E}_{\mathbf{a} \sim \mathbb{P}_U^a, \mathbf{z} \sim \mathcal{N}(\mathbf{0}, \mathbf{I})} \left[\|\mathbf{a} - R(G(\mathbf{a}, \mathbf{z}; \theta_G); \theta_R)\|_2^2 \right], \tag{5}$$

where $\mathbb{P}_S^a$ and $\mathbb{P}_U^a$ denote the distributions of semantic features of the seen and unseen classes, respectively, and $R : \mathcal{X} \to \mathcal{A}$ represents a regressor that estimates the original semantic features from the visual representation generated by $G(.)$.

3.3 Feature Generation

Using the losses proposed in Sects. 3.1 and 3.2, we can propose several feature generators. First, we pre-train the regressor $R(.)$ defined below in (6), by minimizing a loss function computed only from the seen classes, as follows:

$$\ell_{REG}(\theta_R) = \mathbb{E}_{(\mathbf{a}, \mathbf{x}) \sim \mathbb{P}_S^{a, x}} \left[\|\mathbf{a} - R(\mathbf{x}; \theta_R)\|_2^2 \right], \tag{6}$$

where $\mathbb{P}_S^{a, x}$ represents the real joint distribution of image and semantic features present in the seen classes. In practice, this regressor is defined by a multilayer perceptron, whose output activation function depends on the format of the semantic vector.

Our first strategy to build a feature generator consists of pre-training a regressor (using samples from seen classes) optimized by minimizing ℓ_{REG} in (6), which produces θ_R^* and training the generator and discriminator of the WGAN using the following optimization function:

$$\theta_G^*, \theta_D^* = \arg \min_{\theta_G} \max_{\theta_D} \ell_{WGAN}(\theta_G, \theta_D) + \lambda_1 \ell_{CYC}(\theta_R^*, \theta_G), \tag{7}$$

where ℓ_{WGAN} is defined in (2), ℓ_{CYC} is defined in (5), and λ_1 weights the importance of the second optimization term. The optimization in (7) can use both the seen and unseen classes, or it can rely only the seen classes, in which case the loss ℓ_{CYC} in (5) has to be modified so that its second term (that depends on unseen classes) is left out of the optimization. The feature generator model in (7) trained with seen and unseen classes is referred to as **cycle-(U)WGAN**, while the feature generator trained with only seen classes is labeled **cycle-WGAN**.

The second strategy explored in this paper to build a feature generator involves pre-training the regressor in (6) using samples from seen classes to produce θ_R^*, and pre-training a softmax classifier for the seen classes using ℓ_{CLS}, defined in (3), which results in θ_C^*. Then we train the combined loss function:

$$\theta_G^*, \theta_D^* = \arg \min_{\theta_G} \max_{\theta_D} \ell_{WGAN}(\theta_G, \theta_D) + \lambda_1 \ell_{CYC}(\theta_R^*, \theta_G) + \lambda_2 \ell_{CLS}(\theta_C^*, \theta_G). \tag{8}$$

The feature generator model in (8) trained with seen classes is referred to as **cycle-CLSWGAN**.

3.4   Learning and Testing

As shown in [1] the training of a classifier using a potentially unlimited number of samples from the seen and unseen classes generated with $\mathbf{x} \sim G(\mathbf{a}, \mathbf{z}; \theta_G^*)$ produces more accurate classification results compared with multi-modal embedding models [18–21]. Therefore, we train a final softmax classifier $P(y|\mathbf{x}, \theta_C)$, defined in (4), using the generated visual features by minimizing the negative log likelihood loss $\ell_{CLS}(\theta_C, \theta_G^*)$, as defined in (3), where θ_G^* has been learned from one of the feature learning strategies discussed in Sect. 3.3 - the training of the classifier produces θ_C^*. The samples used for training the classifier are generated based on the task to be solved. For instance, for ZSL, we only use generated visual representations from the set of unseen classes; while for GZSL, we use the generated samples from seen and unseen classes.

Finally, the testing is based on the prediction of a class for an input test visual representation $\mathbf{x}$, as follows:

$$y^* = \arg \max_{y \in \widetilde{\mathcal{Y}}} P(y|\mathbf{x}, \theta_C^*), \qquad (9)$$

where $\widetilde{\mathcal{Y}} = \mathcal{Y}$ for GZSL or $\widetilde{\mathcal{Y}} = \mathcal{Y}_U$ for ZSL.

4   Experiments

In this section, we first introduce the datasets and evaluation criteria used in the experiments, then we discuss the experimental set-up and finally show the results of our approach, comparing with the state-of-the-art results.

4.1   Datasets

We evaluate the proposed method on the following ZSL/GZSL benchmark datasets, using the experimental setup of [2], namely: CUB-200-2011 [1,12], FLO [13], SUN [2], and AWA [2,30] – where CUB, FLO and SUN are fine-grained datasets, and AWA coarse. Table 1 shows some basic information about these datasets in terms of number of seen and unseen classes and number of training and testing images. For CUB-200-2011 [1,12] and Oxford-Flowers [13], the semantic feature has 1024 dimensions produced by the character-based CNN-RNN [31] that encodes the textual description of an image containing fine-grained visual descriptions (10 sentences per image). The sentences from the unseen classes are not used for training the CNN-RNN and the per-class sentence is obtained by averaging the CNN-RNN semantic features that belong to the same class. For the FLO dataset [13], we used the same type of semantic feature with 1024 dimensions [31] as was used for CUB (please see description above). For the SUN dataset [2], the semantic features have 102 dimensions. Following the protocol from Xian et al. [2], visual features are represented by the activations of the 2048-dim top-layer pooling units of ResNet-101 [26], obtained from the entire image. For AWA [2,30], we use a semantic feature containing 85

Table 1. Information about the datasets CUB [12], FLO [13], SUN [33], AWA [2], and ImageNet [15]. Column (1) shows the number of seen classes, denoted by $|\mathcal{Y}_S|$, split into the number of training and validation classes (train + val), (2) presents the number of unseen classes $|\mathcal{Y}_U|$, (3) displays the number of samples available for training $|\mathcal{D}^{Tr}|$ and (4) shows number of testing samples that belong to the unseen classes $|\mathcal{D}_U^{Te}|$ and number of testing samples that belong to the seen classes $|\mathcal{D}_S^{Te}|$.

Name	$|\mathcal{Y}_S|$ (train + val)	$|\mathcal{Y}_U|$	$|\mathcal{D}^{Tr}|$	$|\mathcal{D}_U^{Te}| + |\mathcal{D}_S^{Te}|$
CUB	150 (100 + 50)	50	7057	1764 + 2967
FLO	82 (62 + 20)	20	1640	1155 + 5394
SUN	745 (580 + 65)	72	14340	2580 + 1440
AWA	40 (27 + 13)	10	19832	4958 + 5685
ImageNet	1000 (1000 + 0)	100	1.2×10^6	5200 + 0

dimensions denoting per-class attributes. In addition, we also test our approach on *ImageNet* [15], for a split containing 100 classes for testing [32].

The input images do not suffer any pre-processing (cropping, background subtraction, etc.) and we do not use any type of data augmentation. This ResNet-101 is pre-trained on ImageNet with 1K classes [15] and is not fine tuned. For the synthetic visual representations, we generate 2048-dim CNN features using one of the feature generation models, presented in Sect. 3.3.

For CUB, FLO, SUN, and AWA we use the zero-shot splits proposed by Xian et al. [2], making sure that none of the training classes are present on ImageNet [15]. Differently from these datasets (i.e., CUB, FLO, SUN, AWA), we observed that there is a lack of standardized experimental setup for GZSL on *Imagenet*. Recently, papers have used *ImageNet* for GZSL using several splits (e.g., 2-hop, 3-hop), but we noticed that some of the supposedly unseen classes can actually be seen during training (e.g., in split **2-hop**, we note that the class *American mink* is assumed to be unseen, while class *Mink* is seen, but these two classes are arguably the same). Nevertheless, in order to demonstrate the competitiveness of our proposed **cycle-WGAN**, we compare it to the **baseline** using carefully selected 100 unseen classes [32] (i.e., no overlap with 1k training seen classes) from *ImageNet*.

4.2 Evaluation Protocol

We follow the evaluation protocol proposed by Xian et al. [2], where results are based on average per-class top-1 accuracy. For the ZSL evaluation, top-1 accuracy results are computed with respect to the set of unseen classes $\mathcal{Y}_U$, where the average accuracy is independently computed for each class, which is then averaged over all unseen classes. For the GZSL evaluation, we compute the average per-class top-1 accuracy on seen classes $\mathcal{Y}_S$, denoted by s, the average per-class top-1 accuracy on unseen classes $\mathcal{Y}_U$, denoted by u, and their harmonic mean, i.e. $H = 2 \times (s \times u)/(s + u)$.

Table 2. Summary of cross-validated hyper-parameters in our experiments.

	$R(.)$			GAN: $G(.)$ and $D(.)$				Classifier		
	$lr_{R(.)}$	batch	#ep	$lr_{G(.)}$	$lr_{D(.)}$	batch	#ep	lr	batch	#ep
CUB	$1e^{-4}$	64	100	$1e^{-4}$	$1e^{-3}$	64	926	$1e^{-4}$	4096	80
FLO	$1e^{-4}$	64	100	$1e^{-4}$	$1e^{-3}$	64	926	$1e^{-4}$	2048	100
SUN	$1e^{-4}$	64	100	$1e^{-2}$	$1e^{-2}$	64	926	$1e^{-4}$	4096	298
AWA	$1e^{-3}$	64	50	$1e^{-4}$	$1e^{-3}$	64	350	$1e^{-4}$	2048	37
ImageNet	$1e^{-4}$	2048	5	$1e^{-4}$	$1e^{-3}$	256	300	$1e^{-3}$	2048	300

4.3 Implementation Details

In this section, we explain the implementation details of the generator $G(.)$, the discriminator $D(.)$, the regressor $R(.)$, and the weights used for the hyper-parameters in the loss functions in (2), (3), (7) and (8) - all these terms have been formally defined in Sect. 3 and depicted in Fig. 2. The generator consists of a multi-layer perceptron (MLP) with a single hidden layer containing 4096 nodes, where this hidden layer is activated by LeakyReLU [34], and the output layer, with 2048 nodes, has a ReLU activation [35]. The weights of $G(.)$ are initialized with a truncated normal initialization with mean 0 and standard deviation 0.01 and the biases are initialized with 0. The discriminator $D(.)$ is also an MLP consisting of a single hidden layer with 4096 nodes, which is activated by LeakyReLU, and the output layer has no activation. The initialization of $D(.)$ is the same as for $G(.)$. The regressor $R(.)$ is a linear transform from the visual space $\mathcal{X}$ to the semantic space $\mathcal{A}$. Following [1], we set $\lambda = 10$ in (2), $\beta = 0.01$ in (3) and $\lambda_1 = \lambda_2 = 0.01$ in (7) and (8). We ran an empirical evaluation with the training set and noticed that when λ_1 and λ_2 share the same value, the training becomes stable, but a more systematic evaluation to assess the relative importance of these two hyper-parameters is still needed. Table 2 shows the learning rates for each model (denoted by $lr_{\{R(.),G(.),D(.)\}}$), batch sizes (**batch**) and number of epochs (**#ep**) used for each dataset and model – the values for $G(.)$ and $D(.)$ have been estimated to reproduce the published results of our implementation of f-CLSWGAN (explained below), and the values for $R(.)$ have been estimated by cross validation using the training and validation sets.

Regarding the number of visual representations generated to train the classifier, we performed a few experiments and reached similar conclusions, compared to [1]. For all experiments in the paper, we generated 300 visual representations per class [1]. We reached this number after a study that shows that for a small number of representations (below 100), the classification results were not competitive; for values superior to 200 or more, results became competitive, but unstable; and above 300, results were competitive and stable.

Since our approach is based on the f-CLSWGAN [1], we re-implemented this methodology. In the experiments, the results from our implementation of f-CLSWGAN using a softmax classifier is labeled as **baseline**. The results that

Table 3. Comparison between the reported results of **f-CLSWGAN** [1] and our implementation of it, labeled **baseline**, where we show the top-1 accuracy on the unseen test $\mathcal{Y}_U$ (GZSL), the top-1 accuracy for seen test $\mathcal{Y}_S$ (GZSL), the harmonic mean H (GZSL), and the top-1 accuracy for ZSL ($T1_Z$).

Classifier	CUB				FLO				SUN				AWA			
	$\mathcal{Y}_U$	$\mathcal{Y}_S$	H	$T1_Z$	$\mathcal{Y}_U$	$\mathcal{Y}_S$	H	$T1_Z$	$\mathcal{Y}_U$	$\mathcal{Y}_S$	H	$T1_Z$	$\mathcal{Y}_U$	$\mathcal{Y}_S$	H	$T1_Z$
f-CLSWGAN [1]	43.7	57.7	49.7	57.3	59.0	73.8	65.6	67.2	42.6	36.6	39.4	60.8	57.9	61.4	59.6	68.2
baseline	43.8	60.6	50.8	57.7	58.8	70.0	63.9	66.8	47.9	32.4	38.7	58.5	56.0	62.8	59.2	64.1

we obtained from our baseline are very similar to the reported results in [1], as shown in Table 3. For ImageNet, note that we use a split [32] that is different from previous ones used in the literature, as explained above in Sect. 4.1, so it is not possible to have a direct comparison between f-CLSWGAN [1] and our **baseline**. Nevertheless, we show in Table 6 that the results we obtain for the split [32] are in fact similar to the reported results for f-CLSWGAN [1] for similar ImageNet splits. We developed our code[1] and perform all experiments using Tensorflow [36].

5 Results

In this section we show the GZSL and ZSL results using our proposed models **cycle-WGAN**, **cycle-(U)WGAN** and **cycle-CLSWGAN**, the baseline model f-CLSWGAN, denoted by **baseline**, and several other baseline methods previously used in the field for benchmarking [2]. Table 4 shows the **GZSL results** and Table 5 shows the **ZSL results** obtained from our proposed methods, and several baseline approaches on CUB, FLO, SUN and AWA datasets. The results in Table 6 shows that the top-1 accuracy on ImageNet for **cycle-WGAN** and **baseline** [1].

6 Discussion

Regarding the GZSL results in Table 4, we notice that there is a clear trend of all of our proposed feature generation methods (**cycle-WGAN**, **cycle-(U)WGAN**), and **cycle-CLSWGAN**) to perform better than **baseline** on the unseen test set. In particular, it seems advantageous to use the synthetic samples from unseen classes to train the **cycle-(U)WGAN** model since it achieves the best top-1 accuracy results in 3 out of the 4 datasets, with improvements from 0.7% to more than 4%. In general, the top-1 accuracy improvement achieved by our approaches in the seen test set is less remarkable, which is expected given that we prioritize to improve the results for the unseen classes. Nevertheless, our approaches achieved improvements from 0.4% to more than 2.5% for the seen classes. Finally, the harmonic mean results also show that our approaches

---

[1] Code is available at: https://github.com/rfelixmg/frwgan-eccv18.

Table 4. GZSL results using per-class average top-1 accuracy on the test sets of unseen classes $\mathcal{Y}_U$, seen classes $\mathcal{Y}_S$, and the harmonic mean result H – all results shown in percentage. Results from previously proposed methods in the field extracted from [2].

Classifier	CUB			FLO			SUN			AWA		
	$\mathcal{Y}_U$	$\mathcal{Y}_S$	H	$\mathcal{Y}_U$	$\mathcal{Y}_S$	H	$\mathcal{Y}_U$	$\mathcal{Y}_S$	H	$\mathcal{Y}_U$	$\mathcal{Y}_S$	H
DAP [30]	4.2	25.1	7.2	–	–	–	1.7	67.9	3.3	0.0	**88.7**	0.0
IAP [30]	1.0	37.8	1.8	–	–	–	0.2	**72.8**	0.4	2.1	78.2	4.1
DEVISE [19]	23.8	53.0	32.8	9.9	44.2	16.2	16.9	27.4	20.9	13.4	68.7	22.4
SJE [20]	23.5	59.2	33.6	13.9	47.6	21.5	14.7	30.5	19.8	11.3	74.6	19.6
LATEM [23]	15.2	57.3	24.0	6.6	47.6	11.5	14.7	28.8	19.5	7.3	71.7	13.3
ESZSL [21]	12.6	**63.8**	21.0	11.4	56.8	19.0	11.0	27.9	15.8	6.6	75.6	12.1
ALE [18]	23.7	62.8	34.4	13.3	61.6	21.9	21.8	33.1	26.3	16.8	76.1	27.5
SAE [22]	8.8	18.0	11.8	–	–	–	7.8	54.0	13.6	1.8	77.1	3.5
baseline [1]	43.8	60.6	50.8	58.8	70.0	63.9	47.9	32.4	38.7	56.0	62.8	59.2
cycle-WGAN	46.0	60.3	52.2	59.1	71.1	64.5	48.3	33.1	39.2	56.4	63.5	59.7
cycle-CLSWGAN	45.7	61.0	52.3	59.2	**72.5**	65.1	**49.4**	33.6	**40.0**	56.9	64.0	**60.2**
cycle-(U)WGAN	**47.9**	59.3	**53.0**	**61.6**	69.2	**65.2**	47.2	33.8	39.4	**59.6**	63.4	59.8

Table 5. ZSL results using per-class average top-1 accuracy on the test set of unseen classes $\mathcal{Y}_U$ – all results shown in percentage. Results from previously proposed methods in the field extracted from [2].

Classifier	ZSL			
	CUB	FLO	SUN	AWA
DEVISE [19]	52.0	45.9	56.5	54.2
SJE [20]	53.9	53.4	53.7	65.6
LATEM [23]	49.3	40.4	55.3	55.1
ESZSL [21]	53.9	51.0	54.5	58.2
ALE [18]	54.9	48.5	58.1	59.9
baseline [1]	57.7	66.8	58.5	64.1
cycle-WGAN	57.8	68.6	59.7	65.6
cycle-CLSWGAN	58.4	70.1	**60.0**	66.3
cycle-(U)WGAN	**58.6**	**70.3**	59.9	**66.8**

improve over the **baseline** in a range of between 1% and 2.2%. Notice that this results are remarkable considering the outstanding improvements achieved by f-CLSWGAN [1], represented here by **baseline**. In fact, our proposed methods produce the current state of the art GZSL results for these four datasets.

Analyzing the ZSL results in Table 5, we again notice that, similarly to the GZSL case, there is a clear advantage in using the synthetic samples from unseen classes to train the **cycle-(U)WGAN** model. For instance, top-1 accuracy results show that we can improve over the **baseline** from 0.9% to 3.5%. The results in this table show that our proposed approaches currently hold the best ZSL results for these datasets.

Table 6. ZSL and GZSL ImageNet results using per-class average top-1 accuracy on the test sets of unseen classes $\mathcal{Y}_U$ – all results shown in percentage.

Classifier	ZSL	GZSL
baseline [1]	7.5	0.7
cycle-WGAN	8.7	1.5

It is interesting to see that, compared to GZSL, the ZSL results from previous method in the literature are far more competitive, achieving results that are relatively close to ours and the **baseline**. This performance gap between ZSL and GZSL, shown by previous methods, enforces the argument in favor of using generative models to synthesize images from seen and unseen classes to train GZSL models [1,8,9]. As argued throughout this paper, the performance produced by generative models can be improved further with methods that help the training of GANs, such as the cycle consistency loss [10].

In fact, the experiments clearly demonstrate the advantage of using our proposed multi-modal cycle consistency loss in training GANs for GZSL and ZSL. In particular, it is interesting to see that the use of synthetic examples of unseen classes generated by **cycle-(U)WGAN** to train the GZSL classifier provides remarkable improvements over the **baseline**, represented by f-CLSWGAN [1]. The only exception is with the SUN dataset, where the best result is achieved by **cycle-CLSWGAN**. We believe that **cycle-(U)WGAN** is not the top performer on SUN due to the number of classes and the proportion of seen/unseen classes in this dataset. For CUB, FLO and AWA we notice that there is roughly a $(80\%, 20\%)$ ratio between seen and unseen classes. In contrast, SUN has a $(91\%, 9\%)$ ratio between seen and unseen classes. We also notice a sharp increase in the number of classes from 50 to 817 – GAN models tend not to work well with such a large number of classes. Given the wide variety of GZSL datasets available in the field, with different number of classes and seen/unseen proportions, we believe that there is still lots of room for improvement for GZSL models.

Regarding the large-scale study on ImageNet, the results in Table 6 show that the top-1 accuracy classification results for **Baseline** and **cycle-WGAN** are quite low (similarly to the results observed in [1] for several ImageNet splits), but our proposed approach still shows more accurate ZSL and GZSL classification.

An important question about out approach is whether the regularisation succeeds in mapping the generated visual representations back to the semantic space. In order to answer this question, we show in Fig. 3 the evolution of the reconstruction loss ℓ_{REG} in (6) as a function of the number of epochs. In general, the reconstruction loss decreases steadily over training, showing that our model succeeds at such mapping. Another relevant question is if our proposed methods take more or less epochs to converge, compared to the **Baseline** – Fig. 4 shows the classification accuracy of the generated training samples from the seen classes for the proposed models **cycle-WGAN** and **cycle-CLSWGAN**, and also for the **baseline** (note that **cycle-(U)WGAN** is a fine-tuned model

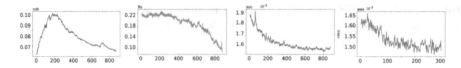

Fig. 3. Evolution of ℓ_{REG} in terms of the number of epochs for CUB, FLO, SUN and AWA.

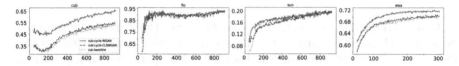

Fig. 4. Convergence of the top-1 accuracy in terms of the number of epochs for the generated training samples from the seen classes for CUB, FLO, SUN and AWA.

from the **cycle-WGAN**, so their loss functions are in fact identical for the seen classes shown in the graph). For three out of four datasets, our proposed **cycle-WGAN** converges faster. However, when the ℓ_{CLS} in included in (7) to form the loss in (8) (transforming **cycle-WGAN** into **cycle-CLSWGAN**), then the convergence of **cycle-CLSWGAN** is comparable to that of the **baseline**. Hence, **cycle-WGAN** tends to converge faster than the **baseline** and **cycle-CLSWGAN**.

7   Conclusions and Future Work

In this paper, we propose a new method to regularize the training of GANs in GZSL models. The main argument explored in the paper is that the use of GANs to generate seen and unseen synthetic examples for training GZSL models has shown clear advantages over previous approaches. However, the unconstrained nature of the generation of samples from unseen classes can produce models that may not work robustly for some unseen classes. Therefore, by constraining the generation of samples from unseen classes, we target to improve the GZSL classification accuracy. Our proposed constraint is motivated by the cycle consistency loss [10], where we enforce that the generated visual representations maps back to their original semantic feature – this represents the multi-modal cycle consistency loss. Experiments show that the use of such loss is clearly advantageous, providing improvements over the current state of the art f-CLSWGAN [1] both in terms of GZSL and ZSL.

As noticed in Sect. 6, GAN-based GZSL approaches offer indisputable advantage over previously proposed methods. However, the reliance on GANs to generate samples from unseen classes is challenging because GANs are notoriously difficult to train, particularly in unconstrained and large scale problems. Therefore, future work in this field should be focused on targeting these problems. In this paper, we provide a solution that addresses the unconstrained problem, but it is clear that other regularization approaches could also be used. In addition, the use of GANs in large scale problems (regarding the number of classes) should also be more intensively studied, particularly when dealing with real-life datasets and scenarios. Therefore, we will focus our future research activities in solving these two issues in GZSL.

References

1. Xian, Y., Lorenz, T., Schiele, B., Akata, Z.: Feature generating networks for zero-shot learning. In: 31st IEEE Conference on Computer Vision and Pattern Recognition (CVPR 2018), Salt Lake City, UT, USA (2018)
2. Xian, Y., Schiele, B., Akata, Z.: Zero-shot learning - the Good, the Bad and the Ugly. In: 30th IEEE Conference on Computer Vision and Pattern Recognition (CVPR 2017), Honolulu, HI, USA, pp. 3077–3086. IEEE Computer Society (2017)
3. Zhang, Z., Saligrama, V.: Zero-shot learning via semantic similarity embedding. In: Proceedings of the IEEE International Conference on Computer Vision,pp. 4166–4174 (2015)
4. Lampert, C.H., Nickisch, H., Harmeling, S.: Attribute-based classification for zero-shot visual object categorization. IEEE Trans. Pattern Anal. Mach. Intell. **36**(3), 453–465 (2014)
5. Qiao, R., Liu, L., Shen, C., van den Hengel, A.: Less is more: zero-shot learning from online textual documents with noise suppression. In: Proceedings of the IEEE Conference on Computer Vision and Pattern Recognition, pp. 2249–2257 (2016)
6. Socher, R., Ganjoo, M., Manning, C.D., Ng, A.: Zero-shot learning through cross-modal transfer. In: Advances in Neural Information Processing Systems, pp. 935–943 (2013)
7. Yu, F.X., Cao, L., Feris, R.S., Smith, J.R., Chang, S.F.: Designing category-level attributes for discriminative visual recognition. In: Proceedings of the IEEE Conference on Computer Vision and Pattern Recognition, pp. 771–778 (2013)
8. Long, Y., Liu, L., Shen, F., Shao, L., Li, X.: Zero-shot learning using synthesised unseen visual data with diffusion regularisation. IEEE Trans. Pattern Anal. Mach. Intell. (2017)
9. Bucher, M., Herbin, S., Jurie, F.: Generating visual representations for zero-shot classification. In: International Conference on Computer Vision (ICCV) Workshops: TASK-CV: Transferring and Adapting Source Knowledge in Computer Vision (2017)
10. Zhu, J.Y., Park, T., Isola, P., Efros, A.A.: Unpaired image-to-image translation using cycle-consistent adversarial networks. In: 2017 IEEE International Conference on Computer Vision (ICCV) (2017)
11. Tran, T., Pham, T., Carneiro, G., Palmer, L., Reid, I.: A Bayesian data augmentation approach for learning deep models. In: Advances in Neural Information Processing Systems, pp. 2794–2803
12. Welinder, P., et al.: Caltech-UCSD birds 200 (2010)
13. Nilsback, M.E., Zisserman, A.: Automated flower classification over a large number of classes. In: Sixth Indian Conference on Computer Vision, Graphics & Image Processing, ICVGIP 2008, pp. 722–729. IEEE (2008)
14. Farhadi, A., Endres, I., Hoiem, D., Forsyth, D.: Describing objects by their attributes. In: IEEE Conference on Computer Vision and Pattern Recognition, CVPR 2009, pp. 1778–1785. IEEE (2009)

15. Deng, J., Dong, W., Socher, R., Li, L.J., Li, K., Fei-Fei, L.: ImageNet: a large-scale hierarchical image database. In: CVPR09 (2009)
16. Chen, L., Zhang, H., Xiao, J., Liu, W., Chang, S.F.: Zero-shot visual recognition using semantics-preserving adversarial embedding networks. In: The IEEE Conference on Computer Vision and Pattern Recognition (CVPR), June 2018
17. Annadani, Y., Biswas, S.: Preserving semantic relations for zero-shot learning. In: The IEEE Conference on Computer Vision and Pattern Recognition (CVPR), June 2018
18. Akata, Z., Perronnin, F., Harchaoui, Z., Schmid, C.: Label-embedding for image classification. IEEE Trans. Pattern Anal. Mach. Intell. **38**(7), 1425–1438 (2016)
19. Frome, A., Corrado, G.S., Shlens, J., Bengio, S., Dean, J., Mikolov, T., et al.: DeVISE: a deep visual-semantic embedding model. In: Advances in Neural Information Processing Systems, pp. 2121–2129 (2013)
20. Akata, Z., Reed, S., Walter, D., Lee, H., Schiele, B.: Evaluation of output embeddings for fine-grained image classification. In: Proceedings of the IEEE Conference on Computer Vision and Pattern Recognition, pp. 2927–2936 (2015)
21. Romera-Paredes, B., Torr, P.: An embarrassingly simple approach to zero-shot learning. In: International Conference on Machine Learning, pp. 2152–2161 (2015)
22. Elyor Kodirov, T.X., Gong, S.: Semantic autoencoder for zero-shot learning. In: IEEE CVPR 2017 (2017)
23. Xian, Y., Akata, Z., Sharma, G., Nguyen, Q., Hein, M., Schiele, B.: Latent embeddings for zero-shot classification. In: Proceedings of the IEEE Conference on Computer Vision and Pattern Recognition, pp. 69–77 (2016)
24. Norouzi, M., et al.: Zero-shot learning by convex combination of semantic embeddings (2014)
25. Changpinyo, S., Chao, W.L., Gong, B., Sha, F.: Synthesized classifiers for zero-shot learning. In: Proceedings of the IEEE Conference on Computer Vision and Pattern Recognition, pp. 5327–5336 (2016)
26. He, K., Zhang, X., Ren, S., Sun, J.: Deep residual learning for image recognition. In: Proceedings of the IEEE Conference on Computer Vision and Pattern Recognition, pp. 770–778 (2016)
27. Mikolov, T., Sutskever, I., Chen, K., Corrado, G.S., Dean, J.: Distributed representations of words and phrases and their compositionality. In: Advances in Neural Information Processing Systems, pp. 3111–3119 (2013)
28. Yan, X., Yang, J., Sohn, K., Lee, H.: Attribute2Image: conditional image generation from visual attributes. In: Leibe, B., Matas, J., Sebe, N., Welling, M. (eds.) ECCV 2016 Part IV. LNCS, vol. 9908, pp. 776–791. Springer, Cham (2016). https://doi.org/10.1007/978-3-319-46493-0_47
29. Arjovsky, M., Chintala, S., Bottou, L.: Wasserstein GAN. arXiv preprint arXiv:1701.07875 (2017)
30. Lampert, C.H., Nickisch, H., Harmeling, S.: Learning to detect unseen object classes by between-class attribute transfer. In: IEEE Conference on Computer Vision and Pattern Recognition, CVPR 2009, pp. 951–958, June 2009
31. Reed, S., Akata, Z., Lee, H., Schiele, B.: Learning deep representations of fine-grained visual descriptions. In: Proceedings of the IEEE Conference on Computer Vision and Pattern Recognition, pp. 49–58 (2016)
32. Wang, P., Liu, L., Shen, C., Huang, Z., van den Hengel, A., Shen, H.T.: Multi-attention network for one shot learning. In: 2017 IEEE Conference on Computer Vision and Pattern Recognition, CVPR, pp. 22–25 (2017)

33. Xiao, J., Hays, J., Ehinger, K.A., Oliva, A., Torralba, A.: SUN database: large-scale scene recognition from abbey to zoo. In: 2010 IEEE conference on Computer Vision and Pattern Recognition (CVPR), pp. 3485–3492, IEEE (2010)

34. Maas, A.L., Hannun, A.Y., Ng, A.Y.: Rectifier nonlinearities improve neural network acoustic models. Proc. ICML. **30**, 3 (2013)

35. Nair, V., Hinton, G.E.: Rectified linear units improve restricted Boltzmann machines. In: Proceedings of the 27th International Conference on Machine Learning (ICML 2010), pp. 807–814 (2010)

36. Abadi, M., et al.: TensorFlow: a system for large-scale machine learning. OSDI **16**, 265–283 (2016)

Key-Word-Aware Network for Referring Expression Image Segmentation

Hengcan Shi, Hongliang Li$^{(\boxtimes)}$, Fanman Meng, and Qingbo Wu

School of Information and Communication Engineering,
University of Electronic Science and Technology of China, Chengdu, China
shihc@std.uestc.edu.cn, {hlli,fmmeng,qbwu}@uestc.edu.cn

Abstract. Referring expression image segmentation aims to segment
out the object referred by a natural language query expression. Without considering the specific properties of visual and textual information, existing works usually deal with this task by directly feeding a
foreground/background classifier with cascaded image and text features,
which are extracted from each image region and the whole query, respectively. On the one hand, they ignore that each word in a query expression makes different contributions to identify the desired object, which
requires a differential treatment in extracting text feature. On the other
hand, the relationships of different image regions are not considered as
well, even though they are greatly important to eliminate the undesired
foreground object in accordance with specific query. To address aforementioned issues, in this paper, we propose a key-word-aware network,
which contains a query attention model and a key-word-aware visual context model. In extracting text features, the query attention model attends
to assign higher weights for the words which are more important for
identifying object. Meanwhile, the key-word-aware visual context model
describes the relationships among different image regions, according to
corresponding query. Our proposed method outperforms state-of-the-art
methods on two referring expression image segmentation databases.

Keywords: Referring expression image segmentation
Key word extraction · Query attention · Key-word-aware visual context

1   Introduction

Image segmentation expects to segment out objects of interest from an image,
which is a fundamental step towards high-level vision tasks, such as object
extraction [14,23,25], image captioning [21,32,34] and visual question answering [21,22,35]. This paper focuses on referring expression image segmentation,
in which the objects of interest are referred by natural language expressions,
as shown in Fig. 1. Beyond traditional semantic segmentation, referring expression image segmentation needs to analyze both the image and natural language,
which is a more challenging task.

© Springer Nature Switzerland AG 2018
V. Ferrari et al. (Eds.): ECCV 2018, LNCS 11210, pp. 38–54, 2018.
https://doi.org/10.1007/978-3-030-01231-1_3

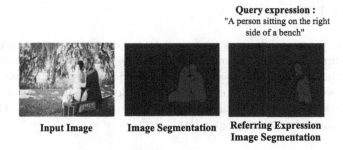

Fig. 1. Example of referring expression image segmentation task. Different from traditional image segmentation, referring expression image segmentation aims at segmenting out the object referred by a natural language query expression.

Previous works [9,10,18] formulate referring expression image segmentation task as a region-wise foreground/background classification problem. They combine each image region feature with whole query feature [9,10] or every word feature [18] to classify the image region. However, each word in a query expression makes different contributions to identify the desired object, which requires a differential treatment in extracting text feature. Extracting key words is helpful to suppress the noise in the query and to highlight the desired objects. In addition, existing methods also ignore the visual context among different image regions. Visual context is important to localize and recognize objects. In Fig. 1 we illustrate an example, which includes two foreground objects, i.e., the bride and the groom. It is clear that the groom is on the right side of the bench, which is important to match the query expression.

In this paper, we propose a key-word-aware network (KWAN) that extracts key words for each image region and models the key-word-aware visual context among multiple image regions in accordance with the natural language query. Firstly, we use a convolutional neural network (CNN) and a recurrent neural network (RNN) to encode the features of every image region and every word, respectively. Based on these features, we then find out the key words for each image region by a query attention model. Next, a key-word-aware visual context model is used to model the visual context among multiple image regions in accordance with corresponding key words. Finally, we classify each image region based on extracted visual features, key-word-aware visual context features and corresponding key word features. We verify the proposed method on the Refer-ItGame and Google-Ref datasets. The results show that our method outperforms previous state-of-the-art methods and achieves the best IoU and precision.

This paper is organized as follows. We introduce the related work in Sect. 2. In Sect. 3, we detail our proposed method for referring expression image segmentation. Experimental results are reported in Sect. 4 to validate the effectiveness of our method. Finally, Sect. 5 concludes this paper.

2   Related Work

In summary, there are three categories of works related with the task of this paper. The first is semantic segmentation, which is one of the most classic tasks in image segmentation and a foundation for referring expression image segmentation. The second is referring expression visual localization, which also needs to search object in an given image from natural language expressions. The third is referring expression image segmentation.

Semantic Segmentation. Semantic segmentation technologies have developed quickly in recent years, on which convolutional neural network (CNN)-based methods achieve state-of-the-art performance. The CNN-based semantic segmentation methods can be mainly divided into two types. The first is hybrid proposal-classifier models [1, 4–7], which first generate a number of proposals from the input image, and then segment out the foreground object in each proposal. The second is fully convolutional networks (FCNs) [2, 20, 27, 36], which segment the whole image end-to-end, without any pre-processing. Some methods [3, 15, 16, 19, 28, 39] leveraged visual context model to boost the semantic segmentation performance, which models the relationships among multiple image regions based on their spatial positions. Wang et al. [31] built an interaction between semantic segmentation and natural language. They extract an object relationship distribution from natural language descriptions, and then use the extracted distribution to constrain the object categories in semantic segmentation predictions. These semantic segmentation methods are foundations for referring expression image segmentation task.

Referring Expression Visual Localization. Referring expression visual localization expects to localize regions in an image from natural language expressions. The goal of this task is to find bounding boxes [11, 24, 26, 37, 38] or attention regions [21, 22, 32, 33, 35] referred by natural language queries. Methods in [11, 24, 26, 37, 38] first restored the natural language expressions from a number of pre-extracted proposals, and then took the proposal with the highest restoration score as the referred object. Methods proposed by [21, 22, 32, 33, 35] used visual attention models to measure the importance of each image region for image captioning [21, 32] or visual question answering [21, 22, 35] task. The most important regions were deemed as attention regions. The similarity between these localization methods and referring expression image segmentation methods is that they both need to find out objects referred by natural language queries. However, these localization methods only focus on generating bounding boxes or coarse attention maps, while referring expression image segmentation methods aim at obtaining fine segmentation masks.

Referring Expression Image Segmentation. Referring expression image segmentation have attracted increasing researchers' interest [9, 10, 18] in recent

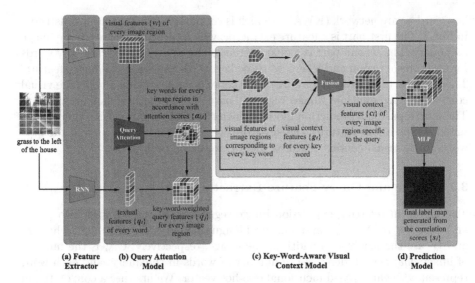

Fig. 2. Our proposed key-word-aware Network (KWAN) consists of four parts: (a) a CNN and an RNN that encode the features of every image region and every word in the nature language query, (b) a query attention model that extracts key words for each image region and use extracted key words to weight the original query, (c) a key-word-aware visual context model that models visual context based on corresponding key words, (d) a prediction model that predict the segmentation results based on visual features, key-word-aware visual context features and key-word-weight query features.

years. Beyond referring expression visual localization and semantic segmentation, referring expression image segmentation aims at generating fine segmentation masks from natural language queries. Hu *et al.* [9,10] combined the features of the natural language query and each image to determine whether the image region belongs to the referred object. Liu *et al.* [18] developed the referring expression image segmentation technologies. Instead of directly using the feature of whole query, they concatenated the features of each word and each image region, and then used a multimodal LSTM to integrate these concatenated features. However, on one hand, these methods ignore that each word in a query makes different contributions to the segmentation. On the other hand, many queries need to compare multiple image regions, while these methods only separately tackle each image region. In contrast to previous methods, we propose a key-word-aware network, which extracts key words to suppress the noise in queries, and models key-word-aware visual context among multiple image regions to better localize and recognize objects.

3   Proposed Method

Overview. Given an image and a natural language query, our goal is to segment out the object referred by the query from the image. To this end, we propose a key-word-aware network (KWAN), which is composed of four parts as illustrated in Fig. 2. The first part is a feature extractor, which encodes features of the image and query. The second part is a query attention model, which extracts key words for each image region and leverages these key words to weight the query feature. The third part is a key-word-aware visual context model, which models the visual context among multiple image regions based on the natural language query. The fourth part is a prediction model, which generates segmentation predictions based on the image features, the key-word-weighted query features and the key-word-aware visual context features. Below, we detail each part.

3.1 Image and Query Feature Extractor

The inputs in referring expression image segmentation task contain two parts: an image $I \in R^{H \times W \times C_{im}}$ and a natural language query $X \in R^{C_{text} \times T}$, where H and W are the height and width of the image, respectively; C_{im} is the number of image channels; T denotes the number of words in the query; and each word represented by an C_{text}-dimensional one-hot vector. We first use a convolutional neural network (CNN) to extract a feature map of the input image as follows:

$$F = CNN(I)$$
$$= \{f_1, f_2, ..., f_{hw}\} \tag{1}$$

where $F \in R^{h \times w \times C_f}$ is the extracted feature map; h and w are the height and width of feature map, respectively; and C_f is the feature dimension. In the feature map F, each feature vector $f_i \in R^{C_f}$ encodes the appearance and semantic information of the i-th image region.

Since the referring expression image segmentation task also needs spatial position information, we extract a position feature from the spatial coordinates of the i-th image region:

$$p_i = [x_i, y_i] \tag{2}$$

where $p_i \in R^2$ is the position feature of the i-th image region, which is concatenated by the normalized horizontal and vertical coordinates x_i and y_i. The operator $[\cdot, \cdot]$ represents the concatenation of features. Therefore, the final visual feature of the i-th image region can be obtained as follows:

$$v_i = [f_i, p_i] \tag{3}$$

where $v_i \in R^{Cv}$ is a Cv-dimensional visual feature vector of the i-th image region, and $Cv = C_f + 2$. The visual feature contains appearance, semantic and spatial position information of the image region.

We use a recurrent neural network (RNN) to encode the feature of natural language query X as follows:

$$Q = RNN(W_e X)$$
$$= \{q_1, q_2, ..., q_T\} \tag{4}$$

where $Q \in R^{C_q \times T}$ is the encoded feature matrix of the query X, in which each feature vector $q_t \in R^{C_q}$ encodes the textual semantic and contextual information for the t-th word. $W_e \in R^{C_e \times C_{text}}$ is a word embedding matrix to reduce the dimensionality of the word features.

3.2   Query Attention Model

After the feature encoding, we then extract key words by a query attention model. For the i-th image region, the query attention can be captured as follows:

$$z_{i,t} = w_z^T tanh(W_q q_t + W_v v_i) \tag{5}$$

$$\alpha_{i,t} = \frac{exp(z_{i,t})}{\sum_{r=1}^T exp(z_{i,r})} \tag{6}$$

where $W_q \in R^{C_z \times C_q}$, $W_v \in R^{C_z \times C_v}$ and $w_z \in R^{C_z}$ are parameters in query attention model; $\alpha_{i,t} \in [0,1]$ is the query attention score of the t-th word for the i-th image region, and $\sum_{t=1}^T \alpha_{i,t} = 1$. A high score $\alpha_{i,t}$ means that the t-th word is important for i-th image region, i.e., word t is a key word for image region i.

Based on the learned query attention scores, the feature of query can be weighted as follows:

$$\hat{q}_i = \sum_{t=1}^T \alpha_{i,t} q_t \tag{7}$$

where $\hat{q}_i \in R^{C_q}$ is the weighted query feature for the i-th image region. In the weighted query feature, words are no longer equally important. Key words make more important contributions.

3.3   Key-Word-Aware Visual Context Model

The key-word-aware visual context model learns the context among multiple image regions for the natural language query. Towards this goal, we first aggregate the visual messages of image regions for each key word:

$$m_t = \begin{cases} \dfrac{\sum_{i=1}^{hw} v_i u(\alpha_{i,t} - Thr)}{\sum_{i=1}^{hw} u(\alpha_{i,t} - Thr)}, & \max\limits_{i=1,...,hw}(\alpha_{i,t}) \geq Thr \\ 0, & otherwise \end{cases} \tag{8}$$

where $m_t \in R^{C_v}$ is the aggregated visual feature vector, and $u(\cdot)$ represents an unit step function. Thr is a threshold to select out the key word. $\alpha_{i,t} \geq Thr$ implies that the t-th word is a key word for the i-th image region. If the t-th word is a key word for at least one image region (i.e., $\max_{i=1,...,hw}(\alpha_{i,t}) \geq Thr$), we average the visual features of image regions which take this word as a key word. Otherwise, the t-th word is a non-key word for whole image, hence the aggregated visual feature m_t is 0. The threshold Thr is set to $1/T$, since $\sum_{t=1}^T \alpha_{i,t} = 1$.

Based on the aggregated visual messages, we then use a fully-connected layer to learn visual context:

$$g_t = ReLU(W_g m_t + b_g) \tag{9}$$

where $g_t \in R^{C_g}$ is the learned visual context feature specific to the t-th word, $W_g \in R^{C_g \times C_v}$ and $b_g \in R^{C_g}$ are the parameters in the fully-connected layer, and ReLU denotes the rectified linear unit activation function.

Finally, we fuse the visual context features specific to each key words into the one specific to whole query as follows:

$$c_i = \sum_{t=1}^{T} g_t u(\alpha_{i,t} - Thr) \tag{10}$$

where $c_i \in R^{C_g}$ is the fused visual context feature specific to the query for the i-th image region.

3.4 Prediction Model and Loss Function

Once we extract the visual feature v_i, the key-word-weighted query feature $\hat{q}_i$ and the key-word-aware visual context feature c_i, a correlation score between the query and each image region can be obtained as follows:

$$s_i = sigmoid(MLP([\hat{q}_i, v_i, c_i])) \tag{11}$$

where MLP denotes a multi-layer perceptron, and sigmoid function are used to normalize the score. $s_i \in (0,1)$ is the normalized correlation score between i-th image region and the natural language query. A high correlation score means that current image region is highly correlative with the query, i.e., this image region is belong to referred foreground object.

Scores of all image regions together form a label map. We upsample the label map into original image size as the segmentation result. A pixel-wise cross entropy loss is used to constrain the training:

$$Loss = -\frac{1}{N} \sum_{n=1}^{N} \frac{1}{H^{(n)} W^{(n)}} \sum_{j=1}^{H^{(n)} W^{(n)}} [y_j^{(n)} \times log s_j^{(n)} \\ + (1 - y_j^{(n)}) \times log(1 - s_j^{(n)})] \tag{12}$$

where N is the number of images in total training set; $H^{(n)}$ and $W^{(n)}$ are the height and width of the n-th image, respectively; $s_j^{(n)}$ denotes the correlation score of the j-th pixel in the n-th image; and $y_j^{(n)} \in \{0,1\}$ is the label indicating whether pixel j belongs to referred object.

4 Experiments

We conduct experiments to evaluate our method on two challenging referring expression image segmentation datasets, including the ReferItGame dataset and the Google-Ref dataset. Objective and subjective results are reported in this section.

Evaluation Metrics. We adopt two typical image segmentation metrics: the intersection-over-union (IoU) and the precision (Pr). The IoU is a ratio between intersection and union areas of segmentation results and ground truth. The precision is the percentage of correctly segmented objects in the total dataset. The correctly segmented objects are defined as objects whose IoU passes a pre-set threshold. We use five different thresholds in experiments: 0.5, 0.6, 0.7, 0.8, 0.9. The precisions with these thresholds are represented by Pr@0.5, Pr@0.6, Pr@0.7, Pr@0.8, Pr@0.9, respectively.

Implementation Details. The proposed method can be implemented with any CNN and RNN. Since state-of-the-art methods [9,18] often choose VGG16 [30] or Deeplab101 [2] as their CNN and use LSTM [8] as their RNN, to fairly compare our method with them, we also implement the proposed method with these CNN and RNN in our experiments. The dimensions of CNN and RNN features are both set to 1000 (i.e., $C_f = C_q = 1000$). The maximum number T of words in a query is 20, thus the key word threshold Thr in the key-word-aware visual context model is set to 0.05 (i.e., $1/T$). We train the proposed method in two stages. The first stage is low resolution training. In this stage, the predictions are not upsampled, and the loss is calculated with down-sampled ground truth. The second stage is high resolution training, in which the predictions are upsampled into the original image size. The model is trained with Adaptive Moment Estimation (Adam) in all stages, and the learning rate is set to 0.0001. We initialize the CNN from the weights pre-trained on ImageNet dataset [29], and initialize other parts from random weights. All experiments are conducted based on the Caffe [12] toolbox on a single Nvidia GTX Titan X GPU with 12G memory.

Table 1. Comparison with state-of-the-art methods on the ReferItGame testing.

Method	IoU	Pr@0.5	Pr@0.6	Pr@0.7	Pr@0.8	Pr@0.9
VGG16						
[9]	48.03%	34.02%	26.71%	19.32%	11.63%	3.92%
[18]	48.84%	**35.79%**	27.53%	20.90%	11.72%	3.83%
Ours	**52.19%**	35.61%	**28.50%**	**21.85%**	**12.87%**	**4.83%**
Deeplab101						
[9]	56.83%	43.86%	35.75%	26.65%	16.75%	6.47%
[18]	57.34%	44.33%	36.13%	27.20%	16.99%	6.43%
Ours	**59.09%**	**45.87%**	**39.80%**	**32.82%**	**23.81%**	**11.79%**

4.1   Results on ReferItGame Dataset

The ReferItGame dataset [13] is a public dataset, with 20000 natural images and 130525 natural language expressions. Totalling 96654 foreground regions

Query Expression : "bottom of picture (shady area)"

Query Expression : "tree above statue"

Query Expression : "ground to the right of the child"

Query Expression : "couple in the middle"

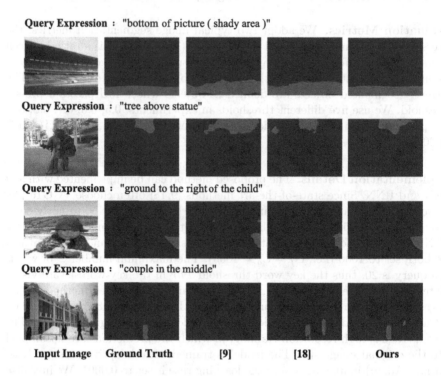

Input Image   Ground Truth   [9]   [18]   Ours

Fig. 3. Referring expression image segmentation results on the ReferItGame testing. Left to right: input images, ground truth, the segmentation results from [9], [18] and our method, respectively. All methods are implemented with *Deeplab101*. In query expressions, the black words mean key words our method predicted for foreground regions (red regions). (Color figure online)

are referred by these expressions, which contain not only objects but also stuff, such as *snow, mountain* and so on. The dataset are split into training, validation and testing sets, containing 9000, 1000, and 10000 images, respectively. Similar to [9,18], we use training and validation sets to train, and use testing set to test our method.

The results are summarized in Table 1. All methods do not use additional training data and post processing like CRF. State-of-the-art methods in [9,18] equally deal with every word in the natural language expressions and do not take into account the visual context. It can be observed from Table 1 that our proposed method outperforms these methods in terms of both IoU and precision, whether implemented with VGG16 or Deeplab101. Moreover, under the precision metric, with higher thresholds, our method achieves more improvements. This superior performance demonstrates the effectiveness of selectively extracting key words for every image region and modeling the key-word-aware visual context.

We depict some subjective referring expression image segmentation results on the ReferItGame dataset in Fig. 3. From the first and third images in Fig. 3, it can be seen that existing methods do not well segment out some objects when the query expression is too long or contains some noise, such as round brackets. Our method selects key words and filters out useless information in the query, therefore can successfully segment out the referred objects in these images. Moreover, it can be observed that previous method localize and segment some desired objects wrongly when the query needs to compare multiple objects, such as the second and fourth images in Fig. 3. A major reason is that previous methods ignore the visual context among objects. Our method can generate better segmentation results by modeling the key-word-aware visual context.

Table 2. Comparison with state-of-the-art methods on the Google-Ref validation.

Method	IoU	Pr@0.5	Pr@0.6	Pr@0.7	Pr@0.8	Pr@0.9
VGG16						
[9]	28.14%	15.25%	8.37%	3.75%	1.29%	0.06%
[18]	28.60%	16.70%	8.77%	4.96%	1.79%	0.38%
Ours	**31.36%**	**17.71%**	**11.12%**	**7.90%**	**3.69%**	**1.07%**
Deeplab101						
[9]	33.08%	25.66%	18.23%	10.82%	4.17%	0.64%
[18]	34.40%	26.19%	18.46%	10.68%	4.28%	0.73%
Ours	**36.92%**	**27.85%**	**21.01%**	**13.42%**	**6.60%**	**1.97%**

4.2 Results on Google-Ref Dataset

The Google-Ref dataset [24] contains 26711 natural images with 54822 objects extracted from the MS COCO dataset [17]. There are 104560 expressions referring to these objects, and the average length of these expressions is longer than that in the ReferItGame dataset. We use the split from [24], which chose 44822 and 5000 objects for training and validation, respectively.

The objective and subjective results are shown in Table 2 and Fig. 4, respectively. From Table 2, it can be seen that our method outperforms previous methods under the both two metrics, IoU and precision. This demonstrates the effectiveness of our method. From Fig. 4, it can be observed that previous methods fail to segment some objects when the queries are too long, such as the first and second images in Fig. 4. In addition, previous methods find some wrong object instances when the queries need to compare different instances with the same class, such as the third and fourth images in Fig. 4. The proposed method can successfully segment out these objects, benefiting from the key word extraction and the key-word-aware visual context.

4.3 Discussion

Ablation Study. To verify the effectiveness of each part in our method, a number of ablation studies are conducted on the ReferItGame dataset. We compare five different models as follows:

Query Expression : "A girl with a cell phone"

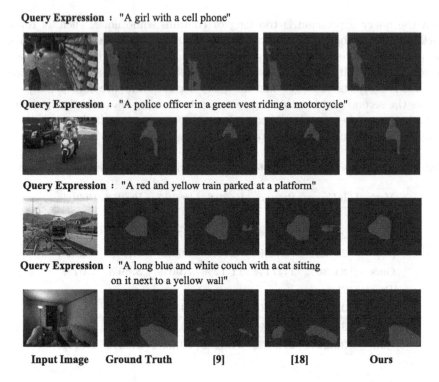

Query Expression : "A police officer in a green vest riding a motorcycle"

Query Expression : "A red and yellow train parked at a platform"

Query Expression : "A long blue and white couch with a cat sitting on it next to a yellow wall"

| Input Image | Ground Truth | [9] | [18] | Ours |

Fig. 4. Referring expression image segmentation results on the Google-Ref validation. Left to right: input images, ground truth, the segmentation results from [9], [18] and our method, respectively. All methods are implemented with *Deeplab101*. In query expressions, the black words mean key words our method predicted for foreground regions (red regions). (Color figure online)

1. **Baseline:** We take the method in [9] as the baseline model, which classify each image region with whole query feature and do not model visual context.
2. **Key-word-model:** Instead of using whole query, we extract key words for every image region, but the visual context is not used in this model.
3. **Context-model:** We extract key words for every image region and leverage spatial pyramid pooling to model visual context, which is only based on the visual information.
4. **Full-model:** Full-model extracts key words for every image region and models key-word-aware visual context, which is not only based on vision but also the nature language query.
5. **Soft-model:** Soft-model also extracts key words and models key-word-aware visual context. In this model, we use a soft attention model to aggregate the context instead of the unit step function described in Sect. 3.3.

The results of ablation studies are shown in Table 3. It can be seen that (1) using key words is better than using whole query; (2) visual context is effective to improve the performance; (3) compared with the context only based on vision,

Query Expression: "laughing person in black shirt"

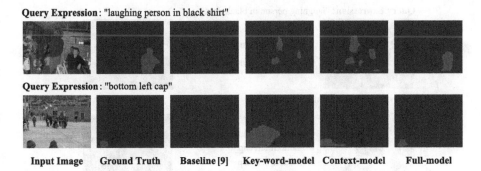

Query Expression: "bottom left cap"

Input Image   Ground Truth   Baseline [9]   Key-word-model   Context-model   Full-model

Fig. 5. Visualized results of the ablation studies on the ReferItGame testing. Left to right: input images, ground truth, the segmentation results from baseline model [9], key-word-model, context-model and full-model, respectively. All models are implemented with *VGG16*.

Table 3. Comparison of different ablation models on the ReferItGame testing. "Soft" means that the key-word-aware visual context is calculated by a soft attention model instead of the unit step function. All models are implemented with *VGG16*.

Method	Query attention	Visual context	Key-word-aware Visual Context	IoU
Baseline [9]				48.03%
Key-word-model	✓			50.28%
Context-model	✓	✓		51.01%
Full-model	✓		✓	**52.19%**
Soft-model	✓		soft	51.93%

key-word-aware visual context can further improve the referring expression image segmentation performance; (4) the performance of soft-attention-based model is comparable with that of the unit-step-function-based model. However, the computation cost of soft attention is much higher than that of unit step function. Therefore, we use the unit step function instead of the soft attention.

We visualize some results of different ablation models in Fig. 5. It can observed that the baseline model almost does not predict any foreground object region for some queries, due to that it fails to mine semantic from these query expressions. Key-word-model mines key words from the queries, thus it generates some foreground predictions. However, key-word-model still cannot segment out the referred objects, because it separately classify each image region, while these queries need to compare multiple regions. Context-model improves the segmentation results by modeling visual context among image regions, but it also fails to segment out these objects. A major reason is that the context-model ignores the relationship between visual context and the natural language queries. Our full-model extracts key words and models key-word-aware visual context, therefore successfully segments out these objects.

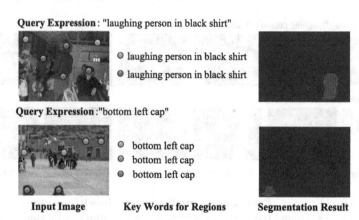

Fig. 6. Visualization of key words for some image regions on the ReferItGame testing. Left to right: input images, key words (black words) for image regions (red, green and blue points), and segmentation results from our full model implemented with *VGG16* (Color figure online).

Table 4. IoU for queries of different lengths on the ReferItGame testing. All methods are implemented with *VGG16*.

IoU⟍Length Method	1	2-3	4-6	7-20
[9]	62.64%	44.48%	34.56%	20.09%
[18]	63.19%	46.08%	35.43%	22.25%
Ours	**65.59%**	**48.03%**	**38.03%**	**26.61%**

Key Word. Tables 4 and 5 show the segmentation performance for queries of different lengths. It can be observed that compared with existing methods, the proposed method yields more gains when deals with longer queries. This demonstrates that using key words instead of whole queries is effective, especially when tackling long queries. Figure 6 depicts visualized examples of extracted key words for some image regions. For example, in the second image in Fig. 6, only according to the word *cap*, the green regions can be eliminated from the desired foreground object, because they are not caps.

Failure Case. Some failure cases are shown in Fig. 7. One type of failures occurs when queries contain low-frequency or new words. For example, in the first image in Fig. 7, *blanket* rarely appears in the training data. As a result, our method does not segment out the *blanket*, although it has already highlighted the *right white* regions in the *background*. Another case is that our method sometimes fails to segment out small objects. For instance, in the second image in Fig. 7, our method highlights the *left* of the *background*, but does not segment out the

Table 5. IoU for different length queries on Google-Ref validation. All methods are implemented with *VGG16*.

IoU \ Length Method	1-5	6-7	8-10	11-20
[9]	28.67%	23.69%	23.44%	23.22%
[18]	31.05%	27.32%	26.23%	25.25%
Ours	**34.15%**	**28.79%**	**29.90%**	**28.33%**

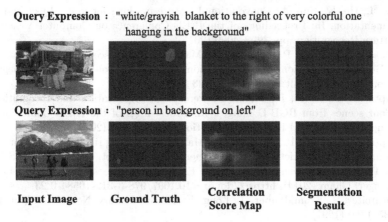

Query Expression : "white/grayish blanket to the right of very colorful one hanging in the background"

Query Expression : "person in background on left"

| Input Image | Ground Truth | Correlation Score Map | Segmentation Result |

Fig. 7. Failure cases on the ReferItGame dataset. Left to right: input images, ground truth, correlation score maps and segmentation results from our method implemented with *VGG16*.

person, because it is very small. This problem may be alleviated by enlarging the scale of input images.

5   Conclusion

This paper has presented key-word-aware network (KWAN) for referring expression image segmentation. KWAN extracts key words by a query attention model, to suppress the noise in the query and to highlight the desired objects. Moreover, a key-word-aware visual context model is used to learn the relationships of multiple visual objects based on the nature language query, which is important to localize and recognize objects. Our method outperforms state-of-the-art methods on two common referring expression image segmentation databases. In the future, we plan to improve the capacity of the network to tackle objects of different sizes.

Acknowledgement. This work was supported in part by National Natural Science Foundation of China (No. 61525102, 61601102 and 61502084).

References

1. Caesar, H., Uijlings, J., Ferrari, V.: Region-based semantic segmentation with end-to-end training. In: Leibe, B., Matas, J., Sebe, N., Welling, M. (eds.) ECCV 2016 Part I. LNCS, vol. 9905, pp. 381–397. Springer, Cham (2016). https://doi.org/10.1007/978-3-319-46448-0_23
2. Chen, L.C., Papandreou, G., Kokkinos, I., et al.: Deeplab: Semantic image segmentation with deep convolutional nets, atrous convolution, and fully connected CRFs. IEEE Trans. Pattern Anal. Mach. Intell. **40**(4), 834–848 (2018)
3. Chen, L.C., Papandreou, G., Schroff, F., Adam, H.: Rethinking atrous convolution for semantic image segmentation. CoRR (2017)
4. Dai, J., He, K., Sun, J.: Convolutional feature masking for joint object and stuff segmentation. In: Proceedings of the IEEE Conference on Computer Vision and Pattern Recognition, pp. 3992–4000 (2015)
5. Gupta, S., Arbeláez, P., Girshick, R., Malik, J.: Indoor scene understanding with RGB-D images: bottom-up segmentation, object detection and semantic segmentation. Int. J. Comput. Vis. **112**(2), 133–149 (2015)
6. Gupta, S., Arbelaez, P., Malik, J.: Perceptual organization and recognition of indoor scenes from RGB-D images. In: Proceedings of the IEEE Conference on Computer Vision and Pattern Recognition, pp. 564–571 (2013)
7. Gupta, S., Girshick, R., Arbeláez, P., Malik, J.: Learning rich features from RGB-D images for object detection and segmentation. In: Fleet, D., Pajdla, T., Schiele, B., Tuytelaars, T. (eds.) ECCV 2014 Part VII. LNCS, vol. 8695, pp. 345–360. Springer, Cham (2014). https://doi.org/10.1007/978-3-319-10584-0_23
8. Hochreiter, S., Schmidhuber, J.: Long short-term memory. Neural Comput. **9**(8), 1735–1780 (1997)
9. Hu, R., Rohrbach, M., Darrell, T.: Segmentation from natural language expressions. In: European Conference on Computer Vision (2016)
10. Hu, R., Rohrbach, M., Venugopalan, S., Darrell, T.: Utilizing large scale vision and text datasets for image segmentation from referring expressions. CoRR (2016)
11. Hu, R., Xu, H., Rohrbach, M., Feng, J., Saenko, K., Darrell, T.: Natural language object retrieval. In: Computer Vision and Pattern Recognition, pp. 4555–4564 (2016)
12. Jia, Y., et al.: Caffe: convolutional architecture for fast feature embedding. In: Proceedings of the 22nd ACM International Conference on Multimedia, pp. 675–678. ACM (2014)
13. Kazemzadeh, S., Ordonez, V., Matten, M., Berg, T.: ReferitGame: referring to objects in photographs of natural scenes. In: Conference on Empirical Methods in Natural Language Processing, pp. 787–798 (2014)
14. Li, H., Meng, F., Wu, Q., Luo, B.: Unsupervised multiclass region cosegmentation via ensemble clustering and energy minimization. IEEE Trans. Circuits Syst. Video Technol. **24**(5), 789–801 (2014)
15. Li, Z., Gan, Y., Liang, X., Yu, Y., Cheng, H., Lin, L.: LSTM-CF: unifying context modeling and fusion with LSTMs for RGB-D scene labeling. In: Leibe, B., Matas, J., Sebe, N., Welling, M. (eds.) ECCV 2016 Part II. LNCS, vol. 9906, pp. 541–557. Springer, Cham (2016). https://doi.org/10.1007/978-3-319-46475-6_34
16. Liang, X., Shen, X., Feng, J., Lin, L., Yan, S.: Semantic object parsing with graph LSTM. In: Leibe, B., Matas, J., Sebe, N., Welling, M. (eds.) ECCV 2016 Part I. LNCS, vol. 9905, pp. 125–143. Springer, Cham (2016). https://doi.org/10.1007/978-3-319-46448-0_8

17. Lin, T.-Y., et al.: Microsoft COCO: common objects in context. In: Fleet, D., Pajdla, T., Schiele, B., Tuytelaars, T. (eds.) ECCV 2014 Part V. LNCS, vol. 8693, pp. 740–755. Springer, Cham (2014). https://doi.org/10.1007/978-3-319-10602-1_48
18. Liu, C., Lin, Z., Shen, X., Yang, J., Lu, X., Yuille, A.: Recurrent multimodal interaction for referring image segmentation. In: IEEE International Conference on Computer Vision (2017)
19. Liu, W., Rabinovich, A., Berg, A.C.: ParseNet: looking wider to see better. CoRR abs/1506.04579 (2015)
20. Long, J., Shelhamer, E., Darrell, T.: Fully convolutional networks for semantic segmentation. In: Proceedings of the IEEE Conference on Computer Vision and Pattern Recognition, pp. 3431–3440 (2015)
21. Lu, J., Xiong, C., Parikh, D., Socher, R.: Knowing when to look: adaptive attention via a visual sentinel for image captioning. In: Proceedings of the IEEE Conference on Computer Vision and Pattern Recognition (2016)
22. Lu, J., Yang, J., Batra, D., Parikh, D.: Hierarchical question-image co-attention for visual question answering. In: NIPS (2016)
23. Luo, B., Li, H., Meng, F., Wu, Q., Huang, C.: Video object segmentation via global consistency aware query strategy. IEEE Trans. Multimed. **PP**(99), 1 (2017)
24. Mao, J., Huang, J., Toshev, A., Camburu, O., Yuille, A., Murphy, K.: Generation and comprehension of unambiguous object descriptions. In: CVPR (2016)
25. Meng, F., Li, H., Wu, Q., Luo, B., Huang, C., Ngan, K.: Globally measuring the similarity of superpixels by binary edge maps for superpixel clustering. IEEE Trans. Circuits Syst. Video Technol. **PP**(99), 1 (2016)
26. Nagaraja, V.K., Morariu, V.I., Davis, L.S.: Modeling context between objects for referring expression understanding. In: Leibe, B., Matas, J., Sebe, N., Welling, M. (eds.) ECCV 2016 Part IV. LNCS, vol. 9908, pp. 792–807. Springer, Cham (2016). https://doi.org/10.1007/978-3-319-46493-0_48
27. Noh, H., Hong, S., Han, B.: Learning deconvolution network for semantic segmentation. In: Proceedings of the IEEE International Conference on Computer Vision, pp. 1520–1528 (2015)
28. Peng, Z., Zhang, R., Liang, X., Liu, X., Lin, L.: Geometric scene parsing with hierarchical LSTM. In: Proceedings of the Twenty-Fifth International Joint Conference on Artificial Intelligence, pp. 3439–3445 (2016)
29. Russakovsky, O., et al.: Imagenet large scale visual recognition challenge. Int. J. Comput. Vis. **115**(3), 211–252 (2015)
30. Simonyan, K., Zisserman, A.: Very deep convolutional networks for large-scale image recognition. In: International Conference on Learning Representations (2015)
31. Wang, G., Luo, P., Lin, L., Wang, X.: Learning object interactions and descriptions for semantic image segmentation. In: CVPR (2017)
32. Xu, K., et al.: Show, attend and tell: neural image caption generation with visual attention. In: International Conference on Machine Learning, pp. 2048–2057 (2015)
33. Yang, Z., He, X., Gao, J., Deng, L., Smola, A.: Stacked attention networks for image question answering. In: Proceedings of the IEEE Conference on Computer Vision and pattern Recognition (2016)
34. Yao, B.Z., Yang, X., Lin, L., Lee, M.W., Zhu, S.C.: I2T: image parsing to text description. Proc. IEEE **98**(8), 1485–1508 (2010)
35. Yu, D., Fu, J., Rui, Y., Mei, T.: Multi-level attention networks for visual question answering. In: Proceedings of the IEEE Conference on Computer Vision and Pattern Recognition, July 2017

36. Yu, F., Koltun, V.: Multi-scale context aggregation by dilated convolutions. In: International Conference on Learning Representations (2016)
37. Yu, L., Poirson, P., Yang, S., Berg, A.C., Berg, T.L.: Modeling context in referring expressions. In: Leibe, B., Matas, J., Sebe, N., Welling, M. (eds.) ECCV 2016 Part II. LNCS, vol. 9906, pp. 69–85. Springer, Cham (2016). https://doi.org/10.1007/978-3-319-46475-6_5
38. Zhang, Y., Yuan, L., Guo, Y., He, Z., Huang, I., Lee, H.: Discriminative bimodal networks for visual localization and detection with natural language queries. In: Proceedings of the IEEE Conference on Computer Vision and Pattern Recognition (2017)
39. Zhao, H., Shi, J., Qi, X., Wang, X., Jia, J.: Pyramid scene parsing network. In: Proceedings of the IEEE Conference on Computer Vision and Pattern Recognition (2017)

A Segmentation-Aware Deep Fusion Network for Compressed Sensing MRI

Zhiwen Fan[1], Liyan Sun[1], Xinghao Ding[1(✉)], Yue Huang[1], Congbo Cai[1], and John Paisley[2]

[1] Fujian Key Laboratory of Sensing and Computing for Smart City,
Xiamen University, Xiamen, Fujian, China
dxh@xmu.edu.cn
[2] Department of Electrical Engineering, Columbia University, New York, NY, USA

Abstract. Compressed sensing MRI is a classic inverse problem in the field of computational imaging, accelerating the MR imaging by measuring less k-space data. The deep neural network models provide the stronger representation ability and faster reconstruction compared with "shallow" optimization-based methods. However, in the existing deep-based CS-MRI models, the high-level semantic supervision information from massive segmentation-labels in MRI dataset is overlooked. In this paper, we proposed a segmentation-aware deep fusion network called SADFN for compressed sensing MRI. The multilayer feature aggregation (MLFA) method is introduced here to fuse all the features from different layers in the segmentation network. Then, the aggregated feature maps containing semantic information are provided to each layer in the reconstruction network with a feature fusion strategy. This guarantees the reconstruction network is aware of the different regions in the image it reconstructs, simplifying the function mapping. We prove the utility of the cross-layer and cross-task information fusion strategy by comparative study. Extensive experiments on brain segmentation benchmark MRBrainS and BratS15 validated that the proposed SADFN model achieves state-of-the-art accuracy in compressed sensing MRI. This paper provides a novel approach to guide the low-level visual task using the information from mid- or high-level task.

Keywords: Compressed sensing · Magnetic resonance imaging
Medical image segmentation · Deep neural network

1 Introduction

Magnetic resonance imaging (MRI) is a medical imaging technique used in radiology to produce the anatomical images in human body with the advantages of low

---

Z. Fan and L. Sun—The co-first authors contributed equally.

Electronic supplementary material The online version of this chapter (https://doi.org/10.1007/978-3-030-01231-1_4) contains supplementary material, which is available to authorized users.

© Springer Nature Switzerland AG 2018
V. Ferrari et al. (Eds.): ECCV 2018, LNCS 11210, pp. 55–70, 2018.
https://doi.org/10.1007/978-3-030-01231-1_4

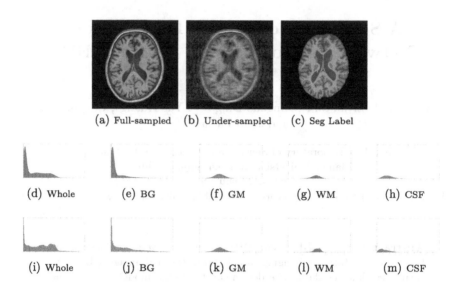

Fig. 1. A full-sampled MR image in Fig. (a), its under-sampled counterpart in Fig. (b) and segmentation labels in Fig. (c). We plot the histograms of under-sampled MRI (second row) and full-sampled MRI (third row) on training MRI datasets. (Color figure online)

radiation, high resolution in soft tissues and multiple imaging modalities. However, the major limitation in MRI is the slow imaging speed which causes motion artifacts [1] when the imaging subject moves consciously or unconsciously. The high resolution in k-t space is also difficult to be achieved in dynamic MRI because of long imaging period [2]. Thus compressed sensing technique is introduced to accelerate the MRI by measuring less k-space samples called compressed sensing MRI (CS-MRI) [3]. The CS-MRI is a classic inverse problem in computation imaging requiring proper regularization for accurate reconstruction.

The standard CS-MRI can be formulated as

$$\hat{x} = \arg\min_{x} \|F_u x - y\|_2^2 + \sum_i \alpha_i \Psi_i(x), \tag{1}$$

where $x \in C^{P \times 1}$ is the complex-valued MR image to be reconstructed, $F_u \in C^{M \times P}$ is the under-sampled Fourier operator and $y \in C^{M \times 1}$ ($M \ll P$) are the k-space measurements by the MRI machine, Ψ_i represents a certain prior transform, α_i is the parameter balancing the data fidelity term and the prior term. The first data fidelity term ensures consistency between the Fourier coefficients of the reconstructed image and the measured k-space data, while the second prior term regularizes the reconstruction to encourage certain image properties such as sparsity in a transform domain.

In conventional CS-MRI methods, the sparse and nonlocal are common priors for the inverse recovery in situ, which brings three limitations: (1) The common complex patterns hiding massive MRI datasets are overlooked in the capacity-limited "shallow" prior [4]. (2) The sparse or nonlocal regularization lacks semantic representation ability, which is difficult to distinguish between the image structure details and structural artifacts brought by under-sampling. (3) The optimization for conventional priors requires long time to iterate to reach convergence, which brings long reconstruction time consumption [5].

Recently, the deep neural network models are introduced in the field of CS-MRI to overcome the limitations of conventional CS-MRI methods. Where the information from massive training MRI datasets can be encoded in the network architecture in training phase with large model capacity. Once the network is well-trained, the forward reconstruction for test MRI data is much faster compared with methods based on conventional sparse priors because no iteration is required. More importantly, the deep neural network models enjoy the benefit of modeling the semantic information in the image, providing an appropriate approach to integrate information for different visual tasks, however, which is rarely considered in the existing models for inverse problem, leaving high-level supervision information poorly utilized, causing negative effect on the later automatic analysis phase.

We take segmentation information for example to prove the benefits of introducing high-level supervision information into reconstruction. Usually different tissues in the MR image not only have different diagnostic information, but also show different statistical properties. In Fig. 1(a) and (b), we show a full-sampled and corresponding under-sampled T1-weighted brain MR image which contains three different labeled tissues: gray matter (GM), white matter (WM) and cerebrospinal fluid (CSF). The corresponding GM, WM and CSF labels are shown in green, yellow and red in the segmentation label map in Fig. 1(c). Clearly, different regions show different intensity scales. To further quantify this phenomenon, we give the statistical histograms of the three tissues, back ground (BG) and the whole images of the under-sampled/full-sampled MRI data in the second/third row in Fig. 1 on all the training MRI data. We observe each of the GM, WM and CSF tissues has simple single-mode distribution on the full-sampled and under-sampled MRI data. Since the deep neural network usually learns the function mapping from the under-sampled MR images to their full-sampled counterparts. The function mapping can be significantly simplified by learning the corresponding relations between the single-mode distributions. However, the distributions of the whole under-sampled and full-sampled MRI in Fig. 1(d) and (i) are much more complicated, making the learning of function mapping more difficult.

In this paper, we propose a segmentation-aware deep fusion network (SADFN) architecture for compressed sensing MRI to fuse the semantic supervision information in the different depth from the segmentation label and propagate the semantic features to each layer in the reconstruction network. The main contribution can be summarized as follows:

- The proposed SADFN model can effectively fuse the information from tasks and depths in different levels. Both the MRI reconstruction and segmentation accuracies are significantly improved under the proposed framework.
- The semantic information from the segmentation network is provided to reconstruction network using a feature fusion strategy, helping the reconstruction network be aware of the content it reconstructs and simplifying the function mapping.

– We adopt the multilayer feature aggregation to effectively collect and extract the information from different depth in the segmentation network.

2   Related Work

2.1   Compressed Sensing MRI

In the study of CS-MRI, the researches focus on proposing appropriate regularization. In the pioneer work SparseMRI [3], the fixed transform operator wavelets and total variation is adopted for regularization in Eq. 1. More methods [6–8] are proposed to address the same objective function efficiently. The variants of wavelet are proposed to exploit the geometric information in MR images adaptively in [9–11]. Dictionary learning techniques are also utilized in situ to model the MR images adaptively [5,12,13]. Nonlocal prior also can be introduced as regularization [14] or combined with sparse prior in [10].

Recently, the deep neural network models are introduced in CS-MRI. A vanilla deep convolutional neural network (CNN) is used to learn the function mapping from the zero-filled MR images to the full-sampled MR images [15]. Furthermore, a modified U-Net architecture is utilized to learn the residual mapping in [17]. The above deep-based CS-MRI models overlooks the accurate information on the sampled positions in the compressive measurements. In [4], a deep cascaded CNN (DC-CNN) is proposed to cascade several basic blocks to learn the mapping with each block containing the nonlinear convolution layers and a nonadjustable data fidelity layer. In data fidelity layers, the reconstructed MR images are corrected by the accurate k-space samples. Despite the state-of-the-art reconstruction quality has been achieved using the DC-CNN model, the high-level supervision information from the manual labels in MRI datasets hasn't been taken into consideration, still leaving room for further improvement on model performance.

2.2   MR Image Segmentation

With the segmentation labels in MRI datasets, different models are proposed to learn to automatically segment the MR images into different tissues from the test set. Compared with conventional segmentation methods based on manually designed features, the deep neural network models can extract image features automatically, leading to better segmentation performance. Recently, the U-shaped network called U-Net trained in end-to-end and pixel-to-pixel manner is proposed in [18], which can take the input of arbitrary size and produce the output of the same size, achieving the state-of-the-art medical image segmentation accuracy and computational efficiency. Its variant where the 2D operations are replaced with 3D ones is proposed in [19] called 3D U-Net. The residual learning is also utilized in the segmentation model in [20]. The recurrent neural network can efficiently model the relation among different frames in the volumetric MR data can introduced in the medical image segmentation [21,22].

Throughout the paper, we use the classic 2D U-Net for single-frame MRI segmentation for the single-frame MRI reconstruction, and the proposed model can be easily extended to volumetric MRI data.

2.3 Multilayer Feature Aggregation

The works [23] on visualization of deep CNN has revealed the feature maps at different layers describe the image in different scales and views. In the conventional deep neural network models, the output is produced based on the deep layers or even the last layer of the model, leaving the features in lower layers containing information from different scales underemphasized. In the field of salient object detection, the multilayer feature aggregation is a popular approach to integrate information from different layers in the network [24–26].

2.4 High-Level Information Guidance for Low-Level Tasks

In [16], the MRI reconstruction and segmentation are integrated into a single objective function, resulting in both improvements on reconstruction and segmentation. However, the sparse-based method is limited by the model capacity and lack of semantic representation. Recently, some works are devoted to combining the low-level task with tasks in higher levels. In the work of [27], a well pre-trained segmentation network is cascaded behind a denoising network, then the loss functions for both segmentation and denoising are optimized to train the denoising network without adjusting the parameters in segmentation network. With this model, the denoising network produces the denoised images with higher segmentation accuracy using automatic segmentation network at the expense of limited improvement in restoration accuracy or even degradation. In the AOD-Net [28], the well-trained dehaze model is jointly optimized with a faster R-CNN, resulting better detection and recognition results.

3   The Proposed Architecture

To incorporate the information from segmentation label into the MRI reconstruction, we proposed the segmentation-aware deep fusion network (SADFN). The network architecture is shown in Fig. 2. The reconstruction network and segmentation network are first pre-trained. Then a segmentation-aware feature extraction module is designed to provide features with rich segmentation information to reconstruction network using a feature fusion strategy.

3.1   The Pre-trained MRI Reconstruction Network

As we introduced above, the DC-CNN architecture achieves the state-of-the-art performance in reconstruction accuracy and computational efficiency. We train a DC-CNN network with N cascaded blocks. Each block contains several convolutional layers and a data fidelity layer. The details of each block in the

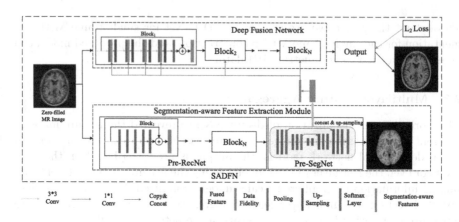

Fig. 2. The network architecture of SADFN model.

DC-CNN architecture is shown in Table 1. The data fidelity layer enforces consistency between k-space value of the reconstructed image and the measured data. The details can also be found in [4]. Note the identity function is used in last convolutional layer to admit the negative values because of the global residual learning in the blocks. We also refer to the DC-CNN architecture as Pre-RecNet for simplicity. The Pre-RecNet with N blocks are called Pre-RecNet$_N$. We train the Pre-RecNet$_N$ using the under-sampled and full-sampled training data pairs by minimizing the following Euclidean loss function

$$\mathcal{L}_{\text{Rec}}\left(y_i, x_i^{fs}; \theta_r\right) = \frac{1}{L_r} \sum_{i=1}^{L_r} \left\| x_i^{fs} - f_{\theta_r}\left(F_u^H y_i\right) \right\|_2^2. \tag{2}$$

where the x_i^{fs} is the full-sampled MR image, y_i is the under-sampled k-space measurements in the training batch. θ_r denotes the network parameter and L_r is the number of MRI data in the training batch.

Table 1. The parameter setting of a block in the Pre-RecNet.

Layer	Input	Filter size	Stride	Number of filters	Activation	Output
Conv$_1$	240 * 240	3 * 3	1	32	ReLU	240 * 240 * 32
Conv$_2$	240 * 240 * 32	3 * 3	1	32	ReLU	240 * 240 * 32
Conv$_3$	240 * 240 * 32	3 * 3	1	32	ReLU	240 * 240 * 32
Conv$_4$	240 * 240 * 32	3 * 3	1	32	ReLU	240 * 240 * 32
Conv$_5$	240 * 240 * 32	3 * 3	1	1	Linear	240 * 240
Data fidelity	240 * 240	N/A	N/A	N/A	N/A	240 * 240

3.2   The MRI Segmentation Network

To fully utilize the segmentation supervision information, we train a automatic segmentation network. We adopt the popular U-Net architecture as the segmentation model called Pre-SegNet. The parameter setting of the Pre-SegNet is shown in Table 2. The pooling operation can help the network extract the image features in different scales and the symmetric concatenation is utilized to propagate the low-layer features to high layers directly, providing accurate localization. We train the Pre-SegNet using the full-sampled MR images and their corresponding segmentation labels as training data pairs by minimizing the following pixel-wise cross-entropy loss function

$$\mathcal{L}_{\mathrm{Seg}}\left(x_i^{fs}, t_i^{gt}; \theta_s\right) = -\sum_{i=1}^{L_s}\sum_{j=1}^{R}\sum_{c=1}^{C} t_{ijc}^{gt} \ln t_{ijc}. \tag{3}$$

where the t_i^{gt} is the segmentation label in the training batch and t_i is the corresponding segmentation result produced by Pre-SegNet. θ_s denotes the network parameter and L_s is the number of MRI data in the training batch. C denotes the number of classes of the label. Taking the brain segmentation for example [29], the brain tissues can be classified into white matter, gray matter, cerebrospinal fluid and background. Thus C is 4 for segmentation.

Table 2. The parameter setting of the Pre-SegNet.

Layer	Input	Filter size	Stride	Number of filters	Activation	Output
Conv$_1$	240 * 240	3 * 3	1	32	ReLU	240 * 240 * 32
Conv$_2$	240 * 240 * 32	3 * 3	1	32	ReLU	240 * 240 * 32
Max Pooling$_1$	240 * 240 * 32	N/A	2	N/A	N/A	120 * 120 * 32
Conv$_3$	120 * 120 * 32	3 * 3	1	64	ReLU	120 * 120 * 64
Conv$_4$	120 * 120 * 64	3 * 3	1	64	ReLU	120 * 120 * 64
Max Pooling$_2$	120 * 120 * 64	N/A	2	N/A	N/A	60 * 60 * 64
Conv$_5$	60 * 60 * 64	3 * 3	1	128	ReLU	60 * 60 * 128
Conv$_6$	60 * 60 * 128	3 * 3	1	128	ReLU	60 * 60 * 128
Deconv$_1$	60 * 60 * 128	3 * 3	1	64	ReLU	120 * 120 * 64
Conv$_7$	120 * 120 * (64 + 64)	3 * 3	1	64	ReLU	120 * 120 * 64
Conv$_8$	120 * 120 * 64	3 * 3	1	64	ReLU	120 * 120 * 64
Deconv$_2$	120 * 120 * 64	3 * 3	1	32	ReLU	240 * 240 * 32
Conv$_9$	240 * 240 * (32 + 32)	3 * 3	1	32	ReLU	240 * 240 * 32
Conv$_{10}$	240 * 240 * 32	3 * 3	1	32	ReLU	240 * 240 * 32
Conv$_{11}$	240 * 240 * 32	3 * 3	1	5	Linear	240 * 240 * 5
Softmax	240 * 240 * 5	N/A	N/A	N/A	N/A	240 * 240

3.3   Deep Fusion Network

With the well-trained Pre-RecNet and Pre-SegNet, we can construct the segmentation-aware deep fusion network with N blocks (SADFN$_N$) by integrating the features from the Pre-RecNet and Pre-SegNet, which involving a cross-layer multilayer feature aggregation strategy and a cross-task feature fusion strategy.

Segmentation-Aware Feature Extraction Module. As we discussed in the related work section, the multilayer feature aggregation can be used to fuse the information from layers in different depth. Here we extract the feature maps from the output of the $Conv_1$, $Conv_2$, $Conv_3$, $Conv_4$, $Conv_5$, $Conv_6$, $Conv_7$, $Conv_8$, $Conv_9$, $Conv_{10}$ and concatenate them into a single "thick" feature map tensor. Note the smaller size feature maps are up-sampled using bilinear interpolation to the same size of features from the Pre-RecNet$_N$. Then the "thick" feature maps of the size $240 * 240 * 640$ $(32 + 32 + 64 + 64 + 128 + 128 + 64 + 64 + 32 + 32)$ are further compressed into a "thin" feature tensor of the size $240 * 240 * 32$ via the 1×1 convolution with ReLU as activation function.

The Feature Fusion Cross Tasks. The compressed feature tensor obtained by the multilayer feature aggregation strategy contains the supervision information from the Pre-SegNet. We concatenate the feature tensor of the size $240 * 240 * 32$ with the feature maps of the size $240 * 240 * 32$ output by convolutional layers in the Pre-RecNet as shown in Fig. 2. Then the concatenated features of the size $240 * 240 * 64$ are further compressed into a feature tensor of the size $240 * 240 * 32$ via 1×1 convolution with ReLU activation function. The information from feature maps can be efficiently fused via such a concatenation and compression strategy. Note the compressed feature tensor is concatenated to the first four convolutional layers in each Pre-RecNet block, the supervision information from segmentation can guide the reconstruction in different depth. Also, in the Fig. 2, the feature fusion strategy is also utilized in each block of the Pre-RecNet.

To prove the supervision information is effectively fused into the reconstruction, we give some feature maps in the fused feature tensor yielded by the 1×1 convolution in Fig. 3. In Fig. 3(a) we show the segmentation label of a certain MRI data. In Fig. 3(b), (c) and (d), we visualize the feature maps selected from the fused feature tensors in the second layer and fourth layer. We observe the feature maps show clear segmentation information, while no such feature maps are observed in the Pre-RecNet$_N$ model.

The Fine-Tuning Strategy. With the well-constructed deep fusion network, we further fine-tune the resulting architecture. Given a zero-filled MR image in the training dataset, a corresponding high-quality MR image can be yielded by the Pre-RecNet$_N$ in Sect. 3.1. Then the MR image is sent to the Pre-SegNet to extract the segmentation features, which are then utilized for the multilayer feature aggregation in Pre-SegNet and feature fusion. Meanwhile, the zero-filled MR image is also input to the deep fusion network. The ℓ_2 Euclidean distance between the output reconstructed MR image and the corresponding full-sampled MR image in the training dataset is minimized. During the optimization, the parameters in the Pre-RecNet$_N$ and Pre-SegNet are kept fixed, while we only adjust the parameters in the deep fusion network.

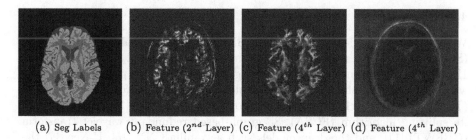

(a) Seg Labels   (b) Feature (2nd Layer) (c) Feature (4th Layer) (d) Feature (4th Layer)

Fig. 3. The selected feature maps from the feature tensors produced by the feature fusion in the deep fusion network.

4   Experiments

4.1   Datasets

We train and test our SADFN model on MRBrainS datasets from Grand Challenge on MR Brain Image Segmentation (MRBrainS) Benchmark [29]. The datasets provides well-aligned multiple modalities MRI including T1, T1-IR and T2-FLAIR with segmentation labels by human experts. For simplicity, we only use the T1 weighted MRI data. In the future work, we plan to extend the model on multi-modalities MRI imaging. Total 5 scans are provided public segmentation labels. We randomly choose four scans for training containing total 172 slices. The training MR images are of size 240×240. We use the remaining MRI scan for testing the model performance containing total 48 slices.

4.2   Implementation Details

We train and test the algorithm on Tensorflow for the Python environment on a NVIDIA Geforce GTX 1080Ti with 11 GB GPU memory and Intel Xeon CPU E5-2683 at 2.00 GHz. The detailed network architectures for Pre-RecNet, Pre-SegNet and SADFN have been introduced in previous section.

The ADAM is used as the optimizer. We train the Pre-RecNet for 32000 iterations using a batch containing four under-sampled and their corresponding full-sampled MR images as training pairs in Eq. 2. The Pre-SegNet is also pre-trained for 32000 iterations using a batch containing 16 randomly cropped fully-sampled 128×128 patches and their segmentation labels. Again, we note that during the fine-tuning of the SADFN model, compressed feature tensor is yielded by multilayer features aggregation (MLFA) and the feature tensor is propagated to the Pre-RecNet before the feature fusion in each block. The SADFN is fine-tuned 12000 iterations using the same training batchsize as the pre-training of Pre-RecNet. We select the initial learning rate to be 0.001 for pre-trained stage and 0.0001 for fine-tune stage, the first-order momentum to be 0.9 and the second momentum to be 0.999 for both stages. We adopt batch normalization (BN) in Pre-SegNet. We also adopt data augmentation for training as implemented in [30].

4.3 Quantitative Evaluation

We use peak signal-to-noise ratio (PSNR) and structural similarity index (SSIM) [31] for the reconstruction quantitative evaluation. We adopt a 30% 1D Cartesian pattern for under-sampling. We compare the proposed SADFN$_5$ with other state-of-the-art CS-MRI models including transform learning MRI (TLMRI) [12], patch-based nonlocal operator (PANO) [10], fast composite splitting algorithm (FCSA) [8], graph-based redundant wavelet transform (GBRWT) [11], and the deep models such as vanilla CNN [15], U-Net [17] the Pre-RecNet$_5$ (which is also the state-ot-the-art DC-CNN with 5 blocks [4]). For the non-deep CS-MRI methods, we adjust the parameters to their best performance. We also compare the proposed SADFN$_5$ with the model proposed in [27], where the pre-trained Pre-RecNet$_5$ and Pre-SegNet are cascaded during fine-tuning and only the parameters in Pre-RecNet$_5$ are adjusted for optimization. Since no name for the model is provided in the original work, we refer the model as Liu [27]. Besides, we compare the proposed SADFN model with the model without the guidance of segmentation information (SADFN-WOS). For fair comparison, we design the building block of the SADFN-WOS network architecture in Table 3. Note the network architecture is kept unchanged with the only difference is some feature maps in SADFN come from Pre-SegNet while all the features come from the reconstruction network in SADFN$_5$-WOS. In the model Pre-RecNet$_5$ and SADFN$_5$-WOS, no segmentation label is utilize for training, meaning the corresponding supervision information is overlooked.

Table 3. The parameter setting of a block in the SADFN-WOS model

Layer	Input	Filter size	Stride	Number of filters	Activation	Output
Conv$_1$	240 * 240	3 * 3	1	64	ReLU	240 * 240 * 64
Conv$_2$	240 * 240 * 64	1 * 1	1	32	ReLU	240 * 240 * 32
Conv$_3$	240 * 240 * 32	3 * 3	1	64	ReLU	240 * 240 * 64
Conv$_4$	240 * 240 * 64	1 * 1	1	32	ReLU	240 * 240 * 32
Conv$_5$	240 * 240 * 32	3 * 3	1	64	ReLU	240 * 240 * 64
Conv$_6$	240 * 240 * 64	1 * 1	1	32	ReLU	240 * 240 * 32
Conv$_7$	240 * 240 * 32	3 * 3	1	64	ReLU	240 * 240 * 64
Conv$_8$	240 * 240 * 64	1 * 1	1	32	ReLU	240 * 240 * 32
Conv$_9$	240 * 240 * 32	3 * 3	1	32	ReLU	240 * 240 * 32
Conv$_{10}$	240 * 240 * 32	3 * 3	1	1	Linear	240 * 240
Data fidelity	240 * 240	N/A	N/A	N/A	N/A	240 * 240

We show the objective evaluation indexes in Fig. 4. Note the deep-based models outperform most non-deep CS-MRI models in reconstruction. We observe the proposed SADFN$_5$ model achieves the optimal performance in PSNR and SSIM indexes among the compared methods. From the standard deviation of the indexes. We note the improvement of the SADFN$_5$ is quite steady for different

MRI test data. We observe the model Liu [27] brings little improvement in objective evaluation indexes compared with the Pre-RecNet₅. We also observe the SADFN₅ model outperforms the comparative SADFN₅-WOS around 1dB in PSNR and 0.03 in SSIM in average, which proves the benefits are brought by introducing the supervision information from the segmentation labels instead of merely increasing the network size.

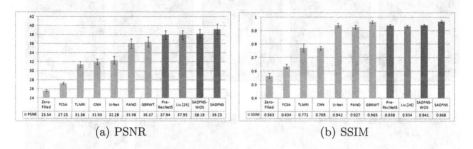

(a) PSNR   (b) SSIM

Fig. 4. The comparison in averaged PSNR and SSIM index on the test MRI data.

4.4 Qualitative Evaluation

We give the qualitative reconstruction results produced by compared CS-MRI methods in Fig. 5. We also plot the reconstruction error maps to better observe their differences. The display range for the error maps is [0 0.12]. We observe the Pre-RecNet₅ (DC-CNN [4]) architecture, produce better reconstruction than the conventional sparse- and nonlocal- regularized CS-MRI models. The model in [27] didn't brought significant improvement in reconstruction. The SADFN₅-WOS with larger network size also brought limited improvement. We observe the proposed SADFN₅ achieves much smaller reconstruction errors compared with other models, which is consistent with our observations in objective index evaluations.

4.5 Running Time

We compare the running time of the compared models in Table 4. As we mentioned in the Sect. 1, the CS-MRI models based on sparse or non-local regularization requires a large number of iterations, resulting slow reconstruction speed. Although the running time of the proposed SADFN model is slower than the other deep-based CS-MRI models, it achieves the state-of-the-art reconstruction accuracy, providing the best balance between running time and reconstruction quality.

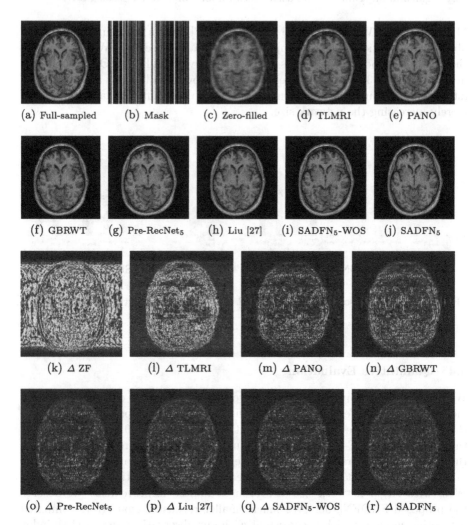

Fig. 5. The reconstruction results of zero-filled (ZF), TLMRI, PANO, GBRWT, Pre-RecNet5, Liu [27], SADFN5-WOS and SADFN5. We also give the corresponding reconstruction error maps Δ with display ranges [0 0.12].

5   Discussions

5.1   The Number of Blocks

In Fig. 6, we discuss how the model performance varies with the different number of blocks from 1 to 5 in the Pre-RecNet5, SADFN5-WOS and SADFN5 models. As expected, the SADFN5 model achieves steady improvement to large margins with different model capacity, meaning the supervision information can robustly improve the reconstruction accuracy.

Table 4. The comparison in runtime (seconds) between the compared models.

	TLMRI	GBRWT	PANO	Pre-RecNet$_5$	Liu[26]	SADFN$_5$-WOS	SADFN$_5$
Runtime	127.67	100.60	11.37	0.03	0.03	0.07	0.07

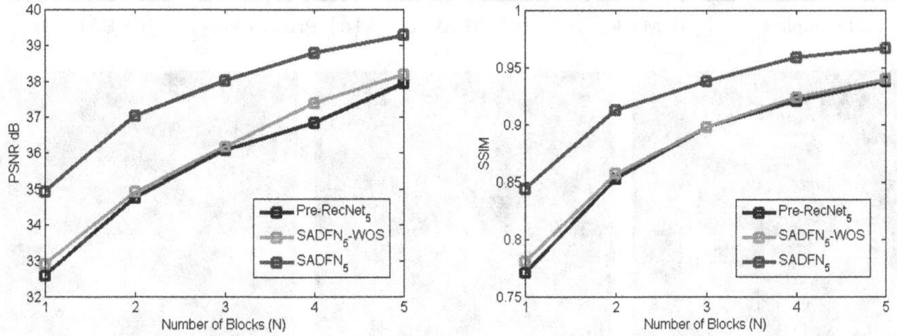

(a) PSNR   (b) SSIM

Fig. 6. The comparison in averaged PSNR and SSIM index on the test MRI data.

5.2 Different Under-Sampling Patterns

We also test the proposed SADFN model on the 20% Random under-sampling mask shown in Fig. 5. The SADFN$_5$ achieves the optimal performance, proving it can be well generalized on various kind of under-sampling patterns.

5.3 The Evaluation on the Segmentation Performance

With the reconstructed MR images produced by different CS-MRI models, we input them into the pre-trained automatic segmentation models in Sect. 3.2 to evaluate the effect of different reconstruction models on the segmentation task. We adopt the Dice Coefficient (DC), the 95th-percentile of the Hausdorff distance (HD) and the absolute volume difference (AVD) as objective evaluation indexes for segmentation as recommended in [29]. The higher DC, lower HD and lower AVD values indicate better segmentation accuracy. Details on evaluation of segmentation performance can be referred to [29]. The segmentation results with full-sampled MR image inputs are the performance upper bounds. We show the averaged segmentation results with compared models on the test MRI data set in Table 5. We observe the proposed SADFN$_5$ achieves the best accuracy on the segmentation task of the compared models.

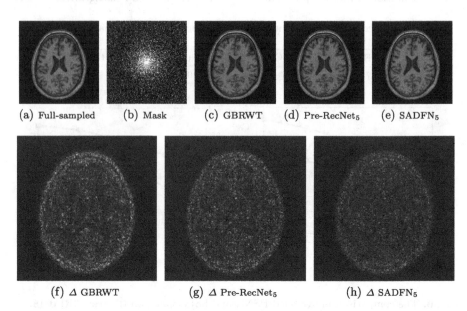

(a) Full-sampled   (b) Mask   (c) GBRWT   (d) Pre-RecNet₅   (e) SADFN₅

(f) Δ GBRWT   (g) Δ Pre-RecNet₅   (h) Δ SADFN₅

Fig. 7. The reconstruction results of zero-filled (ZF), TLMRI, PANO, GBRWT, Pre-RecNet₅, Liu [27], SADFN₅-WOS and SADFN₅ on the 20% random mask. We also give the corresponding reconstruction error maps Δ with display ranges [0 0.1].

Table 5. The averaged DC, HD and AVD values on the test MRI data.

Methods	GM			WM			CSF		
	DC %	HD	AVD	DC %	HD	AVD	DC %	HD	AVD
ZF + Pre-SegNet	64.78	2.587	6.202	54.07	2.085	4.294	57.37	2.221	4.689
TLMRI + Pre-SegNet	76.28	2.093	3.985	63.77	1.870	3.185	68.17	2.072	3.796
PANO + Pre-SegNet	83.73	1.819	2.958	75.72	1.348	1.815	78.93	1.653	2.361
GBRWT + Pre-SegNet	83.66	1.821	2.937	76.14	1.353	1.783	79.39	1.647	2.342
Pre-RecNet₅ + Pre-SegNet	83.63	1.795	2.874	75.16	1.378	1.813	78.99	1.668	2.386
SADFN₅-WOS + Pre-SegNet	83.85	1.782	2.838	75.84	1.357	1.762	79.25	1.661	2.364
Liu [27] + Pre-SegNet	84.08	1.776	2.814	76.30	1.335	1.724	79.37	1.661	2.357
SADFN₅ + Pre-SegNet	**85.76**	**1.690**	**2.579**	**81.29**	**1.143**	**1.381**	**80.08**	**1.649**	**2.305**
Full-sampled + Pre-SegNet	87.30	1.596	2.328	86.89	0.973	1.092	80.76	1.617	2.225

6   Conclusion

In this paper, we proposed a segmentation-aware deep fusion network (SADFN) for compressed sensing MRI. We showed the high-level supervision information can be effectively fused into deep neural network models to help the low-level MRI reconstruction. The multilayer feature aggregation is adopted to fuse cross-layer information in the MRI segmentation network and the feature fusion strategy is utilized to fuse cross-task information in the MRI reconstruction network. We prove the proposed SADFN architecture enables the reconstruction network aware of the contents it reconstructs and the function mapping can be significantly simplified. The SADFN model achieves state-of-the-art performance in CS-MRI and balance between accuracy and efficiency (Fig. 7).

References

1. Atkinson, D., et al.: Automatic compensation of motion artifacts in MRI. Magn. Reson. Med. **41**(1), 163–170 (1999)
2. Jung, H., Sung, K., Nayak, K.S., Kim, E.Y., Ye, J.C.: k-t FOCUSS: a general compressed sensing framework for high resolution dynamic MRI. Magn. Reson. Med. **61**(1), 103–116 (2009)
3. Lustig, M., Donoho, D., Pauly, J.M.: Sparse MRI: the application of compressed sensing for rapid MR imaging. Magn. Reson. Med. **58**(6), 1182–1195 (2007)
4. Schlemper, J., et al.: A deep cascade of convolutional neural networks for MR image reconstruction. In: Niethammer, M., Styner, M., Aylward, S., Zhu, H., Oguz, I., Yap, P.-T., Shen, D. (eds.) IPMI 2017. LNCS, vol. 10265, pp. 647–658. Springer, Cham (2017). https://doi.org/10.1007/978-3-319-59050-9_51
5. Ravishankar, S., Bresler, Y.: MR image reconstruction from highly undersampled k-space data by dictionary learning. IEEE Trans. Med. Imaging **30**(5), 1028–1041 (2011)
6. Ma, S., Yin, W., Zhang, Y., Chakraborty, A.: An efficient algorithm for compressed MR imaging using total variation and wavelets. In: CVPR, pp. 1–8. IEEE (2008)
7. Yang, J., Zhang, Y., Yin, W.: A fast alternating direction method for TVL1-L2 signal reconstruction from partial fourier data. IEEE J. Sel. Top. Sig. Process. **4**(2), 288–297 (2010)
8. Huang, J., Zhang, S., Metaxas, D.: Efficient MR image reconstruction for compressed MR imaging. Med. Image Anal. **15**(5), 670–679 (2011)
9. Qu, X., Guo, D., Ning, B., Hou, Y., Lin, Y., Cai, S., Chen, Z.: Undersampled MRI reconstruction with patch-based directional wavelets. Magn. Reson. Imaging **30**(7), 964–977 (2012)
10. Qu, X., Hou, Y., Lam, F., Guo, D., Zhong, J., Chen, Z.: Magnetic resonance image reconstruction from undersampled measurements using a patch-based non-local operator. Med. Image Anal. **18**(6), 843–856 (2014)
11. Lai, Z., et al.: Image reconstruction of compressed sensing MRI using graph-based redundant wavelet transform. Med. Image Anal. **27**, 93–104 (2016)
12. Ravishankar, S., Bresler, Y.: Efficient blind compressed sensing using sparsifying transforms with convergence guarantees and application to magnetic resonance imaging. SIAM J. Imaging Sci. **8**(4), 2519–2557 (2015)
13. Huang, Y., Paisley, J., Lin, Q., Ding, X., Fu, X., Zhang, X.P.: Bayesian non-parametric dictionary learning for compressed sensing MRI. IEEE Trans. Image Process. **23**(12), 5007–5019 (2014)
14. Dong, W., Shi, G., Li, X., Ma, Y., Huang, F.: Compressive sensing via nonlocal low-rank regularization. IEEE Trans. Image Process. **23**(8), 3618–3632 (2014)
15. Wang, S., et al.: Accelerating magnetic resonance imaging via deep learning. In: ISBI, pp. 514–517. IEEE (2016)
16. Caballero, J., Bai, W., Price, A.N., Rueckert, D., Hajnal, J.V.: Application-driven MRI: joint reconstruction and segmentation from undersampled MRI data. In: Golland, P., Hata, N., Barillot, C., Hornegger, J., Howe, R. (eds.) MICCAI 2014. LNCS, vol. 8673, pp. 106–113. Springer, Cham (2014). https://doi.org/10.1007/978-3-319-10404-1_14

17. Lee, D., Yoo, J., Ye, J.C.: Deep residual learning for compressed sensing MRI. In: ISBI, pp. 15–18. IEEE (2017)
18. Ronneberger, O., Fischer, P., Brox, T.: U-Net: convolutional networks for biomedical image segmentation. In: Navab, N., Hornegger, J., Wells, W.M., Frangi, A.F. (eds.) MICCAI 2015. LNCS, vol. 9351, pp. 234–241. Springer, Cham (2015). https://doi.org/10.1007/978-3-319-24574-4_28
19. Çiçek, Ö., Abdulkadir, A., Lienkamp, S.S., Brox, T., Ronneberger, O.: 3D U-Net: learning dense volumetric segmentation from sparse annotation. In: Ourselin, S., Joskowicz, L., Sabuncu, M.R., Unal, G., Wells, W. (eds.) MICCAI 2016. LNCS, vol. 9901, pp. 424–432. Springer, Cham (2016). https://doi.org/10.1007/978-3-319-46723-8_49
20. Chen, H., Dou, Q., Yu, L., Qin, J., Heng, P.A.: VoxResNet: deep voxelwise residual networks for brain segmentation from 3D MR images. NeuroImage 170, 446–455 (2018)
21. Stollenga, M.F., Byeon, W., Liwicki, M., Schmidhuber, J.: Parallel multi-dimensional LSTM, with application to fast biomedical volumetric image segmentation. In: NIPS, pp. 2998–3006 (2015)
22. Chen, J., Yang, L., Zhang, Y., Alber, M., Chen, D.Z.: Combining fully convolutional and recurrent neural networks for 3D biomedical image segmentation. In: NIPS, pp. 3036–3044 (2016)
23. Zeiler, M.D., Fergus, R.: Visualizing and understanding convolutional networks. In: Fleet, D., Pajdla, T., Schiele, B., Tuytelaars, T. (eds.) ECCV 2014. LNCS, vol. 8689, pp. 818–833. Springer, Cham (2014). https://doi.org/10.1007/978-3-319-10590-1_53
24. Li, G., Yu, Y.: Deep contrast learning for salient object detection. In: CVPR, pp. 478–487 (2016)
25. Zhang, P., Wang, D., Lu, H., Wang, H., Ruan, X.: Amulet: aggregating multi-level convolutional features for salient object detection. In: ICCV, October 2017
26. Hou, Q., Cheng, M.M., Hu, X., Borji, A., Tu, Z., Torr, P.: Deeply supervised salient object detection with short connections. In: CVPR, pp. 5300–5309 (2017)
27. Liu, D., Wen, B., Liu, X., Huang, T.S.: When image denoising meets high-level vision tasks: a deep learning approach. arXiv preprint arXiv:1706.04284 (2017)
28. Li, B., Peng, X., Wang, Z., Xu, J., Feng, D.: AOD-Net: all-in-one dehazing network. In: ICCV, October 2017
29. Mendrik, A.M., et al.: MRBrainS challenge: online evaluation framework for brain image segmentation in 3T MRI scans. Comput. Intell. Neurosci. 2015, 1 (2015)
30. Dong, H., Yang, G., Liu, F., Mo, Y., Guo, Y.: Automatic brain tumor detection and segmentation using U-net based fully convolutional networks. In: Valdés Hernández, M., González-Castro, V. (eds.) MIUA 2017. CCIS, vol. 723, pp. 506–517. Springer, Cham (2017). https://doi.org/10.1007/978-3-319-60964-5_44
31. Wang, Z., Bovik, A.C., Sheikh, H.R., Simoncelli, E.P.: Image quality assessment: from error visibility to structural similarity. IEEE Trans. Process. 13(4), 600–612 (2004)
32. Tai, Y., Yang, J., Liu, X.: Image super-resolution via deep recursive residual network. In: CVPR, pp. 2790–2798 (2017)

Correcting the Triplet Selection Bias
for Triplet Loss

Baosheng Yu[1(✉)], Tongliang Liu[1], Mingming Gong[2,3], Changxing Ding[4],
and Dacheng Tao[1]

[1] UBTECH Sydney AI Centre and SIT, FEIT, The University of Sydney,
Sydney, Australia
`bayu0826@uni.sydney.edu.au`,{`tongliang.liu,dacheng.tao`}`@sydney.edu.au`
[2] Department of Biomedical Informatics, University of Pittsburgh,
Pittsburgh, USA
`mig73@pitt.edu.com`
[3] Department of Philosophy, Carnegie Mellon University,
Pittsburgh, USA
[4] School of Electronic and Information Engineering,
South China University of Technology, Guangzhou, China
`chxding@scut.edu.cn`

Abstract. Triplet loss, popular for metric learning, has made a great
success in many computer vision tasks, such as fine-grained image classification, image retrieval, and face recognition. Considering that the
number of triplets grows cubically with the size of training data, triplet
selection is thus indispensable for efficiently training with triplet loss.
However, in practice, the training is usually very sensitive to the selection of triplets, e.g., it almost does not converge with randomly selected
triplets and selecting the hardest triplets also leads to bad local minima.
We argue that the bias in the selection of triplets degrades the performance of learning with triplet loss. In this paper, we propose a new
variant of triplet loss, which tries to reduce the bias in triplet selection
by adaptively correcting the distribution shift on the selected triplets.
We refer to this new triplet loss as adapted triplet loss. We conduct a
number of experiments on MNIST and Fashion-MNIST for image classification, and on CARS196, CUB200-2011, and Stanford Online Products
for image retrieval. The experimental results demonstrate the effectiveness of the proposed method.

Keywords: Triplet loss · Selection bias · Domain adaptation

1 Introduction

Deep metric learning aims to learn a similarity or distance metric which enjoys
a small intra-class variation and a large inter-class variation [41]. Triplet loss is
a popular loss function for deep metric learning and has made a great success in
many computer vision tasks, such as fine-grained image classification [38], image

© Springer Nature Switzerland AG 2018
V. Ferrari et al. (Eds.): ECCV 2018, LNCS 11210, pp. 71–86, 2018.
https://doi.org/10.1007/978-3-030-01231-1_5

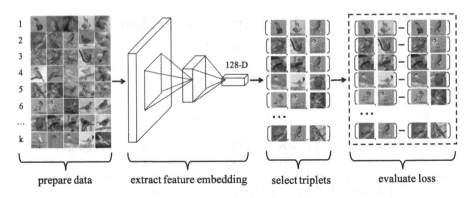

Fig. 1. The pipeline of triplet loss based deep metric learning. In the first stage, a mini-batch is sampled from the training data, which usually contains k identities with several images per identity. Deep neural networks then are used to learn a feature embedding, e.g., a 128-D feature vector. In the third stage, a subset of triplets are selected using some triplet selection methods. Lastly, the loss is evaluated using the selected triplets.

retrieval [16,21], person re-identification [5,13], and face recognition [30,33]. Recently, deep metric learning approaches employing triplet loss have attracted a lot of attention due to their efficiency for dealing with enormous of labels, e.g., the extreme multi-label classification problem [31]. More specifically, for conventional classification approaches, the number of parameters will increase linearly with the number of labels, and it is impractical to learn an N-way soft-max classifier with millions of labels [28]. However, with triplet loss, deep metric learning is able to efficiently deal with an extreme multi-label classification problem by learning a compact embedding, which is known as the large margin nearest neighbor (LMNN) classification [41]. As a result, deep metric learning exploiting triplet loss is very efficient for applications with enormous labels, e.g., the number of objects in image retrieval [16], the number of identities in face recognition [33] and person re-identification [13].

To learn a discriminative feature embedding, triplet loss maximizes the margin between the intra-class distance and the inter-class distance. As a result, for each triplet (x^a, x^p, x^n), where x^a is called the anchor point, x^p is called the positive point having the same label with x^a, and x^n is called the negative point having a different label, the intra-class distance $d(x^a, x^p)$ will be smaller than the inter-class distance $d(x^a, x^n)$ in the learned embedding space. As the number of triplets grows cubically with the size of training data, triplet selection thus is indispensable for efficiently training with triplet loss. Specifically, triplet selection usually works in an online manner, i.e., triplets are constructed within each mini-batch [33], and we describe a typical pipeline of deep metric learning using triplet loss in Fig. 1.

However, the performance of triplet loss is heavily influenced by triplet selection methods [5,13], i.e., training with randomly selected triplets almost does not converge while training with the hardest triplets often leads to a bad local

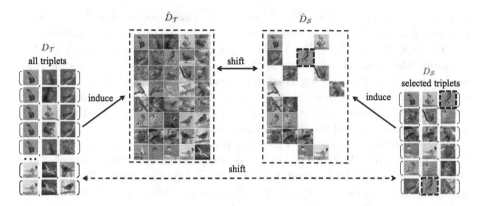

Fig. 2. An example illustrating the distribution shift in triplet selection. In online triplet selection, all triplets D_T are constructed from each mini-batch and will induce a dataset $\hat{D}_T$. For the selected triplets D_S, they also induce a dataset $\hat{D}_S$. We evaluate the distribution shift between D_S and D_T using the distribution shift between $\hat{D}_S$ and $\hat{D}_T$.

solution [33]. To ensure fast convergence, it is crucial to select "good" hard triplets [33] and a variety of triplet selection methods have been designed in different applications [13,16,33,38]. Although selecting hard triplets leads to fast convergence, it has the risk of introducing a selection bias, which is an essential problem for learning. A triplet selection method thus needs to balance the trade-off between mining hard triplets and introducing selection bias. In contrast to struggling with this trade-off by carefully selecting triplets, we address this problem by directly minimizing the selection bias. More specifically, let D_T denote all possible triplets and D_S indicate the subset of selected triplets from D_T. If the triplet selection is unbiased, D_S and D_T then share the same distribution. Otherwise, we can correct the bias in triplet selection by minimizing the distribution shift between D_S and D_T.

The problem of distribution shift falls within the scope of domain adaption [3, 15], which arises when learning a predictor from the source domain $\mathcal{S}$ while the target domain $\mathcal{T}$ changes. In learning with triplet loss, the model is trained using selected triplets D_S while the target is to learn a model using all possible triplets D_T. To measure the distribution shift between D_S and D_T, we define a set of triplet-induced data, i.e., given a set of triplets, e.g., D_S, the triplet-induced data $\hat{D}_S$ is defined as follows:

$$\hat{D}_S = \{(x_i^a, y_i^a), (x_i^p, y_i^p), (x_i^n, y_i^n)|\ \forall (x_i^a, x_i^p, x_i^n) \in D_S\}, \tag{1}$$

where y_i are the corresponding labels of x_i. The induced data $\hat{D}_T$ can be defined similarly. We give an example of the distribution shift between D_S and D_T in Fig. 2. To deal with the problem of distribution shift, distribution matching approaches learn a domain invariant representation and have been widely employed [2,3,29]. Due to triplet loss often involves lots of labels and inspired by the methods in [10,47], we try to minimize the distribution shift between $\hat{D}_S$ and $\hat{D}_T$ by learning a conditional invariant representation $\Phi(X)$, i.e., $P^S(\Phi(X)|Y) \approx P^T(\Phi(X)|Y)$, where X and Y stand the random variables for data and label, respectively. More specifically, we propose a distribution matching loss function by employing Maximum Mean Discrepancy (MMD) [15], which measures the difference between $P^S(\Phi(X)|Y)$ and $P^T(\Phi(X)|Y)$. As a result, we learn a discriminative and conditional invariant embedding by jointly training with the triplet loss and the distribution matching loss.

In this paper, we first introduce the problem of triplet selection bias for learning with triplet loss. We then address this problem by reducing distribution shift between the triplet-induced data $\hat{D}_S$ and $\hat{D}_T$. As the proposed distribution matching loss adaptively corrects the distribution shift, we refer to this new variant of triplet loss as adapted triplet loss. Lastly, we conduct a number of experiments on MNIST [22] and Fashion-MNIST [44] for image classification, on CARS196 [19], CUB200-2011 [37], and Stanford Online Products [28] for image retrieval. The experimental results demonstrate the effectiveness of the proposed method.

2   Related Work

Deep Metric Learning and Triplet Loss. Many problems in machine learning and computer vision depend heavily on learning a distance metric [41]. Inspired by the great success of deep learning [20], deep neural networks have been widely used to learn a discriminative feature embedding [14,38]. Deep metric learning employing triplet loss raises a lot of attention due to its impressive performance on FaceNet [33] for face verification and recognition. After that, triplet loss has been widely used to learn a discriminative embedding for a variety of applications, such as image classification [38] and image retrieval [11,16,21,46,48]. A majority of applications for triplet loss lies in visual object recognition, such as action recognition [32], vehicle recognition [25], place recognition [1], 3d pose recognition [42], face recognition [8,30,33], and person re-identification [4,5,9,13,24,45].

Triplet Selection Methods. Triplet selection is the key for the success of triplet loss and a variety of triplet selection methods have been used in different applications [6,14,30,33,38,39]. More specifically, in the deep ranking model proposed by [38], triplets are selected according to the pair-wise relevance score. In [39], the triplets are selected using the top k triplets in each mini-batch based on the margin $d(x^a, x^p) - d(x^a, x^n)$. In [14], it selects only hard triplets, i.e., $d(x^a, x^p) < d(x^a, x^n)$, while [30,33] select semi-hard triplets which violate the triplet constraint, i.e., $d(x^a, x^p) + \alpha < d(x^a, x^n)$, where α is a positive scalar. Unlike [33], which defines semi-hard triplet using moderate negatives, [34] select semi-hard triplets based on moderate positives. [6] proposes an online hard negative mining method for triplet selection to boost the performance on triplet loss. In [13], it proposes a batch-hard triplet selection method, i.e., it first select a set of hard anchor-positive pairs, and it then select hardest negatives within the mini-batch. Recently, [43] proposes a weighted sampling method to address the sampling matters in deep metric learning.

Domain Adaptation. Domain adaptation methods can be divided into four categories due to different assumptions about how the distribution shifts across domains. (1) Covariate shift [15] assumes the marginal distribution $P(X)$ changes across domains while the conditional distribution $P(Y|X)$ stays the same. (2) Model shift [40] assumes that both $P(X)$ and $P(Y|X)$ independently change across domains. (3) Target shift [47] assumes that the marginal distribution $P(Y)$ shifts wile $P(X|Y)$ stays the same. (4) Generalized target shift [10,23,26] assumes that both $P(Y)$ and $P(X|Y)$ independently change. Since triplet loss is widely used for extreme multi-label classification problems, we model the triplet selection bias by the change of $P(X|Y)$ in this paper.

3 Formulation

In this section, we first introduce triplet loss for deep metric learning and a widely used triplet selection method, i.e., semi-hard triplets [33]. We then formulate the problem of triplet selection bias as the distribution shift problem on triplet induced data. To minimize the distribution shift, we propose a distribution matching loss, which jointly works with the triplet loss to adaptively correct the distribution shift. As a result, we refer to this new triplet loss as adapted triplet loss.

3.1 Triplet Loss for Deep Metric Learning

Let X, Y denote two random variables, which indicate data and label, respectively. Let D denote a set of training data sampled from $P(X,Y)$, i.e., $D = \{(x_i, y_i)| (x_i, y_i) \sim P(X,Y)\}$. Metric learning aims to learn a distance function that assigns small (or large) distance to a pair of similar (or dissimilar) examples. A widely used distance metric, i.e., the Mahalanobis distance, is defined as follows:

$$d_K^2(x_i, x_j) = (x_i - x_j)^\top K(x_i - x_j), \qquad (2)$$

where K is a symmetric positive semi-definite matrix. As K can be decomposed as $K = L^\top L$, we then have

$$d_K^2(x_i, x_j) = \|L(x_i - x_j)\|_2^2 = \|x_i' - x_j'\|_2^2, \qquad (3)$$

where $x_i' = Lx_i$ and $x_j' = Lx_j$. Inspired by this, deep metric learning uses deep neural networks to learn a feature embedding $x' = \Phi(x)$, which generalizes the linear transformation $x' = Lx$ to a non-linear transformation $\Phi(x)$. That is, the learned distance metric is

$$d_K^2(x_i, x_j) = \|\Phi(x_i) - \Phi(x_j)\|_2^2. \qquad (4)$$

To learn a discriminative feature embedding $\Phi(x)$, i.e., intra-class distance is smaller than inter-class distance [41], triplet loss is defined as follows:

$$\mathcal{L}^*_{triplet} = \sum_{(x^a, x^p, x^n) \in D_T} [d_K^2(x^a, x^p) - d_K^2(x^a, x^n) + \alpha]_+, \tag{5}$$

where $[\cdot]_+ = \max(0, \cdot)$, $\alpha \geq 0$ is the margin, and D_T is a set of triplets constructed from the original training data D, i.e.,

$$D_T = \{(x^a, x^p, x^n) | \ y^a = y^p \text{ and } y^a \neq y^n\}. \tag{6}$$

3.2   Triplet Selection Bias

Let D_T denote all possible triplets constructed within a mini-batch and D_S denote the subset of selected triplets, i.e., $D_S \subseteq D_T$. More specifically, given a mini-batch of training data with k identities and c images per identity, there will be $k(k-1)c^2(c-1)$ possible triplets in total. As the number of triplets grows cubically with the number of training data, triplet loss usually is evaluated using only a selected subset of the total triplets. A typical triplet selection methods used in [33], which is referred to as semi-hard triplet selection, can be described as follows: it uses all possible anchor-positive pairs, i.e., $kc(c-1)$ pairs in total. For each anchor-positive pair (x^a, x^p), a semi-hard negative x^n then is randomly selected from all negatives under the constraint

$$d_K^2(x^a, x^p) \leq d_K^2(x^a, x^n) < d_K^2(x^a, x^p) + \alpha. \tag{7}$$

That is, triplet loss is evaluated on D_S, i.e.,

$$\mathcal{L}_{triplet} = \sum_{(x^a, x^p, x^n) \in D_S} [d_K^2(x^a, x^p) - d_K^2(x^a, x^n) + \alpha]_+, \tag{8}$$

As a result, there will be always a distribution shift between D_S and D_T. To measure the distribution shift between D_S and D_T, we define the triplet-induced data $\hat{D}_S$ for D_S as follows:

$$\hat{D}_S = \{(x^a, y^a), (x^p, y^p), (x^n, y^n) | \ \forall (x^a, x^p, x^n) \in D_S\}. \tag{9}$$

Similarly, we also define $\hat{D}_T$ as the data induced by D_T. If D_S and D_T shares the same distribution $P(x^a, x^p, x^n)$, we then have, $\forall x \in \hat{D}_S$,

$$P^S(x) = \sum_{i \in \{a,p,n\}} P(x^i) * \mathbf{1}\{x = x^i\} = P^T(x). \tag{10}$$

where $P^S(x)$ and $P^T(x)$ are the probability density functions for $\hat{D}_S$ and $\hat{D}_T$ respectively. That is, there will be no distribution shift between the triplet-induced data $\hat{D}_S$ and $\hat{D}_T$. As a result, we use the difference between $\hat{D}_S$ and $\hat{D}_T$ as a measure the distribution shift in triplet loss.

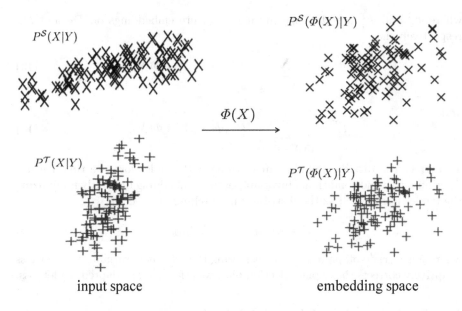

Fig. 3. An example illustrating the conditional invariant representation. There is a distribution shift between the source domain and the target domain in the input space, i.e., $P^S(X|Y) \neq P^T(X|Y)$. By learning a conditional invariant representation $\Phi(x)$, both source domain and target domain shares similar distribution in the embedding space, i.e., $P^S(\Phi(X)|Y) = P^T(\Phi(X)|Y)$. That is, the embedding $\Phi(x)$ generalizes well on the target domain while it is learned on source domain. Intuitively, the source domain consists of the selected triplets D_S while the target domain consists of all triplets D_T. That is, we learn a conditional invariant embedding using selected triplets and it will generalize well on all triplets.

3.3   Adapted Triplet Loss

To correct the triplet selection bias, we thus try to minimize the distribution shift between $\hat{D}_S$ and $\hat{D}_T$ during learning the representation. Let $x \in X$ denote an input data and $\Phi(x)$ denote the representation learned by deep neural networks, i.e., a dimension fixed feature vector. Inspired by [10,47], we learn a shared conditional invariant representation between $\hat{D}_S$ and $\hat{D}_T$, i.e.,

$$P^S(\Phi(X)|Y) = P^T(\Phi(X)|Y). \tag{11}$$

See Fig. 3 for an example of the conditional invariant representation. Maximum Mean Discrepancy (MMD) has been widely used to estimate the difference between two distributions [15] and we thus use the conditional mean feature embedding to estimate the difference between $P^S(\Phi(X)|Y)$ and $P^T(\Phi(X)|Y)$. As a result, the distribution matching loss can be defined as follows:

$$\mathcal{L}_{match} = \sum_y \|\Phi_y^S - \Phi_y^T\|_2^2, \tag{12}$$

where Φ_y^S and Φ_y^T are class-specific mean feature embeddings on $\hat{D}_S$ and $\hat{D}_T$ respectively, i.e.,

$$\Phi_y^S = \sum_{(X,Y=y)\in\hat{D}_S} P^S(\Phi(X)|Y) * \Phi(X) \tag{13}$$

and

$$\Phi_y^T = \sum_{(X,Y=y)\in\hat{D}_T} P^T(\Phi(X)|Y) * \Phi(X). \tag{14}$$

To correct the distribution shift in learning with triplet loss, we thus learn a discriminative and conditional invariant feature embedding by jointly minimizing the triplet loss as well as the distribution matching loss, i.e.,

$$\mathcal{L} = \mathcal{L}_{triplet} + \lambda * \mathcal{L}_{match}, \tag{15}$$

where λ is a trade-off parameter. Considering that this new variant of triplet loss adaptively corrects the triplet selection bias, we refer to it as adapted triplet loss.

3.4   Semi-supervised Adapted Triplet Loss

Unlabeled data are usually very helpful for domain adaptation. We believe that the unlabeled data will also be helpful for correcting the triplet selection bias. To scale the adapted triplet loss for exploiting large scale unlabeled data, we extend it for the semi-supervised setting.

Given a set of labeled data D_1 and a set of unlabeled data D_2. Let D_{T_1} denote the all triplets constructed from D_1 and D_S denote the subset of selected triplets, i.e., $D_S \subseteq D_{T_1}$. Let D_{T_2} be the latent triplets constructed using the unlabeled data D_2, which is actually unavailable since we do not know the latent labels of D_2. Different from the supervised setting, in which we learn a conditional invariant representation among D_S and D_{T_1}, we consider how to learn a conditional invariant representation between D_S, D_{T_1}, and D_{T_2}, i.e.,

$$P^S(\Phi(X)|Y) = P^{T_1}(\Phi(X)|Y) = P^{T_2}(\Phi(X)|Y). \tag{16}$$

Given the target $P^S(\Phi(X)|Y) = P^{T_2}(\Phi(X)|Y)$, we then have

$$\sum_y P^{T_2}(\Phi(X)|Y)P^{T_2}(Y) = \sum_y P^S(\Phi(X)|Y)P^{T_2}(Y). \tag{17}$$

That is, if we know the class ratio $P^{T_2}(Y)$ for triplet-induced data $\hat{D}_{T_2}$, we are able to estimate the difference between $P^S(\Phi(X)|Y)$ and $P^{T_2}(\Phi(X)|Y)$. Inspired by [17], we estimate the class ratio $P^{T_2}(Y)$ by converting it into an optimization problem, i.e.,

$$\theta^{T_2} = \arg\min_\theta \|\sum_y \theta_y^{T_2} * \Phi_y^S - \Phi^{T_2}\|_2^2, \ s.t. \sum_y \theta_y = 1, \tag{18}$$

where $\Phi^{T_2} = \mathbb{E}_{P_X^{T_2}}[\Phi(X)]$ and $\theta_y^{T_2} = P^{T_2}(Y = y)$. This optimization problem can be solved as follows:

$$\theta_{1:|Y|-1}^{T_2} = (A^\top A)^{-1} A^\top B, \text{ and } \theta_0^{T_2} = 1 - \sum_{y=1}^{|Y|-1} \theta_y^{T_2}, \tag{19}$$

where $A = [\Phi_1^S - \Phi_0^S, \ldots, \Phi_{|Y|-1}^S - \Phi_0^S]$ and $B = \Phi^{T_2}$. We can then define the distribution matching loss in a semi-supervised manner, i.e.,

$$\mathcal{L}_{semi-match} = \| \sum_y \theta_y^{T_2} * \Phi_y^S - \Phi^{T_2} \|_2^2. \tag{20}$$

4 Experiment

In this section, we evaluate the proposed adapted triplet loss function on image classification and retrieval. For image classification, we use MNIST [22] and Fashion-MNIST [44] datasets. The MNIST dataset contains 60,000 training examples and 10,000 test examples, in which all examples are 28×28 grayscale images of handwritten digits. The Fashion-MNIST dataset contains a set of 28×28 grayscale article images and shares the same structure with the MNIST dataset, i.e., 60,000 training examples and 10,000 test examples. For image retrieval, we use three popular datasets, CARS196 [19], CUB200-2011 [37], and Stanford Online Products [28]. The CARS196 dataset contains 16,185 images of 196 different car models, the CUB200-2011 dataset contains 11,788 images of 200 different species of birds, and the Stanford Online Products contains 120,053 images of 22,634 different products.

4.1 Implementation Details

We implement the proposed method using Caffe [18]. Following [33], we always use a L2 normalization layer before the triplet loss layer. We use the margin $\alpha = 0.2$ in all experiments. We train our models using the stochastic gradient descent (SGD) algorithm with momentum 0.9 and weight decay 2e−5. For experiments on MNIST and Fashion-MNIST datasets, we learn 64-D feature embeddings using a modified LeNet [22]. More specifically, we use 3×3 filters in all convolutional layers and replace all activation layers with the PReLU [12] layer. The batch size is set to 256, which is large enough for both MNIST and Fashion-MNIST datasets, i.e., we are able to select enough triplets from each mini-batch. We use the learning rate 0.001 and the maximum iterations are set to 20k and 50k for MNIST and Fashion-MNIST, respectively.

For experiments on CARS196, CUB200-2011, and Stanford Online Products, we use GoogLeNet [36] as our base network and all layers except the last fully connected layer are initialized from the model trained on ImageNet [7]. The last fully connected layer is changed to learn 128-D feature embeddings and is initialized with random weights. All training images are resized to 256×256 and randomly cropped to 224×224. We use a learning rate 0.0005 with the batch size 120 and the maximum training iterations are set to 15k iterations on CARS196, 20k iterations on CUB200-2011, and 50k iterations on Stanford Online Products datasets. To ensure enough triplets in each mini-batch, we prepare the training data using a similar method with [33], i.e., each mini-batch is randomly sampled from 20 classes with 6 images per class.

4.2 Experiment on Image Classification

In this subsection, we describe the experimental results on MNIST and Fashion-MNIST datasets. To demonstrate the effectiveness of the proposed method, we compare the classification accuracy of models trained using the original triplet loss function (baseline) and the adapted triplet loss function. The evaluation metric can be described as follows: to learn a fixed dimensional feature embedding $\Phi(x)$, we train our models using the original triplet loss function and the adapted triplet loss function respectively.

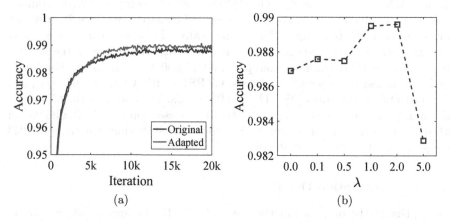

(a)   (b)

Fig. 4. Results on MNIST dataset. In figure (a), we use $\lambda = 2.0$ for adapted triplet loss and compare its performance with the original triplet loss for every 100 iterations. In figure (b), we compare the test accuracy for using different λ.

For testing, we first evaluate the conditional mean embedding $\mathbb{E}\left[\Phi(x)|y\right]$, i.e., the mean point in embedding space, for each class y using the training data. For each input x in test set, we then assign it to a class $\hat{y}$ according to the nearest mean point, i.e.,

$$\hat{y} = \arg\min_{y} \|\Phi(x) - \mathbb{E}[(\Phi(x)|y)]\|_2^2 \tag{21}$$

We demonstrate the results on MNIST dataset in Fig. 4. More specifically, we find that: in figure (a), the adapted triplet loss brings improvement after 5k iterations. Possible explanations for this improvement can be described as follows: for the original triplet loss, the gradient might be dominated by the noise triplets or the hard triplets from some specific classes while the distribution matching loss can adaptively corrects the triplet selection bias between selected triplets and all possible triplets. That is, the adapted triplet loss will generate more balanced gradients for each iteration. Another reason is that the distribution matching loss acts as a regularizer for the original triplet loss, which reduces the risk of overfitting. We evaluate the performance for the adapted triplet loss using different loss weight λ, i.e., $\lambda = 0, 0.1, 0.5, 1.0, 2.0, 5.0$ in figure (b). Specifically, we use $\lambda = 0$ for the original triplet loss, which is a special case of the adapted triplet loss. We find that a trade-off on λ are required for using adapted triplet loss to learn a discriminative and conditional invariant embedding. Furthermore, we demonstrate similar results on Fashion-MNIST in Fig. 5.

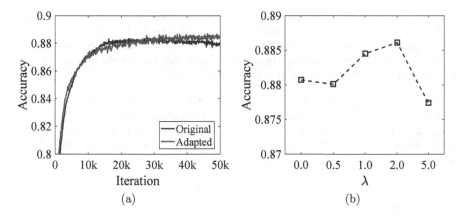

Fig. 5. Results on Fashion-MNIST dataset. In figure (a), we use $\lambda = 2.0$. For the original triplet loss, the test accuracy is reduced after $40k$ iterations, while the adapted triplet loss does not suffer from the problem of overfitting.

To demonstrate the feature embeddings learned by both the original triplet loss and the adapted triplet loss, we use t-SNE [27], which has been widely used for the visualization of high dimensional data, to convert embeddings into 2D space. In Fig. 6, we show the embeddings learned by the adapted triplet loss. Comparing with the embeddings learned by the original triplet loss, we find that the embedding learned by the adapted triplet loss forms uniform margins between different classes, while the embedding learned by the original triplet loss fails to keep a clear margins between some classes.

4.3 Experiment on Image Retrieval

In this subsection, we evaluate the adapted triplet loss on image retrieval. For CARS196, CUB200-2011, and Stanford Online Products datasets, we use similar train/test splits with [28]. More specifically, for CARS196 dataset, we use all 8054 images from the first 98 classes as the training data and the rest as test data

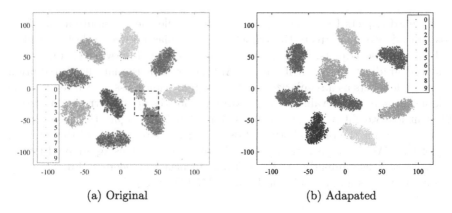

(a) Original   (b) Adapated

Fig. 6. An example for the visualization of feature embeddings learned by the adapted triplet loss as well as the baseline model, i.e., the original triplet loss. We use the model trained on the training set of MNIST and show the learned embeddings on the test set. For the embedding learned by the original triplet loss, the margin between the two classes in the dash-line rectangle area is not large enough.

Table 1. Recall rate on CARS196, CUB200-2011, and Stanford Online Products datasets. For the adapted triplet loss, we train multiple models on all datasets using different λ, i.e., we use $\lambda = 0.001, 0.005, 0.01, 0.05, 0.1$ on CARS196, $\lambda = 0.005, 0.01, 0.1, 0.5$ on CUB200-2011, and $\lambda = 0.01, 0.05, 0.1$ on Stanford Online Products. For the original triplet loss, we use the adapted triplet loss with $\lambda = 0$.

Loss function	R@1	R@2	R@3	R@4	R@5	R@10	R@20
(a) CARS196							
Original ($\lambda = 0$)	0.7781	0.8582	0.8903	0.9105	0.9217	0.9523	0.9716
Adapted ($\lambda = 0.001$)	0.7858	0.8587	0.8921	0.9094	0.9228	0.9525	0.9715
Adapted ($\lambda = 0.005$)	0.7912	**0.8666**	**0.8966**	0.9133	0.9250	0.9535	0.9716
Adapted ($\lambda = 0.010$)	**0.7917**	0.8627	0.8939	**0.9135**	**0.9237**	**0.9570**	**0.9745**
Adapted ($\lambda = 0.050$)	0.7917	0.8627	0.8939	0.9135	0.9237	0.9570	0.9745
Adapted ($\lambda = 0.100$)	0.7631	0.8463	0.8774	0.8996	0.9130	0.9449	0.9665
(b) CUB200-2011							
Original ($\lambda = 0$)	0.4450	0.5724	0.6435	0.6913	0.7275	0.8207	0.8893
Adapted ($\lambda = 0.005$)	0.4439	0.5763	0.6464	0.6884	0.7250	0.8253	0.8964
Adapted ($\lambda = 0.010$)	**0.4660**	**0.5861**	**0.6555**	**0.6997**	**0.7343**	**0.8288**	**0.9024**
Adapted ($\lambda = 0.100$)	0.4512	0.5768	0.6475	0.6904	0.7230	0.8160	0.8902
Adapted ($\lambda = 0.500$)	0.4483	0.5682	0.6381	0.6879	0.7245	0.8114	0.8890
(c) Stanford Online Products							
Original ($\lambda = 0$)	0.6274	0.6865	0.7170	0.7384	0.7524	0.7955	0.9050
Adapted ($\lambda = 0.010$)	**0.6303**	**0.6882**	**0.7206**	**0.7416**	**0.7550**	**0.7982**	**0.9071**
Adapted ($\lambda = 0.050$)	0.6303	0.6876	0.7191	0.7386	0.7530	0.7964	0.9063
Adapted ($\lambda = 0.100$)	0.6297	0.6874	0.7183	0.7378	0.7526	0.7957	0.9044

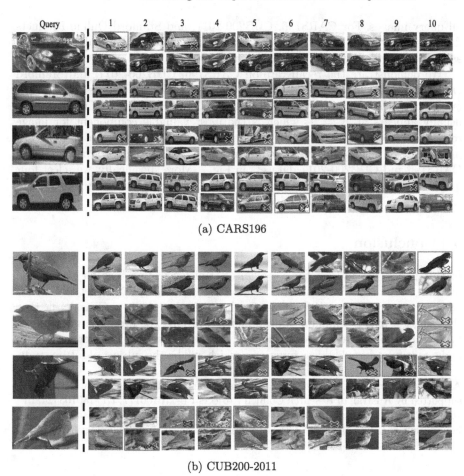

(a) CARS196

(b) CUB200-2011

Fig. 7. Retrieval results on CARS196 and CUB200-2011. The first column is the query image. For each query image, the first row contains 10 nearest neighbors for the original triplet loss; the second row contains 10 nearest neighbors for the adapted triplet loss. We highlight false positive examples with a white/black cross (best view in color).

(8131 images); For CUB200-2011 dataset, we use the data from the first 100 classes as the training data (5864 images) and the rest 5924 images for test; For Stanford Online Products dataset, we use the standard train/test split provided in the dataset, i.e., 59,551 images of the first 11,318 classes for training and the rest 60,502 images of 11,316 classes for testing.

For all experiments on image retrieval, we use the standard Recall@K metric, i.e., the same protocol used in [28]. More specifically, the Recall@K metric can be described as follows: given a query image and its K nearest neighbors, if at least one example hit the query image, i.e., with the same label, the recall rate is equal to 1, otherwise the recall rate is 0. We then report the mean recall rate on all query images. For CARS196, CUB200-2011, and Stanford Online Products datasets, we train all models using only the training split and use all test images as the query images to evaluate the recall rate.

We demonstrate the recall rate on CARS196, CUB200-2011, and Stanford Online Products datasets in Table 1. We can see that the adapted triplet loss outperforms the baseline with all different K values. The maximum improvement usually appears at $K = 1$, which is the most valuable component for image retrieval. Another observation is that the adapted triplet loss usually recalls more positive neighbors. Furthermore, we demonstrate the retrieval results on CARS196 and CUB200-2011 datasets in Fig. 7. More specifically, we select four query images and 10 retrieval results for each query image using the adapted triplet loss and the original triplet loss respectively.

5   Conclusion

In this paper, we address the problem of triplet selection bias for triplet loss by using a domain adaption method. We propose an adapted triplet loss, which adaptively corrects the selection bias for the original triplet loss. Considering that the selection bias is common in deep metric learning, the proposed method can be extended to a variety of loss functions, e.g., pair-based [35], triplet-based [28], and quadruplet-based [4] loss functions, which will be the subject of future study.

Acknowledgement. Baosheng Yu, Tongliang Liu, and Dacheng Tao were partially supported by Australian Research Council Projects FL-170100117, DP-180103424, LP-150100671. Changxing Ding was partially supported by the National Natural Science Foundation of China (Grant No.: 61702193) and Science and Technology Program of Guangzhou (Grant No.: 201804010272).

References

1. Arandjelovic, R., Gronat, P., Torii, A., Pajdla, T., Sivic, J.: NetVLAD: CNN architecture for weakly supervised place recognition. In: CVPR (2016)
2. Ben-David, S., Blitzer, J., Crammer, K., Kulesza, A., Pereira, F., Vaughan, J.W.: A theory of learning from different domains. Mach. Learn. **79**(1), 151–175 (2010)
3. Ben-David, S., Blitzer, J., Crammer, K., Pereira, F., et al.: Analysis of representations for domain adaptation. In: NIPS, vol. 19, p. 137 (2007)
4. Chen, W., Chen, X., Zhang, J., Huang, K.: Beyond triplet loss: a deep quadruplet network for person re-identification. In: CVPR (2017)
5. Cheng, D., Gong, Y., Zhou, S., Wang, J., Zheng, N.: Person re-identification by multi-channel parts-based CNN with improved triplet loss function. In: CVPR, pp. 1335–1344 (2016)
6. Cui, Y., Zhou, F., Lin, Y., Belongie, S.: Fine-grained categorization and dataset bootstrapping using deep metric learning with humans in the loop. In: CVPR, pp. 1153–1162 (2016)
7. Deng, J., Dong, W., Socher, R., Li, L.J., Li, K., Fei-Fei, L.: ImageNet: a large-scale hierarchical image database. In: CVPR, pp. 248–255. IEEE (2009)

8. Ding, C., Tao, D.: Trunk-branch ensemble convolutional neural networks for video-based face recognition. IEEE T-PAMI (2017)
9. Ding, S., Lin, L., Wang, G., Chao, H.: Deep feature learning with relative distance comparison for person re-identification. Pattern Recogn. **48**(10), 2993–3003 (2015)
10. Gong, M., Zhang, K., Liu, T., Tao, D., Glymour, C., Schölkopf, B.: Domain adaptation with conditional transferable components. In: ICML, pp. 2839–2848 (2016)
11. Gordo, A., Almazán, J., Revaud, J., Larlus, D.: Deep image retrieval: learning global representations for image search. arXiv preprint arXiv:1604.01325 (2016)
12. He, K., Zhang, X., Ren, S., Sun, J.: Delving deep into rectifiers: surpassing human-level performance on imagenet classification. In: ICCV, pp. 1026–1034 (2015)
13. Hermans, A., Beyer, L., Leibe, B.: In defense of the triplet loss for person re-identification. arXiv preprint arXiv:1703.07737 (2017)
14. Hoffer, E., Ailon, N.: Deep metric learning using triplet network. arXiv preprint arXiv:1412.6622 (2014)
15. Huang, J., Gretton, A., Borgwardt, K.M., Schölkopf, B., Smola, A.J.: Correcting sample selection bias by unlabeled data. In: NIPS, pp. 601–608 (2007)
16. Huang, J., Feris, R.S., Chen, Q., Yan, S.: Cross-domain image retrieval with a dual attribute-aware ranking network. In: ICCV, pp. 1062–1070 (2015)
17. Iyer, A., Nath, S., Sarawagi, S.: Maximum mean discrepancy for class ratio estimation: convergence bounds and kernel selection. In: ICML, pp. 530–538 (2014)
18. Jia, Y., et al.: Caffe: convolutional architecture for fast feature embedding. arXiv preprint arXiv:1408.5093 (2014)
19. Krause, J., Stark, M., Deng, J., Fei-Fei, L.: 3D object representations for fine-grained categorization. In: 3dRR (Workshop) (2013)
20. Krizhevsky, A., Sutskever, I., Hinton, G.E.: Imagenet classification with deep convolutional neural networks. In: NIPS, pp. 1097–1105 (2012)
21. Lai, H., Pan, Y., Liu, Y., Yan, S.: Simultaneous feature learning and hash coding with deep neural networks. In: CVPR, pp. 3270–3278 (2015)
22. LeCun, Y., Bottou, L., Bengio, Y., Haffner, P.: Gradient-based learning applied to document recognition. Proc. IEEE **86**(11), 2278–2324 (1998)
23. Li, Y., Gong, M., Tian, X., Liu, T., Tao, D.: Domain generalization via conditional invariant representations. In: AAAI (2018)
24. Liu, H., Feng, J., Qi, M., Jiang, J., Yan, S.: End-to-end comparative attention networks for person re-identification. IEEE T-IP (2017)
25. Liu, H., Tian, Y., Yang, Y., Pang, L., Huang, T.: Deep relative distance learning: tell the difference between similar vehicles. In: CVPR (2016)
26. Liu, T., Yang, Q., Tao, D.: Understanding how feature structure transfers in transfer learning. In: IJCAI, pp. 2365–2371 (2017)
27. van dar Maaten, L., Hinton, G.: Visualizing data using t-SNE. JMLR **9**(Nov), 2579–2605 (2008)
28. Oh Song, H., Xiang, Y., Jegelka, S., Savarese, S.: Deep metric learning via lifted structured feature embedding. In: CVPR, pp. 4004–4012 (2016)
29. Pan, S.J., Tsang, I.W., Kwok, J.T., Yang, Q.: Domain adaptation via transfer component analysis. IEEE T-NN **22**(2), 199–210 (2011)
30. Parkhi, O.M., Vedaldi, A., Zisserman, A.: Deep face recognition. In: BMVC, vol. 1, p. 6 (2015)
31. Prabhu, Y., Varma, M.: FastXML: a fast, accurate and stable tree-classifier for extreme multi-label learning. In: SIGKDD, pp. 263–272. ACM (2014)
32. Ramanathan, V., et al.: Learning semantic relationships for better action retrieval in images. In: CVPR (2015)

33. Schroff, F., Kalenichenko, D., Philbin, J.: FaceNet: a unified embedding for face recognition and clustering. In: CVPR, pp. 815–823 (2015)
34. Shi, H., et al.: Embedding deep metric for person re-identification: a study against large variations. In: Leibe, B., Matas, J., Sebe, N., Welling, M. (eds.) ECCV 2016. LNCS, vol. 9905, pp. 732–748. Springer, Cham (2016). https://doi.org/10.1007/978-3-319-46448-0_44
35. Sohn, K.: Improved deep metric learning with multi-class N-pair loss objective. In: NIPS, pp. 1857–1865 (2016)
36. Szegedy, C., et al.: Going deeper with convolutions. In: CVPR (2015)
37. Wah, C., Branson, S., Welinder, P., Perona, P., Belongie, S.: The caltech-UCSD birds-200-2011 dataset (2011)
38. Wang, J., et al.: Learning fine-grained image similarity with deep ranking. In: CVPR, pp. 1386–1393 (2014)
39. Wang, L., Li, Y., Lazebnik, S.: Learning deep structure-preserving image-text embeddings. In: CVPR (2016)
40. Wang, X., Huang, T.K., Schneider, J.: Active transfer learning under model shift. In: ICML, pp. 1305–1313 (2014)
41. Weinberger, K.Q., Saul, L.K.: Distance metric learning for large margin nearest neighbor classification. JMLR 10(Feb), 207–244 (2009)
42. Wohlhart, P., Lepetit, V.: Learning descriptors for object recognition and 3D pose estimation. In: CVPR, pp. 3109–3118 (2015)
43. Wu, C.Y., Manmatha, R., Smola, A.J., Krahenbuhl, P.: Sampling matters in deep embedding learning. In: CVPR, pp. 2840–2848 (2017)
44. Xiao, H., Rasul, K., Vollgraf, R.: Fashion-MNIST: a novel image dataset for benchmarking machine learning algorithms. arXiv preprint arXiv:1708.07747 (2017)
45. Xiao, T., Li, H., Ouyang, W., Wang, X.: Learning deep feature representations with domain guided dropout for person re-identification. In: CVPR, pp. 1249–1258 (2016)
46. Yuan, Y., Yang, K., Zhang, C.: Hard-aware deeply cascaded embedding. In: ICCV, pp. 814–823. IEEE (2017)
47. Zhang, K., Schölkopf, B., Muandet, K., Wang, Z.: Domain adaptation under target and conditional shift. In: ICML, pp. 819–827 (2013)
48. Zhuang, B., Lin, G., Shen, C., Reid, I.: Fast training of triplet-based deep binary embedding networks. In: CVPR, pp. 5955–5964 (2016)

CrossNet: An End-to-End Reference-Based Super Resolution Network Using Cross-Scale Warping

Haitian Zheng[1], Mengqi Ji[1,2], Haoqian Wang[1], Yebin Liu[3], and Lu Fang[1(✉)]

[1] Tsinghua-Berkeley Shenzhen Institute, Tsinghua University, Beijing, China
fanglu@sz.tsinghua.edu.cn
[2] Hong Kong University of Science and Technology, Clear Water Bay, Hong Kong
[3] Department of Automation, Tsinghua University, Beijing, China

Abstract. The Reference-based Super-resolution (RefSR) super-resolves a low-resolution (LR) image given an external high-resolution (HR) reference image, where the reference image and LR image share similar viewpoint but with significant resolution gap ($8\times$). Existing RefSR methods work in a cascaded way such as patch matching followed by synthesis pipeline with two independently defined objective functions, leading to the inter-patch misalignment, grid effect and inefficient optimization. To resolve these issues, we present CrossNet, an end-to-end and fully-convolutional deep neural network using cross-scale warping. Our network contains image encoders, cross-scale warping layers, and fusion decoder: the encoder serves to extract multi-scale features from both the LR and the reference images; the cross-scale warping layers spatially aligns the reference feature map with the LR feature map; the decoder finally aggregates feature maps from both domains to synthesize the HR output. Using cross-scale warping, our network is able to perform spatial alignment at pixel-level in an end-to-end fashion, which improves the existing schemes [1,2] both in precision (around $2\,\mathrm{dB}$–$4\,\mathrm{dB}$) and efficiency (more than 100 times faster).

Keywords: Reference-based Super Resolution · Light field imaging
Image synthesis · Encoder-decoder · Optical flow

L. Fang—This work is supported in part by Natural Science Foundation of China (NSFC) under contract No. 61722209, 61331015 and 61522111, in part by the National key foundation for exploring scientific instrument of China No. 2013YQ140517.

Electronic supplementary material The online version of this chapter (https://doi.org/10.1007/978-3-030-01231-1_6) contains supplementary material, which is available to authorized users.

V. Ferrari et al. (Eds.): ECCV 2018, LNCS 11210, pp. 87–104, 2018.
https://doi.org/10.1007/978-3-030-01231-1_6

1   Introduction

Reference-based super-resolution (RefSR) methods [2] utilizes an extra high resolution (HR) reference image to help super-resolve the low resolution (LR) image that shares similar viewpoint. Benefit from the high resolution details in reference image, RefSR usually leads to competitive performance compared to single-image SR (SISR). While RefSR has been successfully applied in light-field reconstruction [1–3] and giga-pixel video synthesis [4], it remains a challenging and unsolved problem, due to the parallax and the huge resolution gap (8x) exist between HR reference image and LR image. Essentially, how to transfer the high-frequency details from the reference image to the LR image is the key to the success of RefSR. This leads to the two critical issues in RefSR, i.e., image correspondence between the two input images and high resolution synthesis of the LR image.

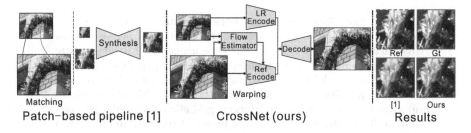

Fig. 1. Left: the 'patch maching + synthesis' pipeline of [2], middle: the proposed end-to-end CrossNet, right: results comparisons.

In the initial work of [1], to develop image correspondences between the two inputs, the gradient features on the down-sampled patches in the HR reference are used for patch-based matching, while patch averaging is designed for the image synthesis. However, the oversimplified and down-sampled correspondence estimation of [1] does not take advantage of the high frequency information for matching, while the synthesizing step does not utilize high resolution image prior for better fusion. To address the above two limitations, a recent work [2] replaces the gradient feature of [1] with the convolutional neural network (CNN) learned features to improve the matching accuracy, and then proposes an additional CNN which utilizes the state-of-the-art single image super-resolution (SISR) algorithm [5] for patch synthesis. However, the 'patch matching + patch synthesis' scheme of [1,2] are fundamentally limited. Firstly, the adopted sliding averaging blurs the output image and causes grid artifacts. Moreover, patch-based synthesis is inherently incapable in handling the non-rigid image deformation caused by viewpoint changes. To impose the non-rigid deformation to patch-based algorithms, [3] enriches the reference images by iteratively applying non-uniform warping before the patch synthesis. However, directly warping between the low and high resolution images is inaccurate. In addition, such iterative combination of patch matching and warping introduces heavy computational burden, e.g. around 30 min for synthesizing an image.

In this paper, we propose CrossNet, an end-to-end convolutional neural network based on the idea of 'warping + synthesis' for reference-based image super-resolution. We discard the idea of 'patch matching' and replace it with 'warping', which enables the design of 'Encoder-Warping-Decoder' structure, as shown in Fig. 1. Such structure contains two encoders to extract multi-scale features from LR and reference image respectively. We take advantage of the warping module originated from spatial transformer network (STN) [6], and integrate it to our HR reference image encoder. Compared with the patch matching based methods, warping naturally supports non-rigid deformation to overcome the parallax challenge in RefSR. More over, we extract multi-scale features in the encoder, and then perform multi-scale spatial alignment using warping, as shown in Fig. 1. The introduced multi-scale features capture the complementary scale information from two images, which help to alleviate the huge resolution gap challenge in RefSR. Finally, the decoder aggregates features to synthesize the HR output. Overall, our model is fully end-to-end trainable and does not require pretraining the flow estimator.

Extensive experiments have shown the superior performance of CrossNet (around 2 dB–4 dB gain) compared to state-of-the-art SISR and RefSR methods, under different datasets with large/small viewpoint disparities and different scales. Our trained model that generalized to external dataset including Stanford light field maintains the ability to retain high frequency details. More importantly, CrossNet is efficient in terms that it generates a 320 × 512 image within one second, while [1,2] and [3] take 86.3 s, 105.0 s and around 30 min to perform the same task, respectively.

2   Related Work

2.1   Single-Image Super-Resolution

The single-image super-resolution (SISR) problem aims to super-resolve an LR image without additional references. Despite that, the SISR problems are closely related to the Reference-based Super-resolution (RefSR) problem. In the early days, approaches based on adaptive sampling [7,8] has been applied to SISR. However, such approaches did not utilize the statistics of nature images. In contrast, model-based approaches try to design image prior which helps to super-resolve the image-specific patterns. Such works usually utilize edge prior [9], total variation model [10], hyper-Laplacian prior [11], sparsity priors [12–15], or exemplar patches [16,17].

More recently, the SISR problem was casted into a supervised regression problem, which try to learn a mapping function from LR patches to HR patches. Those works relies on varieties of learning techniques including nearest-neighbor search [18,19], decision tree [20], random forests [21], simple function [22,23], Gaussian process regression [24], and deep neural networks.

With the increasing model capacity of the deep neural networks, the SISR performance has been rapidly improved. Since the appearance of the first deep learning-based SR method [25], a large number of works have been proposed to further improve the SISR performance. For example, Dong et al. [26] and Shi et al. [27] accelerate the efficiency of SISR by computing features on low-resolution domains. Kim et al. [28] proposed a 20-layers deep network for predicting the bicubic upsampling residue. Ledig et al. [5] proposed a deep residue network with adversarial training for SISR. Lai et al. [29] reconstructed the sub-band residuals using a multi-stage Laplacian network. Lim et al. [30] improved [5] by introducing a multi-scale feature extraction residue block for better performance. Because of the impressive performance of the MDSR network from [30], we employ MDSR as a sub-module for LR images feature extraction and RefSR synthesis.

2.2   Reference-Based Super-Resolution

Recent works such as [1–3,31–33] uses additional reference images from different viewpoints to help super-resolving the LR input, which forms a new kind of SR method called RefSR. Specifically, Boominathan et al. [1] used an DSLR captured high-definition image as reference, and applies a patch-based synthesizing algorithm using non-local mean [19] for super-resolving the low-definition light-field images. Wu et al. [33] improved such algorithm by employing patch registration before the nearest neighbor searching, then applies dictionary learning for reconstruction. Wang et al. [3] iterate the patch synthesizing step of [1] for enriching the exemplar database. Zheng et al. [34] decompose images into subbands by frequencies and apply patch matching for high-frequency subband reconstruction. Recently, Zheng et al. [2] proposed a deep learning-based approach for the cross-resolution patch matching and synthesizing, which significantly boosts the accuracy of RefSR. However, the patch-based synthesizing algorithms are inherently incapable in handling the non-rigid image deformation that is often caused by the irregular foreground shapes. Under such cases, patch-based synthesize causes issues such as blocky artifact and blurring effect. Despite that sliding windows [1,2] or iterative refinement [3] mitigate such difficulties to some extends, these strategies usually introduce heavy computational cost. On the contrary, our fully convolutional network makes it possible to achieve more than 100 times speedup compared to existing RefSR approaches, allowing the model to be applicable for real-time applications.

2.3   Image/Video Synthesis Using Warping

Our task is also related to image/video synthesis tasks that use additional images from other viewpoints or frames. Such tasks include view synthesis [35,36], video denoising [37], super-resolution [37–39], interpolation or extrapolation [40,41]. To solve this type of problems, deep neural networks based of the design of "warping and synthesis" has been recently proposed. Specifically, the additional images are backward warped to the target image using the estimated flow. Afterward, the warped image is used for image/frame synthesis using an additional synthesis module. We follow such "warping and synthesis" pipeline. However, our approach is different from existing works in the following ways: (1) in stead of the common practice where warping was performed on image-domain at pixel-scale [35,36,

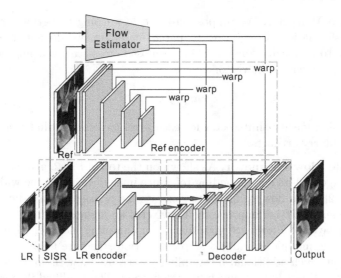

Fig. 2. Network structure of our proposed CrossNet.

40,41], our approach performs multi-scale warping on feature domain, which accelerates the model convergence by allowing flow to be globally updated at higher scales. (2) after the warping operations, a novel fusion scheme is proposed for image synthesis. Our fusion scheme is different from the existing synthesizing practices that include image-domain early fusion (concatenation) [36,40] and linearly combining images [35,41].

3 Approach

Our reference-based super resolution scheme, named CrossNet, is based on a fully convolutional cross-scale alignment module that spatially aligns the reference image information to the LR image domain. Along with the cross-scale alignment module, an encoder-decoder structure is proposed to directly synthesize the RefSR output in an end-to-end, and fully convolutional fashion. The entire network is plotted in Fig. 2. In Sect. 3.1, we introduce the designs and properties of the fully convolutional cross scale alignment module. In Sect. 3.2, the end-to-end network structure is described, followed by the image synthesis loss function depicted in Sect. 3.3.

3.1 Fully Convolutional Cross-Scale Alignment Module

Since the reference image is captured at different view points from LR image, it is necessary to perform spatial alignment. In [1–3], such correspondence is estimated by matching every LR patches with its surrounding reference patches. However, such sparsely-sampled and non-rigidly upsampled correspondence can easily fail around the region with varying depth or disparity.

Cross-Scale Warping. We propose cross-scale warping to perform non-rigid image transformation. Comparing to patch matching, we do not assume the depth plane to be locally constant. Our proposed cross-scale warping operation considers a pixel-wise shift vector V:

$$I_o = warp(y_{Ref}, V), \tag{1}$$

which assigns a specific shift vector for each pixel location, so that it avoids the blocky and blurry artifacts.

Cross-Scale Flow Estimator. As shown on the top of Fig. 2, given an upsampled LR image and its corresponding reference image, we adopt the widely used FlowNetS [42] as our flow estimator to generate the cross-scale correspondence at multiple scale. To further improve the FlowNetS, we replace the final ×4 bilinear upsampling layer of FlownetS with two ×2 upsampling module, whereas each ×2 upsampling module contains a skip connection structure following a deconvolution layer. Such additional upsampling procedure allow the modified model to predict the flow-field with much finer definition. The modified flow estimator works to generate the multi-scale flow-fields as follows:

$$\{V^{(3)}, V^{(2)}, V^{(1)}, V^{(0)}\} = Flow(I_{LR\uparrow}, I_{REF}), \tag{2}$$

where the I_{REF} denotes the reference image, and $I_{LR\uparrow}$ denotes an representative Single-Image SR (SISR) approach [30] upsampled the LR image (I_{LR}):

$$I_{LR\uparrow} = SISR(I_{LR}). \tag{3}$$

More discussions on the choice of flow estimator are presented in discussion in Sect. 4.3.

3.2　End-to-End Network Structure

The patch matching calculates pixel-wise flow using a sliding window scheme. Such matching is computationally expensive, compared with the proposed fully convolutional network for cross-scale flow field estimation.

Resorting the cross-scale warping as a key component for spatial alignment, we propose an end-to-end network for RefSR synthesis. Our network, contains a **LR image encoder** which extracts multi-scale feature maps from the LR image I_L, a **reference image encoder** which extracts and aligns the reference image feature maps at multiple scales, and a **decoder** which perform multi-scale feature fusion and synthesis using the U-Net [43] structure. Figure 2 summarizes the structure of our proposed CrossNet. The major modules, i.e., encoder, estimator and decoder, are elaborated as follows.

LR Image Encoder. Given the LR image I_L, we design a LR image encoder to extract reference feature maps at 4 scales. Specifically, we utilize SISR approach in Eq. 3 to upsample the LR image. After that, we convolve the upsampled images with 64 filters (of size 5 × 5) with stride 1 to extract feature map at scale

0. We repeatedly convolve the feature map at the scale $i - 1$ (for $0 < i \leq 3$) with 64 filters (of size 5×5) with stride 2 to extract feature map at scale i. Such operations can be represented as

$$
\begin{aligned}
F_{LR}^{(0)} &= \sigma(\boldsymbol{W}_{LR}^{(0)} * I_{LR\uparrow} + \boldsymbol{b}_{LR}^{(0)}), \\
F_{LR}^{(i)} &= \sigma(\boldsymbol{W}_{LR}^{(i)} * F_{LR}^{(i-1)} + \boldsymbol{b}_{LR}^{(i)})\Downarrow_2, \ i = 1, 2, 3,
\end{aligned}
\tag{4}
$$

where $F_{LR}^{(i)}$ is the LR feature map at scale i, σ stands for the activation function of rectified linear unit (ReLU) [44], $*$ denotes convolution, and $\Downarrow_2$ denotes 2D sampling with stride 2.

Note that resorting independent SISR approaches (such as [30]) to encode LR image owns two advantages. First, the SISR approaches that are validated on large-scale external datasets help the LR image encoder to generalize better on unseen scenes. Second, new state-of-the-art SISR approaches can be easily integrated into our system to improve the performance without changing our network structures.

Reference Image Encoder. Given the raw reference image I_R, a 4 scale feature extraction network with the exact structure from Eq. 4 are used to sequentially extract reference image features $\{F_{REF}^{(0)}, F_{REF}^{(1)}, F_{REF}^{(2)}, F_{REF}^{(3)}\}$ from multiple scales. We allow the reference feature extractor and the LR feature extractor to learn different weights, which helps the two sets of features to complement each other.

After that, we perform backward warping operation on the reference image features $F_R^{(i)}$ using the cross-scale flow $V^{(i)}$ in Eq. 2, to generate the spatially aligned feature $\hat{F}_R^{(i)}$.

$$
\hat{F}_{REF}^{(i)} = warp(F_{REF}^{(i)}, V^{(i)}), \ i = 0, 1, 2, 3.
\tag{5}
$$

More discussions on the multi-scale warping are presented in Sect. 4.3.

Decoder. After extracting the LR image feature and the warped reference image feature at different scales, a U-Net like decoder is proposed to perform fusion and SR synthesis. Specifically, the warped features and the LR image features at scale i (for $0 \leq i \leq 3$), as well as the decoder feature from scale $i - 1$ (if any) are concatenated following a deconvolution layer with 64 filters (of size 4×4) and stride 2 to generate decoder features at scale i,

$$
\begin{aligned}
F_D^{(3)} &= \sigma(\boldsymbol{W}_D^{(3)} \star (F_{LR}^{(3)}, \hat{F}_{REF}^{(3)}) + \boldsymbol{b}_D^{(3)}), \\
F_D^{(i)} &= \sigma(\boldsymbol{W}_D^{(i)} \star (F_{LR}^{(i+1)}, \hat{F}_{REF}^{(i+1)}, F_D^{(i+1)}) + \boldsymbol{b}_D^{(i)}), \ i = 2, 1, 0,
\end{aligned}
\tag{6}
$$

where $\star$ denotes the deconvolution operation.

After generating the decoder feature at scale 0, three additional convolution layers with filter sizes 5×5 and filter number $\{64, 64, 3\}$ are added to perform post-fusion and to generate the SR output,

$$\begin{aligned} F_1 &= \sigma(\boldsymbol{W}_1 * F_D^{(0)} + \boldsymbol{b}_1), \\ F_2 &= \sigma(\boldsymbol{W}_2 * F_1 + \boldsymbol{b}_2), \\ I_p &= \sigma(\boldsymbol{W}_p * F_2 + \boldsymbol{b}_p). \end{aligned} \tag{7}$$

3.3 Loss Function

Our network can be directly trained to synthesize the SR output. Given the network prediction I_p, and the ground truth high-resolution image I_{HR}, the loss function can be written as

$$\mathcal{L} = \frac{1}{N} \sum_{i=1}^{N} \sum_s \rho(I_{HR}^{(i)}(s) - I_p^{(i)}(s)), \tag{8}$$

where $\rho(x) = \sqrt{x^2 + 0.001^2}$ is the Charbonnier penalty function [45], N is the number of samples, i and s iterate over training samples and spatial locations, respectively.

4 Experiment

4.1 Dataset

The representative Flower dataset [46] and Light Field Video (LFVideo) dataset [41] are used here. The Flower dataset [46] contains 3343 flowers and plants light-field images captured by Lytro ILLUM camera, whereas each light field image has 376×541 spatial samples, and 14×14 angular samples. Following [46], we extract the central 8×8 grid of angular sample to avoid invalid images, and randomly divide the dataset into 3243 images for training and 100 images for testing. The LFVideo dataset [41] contains real-scene light-field image captured by Lytro ILLUM camera. Similar to the Flower dataset, each light field image has 376×541 spatial samples and 8×8 angular samples. There are in total 1080 light-field samples for training and 270 light-field samples for testing.

For model training using these two dataset, the LR and reference images are randomly selected from the 8×8 angular grid. While for testing, the LR images at angular position $(i, i), 0 < i \leq 7$ and reference images at position $(0, 0)$ are selected for evaluating RefSR algorithms. As our model requires the input size being a factor of 32, the images from the two dataset are cropped to 320×512 for training and validation.

To validate the generalization ability of CrossNet, we also test it on the images from Stanford Light Field dataset [47] and Scene Light Field dataset [48], where we apply our trained model using sliding windows approach, with windows size being 512×512 and stride being 256 to output the SR result of the entire image. More details are presented in the generalization analysis in 4.2.

Table 1. Quantitative evaluation of the state-of-the-art SISR and RefSR algorithms, in terms of PSNR/SSIM/IFC for scale factors ×4 and ×8 respectively.

Algorithm	Scale	Flower (1, 1) PSNR/SSIM/IFC	Flower (7, 7) PSNR/SSIM/IFC	LFVideo (1, 1) PSNR/SSIM/IFC	LFVideo (7, 7) PSNR/SSIM/IFC
SRCNN [25]	×4	32.76/0.89/2.46	32.96/0.90/2.49	32.98/0.86/2.07	33.27/0.86/2.08
VDSR [28]	×4	33.34/0.90/2.73	33.58/0.91/2.76	33.58/0.87/2.29	33.87/0.88/2.30
MDSR [30]	×4	34.40/0.92/3.04	34.65/0.92/3.07	34.62/0.89/2.62	34.91/0.90/2.63
PatchMatch [1]	×4	38.03/0.97/5.11	35.23/0.94/3.85	38.22/0.95/4.60	37.08/0.94/3.99
CrossNet (ours)	×4	**42.09/0.98/6.70**	**38.49/0.97/5.02**	**42.21/0.98/5.96**	**39.03/0.96/4.61**
SRCNN [25]	×8	28.17/0.77/0.98	28.25/0.77/1.00	29.43/0.75/0.82	29.63/0.76/0.82
VDSR [28]	×8	28.58/0.78/1.04	28.68/0.78/1.06	29.83/0.77/0.89	30.04/0.77/0.89
MDSR [30]	×8	29.15/0.79/1.17	29.26/0.80/1.19	30.43/0.78/1.04	30.65/0.79/1.05
PatchMatch [1]	×8	35.26/0.95/4.00	30.41/0.85/2.07	36.72/0.94/3.81	34.48/0.91/2.84
SS-Net [2]	×8	37.46/0.97/4.72	32.42/0.91/2.95	37.93/0.95/4.06	35.81/0.93/3.30
CrossNet (ours)	×8	**40.31/0.98/5.74**	**34.37/0.93/3.45**	**41.26/0.97/5.22**	**36.48/0.93/3.43**

4.2   Evaluation

We train the CrossNet for 200K iterations on the Flower and LFVideo datasets for ×4 and ×8 SR respectively. The learning rates are initially set to 1e−4 and 7e−5 for the two dataset respectively, and decay to 1e−5 and 7e−6 after 150k iterations. As optimizer, the Adam [49] is used with $\beta_1 = 0.9$, and $\beta_1 = 0.999$. In comparison to CrossNet, we also test the latest RefSR algorithms SS-Net [2] and PatchMatch [1], and the representative SISR approaches including SRCNN [25], VDSR [28] and MDSR [30].

We evaluate the results using three image quality metrics: PSNR, SSIM [50], and IFC [51]. Table 1 shows quantitative comparisons for ×4 and ×8 RefSR under the two parallax settings, where the reference images are sampled at position $(0, 0)$ while LR images are sampled at position $(1, 1)$ and $(7, 7)$. Examining Table 1, the proposed CrossNet outperforms the previous approaches considerably under various settings including small/large parallax, different upsampling scales and different datasets, achieving 2 dB–4 dB gain in general.

For better comparison, we also visualize the PSNR performance under different parallax setting in Fig. 3. As expected, the RefSR approaches such as Cross-Net, PatchMatch, SS-Net outperform SISR approaches owe to the high-frequency details provided by reference images. However, RefSR results deteriorate as the parallax enlarges, due to the fact that the correspondence searching is more difficult for large parallax. In contrast, the performance of SISR approaches appears as 'U-shape' for different views, i.e., at the corners of LF image for disparity being (1, 1) and (7, 7), the SISR performs slightly better. This is probably due to the occurrence of easily super-resolved invalid region becomes larger at corners. Finally, it can be seen that the proposed CrossNet consistently outperforms the resting approaches under different disparities, datasets and scales.

Figure 4 presents the visual comparisons of CrossNet with SISR approaches including SRCNN, VDSR, MDSR and RefSR approaches including PatchMatch and SS-Net under the challenging ×8 scale setting. Benefiting from the reference image, RefSR approaches show competitive results compared to the SISR

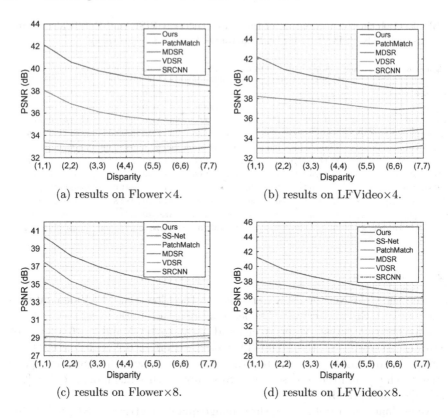

(a) results on Flower×4.

(b) results on LFVideo×4.

(c) results on Flower×8.

(d) results on LFVideo×8.

Fig. 3. The PSNR measurement under different parallax settings: the reference images are select at $(0,0)$ LF grid, while the LR image are selected at (i,i) LR grid $((i,i), 0 < i \le 8)$.

methods, where the high frequency details are explicitly retained. Among them, the proposed CrossNet can further provide finer details, resembling the details in ground truth image. More visual comparison are shown in the supplementary material and supplementary video[1].

Generalization: To further estimate the cross-dataset generalization capacity of our model, we report the results on Stanford light field dataset (Lego Gantry) [47] and the Scene Light Field dataset [48], where the former one contains light field images captured by a Canon Digital Rebel XTi that set on a movable Mindstorms motors on the Lego gantry, and images from the latter one are also captured on a motorized stage with a standard DSLR camera. Under such equipment settings, the captured light-field images of the two datasets have much large parallax comparing to the ones captured by Lytro ILLUM cameras. The parallax discrepancy between datasets yields difficulty to our trained model, as our model is not particularly trained with large parallax.

---

[1] https://youtu.be/7htEaaNkxG8.

Fig. 4. Visual comparison for ×8 RefSR on LFVideo (1, 1), LFVideo (3, 3), Flower (1, 1). In the experiment, our approach is compared against SRCNN [25], VDSR [28], MDSR [30], PatchMatch [1], and SS-Net [2].

To handle these two datasets, we employ a parallax augmentation procedure during training, which randomly offsets the reference input by $[-15, 15]$ pixels both horizontally and vertically. We take the pre-trained model parameters using LFVideo dataset (in Sect. 4.2) as the initialization, and re-train the CrossNet on the Flower dataset for 200K iterations in order to achieve better generalization. We use 7e−5 as the initial learning rate, and decay the learning rate using factors 0.5, 0.2, 0.1 at 50K, 100K, 150K iterations.

Table 2. ×8 super-resolution experiment on the Stanford light field dataset [47].

Image, parallax=(1/3/5, 0)	MDSR [30]	PatchMatch [1]	SS-Net [2]	Ours
Amethyst	29.64/29.66/29.74	36.44/34.71/33.20	36.91/34.97/33.35	**39.52/36.92/35.13**
Bracelet	24.66/24.68/24.64	35.66/33.71/25.47	36.33/34.19/**32.53**	**38.19/34.27**/27.20
Chess	30.39/30.42/30.39	38.68/36.68/34.99	39.85/38.64/37.12	**41.85/40.68/39.34**
Flowers	30.01/30.00/29.98	33.74/33.24/32.58	37.46/35.44/34.09	**39.50/36.53/34.56**
JellyBeans	41.09/41.00/41.15	39.48/38.68/37.19	37.98/36.60/35.14	**43.81/42.29/40.11**
LegoBulldozer	29.58/29.56/29.58	35.60/31.39/28.87	35.99/33.26/31.86	**38.79/35.00/32.61**
LegoGantry	26.58/26.52/26.58	31.73/29.86/27.15	32.68/**30.97/30.06**	**33.42**/30.83/29.96
LegoKnights	29.49/29.48/29.46	33.57/30.73/27.57	33.48/31.45/30.20	**37.60/34.40/32.11**
LegoTruck	30.82/30.80/30.67	34.96/34.22/33.30	37.80/36.44/34.87	**39.87/38.51/37.17**
TarotCardsLarge	22.91/22.89/22.86	27.98/20.90/20.40	29.69/**26.71/24.63**	**31.27**/23.69/22.16
TarotCardsSmall	23.98/23.98/23.97	30.08/29.30/27.60	32.92/**31.44/30.70**	**35.48**/31.42/28.22
StanfordBunny	36.82/36.90/36.96	37.39/37.15/36.75	40.36/39.77/39.09	**41.99/41.48/40.88**
Average	29.66/29.66/29.67	34.61/32.55/30.42	35.96/34.16/32.81	**38.44/35.50/33.29**

Table 3. ×8 super-resolution experiment on the Scene light field dataset [48].

Image, parallax = (1, 0)	MDSR [30]	PatchMatch [1]	SS-Net [2]	Ours
Bikes	28.38	36.70	36.36	**37.91**
Church	36.04	41.89	40.10	**43.68**
Couch	32.52	33.93	35.86	**39.83**
Mansion	28.03	32.83	33.39	**36.38**
Statue	29.72	35.96	35.21	**37.30**
Average	30.94	36.26	36.18	**39.02**

Tables 2 and 3 compare in PSNR measurement our re-trained model with PatchMatch [1], SS-Net [2] for ×8 RefSR on the Stanford light-field dataset and the Scene Light Field dataset respectively. It can be seen that our approach outperforms the resting approaches with different parallax settings on the Stanford dataset. On average, our approach outperforms the competitive SS-Net by 1.79–2.50 dB on the Stanford light-field dataset and 2.84 dB on the Stanford light-field dataset.

Efficiency: It is worth mentioning that the proposed CrossNet generates an 320×512 image for ×8 RefSR within 1 s, i.e., 0.75 s to perform SISR preprocessing using the MDSR [30] model, and 0.12 s to synthesize the final output. In contrast, the PatchMatch [1] takes 86.3 s to run on Matlab2016 using GPU parallelization while the SS-Net [2] takes on average 105.6 s running on GPU. The above running times are profiled using a machine with 8 Intel Xeon CPU (3.4 GHz) and a GeForce GTX 1080 GPU, while the model inferences of our CrossNet and SS-Net [2] are implemented on Python with Theano deep learning package [52].

Fig. 5. Flow visualization and comparison for sample #1, #99 in the flower ×8 testing set. (a) the HR image, (b) (c) (d) flow visualization of PatchMatch [1], SS-Net [2], and our approach respectively. In (d), the flow is visualized at scales ×1, ×2, ×4 (row 1), and ×8, ×32, ×64 (row 2).

4.3 Discussions

One may concern that our loss is designed for image synthesis, and does not explicitly define terms for flow estimation. However, since the correctly aligned features are extremely informative for decoder to reconstruct high-frequency details, our model actually learns to predict optical flow by aligning features maps in an unsupervised fashion. To validate the effectiveness of the learned flow by aligning feature, we visualize the intermediate flow field at all scales in Fig. 5(d), where flow predictions at scales $0, 1, 2, 3(\times 1, \times 2, \times 4, \times 8)$ are reasonably coherent, yet noisy flow predictions are observed at scales $4, 5(\times 16, \times 32)$, because the flow at scale $4, 5$ are not used for the feature-domain warping.

In addition to the multi-scale feature warping module proposed in this paper, we investigate a single-scale image warping counterpart which performs reference image warping **before** the following image encoder for feature extraction. This counterpart is inspired by the common practice in [35,41] that performs image warping before synthesis. More concretely, our single-scale image warping counterpart performs image warping using the flow from scale 0: $\hat{I}_{REF} = warp(I_{REF}, V^{(0)})$. After that, reference image encoder with the same structure is used to extract features from the warped reference image. Without changing the structure of encoder and decoder, such image warping counterpart CrossNet-iw has the same model size as CrossNet.

We train both CrossNet-iw and CrossNet according to the same procedure in Sect. 4.2. We also adopt a pretraining strategy to train CrossNet-iw. We pretrain the flow estimator of WS-SRNet with image warping task for 100K iterations, and then apply the joint training for another 100K iterations, resulting the CrossNet-iw-p model. Figure 6 shows the PSNR convergence curves on training set for ×8RefSR on the Flower and LFVideo dataset. It can be noticed that our CrossNet converges faster than the CrossNet-iw counterparts. At the end of the training, CrossNet outperforms CrossNet-iw 0.20 dB and 0.27 dB on training set. Table 4 shows the RefSR precision on the test sets with three representative point views. CrossNet outperforms CrossNet-iw, especially on small parallax setting. It is reasonable because the training uses random sampled pairs from the LF grid, which are mostly took up by small parallax training pairs.

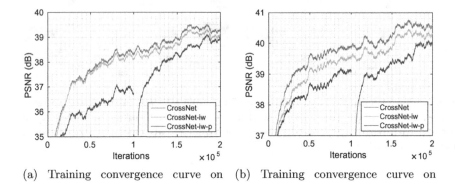

(a) Training convergence curve on Flower×8.

(b) Training convergence curve on LFVideo×8.

Fig. 6. The convergence analysis on our feature domain warping scheme (CrossNet) versus image warping schemes. Our model (CrossNet, red) converges faster than the image-domain warping counterpart (CrossNet-iW) with or without pre-training. (Color figure online)

As our method relies on the cross-scale flow estimators, it is also important to study the flow predicting capacities of different flow estimator. For such purpose, we train the FlowNetS and our modified model (FlowNetS+) on the Flower and the LFVideo dataset for warping the reference images to the ground truth images given the reference and LR image as input. As shown In Table 5, while the FlowNetS+ contains 2% more parameters in comparison to FlowNetS, the additional upscaling layers of FlowNetS+ reasonably improves the warping precision in both the Flower dataset [46] and the LFVideo dataset [41], as they help to generate finer flow field. In addition, we also observe that by plain warping, the FlowNetS+ achieves notably better compatible performance compared to SS-Net [2], as depicted by the SS-Net (×8) row in Table 1.

Table 4. Ablation study to evaluate the effectiveness of multi-scale feature warping.

Model	Parameter size	Flower×8 (1, 1) PSNR/SSIM/IFC	Flower×8 (3, 3) PSNR/SSIM/IFC	Flower×8 (7, 7) PSNR/SSIM/IFC
CrossNet	41M	**40.31/0.98/5.74**	**36.95/0.96/4.61**	34.37/0.93/3.45
CrossNet-iw	41M	40.14/0.98/5.75	36.94/0.96/4.59	**34.49/0.93/3.52**
CrossNet-iw-p	41M	40.01/0.98/5.75	36.85/0.96/4.58	34.35/0.93/3.49
		LFVideo×8 (1, 1) PSNR/SSIM/IFC	LFVideo×8 (3, 3) PSNR/SSIM/IFC	LFVideo×8 (7, 7) PSNR/SSIM/IFC
CrossNet	41M	**41.26/0.97/5.22**	**38.69/0.96/4.32**	**36.48/0.93/3.43**
CrossNet-iw	41M	41.12/0.97/5.20	38.61/0.96/4.32	36.32/0.93/3.43
CrossNet-iw-p	41M	40.96/0.97/5.16	38.47/0.96/4.29	36.11/0.93/3.43

Table 5. Quantitative evaluation and the parameter sizes comparison, using different flow estimators to warp the reference image. The LR images are located at angular position $(3, 3)$.

Model	# of parameters	Flower×8(1, 1) PSNR/SSIM/IFC	Flower×8(7, 7) PSNR/SSIM/IFC	LFVideo×8(1, 1) PSNR/SSIM/IFC	LFVideo×8(7, 7) PSNR/SSIM/IFC
FlownetS	31.9 million	37.78/0.97/5.41	31.23/0.90/3.02	**39.39/0.97/4.97**	34.94/0.92/3.30
FlownetS+	32.6 million	**38.04/0.97/5.46**	**31.66/0.90/3.11**	39.37/0.97/4.88	**35.85/0.93/3.54**

5 Conclusion

Aiming for the challenge large-scale (8×) super-resolution problem, we propose an end-to-end reference-based super resolution network named as CrossNet, where the input is a low-resolution (LR) image and a high-resolution (HR) reference image that shares similar view-point, the output is the super-resolved (4× or 8×) result of LR image. The pipeline of CrossNet is full-convolutional, containing encoder, cross-scale warping, and decoder respectively. Extensive experiment on several large-scale datasets demonstrate the superior performance of CrossNet (around 2 dB–4 dB) compared to previous methods. More importantly, CrossNet achieves a speedup of more than 100 times compared to existing RefSR approaches, allowing the model to be applicable for real-time applications.

References

1. Boominathan, V., Mitra, K., Veeraraghavan, A.: Improving resolution and depth-of-field of light field cameras using a hybrid imaging system. In: ICCP, pp. 1–10. IEEE (2014)
2. Zheng, H., Ji, M., Wang, H., Liu, Y., Fang, L.: Learning cross-scale correspondence and patch-based synthesis for reference-based super-resolution. In: BMVC (2017)
3. Wang, Y., Liu, Y., Heidrich, W., Dai, Q.: The light field attachment: turning a DSLR into a light field camera using a low budget camera ring. IEEE Trans. Vis. Comput. Graph. (2016)
4. Yuan, X., Lu, F., Dai, Q., Brady, D., Yebin, L.: Multiscale gigapixel video: a cross resolution image matching and warping approach. In: IEEE International Conference on Computational Photography (2017)
5. Ledig, C., et al.: Photo-realistic single image super-resolution using a generative adversarial network. arXiv preprint arXiv:1609.04802 (2016)
6. Jaderberg, M., Simonyan, K., Zisserman, A., et al.: Spatial transformer networks. In: Advances in Neural Information Processing Systems, pp. 2017–2025 (2015)
7. Li, X., Orchard, M.T.: New edge-directed interpolation. IEEE Trans. Image Process. **10**(10), 1521–1527 (2001)
8. Zhang, L., Wu, X.: An edge-guided image interpolation algorithm via directional filtering and data fusion. IEEE Trans. Image Process. **15**(8), 2226–2238 (2006)
9. Tai, Y.W., Liu, S., Brown, M.S., Lin, S.: Super resolution using edge prior and single image detail synthesis. In: 2010 IEEE Conference on Computer Vision and Pattern Recognition (CVPR), pp. 2400–2407. IEEE (2010)

10. Babacan, S.D., Molina, R., Katsaggelos, A.K.: Total variation super resolution using a variational approach. In: 2008 15th IEEE International Conference on Image Processing, ICIP 2008, pp. 641–644. IEEE (2008)
11. Krishnan, D., Fergus, R.: Fast image deconvolution using hyper-Laplacian priors. In: Advances in Neural Information Processing Systems, pp. 1033–1041 (2009)
12. Yang, J., Wright, J., Huang, T., Ma, Y.: Image super-resolution as sparse representation of raw image patches. In: CVPR. IEEE (2008) 1–8
13. Yang, J., Wright, J., Huang, T.S., Ma, Y.: Image super-resolution via sparse representation. IEEE Trans. Image Process. 19(11), 2861–2873 (2010)
14. Kim, K.I., Kwon, Y.: Single-image super-resolution using sparse regression and natural image prior. TPAMI 32(6), 1127–1133 (2010)
15. Yang, J., Wang, Z., Lin, Z., Cohen, S., Huang, T.: Coupled dictionary training for image super-resolution. IEEE Trans. Image Process. 21(8), 3467–3478 (2012)
16. Glasner, D., Bagon, S., Irani, M.: Super-resolution from a single image. In: ICCV, pp. 349–356. IEEE (2009)
17. Freeman, W.T., Jones, T.R., Pasztor, E.C.: Example-based super-resolution. IEEE Comput. Graph. Appl. 22(2), 56–65 (2002)
18. Chang, H., Yeung, D.Y., Xiong, Y.: Super-resolution through neighbor embedding. In: CVPR, vol. 1, p. I. IEEE (2004)
19. Buades, A., Coll, B., Morel, J.M.: A non-local algorithm for image denoising. In: 2005 IEEE Computer Society Conference on Computer Vision and Pattern Recognition, CVPR 2005, vol. 2, pp. 60–65. IEEE (2005)
20. Salvador, J., Pérez-Pellitero, E.: Naive bayes super-resolution forest. In: ICCV, pp. 325–333 (2015)
21. Schulter, S., Leistner, C., Bischof, H.: Fast and accurate image upscaling with super-resolution forests. In: CVPR, pp. 3791–3799 (2015)
22. Yang, C.Y., Yang, M.H.: Fast direct super-resolution by simple functions. In: ICCV, pp. 561–568 (2013)
23. Yang, J., Lin, Z., Cohen, S.: Fast image super-resolution based on in-place example regression. In: CVPR, pp. 1059–1066 (2013)
24. He, H., Siu, W.C.: Single image super-resolution using Gaussian process regression. In: CVPR, pp. 449–456. IEEE (2011)
25. Dong, C., Loy, C.C., He, K., Tang, X.: Learning a deep convolutional network for image super-resolution. In: Fleet, D., Pajdla, T., Schiele, B., Tuytelaars, T. (eds.) ECCV 2014. LNCS, vol. 8692, pp. 184–199. Springer, Cham (2014). https://doi.org/10.1007/978-3-319-10593-2_13
26. Dong, C., Loy, C.C., Tang, X.: Accelerating the super-resolution convolutional neural network. In: Leibe, B., Matas, J., Sebe, N., Welling, M. (eds.) ECCV 2016. LNCS, vol. 9906, pp. 391–407. Springer, Cham (2016). https://doi.org/10.1007/978-3-319-46475-6_25
27. Shi, W., et al.: Real-time single image and video super-resolution using an efficient sub-pixel convolutional neural network. In: CVPR, pp. 1874–1883 (2016)
28. Kim, J., Kwon Lee, J., Mu Lee, K.: Accurate image super-resolution using very deep convolutional networks. In: CVPR, pp. 1646–1654 (2016)
29. Lai, W.S., Huang, J.B., Ahuja, N., Yang, M.H.: Deep Laplacian pyramid networks for fast and accurate super-resolution. In: CVPR, pp. 624–632 (2017)
30. Lim, B., Son, S., Kim, H., Nah, S., Lee, K.M.: Enhanced deep residual networks for single image super-resolution. In: CVPRW, vol. 1, p. 3 (2017)

31. Wanner, S., Goldluecke, B.: Spatial and angular variational super-resolution of 4D light fields. In: Fitzgibbon, A., Lazebnik, S., Perona, P., Sato, Y., Schmid, C. (eds.) ECCV 2012. LNCS, vol. 7576, pp. 608–621. Springer, Heidelberg (2012). https://doi.org/10.1007/978-3-642-33715-4_44

32. Mitra, K., Veeraraghavan, A.: Light field denoising, light field superresolution and stereo camera based refocussing using a GMM light field patch prior. In: 2012 IEEE Computer Society Conference on Computer Vision and Pattern Recognition Workshops (CVPRW), pp. 22–28. IEEE (2012)

33. Wu, J., Wang, H., Wang, X., Zhang, Y.: A novel light field super-resolution framework based on hybrid imaging system. In: 2015 Visual Communications and Image Processing (VCIP), pp. 1–4. IEEE (2015)

34. Zheng, H., Guo, M., Wang, H., Liu, Y., Fang, L.: Combining exemplar-based approach and learning-based approach for light field super-resolution using a hybrid imaging system. In: Proceedings of the IEEE Conference on Computer Vision and Pattern Recognition, pp. 2481–2486 (2017)

35. Kalantari, N.K., Wang, T.C., Ramamoorthi, R.: Learning-based view synthesis for light field cameras. ACM Trans. Graph. (TOG) 35(6), 193 (2016)

36. Ji, D., Kwon, J., McFarland, M., Savarese, S.: Deep view morphing. Technical report (2017)

37. Xue, T., Chen, B., Wu, J., Wei, D., Freeman, W.T.: Video enhancement with task-oriented flow. arXiv preprint arXiv:1711.09078 (2017)

38. Sajjadi, M.S., Vemulapalli, R., Brown, M.: Frame-recurrent video super-resolution. In: Proceedings of the IEEE Conference on Computer Vision and Pattern Recognition, pp. 6626–6634 (2018)

39. Tao, X., Gao, H., Liao, R., Wang, J., Jia, J.: Detail-revealing deep video super-resolution

40. Liu, Z., Yeh, R., Tang, X., Liu, Y., Agarwala, A.: Video frame synthesis using deep voxel flow. In: ICCV, vol. 2 (2017)

41. Wang, T.C., Zhu, J.Y., Kalantari, N.K., Efros, A.A., Ramamoorthi, R.: Light field video capture using a learning-based hybrid imaging system. ACM Trans. Graph. (TOG) 36(4), 133 (2017)

42. Fischer, P., et al.: FlowNet: learning optical flow with convolutional networks. arXiv preprint arXiv:1504.06852 (2015)

43. Ronneberger, O., Fischer, P., Brox, T.: U-Net: convolutional networks for biomedical image segmentation. In: Navab, N., Hornegger, J., Wells, W.M., Frangi, A.F. (eds.) MICCAI 2015. LNCS, vol. 9351, pp. 234–241. Springer, Cham (2015). https://doi.org/10.1007/978-3-319-24574-4_28

44. Nair, V., Hinton, G.E.: Rectified linear units improve restricted Boltzmann machines. In: Proceedings of the 27th International Conference on Machine Learning (ICML 2010), pp. 807–814 (2010)

45. Bruhn, A., Weickert, J., Schnörr, C.: Lucas/Kanade meets Horn/Schunck: combining local and global optic flow methods. IJCV 61(3), 211–231 (2005)

46. Srinivasan, P.P., Wang, T., Sreelal, A., Ramamoorthi, R., Ng, R.: Learning to synthesize a 4D RGBD light field from a single image. In: ICCV, vol. 2, p. 6 (2017)

47. The (new) stanford light field archive. http://lightfield.stanford.edu/lfs.html

48. Kim, C., Zimmer, H., Pritch, Y., Sorkine-Hornung, A., Gross, M.H.: Scene reconstruction from high spatio-angular resolution light fields. ACM TOG (2013)

49. Kingma, D., Ba, J.: Adam: a method for stochastic optimization. arXiv preprint arXiv:1412.6980 (2014)

50. Wang, Z., Bovik, A.C., Sheikh, H.R., Simoncelli, E.P.: Image quality assessment: from error visibility to structural similarity. IEEE Trans. Image Process. **13**(4), 600–612 (2004)

51. Sheikh, H.R., Bovik, A.C., De Veciana, G.: An information fidelity criterion for image quality assessment using natural scene statistics. IEEE Trans. Image Process. **14**(12), 2117–2128 (2005)

52. Bergstra, J., et al.: Theano: a CPU and GPU math compiler in Python

Single Image Water Hazard Detection Using FCN with Reflection Attention Units

Xiaofeng Han[1], Chuong Nguyen[2,3,4], Shaodi You[2,3], and Jianfeng Lu[1(✉)]

[1] Nanjing University of Science and Technology, Nanjing 210094, Jiangsu, China
lujf@njust.edu.cn
[2] Australian National University, Canberra, ACT 2600, Australia
[3] CSIRO DATA61, Canberra, ACT 2601, Australia
[4] Australian Centre of Excellence for Robotic Vision,
2 George Street, Brisbane 4001, Australia

Abstract. Water bodies, such as puddles and flooded areas, on and off road pose significant risks to autonomous cars. Detecting water from moving camera is a challenging task as water surface is highly refractive, and its appearance varies with viewing angle, surrounding scene, weather conditions. In this paper, we present a water puddle detection method based on a Fully Convolutional Network (FCN) with our newly proposed Reflection Attention Units (RAUs). An RAU is a deep network unit designed to embody the physics of reflection on water surface from sky and nearby scene. To verify the performance of our proposed method, we collect 11455 color stereo images with polarizers, and 985 of left images are annotated and divided into 2 datasets: On Road (ONR) dataset and Off Road (OFR) dataset. We show that FCN-8s with RAUs improves significantly precision and recall metrics as compared to FCN-8s, DeepLab V2 and Gaussian Mixture Model (GMM). We also show that focal loss function can improve the performance of FCN-8s network due to the extreme imbalance of water versus ground classification problem.

Keywords: Water puddle detection · Road hazard detection
Fully convolutional network · Deep learning · Reflection attention unit

1 Introduction

It is well-known that adverse weather conditions affect traffic safety [10,11,20, 30]. Weather-related driving risks are elevated in wet weather not only for human but also for autonomous cars [3,15]. Water and reflection on water surface can cause serious problems in many scenarios. Running into deep water puddle could cause damages to mechanical and electronic parts of the vehicle.

Electronic supplementary material The online version of this chapter (https:// doi.org/10.1007/978-3-030-01231-1_7) contains supplementary material, which is available to authorized users.

V. Ferrari et al. (Eds.): ECCV 2018, LNCS 11210, pp. 105–121, 2018.
https://doi.org/10.1007/978-3-030-01231-1_7

Detection of water puddles on road is, however, not a trivial task because of the wide varieties of appearance and reflection of surrounding environment. Many existing methods rely on special sensors such as dual-polarized cameras [25], near field Radar [2]. However, such devices are not general applicable for normal autonomous cars and are not providing sufficient detection accuracy.

Existing image based detection methods simplify the problem by utilizing multi images along with hand-crafted features, such as average brightness [8], Gaussian fitting of brightness and saturation [16]. However, the water puddle detection are highly ill-posed for hand-crafted features because the real outdoor environments are far too complex to be properly modeled with those hand-crafted features. For example, in Fig. 1, the reflections are coming from sky, clouds and a variety of environment objects.

On the other hand, Deep neural nets can learn features autonomously and have achieved great performance in outdoor navigation nowadays. However, to the best of our knowledge, there is no existing work using deep nets to tackle the water hazard detection. Note that it is not a trivial task because water puddles do not have a well-defined appearance which varies drastically with surrounding environment. Furthermore, there is no existing dataset that is large enough for the training of deep nets.

In this paper, we propose a water detection method based on a Fully Convolutional Network (FCN) with reflection attention units (RAUs). The RAUs are designed to allow the network to capture reflection correspondences between different parts of the images. Because the reflection correspondences are mostly vertical, feature maps in multi-scales are divided into several patches along vertical directions. Then average of each patch is calculated. All the pixels are compared with the averages in the same column to determine whether it is a reflection of a certain patch. As shown in Fig. 1(c), since the X_8 is the reflection of X_6, the subtraction results between pixels in X_8 and the average of X_6 should be lower than that of other pairs. Figure 1 also shows the water hazard detection results of our method (d) and FCN-8s (e). Because the reflections on the water surface are detected by (c), our method clearly outperforms FCN-8s. In addition we propose to replace cross entropy loss function by focal loss [12] to deal with the data imbalance problem, as the size of the water puddle various tremendously between images.

Furthermore, in order to verify the performance of our proposed method and encouraging new research, we propose the 'Puddle-1000' Dataset. We collect 11455 color stereo images with polarizers, and 985 of left images are annotated and divided into 2 datasets: On Road (ONR) sub-dataset and Off Road (OFR) sub-dataset.

As far as we know, this is the first work to exploit deep neural networks on water hazard detection. And our main contributions are as follows:

- We propose a reflection attention unit (RAU), and insert it after every last convolutional layer of 5 group layers in the FCN-8s network [13]. These units are designed to pick up reflection correspondences relationships between different vertical parts of images.

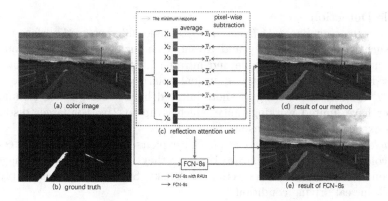

Fig. 1. Single image water hazard detection using a deep net with and without RAUs. (c) illustrates the proposed reflection attention unit (RAU) to automatically learn the reflection relationship within a single image. (Color figure online)

- We take the advantage of focal loss [12] to deal with this imbalanced water detection problem where water puddles account for a small fraction of total number of pixels.
- To the best of knowledge, we propose the first single image deep neural net based method on water hazard detection in real driving scenes. And the proposed method achieves the state-of-the-art performance.
- We have pixel-wise annotated 985 images mostly containing water puddles. These include 357 on road images and 628 off road images. This newly annotated dataset and source codes of deep networks are available to public.

2   Related Work

Traversable Area Detection and Semantic Segmentation Deep Neural Networks

Water hazard detection is often considered as complementary to the traversable area detection, or the road detection. Traditional methods are based on hand-crafted features and color priors. For example, Lu et al. [14] used Gaussian Mixture Model (GMM) to estimate the priors.

Recently, CNN based semantic segmentation methods have demonstrated a superior performance. Long *et al.* [13] first proposed a fully convolutional network (FCN). And after that, by taking the benefit from ResNet [7], Chen *et al.* [4] proposed the Deeplab and futher improved the performance. Zhao *et al.* [31] proposed a new network structure, called pyramid pooling module, to exploit global context information. Recently, Han *et al.* [6] proposed a semi-supervised learning semantic segmentation method based on generative adversarial network (GAN). However, the hyper-parameters of GAN were selected empirically which are not robust to various water detection scenes.

Puddle Detection

Active Imaging Based Methods: To determine different road surface conditions such as dry, wet, snowy and frozen, Fukamizu *et al.* [5] relied on the reflectance of a projected visible and infrared light source. Viikari *et al.* [25] proposed to use the backscattering of dual polarized RADARs, while Bertozzi *et al.* [2] used backscattering of short infrared light source. These techniques however have limited working range which is up to 2 m. For larger distance, images extracted from cameras are required.

Single Image Method: Zhao *et al.* [32] exploits the water region detection using color constancy and texture. However they assume a close-up image of water puddles with uniform reflection of the sky. Such assumptions simply do not hold in real driving conditions.

Stereo Images/Video Based Methods: Texture cues of water surface have been used including smoothness descriptor [29], and local binary pattern [17,18]. Color cue in HSV space have also been used by Yan [29]. Rankin and Matthies [21] further showed that color of water puddle varies with viewing distance and angle. Temporal fluctuation (or dynamic texture) of water surface was also exploited by Santana *et al.* [23] (optical flow), and Mettes *et al.* [17,18] (temporal deviation and L1-norm FFT) to successfully detect running water bodies or still water under windy condition from a fixed camera position. Stereo depth was also exploited by Matthies *et al.* [16], Yan [29], and Kim *et al.* [9]. As light reflected from water surfaces is polarized [26], this provides a strong cue to detect water puddles as used in several works [9,19,24,28,29]. While Xie *et al.* [28] used 3 cameras, others used stereo cameras attached to horizontal and vertical polarizers. Nguyen *et al.* [19] further showed that sky polarization strongly effect the appearance of water.

Other imaging wavelengths including infrared and thermal imaging are also used by [2,16,22] to allow water detection at any time without active light sources. Rankin *et al.* [22] also showed that the relative intensity of water versus ground changes distinctively between night and day and this provide a strong cue of water.

Classification Techniques

From obtained cues of water, different classification techniques have been utilized including hard coded and adaptive thresholding [9,21,28,29], K-means [23], decision forest [17], support vector machine [9], and Gaussian mixture model [19].

To exploit temporal constraint, state propagation techniques have been used including segmentation guided label [23] and Markov random field [17].

3   Problem Formation and Physical Insights

In this section, we formulate the problem and explicitly explain why water puddle detection in a single image is a challenging problem. Also, we introduce concept on reflection attention.

Fig. 2. Examples from the proposed 'Puddle-1000' dataset. Water on ground could have different reflections, colors, brightness, and shapes. Water surface can be still or moving. (Color figure online)

Appearance of Water Puddle: Reflection. Detecting water hazard from distance is challenging due to the very nature of reflection on water surface. Examples of water are given in Fig. 2. In (a) the shape and boundary of puddles are very irregular. In (b) even though there are only reflections of sky, the colors of water surfaces change with the distances. Both in (a) and (b), reflections of puddles far away are very bright. In (c) the reflections are mainly about clouds and trees, while in (d) they consist of blue sky, red fences, clouds and trees, which makes the puddles look very different. The colors of the puddles in (a) and (b) are different from those in (c) and (d), as the latter ones have more soil sediments. In (e) the right puddle has waves due to the wind. The left puddle in (f) looks very similar with road areas. (g) and (h) contain the same puddle but captured at different distances. The puddle reflects of different parts of trees, therefore the textures on puddle surface are quite different.

Appearance of Water Puddle: Inter Reflection/Refraction and Scattering. The process of light reflecting and scattering from a water puddle is illustrated in Fig. 3. Modeling the appearance of a puddle with a provided environmental luminance is, yet, ill-posed. Light source S_1 from the sky or nearby objects hit water surface at O_1. It partially reflects back into the air and partially refracts into water column as shown in the left of the figure. What we see from the water puddle is a summation of (a) reflection of the light source as at O_1, and (b) the fraction from inside the water as at O_2 and O_3. Reflection as shown in the top right in fact is the combination of specular reflection (i.e. clear image) $R_{reflect}$ and scatter reflection (i.e. blurry image) $R_{scatter}$. Similarly, the refraction as shown in the bottom right is the combination of light coming straight from the ground bottom R_{bottom} as at S_3 and light from sediment particles $R_{particles}$ as at S_2. This process is expressed as the following summation:

$$R_{total} = R_{reflect} + R_{scatter} + R_{bottom} + R_{particles} \qquad (1)$$

An important property of reflection is that the light source and its reflected image lie on a straight line perpendicular to the water surface (or the ground) and that they have same height from the ground as shown in Fig. 4. Perspective view and imperfect camera lens introduce some distortions to captured images. The line connecting the source and its reflection may not be exactly vertical in

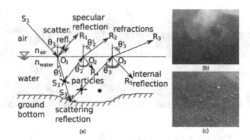

Fig. 3. (a) shows the process of water reflection $(S_1 O_1 R_1)$, refraction $(S_2 O_2 R_2$ and $S_3 O_3 R_3)$ and scattering $(O_1 S_2 O_2$ and $O_1 S_3 O_3)$ at a water puddle. (b) and (c) show light components from the same water puddle. (b) shows reflection light on water surface, magnified by passing through horizontal polariser. (c) shows fraction light from inside water puddle, magnified passing through vertical polariser (wikipedia.org).

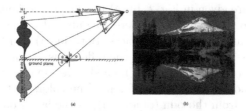

Fig. 4. (a) shows image formation of an object and its reflection. The light source and its image is on a line SS" perpendicular at ground G where GS = GS". However the pixel distances on camera image are different, G'S' ≠ G'R'. (b) shows reflection on water with vertical correspondences between tree tops and their reflections (wikipedia.org).

the image, and the distances of the source and its reflection to the ground are not exactly the same. As the distance from the camera increases, the different in the height of the object and its reflection reduces. We aim to design a deep network that captures this reflection effect and tolerates the distortion and camera rotation.

Mining Visual Priors Through Deep Learning. With recent rapid advancements of Convolutional Neural Network (CNN) to effectively solve various traditional computer vision problems, we aim to apply this powerful tool to the problem of water hazard detection. CNN in general and Fully Convolutional Network (FCN) in particular recognise objects with distinct structures and patterns. Therefore these networks do not work well with water reflection which varies drastically depending on what is reflected. As a result, we want to extend the networks recognise the physics of the reflection phenomenon. The main characteristics of reflection on water surface is that the reflection is a inverted and disturbed transform of the sky or nearby objects above the water surface. Specifically, we propose in this paper a new network module called Reflection Attention Unit (RAU) that matches image pattern in the vertical direction.

4   Fully Convolutional Network with Reflection Attention Units

Water hazard is hard to recognize for existing semantic segmentation methods because of the reflections on the water surface. Therefore, we want to exploit more information about local and global reflection contexts especially in the vertical direction. The proposed Reflection Attention Units (RAUs) are then used to learn the reflection relationships.

4.1   Reflection Attention Unit

We propose RAU based on a strong cue in a single image that water puddles usually contain vertical reflections. As illustrated by Fig. 4, a reflection and its source lies along a line nearly vertical in the image. Therefore to detect water puddles, we can search for reflections by matching image regions along pixel columns of an image. Furthermore, to tolerate perspective distortion, small camera rotation (angle with line of horizon) and blurry reflection, multiple resolutions or scales are used in the vertical matching.

The architecture of the proposed RAU is illustrated in Fig. 5. Given an input feature map I of size $[h, w, c]$, horizontal average pooling is applied to I reduce to size $[h, w/2, c]$. Then vertical average pooling is applied to reduce this to X of size $[n, w/2, c]$. In Fig. 5, n is set to be 8 for illustration purpose. After that, each row X_i sized $[1, w/2]$ of X is tiled or self replicated to size $[n, w/2]$. Those obtained from all rows are concatenated along the feature axis into a new feature map of size of $[n, w/2, c * n]$. Then, this feature map are up-sampled to size $[h, w, c * n]$ and denoted as X'. We then concatenate n times of I along the feature axis to get I' with size $[h, w, c * n]$. I' is subtracted from X' to produce D with size $[h, w, c * n]$ which encode the reflection relationships. The subtracted feature map is concatenated with I again, fed into a convolutional layer and activated by ReLU function to generate the final output of the same size as I.

Figure 6 illustrate how the RAU computes the similarities between one pixel and the averages of other different parts along vertical direction in the neighboring 2 columns in a certain scale. Take the first channel of X' as an example. This single-channel image has 16 tiled rows and pixels along each column are the same. A single row represents the blurry version of the top rows of the first channel of I. Because the top rows of I contain mostly clouds, therefore in the difference D, the clouds and reflection of clouds on the water surface has lower intensity than ground, fences and trees. Furthermore, as the reflection lines are not strictly vertical due to distortion and image rotation, the two average poolings allow for such misalignments from these. In addition, such misalignments are also taken account for when several RAUs are applied to feature maps of different scales as outputs of successive convolutional layer groups.

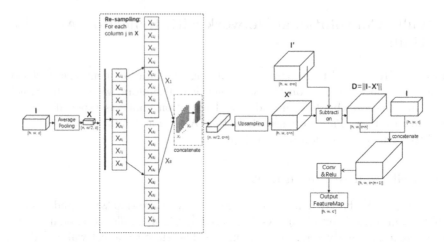

Fig. 5. Illustration of a Reflection Attention Unit (RAU).

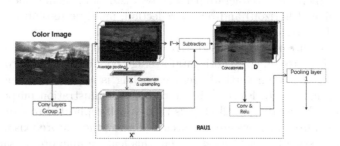

Fig. 6. Working principle of a Reflection Attention Unit. After the convolutional layer group 1, the input color image is transformed to a feature map I, and average pooling is applied to I to get the downsampled feature map X. Then, self replication, concatenation and upsampling of I produce feature map X'. I are concatenated to get I'. I' is subtracted from X' to produce a difference map D. Finally, D and I are concatenated and fed into a convolutional layer and a ReLU to output a new feature map of the same size as I. This is fed to pooling layer 1 of a normal convolutional layer group. (Color figure online)

4.2 Network Architecture

Figure 7 shows the network architectures of standard FCN-8s [27] (a) and our method (b). To study the usefulness of different RAUs in a FCN-8s network, we increasingly insert 5 RAUs after each group of convolutional layers to enable the reflection awareness at different scales.

4.3 Focal Loss

The area of water puddles is found much smaller than that of the ground. Particularly, in ONR dataset and OFR dataset, introduced in the next section, the

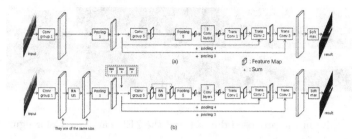

Fig. 7. Architectures of FCN-8s and our proposed FCN-8s with RAUs. For compactness, we only show 2 out of 5 groups of convolutional layers and their corresponding RAUs.

ratios between the pixel number of water and non-water are approximately 1:61 and 1:89. These lead to skewed training when using a common loss function, such as cross entropy loss.

To deal with unbalanced classification, we propose to use focal loss [12] with our network. Given such a binary classification problem, we define $y = \{0, 1\}$ as the ground truth classes and p as the probability that one sample belongs to class $y = 1$. Then standard cross entropy loss is defined as follows:

$$CE(p, y) = \begin{cases} -log(p) & if\ y = 1 \\ -log(1 - p)\ otherwise \end{cases} \tag{2}$$

If we define p_t as follows:

$$p_t = \begin{cases} p & if\ y = 1 \\ 1 - p\ otherwise \end{cases} \tag{3}$$

Then Eq. 2 can be rewritten as:

$$CE(p, y) = CE(p_t) = -log(p_t) \tag{4}$$

The focal loss is defined as follows to down-weight easy examples and focus on hard examples:

$$FL(p_t) = -(1 - p_t)^\gamma log(p_t) \tag{5}$$

where $-(1 - p_t)^\gamma$ is the modulating factor and $\gamma \geq 0$ is a tunable focusing parameter. γ is chosen to be 2 in this paper.

5   Puddle-1000 Dataset

To enable deep learning based methods and systematical tests, in this paper we present a new and practical water puddle detection dataset. Note that a previous dataset of water puddles was published by [19] recorded at two different locations for on road and off road conditions near Canberra city, Australia. This dataset only contains 126 and 157 annotated left frames for on road sequence (ONR) and off road sequence (OFR). For this paper, the annotated frame are too limited for training deep networks.

(a) on road images   (b) off road images   (c) on road groud truths   (d) off road ground truths   (e) our camera

Fig. 8. Examples in the proposed dataset and the ZED camera. (Color figure online)

Proposed Dataset. In this paper, we extend the existing dataset with 5 times more pixel-wise labeled images. The labeled data are all from the above dataset captured by the ZED stereo camera, and since we aim for a single image solution, only left images are annotated and used to validate the performance of different networks. Specifically, ONR now has 357 annotated frames, while OFR now has 628 annotated frames. Figure 8(a) and (b) show color images from ONR and OFR datasets, and (c) and (d) show examples of the pixel-wise annotation masks with two classes. In the ONR dataset, the waters are very muddy and the reflections are mainly from sky, clouds, pillars and fences, while in the OFR dataset the water surfaces are the combined reflections of blue sky, clouds, trees, telegraphs, buildings and some fences. The appearances of ground and other obstacles in those two datasets are also much different. In ONR, there are asphalt roads with moving cars and containers. In OFR the grounds are just wet dirt roads, however it has more different kinds of obstacles, such as fences, buildings, many kinds of trees, mounds and building materials. Therefore there are significant differences in water reflections. These new annotated frames are also released to the public.

6   Experiments

We systematically evaluate the proposed network using the proposed dataset. We compare with existing single image based methods and also compare with a various of existing network structures. We also provide detailed analysis on training time, robustness to over-fitting in the supplementary material (because of the length limit.)

6.1   Implementation Details

Our network is implemented using Tensorflow [1] framework and is trained on an NVIDIA TITAN XP GPU with 12 GB of memory. In experiments, the resolution of images and ground truths are downsampled to 360px × 640px. The batch size is 1 during training. Learning rate is set to 10^{-6} at first, and decreases by a factor of 0.2 every 5K iterations after 20K iterations. The number of training iteration of both FCN-8s and FCN-8S-focal-loss is 100K, and that of both Deeplab-V2 and our proposed network is 60K.

Table 1. Details of RAUs

Name	N	Convolutional kernel			Feature map size
		Input channels	Output channels	kernel size	
RAU1	16	$64 * (16 + 1)$	64	[3, 3]	360×640
RAU2	16	$128 * (16 + 1)$	128	[3, 3]	180×320
RAU3	16	$256 * (16 + 1)$	256	[3, 3]	90×160
RAU4	16	$512 * (16 + 1)$	512	[3, 3]	45×80
RAU5	8	$512 * (8 + 1)$	512	[3, 3]	23×40

Table 2. Performances of the networks with different number of RAUs.

Dataset	Method	F-measure	Precision	Recall	Accuracy
ONR	FCN-8s-FL-5Conv	55.76%	55.68%	55.85%	99.06%
	FCN-8s-FL-1RAU	59.63%	61.64%	57.75%	99.17%
	FCN-8s-FL-3RAU	61.97%	63.43%	60.57%	99.20%
	FCN-8s-FL-5RAU	**70.11%**	**67.78%**	**72.61%**	**99.35%**
OFR	FCN-8s-FL-5Conv	78.56%	89.33%	70.11%	99.32%
	FCN-8s-FL-1RAU	71.67%	87.45%	60.71%	99.14%
	FCN-8s-FL-3RAU	79.09%	**91.36%**	69.72%	99.34%
	FCN-8s-FL-5RAU	**81.67%**	87.21%	**76.79%**	**99.38%**
BOTH	FCN-8s-FL-5Conv	63.44%	62.52%	64.44%	99.21%
	FCN-8s-FL-1RAU	67.64%	74.66%	61.82%	99.14%
	FCN-8s-FL-3RAU	67.63%	75.27%	64.40%	99.15%
	FCN-8s-FL-5RAU	**76.91%**	**78.03%**	**75.81%**	**99.34%**

The ONR and OFR datasets are randomly divided into training and testing categories in the following experiments. For ONR dataset, we use 272 images to train the networks, and 85 images to verify the performances. As for OFR dataset, 530 images are used for training and 98 images for testing. Furthermore, we also carry out the experiments on both datasets combined together. The metrics used for evaluation are F-measure, precision, recall and accuracy. In all experiments, we do not use data augmentation.

The details of 5 RAUs are shown in Table 1.

6.2 Validation of the Reflection Attention Units

We train four different networks on the dataset. Three of them are FCN-8s with RAUs, the difference is that, the number of RAUs in these networks are 1, 3 and 5 respectively. They are named as FCN-8s-FL-1RAU, FCN-8s-FL-3RAU and FCN-8s-FL-5RAU. In FCN-8s-FL-1RAU the single RAU is placed before the first pooling layer. In FCN-8s-FL-3RAU the RAUs are added before the first, the third

Table 3. Performances of FCN-8s with and without focal loss.

Dataset	Method	F-measure	Precision	Recall	Accuracy
ONR	FCN-8s	56.99%	**59.01%**	55.11%	**99.12%**
	FCN-8s-FL	**57.85%**	50.49%	**67.71%**	98.96%
OFR	FCN-8s	64.33%	78.18%	54.64%	98.92%
	FCN-8s-FL	**74.05%**	**84.88%**	**65.66%**	**99.18%**
BOTH	FCN-8s	65.21%	69.81%	61.18%	99.05%
	FCN-8s-FL	**70.62%**	**74.38%**	**67.22%**	**99.19%**

Table 4. Performances of different methods on cross dataset validations.

Testing dataset	Training dataset	Method	F-measure	Precision	Recall	Accuracy
ONR	OFR	FCN-8s-FL	9.16%	15.80%	6.45%	98.65%
		FCN-8s-FL-RAU	**31.43%**	**50.99%**	**22.72%**	**98.95%**
OFR	ONR	FCN-8s-FL	22.98%	27.20%	19.89%	97.62%
		FCN-8s-FL-RAU	**36.60%**	**60.71%**	**26.20%**	**98.38%**

and the fifth pooling layers. And FCN-8s-FL-5RAU is the proposed network. In the last network we do not use RAUs and only add 5 more convolutional layers. In all the networks we use the focal loss. Table 2 shows that, the performances are improved with increasing using of RAUs.

6.3   Validation of the Focal Loss

We train the FCN-8s with the cross entropy loss function and the focal loss, respectively. The results are shown in Table 3. From this table, we can see that using focal loss can get obviously better performances on OFR and BOTH datasets. The reason why there is no significant improvement on ONR dataset is because the data imbalance of ONR dataset is much smaller than that of OFR dataset. Even so, the FCN-8s-FL still gets better F-measure and Recall.

6.4   Cross Dataset Validation

To further validate the robustness of our method, we train two networks on ONR and OFR dataset, and verify them on the other datasets. The results (Table 4) of our method are better than the FCN-8s-FL in all the experiments. This indicates our method has much better generalization performance on different datasets.

6.5   Comparison with Existing Methods

For further comparison, we implement and re-train other image segmentation networks including FCN-8s, FCN-8s-FL, FCN-8s-5Conv and DeepLab (version 2) [4]. We also compared our method with the non deep learning method,

Table 5. Performance comparison between our proposed network and others.

Dataset	Method	F-measure	Precision	Recall	Accuracy	Time
ONR	FCN-8s-FL-RAU (ours)	**70.11%**	**67.78%**	72.61%	**99.35%**	0.32 s
	FCN-8s-FL	57.85%	50.49%	67.71%	98.96%	0.06 s
	FCN-8s [27]	56.99%	59.01%	55.11%	99.12%	0.06 s
	DeepLab [4]	21.97%	37.18%	15.60%	98.83%	0.27 s
	FCN-8s-FL-5Conv	55.76%	55.68%	55.85%	99.06%	0.07 s
	GMM & polarisation [19]	31.0%	18.7%	**90.2%**	96.5%	NA
OFR	FCN-8s-FL-RAU (ours)	**81.67%**	87.21%	76.79%	**99.38%**	0.32 s
	FCN-8s-FL	74.05%	84.88%	65.66%	99.18%	0.06 s
	FCN-8s [27]	64.33%	78.18%	54.64%	98.92%	0.06 s
	DeepLab [4]	45.05%	71.31%	32.92%	98.56%	0.27 s
	FCN-8s-FL-5Conv	78.56%	**89.33%**	70.11%	99.32%	0.07 s
	GMM & polarization [19]	28.1%	16.8%	**85.4%**	95.2%	NA
BOTH	FCN-8s-FL-RAU (ours)	76.91%	**78.03%**	**75.81%**	99.34%	0.32 s
	FCN-8s-FL	70.62%	74.38%	67.22%	99.19%	0.06 s
	FCN-8s [27]	65.21%	69.81%	61.18%	99.05%	0.06 s
	DeepLab [4]	30.36%	53.52%	21.19%	98.59%	0.27 s
	FCN-8s-FL-5Conv	63.44%	62.52%	64.44%	99.21%	0.07 s

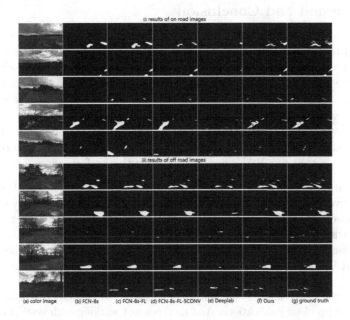

Fig. 9. Water hazards detection results trained on both datasets. (Color figure online)

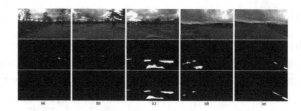

Fig. 10. The challenging cases for water hazard detection by our method. The first row are the color images, the second row are the ground truths and the last row are our results. (Color figure online)

such as GMM&polarisation [19]. For DeepLab, we fine-tune it based on a pre-trained Resnet101 model provided by Deeplab, and we do not apply CRF after the inference.[1]

Table 5 shows the performances of different methods and the average inference time for one frame. Figure 9 demonstrates the water hazard detection results of them. We can see that our RAUs help improve the performances a lot. The precision and recall have great improvements, showing that our RAUs can help the networks to reduce the false-positives and false-negatives. Figure 9 also demonstrates that improvements too.[2]

7   Discussion and Conclusion

Challenging Cases. Even with the help with RAUs, the water hazard detection is still very challenging in various cases. Figure 10 shows some examples. As shown in red rectangles, some puddle areas are too small to be recognized, because they only contain a few pixels. Besides, the wet areas are very similar with puddles, as we present in blue rectangles in (c) and (e). Lastly, in (d) the green rectangles show that some of the water surfaces almost look the same with the road. In all these cases, the water surfaces contain very little reflection information, so that our RAUs can not improve the performances.

Conclusion. We propose a robust single image water hazard detection based on fully convolutional networks with reflection attention units (RAUs) and focal loss. We also collect on road and off road color images with water hazards, and pixel-wisely annotate 985 images of them to build a dataset and verify the performances. We apply RAUs on multi-scale feature maps. In this novelly proposed RAUs, we calculate the distances between one pixel and the averages

---

[1] We respectfully mention that we don't have access to source codes and datasets from some other previous publications. And methods not working with single images are not compared too.

[2] The accuracy does not increase significantly because the number of water pixels is much smaller than that of non-water pixels, however, when we calculate the accuracy, we count the detection accuracies both of water and non-water pixels.

of different patches in each 2 columns along vertical direction. The focal loss is also used to deal with the serious data imbalance. Experiments of several deep neural networks and one traditional method on these datasets are carried out, and the results show the great effectiveness of our proposed method.

Acknowledgement. New ground-truth video frames were made possible thanks to the support from National Natural Science Foundation of China under the grant No. 61703209 of Dr Huan Wang, and the help from his students Zhaochen Fan, Zhijian Zheng, Renjie Sun, Yuchen Zhang, Jingyi Li and Laijingben Yang. Xiaofeng Han and Prof Jianfeng Lu would like to acknowledge funding from National Key R&D Program of China under contract No. 2017YFB1300205 and National Science and Technology Major Project under contract No. 2015ZX01041101. The capture of original video data was supported by the Australian Centre of Excellence for Robotic Vision (CE140100016) www.roboticvision.org. Special thanks also go to Dr Anoop Cherian, Dr Basura Fernando, Dr Laurent Kneip, A/Prof Hongdong Li, Prof Michael Milford and Prof Robert Mahony of ACRV, and James Nobles of Australian National University for their earlier supports.

References

1. Abadi, M., et al.: TensorFlow: large-scale machine learning on heterogeneous distributed systems (2016)
2. Bertozzi, M., Fedriga, R.I., D'Ambrosio, C.: Adverse driving conditions alert: investigations on the SWIR bandwidth for road status monitoring. In: Petrosino, A. (ed.) ICIAP 2013. LNCS, vol. 8156, pp. 592–601. Springer, Heidelberg (2013). https://doi.org/10.1007/978-3-642-41181-6_60
3. Byrne, K.: Self-driving cars: will they be safe during bad weather? (2016). https://www.accuweather.com/en/weather-news/self-driving-cars-will-they-be-safe-during-bad-weathr/60524998
4. Chen, L.C., Papandreou, G., Kokkinos, I., Murphy, K., Yuille, A.L.: DeepLab: semantic image segmentation with deep convolutional nets, atrous convolution, and fully connected CRFS. arXiv:1606.00915 (2016)
5. Fukamizu, H., Nakano, M., Iba, K., Yamasaki, T., Sano, K.: Road surface condition detection system, 1 September 1987. US Patent 4,690,553
6. Han, X., Lu, J., Zhao, C., You, S., Li, H.: Semi-supervised and weakly-supervised road detection based on generative adversarial networks. IEEE Signal Process. Lett. (in press)
7. He, K., Zhang, X., Ren, S., Sun, J.: Deep residual learning for image recognition, pp. 770–778 (2015)
8. Iqbal, M., Morel, O., Meriaudeau, F., Raya, J.M., Gunadarma, U., Fakultas, I.: A survey on outdoor water hazard detection. Institus Teknologi Sepuluh November **33**, 2085–1944 (2009)
9. Kim, J., Baek, J., Choi, H., Kim, E.: Wet area and puddle detection for advanced driver assistance systems (ADAS) using a stereo camera. Int. J. Control., Autom. Syst. **14**(1), 263–271 (2016)
10. Koetse, M.J., Rietveld, P.: The impact of climate change and weather on transport: an overview of empirical findings. Transp. Res. Part D: Transp. Environ. **14**(3), 205–221 (2009)

11. Li, Y., You, S., Brown, M.S., Tan, R.T.: Haze visibility enhancement: a survey and quantitative benchmarking. ComComput. Vis. Image Underst. (2016)
12. Lin, T.Y., Goyal, P., Girshick, R., He, K., Dollár, P.: Focal loss for dense object detection. arXiv preprint arXiv:1708.02002 (2017)
13. Long, J., Shelhamer, E., Darrell, T.: Fully convolutional networks for semantic segmentation. In: Proceedings of the IEEE Conference on Computer Vision and Pattern Recognition, pp. 3431–3440 (2015)
14. Lu, K., Li, J., An, X., He, H.: A hierarchical approach for road detection. In: IEEE International Conference on Robotics and Automation, pp. 517–522 (2014)
15. Marshall, A.: To let self-driving cars go anywhere, train them everywhere (2017). https://www.wired.com/story/waymo-self-driving-michigan-testing/
16. Matthies, L.H., Bellutta, P., McHenry, M.: Detecting water hazards for autonomous off-road navigation. In: Unmanned Ground Vehicle Technology V, vol. 5083, pp. 231–243. International Society for Optics and Photonics (2003)
17. Mettes, P., Tan, R.T., Veltkamp, R.: On the segmentation and classification of water in videos. In: 2014 International Conference on Computer Vision Theory and Applications (VISAPP), vol. 1, pp. 283–292. IEEE (2014)
18. Mettes, P., Tan, R.T., Veltkamp, R.C.: Water detection through spatio-temporal invariant descriptors. Comput. Vis. Image Underst. **154**, 182–191 (2017)
19. Nguyen, C.V., Milford, M., Mahony, R.: 3D tracking of water hazards with polarized stereo cameras. In: International Conference on Robotics and Automation (ICRA), pp. 5251–5257. IEEE (2017)
20. Office of Operation: How do weather events impact roads? (2017). https://ops.fhwa.dot.gov/weather/q1_roadimpact.htm
21. Rankin, A., Matthies, L.: Daytime water detection based on color variation. In: 2010 IEEE/RSJ International Conference on Intelligent Robots and Systems (IROS), pp. 215–221. IEEE (2010)
22. Rankin, A.L., Matthies, L.H., Bellutta, P.: Daytime water detection based on sky reflections. In: 2011 IEEE International Conference on Robotics and Automation (ICRA), pp. 5329–5336. IEEE (2011)
23. Santana, P., Mendonça, R., Barata, J.: Water detection with segmentation guided dynamic texture recognition. In: 2012 IEEE International Conference on Robotics and Biomimetics (ROBIO), pp. 1836–1841. IEEE (2012)
24. Sarwal, A., Nett, J., Simon, D.: Detection of small water-bodies. Technical report, DTIC Document (2004)
25. Viikari, V.V., Varpula, T., Kantanen, M.: Road-condition recognition using 24-GHz automotive radar. IEEE Trans. Intell. Transp. Syst. **10**(4), 639–648 (2009)
26. Wehner, R.: Polarization vision – a uniform sensory capacity? J. Exp. Biol. **204**(14), 2589–2596 (2001)
27. Wu, X.: Fully convolutional networks for semantic segmentation. In: Computer Science (2015)
28. Xie, B., Pan, H., Xiang, Z., Liu, J.: Polarization-based water hazards detection for autonomous off-road navigation. In: 2007 International Conference on Mechatronics and Automation, pp. 1666–1670. IEEE (2007)
29. Yan, S.H.: Water body detection using two camera polarized stereo vision. Int. J. Res. Comput. Eng. Electron. **3**(3) (2014)

30. You, S., Tan, R., Kawakami, R., Mukaigawa, Y., Ikeuchi, K.: Adherent raindrop modeling, detection and removal in video. IEEE Trans. Pattern Anal. Mach. Intell. **38**(9), 1721–1733 (2016)
31. Zhao, H., Shi, J., Qi, X., Wang, X., Jia, J.: Pyramid scene parsing network. In: IEEE Conference on Computer Vision and Pattern Recognition, pp. 6230–6239 (2017)
32. Zhao, Y., Deng, Y., Pan, C., Guo, L.: Research of water hazard detection based on color and texture features. Sens. Transducers **157**(10), 428 (2013)

Bidirectional Feature Pyramid Network with Recurrent Attention Residual Modules for Shadow Detection

Lei Zhu[1,2,5], Zijun Deng[3], Xiaowei Hu[1], Chi-Wing Fu[1,5(✉)], Xuemiao Xu[4], Jing Qin[2], and Pheng-Ann Heng[1,5]

[1] The Chinese University of Hong Kong, Hong Kong, China
cwfu@cse.cuhk.edu.hk
[2] The Hong Kong Polytechnic University, Hong Kong, China
[3] South China University of Technology, Guangzhou, China
[4] Guangdong Provincial Key Lab of Computational Intelligence and Cyberspace Information, South China University of Technology, Guangzhou, China
[5] Shenzhen Key Laboratory of Virtual Reality and Human Interaction Technology, Shenzhen Institutes of Advanced Technology, Chinese Academy of Sciences, Shenzhen, China

Abstract. This paper presents a network to detect shadows by exploring and combining global context in deep layers and local context in shallow layers of a deep convolutional neural network (CNN). There are two technical contributions in our network design. First, we formulate the *recurrent attention residual* (RAR) module to combine the contexts in two adjacent CNN layers and learn an attention map to select a residual and then refine the context features. Second, we develop a bidirectional feature pyramid network (BFPN) to aggregate shadow contexts spanned across different CNN layers by deploying two series of RAR modules in the network to iteratively combine and refine context features: one series to refine context features from deep to shallow layers, and another series from shallow to deep layers. Hence, we can better suppress false detections and enhance shadow details at the same time. We evaluate our network on two common shadow detection benchmark datasets: SBU and UCF. Experimental results show that our network outperforms the best existing method with 34.88% reduction on SBU and 34.57% reduction on UCF for the balance error rate.

1 Introduction

Shadows are regions that receive less illumination than the surroundings, due to lights occluded by associated objects in the scene. To detect shadows in images,

---

L. Zhu and Z. Deng—Joint first authors.

Electronic supplementary material The online version of this chapter (https://doi.org/10.1007/978-3-030-01231-1_8) contains supplementary material, which is available to authorized users.

© Springer Nature Switzerland AG 2018
V. Ferrari et al. (Eds.): ECCV 2018, LNCS 11210, pp. 122–137, 2018.
https://doi.org/10.1007/978-3-030-01231-1_8

early works develop physical models with heuristic priors [1,2] or take a machine learning approach based on hand-crafted features. However, image priors and hand-crafted features are not effective for extracting high-level semantics.

More recently, methods based on the convolutional neural network (CNN) [3–7] show distinct performance on various shadow detection benchmarks, e.g., [4,8]. A key factor for the successes is that CNN is able to learn the global spatial contexts in shadow images, as demonstrated in very recent works [5–7].

To further explore the spatial contexts and improve the shadow detection performance, it requires an understanding of the *global contexts* about the objects and illumination conditions in the scene, the *local contexts* about the details in the shadow shapes, as well as an *integration of various contexts* extracted in different scales. This drives us to explore shadow contexts over different CNN layers, where the shallow layers help reveal local contexts and the deep layers help reveal the global contexts due to a large receptive field.

In this work, we design a *bidirectional feature pyramid network* (BFPN), which extends over the feature pyramid network architecture [9]. Particularly, we aim to leverage the spatial contexts across deep and shallow layers, as well as iteratively integrate the contexts for maximized shadow detection performance. In detail, we have the following technical contributions in this work:

- First, we develop the *recurrent attention residual module*, or RAR module for short, to combine and process spatial contexts in two adjacent CNN layers. Inside the module, an attention map is learnt and predicted by the network to select a residual and to refine the context features.
- Second, we design our *bidirectional feature pyramid network* (BFPN) by taking the RAR modules as building blocks. Inside the BFPN, we first apply the convolutional neural network (CNN) to generate a set of feature maps (i.e., spatial contexts) in different resolutions, and then use two series of RAR modules to iteratively integrate spatial contexts over the CNN layers: one series of RAR modules from deep to shallow layers and another series from shallow to deep layers. Lastly, the prediction results from the two directions are further integrated by means of an attention mechanism.

To demonstrate the performance of our network, we evaluate it on two common benchmarks, i.e., SBU [4] and UCF [8], and compare its performance against several state-of-the-art methods designed for shadow detection, shadow removal, saliency detection and semantic segmentation. Results show that our model clearly outperforms the best existing method with over 34.88% reduction on SBU and 34.57% reduction on UCF in terms of the balance error rate. The code and models of our method are available at https://github.com/zijundeng/BDRAR.

2   Related Work

Shadows in natural images have been employed as hints in various computer vision problems for extracting the scene geometry [10,11], light direction [12], and camera location and parameters [13]. On the other hand, shadows are also beneficial to a variety of high-level image understanding tasks, e.g., image segmentation [14], object detection [15], and object tracking [16].

In the literature, a number of single-image shadow detection methods have been proposed. Early works [1,2,17] focused on illumination models and color information to detect shadows from inputs, but just worked well for wide dynamic range images [5,18]. Data-driving statistical learning is another popular strategy for shadow detection by learning shadow properties from images with annotated ground truths. These methods usually began by first designing some hand-crafted features [8,18–21] and then employing some classifiers [8,18–21] for shadow detection. While showing the performance improvement on the shadow detection, they often failed in complex cases, due to the limited discriminative capability of the hand-crafted features.

Compared with traditional methods based on hand-crafted features, deep convolutional neural network (CNN) based methods have refreshed many computer vision tasks [6,7,9,22,23], including shadow detection. For instance, Khan et al. [3] was the first one to use deep learning to automatically learn features for shadow detection with a significant improvement. They trained one CNN to detect shadow regions and another CNN to detect shadow boundaries, and then fed the prediction results to a conditional random field (CRF) for classifying image pixels as shadows/non-shadows. Later, a stacked CNN [4] was presented to detect shadows by considering the global prediction of an image and the shadow predictions of image patches. They first trained a fully convolutional network to obtain an image-level shadow prior, which was combined with local image patches to train a patch-based CNN for the final shadow map prediction.

Recently, a fast deep shadow detection network [24] was introduced by obtaining a shadow prior map produced from hand-crafted features and then applying a patch level CNN to compute the improved shadow probability map of the input image. And a generative adversarial network based shadow detector, called scGAN [5], was developed by formulating a conditional generator on input RGB images and learning to predict the corresponding shadow maps. When detecting shadows for a given image, they combined the predicted shadow masks for a large quantity of multi-scale crops for the final shadow mask prediction. The most recent work by Hu et al. [6,7] presented a deep network with direction-aware spatial context modules to analyze the global semantics.

The deep models in state-of-the-art works [5–7] mainly emphasized the importance of inferring global contexts for shadow detection. Compared to these methods, we suggest to develop a network by fully leveraging the global and local contexts in different layers of the CNN to detect shadows. Results show that our method clearly outperforms [5–7] in terms of the BER values on two widely-used benchmark datasets.

3 Methodology

Figure 1 presents the workflow of the overall shadow detection network that employs two series of RAR modules (see Fig. 2(d)) to fully exploit the global

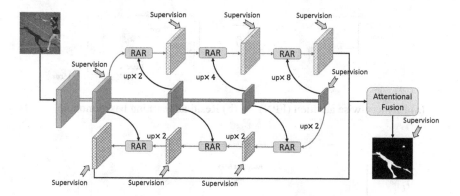

Fig. 1. The schematic illustration of the overall shadow detection network. Best viewed in color.

contexts and the local contexts at two adjacent layers of the convolutional neural network. Our network takes a single image as input and outputs the shadow detection result in an end-to-end manner. First, it leverages a convolutional neural network (CNN) to extract the feature maps with different resolutions. The feature maps in shallow layers discover the fine shadow detail information in the local regions while the feature maps in deep layers capture shadow semantic information of the whole image [25]. Then, we develop RAR modules to progressively refine features at each layer of the CNN by taking two adjacent feature maps as inputs to learn an attention map and to select a residual for the refinement of context features. We embed multiple RAR modules into a bidirectional feature pyramid network (BFPN), which uses two directional pathways to harvest the context information at different layers: one pathway is from shallow layers to deep layers, while another pathway is in the opposite direction. Lastly, we predict the score maps from the features at the last layers of two directional pathways, and then fuse those two score maps in an attentional manner to generate the final shadow detection result.

In the following subsections, we firstly elaborate how the RAR module refine the feature maps at each layer of the CNN, then present the details on how we embed our RAR modules into the shadow detection network (called bidirectional feature pyramid network (BFPN) with RAR modules, *BDRAR* for short), and finally introduce the training and testing strategies of our network.

3.1 Recurrent Attention Residual Module

One of the main issues in our method is to refine the context features at each layer for shadow detection by combining the context features at two adjacent layers of the CNN. A common way is to use an element-wise addition (see Fig. 2(a)) like the original FPN [9] to merge these two adjacent features. It up-samples the low-resolution feature maps and then adds it with the high-resolution feature maps. However, the element-wise addition on the two input context features

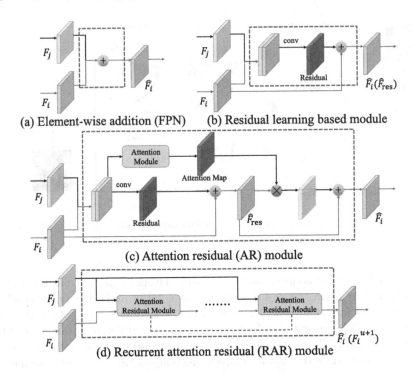

Fig. 2. The schematic illustration of different modules to merge features (F_i and F_j) at two layers for the feature refinement (output refined feature: $\widehat{F}_i$).

simply merges the features at different layers, suffering from a limited ability to suppress non-shadow details in the high-resolution feature maps and introducing the non-shadow regions into the results. To alleviate this problem, we introduce the residual learning technique [26, 27] to improve the feature refinement by learning the residual of input features. As shown in Fig. 2(b), it begins by taking the concatenation of two input feature maps as the inputs and learning to produce the residual maps to refine original features by the element-wise addition. Learning the residual counterpart (see Fig. 2(b)) instead of adding the feature maps directly (see Fig. 2(a)) makes the feature refinement task easier, since it only needs to learn the complementary information from the features at different layers and can preserve the original features.

To further improve the performance of feature refinement, we develop a recurrent attention residual (RAR) module (see Fig. 2(d)), which recurrently applies an attention residual (AR) module (see Fig. 2(c)) to compute the refined context features. Let $\widehat{F}_{res}$ denote the refined output features produced by using the residual learning based module of Fig. 2(b). Our AR module improves the feature enhancement performance by recurrently learning an attention map to select the useful information of $\widehat{F}_{res}$ as the residual, which is added by the original $\widehat{F}_{res}$ as the output refined features. Specifically, the AR module starts by concatenating

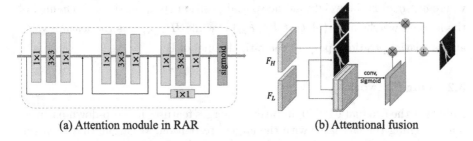

(a) Attention module in RAR   (b) Attentional fusion

Fig. 3. (a) The schematic illustration of the attention module in RAR; (b) the details of attentional fusion for the final shadow detection map; see Sect. 3.2.

the input two adjacent context features, and then utilizes an attention module (see Fig. 3(a)) to produce a weight (or an attention) map from the concatenated features. The attention map works as a feature selector to enhance good features and suppress noise in $\widehat{F}_{res}$. Then, the output refined feature of AR module is obtained by multiplying the learned attention map with the $\widehat{F}_{res}$, and then adding it with $\widehat{F}_{res}$ using an element-wise addition, as shown in Fig. 3(c). Hence, our RAR module computes the refined context features by recurrently employing the AR modules, where the output refined features at the previous recurrent step are used as the input of subsequent AR modules, and the parameters of different AR modules are shared to reduce the risk of overfitting.

Mathematically, our RAR computes the refinement features (denoted as F_i^{u+1}) at the layer i as:

$$F_i^{u+1} = \left(1 + A\big(Cat(F_i^u, F_j)\big)\right) * \left[\Phi\big(Cat(F_i^u, F_j)\big) + F_j\right], \qquad (1)$$

where $u=1,2,\ldots,$ U; U is the number of recurrent steps; F_i^u is the refined features after u recurrent steps, $F_i^1 = F_i$, which is the context features at layer i of the CNN; F_j is the context features at layer j of the CNN; Cat denotes the concatenation operation on F_i and F_j; $A(Cat(F_i, F_j))$ is the learned weight map using the attention mechanism (see the paragraph below for the details); and Φ represents the residual function.

Attention Module in the RAR. Motivated by the attention mechanism used for image classification [23], we develop an attention module (see Fig. 3(a)) to learn a weight map from the concatenated features $(Cat(F_i^u, F_j)$ of Eq. (1)). It starts with three residual blocks, where each block has a 1 * 1 convolution layer, a 3 * 3 dilated convolution layer, and a 1*1 convolutional layer. After that, we compute the weight (attention) map $\left(A\big(Cat(F_i^u, F_j)\big)\right)$ by using a sigmoid function on the feature maps (denoted as H) learned from three residual blocks:

$$a(p, q, c) = \frac{1}{1 + exp\big(-H(p, q, c)\big)}, \qquad (2)$$

where $a(p, q, c)$ is the weight at the spatial position (p, q) of the c-th channel of the learned weight map $\left(A\big(Cat(F_i^u, F_j)\big)\right)$, while $H(p, q, c)$ is the feature value at the spatial position (p, q) of the c-th channel of H.

3.2 Our Network

Note that the original FPN [9] iteratively merges features in a top-down pathway until reaching the last layer with the largest resolution. We argue that such single top-down pathway is not enough to capture the shadow context information spanned in different layers of the CNN. To alleviate this problem, we design a bidirection mechanism to integrate context information of different layers: one (top-down) pathway is to integrate features from low-resolution layers to high-resolution layers, while another (bottom-up) pathway is from high-resolution layers to low-resolution layers, and we use our RAR module (see Sect. 3.1) to refine features at each layer by merging two adjacent features. After that, we, following [28], use an attention mechanism (see Fig. 3(b)) to generate the final shadow detection map by fusing the shadow predictions from the refined features (denoted as F_H) at the last layer in the top-down direction and the features (denoted as F_L) at the last layer in the bottom-up direction. As shown in Fig. 3(b), we first generate two shadow detection maps from the refined features (F_H and F_L) by using a 1×1 convolutional layer. Then, we perform two convolution layers (3×3 and 1×1) on the concatenation of F_H and F_L, and use a sigmoid function to generate attention maps, which are multiplied with the shadow detection maps to produce the final shadow detection result.

The designed bidirection feature pyramid network (BFPN) can effectively use the complementary information of features in two directional pathways for shadow detection. Please refer to the Ablation study in Sect. 4.4 for the comparisons between the original FPN and our BFRN on two shadow detection benchmark datasets.

3.3 Training and Testing Strategies

We implement our network using PyTorch, and adopt ResNeXt101 [29] as the basic convolutional neural network for feature extraction.

Loss Function. As shown in Fig. 1, our network utilizes the deep supervision mechanism [30] to impose supervision signals to the features at each layer of two bidirectional pathways to promote useful information propagation to the shadow regions. During the training process, binary cross-entropy loss is used for each output of the network, and the total loss is the summation of the losses of all the output score maps.

Training Parameters. To accelerate the training procedure and reduce the overfitting risk, we initialize the parameters of the basic convolutional neural network by ResNeXt [29], which has been well-trained for the image classification task

Table 1. Comparing our method (BDRAR) with state-of-the-arts for shadow detection (DSC [6,7], scGAN [5], stacked-CNN [4], patched-CNN [24] and Unary-Pairwise [19]), for shadow removal (DeshadowNet [33]), for saliency detection (SRM [34] and Amulet [35]), and for semantic segmentation (PSPNet [36]).

Method	SBU [4]	UCF [8]
	BER	BER
BDRAR (ours)	**3.64**	**5.30**
DSC [6,7]	5.59	8.10
scGAN [5]	9.10	11.50
stacked-CNN [4]	11.00	13.00
patched-CNN [24]	11.56	-
Unary-Pairwise [19]	25.03	-
DeshadowNet [33]	6.96	8.92
SRM [34]	7.25	9.81
Amulet [35]	15.13	15.17
PSPNet [36]	8.57	11.75

on the ImageNet. Other parameters are initialized by random noise. Stochastic gradient descent (SGD) equipped with momentum of 0.9 and weight decay of 0.0005 is used to optimize the whole network for 3000 iterations. We adjust the learning rate by the poly strategy [31] with the basic learning rate of 0.005 and the power of 0.9. We train our network on the SBU training set, which contains 4089 images. Moreover, we augment the training set by random horizontal flipping. We resize all the images to the same resolution (416 × 416). Our network is trained on a single GTX 1080Ti GPU with a mini-batch size of eight, and the whole training process only takes about 40 min.

Inference. During testing, we first resize the input images to the same resolution as we used in the training stage. Then, we take the output of the attentional fusion module (see Fig. 3(b)) as the final output of the whole network for shadow detection. Finally, we use the fully connected conditional random field (CRF) [32] to further enhance the detection results by optimizing the spatial coherence of each pixel on the output of our network.

4 Experimental Results

4.1 Datasets and Evaluation Metrics

Benchmark Datasets. We evaluate the effectiveness of the proposed network on two widely-used shadow benchmark datasets: SBU [4] and UCF [8]. Each image in both two benchmark datasets has its corresponding annotated binary shadow mark. The SBU dataset is the largest publicly available annotated shadow dataset with 4089 training images and 638 testing images, while

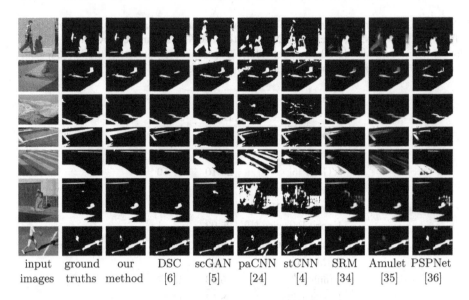

| input images | ground truths | our method | DSC [6] | scGAN [5] | paCNN [24] | stCNN [4] | SRM [34] | Amulet [35] | PSPNet [36] |

Fig. 4. Visual comparison of shadow maps produced by our method and others (4th-10th columns) against ground truths shown in 2nd column. Note that "stCNN" and "paCNN" stand for "stacked-CNN" and "patched-CNN", respectively.

the UCF dataset consists of 145 training images and 76 testing images. In our experiment, we train our shadow detection network using SBU training set, and evaluate our method and competitors on the testing sets of the SBU and UCF. Our network takes 0.056 s to process an image of 416 × 416 resolution.

Evaluation Metrics. We employ a commonly-used metric, which is balance error rate (BER), to quantitatively evaluate the shadow detection performance; please refer to this work [6] for the definition of the BER. Note that better performance is indicated by a lower BER value.

4.2 Comparison with the State-of-the-Art Shadow Detectors

We compare our method with five recent shadow detectors: DSC [6,7], scGAN [5], stacked-CNN [4], patched-CNN [24] and Unary-Pairwise [19]. To make a fair comparison, we obtain other shadow detectors' results either directly from the authors or by using the public implementations provided by the authors with recommended parameter settings.

Table 1 reports the quantitative results of different methods. From the results, we can find that the deep learning based methods [4,6,7,24] usually have better shadow detection results than hand-crafted detectors [19], since they can learn more powerful features for shadow detection from the annotated training set. DSC [6,7] achieves a superior performance than other existing deep learning models [4,5,24] by analyzing the directional contexts to understand the global

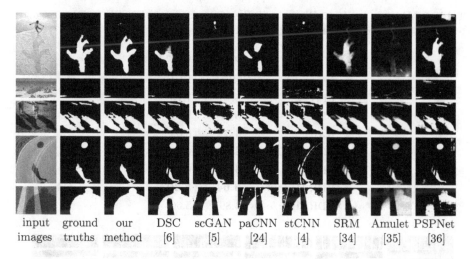

input   ground   our   DSC   scGAN paCNN   stCNN   SRM   Amulet PSPNet
images   truths   method   [6]   [5]   [24]   [4]   [34]   [35]   [36]

Fig. 5. Visual comparison of shadow maps produced by our method and others (4th-10th columns) against ground truths shown in 2nd column. Note that "stCNN" and "paCNN" stand for "stacked-CNN" and "patched-CNN", respectively.

image semantics to infer shadows. Compared to DSC, our method has 34.88% reduction on SBU and 34.57% reduction on UCF in terms of BER, demonstrating that our method (BDRAR) outperforms the others on both benchmark datasets. Although our shadow detection network is trained on the SBU training set [4], it still has a superior performance over the others on the UCF dataset, which demonstrates the generalization capability of our network.

In Figs. 4 and 5, we provide visual comparison results on different input images. From the results, we can find that our method (3rd column of Figs. 4 and 5) can effectively locate shadows under various backgrounds and avoid false positives, and thus has the best performance among all the shadow detectors. Moreover, for high-contrast objects in a large shadow region, our method still recognizes them as shadows; see the last two rows of Fig. 5.

4.3   Comparison with Methods of Shadow Removal, Saliency Detection and Semantic Segmentation

Note that deep networks designed for shadow removal, saliency detection and semantic image segmentation can be re-trained for shadow detection by using annotated shadow datasets. To further evaluate the effectiveness of our method, another experiment is conducted by comparing our method with a recent shadow removal model, i.e., DeshadowNet [33], two recent deep saliency detection models, i.e., SRM [34] and Amulet [35], and a recent semantic segmentation model, i.e., PSPNet [36].

Since we cannot obtain the original code of DeshadowNet [33], we carefully follow the published paper of DeshadowNet to implement it with our best efforts

Table 2. Ablation analysis. We train all the networks using the SBU training set and test them using the SBU testing set [4], and UCF testing set [8].

	SBU [4]	UCF [8]
Network	BER	BER
FPN	5.78	7.70
BD	5.37	7.11
RAR	4.33	6.09
BDR	4.23	6.71
BDAR	3.74	6.19
BDRAR (ours)	**3.64**	**5.30**
BDRAR_w/o_sw	3.89	5.66

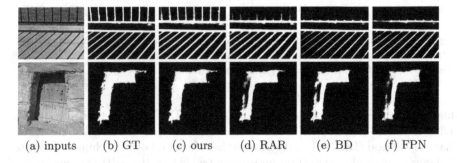

(a) inputs   (b) GT   (c) ours   (d) RAR   (e) BD   (f) FPN

Fig. 6. Comparing the shadow maps produced by our method (c) and by the other three models (d)-(f) against the ground truths (denoted as "GT") in (b).

and train the model for shadow detection on the SBU training set. For the other three methods, we obtain the code of these methods from their project webpages, and re-train their models on the SBU training set. For a fair comparison, we try our best to tune their training parameters and select the best shadow detection results. The last four rows in Table 1 report the BER values of these methods. Even though they have better BER values than some existing shadow detectors, our method still demonstrates a superior shadow detection performance over them on both benchmark datasets. On the other hand, the last three columns in Figs. 4 and 5 present the predicted shadow maps, showing that our network can consistently produce better shadow detection maps than the other methods.

4.4   Ablation Analysis

We perform experiments to evaluate the bidirectional feature integration in the FPN and the effectiveness of the RAR module design. The basic model is the original "FPN [9]," which only uses the top-down direction to integrate features and removes all the RAR modules shown in Fig. 1. The second model (denoted

Table 3. RAR module with different recurrent steps.

Number of recurrent steps	SBU [4]		UCF [8]	
	BER	Improvement	BER	Improvement
1 (BDRA)	3.74	-	6.19	-
2	3.64	2.67%	5.30	14.38%
3	3.89	−6.87%	5.66	−6.79%

as "BD") is similar to the "FPN," but it uses our bidirectional pathway to merge features at different layers of the CNN. The third model (denoted as "RAR") is the "FPN" with the RAR modules only. The fourth model (denoted as "BDR") replaces all the RAR modules of our network with residual learning based modules (see Fig. 2(b)), while the fifth model (denoted as "BDAR") replaces all our RAR modules with the attention residual learning modules (see Fig. 2(c)), which means that this model is constructed by removing the recurrent mechanism from our RAR modules. The last model (denoted as "BDRAR_w/o_sw") has a similar structure with our BDRAR, but it uses independent weights at each recurrent step in our RAR modules.

Table 2 summaries the compared BER values on both benchmark datasets. From the results, we can see that both "replacing the single top-down pathway of the FPN with the bidirectional pathways" and "adopting the RAR modules" lead to an obvious improvement. Compared to results of our network with the residual learning based module (see Fig. 2(b)) and attention residual module (see Fig. 2(c)), our RAR modules (see Fig. 2(d)) have better performance on shadow detection, since it can recurrently learn a set of attention weights to select good residual features to refine the integrated features, as shown in Table 2. Moreover, we provide visual analysis to evaluate how RAR and bidirectional feature integration contribute by conducting an experiment by comparing our method with three models: "FPN", "BD", and "RAR." Fig. 6 shows the comparisons on two input images, showing that RAR and BD can detect more shadow regions, as shown in Fig. 6(d–f). More importantly, our method with both RAR and bidirectional integration produces the best performance, and our predicted shadow maps are more similar to the ground truths (GT). Lastly, our method also outperforms "BDRAR_w/o_sw", showing that sharing weights in the RAR modules can reduce the learning parameters of the network, and thus leads to better shadow detection results.

Note that our RAR module (see Fig. 2(d)) recurrently employs the AR module (see Fig. 2(c)) to refine features at each layer by merging two adjacent features. Hence, a basic question of configuring our network is how many recurrent steps we use in our RAR modules. We adopt the network with the RAR modules as the baseline (BDAR), which has only one recurrent step (see Table 2); We conduct an experiment for comparisons by modifying our network with different rounds of recurrent steps (the round of AR modules; see Fig. 2(c) in our RAR), and Table 3 reports the results. As shown in Table 3, we can find that having two

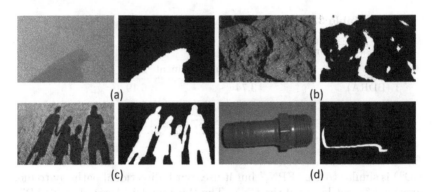

Fig. 7. More results produced from our network.

input images   ground truths   our results

Fig. 8. Failure cases of our network.

recurrent steps in the RAR module achieves the best performance on shadow detection. Compared to only one AR module, the network with two rounds of AR models can enhance the quality of the refined features at each layer by further integrating the adjacent features. However, when there are three rounds of AR modules in our RAR, it largely increases the complexity of our network, thus making the network training more difficult.

4.5 More Shadow Detection Results

In Fig. 7, we show more shadow detection results: (a) low-contrast shadow boundary; (b) unconnected shadows with a black background; (c) multiple human objects; and (d) tiny and irregular shadows. From the results, we can see that our method can still detect these shadows fairly well. Note that our method also has its limitations, and tends to fail in some extreme cases, such as the soft shadows (see Fig. 8 (top)), and shadows with tiny details (see Fig. 8 (bottom)).

Table 4. Comparison with the state-of-the-art methods on saliency detection.

Method	ECSSD		HKU-IS		PASCAL-S		DUT-OMRON	
	F_β	MAE	F_β	MAE	F_β	MAE	F_β	MAE
NLDF [39]	0.905	0.063	0.902	0.048	0.831	0.099	0.753	0.080
UCF [40]	0.910	0.078	0.886	0.073	0.821	0.120	0.735	0.131
DSS [37]	0.916	0.053	0.911	0.040	0.829	0.102	0.771	0.066
Amulet [35]	0.913	0.059	0.887	0.053	0.828	0.095	0.737	0.083
SRM [34]	0.917	0.056	0.906	0.046	0.844	**0.087**	0.769	0.069
RADF [38]	0.924	0.049	0.914	0.039	0.832	0.102	0.789	0.060
BDRAR (ours)	**0.935**	**0.045**	**0.916**	**0.038**	**0.846**	0.109	**0.808**	**0.058**

4.6 Saliency Detection

Our deep model has the potential to handle other vision tasks. Here, we take the saliency detection as an example. To evaluate the saliency detection performance of our deep model, we first re-trained our model on "MSRA10k," which is a widely-used dataset for saliency object detection, and then tested the trained model on four widely-used benchmark datasets, including ECSSD, HKU-IS, PASCAL-S, and DUT-OMRON; please refer to [37,38] for the details of these datasets. Moreover, we used two common metrics (F_β and MAE; see [37] for their definitions) for the quantitative comparisons among different saliency detectors. Table 4 shows the quantitative comparisons between our model and several state-of-the-art saliency detectors. From the table, we can see that our model produces the best performance on almost all the four benchmarks in terms of F_β and MAE, showing that our model predicts more accurate saliency maps.

5   Conclusion

This paper presents a novel network for single-image shadow detection. Two new techniques, recurrent attention residual (RAR) module and bidirectional feature pyramid network (BFPN), are presented to fully explore the global and local context information encoded in different layers of the convolutional neural network (CNN). The RAR module presents a novel feature refinement strategy for the context features at adjacent layers by learning the attention weights to select a residual in a recurrent manner, while the BFPN aggregates the shadow context features at different layers in two directions, and it can enhance the shadow boundaries as well as suppress the non-shadow regions. In the end, our network achieves the state-of-the-art performance on two benchmark datasets and outperforms other methods by a significant margin.

Acknowledgments. The work is supported by the National Basic Program of China, 973 Program (Project no. 2015CB351706), the Research Grants Council of the Hong Kong Special Administrative Region (Project no. CUHK 14225616),

Shenzhen Science and Technology Program (No. JCYJ20160429190300857 and JCYJ20170413162617606), the CUHK strategic recruitment fund, the NSFC (Grant No. 61272293, 61300137, 61472145, 61233012) and NSFG (Grant No. S2013010014973), RGC Fund (Grant No. CUHK14200915), Science and Technology Planning Major Project of Guangdong Province (Grant No. 2015A070711001), and Open Project Program of Guangdong Key Lab of Popular High Performance Computers and Shenzhen Key Lab of Service Computing and Applications (Grant No. SZU-GDPHPCL2015). Xiaowei Hu is funded by the Hong Kong Ph.D. Fellowship.

References

1. Finlayson, G.D., Hordley, S.D., Lu, C., Drew, M.S.: On the removal of shadows from images. IEEE Trans. Pattern Anal. Mach. Intell. **28**(1), 59–68 (2006)
2. Finlayson, G.D., Drew, M.S., Lu, C.: Entropy minimization for shadow removal. Int. J. Comput. Vis. **85**(1), 35–57 (2009)
3. Khan, S.H., Bennamoun, M., Sohel, F., Togneri, R.: Automatic feature learning for robust shadow detection. In: CVPR, pp. 1939–1946 (2014)
4. Vicente, T.F.Y., Hou, L., Yu, C.-P., Hoai, M., Samaras, D.: Large-scale training of shadow detectors with noisily-annotated shadow examples. In: Leibe, B., Matas, J., Sebe, N., Welling, M. (eds.) ECCV 2016. LNCS, vol. 9910, pp. 816–832. Springer, Cham (2016). https://doi.org/10.1007/978-3-319-46466-4_49
5. Nguyen, V., Vicente, T.F.Y., Zhao, M., Hoai, M., Samaras, D.: Shadow detection with conditional generative adversarial networks. In: ICCV, pp. 4510–4518 (2017)
6. Hu, X., Zhu, L., Fu, C.W., Qin, J., Heng, P.A.: Direction-aware spatial context features for shadow detection. In: CVPR, pp. 7454–7462 (2018)
7. Hu, X., Fu, C.W., Zhu, L., Qin, J., Heng, P.A.: Direction-aware spatial context features for shadow detection and removal. arXiv preprint arXiv:1805.04635 (2018)
8. Zhu, J., Samuel, K.G., Masood, S.Z., Tappen, M.F.: Learning to recognize shadows in monochromatic natural images. In: CVPR, pp. 223–230 (2010)
9. Lin, T.Y., Dollár, P., Girshick, R., He, K., Hariharan, B., Belongie, S.: Feature pyramid networks for object detection. In: CVPR, pp. 2117–2125 (2017)
10. Okabe, T., Sato, I., Sato, Y.: Attached shadow coding: estimating surface normals from shadows under unknown reflectance and lighting conditions. In: ICCV, pp. 1693–1700 (2009)
11. Karsch, K., Hedau, V., Forsyth, D., Hoiem, D.: Rendering synthetic objects into legacy photographs. ACM Trans. Graph. (SIGGRAPH Asia) **30**(6), 157:1–157:12 (2011)
12. Lalonde, J.F., Efros, A.A., Narasimhan, S.G.: Estimating natural illumination from a single outdoor image. In: ICCV, pp. 183–190 (2009)
13. Junejo, I.N., Foroosh, H.: Estimating geo-temporal location of stationary cameras using shadow trajectories. In: Forsyth, D., Torr, P., Zisserman, A. (eds.) ECCV 2008. LNCS, vol. 5302, pp. 318–331. Springer, Heidelberg (2008). https://doi.org/10.1007/978-3-540-88682-2_25
14. Ecins, A., Fermuller, C., Aloimonos, Y.: Shadow free segmentation in still images using local density measure. In: ICCP, pp. 1–8 (2014)
15. Cucchiara, R., Grana, C., Piccardi, M., Prati, A.: Detecting moving objects, ghosts, and shadows in video streams. IEEE Trans. Pattern Anal. Mach. Intell. **25**(10), 1337–1342 (2003)
16. Nadimi, S., Bhanu, B.: Physical models for moving shadow and object detection in video. IEEE Trans. Pattern Anal. Mach. Intell. **26**(8), 1079–1087 (2004)

17. Tian, J., Qi, X., Qu, L., Tang, Y.: New spectrum ratio properties and features for shadow detection. Pattern Recogn. **51**, 85–96 (2016)
18. Lalonde, J.-F., Efros, A.A., Narasimhan, S.G.: Detecting ground shadows in outdoor consumer photographs. In: Daniilidis, K., Maragos, P., Paragios, N. (eds.) ECCV 2010. LNCS, vol. 6312, pp. 322–335. Springer, Heidelberg (2010). https://doi.org/10.1007/978-3-642-15552-9_24
19. Guo, R., Dai, Q., Hoiem, D.: Single-image shadow detection and removal using paired regions. In: CVPR, pp. 2033–2040 (2011)
20. Huang, X., Hua, G., Tumblin, J., Williams, L.: What characterizes a shadow boundary under the sun and sky? In: ICCV, pp. 898–905 (2011)
21. Vicente, Y., Tomas, F., Hoai, M., Samaras, D.: Leave-one-out kernel optimization for shadow detection. In: ICCV, pp. 3388–3396 (2015)
22. Tai, Y., Yang, J., Liu, X.: Image super-resolution via deep recursive residual network. In: CVPR, pp. 3147–3155 (2017)
23. Wang, F., et al.: Residual attention network for image classification. In: CVPR, pp. 3156–3164 (2017)
24. Hosseinzadeh, S., Shakeri, M., Zhang, H.: Fast shadow detection from a single image using a patched convolutional neural network. arXiv preprint arXiv:1709.09283 (2017)
25. Bell, S., Zitnick, C.L., Bala, K., Girshick, R.: Inside-outside net: detecting objects in context with skip pooling and recurrent neural networks. In: CVPR, pp. 2874–2883 (2016)
26. He, K., Zhang, X., Ren, S., Sun, J.: Deep residual learning for image recognition. In: CVPR, pp. 770–778 (2016)
27. Deng, Z., et al.: R^3Net: recurrent residual refinement network for saliency detection. In: IJCAI, pp. 684–690 (2018)
28. Li, G., Xie, Y., Lin, L., Yu, Y.: Instance-level salient object segmentation. In: CVPR, pp. 247–256 (2017)
29. Xie, S., Girshick, R., Dollár, P., Tu, Z., He, K.: Aggregated residual transformations for deep neural networks. In: CVPR, pp. 5987–5995 (2017)
30. Xie, S., Tu, Z.: Holistically-nested edge detection. In: ICCV, pp. 1395–1403 (2015)
31. Liu, W., Rabinovich, A., Berg, A.C.: ParseNet: looking wider to see better. arXiv preprint arXiv:1506.04579 (2015)
32. Krähenbühl, P., Koltun, V.: Efficient inference in fully connected CRFs with Gaussian edge potentials. In: NIPS, pp. 109–117 (2011)
33. Qu, L., Tian, J., He, S., Tang, Y., Lau, R.W.: DeshadowNet: a multi-context embedding deep network for shadow removal. In: CVPR, pp. 4067–4075 (2017)
34. Wang, T., Borji, A., Zhang, L., Zhang, P., Lu, H.: A stagewise refinement model for detecting salient objects in images. In: ICCV, pp. 4019–4028 (2017)
35. Zhang, P., Wang, D., Lu, H., Wang, H., Ruan, X.: Amulet: aggregating multi-level convolutional features for salient object detection. In: ICCV, pp. 202–211 (2017)
36. Zhao, H., Shi, J., Qi, X., Wang, X., Jia, J.: Pyramid scene parsing network. In: CVPR, pp. 2881–2890 (2017)
37. Hou, Q., Cheng, M.M., Hu, X.W., Borji, A., Tu, Z., Torr, P.: Deeply supervised salient object detection with short connections. In: CVPR, pp. 3203–3212 (2017)
38. Hu, X., Zhu, L., Qin, J., Fu, C.W., Heng, P.A.: Recurrently aggregating deep features for salient object detection. In: AAAI, pp. 6943–6950 (2018)
39. Luo, Z., Mishra, A., Achkar, A., Eichel, J., Li, S., Jodoin, P.M.: Non-local deep features for salient object detection. In: CVPR, pp. 6609–6617 (2017)
40. Zhang, P., Wang, D., Lu, H., Wang, H., Yin, B.: Learning uncertain convolutional features for accurate saliency detection. In: ICCV, pp. 212–221 (2017)

Fast Light Field Reconstruction
with Deep Coarse-to-Fine Modeling
of Spatial-Angular Clues

Henry Wing Fung Yeung[1], Junhui Hou[2(✉)], Jie Chen[3], Yuk Ying Chung[1],
and Xiaoming Chen[4]

[1] School of Information Technologies, University of Sydney, Sydney, Australia
[2] Department of Computer Science, City University of Hong Kong,
Kowloon, Hong Kong
jh.hou@cityu.edu.hk
[3] School of Electrical and Electronics Engineering, Nanyang Technological
University, Singapore, Singapore
[4] School of Information Science and Technology,
University of Science and Technology of China, Hefei, China

Abstract. Densely-sampled light fields (LFs) are beneficial to many
applications such as depth inference and post-capture refocusing. However, it is costly and challenging to capture them. In this paper, we
propose a learning based algorithm to reconstruct a densely-sampled LF
fast and accurately from a sparsely-sampled LF in one forward pass. Our
method uses computationally efficient convolutions to deeply characterize the high dimensional spatial-angular clues in a coarse-to-fine manner.
Specifically, our end-to-end model first synthesizes a set of intermediate
novel sub-aperture images (SAIs) by exploring the coarse characteristics
of the sparsely-sampled LF input with spatial-angular alternating convolutions. Then, the synthesized intermediate novel SAIs are efficiently
refined by further recovering the fine relations from all SAIs via guided
residual learning and stride-2 4-D convolutions. Experimental results on
extensive real-world and synthetic LF images show that our model can
provide more than 3 dB advantage in reconstruction quality in average
than the state-of-the-art methods while being computationally faster by
a factor of 30. Besides, more accurate depth can be inferred from the
reconstructed densely-sampled LFs by our method.

Keywords: Light field · Deep learning
Convolutional neural network · Super resolution · View synthesis

1 Introduction

Compared with traditional 2-D images, which integrate the intensity of the light
rays from all directions at a pixel location, LF images separately record the light

---

H.W.F. Yeung and J. Hou—Equal Contributions.

V. Ferrari et al. (Eds.): ECCV 2018, LNCS 11210, pp. 138–154, 2018.
https://doi.org/10.1007/978-3-030-01231-1_9

ray intensity from different directions, thus providing additional information on the 3-D scene geometry. Such information is proportional to the angular resolution, i.e. the number of directions of the light rays, captured by the LF image. Densely sampled LF, with high resolution in the angular domain, contains sufficient information for accurate depth inference [1–4], post-capture refocusing [5] and 3D display [6,7].

LF images [8,9] can be acquired in a single shot using camera arrays [10] and consumer hand-held LF cameras such as Lytro [11] and Raytrix [12]. The former, due to the large number of sensors, can capture LF with higher spatial resolution while being expensive and bulky. Through multiplexing the angular domain into the spatial domain, the later is able to capture LF images with a single sensor, and thus are cheaper and portable. However, due to the limited sensor resolution, there is a trade-off between spatial and angular resolution. As a result, these cameras cannot densely sample in both the spatial and angular domains.

Reconstruction of a densely-sampled LF from a sparsely-sampled LF input is an on-going problem. Recent development in deep learning based LF reconstruction models [13,14] have achieved far superior performance over the traditional approaches [1–4]. Most notably, Kalantari et al. [13] proposed a sequential convolutional neural network (CNN) with disparity estimation and Wu et al. [14] proposed to use a blur-deblur scheme to counter the problem of information asymmetry between angular and spatial domain and a single CNN is used to map the blurred epipolar-plane images (EPIs) from low to high resolution. However, both approaches require heavy pre- or post-processing steps and long runtime, making them impractical to be applied in consumer LF imaging system.

In this paper, we propose a novel learning based model for fast reconstruction of a densely-sampled LF from a very sparsely-sampled LF. Our model, an end-to-end CNN, is composed of two phases, i.e., view synthesis and refinement, which are realized by computationally efficient convolutions to deeply characterize the spatial-angular clues in a coarse-to-fine manner. Specifically, the view synthesis network is designed to synthesize a set of intermediate novel sub-aperture images (SAIs) based on the input sparsely-sampled LF and the view refinement network is deployed for further exploiting the intrinsic LF structure among the synthesized novel SAIs. Our model does not require disparity warping nor any computationally intensive pre- and post-processing steps. Moreover, reconstruction of all novel SAIs are performed in one forward pass during which the intrinsic LF structural information among them is fully explored. Hence, our model fully preserves the intrinsic structure of reconstructed densely-sampled LF, leading to better EPI quality that can contribute to more accurate depth estimation.

Experimental results show that our model provides over 3 dB improvement in the average reconstruction quality while requiring less than 20 s on CPU, achieving over 30× speed up, compared with the state-of-the-art methods in synthesizing a densely-sampled LF from a sparsely-sampled LF. Experiment also shows that the proposed model can perform well on large baseline LF inputs and provides substantial quality improvement of over 3 dB with extrapolation. Our algorithm not only increases the number of samples for depth inference and post-capture refocusing, it can also enable LF to be captured with higher spatial resolution from hand-held LF cameras and potentially be applied in compression of LF images.

2 Related Work

Early works on LF reconstruction are based on the idea of warping the given SAIs to novel SAIs guided by an estimated disparity map. Wanner and Goldluecke [1] formulated the SAI synthesis problem as an energy minimization problem with a total variation prior, where the disparity map is obtained through global optimisation with a structure tensor computed on the 2-D EPI slices. Their approach considers disparity estimation as a separate step from SAI synthesis, which makes the reconstructed LF heavily dependent on the quality of the estimated disparity maps. Although subsequent research [2–4] has shown significantly better disparity estimations, ghosting and tearing effects are still present when the input SAIs are sparse.

Kalantari et al. [13] alleviated the drawback of Wanner and Goldluecke [1] by synthesizing the novel SAIs with two sequential CNNs that are jointly trained end-to-end. The first CNN performs disparity estimation based on a set of depth features pre-computed from the given input SAIs. The estimated disparities are then used to warp the given SAIs to the novel SAIs for the second CNN to perform color estimation. This approach is accurate but slow due to the computation intensive depth features extraction. Furthermore, each novel SAI is estimated at a separate forward pass, hence the intrinsic LF structure among the novel SAIs is neglected. Moreover, the reconstruction quality depends heavily upon the intermediate disparity warping step, and thus the synthesized SAIs are prone to occlusions.

Advancement in single image super-resolution (SISR) is recently made possible by the adoption of deep CNN models [15–18]. Following this, Yoon et al. [19,20], developed a CNN model that jointly super-resolves the LF in both the spatial and angular domain. This model concatenates at the channel dimension a subset of the spatially super-resolved SAIs from a CNN that closely resembles the model proposed in [15]. The concatenated SAIs are then passed into a second CNN for angular super-resolution. Their approach is designed specificity for scale 2 angular super-resolution and can not flexibly adapt to perform on very sparsely-sampled LF input.

Recently, Wu et al. [14] developed a CNN model that inherits the basic architecture of [15] with an addition residual learning component as in [16]. Using the idea of SISR, their model focuses on recovering the high frequency details of the bicubic upsampled EPI while a blur-deblur scheme is proposed to counter the information asymmetry problem caused by sparse angular sampling. Their model is adaptable to different devices. Since each EPI is a 2-D slice in both the spatial and angular domains of the 4-D LF, EPI based model can only utilize

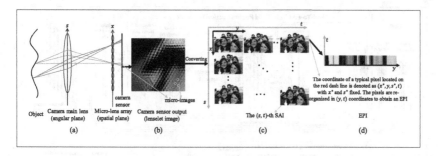

Fig. 1. LF captured with a single sensor device. The angular information of an LF is captured via the separation of light rays by the micro-lens array. The resulting LF can be parameterized by the spatial coordinates and the angular coordinates, i.e. the position of the SAI.

SAIs from the same horizontal or vertical angular coordinate of the sparsely-sampled LF to recover the novel SAIs in between, thus severely restricting the accessible information of the model. For the novel SAIs that do not fall within the same horizontal or vertical angular coordinate as the input SAIs, they are reconstructed based on the previously estimated SAIs. As a result, these SAIs are biased due to input errors. Moreover, due to the limitation in the blurring kernel size and bicubic interpolation, this method cannot be applied to sparsely-sampled LF with only 2×2 SAIs or with disparity larger than 5 pixels.

3   The Proposed Approach

3.1   4-D Light Field and Problem Formulation

4-D LF can be represented using the two-plane parameterization structure, as illustrated in Fig. 1, where the light ray travels and intersects the angular plane (s, t) and the spatial plane (x, y) [21]. Let $\mathcal{I} \in \mathbb{R}^{W \times H \times M \times N \times 3}$ denote an LF with $M \times N$ SAIs of spatial dimension $W \times H \times 3$, and $\mathcal{I}(:, :, s, t, :) \in \mathbb{R}^{W \times H \times 3}$ be the (s, t)-th SAI $(1 \leq s \leq M, 1 \leq t \leq N)$.

Densely-sampled LF reconstruction aims to construct an LF $\mathcal{I}' \in \mathbb{R}^{W \times H \times M' \times N' \times 3}$ including a large number of SAIs, from an LF $\mathcal{I}$ containing a small number of SAIs , where $M' > M$ and $N' > N$. Since the densely-sampled LF $\mathcal{I}'$ also contains the set of input SAIs, denoted as $\mathcal{K}$, the SAIs to be estimated is therefore reduced to the set of $(M' \times N' - M \times N)$ novel SAIs, denoted as $\mathcal{N}$.

Efficient modelling of the intrinsic structure of LF , i.e. photo-consistency, defined as the relationship of pixels from different SAIs that represent the same scene point, is crucial for synthesising high quality LF SAIs. However, real-world scenes usually contain factors such as occlusions, specularities and

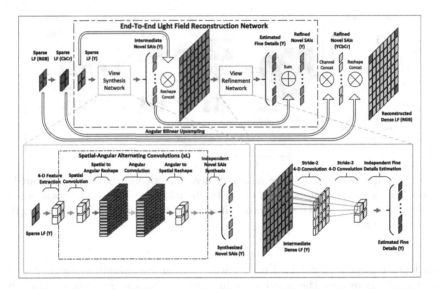

Fig. 2. The workflow of reconstructing a densely-sampled LF with 8×8 SAIs from a sparsely-sampled LF with 2×2 SAIs. Our proposed model focuses on reconstructing the luma components (Y) of the novel SAIs, while angular bilinear interpolation recovers the other two chrominance components (Cb and Cr). Note that the reshape operations in the view synthesis network are included for understanding of the data flow and are not required in actual implementation.

non-Lambertian lighting, making it challenging to characterize this structure accurately. In this paper, we propose a CNN based approach for efficient characterisation of spatial-angular clues for high quality reconstruction of densely sampled LFs.

3.2   Overview of Network Architecture

As illustrated in Fig. 2, we propose a novel CNN model to provide direct end-to-end mapping between the luma component of the input SAIs, denoted as $\mathcal{K}_Y$, and that of the novel SAIs, denoted as $\widehat{\mathcal{N}}_Y$. Our proposed network consists of two phases: view synthesis and view refinement. The view synthesis network, denoted as $f_S(.)$, first synthesizes the whole set of intermediate novel SAIs based on all input SAIs. The synthesized novel SAIs are then combined with the input SAIs to form a 4-D LF structure using a customised reshape-concat layer. This intermediate LF is then fed into the refinement network, denoted as $f_R(.)$, for recovering the fine details. At the end, the estimated fine details are added to the intermediate synthesized SAIs in an pixel-wise manner to give the final prediction of the novel SAIs $\widehat{\mathcal{N}}_Y$. The relations between the inputs and outputs of our model is represented as:

$$\widehat{\mathcal{N}}_Y = f_S(\mathcal{K}_Y) + f_R(f_S(\mathcal{K}_Y), \mathcal{K}_Y). \tag{1}$$

Note that the full color novel SAIs $\hat{\mathcal{N}}$ are obtained from combining $\hat{\mathcal{N}}_Y$ with angular bilinear interpolation of the other two chrominance components, i.e., Cb and Cr. Contrary to the previous approaches that synthesize a particular novel SAI at a each forward pass [13], and an EPI of a row or column of novel SAIs at each forward pass [14], our approach is capable of jointly producing all novel SAIs at one pass to preserve the intrinsic LF structure among them. Our network is full 4-D convolutional and uses Leaky Relu with the parameter of 0.2 for activation. Table 1 provides a summary of the network architecture.

3.3 View Synthesis Network

The view synthesis network estimates a set of intermediate novel SAIs by uncovering the coarse spatial-angular clues carried by the limited number of SAIs of the input sparsely-sampled LF. This step takes in all input SAIs from the given LF for the estimation of novel SAIs, and thus it can make full use of available information on the structural relationship among SAIs. For achieving this, it is necessary to perform convolution on all both the spatial and the angular dimensions of the input LF.

4-D convolution is a straightforward choice for this task. However, for this particular problem, the computational cost required by 4-D convolution makes training such a model impossible in a reasonable amount of time. Pseudo filters or separable filters, which reduce model complexity by approximating a high dimensional filter with filters of lower dimension, have been applied to solve different computer vision problems, such as image structure extraction [22], 3-D rendering [23] and video frame interpolation [24]. This is recently adopted in [25] for LF material classification, which verifies that the pseudo 4-D filters can achieve similar performance as 4-D filters.

For preventing potential overfitting and long training time from the use of full 4-D filter while characterizing 4-D information of LF, we adopt the pseudo 4-D filter which approximates a single 4-D filtering step with two 2-D filters that perform convolution on the spatial and the angular dimensions of the LF in an alternating manner. Such a design requires only the computation of $2/n^2$ of a 4-D convolution while still utilizing all available information from the input SAIs.

In the synthesis network, spatial-angular alternating convolutions are adopted only for intermediate feature extraction. For the initial feature extraction step and the novel SAIs synthesis step, 4-D convolution is applied since the computational complexity is less. Such a design obtains a significant reduction in parameter size as well as computational cost. Moreover, the low computational cost also benefits from that feature extraction is performed at the coarse angular resolution of $M \times N$ as opposed to [14] at the fine level of $M' \times N'$.

Table 1. Model specification for reconstructing a densely-sampled LF with 8×8 SAIs from a sparsely-sampled LF with 2×2 SAIs on the luma component. The first two dimensions of the filters, input and output data tensor correspond to the spatial dimension whereas the third and the forth dimension correspond to the angular dimension. The fifth dimension of the output tensor denotes the number of feature maps in the intermediate convolutional layers while representing the number of novel SAIs at the final layer. Stride and Paddings are given in the form of (Spatial/Angular). All convolutional layers contain biases. Note that the intermediate LF reconstruction step is performed with reshape and concatenation operations to enable back-propagation of loss from the view refinement network to the view synthesis network.

	Filter size/operation	Input Size	Output Size	Stride	Pad
sparsely-sampled LF input	-	-	$(64, 64, 2, 2, 1)$	-	-
View synthesis netowrk					
Feature extraction	$(3, 3, 3, 3, 1, 64)$	$(64, 64, 2, 2, 1)$	$(64, 64, 2, 2, 64)$	1/1	1/1
Alternating filtering $(\times L)$					
Spatial $S_l, l \in \{1, ..., L\}$	$(3, 3, 1, 1, 64, 64)$	$(64, 64, 2, 2, 64)$	$(64, 64, 2, 2, 64)$	1/1	1/0
Angular $A_l, l \in \{1, ..., L\}$	$(1, 1, 3, 3, 64, 64)$	$(64, 64, 2, 2, 64)$	$(64, 64, 2, 2, 64)$	1/1	0/1
Novel SAIs synthesis	$(3, 3, 2, 2, 64, 60)$	$(64, 64, 2, 2, 64)$	$(64, 64, 1, 1, 60)$	1/1	1/0
Intermediate LF	Reshape & concat	$(64, 64, 2, 2, 1)$	$(64, 64, 8, 8, 1)$	-	-
Reconstruction		$(64, 64, 1, 1, 60)$			
View refinement network					
Angular Dim. Reduction 1	$(3, 3, 2, 2, 1, 16)$	$(64, 64, 8, 8, 1)$	$(64, 64, 4, 4, 16)$	1/2	1/0
Angular Dim. Reduction 2	$(3, 3, 2, 2, 16, 64)$	$(64, 64, 4, 4, 16)$	$(64, 64, 2, 2, 64)$	1/2	1/0
Fine details recovery	$(3, 3, 2, 2, 64, 60)$	$(64, 64, 2, 2, 64)$	$(64, 64, 1, 1, 60)$	1/1	1/0
Novel SAIs reconstruction	Element-wise sum	$(64, 64, 1, 1, 60)$	$(64, 64, 1, 1, 60)$	-	-
		$(64, 64, 1, 1, 60)$			

3.4 View Refinement Network

In the view synthesis phase, novel SAIs are independently synthesized, and the relationship among them is not taken into account. Therefore, a view refinement network is designed to further exploit the relationship among the synthesized novel SAIs from the intermediate LF, which is expected to contribute positively to the reconstruction quality of the densely-sampled LF. This can be considered as a regularizer that imposes the LF structure on the synthesized SAIs.

Inspired by the success of residual learning on image reconstruction [14,16–18], we equip our view refinement network with guided residual learning that is specifically designed for the LF data structure. Typical residual learning attempts to learn a transformation $R(\cdot)$ to recover the residual $R(\mathcal{I}')$ for the input data $\mathcal{I}'$, i.e. the intermediate LF, as shown in Eq. (2). However, the input to the refinement network consists of a set of SAIs $\mathcal{K}_Y \subset \mathcal{I}'$ from the given sparsely-sampled LF, which is absolutely correct, i.e. $R(\mathcal{K}_Y) = 0$, and a set of synthesized SAIs $\mathcal{N}'_Y = f_S(\mathcal{K}_Y) \subset \mathcal{I}'$, which is erroneous. Hence, residual learning on $\mathcal{K}_Y$ is unnecessary. Guided residual learning can be formulated as a typical residual learning on $\mathcal{N}'_Y$ with the guidance from the additional input, $\mathcal{K}_Y$, as shown in Eq. (3).

$$\widehat{\mathcal{I}}_Y = \mathcal{I}' + R(\mathcal{I}') \tag{2}$$

$$\widehat{\mathcal{N}}_Y = \mathcal{N}'_Y + R(\mathcal{N}'_Y | \mathcal{K}_Y) \tag{3}$$

Guided residual learning has the following benefits: (i) $\mathcal{K}_Y$, as a set of ground-truth SAIs, offers correct complementary information of the scene; (ii) learning 0 residuals for $\mathcal{K}_Y$ is not performed; and (iii) By placing $\mathcal{K}_Y$ and $\mathcal{N}'_Y$ in the form of $\mathcal{I}'$, a densely sampled intermediate LF, for input to the second stage refinement network, it encourages the first stage, i.e., view synthesis network, to generate SAIs that preserve the LF structure exhibiting in the EPI shown in Fig. 1(d).

Since the angular dimension increases significantly from $M \times N$ to $M' \times N'$ after the view synthesis processes, alternating convolution will incur a substantially higher computation cost that increases linearly in angular dimension. For reducing the computation to a manageable level, stride-2 4-D convolution is used for efficient angular dimension reduction while the feature map number is set to increase gradually. Note that to allow back-propagation, an intermediate 4-D LF is reconstructed from the previously synthesized novel SAIs and the input SAIs via a customised reshape-concat layer. The refinement details of all novel SAIs are independently estimated at the final 4-D convolution layer and are added to the previously synthesized intermediate novel SAIs to give the final reconstructed novel SAIs.

3.5 Training Details

The training objective is to minimise the $\mathcal{L}_2$ distance between all reconstructed novel SAIs $\widehat{\mathcal{N}}_Y$ and their respective ground-truth $\mathcal{N}_Y$:

$$\mathcal{L}_2(\mathcal{N}_Y, \widehat{\mathcal{N}}_Y) = \sum_x \sum_y \sum_s \sum_t \left(\widehat{\mathcal{N}}_Y(x, y, s, t) - \mathcal{N}_Y(x, y, s, t) \right)^2 .$$

We trained a model for each task on the training set with 100 scenes provided by Kalantari et al. [13][1]. All images were taken with a Lytro Illum camera and were decoded to 14×14 SAIs with spatial resolution 376×541. Since the three SAIs from each side are usually black, we only adopted the middle 8×8 SAIs for training and testing as done in [13].

Training LFs were spatially cropped to 64×64 patches with stride 1, giving a maximum of approximately 15,000,000 training samples. Moreover, we adopted stochastic gradient descent to optimize the model, and the batch size was set to 1. The spatial resolution of the model output is kept unchanged at 64×64 with padding of zeros.

We implemented the model with the MatConvNet toolbox [26] in MATLAB and trained it with the GTX 1080 Ti GPU. Random filter weights under the MSRA method [27] were used to initialize our model, while biases were initialized to 0. Throughout training, momentum parameter was set to 0.9. Depending

---

[1] http://cseweb.ucsd.edu/~viscomp/projects/LF/papers/SIGASIA16.

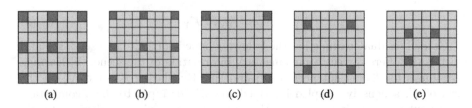

Fig. 3. Illustration of inputs (red blocks) and outputs (yellow blocks) for different tasks. From left to right: (a) $3 \times 3 - 7 \times 7$, (b) $3 \times 3 - 9 \times 9$, (c) $2 \times 2 - 8 \times 8$, (d) $2 \times 2 - 8 \times 8$ extrapolation-1, (e) $2 \times 2 - 8 \times 8$ extrapolation-2. (Color figure online)

on model depth, a learning rate between $1e-6$ to $2e-5$ was applied without weight decay, and epoch number was set between 8000 to 12000 each with 1000 iterations. Training time increases linearly with the number of alternating convolutions, ranging from around 1 day for model with 1 alternating convolution and 10 days for model with 16 alternating convolutions.

4   Experimental Results

Our model was compared with two state-of-the-art CNN based methods that are specifically designed for densely-sampled LF reconstruction, i.e., Kalantari et al. [13] and Wu et al. [14]. Comparisons were performed over three different tasks, shown in Fig. 3: $3 \times 3 - 7 \times 7$, $3 \times 3 - 9 \times 9$ and $2 \times 2 - 8 \times 8$. Task $M \times N - M' \times N'$ stands for reconstructing densely-sampled LFs with $M' \times N'$ SAIs from sparsely-sampled LFs with $M \times N$ SAIs. Moreover, we investigated the effect of the positions of SAIs involved in the sparsely-sampled LF input on the reconstruction quality via task $2 \times 2 - 8 \times 8$.

Both quantitative and qualitative results will be shown in the following subsections. Reconstruction quality is measured with PSNR and SSIM, averaged over all synthesised novel SAIs. Due to limited space, we only report the average result for all data entries in each dataset. The $(5,5)$-th SAI of the reconstructed densely-sampled LF is chosen for display. Both training and testing codes are publicly available[2].

4.1 $3 \times 3 - 7 \times 7$ Light Field Reconstruction

For the task $3 \times 3 - 7 \times 7$, we compared with Kalantari et al. [13] and Wu et al. [14]. We set the number of spatial-angular alternating convolutional layers to 4. Comparisons were performed on the *30 Scenes* dataset [13], the *reflective-29* and *occlusion-16* LFs from the Stanford Lytro Lightfield Archive [28] and *Neurons 20×* from the Stanford Light Field microscope dataset [29]. The reconstruction

---

[2] https://github.com/angularsr/LightFieldAngularSR.

Table 2. Quantitative comparisons of the reconstruction quality of the proposed model and the state-of-the-art methods under the task $3 \times 3 - 7 \times 7$.

Algorithm	30 scenes	Reflective-29	Occlusions-16	Neurons 20×	Average
Wu et al. [14]	41.02/0.9875	46.10/0.9929	38.86/0.9852	29.34/0.9378	40.75/0.9861
Kalantari et al. [13]	43.73/0.9891	46.54/0.9953	37.97/0.9827	28.45/0.9274	43.18/0.9872
Ours 4L	**44.53/0.9900**	**47.85/0.9960**	**39.53/0.9873**	**30.69/0.9518**	**44.06/0.9889**

Table 3. Quantitative comparisons of reconstruction quality of the proposed model, Kalantari et al. and Wu et al. over Buddha and Mona from the HCI dataset.

Algorithm	Buddha	Mona	Average
Wu et al. [14]/SC	41.67/0.9975	42.39/0.9973	42.03/0.9974
Wu et al. [14]/SRCNN	41.50/0.9971	42.64/0.9976	42.07/0.9974
Wu et al. [14]	43.20/**0.9980**	44.37/**0.9982**	43.79/**0.9981**
Kalantari et al. [13]	42.73/0.9844	42.42/0.9858	42.58/0.9851
Ours 8L	**43.77**/0.9872	**45.67**/0.9920	**44.72**/0.9896

quality measured in PSNR and SSIM is shown in Table 2. For each LF, the results are the average of the luma component of all 40 novel SAIs. Our proposed model performs better for all datasets than the two comparing methods: with 0.88 dB and 3.31 dB reconstruction advantage over Kalantari et al. [13] and Wu et al. [14], respectively. A 2.3 dB advantage for the Neurons 20× dataset shows that the proposed LF reconstruction model generalizes well to different LF capturing devices.

4.2 $3 \times 3 - 9 \times 9$ Reconstruction on Large Disparity Light Field

To demonstrate that our model can work on LFs with larger disparities, the proposed model was modified for task $3 \times 3 - 9 \times 9$ and was trained with LFs from the HCI dataset [30], which are created with Blender software [31], with larger disparities compared with Lytro Illum captures. The LFs Budda and Mona are used for testing and the rest are used for training. For this task, we set the number of spatial-angular alternating convolution layers to 8. Due to limited number of training images, data augmentation was applied for obtaining more data training samples.

Comparison results with [14] are reported in Table 3. Using only 7 training LFs, our proposed method provides superior reconstruction quality on the luma component, averaged across all 72 novel SAIs.

4.3 $2 \times 2 - 8 \times 8$ Light Field Reconstruction

We carried out comparison with the method by Kalantari et al. [13] retrained with the same training dataset as ours. The method by Wu et al. [14] cannot be compared since their approach requires 3 views in each angular dimension

Table 4. Quantitative comparisons of reconstruction quality of the proposed model and Kalantari *et al.* under task $2 \times 2 - 8 \times 8$ over 222 real-world LFIs.

Algorithm	30 Scenes	EPFL	Reflective	Occlusions	Average
Kalantari *et al.* [13]	38.21/0.9736	38.70/0.9574	35.84/0.9416	31.81/0.8945	36.90/0.9452
Ours 16L	**39.22/0.9773**	**39.57/0.9637**	**36.47/0.9472**	**32.68/0.9061**	**37.76/0.9521**

to provide enough information for the bicubic interpolation step. Our testing dataset contains 30 test scenes from [13] (See footnote 1) and 118 LFs from the EPFL dataset [32][3] with diversified real-world scenes. To further evaluate the robustness of the algorithms, we also included the *Refractive and Reflective Surfaces* and the *Occlusions* categories from the Stanford Lytro Lightfield Archive [28], which contain 31 and 43 LFs, respectively. Note that the 8 LFs from the *Occlusions* category and 1 LF from the *Refractive and Reflective Surfaces* category were removed from testing as they were used for training. This test set contains 222 LFs which is sufficient to provide objective evaluation of model performance.

Reconstruction quality is measured with PSNR and SSIM averaged over the RGB channels, and over all 60 novel SAIs. As shown in Table 4, our proposed model with 16 alternating convolutions in the synthesis network obtains an average of 37.76 dB, 0.86 higher than that of Kalantari *et al.* [13].

Figure 4 further visually demonstrates that our algorithm is able to obtain better reconstruction quality compare with the state-of-the-art. As shown in the error maps, Kalantari *et al.* produces artifacts near the boundaries of the foreground objects. In most cases, thin edges cannot be reconstructed correctly, leaving blurred and overlapped regions between occluders and the background. Moreover, since our method fully explores the relationship among all SAIs in the reconstruction process, the LF structure is well preserved, leading to better EPI quality that can contribute to more accurate depth estimation.

4.4 $2 \times 2 - 8 \times 8$ Light Field Reconstruction with Extrapolation

Figures 5(a) and (b) show the average quality of each novel SAIs by Kalantari *et al.* [13] and the proposed approach under the task $2 \times 2 - 8 \times 8$, where it can be observed that reconstruction quality of the center SAIs has significantly worse quality compared with the novel SAIs near the input SAIs. The central view is furthest away from any of the input SAIs, therefore it poses greatest challenge to correctly infer the details. Based on this analysis, we investigated the possibility of combing interpolation and extrapolation for the LF reconstruction, which can make the average distances from all novel SAIs shorter to the input SAIs.

---

[3] https://jpeg.org/plenodb/lf/epfl/.

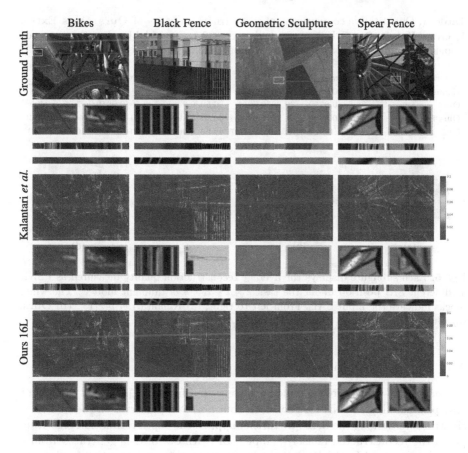

Fig. 4. Visual comparison of our proposed approach with Kalantari *et al.* [13] on the (5, 5)-th synthesised novel SAI for the task $2 \times 2 - 8 \times 8$. Selected regions have been zoomed on for better comparison. Digital zoom-in is recommended for more visual details.

We trained two models with the exact same network architecture as **Ours 8L**, however, with different input view position configurations as shown in Fig. 3(d) and (e), which we name as **Ours Extra. 1** and **Ours Extra. 2**, respectively. Note that for the first model, 1 row and column of SAIs are extrapolated while for the second model, 2 rows and columns of SAIs are extrapolated.

As shown in Table 5, when our model combines interpolation and extrapolation, an average of 2.5 dB improvement can be achieved for all novel SAIs on the 222 LFs dataset. Figures 5(c) and (d) also show the average quality of each novel SAIs by **Ours Extra. 1** and **Ours Extra. 2**, respectively. The significant gain in reconstruction quality indicates the potential for the proposed algorithm to be applied on LF compression [33,34].

Table 5. Quantitative comparisons of reconstruction quality of **Ours, Ours Extra. 1, Ours Extra. 2** and Kalantari *et al.* over 222 real-world LFs. For the proposed models, the number of spatial-angular alternating convolutions is set to 8.

Algorithm	30 Scenes	EPFL	Reflective	Occlusions	Average
Kalantari *et al.* [13]	38.21/0.9736	38.70/0.9574	35.84/0.9416	31.81/0.8945	36.90/0.9452
Ours	38.88/0.9750	39.29/0.9611	36.52/0.9466	32.58/0.9019	37.55/0.9495
Ours Extra. 1	40.79/0.9820	41.25/0.9705	**40.16/0.9667**	35.54/**0.9275**	39.93/**0.9632**
Ours Extra. 2	**40.93/0.9827**	**41.46/0.9717**	40.02/0.9651	**35.79**/0.9246	**40.09**/0.9631

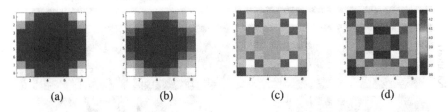

(a)   (b)   (c)   (d)

Fig. 5. Each subfigure displays the average reconstruction quality measured as PSNR at different SAI position under the task $2 \times 2 - 8 \times 8$ of different models. The white blocks indicate the input SAIs. From left to right: (a) Kalantari *et al.* [13], (b) **Ours**, (c) **Ours Extra. 1** and (d) **Ours Extra. 2**.

4.5   Depth Estimation

To verify that the densely-sampled LF generated from our proposed model not only produces high PSNR for each SAIs, but also well preserves the 3-D geometric structures among the SAIs, we further applied the depth estimation algorithm [3] on the reconstructed densely-sampled LF with 8×8 SAIs generated from a sparsely-sampled LF with 2×2 SAIs. Figure 6 shows in each row the depth maps based on the sparsely-sampled LFs, the densely-sampled LFs from Kalantari *et al.*, the densely-sampled LFs from our model and the ground-truth densely-sampled LFs. It can be observed that the depth maps from **Ours Extra. 1** are more accurate than those by Kalantari *et al.*

4.6   Runtime and Reconstruction Quality vs. Model Depth

The runtime and performance trade-off of our proposed model with different numbers of alternating convolutions are shown in Fig. 7. We can observe that the reconstruction quality by our model increases rapidly with the number of alternating convolutions increasing. Furthermore, the adoption of extrapolation leads to a significant improvement in reconstruction with a runtime of around 11 s, over 30× speed up compared with Kalantari *et al.* [13], on an Intel i7-6700K CPU @ 4.00 GHz without GPU acceleration. Moreover, the scalable structure in the synthesis network enables a trade-off between the reconstruction quality

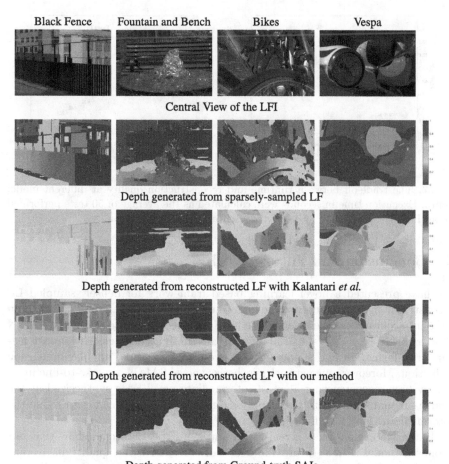

Fig. 6. Visual comparison of the depth estimation results from a sparsely-sampled LF, reconstructed densely-sampled LF from our proposed approach and Kalantari *et al.* [13] and a ground-truth densely-sampled LF.

and speed. For task $2 \times 2 - 8 \times 8$, our model with 16 alternating convolutions needs approximately 20 s. If speed is of priority, at similar reconstruction quality to Kalantari *et al.*, our model with 1 alternating convolution can provide over $130\times$ speed up, taking only 3.15 s to process an LF.

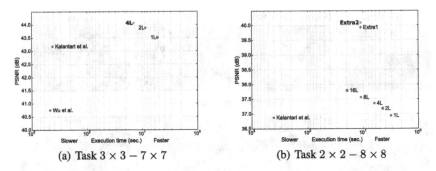

(a) Task $3 \times 3 - 7 \times 7$ (b) Task $2 \times 2 - 8 \times 8$

Fig. 7. The trade-off between runtime and reconstruction quality at different model depth. Execution time in seconds were calculated as the average of 50 tests performed on an Intel i7-6700K CPU @ 4.00 GHz **without** GPU acceleration.

5   Conclusion and Future Work

We have presented a novel learning based framework for densely-sampled LF reconstruction. To characterize the high-dimensional spatial-angular clues within LF data accurately and efficiently, we have designed an end-to-end trained CNN that extensively employs spatial-angular alternating convolutions for fast feature transformation and stride-2 4-D convolutions for rapid angular dimension reduction. Moreover, our network synthesizes novel SAIs in a coarse-to-fine manner by first reconstructing a set of intermediate novel SAIs synthesized at the coarse angular dimension, then applying guided residual learning to refine the intermediate views at a finer level.

Extensive evaluations on real-world and synthetic LF scenes show that our proposed model is able to provide over 3 dB reconstruction quality in average than the state-of-the-art methods while being over 30× faster. Especially, our model can handle complex scenes with serious occlusions well. Moreover, our model is able to perform well under LFs with larger disparities, and more accurate depth can be inferred from the reconstructed densely-sampled LFs by our method. Considering the efficiency and effectiveness of the proposed CNN model in processing LF data, we believe such a design has great potential on LF compression, as well as a wide range of LF image processing tasks, including but not limited to LF spatial super-resolution, temporal super-resolution and depth estimation.

Acknowledgements. This work was supported in part by the CityU Start-up Grant for New Faculty under Grant 7200537/CS and in part by the Hong Kong RGC Early Career Scheme Funds 9048123 (CityU 21211518).

References

1. Wanner, S., Goldluecke, B.: Variational light field analysis for disparity estimation and super-resolution. IEEE Trans. Pattern Anal. Mach. Intell. **36**(3), 606–619 (2014)
2. Jeon, H.G., et al.: Accurate depth map estimation from a lenslet light field camera. In: Proceedings of the IEEE Conference on Computer Vision and Pattern Recognition, pp. 1547–1555 (2015)
3. Wang, T.C., Efros, A.A., Ramamoorthi, R.: Occlusion-aware depth estimation using light-field cameras. In: Proceedings of the IEEE International Conference on Computer Vision, pp. 3487–3495 (2015)
4. Chen, J., Hou, J., Ni, Y., Chau, L.P.: Accurate light field depth estimation with superpixel regularization over partially occluded regions. IEEE Trans. Image Process. **27**(10), 4889–4900 (2018)
5. Fiss, J., Curless, B., Szeliski, R.: Refocusing plenoptic images using depth-adaptive splatting. In: Proceedings of IEEE International Conference on Computational Photography, pp. 1–9 (2014)
6. Levoy, M., Hanrahan, P.: Light field rendering. In: Proceedings of the 23rd Annual Conference on Computer Graphics and Interactive Techniques, pp. 31–42. ACM (1996)
7. Jones, A., McDowall, I., Yamada, H., Bolas, M., Debevec, P.: Rendering for an interactive 360 light field display. ACM Trans. Graph. **26**(3), 40 (2007)
8. Ihrke, I., Restrepo, J., Mignard-Debise, L.: Principles of light field imaging: briefly revisiting 25 years of research. IEEE Sig. Process. Mag. **33**(5), 59–69 (2016)
9. Wu, G., et al.: Light field image processing: an overview. IEEE J. Sel. Top. Sig. Process. **11**(7), 926–954 (2017)
10. Wilburn, B., et al.: High performance imaging using large camera arrays. ACM Trans. Graph. **24**(3), 765–776 (2005)
11. Lytro Illum. https://www.lytro.com/
12. Raytrix. https://www.raytrix.de/
13. Kalantari, N.K., Wang, T.C., Ramamoorthi, R.: Learning-based view synthesis for light field cameras. ACM Trans. Graph. **35**(6), 193 (2016)
14. Wu, G., Zhao, M., Wang, L., Dai, Q., Chai, T., Liu, Y.: Light field reconstruction using deep convolutional network on EPI. In: Proceedings of the IEEE Conference on Computer Vision and Pattern Recognition, pp. 6319–6327 (2017)
15. Dong, C., Loy, C.C., He, K., Tang, X.: Learning a deep convolutional network for image super-resolution. In: Fleet, D., Pajdla, T., Schiele, B., Tuytelaars, T. (eds.) ECCV 2014. LNCS, vol. 8692, pp. 184–199. Springer, Cham (2014). https://doi.org/10.1007/978-3-319-10593-2_13
16. Kim, J., Kwon Lee, J., Mu Lee, K.: Accurate image super-resolution using very deep convolutional networks. In: Proceedings of the IEEE Conference on Computer Vision and Pattern Recognition, pp. 1646–1654 (2016)
17. Lai, W.S., Huang, J.B., Ahuja, N., Yang, M.H.: Deep laplacian pyramid networks for fast and accurate super-resolution. In: Proceedings of the IEEE Conference on Computer Vision and Pattern Recognition, no. 3, pp. 5835–5843 (2017)
18. Tai, Y., Yang, J., Liu, X.: Image super-resolution via deep recursive residual network. In: Proceedings of the IEEE Conference on Computer Vision and Pattern Recognition, pp. 2790–2798 (2017)
19. Yoon, Y., Jeon, H.G., Yoo, D., Lee, J.Y., So Kweon, I.: Learning a deep convolutional network for light-field image super-resolution. In: Proceedings of the IEEE International Conference on Computer Vision Workshops, pp. 24–32 (2015)

20. Yoon, Y., Jeon, H.G., Yoo, D., Lee, J.Y., Kweon, I.S.: Light-field image super-resolution using convolutional neural network. IEEE Sig. Process. Lett. **24**(6), 848–852 (2017)
21. Ng, R., Levoy, M., Brédif, M., Duval, G., Horowitz, M., Hanrahan, P.: Light field photography with a hand-held plenoptic camera. Comput. Sci. Tech. Rep. CSTR **2**(11), 1–11 (2005)
22. Rigamonti, R., Sironi, A., Lepetit, V., Fua, P.: Learning separable filters. In: Proceedings of the IEEE International Conference on Computer Vision, pp. 2754–2761 (2013)
23. Yan, L.Q., Mehta, S.U., Ramamoorthi, R., Durand, F.: Fast 4D sheared filtering for interactive rendering of distribution effects. ACM Trans. Graph. **35**(1), 7 (2015)
24. Niklaus, S., Mai, L., Liu, F.: Video frame interpolation via adaptive separable convolution. In: Proceedings of the IEEE International Conference on Computer Vision, pp. 261–270 (2017)
25. Wang, T.C., Zhu, J.Y., Hiroaki, E., Chandraker, M., Efros, A.A., Ramamoorthi, R.: A 4D light-field dataset and CNN architectures for material recognition. In: Proceedings of the European Conference on Computer Vision, pp. 121–138 (2016)
26. Vedaldi, A., Lenc, K.: MatConvNet - convolutional neural networks for MATLAB. In: Proceedings of the ACM International Conference on Multimedia, pp. 689–692 (2015)
27. He, K., Zhang, X., Ren, S., Sun, J.: Delving deep into rectifiers: surpassing human-level performance on ImageNet classification. In: Proceedings of the IEEE International Conference on Computer Vision, pp. 1026–1034 (2015)
28. Raj, A.S., Lowney, M., Shah, R., Wetzstein, G.: Stanford Lytro light field archive. http://lightfields.stanford.edu/
29. Levoy, M., Ng, R., Adams, A., Footer, M., Horowitz, M.: Light field microscopy. ACM Trans. Graph. **25**(3), 924–934 (2006)
30. Wanner, S., Meister, S., Goldluecke, B.: Datasets and benchmarks for densely sampled 4D light fields. In: VMV, pp. 225–226. Citeseer (2013)
31. Blender Online Community: Blender - a 3D modelling and rendering package. Blender Foundation, Blender Institute, Amsterdam
32. Rerabek, M., Ebrahimi, T.: New light field image dataset. In: Proceedings of the 8th International Conference on Quality of Multimedia Experience. Number EPFL-CONF-218363 (2016)
33. Hou, J., Chen, J., Chau, L.P.: Light field image compression based on bi-level view compensation with rate-distortion optimization. IEEE Trans. Circ. Syst. Video Technol. 1 (2018)
34. Chen, J., Hou, J., Chau, L.P.: Light field compression with disparity-guided sparse coding based on structural key views. IEEE Trans. Image Process. **27**(1), 314–324 (2018)

Image Reassembly Combining Deep Learning and Shortest Path Problem

Marie-Morgane Paumard[1], David Picard[1,2]([✉]), and Hedi Tabia[1]

[1] ETIS, UMR 8051, Université Paris Seine, Université Cergy-Pontoise, ENSEA,
CNRS, Cergy-Pontoise, France
{marie-morgane.paumard,picard,hedi.tabia}@ensea.fr
[2] Sorbonne Université, CNRS, Laboratoire d'Informatique de Paris 6,
75005 Paris, France

Abstract. This paper addresses the problem of reassembling images from disjoint fragments. More specifically, given an unordered set of fragments, we aim at reassembling one or several possibly incomplete images. The main contributions of this work are: (1) several deep neural architectures to predict the relative position of image fragments that outperform the previous state of the art; (2) casting the reassembly problem into the shortest path in a graph problem for which we provide several construction algorithms depending on available information; (3) a new dataset of images taken from the Metropolitan Museum of Art (MET) dedicated to image reassembly for which we provide a clear setup and a strong baseline.

Keywords: Fragments reassembly · Jigsaw puzzle
Image classification · Cultural heritage · Deep learning

1 Introduction

The problem of automatic object reconstruction is very important in computer vision, as it has many potential applications in, e.g. cultural heritage and archaeology. For instance, given numerous fragments of an art masterpiece, archaeologists may spend a long time searching their correct configuration. In recent years, vision-related tasks such as classification [1], captioning [2] or image retrieval [3] have been tremendously improved thanks to deep neural network architectures, and the automatic reassembly of fragments can also be cast as a vision task and improved using the same deep learning methods.

In this paper, we focus on global image reassembly. The fragments are 2D-tiles and the problem consists in finding their approximated position, as shown in Fig. 1. To solve the problem, we build on the method proposed by Doersch et al. [4] that proposes to train a classifier able to predict the relative position of a fragment with respect to another one. We show that solving the reassembly

---

H. Tabia—This work is supported by the Fondation des sciences du patrimoine, LabEx PATRIMA ANR-10-LABX-0094-01.

V. Ferrari et al. (Eds.): ECCV 2018, LNCS 11210, pp. 155–169, 2018.
https://doi.org/10.1007/978-3-030-01231-1_10

problem from an unordered list of fragments can be expressed as a shortest path problem in a carefully designed graph. The structure of the graph heavily depends on the properties of the puzzle such as its geometry (number of positions and their layout), its completeness (a fragment for each available positions) and its homogeneity (all fragments have a correct position in the puzzle).

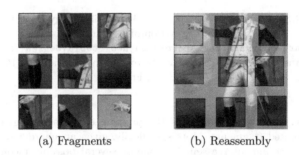

(a) Fragments   (b) Reassembly

Fig. 1. Example of the reassembly task on the MET dataset

Our contributions are the following. First, we propose several deep convolutional neural network architectures for predicting the relative position of a square-cropped fragment with respect to another. The crop allows us to ignore the borders of each piece and to focus on the content in order to achieve a global positioning. Second, we propose several graph construction algorithms that implement the reassembly problem corresponding to the different cases of puzzles depending on the aforementioned properties. Third, we perform extensive experiments of the different neural network and shortest path graph problem combinations on ImageNet [5] and on a new dataset composed of 14,000 images from the Metropolitan Museum of Art (MET). For this new dataset, we provide a clear setup and evaluation procedure that allows future works on the reassembly problem to be compared.

This paper is organized as follows: in Sect. 2, we present related work on puzzle solving and fragment reassembly as well as relevant literature on feature combination as it is an essential step of the relative position prediction. Next, we detail our propositions for the deep neural network building block and the graph construction algorithms that correspond to the different image reassembly problems. In Sect. 4, we present our experimental setups and analyze the results obtained for different combinations of deep neural networks and graphs.

2   Related Work

In this section, we first present the related work on puzzle solving. Then we detail the relevant literature on feature combination.

2.1   Puzzle Solving

The reconstruction of archaeological pieces of art leads to better understanding of our history and thus attracts numerous researchers, as Rasheed and Nordin described in their surveys [6,7]. Most publications of this field rely on the border irregularities and aim for precise alignment. They focus on automated reconstruction, such as [8–10] and consider jigsaw puzzle solving with missing fragments or with differently sized tiles [11–13]. These methods perform well on a small dataset with only one source of fragments. On the downside, they stall when fragments come from various sources and they require costly human made annotations. Moreover, they are fragile towards erosion and fragment loss.

Without being interested in jigsaw puzzle solving, Doersch et al. proposed a deep neural network to predict the relative position of two adjacent fragments in [4]. The end goal of the authors is to use this task as a pretraining step of deep convolutional neural network (CNN), harnessing the vast amounts of unlabeled images since the ground truth for such task can be automatically generated. The intuitions for training features able to predict their context are the same as what is found in the text literature with word2vec [14] or skip-thought [15]. In [4], the authors show their proposed task outperforms all other unsupervised pretraining methods. Based on [4], Noroozi and Favaro [16] introduce a network that compares all the nine tiles at the same time. They claim that the complete representation obtained allows discarding the ambiguities that may have been learned with the algorithm proposed by Doersch et al. Gur et al. [17] consider missing fragments, but heavily rely on border to solve the puzzle.

In this paper, we focus on solving the jigsaw puzzle and not on the building of generic images features. In cultural heritage, we have missing pieces, as well as pieces from various images. Therefore, the setup of [16] is impractical, as it requires exactly the nine correct fragments to make a prediction. For this reason, we base our work on the method proposed in [4], but we do not share the same objective and we bring two significant innovations. First, we consider the correlations between localized parts of the fragments when merging the features, something that is difficult to achieve in [4]. We believe these correlations are important, since, e.g., we expect the right part of the baseline fragment to be correlated with the left part of the right fragment. Second, we look for a complete fragment reassembly, which we perform by using the deep neural network predictions to build a shortest path graph problem.

2.2   Feature Combination

Doersch et al. [4] separately processed fragments using a deep CNN with shared weights which output comparable features. These features are then serially concatenated and fed to a multi-layer perceptron (MLP) that performs the classification. The full network has been trained in an end-to-end fashion with standard back-propagation using stochastic gradient descent.

In Doersch et al. [4] formulation, the cross-covariance between the features of both fragments is neglected. Indeed, the output of the CNN can be viewed as localized pattern activations. The prediction of the relative position depends on the conjunction of specific patterns occurring at specific positions in the first fragment and specific patterns occurring at specific positions in the second fragment. It can be argued that a sufficiently deep MLP can model these cross-covariances, but it also seems easier to model them directly.

In [18], the authors suggest modeling these co-occurrences of patterns using a bilinear model which can be computed using the Kronecker product of the feature vectors. They report improved accuracy on fine-grained classification. However, using the Kronecker product leads to high dimensional features that are intractable in practice. To overcome this burden, the authors of [19] propose to use random projections combined with the Hadamard (element-wise) product to approximate the bilinear model. This strategy is further extended in [20] where the projections are trained in true deep learning fashion. Another factorization based on the Tucker decomposition is also proposed in [21] which allows controlling the rank of the considered co-occurrences.

3   Method

In this section, we detail our proposed method. We start by presenting the deep CNN model upon which we build to solve the image reassembly problem.

3.1   Relative Position Prediction

To solve a puzzle, we need to pick the fragments to use. We compare each selected fragment with the central fragment and compute their relative position. We examine several ways to articulate this problem.

Problem Formulation. The first step towards reassembly consists in discriminating between the fragments that may be of use and the others. On our puzzle, it means that we predict which fragments are allegedly extracted from the same image as a given central fragment, which is a binary classification problem. Once only relevant fragments are selected, we model the position prediction as an 8-classes classification problem, as shown in Fig. 2. Both these classification tasks are performed by a deep CNN described later.

We also propose an alternative model by merging these two networks into a single network. This single network predicts the relative position of the second fragment among the 8 possible positions and a 9th class, activated if the fragment is not part of the same image.

Network Architecture. The global network architecture is described in Fig. 3. Given two input fragments, we first extract fragment representations using a shared feature extraction network (FEN). We tested the most common architectures and empirically found out that a VGG-like [22] network works the best. Therefore, the FEN architecture is inspired by a simplified version of VGG [22]

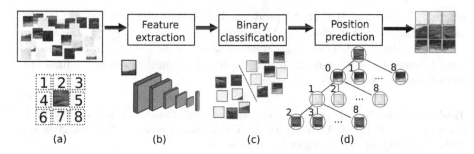

Fig. 2. Overview of our method. Knowing a central fragment, we are looking for the correct arrangement to reassemble the image (a). We extract the feature of all the fragments (b) and we compare them to the features of the central fragment. We predict which fragments are part of the image (c). We retrieve the top eight fragments and we predict their relative position with respect to the central one. We turn the prediction into a graph (d). We then run a shortest path algorithm to reconstruct the image

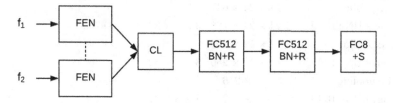

Fig. 3. General network architecture block diagram

and is shown on Table 1. The network is composed of sequences of a 3×3 convolution followed by batch-normalization [23], ReLU activation [24] and max-pooling. We also tried other models based on more recent architectures such as Resnet [25], but we empirically found that they were underperforming compared to the simpler architecture. This can be explained by the fact that contrarily to full images, fragments do not contain as much semantic information and thus require less involved features. Remark also that there is no global pooling [26] in the FEN and thus spatial information is preserved, which we believe is important for the relative position prediction.

The features of each fragment are then combined in a combination layer (CL). Contrarily to the concatenation that is proposed at this stage in [4], we explore variations on the bilinear product in order to model cross-covariances among the features. With $\phi_{\text{FEN}}(f)$ the output of the FEN for fragment f, the full bilinear product is obtained by using the Kronecker product of the features [18]:

$$y_{kron} = \phi_{\text{FEN}}(f_1) \otimes \phi_{\text{FEN}}(f_2). \tag{1}$$

However, this leads to very high dimensional vectors. Similarly to [20], we explore a compressed version using the entry-wise product:

$$y_{had} = (W^\top \phi_{\text{FEN}}(f_1)) \circ (W^\top \phi_{\text{FEN}}(f_2)), \tag{2}$$

where ∘ denotes the Hadamard product. This compressed version can be efficiently implemented by changing the output size of the last layer in the FEN.

Finally, the classification stage consists of two sequences of a fully connected layer followed by a batch-normalization and a ReLU activation, and a final prediction layer with softmax activation.

Table 1. Architecture of the feature extraction network. Conv: convolution, BN: Batch-Normalization, ReLU: ReLU activation. OUT is chosen among 512, 1024, 2048 and 4096, depending on what merging function we use

Layer	Output shape	Parameters shape	Parameters count
Input	$96 \times 96 \times 3$		0
Conv+BN+ReLU	$96 \times 96 \times 32$	$3 \times 3 \times 32$	1k
Maxpooling	$48 \times 48 \times 32$		–
Conv+BN+ReLU	$48 \times 48 \times 64$	$3 \times 3 \times 32$	19k
Maxpooling	$24 \times 24 \times 64$		–
Conv+BN+ReLU	$24 \times 24 \times 128$	$3 \times 3 \times 32$	74k
Maxpooling	$12 \times 12 \times 128$		–
Conv+BN+ReLU	$12 \times 12 \times 256$	$3 \times 3 \times 32$	296k
Maxpooling	$6 \times 6 \times 256$		–
Conv+BN+ReLU	$6 \times 6 \times 512$	$3 \times 3 \times 32$	1.2M
Maxpooling	$3 \times 3 \times 512$		–
Fully connected+BN	OUT		$OUT_{nb\ param}$

3.2 Puzzle Resolution

Once the position is predicted by the neural network for each fragment, we can solve the puzzle, which consists in assigning fragments to a position in the image. We consider several cases depending on whether we already have a well-positioned fragment, and whether we have supernumerary fragments.

Problem Formulation. We first consider the case where we are given the central fragment as well as an unordered list of 8 fragments corresponding to the possible neighbors of the central fragment. Solving the puzzle then consists in solving the assignment problem where each fragment i has to be associated with a position j. Given the relevance $p_{i,j}$ of fragment i at position j, and the assignment variable $x_{i,j} = 1$ if fragment i is at position j, we want to maximize:

$$\max_{x_{i,j}} \sum_{i,j} p_{i,j} \cdot x_{i,j} \tag{3}$$

under the constraints:

$$\forall j, \sum_{i=0}^{8} x_{i,j} = 1 \,, \tag{4}$$

$$\forall i, \sum_{j=0}^{8} x_{i,j} = 1 \,, \tag{5}$$

$$\forall i, j, x_{i,j} \in \{0,1\}. \tag{6}$$

Remark that only one fragment can occupy a position (Eq. 4) and a fragment can be placed only once (Eq. 5).

Then, if we allow the puzzle to be uncompleted (i.e. some positions are not used), we replace the constraint 4 with:

$$\forall j, \sum_{i=0}^{8} x_{i,j} \leq 1. \tag{7}$$

Similarly, if we have supernumerary fragments (i.e. some fragments are not used), we replace the constraint 5 with:

$$\forall i, \sum_{j=0}^{N} x_{i,j} \leq 1. \tag{8}$$

Finally, if we do not know which fragment is the central fragment, we have to solve the extended assignment problem where one fragment has to be assigned to the central position and the remaining fragment are assigned to the relative positions. This leads to the following problem:

$$\max_{c,x_{i,j}} \sum_{i,j} p_{i,j,c} \cdot x_{i,j,c} \tag{9}$$

under the following constraints:

$$\forall c, j, \sum_{i=0}^{N} x_{i,j,c} \leq 1; \forall c, i \neq c, \sum_{j=0}^{8} x_{i,j,c} \leq 1; \forall c, j, \forall i \neq c, x_{i,j,c} \in \{0,1\};$$

$$\forall c, j, \forall i = c, x_{i,j,c} = 0.$$

3.3   Graph Formulation

Solving the mentioned problem can be done by finding the shortest path in a corresponding directed graph, which can be done using Dijkstra's algorithm or any of its variants. In this section, we show how to construct such graphs.

Each graph starts with a source S and ends with a sink T. Each subsequent depth level from S corresponds to a fragment. All nodes at a given depth i from S correspond to the position that could be assigned to a fragment i given all previous assignments. Each edge receives the corresponding classification score as the weight.

Algorithm 1. Graph building from central fragment

1: **procedure** CONSTRUCT_EDGES(Y)   ▷ Y is the predicted values matrix for i, j
2:     $empty\_pos \leftarrow [1..9]$
3:     $used\_pos \leftarrow [S]$
4:     $next\_frag \leftarrow 1$
5:     $tree \leftarrow$ ADD CHILDREN($Y, empty\_pos, used\_pos, next\_frag$)
6:     **return** $tree$ ▷ The list of the edges: related fragment, position of the previous node, position of the current node, cost of the edge.
7: **end procedure**

1: **procedure** ADD_CHILDREN($Y, empty\_pos, used\_pos, next\_frag$)
2:     $edges \leftarrow [\ ]$
3:     **if** $empty\_pos$ is empty **then**
4:         $edges \leftarrow [(None, last(used\_pos), T, 0)]$ ▷ Append the $j \rightarrow T$ edge
5:         **return** $edges$
6:     **end if**
7:     **for** pos in $empty\_pos$ **do**
8:         $edges \leftarrow edges \cup [(next\_frag, last(used\_pos), pos, Y[next\_fragment, pos])]$
9:         $empty\_pos \leftarrow empty\_pos \setminus pos$
10:        $used\_pos \leftarrow used\_pos \cup pos$
11:        $edges \leftarrow edges \cup (\text{ADD CHILDREN}(Y, empty\_pos, used\_pos, next\_frag + 1))$
12:    **end for**
13:    **return** $edges$
14: **end procedure**

When the central fragment is known and we have the exact number of missing fragments, the construction procedure is given in Algorithm 1. We also give a very simple example with only two relative positions in Fig. 4a.

In the case where the central fragment is known, the size of the resulting graph is $|E| = \frac{n!}{(n-p)!} + \sum_{i=n-p}^{n-1} \frac{n!}{i!}$ for the number of edges and $|N| = 2 + \sum_{i=n-p}^{n-1} \frac{n!}{i!}$ for the number of vertices, with n the number of fragments and p the number of positions. With 8 fragments and positions, this corresponds to $|E| = 150k$ and $|N| = 100k$.

In the case where we do not know the central fragment, we simply perform the central fragment selection as a first step. The first expansion from S consists in all the possible cases where each fragment is used as the central fragment. The corresponding subgraphs are the built using Algorithm 1. The size of the resulting graph is unchanged, except we have $n + 1$ fragments, with n the number of the fragment to be assigned to a relative position. With $n = 8$, we obtain $|N| = 1M$ and $|E| = 1.3M$. We show in Fig. 4b a simplified example with 3 fragments and 2 relative positions.

Finally, we now consider the case where the puzzle may not be solved with all the fragments we have. This means that we can have more than 8 fragments, coming from various sources. We also may have missing fragments, and consequently, we prefer an algorithm that proposes an incomplete solution than a wrong reassembly. We construct a graph allowing such configurations by enabling the algorithm to pick no fragment. A simplified example of the graph shown in Fig. 5.

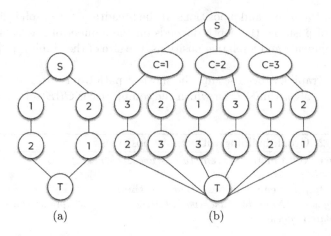

Fig. 4. Examples of graphs for a complete problem with known and unknown central fragment, for empty 2 positions

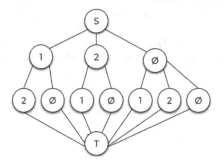

Fig. 5. Example of a graph allowing empty positions

The graph building algorithm is similar to the Algorithm 1; if we add a position ∅ at the *antecedents* list, we do not exclude it from the further available choices, as detailed in Algorithm 2. This graph has:

$$|N| = 2 + \sum_{l=0}^{n} \sum_{k=p-l}^{p} \binom{l}{p-k} \frac{(k+1)p!}{k!} \tag{10}$$

vertices and

$$|E| = \sum_{k=p-n}^{p} \binom{l}{p-k} \frac{(k+1)p!}{k!} + \sum_{l=0}^{n} \sum_{k=p-l}^{p} \binom{l}{p-k} \frac{(k+1)p!}{k!} \tag{11}$$

edges, with n fragments and p positions. If the breadth of the graph is limited by the number of position, the depth depends on the number of fragments. In the case of 10 fragments and 8 relative positions, the size of the graph is $|E| = 5 \cdot 10^9$ and $|N| = 4 \cdot 10^8$.

Once the graph has been set up, the shortest path from S to T can be found with Dijkstra's algorithm [27] for which the complexity is $\mathcal{O}(|E| + |N| \times \log(N))$.

Algorithm 2. Graph building with empty positions

1: **procedure** ADD_CHILDREN($Y, empty\_pos, used\_pos, next\_frag$)
2:    $edges \leftarrow [\,]$
3:    **if** $empty\_pos$ is empty or $next\_frag > n$ **then**
4:        $edges \leftarrow [(None, last(used\_pos), T, 0)]$ ▷ Append the $j \to T$ edge
5:        **return** $edges$
6:    **end if**
7:    **for** pos in $empty\_pos \cup \emptyset$ **do**
8:        $edges \leftarrow edges \cup [(next\_frag, last(used\_pos), pos, Y[next\_fragment, pos])]$
9:        **if** pos in $empty\_pos$ **then**
10:            $empty\_pos \leftarrow empty\_pos \setminus pos$
11:        **end if**
12:        $used\_pos \leftarrow used\_pos \cup pos$
13:        $edges \leftarrow edges \cup (\text{ADD CHILDREN}(Y, empty\_pos, used\_pos, next\_frag + 1))$
14:    **end for**
15:    **return** $edges$
16: **end procedure**

Greedy Method. We implement a greedy method to enable us to benchmark the Dijkstra algorithm. We solve iteratively the puzzle, picking at each step the top value from the neural network predictions. We expect this method will make worst choices than Dijkstra's considering the dependencies between the steps.

4   Experiments

In this section, we first describe our experimental setup as well as our new dataset related to cultural heritage. Then, we give experimental results on the classification task and on full image reassembly.

4.1   Experimental Setup

The neural networks are trained using fragments from 1.2M images of ImageNet. We use 50k images to evaluate the classification accuracy. Each image is resized and square-cropped to 398×398 pixels, and divided into 9 parts separated by a 48-pixel margin, corresponding to the erosion of the fragments. Each fragment has a size of 96 × 96 pixels and has to be contained in one of the 9 parts, which means that it can be chosen within a ±7-pixels range in each direction.

For the reassembly, the neural networks are then fine-tuned on a cultural heritage dataset, consisting of 14,000 open-source images from the Metropolitan Museum of Art. Such dataset is close to our aimed application, puzzle solving for cultural heritage

4.2   Classification

To evaluate our proposed architectures for classification, we reproduce the architecture Doersch et al. detailed in [4]. The authors reported a 40% accuracy on ImageNet for the 8-classes classification task. Replicating the architecture of their neural network, we obtain an accuracy of 57%. This may be explained by the tuning of the hyperparameters.

In Table 2, we report the accuracy for the different combination layers on the 8-classes problem on ImageNet validation images. As we can see, the Kronecker product obtain slightly better results than the concatenation. However, using the low-rank approximation of [20] yields lower results which means that the full covariances are needed to obtain the best performances. Remark that all of our architecture outperforms the architecture proposed in [4].

Table 2. Accuracy for different fusion strategies, for the 8-classes classification problem on ImageNet validation. *denotes our implementation

Fusion	Accuracy
Doersch et al. [4]*	57.0%
Concatenation	64.6%
Kronecker product	66.4%
Hadamard product	59.2%

We show the results of the sequential classification approach (2 classes, then 8 classes) and the joint classification approach (9 classes) on Table 3. For the binary classification problem, we set the proportion of fragments belonging to the same image to 50% and we obtain 92.5% accuracy. which means that deciding whether two fragments belong to the same image seems to be an easy problem. For the 8 classes problem, we obtain 66.4% accuracy. It is not surprising to reach around 33% error since many fragments are ambiguous with respect to the precise location among three positions. For example, sky fragments are easy to classify on top with respect to the central fragment, but which of the three top positions is often difficult to guess. Finally, the joint classification problem achieves 64.2% (the proportion of fragment belonging to the same image was set to 70%), which indicates that solving the joint problem is not harder than solving the sequence of simpler problems.

Table 3. Classification accuracy for the 2-classes, 8-classes and 9-classes problems on Imagenet, using the Kronecker combination layer

Problem	Accuracy
2-classes neighborhood classifier	92.5%
8-classes position classifier	66.4%
9-classes classifier	64.2%

4.3 Reassembly

In Table 4, we compare various cases of reassembly tasks, using two different accuracy measures. The reconstruction accuracy describe if the puzzle is perfectly solved. The position accuracy counts how many fragments are well placed.

Table 4. Reconstruction accuracies and position accuracies for different reassembly problems

Problem	Reconstruction accuracy		Position accuracy	
	Greedy	Dijkstra	Greedy	Dijkstra
Central known, complete puzzle	41.0	44.4	87.7	89.9
Central unknown, complete puzzle	36.2	39.2	69.5	71.1
Central known, incomplete puzzle	26.5	29.5	80.5	82.4

As we can see, in the case of the complete puzzle where the central fragment is known, we are able to perfectly reassemble the image in 44.4% of the cases using Dijkstra's algorithm, which represent a 3% improvement over the greedy algorithm, which is closer to the optimal solution than one might think. Remark that the position accuracy is around 90%, which is much better than the 66.4% accuracy of the neural network used to solve the task. This shows that solving the reassembly problem can remove some uncertainty the classifier has.

When the central fragment is not know, the reassembly accuracy drops only to 39.2% and the position accuracy drops to 71.1%. This means that reassembling the image without knowing the central fragment is not much more complicated than with the central fragment known, however, if that first step is missed, then all subsequent assignments are likely to be wrong.

We consider adding outsider fragments to the puzzle (Table 5), making the accuracy drop. The increase of computation time triggered by the addition is reasonable as long as the puzzle still contains 9 pieces. Any increment of the number of pieces leads to an factorial increase of the number of solution, making the problem quickly intractable. Nonetheless, any puzzle can be divided into 3×3 puzzles, that would be solved individually and fused.

Table 5. Position and reconstruction accuracies with additional fragments

Number of additional fragments	0	1	2
Reassembly accuracy (Dijkstra)	44.4%	26.3%	14.3%
Position accuracy (Dijkstra)	89.9%	75.3%	64.8%

In Fig. 6, we selected few reconstructions with unknown central fragment. The two first images illustrate a significant part of our dataset in which it is easy to misplace background fragments. Most of our reconstruction errors are due to similar reversals. The type of error illustrated by the right image is rare; but, when the central fragment is misplaced, all the other fragments are shifted.

Fig. 6. Examples of reconstructions with unknown central fragment. The red outlined fragments are misplaced (Color figure online)

Finally, we study the case where we have missing fragments (Table 4, last row). In that scenario, only 4 fragment are taken from the image while 8 positions are available. We are still able to predict the position with high accuracy (surprisingly better than in the case where the central fragment is unknown), but perfectly reassembling the image is very difficult. This means that the algorithm tends to drop fragments instead of assigning them to an uncertain location. Figure 7 shows examples of reconstructions in the case of missing fragments.

Fig. 7. Examples of reconstructions with 4 missing fragments. The red outlined fragments are misplaced (Color figure online)

5   Conclusion

In this paper, we tackled the image reassembly problem where given a unordered list of image fragments, we want to recover the original image. To that end, we proposed a deep neural network architecture that predicts the relative position of a given pair of fragments. Then, we cast the reassembly problem into a shortest path in a graph algorithm for which we propose several construction algorithms depending on whether the puzzle is complete or if there are missing pieces. We propose a new dataset containing 14,000 images to test several reassembly tasks and we show that we are able to perfectly reassemble the image 44.4% of the time in the simpler case and 29.5% of the time if there are missing pieces.

References

1. Krizhevsky, A., Sutskever, I., Hinton, G.: ImageNet classification with deep convolutional neural networks. NIPS **1**, 1097–1105 (2012)
2. Johnson, J., Karpathy, A., Fei-Fei, L.: DenseCap: fully convolutional localization networks for dense captioning. In: CVPR (2016)
3. Gordo, A., Almazán, J., Revaud, J., Larlus, D.: Deep image retrieval: learning global representations for image search. In: Leibe, B., Matas, J., Sebe, N., Welling, M. (eds.) ECCV 2016. LNCS, vol. 9910, pp. 241–257. Springer, Cham (2016). https://doi.org/10.1007/978-3-319-46466-4_15
4. Doersch, C., Gupta, A., Efros, A.: Unsupervised visual representation learning by context prediction. In: ICCV (2015)
5. Russakovsky, O., et al.: ImageNet large scale visual recognition challenge. IJCV **115**(3), 211–252 (2015)

6. Rasheed, N., Nordin, M.J.: A survey of classification and reconstruction methods for the 2D archaeological objects. In: ISTMET, pp. 142–147, August 2015

7. Rasheed, N., Nordin, M.J.: A survey of computer methods in reconstruction of 3D archaeological pottery objects. Int. J. Adv. Res. **3**, 712–714 (2015)

8. McBride, J., Kimia, B.: Archaeological fragment reconstruction using curve-matching. In: CVPRW (2003)

9. Jampy, F., Hostein, A., Fauvet, E., Laligant, O., Truchetet, F.: 3D puzzle reconstruction for archeological fragments. In: 3DIPM (2015)

10. Zhu, L., Zhou, Z., Zhang, J., Hu, D.: A partial curve matching method for automatic reassembly of 2D fragments. In: Huang, D.S., Li, K., Irwin, G.W. (eds.) Intelligent Computing in Signal Processing and Pattern Recognition. LNCIS, vol. 345, pp. 645–650. Springer, Berlin (2006). https://doi.org/10.1007/978-3-540-37258-5_70

11. Hammoudeh, Z., Pollett, C.: Clustering-based, fully automated mixed-bag jigsaw puzzle solving. In: Felsberg, M., Heyden, A., Krüger, N. (eds.) CAIP 2017. LNCS, vol. 10425, pp. 205–217. Springer, Cham (2017). https://doi.org/10.1007/978-3-319-64698-5_18

12. Andaló, F., Taubin, G., Goldenstein, S.: PSQP: puzzle solving by quadratic programming. IEEE TPAMI **39**, 385–396 (2017)

13. Lifang, C., Cao, D., Liu, Y.: A new intelligent jigsaw puzzle algorithm base on mixed similarity and symbol matrix. IJPRAI **32**, 1859001 (2018)

14. Mikolov, T., Sutskever, I., Chen, K., Corrado, G.S., Dean, J.: Distributed representations of words and phrases and their compositionality. In: NIPS, pp. 3111–3119 (2013)

15. Kiros, R., et al.: Skip-thought vectors. In: NIPS, pp. 3294–3302 (2015)

16. Noroozi, M., Favaro, P.: Unsupervised learning of visual representations by solving jigsaw puzzles (2015)

17. Gur, S., Ben-Shahar, O.: From square pieces to brick walls: the next challenge in solving jigsaw puzzles. In: ICCV (2017)

18. Lin, T.Y., RoyChowdhury, A., Maji, S.: Bilinear CNN models for fine-grained visual recognition. In: ICCV, pp. 1449–1457 (2015)

19. Gao, Y., Beijbom, O., Zhang, N., Darrell, T.: Compact bilinear pooling. In: IEEE CVPR, pp. 317–326 (2016)

20. Kim, J.H., On, K.W., Lim, W., Ha, J., Zhang, B.-T.: Hadamard product for low-rank bilinear pooling. In: ICLR (2017)

21. Ben-younes, H., Cadene, R., Cord, M., Thome, N.: MUTAN: multimodal tucker fusion for visual question answering, pp. 2612–2620 (2017)

22. Simonyan, K., Zisserman, A.: Very deep convolutional networks for large-scale image recognition. In: ILSVRC (2014)

23. Ioffe, S., Szegedy, C.: Batch normalization: accelerating deep network training by reducing internal covariate shift. In: ICML (2015)

24. Nair, V., Hinton, G.: Rectified linear units improve restricted Boltzmann machines. In: ICML (2010)

25. He, K., Zhang, X., Ren, S., Sun, J.: Deep residual learning for image recognition. In: IEEE CVPR, pp. 770–778 (2016)

26. Lin, M., Chen, Q., Yan, S.: Network in network. arXiv preprint arXiv:1312.4400 (2013)

27. Dijkstra, E.: A note on two problems in connexion with graphs. Numerische Mathematik **1**, 269–271 (1959)

BusterNet: Detecting Copy-Move Image Forgery with Source/Target Localization

Yue Wu[1]([✉]), Wael Abd-Almageed[1], and Prem Natarajan[1,2]

[1] USC Information Sciences Institute, Marina del Rey, CA 90292, USA
{yue_wu,wamageed,pnataraj}@isi.edu
[2] Amazon Alexa, 101 Main Street, Cambridge, MA 02142, USA

Abstract. We introduce a novel deep neural architecture for image copy-move forgery detection (CMFD), code-named *BusterNet*. Unlike previous efforts, BusterNet is a pure, end-to-end trainable, deep neural network solution. It features a two-branch architecture followed by a fusion module. The two branches localize potential manipulation regions via visual artifacts and copy-move regions via visual similarities, respectively. To the best of our knowledge, this is the first CMFD algorithm with discernibility to localize source/target regions. We also propose simple schemes for synthesizing large-scale CMFD samples using out-of-domain datasets, and stage-wise strategies for effective BusterNet training. Our extensive studies demonstrate that BusterNet outperforms state-of-the-art copy-move detection algorithms by a large margin on the two publicly available datasets, CASIA and CoMoFoD, and that it is robust against various known attacks.

Keywords: Copy-move · Image forgery detection · Deep learning

1 Introduction

Fake news, often utilizing tampered images, has lately become a global epidemic, especially with the massive adoption of social media as a contemporary alternative to classic news outlets. This phenomenon can be largely attributed to the following: (i) the rapidly declining cost of digital cameras and mobile phones, which leads to a proliferation of digital images, and (ii) the availability and ease-of-use of image-editing software (e.g., mobile phone applications and open source tools) which make images editing or manipulating profoundly easy, whether it is for innocent or malicious intent.

This work is based on research sponsored by the Defense Advanced Research Projects Agency under agreement number FA8750-16-2-0204. The U.S. Government is authorized to reproduce and distribute reprints for Governmental purposes notwithstanding any copyright notation thereon. The views and conclusions contained herein are those of the authors and should not be interpreted as necessarily representing the official policies or endorsements, either expressed or implied, of the Defense Advanced Research Project Agency or the U.S. Government.

© Springer Nature Switzerland AG 2018
V. Ferrari et al. (Eds.): ECCV 2018, LNCS 11210, pp. 170–186, 2018.
https://doi.org/10.1007/978-3-030-01231-1_11

Fig. 1. Whom in photo is *not* manipulated? BusterNet answers this question by not only detecting copy-move regions but also differentiating source (green) and target (red) copies. (a) tweet snapshot of a manipulated photo by James Fridman; (b) input region for analysis; (c) raw BusterNet output; (d) BusterNet output by applying majority rule; (e) overlaid result of (c) on (b); and (f) tweet snapshot of the original photo. (Color figure online)

Copy-move image forgery is one of the most common and easiest-to-perform image tampering schemes (see Fig. 1), in which an image patch, regular or irregular shape, is copied and cloned into the same image. Since the cloned image patch comes from the same image, the photometric characteristic remains largely consistent, which increases the difficulty of detecting this type of image forgery.

The objective of copy-move forgery detection (CMFD) is to determine whether a probe (*i.e.* query) image contains *cloned regions*, as evidence of potential malicious intent. Based on the sophistication of the cloning process, we can generally classify copy-move manipulations as *plain, affine* and *complex* forgeries. Let S and T denote the source and target regions, respectively. Plain cloning means that T is simply a translated version of S, i.e., copy S and directly paste it to a new location as T. This is the simplest cloning, which can be done with very basic image editing tools. In contrast, affine cloning means that T is an affine-transformed version of S, implying that additional scaling and rotation changes have been made on S. Similarly, this type of copy-move tampering can be easily performed with image editing tools supporting affine transformations. Finally, complex cloning entails a more complicated relationship between D and T, often with extra diffusion estimation, edge blending, color change or other more sophisticated image processing steps. Complex cloning requires advancing image editing tools, such as *Adobe Photoshop* or *GIMP*.

In this paper we present a novel deep neural architecture for detecting copy-move image forgeries. The proposed architecture addresses two major limitations of state-of-the-art CMFD algorithms—(i) it is an end-to-end DNN solution, and thus can be optimized directly w.r.t. copy-move forgery detection task; and (ii) it not only detects copy-move forgeries, but also produces source and target region masks, as shown in Fig. 1. To the best of our knowledge, our proposed technology is the first to feature this capability. Discriminating between source and target regions could be significant for forensic investigations. Consider, for example, two people each holding a pistol in a criminal investigation. We not only are interested in knowing that image is manipulated, but also which gun is the original and which is the clone.

The remainder of this paper is organized as follows. Section 2 briefly discusses existing approaches and their limitations. Section 3 introduces the proposed BusterNet. Section 4 discusses BusterNet training details. Section 5 shows extensive experimental results and analysis. Finally, we conclude the paper in Sect. 6.

2 Related Work

Early CMFD work can be traced back to the early 2000s [12,15] when most of the research work focused on plain cloning. As mentioned in Sect. 1, the increasing volume of digital images and availability of editing software meant that *"Doctoring digital photos is easy. Detecting it can be hard"* [11].

Without loss of generality, a general copy-move detection framework consists of three major steps [9]: namely (i) *feature extraction* which basically converts an input image X to a set of features of interests $\mho = \{f_1, \cdots, f_k\}$, (ii) *feature matching* which measures the similarity (or distance) between two features f_i and f_j for all $f_i, f_j \in \mho$, and (iii) *post-processing* which usually uses a set of heuristics to further improve CMFD performance, e.g., considering holistic matching between set of features on a higher level of consistency to reduce false alarms and to improve true positive. Copy-move detection frameworks can be broadly classified, based on the underlying feature extraction and subsequent matching schemes, into three main categories: patch/block-based methods such as chroma features [4,9], PCA feature [14], Zernike moments [26], blur moments [20], DCT [21]; keypoint-based methods such as SIFT [1,8,36], ORB [40], triangles [2], SURF [22,27,28], and irregular region-based methods [16,25].

Each category has its own advantages and disadvantages in CMFD. For example, block-based methods are known to be simple but computationally expensive. In contrast, keypoint-based methods are fast and robust against affine transformation. However, keypoint-based method often fail when S and D are homogeneous. This general architecture for CMFD pipelines suffers three inherent limitations: (i) each module is optimized independently, (ii) dependence on hand-crafted features that may not be optimal for the downstream task, and (iii) inclusion of one or more heuristics or manually tuned thresholds in order to reduce false alarm and increase detection rates. For a detailed comparison of existing methods, the reader is referred to [3,5,30,32].

Recently, deep neural network (DNN) has been applied to the image forgery detection research. [18] uses DNN for feature extraction in CMFD. [6] detects manipulated regions via a DNN-based patch classifier. [34] proposes an end-to-end DNN solution for splicing detection and localization. [39] uses DNN to detect tampered faces.

3 Copy-Move Forgery Detection via BusterNet

3.1 BusterNet Overview

To overcome the drawbacks of classic CMFD pipelines, as discussed in Sect. 2, our goal is to design a DNN pipeline that is (i) end-to-end trainable, such that it does not include manually tuned parameters and/or decision rules and (ii) capable of producing distinct source and target manipulation masks (which could be used for forensic analysis).

To achieve the above goals, a valid DNN solution should attain two feature properties simultaneously, (i) source and target features are dissimilar enough to distinguish source from target, and (ii) they are also more similar than those in pristine regions. Of course, one can train a naive DNN, while hoping it could attain these properties magically. However, a better idea is to explicitly consider these properties, and we therefore propose *BusterNet*, a two-branch DNN architecture as shown in Fig. 2.

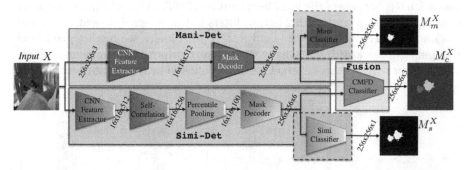

Fig. 2. Overview of the proposed two-branch DNN-based CMFD solution. Dashed blocks are only activated during branch training. Output mask of the main task, *i.e.* M_c^X, is color coded to represent pixel classes, namely *pristine* (blue), *source copy* (green), and *target copy* (red). Output masks of auxiliary tasks, *i.e.* M_m^X and M_s^X, are binary where white pixels indicates manipulated/similar pixels of interests, respectively. (Color figure online)

Specifically, we design `Mani-Det` branch to detect manipulated regions such that its feature is good for property (i), while `Simi-Det` branch to detect cloned regions such that its feature attains property (ii), and finally use both features in `Fusion` to predict pixel-level copy-move masks differentiating *pristine, source copy*, and *target copy* classes. To ensure these two branches achieve the desired functionality, we define each branch an auxiliary task, as indicated by the dashed blocks in Fig. 2. More precisely, `Mani-Det`'s and `Simi-Det`'s tasks are to predict a binary manipulation mask M_m^X and a binary copy-move mask M_s^X, respectively, and both binary masks can be derived from the 3-class mask M_c^X.

To simplify discussions, we assume our input image is of size $256 \times 256 \times 3$, but BusterNet is capable of handling images of other sizes.

3.2   Manipulation Detection Branch

The manipulation detection branch (*i.e.* `Mani-Det` as shown by red shaded regions in Fig. 2) can be thought of as a special segmentation network [19] whose aim is to segment manipulated regions. More precisely, it takes input image X, extracts features using `CNN Feature Extractor`, upsamples the feature maps to the original image size using `Mask Decoder`, and applies `Binary Classifier` to fulfill the auxiliary task, *i.e.* producing a manipulation mask M_m^X.

Any convolutional neural network (CNN) can serve as `CNN Feature Extractor`. Here, we use the first four blocks of the VGG16 architecture [29] for its simplicity. The resulting CNN feature f_m^X is of size $16 \times 16 \times 512$, whose resolution is much lower than that is required by the manipulation mask. We therefore need to decode this feature, and apply deconvolution [23] to restore the original resolution via the `Mask Decoder` as shown Fig. 3, which applies `BN-Inception` and `BilinearUpPool2D` [33] in an alternating way and eventually produces a tensor d_m^X of shape $256 \times 256 \times 6$. To be clear, 16 times of the spatial dimension increase is due to the 4 times of `BilinearUpPool2D` (*i.e.* $2^4 = 16$), and the output filter dimension 6 is because of the last `BN-Inception(2@[5,7,11])`, which concatenates 3 `Conv2D` responses, each with 2 output filters but uses kernel sizes at $(5, 5)$, and $(7, 7)$ and $(11, 11)$, respectively (*i.e.* $3 \times 2 = 6$). Finally, we predict pixel-level manipulation mask M_m^X via `Binary Classifier`, which is as simple as a single `Conv2D` layer with 1 filters of kernel size $(3, 3)$ followed by the `sigmoid` activation.

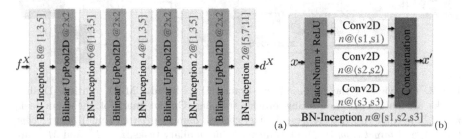

Fig. 3. Inception-based mask deconvolution module. (a) Mask deconvolution network and (b) parametric BN-inception module, where $s1, s2$ and $s3$ indicates the kernel sizes used in three `Conv2D` layers, respectively, and n stands for the number of filters.

3.3   Similarity Detection Branch

The similarity detection branch (*i.e.* `Simi-Det` as shown by blue shaded regions in Fig. 2) takes an input image X, extracts features using `CNN Feature Extractor`, computes feature similarity via `Self-Correlation` module, collects useful statistics via `Percentile Pooling`, upsamples feature maps to the original image size using `Mask Decoder`, and applies `Binary Classifier` to fulfill the auxiliary task, *i.e.* producing a copy-move mask M_m^X at the same resolution of X. It is worthy to stress that modules shared in both branches, *e.g.* `CNN Feature Extractor`, only share the network architecture, but not weights.

Like `Mani-Det` branch, `Simi-Det` branch starts with feature representation via `CNN Feature Extractor`. It again produces a feature tensor f_s^X of size $16 \times 16 \times 512$, which can be also viewed as 16×16 patch-like features, *i.e.* $f_s^X = \{f_s^X[i_r, i_c]\}_{i_r, i_c \in [0, \cdots, 15]}$, and each with 512 dimensions. Since our goal is to recover the potential copy-move regions, we have to mine useful information to decide what are matched patch-like features. To do so, we first compute all-to-all feature similarity score using `Self-Correlation`, and collect meaningful statistics to identify matched patches via `Percentile Pooling`.

Specifically, given two patch-like feature $f_m^X[i]$ and $f_m^X[j]$ where $i = (i_r, i_c)$ and $j = (j_r, j_c)$, we use the Pearson correlation coefficient ρ to quantify the feature similarity as shown in Eq. (1)

$$\rho(i, j) = (\tilde{f}_m^X[i])^T \tilde{f}_m^X[j]/512 \tag{1}$$

where $(\cdot)^T$ is the transpose operator, and $\tilde{f}_m^X[i]$ is the normalized version of $f_m^X[i]$ by subtracting its mean $\mu_m^X[i]$ and dividing by its standard deviation $\sigma_m^X[i]$ as shown in Eq. (2).

$$\tilde{f}_m^X[i] = (f_m^X[i] - \mu_m^X[i])/\sigma_m^X[i] \tag{2}$$

For a given $f_m^X[i]$, we repeat the process over all possible $f_m^X[j]$, and form a score vector $S^X[i]$, namely

$$S^X[i] = [\rho(i, 0), \cdots, \rho(i, j), \cdots, \rho(i, 255)] \tag{3}$$

As a result, `Self-Correlation` outputs a tensor S^X of shape $16 \times 16 \times 256$.

When f_m^X and Pearson correlation coefficient are both meaningful, it is clear that if $f_m^X[i]$ is matched, some score $S^X[i][j]$ with $j \neq i$ should be significantly greater than the rest of the scores $S^X[i][k]$ with $k \notin \{i, j\}$. Since we do not know the corresponding $f_m^X[j]$ in advance, it is difficult to check this pattern in the context of DNN. Alternatively, it is easier to check this pattern in a sorted score vector. Specifically, `Percentile Pooling` first sorts a score vector $S^X[i]$ to $S'^X[i]$ in the descending order as shown Eq. (4).

$$S'^X[i] = \text{sort}(S^X[i]) \tag{4}$$

Imagining plotting a curve about $(k, S'^X[i][k])$ for $k \in [0, \cdots, 255]$, we are supposed to see a monotonic decreasing curve with an abrupt drop at some point if $f_m^X[i]$ is matched. This indicates that this sorted version of score vector contains sufficient information to decide what feature is matched in future stages.

One can directly feed S'^X to future modules to decide matched features. However one drawback of doing so is that the resulting network loses the capability of accepting an input of an arbitrary size, because the length of score vector is dependent on the input size. To remove this dependency, `Percentile Pooling` also standardize the sorted score vector by only picking those scores at percentile ranks of interests. In other words, regardless the length L of raw sorted score vector, we always pick K scores to form a pooled percentile score vector $P^X[i]$ as shown in Eq. (5)

$$P^X[i][k] = S'^X[i][k'] \tag{5}$$

where $k \in [0, \cdots, K-1]$, and k' is the index of raw sorted score vector after mapping a predefined percentile $p_k \in [0,1]$ according to L as shown in Eq. (6)

$$k' = \text{round}(p_k \cdot (L-1)) \qquad (6)$$

Another advantage of the above standardization is dimension reduction, because only a small portion of all scores is kept. Once `Percentile Pooling` is done, we use `Mask Decoder` to gradually upsample feature P^X to the original image size as d_s^X, and `Binary Classifier` to produce a copy-move mask M_s^X to fulfill the auxiliary task. Again, both `Mask Decoder` and `Binary Classifier` only have the same architecture as those in `Mani-Det`, but with distinctive weights.

3.4   BusterNet Fusion

As illustrated in Fig. 2, `Fusion` module takes inputs of the `Mask Decoder` features from both branches, namely d_m^X and d_s^X, and jointly considers these two branches and make the final CMFD prediction. More precisely, we (i) concatenate feature d_m^X and d_s^X, (ii) fuse feature using the `BN-Inception` with parameter set 3@[1,3,5] (see Fig. 3(b)), and (iii) predict the three-class CMFD mask using a `Conv2D` with one filter of kernel size 3×3 followed by the `softmax` activation.

4   BusterNet Implementation and Training

4.1   Custom Layer Implementation

It is clear that except `Self-Correlation` and `Percentile Pooling` modules, all other modules are either standard or can be built from standard layers. `Self-Correlation` requires implementing Eqs. (1) and (2). We compute (i) tensor $\tilde{f}_m^X$ using Eq. (2), and (ii) correlation scores for all i, j pairs in one-shot via tensor dot product operator[1], instead of computing Eq. (1) one by one. Both operations are differentiable.

   `Percentile Pooling` is essentially a pooling layer, which has no trainable parameters but a deterministic pooling function. As one may notice, neither Eq. (4) nor (5) is differentiable. However, all we need to do is to perform backpropagation similar to that is performed in standard `MaxPooling` (*i.e.* only the neuron corresponding to the max receives the gradient).

4.2   Training Details

As shown in Table 1 of [38], and Table 12 of [32], publicly available dataset are very small (typically around a few thousands). More importantly, none of existing CMFD dataset provides ground truth masks differentiating source and target copies. We therefore create a synthetic dataset for training BusterNet.

   Inspired by [13] and also [10], we start with an original image X with an associated object mask M_s, randomly generate an affine matrix m to transform both the source mask and the source object image. We then use the transformed mask as the target mask M_t, paste the transformed object back to image

---

[1] This operator is known as `batched_tensordot` in Theano, and `matmul` in TensorFlow.

X and obtain a copy-move forgery sample X'. In particular, we use the MIT SUN2012 dataset [35], and the Microsoft COCO dataset [17] as image sources. All generated manipulation are either affine [34] or complex[2]. Complex clones use *Poisson image editing* [24], and perform complicated blending far beyond naive region pasting. Parameters used in affine matrix are: rotation $\in [-30°, 30°]$, scale $\in [0.5, 2]$, and translation is also uniformly picked within regions.

To further encourage more real-like training samples, we train a binary classifier to predict whether a sample is real unmanipulated or synthetic copy-move forged. Synthetic samples that fail to fool this classifier are not used for training BusterNet. Figure 4 shows some synthetic samples of our dataset, and they look quite natural in general. This dataset can be provided upon request.

Fig. 4. Synthetic CMFD samples with ground truth masks. Pixel colors blue, green and red in masks denotes *pristine, source* and *target copy* classes, respectively. (Color figure online)

In total, we collected 100,000 quality synthetic samples for copy-move detection, each with one three-class mask distinguishing source and destination copies and two binary masks auxiliary task training. The synthetic training data is split into training, validation and testing splits with 8:1:1 ratio. This synthetic dataset is used to train both auxiliary tasks and the main task of BusterNet.

It is worth noting that external image manipulation dataset from IEEE IFS-TC First Image Forensics Challenge[3] and the Wild Web tampered image dataset [37] are also used for training Mani-Det branch, because we want Mani-Det learns to identify more manipulated regions beyond the fixed set of manipulations in our synthetic dataset.

To train BusterNet, we initialize all parameters from random weights except for using a pretrained VGG16 on ImageNet for CNN Feature Extractor in Simi-Det. Instead of training BusterNet all modules together, we adopt a three-stage training strategy—(i) train each branch with its auxiliary task independently, (ii) freeze both branches and train fusion module, and (iii) unfreeze entire network and fine tune BusterNet end-to-end. Specifically, for auxiliary tasks, we use Adam optimizer with initial learning rate of 1e−2 and binary_crossentropy loss. Whenever validation loss reaches plateaus after 10

---

[2] https://github.com/fbessho/PyPoi.git.

[3] http://ifc.recod.ic.unicamp.br/.

epochs, we reduce learning rate by half until improvement stops for 20 epochs. For main task, we also `Adam` optimizer with `categorical_crossentropy` loss, but use initial learning rate of 1e−2 for `fusion` training while 1e−5 for finetuning. Pretrained models can be also found in our open repository https://github.com/isi-vista/BusterNet.git.

Table 1. Comparing different training strategies on Synthetic 10K testing set

Metrics	Recall			Accuracy
Class	Pristine	Source	Target	3-Class
Simi-Det Only	92.57%	32.28%	38.97%	92.57%
Direct BusterNet	93.70%	34.12%	47.37%	92.74%
Stage-wise BusterNet	93.83%	41.64%	53.61%	93.02%

This stage-wise training strategy is important to ensure the functionality of each branch, and further to achieve BusterNet's goals. Table 1 compares BusterNet performance on our synthetic testing dataset. Specifically, *Simi-Det Only* denotes to perform the main task but only use the `Simi-Det` branch (in other words, a naive solution as we discussed in Sect. 3.1), *Direct BusterNet* means to train BusterNet without auxiliary tasks, and *Stage-wise BusterNet* is our proposed training strategy. As one can see, it is easier to predict target copies than source copies in general, possibly because target copies may contain visual artifacts to help classification; and differences of prediction accuracy between systems are small, due to the dominant *pristine* class. However, the impact of two-branch design and stage-wise training should not be under-looked. As shown in Table 1, it turns out that two-branch model(*Direct BusterNet*) outperforms one-branch model (*Simi-Det Only*), and stage-wise training further improves recall on all classes by a large margin, especially on source and target classes.

5   Experimental Evaluation

5.1   Metrics and Baseline Settings

We use precision, recall and F_1 scores to report CMFD performance [7,9,34]. For a testing image, we compute the true positive (TP), false positive (FP) and false negative (FN) at pixel level. Of course, we have to treat pixels classified to source and target both as *forged*, so that the proposed BusterNet could be fairly compared with all classic CMFD methods which only predict binary masks.

Based on how F_1 is calculated, two protocols are used for **pixel-level evaluation**: (A) aggregate all TP, FP, and FN numbers over the whole dataset, and report precision, recall and F_1 scores [7,34]; and (B) compute precision, recall, F_1 scores for each image, and report the averaged scores [25]. Protocol A better captures overall performance including non-forged images, while protocol B only works for a subset of forged images (F_1 score is ill-defined when TP is zero), but better quantifies the localization performance. We use both protocols in our evaluations. If any pixels in a testing image are detected as forged, the testing image is labeled as forged. We compare a predicted image label with its ground truth to compute image-level TP, FP, and FN, and report precision, recall and F_1 scores over an entire dataset as **image-level evaluation protocol.**

Furthermore, we use *area under the receiver operating characteristic (ROC) curve (AUC)* to evaluate overall performance, where the ROC curve is a function of *true positive rate (TPR)* in terms of *false positive rate (FPR)*. AUC quantifies the overall ability of the network to discriminate between two classes.

We use four methods as baselines for comparison—a block-based CMFD with the Zernike moment feature [26], a keypoint-based CMFD with the SIFT feature [7], a dense field-based CMFD [9], and a deep matching and validation network (DMVN) [34]. All method implementations are either provided by paper authors or from reliable third-party implementation in [7]. Since DMVN is originally designed for image splicing detection where the input is a pair of images, we recursively split the input image into two halves X_1 and X_2 along X's longer axis, and feed DMVN this pair of (X_1, X_2). If DMVN finds anything spliced, this means X contains copy-move regions (one in X_1 and the other in X_2). If not, we then split X_1 and X_2 into halves again, and apply DMVN to detect whether splicing has happened within X_1 and X_2. This recursion continues until it reaches the smallest patch size (we use 16×16) for analysis or successfully finding splicing regions. Default parameters are used for all baseline methods without any preprocessing. Speed measurement is based on an Intel Xeon CPU E52695@2.4GHz with a single Nivdia Titan-X GPU.

5.2   Evaluation Data

We use two standard datasets for evaluation. The first dataset is the CASIA TIDEv2.0 dataset,[4] which is the largest public accessible image forgery detection benchmark, in which all manipulations are created manually. It contains 7491 authentic and 5123 tampered color images. However, it does not specify which images are manipulated in a copy-move manner and does not provide ground truth manipulation masks. We therefore manually verify that 1313 out of 5123 tampered samples are of copy-move forgery. These 1313 CMFD samples and their authentic counterparts together form the testing dataset (total 2626 samples) we used later. We refer to it as the CASIA CMFD dataset.

The second dataset is the CoMoFoD dataset [31], which contains 200 base forged images and 25 categories (total 5000 images). Each category is made by applying postprocessing/attacks to the **base** category images to hide forgery clues (e.g., JPEG compression, etc.). Detailed attack descriptions and settings can be found in [31].

Finally, to evaluate BusterNet discernibility, we need testing data with ground truth masks distinguishing source and target. However, neither the

---

[4] http://forensics.idealtest.org/casiav2

CASIA CMFD nor the CoMoFoD datasets provide such masks. We therefore synthesize them by comparing a forged image with its authentic counterpart for both datasets. All synthesized masks are manually verified, and can be found in our code repository.

5.3   Overall CMFD Performance Analysis

Table 2 shows the overall performance on the CASIA CMFD dataset. Buster-Net's F_1 score outperforms all others by a large margin on all three evaluation protocols; it is also is the fastest solution. By comparing the performance of Simi-Det branch and the full BusterNet, one can see that end-to-end fine-tuning improves AUC by 3–4% at both pixel- and image-level as shown in Fig. 5.

Table 2. Performance analysis on CASIA CMFD dataset.

	Methods				Ours	
	[26]	[7]	[9]	[34]	Simi. Det.	BusterNet
Image level evaluation protocol						
Precision	97.01%	68.49%	**99.51%**	66.37%	71.53%	78.22%
Recall	24.47%	67.82%	30.61%	73.59%	**80.73%**	73.89%
F-score	39.08%	68.15%	46.82%	69.80%	75.85%	**75.98%**
Pixel level evaluation protocol - A						
Precision	**94.46%**	64.84%	83.12%	17.06%	56.52%	77.38%
Recall	25.05%	0.17%	51.28%	10.60%	**62.06%**	59.15%
F-score	39.59%	0.34%	63.43%	13.08%	59.16%	**67.05%**
Pixel level evaluation protocol - B						
Precision	22.71%	37.09%	24.92%	23.97%	47.23%	**55.71%**
Recall	13.36%	0.14%	26.81%	13.79%	**48.44%**	43.83%
F-score	16.40%	0.23%	25.43%	14.64%	43.72%	**45.56%**
Processing speed						
Sec./Img.	5.11	0.97	1.78	0.95	**0.44**	0.62

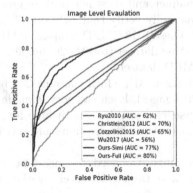
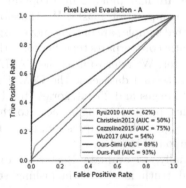

Fig. 5. AUC performance comparison on CASIA CMFD dataset.

5.4   BusterNet Robustness Analysis

To evaluate BusterNet robustness against various attacks/postprocessing, we test it and all baseline methods on the CoMoFoD dataset. Table 3 shows the number of *correctly detected* images under each attack (containing 200 samples). An image is to referred as *correctly detected* if its pixel-level F_1 score is higher than 0.5 [31]. BusterNet outperforms baseline methods on all but one attack.

To better understand the BusterNet performance against the state-of-the-art, we conduct performance analysis over the entire dataset. Figure 6 shows the detailed pixel-level F_1 scores under protocol B for all attacks. As one can see, except for attacks of severe JPEG compression (*e.g.* JC1 compression quality 10), BusterNet is quite robust against various attacks. The performance analysis on the base category (i.e., no attack) is shown in Table 3. On the left half of the table, we follow the modified protocol used by [18,31] to report average scores only on the correctly detected subset, while on the right half of table we continuously report our performance using pixel-level protocol B. It is worthy to mention that although [9] leads the proposed BusterNet by 7% in F_1 score when only considering correctly detected samples, BusterNet correctly detected 24 more

Table 3. Number of correctly detected images on CoMoFoD dataset under attacks.

Attack	Methods							
	[31]	[26]	[16]	[28]	[18]	[9]	[34]	Ours
Base	53	90	102	88	97	93	53	**117**
BC1	-	91	-	-	-	94	50	**116**
BC2	-	89	-	-	-	94	53	**115**
BC3	42	89	99	90	94	88	48	**109**
CA1	-	93	-	-	-	98	50	**117**
CA2	-	93	-	-	-	96	50	**116**
CA3	45	92	99	90	94	96	48	**116**
CR1	44	92	90	82	72	97	51	**117**
CR2	-	91	-	-	-	95	50	**116**
CR3	-	90	-	-	-	92	54	**116**
IB1	-	90	91	94	104	91	53	**113**
IB2	47	87	-	-	-	88	32	**98**
IB3	-	84	-	-	-	84	26	**93**
JC1	-	43	-	-	-	69	18	60
JC2	-	63	-	-	-	73	21	**77**
JC3	-	72	-	-	-	75	26	**86**
JC4	5	73	-	-	-	77	29	**103**
JC5	-	76	-	-	-	81	38	**99**
JC6	-	80	-	-	-	83	33	**101**
JC7	-	86	-	-	-	87	42	**107**
JC8	-	88	-	-	-	92	42	**109**
JC9	-	81	89	31	78	87	36	**106**
NA1	-	24	-	-	-	41	38	**100**
NA2	3	42	-	-	-	66	39	**102**

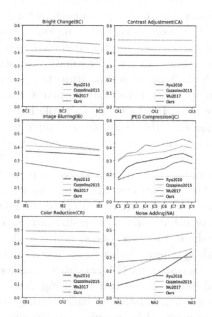

Fig. 6. Pixel-level F1 scores (y-axis) on CoMoFoD under attacks (x-axis).

Table 4. CMFD performance comparisons on CoMoFoD dataset with no attack.

Methods	Correctly detected average				Protocol B (overall average)		
	#Passed	Precision	Recall	F1	Precision	Recall	F1
[31]	50	**96.77%**	83.91%	**88.72%**	-	-	-
[26]	90	96.27%	69.84%	79.93%	45.78%	34.35%	37.37%
[16]	102	54.46%	85.04%	59.54%	-	-	-
[28]	100	54.37%	74.19%	54.60%	-	-	-
[18]	97	59.27%	82.20%	63.18%	-	-	-
[9]	93	84.22%	**93.58%**	87.82%	39.92%	47.61%	41.83%
[34]	53	61.11%	71.48%	63.13%	36.29%	40.41%	31.13%
Ours	**117**	83.52%	78.75%	80.09%	**57.34%**	**49.39%**	**49.26%**

samples than [9], indicting BusterNet is better in general. Indeed,BusterNet outperforms [9] by 7% on the performance over the entire dataset (Table 4).

5.5   Source/Target Discernibility Analysis

To the best of our knowledge, none of CMFD state-of-the-art methods is capable of localizing, and differentiating between, the source and target of the manipulation. One of the prominent features of BusterNet, however, is the ability to localize source and target regions. In order to evaluate the accuracy of localization, we compare the predicted forgery region labels with those from ground truth. For each predicted mask, we merge the source and destination channels to find all forged regions using the connected component (CC) analysis, and use the dominant class of all its pixels as the label of a CC. If no CC is found, this is a miss. If all CCs in a sample have the same label, we opt-out this sample. Otherwise, this is an opt-in sample for analysis, and we label it "correct" only when both source and target forgery regions are correctly classified.

Visual examples are shown in Fig. 7. Table 5 summarizes the discernibility performance of BusterNet on both the CASIA CMFD (manipulated only) and CoMoFoD datasets, where *miss* indicates those missed samples, *overall accuracy* is the ratio of corrected samples to total samples, and opt-in accuracy is the ratio of corrected samples to opt-in samples. The overall ~12% accuracy does not seem not high. However, one should consider the fact that BusterNet is only trained with synthetic data with a limited number of real manipulation samples, and the used simple CC-based label assignment scheme is also simple for complicated real cases. As one can see in Fig. 7(b), BusterNet sometimes correctly captures target manipulation at least partially (*e.g.*, the left-most bird sample and the right-most spider sample), but the simple CC-based label scheme fails to assign correct labels. Indeed, if we consider the accuracy only for opt-in samples, the accuracy of the proposed BusterNet jumps to 78% as shown in Table 5.

Table 5. Source/target discernibility performance of BusterNet.

Dataset	Number of images					Accuracy	
	Total	Miss	Opt-out	Opt-in	Corr.	Overall	Opt-in
CASIA CMFD	1313	542	581	190	146	11.11%	76.84%
CoMoFoD	200	83	76	41	33	16.50%	80.49%
Overall	1513	625	657	231	179	11.83%	77.49%

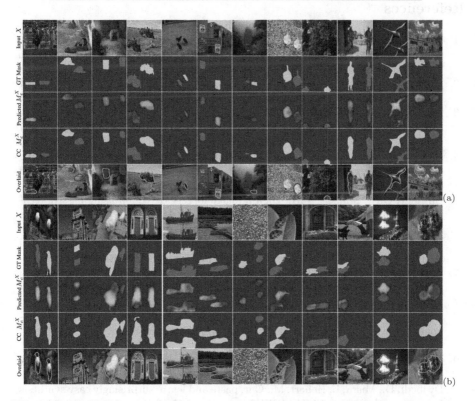

(a)

(b)

Fig. 7. BusterNet detection results on testing dataset. (a) samples that BusterNet correctly distinguishes source/target copies; and (b) samples that BusterNet fails to distinguish source/target copies. blue: *pristine*, green: *source copy* and red: *target copy*. Note many object classes, *e.g. flower*, *sand*, and *ladybug*, are not included in SUN or COCO dataset, indicating the generalizability of BusterNet to unseen classes. (Color figure online)

6   Conclusion

We introduce BusterNet, an end-to-end DNN solution to detecting copy-move forged images with source/target localization with two branches as shown in Fig. 2. We show how to design auxiliary tasks for each branch to ensure its functionality and feature properties. We also demonstrate how to overcome the training data shortage by synthesizing a large scale of realistic and quality CMFD samples from out-of-domain datasets. Our evaluation results demonstrate that BusterNet outperforms state-of-the arts methods by a large margin, and is also robust against various known CMFD attacks. More importantly, BusterNet has the prominent advantage, over any existing CMFD solutions, of distinguishing source/target copies. This is a desired capability for forensic experts.

References

1. Amerini, I., Ballan, L., Caldelli, R., Del Bimbo, A., Serra, G.: A SIFT-based forensic method for copy-move attack detection and transformation recovery. IEEE Trans. Inf. Forensics Secur. **6**(3), 1099–1110 (2011)
2. Ardizzone, E., Bruno, A., Mazzola, G.: Copy-move forgery detection by matching triangles of keypoints. IEEE Trans. Inf. Forensics Secur. **10**(10), 2084–2094 (2015)
3. Asghar, K., Habib, Z., Hussain, M.: Copy-move and splicing image forgery detection and localization techniques: a review. Aust. J. Forensic Sci. **49**(3), 281–307 (2017)
4. Bayram, S., Sencar, H.T., Memon, N.: An efficient and robust method for detecting copy-move forgery. In: IEEE International Conference on Acoustics, Speech and Signal Processing, ICASSP 2009, pp. 1053–1056. IEEE (2009)
5. Birajdar, G.K., Mankar, V.H.: Digital image forgery detection using passive techniques: a survey. Digit. Investig. **10**(3), 226–245 (2013)
6. Bunk, J., et al.: Detection and localization of image forgeries using resampling features and deep learning. In: 2017 IEEE Conference on Computer Vision and Pattern Recognition Workshops (CVPRW), pp. 1881–1889. IEEE (2017)
7. Christlein, V., Riess, C., Jordan, J., Riess, C., Angelopoulou, E.: An evaluation of popular copy-move forgery detection approaches. IEEE Trans. Inf. Forensics Secur. **7**(6), 1841–1854 (2012)
8. Costanzo, A., Amerini, I., Caldelli, R., Barni, M.: Forensic analysis of SIFT keypoint removal and injection. IEEE Trans. Inf. Forensics Secur. **9**(9), 1450–1464 (2014)
9. Cozzolino, D., Poggi, G., Verdoliva, L.: Efficient dense-field copy-move forgery detection. IEEE Trans. Inf. Forensics Secur. **10**(11), 2284–2297 (2015)
10. Dwibedi, D., Misra, I., Hebert, M.: Cut, paste and learn: surprisingly easy synthesis for instance detection. In: The IEEE International Conference on Computer Vision (ICCV), October 2017
11. Farid, H.: Seeing is not believing. IEEE Spectr. **46**(8) (2009)
12. Fridrich, A.J., Soukal, B.D., Lukáš, A.J.: Detection of copy-move forgery in digital images. In: Proceedings of Digital Forensic Research Workshop. Citeseer (2003)
13. Gupta, A., Vedaldi, A., Zisserman, A.: Synthetic data for text localisation in natural images. In: IEEE Conference on Computer Vision and Pattern Recognition (2016)
14. Huang, D.Y., Huang, C.N., Hu, W.C., Chou, C.H.: Robustness of copy-move forgery detection under high JPEG compression artifacts. Multimed. Tools Appl. **76**(1), 1509–1530 (2017)
15. Ke, Y., Sukthankar, R., Huston, L.: An efficient parts-based near-duplicate and sub-image retrieval system. In: Proceedings of the 12th Annual ACM International Conference on Multimedia, pp. 869–876. ACM (2004)

16. Li, J., Li, X., Yang, B., Sun, X.: Segmentation-based image copy-move forgery detection scheme. IEEE Trans. Inf. Forensics Secur. **10**(3), 507–518 (2015)
17. Lin, T.-Y., et al.: Microsoft COCO: common objects in context. In: Fleet, D., Pajdla, T., Schiele, B., Tuytelaars, T. (eds.) ECCV 2014. LNCS, vol. 8693, pp. 740–755. Springer, Cham (2014). https://doi.org/10.1007/978-3-319-10602-1_48
18. Liu, Y., Guan, Q., Zhao, X.: Copy-move forgery detection based on convolutional kernel network. Multimed. Tools Appl. 1–25 (2017)
19. Long, J., Shelhamer, E., Darrell, T.: Fully convolutional networks for semantic segmentation. In: Proceedings of the IEEE Conference on Computer Vision and Pattern Recognition, pp. 3431–3440 (2015)
20. Mahdian, B., Saic, S.: Detection of copy-move forgery using a method based on blur moment invariants. Forensic Sci. Int. **171**(2), 180–189 (2007)
21. Mahmood, T., Nawaz, T., Irtaza, A., Ashraf, R., Shah, M., Mahmood, M.T.: Copy-move forgery detection technique for forensic analysis in digital images. Math. Probl. Eng. **2016**, 1–13 (2016)
22. Manu, V.T., Mehtre, B.M.: Detection of copy-move forgery in images using segmentation and SURF. In: Thampi, S., Bandyopadhyay, S., Krishnan, S., Li, K.C., Mosin, S., Ma, M. (eds.) Advances in Signal Processing and Intelligent Recognition Systems. AISC, vol. 425, pp. 645–654. Springer, Cham (2016). https://doi.org/10.1007/978-3-319-28658-7_55
23. Noh, H., Hong, S., Han, B.: Learning deconvolution network for semantic segmentation. In: Proceedings of the IEEE International Conference on Computer Vision, pp. 1520–1528 (2015)
24. Pérez, P., Gangnet, M., Blake, A.: Poisson image editing. ACM Trans. Graph. (TOG) **22**, 313–318 (2003)
25. Pun, C.M., Yuan, X.C., Bi, X.L.: Image forgery detection using adaptive oversegmentation and feature point matching. IEEE Trans. Inf. Forensics Secur. **10**(8), 1705–1716 (2015)
26. Ryu, S.-J., Lee, M.-J., Lee, H.-K.: Detection of copy-rotate-move forgery using Zernike moments. In: Böhme, R., Fong, P.W.L., Safavi-Naini, R. (eds.) IH 2010. LNCS, vol. 6387, pp. 51–65. Springer, Heidelberg (2010). https://doi.org/10.1007/978-3-642-16435-4_5
27. Shivakumar, B., Baboo, S.: Detection of region duplication forgery in digital images using SURF. Int. J. Comput. Sci. Issues **8**(4), 199–205 (2011)
28. Silva, E., Carvalho, T., Ferreira, A., Rocha, A.: Going deeper into copy-move forgery detection: exploring image telltales via multi-scale analysis and voting processes. J. Vis. Commun. Image Represent. **29**, 16–32 (2015)
29. Simonyan, K., Zisserman, A.: Very deep convolutional networks for large-scale image recognition. CoRR abs/1409.1556 (2014)
30. Soni, B., Das, P., Thounaojam, D.: CMFD: a detailed review of block based and key feature based techniques in image copy-move forgery detection. IET Image Process. **12**, 167–178 (2017)
31. Tralic, D., Zupancic, I., Grgic, S., Grgic, M.: CoMoFod—new database for copy-move forgery detection. In: 2013 55th International Symposium on ELMAR, pp. 49–54. IEEE (2013)
32. Warif, N.B.A., et al.: Copy-move forgery detection: survey, challenges and future directions. J. Netw. Comput. Appl. **75**, 259–278 (2016)
33. Wojna, Z., et al.: The devil is in the decoder (2017)

34. Wu, Y., Abd-Almageed, W., Natarajan, P.: Deep matching and validation network: an end-to-end solution to constrained image splicing localization and detection. In: Proceedings of the 2017 ACM on Multimedia Conference, MM 2017, pp. 1480–1502 (2017)

35. Xiao, J., Hays, J., Ehinger, K.A., Oliva, A., Torralba, A.: Sun database: large-scale scene recognition from abbey to zoo. In: 2010 IEEE conference on Computer Vision and Pattern Recognition (CVPR), pp. 3485–3492. IEEE (2010)

36. Yang, B., Sun, X., Guo, H., Xia, Z., Chen, X.: A copy-move forgery detection method based on CMFD-SIFT. Multimed. Tools Appl. **77**, 1–19 (2017)

37. Zampoglou, M., Papadopoulos, S., Kompatsiaris, Y.: Detecting image splicing in the wild (web). In: 2015 IEEE International Conference on Multimedia & Expo Workshops (ICMEW), pp. 1–6. IEEE (2015)

38. Zampoglou, M., Papadopoulos, S., Kompatsiaris, Y.: Large-scale evaluation of splicing localization algorithms for web images. Multimed. Tools Appl. **76**(4), 4801–4834 (2017)

39. Zhou, P., Han, X., Morariu, V.I., Davis, L.S.: Two-stream neural networks for tampered face detection. In: 2017 IEEE Conference on Computer Vision and Pattern Recognition Workshops (CVPRW), pp. 1831–1839. IEEE (2017)

40. Zhu, Y., Shen, X., Chen, H.: Copy-move forgery detection based on scaled ORB. Multimed. Tools Appl. **75**(6), 3221–3233 (2016)

To Learn Image Super-Resolution, Use a GAN to Learn How to Do Image Degradation First

Adrian Bulat, Jing Yang[(✉)], and Georgios Tzimiropoulos

Computer Vision Laboratory, University of Nottingham, Nottingham, UK
{adrian.bulat,jing.yang2,yorgos.tzimiropoulos}@nottingham.ac.uk

Abstract. This paper is on image and face super-resolution. The vast majority of prior work for this problem focus on how to increase the resolution of low-resolution images which are artificially generated by simple bilinear down-sampling (or in a few cases by blurring followed by down-sampling). We show that such methods fail to produce good results when applied to real-world low-resolution, low quality images. To circumvent this problem, we propose a two-stage process which firstly trains a High-to-Low Generative Adversarial Network (GAN) to learn how to degrade and downsample high-resolution images requiring, during training, only *unpaired* high and low-resolution images. Once this is achieved, the output of this network is used to train a Low-to-High GAN for image super-resolution using this time *paired* low- and high-resolution images. Our main result is that this network can be now used to effectively increase the quality of real-world low-resolution images. We have applied the proposed pipeline for the problem of face super-resolution where we report large improvement over baselines and prior work although the proposed method is potentially applicable to other object categories.

Keywords: Image and face super-resolution
Generative Adversarial Networks · GANs

1 Introduction

This paper is on enhancing the resolution and quality of low-resolution, noisy, blurry, and corrupted by artefacts images. We collectively refer to all these tasks as image super-resolution. This is a challenging problem with a multitude of applications from image enhancement and editing to image recognition and object detection to name a few.

A. Bulat and J. Yang—Equal contribution.

Electronic supplementary material The online version of this chapter (https://doi.org/10.1007/978-3-030-01231-1_12) contains supplementary material, which is available to authorized users.

© Springer Nature Switzerland AG 2018
V. Ferrari et al. (Eds.): ECCV 2018, LNCS 11210, pp. 187–202, 2018.
https://doi.org/10.1007/978-3-030-01231-1_12

Fig. 1. Super-resolution results produced by our system on real-world low-resolution faces from Widerface [1]. Our method is compared against SRGAN [2] and CycleGan [3].

Our main focus is on the problem of super-resolving *real-world low-resolution* images *for a specific object category*. We use faces in our case noting however that the proposed method is potentially applicable to other object categories. Although there is a multitude of papers on image and face super-resolution, the large majority of them use as input low-resolution images which are artificially generated by simple bilinear down-sampling or in a few cases by blurring followed by down-sampling. On the contrary, the real-world setting has received little attention by the community. To our knowledge, this paper presents one of the very first attempts towards real-world image super-resolution. A few results produced by our system are shown in Fig. 1.

Main Idea. There is a large list of nuisance factors which one needs to take into account when doing real-world image super-resolution, including blur (e.g. motion or defocus), compression artefacts, colour and sensor noise. These nuisance factors are usually unknown (e.g. motion blur) and sometimes hard to effectively model (e.g. the case of multiple degradations). If the true image degradation model is different from the one assumed and modeled, inevitably, this leads to poor performance during test time. To alleviate this, in this paper, rather than trying to model the image degradation process, we propose to learn it using a High-to-Low Generative Adversarial Network (GAN). Notably, the proposed network uses unpaired image data during training and hence it does not require pairs of low and high-resolution images but just two unrelated sets of low- and high-resolution images with no correspondence. Once this is achieved, we can use the High-to-Low GAN to "realistically" degrade and downsample high-resolution images and use these images as input to learn super-resolution under a "paired" image setting. The proposed architecture is shown in Fig. 2.

In summary our **contributions** are:

1. We present one of the first attempts to super-resolve real-world low-resolution images for a given object category, namely faces in this paper.

2. To this end, and inspired by [3], we propose to train a High-to-Low GAN using unpaired low- and high-resolution images which can be used to effectively simulate the image degradation process. Following this, we use the High-to-Low GAN to create paired low and high-resolution images which can be used to train a Low-to-High GAN for real-world super-resolution.

3. In recent works on image super-resolution, the L_2 pixel loss dominates the GAN loss which plays a refinement role in making the images look sharper. In this work, we propose a GAN-centered approach in which the GAN loss drives the image generation process. We note that the GAN loss used plays a reciprocal role in High-to-Low and Low-to-High. In High-to-Low, it is used to contaminate the high-resolution input image with noise and artefacts coming from the Widerface dataset [1], whereas in Low-to-High it is used for denoising. In both networks, the role of the L_2 pixel loss is reduced to that of helping the generator preserve the face characteristics (e.g. identity, pose, expression).

4. We have applied the proposed pipeline to the problem of face super-resolution where we report large improvement over baselines and prior work on real-world, low-quality, low-resolution images from the Widerface dataset.

2   Closely Related Work

There is a very long list of image and face super-resolution papers and a detailed review of the topic is out of the scope of this section. Herein, we focus on related recent work based on Convolutional Neural Networks (CNNs).

The standard approach to super-resolution using CNNs is to use a fully supervised approach where a low-resolution (LR) image is processed by a network comprising convolutional and upsampling layers in order to produce a high-resolution (HR) image which is then matched against the original HR image using an appropriate loss function. We call this paired setting as it uses pairs of LR and corresponding HR images for training.

We emphasize that the large majority of prior work use LR images which are artificially generated by simple bilinear down-sampling of the corresponding HR images (or in a few cases by blurring followed by down-sampling). No matter the approach taken, the vast majority of image and face super-resolution methods reviewed below are based on this setting. Notably, a recent challenge on super-resolution [4] is also based on this setting. As it was recently shown in [5] and also validated in this work, this setting cannot produce good results for real-world low-resolution images.

Image Super-Resolution. Early attempts based on the aforementioned setting [6,7] use various L_p losses between the generated and the ground truth HR images for training the networks which however result in blurry super-resolved images. A notable improvement is the so-called perceptual loss [8] which applies an L_2 loss over feature maps calculated using another pre-trained network (e.g. VGG [9]). More advanced deep architectures for super-resolution including recursive, laplacian and dense networks have been recently proposed in [10–12].

More recently, and following the introduction of GANs [13], the authors of [2] proposed a super-resolution approach which, on top of pixel- and/or feature-based losses, it also uses a discriminator to differentiate between the generated and the original HR images which is found to produce more photo-realistic results. Notably, [14], which is an improved version of [2], won the first place in the challenge of [4]. More recently, [15] proposed a patch-based texture loss which is found to improve the reconstruction quality. Different from the aforementioned methods is [16] which does not use a GAN but proposes a pixel recursive super-resolution method which is based on PixelCNNs [17].

From the aforementioned works, our method has similar objectives to those of [5] which also targets the case of real-world image super-resolution. However, the methodology used in [5] and the one proposed in this paper are completely different. While [5] proposes to capitalize on internal image statistics to do real-world super-resolution, our method proposes to use unpaired LR and HR images to learn the image degradation process, and then use it to learn super-resolution.

Face Super-Resolution. Face super-resolution is super-resolution applied to faces. Similarly to image super-resolution, the vast majority of face super-resolution methods [18–23] are based on a paired setting for training and evaluation which is typically done on frontal datasets (e.g. CelebA [24], Helen [25], LFW [26], BioID [27]).

The method of [21] performs super-resolution and dense landmark localization in an alternating manner which is shown to improve the quality of the super-resolved faces. The authors of [19] propose a patch-based super-resolution method in which the facial regions to be enhanced are sequentially discovered using deep reinforcement learning. Rather than directly generating the HR image, the method of [20] proposes to combine CNNs with the Wavelet Transform for predicting a series of corresponding wavelet coefficients. The recent work of [22] is a GAN-based approach similar to the one proposed in [2]. In [18], a two-step decoder-encoder-decoder architecture is proposed also incorporating a spatial transformer network to undo face misalignment.

To our knowledge, the only method that reports face super-resolution results for real-world LR facial images is the very recent work of [28] which presents impressive qualitative results on more than 200 facial images taken from the Widerface dataset [1]. However, [28] is face-specific making use of facial landmarks for producing these results, rendering the approach inapplicable for other object categories for which landmarks are not available or landmark localization is not so effective. Contrary to many face super-resolution methods, the proposed pipeline is potentially applicable to other object categories.

3   Method

3.1   Overall Architecture

Given a LR facial image of size 16×16, our system uses a super-resolution network, which we call Low-to-High, to super-resolve it into a HR image of

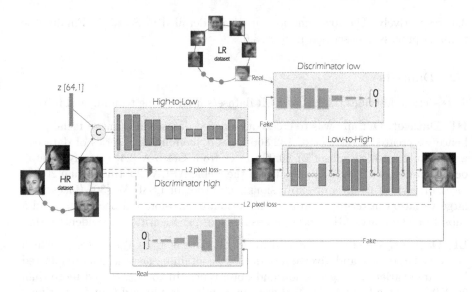

Fig. 2. Overall proposed architecture and training pipeline. See also Sect. 3.1.

64×64. This Low-to-High network is trained with paired LR and HR facial images. One first fundamental difference between this paper and prior work on super-resolution is how the LR images are produced. In most prior work, the LR images are produced by bilinearly downsampling the corresponding (original) HR images, which completely ignores the degradation process (e.g. motion blur, compression artefacts etc.). To alleviate this, and inspired by [3], in this work, we propose to learn both degrading and downsampling a HR facial image using another network which we call High-to-Low. Notably, High-to-Low is trained using unpaired data from 2 completely different and disjoint datasets. The first of these datasets contains HR facial images from a number of face alignment datasets. The second dataset contains blurry and low quality LR facial images from Widerface.

A second fundamental difference between this paper and previous work is how the losses used to train both networks are combined with our paper putting more emphasis on the GAN over the L_2 pixel loss. In particular, while prior methods also use a combination of a pixel loss and GAN loss (and in some cases a feature loss), the GAN simply plays the role of making the images sharper. On the contrary, our proposed method is fully GAN-driven, with the pixel loss having the sole role of accelerating the convergence speed, especially early in the training process and helping the GAN to preserve the identity and the overall facial characteristics (e.g. pose, facial expression).

The overall architecture, which is end-to-end trainable, is shown in Fig. 2. Note that at test time only the generator part of the Low-to-High network is used. The datasets used for training and testing are described in Sect. 3.2. The High-to-Low and Low-to-High networks are described in detail in Sects. 3.3 and

3.4, respectively. The loss functions used are detailed in Sect. 3.5. Finally, the training process is described in Sect. 3.6.

3.2 Datasets

This section describes the HR and LR datasets used during training and testing.

HR Dataset. Our aim was to create a balanced dataset in terms of facial pose, hence we created a dataset of 182,866 faces by combining a series of datasets: a randomly selected subset of 60,000 faces from Celeb-A [24] (mainly frontal, occlusion-free, with good illumination), the whole AFLW [29] (more than 20,000 faces in various poses and expressions), a subset of LS3D-W [30] (faces with large variation in terms of pose, illumination, expression and occlusion), and a subset of VGGFace2 [31] (10 large pose images per identity; 9,131 identities).

LR Dataset. We created our real-world LR dataset from Widerface [1] which is a very large scale and diverse face dataset, containing faces which are affected by a large variety of degradation and noise types. In total, we used more than 50,000 images out of which 3,000 were randomly selected and kept for testing.

3.3 High-to-Low

In this section, we describe the overall architecture used for the High-to-Low network. Both the generator and the discriminator are based on ResNet architectures [32,33] using the basic block with pre-activation introduced in [33].

High-to-Low Generator. The generator uses input images from the HR dataset. Its architecture is similar to the ones used in [2,28] with the main difference being that the first layer takes as input the HR image concatenated with a noise vector that was projected and then reshaped using a fully connected layer in order to have the same size as one image channel. This is because the problem at hand is one-to-many, i.e. a HR image can have multiple corresponding LR ones, due to the fact that it can be affected by multiple types of noise coming from different sources and applied in different amounts and ways. We model this by concatenating the above-mentioned noise vector along with the HR image. This is similar in nature to a conditional GAN [34], in which the label is the HR image. A few visual examples illustrating the various noise types learned by the proposed network are shown in Fig. 3.

The network has an encoder-decoder structure and consists of 12 residual blocks equally distributed in 6 groups. Resolution is dropped 4 times using pooling layers, from 64×64 to 4×4 px, and then it is increased twice to 16×16 using pixel shuffle layers. The High-to-Low generator is shown in Fig. 4a.

High-to-Low Discriminator. The discriminator, shown in Fig. 5, follows the ResNet-based architecture used in [35–37] and consists of 6 residual blocks (without batch normalization), followed by a fully connected layer. Since the input resolution of the High-to-Low discriminator is 16×16, the resolution is dropped for the last two blocks only using max-pooling.

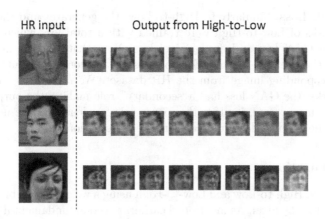

Fig. 3. Examples of different low-resolution samples produced by our High-to-Low network (described in Sect. 3.3) for different input noise vectors. Notice that our network can model a large variety of image degradation types, in various degrees, such as illumination, blur, colour and jpeg artefacts. Moreover, it learns what types of noise are more likely to be found given the input image type (e.g. gray-scale vs colour images). Best viewed in electronic format.

High-to-Low Loss. The generator and the discriminator networks of the High-to-Low network were trained with a total loss which is a combination of a GAN loss and an L_2 pixel loss. These are further described in Eq. 1 and detailed in Sect. 3.5. For the GAN loss, we used an "unpaired" training setting: in particular, we used real images from the LR dataset, i.e. real-world LR images from Widerface, therefore enforcing the output of the generator (whose input are images from the HR dataset) to be contaminated with real-world noisy artefacts. We also used an L_2 pixel loss between the output of the generator and the HR image after passing it through an average pooling layer (so that the image resolutions match) to enforce that the output of the generator has similar content (i.e. face identity, pose and expression) with the original HR image.

3.4 Low-to-High

Low-to-High Generator. The generator accepts as input the output of the High-to-Low network. The network consists of 17 residual blocks distributed in 3 groups: 2, 3 and 12. Each group has a skip connection that connects the first and the last block within the group. Resolution is increased 4 times using bilinear interpolation, from 16×16 to 64×64 px. The generator is shown in Fig. 4b. We note that because sample diversity is already obtained at the previous stage with the help of the noise vector used in the input of the High-to-Low, we did not use an additional noise vector at this stage.

Low-to-High Discriminator. The discriminator, shown in Fig. 5, is the same as the one used in High-to-Low, with the exception of adding two new max-pooling layers to accommodate for the increase in resolution.

Low-to-High Loss. Similarly to High-to-Low, the generator and the discriminator networks of Low-to-High were trained with a total loss which is a combination of a GAN loss and an L_2 pixel loss. Note that training in this case fully follows the "paired" setting: For both losses, and for each input image, we use the corresponding image from the HR dataset. We note that, although in previous works, the GAN loss had a "secondary" role making the output image look sharper, in our case, it plays the major role for denoising the noisy input LR image. The L_2 pixel loss enforces content preservation.

3.5   Loss Functions

We trained *both* High-to-Low and Low-to-High using a weighted combination of a GAN loss and an L_2 pixel. As mentioned earlier, a second fundamental difference between this paper and previous work is how these losses are combined. While recent works on image super-resolution also use such a combination (in many cases there is also a feature loss), in these works, the L_2 pixel loss dominates with the GAN loss playing a refinement role for making the images look sharper and more realistic (as the L_2 pixel loss is known to generate blurry images).

On the contrary, in this work, we propose a GAN-centered approach in which the GAN loss drives the image generation process. We note that the GAN loss used plays a reciprocal role in High-to-Low and Low-to-High. In High-to-Low, it is used to contaminate the HR input with noise and artefacts coming from the Widerface dataset, whereas in Low-to-High it is used for denoising. In both networks, the role of the L_2 pixel loss is reduced to that of helping the generator preserve the face characteristics (e.g. identity, pose, expression).

For *each network*, we used a loss defined as:

$$l = \alpha l_{pixel} + \beta l_{GAN}, \tag{1}$$

where α and β are the corresponding weights and $\beta l_{GAN} > \alpha l_{pixel}$ in general.

For both networks, for the GAN loss, we made use of the recent advancements in the field and experimented with both the Improved Wasserstein [35] and the Spectral Normalization GAN [36]. From our experiments, we found that they both generated samples of similar visual quality. We note that, for our final results, we used the latter one, due to the faster training.

Following [36], we used the hinge loss defined as:

$$l_{GAN} = \mathop{\mathbb{E}}_{x \sim \mathbb{P}_r} [\min(0, -1 + D(x))] + \mathop{\mathbb{E}}_{\hat{x} \sim \mathbb{P}_g} [\min(0, -1 - D(\hat{x}))], \tag{2}$$

where $\mathbb{P}_r$ is the data distribution and $\mathbb{P}_g$ is the generator G distribution defined by $\hat{x} = G(x)$. For High-to-Low, $\mathbb{P}_r$ denotes the LR dataset (i.e. the LR Widerface images), while for Low-to-High the HR dataset. See also Sect. 3.2.

The weights W of the discriminator D are normalized in order to satisfy the Lipschitz constraint $\sigma(W) = 1$ as follows:

$$W_{SN}(W) = W/\sigma(W). \tag{3}$$

Finally, the L_2 pixel loss used minimizes the L_2 distance between the predicted and the ground truth image and is defined as follows:

$$l_{pixel} = \frac{1}{WH} \sum_{i=1}^{W} \sum_{j=1}^{H} (F(I^{hr})_{i,j} - G_{\theta_G}(I^d)_{i,j})^2, \tag{4}$$

where W, H denote the size of the generated output image and F is a function that maps the corresponding original HR image I^{hr} to the output resolution. For High-to-Low, this function is implemented using an average pooling layer, while, for Low-To-High, it is simply the identity function.

3.6 Training

To crop all facial images in a consistent manner, we ran the face detector [38] on all datasets. To further increase the diversity, we augmented the data during training by applying random image flipping, scaling, rotation and colour jittering. In order to train the Low-to-High network, we generated on-the-fly LR images, each time providing as input a different random noise vector to High-to-Low, sampled from a normal distribution, in order to simulate a large variety of image degradation types. Both the High-to-Low and Low-to-High networks were trained for 200 epochs (about 570,000 generator updates), with an update ratio 5:1 between the discriminator and the generator. In the end, we fine-tuned them together for another 2,000 generator updates. The learning rate was kept to $1e-4$ for the entire duration of the training process. We used $\alpha = 1$ and $\beta = 0.05$ in Eq. 1. All of our models were trained using PyTorch [39] and optimized with Adam [40] ($\beta_1 = 0$ and $\beta_2 = 0.9$).

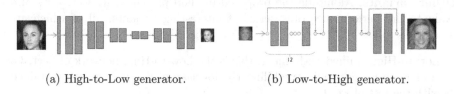

(a) High-to-Low generator.   (b) Low-to-High generator.

Fig. 4. The generator architecture used for the (a) High-to-Low and (b) Low-to-High networks. The residual block used is shown in Fig. 6b.

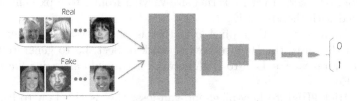

Fig. 5. The discriminator architecture used for both High-to-Low and Low-to-High networks. Note that, for High-to-Low, the first two max-pooling layers are omitted since the input resolution is 16×16. The residual block used is shown in Fig. 6a.

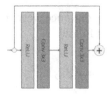   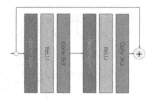

(a) Residual block with pre-activation and without batchnorm.

(b) Residual block with pre-activation and batch normalization as defined in [33].

Fig. 6. The residual blocks used for the discriminator (a) and the generator (b).

4   Results

In this section, we evaluate the performance of our system, and compare it with that of a few interesting variants and related state-of-the-art methods. Our main results are on the 3,000 images of our LR test set which contains images from the Widerface dataset. For this experiment, and because there are no corresponding ground-truth HR images, besides visual results, we numerically assess the quality of the generated samples using the Fréchet Inception Distance (FID) [41]. Finally, for completeness, we also provide PSNR results on 1,000 test images from the LS3D-W dataset using bilinearly downsampled images as input. This is the standard super-resolution experimental setting used in prior work.

4.1   Methods Compared

Other variants. Alongside the proposed method presented in Sect. 3, we also evaluate the performance of a series of interesting variants, all of which are detailed as follows:

1. Low-to-High-trained-on-bilinear: this is the Low-to-High network of Sect. 3.4 trained on images that were bilinearly downsampled. The network is trained with the loss of Eq. 1.
2. Low-to-High-trained-on-bilinear-blur: this is the Low-to-High network of Sect. 3.4 trained on bilinearly downsampled images after being blurred with a random blur kernel with a kernel size varying from 2 to 6 px. The network is trained with the loss of Eq. 1.
3. Low-to-High+Low-to-High-pixel-loss: this is the Low-to-High network of Sect. 3.4 that uses the High-to-Low network of Sect. 3.3 to generate the LR training samples. The Low-to-High network is trained *only using the L_2 pixel loss* in Eq. 4.
4. Low-to-High+High-to-Low-pixel-and-gan-loss: this is the Low-to-High network of Sect. 3.4 that uses the High-to-Low network of Sect. 3.3 to generate the LR training samples. The network is trained using the loss defined in Eq. 1. *This is the full implementation of the proposed method.*

Table 1. (a) FID-based performance on our real-world LR test set. Lower is better. (b) PSNR results on LS3D-W (the input LR images are bilinearly downsampled images).

Method	FID	PSNR
	LR test set	LS3D-W
SRGAN [2]	104.80	23.19
CycleGan [3]	19.01	16.10
DeepDeblur [43]	294.96	19.62
Wavelet-SRNet [20]	149.46	**23.98**
FSRNet [42]	157.29	19.45
Low-to-High (trained on bilinear)	85.59	23.50
Low-to-High (trained on blur + bilinear)	84.68	22.87
High-to-Low+Low-to-High (pixel loss only)	87.91	23.22
Ours	**14.89**	19.30

State-of-the-Art. Our method is compared both numerically and qualitatively with 5 related state-of-the-art methods: 1 image super-resolution method, namely SRGAN [2], 2 face super-resolution methods, namely Wavelet-SRNet [20] and FSRNet [42], 1 unpaired image translation method, namely CycleGan [3], and 1 deblurring method, namely DeepDeblur [43]. SRGAN and Wavelet-SRNet were trained on our training set using pairs of bilinearly downsampled - HR images. FSRNet provides only testing code (trained on their dataset using pairs of bilinearly downsampled - HR images). CycleGan was trained similarly to our method. Finally, for DeepDeblur we had 2 options: either use the pre-trained model trained on their data (pairs of blurred - clear images) or re-train it on our training set using pairs of bilinearly downsampled - HR images. The latter option would make it very similar to SRGAN, hence we used the former option.

4.2   Super-Resolution Results

Quantitative results on our LR test set in terms of FID are shown in Table 1. Qualitative results for several images are shown in Figs. 7 and 8. The visual results for *all 3,000* test images can be found in the supplementary material. Moreover, we provide PSNR results on LS3D-W in Table 1. Our method clearly outperforms all other variants and methods considered both numerically (in terms of FID) and (more importantly) visually.

Comparison with Other Variants. As expected, the Low-to-High trained on bilinearly downsampled images (Low-to-High-trained-on-bilinear) does not perform well and neither does the Low-to-High trained on bilinearly downsampled images after blurring them with various blur kernels (Low-to-High-trained-on-bilinear-blur). Overall, the results obtained by these methods are both noisy and blurry. Because of this, we propose to learn the noise distribution from Widerface images using the High-to-Low network. Directly training however such network

Fig. 7. Detailed qualitative results on our LR test set from Widerface. The methods compared are described in Sect. 4.1.

using an L_2 pixel loss does not work well (Low-to-High+Low-to-High-pixel-loss). We conclude that the L_2 loss alone is not able to denoise the input and produce good results. However, once the GAN loss (proposed method) is added, the network is successfully able to both (a) produce high quality samples and (b) denoise the images for most of the cases.

In addition to the above results, we also tried to quantify how close the generated by the High-to-Low network images resemble the original LR images from Widerface. To this end, their FID was found equal to 15.27 while the FID between bilinearly downsampled and original LR images was found equal to 23.15. This result clearly illustrates the effectiveness of the proposed High-to-Low network in producing images that faithfully represent real-world degradations.

Comparison with the State-of-the-Art. In terms of FID, our method largely outperforms all other methods. Moreover, from Figs. 7 and 8, we observe that our method produces the most appealing visual results. Both results show that, in

Fig. 8. Additional qualitative results on our LR test set from Widerface. The methods compared are described in Sect. 4.1.

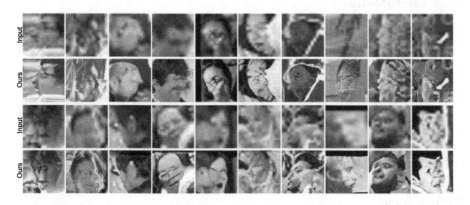

Fig. 9. Examples of failure cases. The input images are shown in the first and third row while the output images produced by our method in the second and fourth row, respectively. The images shown in the second row do not resemble a face. The images in the fourth row do resemble a face but they are heavily distorted.

contrary to all other methods considered, our High-to-Low network can model the image degradation in real LR datasets. Although CycleGan also achieves relatively low FID, from Figs. 7 and 8, it can be observed that visually the produced results are of low quality. This is because the cycle consistency loss emphasizes too much on pixel-level similarity, creating a lot of noise artifacts in the final output.

Finally, regarding our experiment on LS3D-W, as all other methods were trained on pairs of bilinearly downsampled and original HR images, they have an advantage and outperform our method. Our method however (trained using the output of High-to-Low) provides competitive results (PSNR $\approx$ 20 dB).

4.3   Failure Cases

By no-means we claim that the proposed method solves the real-world image and face super-resolution problem. We show several failure cases of our method in Fig. 9. We can group failures into two groups: the first one contains cases of complete failures where the produced image does not resemble a face. For many of these cases, we note that the input does not resemble a face either. Examples of these cases are shown in the first two rows of Fig. 9. The second group contains cases that the produced super-resolved face is distorted. These are mostly cases of extreme blur, occlusion and large pose. Examples of these cases are shown in the last two rows of Fig. 9. We need to emphasize here that many of the large pose facial images of the HR dataset used for training are synthetically warped into these poses (see [30]), and this is expected to have some negative impact on performance. In total, we found that the percentage of fail cases in our test set is about 10%.

5   Conclusions

We presented a method for image and face super-resolution which does not assume as input artificially generated LR images but aims to produce good results when applied to real-world, LR, low quality images. To this end, we proposed a two-stage process which firstly uses a High-to-Low network to learn how to downgrade high-resolution images requiring only *unpaired* high- and low-resolution images and uses the output of this network to train a Low-to-High network for image super-resolution. We showed that our pipeline can be used to effectively increase the quality of real-world LR images. We reported large improvement over baselines and prior work.

References

1. Yang, S., Luo, P., Loy, C.C., Tang, X.: Wider face: a face detection benchmark. In: CVPR (2016)
2. Ledig, C., et al.: Photo-realistic single image super-resolution using a generative adversarial network. In: CVPR (2017)

3. Zhu, J.Y., Park, T., Isola, P., Efros, A.A.: Unpaired image-to-image translation using cycle-consistent adversarial networks. In: ICCV (2017)
4. Timofte, R., et al.: Ntire 2017 challenge on single image super-resolution: methods and results. In: CVPR-W (2017)
5. Shocher, A., Cohen, N., Irani, M.: "Zero-shot" super-resolution using deep internal learning. arXiv (2017)
6. Dong, C., Loy, C.C., He, K., Tang, X.: Image super-resolution using deep convolutional networks. IEEE TPAMI (2016)
7. Kim, J., Kwon Lee, J., Mu Lee, K.: Accurate image super-resolution using very deep convolutional networks. In: CVPR (2016)
8. Johnson, J., Alahi, A., Fei-Fei, L.: Perceptual losses for real-time style transfer and super-resolution. In: Leibe, B., Matas, J., Sebe, N., Welling, M. (eds.) ECCV 2016. LNCS, vol. 9906, pp. 694–711. Springer, Cham (2016). https://doi.org/10.1007/978-3-319-46475-6_43
9. Simonyan, K., Zisserman, A.: Very deep convolutional networks for large-scale image recognition. arXiv (2014)
10. Lai, W.S., Huang, J.B., Ahuja, N., Yang, M.H.: Deep Laplacian pyramid networks for fast and accurate super-resolution. In: CVPR (2017)
11. Tai, Y., Yang, J., Liu, X.: Image super-resolution via deep recursive residual network. In: CVPR (2017)
12. Tong, T., Li, G., Liu, X., Gao, Q.: Image super-resolution using dense skip connections. In: ICCV (2017)
13. Goodfellow, I., et al.: Generative adversarial nets. In: NIPS, pp. 2672–2680 (2014)
14. Lim, B., Son, S., Kim, H., Nah, S., Lee, K.M.: Enhanced deep residual networks for single image super-resolution. In: CVPR-W (2017)
15. Sajjadi, M.S., Scholkopf, B., Hirsch, M.: EnhanceNet: single image super-resolution through automated texture synthesis. In: ICCV (2017)
16. Dahl, R., Norouzi, M., Shlens, J.: Pixel recursive super resolution. In: ICCV (2017)
17. van den Oord, A., Kalchbrenner, N., Kavukcuoglu, K.: Pixel recurrent neural networks. arXiv (2016)
18. Yu, X., Porikli, F.: Hallucinating very low-resolution unaligned and noisy face images by transformative discriminative autoencoders. In: CVPR (2017)
19. Cao, Q., Lin, L., Shi, Y., Liang, X., Li, G.: Attention-aware Face Hallucination via deep reinforcement learning. In: CVPR (2017)
20. Huang, H., He, R., Sun, Z., Tan, T.: Wavelet-SRNet: a wavelet-based CNN for multi-scale face super resolution. In: ICCV (2017)
21. Zhu, S., Liu, S., Loy, C.C., Tang, X.: Deep cascaded bi-network for Face Hallucination. In: Leibe, B., Matas, J., Sebe, N., Welling, M. (eds.) ECCV 2016. LNCS, vol. 9909, pp. 614–630. Springer, Cham (2016). https://doi.org/10.1007/978-3-319-46454-1_37
22. Yu, X., Porikli, F.: Ultra-resolving face images by discriminative generative networks. In: Leibe, B., Matas, J., Sebe, N., Welling, M. (eds.) ECCV 2016. LNCS, vol. 9909, pp. 318–333. Springer, Cham (2016). https://doi.org/10.1007/978-3-319-46454-1_20
23. Yang, C.Y., Liu, S., Yang, M.H.: Structured Face Hallucination. In: CVPR (2013)
24. Liu, Z., Luo, P., Wang, X., Tang, X.: Deep learning face attributes in the wild. In: ICCV (2015)
25. Le, V., Brandt, J., Lin, Z., Bourdev, L., Huang, T.S.: Interactive facial feature localization. In: Fitzgibbon, A., Lazebnik, S., Perona, P., Sato, Y., Schmid, C. (eds.) ECCV 2012. LNCS, vol. 7574, pp. 679–692. Springer, Heidelberg (2012). https://doi.org/10.1007/978-3-642-33712-3_49

26. Huang, G.B., Ramesh, M., Berg, T., Learned-Miller, E.: Labeled faces in the wild: a database for studying face recognition in unconstrained environments. Technical report 07–49, University of Massachusetts, Amherst, October 2007
27. Jesorsky, O., Kirchberg, K.J., Frischholz, R.W.: Robust face detection using the Hausdorff distance. In: Bigun, J., Smeraldi, F. (eds.) AVBPA 2001. LNCS, vol. 2091, pp. 90–95. Springer, Heidelberg (2001). https://doi.org/10.1007/3-540-45344-X_14
28. Bulat, A., Tzimiropoulos, G.: Super-FAN: integrated facial landmark localization and super-resolution of real-world low resolution faces in arbitrary poses with GANs. arXiv (2017)
29. Köstinger, M., Wohlhart, P., Roth, P.M., Bischof, H.: Annotated facial landmarks in the wild: a large-scale, real-world database for facial landmark localization. In: ICCV-W (2011)
30. Bulat, A., Tzimiropoulos, G.: How far are we from solving the 2D & 3D face alignment problem? (and a dataset of 230,000 3D facial landmarks). In: ICCV (2017)
31. Cao, Q., Shen, L., Xie, W., Parkhi, O.M., Zisserman, A.: VGGFace2: a dataset for recognising faces across pose and age. In: FG (2018)
32. He, K., Zhang, X., Ren, S., Sun, J.: Deep residual learning for image recognition. In: CVPR (2016)
33. He, K., Zhang, X., Ren, S., Sun, J.: Identity mappings in deep residual networks. In: Leibe, B., Matas, J., Sebe, N., Welling, M. (eds.) ECCV 2016. LNCS, vol. 9908, pp. 630–645. Springer, Cham (2016). https://doi.org/10.1007/978-3-319-46493-0_38
34. Mirza, M., Osindero, S.: Conditional generative adversarial nets. arXiv (2014)
35. Gulrajani, I., Ahmed, F., Arjovsky, M., Dumoulin, V., Courville, A.: Improved training of wasserstein GANs. arXiv (2017)
36. Miyato, T., Kataoka, T., Koyama, M., Yoshida, Y.: Spectral normalization for generative adversarial networks. arXiv (2018)
37. Arjovsky, M., Chintala, S., Bottou, L.: Wasserstein GAN. arXiv (2017)
38. Zhang, S., Zhu, X., Lei, Z., Shi, H., Wang, X., Li, S.Z.: S 3FD: single shot scale-invariant face detector. In: ICCV (2017)
39. Paszke, A., Gross, S., Chintal, S.: Pytorch. http://github.com/pytorch/pytorch
40. Kingma, D.P., Ba, J.: Adam: a method for stochastic optimization. arXiv (2014)
41. Heusel, M., Ramsauer, H., Unterthiner, T., Nessler, B., Hochreiter, S.: GANs trained by a two time-scale update rule converge to a local nash equilibrium. In: NIPS (2017)
42. Chen, Y., Tai, Y., Liu, X., Shen, C., Yang, J.: FSRNet: end-to-end learning face super-resolution with facial priors. In: CVPR (2018)
43. Nah, S., Kim, T.H., Lee, K.M.: Deep multi-scale convolutional neural network for dynamic scene deblurring. In: CVPR (2017)

FloorNet: A Unified Framework for Floorplan Reconstruction from 3D Scans

Chen Liu[1]([✉]), Jiaye Wu[1], and Yasutaka Furukawa[2]

[1] Washington University in St. Louis, St. Louis, USA
{chenliu,jiaye.wu}@wustl.edu
[2] Simon Fraser University, Burnaby, Canada
furukawa@sfu.ca

Abstract. This paper proposes a novel deep neural architecture that automatically reconstructs a floorplan by walking through a house with a smartphone, an ultimate goal of indoor mapping research. The challenge lies in the processing of RGBD streams spanning a large 3D space. The proposed neural architecture, dubbed FloorNet, effectively processes the data through three neural network branches: (1) PointNet with 3D points, exploiting 3D information; (2) CNN with a 2D point density image in a top-down view, enhancing local spatial reasoning; and (3) CNN with RGB images, utilizing full image information. FloorNet exchanges intermediate features across the branches to exploit all the architectures. We have created a benchmark for floorplan reconstruction by acquiring RGBD video streams for 155 residential houses or apartments with Google Tango phones and annotating complete floorplan information. Our qualitative and quantitative evaluations demonstrate that the fusion of three branches effectively improves the reconstruction quality. We hope that the paper together with the benchmark will be an important step towards solving a challenging vector-graphics floorplan reconstruction problem.

Keywords: Floorplan reconstruction · 3D Computer Vision · 3D CNN

1 Introduction

Architectural floorplans play a crucial role in designing, understanding, and remodeling indoor spaces. Their drawings are effective in conveying geometric and semantic information of a scene. For instance, we can quickly identify room extents, the locations of doors, or object arrangements. We can also recognize the types of rooms, doors, or objects easily through texts or icon styles. Unfortunately, more than 90% of houses in North America do not have floorplans. The ultimate goal of indoor mapping research is to enable automatic reconstruction of a floorplan simply by walking through a house with a smartphone.

C. Liu and J. Wu—The first two authors contribute equally on this work.

© Springer Nature Switzerland AG 2018
V. Ferrari et al. (Eds.): ECCV 2018, LNCS 11210, pp. 203–219, 2018.
https://doi.org/10.1007/978-3-030-01231-1_13

The Consumer-grade depth sensors have revolutionized indoor 3D scanning with successful products. Matterport [1] produces detailed texture mapped models of indoor spaces by acquiring a set of panorama RGBD images with a specialized hardware. Google Project Tango phones [14] convert RGBD image streams into 3D or 2D models. These systems produce detailed geometry, but fall short as floorplans or architectural blue-prints, whose geometry must be concise and respect underlying scene segmentation and semantics.

Reconstruction of the floorplan for an entire house or an apartment with multiple rooms poses fundamental challenges to existing techniques due to its large 3D extent. A standard approach projects 3D information onto a 2D lateral domain [10], losing the information of height. PointNet [26,28] consumes 3D information directly but suffers from the lack of local neighborhood structures. A multi-view representation [27,34] avoids explicit 3D space modeling, but has been mostly demonstrated for objects, rather than large scenes and complex camera motions. 3D Convolutional Neural Networks (CNNs) [29,36] also show promising results but have been so far limited to objects or small-scale scenes.

This paper proposes a novel deep neural network (DNN) architecture Floor-Net, which turns a RGBD video covering a large 3D space into pixel-wise predictions on floorplan geometry and semantics, followed by an existing Integer Programming formulation [17] to recover vector-graphics floorplans. FloorNet consists of three DNN branches. The first branch employs PointNet with 3D points, exploiting the 3D information. The second branch uses a CNN with a 2D point density image in a top-down floorplan view, enhancing the local spatial reasoning. The third branch uses a CNN with RGB images, utilizing the full image information. The PointNet branch and the point-density branch exchange features between the 3D points and their corresponding cells in the top-down view. The image branch contributes deep image features into the corresponding cells in the top-down view. This hybrid DNN design exploits the best of all the architectures and effectively processes the full RGBD video covering a large 3D scene with complex camera motions.

We have created a benchmark for floorplan reconstruction by acquiring RGBD video streams for 155 residential houses or apartments with Google Tango phones and annotated their complete floorplan information including architectural structures, icons, and room types. Extensive qualitative and quantitative evaluates demonstrate the effectiveness of our approach over competing methods.

In summary, the main contributions of this paper are two-fold: (1) Novel hybrid DNN architecture for RGBD videos, which processes the 3D coordinates directly, models local spatial structures in the 2D domain, and incorporates the full image information; and (2) A new floorplan reconstruction benchmark with RGBD videos, where many indoor scene databases exist [1,4,33] but none tackles a vector-graphics reconstruction problem, which has immediate impact on digital mapping, real estate, or civil engineering applications.

2   Related Work

We discuss the related work in three domains: indoor scene reconstruction, 3D deep learning, and indoor scan datasets.

Indoor Scene Reconstruction: The advancements in consumer-grade depth sensors have brought revolutionary changes to indoor 3D scanning. KinectFusion [23] enables high-fidelity 3D scanning for objects and small-scale scenes. Whelan et al. [40] extends the work to building-scale scans. While being accurate with details, these dense reconstructions fall short as CAD models, which must have (1) concise geometry for efficient data transmission and (2) proper segmentations/semantics for architectural analysis or effective visualization.

Towards CAD-quality reconstructions, researchers have applied model-based approaches by representing a scene with geometric primitives. Utilizing the 2.5D property of indoor building structures, rooms can be separated by fitting lines to points in a top-down view [25,35,37]. Primitive types have been extended to planes [5,6,22,31,43] or cuboids [42]. While they produce promising results for selected scans, their heuristic-based primitive detection faces challenges with noisy and incomplete 3D data. Our approach conducts global analysis of the entire input by DNNs to detect primitive structures much more robustly.

Another line of research studies the top-down scene reconstruction with shape grammars from a single image [47] or a set of panorama RGBD images [10,21]. Crowdsensing data such as images and WiFi-fingerprints are also exploited in building scene graphs [7,8,12,19]. While semantic segmentation [4,26,28] and scene understanding [45] are popular for indoor scenes, there has been no robust learning-based method for vector-graphics floorplan reconstruction. This paper provides such a method and its benchmark with the ground-truth.

One way to recover the mentioned vector-graphics floorplan models is from rasterized floorplan images [17]. We share the same reconstruction target, and we utilize their Integer Programming formulation in our last step to recover the final floorplan. Nevertheless, instead of a single image as input, our input is a RGBD video covering a large 3D space, which requires a fundamentally different approach to process the input data effectively.

3D Deep Learning: The success of CNN on 2D images has inspired research on 3D feature learning via DNNs. Volumetric CNNs [20,27,41] are straightforward extensions of CNN to a 3D domain, but there are two main challenges: (1) data sparsity and (2) computational cost of 3D convolutions. FPNN [15] and Vote3D [38] attempt to solve the first challenge, while OctNet [29] and O-CNN [39] address the computational costs via octree representations.

2D CNNs with multi-view renderings have been successful for object recognition [27,34] and part segmentation [16]. They effectively utilize all the image information but are so far limited to regular (or fixed) camera arrangements. The extension to larger scenes with complex camera motions is not trivial.

PointNet [26] directly uses 3D point coordinates to exploit the sparsity and avoid quantization errors, but it does not provide an explicit local spatial reasoning. PointNet++ [28] hierarchically groups points and adds spatial structures by farthest point sampling. Kd-Networks [13] similarly group points by a KD-tree. These techniques incur additional computational expenses due to the grouping and have been limited at object-scale. For scenes, they need to split the space into smaller regions (e.g., $1\,\mathrm{m} \times 1\,\mathrm{m}$ blocks) and process each region independently [26,28], hurting global reasoning (e.g., identifying long walls for corridors).

Indoor Scan Dataset: Affordable depth sensing hardware enables researchers to build many indoor scan datasets. The ETH3D dataset contains only 16 indoor scans [30], and its purpose is for multi-view stereo rather than 3D point-cloud processing. The ScanNet dataset [4] and the SceneNN dataset [9] capture a variety of indoor scenes. However, most of their scans contain only one or two rooms, not suitable for the floorplan reconstruction problem.

Matterport3D [3] builds high quality panorama RGBD image sets for 90 luxurious houses. 2D-3D-S dataset [2] provides 6 large-scale indoor scans of office spaces by using the same Matterport camera. However, they focus on 2D and 3D semantic annotations, and do not address a vector-graphics reconstruction problem. Meanwhile, they require an expensive specialized hardware (i.e., Matterport camera) for high-fidelity 3D scanning, while we aim to tackle the challenge by consumer-grade smartphones with low data quality.

Lastly, a large-scale synthetic dataset, SUNCG [32], offers a variety of indoor scenes with CAD-quality geometry and annotations. However, they are synthetic and cannot model the complexity of real scenes or replace the real photographs. We provide the benchmark with full floorplan annotations and the corresponding RGBD videos from smartphones for 155 residential units.

3   FloorNet

The proposed FloorNet converts a RGBD video with camera poses into pixel-wise floorplan geometry and semantics information, which is an intermediate floorplan representation introduced by Liu et al. [17]. We first explain the intermediate representation for being self-contained, then provide the details.

3.1   Preliminaries

The intermediate representation consists of the geometry and the semantics information. The geometry part contains room-corners, object icon-corners, and door/window end-points, where the locations of each corner/point type are estimated by a 256×256 heatmap in the 2D floorplan image domain, followed by a standard non-maximum suppression. For example, a room corner is either I-, L-, T-, or X-shaped depending on the number of incident walls, making the total number of feature maps to be 13 considering their rotational variants. The semantics part is modeled as (1) 12 feature maps as a probability distribution function (PDF) over 12 room types, and (2) 8 feature maps as a PDF over 8 icon types. We follow their approach and use their Integer Programming formulation to reconstruct a floorplan from this representation at the end.

3.2 Triple-Branch Hybrid Design

Floornet consists of three DNN branches. We employ existing DNN architectures in each branch without modifications. Our contribution lies in its hybrid design: how to combine them and share intermediate features (See Fig. 1).

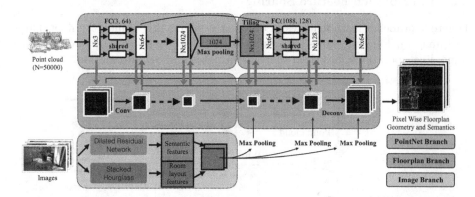

Fig. 1. FloorNet consists of three DNN branches. The first branch uses PointNet [26] to directly consume 3D information. The second branch takes a top-down point density image in a floorplan domain with a fully convolutional network [18], and produces pixel-wise geometry and semantics information. The third branch produces deep image features by a dilated residual network trained on the semantic segmentation task [44] as well as a stacked hourglass CNN trained on the room layout estimation [24]. The PointNet branch and the floorplan branch exchanges intermediate features at every layer, while the image branch contributes deep image features into the decoding part of the floorplan branch. This hybrid DNN architecture effectively processes an input RGBD video with camera poses, covering a large 3D space.

PointNet Branch: The first branch is PointNet [26] with the original architecture except that each 3D point is represented by XYZ and RGB values without the normalized position. We randomly subsample 50,000 points for each data. We manually rectify the rotation and align the gravity direction with the Z-axis. We add translation to move the center of mass to the origin.

Floorplan Branch: The second branch is a fully convolutional network (FCN) [18] with skip connections between the encoder and the decoder, which takes a point-density image with RGB values in the top-down view. The RGB value in each cell is computed as the average over the 3D points. We compute a 2D axis-aligned bounding box of the Manhattan-rectified 3D points to define a rectangular floorplan domain, while ignoring the 2.5% outlier points and expanding the rectangle by 5% in each of the four directions. The rectangle is placed in the middle of the 256×256 square image in which the geometry and semantics feature maps are produced. The input to the branch is a point-density image in the same domain.

Image Branch: The third branch computes deep image features through two CNN architectures: (1) Dilated residual network (DRN) [44] trained on semantic segmentation using the ScanNet dataset [4]; and (2) stacked hourglass CNN (SH) [24] trained on room layout estimation using the LSUN dataset [46].

3.3   Inter-branch Feature Sharing

Different branches learn features in different domains (3D points, the floorplan, and images). Figure 2 shows three inter-branch feature sharing by pooling and unpooling operations, based on the camera poses and 3D information.

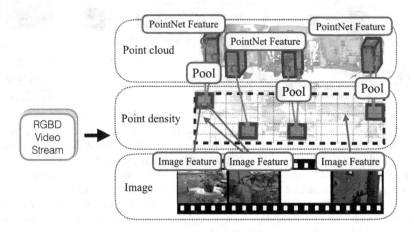

Fig. 2. FloorNet shares features across branches to exploit the best of all the architectures. PointNet features at 3D points are pooled into corresponding 2D cells in the floorplan branch. Floorplan features at 2D cells are unpooled to the corresponding 3D points in the PointNet branch. Deep image features are pooled into corresponding 2D cells in the floorplan branch, based on the depthmap and the camera pose information.

PointNet to Floorplan Pooling: This pooling module takes features of unordered points from each layer of the PointNet branch and produces a 2D top-down feature map in the corresponding layer of the floorplan branch. The module simply projects 3D point features into cells in the floorplan feature map, then aggregates the features in each cell by either summation or maximum operation. We use the summation operation in the first three convolution layers to keep more information while taking the maximum in the rest layers to introduce competition. A constructed feature map has the same dimension as the feature map in the floorplan branch. We have explored several different aggregation schemes between the feature map from the pointnet branch and the feature map at the floorplan branch. We found that a sum-pooling (i.e., element-wise addition) works the best. The time complexity of the projection pooling module is linear in the number of 3D points.

Floorplan to PointNet Unpooling: This module reverses the above pooling operation. It simply copies and adds a feature of the floorplan cell into each of the corresponding 3D points that project inside the cell. The time complexity is again linear in the number of points.

Table 1. Dataset statistics. From left to right: the number of rooms, the number of icons, the number of openings (i.e., doors or windows), the number of room-corners, and the total area. The average and the standard deviation are reported for each entry.

	#room	#icon	#opening	#corner	Area
Average	5.2	9.1	9.9	18.1	$63.8\,[\mathrm{m}^2]$
Std	1.8	4.5	2.9	4.2	$13.0\,[\mathrm{m}^2]$

Image to Floorplan Pooling: The image branch produces two deep image features of dimensions $512 \times 32 \times 32$ and $256 \times 64 \times 64$ from DRN and SH for each video frame. We first unproject image features to 3D points by their depthmaps and camera poses, then apply the same 3D to floorplan pooling above. One modification is that we use max-pooling at all the layers in projecting 3D points onto the floorplan domain to be simple, instead of the mix of sum and max poolings. The reason is that we use pre-trained models for image feature encoding, and more complex hybrid pooling would have less effects. We conduct the image branch pooling for every 10 frames in the video sequence.

3.4 Loss Functions

Our network outputs pixel-wise predictions on the floorplan geometry and semantics information in the same resolution 256×256. For geometry heatmaps (i.e., room corners, object icon-corners, and door/window end-points), a sigmoid cross entropy loss is used. The ground-truth heatmap is prepared by putting a value of 1.0 inside a disk of radius 11 pixels around each ground-truth pixel. For semantic classification feature maps (i.e., room types and object icon types), a pixel-wise softmax cross entropy loss is used.

4   Floorplan Reconstruction Benchmark

This paper creates a benchmark for the vector-graphics floorplan reconstruction problem from RGBD videos with camera poses. We have acquired roughly two-hundreds 3D scans of residential units in the United States and China using Google Tango phones (Lenovo Phab 2 Pro and Asus ZenFone AR) (See Fig. 3). After manually removing poor quality scans, we have annotated the complete floorplan information for the remaining 155 scans: (1) room-corners as points, (2) walls as pairs of room-corners, (3) object icons and types as axis-aligned rectangles and classification labels, 4) doors and windows (i.e., openings) as

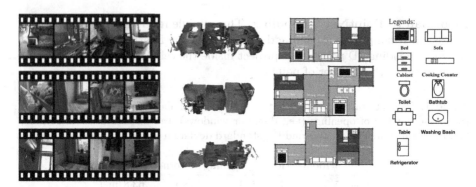

Fig. 3. Floorplan reconstruction benchmark. From left to right: subsampled video frames, colored 3D point clouds, and ground-truth floorplan data. The floorplan data is stored in a vector-graphics representation, which is visualized with a simple rendering engine (e.g., rooms are assigned different colors based on their types, and objects are shown as canonical icons). (Color figure online)

line-segments on walls, and 5) room types as classification labels for polygonal areas enclosed by walls. The list of object types is {*counter, bathtub, toilet, sink, sofa, cabinet, bed, table, refrigerator*}. The list of room types is {*living room, kitchen, bedroom, bathroom, closet, balcony, corridor, dining room*}. Table 1 provides statistics of our data collections.

Reconstructed floorplans are evaluated on three different levels of geometric and semantic consistency with the ground-truth. We follow the work by Liu et al. [17] and define the low- and mid-level metrics as follows.

- The low-level metric is the precision and recall of room corner detections. A corner detection is declared a success if its distance to the ground-truth is below 10 pixels and the closest among all the other room corners.
- The mid-level metric is the precision and recall of detected openings (i.e., doors and windows), object-icons, and rooms. The detection of an opening is declared a success if the largest distance of the corresponding end-points is less than 10 pixels. The detection of an object (resp. a room) is declared a success if the intersection-over-union (IOU) with the ground-truth is above 0.5 (resp. 0.7).
- Relationships of architectural components play crucial roles in evaluating indoor spaces. For example, one may look for apartments where bedrooms are not connected to a kitchen. A building code may enforce every bedroom to have a quick evacuation route to outside through windows or doors in case of fire. We introduce the high-level metric as the ratio of rooms that have the correct relationships with the neighboring rooms. More precisely, we declare that a room has a correct relationship if (1) it is connected to the correct set of rooms through doors, where two rooms are connected if their common walls contain at least one door, (2) the room has an IOU score larger than 0.5 with the corresponding ground-truth, and (3) the room has the correct room type.

5   Implementation Details

5.1   DNN Training

Among the 155 scans we collected, we randomly sample 135 for training and leave 20 for testing. We perform data augmentation by random scaling and rotation every time we feed a training sample. First, we apply rescaling to the point-cloud and the annotation with a random factor uniformly sampled from a range $[0.5, 1.5]$. Second, we randomly apply the rotation around the z axis by either $0°, 90°, 180°$, or $270°$.

We have utilized the official code for the two image encoders DRN [44] and SH [24]. We pre-trained DRN on the semantic segmentation task with ScanNet database [4] and SH on the room layout estimation task with LSUN [46]. DRN and SH are fixed during the FloorNet training. We implemented the remaining DNN modules by ourselves in TensorFlow with the modern APIs, that is, PointNet [26] for the Pointnet branch and FCN [18] for the Floorplan branch.

Training of FloorNet takes around 2 h with a TitanX GPU. We set the batch size to 6. FloorNet has three types of loss functions. To avoid overfitting with the icon loss, we trained icon-loss separately for at most 600 epochs with early-stopping based on the testing loss. The others losses are trained jointly for 600 epochs.[1] The training consumes $81,000 = 135(\text{samples}) \times 600(\text{epochs})$ augmented training samples. It is initially to our surprise that FloorNet generalizes even from a small number of 3D scans. However, FloorNet makes pixel-wise low-level predictions. Each 3D scan contains about 10 object-icons, 10 openings, and a few dozen room corners, which probably lead to the good generalization performance together with data augmentation, where similar phenomena were observed by Liu et al. [17].

5.2   Enhancement Heuristics

We augment the Integer Programming Formulation [17] with the following two enhancement heuristics to deal with more challenging input data (i.e., large-scale raw sensor data) and hence more noise in the network predictions.

Primitive Candidate Generation: Standard non-maximum suppression often detects multiple room corners around a single ground-truth. After thresholding the room-corner heatmap by a value 0.5, we simply extract the highest peak from each connected component, whose area is more than 5 pixels. To handle localization errors, we connect two room-corners and generate a wall candidate when their corresponding connected components overlap along X or Y direction. We do not augment junctions to keep the number of candidates tractable.

---

[1] We considered synthetic dataset SUNCG [32] and real dataset Matterport3D [3] for training with the icon loss, while using their semantic segmentation information to produce icon annotations. However, the joint-training still experiences overfitting, while this simple early-stopping heuristic works well in our experiments.

Objective Function: Wall and opening candidates are originally assigned uniform weights in the objective function [17]. We calculate the confidence of a wall (resp. opening) candidate by taking the average of the semantic heatmap scores of type "wall" along the line with width 7 pixels (resp. 5 pixels). We set the weight of each primitive by the confidence score minus 0.5, so that a primitive is encouraged to be chosen only when the confidence is at least 0.5.

6   Experiments

Figure 4 shows our reconstruction results on some representative examples. Our approach successfully recovers complex vector-graphics floorplan data including room geometries and their connectivities through doors. One of the major failure modes is in the icon detection, as object detection generally requires more training data than low-level geometry detection [17]. We believe that more training data will overcome this issue. Another typical failures come from missing room corners due to clutter or incomplete scanning. The successful reconstruction of a room requires successful detection of every room corner. This is a challenging problem and the introduction of higher level constraints may reveal a solution (Fig. 5).

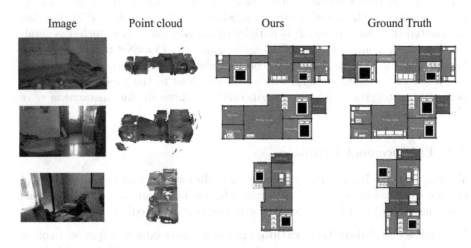

| Image | Point cloud | Ours | Ground Truth |

Fig. 4. Floorplan reconstruction results.

Figure 6 and Table 2 qualitatively and quantitatively compare our method against competing techniques, namely, OctNet [29], PointNet [26], and a few variants of our FloorNet. OctNet and PointNet represent state-of-the-art 3D DNNs. More precisely, we implement the voxel semantic segmentation network based on the official OctNet library,[2] which takes $256 \times 256 \times 256$ voxels as input and outputs 3D voxels of the same resolution. We then add three separate $5 \times 3 \times 3$ convolution layers with strides $4 \times 1 \times 1$ to predict the same pixel-wise geometry and

---

[2] OctNet library: https://github.com/griegler/octnet.

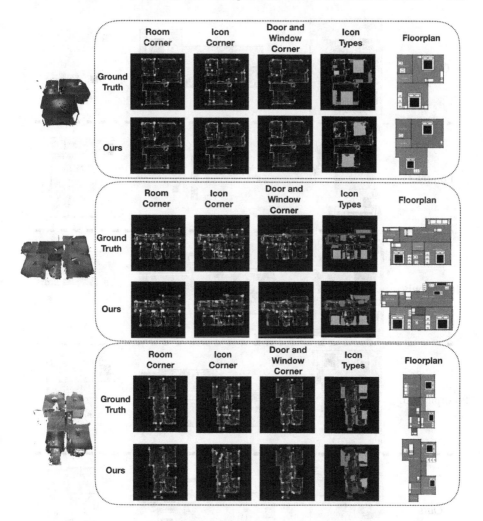

Fig. 5. Intermediate results. For each example, we show raw outputs of the networks (room corners, icon corners, opening corners, and icon types) compared against the ground-truth. In the second example, we produce a fake room (blue color) at the top due to poor quality 3D points. In the third example, reconstructed rooms have inaccurate shapes near the bottom left again due to noisy 3D points, illustrating the challenge of our problem. (Color figure online)

semantics feature-maps with the same set of loss functions. PointNet is simply our FloorNet without the point density or the image input. Similarly, we construct a FloorNet variant by enabling only the 3D points (for the PointNet branch) or the point density image (for the floorplan branch) as the input.

The table shows that the floorplan branch is the most informative as it is the most natural representation for floorplan reconstruction task, while PointNet

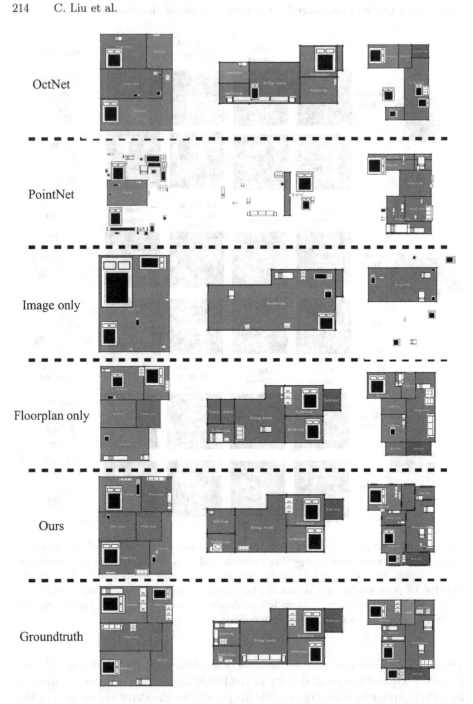

Fig. 6. Qualitative comparisons against competing methods. The top is OctNet [29], a state-of-the-art 3D CNN architecture. The next three rows show variants of our FloorNet, where only one branch is enabled. FloorNet with all the branches overall produce more complete and accurate floorplans.

Table 2. Quantitative evaluations on low-, mid-, and high-level metrics against competing methods and our variants. The orange and cyan color indicates the best and the second best result for each entry.

	Wall	Door	Icon	Room	Relationship
PointNet [26]	25.8/42.5	11.5/38.7	22.5/27.9	27.0/40.2	5.0
Floorplan-branch	90.2/88.7	70.5/78.0	43.4/42.8	76.3/75.3	50.0
Image-branch	40.0/83.3	15.4/47.1	21.4/17.4	25.0/57.1	0.0
OctNet [29]	75.4/89.2	36.6/82.3	32.8/48.8	62.1/72.0	13.5
Ours w/o PointNet-Unpooling	92.6/92.1	75.8/76.8	55.1/51.9	80.9/77.4	52.3
Ours w/o PointNet-Pooling	88.4/93.0	73.0/87.2	50.0/42.2	75.0/80.6	52.8
Ours w/o Image-Pooling	92.6/89.7	77.1/74.4	50.5/57.8	84.2/83.1	56.8
Ours	92.1/92.8	76.7/80.2	56.1/57.8	83.6/85.2	56.8

branch or Image branch alone does not work well. We also split the entire point clouds into 1 m × 1 m blocks, train the PointNet-only model that makes predictions per block separately, followed by a simple merging. However, this performs much worse. OctNet performs reasonably well across low- to mid-level metrics, but does poorly on the high-level metric, where all the rooms and relevant doors must be reconstructed at high precision to report good numbers.

To further evaluate the effectiveness of the proposed FloorNet architecture, we conduct ablation studies by disabling each of the inter-branch pooling/unpooling operations. The bottom of Table 2 shows that the feature sharing overall leads to better results, especially for mid- to high-level metrics.

Table 3 compares different inter-branch pooling/unpooling schemes for the PointNet to floorplan pooling. The table shows that the max operation in early layers loses too much information and leads to worse performance.

Finally, Fig. 7 compares against a build-in Tango Navigator App [11], which generates a floorplan image real-time on the phone. Note that their system does not (1) produce room segmentations, (2) recognize room types, (3) detect objects, (4) recognize object types, or (5) produce CAD-quality geometry. Therefore, we quantitatively evaluate only the geometry information by measuring the line distances between the ground-truth walls and predicted walls. More precisely, we (1) sample 100 points from each wall line segment, (2) for each sampled point, find the closest one in the other line segment, and (3) compute the mean distance over all the sampled points and line segments. The average line distances are 2.72 [pixels] and 1.66 [pixels] for Tango Navigator App and our FloorNet, respectively. This is a surprising result, because our algorithm

Table 3. In the PointNet to floorplan inter-branch pooling, we use a mix of sum and max pooling in projecting 3D points onto the 2D floorplan domain. To validate this hybrid scheme, we have also evaluated the performance when only the max-pooling or the sum-pooling is used at all the layers.

Pooling method	Wall	Door	Icon	Room	Relationship
Max	88.0/89.9	70.9/86.6	59.1/47.8	76.3/77.3	47.0
Sum	88.3/97.0	69.6/85.9	55.6/53.4	76.3/82.9	52.3
Sum/max (default)	92.1/92.8	76.7/80.2	56.1/57.8	83.6/85.2	56.8

drops many confident line segments during Integer Programming, when the corresponding room is not reconstructed. On the other hand, it is an expected result as our approach utilizes all the geometry and image information.

Fig. 7. Comparison against a commercial floorplan generator, Tango Navigator App. Top: floorplan image from Tango. Bottom: our results.

7   Conclusion

This paper proposes a novel DNN architecture FloorNet that reconstructs vector-graphics floorplans from RGBD videos with camera poses. FloorNet takes a hybrid approach and exploits the best of three DNN architectures to effectively process a RGBD video covering a large 3D space with complex camera motions. The paper also provides a new benchmark for a new vector-graphics reconstruction problem, which is missing in the recent indoor scene databases of Computer Vision. Two main future works are ahead of us. The first one is to learn to enforce higher level constraints inside DNNs as opposed to inside a separate post-processing (e.g., Integer Programming). Learning high-level constraints likely require more training data and the second future work is to acquire more scans.

More than 90% of houses in North America do not have floorplans. We hope that this paper together with the benchmark will be an important step towards solving this challenging vector-graphics reconstruction problem, and enabling the reconstruction of a floorplan just by walking through a house with a smartphone. We publicly share our code and data to promote further research.

Acknowledgement. This research is partially supported by National Science Foundation under grant IIS 1540012 and IIS 1618685, Google Faculty Research Award, Adobe gift fund, and Zillow gift fund. We thank Nvidia for a generous GPU donation.

References

1. Matterport. https://matterport.com/
2. Armeni, I., et al.: 3D semantic parsing of large-scale indoor spaces. In: Proceedings of the IEEE Conference on Computer Vision and Pattern Recognition, pp. 1534–1543 (2016)
3. Chang, A., et al.: Matterport3D: learning from RGB-D data in indoor environments. arXiv preprint arXiv:1709.06158 (2017)
4. Dai, A., Chang, A.X., Savva, M., Halber, M., Funkhouser, T., Nießner, M.: ScanNet: richly-annotated 3D reconstructions of indoor scenes. In: Proceedings of IEEE Conference on Computer Vision and Pattern Recognition (CVPR), vol. 1 (2017)
5. Furukawa, Y., Curless, B., Seitz, S.M., Szeliski, R.: Manhattan-world stereo. In: IEEE Conference on Computer Vision and Pattern Recognition, CVPR 2009, pp. 1422–1429. IEEE (2009)
6. Furukawa, Y., Curless, B., Seitz, S.M., Szeliski, R.: Reconstructing building interiors from images. In: 2009 IEEE 12th International Conference on Computer Vision, pp. 80–87. IEEE (2009)
7. Gao, R., et al.: Multi-story indoor floor plan reconstruction via mobile crowdsensing. IEEE Trans. Mob. Comput. **15**(6), 1427–1442 (2016)
8. Gao, R., et al.: Jigsaw: indoor floor plan reconstruction via mobile crowdsensing. In: Proceedings of the 20th Annual International Conference on Mobile Computing and Networking, pp. 249–260. ACM (2014)
9. Hua, B.S., Pham, Q.H., Nguyen, D.T., Tran, M.K., Yu, L.F., Yeung, S.K.: SceneNN: a scene meshes dataset with annotations. In: 2016 Fourth International Conference on 3D Vision (3DV), pp. 92–101. IEEE (2016)
10. Ikehata, S., Yang, H., Furukawa, Y.: Structured indoor modeling. In: Proceedings of the IEEE International Conference on Computer Vision, pp. 1323–1331 (2015)
11. Google Inc.: Project tango. https://developers.google.com/tango/
12. Jiang, Y., et al.: Hallway based automatic indoor floorplan construction using room fingerprints. In: Proceedings of the 2013 ACM International Joint Conference on Pervasive and Ubiquitous Computing, pp. 315–324. ACM (2013)
13. Klokov, R., Lempitsky, V.: Escape from cells: deep KD-networks for the recognition of 3D point cloud models. In: 2017 IEEE International Conference on Computer Vision (ICCV), pp. 863–872. IEEE (2017)
14. Lee, J., Dugan, R., et al.: Google project tango
15. Li, Y., Pirk, S., Su, H., Qi, C.R., Guibas, L.J.: FPNN: field probing neural networks for 3D data. In: Advances in Neural Information Processing Systems, pp. 307–315 (2016)

16. Limberger, F.A., et al.: SHREC'17 track: point-cloud shape retrieval of non-rigid toys. In: 10th Eurographics Workshop on 3D Object Retrieval, pp. 1–11 (2017)
17. Liu, C., Wu, J., Kohli, P., Furukawa, Y.: Raster-to-vector: revisiting floorplan transformation. In: Proceedings of the IEEE Conference on Computer Vision and Pattern Recognition, pp. 2195–2203 (2017)
18. Long, J., Shelhamer, E., Darrell, T.: Fully convolutional networks for semantic segmentation. In: Proceedings of the IEEE Conference on Computer Vision and Pattern Recognition, pp. 3431–3440 (2015)
19. Luo, H., Zhao, F., Jiang, M., Ma, H., Zhang, Y.: Constructing an indoor floor plan using crowdsourcing based on magnetic fingerprinting. Sensors 17(11), 2678 (2017)
20. Maturana, D., Scherer, S.: VoxNet: a 3D convolutional neural network for real-time object recognition. In: 2015 IEEE/RSJ International Conference on Intelligent Robots and Systems (IROS), pp. 922–928. IEEE (2015)
21. Mura, C., Mattausch, O., Pajarola, R.: Piecewise-planar reconstruction of multi-room interiors with arbitrary wall arrangements. In: Computer Graphics Forum, vol. 35, pp. 179–188. Wiley Online Library (2016)
22. Mura, C., Mattausch, O., Villanueva, A.J., Gobbetti, E., Pajarola, R.: Automatic room detection and reconstruction in cluttered indoor environments with complex room layouts. Comput. Graph. 44, 20–32 (2014)
23. Newcombe, R.A., et al.: KinectFusion: real-time dense surface mapping and tracking. In: 2011 10th IEEE International Symposium on Mixed and Augmented Reality (ISMAR), pp. 127–136. IEEE (2011)
24. Newell, A., Yang, K., Deng, J.: Stacked hourglass networks for human pose estimation. In: Leibe, B., Matas, J., Sebe, N., Welling, M. (eds.) ECCV 2016. LNCS, vol. 9912, pp. 483–499. Springer, Cham (2016). https://doi.org/10.1007/978-3-319-46484-8_29
25. Okorn, B., Xiong, X., Akinci, B., Huber, D.: Toward automated modeling of floor plans. In: Proceedings of the Symposium on 3D Data Processing, Visualization and Transmission, vol. 2 (2010)
26. Qi, C.R., Su, H., Mo, K., Guibas, L.J.: PointNet: deep learning on point sets for 3D classification and segmentation. arXiv preprint arXiv:1612.00593 (2016)
27. Qi, C.R., Su, H., Nießner, M., Dai, A., Yan, M., Guibas, L.J.: Volumetric and multi-view CNNs for object classification on 3D data. In: Proceedings of the IEEE Conference on Computer Vision and Pattern Recognition, pp. 5648–5656 (2016)
28. Qi, C.R., Yi, L., Su, H., Guibas, L.J.: PointNet++: deep hierarchical feature learning on point sets in a metric space. In: Advances in Neural Information Processing Systems, pp. 5105–5114 (2017)
29. Riegler, G., Ulusoys, A.O., Geiger, A.: OctNet: learning deep 3D representations at high resolutions. arXiv preprint arXiv:1611.05009 (2016)
30. Schöps, T., et al.: A multi-view stereo benchmark with high-resolution images and multi-camera videos. In: Proceedings of CVPR, vol. 3 (2017)
31. Sinha, S., Steedly, D., Szeliski, R.: Piecewise planar stereo for image-based rendering (2009)
32. Song, S., Yu, F., Zeng, A., Chang, A.X., Savva, M., Funkhouser, T.: Semantic scene completion from a single depth image. arXiv preprint arXiv:1611.08974 (2016)
33. Song, S., Yu, F., Zeng, A., Chang, A.X., Savva, M., Funkhouser, T.: Semantic scene completion from a single depth image. In: IEEE Conference on Computer Vision and Pattern Recognition (2017)
34. Su, H., Maji, S., Kalogerakis, E., Learned-Miller, E.: Multi-view convolutional neural networks for 3D shape recognition. In: Proceedings of the IEEE International Conference on Computer Vision, pp. 945–953 (2015)

35. Sui, W., Wang, L., Fan, B., Xiao, H., Wu, H., Pan, C.: Layer-wise floorplan extraction for automatic urban building reconstruction. IEEE Trans. Vis. Comput. Graph. **22**(3), 1261–1277 (2016)

36. Tatarchenko, M., Dosovitskiy, A., Brox, T.: Octree generating networks: efficient convolutional architectures for high-resolution 3D outputs. arXiv preprint arXiv:1703.09438 (2017)

37. Turner, E., Cheng, P., Zakhor, A.: Fast, automated, scalable generation of textured 3D models of indoor environments. IEEE J. Sel. Top. Sig. Process. **9**(3), 409–421 (2015)

38. Wang, D.Z., Posner, I.: Voting for voting in online point cloud object detection. In: Robotics: Science and Systems (2015)

39. Wang, P.S., Liu, Y., Guo, Y.X., Sun, C.Y., Tong, X.: O-CNN: octree-based convolutional neural networks for 3D shape analysis. ACM Trans. Graph. (TOG) **36**(4), 72 (2017)

40. Whelan, T., Kaess, M., Fallon, M., Johannsson, H., Leonard, J., McDonald, J.: Kintinuous: spatially extended kinectfusion (2012)

41. Wu, Z., et al.: 3D ShapeNets: a deep representation for volumetric shapes. In: Proceedings of the IEEE Conference on Computer Vision and Pattern Recognition, pp. 1912–1920 (2015)

42. Xiao, J., Furukawa, Y.: Reconstructing the worlds museums. Int. J. Comput. Vis. **110**(3), 243–258 (2014)

43. Xiong, X., Adan, A., Akinci, B., Huber, D.: Automatic creation of semantically rich 3D building models from laser scanner data. Autom. Constr. **31**, 325–337 (2013)

44. Yu, F., Koltun, V., Funkhouser, T.: Dilated residual networks. In: Computer Vision and Pattern Recognition, vol. 1 (2017)

45. Zhang, Y., Bai, M., Kohli, P., Izadi, S., Xiao, J.: DeepContext: context-encoding neural pathways for 3D holistic scene understanding. arXiv preprint arXiv:1603.04922 (2016)

46. Zhang, Y., Yu, F., Song, S., Xu, P., Seff, A., Xiao, J.: Large-scale scene understanding challenge: room layout estimation (2015). Accessed Sept 2015

47. Zhao, Y., Zhu, S.C.: Image parsing with stochastic scene grammar. In: Advances in Neural Information Processing Systems, pp. 73–81 (2011)

Transferring GANs: Generating Images from Limited Data

Yaxing Wang$^{(\boxtimes)}$, Chenshen Wu, Luis Herranz, Joost van de Weijer, Abel Gonzalez-Garcia, and Bogdan Raducanu

Computer Vision Center, Universitat Autònoma de Barcelona, Barcelona, Spain
{yaxing,chenshen,lherranz,joost,agonzgarc,bogdan}@cvc.uab.es

Abstract. Transferring knowledge of pre-trained networks to new domains by means of fine-tuning is a widely used practice for applications based on discriminative models. To the best of our knowledge this practice has not been studied within the context of generative deep networks. Therefore, we study domain adaptation applied to image generation with generative adversarial networks. We evaluate several aspects of domain adaptation, including the impact of target domain size, the relative distance between source and target domain, and the initialization of conditional GANs. Our results show that using knowledge from pre-trained networks can shorten the convergence time and can significantly improve the quality of the generated images, especially when target data is limited. We show that these conclusions can also be drawn for conditional GANs even when the pre-trained model was trained without conditioning. Our results also suggest that density is more important than diversity and a dataset with one or few densely sampled classes is a better source model than more diverse datasets such as ImageNet or Places.

Keywords: Generative adversarial networks · Transfer learning
Domain adaptation · Image generation

1 Introduction

Generative Adversarial Networks (GANs) can generate samples from complex image distributions [13]. They consist of two networks: a discriminator which aims to separate real images from fake (or generated) images, and a generator which is simultaneously optimized to generate images which are classified as real by the discriminator. The theory was later extended to the case of conditional GANs where the generative process is constrained using a conditioning prior [29] which is provided as an additional input. GANs have further been widely applied in applications, including super-resolution [26], 3D object generation and reconstruction [40], human pose estimation [28], and age estimation [47].

Electronic supplementary material The online version of this chapter (https://doi.org/10.1007/978-3-030-01231-1_14) contains supplementary material, which is available to authorized users.

© Springer Nature Switzerland AG 2018
V. Ferrari et al. (Eds.): ECCV 2018, LNCS 11210, pp. 220–236, 2018.
https://doi.org/10.1007/978-3-030-01231-1_14

Deep neural networks have obtained excellent results for discriminative classification problems for which large datasets exist; for example on the ImageNet dataset which consists of over 1M images [25]. However, for many problems the amount of labeled data is not sufficient to train the millions of parameters typically present in these networks. Fortunately, it was found that the knowledge contained in a network trained on a large dataset (such as ImageNet) can easily be transferred to other computer vision tasks. Either by using these networks as off-the-shelf feature extractors [3], or by adapting them to a new domain by a process called fine tuning [33]. In the latter case, the pre-trained network is used to initialize the weights for a new task (effectively transferring the knowledge learned from the source domain), which are then fine tuned with the training images from the new domain. It has been shown that much fewer images were required to train networks which were initialized with a pre-trained network.

GANs are in general trained from scratch. The procedure of using a pre-trained network for initialization – which is very popular for discriminative networks – is to the best of our knowledge not used for GANs. However, like in the case of discriminative networks, the number of parameters in a GAN is vast; for example the popular DC-GAN architecture [36] requires 36M parameters to generate an image of 64×64. Especially in the case of domains which lack many training images, the usage of pre-trained GANs could significantly improve the quality of the generated images.

Therefore, in this paper, we set out to evaluate the usage of pre-trained networks for GANs. The paper has the following contributions:

1. We evaluate several transfer configurations, and show that pre-trained networks can effectively accelerate the learning process and provide useful prior knowledge when data is limited.
2. We study how the relation between source and target domains impacts the results, and discuss the problem of choosing a suitable pre-trained model, which seems more difficult than in the case of discriminative tasks.
3. We evaluate the transfer from unconditional GANs to conditional GANs for two commonly used methods to condition GANs.

2   Related Work

Transfer Learning/Domain Transfer: Learning how to transfer knowledge from a source domain to target domain is a well studied problem in computer vision [34]. In the deep learning era, complex knowledge is extracted during the training stage on large datasets [38,48]. Domain adaptation by means of fine tuning a pre-trained network has become the default approach for many applications with limited training data or slow convergence [9,33].

Several works have investigated transferring knowledge to unsupervised or sparsely labeled domains. Tzeng et al. [43] optimized for domain invariance, while transferring task information that is present in the correlation between the classes of the source domain. Ganin et al. [12] proposed to learn domain invariant features by means of a gradient reversal layer. A network simultaneously trained on these invariant features can be transfered to the target domain. Finally, domain transfer has also been studied for networks that learn metrics [18]. In contrast to these methods, we do not focus on transferring discriminative features, but transferring knowledge for image generation.

GAN: Goodfellow et al. [13] introduced the first GAN model for image generation. Their architecture uses a series of fully connected layers and thus is limited to simple datasets. When approaching the generation of real images of higher complexity, convolutional architectures have shown to be a more suitable option. Shortly afterwards, Deep Convolutional GANs (DC-GAN) quickly became the standard GAN architecture for image generation problems [36]. In DC-GAN, the generator sequentially up-samples the input features by using fractionally-strided convolutions, whereas the discriminator uses normal convolutions to classify the input images. Recent multi-scale architectures [8,20,22] can effectively generate high resolution images. It was also found that ensembles can be used to improve the quality of the generated distribution [44].

Independently of the type of architecture used, GANs present multiple challenges regarding their training, such as convergence properties, stability issues, or mode collapse. Arjovksy et al. [1] showed that the original GAN loss [13] are unable to properly deal with ill-suited distributions such as those with disjoint supports, often found during GAN training. Addressing these limitations the Wassertein GAN [2] uses the Wasserstein distance as a robust loss, yet requiring the generator to be 1-Lipschitz. This constrain is originally enforced by clipping the weights. Alternatively, an even more stable solution is adding a gradient penalty term to the loss (known as WGAN-GP) [15].

cGAN: Conditional GANs (cGANs) [29] are a class of GANs that use a particular attribute as a prior to build conditional generative models. Examples of conditions are class labels [14,32,35], text [37,46], another image (image translation [23,50] and style transfer [11]).

Most cGAN models [10,29,41,46] apply their condition in both generator and discriminator by concatenating it to the input of the layers, i.e. the noise vector for the first layer or the learned features for the internal layers. Instead, in [11], they include the conditioning in the batch normalization layer. The AC-GAN framework [32] extends the discriminator with an auxiliary decoder to reconstruct class-conditional information. Similarly, InfoGAN [5] reconstructs a subset of the latent variables from which the samples were generated. Miyato et al. [30] propose another modification of the discriminator based on a projection layer that uses the inner product between the conditional information and the intermediate output to compute its loss.

3   Generative Adversarial Networks

3.1   Loss Functions

A GAN consists of a generator G and a discriminator D [13]. The aim is to train a generator G which generates samples that are indistinguishable from the real data distribution. The discriminator is optimized to distinguish samples from the real data distribution p_{data} from those of the fake (generated) data distribution p_g. The generator takes noise $z \sim p_z$ as input, and generates samples $G(z)$ with a distribution p_g. The networks are trained with an adversarial objective. The generator is optimized to generate samples which would be classified by the discriminator as belonging to the real data distribution. The objective is:

$$G^* = \operatorname*{argmin}_{G} \max_{D} \mathcal{L}_{GAN}(G, D) \tag{1}$$

$$\mathcal{L}_{GAN}(G, D) = \mathbb{E}_{x \sim p_{data}}[\log D(x)] + \mathbb{E}_{z \sim p_z}[\log(1 - D(G(z)))] \tag{2}$$

In the case of WGAN-GP [15] the two loss functions are:

$$\mathcal{L}_{WGAN\text{-}GP}(D) = -\mathbb{E}_{x \sim p_{data}}[D(x)] + \mathbb{E}_{z \sim p_z}[D(G(z))]$$
$$+ \lambda \mathbb{E}_{x \sim p_{data}, z \sim p_z, \alpha \sim (0,1)} \left[(\|\nabla D(\alpha x + (1 - \alpha) G(z))\|_2 - 1)^2 \right] \tag{3}$$

$$\mathcal{L}_{WGAN\text{-}GP}(G) = -\mathbb{E}_{z \sim p_z}[D(G(z))] \tag{4}$$

3.2 Evaluation Metrics

Evaluating GANs is notoriously difficult [42] and there is no clear agreed reference metric yet. In general, a good metric should measure the quality and the diversity in the generated data. Likelihood has been shown to not correlate well with these requirements [42]. Better correlation with human perception has been found in the widely used Inception Score [39], but recent works have also shown its limitations [49]. In our experiments we use two recent metrics that show better correlation in recent studies [4,21]. While not perfect, we believe they are satisfactory enough to help us to compare the models in our experiments.

Fréchet Inception Distance [17]. The similarity between two sets is measured as their Fréchet distance (also known as Wasserstein-2 distance) in an embedded space. The embedding is computed using a fixed convolutional network (an Inception model) up to a specific layer. The embedded data is assumed to follow a multivariate normal distribution, which is estimated by computing their mean and covariance. In particular, the FID is computed as

$$\mathrm{FID}(\mathcal{X}_1, \mathcal{X}_2) = \|\mu_1 - \mu_2\|_2^2 + \mathrm{Tr}\left(\Sigma_1 + \Sigma_2 - 2(\Sigma_1 \Sigma_2)^{\frac{1}{2}}\right) \tag{5}$$

Typically, $\mathcal{X}_1$ is the full dataset with real images, while $\mathcal{X}_2$ is a set of generated samples. We use FID as our primary metric, since it is efficient to compute and correlates well with human perception [17].

Independent Wasserstein (IW) Critic [7]. This metric uses an independent critic $\hat{D}$ only for evaluation. This independent critic will approximate the Wasserstein distance [1] between two datasets $\mathcal{X}_1$ and $\mathcal{X}_2$ as

$$\text{IW}\left(\mathcal{X}_1, \mathcal{X}_2\right) = \mathbb{E}_{x \sim \mathcal{X}_1}\left(\hat{D}\left(x\right)\right) - \mathbb{E}_{x \sim \mathcal{X}_2}\left(\hat{D}\left(x\right)\right) \tag{6}$$

In this case, $\mathcal{X}_1$ is typically a validation set, used to train the independent critic. We report IW only in some experiments, due to the larger computational cost that requires training a network for each measurement.

Table 1. FID/IW (the lower the better/the higher the better) for different transfer configurations. ImageNet was used as source dataset and LSUN Bedrooms as target (100K images).

Generator	Scratch		Pre-trained	
Discriminator	Scratch	Pre-trained	Scratch	Pre-trained
FID $\left(\mathcal{X}_{data}^{tgt}, \mathcal{X}_{gen}^{tgt}\right)$	32.87	30.57	56.16	**24.35**
IW $\left(\mathcal{X}_{val}^{tgt}, \mathcal{X}_{gen}^{tgt}\right)$	−4.27	−4.02	−6.35	**−3.88**

4   Transferring GAN Representations

4.1   GAN Adaptation

To study the effect of domain transfer for GANs we will use the WGAN-GP [15] architecture which uses ResNet in both generator and discriminator. This architecture has been experimentally demonstrated to be stable and robust against mode collapse [15]. The generator consists of one fully connected layer, four Residual Blocks and one convolution layer, and the Discriminator has same setting. The same architecture is used for conditional GAN.

Implementation Details. We generate images of 64×64 pixels, using standard values for hyperparameters. The source models[1] are trained with a batch of 128 images during 50K iterations (except 10K iterations for CelebA) using Adam [24] and a learning rate of 1e−4. For fine tuning we use a batch size of 64 and a learning rate of 1e−4 (except 1e−5 for 1K target samples). Batch normalization and layer normalization are used in the generator and discriminator respectively.

4.2   Generator/Discriminator Transfer Configuration

The two networks of the GAN (generator and discriminator) can be initialized with either random or pre-trained weights (from the source networks). In a first

---

[1] The pretrained models are available at https://github.com/yaxingwang/Transferring-GANs.

experiment we consider the four possible combinations using a GAN pre-trained with ImageNet and 100K samples of LSUN bedrooms as target dataset. The source GAN was trained for 50K iterations. The target GAN was trained for (additional) 40K iterations.

Table 1 shows the results. Interestingly, we found that transferring the discriminator is more critical than transferring the generator. The former helps to improve the results in both FID and IW metrics, while the latter only helps if the discriminator was already transferred, otherwise harming the performance. Transferring both obtains the best result. We also found that training is more stable in this setting. Therefore, in the rest of the experiments we evaluated either training both networks from scratch or pre-training both (henceforth simply referred to as *pre-trained*).

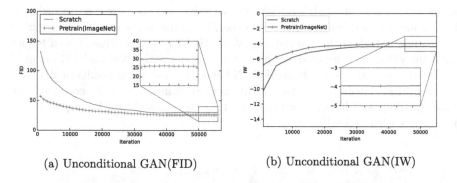

(a) Unconditional GAN(FID)   (b) Unconditional GAN(IW)

Fig. 1. Evolution of evaluation metrics when trained from scratch or using a pre-trained model for unconditional GAN measured with (a) FID and (b) IW (source: ImageNet, target: LSUN Bedrooms, metrics: FID and IW). The curves are smoothed for easier visualization by averaging in a window of a few iterations.

Table 2. FID/IW for different sizes of the target set (LSUN Bedrooms) using ImageNet as source dataset.

Target samples	1K	5K	10K	50K	100K	500K	1M
From scratch	256.1/−33.3	86.0/−18.5	73.7/−15.3	45.5/−7.4	32.9/−4.3	24.9/−3.6	21.0/−2.9
Pre-trained	93.4/−22.5	74.3/−16.3	47.0/−7.0	29.6/−4.56	24.4/−4.0	21.6/−3.2	18.5/−2.8

Figure 1 shows the evolution of FID and IW during the training process with and without transfer. Networks adapted from a pre-trained model can generate images of given scores in significantly fewer iterations. Training from scratch for a long time manages to reduce this gap significantly, but pre-trained GANs can generate images with good quality already with much fewer iterations. Figures 2 and 4 show specific examples illustrating visually these conclusions.

4.3 Size of the Target Dataset

The number of training images is critical to obtain realistic images, in particular as the resolution increases. Our experimental settings involve generating images of 64 × 64 pixels, where GANs typically require hundreds of thousands of training images to obtain convincing results. We evaluate our approach in a challenging setting where we use as few as 1000 images from the LSUN Bedrooms dataset, and using ImageNet as source dataset. Note that, in general, GANs evaluated on LSUN Bedrooms use the full set of 3M million images.

Table 2 shows FID and IW measured for different amounts of training samples of the target domain. As the training data becomes scarce, the training set implicitly becomes less representative of the full dataset (i.e. less diverse). In this experiment, a GAN adapted from the pre-trained model requires roughly between two and five times fewer images to obtain a similar score than a GAN trained from scratch. FID and IW are sensitive to this factor, so in order to have a lower bound we also measured the FID between the specific subset used as training data and the full dataset. With 1K images this value is even higher than the value for generated samples after training with 100K and 1M images.

Intializing with the pre-trained GAN helps to improve the results in all cases, being more significant as the target data is more limited. The difference with the lower bound is still large, which suggests that there is still field for improvement in settings with limited data.

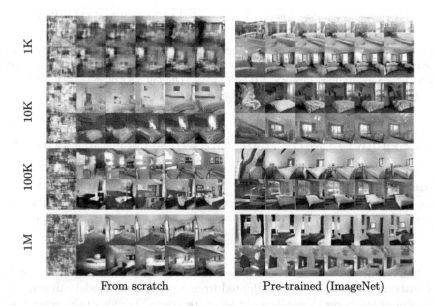

From scratch   Pre-trained (ImageNet)

Fig. 2. Images generated at different iterations (from 0 and 10000, step 2000) for LSUN bedrooms training from scratch and from a pre-trained network. Better viewed in electronic version.

Figure 2 shows images generated at different iterations. As in the previous case, pre-trained networks can generate high quality images already in earlier iterations, in particular with sharper and more defined shapes and more realistic fine details. Visually, the difference is also more evident with limited data, where learning to generate fine details is difficult, so adapting pre-trained networks can transfer relevant prior information.

4.4 Source and Target Domains

The domain of the source model and its relation with the target domain are also a critical factor. We evaluate different combinations of source domains and target domains (see Table 3 for details). As source datasets we used ImageNet, Places, LSUN Bedrooms and CelebA. Note that both ImageNet and Places cover wide domains, with great diversity in objects and scenes, respectively, while LSUN Bedrooms and CelebA cover more densely a narrow domain. As target we used smaller datasets, including Oxford Flowers, LSUN Kitchens (a subset of 50K out of 2M images), Label Faces in the Wild (LFW) and CityScapes.

Table 3. Datasets used in the experiments.

Source datasets	ImageNet [38]	Places [48]	Bedrooms [45]	CelebA [27]
Number of images	1M	2.4M	3M	200K
Number of classes	1000	205	1	1
Target datasets	Flower [31]	Kitchens [45]	LFW [19]	Cityscapes [6]
Number of images	8K	50K	13K	3.5K
Number of classes	102	1	1	1

Table 4. Distance between target real data and target generated data FID/IW $\left(\mathcal{X}_{data}^{tgt}, \mathcal{X}_{gen}^{tgt}\right)$.

Source → Target ↓	Scratch	ImageNet	Places	Bedrooms	CelebA
Flowers	71.98/−13.62	**54.04/−3.09**	66.25/−5.97	56.12/−5.90	67.96/−12.64
Kitchens	42.43/−7.79	34.35/−4.45	34.59/−**2.92**	**28.54**/−3.06	38.41/−4.98
LFW	19.36/−8.62	9.65/−5.17	15.02/−6.61	7.45/−3.61	**7.16/−3.45**
Cityscapes	155.68/−9.32	**122.46**/−9.00	151.34/−8.94	123.21/−8.44	130.64/−**6.40**

We pre-trained GANs for the four source datasets and then trained five GANs for each of the four target datasets (from scratch and initialized with each of the source GANs). The FID and IW after fine tuning are shown in Table 4. Pre-trained GANs achieve significantly better results. Both metrics generally agree but there are some interesting exceptions. The best source model for Flowers as target is ImageNet, which is not surprising since it contains also flowers, plants and objects in general. It is more surprising that Bedrooms is also competitive according to FID (but not so much according to IW). The most interesting case is perhaps Kitchens, since Places has several thousands of kitchens in the dataset, yet also many more classes that are less related. In contrast, bedrooms and kitchens are not the same class yet still very related visually and structurally, so the much larger set of related images in Bedrooms may be a better choice. Here FID and IW do not agree, with FID clearly favoring Bedrooms, and even the less related ImageNet, over Places, while IW preferring Places by a small margin. As expected, CelebA is the best source for LFW, since both contain faces (with different scales though), but Bedroom is surprisingly very close to the performance in both metrics. For Cityscapes all methods have similar results (within a similar range), with both high FID and IW, perhaps due to the large distance to all source domains (Fig. 3).

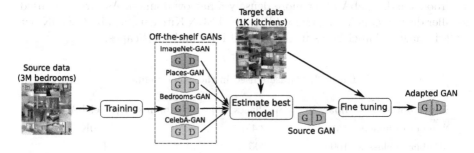

Fig. 3. Transferring GANs: training source GANs, estimation of the most suitable pre-trained model and adaptation to the target domain.

Table 5. Distance between source generated data $\mathcal{X}_{gen}^{src}$ and target real data $\mathcal{X}_{data}^{tgt}$, and distance between source real $\mathcal{X}_{data}^{src}$ and generated data $\mathcal{X}_{gen}^{src}$.

	Source → Target ↓	ImageNet	Places	Bedrooms	CelebA
FID $\left(\mathcal{X}_{gen}^{src}, \mathcal{X}_{data}^{tgt}\right)$	Flowers	**237.04**	251.93	278.80	284.74
	Kitchens	183.27	180.63	**70.06**	254.12
	LFW	333.54	333.38	329.92	**151.46**
	Cityscapes	233.45	**181.72**	227.53	292.66
FID $\left(\mathcal{X}_{gen}^{src}, \mathcal{X}_{data}^{src}\right)$	Source	63.46	55.66	17.30	75.84

4.5 Selecting the Pre-trained Model

Selecting a pre-trained model for a discriminative task (e.g. classification) is reduced to simply selecting either ImageNet, for object-centric domains, or Places, for scene-centric ones. The target classifier or fine tuning will simply learn to ignore non-related features and filters of the source network.

However, this simple rule of thumb does not seem to apply so clearly in our GAN transfer setting due to generation being a much more complex task than discrimination. Results in Table 4 show that sometimes unrelated datasets may perform better than other apparently more related. The large number of unrelated classes may be an important factor, since narrow yet dense domains also seem to perform better even when they are not so related (e.g. Bedrooms). There are also non-trivial biases in the datasets that may explain this behavior. Therefore, a way to estimate the most suitable model for a given target dataset is desirable, given a collection of pre-trained GANs.

Perhaps the most simple way is to measure the distance between the source and target domains. We evaluated the FID between the (real) images in the target and the source datasets (results included in the supplementary material). While showing some correlation with the FID of the target generated data, it has the limitation of not considering whether the actual pre-trained model is able or not to accurately sample from the real distribution. A more helpful metric is the distance between the target data and the *generated* samples by the pre-trained model. In this way, the quality of the model is taken into account. We estimate this distance also using FID. In general, there seem to roughly correlate with the final FID results with target generated data (compare Tables 4 and 5). Nevertheless, it is surprising that Places is estimated as a good source dataset but does not live up to the expectation. The opposite occurs for Bedrooms, which seems to deliver better results than expected. This may suggest that density is more important than diversity for a good transferable model, even for apparently unrelated target domains.

In our opinion, the FID between source generated and target real data is a rough indicator of suitability rather than accurate metric. It should taken into account jointly with others factors (e.g. quality of the source model) to decide which model is best for a given target dataset.

4.6   Visualizing the Adaptation Process

One advantage of the image generation setting is that the process of shifting from the source domain towards the target domain can be visualized by sampling images at different iterations, in particular during the initial ones. Figure 4 shows some examples of the target domain Kitchens and different source domains (iterations are sampled in a logarithmic scale).

Trained from scratch, the generated images simply start with noisy patterns that evolve slowly, and after 4000 iterations the model manages to reproduce the global layout and color, but still fails to generate convincing details. Both the GANs pre-trained with Places and ImageNet fail to generate realistic enough source images and often sample from unrelated source classes (see iteration 0). During the initial adaptation steps, the GAN tries to generate kitchen-like patterns by matching and slightly modifying the source pattern, therefore preserving global features such as colors and global layout, at least during a significant number of iterations, then slowly changing them to more realistic ones. Nevertheless, the textures and edges are sharper and more realistic than from scratch.

The GAN pre-trained with Bedrooms can already generate very convincing bedrooms, which share a lot of features with kitchens. The larger number of training images in Bedrooms helps to learn transferable fine grained details that other datasets cannot. The adaptation mostly preserves the layout, colors and perspective of the source generated bedroom, and slowly transforms it into kitchens by changing fine grained details, resulting in more convincing images than with the other source datasets. Despite being a completely unrelated domain, CelebA also manages to help in speeding up the learning process by providing useful priors. Different parts such as face, hair and eyes are transformed into different parts of the kitchen. Rather than the face itself, the most predominant feature remaining from the source generated image is the background color and shape, that influences in the layout and colors that the generated kitchens will have.

5   Transferring to Conditional GANs

Here we study the transferring the representation learned by a pre-trained unconditional GAN to a cGAN [29]. cGANs allow us to condition the generative model on particular information such as classes, attributes, or even other images. Let y be a conditioning variable. The discriminator $D(x, y)$ aims to distinguish pairs of real data x and y sampled from the joint distribution $p_{data}(x, y)$ from pairs of generated outputs $G(z, y')$ conditioned on samples y' from y's marginal $p_{data}(y)$.

5.1   Conditional GAN Adaptation

For the current study, we adopt the Auxiliary Classifier GAN (AC-GAN) framework of [32]. In this formulation, the discriminator has an 'auxiliary classifier' that outputs a probability distribution over classes $P(C = y|x)$ conditioned on the input x. The objective function is then composed of the conditional version of the GAN loss $\mathcal{L}_{GAN}$ (Eq. (1)) and the log-likelihood of the correct class. The final loss functions for generator and discriminator are:

$$\mathcal{L}_{AC-GAN}(G) = \mathcal{L}_{GAN}(G) - \alpha_G \mathbb{E}\left[\log\left(P\left(C = y'|G(z, y')\right)\right)\right], \qquad (7)$$

$$\mathcal{L}_{AC-GAN}(D) = \mathcal{L}_{GAN}(D) - \alpha_D \mathbb{E}\left[\log\left(P\left(C = y|x\right)\right)\right], \qquad (8)$$

respectively. The parameters α_G and α_D weight the contribution of the auxiliary classifier loss with respect to the GAN loss for the generator and discriminator. In our implementation, we use Resnet-18 [16] for both G and D, and the WGAN-GP loss from the Eqs. (3) and (4) as the GAN loss. Overall, the implementation details (batch size, learning rate) are the same as introduced in Sect. 4.1.

In AC-GAN, the conditioning is performed only on the generator by appending the class label to the input noise vector. We call this variant 'Cond Concat'. We randomly initialize the weights which are connected to the conditioning prior. We also used another variant following [11], in which the conditioning prior is embedded in the batch normalization layers of the generator (referred to as 'Cond BNorm'). In this case, there are different batch normalization parameters for each class. We initialize these parameters by copying the values from the unconditional GAN to all classes.

5.2   Results

We use Places [48] as the source domain and consider all the ten classes of the LSUN dataset [45] as target domain. We train the AC-GAN with 10K images per class for 25K iterations. The weights of the conditional GAN can be transferred from the pre-trained unconditional GAN (see Sect. 3.1) or initialized at random. The performance is assessed in terms of the FID score between target domain and generated images. The FID is computed class-wise, averaging over all classes and also considering the dataset as a whole (class-agnostic case). The classes in the target domain have been generated uniformly. The results are presented in Table 6, where we show the performance of the AC-GAN whose weights have been transferred from pre-trained network vs. an AC-GAN initialized randomly. We computed the FID for 250, 2500 and 25000 iterations. At the beginning of the learning process, there is a significant difference between the two cases. The gap is reduced towards the end of the learning process but a significant performance gain still remains for pre-trained networks. We also consider the case with fewer images per class. The results after 25000 iterations for 100 and 1K images per class are provided in the last column of Table 7. We can observe how the difference between networks trained from scratch or from pre-trained weights is more significant for smaller sample sizes. This confirms the trend observed in Sect. 4.3: transferring the pre-trained weights is especially advantageous when only limited data is available.

The same behavior can be observed in Fig. 5 (left) where we compare the performance of the AC-GAN with two unconditional GANs, one pre-trained on the source domain and one trained from scratch, as in Sect. 4.2. The curves correspond to the class-agnostic case (column 'All' in the Table 6). From this plot, we can observe three aspects: (i) the two variants of AC-GAN perform similarly (for this reason, for the remaining of the experiments we consider only 'Cond BNorm'); (ii) the network initialized with pre-trained weights converges faster than the network trained from scratch, and the overall performance is better; and (iii) AC-GAN performs slightly better than the unconditional GAN.

Table 6. Per-class and overall FID for AC-GAN. Source: Places, target: LSUN

Init	Iter	Bedr	Bridge	Church	Classr	Confer	Dining	Kitchen	Living	Rest	Tower	Avg	All
Scratch	250	298.4	310.3	314.4	376.6	339.1	294.9	314.2	316.5	324.4	301.0	319.0	352.4
	2500	195.9	135.0	133.0	218.6	185.3	173.9	167.9	189.3	159.5	125.6	168.4	137.3
	25000	72.9	78.0	52.4	106.7	76.9	40.1	53.9	56.1	74.7	59.8	67.2	49.6
Pre-trained	250	168.3	122.1	148.1	145.0	151.6	144.2	156.9	150.1	113.3	129.7	142.9	107.2
	2500	140.8	96.8	77.4	136.0	136.8	84.6	85.5	94.9	77.0	69.4	99.9	74.8
	25000	59.9	68.6	48.2	79.0	68.7	35.2	48.2	47.9	44.4	49.9	55.0	42.7

Next, we evaluate the AC-GAN performance on a classification experiment. We train a reference classifier on the 10 classes of LSUN (10K real images per class). Then, we evaluate the quality of each model trained for 25K iterations by generating 10K images per class and measuring the accuracy of the reference

Table 7. Accuracy of AC-GAN for the classification task and overall FID for different sizes of the target set (LSUN).

#images	Method	Accuracy (%)											FID
		Bedr	Bridge	Church	Classr	Confer	Dining	Kitchen	Living	Rest	Tower	Avg.	
100/class	Scratch	23.0	**88.2**	**55.1**	29.2	3.6	24.9	20.8	8.4	**89.3**	**61.6**	40.4	162.9
	Pre-trained	**35.7**	72.7	45.7	**59.4**	**7.9**	**38.2**	**36.3**	**20.1**	81.0	56.6	**45.4**	**119.1**
1K/class	Scratch	49.9	78.1	**75.1**	51.8	14.6	51.2	31.2	23.2	**90.7**	61.5	52.7	117.3
	Pre-trained	**76.4**	**82.5**	69.1	**80.6**	**34.2**	**52.6**	**62.4**	**52.9**	80.5	**67.5**	**65.9**	**77.5**
10K/class	Scratch	**94.9**	94.3	89.6	85.0	82.4	**91.2**	88.0	86.9	91.3	83.5	88.7	49.6
	Pre-trained	87.1	**95.7**	**90.8**	**95.1**	**86.8**	90.2	**88.9**	**90.1**	**93.0**	**88.9**	**90.8**	**42.7**

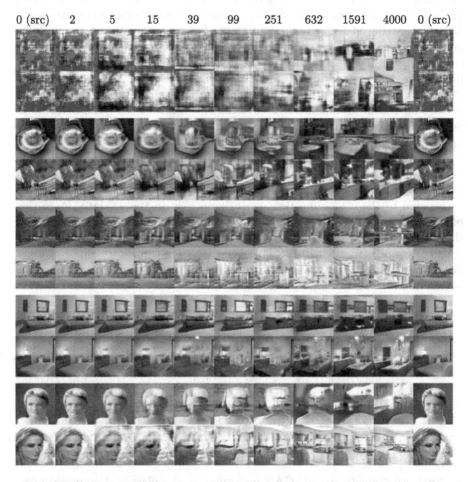

0 (src)   2   5   15   39   99   251   632   1591   4000   0 (src)

Fig. 4. Evolution of generated images (in logarithmic scale) for LSUN kitchens with different source datasets (from top to bottom: from scratch, ImageNet, Places, LSUN bedrooms, CelebA). Better viewed in electronic version.

classifier for 100, 1K and 10K images per class. The results show an improvement when using pre-trained models, with higher accuracy and lower FID in all settings, suggesting that it captures better the real data distribution of the dataset compared to training from scratch.

Finally, we perform a psychophysical experiment with generated images by AC-GAN with LSUN as target. Human subjects are presented with two images: pre-trained vs. from scratch (generated from the same condition <class>), and asked 'Which of these two images of <class> is more realistic?' Subjects were also given the option to skip a particular pair should they find very hard to decide for one of them. We require each subject to provide 100 valid assessments. We use 10 human subjects which evaluate image pairs for different settings (100, 1K, 10K images per class). The results (Fig. 5 right) clearly show that the images based on pre-trained GANs are considered to be more realistic in the case of 100 and 1K images per class (e.g. pre-trained is preferred in 67% of cases with 1K images). As expected the difference is smaller for the 10K case.

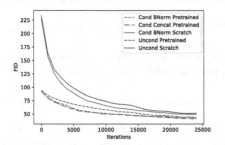 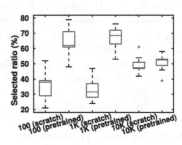

Fig. 5. (Left) FID score for Conditional and Unconditional GAN (source: Places, target: LSUN 10 classes). (Right) Human evaluation of image quality.

6   Conclusions

We show how the principles of transfer learning can be applied to generative features for image generation with GANs. GANs, and conditional GANs, benefit from transferring pre-trained models, resulting in lower FID scores and more recognizable images with less training data. Somewhat contrary to intuition, our experiments show that transferring the discriminator is much more critical than the generator (yet transferring both networks is best). However, there are also other important differences with the discriminative scenario. Notably, it seems that a much higher density (images per class) is required to learn good transferable features for image generation, than for image discrimination (where diversity seems more critical). As a consequence, ImageNet and Places, while producing excellent transferable features for discrimination, seem not dense enough for generation, and LSUN data seems to be a better choice despite its limited diversity. Nevertheless, poor transferability may be also related to the limitations of current GAN techniques, and better ones could also lead to better transferability.

Our experiments evaluate GANs in settings rarely explored in previous works and show that there are many open problems. These settings include GANs and evaluation metrics in the very limited data regime, better mechanisms to estimate the most suitable pre-trained model for a given target dataset, and the design of better pre-trained GAN models.

Acknowledgement. Y. Wang and C. Wu acknowledge the Chinese Scholarship Council (CSC) grant No. 201507040048 and No. 201709110103. L. Herranz acknowledges the European Union research and innovation program under the Marie Skodowska-Curie grant agreement No. 6655919. This work was supported by TIN2016-79717-R, and the CHISTERA project M2CR (PCIN-2015-251) of the Spanish Ministry, the CERCA Program of the *Generalitat de Catalunya*. We also acknowledge the generous GPU support from NVIDIA.

References

1. Arjovsky, M., Bottou, L.: Towards principled methods for training generative adversarial networks. In: ICLR (2017)
2. Arjovsky, M., Chintala, S., Bottou, L.: Wasserstein generative adversarial networks. In: ICML, pp. 214–223 (2017)
3. Azizpour, H., Razavian, A.S., Sullivan, J., Maki, A., Carlsson, S.: Factors of transferability for a generic convnet representation. IEEE Trans. PAMI **38**(9), 1790–1802 (2016)
4. Borji, A.: Pros and Cons of GAN evaluation measures. arXiv preprint arXiv:1802.03446 (2018)
5. Chen, X., Duan, Y., Houthooft, R., Schulman, J., Sutskever, I., Abbeel, P.: Infogan: interpretable representation learning by information maximizing generative adversarial nets. In: NIPS (2016)
6. Cordts, M., et al.: The cityscapes dataset for semantic urban scene understanding. In: CVPR, pp. 3213–3223 (2016)
7. Danihelka, I., Lakshminarayanan, B., Uria, B., Wierstra, D., Dayan, P.: Comparison of maximum likelihood and GAN-based training of real NVPs. arXiv preprint arXiv:1705.05263 (2017)
8. Denton, E.L., Chintala, S., Fergus, R., et al.: Deep generative image models using a Laplacian pyramid of adversarial networks. In: NIPS, pp. 1486–1494 (2015)
9. Donahue, J., et al.: DeCAF: a deep convolutional activation feature for generic visual recognition. In: ICML, pp. 647–655 (2014)
10. Dumoulin, V., et al.: Adversarially learned inference. In: ICLR (2017)
11. Dumoulin, V., Shlens, J., Kudlur, M.: A learned representation for artistic style. In: ICLR (2017)
12. Ganin, Y., et al.: Domain-adversarial training of neural networks. JMLR **17**(1), 2030–2096 (2016)
13. Goodfellow, I., et al.: Generative adversarial nets. In: NIPS, pp. 2672–2680 (2014)
14. Grinblat, G.L., Uzal, L.C., Granitto, P.M.: Class-splitting generative adversarial networks. arXiv preprint arXiv:1709.07359 (2017)
15. Gulrajani, I., Ahmed, F., Arjovsky, M., Dumoulin, V., Courville, A.C.: Improved training of Wasserstein GANs. In: NIPS, pp. 5769–5779 (2017)
16. He, K., Zhang, X., Ren, S., Sun, J.: Deep residual learning for image recognition. In: CVPR, pp. 770–778 (2016)

17. Heusel, M., Ramsauer, H., Unterthiner, T., Nessler, B., Klambauer, G., Hochreiter, S.: GANs trained by a two time-scale update rule converge to a Nash equilibrium. In: NIPS (2017)
18. Hu, J., Lu, J., Tan, Y.P.: Deep transfer metric learning. In: CVPR, pp. 325–333. IEEE (2015)
19. Huang, G.B., Mattar, M., Berg, T., Learned-Miller, E.: Labeled faces in the wild: a database for studying face recognition in unconstrained environments. In: Workshop on Faces in 'Real-Life' Images: Detection, Alignment, and Recognition (2008)
20. Huang, X., Li, Y., Poursaeed, O., Hopcroft, J., Belongie, S.: Stacked generative adversarial networks. In: CVPR, vol. 2, p. 4 (2017)
21. Im, D.J., Ma, H., Taylor, G., Branson, K.: Quantitatively evaluating GANs with divergences proposed for training. In: ICLR (2018)
22. Karras, T., Aila, T., Laine, S., Lehtinen, J.: Progressive growing of GANs for improved quality, stability, and variation. In: ICLR (2018)
23. Kim, T., Cha, M., Kim, H., Lee, J., Kim, J.: Learning to discover cross-domain relations with generative adversarial networks. In: ICML, pp. 1857–1865 (2017)
24. Kingma, D.P., Ba, J.: Adam: a method for stochastic optimization. In: ICLR (2014)
25. Krizhevsky, A., Sutskever, I., Hinton, G.E.: Imagenet classification with deep convolutional neural networks. In: NIPS, pp. 1097–1105 (2012)
26. Ledig, C., et al.: Photo-realistic single image super-resolution using a generative adversarial network. In: CVPR (2016)
27. Liu, Z., Luo, P., Wang, X., Tang, X.: Deep learning face attributes in the wild. In: ICCV, pp. 3730–3738 (2015)
28. Ma, L., Jia, X., Sun, Q., Schiele, B., Tuytelaars, T., Van Gool, L.: Pose guided person image generation. In: NIPS, pp. 405–415 (2017)
29. Mirza, M., Osindero, S.: Conditional generative adversarial nets. arXiv preprint arXiv:1411.1784 (2014)
30. Miyato, T., Koyama, M.: CGANs with projection discriminator. In: ICLR (2018)
31. Nilsback, M.E., Zisserman, A.: Automated flower classification over a large number of classes. In: ICVGIP, pp. 722–729. IEEE (2008)
32. Odena, A., Olah, C., Shlens, J.: Conditional image synthesis with auxiliary classifier GANs. In: ICML (2016)
33. Oquab, M., Bottou, L., Laptev, I., Sivic, J.: Learning and transferring mid-level image representations using convolutional neural networks. In: CVPR, pp. 1717–1724. IEEE (2014)
34. Pan, S.J., Yang, Q.: A survey on transfer learning. IEEE Trans. Knowl. Data Eng. **22**(10), 1345–1359 (2010)
35. Perarnau, G., van de Weijer, J., Raducanu, B., Álvarez, J.M.: Invertible conditional GANs for image editing. In: NIPS 2016 Workshop on Adversarial Training (2016)
36. Radford, A., Metz, L., Chintala, S.: Unsupervised representation learning with deep convolutional generative adversarial networks. In: ICLR (2015)
37. Reed, S., Akata, Z., Yan, X., Logeswaran, L., Schiele, B., Lee, H.: Generative adversarial text to image synthesis. In: ICML, pp. 1060–1069 (2016)
38. Russakovsky, O., et al.: Imagenet large scale visual recognition challenge. IJCV **115**(3), 211–252 (2015)
39. Salimans, T., Goodfellow, I., Zaremba, W., Cheung, V., Radford, A., Chen, X.: Improved techniques for training GANs. In: NIPS, pp. 2234–2242 (2016)
40. Smith, E., Meger, D.: Improved adversarial systems for 3D object generation and reconstruction. arXiv preprint arXiv:1707.09557 (2017)
41. Sricharan, K., Bala, R., Shreve, M., Ding, H., Saketh, K., Sun, J.: Semi-supervised conditional GANs. arXiv preprint arXiv:1708.05789 (2017)

42. Theis, L., van den Oord, A., Bethge, M.: A note on the evaluation of generative models. In: ICLR (2015)
43. Tzeng, E., Hoffman, J., Darrell, T., Saenko, K.: Simultaneous deep transfer across domains and tasks. In: CVPR, pp. 4068–4076 (2015)
44. Wang, Y., Zhang, L., van de Weijer, J.: Ensembles of generative adversarial networks. In: NIPS 2016 Workshop on Adversarial Training (2016)
45. Yu, F., Zhang, Y., Song, S., Seff, A., Xiao, J.: Construction of a large-scale image dataset using deep learning with humans in the loop. arXiv preprint arXiv:1506.03365 (2015)
46. Zhang, H., et al.: StackGAN: text to photo-realistic image synthesis with stacked generative adversarial networks. In: ICCV, pp. 5908–5916 (2017)
47. Zhang, Z., Song, Y., Qi, H.: Age progression/regression by conditional adversarial autoencoder. In: CVPR, vol. 2 (2017)
48. Zhou, B., Lapedriza, A., Xiao, J., Torralba, A., Oliva, A.: Learning deep features for scene recognition using places database. In: NIPS, pp. 487–495 (2014)
49. Zhou, Z., et al.: Activation maximization generative adversarial nets. In: ICLR (2018)
50. Zhu, J.Y., Park, T., Isola, P., Efros, A.A.: Unpaired image-to-image translation using cycle-consistent adversarial networks. In: ICCV, pp. 2242–2251 (2017)

Saliency Preservation in Low-Resolution Grayscale Images

Shivanthan Yohanandan[1]([⊠]), Andy Song[1], Adrian G. Dyer[1], and Dacheng Tao[2]

[1] RMIT University, Melbourne, Australia
{shivanthan.yohanandan,andy.song,adrian.dyer}@rmit.edu.au
[2] UBTECH Sydney AI Centre, SIT, FEIT, The University of Sydney,
Sydney, Australia
dacheng.tao@sydney.edu.au

Abstract. Visual salience detection originated over 500 million years ago and is one of nature's most efficient mechanisms. In contrast, many state-of-the-art computational saliency models are complex and inefficient. Most saliency models process high-resolution color images; however, insights into the evolutionary origins of visual salience detection suggest that achromatic low-resolution vision is essential to its speed and efficiency. Previous studies showed that low-resolution color and high-resolution grayscale images preserve saliency information. However, to our knowledge, no one has investigated whether saliency is preserved in low-resolution grayscale (LG) images. In this study, we explain the biological and computational motivation for LG, and show, through a range of human eye-tracking and computational modeling experiments, that saliency information is preserved in LG images. Moreover, we show that using LG images leads to significant speedups in model training and detection times and conclude by proposing LG images for fast and efficient salience detection.

Keywords: Saliency detection · Fully convolutional network
Peripheral vision

1 Introduction

Visual scenes often contain more items than can be processed concurrently due to the visual system's limited processing capacity [1]. Visual salience (or attention) detection is a cognitive mechanism that efficiently deals with this capacity limitation by selecting relevant or salient information, while ignoring irrelevant information [1]. Salience detection is a fundamental vision mechanism present in many sighted organisms. Even insects, despite having significantly smaller brains and dissimilar eyes to vertebrates, can detect salient stimuli in their visual field [2–4]. Salience detection can be crudely divided into bottom-up and top-down mechanisms. Bottom-up salience is stimulus and feature-driven, and responsible

© Springer Nature Switzerland AG 2018
V. Ferrari et al. (Eds.): ECCV 2018, LNCS 11210, pp. 237–254, 2018.
https://doi.org/10.1007/978-3-030-01231-1_15

for automatic, involuntary rapid shifts in attention and gaze. In contrast, top-down salience is task-driven, experience-based, and varies between individuals [5].

Recently, deep neural networks have achieved state-of-the-art performance on various saliency benchmarks [6–9]. Nevertheless, this success comes at high computational costs [10,11]. Training and running these networks is time- and resource-intensive, which is not easily scalable to resource-limited devices [10]. Processing high-resolution or stacked multi-resolution color images contributes to these limitations [12]. In contrast, natural visual salience detection proves to be much more efficient. A deeper understanding of the evolutionary origins of visual salience detection suggests that bottom-up saliency is computed from achromatic low-resolution information [13].

Previous studies have shown that low-resolution *color* (LC) [14–16] and *high-resolution* grayscale (HG) [17–22] images preserve saliency information, yet are significantly more computationally attractive than high-resolution color (HC) images. Low-resolution grayscale (LG) images are even more computationally attractive, compared to LC and HG images. Nevertheless, to our knowledge, no one has investigated whether saliency information is preserved in LG images. In this study, we therefore investigate saliency preservation in LG images, and present the following three contributions: (1) linking low-resolution grayscale information with the bio-inspired evolutionary origins of visual saliency, (2) assessing the preservation of saliency information in low-resolution grayscale images, and (3) proposing low-resolution grayscale images for fast and efficient saliency detection. Therefore, based on a deeper understanding of the evolutionary origins of visual saliency, together with knowledge gained from studies investigating salience preservation in LC and HG images, we hypothesize that saliency information is well-preserved in LG images.

2   Related Work

2.1   Fixations on Low-Resolution Images

Judd *et al.* [14] investigated how well fixations on LC images predict fixations on the same images in HC. They found that fixations on LC images (76×64 pixels) can predict fixations on HC images (610×512 pixels) quite well (AUC-Judd [14] > 0.85). However, they did not investigate the HC fixation-predictability of LG images, nor did they mention any biological plausibility for deciding to investigate fixations in LC images. Nevertheless, they concluded that working with fixations on LC instead of HC images could be perceptually adequate and computationally attractive, which is part of our motivation for pursuing this study.

2.2   Multi-resolution Approaches

Deep artificial neural networks are not inherently scale-invariant [23]. Therefore, multi-resolution models are often used to capture saliency at different scales. Advani *et al.* [24] presented a multi-resolution framework for detecting visual salience where resolution degrades further away from the point of fixation represented as a three-level architecture: a central high-resolution fovea (960 × 960 pixels), a mid-resolution filter (640 × 640 pixels), and a low-resolution region (480 × 480 pixels). They found significant computational benefits using this model, but only investigated color images and ignored the achromaticity of peripheral vision.

Shen *et al.* [15] went a step further and modeled the visual acuity of the parafovea and periphery as a stack of multi-scale inputs. They extracted multi-resolution image patches in multiple visual acuity on the same image from fixation targets and non-target locations based on the "sunflower" model of retina [25–27]. However, despite finding comparable performance to higher-resolution models, they too only investigated color images, and overlooked the fact that the parafovea and periphery predominantly processes achromatic information [13]. Furthermore, multi-scale models need to process and train on the same image multiples times at different resolutions, which is computationally unattractive. Therefore, the ideal input image has the lowest resolution and smallest color space that preserves saliency.

2.3   Fixations in Grayscale

Colour processing in chromatic vision conveys processing advantages when combined with brightness information and higher level cognitive influences (e.g. top-down task-driven visual search [28]). Nevertheless, colour information alone is poor at object detection tasks or enabling spatial resolution [29–31].

Hamel *et al.* [19] investigated the role of color in visual attention by comparing eye movements across different participants viewing color and grayscale videos. They found color to only have a modest effect in predicting salience. However, they only investigated high-resolution images, leaving the influence of color in low-resolution images a gap for us to fill.

Yang *et al.* [32] also investigated whether saliency information is preserved in grayscale images using a novel minimization function. They showed that saliency is well-preserved in grayscale images of the same resolution, but did not extend their investigation to lower resolutions, which our study aims to do.

3   Evolutionary Origin of Visual Saliency

In the beginning, life was blind. Then, around 600 million years ago, the first eyes discriminated night and day (Fig. 1(a)) [34]. Light-source localization followed a few million years later (Fig. 1(b)), heralding eyes capable of distinguishing light from shadow, thus crudely making-out objects in their vicinity (Fig. 1(c)), including those to eat, and those that might eat it. This was likely the birth of stimulus-driven, bottom-up visual salience detection – the mechanism thought to be primarily responsible for the Cambrian explosion [13]. Later, things became

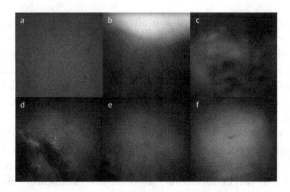

Fig. 1. Hypothetical stages of the evolution of vertebrate vision. This figure panel shows a series of photographic reconstructions of how the vertebrate eye is hypothesized to have evolved, and what that vision hypothetically looked like from an animal's point of view. Static images adapted from *Cosmos: A Spacetime Odyssey (Some of the Things that Molecules do)* [33].

a little clearer. The eye's opening contracted to a pinhole covered by a protective transparent membrane, allowing just enough light to paint a dim image on the sensitive inner surface of the eye [35]. Then came focus-sharpening lenses (Fig. 1(d)), foveated central vision (Fig. 1(e)), and finally, color (Fig. 1(f)). However, despite the arrival of high-acuity chromatic central vision, blurry achromatic peripheral vision dominates over 90% of our visual field, and is still the primary information source for bottom-up salience detection – a relic mechanism conserved through evolution in many species because of its apparent speed and efficiency [13]. Furthermore, many sighted animals completely lack chromatic vision, yet are able to rapidly detect obstacles and avoid collisions in complex environments [36].

The ability then of an organism's pupil to rapidly shift foveal gaze to salient regions suggests that it is peripheral vision that points the sharper, high-resolution foveated (sometimes chromatic) vision to investigate objects and regions further. Eye movements align objects with the high-acuity fovea of the retina, making it possible to gather detailed information about the world [35]. Therefore, bottom-up visual salience detection is predominantly a peripheral vision information processing task.

4   Peripheral Vision

A key to the speed and efficiency in bottom-up salience detection lies in the distribution of rod and cone photoreceptor cells in the human retina (Fig. 2(a)), and the information processing pipeline of typical vertebrate peripheral vision (Fig. 2(b)). Rods primarily encode achromatic luminance (brightness) information, and have a higher distribution outside the fovea. In contrast, cones encode chrominance (color), and are concentrated in the fovea (center of the retina)

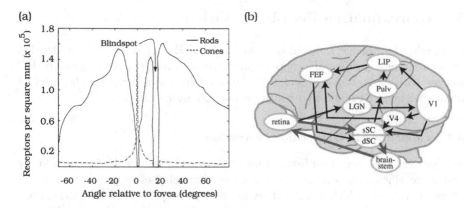

Fig. 2. (a) The human retina's distribution of rod and cone photoreceptors is shown in degrees of visual angle relative to the position of the fovea for the left eye. Cones, concentrated in the fovea, encode high-resolution color. Rod photoreceptors distributed outside the fovea encode low-resolution grayscale information [37]. (b) Macaque brain information flow from retinal input to eye movement output. Visual signals from the retina to the cerebral cortex are mediated through the primary visual cortex (V1) and the superior colliculus (sSC and dSC). There is also a shortcut from the superficial (sSC) to the deep (dSC) superior colliculus, which then sends outputs directly to the brainstem oculomotor nuclei, resulting in rapid saccades (red pathway) (Color figure online) [38].

[37]. Moreover, multiple rods converge to and activate a single retinal ganglion neuron, which is why rod vision has lower spatial resolution compared to information encoded by cones, despite having a high peripheral distribution. In contrast, each cone activates multiple ganglion neurons, resulting in higher acuity vision [39]. Therefore, afferent ganglion neurons, not photoreceptors, from the retina determine the perceived image resolution.

The sparse retinal output of peripheral vision (only 10% of all ganglion cells leaving the eye) enters a structure called the optic tectum (or superior colliculus (SC) in higher-order animals, Fig. 2(b)). This structure has only recently emerged as a likely candidate for encoding the saliency map "– a well-known precursor for bottom-up salience detection [38,40,41]. Furthermore, the SC has direct control of eye muscles. In their study, Veale *et al.* [38] explain that direct retinal input into the SC of a macaque brain can trigger reflex-like saccades via brainstem oculomotor nuclei (red pathway in Fig. 2(b)). This could explain why bottom-up saliency detection is rapid and reflex-like, which makes sense since it is processing predominantly achromatic information from fewer afferent neurons, compared to foveated vision, which is processed downstream of the SC and in larger complex brain regions, therefore taking longer. This means far fewer neurons enter the SC, which is analogous to a low-resolution grayscale digital image. Therefore, this sparse achromatic peripheral output could be approximated using low-resolution grayscale images in the digital domain.

5   Approximating Peripheral Vision

Leveraging knowledge from Judd *et al.* [14] and Hamel *et al.* [19], we decided
to approximate peripheral vision by first transforming the color space of HC
images to 8-bit grayscale (Sect. 5.1), followed by down-sampling the original
image height to 64 pixels and width proportionally (Sect. 5.2).

5.1   Colorimetric Grayscale Conversion

Images were first converted from 24-bit sRGB to 8-bit grayscale since it is faster
and more efficient to consolidate the three channels before performing subsequent operations, which would otherwise need to be performed thrice (i.e. once
per channel). Color to grayscale conversion is a lossy operation, resulting in
luminance degradation, which may affect saliency [17]. To avoid such systematic
errors, the grayscale conversion must at least preserve the brightness features of
the original stimuli (i.e. the luminosity of grayscale pixels must be identical to
the original color image). The HC images used in this study are stored in the
sRGB (standard Red Green Blue) color space, which also defines a nonlinear
transformation (gamma correction) between the luminosity of these primaries
and the actual number stored.

To convert the 24-bit sRGB gamma-compressed color model I_{HC} to an 8-bit
grayscale representation of its luminance I_{HG}, the gamma compression function
must first be removed via gamma expansion to transform the image to a linear
RGB color space [42], so that the appropriate weighted sum can be applied to
the linear color components $R_{linear}, G_{linear}, B_{linear}$. For the sRGB color space,
gamma expansion is defined as

$$C_{linear} = \begin{cases} \frac{C_{sRGB}}{12.92} & C_{sRGB} \leq 0.04045 \\ (\frac{C_{sRGB}+0.055}{1.055})^{2.4} & C_{sRGB} > 0.04045 \end{cases} \tag{1}$$

where C_{sRGB} represents any of the three gamma-compressed sRGB primaries
(R_{sRGB}, G_{sRGB}, and B_{sRGB}, each in range $[0, 1]$) and C_{linear} is the corresponding linear-intensity value (R_{linear}, G_{linear}, and B_{linear}, also in range $[0, 1]$). Then,
I_{HG} is calculated as a weighted sum of the three linear-intensity values, which
is given by

$$I_{HG} = 0.2126 \times R_{linear} + 0.7152 \times G_{linear} + 0.0722 \times B_{linear}. \tag{2}$$

These three coefficients represent the intensity (luminance) perception of a standard observer trichromat human to light of the precise Rec. 709 [43] additive
primary colors that are used in the definition of sRGB.

5.2   Down-Sampling Image Resolution

We chose 64 pixels as our low-resolution height since Judd *et al.* [14] found
this to be the resolution with the best resolution-saliency compromise compared

to other resolutions. According to the Nyquist theorem, down-sampling from a higher-resolution image can only be carried out after applying a suitable 2D anti-aliasing filter to prevent aliasing artifacts. To reduce the height of each image down to 64 pixels, we used the same method as Torralba *et al.* [44]: we first applied a low-pass 5×5 binomial filter to I_{HG} and then down-sampled the resulting image using bicubic interpolation by a factor of two, until the desired image height of 64 pixels was reached (corresponding width was maintained based on the original aspect ratio), forming I_{LG}. This also had the effect of providing a clear upper bound on the amount of visual information available [44].

6 Experiments

This section assesses how well saliency information is preserved after transforming HC images to LG images using methods outlined above. Furthermore, it investigates if there are any computational benefits using LG over HC. A fixation map is a two-dimensional spatial record of discrete image locations fixated by an observer, and is collected using an eye-tracker [45]. Previous studies used fixation maps to compare saliency similarity between images [14,46]. Saliency similarity can also be quantified using fixation-map inter-observer visual congruency (agreement) [46]. To that end, we designed and conducted three separate experiments: Sect. 6.1 assesses LG and HC fixation-map similarity; Sect. 6.2 assesses LG vs. HC fixation-map inter-observer congruency; and Sect. 6.3 compares accuracy, training and detection speed performance between saliency models trained on HC and LG data.

6.1 HC and LG Fixation-Map Similarity

Dataset. A subset I_{HC} of 20 HC images (1920×1080 pixels, sRGB) along with the corresponding aggregated eye fixations F_{HC} from 18 observers were randomly sampled from the publicly-available CAT2000 benchmark dataset [47]. This dataset contains 4000 images selected from a wide variety of categories such as *art, cartoons, indoor, jumbled, line drawings, random, satellite, and outdoor*. Overall, this dataset contains 20 different categories with 200 images from each category. Only 20 images were evaluated since the sample size of observers was sufficient to determine the statistical significance of fixation-map similarity. Using methods outlined in Sect. 5, images from I_{HC} were first converted to grayscale, then down-sampled to 120×64 pixels. This resulted in a set of images I_{LG} that were a mere 0.12% of the original size, thus significantly reducing computational costs. For human visualization on the eye-tracker screen, I_{LG} images were up-sampled back to their original resolution using the same bicubic interpolation rescaling method outlined in Sect. 5.2.

Eye Tracking. Eye fixations F_{LG} were collected using a Tobii T60 eye-tracker by allowing a separate cohort of 18 consenting participants to free-view each

I_{LG} image for 3 sfrom a viewing distance of 60 cm, consistent with the CAT2000 study. Such a viewing duration typically elicits 4–6 fixations from each observer. This is sufficient to highlight a few points of interest per image, and offers a reasonable testing ground for saliency models [48]. Each observer underwent an initial five-point calibration procedure to minimize eye-tracking calibration errors. Every pair of LG/HC images was displayed at least 2 images apart to minimize the effect of priming.

Evaluation Metrics. We compared F_{HC} and F_{LG} fixation map similarity as a function of six recommended "gold standard" metrics: Normalized Scanpath Saliency (NSS) [49], Kullback-Leibler divergence (KL) [50], Judd Area under ROC Curve (jAUC) [51], Shuffled AUC (sAUC) [52], Pearson's Correlation Coefficient (CC) [53], and Similarity or histogram intersection (SIM) [54]. NSS is computed as the average normalized saliency at fixated locations. KL divergence measures the difference between two probability distributions. jAUC measures the area under the Receiver Operating Characteristic curve representing the trade-off between true and false positives at various discrimination thresholds. The sAUC samples negatives from fixation locations from other images, which has the effect of sampling negatives predominantly from the image center. This is because averaging fixations over many images results in the natural emergence of a central Gaussian distribution. Models only predicting the center achieve an sAUC score $\leq 0{:}5$ because at all thresholds they capture as many fixations on the target image as on other images. CC measures statistical Pearson's correlation between two saliency maps. Finally, SIM measures the similarity between two distributions, viewed as histograms. These metrics have been used in the past to evaluate fixation map similarity because of their easy interpretability [48,52]. We skip explaining these metrics in detail for brevity, and refer readers to the relevant publications.

Discrete fixations from F_{HC} and F_{LG} are converted into continuous distribution maps M_{HC} and M_{LG}, respectively, by smoothing, which acts as regularization, allowing for uncertainty in the ground truth measurements to be incorporated. A blur value σ is required for the Gaussian low-pass filter in the Fourier domain. We follow common practice [48], and blur each fixation location using a Gaussian with σ ranging from 1 to 100, resulting in 100 fixation maps for each HC and LG image per participant. For highly similar fixation maps, all evaluation metrics rise (except KL, which falls) rapidly towards a large maximum as $\sigma \rightarrow 100$. Conversely, for highly dissimilar fixation maps, evaluation metrics decrease with an increasing σ [55]. We calculated these metrics using MATLAB scripts from [48], and plot the median across all participants for each metric (Fig. 4).

Results. From visual inspection (Fig. 3), we can see that increasing σ smooths the fixation density map and has the effect of filtering out stray fixations with low inter-observer congruency, leaving behind high-confidence fixations. These results suggest that M_{HC} and M_{LG} are highly similar, attaining high jAUC (0.88), SIM (0.85) and CC (0.92) as $\sigma \rightarrow 100$ (Fig. 4). Moreover, this result confirms saliency preservation in LG images in terms of fixation map similarity.

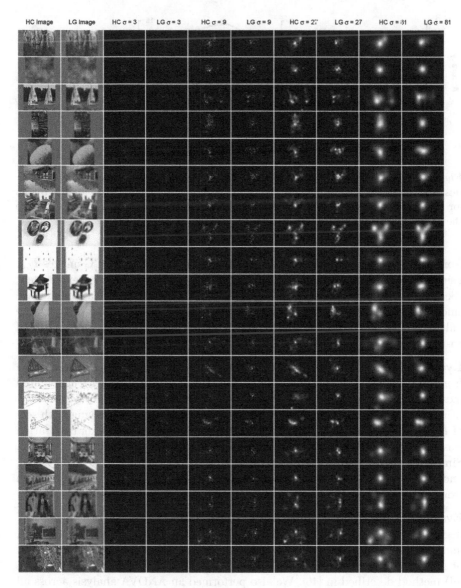

Fig. 3. Twenty images from the CAT2000 dataset [46] in high-resolution color (HC) and low-resolution grayscale (LG), and their corresponding fixation maps (from 18 observers each) as a function of σ, where $\sigma \in \{3, 9, 27, 81\}$, from Experiment 1 analyses (Sect. 6.1).

6.2 HC vs. LG Inter-observer Consistency

Dataset. To determine LG and HC inter-observer congruency (agreement), a subset I_{HC} of 10 HC (1280 × 1024 pixels, sRGB) images were randomly sampled

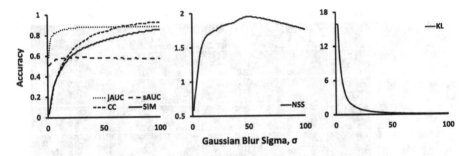

Fig. 4. Low-resolution grayscale and high-resolution color fixation-map similarity metrics as a function of the Gaussian blur σ. Plots represent medians across all participants for all 20 images. Note: NSS y-axis range is constrained to min/max and all plots share the x-axis.

from the Internet (Google Images) and converted to 120×64 pixel LG images I_{LG} using the same methods described in Sect. 5. As with the previous experiment (Sect. 6.1), 10 images were deemed sufficient to determine statistical significance since the sample size of observers was large. This resulted in images that were only 0.19% of the original size; once again, significantly reducing computational costs.

Eye Tracking. To conduct this analysis, we required separate fixation data from each observer, which was lacking from the CAT2000 dataset's aggregated fixations. To that end, we collected eye-tracking fixation data F_{HC} and F_{LG} using the same Tobii eye-tracker from 35 consenting observers viewing both sets of I_{HC} and I_{LG} images, respectively. Standard five-point eye-tracker calibration was performed at the start of each trial for each participant as standard practice. Similar to the previous experiment in §6.1, images were presented for 3 s each, and participants were instructed to freely view images, while seated 60 cm in front of the screen.

Evaluation Metrics. We chose a Gaussian blur σ of 30, which corresponds to 1 degree of visual angle [48], generated continuous fixation maps, M_{HC} and M_{LG}, and calculated inter-observer congruency as a function of the same previous set of 6 metrics within the F_{HC} and F_{LG} sets using the leave-one-out (one-vs-all) method described in [46]. We also performed an ANOVA analysis across all co-variates.

Results. Figure 6 show that the LG fixation data does not show a higher dispersion between observers' eye tracking data compared to HG fixations. Furthermore, the ANOVA analysis found no significant difference between HC and LG inter-observer consistency ($p > 0.05$). This result suggests that LG fixation data is as accurate as expected for substituting HC fixation data [46]. Moreover, this result further confirms saliency preservation in LG images in terms of fixation map inter-observer congruency.

HC Image   LG Image   HC σ = 30   LG σ = 30

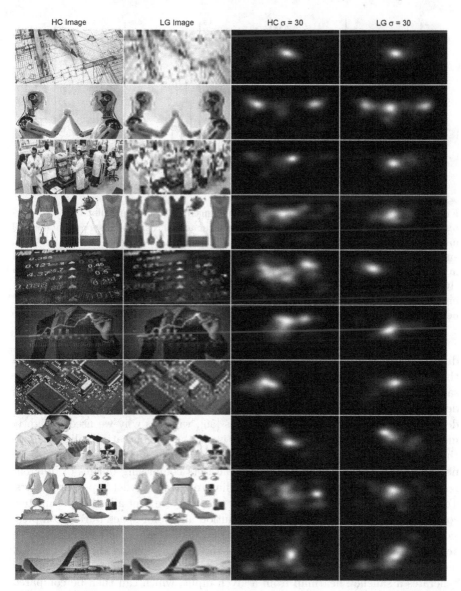

Fig. 5. Full set of 10 images in high-resolution color (HC) and low-resolution grayscale (LG), and their corresponding fixation maps (from 35 observers each) as a function of $\sigma = 30$, from Experiment 2 analyses (Sect. 6.2).

6.3 HC vs. LG Saliency Detection Models

Model Architecture. Conventional convolutional neural networks (CNNs) used for image classification consists of convolutional layers followed by fully connected layers, which takes an image of fixed spatial size as input and pro-

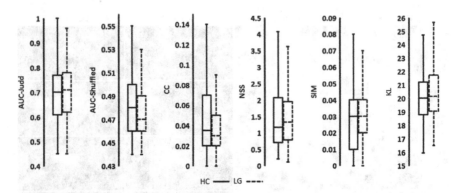

Fig. 6. Experiment 2 (Sect. 6.2) boxplots showing high-resolution color (HC) vs. low-resolution grayscale (LG) inter-observer congruency across 35 observers across 10 images (in HC and LG) as a function of AUC-Judd, AUC-Shuffled, CC, NSS, SIM, and KL. A σ of 30 was chosen from Experiment 1 to generate the fixation maps used in this analysis. ANOVA analysis revealed no statistically significant difference between HC and LG across all 6 metrics. Note: y–axes have been cropped and scaled for viewing convenience; boxplot key (from bottom): minimum, 25th percentile, median, 75th percentile, and maximum.

duces a single-dimensional vector indicating the class-probability or category of the input image. For tasks requiring spatial labels, like generating pixel-wise saliency heatmaps, we consider fully convolutional neural networks (FCNs) with deconvolutional layers. This architecture has been previously used for saliency detection in video with enormous success [56], which is why we used a slightly modified version in our study (Fig. 7). It is capable of generating saliency maps the same size as the input image, which was ideal for our experiment since we needed to compare the same model on datasets comprising images of different resolutions and color spaces without needing to change model hyperparameters. To test if HC and LG models have similar accuracy, we kept all other parameters constant and only varied the image resolution and color space during compression. We were only interested in a HC saliency detection model with comparable accuracy and performance to the state-of-the-art so we could show that an LG model can achieve the same performance faster and more efficiently. The model generates a saliency heatmap from a given input, which can then be compared with the ground-truth density map, just as in the above experiments.

Dataset. The 2000 labeled images from the same CAT2000 saliency benchmark dataset used previously was split into training (1800 images) and validation (200 images) sets. These sets were duplicated and preprocessed to produce four new sets: high-resolution 24-bit color training and validation sets, T_{HC} and V_{HC}, created by downsampling the original resolution to 512×512 pixels (typical resolution used by many state-of-the-art saliency detection models) using methods described in Sect. 5.2, and low-resolution (64×64 pixels) 8-bit grayscale sets, T_{LG} and V_{LG}, generated using methods outlined above.

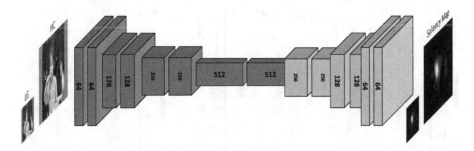

Fig. 7. Fully convolutional neural network architecture. The network takes an HC or LG image as input, adopts convolution layers (blue) with 3×3 kernels and a stride of 1 to transform the image into multidimensional feature representations, then applies a stack of deconvolution layers (orange) for upsampling the extracted coarse features. Finally, a fully convolution layer with a 1×1 kernel and sigmoid activation function outputs a pixel-wise probability (saliency) map the same size as the input, where larger values correspond to higher saliency. Numbers represent convolutional filters. (Color figure online)

Model Training. The Python Keras API with the TensorFlow framework back-end was used to implement and train HC and LG FCN models, M_{HC} and M_{LG}, on the respective 1800 training images end-to-end and from scratch (i.e. random-ized initial weights). Network weights and parameters were initialized by seeding a pseudo-random number generator with the same seed for all training sessions and models to ensure everything else remained constant. The training images were propagated through the FCN in batches of 8 and 64 for M_{HC} and M_{LG}, respectively. Due to the FCN's large parameter space, M_{HC} batch size was restricted to 8 so that the 512×512 images could be accommodated by the available memory (12 GB) and resources. Weights were learned using slow gra-dient decent (RMSProp) over 100 epochs totaling 180,000 iterations. The base learning rate was set to 0.05, and decreased by a factor of 10 after 2000 itera-tions. A mean-squared error loss function was implemented to compute loss for gradient descent. An NVIDIA Tesla K80 GPU was used for training and infer-ence. Training time (i.e. the time taken to complete all iterations to completion) for each model was recorded.

Evaluation Metrics. M_{HC} and M_{LG} were tested on their respective held-out validation sets, V_{HC} and V_{LG}. The predicted labels from the models' output were up-sampled to match the original dimensions of the ground truth labels (1920×1080 pixels) for a fair accuracy evaluation. Model accuracy was defined as a function of NSS, Judd-AUC, SIM, and CC, described above, and computed using MATLAB code from the MIT saliency benchmark GitHub repository [14]. Furthermore, detection time, defined as the average time taken by the model to generate a predicted saliency map based on each of the 200 test images, was also measured for M_{HC} and M_{LG}. Two-tailed paired Student's t-tests were performed between HC and LG result pairs to determine if differences were

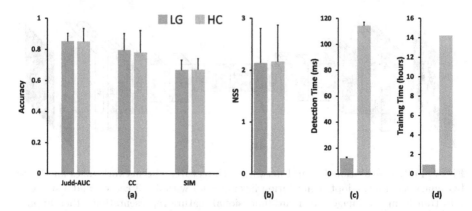

Fig. 8. (a) HC and LG model accuracy as a function of Judd-AUC, CC, SIM, and (b) NSS. (c) HC vs. LG training time. (d) HC vs. LG detection time. Bar plots represent means and error bars represent standard deviations across the 200 test results per model.

statistically significant. Finally, to rule out centre bias [57] we applied a 2D Gaussian located at the image centre and statistically compared (using paired Student's t-tests) its sAUC with our LG and HC models on 200 test images.

Results. Figures 8(a) and (b) show no statistically significant difference between M_{HC} and M_{LG} accuracy across all evaluation metrics ($p > 0.05$). Furthermore, these accuracies are comparable to state-of-the-art models. The centre-bias sAUC results (2D Gaussian HC = 0.45 and LG = 0.44; our FCN HC = 0.58 and LG = 0.57; p-value < 0.05) discard the hypothesis that our models only predict central saliency. Moreover, an sAUC of 0.58 is highly comparable to state-of-the-art models [58]. Therefore, this is further evidence suggesting saliency is well-preserved in LG images. Figures 8(c) and (d) show a significant difference between M_{HC} and M_{LG} training and detection times ($p < 0.05$). M_{LG} trained more than 14× faster than its HC counterpart, M_{HC}. Furthermore, M_{LG} is capable of generating a predicted saliency map almost 10× faster than M_{HC} (12 vs. 114 ms). Considering these significant speedups come at negligible accuracy cost, the implications of using LG images over HC are substantial; thus, the motivation to use LG images in saliency detection should now be more obvious and appealing.

7   Conclusion

In this study, we explained and demonstrated the biological and computational motivation for using LG images in salience detection. We learned, through evolutionary insights, that bottom-up visual salience detection is predominantly a peripheral vision mechanism. We also learned that peripheral vision information is primarily achromatic and low-resolution, and can be approximated in the digital domain using a simple LG transformation. Through eye-tracking experiments, we found high similarity between LG and HC fixations. The results of this study also showed no significant difference in inter-observer congruency between LG and HC groups. Additionally, we trained fully convolutional neural networks for saliency detection using LG and HC data from a benchmark dataset and found no significant difference between HC, LG and state-of-the-art model accuracy. However, we found that the LG model required significantly less (1/14) training time and is much faster (almost 10×) performing detection compared to the same network trained and evaluated on HC images. Therefore, these results confirm our hypothesis that saliency information is preserved in LG images, and we conclude by proposing LG images for fast and efficient saliency detection. Future research will extend this work by investigating the use of LG images in other computer vision tasks, such as object detection, pose tracking and background subtraction, since we have reason to believe that many vision tasks could just as easily be done using peripheral vision and hence, low-resolution grayscale information.

Acknowledgements. This research was supported by an Australian Postgraduate Award scholarship, the Professor Robert and Josephine Shanks scholarship, and Australian Research Council grants FL-170100117, DP-180103424, and LP-150100671. The authors wish to thank the eye tracking participants for volunteering their time and Mr Wei Li for helping with the experiments.

References

1. McMains, S.A., Kastner, S.: Visual attention. In: Binder, M.D., Hirokawa, N., Windhorst, U. (eds.) Encyclopedia of Neuroscience, pp. 4296–4302. Springer, Heidelberg (2009). https://doi.org/10.1007/978-3-540-29678-2

2. Morawetz, L., Spaethe, J.: Visual attention in a complex search task differs between honeybees and bumblebees. J. Exp. Biol. **215**(Pt 14), 2515–2523 (2012)

3. Avarguès-Weber, A., Dyer, A.G., Ferrah, N., Giurfa, M.: The forest or the trees: preference for global over local image processing is reversed by prior experience in honeybees. Proc. Roy. Soc. B Biol. Sci. **282**(1799), 20142384 (2015)

4. Morawetz, L., Svoboda, A., Spaethe, J., Dyer, A.G.: Blue colour preference in honeybees distracts visual attention for learning closed shapes. J. Comp. Physiol. A Neuroethol. Sens. Neural Behav. Physiol. **199**(10), 817–827 (2013)

5. Hou, W., Gao, X., Tao, D., Li, X.: Visual saliency detection using information divergence. Pattern Recogn. **46**(10), 2658–2669 (2013)

6. Kümmerer, M., Wallis, T.S.A., Bethge, M.: DeepGaze II: reading fixations from deep features trained on object recognition. arXiv:1610.01563 [cs, q-bio, stat], October 2016

7. Huang, X., Shen, C., Boix, X., Zhao, Q.: SALICON: reducing the semantic gap in saliency prediction by adapting deep neural networks. In: 2015 IEEE International Conference on Computer Vision (ICCV), pp. 262–270, December 2015

8. Kruthiventi, S.S.S., Ayush, K., Babu, R.V.: DeepFix: a fully convolutional neural network for predicting human eye fixations. IEEE Trans. Image Process. **26**(9), 4446–4456 (2017)

9. Cornia, M., Baraldi, L., Serra, G., Cucchiara, R.: Predicting human eye fixations via an LSTM-based saliency attentive model. arXiv:1611.09571 [cs], November 2016

10. Rajankar, O.S., Kolekar, U.D.: Scale space reduction with interpolation to speed up visual saliency detection. Int. J. Image Graph. Sig. Process. (IJIGSP) **7**(8), 58 (2015)

11. Wang, W., Shen, J.: Deep visual attention prediction. arXiv:1705.02544 [cs], May 2017

12. Vo, A.V., et al.: Processing of extremely high resolution LiDAR and RGB data. IEEE J. Sel. Top. Appl. Earth Obs. Remote Sens. **9**(12), 5560–5575 (2016)

13. Lamb, T.D.: Evolution of phototransduction, vertebrate photoreceptors and retina. In: Kolb, H., Fernandez, E., Nelson, R. (eds.) Webvision: The Organization of the Retina and Visual System. University of Utah Health Sciences Center, Salt Lake City (UT) (1995)

14. Judd, T., Durand, F., Torralba, A.: Fixations on low-resolution images. J. Vis. **11**(4), 1–20 (2011)

15. Shen, C., Huang, X., Zhao, Q.: Learning of proto-object representations via fixations on low resolution. ArXiv e-prints, December 2014. arXiv:1412.7242

16. Ho-Phuoc, T., Guyader, N., Landragin, F., Guérin-Dugué, A.: When viewing natural scenes, do abnormal colors impact on spatial or temporal parameters of eye movements? J. Vis. **12**(2), 4 (2012)

17. Hamel, S., Guyader, N., Pellerin, D., Houzet, D.: Contribution of color information in visual saliency model for videos. In: Elmoataz, A., Lezoray, O., Nouboud, F., Mammass, D. (eds.) ICISP 2014. LNCS, vol. 8509, pp. 213–221. Springer, Cham (2014). https://doi.org/10.1007/978-3-319-07998-1_24

18. Hamel, S., Guyader, N., Pellerin, D., Houzet, D.: Contribution of color in saliency model for videos. Sig. Image Video Process. **10**(3), 423–429 (2016)

19. Hamel, S., Houzet, D., Pellerin, D., Guyader, N.: Does color influence eye movements while exploring videos? J. Eye Mov. Res. **8**(1) (2015)

20. Frey, H.P., Honey, C., König, P.: What's color got to do with it? The influence of color on visual attention in different categories. J. Vis. **8**(14), 6 (2008)

21. Baddeley, R.J., Tatler, B.W.: High frequency edges (but not contrast) predict where we fixate: a Bayesian system identification analysis. Vis. Res. **46**(18), 2824–2833 (2006)

22. Dorr, M., Vig, E., Barth, E.: Colour saliency on video. In: Suzuki, J., Nakano, T. (eds.) BIONETICS 2010. LNICST, vol. 87, pp. 601–606. Springer, Heidelberg (2012). https://doi.org/10.1007/978-3-642-32615-8_59

23. Xu, Y., Xiao, T., Zhang, J., Yang, K., Zhang, Z.: Scale-invariant convolutional neural networks. arXiv:1411.6369 [cs], November 2014

24. Advani, S., Sustersic, J., Irick, K., Narayanan, V.: A multi-resolution saliency framework to drive foveation. In: 2013 IEEE International Conference on Acoustics, Speech and Signal Processing, pp. 2596–2600, May 2013

25. Lindeberg, T., Florack, L.: Foveal Scale-space and the Linear Increase of Receptive Field Size as a Function of Eccentricity. KTH Royal Institute of Technology, Stockholm (1994)

26. Koenderink, J.J., Doorn, A.J.V.: Visual detection of spatial contrast; Influence of location in the visual field, target extent and illuminance level. Biol. Cybern. **30**(3), 157–167 (1978)

27. Romeny, B.M.H.: Front-End Vision and Multi-Scale Image Analysis: Multi-scale Computer Vision Theory and Applications, Written in Mathematica. Springer, Heidelberg (2008)

28. Treisman, A.M., Gelade, G.: A feature-integration theory of attention. Cogn. Psychol. **12**(1), 97–136 (1980)
29. Humphrey, G.K., Goodale, M.A., Jakobson, L.S., Servos, P.: The role of surface information in object recognition: studies of a visual form agnosic and normal subjects. Perception **23**(12), 1457–1481 (1994)
30. Gegenfurtner, K.R., Rieger, J.: Sensory and cognitive contributions of color to the recognition of natural scenes. Curr. Biol. **10**(13), 805–808 (2000)
31. Lennie, P.: Color vision: putting it together. Curr. Biol. **10**(16), R589–R591 (2000)
32. Yang, Y., Song, M., Bu, J., Chen, C., Jin, C.: Color to gray: attention preservation. In: 2010 Fourth Pacific-Rim Symposium on Image and Video Technology, pp. 337–342, November 2010
33. Pope, B., Druyan, A., Soter, S., deGrasse Tyson, N., Hanich, L., Holtzman, S.: Cosmos: A Spacetime Odyssey (episode 2: some of the things that molecules do) (2014)
34. Nilsson, D.E.: The evolution of eyes and visually guided behaviour. Philos. Trans. Roy. Soc. Lond. B: Biol. Sci. **364**(1531), 2833–2847 (2009)
35. Potter, M.C., Wyble, B., Hagmann, C.E., McCourt, E.S.: Detecting meaning in RSVP at 13 ms per picture. Atten. Percept. Psychophys. **76**(2), 270–279 (2014)
36. Stojcev, M., Radtke, N., D'Amaro, D., Dyer, A.G., Neumeyer, C.: General principles in motion vision: color blindness of object motion depends on pattern velocity in honeybee and goldfish. Vis. Neurosci. **28**(4), 361–370 (2011)
37. Wandell, B.A.: Foundations of Vision. Sinauer Associates, Sunderland (1995)
38. Veale, R., Hafed, Z.M., Yoshida, M.: How is visual salience computed in the brain? Insights from behaviour, neurobiology and modelling. Philos. Trans. Roy. Soc. B: Biol. Sci. **372**(1714), 20160113 (2017)
39. Okawa, H., Sampath, A.P.: Optimization of single-photon response transmission at the rod-to-rod bipolar synapse. Physiology (Bethesda, Md.) **22**, 279–286 (2007)
40. White, B.J., Kan, J.Y., Levy, R., Itti, L., Munoz, D.P.: Superior colliculus encodes visual saliency before the primary visual cortex. Proc. Nat. Acad. Sci. **114**(35), 9451–9456 (2017)
41. Krauzlis, R.J., Lovejoy, L.P., Zénon, A.: Superior colliculus and visual spatial attention. Ann. Rev. Neurosci. **36**(1), 165–182 (2013)
42. Poynton, C.A.: Rehabilitation of gamma. Int. Soc. Opt. Photonics **3299**, 232–250 (1998)
43. Poynton, C., Funt, B.: Perceptual uniformity in digital image representation and display. Color Res. Appl. **39**(1), 6–15 (2014)
44. Torralba, A.: How many pixels make an image? Vis. Neurosci. **26**(1), 123–131 (2009)
45. Wooding, D.S.: Fixation maps: quantifying eye-movement traces. In: Proceedings of the 2002 Symposium on Eye Tracking Research & Applications, pp. 31–36 (2002)
46. Tavakoli, H.R., Ahmed, F., Borji, A., Laaksonen, J.: Saliency revisited: analysis of mouse movements versus fixations. arXiv:1705.10546 [cs], May 2017
47. Borji, A., Itti, L.: CAT2000: a large scale fixation dataset for boosting saliency research. arXiv:1505.03581 [cs], May 2015
48. Bylinskii, Z., Judd, T., Oliva, A., Torralba, A., Durand, F.: What do different evaluation metrics tell us about saliency models? arXiv:1604.03605 [cs], April 2016
49. Peters, R.J., Iyer, A., Itti, L., Koch, C.: Components of bottom-up gaze allocation in natural images. Vis. Res. **45**(18), 2397–2416 (2005)
50. Liang, J., Zhang, Y.: Top down saliency detection via Kullback-Leibler divergence for object recognition. In: 2015 International Symposium on Bioelectronics and Bioinformatics (ISBB), pp. 200–203, October 2015

51. Judd, T., Ehinger, K., Durand, F., Torralba, A.: Learning to predict where humans look. In: 2009 IEEE 12th International Conference on Computer Vision, pp. 2106–2113, September 2009
52. Borji, A., Tavakoli, H.R., Sihite, D.N., Itti, L.: Analysis of scores, datasets, and models in visual saliency prediction. In: 2013 IEEE International Conference on Computer Vision, pp. 921–928, December 2013
53. Le Meur, O., Le Callet, P., Barba, D.: Predicting visual fixations on video based on low-level visual features. Vis. Res. **47**(19), 2483–2498 (2007)
54. Koch, C., Ullman, S.: Shifts in selective visual attention: towards the underlying neural circuitry. Hum. Neurobiol. **4**(4), 219–227 (1985)
55. Engelke, U., et al.: A comparative study of fixation density maps. IEEE Trans. Image Process. **22**(3), 1121–1133 (2013)
56. Wang, W., Shen, J., Shao, L.: Video salient object detection via fully convolutional networks. IEEE Trans. Image Process. **27**(1), 38–49 (2018)
57. Tatler, B.W.: The central fixation bias in scene viewing: selecting an optimal viewing position independently of motor biases and image feature distributions. J. Vis. **7**(14), 4.1–17 (2007)
58. Judd, T., Durand, F., Torralba, A.: A benchmark of computational models of saliency to predict human fixations

Proxy Clouds for Live RGB-D Stream Processing and Consolidation

Adrien Kaiser[1]([⊠]), Jose Alonso Ybanez Zepeda[2], and Tamy Boubekeur[1]

[1] LTCI, Telecom ParisTech, Paris-Saclay University, Paris, France
{adrien.kaiser,tamy.boubekeur}@telecom-paristech.fr
[2] Ayotle, Le Kremlin Bicetre, France
alonso@hayo.io

Abstract. We propose a new multiplanar superstructure for unified real-time processing of RGB-D data. Modern RGB-D sensors are widely used for indoor 3D capture, with applications ranging from modeling to robotics, through augmented reality. Nevertheless, their use is limited by their low resolution, with frames often corrupted with noise, missing data and temporal inconsistencies. Our approach, named *Proxy Clouds*, consists in generating and updating through time a single set of compact local statistics parameterized over detected planar proxies, which are fed from raw RGB-D data. *Proxy Clouds* provide several processing primitives, which improve the quality of the RGB-D stream on-the-fly or lighten further operations. Experimental results confirm that our light weight analysis framework copes well with embedded execution as well as moderate memory and computational capabilities compared to state-of-the-art methods. Processing of RGB-D data with *Proxy Clouds* includes noise and temporal flickering removal, hole filling and resampling. As a substitute of the observed scene, our *proxy cloud* can additionally be applied to compression and scene reconstruction. We present experiments performed with our framework in indoor scenes of different natures within a recent open RGB-D dataset.

Keywords: RGB-D stream · 3D geometric primitives
Data reinforcement · Depth improvement · Online processing
Scene reconstruction

1 Introduction

Context. The real time RGB-D stream output of modern commodity consumer depth cameras can feed a growing set of end applications, from human computer interaction and augmented reality to industrial design. Although such devices are constantly improving, the limited quality of their stream still restraints their impact spectrum. This mostly originates in the low resolution of the frames and

Electronic supplementary material The online version of this chapter (https://doi.org/10.1007/978-3-030-01231-1_16) contains supplementary material, which is available to authorized users.

© Springer Nature Switzerland AG 2018
V. Ferrari et al. (Eds.): ECCV 2018, LNCS 11210, pp. 255–271, 2018.
https://doi.org/10.1007/978-3-030-01231-1_16

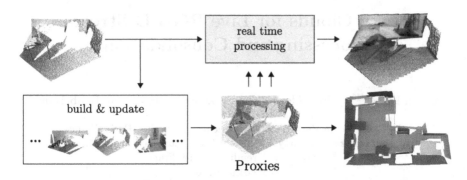

Fig. 1. Proxy clouds overview. From a stream of RGB-D frames (left), proxies are built on-the-fly and updated over time (bottom) and used to apply different real-time processing primitives to the incoming RGB-D frames (top). The system outputs an enhanced data stream and a planar model of the observed scene (right). The "build & update" procedure is detailed in Fig. 4.

the inherent noise, incompleteness and temporal inconsistency stemming from single view capture. With *Proxy Clouds*, we aim at improving real time RGB-D streams by analyzing them. A sparse set of detected 3D planes are parameterized to record statistics extracted from the stream and form a structure that we call *proxy*. This superstructure substitutes the RGB-D data and approximates the geometry of the scene. Using these time-evolving statistics, our plane-based framework improves the RGB-D stream on the fly by reinforcing features, removing noise and outliers or filling missing parts, under the memory-limited and real time embedded constraints of mobile capture in indoor environments (Fig. 1). We design such a lightweight planar superstructure to be stable through time and space, which gives priors to apply several signal-inspired processing primitives to the RGB-D frames. They include filtering to remove noise and temporal flickering, hole filling or resampling (Sect. 4). This allows structuring the data and simplifying or lightening subsequent operations, e.g. tracking and mapping, measurements, data transmission, rendering or physical simulations. While our primary goal is the enhancement of the RGB-D data stream, our framework can additionally be applied to compression and scene reconstruction (Sect. 6), as the generated structure is a representation of the observed scene.

Overview. In practice, our system takes a raw RGB-D stream as input to build and update a set of planar proxies on-the-fly. It outputs an enhanced stream together with a model of planar areas in the observed scene (see Fig. 2). On the contrary to previous approaches, which mostly rely on a full volumetric reconstruction to consolidate data, our approach is light weight, with a moderate memory footprint and a transparent interfacing to any higher-level RGB-D pipeline. To summarize, our contributions are:

- a stable and lightweight multiplanar superstructure for RGB-D data,
- construction and updating methods which are spatially and temporally consistent,
- a collection of RGB-D enhancement methods based on our structure which run on-the-fly.

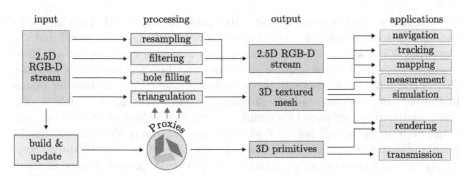

Fig. 2. Proxy clouds workflow. From a stream of 2.5D RGB-D frames, proxies are built on-the-fly and updated through time (Sect. 3). They are used as priors to process incoming frames through filtering, resampling or hole filling which allows better tracking, mapping, automated navigation or measurement. A selection of proxies based on the current RGB-D frame can be used for lightened transmission of the data. Proxies can be used as priors for triangulation and fast depth data meshing, with application to rendering or simulation. Eventually, the consolidation of the depth stream within the proxies leads to a reconstruction of planar areas in the observed scene. Processing modules are described in Sect. 4 and the consolidation of data is presented in Sect. 6.

2   Previous Work

Camera Motion Estimation. Endres et al. [1] describe an egomotion estimation method that uses point features detected in the color component of the RGB-D frame. After detecting and matching SIFT, SURF or ORB features in subsequent color images, their 3D position in both frames is computed using the depth component. Using these matching 3D points, a robust RANSAC-based [2] estimation of the motion matrix allows discarding false positive matches. Sets of three matching points are randomly picked and the matrix transforming a set in the first frame into the second set is computed using a Least-Squares method [3]. Inliers of the transformation are estimated using their 3D position and orientation and the one giving the most inliers is kept. It is important to note that any existing method or device that localizes an RGB-D camera in its environment can be used instead. Some of them are presented in Sect. 2.

Plane Detection in RGB-D Stream. Methods that build high level models of captured 3D data are mostly based on *RANSAC* [2], the *Hough transform* [4] or *Region Growing* algorithms. In our embedded, real time, memory-limited context, we take inspiration from the RANSAC-based method of Schnabel et al. [5] for its time and memory efficiency, by repeating plane detection through time to acquire a consistent model and cope with the stochastic nature of RANSAC.

   Their *Efficient RANSAC* implementation gives stochastic improvements to the critical steps of the algorithm in terms of complexity. For a regular RANSAC-based plane detection, minimal sets of three points would be randomly picked a fixed and large number of times. Then, the shape parameters are estimated from this minimal set and inliers of the estimated plane are computed. The shape with the highest score is kept, its inliers are removed from the point cloud and the algorithm is ran again on the remaining data. Schnabel et al. replace the fixed number of loops with a stochastic condition, based on the number of detected shapes and number of randomly picked minimal sets, to stop looking for planes in the dataset. Also, instead of searching the full point cloud for inliers of a given shape, they estimate this count in a random subset of the dataset and extrapolate it to the full point cloud. Other modifications allow improving the quality of detected shapes with a localized sampling and specific post-processing.

Again, our framework is not attached to a particular plane detection method, and other algorithms such as *point clustering* [6] or *agglomerative hierarchical clustering* [7], could be used. For a complete overview of plane detection methods in captured 3D data, we refer the reader to our survey [8].

Depth Processing. Depth maps can be denoised using spatial filters [9] e.g., Gaussian, median, bilateral [10–12], adaptive or anisotropic [13,14] filters, often refined through time, with the resulting enhanced stream potentially used for a full 3D reconstruction [15]. Other methods include non-local means [16], bilateral filters with time [12], Kalman filters [17], over-segmentation [18] and region-growing [19]. Wu et al. [20] present a shape-from-shading method using the color component to improve the geometry, which allows adding details to the low quality input depth. They show applications of their method to improve volumetric reconstruction on multiple small scale and close range scenes. Depth maps can be upsampled using cross bilateral filters such as *joint bilateral upsampling* [21] or *weighted mode filtering* [22]. Such methods are particularly useful to recover sharp depth regions boundaries and enforce depth-based segmentation.

Hole Filling. Depth sensing range limits and high noise levels often create holes in RGB-D data. Given the material of observed objects and the type of technology used, e.g. *time of flight*, *light coding* or *stereo vision*, some surfaces are harder to detect. The orientation of the surface with regards to the sensor and the perturbations due to light sources can also lower the quality of certain areas. In order to fill these holes in the depth component, one can use the same spatial filters as those used for denoising [16], or morphological filters [13,14].

Inpainting methods [23], over-segmentation [24] or multiscale [25] processing are also used to fill holes for e.g., *depth image-based rendering* (DIBR) under close viewing conditions.

Plane-Based Depth Processing. A set of 3D planes offers a faithful yet lightweight approximation for many indoor environments. Surprisingly, only a few methods have used planar proxies as priors to process 2.5D data, with in particular Schnabel et al. [26] who detect limits of planes to fill in holes in static 3D point clouds. *Fast Sampling Plane Filtering* [27] detects and merges planar patches in static indoor scenes. The detected planes allow filtering the planar surfaces of the input point cloud, however the primitives seem quite sensitive to the depth sensor noise and lack spatial consistency.

Dense SLAM. Online dense *Simultaneous Localization And Mapping (SLAM)* methods accumulate points within a map of the environment, while continuously localizing the sensor in this map. Recent dense SLAM systems include *RGB-D SLAM* [1], *RTAB-Map* [28], *KDP SLAM* [29] or *ORB-SLAM2* [30]. Point-based fusion [31] is also used to accumulate points without the need of a full volumetric representation. Several methods have been developed to include planar primitives in the SLAM system, either to smooth and improve the reconstruction [32,33] or improve the localization of the sensor [34–36]. Finally, a recent offline method [37] makes use of planes to estimate the geometry of a room in order to remove furnitures and model the lighting of the environment. This allows the user to re-light and re-furnish the room as desired.

Volumetric Depth Fusion. Online scene reconstruction methods using volumetric fusion were pioneered by *KinectFusion* [15], then made more efficient with *VoxelHashing* [38], and more accurate with *BundleFusion* [39]. However, the need for a voxel grid representing the space leads to high requirements of memory. Recent algorithms make use of planes to smooth and complete the data within the volume, such as methods by Zhang et al. [40] or Dzitsiuk et al. [41]. Offline improvement methods have been developed based on the volumetric representation of the scene, such as *3DLite* [42] that builds a planar model of the observed scene and optimizes it to achieve a high quality texturing of the surfaces.

3   Proxy Clouds

Model. Basically, *Proxy Clouds* model RGB-D data which is often seen and consistent through frames and space, hence revealing the dominant structural elements in the scene. To do so, they take the form of a multiplanar superstructure, where each proxy is equipped with a local frame, bounds and, within the bounds, a regular 2D grid of rich statistics, mapped on the plane and gathered from the RGB-D data.

Each cell of the grid includes an occupancy probability as well as a statistical model of the depth values. We choose to represent this local distribution using *smoothed local histograms* [43] made of Gaussian kernels. The contribution of an inlier p of distance $d(p)$ to the proxy is given in Eq. 1.

$$h_p(s) = \frac{1}{\sigma\sqrt{2\pi}}e^{\frac{(s-d(p))^2}{2\sigma^2}} \qquad h'_p(s) = -\frac{s-d(p)}{\sigma^2}h_p(s) \qquad (1)$$

This compressed model stores the repartition of plane inliers distances to the proxy and makes possible estimating the diversity of the values within each cell by counting the number of modes in the distribution. If it has a single mode, then all values are similar and the surface of the proxy within the cell is most likely flat. If the distribution has two or more modes, then the values belong to different groups and the cell likely overlaps a salient area of the surface.

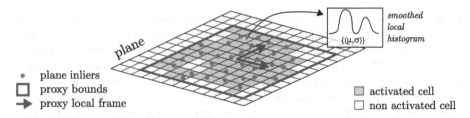

Fig. 3. Planar proxy model. Built upon a plane in 3D space, our proxy model is made of a local frame, bounds and a grid of cells which contain statistics. These statistics are the occupancy probability as well as a collection of mean μ and variance σ values for depth, representing a *smoothed local histogram* and gathered from the RGB-D data. Activated cells are the ones containing inliers from many frames.

Cells have a fixed size of $5\,\mathrm{cm} \times 5\,\mathrm{cm}$, which corresponds to about four times the area of a depth pixel at a typical distance of 8 meters[1]. Hence, this size ensures a minimum sampling of proxy cells by depth points even at far capture distances.

Cells are activated when their visitation percentage over the recent frames (the last 100 frames in our experiments) is greater than a threshold (25% in practice). Once activated, a cell stays so until the end of the processing. We consider a cell as visited as soon as it admits at least one inlier data point i.e., a data point located within a threshold distance to the cell under a projection in the direction from the sensor origin to the point. This activation threshold allows modeling the actual geometry of the observed scene, while discarding outliers observations due to the low quality of the sensor. Figure 3 gives visual insight of a planar proxy.

Building Proxies. We build planar proxies on-the-fly and update them through time using solely incoming raw RGB-D frames from the live stream. More precisely, for each new RGB-D image $X_t = \{I_t, D_t\}$ (color and depth), we run the procedure described in Algorithm 1 and Fig. 4.

The initial depth filtering (step 1) is based on a bilateral convolution [10] of the depth map using a Gaussian kernel associated with a range check to discard points further than a depth threshold from the current point, which could create artificial depth values if taken into account. In our experiments, we choose to set this threshold to $20\,\mathrm{cm}$, which allows filtering together parts of the same object, while ignoring the influence of unrelated objects. Due to the embedded processing constraint, we estimate the normal field (step 2) through the simple computation of the depth gradient at each pixel, using the sensor topology as domain. The estimation of the camera motion from the previous frame (step 3) is inspired from the method introduced by Endres et al. [1], using point features from I_t. As previously stated, any egomotion estimation algorithm can be used at this step, as all we need is the values of the six degrees

---

[1] The area of a pixel at given depth Z is given by $a(Z) = tan(\frac{fov_H}{res_H})tan(\frac{fov_V}{res_V})Z^2$. With $fov = (60°, 45°)$ and $res = (320, 240)$, we have $a(8\,\mathrm{m}) \approx 0.00068539\,\mathrm{m}^2 \approx (2.6\,\mathrm{cm})^2$.

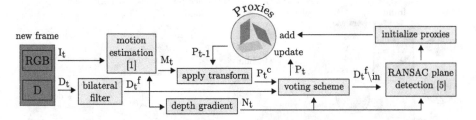

Fig. 4. Building proxies. This procedure is ran for each new RGB-D image X_t at frame t, made of a color image I_t and a depth map D_t. D_t^f: low-pass filtered version of D_t; M_t: camera motion matrix; N_t: normal vectors associated with D_t; P_{t-1}: proxies detected at frame $t-1$; P_t^c: candidate proxies; P_t: proxies at frame t; $D_t^f|_{in}$: low-pass filtered depth points without inliers from P_t;

Algorithm 1. Building Proxies

Notations: X_t: current RGB-D frame; I_t: current RGB frame; D_t: current depth frame; P_t: current proxies;

$P_t \leftarrow \varnothing$
function BUILDPROXIES($X_t = \{I_t, D_t\}$)

1. filter D_t with a bilateral color/depth convolution;
2. estimate the normal field N_t from D_t;
3. estimate the camera motion M_t from X_{t-1} [1];
4. search for previous proxies in X_t:

    4.1 register previous frame proxies to X_t using M_t;
    4.2 cast votes from samples of X_t to previous proxies;
    4.3 given the vote count for each previous proxy:

        keep it, update it with X_t and add it to P_t;
        discard it and place it in probation state;
        purge it if it has been discarded for too long.

5. detect new proxy planes in $X_t \setminus inliers(P_t)$:

    5.1 RANSAC-based plane detection [5];
    5.2 post-detection plane fusion;
    5.3 compute the local frame;
    5.4 initialize the new proxy with X_t.
    5.5 register new proxy to global space using M_t.

    return P_t
end function

---

of freedom modeling the camera motion. Examples of such algorithms are given in Sect. 2. In order to keep or discard previously detected proxies (step 4.2), we define a voting scheme where samples of X_t which are inliers of a given previous proxy cast their vote to this proxy and are marked. Then, the per-proxy vote count indicates whether the proxy is preserved or discarded (step 4.3). Preserved proxies are updated with X_t, hence see their parameters refined and occupancy statistics updated with new inliers. Discarded proxies are placed in *probation*

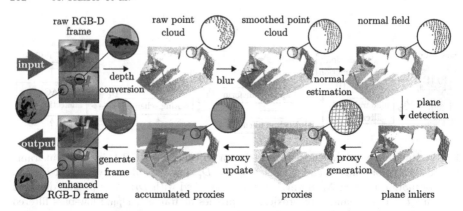

Fig. 5. Proxy building procedure. The input RGB-D frame is converted into a raw point cloud on which a low-pass filter is applied, followed by normal estimation (top). RANSAC-based plane detection [5] is applied and used as a basis for the construction or the update of our proxies, following the structure shown in Fig. 3 (bottom right). Accumulated proxy cells (bottom) are visualized with colors weighted by their occupancy probabilities: darker cells have a low probability and represent low confidence areas, whereas brighter cells represent areas with high confidence. Proxies are then used to generate enhanced RGB-D frames. The whole process runs on-the-fly.

state for near-future recheck with new incoming frames, and purged if discarded for too long. However, in order to avoid losing information on non-observed parts of the scene, we do not purge proxies that have been seen long enough, which stay in probation instead. When new proxies have been detected (step 5.1), similar ones are merged together in order to avoid modeling different parts of planar surfaces with multiple proxy instances (step 5.2). The proxy is then generated (step 5.3) with a bounding rectangle and a local frame computed to be aligned with the scene orientation (more details in the supplemental material). Using the global scene axes to compute the local frame leads to a fixed resolution and spatial consistency for the grid of all proxies and allows efficient recovery and fusion (step 5.2). Finally, occupancy statistics are initialized using X_t (step 5.4). In order to take into account the point of view when modeling the scene, inlier depth points are projected upon the detected shape following the direction between the camera and the point. The coordinates of the corresponding cell of the proxy grid are then recovered to update its statistics. As a last step, proxies are transformed from local depth frame into global 3D space in order to be tracked in the next frames (step 5.5).

Figure 5 shows the different steps of the construction of the proxy cloud on one specific example.

4   RGB-D Stream Processing

Our *Proxy Cloud* allows online recovery of the underlying structure of piecewise planar scenes (e.g., indoor) and is used as a prior to run on-the-fly processing on the incoming RGB-D frames. The different processing modules applied to the frames are presented below.

Filtering. While projecting the sensor's data points onto their associated proxy would allow removing the acquisition noise and quantization errors due to the sensor, this would lead to the flattening of all plane inliers. In order to minimize the loss of details on the planar surfaces while keeping a lightweight data structure, we instead use the planar proxies as a simple collaborative filter model. To that end, we designed a custom filter to leverage the *smoothed local histograms* stored in each cell of the proxies. As explained in Sect. 3, the number of detected modes allows distinguishing flat areas of the proxy surface from salient ones. For flat cells whose distribution has a single mode, we project the depth points on the plane along the direction between the camera and the point. We offset the points of the average distance to the plane only if it is above the noise threshold at the corresponding distance to the camera (see details on the noise threshold in the supplemental material). This allows smoothing surface areas that are exactly on the plane while keeping flat areas offset from the plane as they are in the scene. For flat cells whose distribution has two or more modes, we do not perform any projection in order to keep the saliency of the surface.

Equation 2 details the *smoothed local histograms*-based filtering of inlier $\mathbf{p}$ to $\mathbf{p}_f$, belonging to cell c with m_c modes and an average distance to the proxy of d_c, and a noise threshold of α. The proxy is based on a plane of normal $\mathbf{N}$ and distance to origin l.

$$\mathbf{p}_f = \begin{cases} \frac{l}{\mathbf{p}.\mathbf{N}}\mathbf{p} & \text{if } m_c = 1 \text{ and } d_c \leq \alpha \\ \frac{l}{\mathbf{p}.\mathbf{N}}\mathbf{p} + d_c\mathbf{N} & \text{if } m_c = 1 \text{ and } d_c > \alpha \\ \mathbf{p} & \text{if } m_c \neq 1 \end{cases} \tag{2}$$

The proxy can also be used as a high level range space for cross bilateral filtering [21], where inliers of different proxies will not be processed together.

Based on time-evolving data points, the proxies consolidate the stable geometry of the scene by accumulating observations in multiple frames. Averaging those observations over time removes temporal flickering, after a few frames only.

Hole Filling. Missing data in depth is often due to specular and transparent surfaces such as glass or screens. With our *Proxy Cloud*, observed data is reinforced over multiple frames from the support of stable proxies, augmenting the current frame with missing samples from previous ones. In practice, the depth data that is often seen in incoming frames creates activated cells with sufficient occupancy probability to survive within the model even when samples for these cells are missing.

This hole filling, stemming naturally from the proxy structure, is completed by two additional steps. First, the extent of the proxies is extrapolated to the intersection of adjacent proxies - this is particularly useful to complete unseen areas under furniture for example. Second, we perform a morphological closing [44] on the grid of cells, with a square structural element having a fixed side of seven cells. This corresponds to closing holes of maximum 35 cm by 35 cm, which allows filling missing data due to small specular surfaces, e.g. computer screens or glass-door cabinets, while keeping larger openings such as windows or doors.

Resampling. RGB-D streams can be *super-sampled* on the fly, by enriching their low definition geometric component using the higher resolution color component structured in the proxies to guide the process. This results in high definition RGB-D data with controllable point density on the surface of the shapes.

Lossy Compression. Compression of the input data is achieved by using directly the proxy cloud as a compressed, lightweight geometric substitute to the huge amount of depth data carried in the stream, avoiding storing uncertain and highly noisy depth regions, while still being able to upsample back to high resolution depth using a bilateral upsampling. In particular, this is convenient to broadcast captures of indoor scenes where planar regions are frequent.

5 Experiments

Proxy Clouds are implemented through hardware and software components. The hardware setup is made of a computer with Intel Core i7 at 3.5 GHz and 10 GB memory. No GPU is used. The software setup has a client-server architecture, where the server runs in a single thread within an embedded environment with low computational power and limited memory to trigger the sensor and process the data. The client's graphical user interface allows controlling the processing parameters and getting a real time feedback of the stream. A limited range of intuitive parameters allow the user to control the trade-off between quality of the output and performance of the processing.

We run all of our experiments on the *3DLite* [42] dataset[2], containing 10 scenes acquired with a Structure sensor[3] under the form of RGB-D image sequences. This choice was motivated by the availability of ground truth poses along with the visual data, as well as result meshes and performance metrics provided from processing with both *BundleFusion* [39] and *3DLite* [42], with which we compare our method in Sect. 6.

Geometric statistics on the generated proxies are available as supplemental material for all processed scenes (Table 1). We also provide in Fig. 1 of the supplemental material, a plot of the increment of the average depth over time, to show the fast convergence of the proxy statistics after about 30 accumulated samples. The accuracy of the proxy representation can be quantitatively assessed through the PSNR values in Table 1.

Performance. The current time required to build and update planar proxies using our (single-threaded) implementation is around 130 ms for an input depth image of 320×240 pixels. A detailed graph presenting the time needed for all steps is available as supplemental material (Fig. 2).

---

[2] 3DLite dataset: http://graphics.stanford.edu/projects/3dlite/#data.

[3] Structure sensor: http://structure.io.

Live RGB-D Stream Processing. Figure 6 shows examples of data improvement using the processing modules of our framework. Experiments show that the *Proxy Cloud* is particularly efficient to remove noise over walls and floors while keeping salient parts, and helps reducing holes due to unseen areas, specular areas, such as lights or glass, and low confidence areas, such as distant points. Resampling the point cloud allows recovering structure if the sensor did not give enough data samples, e.g. on lateral planar surfaces. More examples of RGB-D stream improvement on other scenes are available as supplemental material.

raw RGB-D   filtering   hole filling   resampling

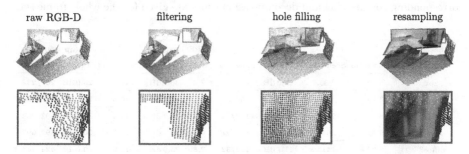

Fig. 6. Data improvement. Raw RGB-D and *Proxy Clouds*-improved data showing results of real time filtering, hole filling and resampling. The texture applied to the completed data is extracted from the raw color frame, which does not make sense for all parts of unseen geometry, as we can see on the hole filling and resampling examples. (Color figure online)

Compression. Substituting the *Proxy Cloud* to the RGB-D stream provides a simple yet effective lossy compression scheme for transmission, with the practical side effect of removing many outliers. Our efficient data structure leads to good compression ratios while keeping high Peak Signal-to-Noise Ratio (PSNR) and being fast for compression and decompression (see Table 1 for evaluation metrics of the compression using proxies). The proxies are stored as simple grids of statistics with a local frame and bounding rectangle. As such, the compressed structure itself, i.e. the proxies, can benefit from image-based compression schemes such as JPEG [45] for offline export and storage, for which we report compression ratios and PSNR values in Table 1. In addition to the bandwidth saving, the compressed *Proxy Cloud* representation enables smooth super-sampling of the geometric data, where the output point cloud density over proxy surfaces *can be increased as desired.* The planar parameterization of each proxy offers a suitable domain for point upsampling operators, while a similar approach performed directly on the RGB-D stream is blind to the scene structure.

6   RGB-D Stream Consolidation

While being lightweight and fast to compute, the *Proxy Cloud* represents a superstructure modeling the dominant planar elements of an indoor scene. In

Table 1. Compression metrics for all processed scenes. Compression ratios are based on the raw size of a 320 × 240 depth map and the size of the proxies without the outliers. The JPEG export ratio is between the sizes of the raw and exported proxy clouds. The export and load procedure for all proxies takes an average of about 40 ms. The Peak Signal-to-Noise Ratio (PSNR) is computed using the average Root Mean Square Error (RMSE) between raw depth points and *proxy*-filtered ones. The time values correspond to the compression and decompression. The former is the building of proxies averaged over all frames, while the latter is the generation of a depth map by applying visibility tests to the proxies. We compare our compression performance to a state-of-the-art method based on H.264 [46] with a quality profile of 50. The corresponding compression and decompression times are given for the whole frame set.

Scene	Proxy clouds				JPEG export		H.264 [46] (qp = 50)		
	Frame ratio	Scene ratio	PSNR	Time (ms)	Ratio	PSNR	Scene ratio	PSNR	Time (s)
apt	5.19	835.7	43.0 dB	147/32	7.65	36.7 dB	11.1	25.0 dB	267/232
offices	3.75	945.5	42.0 dB	154/30	11.5	36.0 dB	10.5	22.1 dB	828/926
office0	8.72	2324.5	42.4 dB	122/19	6.75	35.7 dB	14.4	30.3 dB	692/902
office1	6.61	1944.8	40.8 dB	116/27	6.30	34.5 dB	10.5	26.9 dB	693/692
office3	8.02	1415.8	41.7 dB	122/32	7.80	35.9 dB	12.3	29.0 dB	424/444
scene0220_02	5.26	707.3	39.0 dB	127/41	7.25	33.1 dB	11.1	18.3 dB	165/175
scene0271_01	5.45	942.0	37.5 dB	119/39	6.04	33.4 dB	10.5	18.8 dB	165/162
scene0294_02	3.99	1113.4	41.9 dB	133/39	6.69	36.1 dB	9.4	17.2 dB	238/200
scene0451_05	3.59	674.7	37.1 dB	128/41	5.61	32.3 dB	7.9	15.5 dB	190/138
scene0567_01	6.09	806.5	40.6 dB	137/28	8.13	35.5 dB	15.6	20.0 dB	170/151

addition to being used to filter the input point cloud and generate an enhanced RGB-D stream as output, proxies themselves are a way to consolidate the input RGB-D frames. Hence, meshing the proxy cells leads to a lightened organized structure and aggregating all proxies in the global space allows reconstructing a higher quality surface model of the observed scene, generated on-the-fly. In this section, we compare the performance and quality of scene reconstruction using *Proxy Clouds* to state-of-the-art methods *BundleFusion* [39] and *3DLite* [42].

Qualitative Results. Figure 7 presents the reconstructed planar models based on the corresponding *Proxy Cloud*. More reconstructed scenes are available as supplemental material. As we can see, most large planar surfaces such as walls and floors are modeled with a single proxy instance.

Quantitative Results. Tables 2 and 3 present performance and quality metrics for the 10 scenes of the dataset. The reconstruction using proxies can be quantitatively assessed and compared to *3DLite* through the values of RMSE with *BundleFusion*. These metrics show that the lightweight and simple structure of the *Proxy Cloud* leads to better performance both in timing and memory consumption, while keeping a quality comparable to that of state-of-the art methods.

apt   office0   scene0220_02

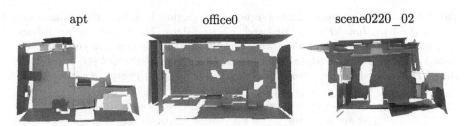

Fig. 7. Scene reconstruction. Examples of reconstructed scenes of the *3DLite* [42] dataset using *Proxy Clouds*. The meshes are made of quads when four activated cells are adjacent, and triangles otherwise.

With its low runtime and memory needs, *Proxy Clouds* offer a lighter alternative to most recent reconstruction methods characterized by *volumetric* or *deep learning* approaches, which have high requirements in computation costs and memory consumption. The generic format and implementation of the proxies avoid the need for tedious platform-specific tuning and make them well suited for embedded operation and modern mobile applications. In addition to the fact that our proxies are built and updated on the fly, the processing runs in a single thread and requires far less memory than modern embedded devices offer.

Table 2. Quantitative comparison of scene reconstruction processing. The metrics are compared between *BundleFusion* (BF), *3DLite* (3DL) and our *Proxy Clouds* (PC). The processing time to process one frame is averaged over all frames in the scene. The memory consumption is the maximum used memory during processing.

Scene	#Frames	Processing time			Memory consumption	
		BF	3DL	PC	BF	PC
apt	2865	–	5.5 h	**147 ms**	–	**135 MB**
offices	8518	–	10.8 h	**154 ms**	–	**251 MB**
office0	6159	26.4 ms	3.6 h	**122 ms**	21.4 GB	**136 MB**
office1	5730	27.7 ms	3.1 h	**116 ms**	21.1 GB	**138 MB**
office3	3820	27.7 ms	4.5 h	**122 ms**	16.9 GB	**218 MB**
scene0220_02	2026	–	2.8 h	**127 ms**	–	**119 MB**
scene0271_01	1904	–	3.0 h	**119 ms**	–	**105 MB**
scene0294_02	2369	–	5.0 h	**133 ms**	–	**110 MB**
scene0451_05	1719	–	5.1 h	**128 ms**	–	**126 MB**
scene0567_01	2066	–	3.1 h	**137 ms**	–	**206 MB**

Table 3. Quantitative comparison of scene reconstruction data. We compare our *Proxy Clouds* (PC) to *BundleFusion* (BF) and *3DLite* (3DL). The model size for BF and 3DL includes texture information, while the PC model only contains geometry. The Root Mean Square Error (RMSE) is computed using the *Metro* tool [47] between the *BundleFusion* mesh, taken as reference, and the *3DLite* and *Proxy Clouds* meshes.

Scene	Geometry size (vertices/faces)			Model size			RMSE with BF	
	BF	3DL	PC	BF	3DL	PC	3DL	PC
apt	1.7M/3.3M	62K/93K	**58K/55K**	70 MB	9.8 MB	**4.5 MB**	**3.65 m**	5.26 m
offices	1.4M/2.8M	**116K/174K**	153K/144K	58 MB	19 MB	**12.7 MB**	**3.81 m**	4.72m
office0	5.7M/11.3M	**42K/63K**	45K/42K	238 MB	6.3 MB	**3.6 MB**	**0.10 m**	0.29m
office1	6.0M/11.8M	**46K/69K**	50K/46K	251 MB	7.2 MB	**4.5 MB**	**0.19 m**	0.45m
office3	6.4M/12.6M	**42K/64K**	46K/43K	266 MB	6.2 MB	**3.9 MB**	0.30 m	**0.24 m**
scene0220_02	0.3M/0.6M	55K/83K	**49K/46K**	12 MB	9.1B	**3.7 MB**	**2.84 m**	3.75m
scene0271_01	0.2M/0.4M	39K/59K	**34K/33K**	9 MB	5.8 MB	**2.7 MB**	2.32 m	**2.31 m**
scene0294_02	0.3M/0.5M	39K/59K	**36K/34K**	10 MB	6.1MB	**3 MB**	2.75 m	**2.74 m**
scene0451_05	0.3M/0.6M	60K/90K	**43K/39K**	12 MB	9.2 MB	**3.9 MB**	5.01 m	**3.84 m**
scene0567_01	0.3M/0.4M	**29K/43K**	44K/41K	9 MB	4.5 MB	**3.4 MB**	2.21 m	**1.67 m**

7   Conclusion and Future Work

We introduced *Proxy Clouds*, a unified plane-based framework for real-time processing of RGB-D streams. It takes the form of stable proxies modeling the dominant geometric scene structure through a set of rich statistics. Our method provides a compact, lightweight and consistent spatio-temporal support for the processing primitives designed to enhance data or lighten subsequent operations. It runs at interactive rates on mobile platforms and allows fast enhancement and transmission of the captured data. Our structure can be meshed and used as a model of the observed scene, generated on-the-fly. Its implementation makes possible real-time feedback and its control relies on a limited range of parameters. Compared to *BundleFusion* and *3DLite*, *Proxy Clouds* provide a good balance between processing time, memory consumption and approximation quality.

In the future, we plan to develop a parallel implementation using multi-core CPU and mobile GPUs to achieve a higher processing rate on embedded platforms. To that end, the primitives we use in our algorithm are naturally parallel scalable. While our current proxy model stores statistics on a uniform (yet sparse) grid, it could be improved using a sparse adaptive structure [48]. We also plan to extend the geometry of proxies to other simple shapes, such as boxes, spheres and cylinders, while still maintaining a unified representation for all of them, interfacing them seamlessly to the processing primitives. Last, we plan to use our stable proxies to estimate the position and orientation of the camera and track it within the scene, in a similar spirit to Raposo et al. [49].

Acknowledgements.. This work is partially supported by the French National Research Agency under grant ANR 16-LCV2-0009-01 ALLEGORI and by BPI France, under grant PAPAYA. We also wish to thank the authors of *3DLite* [42], *BundleFusion* [39] and *ScanNet* [50] for providing the dataset we use.

References

1. Endres, F., Hess, J., Sturm, J., Cremers, D., Burgard, W.: 3-D mapping with an RGB-D camera. IEEE Trans. Robot. **30**(1), 177–187 (2014)
2. Fischler, M.A., Bolles, R.C.: Random sample consensus: a paradigm for model fitting with applications to image analysis and automated cartography. Commun. ACM **24**(6), 381–395 (1981)
3. Umeyama, S.: Least-squares estimation of transformation parameters between two point patterns. IEEE Trans. Pattern Anal. Mach. Intell. **13**(4), 376–380 (1991)
4. Hulik, R., Spanel, M., Smrz, P., Materna, Z.: Continuous plane detection in point-cloud data based on 3D Hough transform. J. Vis. Commun. Image Representation **25**(1), 86–97 (2014)
5. Schnabel, R., Wahl, R., Klein, R.: Efficient RANSAC for point-cloud shape detection. Comput. Graph. Forum **26**(2), 214–226 (2007)
6. Holz, D., Holzer, S., Rusu, R.B., Behnke, S.: Real-time plane segmentation using RGB-D cameras. In: Röfer, T., Mayer, N.M., Savage, J., Saranlı, U. (eds.) RoboCup 2011. LNCS (LNAI), vol. 7416, pp. 306–317. Springer, Heidelberg (2012). https://doi.org/10.1007/978-3-642-32060-6_26
7. Feng, C., Taguchi, Y., Kamat, V.R.: Fast plane extraction in organized point clouds using agglomerative hierarchical clustering. In: IEEE International Conference on Robotics and Automation (ICRA), pp. 6218–6225. IEEE (2014)
8. Kaiser, A., Ybanez Zepeda, J.A., Boubekeur, T.: A survey of simple geometric primitives detection methods for captured 3D data. In: Computer Graphics Forum (2018, to appear)
9. Li, L.: Filtering for 3D time-of-flight sensors. Technical report SLOA230, Texas Instruments, January 2016
10. Tomasi, C., Manduchi, R.: Bilateral filtering for gray and color images. In: Sixth International Conference on Computer Vision, pp. 839–846. IEEE (1998)
11. Shao, L., Han, J., Kohli, P., Zhang, Z. (eds.): Computer Vision and Machine Learning with RGB-D Sensors. Advances in Computer Vision and Pattern Recognition. Springer, Heidelberg (2014). https://doi.org/10.1007/978-3-319-08651-4
12. Essmaeel, K., Gallo, L., Damiani, E., De Pietro, G., Dipandà, A.: Temporal denoising of kinect depth data. In: Eighth International Conference on Signal Image Technology and Internet Based Systems (SITIS), pp. 47–52. IEEE (2012)
13. Liu, S., Chen, C., Kehtarnava, N.: A computationally efficient denoising and hole-filling method for depth image enhancement. In: Kehtarnavaz, N., Carlsohn, M.F. (eds.) SPIE Conference on Real-Time Image and Video Processing, SPIE, April 2016
14. Le, A.V., Jung, S.W., Won, C.S.: Directional joint bilateral filter for depth images. Sensors **14**(7), 11362–11378 (2014)
15. Newcombe, R.A., et al.: Kinectfusion: real-time dense surface mapping and tracking. In: IEEE International Symposium on Mixed and Augmented Reality (ISMAR), pp. 127–136. IEEE, October 2011

16. Bapat, A., Ravi, A., Raman, S.: An iterative, non-local approach for restoring depth maps in RGB-D images. In: Twenty First National Conference on Communications (NCC), pp. 1–6. IEEE (2015)
17. Camplani, M., Salgado, L.: Adaptive spatio-temporal filter for low-cost camera depth maps. In: IEEE International Conference on Emerging Signal Processing Applications (ESPA), pp. 33–36. IEEE (2012)
18. Schmeing, M., Jiang, X.: Color segmentation based depth image filtering. In: Jiang, X., Bellon, O.R.P., Goldgof, D., Oishi, T. (eds.) WDIA 2012. LNCS, vol. 7854, pp. 68–77. Springer, Heidelberg (2013). https://doi.org/10.1007/978-3-642-40303-3_8
19. Chen, L., Lin, H., Li, S.: Depth image enhancement for kinect using region growing and bilateral filter. In: 21st International Conference on Pattern Recognition (ICPR), pp. 3070–3073. IEEE (2012)
20. Wu, C., Zollhöfer, M., Nießner, M., Stamminger, M., Izadi, S., Theobalt, C.: Real-time shading-based refinement for consumer depth cameras. ACM Trans. Graph. (TOG) 33(6), 200 (2014)
21. Kopf, J., Cohen, M.F., Lischinski, D., Uyttendaele, M.: Joint bilateral upsampling. ACM Trans. Graph. (ToG) 26(3), 96 (2007)
22. Min, D., Lu, J., Do, M.N.: Depth video enhancement based on weighted mode filtering. IEEE Trans. Image Process. 21(3), 1176–1190 (2012)
23. Liu, R., et al.: Hole-filling based on disparity map and inpainting for depth-image-based rendering. Int. J. Hybrid Inf. Technol. 9(5), 145–164 (2016)
24. Buyssens, P., Daisy, M., Tschumperlé, D., Lézoray, O.: Superpixel-based depth map inpainting for RGB-D view synthesis. In: IEEE International Conference on Image Processing (ICIP), pp. 4332–4336. IEEE (2015)
25. Solh, M., AlRegib, G.: Hierarchical hole-filling for depth-based view synthesis in FTV and 3D video. IEEE J. Sel. Topics Sig. Process. 6(5), 495–504 (2012)
26. Schnabel, R., Degener, P., Klein, R.: Completion and reconstruction with primitive shapes. Comput. Graph. Forum 28(2), 503–512 (2009)
27. Biswas, J., Veloso, M.: Planar polygon extraction and merging from depth images. In: IEEE/RSJ International Conference on Intelligent Robots and Systems (IROS), pp. 3859–3864. IEEE (2012)
28. Labbé, M., Michaud, F.: Online global loop closure detection for large-scale multi-session graph-based slam. In: IEEE/RSJ International Conference on Intelligent Robots and Systems (IROS), pp. 2661–2666. IEEE, September 2014
29. Hsiao, M., Westman, E., Zhang, G., Kaess, M.: Keyframe-based dense planar slam. In: IEEE International Conference on Robotics and Automation (ICRA), pp. 5110–5117. IEEE, May 2017
30. Mur-Artal, R., Tardós, J.D.: ORB-SLAM2: an open-source SLAM system for monocular, stereo, and RGB-D cameras. IEEE Trans. Robot. 33(5), 1255–1262 (2017)
31. Keller, M., Lefloch, D., Lambers, M., Izadi, S., Weyrich, T., Kolb, A.: Real-time 3D reconstruction in dynamic scenes using point-based fusion. In: International Conference on 3D Vision (3DV), pp. 1–8. IEEE, June 2013
32. Salas-Moreno, R.F., Glocken, B., Kelly, P.H., Davison, A.J.: Dense planar slam. In: IEEE International Symposium on Mixed and Augmented Reality (ISMAR), pp. 157–164. IEEE, September 2014
33. Elghor, H.E., Roussel, D., Ababsa, F., Bouyakhf, E.H.: Planes detection for robust localization and mapping in RGB-D slam systems. In: International Conference on 3D Vision (3DV), pp. 452–459. IEEE, October 2015

34. Dou, M., Guan, L., Frahm, J.-M., Fuchs, H.: Exploring high-level plane primitives for indoor 3D reconstruction with a hand-held RGB-D camera. In: Park, J.-I., Kim, J. (eds.) ACCV 2012. LNCS, vol. 7729, pp. 94–108. Springer, Heidelberg (2013). https://doi.org/10.1007/978-3-642-37484-5_9

35. Kaess, M.: Simultaneous localization and mapping with infinite planes. In: IEEE International Conference on Robotics and Automation (ICRA), pp. 4605–4611. IEEE, May 2015

36. Gao, X., Zhang, T.: Robust RGB-D simultaneous localization and mapping using planar point features. Robot. Auton. Syst. **72**, 1–14 (2015)

37. Zhang, E., Cohen, M.F., Curless, B.: Emptying, refurnishing, and relighting indoor spaces. ACM Trans. Graph. (TOG) **35**(6), 174 (2016)

38. Nießner, M., Zollhöfer, M., Izadi, S., Stamminger, M.: Real-time 3D reconstruction at scale using voxel hashing. ACM Trans. Graph. (ToG) **32**(6), 169 (2013)

39. Dai, A., Nießner, M., Zollhöfer, M., Izadi, S., Theobalt, C.: Bundlefusion: real-time globally consistent 3D reconstruction using on-the-fly surface reintegration. ACM Trans. Graph. (TOG) **36**(3), 24 (2017)

40. Zhang, Y., Xu, W., Tong, Y., Zhou, K.: Online structure analysis for real-time indoor scene reconstruction. ACM Trans. Graph. (TOG) **34**(5), 159 (2015)

41. Dzitsiuk, M., Sturm, J., Maier, R., Ma, L., Cremers, D.: De-noising, stabilizing and completing 3D reconstructions on-the-go using plane priors. In: IEEE International Conference on Robotics and Automation (ICRA), pp. 3976–3983. IEEE, May 2017

42. Huang, J., Dai, A., Guibas, L., Niessner, M.: 3Dlite: towards commodity 3D scanning for content creation. ACM Trans. Graph. (TOG) **36**(6), 203 (2017)

43. Kass, M., Solomon, J.: Smoothed local histogram filters. ACM Trans. Graph. (TOG) **29**(4), 100 (2010)

44. Serra, J.: Image Analysis and Mathematical Morphology. Academic Press, Inc., Cambridge (1983)

45. Wallace, G.K.: The JPEG still picture compression standard. IEEE Trans. Consum. Electron. **38**(1), xviii–xxxiv (1992)

46. Nenci, F., Spinello, L., Stachniss, C.: Effective compression of range data streams for remote robot operations using H. 264. In: IEEE/RSJ International Conference on Intelligent Robots and Systems (IROS), pp. 3794–3799. IEEE, September 2014

47. Cignoni, P., Rocchini, C., Scopigno, R.: Metro: measuring error on simplified surfaces. Comput. Graph. Forum **17**(2), 167–174 (1998)

48. Lefebvre, S., Hoppe, H.: Compressed random-access trees for spatially coherent data. In: Kautz, J., Pattanaik, S. (eds.) Proceedings of the 18th Eurographics Conference on Rendering Techniques, pp. 339–349. Eurographics Association (2007)

49. Raposo, C., Lourenco, M., Goncalves Almeida Antunes, M., Barreto, J.P.: Plane-based odometry using an RGB-D camera. In: British Machine Vision Conference (BMVC). Elsevier, September 2013

50. Dai, A., Chang, A.X., Savva, M., Halber, M., Funkhouser, T., Nießner, M.: Scannet: richly-annotated 3D reconstructions of indoor scenes. In: IEEE Conference on Computer Vision and Pattern Recognition (CVPR). IEEE, July 2017

Deep Metric Learning with Hierarchical Triplet Loss

Weifeng Ge[1,2,3], Weilin Huang[1,2(✉)], Dengke Dong[1,2], and Matthew R. Scott[1,2]

[1] Malong Technologies, Shenzhen, China
{terrencege,whuang,dongdk,mscott}@malong.com
[2] Shenzhen Malong Artificial Intelligence Research Center, Shenzhen, China
[3] The University of Hong Kong, Pok Fu Lam, Hong Kong

Abstract. We present a novel hierarchical triplet loss (HTL) capable of automatically collecting informative training samples (triplets) via a defined hierarchical tree that encodes global context information. This allows us to cope with the main limitation of random sampling in training a conventional triplet loss, which is a central issue for deep metric learning. Our main contributions are two-fold. (i) we construct a hierarchical class-level tree where neighboring classes are merged recursively. The hierarchical structure naturally captures the intrinsic data distribution over the whole dataset. (ii) we formulate the problem of triplet collection by introducing a new violate margin, which is computed dynamically based on the designed hierarchical tree. This allows it to automatically select meaningful hard samples with the guide of global context. It encourages the model to learn more discriminative features from visual similar classes, leading to faster convergence and better performance. Our method is evaluated on the tasks of image retrieval and face recognition, where it outperforms the standard triplet loss substantially by 1%–18%, and achieves new state-of-the-art performance on a number of benchmarks.

Keywords: Deep metric learning · Image retrieval · Triplet loss
Anchor-neighbor sampling

1 Introduction

Distance metric learning or similarity learning is the task of learning a distance function over images in visual understanding tasks. It has been an active research topic in computer vision community. Given a similarity function, images with similar content are projected onto neighboring locations on a manifold, and images with different semantic context are mapped apart from each other. With the boom of deep neural networks (DNN), metric learning has been turned from learning distance functions to learning deep feature embeddings that better fits a simple distance function, such as Euclidean distance or cosine distance. Metric learning with DNNs is referred as deep metric learning, which has recently

© Springer Nature Switzerland AG 2018
V. Ferrari et al. (Eds.): ECCV 2018, LNCS 11210, pp. 272–288, 2018.
https://doi.org/10.1007/978-3-030-01231-1_17

achieved great success in numerous visual understanding tasks, including images or object retrieval [26,30,34], single-shot object classification [30,32,34], keypoint descriptor learning [12,24], face verification [20,22], person re-identification [23,30], object tracking [29] and etc.

Recently, there is a number of widely-used loss functions developed for deep metric learning, such as contrastive loss [6,27], triplet loss [22] and quadruplet loss [5]. These loss functions are calculated on correlated samples, with a common goal of encouraging samples from the same class to be closer, and pushing samples of different classes apart from each other, in a projected feature space. The correlated samples are grouped into contrastive pairs, triplets or quadruplets, which form the training samples for these loss functions on deep metric learning. Unlike softmax loss used for image classification, where the gradient is computed on each individual sample, the gradient of a deep metric learning loss often depends heavily on multiple correlated samples. Furthermore, the number of training samples will be increased exponentially when the training pairs, triplets or quadruplets are grouped. This generates a vast number of training samples which are highly redundant and less informative. Training that uses random sampling from them can be overwhelmed by redundant samples, leading to slow convergence and inferior performance.

Deep neural networks are commonly trained using online stochastic gradient descent algorithms [19], where the gradients for optimizing network parameters are computed *locally* with mini-batches, due to the limitation of computational power and memory storage. It is difficult or impossible to put all training samples into a single mini-batch, and the networks can only focus on local data distribution within a mini-batch, making it difficult to consider global data distribution over the whole training set. This often leads to local optima and slow convergence. This common challenge will be amplified substantially in deep metric learning, due to the enlarged sample spaces where the redundancy could become more significant. Therefore, collecting and creating meaningful training samples (e.g., in pairs, triplets or quadruplets) has been a central issue for deep metric learning, and an efficient sampling strategy is of critical importance to this task. This is also indicated in recent literature [1,20,22,35].

Our goal of this paper is to address the sampling issue of conventional triplet loss [22]. In this work, we propose a novel hierarchical triplet loss (HTL) able to automatically collect informative training triplets via an adaptively-learned hierarchical class structure that encodes global context in an elegant manner. Specifically, we explore the underline data distribution on a manifold sphere, and then use this manifold structure to guide triplet sample generation. Our intuition of generating meaningful samples is to encourage the training samples within a mini-batch to have similar visual appearance but with different semantic content (e.g., from different categories). This allows our model to learn more discriminative features by identifying subtle distinction between the close visual concepts. Our main contribution are described as follows.

- We propose a novel hierarchical triplet loss that allows the model to collect informative training samples with the guide of a global class-level hierarchical tree. This alleviates main limitation of random sampling in training of deep metric learning, and encourages the model to learn more discriminative features from visual similar classes.

- We formulate the problem of triplet collection by introducing a new violate margin, which is computed dynamically over the constructed hierarchical tree. The new violate margin allows us to search informative samples, which are hard to distinguish between visual similar classes, and will be merged into a new class in next level of the hierarchy. The violate margin is automatically updated, with the goal of identifying a margin that generates gradients for violate triplets, naturally making the collected samples more informative.

- The proposed HTL is easily implemented, and can be readily integrated into the standard triplet loss or other deep metric learning approaches, such as contrastive loss, quadruplet loss, recent HDC [38] and BIER [17]. It significantly outperforms the standard triplet loss on the tasks of image retrieval and face recognition, and obtains new state-of-art results on a number of benchmarks.

2   Related Work

Deep Metric Learning. Deep metric learning maps an image into a feature vector in a manifold space via deep neural networks. In this manifold space, the Euclidean distance (or the cosine distance) can be directly used as the distance metric between two points. The contribution of many deep metric learning algorithms, such as [2,3,5,22,26], is the design of a loss function that can learn more discriminant features. Since neural networks are usually trained using the stochastic gradient descent (SGD) in mini-batches, these loss functions are difficult to approximate the target of metric learning - pull samples with the same label into nearby points and push samples with different labels apart.

Informative Sample Selection. Given N training images, there are about $O(N^2)$ pairs, $O(N^3)$ triplets, and $0(N^4)$ quadruplets. It is infeasible to traverses all these training tuples during training. Schroff *et al.* [22] constructed a mini-batch of with 45 identities and each of which has 40 images. There are totally 1800 images in a mini-batch, and the approach obtained the state-of-art results on LFW face recognition challenge [8]. While it is rather inconvenient to take thousands of images in a mini-batch with a large-scale network, due to the limitation of GPU memory. For deep metric learning, it is of great importance to selecting informative training tuples. Hard negative mining [4] is widely used to select hard training tuples. Our work is closely related to that of [7,35] which inspired the current work. Distance distribution was applied to guide tuple sampling for deep metric learning [7,35]. In this work, we strive to a further step by constructing a hierarchical tree that aggregates class-level global context, and formulating tuple selection elegantly by introducing a new violate margin.

(a) Caltech-UCSD Bird Species Dataset   (b) Data Distribution and Triplets in a Mini-Batch

Fig. 1. (a) Caltech-UCSD Bird Species Dataset [31]. Images in each row are from the same class. There are four classes in different colors—red, green, blue and yellow. (b) Data distribution and triplets in a mini-batch. Triplets in the top row violate the triplet constrain in the traditional triplet loss. Triplets in the bottom row are ignored in the triplet loss, but are revisited in the hierarchical triplet loss. (Color figure online)

3   Motivation: Challenges in Triplet Loss

We start by revisiting the main challenges in standard triplet loss [22], which we believe have a significant impact to the performance of deep triplet embedding.

3.1   Preliminaries

Let $(\boldsymbol{x}_i, y_i)$ be the i-th sample in the training set $\mathcal{D} = \{(\boldsymbol{x}_i, y_i)\}_{i=1}^{N}$. The feature embedding of $\boldsymbol{x}_i$ is represented as $\phi(\boldsymbol{x}_i, \boldsymbol{\theta}) \in \mathbb{R}^d$, where $\boldsymbol{\theta}$ is the learnable parameters of a differentiable deep networks, d is the dimension of embedding and y_i is the label of $\boldsymbol{x}_i$. $\phi(\cdot, \boldsymbol{\theta})$ is usually normalized into unit length for the training stability and comparison simplicity as in [22]. During the neural network training, training samples are selected and formed into triplets, each of which $\mathcal{T}_z = (\boldsymbol{x}_a, \boldsymbol{x}_p, \boldsymbol{x}_n)$ are consisted of an anchor sample $\boldsymbol{x}_a$, a positive sample $\boldsymbol{x}_p$ and a negative sample $\boldsymbol{x}_n$. The labels of the triplet $\mathcal{T}_z = (\boldsymbol{x}_a^z, \boldsymbol{x}_p^z, \boldsymbol{x}_n^z)$ satisfy $y_a = y_p \neq y_n$. Triplet loss aims to pull samples belonging to the same class into nearby points on a manifold surface, and push samples with different labels apart from each other. The optimization target of the triplet $\mathcal{T}_z$ is,

$$l_{tri}(\mathcal{T}_z) = \frac{1}{2}\left[\left\|\boldsymbol{x}_a^z - \boldsymbol{x}_p^z\right\|^2 - \left\|\boldsymbol{x}_a^z - \boldsymbol{x}_n^z\right\|^2 + \alpha\right]_+ .$$

$[\cdot]_+ = \max(0, \cdot)$ denotes the hinge loss function, and α is the violate margin that requires the distance $\left\|\boldsymbol{x}_a^z - \boldsymbol{x}_n^z\right\|^2$ of negative pairs to be larger than the distance $\left\|\boldsymbol{x}_a^z - \boldsymbol{x}_p^z\right\|^2$ of positive pairs. For all the triplets $\mathcal{T}$ in the training set $\mathcal{D} = \{(\boldsymbol{x}_i, y_i)\}_{i=1}^{N}$, the final objective function to optimize is,

$$\mathcal{L} = \frac{1}{Z}\sum_{\mathcal{T}^z \in \mathcal{T}} l_{tri}(\mathcal{T}_z),$$

where Z is the normalization term. For training a triplet loss in deep metric learning, the violate margin plays a key role to sample selection.

3.2   Challenges

Challenge 1: Triplet Loss with Random Sampling. For many deep metric learning loss functions, such as contrastive loss [6], triplet loss [22] and quadruplet loss [5], all training samples are treated equally with a constant violate margin, which only allows training samples that violate this margin to produce gradients. For a training set $\mathcal{D} = \{(x_i, y_i)\}_{k=1}^{N}$ with N samples, training a triplet loss will generate $O\left(N^3\right)$ triplets, which is infeasible to put all triplets into a single mini-batch. When we sample the triplets over the whole training set randomly, it has a risk of slow convergence and pool local optima. We identify the problem that most of training samples obey the violate margin when the model starts to converge. These samples can not contribute gradients to the learning process, and thus are less informative, but can dominate the training process, which significantly degrades the model capability, with a slow convergence. This inspired current work that formulates the problem of sample selection via setting a dynamic violate margin, which allows the model to focus on a small set of informative samples.

However, identifying informative samples from a vast number of the generated triplets is still challenging. This inspires us to strive to a further step, by sampling meaningful triplets from a structural class tree, which defines class-level relations over all categories. This transforms the problem of pushing hard samples apart from each other into encouraging a larger distance between two confusing classes. This not only reduces the search space, but also avoid overfitting the model over individual samples, leading to a more discriminative model that generalizes better.

Challenge 2: Risk of Local Optima. Most of the popular metric learning algorithms, such as the contrastive loss, the triplet loss, and the quadruplet loss, describe similarity relationship between individual samples locally in a mini-batch, without considering global data distribution. In triplet loss, all triplet is treated equally. As shown in Fig. 1, when the training goes after several epoches, most of training triplets dose not contribute to the gradients of learnable parameters in deep neural networks. There has been recent work that aims to solve this problem by re-weighting the training samples, as in [36]. However, even with hard negative mining or re-weighting, the triplets can only see a few samples within a mini-batch, but not the whole data distribution. It is difficult for the triplet loss to incorporate the global data distribution on the target manifold space. Although the data structure in the deep feature space are changed dynamically during the training process, the relative position of data points can be roughly preserved. This allows us to explore the data distribution obtained in the previous iterations to guide sample selection in the current stage. With this prior knowledge of data structure, a triplet, which does not violate the original margin α, is possible to generate gradients that contribute to the network training, as shown in Fig. 1. Discriminative capability can be enhanced by learning from these hard but informative triplets.

4   Hierarchical Triplet Loss

We describe details of the proposed hierarchical triplet loss, which contains two main components, constructing a hierarchical class tree and formulating the hierarchical triplet loss with a new violate margin. The hierarchical class tree is designed to capture global data context, which is encoded into triplet sampling via the new violate margin, by formulating the hierarchical triplet loss.

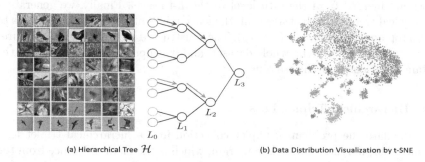

(a) Hierarchical Tree $\mathcal{H}$ (b) Data Distribution Visualization by t-SNE

Fig. 2. (a) A toy example of the hierarchical tree $\mathcal{H}$. Different colors represent different image classes in CUB-200-2011 [31]. The leaves are the image classes in the training set. Then they are merged recursively until to the root node. (b) The training data distribution of 100 classes visualized by using t-SNE [16] to reduce the dimension of triplet embedding from 512 to 2.

4.1   Manifold Structure in Hierarchy

We construct a global hierarchy at the class level. Given a neural network $\phi_t\left(\cdot, \boldsymbol{\theta}\right)(\in \mathbb{R}^d)$ pre-trained using the traditional triplet loss, we get the hierarchical data structure based on sample rules. Denote the deep feature of a sample $\boldsymbol{x}_i$ as $\boldsymbol{r}_i = \phi_t\left(\boldsymbol{x}_i, \boldsymbol{\theta}\right)$. We first calculate a distance matrix of $\mathcal{C}$ classes in the whole training set $\mathcal{D}$. The distance between the p-th class and the q-th class is computed as,

$$d\left(p, q\right) = \frac{1}{n_p n_q} \sum_{i \in p, j \in q} \|\boldsymbol{r}_i - \boldsymbol{r}_j\|^2,$$

where n_p and n_q are the numbers of training samples in the p-th and the q-th classes respectively. Since the deep feature $\boldsymbol{r}_i$ is normalized into unit length, the value of the interclass distance $d\left(p, q\right)$ varies from 0 to 4.

We build hierarchical manifold structure by creating a hierarchical tree, according to the computed interclass distances. The leaves of the hierarchical tree are the original image classes, where each class represents a leave node at the 0-th level. Then hierarchy is created by recursively merging the leave notes at different levels, based on the computed distance matrix. The hierarchical tree is set into L levels, and the average inner distance d_0 is used as the threshold for merging the nodes at the 0-th level.

$$d_0 = \frac{1}{C} \sum_{c=1}^{C} \left(\frac{1}{n_c^2 - n_c} \sum_{i \in c, j \in c} \| r_i - r_j \|^2 \right).$$

where n_c is the number of samples in the c-th class. Then the nodes are merged with different thresholds. At the l-th level of the hierarchical tree, the merging threshold is set to $d_l = \frac{l(4-d_0)}{L} + d_0$. Two classes with a distance less than d_l are merged into a node at the l-th level. The node number at the l-th level is N_l. The nodes are merged from the 0-th level to the L-th level. Finally, we generate a hierarchical tree $\mathcal{H}$ which starts from the leave nodes of original image classes to a final top node, as shown in Fig. 2(a). The constructed hierarchical tree captures class relationships over the whole dataset, and it is updated interactively at the certain iterations over the training.

4.2   Hierarchical Triplet Loss

We formulate the problem of triplet collection into a hierarchical triplet loss. We introduce a dynamical violate margin, which is the main difference from the conventional triplet loss using a constant violate margin.

Anchor Neighbor Sampling. We randomly select l' nodes at the 0-th level of the constructed hierarchical tree $\mathcal{H}$. Each node represents an original class, and collecting classes at the 0-th level aims to preserve the diversity of training samples in a mini-batch, which is important for training deep networks with batch normalization [9]. Then $m - 1$ nearest classes at the 0-th level are selected for each of the l' nodes, based on the distance between classes computed in the feature space. The goal of collecting nearest classes is to encourage model to learn discriminative features from the visual similar classes. Finally, t images for each class are randomly collected, resulting in n ($n = l'mt$) images in a mini-batch $\mathcal{M}$. Training triplets within each mini-batch are generated from the collected n images based on class relationships. We write the anchor-neighbor sampling into A-N sampling for convenience (Fig. 3).

Triplet Generation and Dynamic Violate Margin. Hierarchical triplet loss (computed on a mini-batch of $\mathcal{M}$) can be formulated as,

$$\mathcal{L}_{\mathcal{M}} = \frac{1}{2Z_{\mathcal{M}}} \sum_{T^z \in \mathcal{T}^{\mathcal{M}}} \left[\| x_a^z - x_p^z \| - \| x_a^z - x_n^z \| + \alpha_z \right]_+ .$$

where $\mathcal{T}^{\mathcal{M}}$ is all the triplets in the mini-batch $\mathcal{M}$, and $Z_{\mathcal{M}} = A_{l'm}^2 A_t^2 C_t^1$ is the number of triplets. Each triplet is constructed as $\mathcal{T}_z = (x_a, x_p, x_n)$, and the training triplets are generated as follows. $A_{l'm}^2$ indicates randomly selecting two classes - a positive class and a negative class, from all $l'm$ classes in the mini-batch. A_t^2 means selecting two samples - a anchor sample (x_a^z) and a positive sample (x_p^z), from the positive class, and C_t^1 means randomly selecting a negative sample (x_n^z) from the negative class. $A_{l'm}^2$, A_t^2 and C_t^1 are notations in combinatorial mathematics. See reference [13] for details.

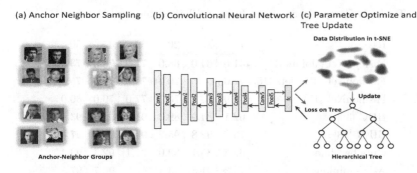

Fig. 3. (a) Sampling strategy of each mini-batch. The images in red stand for anchors and the images in blue stand for the nearest neighbors. (b) Train CNNs with the hierarchical triplet loss. (c) Online update of the hierarchical tree. (Color figure online)

α_z is a dynamic violate margin, which is different from the constant margin of traditional triplet loss. It is computed according to the class relationship between the anchor class y_a and the negative class y_n over the constructed hieratical class tree. Specifically, for a triplet $\mathcal{T}_z$, the violate margin α_z is computed as,

$$\alpha_z = \beta + d_{\mathcal{H}(y_a, y_n)} - s_{y_a},$$

where β (= 0.1) is a constant parameter that encourages the image classes to reside further apart from each other than the previous iterations. $\mathcal{H}(y_a, y_n)$ is the hierarchical level on the class tree, where the class y_a and the class y_n are merged into a single node in the next level. $d_{\mathcal{H}(y_a, y_n)}$ is the threshold for merging the two classes on $\mathcal{H}$, and $s_{y_a} = \frac{1}{n_{y_a}^2 - n_{y_a}} \sum_{i,j \in y_a} \|r_i - r_j\|^2$ is the average distance between samples in the class y_a. In our hierarchical triplet loss, a sample x_a is encouraged to push the nearby points with different semantic meanings apart from itself. Furthermore, it also contributes to the gradients of data points which are very far from it, by computing a dynamic violate margin which encodes global class structure via $\mathcal{H}$. For every individual triplet, we search on $\mathcal{H}$ to encode the context information of the data distribution for the optimization objective. Details of training process with the proposed hierarchical triplet loss are described in Algorithm 1.

Implementation Details. All our experiments are implemented using Caffe [10] and run on an NVIDIA TITAN X(Maxwell) GPU with 12 GB memory. The network architecture is a GoogLeNet [28] with batch normalization [9] which is pre-trained on the ImageNet dataset [21]. The 1000-way fully connected layer is removed, and replace by a d dimensional fully connected layer. The new added layer is initialized with random noise using the "Xaiver" filler. We modify the memory management of Caffe [10] to ensure it can take 650 images in a mini-batch for GoogLeNet with batch normalization. The input images are resized and cropped into 224 × 224, and then subtract the mean value. The optimization method used is the standard SGD with a learning rate $1e^{-3}$.

Table 1. Comparisons on the In-Shop Clothes Retrieval Dataset [15].

R@	1	10	20	30	40	50
FashionNet+Joints [15]	41.0	64.0	68.0	71.0	73.0	73.5
FashionNet+Poselets [15]	42.0	65.0	70.0	72.0	72.0	75.0
FashionNet [15]	53.0	73.0	76.0	77.0	79.0	80.0
HDC [38]	62.1	84.9	89.0	91.2	92.3	93.1
BIER [18]	76.9	92.8	95.2	96.2	96.7	97.1
Ours baseline	62.3	85.1	89.0	91.1	92.4	93.4
A-N sampling	75.3	91.8	94.3	96.2	96.7	97.5
HTL	**80.9**	**94.3**	**95.8**	**97.2**	**97.4**	**97.8**

Algorithm 1. Training with hierarchical triplet loss

Input: Training data $\mathcal{D} = \{(\boldsymbol{x}_i, y_i)\}_{k=1}^{N}$. Network $\phi\left(\cdot, \boldsymbol{\theta}\right)$ is initialized with a pretrained ImageNet model. The hierarchical class tree $\mathcal{H}$ is built according to the features of the initialized model. The margin α_z for any pair of classes is set to 0.2 at the beginning.
Output: The learnable parameters θ of the neural network $\phi\left(\cdot, \boldsymbol{\theta}\right)$.

1 **while** *not converge* **do**
2 | $t \leftarrow t + 1$;
3 | Sample anchors randomly and their neighborhoods according to $\mathcal{H}$;
4 | Compute the violate margin for different pairs of image classes by searching through the hierarchical tree $\mathcal{H}$;
5 | Compute the hierarchical triplet loss in a mini-batch $\mathcal{L}_{\mathcal{M}}$;
6 | Backpropagate the gradients produced at the loss layer and update the learnable parameters ;
7 | At each epoch, update the hierarchical tree $\mathcal{H}$ with current model.

---

5   Experimental Results and Comparisons

We evaluate the proposed hierarchical triplet loss on the tasks of image retrieval and face recognition. Extensive experiments are conducted on a number of benchmarks, including *In-Shop Clothes Retrieval* [15] and *Caltech-UCSD Birds 200* [31] for image retrieval, and LFW [8] for face verification. Descriptions of dataset and implementation details are presented as follows.

5.1   In-Shop Clothes Retrieval

Datasets and Performance Measures. The *In-Shop Clothes Retrieval* dataset [15] is very popular in image retrieval. It has 11735 classes of clothing items and 54642 training images. Following the protocol in [15,38], 3997

Fig. 4. Anchor-Neighbor visualization on *In-Shop Clothes Retrieval* training set [15]. Each row stands for a kind of fashion style. The row below each odd row is one of neighborhoods of the fashion style in the odd row.

classes are used for training (25882 images) and 3985 classes are for testing (28760 images). The test set are partitioned into the query set and the gallery set, both of which has 3985 classes. The query set has 14218 images and the gallery set has 12612 images. As in Fig. 4, there are a lot image classes that have very similar contents.

For the evaluation, we use the most common Recall@K metric. We extract the features of each query image and search the K most similar images in the gallery set. If one of the K retrieved images have the same label with the query image, the recall will increase by 1, otherwise will be 0. We evaluate the recall metrics with $K \in \{1, 2, 4, 8, 16, 32\}$.

Implementation Details. Our network is based on GoogLeNet V2 [9]. The dimension d of the feature embedding is 128. The triplet violate margin is set to 0.2. The hierarchical tree has 16 levels including the leaves level which contains the images classes. At the first epoch, the neural network is trained with the standard triplet loss which samples image classes for mini-batches randomly. Then during the training going on, the hierarchical tree is updated and used in the following steps. Since there are 3997 image classes for training and there many similar classes, the whole training needs 30 epoch and the batch size is set to 480. For every 10 epoch, we decrease the learning rate by multiplying 0.1. The testing codes are gotten from HDC [38].

Result Comparison. We compare our method with existing state-of-the-art algorithms and our baseline—triplet loss. Table 1 lists the results of image retrieval on *In-Shop Clothes Retrieval*. The proposed method achieves 80.9% Recall@1, and outperforms the baseline algorithm—triplet loss by 18.6%. It indicates that our algorithm can improve the discriminative power of the original

Table 2. Comparison with the state-of-art on the CUB-200-2011 dataset [31].

R@	1	2	4	8	16	32
LiftedStruct [26]	47.2	58.9	70.2	80.2	89.3	93.2
Binomial deviance [30]	52.8	64.4	74.7	83.9	90.4	94.3
Histogram loss [30]	50.3	61.9	72.6	82.4	88.8	93.7
N-Pair-Loss [25]	51.0	63.3	74.3	83.2	-	-
HDC [38]	53.6	65.7	77.0	85.6	91.5	95.5
BIER [18]	55.3	67.2	76.9	85.1	91.7	95.5
Ours baseline	55.9	68.4	78.2	86.0	92.2	95.5
HTL	**57.1**	**68.8**	**78.7**	**86.5**	**92.5**	**95.5**

triplet loss by a large margin. State-of-the-art algorithms, including HDC [38], and BIER [18], used boosting and ensemble method to take the advantage of different features and get excellent results. Our method demonstrates that by incorporate the global data distribution into deep metric learning, the performance will be highly improved. The proposed hierarchical loss get 80.9% Recall@1, which is 4.0% higher than BIER [18] and 18.8% higher than HDC [38].

5.2   Caltech-UCSD Birds 200-2011

Datasets and Performance Measures. The *Caltech-UCSD Birds 200* dataset (CUB-200-2011) [31] contains photos of 200 bird species with 11788 images. CUB-200-2011 serves as a benchmark in most existing work on deep metric learning and image retrieval. The first 100 classes (5864 images) are used for training, and the rest (5924 images) of classes are used for testing. The rest images are treated as both the query set and the gallery set. For the evaluation, we use the same Recall@K metric as in Section *In-Shop Clothes Retrieval*. Here, $K \in \{1, 2, 4, 8, 16, 32\}$.

Implementation Details. The dimension d of the feature embedding is 512. The triplet violate margin is set to 0.2. As in the previous section, the hierarchical tree is still set to 16 levels. All the training details are almost the same with the *In-Shop Clothes Retrieval* dataset. But since there are only 100 image classes for training, the dataset is very easy to get overfitting. When we train 10 epoches, the training stopped. The batch size is set to 50. For every 3 epoch, we decrease the learning rate by multiplying 0.1.

Result Comparison. Table 2 lists the results of image retrieval on *Caltech-UCSD Birds 200-2011*. The baseline—triplet loss already get the state-of-art results with 55.9% Recall@1 compared with the previous state-of-art HDC 54.6% and BIER 55.3%. If we use the anchor-neighbor sampling and the hierarchical loss, we get 57.1% Recall@1. Since there are only 100 classes and 6000 images for training, the network is very easy to get overfitting. The performance gain gotten by the hierarchical loss is only 1.2% Recall@1.

5.3   Cars-196 [11] and Stanford Online Products [26]

Details of the Cars-196 and Stanford Online Products [26] are described in [11, 26]. The dimension of the feature embedding is set to 512. The triplet violate margin is set to 0.2, with a hierarchical tree of *depth* = 16. The whole training needs 30 epoch and the batch size is set to 50. For every 10 epoch, we decrease the learning rate by multiplying 0.1.

Results are presented in Table 3, where the proposed HTL outperforms our baseline, BIER and HDC, with clear margins on both datasets. Specifically, on the Cars-196, HTL achieves 81.4% Recall@1, which outperforms original triplet loss by 2.2%, and previous state-of-art by 3.4%. On the Stanford Online Products, HTL achieves 74.8% Recall@1, outperforming triplet loss by 2.2%, and previous state-of-art by 2.1%. These results demonstrate that the proposed HTL can improve original triplet loss efficiently, and further proved the generalization ability of HTL.

Table 3. Comparison with the state-of-art on the cars-196 and Stanford products.

R@	Cars-196						Stanford online products			
	1	2	4	8	16	32	1	10	100	100
HDC	73.7	83.2	89.5	93.8	96.7	98.4	69.5	84.4	92.8	97.7
BIER	78.0	85.8	91.1	95.1	97.3	98.7	72.7	86.5	94.0	98.0
Baseline	79.2	87.2	92.1	95.2	97.3	98.6	72.6	86.2	93.8	98.0
HTL(depth = 16)	**81.4**	**88.0**	**92.7**	**95.7**	**97.4**	**99.0**	**74.8**	**88.3**	**94.8**	**98.4**

5.4   LFW Face Verification

Datasets and Performance Measures. The *CASIA-WebFace* dataset [37] is one of the publicly accessible datasets for face recognition. It has been the most popular dataset for the training of face recognition algorithms, such as in [1,14,33]. *CASIA-WebFace* has 10575 identities and 494414 images. We following the testing protocol in [37] to test the performance of our algorithms. The face verification results on LFW dataset [8] is reported.

Implementation Details. Since the triplet loss is very sensitive to the noise, we clear the CASIA-WebFace using the pre-trained model of VGG-Face [20] and manually remove some noises. About 10% images are removed. Then the remained faces are used to train a SoftMax classifier. The network parameters are initialized by a pre-trained ImageNet model. We fine-tune the pre-trained classification network for face recognition using the hierarchical loss.

Result Comparison. The triplet loss gets 98.3% accuracy on the LFW face verification task, which is 1.12% lower than the SpereFace [14]—99.42% which uses the same dataset for training. When we substitute the triplet loss with the hierarchical triplet loss, the results comes to 99.2. It's comparable with state-of-art results. This indicates that the hierarchical triplet loss has stronger discriminative power than triplet loss. While, since the triplet based method are very sensitive to noise, the hierarchical triplet loss get inferior performance compared with SphereFace [14] 99.42% and FaceNet [22] 99.65%.

5.5   Sampling Matter and Local Optima

Sampling Matter. We investigate the influence of batch size on the test set of *In-Shop Clothes Retrieval*. Figure 5(a) shows that when the batch size grows from 60 to 480, the accuracy increases in the same iterations. When the training continues, the performance will fluctuates heavily and get overfitting. Besides, when come to the same results at 60% Recall@1, both the anchor-neighbor sampling with triplet loss and the hierarchical loss converge at about 2 times faster than random sampling (Batch Size = 480). Figure 5(b) shows the compares the convergence speed of the triplet loss (our baseline), the hierarchical triplet loss and the HDC [38] on the test set of *Caltech-UCSD Birds 200*. Compared to the 60000 iterations (see in [38]), the hierarchical triplet loss converges in 1000 iterations. The hierarchical triplet loss with anchor-Neighborhood sampling converge faster traditional and get better performance than HDC [38].

Pool Local Optima. In Tables 1 and 2, we can find that the triplet loss get inferior performance than the hierarchical triplet loss on both the *In-Shop Clothes Retrieval* and *Caltech-UCSD Birds 200*. In the Fig. 5, the accuracy of the triplet loss start to fluctuate when the training continues going after the loss drops to very low. In fact, there are always very few or zeros triplets in mini-batch even when the network isn't gotten the best results. Then they don't produce gradients and will decay the learnable parameters in networks by SGD [19]. So we incorporate the hierarchical structure to make points in the mini-batch know the position of point that are already far away, and then attempt to push them further from itself and its neighborhood classes.

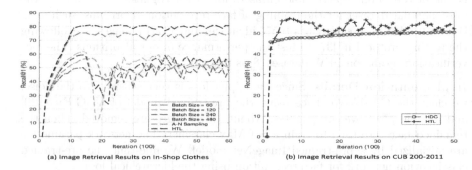

(a) Image Retrieval Results on In-Shop Clothes   (b) Image Retrieval Results on CUB 200-2011

Fig. 5. (a) Image retrieval results on In-Shop Clothes [15] with various batch sizes. (b) Image retrieval results on CUB-200-2011 [31].

5.6   Ablation Study

We perform ablation studies on In-Shop Clothes and CUB-200-2011, as reported in Table 4. First, directly applying hard negative sampling (HNS) to the whole training set is difficult to obtain a performance gain. Actually, our baseline model applies a semi-HNS, which outperforms HNS. We design a strong class-level constrain - Anchor-Neighbor Sampling of HTL, which encourages the model to learn discriminative features from visual similar classes. This is the key to performance boost. Second, we integrated the proposed anchor-neighbor sampling and dynamic violate margin into HDC where a contrastive loss is used. As shown in Table 4 (bottom), HDC+ got an improvement of 7.3% R@1 on the In-Shop Clothes Retrieval, suggesting that our methods work practically well with a contrastive loss and HDC. Third, HTL with a depth of 16 achieves best performance at R@1 of 80.9%. This is used as default setting in all our experiments. We also include results of "flat" tree with depth = 1. Results suggest that the "flat" tree with the proposed dynamic violate margin improves the R@1 from 75.3% to 78.9%, and hierarchy tree improves it further to 80.9%.

Table 4. Ablation studies on In-Shop Clothes Retrieval and CUB-200-2011.

	In-shop clothes						CUB-200-2011					
R@	1	10	20	30	40	50	1	2	4	8	16	32
On triplets with sampling												
Random sampling	59.3	83.5	87.9	90.5	91.3	93.0	51.4	63.9	74.8	83.4	90.0	94.3
Hard negative mining	60.1	84.3	88.2	90.2	91.5	92.6	51.6	63.9	74.2	84.4	89.9	94.6
Semi-hard negative mining	62.3	85.1	89.0	91.1	92.4	93.4	55.9	68.4	78.2	86.0	92.2	95.5
Anchor-neighbor sampling (HTL)	75.3	91.8	94.3	96.2	96.7	97.5	56.4	68.5	78.5	86.2	92.4	95.5
HTL with A-N sampling + dynamic violate margin(α_z)												
Class proxy(flat/depth = 1)	78.9	93.4	94.8	96.0	96.5	97.5	56.0	68.1	78.2	86.2	92.3	95.5
HTL(depth = 8)	78.7	93.3	94.6	96.2	96.9	97.4	56.2	68.5	78.3	86.1	92.3	95.5
HTL(depth = 16)	**80.9**	**94.3**	**95.8**	**97.2**	**97.4**	**97.8**	**57.1**	**68.8**	**78.7**	**86.5**	**92.5**	**95.5**
HTL(depth = 32)	79.3	93.8	95.0	96.9	97.1	97.5	56.4	68.5	78.5	86.2	92.3	95.5
HDC+: contrastive loss with A-N sampling + dynamic violate margin(α_z)												
HDC	62.1	84.9	89.0	91.2	92.3	93.1	53.6	65.7	77.0	85.6	91.5	95.5
HDC+	69.4	88.6	93.4	94.1	95.3	96.5	54.1	66.3	77.2	85.6	91.7	95.5

6   Conclusion

We have presented a new hierarchical triplet loss (HTL) which is able to select informative training samples (triplets) via an adaptively-updated hierarchical tree that encodes global context. HTL effectively handles the main limitation of random sampling, which is a critical issue for deep metric learning. First, we construct a hierarchical tree at the class level which encodes global context information over the whole dataset. Visual similar classes are merged recursively to form the hierarchy. Second, the problem of triplet collection is formulated by proposing a new violate margin, which is computed dynamically based on the designed hierarchical tree. This allows it to learn from more meaningful hard samples with the guide of global context. The proposed HTL is evaluated on the tasks of image retrieval and face recognition, where it achieves new state-of-the-art performance on a number of standard benchmarks.

References

1. Amos, B., Ludwiczuk, B., Satyanarayanan, M.: Openface: a general-purpose face recognition library with mobile applications. CMU School of Computer Science (2016)
2. Bai, S., Bai, X., Tian, Q., Latecki, L.J.: Regularized diffusion process for visual retrieval. In: AAAI, pp. 3967–3973 (2017)
3. Bai, S., Zhou, Z., Wang, J., Bai, X., Latecki, L.J., Tian, Q.: Ensemble diffusion for retrieval. In: Proceedings of the IEEE Conference on Computer Vision and Pattern Recognition, pp. 774–783 (2017)
4. Bucher, M., Herbin, S., Jurie, F.: Hard negative mining for metric learning based zero-shot classification. In: Hua, G., Jégou, H. (eds.) ECCV 2016. LNCS, vol. 9915, pp. 524–531. Springer, Cham (2016). https://doi.org/10.1007/978-3-319-49409-8_45
5. Chen, W., Chen, X., Zhang, J., Huang, K.: Beyond triplet loss: a deep quadruplet network for person re-identification. In: The IEEE Conference on Computer Vision and Pattern Recognition (CVPR), July 2017
6. Hadsell, R., Chopra, S., LeCun, Y.: Dimensionality reduction by learning an invariant mapping. In: 2006 IEEE Computer Society Conference on Computer Vision and Pattern Recognition, vol. 2, pp. 1735–1742. IEEE (2006)
7. Harwood, B., Kumar, B.G.V., Carneiro, G., Reid, I., Drummond, T.: Smart mining for deep metric learning. In: The IEEE International Conference on Computer Vision (ICCV), October 2017
8. Huang, G.B., Ramesh, M., Berg, T., Learned-Miller, E.: Labeled faces in the wild: a database for studying face recognition in unconstrained environments. Technical report 07–49, University of Massachusetts, Amherst, October 2007
9. Ioffe, S., Szegedy, C.: Batch normalization: accelerating deep network training by reducing internal covariate shift. In: International Conference on Machine Learning, pp. 448–456 (2015)
10. Jia, Y., et al.: Caffe: convolutional architecture for fast feature embedding. In: Proceedings of the 22nd ACM International Conference on Multimedia, pp. 675–678. ACM (2014)
11. Krause, J., Stark, M., Deng, J., Fei-Fei, L.: 3D object representations for fine-grained categorization. In: 4th IEEE Workshop on 3D Representation and Recognition, ICCV (2013)
12. Kumar, B., Carneiro, G., Reid, I., et al.: Learning local image descriptors with deep siamese and triplet convolutional networks by minimising global loss functions. In: Proceedings of the IEEE Conference on Computer Vision and Pattern Recognition, pp. 5385–5394 (2016)
13. van Lint, J.H., Wilson, R.M.: A Course in Combinatorics. Cambridge University Press, Cambridge (2001)
14. Liu, W., Wen, Y., Yu, Z., Li, M., Raj, B., Song, L.: Sphereface: deep hypersphere embedding for face recognition. In: The IEEE Conference on Computer Vision and Pattern Recognition (CVPR), vol. 1 (2017)

15. Liu, Z., Luo, P., Qiu, S., Wang, X., Tang, X.: Deepfashion: powering robust clothes recognition and retrieval with rich annotations. In: Proceedings of the IEEE Conference on Computer Vision and Pattern Recognition, pp. 1096–1104 (2016)
16. van der Maaten, L., Hinton, G.: Visualizing data using t-SNE. J. Mach. Learn. Res. 9(Nov), 2579–2605 (2008)
17. Opitz, M., Waltner, G., Possegger, H., Bischof, H.: Bier - boosting independent embeddings robustly. In: The IEEE International Conference on Computer Vision (ICCV), October 2017
18. Opitz, M., Waltner, G., Possegger, H., Bischof, H.: Bier-boosting independent embeddings robustly. In: Proceedings of the IEEE Conference on Computer Vision and Pattern Recognition, pp. 5189–5198 (2017)
19. Orr, G.B., Müller, K.R.: Neural Networks: Tricks of the Trade. Springer, Heidelberg (2003). https://doi.org/10.1007/978-3-642-35289-8
20. Parkhi, O.M., Vedaldi, A., Zisserman, A., et al.: Deep face recognition. In: BMVC, vol. 1, p. 6 (2015)
21. Russakovsky, O., et al.: ImageNet large scale visual recognition challenge. Int. J. Comput. Vis. (IJCV) 115(3), 211–252 (2015). https://doi.org/10.1007/s11263-015-0816-y
22. Schroff, F., Kalenichenko, D., Philbin, J.: Facenet: a unified embedding for face recognition and clustering. In: Proceedings of the IEEE Conference on Computer Vision and Pattern Recognition, pp. 815–823 (2015)
23. Shi, H., et al.: Embedding deep metric for person re-identification: a study against large variations. In: Leibe, B., Matas, J., Sebe, N., Welling, M. (eds.) ECCV 2016. LNCS, vol. 9905, pp. 732–748. Springer, Cham (2016). https://doi.org/10.1007/978-3-319-46448-0_44
24. Simo-Serra, E., Trulls, E., Ferraz, L., Kokkinos, I., Fua, P., Moreno-Noguer, F.: Discriminative learning of deep convolutional feature point descriptors. In: 2015 IEEE International Conference on Computer Vision (ICCV), pp. 118–126. IEEE (2015)
25. Sohn, K.: Improved deep metric learning with multi-class n-pair loss objective. In: Advances in Neural Information Processing Systems, pp. 1857–1865 (2016)
26. Song, H.O., Xiang, Y., Jegelka, S., Savarese, S.: Deep metric learning via lifted structured feature embedding. In: 2016 IEEE Conference on Computer Vision and Pattern Recognition (CVPR), pp. 4004–4012. IEEE (2016)
27. Sun, Y., Chen, Y., Wang, X., Tang, X.: Deep learning face representation by joint identification-verification. In: Advances in Neural Information Processing Systems, pp. 1988–1996 (2014)
28. Szegedy, C., et al.: Going deeper with convolutions. In: CVPR (2015)
29. Tao, R., Gavves, E., Smeulders, A.W.: Siamese instance search for tracking. In: 2016 IEEE Conference on Computer Vision and Pattern Recognition (CVPR), pp. 1420–1429. IEEE (2016)
30. Ustinova, E., Lempitsky, V.: Learning deep embeddings with histogram loss. In: Advances in Neural Information Processing Systems, pp. 4170–4178 (2016)
31. Wah, C., Branson, S., Welinder, P., Perona, P., Belongie, S.: The Caltech-UCSD birds-200-2011 dataset (2011)
32. Waltner, G., Opitz, M., Bischof, H.: BaCoN: building a classifier from only n samples. In: Proceedings of CVWW, vol. 1 (2016)
33. Wen, Y., Zhang, K., Li, Z., Qiao, Y.: A discriminative feature learning approach for deep face recognition. In: Leibe, B., Matas, J., Sebe, N., Welling, M. (eds.) ECCV 2016. LNCS, vol. 9911, pp. 499–515. Springer, Cham (2016). https://doi.org/10.1007/978-3-319-46478-7_31

34. Wohlhart, P., Lepetit, V.: Learning descriptors for object recognition and 3D pose estimation. In: Proceedings of the IEEE Conference on Computer Vision and Pattern Recognition, pp. 3109–3118 (2015)
35. Wu, C.Y., Manmatha, R., Smola, A.J., Krahenbuhl, P.: Sampling matters in deep embedding learning. In: The IEEE International Conference on Computer Vision (ICCV), October 2017
36. Wu, C.Y., Manmatha, R., Smola, A.J., Krähenbühl, P.: Sampling matters in deep embedding learning. arXiv preprint arXiv:1706.07567 (2017)
37. Yi, D., Lei, Z., Liao, S., Li, S.Z.: Learning face representation from scratch. arXiv preprint arXiv:1411.7923 (2014)
38. Yuan, Y., Yang, K., Zhang, C.: Hard-aware deeply cascaded embedding. In: The IEEE International Conference on Computer Vision (ICCV), October 2017

Joint Learning of Intrinsic Images and Semantic Segmentation

Anil S. Baslamisli[1]([⊠]), Thomas T. Groenestege[1,2], Partha Das[1,2],
Hoang-An Le[1], Sezer Karaoglu[1,2], and Theo Gevers[1,2]

[1] University of Amsterdam, Amsterdam, The Netherlands
{a.s.baslamisli,h.a.le,th.gevers}@uva.nl
[2] 3DUniversum B.V., Amsterdam, The Netherlands
s.karaoglu@3duniversum.com

Abstract. Semantic segmentation of outdoor scenes is problematic
when there are variations in imaging conditions. It is known that albedo
(reflectance) is invariant to all kinds of illumination effects. Thus, using
reflectance images for semantic segmentation task can be favorable. Additionally, not only segmentation may benefit from reflectance, but also
segmentation may be useful for reflectance computation. Therefore, in
this paper, the tasks of semantic segmentation and intrinsic image decomposition are considered as a combined process by exploring their mutual
relationship in a joint fashion. To that end, we propose a supervised end-
to-end CNN architecture to jointly learn intrinsic image decomposition
and semantic segmentation. We analyze the gains of addressing those two
problems jointly. Moreover, new cascade CNN architectures for intrinsic-
for-segmentation and segmentation-for-intrinsic are proposed as single
tasks. Furthermore, a dataset of 35K synthetic images of natural environments is created with corresponding albedo and shading (intrinsics),
as well as semantic labels (segmentation) assigned to each object/scene.
The experiments show that joint learning of intrinsic image decomposition and semantic segmentation is beneficial for both tasks for natural
scenes. Dataset and models are available at: (https://ivi.fnwi.uva.nl/cv/
intrinseg).

1 Introduction

Semantic segmentation of outdoor scenes is a challenging problem in computer vision. Variations in imaging conditions may negatively influence the segmentation process. These varying conditions include shading, shadows, inter-
reflections, illuminant color and its intensity. As image segmentation is the process of identifying and semantically grouping pixels, drastic changes in pixel
values may hinder a successful segmentation. To address this problem, several
methods are proposed to mitigate the effects of illumination to obtain more
robust image features to help semantic segmentation [1–4]. Unfortunately, these

Electronic supplementary material The online version of this chapter (https://
doi.org/10.1007/978-3-030-01231-1_18) contains supplementary material, which is
available to authorized users.

V. Ferrari et al. (Eds.): ECCV 2018, LNCS 11210, pp. 289–305, 2018.
https://doi.org/10.1007/978-3-030-01231-1_18

methods provide illumination invariance artificially by hand crafted features. Instead of using narrow and specific invariant features, in this paper, we focus on image formation invariance induced by a full intrinsic image decomposition.

Intrinsic image decomposition is the process of decomposing an image into its image formation components such as albedo (reflectance) and shading (illumination) [5]. The reflectance component contains the true color of objects in a scene. In fact, albedo is invariant to illumination, while the shading component heavily depends on object geometry and illumination conditions in a scene. As a result, using reflectance images for semantic segmentation task can be favorable, as they do not contain any illumination effect. Additionally, not only segmentation may benefit from reflectance, but also segmentation may be useful for reflectance computation. Information about an object reveals strong priors about its intrinsic properties. Each object label constrains the color distribution and is expected to reflect that property to class specific reflectance values. Therefore, distinct object labels provided by semantic segmentation can guide intrinsic image decomposition process by yielding object specific color distributions per label. Furthermore, semantic segmentation process can act as an object boundary guidance map for intrinsic image decomposition by enhancing cues that differentiate between reflectance and occlusion edges in a scene. In addition, homogeneous regions (i.e. in terms of color) within an object segment should have similar reflectance values. Therefore, in this paper, the tasks of semantic segmentation and intrinsic image decomposition are considered as a combined process by exploring their mutual relationship in a joint fashion.

To this end, we propose a supervised end-to-end convolutional neural network (CNN) architecture to jointly learn intrinsic image decomposition *and* semantic segmentation. The joint learning includes an end-to-end trainable encoder-decoder CNN with one shared encoder and three separate decoders: one for reflectance prediction, one for shading prediction, and one for semantic segmentation prediction. In addition to joint learning, we explore new cascade CNN architectures to use reflectance to improve semantic segmentation, and semantic segmentation to steer the process of intrinsic image decomposition.

To train the proposed supervised network, a large dataset is needed with ground-truth images for both image semantic segmentation (i.e. class labels) and intrinsic properties (i.e. reflectance and shading). However, there is no such a dataset. Therefore, we have created a large-scale dataset featuring plants and objects under varying illumination conditions that are mostly found in natural environments. The dataset is at scene-level considering natural environments containing intrinsic image decomposition and semantic segmentation ground-truths. The dataset contains 35K synthetic images with corresponding albedo and shading (intrinsics), as well as semantic labels (segmentation) assigned to each object/scene.

Our contributions are: (1) a CNN architecture for joint learning of intrinsic image decomposition and semantic segmentation, (2) analysis on the gains of addressing those two problems jointly, (3) new cascade CNN architectures for intrinsic-for-segmentation and segmentation-for-intrinsic, and (4) a very large-scale dataset of synthetic images of natural environments with scene level intrinsic image decomposition and semantic segmentation ground-truths.

2   Related Work

Intrinsic Image Decomposition. Intrinsic image decomposition is an ill-posed and under-constrained problem since an infinite number of combinations of photometric and geometric properties of a scene can produce the same 2D image. Therefore, most of the work on intrinsic image decomposition considers priors about scene characteristics to constrain a pixel-wise optimization task. For instance, both [6] and [7] use non-local texture cues, whereas [8] and [9] constrain the problem with the assumption of sparsity of reflectance. In addition, the use of multiple images helps to resolve the ambiguity where the reflectance is constant and the illumination changes [10,11]. Nonetheless, with the success of supervised deep CNNs [12,13], more recent research on intrinsic image decomposition has shifted towards using deep learning. [14] is the first work that uses end-to-end trained CNNs to address the problem. They argue that the model should learn both local and global cues together with a multi-scale architecture. In addition, [15] proposes a model by introducing inter-links between decoder modules, based on the expectation that intrinsic components are correlated. Moreover, [16] demonstrates the capability of generative adversarial networks for the task. On the other hand, in more recent work, [17] considers an image formation loss together with gradient supervision to steer the learning process to achieve more vivid colors and sharper edges.

In contrast, our proposed method jointly learns intrinsic properties and segmentation. Additionally, the success of supervised deep CNNs not only depends on a successful model, but also on the availability of annotated data. Generating ground-truth intrinsic images is only possible in a fully-controlled setup and it requires enormous effort and time [18]. To that end, the most popular real-world dataset for intrinsic image decomposition includes only 20 object-centered images with their ground-truth intrinsics [18], which alone is not feasible for deep learning. On the other hand, [19] presents scene-level real world relative reflectance comparisons over point pairs of indoor scenes. However, it does not include ground-truth intrinsic images. The most frequently used scene-level synthetic dataset for intrinsic image decomposition is the MPI Sintel Dataset [20]. It provides around a thousand of cartoon-like images with their ground-truth intrinsics. Therefore, a new dataset is created consisting of 35K synthetic (outdoor) images with 16 distinct object types/scenes which are recorded under different illumination conditions. The dataset contains intrinsic properties and object segmentation ground-truth labels. The dataset is described in detail in the experimental section.

Semantic Segmentation. Traditional semantic segmentation methods design hand-crated features to achieve per-pixel classification with the use of an external classifier such as support vector machines [21–23]. On the other hand, contemporary semantic segmentation methods such as [24–26] benefit from the powerful CNN models and large-scale datasets such as [27,28]. A detailed review on deep learning techniques applied to semantic segmentation task can be found in [29].

Photometric changes, which are due to varying illumination conditions, cause changes in the appearance of objects. Consequently, these appearance changes create problems for the semantic segmentation task. Therefore, several methods are proposed to mitigate the effects of varying illumination to accomplish a more robust semantic segmentation by incorporating illumination invariance in their algorithms [1–4]. However, these methods provide invariance artificially by hand crafted features. Therefore, they are limited in compensating for possible changes in photometry (i.e. illumination). Deep learning based methods may learn to accommodate photometric changes through data exploration. However, they are constrained by the amount of data. In this paper, we propose to use the intrinsic reflectance property (i.e. fully illumination invariance) to be used for semantic segmentation.

Joint Learning. Semantic segmentation has been used for joint learning tasks as it provides useful cues about objects and scenes. For instance, [30–32] propose joint depth prediction and semantic segmentation models. Joint semantic segmentation and 3D scene reconstruction is proposed by [33]. Furthermore, [34] formulates dense stereo reconstruction and semantic segmentation in a joint framework.

For intrinsic image decomposition, [35] introduces the first unified model for recovering shape, reflectance, and chromatic illumination in a joint optimization framework. Other works [36,37], jointly predict depth and intrinsic property. Finally, [38] exploits the relation between the intrinsic property and objects (i.e. attributes and segments). The authors propose to address these problems in a joint optimization framework. Using hand crafted priors, [38] designs energy terms per component and combines them in one global energy to be minimized. In contrast to previous methods, our proposed method is an end-to-end solution and does not rely on any hand crafted priors. Additionally, [38] does not optimize their energy function for each component separately. Therefore, the analysis on the influence of intrinsic image decomposition on semantic segmentation is omitted. In this paper, an in-depth analysis for each component is given.

3   Approach

3.1   Image Formation Model

To formulate our intrinsic image decomposition, the diffuse reflectance component is considered [39]. Then, an *RGB* image, I, over the visible spectrum ω, is defined by:

$$I = m_b(\boldsymbol{n}, \boldsymbol{s}) \int_\omega f_c(\lambda)\, e(\lambda)\, \rho_b(\lambda)\, \mathrm{d}\lambda. \tag{1}$$

In the equation, $\boldsymbol{n}$ denotes the surface normal, whereas $\boldsymbol{s}$ is the light source direction; together forming the geometric dependencies m, which in return forms the shading component $S(\boldsymbol{x})$ under white light. Additionally, λ represents the wavelength, $f_c(\lambda)$ is the camera spectral sensitivity, $e(\lambda)$ specifies the spectral power distribution of the illuminant, and ρ_b represents the diffuse surface reflectance

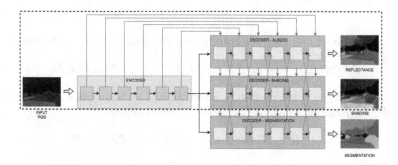

Fig. 1. Model architecture for jointly solving intrinsic image decomposition and semantic segmentation with one shared encoder and three separate decoders: one for shading, one for reflectance, and one for semantic segmentation prediction. The part in the dotted rectangle denotes the baseline ShapeNet model of [15].

$R(x)$. Then, using narrow band filters and considering a linear sensor response under white light, intrinsic image decomposition can be formulated as:

$$I(x) = R(x) \times S(x). \tag{2}$$

Then, for a position x, $I(x)$ can be approximated by the element-wise product of its intrinsic components. When the light source is colored, it is also included in the shading component.

3.2 Baseline Model Architectures

Intrinsic Image Decomposition. We use the model proposed by [15], *ShapeNet*, without the specular highlight module. The model is shown in the dotted rectangle part of Fig. 1. The model provides state-of-the results for intrinsic image decomposition task. Early features in the encoder block are connected with the corresponding decoder layers, which are called *mirror links*. That proves to be useful for keeping visual details and producing sharp outputs. Furthermore, the features across the decoders are linked to each other (*inter-connections*) to further strengthen the correlation between the components.

To train the model for intrinsic image decomposition task, we use a combination of the standard L_2 reconstruction loss (MSE) with its scale invariant version (SMSE). Let J be the prediction of the network and $\hat{J}$ be the ground-truth intrinsic image. Then, the standard L_2 reconstruction loss $\mathcal{L}_{MSE}$ is given by:

$$\mathcal{L}_{MSE}(J, \hat{J}) = \frac{1}{n} \sum_{x,c} ||\hat{J} - J||_2^2, \tag{3}$$

where x denotes the pixel coordinate, c is the color channel index and n is the total number of evaluated pixels. Then, SMSE scales J first and compares MSE with $\hat{J}$:

$$\mathcal{L}_{SMSE}(J, \hat{J}) = \mathcal{L}_{MSE}(\alpha J, \hat{J}), \tag{4}$$

$$\alpha = argmin \; \mathcal{L}_{MSE}(\alpha J, \hat{J}). \tag{5}$$

Then, the combined loss $\mathcal{L}_{CL}$ for training an intrinsic component becomes:

$$\mathcal{L}_{CL}(J, \hat{J}) = \gamma_{SMSE} \; \mathcal{L}_{SMSE}(J, \hat{J}) + \gamma_{MSE} \; \mathcal{L}_{MSE}(J, \hat{J}), \tag{6}$$

where the γs are the corresponding loss weights. The final loss $\mathcal{L}_{IL}$ for training the model for intrinsic image decomposition task becomes:

$$\mathcal{L}_{IL}(R, \hat{R}, S, \hat{S}) = \gamma_R \; \mathcal{L}_{CL}(R, \hat{R}) + \gamma_S \; \mathcal{L}_{CL}(S, \hat{S}). \tag{7}$$

Semantic Segmentation. The same architecture is used as the baseline for semantic segmentation task. However, one of the decoders is removed from the architecture, because there is only one task. As a consequence, inter-connection links are not used for the semantic segmentation task. Furthermore, as a second baseline, we train an off-the-shelf segmentation algorithm [24], *SegNet*, that is specifically engineered for semantic segmentation task.

To train the model for semantic segmentation, we use the cross entropy loss:

$$\mathcal{L}_{CE} = -\frac{1}{n} \sum_{x} \sum_{L \in O_x} log(p_x^L) , \tag{8}$$

where p is the output of the softmax function to compute the posterior probability of a given pixel x belonging to L^{th} class, where $L \in O_x$ and $O_x = \{0, 1, 2, \cdots, C\}$ as the category set for pixel level class label.

3.3   Joint Model Architecture

In this section, a new joint model architecture is proposed. It is an extension of the base model architecture for intrinsic image decomposition task, *ShapeNet* [15], that combines the two tasks i.e. intrinsic image decomposition and semantic segmentation. We modify the baseline model architecture to have one encoder and three distinct decoders i.e. one for reflectance prediction, one for shading prediction, and one for semantic segmentation prediction. We maintain the mirror links and inter-connections. That allows for the network to be constrained with different outputs, and thus reinforce the learned features from different tasks. As a result, the network is forced to learn joint features for the two tasks at hand not only in the encoding phase, but also in the decoding phase. Both encoder and decoder parts contain both intrinsic properties and semantic segmentation characteristics. This setup is expected to be exploited by individual decoder blocks to learn extra cues for the task at hand. Figure 1 illustrates the joint model architecture. To train the model jointly, we combine the task specific loss functions by summing them together:

$$\mathcal{L}_{JL}(I, R, \hat{R}, S, \hat{S}) = \gamma_{CE} \; \mathcal{L}_{CE} + \gamma_{IL} \; \mathcal{L}_{IL}(R, \hat{R}, S, \hat{S}). \tag{9}$$

The effect of the gamma parameters of Eq. 6 and more implementation details can be found in the supplementary materials.

4   Experiments

4.1   New Synthetic Dataset of Natural Environments

A large set of synthetic images is created featuring plants and objects that are mostly found in natural environments such as parks and gardens. The dataset contains different species of vegetation such as trees and flowering plants with different types of terrains and landscapes under different lighting conditions. Furthermore, scenarios are created which involves human intervention such as the presence of bushes (like rectangular hedges or spherical topiaries), fences, flowerpots and planters, and etc. (16 classes in total). There is a substantial variety of object colors and geometry. The dataset is constructed by using the parametric tree models [40] (implemented as add-ons in Blender software), and several manually-designed models from the Internet that aim for realistic natural scenes and environments. Ambient lighting is provided by real HDR sky images with a parallel light source. Light source properties are designed to correspond to daytime lighting conditions such as clear sky, cloudy, sunset, twilight, etc. For each virtual park/garden, we captured the scene from different perspectives with motion blur effects. Scene are rendered with the physics-based Blender Cycles[1] engine. To obtain annotations, the rendering pipeline is modified to output *RGB* images, their corresponding albedo and shading profiles (intrinsics) and semantic labels (segmentation). The dataset consists of 35K images, depicted 40 various parks/gardens under 5 lighting conditions. A number of samples are shown in Fig. 2. For the experiments, the dataset is randomly split into 80% training and 20% testing (scene split).

4.2   Error Metrics

To evaluate our method for intrinsic image decomposition task, we report on mean squared error (MSE), its scale invariant version (SMSE), local mean squared error (LMSE), and dissimilarity version of the structural similarity index (DSSIM). DSSIM accounts for the perceptual visual quality of the results. Following [18], for MSE, the absolute brightness of each image is adjusted to minimize the error. Further, $k = 20$ is used for the window size of LMSE. For semantic segmentation task, we report on global pixel accuracy, mean class accuracy and mean intersection over union (mIoU).

5   Evaluation

5.1   Influence of Reflectance on Semantic Segmentation

In this experiment, we evaluate the performance of reflectance and RGB color images as input for semantic segmentation task. We train an off-the-shelf segmentation algorithm *SegNet* [24] using (i) ground-truth reflectance

---

[1] https://www.blender.org/.

Fig. 2. Sample images from the Natural Environment Dataset (NED) featuring plants and objects under varying illumination conditions with ground-truth components

(*Albedo − SegNet*) and (ii) *RGB* color images (*RGB − SegNet*); separately, and (iii) *RGB* + reflectance (*Comb. − SegNet*); together, as input. The results are summarized in Table 1 and illustrated in Fig. 3. Further, confusion matrices for (*RGB − SegNet*) and (*Albedo − SegNet*) are provided in Fig. 4.

Table 1. Semantic segmentation accuracy using albedo and *RGB* images as inputs. Using albedo images significantly outperforms *RGB* images

Methodology	Global pixel	Class average	mIoU
RGB − SegNet	0.8743	0.6259	0.5217
Comb. − SegNet	0.8958	0.6607	0.5577
Albedo − SegNet	**0.9147**	**0.6739**	**0.5810**

The results show that semantic segmentation algorithm highly benefits from illumination invariant intrinsic properties (i.e. reflectance). The combination (*Comb. − SegNet*) outperforms single RGB input (*RGB − SegNet*). On the other hand, the results with reflectance as single input (*Albedo − SegNet*) are superior to the results with inputs including *RGB* color images in all metrics. The combined input (*Comb. − SegNet*) is not better than using only reflectance (*Albedo − SegNet*), because the network may be negatively influenced by the varying photometric cues introduced by the RGB input. Although the CNN framework may learn, to a certain degree, illumination invariance, it is not possible to cover all the variations caused by the illumination. Therefore, a full illumination invariant representation (i.e. reflectance) helps the CNN to improve semantic segmentation performance. Moreover, the confusion matrices show that the network is unable to distinguish a number of classes based on RGB input.

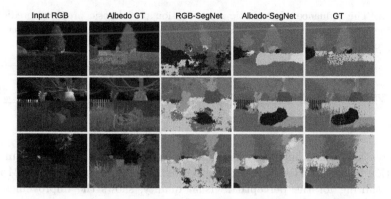

Fig. 3. Qualitative evaluation of the influence of reflectance on semantic segmentation. The results show that the semantic segmentation algorithm highly benefits from illumination invariant intrinsic properties (i.e. reflectance)

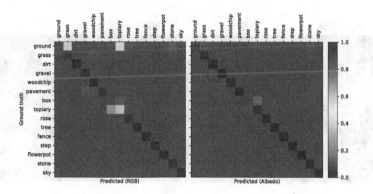

Fig. 4. Confusion matrices for ($RGB - SegNet$) and ($Albedo - SegNet$)

Using reflectance, the same network gains the ability to correctly classify the ground class, as well as making fewer mistakes with similar-looking box and topiary classes.

5.2 Influence of Semantic Segmentation on Intrinsic Decomposition

In this experiment, we evaluate the performance of intrinsic image decomposition using ground-truth semantic segmentation labels as an extra source of information to the RGB images. We compare the performance of intrinsic image decomposition trained with RGB images (RGB) only as input and intrinsic decomposition trained with RGB images and ground-truth semantic segmentation labels ($RGB + SegGT$) together as their input. As for $RGB + SegGT$, four input channels (i.e. RGB color image and semantic segmentation labels) are provided as input. The results are summarized in Table 2.

Table 2. The influence of semantic segmentation on intrinsic property prediction. Providing segmentation as an additional input ($RGB + SegGT$) clearly outperforms the approach of using only RGB color images as their input

	MSE		LMSE		DSSIM	
	Alb	Shad	Alb	Shad	Alb	Shad
RGB	0.0094 ± 0.008	0.0088 ± 0.0078	0.0679 ± 0.0412	0.0921 ± 0.0582	0.1310 ± 0.0535	**0.1303 ± 0.0495**
$RGB + SegGT$	**0.0076 ± 0.0063**	**0.0078 ± 0.0064**	**0.0620 ± 0.0384**	**0.0901 ± 0.0613**	**0.1141 ± 0.0472**	0.1312 ± 0.0523

As shown in Table 2, intrinsic image decomposition clearly benefits from segmentation labels. $RGB + SegGT$ outperforms RGB in all metrics. DSSIM metric, accounting for the perceptual visual quality, shows the improvement on reflectance predictions, which indicates that the semantic segmentation process can act as an object boundary guidance map for reflectance prediction. A number of qualitative comparisons are shown for RGB and $RGB + SegGT$ in Fig. 5.

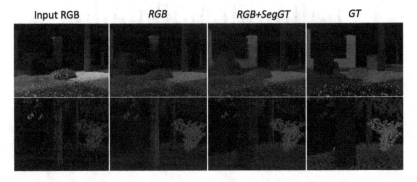

Fig. 5. Columns 2 and 3 show that $RGB + SegGT$ is better in removing shadows and shading from the reflectance images, as well as preserving sharp object boundaries and vivid colors, and therefore is more similar to the ground truth

5.3 Joint Learning of Semantic Segmentation and Intrinsic Decomposition

In this section, we evaluate the influence of joint learning on intrinsic image decomposition and semantic segmentation performances. We perform three experiments. First, we evaluate the effectiveness of joint learning of intrinsic properties and semantic segmentation considering semantic segmentation performance. Second, we evaluate the effectiveness of joint learning of intrinsic property and semantic segmentation to obtain intrinsic property prediction. Finally, we study the effects of the weights of the loss functions for the tasks.

Experiment I. In this experiment, we evaluate the performance of the proposed joint learning-based semantic segmentation algorithm (*Joint*), an off-the-shelf

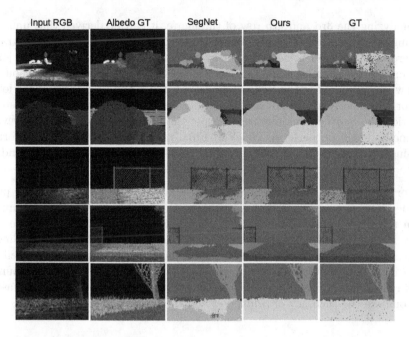

Fig. 6. Proposed joint learning framework outperforms single task framework *SegNet*. Our method preserves the object shapes and boundaries better and is robust against varying lighting conditions

semantic segmentation algorithm [24] (*SegNet*) and the baseline of one encoder one decoder ShapeNet [15] (*Single*). All CNNs receive *RGB* color images as their input. *SegNet* and *Single* output only pixel level object class label predictions, whereas the proposed method predicts intrinsic property (i.e. reflectance and shading) in addition to the object class labels. We compare the accuracy of the models in Table 3. As shown in Table 3, the proposed joint learning framework outperforms the single task frameworks in all metrics. Further, visual comparison between *SegNet* and the proposed *joint* framework is provided in Fig. 6. In addition, confusion matrices are provided in the supplementary material.

Table 3. Comparison of the semantic segmentation accuracy. The proposed joint learning framework outperforms the single task frameworks in all metrics

Methodology	Global pixel	Class average	mIoU
Single	0.8022	0.4584	0.3659
SegNet	0.8743	0.6259	0.5217
Joint	**0.9302**	**0.7055**	**0.6332**

By analyzing the 3rd and 4th row of the figure, it can be derived that unusual lighting conditions negatively influence the results of the *SegNet*. In contrast, our proposed method is not effected by varying illumination due to the joint learning scheme. Furthermore, our method preserves object shapes and boundaries when compared to the *SegNet* model (rows 1, 2 and 5). Note that the joint network does not perform any additional fine-tuning operations (e.g. CRF etc.). Additionally, *SegNet* architecture is deeper than our proposed model. However, our method still outperforms *SegNet*. Finally, the joint network outperforms the single task cascade network; for mIoU 0.6332 vs. 0.5810, see Tables 1 and 3, as the joint scheme enforces to augment joint features.

Experiment II. In this experiment, we evaluate the performance of the proposed joint learning-based and the state-of-the-art intrinsic image decomposition algorithms [15] (*ShapeNet*). Both CNNs receive *RGB* color images as input. *ShapeNet* outputs only intrinsic properties (i.e. reflectance and shading), whereas the proposed method predicts pixel level object class labels as well as intrinsic properties. We train *ShapeNet* and the proposed method using ground-truth reflectance and shading labels on the training set of the proposed dataset. We compare the accuracy of *ShapeNet* and the proposed method in Table 4.

Table 4. Influence of joint learning on intrinsic property prediction

	MSE		LMSE		DSSIM	
	Alb	Shad	Alb	Shad	Alb	Shad
ShapeNet	0.0094 ± 0.0080	0.0088 ± 0.0078	0.0679 ± 0.0412	0.0921 ± 0.0582	0.1310 ± 0.0535	0.1303 ± 0.0495
Int.-Seg. Joint	**0.0030 ± 0.0040**	**0.0030 ± 0.0024**	**0.0373 ± 0.0356**	**0.0509 ± 0.0395**	**0.0753 ± 0.0399**	**0.0830 ± 0.0381**

As shown in Table 4, the performance of the proposed joint learning framework outperforms single task learning (*ShapeNet*) in all the metrics for reflectance (albedo) and shading estimation. Further, our joint model obtains lower standard deviation values. To give more insight on reflectance prediction performances, a number of visual comparisons between *ShapeNet* and the proposed *joint* framework are given in Fig. 7. In the figure, (the first two columns) it can be derived that the semantic segmentation process acts as an object boundary guidance map for the intrinsic image decomposition task by enhancing cues to differentiate between reflectance and occlusion edges in a scene. Hence, object boundaries are better preserved by the proposed method (e.g. the separation between pavement and ground in the first image and the space between fences in the second image). In addition, information about an object reveals strong priors about it's intrinsic properties. Each object label adopts to a constrained color distribution. That can be observed in third and fourth columns. Semantic segmentation guides intrinsic image decomposition process by yielding the trees to be closer to green and flowers to be closer to pink. Moreover, for class-level intrinsics, the best improvement (3.3 times better) is obtained by *concrete step blocks*, which have achromatic colors. Finally, as in segmentation, the joint network outperforms the single task cascade network, see Tables 2 and 4.

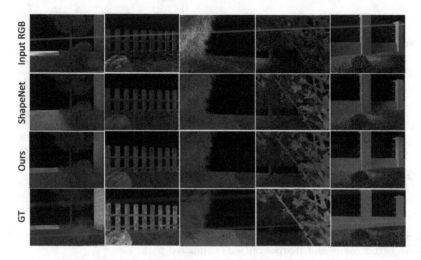

Fig. 7. The first two columns illustrate that the proposed method provides sharper outputs especially at object boundaries than *ShapeNet*. The 3rd and 4th columns show that the proposed method predicts colours that are closer to the ground truth reflectance. The last column shows that the proposed method handles sharp cast shadows better than *ShapeNet* (Color figure online)

Experiment III. In this experiment, we study the effects of the weightings of the loss functions. As the cross entropy loss is an order of magnitude higher than the SMSE loss, we first normalize them by multiplying the intrinsic loss by 100. Then, we evaluate different weights on top of the normalization ($SMSE \times 100 \times w$). See Table 5 for the results. If higher weights are assigned to intrinsics, they both jointly increase. However, weights which are too high, negatively influence the mIoU values. Therefore, $w = 2$ appears to be the proper setting for both tasks.

Table 5. Influence of the weighting of the loss functions. SMSE loss is weighted by ($SMSE \times 100 \times w$). $w = 2$ appears to be the proper setting for both tasks

ω	Segmentation		MSE		LMSE		DSSIM	
	Global	mIoU	Alb	Shad	Alb	Shad	Alb	Shad
0.01	0.9179	0.567	0.0083 ± 0.0068	0.0083 ± 0.0072	0.0650 ± 0.0412	0.0920 ± 0.0611	0.1224 ± 0.0498	0.1343 ± 0.0545
0.5	0.7038	0.512	0.0038 ± 0.0037	0.0035 ± 0.0027	0.0398 ± 0.0311	0.0550 ± 0.0416	0.1633 ± 0.0538	0.1353 ± 0.0497
1	0.9048	0.533	0.0044 ± 0.0041	0.0044 ± 0.0036	0.0477 ± 0.0352	0.0655 ± 0.0474	0.0926 ± 0.0445	0.1040 ± 0.0421
2	0.9302	0.633	0.0030 ± 0.0040	0.0030 ± 0.0024	0.0373 ± 0.0356	0.0509 ± 0.0395	0.0753 ± 0.0399	0.0830 ± 0.0381
4	0.9334	0.611	0.0028 ± 0.3300	0.0028 ± 0.0023	0.0356 ± 0.02997	0.0491 ± 0.04081	0.0716 ± 0.03804	0.0695 ± 0.0357

5.4   Real World Outdoor Dataset

Finally, our model is evaluated on real world garden images provided by the *3D Reconstruction meets Semantics challenge* [41]. The images are captured by

Fig. 8. Evaluation on real world garden images. We observe that our proposed method capture better colors and sharper outputs compared with [15]

a robot driving through a semantically-rich garden with fine geometric details. Results of [15] are provided as a visual comparison on the performance in Fig. 8. It shows that our method generates better results on real images with sharper reflectance images having more vivid and realistic colors. Moreover, our method mitigates sharp shadow effects better. Note that our model is trained fully on synthetic images and still provides satisfactory results on real, natural scenes. For semantic segmentation comparison, we fine-tuned SegNet [24] and our approach on the real world dataset after pre-training on the garden dataset. Since we only have the ground-truth for segmentation, we (only) unfreeze the segmentation branch. Results show that SegNet and our approach obtain 0.54 and 0.54 for mIoU and a global pixel accuracy of 0.85 and 0.88 respectively. Note that our model is much smaller in size and predicts the intrinsics together with the segmentation. More results are provided in the supplementary material.

6   Conclusion

Our approach jointly learns intrinsic image decomposition and semantic segmentation. New CNN architectures are proposed for joint learning, and single intrinsic-for-segmentation and segmentation-for-intrinsic learning. A dataset of 35K synthetic images of natural environments has been created with corresponding albedo and shading (intrinsics), and semantic labels (segmentation). The experiments show joint performance benefit when performing the two tasks (intrinsics and semantics) in joint manner for natural scenes.

Acknowledgements. This project was funded by the EU Horizon 2020 program No. 688007 (TrimBot2020). We thank Gjorgji Strezoski for his contributions to the website.

References

1. Upcroft, B., McManus, C., Churchill, W., Maddern, W., Newman, P.: Lighting invariant urban street classification. In: IEEE International Conference on Robotics and Automations (2014)
2. Wang, C., Tang, Y., Zou, X., Situ, W., Feng, W.: A robust fruit image segmentation algorithm against varying illumination for vision system of fruit harvesting robot. Opt.-Int. J. Light Electron Opt. **131**, 626–631 (2017)
3. Suh, H.K., Hofstee, J.W., van Henten, E.J.: Shadow-resistant segmentation based on illumination invariant image transformation. In: International Conference of Agricultural Engineering (2014)
4. Ramakrishnan, R., Nieto, J., Scheding, S.: Shadow compensation for outdoor perception. In: IEEE International Conference on Robotics and Automation (2015)
5. Land, E.H., McCann, J.J.: Lightness and retinex theory. J. Opt. Soc. Am. **61**, 1–11 (1971)
6. Shen, L., Tan, P., Lin, S.: Intrinsic image decomposition with non-local texture cues. In: IEEE Conference on Computer Vision and Pattern Recognition (2008)
7. Zhao, Q., Tan, P., Dai, Q., Shen, L., Wu, E., Lin, S.: A closed-form solution to retinex with nonlocal texture constraints. IEEE Trans. Pattern Anal. Mach. Intell. **34**, 1437–1444 (2012)
8. Gehler, P.V., Rother, C., Kiefel, M., Zhang, L., Schölkopf, B.: Recovering intrinsic images with a global sparsity prior on reflectance. In: Advances in Neural Information Processing Systems (2011)
9. Shen, L., Yeo, C.: Intrinsic images decomposition using a local and global sparse representation of reflectance. In: IEEE Conference on Computer Vision and Pattern Recognition (2011)
10. Weiss, Y.: Deriving intrinsic images from image sequences. In: IEEE International Conference on Computer Vision (2001)
11. Matsushita, Y., Lin, S., Kang, S.B., Shum, H.-Y.: Estimating intrinsic images from image sequences with biased illumination. In: Pajdla, T., Matas, J. (eds.) ECCV 2004. LNCS, vol. 3022, pp. 274–286. Springer, Heidelberg (2004). https://doi.org/10.1007/978-3-540-24671-8_22
12. Simonyan, K., Zisserman, A.: Very deep convolutional networks for large-scale image recognition. In: International Conference on Learning Representations (2015)
13. Girshick, R., Donahue, J., Darrell, T., Malik, J.: Rich feature hierarchies for accurate object detection and semantic segmentation. In: IEEE Conference on Computer Vision and Pattern Recognition (2014)
14. Narihira, T., Maire, M., Yu, S.X.: Direct intrinsics: learning albedo-shading decomposition by convolutional regression. In: IEEE International Conference on Computer Vision (2015)
15. Shi, J., Dong, Y., Su, H., Yu, S.X.: Learning non-Lambertian object intrinsics across shapenet categories. In: IEEE Conference on Computer Vision and Pattern Recognition (2017)
16. Lettry, L., Vanhoey, K., Gool, L.V.: Darn: a deep adversarial residual network for intrinsic image decomposition. In: IEEE Winter Conference on Applications of Computer Vision (2018)
17. Baslamisli, A.S., Le, H.A., Gevers, T.: CNN based learning using reflection and retinex models for intrinsic image decomposition. In: IEEE Conference on Computer Vision and Pattern Recognition (2018)

18. Grosse, R., Johnson, M.K., Adelson, E.H., Freeman, W.T.: Ground truth dataset and baseline evaluations for intrinsic image algorithms. In: IEEE International Conference on Computer Vision (2009)

19. Bell, S., Bala, K., Snavely, N.: Intrinsic images in the wild. In: ACM Transactions on Graphics (TOG) (2014)

20. Butler, D.J., Wulff, J., Stanley, G.B., Black, M.J.: A naturalistic open source movie for optical flow evaluation. In: Fitzgibbon, A., Lazebnik, S., Perona, P., Sato, Y., Schmid, C. (eds.) ECCV 2012. LNCS, vol. 7577, pp. 611–625. Springer, Heidelberg (2012). https://doi.org/10.1007/978-3-642-33783-3_44

21. Fulkerson, B., Vedaldi, A., Soatto, S.: Class segmentation and object localization with superpixel neighborhoods. In: IEEE International Conference on Computer Vision (2009)

22. Csurka, G., Perronnin, F.: An efficient approach to semantic segmentation. Int. J. Comput. Vis. **95**(2), 198–212 (2011)

23. Shotton, J., Winn, J., Rother, C., Criminisi, A.: Textonboost for image understanding: multi-class object recognition and segmentation by jointly modeling texture, layout, and context. Int. J. Comput. Vis. **95**(2), 2–23 (2009)

24. Badrinarayanan, V., Kendall, A., Cipolla, R.: SegNet: a deep convolutional encoder-decoder architecture for image segmentation. IEEE Trans. Pattern Anal. Mach. Intell. **39**, 2481–2495 (2017)

25. Long, J., Shelhamer, E., Darrell, T.: Fully convolutional networks for semantic segmentation. In: IEEE Conference on Computer Vision and Pattern Recognition (2015)

26. Chen, L.C., Papandreou, G., Kokkinos, I., Murphy, K., Yuille, A.L.: Deeplab: semantic image segmentation with deep convolutional nets, atrous convolution, and fully connected CRFs. arXiv preprint arXiv:1606.00915 (2016)

27. Everingham, M., Eslami, S.M.A., van Gool, L., Williams, C.K.I., Winn, J., Zisserman, A.: The Pascal visual object classes challenge: a retrospective. Int. J. Comput. Vis. **111**(1), 98–136 (2015)

28. Cordts, M., et al.: The cityscapes dataset for semantic urban scene understanding. In: IEEE Conference on Computer Vision and Pattern Recognition (2016)

29. Garcia-Garcia, A., Orts-Escolano, S., Oprea, S.O., Villena-Martinez, V., Garcia-Rodriguez, J.: A survey on deep learning techniques for image and video semantic segmentation. Appl. Soft Comput. **70**, 41–65 (2018)

30. Jafari, O.H., Groth, O., Kirillov, A., Yang, M.Y., Rother, C.: Analyzing modular CNN architectures for joint depth prediction and semantic segmentation. In: IEEE International Conference on Robotics and Automation (2017)

31. Eigen, D., Fergus, R.: Predicting depth, surface normals and semantic labels with a common multi-scale convolutional architecture. In: IEEE International Conference on Computer Vision (2015)

32. Mousavian, A., Pirsiavash, H., Kosecka, J.: Joint semantic segmentation and depth estimation with deep convolutional networks. In: IEEE International Conference on 3D Vision (2016)

33. Kundu, A., Li, Y., Dellaert, F., Li, F., Rehg, J.M.: Joint semantic segmentation and 3D reconstruction from monocular video. In: Fleet, D., Pajdla, T., Schiele, B., Tuytelaars, T. (eds.) ECCV 2014. LNCS, vol. 8694, pp. 703–718. Springer, Cham (2014). https://doi.org/10.1007/978-3-319-10599-4_45

34. Ladicky, L., et al.: Joint optimization for object class segmentation and dense stereo reconstruction. Int. J. Comput. Vis. **100**(2), 122–133 (2012)

35. Barron, J.T., Malik, J.: Color constancy, intrinsic images, and shape estimation. In: Fitzgibbon, A., Lazebnik, S., Perona, P., Sato, Y., Schmid, C. (eds.) ECCV 2012. LNCS, vol. 7575, pp. 57–70. Springer, Heidelberg (2012). https://doi.org/10.1007/978-3-642-33765-9_5
36. Kim, S., Park, K., Sohn, K., Lin, S.: Unified depth prediction and intrinsic image decomposition from a single image via joint convolutional neural fields. In: IEEE Conference on Computer Vision and Pattern Recognition (2016)
37. Shelhamer, E., Barron, J.T., Darrell, T.: Scene intrinsics and depth from a single image. In: IEEE International Conference on Computer Vision Workshop (2015)
38. Vineet, V., Rother, C., Torr, P.H.S.: Higher order priors for joint intrinsic image, objects, and attributes estimation. In: Advances in Neural Information Processing Systems (2013)
39. Shafer, S.: Using color to separate reflection components. Color Res. Appl. **10**, 210–218 (1985)
40. Weber, J., Penn, J.: Creation and rendering of realistic trees. In: Proceedings of the 22nd Annual Conference on Computer Graphics and Interactive Techniques (SIGGRAPH) (1995)
41. Sattler, T., Tylecek, R., Brok, T., Pollefeys, M., Fisher, R.B.: 3D reconstruction meets semantics - reconstruction challange 2017. In: IEEE International Conference on Computer Vision Workshop (2017)

Recurrent Tubelet Proposal and Recognition Networks for Action Detection

Dong Li[1], Zhaofan Qiu[1], Qi Dai[2(✉)], Ting Yao[3], and Tao Mei[3]

[1] University of Science and Technology of China, Hefei, China
dongli1995.ustc@gmail.com, zhaofanqiu@gmail.com
[2] Microsoft Research, Beijing, China
qid@microsoft.com
[3] JD AI Research, Beijing, China
tingyao.ustc@gmail.com,tmei@live.com

Abstract. Detecting actions in videos is a challenging task as video is an information intensive media with complex variations. Existing approaches predominantly generate action proposals for each individual frame or fixed-length clip independently, while overlooking temporal context across them. Such temporal contextual relations are vital for action detection as an action is by nature a sequence of movements. This motivates us to leverage the localized action proposals in previous frames when determining action regions in the current one. Specifically, we present a novel deep architecture called Recurrent Tubelet Proposal and Recognition (RTPR) networks to incorporate temporal context for action detection. The proposed RTPR consists of two correlated networks, i.e., Recurrent Tubelet Proposal (RTP) networks and Recurrent Tubelet Recognition (RTR) networks. The RTP initializes action proposals of the start frame through a Region Proposal Network and then estimates the movements of proposals in next frame in a recurrent manner. The action proposals of different frames are linked to form the tubelet proposals. The RTR capitalizes on a multi-channel architecture, where in each channel, a tubelet proposal is fed into a CNN plus LSTM to recurrently recognize action in the tubelet. We conduct extensive experiments on four benchmark datasets and demonstrate superior results over state-of-the-art methods. More remarkably, we obtain mAP of 98.6%, 81.3%, 77.9% and 22.3% with gains of 2.9%, 4.3%, 0.7% and 3.9% over the best competitors on UCF-Sports, J-HMDB, UCF-101 and AVA, respectively.

Keywords: Action detection · Action recognition

Electronic supplementary material The online version of this chapter (https://doi.org/10.1007/978-3-030-01231-1_19) contains supplementary material, which is available to authorized users.

V. Ferrari et al. (Eds.): ECCV 2018, LNCS 11210, pp. 306–322, 2018.
https://doi.org/10.1007/978-3-030-01231-1_19

1 Introduction

Action detection with accurate spatio-temporal location in videos is one of the most challenging tasks in video understanding. Compared to action recognition, this task is more difficult due to complex variations and large spatio-temporal search space. The solutions to this problem have evolved from handcrafted feature-based methods [18,34,40] to deep learning-based approaches [7]. Promising progresses have been made recently [22,28,36,39] with the prevalence of deep Convolutional Neural Networks (CNN) [10,16,30].

Fig. 1. Action detection comparisons on traditional method (first row) and ours (second row). Traditional method extracts per-frame proposals independently, which may result in some failures. In the example of *horse riding* (left), it fails when the person is partially blocked by the fence. In the example of *long jump* (right), an unwanted person (red bounding box) is also detected. In contrast, our approach can solve these problems by utilizing the temporal context across frames. (Color figure online)

Inspired by the recent advances of CNN based image object detection methods [4,6,26], previous action detection approaches first detect either frame-level [22,39] or clip-level proposals [11] independently. Then these fragmental proposals are associated to generate a complete action proposal by linking or tracking based approaches. However, such methods rarely exploit the temporal relations across frames or clips, which may result in unstable proposals when the single detection is unreliable. Figure 1 illustrates two examples of such limitations. In the example of *horse riding*, detection fails in the second frame where the person is partially blocked by the fence. In the other example of *long jump*, an unwanted person (red bounding box) is also detected, bringing in noises for future proposal recognition. Such noise is long-standing and inevitable due to independent detection on each frame or clip. One possible way to solve the above problems is to model the action by leveraging temporally contextual relations. For example, when the person is blocked in current frame, we could leverage the proposals in previous frames to infer the current ones. Motivated by this idea, we consider exploiting the action proposals in previous frames plus the corresponding contextual information when determining the action regions in current one, instead of detecting proposals from each frame or clip independently. Through involving the temporal context, the inevitable failures in per frame or clip proposal generation scheme could be mostly alleviated.

In this paper we present Recurrent Tubelet Proposal and Recognition (RTPR) networks—a novel architecture for action detection, as shown in Fig. 2. Our proposed RTPR networks consist of two components: Recurrent Tubelet Proposal (RTP) networks and Recurrent Tubelet Recognition (RTR) networks. The RTP produces action proposals in a recurrent manner. Specifically, it initializes action proposals of the start frame through a Region Proposal Network (RPN) [26] on the feature map. Then the movement of each proposal in next frame is estimated from three inputs: feature maps of both current and next frames, and the proposal in current frame. Simultaneously, a sibling proposal classifier is utilized to infer the actionness of the proposal. To form the tubelet proposals, action proposals in two consecutive frames are linked by taking both their actionness and overlap ratio into account, followed by the temporal trimming on it. The RTR capitalizes on a multi-channel architecture for tubelet proposal recognition. For each proposal, we extract three different semantic-level features, i.e., the features on proposal-cropped image, the features with RoI pooling on proposal, and the features on whole frame. These features implicitly encode the spatial context and scene information, which enhance the recognition capability on specific categories. After that, each of them is fed into a Long Short-Term Memory (LSTM) network to model the temporal dynamics. With both RTP and RTR, our approach can generate better tubelets and boost recognition, thus leading to promising detection results as shown in Fig. 1.

The main contribution of this work is the proposal of RTPR networks for addressing the issue of action detection. The solution also leads to the elegant views of what kind of temporal context should be exploited and how to model the temporal relations in a deep learning framework particularly for the task of action detection, which are problems not yet fully understood in the literature.

2   Related Work

Object detection in images is a fundamental computer vision task and has been studied in a plethora of publications. Most object detection techniques are developed based on region mechanism, such as R-CNN [5], Fast R-CNN [4], and Faster R-CNN [26]. These methods first generate a set of object proposals and then do per-proposal classification and bounding box regression. To overcome the speed limit of such two-stage frameworks, YOLO [25] and SSD [21] are proposed to directly classify and regress the anchor boxes in only one step. In our method, we utilize RPN [26] introduced by Faster R-CNN to initialize action proposals in the start frame. It outputs a set of action proposals, each with an actionness score. Besides, RoI pooling [4] is exploited to extract feature for each proposal.

Video action recognition has been extensively studied recently due to its importance in many application areas, such as video surveillance and robotics. Many progresses have been achieved by leveraging the recent advances of CNN, including discriminative feature learning (e.g., Fusion-CNN [15], C3D [35], FV-VAE [23], P3D [24]) and effective architecture design (e.g., Two-Stream CNN [29], SR-CNN [37]). In particular, LSTM is employed in several works [1,19,20,33,41] to model the long-term temporal clues in videos. In our work, we also exploit LSTM model in RTR for tubelet proposal recognition. In addition, both [37] and our RTR capitalize on a multi-channel architecture to capture different semantic-level information. However, ours uniquely designs a *human only* channel, which is potentially more effective than [37] on recognizing human-driven actions.

Video action detection aims to spatio-temporally localize a recognized action within a video. Most recent approaches rely on object detectors which are trained to discriminate human action classes at frame level, including R-CNN based methods [7,38], Faster R-CNN based methods [22,28], and SSD based methods [31]. Typically, 2D action regions are detected in each frame, upon which 3D action volumes are generated [2]. For example, TrackLocalization [38] tracks current proposals to obtain anchor ones in next frame by leveraging optical flow, and selects the best regions in the neighborhood of anchors using a sliding window. However, distinguishing actions from single frame could be ambiguous. To address this issue, ACT [14] takes as input a sequence of frames and outputs tube proposals instead of operating on single frames. T-CNN [11] further extends 2D Region-of-Interest pooling to 3D Tube-of-Interest (ToI) pooling with 3D convolution. It directly generates tube proposals on each fixed-length clip.

The aforementioned action detection methods treat each frame or clip independently, while ignoring the temporally contextual relations. Instead, our approach generates the tubelet proposals in a recurrent manner, which fully leverages the temporal information in videos. The most closely related work is CPLA [39], which solely relies on the detected proposals of current frame to estimate the proposal movements in the next frame. Ours is different from [39] in the way that we effectively model the temporal correlations of proposals between two consecutive frames to predict movements. Moreover, Faster R-CNN is required for each frame in [39], while our approach only runs RPN at initialization. In addition, our work also contributes by reliably capturing different semantic-level information and long-term temporal dynamics for recognition.

3   Recurrent Tubelet Proposal and Recognition Networks

In this section we present our proposed Recurrent Tubelet Proposal and Recognition (RTPR) networks for video action detection. An overview of our framework is shown in Fig. 2. It consists of two main components: Recurrent Tubelet Proposal (RTP) networks and Recurrent Tubelet Recognition (RTR) networks. In RTP, we first utilize CNNs for feature extraction. The RPN is applied on the feature map of the start frame for proposal initialization. Our RTP then generates proposals of subsequent frames in a recurrent manner. In particular, given action proposals in current frame, RTP estimates the movements of them to produce proposals in the next frame. Furthermore, action proposals from consecutive frames are linked according to their actionness and overlap ratio to form video-level tubelet proposals, followed by temporal trimming on tubelets. The obtained tubelets are finally fed into RTR for recognition. RTR employs a

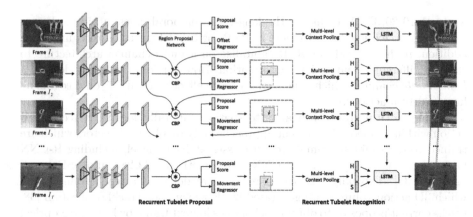

Fig. 2. The overview of RTPR networks. It consists of two components: RTP networks and RTR networks. CNNs are first utilized in RTP for feature extraction. Then RPN is applied on the start frame for proposal initialization. RTP estimates the movements of proposals in current frame to produce proposals in next frame. After proposal linking and temporal trimming, obtained tubelet proposals are fed into RTR. The RTR employs a multi-channel architecture to capture different semantic-level information, where an individual LSTM is utilized to model temporal dynamics on each channel.

multi-channel architecture to capture different semantic-level information, where an individual LSTM is utilized to model temporal dynamics on each channel.

3.1 Recurrent Tubelet Proposal Networks

The RTP aims to generate action proposals for all frames. Instead of producing proposals in each frame independently, we exploit the localized proposals in previous frame when determining the action regions in current one. Such scheme could help avoid the failures caused by unreliable single detection. Note that RTP only indicates the locations where an action exists irrespective of the category.

Architecture. The RTP begins with the initial anchor action proposals obtained by RPN on the start frame, and then produces the action proposals of subsequent frames in a recurrent manner. Given the video frame I_t and its proposal set $B_t = \{b_t^i | i = 1, ..., N\}$ at time t, RTP aims to generate the proposal set B_{t+1} for the next frame I_{t+1}. Let $b_t^i = (x_t^i, y_t^i, w_t^i, h_t^i)$ denote the i-th proposal at time t, where x, y, w and h represent two coordinates of the proposal center, width and height of it. As shown in Fig. 3(a), two consecutive frames, I_t and I_{t+1}, are first fed into a shared CNN to extract features. To predict the i-th proposal b_{t+1}^i at time $t+1$, we need to estimate the movement $m_{t+1}^i = (\Delta x_{t+1}^i, \Delta y_{t+1}^i, \Delta w_{t+1}^i, \Delta h_{t+1}^i)$ between b_{t+1}^i and b_t^i, which is defined as

$$\Delta x_{t+1}^i = (x_{t+1}^i - x_t^i)/w_t^i, \quad \Delta y_{t+1}^i = (y_{t+1}^i - y_t^i)/h_t^i,$$
$$\Delta w_{t+1}^i = \log(w_{t+1}^i/w_t^i), \quad \Delta h_{t+1}^i = \log(h_{t+1}^i/h_t^i). \tag{1}$$

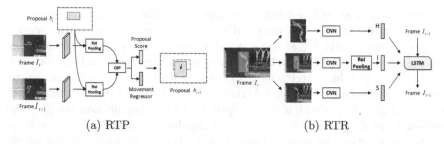

(a) RTP   (b) RTR

Fig. 3. (a) RTP networks. Two consecutive frames I_t and I_{t+1} are first fed into CNNs. Given the proposal b_t in current frame I_t, we perform RoI pooling on both I_t and I_{t+1} w.r.t. the same proposal b_t. The two pooled features are fed into a CBP layer to generate the correlation features, which are used to estimate the movement of proposal b_t and the actionness score. (b) RTR networks. We capitalize on a multi-channel network for tubelet recognition. Three different semantic clues, i.e., *human only* (H), *human-object interaction* (I), and *scene* (S), are exploited, where the features on proposal-cropped image, the features with RoI pooling on the proposal, and the features on whole frame are extracted. Each of them is fed into an LSTM to model the temporal dynamics.

Instead, to estimate this movement, visual features of proposals b_{t+1}^i and b_t^i are required. It is a chicken-and-egg problem, as we do not have the exact location of b_{t+1}^i in advance. Observing the fact that the receptive fields of deep convolutional layers are generally large enough to capture possible movements, we then solve the problem by simply performing RoI pooling at the same proposal location as b_t^i, as shown in Fig. 3(a).

Formally, suppose F_t^i and $F_{t+1}^i \in \mathbb{R}^{W \times H \times D}$ denote the RoI pooled features of I_t and I_{t+1} w.r.t. the same location of proposal b_t^i, where W, H and D are the width, height and channel numbers. The objective is to estimate the proposal movement m_{t+1}^i based on F_t^i and F_{t+1}^i. The movement between two consecutive frames could be characterized by the comparison between feature maps of two frames on the same spatial region. Specifically, we adopt Compact Bilinear Pooling (CBP) [3] to capture the pairwise correlations and model spatial interactions between frames, which can be formulated with the kernelized comparison as

$$CBP(F_t^i, F_{t+1}^i) = \sum_{j=1}^{S} \sum_{k=1}^{S} \left\langle \phi(F_{t,j}^i), \phi(F_{t+1,k}^i) \right\rangle, \tag{2}$$

where $S = W \times H$ is the size of the feature map, $\phi(\cdot)$ is a low dimensional projection function, and $\langle \cdot \rangle$ is the second order polynomial kernel. Finally, the outputs of CBP are fed into two sibling fully connected layers. One is the regression layer that predicts the movement m_{t+1}^i, and the other is the classification layer that predicts the actionness confidence score of b_{t+1}^i.

Training Objective. When training RTP, the network inputs include two consecutive frames I_t and I_{t+1}, the proposal set B_t of I_t obtained by RPN, and the ground-truth bounding boxes $\hat{B}_{t+1}$. Assuming that the action movement across two consecutive frames is not big, those correctly extracted proposals in B_t will have large Intersection-over-Union (IoU) ratios with one ground-truth proposal in $\hat{B}_{t+1}$. Consequently, we assign a positive label to the proposals b_t^i if: (a) b_t^i has an IoU overlap higher than 0.7 with any ground-truth box in $\hat{B}_{t+1}$, or (b) b_t^i is with the highest IoU overlap with a ground-truth box in $\hat{B}_{t+1}$. Otherwise, we assign a negative label to b_t^i if its IoU ratio is lower than 0.3 with all ground-truth boxes in $\hat{B}_{t+1}$. The network is jointly optimized with classification loss $\mathcal{L}_{cls}$ and regression loss $\mathcal{L}_{reg}$. For classification, the standard log loss $\mathcal{L}_{cls}(b_t^i)$ is utilized. It outputs an actionness score in range $[0, 1]$ for the output proposal. For regression, the smooth L_1 loss [4] $\mathcal{L}_{reg}(m_{t+1}^i)$ is exploited. It forces the proposal b_t^i to move towards a nearby ground-truth proposal in the next frame. The overall objective $\mathcal{L}$ is formulated as

$$\mathcal{L} = \frac{1}{N} \sum_i \mathcal{L}_{cls}(b_t^i) + \lambda \frac{1}{N_{reg}} \sum_i y_t^i \mathcal{L}_{reg}(m_{t+1}^i), \qquad (3)$$

where N is the number of proposals in B_t, N_{reg} is the number of positive proposals in B_t, λ is the parameter for balancing classification and regression, and y_t^i is an indicator that $y_t^i = 1$ if b_t^i is assigned a positive label, otherwise 0.

Prediction. Given a video, we initialize action proposals of its start frame by utilizing RPN on the feature map. Among all the proposals, we keep the top N_1 proposals $B_1 = \{b_1^i\}_{i=1}^{N_1}$ according to their confidence scores. Then, our RTP generates the proposals frame by frame. At time $t+1$, we predict the movements of N_t proposals of frame I_t, and also obtain N_t regions on frame I_{t+1}. Similar in spirit, we only keep N_{t+1} positive ones (actionness score > 0.7), which are further exploited in the next iteration. The process is repeated until the proposal number $N_{t'}$ at time t' is smaller than N_{min}, which indicates that there are not enough action regions to track. In this case, we utilize RPN to re-initialize anchor proposals for t'-th frame and restart RTP on the next frames till the end, making RTP robust to bad initialization. Finally, a set of proposals can be obtained for each frame, which will be utilized in the tubelet generation.

3.2   Action Tubelet Generation

Given frame-level proposals with associated actionness scores, linking them in spatial and temporal dimensions is essential for generating action tubelets. It has two steps: (i) linking action proposals based on their actionness scores and spatial overlaps in between to form tubelet proposals, which span the entire video duration, (ii) temporally trimming tubelets to identify their temporal boundaries.

Tubelet Linking. We formulate the linking problem as a path finding problem, which is to produce K connected paths across the whole video and K is the minimum number of action proposals in one frame. The linking score between two temporally consecutive proposals b_t^i and b_{t+1}^j is given by

$$S(b_t^i, b_{t+1}^j) = \{a_t^i + a_{t+1}^j + \gamma \, iou(b_t^i, b_{t+1}^j)\} \cdot \psi(iou), \qquad (4)$$

where a_t^i and a_{t+1}^j are the actionness scores of b_t^i and b_{t+1}^j, $iou(\cdot)$ is the IoU overlap ratio of two proposals, and γ is a scalar parameter for balancing the actionness scores and overlaps. We define $\psi(iou)$ as the following threshold function:

$$\psi(iou) = \begin{cases} 1, & \text{if } iou(b_t^i, b_{t+1}^j) > \tau, \\ 0, & \text{otherwise.} \end{cases} \tag{5}$$

According to Eq. (4), two proposals b_t^i and b_{t+1}^j will be linked if their spatial regions significantly overlap and their actionness scores are both high.

To find the optimal path across the video, we maximize the linking scores over the duration T of the video, which is calculated by

$$P^* = \arg\max_P \frac{1}{T-1} \sum_{t=1}^{T-1} S(b_t, b_{t+1}). \tag{6}$$

We solve it with Viterbi algorithm, whose complexity is $O(T \times N^2)$, where N is the average number of proposals per frame. Once an optimal path is found, we remove all the proposals in it and seek the next one from the remaining proposals.

Temporal Trimming. The above tubelet linking produces tubelets spanning the whole video. In realistic videos, human actions typically occupy only a fraction. In order to determine the temporal extent of an action instance within the tubelet, we employ a similar temporal trimming approach as in [28], which solves an energy maximization problem via dynamic programming. The idea behind is to restrict consecutive proposals to have smooth actionness scores. Note that temporal trimming is only performed on untrimmed datasets in this work.

3.3   Recurrent Tubelet Recognition Networks

Recent detection works always exploit RoI pooling features for action classification directly, which have two main drawbacks. First, the long-term temporal information is not incorporated for action recognition. Second, some action-related semantic clues, such as scene context, are neglected by only utilizing RoI features. To address the issues, we propose Recurrent Tubelet Recognition (RTR) networks with multiple semantic channels to recognize the generated tubelets.

RTR capitalizes on a three-channel architecture for recognition, as illustrated in Fig. 3(b). It leverages three different semantic-level information, i.e., *human only*, *human-object interaction*, and *scene*. **Human only** (H) channel takes proposal-cropped images as input. It focuses on human region and is expected to be capable of classifying "body motion only" actions, such as "walking" and "jumping." **Human-object interaction** (I) channel exploits the RoI pooling layer to extract a fixed-length feature vector for each proposal. Since the receptive fields of deep convolutional layers are generally large, this channel is able to incorporate surrounding contexts. Such information can be utilized to model the relationships between human and nearby objects, which potentially improves the performance for actions involving objects such as "shooting gun." **Scene** (S) channel handles the whole frame and is devised to capture the global context. It provides additional scene information and facilitates the recognition for particular action categories. For example, if a pool is observed, the probability that the action "diving" exists is high. For each channel, an individual LSTM is used to model the temporal dynamics and produces a score vector. We apply late fusion on the scores from different channels to obtain the final action score of a tubelet.

4   Implementations

Details of RTPR networks. For RTP networks, we adopt the pre-trained VGG-16 [30] as our basic CNN model, and build RTP at the top of its last convolutional layer. Following [22], we exploit a two-stream pipeline for utilizing multiple modalities, where the RGB frame and the stacked optical flow "image" are considered. To fuse their proposal results, we simply merge the proposal bounding boxes with non-maximum suppression (NMS). RPN [26] is exploited for proposal initialization, which is fine-tuned on the target datasets. During training, we randomly sample a set of two consecutive frames. For each pair, we use RPN to extract region proposals of the previous frame, and keep the top $N = 300$ proposals after NMS operation. These proposals plus the pair of frames are exploited for training. The output dimension d_c of CBP layer is $4,096$. λ in Eq. (3) is set to 1. In testing, we initialize the proposals of the first frame with top $N_1 = 300$ ones generated from RPN. N_{min} is set to 150. When linking the frame-level proposals to form tubelets, γ and τ are set to 1 and 0.2, respectively. All the above parameters are determined via cross validation.

For RTR networks, we also exploit the pre-trained VGG-16 [30] for feature extraction. Similar to RTP, the two-stream pipeline is employed and late fusion strategy is utilized to fuse the two streams. For all channels, we employ the output of $fc6$ layer as the input of LSTM. Specifically, for channel I, we apply the RoI pooling on the feature maps of the last convolutional layer. The grid of RoI pooling layer is fixed to 7×7. The number of hidden states in LSTM is fixed to $1,024$. Both RTP and RTR networks are trained in an end-to-end manner.

Training Strategy. Our method is implemented on Caffe [13]. We utilize mini-batch SGD algorithm to train the model. Following [4], we re-scale the frames, making their shorter sides 600 pixels. The batch size is 256 and 128 for RTP and RTR, respectively. The momentum and weight decay are set to 0.9 and 0.0005 for both networks. The initial learning rate is 0.001 and we decrease to its 10% after 8 epochs. The whole training procedure stops at 12 epoches.

5   Experiments

5.1   Datasets and Evaluation Metrics

We empirically evaluate our proposed framework on four datasets: UCF-Sports, J-HMDB, UCF-101 and AVA. **UCF-Sports** [27] consists of 150 short videos

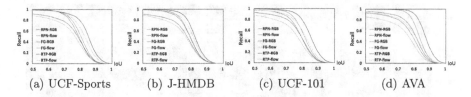

(a) UCF-Sports   (b) J-HMDB   (c) UCF-101   (d) AVA

Fig. 4. The frame-level Recall vs. IoU curves of different action proposal methods on UCF-Sports, J-HMDB (split 1), UCF-101, and AVA datasets.

from 10 sports categories. Videos are truncated to actions and bounding box annotations are available for all frames. Following [17], 103 and 47 videos are used for training and testing, respectively. **J-HMDB** [12] contains 928 well trimmed video clips of 21 actions. The bounding box annotations are inferred from human silhouettes. It provides three training/test splits for evaluation. Following [29], we conduct analysis of different components on the first split, and report the average results over three splits when comparing to the state-of-the-arts.

UCF-101 [32] is an action recognition dataset of realistic videos. For detection, a subset of 24 classes with 3,207 videos are provided with spatio-temporal ground truths. Unlike UCF-Sports and J-HMDB in which the whole videos are truncated to actions, videos in UCF-101 are untrimmed, and additional annotations of action temporal range are available. Following [22,28,39], all experiments are conducted on the first split. **AVA** [8] is a challenging dataset published very recently. It densely annotates 80 atomic visual actions in $57.6K$ video segments collected from 192 movies. The duration of each segment is 3 s. Different from the above datasets where annotations are provided for all frames, only the middle frame of each 3-second-long video segment is annotated in AVA. To take full advantage of the temporal information around the annotated key-frame, 15 consecutive frames (i.e., the key-frame, 7 frames before it, and 7 frames after it) are treated as a video clip to be processed in our framework. Note that each bounding box may be associated with multiple action categories, making the dataset more challenging. Experiments are performed on the standard splits [8].

Evaluation Metrics. We adopt both *frame-mAP* and *video-mAP* as our evaluation metrics [7,22]. A frame or tubelet detection is treated as positive if its IoU with the ground-truth is greater than a threshold δ and the predicted label is correct. Specifically, for UCF-Sports, J-HMDB, and UCF-101, we follow [9,11,22] to exploit video-mAP as evaluation metric. And for AVA, we follow the standard evaluation scheme in [8] to measure frame-mAP. The reported metric is the mAP at IoU threshold $\delta = 0.5$ for spatial localization (UCF-Sports, J-HMDB and AVA) and $\delta = 0.2$ for spatio-temporal localization (UCF-101) by default.

5.2 Performance Evaluations and Experimental Analysis

Evaluation on Recurrent Tubelet Proposal. We first validate the RTP networks and compare with two other proposal generation methods: RPN [26]

Fig. 5. An example of proposal generation results with three methods on action "Run."

Table 1. Evaluation on RTR networks with different channels on the four datasets.

Model	H	I	S	HI	IS	HS	HIS	H	I	S	HI	IS	HS	HIS
	UCF-Sports							J-HMDB (split 1)						
RGB	81.5	85.7	82.5	86.4	87.2	83.7	**87.6**	45.2	59.1	46.5	59.9	60.7	53.2	**61.7**
Flow	90.8	95.4	91.2	95.8	96.1	93.4	**96.5**	61.6	76.4	63.6	77.4	77.3	68.5	**78.1**
Fusion	92.3	96.8	93.4	97.4	97.1	95.1	**97.8**	66.3	78.5	70.8	79.8	80.0	74.3	**80.7**
	UCF-101							AVA						
RGB	54.8	59.2	56.3	59.4	59.8	58.0	**60.4**	14.4	18.2	13.7	18.9	18.7	17.2	**19.4**
Flow	65.6	71.5	68.1	72.0	72.7	70.5	**73.4**	11.2	13.7	9.4	15.2	14.9	12.5	**15.6**
Fusion	69.3	74.9	71.2	75.2	75.8	72.1	**76.3**	16.3	18.9	15.1	19.7	19.5	18.1	**20.1**

and Flow-Guided (FG) region tracking. RPN extracts region proposals of each frame or stacked optical flow "image" separately and then links the proposals in each frame or flow "image" to form tubelet. FG is initialized with proposals of the start frame or stacked optical flow "image" extracted from RPN. Then FG simply tracks each proposal according to the average optical flow over pixels within the proposal region. For fair comparison, we also utilize VGG-16 network for RPN and FG. RPN is fine-tuned on target datasets for both methods.

Figure 4 shows the frame-level Recall vs. IoU curve comparisons on the four datasets. RTP consistently outperforms the others significantly on both RGB and Flow streams, especially at high IoU area. The results demonstrate the effectiveness of incorporating long-term temporal coherence in proposal generation. It is not surprising that FG performs the worst among all. This somewhat reveals the weakness of the straightforward tracking scheme that only exploits very few temporal clues, making FG sensitive to noise. Another observation is that RGB stream outperforms Flow stream. The reason is that Flow stream only focuses on salient motion regions (e.g., waving arm of a person), while the target proposals are human-centered bounding boxes which cover the entire person.

Figure 5 shows the comparison of three methods with RGB stream on an exemplar action "Run" in UCF-Sports. RPN generally works well but fails when the person is blocked by the obstacle. FG generates accurate proposals for former frames. Once the noise (occlusion) occurs, the error is aggregated and the model

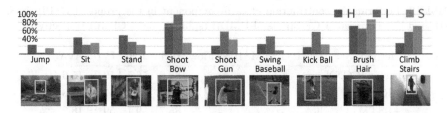

Fig. 6. Performance comparison of *human only* (H) channel, *human-object interaction* (I) channel, and *scene* (S) channel on nine action classes in J-HMDB (split 1).

is then unable to localize the proposals well. RTP, in comparison, benefited from the temporal context and could predict precise proposals in current frame by leveraging those in previous frames.

Evaluation on Recurrent Tubelet Recognition. Next, we turn to measure the performance of the RTR networks on each of designed channels, i.e., *human only* (H) channel, *human-object interaction* (I) channel, and *scene* (S) channel, based on the tubelets generated by RTP. All possible combination schemes between three channels are considered. Table 1 summarizes the comparisons across different modalities. As indicated by our results, the channel I achieves the highest performance among the three channels, as the majority of action classes are related to objects (8 in 10 for UCF-Sports, 14 in 21 for J-HMDB, 20 in 24 for UCF-101, 49 in 80 for AVA). Moreover, the fusion on any two or all three channels could further improve the results, indicating that the three channels are complementary. In addition, combining RGB and Flow streams also leads to considerable improvements. It is worth noting that the channel S performs better than the channel H on UCF-Sports, J-HMDB (split 1) and UCF-101, but worse on AVA. This observation is not surprising because most actions in AVA are collected from similar movie scenes and it is difficult to distinguish them with scene information. Similar in spirit, the performances of Flow stream are superior over RGB stream on UCF-Sports, J-HMDB (split 1) and UCF-101, but inferior on AVA, due to the fact that the actions in the first three datasets have more obvious movements and thus produce salient optical flows.

As described in Sect. 3.3, our multi-channel RTR is devised to capture different semantic-level clues. To verify this, we examine the performance of these channels on several categories from J-HMDB and report the performances on RGB stream in Fig. 6. We observe that the three channels indeed capture different semantic information. Specifically, for "body motion only" actions (e.g., "Jump," "Sit," and "Stand"), channel H performs the best. Similarly, on the object-related categories (e.g., "Shoot Bow," "Shoot Gun," "Swing Baseball," and "Kick Ball"), channel I achieves the best results and channel S outperforms other two on scene-related categories, e.g., "Brush Hair" and "Climb Stairs."

An Ablation Study. Here we study how each design in RTPR influences the overall performance. The basic way is to directly utilize Faster R-CNN on each

Table 2. Performance contribution of each component in the proposed RTPR. U-S, J-H, and U-1 represent UCF-Sports, J-HMDB (split 1), and UCF-101 respectively.

Method	RTP	LSTM	HIS	Flow	U-S	J-H	U-1	AVA
Faster R-CNN					83.8	56.5	56.0	15.6
+RTP	√				85.2	58.2	57.9	16.8
+LSTM	√	√			85.7	59.1	59.2	18.2
+HIS	√	√	√		87.6	61.7	60.4	19.4
RTPR	√	√	√	√	**97.8**	**80.7**	**76.3**	**20.1**

Table 3. Video-mAP comparisons on UCF-Sports, J-HMDB, and UCF-101.

Method	UCF-Sports		J-HMDB					UCF-101			
	0.2	0.5	0.1	0.2	0.3	0.4	0.5	0.05	0.1	0.2	0.3
Gkioxari et al. [7]	-	75.8	-	-	-	-	53.3	-	-	-	-
Weinzaepfe et al. [38]	-	90.5	-	63.1	63.5	62.2	60.7	54.3	51.7	46.8	37.8
Saha et al. [28]	-	-	72.7	72.6	72.6	72.2	71.5	79.1	76.6	66.8	55.5
Peng et al. [22][a]	94.8	94.7	-	74.3	-	-	73.1	78.8	77.3	72.9	65.7
Singh et al. [31]	-	-	-	73.8	-	-	72.0	-	-	73.5	-
Kalogeiton et al. [14]	92.7	92.7	-	74.2	-	-	73.7	-	-	77.2	-
Hou et al. [11][b]	95.2	95.2	-	78.4	-	-	76.9	78.2	77.9	73.1	69.4
Yang et al. [39]	-	-	-	-	-	-	-	79.0	77.3	73.5	60.8
He et al. [9]	96.0	95.7	79.8	79.7	79.3	78.5	77.0	-	-	71.7	-
RTPR											
-w/ VGG-16	97.8	97.8	**83.0**	82.3	82.0	81.2	80.5	81.5	80.7	76.3	70.9
-w/ ResNet-101	**98.6**	**98.6**	**83.0**	**82.7**	**82.3**	**82.3**	**81.3**	**82.1**	**81.3**	**77.9**	**71.4**

[a]Updated result from https://hal.inria.fr/hal-01349107/file/eccv16-pxj-v3.pdf
[b] Updated result from https://arxiv.org/pdf/1712.01111.pdf

RGB frame for both proposal generation and recognition, plus the tubelet generation between them. Average score over all proposals in the tubelet is exploited. **RTP** replaces the independent proposal generation with our recurrent scheme. **LSTM** leverages the temporal dynamics for recognition. **HIS** further employs the multi-channel architecture. **Flow** exploits optical flow stream additionally.

Table 2 details the improvement by considering one more factor at each stage. RTP is an effective method for action tubelet generation. It successfully boosts up the performance with 1.4%, 1.7%, 1.9%, and 1.2% on UCF-Sports, J-HMDB (split 1), UCF-101, and AVA, respectively. LSTM and HIS are two components of our RTR, which also lead to considerable improvement. More specifically, the performance gains range from 0.5% to 1.4% of LSTM, and 1.2% to 2.6% of HIS across the four datasets. In addition, we observe that the Flow stream exhibits significant improvements on UCF-Sports (10.2%), J-HMDB (19.0%) and UCF-101 (15.9%), but marginal gain on AVA (0.7%). As mentioned, this is because the actions in the first three datasets have more intensive motions.

Table 4. Frame-mAP comparisons on AVA.

Method	RGB	Flow	Fusion
[8] w/ ResNet-101	17.1	9.3	18.4
RTPR w/ VGG-16	19.4	15.6	20.1
RTPR w/ ResNet-101	**20.5**	**16.2**	**22.3**

Fig. 7. Four detection examples of our method from UCF-Sports, J-HMDB, UCF-101, and AVA. The proposal score is given for each bounding box. Top predicted action classes for each tubelet are on the right. Red labels indicate ground-truth. (Color figure online)

Comparison with State-of-the-Art. In addition to VGG-16, we also utilize ResNet-101 [10] as our backbone. In Table 3, we summarize the performance comparisons on UCF-Sports, J-HMDB (3 splits) and UCF-101 with different IoU thresholds δ. Early works mainly exploit R-CNN or Faster R-CNN to perform per-frame action detection [7,22,28,38]. T-CNN [11] improves them by utilizing 3D CNN to model short-term temporal information. Our RTPR achieves the best performance in most cases. Specifically, at the standard δ value (0.5 for UCF-Sports/J-HMDB, and 0.2 for UCF-101), our VGG-16 based model makes the improvements over VGG-16 based two-stream networks [9,22] by 2.1%-7.4%. Ours also outperforms T-CNN [11] by 2.6%, 3.6%, and 3.2% on the three datasets respectively. This somewhat reveals the weakness of [11] when the detection data is insufficient to support 3D ConvNets fine-tuning or training from scratch. Compared to the competitor CPLA [39], our approach boosts up the performance from 73.5% to 76.3% on UCF-101 when $\delta = 0.2$. More importantly, from Table 1 we can see that only utilizing the single channel I in RTPR already exceeds most state-of-the-art approaches including CPLA. The results indicate the advantages of modeling the temporal correlations of proposals between consecutive frames to predict movements in RTP rather than relying on RPN for each individual frame in CPLA. In addition, our ResNet-101 based model outperforms the best competitors [9,14] by 2.9%, 4.3% and 0.7% on the three datasets respectively.

Table 4 shows the comparisons on AVA. Since AVA is a very recent dataset, there are very few studies on it and we only compare with [8], which implements Multi-Region Two-Stream CNN [22] with ResNet-101. We can observe that ours with both VGG-16 and ResNet-101 basic models outperform the baseline. Figure 7 showcases four detection examples from UCF-Sports, J-HMDB, UCF-101, and AVA. Even in complex cases, e.g., varying scales (third row) and multi-person plus multi-label (last row), our approach can still work very well.

6 Conclusion

We have presented Recurrent Tubelet Proposal and Recognition (RTPR) networks for video action detection, which is able to incorporate temporal contextual information. Particularly, we study the problem of utilizing the proposals in previous frames to facilitate the detection in current frame through building a recurrent neural network. To verify our claim, we have devised Recurrent Tubelet Proposal networks, which is to estimate the movements of proposals in the next frame in a recurrent manner. Furthermore, a multi-channel architecture is designed for proposal recognition, which leverages different semantic context to enhance recognition. Experiments conducted on four public datasets validate our model and analysis. More remarkably, we achieve the new state-of-the-art performances on all the four datasets.

References

1. Donahue, J., et al.: Long-term recurrent convolutional networks for visual recognition and description. In: CVPR (2015)
2. Feichtenhofer, C., Pinz, A., Zisserman, A.: Detect to track and track to detect. In: CVPR (2017)
3. Gao, Y., Beijbom, O., Zhang, N., Darrell, T.: Compact bilinear pooling. In: CVPR (2016)
4. Girshick, R.: Fast r-cnn. In: ICCV (2015)
5. Girshick, R., Donahue, J., Darrell, T., Malik, J.: Rich feature hierarchies for accurate object detection and semantic segmentation. In: CVPR (2014)
6. Gkioxari, G., Girshick, R., Malik, J.: Contextual action recognition with R*CNN. In: ICCV (2015)
7. Gkioxari, G., Malik, J.: Finding action tubes. In: CVPR (2015)
8. Gu, C., et al.: Ava: a video dataset of spatio-temporally localized atomic visual actions. arXiv preprint arXiv:1705.08421 (2017)
9. He, J., Ibrahim, M.S., Deng, Z., Mori, G.: Generic tubelet proposals for action localization. In: WACV (2018)
10. He, K., Zhang, X., Ren, S., Sun, J.: Deep residual learning for image recognition. In: CVPR (2016)
11. Hou, R., Chen, C., Shah, M.: Tube convolutional neural network (T-CNN) for action detection in videos. In: ICCV (2017)
12. Jhuang, H., Gall, J., Zuffi, S., Schmid, C., Black, M.J.: Towards understanding action recognition. In: ICCV (2013)
13. Jia, Y., et al.: Caffe: convolutional architecture for fast feature embedding. In: ACM MM (2014)

14. Kalogeiton, V., Weinzaepfel, P., Ferrari, V., Schmid, C.: Action tubelet detector for spatio-temporal action localization. In: ICCV (2017)
15. Karpathy, A., Toderici, G., Shetty, S., Leung, T., Sukthankar, R., Fei-Fei, L.: Large-scale video classification with convolutional neural networks. In: CVPR (2014)
16. Krizhevsky, A., Sutskever, I., Hinton, G.E.: Imagenet classification with deep convolutional neural networks. In: NIPS (2012)
17. Lan, T., Wang, Y., Mori, G.: Discriminative figure-centric models for joint action localization and recognition. In: ICCV (2011)
18. Laptev, I., Pérez, P.: Retrieving actions in movies. In: ICCV (2007)
19. Li, Q., Qiu, Z., Yao, T., Mei, T., Rui, Y., Luo, J.: Action recognition by learning deep multi-granular spatio-temporal video representation. In: ICMR (2016)
20. Li, Q., Qiu, Z., Yao, T., Mei, T., Rui, Y., Luo, J.: Learning hierarchical video representation for action recognition. IJMIR 6(1), 85–98 (2017)
21. Liu, W., et al.: SSD: single shot multibox detector. In: Leibe, B., Matas, J., Sebe, N., Welling, M. (eds.) ECCV 2016. LNCS, vol. 9905, pp. 21–37. Springer, Cham (2016). https://doi.org/10.1007/978-3-319-46448-0_2
22. Peng, X., Schmid, C.: Multi-region two-stream R-CNN for action detection. In: Leibe, B., Matas, J., Sebe, N., Welling, M. (eds.) ECCV 2016. LNCS, vol. 9908, pp. 744–759. Springer, Cham (2016). https://doi.org/10.1007/978-3-319-46493-0_45
23. Qiu, Z., Yao, T., Mei, T.: Deep quantization: encoding convolutional activations with deep generative model. In: CVPR (2017)
24. Qiu, Z., Yao, T., Mei, T.: Learning spatio-temporal representation with pseudo-3D residual networks. In: ICCV (2017)
25. Redmon, J., Divvala, S., Girshick, R., Farhadi, A.: You only look once: unified, real-time object detection. In: CVPR (2016)
26. Ren, S., He, K., Girshick, R., Sun, J.: Faster R-CNN: towards real-time object detection with region proposal networks. In: NIPS (2015)
27. Rodriguez, M.D., Ahmed, J., Shah, M.: Action MACH a spatio-temporal maximum average correlation height filter for action recognition. In: CVPR (2008)
28. Saha, S., Singh, G., Sapienza, M., Torr, P.H., Cuzzolin, F.: Deep learning for detecting multiple space-time action tubes in videos. In: BMVC (2016)
29. Simonyan, K., Zisserman, A.: Two-stream convolutional networks for action recognition in videos. In: NIPS (2014)
30. Simonyan, K., Zisserman, A.: Very deep convolutional networks for large-scale image recognition. In: ICLR (2015)
31. Singh, G., Saha, S., Cuzzolin, F.: Online real time multiple spatiotemporal action localisation and prediction. In: ICCV (2017)
32. Soomro, K., Zamir, A.R., Shah, M.: Ucf101: a dataset of 101 human actions classes from videos in the wild. arXiv preprint arXiv:1212.0402 (2012)
33. Srivastava, N., Mansimov, E., Salakhudinov, R.: Unsupervised learning of video representations using LSTMs. In: ICML (2015)
34. Tian, Y., Sukthankar, R., Shah, M.: Spatiotemporal deformable part models for action detection. In: CVPR (2013)
35. Tran, D., Bourdev, L., Fergus, R., Torresani, L., Paluri, M.: Learning spatiotemporal features with 3D convolutional networks. In: ICCV (2015)
36. Wang, L., Qiao, Y., Tang, X., Van Gool, L.: Actionness estimation using hybrid fully convolutional networks. In: CVPR (2016)
37. Wang, Y., Song, J., Wang, L., Van Gool, L., Hilliges, O.: Two-stream SR-CNNs for action recognition in videos. In: BMVC (2016)
38. Weinzaepfel, P., Harchaoui, Z., Schmid, C.: Learning to track for spatio-temporal action localization. In: ICCV (2015)

39. Yang, Z., Gao, J., Nevatia, R.: Spatio-temporal action detection with cascade proposal and location anticipation. In: BMVC (2017)
40. Yuan, J., Liu, Z., Wu, Y.: Discriminative subvolume search for efficient action detection. In: CVPR (2009)
41. Yue-Hei Ng, J., Hausknecht, M., Vijayanarasimhan, S., Vinyals, O., Monga, R., Toderici, G.: Beyond short snippets: deep networks for video classification. In: CVPR (2015)

Beyond Local Reasoning for Stereo Confidence Estimation with Deep Learning

Fabio Tosi, Matteo Poggi[✉], Antonio Benincasa, and Stefano Mattoccia

University of Bologna, Viale del Risorgimento 2, Bologna, Italy
{fabio.tosi5,m.poggi,stefano.mattoccia}@unibo.it
http://vision.disi.unibo.it/~ftosi

Abstract. Confidence measures for stereo gained popularity in recent years due to their improved capability to detect outliers and the increasing number of applications exploiting these cues. In this field, convolutional neural networks achieved top-performance compared to other known techniques in the literature by processing local information to tell disparity assignments from outliers. Despite this outstanding achievements, all approaches rely on clues extracted with small receptive fields thus ignoring most of the overall image content. Therefore, in this paper, we propose to exploit nearby and farther clues available from image and disparity domains to obtain a more accurate confidence estimation. While local information is very effective for detecting high frequency patterns, it lacks insights from farther regions in the scene. On the other hand, enlarging the receptive field allows to include clues from farther regions but produces smoother uncertainty estimation, not particularly accurate when dealing with high frequency patterns. For these reasons, we propose in this paper a multi-stage cascaded network to combine the best of the two worlds. Extensive experiments on three datasets using three popular stereo algorithms prove that the proposed framework outperforms state-of-the-art confidence estimation techniques.

Keywords: Confidence measures · Stereo matching · Deep learning

1 Introduction

Stereo is a popular technique to infer the 3D structure of a scene sensed by two cameras and for this reason deployed in several computer vision applications. A stereo setup is typically made of two synchronized cameras and establishing correspondences between homologous points allows inferring depth through simple triangulation. Consequently, stereo literature is extremely vast since it dates back to the '60s and since then has been very popular. Despite this longstanding research activity, due to its ill-posed nature, algorithms aimed at finding stereo correspondences may lead to inaccurate results. In particular, when dealing with occlusions, transparent or reflecting surfaces, texture-less regions. Thus, on the

© Springer Nature Switzerland AG 2018
V. Ferrari et al. (Eds.): ECCV 2018, LNCS 11210, pp. 323–338, 2018.
https://doi.org/10.1007/978-3-030-01231-1_20

Fig. 1. Example of confidence estimation. (a) Reference image from KITTI 2015 dataset [7], (b) disparity map obtained with MC-CNN [8], (c) confidence estimated with a local approach (CCNN [2]) and (d) the proposed local-global framework, highlighting regions on which the latter method provides more reliable predictions (red bounding boxes). (Color figure online)

one hand, we need accurate depth estimation algorithms. On the other hand, given a depth or disparity map, we need an accurate methodology to infer the degree of reliability of each point. This task is referred to as confidence estimation and is of paramount importance when dealing with depth data.

Among the many confidence estimators proposed in the literature, recently reviewed and evaluated by Poggi et al. in [1], methods using as input cue information extracted from the disparity domain only [2–4] proved to be particularly effective. Compared to approaches relying on cues extracted from the cost volume or other strategies known in the literature, these methods currently represent state-of-the-art. Another notable advantage of methods working in the disparity domain, and in particular [2,4], is their ability to cope with depth data inferred by stereo systems not exposing to the user the cost volume, such as those based on closed source software or commercial stereo cameras. Regardless of this fact, machine learning deeply impacted confidence estimation starting from the seminal work of Haeusler et al. [5] aimed at inferring a confidence measure combining conventional confidence measure within a random forest framework. Later, other works successfully followed this strategy and, more recently, methods based on Convolutional Neural Networks (CNNs) achieved outstanding results [1] by inferring a confidence score for each pixel of a disparity map feeding to the deep-network a patch centered on it. In contrast to CNN-based method [3] and approaches based on random-forest, CCNN [2] accomplishes this task without relying on any hand-crafted feature defined beforehand. Currently, CCNN represents state-of-the-art for confidence estimation as recently highlighted in [1]. This strategy was extended in [6] by feeding to the CNN also the input reference image with promising results deploying, however, a larger amount of training samples.

Regardless of the strategy adopted, all these methods estimate confidence with a relatively small receptive field intrinsic in their local patch-based nature.

Increasing such parameter in these methods does not enable significant improvements and may also lead to poor results. Thus, state-of-the-art methods do not take advantage of the whole image and disparity content. Although this strategy is undoubtedly valid, on the other hand, it seems clear that by looking at the whole reference image and disparity map matters for uncertainty estimation. This fact can be readily perceived by observing Fig. 1 in the highlighted areas.

In particular, considering more global reasoning on the whole image and disparity content can improve the prediction for disparity values more unlikely to occur (e.g., objects extremely close to the camera), at the cost of a smoother prediction. This task can be undertaken by architectures with a large receptive field such as encoder-decoder models thus less accurate in the presence of high-frequency noise (e.g., outliers on the output of stereo algorithms such as AD-CENSUS or other matching functions). On the other hand, networks working on patches detect very well this kind of outliers but they are not able to capture farther information.

Therefore, in this paper, we propose to overcome this limitation by combining the best of the two worlds (i.e., networks based on small and large receptive fields). We do this by deploying a CNN-based architecture able to extract nearby and far-sighted cues, in the RGB and disparity domains, and to merge them to obtain a more accurate confidence estimation. By training a multi-modal cascaded architecture we first obtain two confidence predictions by reasoning respectively on local and farther cues, then we further elaborate on them to obtain a final, more accurate prediction. Figure 1 shows qualitatively how this strategy enables to estimate more reliable confidence scores.

To the best of our knowledge, our proposal is the first one enabling to (i) exploit more global context for learning confidence predictions and (ii) combine this novel technique with local approaches to design an effective local-global confidence measure. From now on, we will define as *global*, with abuse of language, a strategy going beyond traditional neighboring boundaries usually adopted in the field of confidence estimation. We extensively evaluate the proposed framework on three popular datasets, KITTI 2012 [9], KITTI 2015 [7] and Middlebury v3 [10] using three popular algorithms used in this field, respectively, AD-CENSUS [11], MC-CNN-fst matching cost [8] and SGM [12]. Such exhaustive evaluation clearly highlights that our proposal is state-of-the-art.

2   Related Work

In this section, we review the literature concerning confidence measures, their applications and the most recent advances in stereo matching using deep learning being all these fields relevant to our proposal.

Confidence Measures for Stereo. Confidence measures have been extensively reviewed by Hu and Mordohai [13] and by Poggi et al. [1] more recently including methods based on machine-learning. While the first review evaluated confidence measures with standard local algorithm using *sum of absolute differences* (SAD) and *normalized cross correlation* (NCC) as matching costs on the Middlebury 2002 dataset [14], the second review considers recent state-of-the-art confidence measures and evaluates them with three popular algorithms (AD-CENSUS [11], MC-CNN [8] and SGM [12]) on KITTI 2012 [9], KITTI 2015 [7] and Middlebury v3 [10] the standard datasets in this and other related fields. Both works follow the evaluation protocol defined in [13], consisting in Area Under the Curve (AUC) analysis from ROC curves. As reported in [1], machine learning enables to obtain more accurate confidence estimation compared to *conventional* strategies. Starting from the seminal work of Hausler et al. [5], other approaches fed hand-crafted features to a random forest classifier [4,5,15,16]. Recently, more accurate confidence estimators were obtained by leveraging on CNNs. In CCNN [2] Poggi and Mattoccia trained the network with raw disparity maps of the reference image while in PBCP [3] Seki and Pollefeys trained the network with pre-processed disparity maps concerned with reference and target images. According to the extensive evaluation reported in [1] both latter methods, and in particular CCNN, outperform any other known confidence measure. Poggi and Mattoccia [17] also proposed an effective strategy to improve confidence measures by exploiting local consistency. In [18] was proposed a method to improve random forest-based approaches for confidence fusion [4,15,16] by using a CNN. Fu et al. [6] extended CCNN [2] by adding the raw RGB image as input to the CCNN network. This strategy improves the final prediction when training on a much larger amount of training data (94 stereo pairs vs 20 images typically deployed with CCNN as in [1]). Some works looked deeper into the learning process of confidence measures, by studying features augmentation [19] or by designing self-supervised techniques to train them on static video sequences [20] or stereo pairs [21]. The latter technique proved to be effective even with CNN-based confidence measure CCNN. Finally, in [22] was proposed an evaluation of conventional confidence measures and their simplifications when targeting embedded systems.

Applications of Confidence Measures. While traditionally confidence measures were used to filter out outliers from disparity maps, some higher-level applications leveraging on them for other purposes have been deployed in the last years. Spyropoulos and Mordohai [15] used estimated confidence to detect very reliable disparity assignments (i.e., Ground Control Points) and setting for them ideal cost curves to improve the results of a further global optimization step. Park and Yoon [16] proposed a cost modulation function based on confidence applied to intermediate DSI (*Disparity Space Image*) before SGM optimization, Poggi and Mattoccia [4] modified the SGM pipeline to reduce the streaking effects along each scanline by penalizing low confidence hypothesis. Seki and Pollefeys [3] acted on P1 and P2 penalties of SGM tuning them according to the estimated confidence. In addition to these approaches, acting inside stereo algorithms to improve their final output, other applications concern sensor fusion [23] and disparity map fusion [24]. Shaked and Wolf [25] embedded confidence estimation inside a deep model stereo matching. Finally, confidence measures were also deployed for unsupervised adaptation of deep models for stereo matching [26] or unsupervised training of machine learning based measures [21], thus not requiring difficult to source disparity ground-truth labels.

Deep Learning for Stereo Matching. The very first attempt to use deep learning in stereo matching was proposed in the seminal work of Zbontar and LeCun [27] aimed at inferring matching cost through a CNN by processing images patches. This technique, known as MC-CNN, is now deployed by many stereo pipelines as reported on the KITTI and Middlebury v3 benchmarks. By working on small image patches only (i.e., 9×9), deep learning based confidence measures [2,3,6] are affine to this approach, being all these methods based on small receptive fields. Recent advances in stereo consist of deploying deep networks embedding all steps of traditional pipelines. These models are typically characterized by encoder-decoder architectures, enabling an extremely large receptive field and thus able to incorporate most of the global image content. The first, seminal work in this direction is DispNet by Mayer et al. [28], followed more recently by GC-Net [29] and CLR [30].

Thus, although deep learning confidence measures working on image patches have been successfully proposed [2,3,6], the literature lacks global approaches for this task. Therefore, inspired by successful attempts based on encoder-decoder architectures for disparity estimation [28–30] and local approaches for confidence estimation, in this paper we combine both strategies to achieve a more robust confidence measure by exploiting cues inferred from local and global contexts.

3   Method Overview

In this section, we introduce our local-global framework for confidence estimation. Driven by the recent success of confidence measures obtained by processing cues in the disparity domain only, and in particular those based on deep learning [2,3,6], we look beyond the small local neighborhood taken into account for each pixel by these methods and we analyze global context from both RGB and disparity domains to obtain a more consistent confidence estimation. Being local and global approaches characterized by complementary strengths, respectively the formers are very effective at detecting high-frequency patterns while the latter can incorporate much more cues from the surrounding pixels, we argued that combining them can further improve confidence estimation by overcoming the specific limitations of the single approaches. To do so, we will deploy two main architectures, respectively in charge of process local and global context. Then, the output of these two networks is combined to obtain the final prediction. In Sect. 3.1 we describe the local network, for which we choose state-of-the-art CCNN measure [2] and its extensions proposed in [6]. In Sect. 3.2 we introduce a novel architecture for *global* confidence estimation referred to as *ConfNet*, inspired by works concerning end-to-end stereo matching [28]. Finally, in Sect. 3.3 we outline our overall local-global framework combining cues generated by local and global approaches.

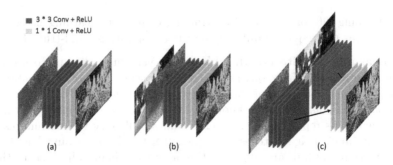

Fig. 2. Local architectures, respectively (a) CCNN [2], (B) EFN [6] and (c) LFN [6]. The networks uses 3 × 3 (blue) and 1 × 1 convolutional layers, all followed by ReLUs except the last one. (Color figure online)

3.1 Local Approaches

With local approaches, we refer to methodologies aimed at estimating the confidence score for a single pixel by looking at nearby pixels laying on a small local neighborhood. PBCP [3], CCNN [2] and multi-modal approaches [6] belongs to this category. We use the two latter techniques in our framework, depicted in Fig. 2, because of the superior outliers detection performance achieved by the first [1] further improved, in some circumstances, by multi-modal networks [6]. Another reason to use CCNN-based networks is that both can be computed without requiring the right disparity map, required by PBCP [3], not always available in some circumstances as previously highlighted.

CCNN. This confidence measure is obtained by processing the disparity map through a shallow network, made of 4 convolutional layers with 3 × 3 kernels producing 64 features map at each level, followed by 2 convolutional layers with 1 × 1 kernels producing 100 features map and a final 1 × 1 convolution followed by Sigmoid activation to obtain confidence scores in $[0, 1]$ interval. All the other layers are followed by ReLU non-linearities. The first 4 layers do not apply any explicit padding to its input, thus reducing input size by 2 pixels on both height and width (i.e., 1 pixel on each side). This makes the single pixel confidence prediction bound to a 9 × 9 local patch, the receptive field of the network, centered on it. The fully convolutional nature of this model allows for training on image patches and then performs a single forward of a full resolution disparity map if properly padded (i.e., applying 4 pixel padding on each side).

Multi-modal Networks. In [6] the authors propose to improve CCNN [2] by feeding to the network additional information from the RGB reference image. To this aim Fu et al. propose two strategies, respectively, the Early Fusion Network (EFN) and the Late Fusion Network (LFN). In the EFN, RGB and disparity patches are concatenated to form a 4-channel input, processed by a shallow network with the same structure of CCNN, but different number of channels at each

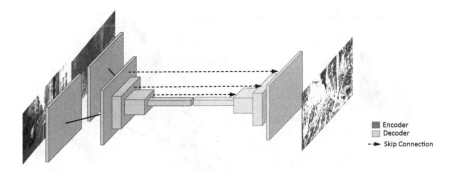

Fig. 3. ConfNet architecture. Encoding blocks (gray) are made by 3 × 3 convolutions followed by batch normalization, ReLU and max-pooling. Decoding blocks (yellow) contains 3 × 3 deconvolutions and 3 × 3 convolutions to reduce grid artifacts. (Color figure online)

layer (i.e., 112 for 3 × 3 and 384 for 1 × 1 convolutions). In the LFN, the information from the two domain is processed into two different streams, obtained by building two towers made of four 3 × 3 convolutional kernels without sharing the weights between them, in order to learn domain specific features representations. The outputs of the two towers are then concatenated and processed by the final 1 × 1 convolutions. Final outputs pass through a Sigmoid activation as for CCNN. The number of channels are the same as for EFN model. Both models have been trained and compared with CCNN, proving to perform better when trained with a much larger amount of samples compared to the amount (i.e., 94 stereo pairs versus 20) typically deployed in this field [1]. The receptive field of both networks is the same of CCNN (9 × 9).

3.2 Proposed Global Approach

In this section, we describe the network architecture designed to infer confidence prediction by looking at the whole image and disparity content.

ConfNet. Inspired by recent works in stereo matching [28–30], we design an encoder/decoder architecture enabling a large receptive field and at the same time maintaining the same input dimensions for the output confidence map. Figure 3 shows an overview of the ConfNet architecture. After concatenating features computed by 3 × 3 convolutional layers from both RGB reference image and disparity map, they are forwarded to the first part of the network, made of 4 encoding blocks. Each of them is made of a 3 × 3 convolutional layer ReLU activations and a 2 × 2 max-pooling used to decimate the input dimension and thus to increase the receptive field. More precisely, after the fourth block the original resolution is reduced by a factor 16, making a 3 × 3 convolution actually processing a 48 × 48 receptive field of the initial input. The number of channels of the convolutional layers in different blocks are respectively 64, 128, 256 and

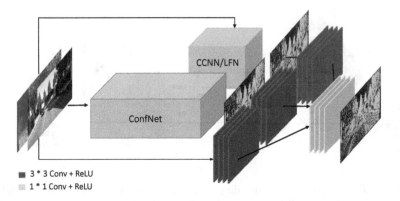

Fig. 4. LGC-net architecture. Given the input reference image and its disparity map, they are forwarded to both local (CCNN or LFN, in orange) and global (ConfNet, green) networks, whose outputs and disparity are processed by 3 independent towers, concatenated to finally infer the output confidence map. (Color figure online)

512, doubling after each max-pooling operator. Then, four decoding block follow in order to restore the original resolution of the input before obtaining the final confidence map. Each block uses a 3×3 deconvolutional layer with stride 2, followed by a 3×3 convolutional layer processing deconvolutional outputs concatenated with features taken from the encoding part at the same resolution. This reduces grid artifacts introduced by deconvolutional layers as suggested in [28], as well as enables to keep fine details present before down-sampling in the encoding part and missing after up-sampling from lower resolutions. The number of channels in each block for both deconvolutional and convolutional layers are respectively 256, 128, 64 and 32. A final 3×3 convolutional layer produces the final, full resolution confidence map followed by a Sigmoid operator to obtain normalized confidence values. The much larger receptive field enables to include much more information when computing per-pixel scores, but also acts as a *regularizer* yielding smoother confidence estimations and this leads to poor accuracy when dealing with high frequency patterns.

3.3 Local-Global Approach

To effectively combine both local and global cues, we introduce a final module acting in cascaded manner after the first two networks by processing their outputs and the initial disparity map. The module in charge of combining these cues is made of three towers processing respectively the local map, the global map and the disparity map. Weights are not shared between towers to extract distinct features from the three domains. Each tower is made of four convolutional layers with kernels 3×3 and 64 channels, their output are then concatenated and forwarded to two final 1×1 convolutional layers producing 100 features map each and a final 1×1 convolution in charge of the final confidence estimation, passed through a Sigmoid layer. Figure 4 describes the overall framework, referred to as Local Global Confidence Network (LGC-Net).

4   Implementation Details and Training Protocol

We implemented our models using the TensorFlow framework. In particular, we deployed CCNN, EFN and LFN using the same configuration proposed in [2]: 64 and 100 channels respectively for 3×3 and 1×1 convolution, for which we report extensive experimental results in the next section. While the entire framework is fully differentiable from the input to the output, thus trainable in end-to-end manner, we first train the local and global networks separately, then we train the cascaded module. As already highlighted in [30], training cascaded models in end-to-end fashion may lead the network to converge at a local minimum, while a reasoned training of each module may enable better overall performance.

Local Networks Training Schedule. Following the guidelines provided in [1], we extract 9×9 image patches from the first 20 stereo pairs in the KITTI 2012 training dataset [9] centered on pixels with available ground-truth disparity used to obtain confidence ground-truths (more details in Sect. 5.1), resulting into about 2.7 million samples. We trained for 14 epochs as proposed in [2,6] using a batch of dimension 128, resulting into nearly 300k iterations. We used Stocastic Gradient Descent optimizer (SGD) to minimize the Binary Cross Entropy (BCE) [2,6], a learning rate of 0.003 decreased by a factor 10 after 11 epochs and a momentum of 0.9.

ConfNet Training Schedule. We train ConfNet on 256×512 images estimating a confidence value for each pixel differently from local approaches that estimate confidence only for the central one in a patch (thus requiring to center the neighborhood on a pixel with available ground-truth). Despite training complex architectures like DispNet requires a large amount of data usually obtained from synthetic datasets [28], we found out that training the same 20 images from KITTI is enough to effectively learn a confidence measure. This is probably due to the simpler task the network is faced with. In fact, finding outliers in a disparity map (i.e., a binary classification of the pixels) is much easier compared to infer depth from a stereo pair. Moreover, the disparity domain is less variegated than its RGB counterpart. Despite RGB data being processed jointly with disparity inside ConfNet, it plays a minor role compared to the latter. Cross-validation on Middlebury v3 dataset [10], with indoor imagery extremely different from outdoor environments observed at training time will confirm this fact. We train ConfNet for 1600 epochs extracting random crops from the training stereo pairs, for a total of about 32k iterations. It is worth to note that, at training time, local networks produce a single pixel prediction versus the 256×512 available from ConfNet. For a single iteration, the minimized loss function encodes the contribution from 128 pixels for local networks (i.e., one for each sample in the batch) and 2^{16} for ConfNet, processing $512\times$ the amount of data. For this reasons only 32k iterations are enough for ConfNet to converge compared to the

300k of local methods. Pixels whose disparity ground-truth is not available are masked when computing the loss function. We used SGD and BCE as for local networks, with an initial learning rate of 0.003, divided by a factor 10 after 1k epochs.

LGC-Net Final Training Schedule. Finally, we train the cascaded module after freezing the weights of the local and global networks. We run additional 14 epochs processing image patches extracted from both disparity, local and global confidence estimations. The same 20 images, SGD, BCE loss, learning rate schedule and momentum are used for this training as well.

5   Experimental Results

In this section, we report extensive experimental results supporting the superior accuracy achieved by the proposed LGC-Net compared to state-of-the-art. We evaluate the newly proposed framework estimating confidence for disparity maps obtained from three popular algorithms standard in this field [1], respectively AD-CENSUS [11], MC-CNN-fst matching cost [8] and SGM [12]. For this latter algorithm, compared to [1], we tuned better P1 and P2 penalties to 3 and 0.03, obtaining more accurate disparities on KITTI datasets slightly reducing accuracy on Middlebury v3 dataset. In Sect. 5.1 we outline the evaluation protocol we follow to validate our method, in Sect. 5.2 we report results on both KITTI 2012 dataset [9] (i.e., on images not involved in training) and KITTI 2015, while in Sect. 5.3 we cross-validate on Middlebury v3 [10] as commonly done by most recent works [1] to measure how well the confidence measures perform on data quite different from the one deployed for training.

5.1   Evaluation Protocol

The standard task on which confidence measures are evaluated is outliers detection [1,13]. It consists in assigning to each disparity assignment a score between 0 an 1 according to their estimated uncertainty. Following the guidelines of standard evaluation benchmarks [7,9,10], each pixel p of an image is considered correctly assigned if its disparity $d(p)$ and its ground-truth label $\tilde{d}(p)$ are distant less than a threshold τ, i.e. $|d(p) - \tilde{d}(p)| < \tau$. The threshold value is assigned according to dataset specifications, in particular for KITTI 2012 and 2015 τ usually it is 3 and for Middlebury v3 it is 1 [1]. The same criterion is used to produce confidence ground-truth labels for training, encoding correct pixels with a score of 1 and outliers with 0. Since in our experiments the training has been always carried out on 20 images of the KITTI 2012 dataset, τ is set to 3 to generate labels. To quantitatively evaluate how well a confidence measure tackles this task, ROC curve analysis represents the standard in this field [1,13]. By plotting the percentage of outliers ε as a function of the amount of pixels sampled from a disparity map in order of decreasing confidence, we can compute the Area Under the Curve (AUC) and average it over the entire evaluation dataset. The lower is the AUC value, the more accurate is the confidence estimation for outliers detection purpose. The lower bound on a single disparity map is obtained according to its error rate ε as

$$AUC_{opt} = \int_{1-\varepsilon}^{\varepsilon} \frac{p - (1 - \varepsilon)}{p} dp = \varepsilon + (1 - \varepsilon) \ln (1 - \varepsilon) \tag{1}$$

5.2 Evaluation on KITTI Datasets

To assess the effectiveness of LGC-Net, we train the networks on the first 20 images of the KITTI 2012 dataset and we report extensive experimental results on the remaining 174 images of the same stereo dataset [9] as well as on the entire KITTI 2015 dataset [7]. This second dataset depicts outdoor environments similar to the first dataset but with the addition of dynamic objects not present in the other. We evaluate confidence measures provided by standalone modules (i.e., CCNN, EFN, LFN and the global architecture ConfNet) as well as those produced by the full local-global framework in two configurations obtained respectively by deploying CCNN [2] or multi-modal architectures [6] as local network. For a fair comparison, all the evaluated models have been trained from scratch following the same protocol described in Sect. 4. Source code is available here https://github.com/fabiotosi92/LGC-Tensorflow.

Table 1 reports experimental results on KITTI 2012. Each row refers to one of the three considered algorithms, respectively AD-CENSUS, MC-CNN and SGM and each column to a confidence measure, reporting AUC values averaged on the entire dataset. In bold, the best AUC for each algorithm. Considering at first single networks, we observe that multi-modal network LFN perform similarly to CCNN being this latter method outperformed by a small margin only with AD-CENSUS. The EFN network has always worse performance compared to CCCN and LFN. These results highlight that, with LFN and EFN networks in this configuration, processing the RGB image does not provide additional information compared to the one inferred from the disparity domain. Looking at ConfNet we can observe how processing global information only leads, as expected, to less accurate results with noisy disparity maps provided by AD-CENSUS but it performs reasonably well, and better than EFN, with smoother disparity maps generated by SGM and MC-CNN. In particular it is always outperformed by CCNN and LFN. According to these results, confirmed also by following evaluations, the global approach alone loses accuracy when dealing with fine details, despite the deployment of skip-connection between encoder and decoder sections, while local approaches performs very well in these cases. Observing LGC-Net results, both configurations outperform all the other evaluated techniques, highlighting how the two complementary cues from local and global networks can be effectively combined to improve confidence estimation moving a step forward optimality for all the three stereo algorithms. By directly comparing the two configurations of LGC-Net, using respectively CCNN or LFN as local network, there is no clear winner highlighting how the contribution given by the RGB image on a small neighborhood seems negligble. In fact, it yields

Table 1. Experimental results on KITTI 2012 dataset [9]. From top to bottom, evaluation concerning AD-CENSUS [11], MC-CNN [8] and SGM [12] algorithms. For each column, average AUC achieved on the entire dataset (i.e., 174 out of 194 stereo pairs) for different confidence measures.

KITTI 2012 [9] (174 images)	CCNN [2]	EFN [6]	LFN [6]	ConfNet	LGC-Net (CCNN)	LGC-Net (LFN)	Optim.
AD-CENSUS [11]	0.1207	0.1261	0.1201	0.1295	**0.1174**	0.1176	0.1067
MC-CNN [8]	0.0291	0.0316	0.0294	0.0311	0.0279	**0.0278**	0.0231
SGM [12]	0.0194	0.0229	0.0198	0.0199	0.0176	**0.0175**	0.0088

Table 2. Experimental results on KITTI 2015 dataset [7]. From top to bottom, evaluation concerning AD-CENSUS [11], MC-CNN [8] and SGM [12] algorithms. For each column, average AUC achieved on the entire dataset (i.e., 200 stereo pairs) for different confidence measures.

KITTI 2015 [7] (200 images)	CCNN [2]	EFN [6]	LFN [6]	ConfNet	LGC-Net (CCNN)	LGC-Net (LFN)	Optim.
AD-CENSUS [11]	0.1045	0.1087	0.1026	0.1128	**0.0999**	0.1004	0.0883
MC-CNN [8]	0.0289	0.0319	0.0292	0.0315	0.0281	**0.0278**	0.0213
SGM [12]	0.0201	0.0239	0.0209	0.0216	0.0193	**0.0190**	0.0091

a 0.0001 difference in terms of average AUC between the two versions, in favor of the first configuration on AD-CENSUS and the second one on MC-CNN and SGM. These experiments highlight that the major benefit is obtained by the proposed strategy exploiting local and global context information.

Table 2 reports experimental results on the KITTI 2015 dataset [7], with AUC values averaged over the available 200 stereo pairs with ground-truth. First of all, we observe that the same trend observed for KITTI 2012 is confirmed also in this case, with CCNN being slightly outperformed by LFN only on AD-CENSUS. CCNN and LFN always provide more accurate estimation accuracy compared to EFN while ConfNet outperforms this latter method on smoother MC-CNN and SGM disparity maps as in previous experiment. Finally, the two LGC-Net versions achieve overall best performance on this dataset, as for KITTI 2012, confirming the effectiveness of the proposed method. Moreover, the same results also highlight once again the negligible margin brought in by using the RGB image with CCNN.

5.3 Cross-Validation on Middlebury V3

Having proved the effectiveness of the proposed LGC-Net on KITTI datasets, we conduct a more challenging evaluation by cross-validating on Middlebury v3 imagery [10] confidence measures trained on the first 20 images of the KITTI 2012 dataset. As done in [1], assessing the performance on a validation dataset quite different from the one used during the training phase effectively measures how robust a confidence measure is with respect to circumstances very likely

Table 3. Experimental results on Middlebury v3 dataset [10]. From top to bottom, evaluation concerning AD-CENSUS [11], MC-CNN [8] and SGM [12] algorithms. For each column, average AUC achieved on the entire dataset (i.e., 15 stereo pairs) for different confidence measures.

Middlebury v3 [10] (15 images)	CCNN [2]	EFN [6]	LFN [6]	ConfNet	LGC-Net (CCNN)	LGC-Net (LFN)	Optim.
AD-CENSUS [11]	0.1131	0.1263	0.1146	0.1206	**0.1099**	0.1109	0.0899
MC-CNN [8]	0.0668	0.0781	0.0645	0.0755	0.0624	**0.0616**	0.0458
SGM [12]	0.0794	0.1005	0.0856	0.0886	**0.0703**	0.0709	0.0431

to occur in practical applications. Being our models trained on KITTI images, depicting outdoor environments concerned with autonomous driving applications, the indoor scenes included in the Middlebury v3 dataset represent a completely different scenario ideal for the kind of cross-validation outlined.

Table 3 quantitatively summarizes the outcome of this evaluation. First and foremost, as in previous experiments, LGC-Net outperforms with both configurations all standalone confidence measures confirming the negligible difference, lower or equal than 0.001, between the two local networks. The trend between single architectures is substantially confirmed with respect to previous experiments, with ConfNet performing always better than EFN in this cross-evaluation even with the noisy AD-CENSUS maps. CCNN and LFF, as for previous experiments, performs quite similarly confirming once again the small impact of RGB cues in local networks with our training configuration.

In Fig. 5 we report a qualitative comparison between local, global (ConfNet) and LGC-Net for two images of the the Middlebury v3 dataset processed with SGM and MC-CNN stereo algorithms. The quantitative advantages reported for LGC-Net in the previous evaluations can be clearly perceived qualitatively by looking, for instance, at texture-less regions on the wall in *PianoL* stereo pair and at the occluded area on the background in *Pipes* stereo pair.

To summarize, exhaustive experiments on three datasets and three stereo algorithms proved that the proposed framework always outperforms both local and global standalone strategy by a significant margin, thus effectively learning to combine local and global cues to obtain more accurate confidence estimation. This trend is also confirmed moving to very different data as reported in the cross evaluation, proving that LGC-Net is more capable to generalize to completely different image contents. Overall, the proposed method always outperforms state-of-the-art methods for confidence estimation.

Fig. 5. Qualitative comparison of confidence maps on selected images from Middlebury v3 dataset [10]. For each sample, we report from top left to bottom right reference image, disparity map, confidence map respectively for CCNN, ConfNet and LGC-net and ground-truth confidence labels. On top *PianoL* pair processed by MC-CNN-fst, on bottom *Pipes* pair processed by SGM.

6 Conclusions

In this paper we propose, for the first time to the best of our knowledge, to leverage on global and local context to infer a confidence measure for stereo. Driven by the outstanding results achieved by CNN-based confidence measures, in this paper we argue that their effectiveness can be improved by changing their intrinsic local nature. To this aim we propose to combine with a CNN cues inferred with two complementary strategies, based on two very different receptive fields. The proposed LGC-Net, a multi-modal cascaded network, merges the outcome of the two complementary approaches enabling more accurate confidence estimation. We extensively evaluated the proposed method on three datasets and three algorithms following standard protocols in this field proving that our proposal outperforms state-of-the-art confidence measures and further moves a step forward optimality.

Acknowledgement. We gratefully acknowledge the support of NVIDIA Corporation with the donation of the Titan X Pascal GPU used for this research. We also thank Alessandro Fusco for his preliminar experiments on the ConfNet architecture.

References

1. Poggi, M., Tosi, F., Mattoccia, S.: Quantitative evaluation of confidence measures in a machine learning world. In: The IEEE International Conference on Computer Vision (ICCV), October 2017
2. Poggi, M., Mattoccia, S.: Learning from scratch a confidence measure. In: Proceedings of the 27th British Conference on Machine Vision, BMVC (2016)
3. Seki, A., Pollefeys, M.: Patch based confidence prediction for dense disparity map. In: British Machine Vision Conference (BMVC) (2016)
4. Poggi, M., Mattoccia, S.: Learning a general-purpose confidence measure based on o(1) features and a smarter aggregation strategy for semi global matching. In: Proceedings of the 4th International Conference on 3D Vision, 3DV (2016)
5. Haeusler, R., Nair, R., Kondermann, D.: Ensemble learning for confidence measures in stereo vision. In: CVPR Proceedings, pp. 305–312 (2013)
6. Fu, Z., Ardabilian, M.: Stereo matching confidence learning based on multi-modal convolution neural networks. In: Representation, Analysis and Recognition of Shape and Motion from Image Data (RFMI) (2017)
7. Menze, M., Geiger, A.: Object scene flow for autonomous vehicles. In: Conference on Computer Vision and Pattern Recognition (CVPR) (2015)
8. Zbontar, J., LeCun, Y.: Stereo matching by training a convolutional neural network to compare image patches. J. Mach. Learn. Res. **17**(1–32), 2 (2016)
9. Geiger, A., Lenz, P., Urtasun, R.: Are we ready for autonomous driving? The KITTI vision benchmark suite. In: 2012 IEEE Conference on Computer Vision and Pattern Recognition (CVPR), pp. 3354–3361. IEEE (2012)
10. Scharstein, D., et al.: High-resolution stereo datasets with subpixel-accurate ground truth. In: Jiang, X., Hornegger, J., Koch, R. (eds.) GCPR 2014. LNCS, vol. 8753, pp. 31–42. Springer, Cham (2014). https://doi.org/10.1007/978-3-319-11752-2_3
11. Zabih, R., Woodfill, J.: Non-parametric local transforms for computing visual correspondence. In: Eklundh, J.-O. (ed.) ECCV 1994. LNCS, vol. 801, pp. 151–158. Springer, Heidelberg (1994). https://doi.org/10.1007/BFb0028345
12. Hirschmuller, H.: Accurate and efficient stereo processing by semi-global matching and mutual information. In: IEEE Computer Society Conference on Computer Vision and Pattern Recognition, CVPR 2005, vol. 2, pp. 807–814. IEEE (2005)
13. Hu, X., Mordohai, P.: A quantitative evaluation of confidence measures for stereo vision. IEEE Trans. Pattern Anal. Mach. Intell. (PAMI) **34**, 2121–2133 (2012)
14. Scharstein, D., Szeliski, R.: A taxonomy and evaluation of dense two-frame stereo correspondence algorithms. Int. J. Comput. Vision **47**(1–3), 7–42 (2002)
15. Spyropoulos, A., Komodakis, N., Mordohai, P.: Learning to detect ground control points for improving the accuracy of stereo matching. In: The IEEE Conference on Computer Vision and Pattern Recognition (CVPR), pp. 1621–1628. IEEE (2014)
16. Park, M.G., Yoon, K.J.: Leveraging stereo matching with learning-based confidence measures. In: The IEEE Conference on Computer Vision and Pattern Recognition (CVPR), June 2015

17. Poggi, M., Mattoccia, S.: Learning to predict stereo reliability enforcing local consistency of confidence maps. In: The IEEE Conference on Computer Vision and Pattern Recognition (CVPR), July 2017

18. Poggi, M., Tosi, F., Mattoccia, S.: Even more confident predictions with deep machine-learning. In: 12th IEEE Embedded Vision Workshop (EVW2017) Held in Conjunction with IEEE Conference on Computer Vision and Pattern Recognition (CVPR), July 2017

19. Kim, S., Min, D., Kim, S., Sohn, K.: Feature augmentation for learning confidence measure in stereo matching. IEEE Trans. Image Process. **26**(12), 6019–6033 (2017)

20. Mostegel, C., Rumpler, M., Fraundorfer, F., Bischof, H.: Using self-contradiction to learn confidence measures in stereo vision. In: 2016 IEEE Conference on Computer Vision and Pattern Recognition, CVPR 2016, Las Vegas, NV, USA, 27–30 June 2016, pp. 4067–4076 (2016)

21. Tosi, F., Poggi, M., Tonioni, A., Di Stefano, L., Mattoccia, S.: Learning confidence measures in the wild. In: 28th British Machine Vision Conference, BMVC 2017, September 2017

22. Poggi, M., Tosi, F., Mattoccia, S.: Efficient confidence measures for embedded stereo. In: Battiato, S., Gallo, G., Schettini, R., Stanco, F. (eds.) ICIAP 2017. LNCS, vol. 10484, pp. 483–494. Springer, Cham (2017). https://doi.org/10.1007/978-3-319-68560-1_43

23. Marin, G., Zanuttigh, P., Mattoccia, S.: Reliable fusion of TOF and stereo depth driven by confidence measures. In: Leibe, B., Matas, J., Sebe, N., Welling, M. (eds.) ECCV 2016. LNCS, vol. 9911, pp. 386–401. Springer, Cham (2016). https://doi.org/10.1007/978-3-319-46478-7_24

24. Poggi, M., Mattoccia, S.: Deep stereo fusion: combining multiple disparity hypotheses with deep-learning. In: Proceedings of the 4th International Conference on 3D Vision, 3DV (2016)

25. Shaked, A., Wolf, L.: Improved stereo matching with constant highway networks and reflective confidence learning. In: The IEEE Conference on Computer Vision and Pattern Recognition (CVPR), July 2017

26. Tonioni, A., Poggi, M., Mattoccia, S., Di Stefano, L.: Unsupervised adaptation for deep stereo. In: The IEEE International Conference on Computer Vision (ICCV), October 2017

27. Zbontar, J., LeCun, Y.: Computing the stereo matching cost with a convolutional neural network. In: Proceedings of the IEEE Conference on Computer Vision and Pattern Recognition, pp. 1592–1599 (2015)

28. Mayer, N., et al.: A large dataset to train convolutional networks for disparity, optical flow, and scene flow estimation. In: The IEEE Conference on Computer Vision and Pattern Recognition (CVPR), June 2016

29. Kendall, A., et al.: End-to-end learning of geometry and context for deep stereo regression. In: The IEEE International Conference on Computer Vision (ICCV), October 2017

30. Pang, J., Sun, W., Ren, J.S., Yang, C., Yan, Q.: Cascade residual learning: a two-stage convolutional neural network for stereo matching. In: The IEEE International Conference on Computer Vision (ICCV), October 2017

Self-supervised Knowledge Distillation
Using Singular Value Decomposition

Seung Hyun Lee⊙, Dae Ha Kim⊙, and Byung Cheol Song$^{(\boxtimes)}$⊙

Inha University, Incheon, Republic of Korea
lsh910703@gmail.com, kdhht5022@gmail.com, bcsong@inha.ac.kr

Abstract. To solve deep neural network (DNN)'s huge training dataset and its high computation issue, so-called teacher-student (T-S) DNN which transfers the knowledge of T-DNN to S-DNN has been proposed. However, the existing T-S-DNN has limited range of use, and the knowledge of T-DNN is insufficiently transferred to S-DNN. To improve the quality of the transferred knowledge from T-DNN, we propose a new knowledge distillation using singular value decomposition (SVD). In addition, we define a knowledge transfer as a self-supervised task and suggest a way to continuously receive information from T-DNN. Simulation results show that a S-DNN with a computational cost of 1/5 of the T-DNN can be up to 1.1% better than the T-DNN in terms of classification accuracy. Also assuming the same computational cost, our S-DNN outperforms the S-DNN driven by the state-of-the-art distillation with a performance advantage of 1.79%. code is available on https://github.com/sseung0703/SSKD_SVD.

Keywords: Statistical methods and learning · Optimization methods Recognition: detection · Categorization · Indexing · Matching

1 Introduction

Recently, DNN has overwhelmed other machine learning methods in the research fields such as classification and recognition [1,2]. As a result of the development of general-purpose graphics processing unit (GP-GPU) with high computational power, DNNs with huge complexity can be implemented and verified, resulting in DNNs that are superior to human recognition capabilities [3–5]. On the other hand, it is still challenging to operate DNN on a mobile device or embedded system due to limited memory and computational capability. Recently, various lightweight DNN models have been proposed to reduce memory burden and computation cost [6,7]. However, these small-size models have less performance than state-of-the-art models like ResNext [5]. Another problem is that not only the conventional DNN but also the lightweight DNN model requires huge data in learning.

As a solution to these two problems, Hinton et al. [8] defined the concept of knowledge distillation and presented a teacher-student (T-S) DNN based

© Springer Nature Switzerland AG 2018
V. Ferrari et al. (Eds.): ECCV 2018, LNCS 11210, pp. 339–354, 2018.
https://doi.org/10.1007/978-3-030-01231-1_21

on it. Then several knowledge distillation techniques have been studied [9,10]. For example, in [10], Yim et al. proposed a method to transfer the correlation between specific feature maps generated by T-DNN as the knowledge of T-DNN to the S-DNN. In this case, the S-DNN learns in two stages: the first stage that initializes the network parameters using the transferred knowledge, and the second stage that learns the main task.

However, the existing T-S knowledge distillation approaches have several limitations as follows: (1) They do not yet extract and distill rich information from the T-DNN. (2) In addition, the structure of T-S-DNN is very limited. (3) Finally, since the knowledge from the T-DNN is learned only for the purpose of initializing the parameters of the S-DNN, it gradually disappears as the learning of the next main task progresses.

In order to solve this problem, this paper approaches two perspectives. The first is a proper manipulation of knowledge for smaller memory and lower computation. So we gracefully compress the knowledge data by utilizing singular value decomposition (SVD), which is mainly applied to dimension reduction of features [11–13] in signal processing domain. We also analyze the correlation between compressed feature maps through a radial basis function (RBF) [14,15], which is often used for kernelized learning. As a result, knowledge distillation using SVD and RBF can distill the information of T-DNN more efficiently than conventional techniques, and can transfer regardless of the spatial resolution of feature maps. Second, the training mechanism [16–18] through self-supervised learning, which learns to create labels by itself, ensures that the transferred knowledge does not vanish and is continuously used. That is, it can figure out the vanishing problem of T-DNN knowledge. In addition, self-supervised learning can be expected to provide additional performance improvement because it allows for more powerful regularization [8].

The experimental results show that when the visual geometry group (VGG) model [19] is applied to the proposed network, T-DNN with 64.4% accuracy for CIFAR-100 can improve the performance of S-DNN with 1/5 computation cost of T-DNN by 65.1%. In addition to VGG, state-of-the-art models such as MobileNet [7] and ResNext [5] are also applied to the proposed knowledge distillation method, confirming similar effects and proving that the proposed method can be generalized. Finally, we introduced self-supervised learning to continuously deliver the T-DNN's knowledge. As a result, we confirmed that the performance of the S-DNN is further improved by a maximum of 1.2%, and finally the performance of the S-DNN becomes superior to the T-DNN by 1.79%.

2   Related Works

2.1   Knowledge Distillation

Knowledge transfer is a technique for transferring information from a relatively complex and deep model, i.e., T-DNN to a smaller DNN model, i.e., S-DNN, ultimately increasing the performance of the S-DNN [8]. FitNet [9] first introduced the two-stage method to re-train the main task of the S-DNN after transferring knowledge of the T-DNN. The S-DNN could have much better initial parameters by learning knowledge distilled from the T-DNN than random initialization. Yim et al. [10] defined the knowledge transferred from the T-DNN to the S-DNN as changes of feature maps rather than layer parameters. They determined a certain layer group in the network and defined the correlation between input and output feature maps of the layer group as a Gram matrix so that the feature correlations of the S- and T-DNN become similar. However, the knowledge defined by the above techniques still lacks information, and knowledge transfer through initialization is still limited.

2.2 SVD and RBF

SVD is mainly used for dimension reduction or for extracting important information from feature maps [11–13]. In [11], Alter et al. showed that it is possible to abstract the information of a dataset by using SVD. Lonescu et al. defined the gradient according to the chain rule for SVD, and proved that end-to-end learning is realizable even in DNN using SVD [13]. They also showed that pooling high-level information in the feature map is very effective in the feature analysis tasks such as recognition and segmentation. RBF is a function that re-maps each feature in a viewpoint of distance from the center so that the feature has a high dimension. RBF can be used for various kernelized learning or RBF network (RBFN) [14,15]. In particular, analyzing features with RBF such as Gaussian function makes it possible to analyze noisy data more robustly. If these two methods can be combined well, it will be possible to extract important information effectively from fuzzy and noisy data. The proposed knowledge distillation method efficiently extracts core knowledge from a given feature map using SVD and effectively computes the correlation between two feature maps using RBF.

2.3 Training Mechanism

Self-supervised learning generates labels and learns them by itself. Recently, various self-supervised learning tasks have been studied [16–18] because they can effectively initialize the network model. In [18], a method to learn various self-supervised tasks at a time by bundling them into a multi-task has been proposed and proved to be more efficient than conventional methods. On the other hand, semi-supervised learning is another learning scheme that uses labeled and unlabeled data at the same time when labeling data is insufficient. In order to solve the fundamental problem of the lack of a training-purpose dataset, various studies on semi-supervised learning have been actively conducted [20,21].

We will introduce the above-mentioned self-supervised learning as a more efficient transfer approach than parameter initialization through knowledge transfer in the existing T-S-DNNs.

3   Method

This section details the proposed knowledge transfer method. Inspired by the idea of [10], we derive a correlation between two feature maps extracted from T-

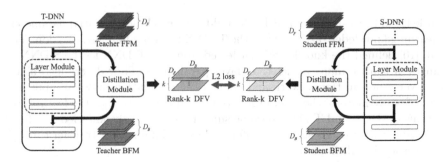

Fig. 1. The concept of the proposed knowledge distillation-based network.

DNN, and transfer it as knowledge. Figure 1 illustrates the proposed knowledge distillation based network. First, both the T-DNN and the S-DNN are composed of a predetermined convolutional layer and a fully-connected layer depending on the purpose. For example, VGG [19], MobileNet [7], ResNext [5], etc. can be adopted as DNN. Then, to extract the feature map characteristic inherent to each DNN, we specify two particular layer points in the DNN and sense the corresponding two feature maps. The layers between the two points are defined as a layer module. The feature map that is sensed at the input of the layer module is called the front-end feature map (FFM) and the feature map that is sensed at the output is called the back-end feature map (BFM). For example, in MobileNet, the layer module can consist of several depth-wise separable convolutions. Let the depths of FFM and BFM be D_F and D_B, respectively. On the other hand, several non-overlapping layer modules may be defined in each DNN for robust distillation. In this paper, the maximum number of layer modules in each DNN is G.

Now we can get the correlation between FFM and BFM of a certain layer module through the distillation module. The distillation module outputs the distillation feature vectors (DFV) having the size of $k \times D_F \times D_B$ from two inputs of FFM and BFM. See Sect. 3.1.

Finally, we propose a novel training mechanism so that the knowledge from the T-DNN does not disappear in the 2nd stage, i.e., main-task learning process. We improve self-supervised learning, which was presented in [8], to enable more effective transfer of knowledge. See Sect. 3.2.

3.1 Proposed Distillation Module

In general, DNNs generate feature maps through multiple layers to suit a given task. In the distillation method of [10], the correlation between feature maps obtained from DNN is first defined as knowledge. The proposed method also accepts the idea of [10] and distillates the knowledge using correlation between feature maps. However, feature maps that are produced through multiple convolution layers are generally too large to be used as they are not only computationally expensive, but also difficult to learn. An intuitive way to solve this problem

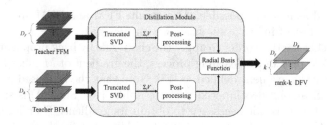

Fig. 2. The proposed knowledge distillation module.

is to reduce the spatial dimensions of the feature maps. We introduce SVD to effectively remove spatial redundancy in feature maps and obtain meaningfully implied feature information in the process of reducing feature dimensions. This section describes in detail how to generate DFV, i.e., knowledge for distillation using SVD.

Figure 2 shows the structure of the proposed knowledge distillation module. Suppose that the input and output feature maps of the layer module defined in T-DNN, i.e., FFM and BFM are inputs to this distillation module. First, we eliminate the spatial redundancy of feature maps by using truncated SVD. Then, the right-hand singular vectors V obtained from the truncated SVD and the singular value matrix are post-processed for easy learning, and then k feature vectors are obtained. Finally, the correlation between feature vectors obtained from FFM and BFM is computed by RBF to obtain a rank-k DFV.

Truncated SVD. As shown in Fig. 3(a), the first step of the distillation module is the truncated SVD which is used to compress the feature map information and lower the dimension simultaneously. Prior to applying SVD, preprocessing is performed to convert the 3D feature map information of $H \times W \times D$ into a 2D matrix M having $(H \times W) \times D$ size. Then M can be a factorization of the form $U\Sigma V^T$ by SVD. V^T is the conjugate transpose of V. The columns of U and the columns of V are called the left-singular vectors and right-singular vectors of M, respectively. The non-zero singular values of M (found on the diagonal entries of Σ) are the square roots of the non-zero eigenvalues of both $M^T M$ and MM^T. On the other hand, U and V decomposed through SVD have different information [11]. U is the unique pattern information of each feature of M, and V can be interpreted as global information of the feature set. And Σ has the scale or energy information of the singular value. Since we aim to obtain compressed feature information, we use only V having global information of the feature map and its energy Σ.

To minimize memory size as well as computational cost, we use truncated SVD. Truncated SVD refers to an SVD that decomposes a given matrix by only a pre-determined rank k. That is, V and Σ have dimensions of $k \times D$ and $k \times 1$, respectively. In this case, since the difference between the re-composed matrix and the original matrix is minimized, the information of the given matrix M can be maintained as much as possible. As a result, FFM and BFM are compressed with minimal loss of information as shown on Fig. 3(a).

On the other hand, in order to apply the chain rule by back propagation to the truncated SVD part in the learning process, the gradient of M must be defined. So, we modify the gradient defined in [13]. Note that the proposed scheme uses only V and Σ among decomposed vectors, unlike [13]. Since Σ is simply used as a scale factor, it is not necessary to obtain its gradient. Therefore, only the gradient for V is obtained and the gradient of M is re-defined as in Eqs. (1)–(2).

$$
\nabla\left(M\right) = \begin{cases} UE^T - U\left(E^TV\right)_{diag} V^T \\ -2U\left(K \circ \left(\Sigma^T \hat{V}^T E\right)\right)_{sym} \Sigma^T V^T, \; \mathrm{HW} \leq D \\ 2U\Sigma\left(K^T \circ \left(V^T\nabla\left(V\right)\right)\right)_{sym} V^T, \qquad otherwise \end{cases} \tag{1}
$$

$$
E = \nabla\left(V\right)\Sigma^{-1}, K = \begin{cases} \frac{1}{\sigma_i^2 - \sigma_j^2}, \; i \neq j, (1 \leq i,j \leq k) \\ 0, \qquad otherwise \end{cases} \tag{2}
$$

where $(A)_{sym} = \frac{1}{2}\left(A^T + A\right)$ and $(A)_{diag}$ is a function that makes all off-diagonal components zero. Also $\circ$ indicates Hadamard product, and σ stands for diagonal component of Σ. We do not need to perform unnecessary operations on $\nabla\left(\Sigma\right)$ and $\nabla\left(U\right)$, and since the dimension of each matrix is low, the computation cost can be minimized as a whole.

Therefore, truncated SVD is a key element of the proposed knowledge distillation module because it effectively reduces the dimension of the feature map. As a result, the proposed knowledge distillation functions to fit the small size network.

Post-processing. Truncated SVD products, V and Σ contain enough FFM and BFM information, but are difficult to use directly because of the following two problems. First, since SVD decomposes a given matrix in decreasing order of energy, the order of singular vectors with similar energy can be reversed. Second, because each element of the singular vector has a value of $[-1,1]$, singular vectors with the same information but the opposite direction may exist. So, even with similar feature maps, the results of decomposing them may seem to be very different.

Therefore, the corresponding singular vectors of T-DNN and S-DNN are post-processed differently based on T-DNN because T-DNN delivers its information to S-DNN. First, post-processing for T-DNN is described in Fig. 3(b). The singular value of T-DNN Σ_T is normalized so that the square sum becomes 1. Normalization is performed by multiplying a normalized Σ_T with singular vector of T-DNN V_T as shown in Eq. (4) to obtain a set of compressed feature vectors F_T as shown in Eq. (3).

$$
F_T = \{f_{T,i} | 1 \leq i \leq k\} \tag{3}
$$

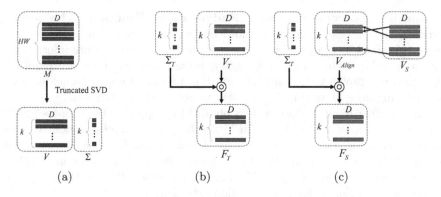

(a)   (b)   (c)

Fig. 3. (a) Truncated SVD (b) post-processing of T-DNN (c) post-processing of S-DNN

$$f_{T,i} = \frac{\sigma_{T,i}}{||\Sigma_T||_2} v_{T,i} \tag{4}$$

where $\sigma_{T,i}$ is the i-th singular value of T-DNN and $v_{T,i}$ is the corresponding singular vector. Since the singular value means the energy of the corresponding singular vector, each singular vector is learned in order of importance.

Next, a singular vector of S-DNN is post-processed as shown in Fig. 3(c). First, we align the student singular vectors based on the teacher singular values. So the student singular vector with the most similar information to the teacher singular vector is aligned in the same order.

Here, the similarity between singular vectors is defined as the absolute value of cosine similarity, which determines the similarity degree through the angles between two vectors so that the similarity between the vectors with opposite directions can be accurately measured. This process is described in Eqs. (5–6).

$$s_j = \underset{j}{argmax} \left(|v_{T,i} \cdot v_{S,j}| \right), (1 \le i \le k), (1 \le j \le k+1) \tag{5}$$

$$v_{Align,i} = sign \left(v_{T,i} \cdot v_{S,s_j} \right) v_{S,s_j} \tag{6}$$

Here $v_{S,j}$ indicates the j-th vector of the S-DNN's V and $v_{Align,i}$ is the i-th vector of the aligned version of the S-DNN's V. Note that for effective alignment, the student feature map decomposes one more vector. Also, the singular vectors of S-DNN are normalized by the singular values of T-DNN, so that a singular vector of higher importance is further learned. This is shown in Eqs. (7–8).

$$F_S = \{f_{S,i} | 1 \le i \le k\}, \tag{7}$$

$$f_{S,i} = \frac{\sigma_{T,i}}{||\Sigma_T||_2} v_{Align,i} \tag{8}$$

Thus, because of the post-processing, noisy and randomly decomposed singular vector information can be used effectively.

Computing Correlation Using Radial Basis Function. This section describes the process of defining knowledge by the correlation of the feature vectors obtained in the previous section. Since the derived feature information from a singular vector is generally noisy, noise-robust methods are required. Therefore, we employ Gaussian RBF, which is a frequently used kernel function for analyzing noisy data [14,15], as a way to obtain the correlation.

On the other hand, feature vectors obtained by applying the proposed SVD and post-processing to FFM and BFM are basically discrete random vectors independent of each other. Thus, we define the correlation between feature vector sets obtained from FFM and BFM as a point-wise L_2 distance as in Eq. (10), and the rank-k DFV are completed by applying Gaussian RBF to the computed correlation as in Eq. (9) for the dimension extension.

$$DFV = \left\{ \exp\left(-\frac{d_{m,n,l}}{\beta} \right), 1 \leq m \leq D_F, 1 \leq n \leq D_B, 1 \leq l \leq k \right\} \quad (9)$$

$$d_{m,n,l} = \left\| f_{m,l}^{FFM} - f_{n,l}^{BFM} \right\|_2^2 \quad (10)$$

β in Eq. (9) is a hyper-parameter for smoothing DFV and it should be properly selected for noise-robust operation.

As mentioned above, the correlation between feature maps composed of noisy and fuzzy data can be effectively obtained through SVD and RBF. Therefore, the distillated knowledge from T-DNN by the proposed scheme can be a very effective guidance for S-DNN. Also, unlike the existing technique, DFV can transfer knowledge regardless of feature map size and therefore it causes consistent performance. The experimental results are discussed in Sect. 4.2.

3.2 Training Mechanism

The remaining step is to learn to improve the performance of S-DNN by transferring distilled knowledge of T-DNN, i.e., DFV, to S-DNN. We need to learn that the S-DNN imitates the T-DNN with the DFV as an intermediary, so we define the L_2 loss function $L_{transfer}(DFV_T, DFV_S)$ of the knowledge pair of T-DNN and S-DNN as Eq. (11).

$$L_{transfer}(DFV_T, DFV_S) = \sum_g^G \frac{\left\| DFV_T^{(g)} - DFV_S^{(g)} \right\|_2^2}{2} \quad (11)$$

where G is the maximum number of layer modules defined in the proposed T-S-DNN. In this case, all layer modules are assumed to have the equivalent importance, and are trained without additional weighting. If S-DNN is initialized by transferring knowledge of T-DNN to S-DNN through learning based on Eq. (11), the learning performance of the main task of S-DNN can be improved (see Sect. 4.2).

However, even though learning the main task of S-DNN after initialization as described above, there is still a problem that the knowledge of T-DNN gradually disappears as learning progresses and the performance improvement is limited. So we introduce self-supervised learning to train both main task and transfer task at the same time. Since the knowledge of T-DNNs learned by S-DNN is a label generated by T-DNN, self-supervised learning is possible using this characteristic. As a result, the final loss function for learning the parameter of S-DNN Θ_S is defined as Eq. (12).

$$L_{total}(\Theta_S) = L_{main}(\Theta_S) + L_{transfer}(DFV_T, DFV_S) \tag{12}$$

As described above, when the main task and the transfer task are learned together by a multi-task learning, it is possible to continuously transfer knowledge of T-DNN to further improve the performance.

On the other hand, if the distillation loss is much larger than the main task loss, the gradient of knowledge transfer becomes too large and the above multi-task learning may not work properly. To solve this problem, it is necessary to limit the effect of the distillation task. So we introduce a gradient clipping [22] to limit the gradient of knowledge transfer.

In general, the threshold for clipping is constant, but we define the L_2-norm ratios of the main task and the transfer task as shown in Eq. (13), and clip the gradient of the knowledge transfer adaptively using this. In addition, since randomly initialized S-DNN is different from T-DNN, it is difficult to follow T-DNN fast. Therefore, we use a sigmoid function as shown in Eq. (14) to design the clipped gradient to grow smoothly as learning progresses.

$$\tau = \frac{\|\nabla(\Theta_S)_{main}\|_2}{\|\nabla(\Theta_S)_{trans}\|_2} \tag{13}$$

$$\nabla(\Theta_S)_{trans}^{clipped} = \begin{cases} \frac{1}{1+\exp(-\tau+p)}\nabla(\Theta_S)_{trans}, & \nabla(\Theta_S)_{trans} < \nabla(\Theta_S)_{main} \\ \nabla(\Theta_S)_{trans} & otherwise \end{cases} \tag{14}$$

In Eq. (14), p means the current epoch. Therefore, the proposed self-supervised learning method can concentrate more on the learning of the main task while learning the two tasks of different nature at the same time. In other words, rich knowledge distillated from T-DNN can be continuously transferred to S-DNN without vanishing. In addition, since the proposed self-supervised learning method has the effect of hard regularization of S-DNN, the performance of S-DNN can be improved without over-fitting (see Sect. 4.3).

4   Experimental Results

In order to evaluate the performance of the proposed knowledge distillation method, we performed the following three experiments. First, we verified the effectiveness of the proposed knowledge itself. To do this, we conducted experiments on so-called small network enhancement that improves the performance

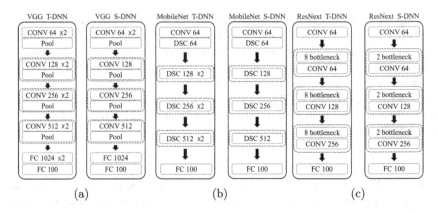

Fig. 4. A pair of T-DNN and S-DNN for an experiment to evaluate small network enhancement. (a) VGG, (b) MobileNet, (c) ResNext. Here dotted boxes indicate layer modules.

of a relatively small S-DNN using T-DNN knowledge (see Sect. 4.2). Second, we examined the performance of the training mechanism proposed in Sect. 3.2 (see Sect. 4.3). Here, the comparison target was Yim et al.'s two-stage approach [10]. Section 4.3 also demonstrates that the proposed method can transfer knowledge robustly even when there is no hard constraint on image information. Third, the performance of the proposed method according to the number of DFVs is experimentally examined in Sect. 4.4.

4.1   Experiment Environments

We implemented the proposed method using Tensorflow [23] on a computer with specification of the Intel Core i7-7700 CPU@3.60 GHz x8, 16 GB RAM, and GeForce GTX 1070. We used CIFAR100 [24]. The CIFAR100 dataset consists of color images with a small size of 32×32, with 50,000 training data and 10,000 test data divided into 100 categories or labels. The augmentations used here are random shift, random rotation, and horizontal flip. The proposed method was tested under the same conditions as [10], and the average of three equivalent experimental results was used as the final result to increase the reliability of the results.

4.2   Small Network Enhancement

In order to verify the effect of knowledge transfer only, we first showed the result of learning in two-stage approach as in [10]. That is, the self-supervised learning of Sect. 3.2 was not used in this experiment. We compared the proposed method and the state-of-the-art knowledge distillation method [10]. In addition, the results of T-DNN alone and S-DNN alone were also shown. All the methods were learned with the CIFAR100 dataset. We employed VGG, MobileNet,

ResNext as the DNN to apply to the proposed method. The T-S-DNNs constructed using these are shown in Fig. 4.

Although VGG is somewhat poorer than the state-of-the-art CNN models in terms of ratio of accuracy and parameter size, it is widely used because of its simple structure and ease of implementation. We used a modified version of the T-DNN for CIFAR100 by removing the last three convolutional layers from the VGG network proposed in [19]. The S-DNN consists of only one convolutional layer with the same filter depth as shown in Fig. 4(a). Here, the layer module is defined as a convolutional layer with the same filter depth.

MobileNet is a CNN with small parameter size and computational cost designed for use in mobile or embedded environments. The MobileNet case shows that the proposed method is capable of improving performance even for small networks. As shown in Fig. 4(b), T-DNN was constructed by removing the last four depth-wise separable convolutional layers (DSC) proposed in [7] to fit CIFAR100. The S-DNN is composed by using the DSC of the same filter depth only once. Here, the layer module is defined by the DSC of the same filter depth.

Finally, ResNext is a network where the convolution layer was divided into several bottleneck layers. Through experiments using ResNext, we show that the proposed method can transfer knowledge effectively even in networks with very complex structures. We used the network proposed in [5] as the T-DNN and the S-DNN is constructed by partially reducing the bottleneck layers. Here, the layer module is defined by combining the bottleneck layer and one convolutional layer (see Fig. 4(c)).

The weight of each network was determined by He's initialization [3] and L_2 regularization. Decay parameter was set to 10^{-4}. Batch size was set to 128, and stochastic gradient descent (SGD) [25] was used for optimization, and Nesterov accelerated gradient [26] was applied. The initial learning rate was set to 10^{-2} and the momentum was set to 0.9. During a total of 200 epochs, the networks were learned and the learning rate was reduced to $1/10$ per 50 epochs. Both stages used the same hyper-parameters. The hyper-parameter of the proposed method k was set to is 1. In other words, only one DFV is used and β of RBF is experimentally fixed to 8.

The experimental results are shown in Table 1, and it can be seen that the proposed method is always better than [10]. In the case of VGG, the proposed method has an outstanding performance improvement of 3.68% compared to S-DNN. It also shows about 0.49% better performance than [10] and 0.61% higher performance than T-DNN alone. In case of Mobilenet, the proposed method improves the performance by about 2% over S-DNN, and 1.62% over [10] and 0.3% over T-DNN. This shows that the proposed method is more suitable for small networks than [10]. In the case of ResNext, the proposed method improves the performance of S-DNN by only 1.43%, which is lower than that of VGG or MobileNet, but has a performance advantage over 1.83% than [10]. This result shows that the proposed method works well in a state-of-the-art network with a complicated structure such as ResNext. Therefore, the proposed method effec-

Table 1. Comparison of the proposed algorithm with [10] for three different networks. Here, FLOPS indicates the sum of the numbers of addition, multiplication, and condition. Params indicates the sum of weights and biases.

Network	Model	FLOPs	Params	Accuracy
VGG	T-DNN	576.3M	10.9M	64.44
	S-DNN	121.3M	3.8M	61.37
	[10]	121.3M	3.8M	64.54
	Proposed	121.3M	3.8M	**65.05**
MobileNet	T-DNN	98.4M	2.3M	57.85
	S-DNN	37.8M	0.82M	56.15
	[10]	37.8M	0.82M	56.53
	Proposed	37.8M	0.82M	**58.15**
ResNext	T-DNN	547.3M	0.66M	66.58
	S-DNN	247.6M	0.34M	64.00
	[10]	247.6M	0.34M	63.60
	Proposed	247.6M	0.34M	**65.43**

Table 2. Sensitivity of the proposed network to spatial resolution of feature map.

Network	Model	FLOPs	Params	Accuracy
VGG	T-DNN	576.3M	10.9M	64.44
	S-DNN	15.6M	3.8M	54.17
	Proposed	15.6M	3.8M	61.15

tively compresses knowledge of T-DNN and transfers the compressed knowledge regardless of network structure.

On the other hand, we constructed another VGG-based S-DNN to show that the proposed method can transfer knowledge regardless of the resolution of feature maps. In the convolutional layer of the S-DNN used above, the padding was not performed and the size of the feature map was reduced by setting the stride of the convolutional layer to 2 instead of pooling. This dramatically reduces the spatial resolution of the feature map as it passes through the convolution layer. The hyper-parameters used for learning were the same as before.

Since knowledge transfer using [10] is impossible in this T-S-DNN structure, Table 2 shows only the results of the proposed method. We can see that the performance of S-DNN with FLOPS of about 0.03 times that of T-DNN is improved by about 6.98%. Therefore, the proposed method can effectively transfer the knowledge of T-DNN regardless of the spatial resolution of the feature map, and is effective for practical applications requiring small size DNNs.

Table 3. Performance evaluation according to training mechanism.

Model	Mechanism	Accuracy
[10]	2 stage	64.54
	1 stage	64.89
Proposed	2 stage	65.05
	1 stage	**65.54**

4.3 Training Mechanism

In this section, we evaluate the training mechanism proposed in Sect. 3.2. The network used for learning is the VGG-based T-S-DNN used in Sect. 4.2. The hyper-parameters are the same as those used in Sect. 4.2.

Table 3 shows the experimental results. The performance improvement was 0.35% when the proposed training mechanism was applied to [10], and the performance improved by 0.49% when the proposed training mechanism was applied together with the proposed knowledge distillation technique. This is because S-DNN is regularized continuously without vanishing of knowledge of T-DNN. In addition, since the number of epochs required for learning is reduced by half compared with the conventional two stage structure, the learning time can be shortened significantly. Therefore, using both the knowledge distillation technique and the training mechanism, the performance improvement is expected to be about 4.17% higher than that of the S-DNN alone. In addition, the proposed method can improve performance up to 1% than [10] and 1.1% over T-DNN. Since the computation cost of S-DNN amounts to only 1/5 of that of T-DNN, we can see that S-DNN is well regularized by the proposed method.

4.4 Performance Evaluation According to the Number of DFVs

The number of DFVs to be transferred in the proposed knowledge distillation has a significant impact on overall performance. For example, using too many DFVs will not only increase cost, but also deliver noisy information, so we need to find an optimal number. In this experiment, we adopted the VGG-based T-DNN used in Sect. 4.2. We took into account two types of S-DNNs for this experiment: S-DNN with pooling and S-DNN with stride.

The experimental results of the proposed method were shown in Table 4. In general, performance was improved regardless of the number of DFVs, but in the case of S-DNN with pooling, we could observe that as the number of DFVs becomes too large, the accuracy rises and drops again. This is because the distillation of too much amount of knowledge may cause transfer of even unnecessary information as mentioned in Sect. 3. However, S-DNN with stride shows a slight increase in performance. This is because the performance of the S-DNN is relatively low compared to that of the T-DNN, so receiving additional knowledge will significantly improve performance. Therefore, a reasonable num-

Table 4. Performance comparison according to the number of DFVs.

VGG	Model	The number of DFVs					
		-	1	2	4	8	16
VGG	S-DNN w/pool	61.37	65.54	**66.33**	66.17	65.38	65.15
	S-DNN w/stride	54.17	61.28	61.54	61.63	61.82	62.00

ber of DFVs should be used depending on the available cost, and the number of DFVs required can be determined according to the structure of the network.

5   Conclusion and Future Work

We propose a novel knowledge distillation method in this paper. The existing knowledge transfer technique (1) was limited to a limited network structure, (2) the quality of knowledge was low, and (3) as the learning progresses, the knowledge of the T-DNN vanished rapidly. We have proposed a method to transfer very rich information by defining novel knowledge using SVD and RBF, which are frequently used in traditional machine learning, without any structural limitations of the network. In addition, self-supervised learning associated with multi-task learning have been applied so that it was able to continue to receive T-DNN's knowledge during the learning process, which could also lead to additional performance enhancement. Experimental results showed that the proposed method has a significant improvement of about 4.96% compared to the 3.17% improvement in terms of accuracy performance based on VGG network [10]. In the future, we will develop a semi-supervised learning scheme by extending self-supervised learning concept through proposed knowledge transfer.

Acknowledgements. This research was supported by National Research Foundation of Korea Grant funded by the Korean Government (2016R1A2B4007353).

References

1. LeCun, Y., Bottou, L., Bengio, Y., Haffner, P.: Gradient-based learning applied to document recognition. Proc. IEEE **86**(11), 2278–2324 (1998)
2. Krizhevsky, A., Sutskever, I., Hinton, G.E.: ImageNet classification with deep convolutional neural networks. In: Advances in Neural Information Processing Systems, pp. 1097–1105 (2012)
3. He, K., Zhang, X., Ren, S., Sun, J.: Deep residual learning for image recognition. In: Proceedings of the IEEE Conference on Computer Vision and Pattern Recognition, pp. 770–778 (2016)
4. Huang, G., Liu, Z., Weinberger, K.Q., van der Maaten, L.: Densely connected convolutional networks. In: Proceedings of the IEEE Conference on Computer Vision and Pattern Recognition, vol. 1, p. 3 (2017)

5. Xie, S., Girshick, R., Dollár, P., Tu, Z., He, K.: Aggregated residual transformations for deep neural networks. In: 2017 IEEE Conference on Computer Vision and Pattern Recognition (CVPR), pp. 5987–5995. IEEE (2017)
6. Zhang, X., Zhou, X., Lin, M., Sun, J.: ShuffleNet: an extremely efficient convolutional neural network for mobile devices. arXiv preprint arXiv:1707.01083 (2017)
7. Howard, A.G., et al.: MobileNets: efficient convolutional neural networks for mobile vision applications. arXiv preprint arXiv:1704.04861 (2017)
8. Hinton, G., Vinyals, O., Dean, J.: Distilling the knowledge in a neural network. arXiv preprint arXiv:1503.02531 (2015)
9. Romero, A., Ballas, N., Kahou, S.E., Chassang, A., Gatta, C., Bengio, Y.: FitNets: hints for thin deep nets. arXiv preprint arXiv:1412.6550 (2014)
10. Yim, J., Joo, D., Bae, J., Kim, J.: A gift from knowledge distillation: fast optimization, network minimization and transfer learning. In: The IEEE Conference on Computer Vision and Pattern Recognition (CVPR) (2017)
11. Alter, O., Brown, P.O., Botstein, D.: Singular value decomposition for genome-wide expression data processing and modeling. Proc. Natl. Acad. Sci. **97**(18), 10101–10106 (2000)
12. Zhang, Z., Ely, G., Aeron, S., Hao, N., Kilmer, M.: Novel methods for multilinear data completion and de-noising based on tensor-SVD. In: Proceedings of the IEEE Conference on Computer Vision and Pattern Recognition, pp. 3842–3849 (2014)
13. Ionescu, C., Vantzos, O., Sminchisescu, C.: Matrix backpropagation for deep networks with structured layers. In: Proceedings of the IEEE International Conference on Computer Vision, pp. 2965–2973 (2015)
14. Kim, N., Byun, H.G., Kwon, K.H.: Learning behaviors of stochastic gradient radial basis function network algorithms for odor sensing systems. ETRI J. **28**(1), 59–66 (2006)
15. Wang, X.X., Chen, S., Harris, C.J.: Using the correlation criterion to position and shape RBF units for incremental modelling. Int. J. Autom. Comput. **3**(4), 392–403 (2006)
16. Larsson, G., Maire, M., Shakhnarovich, G.: Learning representations for automatic colorization. In: Leibe, B., Matas, J., Sebe, N., Welling, M. (eds.) ECCV 2016 Part IV. LNCS, vol. 9908, pp. 577–593. Springer, Cham (2016). https://doi.org/10.1007/978-3-319-46493-0_35
17. Noroozi, M., Favaro, P.: Unsupervised learning of visual representations by solving jigsaw puzzles. In: Leibe, B., Matas, J., Sebe, N., Welling, M. (eds.) ECCV 2016 Part VI. LNCS, vol. 9910, pp. 69–84. Springer, Cham (2016). https://doi.org/10.1007/978-3-319-46466-4_5
18. Doersch, C., Zisserman, A.: Multi-task self-supervised visual learning. In: The IEEE International Conference on Computer Vision (ICCV) (2017)
19. Simonyan, K., Zisserman, A.: Very deep convolutional networks for large-scale image recognition. arXiv preprint arXiv:1409.1556 (2014)
20. Zhou, X., Belkin, M.: Semi-supervised learning. In: Academic Press Library in Signal Processing, vol. 1, pp. 1239–1269. Elsevier (2014)
21. Su, H., Zhu, J., Yin, Z., Dong, Y., Zhang, B.: Efficient and robust semi-supervised learning over a sparse-regularized graph. In: Leibe, B., Matas, J., Sebe, N., Welling, M. (eds.) ECCV 2016 Part VIII. LNCS, vol. 9912, pp. 583–598. Springer, Cham (2016). https://doi.org/10.1007/978-3-319-46484-8_35
22. Pascanu, R., Mikolov, T., Bengio, Y.: On the difficulty of training recurrent neural networks. In: International Conference on Machine Learning, pp. 1310–1318 (2013)
23. Abadi, M., et al.: TensorFlow: large-scale machine learning on heterogeneous systems (2015). tensorflow.org

24. Krizhevsky, A., Hinton, G.: Learning multiple layers of features from tiny images (2009)
25. Kiefer, J., Wolfowitz, J.: Stochastic estimation of the maximum of a regression function. Ann. Math. Stat. **23**, 462–466 (1952)
26. Nesterov, N.: A method for unconstrained convex minimization problem with the rate of convergence o $(1/k^2)$. Doklady AN USSR **269**, 543–547 (1983)

PARN: Pyramidal Affine Regression Networks for Dense Semantic Correspondence

Sangryul Jeon[1], Seungryong Kim[1], Dongbo Min[2], and Kwanghoon Sohn[1]($\boxtimes$)

[1] Yonsei University, Seoul, South Korea
{cheonjsr,srkim89,khsohn}@yonsei.ac.kr
[2] Ewha Womans University, Seoul, South Korea
dbmin@ewha.ac.kr

Abstract. This paper presents a deep architecture for dense semantic correspondence, called pyramidal affine regression networks (PARN), that estimates locally-varying affine transformation fields across images. To deal with intra-class appearance and shape variations that commonly exist among different instances within the same object category, we leverage a pyramidal model where affine transformation fields are progressively estimated in a coarse-to-fine manner so that the smoothness constraint is naturally imposed within deep networks. PARN estimates residual affine transformations at each level and composes them to estimate final affine transformations. Furthermore, to overcome the limitations of insufficient training data for semantic correspondence, we propose a novel weakly-supervised training scheme that generates progressive supervisions by leveraging a correspondence consistency across image pairs. Our method is fully learnable in an end-to-end manner and does not require quantizing infinite continuous affine transformation fields. To the best of our knowledge, it is the first work that attempts to estimate dense affine transformation fields in a coarse-to-fine manner within deep networks. Experimental results demonstrate that PARN outperforms the state-of-the-art methods for dense semantic correspondence on various benchmarks.

Keywords: Dense semantic correspondence · Hierarchical graph model

1 Introduction

Establishing dense correspondences across semantically similar images is essential for numerous computer vision and computational photography applications, such as scene parsing, semantic segmentation, and image editing [1–5].

Electronic supplementary material The online version of this chapter (https://doi.org/10.1007/978-3-030-01231-1_22) contains supplementary material, which is available to authorized users.

© Springer Nature Switzerland AG 2018
V. Ferrari et al. (Eds.): ECCV 2018, LNCS 11210, pp. 355–371, 2018.
https://doi.org/10.1007/978-3-030-01231-1_22

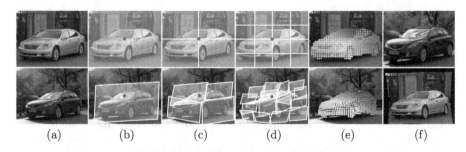

(a)   (b)   (c)   (d)   (e)   (f)

Fig. 1. Visualization of pyramidal model in the PARN: (a) source and target images, estimated affine field at (b) level 1, (c) level 2, (d) level 3, (e) pixel-level, and (f) warped images. In each grid at each level, PARN estimates corresponding affine transformation field regularized with the estimated transformation field at previous level.

Unlike classical dense correspondence tasks such as stereo matching [6] or optical flow estimation [7] that have been dramatically advanced, semantic correspondence estimation still remains unsolved due to severe intra-class appearance and shape variations across images. Several recent approaches [8,9] have been proposed by leveraging deep convolutional neural networks (CNNs), providing satisfactory performances in capturing reliable matching evidences under intra-class appearance variations. However, they still consider geometric variations in just a limited manner such as those used for stereo matching or optical flow estimation [6,7]. In some approaches [9,10], more complex geometric variations such as scale or rotation were addressed, but they seek the labeling solution from only a set of scales and/or rotations quantized within pre-defined ranges. Recently, the discrete-continuous transformation matching (DCTM) framework [10] combined with the fully convolutional self-similarity (FCSS) [8] descriptor exhibits much improved performance by estimating locally-varying affine transformation fields on continuous and discrete domains in an alternative manner. Although DCTM has shown the state-of-the-art performance in dealing with non-rigid shape deformations, it is formulated with handcrafted smoothness constraint model and optimization technique, and thus it cannot guarantee optimal results when the geometric variation is relatively large.

In addition to the effort at measuring reliable matching evidences across images under intra-class appearance variations, recent CNN-based approaches have begun directly regressing geometric deformation fields through deep networks [11,12]. As pioneering works, spatial transformer networks (STNs) [13] and its variant, inverse compositional spatial transformer networks (IC-STNs) [14], offer a way to deal with geometric variations within CNNs. Rocco et al. [12] and Schneider et al. [15] developed a CNN architecture for geometry-invariant matching that estimates transformation parameters across semantically similar images and different modalities. However, these methods assume the global transformation model, and thus they cannot deal with spatially-varying geometric variations, which frequently appear in dense semantic correspondence. More recently, some methods such as universal correspondence network (UCN)

[9] and deformable convolutional networks (DCN) [16] were proposed to encode locally-varying geometric variations in CNNs, but they do not have smoothness constraints with neighboring points, and cannot guarantee reliable performance under relatively large geometric variations. An additional challenge lies in the lack of training data with ground-truth for semantic correspondence, making the use of supervised training approaches difficult.

In this paper, we present a novel CNN architecture, called pyramidal affine regression networks (PARN), that estimates locally-varying affine transformation fields across semantically similar images in a coarse-to-fine fashion, as shown in Fig. 1. Inspired by pyramidal graph models [3,17] that impose the hierarchical smoothness constraint on labeling results, our approach first estimates a global affine transformation over an entire image, and then progressively increases the degree of freedom of the transformation in a form of quad-tree, finally producing pixel-wise continuous affine transformation fields. The regression networks estimate residual affine transformations at each level and these are composed to provide final affine transformation fields. To overcome the limitations of insufficient training data for semantic correspondence, we propose a novel weakly-supervised training scheme that generates progressive supervisions by leveraging the correspondence consistency. Our method works in an end-to-end manner, and does not require quantizing the search space, different from conventional methods [17,18]. To the best of our knowledge, it is the first attempt to estimate the locally-varying affine transformation fields through deep network in a coarse-to-fine manner. Experimental results show that the PARN outperforms the latest methods for dense semantic correspondence on several benchmarks including Taniai dataset [19], PF-PASCAL [20], and Caltech-101 [21].

2   Related Works

Dense Semantic Correspondence. Liu et al. [2] pioneered the idea of dense correspondence across different scenes, and proposed SIFT Flow. Inspired by this, Kim et al. [3] proposed the deformable spatial pyramid (DSP) which performs multi-scale regularization within a hierarchical graph. More recently, Yang et al. [22] proposed the object-aware hierarchical graph (OHG) to regulate matching consistency over whole objects. Among other methods are those that take an exemplar-LDA approach [23], employ joint image set alignment [5], or jointly solve for cosegmentation [19]. As all of these techniques use handcrafted descriptors such as SIFT [24] or DAISY [18], they lack the robustness to deformations that is possible with deep CNNs.

Recently CNN-based descriptors have been used to establish dense semantic correspondences because of their high invariance to appearance variations. Zhou et al. [25] proposed a deep network that exploits cycle-consistency with a 3-D CAD model [26] as a supervisory signal. Choy et al. [9] proposed the universal correspondence network (UCN) based on fully convolutional feature learning. Novotny et al. [27] proposed AnchorNet that learns geometry-sensitive features for semantic matching with weak image-level labels. Kim et al. [8] proposed the

FCSS descriptor that formulates local self-similarity within a fully convolutional network. However, none of these methods is able to handle severe non-rigid geometric variations.

Transformation Invariance. Several methods have aimed to alleviate geometric variations through extensions of SIFT Flow, including scale-less SIFT Flow (SLS) [28], scale-space SIFT Flow (SSF) [29], and generalized DSP [17]. However, these techniques have a critical and practical limitation that their computational cost increases linearly with the search space size. HaCohen et al. [1] proposed in a non-rigid dense correspondence (NRDC) algorithm, but it employs weak matching evidence that cannot guarantee reliable performance. Geometric invariance to scale and rotation is provided by DAISY Filer Flow (DFF) [4], but its implicit smoothness constraint often induces mismatches. Recently, Ham et al. [30] presented the Proposal Flow (PF) algorithm to estimate correspondences using object proposals. Han et al. [31] proposed SCNet to learn the similarity function and geometry kernel of PF algorithm within deep CNN. While these aforementioned techniques provide some amount of geometric invariance, none of them can deal with affine transformations across images, which frequently occur in dense semantic correspondence. More recently, Kim et al. [10] proposed DCTM framework where dense affine transformation fields are inferred using a handcrafted energy function and optimization.

STNs [13] offer a way to deal with geometric variations within CNNs by warping features through a global parametric transformation. Lin et al. [14] proposed IC-STNs that replaces the feature warping with transformation parameter propagation. Rocco et al. [12] proposed a CNN architecture for estimating a geometric model such as an affine transformation for semantic correspondence estimation. However, it only estimates globally-varying geometric fields, and thus exhibits limited performance for dealing with locally-varying geometric deformations. Some methods such as UCN [9] and DCN [16] were proposed to encode locally-varying geometric variations in CNNs, but they do not have the smoothness constraints with neighboring points and cannot guarantee reliable performance for images with relatively large geometric variations [10].

3   Method

3.1   Problem Formulation and Overview

Given a pair of images I and I', the objective of dense correspondence estimation is to establish a correspondence i' for each pixel $i = [i_{\mathbf{x}}, i_{\mathbf{y}}]$. In this work, we infer a field of affine transformations, each represented by a 2×3 matrix

$$\mathbf{T}_i = \begin{bmatrix} \mathbf{T}_{i,\mathbf{x}} \\ \mathbf{T}_{i,\mathbf{y}} \end{bmatrix} \tag{1}$$

that maps pixel i to $i' = \mathbf{T}_i \mathbf{i}$, where $\mathbf{i}$ is pixel i represented in homogeneous coordinates such that $\mathbf{i} = [i, 1]^T$.

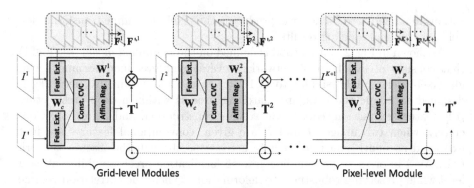

Fig. 2. Network configuration of the PARN, which is defined on the pyramidal model and consists of several grid-level modules and a single pixel-level module. Each module is designed to mimic the standard matching process within a deep architecture, including feature extraction, cost volume construction, and regression.

Compared to the constrained geometric transformation model (i.e. only translational motion) commonly used in the stereo matching or optical flow estimation, the affine transformation fields can model the geometric variation in a more principled manner. Estimating the pixel-wise affine transformation fields, however, poses additional challenges due to its infinite and continuous solution space. It is well-known in stereo matching literatures that global approaches using the smoothness constraint defined on the Markov random field (MRF) [32] tend to achieve higher accuracy on the labeling optimization, compared to local approaches based on the structure-aware cost aggregation [33]. However, such global approaches do not scale very well to our problem in terms of computational complexity, as the affine transformation is defined over the 6-D continuous solution space. Additionally, it is not easy to guarantee the convergence of affine transformation fields estimated through the discrete labeling optimization due to extremely large label spaces. Though randomized search and propagation strategy for labeling optimization [32,34] may help to improve the convergence of labeling optimization on high-dimensional label space, most approaches just consider relatively lower-dimensional label space, e.g. 4-D label space consisting of translation, rotation, and scale.

Inspired by the pyramidal graph model [3,17,35] and the parametric geometry regression networks [11,12], we propose a novel deep architecture that estimates dense affine transformation fields in a coarse-to-fine manner. Our key observation is that affine transformation fields estimated at a coarse scale tend to be robust to geometric variations while the results at a fine scale preserve fine-grained details of objects better. While conventional approaches that employ the coarse-to-fine scheme in dense correspondence estimation [2,36] focus on *image scales*, our approach exploits *semantic scales* within the hierarchy of deep convolutional networks. Our method first estimates an image-level affine transformation using the deepest convolutional activations and then progressively localizes the affine transformation field additionally using the shallower convolutional activations in a quad-tree framework, producing the pixel-level affine transformation fields as the final labeling results.

As shown in Fig. 2, our method is defined on the *pyramidal model* (see Fig. 1) that consists of two kind of networks, several grid-level modules and a single pixel-level module, similar to [3,17]. Each module within two networks is designed to mimic the standard matching process within a deep architecture [12]: feature extraction, correlation volume construction, and regression. Concretely, when two images I and I' are given, convolutional features are first extracted as multi-level intermediate activations through the feature network (with $\mathbf{W}_c$) in order to provide fine-grained localization precision ability at each level while preserving robustness to deformations. Then, the correlation volume is constructed between these features at the cost volume construction layer of Fig. 2. Finally the affine transformation fields are inferred by passing the correlation volume to the regression network (with $\mathbf{W}_g^k$, $\mathbf{W}_p$ of Fig. 2). This procedure is repeated for K grid-level modules and a single pixel-level module.

3.2   Pyramidal Affine Regression Networks

Each module of our pyramidal model has three main components. The first one extracts *hierarchically* concatenated features from the input images and the second computes a cost volume within *constrained* search windows. Lastly, from the third one, a *locally-varying* affine field is densely estimated for all pixels.

Feature Extraction. While conventional CNN-based descriptors have shown the excellent capabilities in handling intra-class appearance variations [37,38], they have difficulties in yielding both semantic robustness and matching precision ability at the same time. To overcome this limitation, our networks are designed to leverage the inherent hierarchies of CNNs where multi-level intermediate convolutional features are extracted through a shared siamese network. We concatenate some of these convolutional feature maps such that

$$\mathbf{F}^k = \bigcup_{n \in M(k)} \mathcal{F}(I^k; \mathbf{W}_c^n) \tag{2}$$

where $\bigcup$ denotes the concatenation operator, $\mathbf{W}_c^n$ is the feature extraction network parameter until n-th convolutional layer and $M(k)$ is the sampled indices of convolutional layers at level k. This is illustrated by the upper of Fig. 2.

Moreover, iteratively extracting the features along our pyramidal model provides evolving receptive fields which is a key ingradient for the geometric invariance [4,10]. By contrast, existing geometry regression networks [11,12] face a tradeoff between appearance invariance and localization precision due to the fixed receptive field of extracted features. Note that we obtained I^k with the outputs from the previous level by warping I^{k-1} with $\mathbf{T}^{k-1}$ through bilinear samplers [13] which facilitate an end-to-end learning framework.

Constrained Cost Volume Construction. To estimate geometry between image pairs I^k and I', the matching cost according to search spaces should be

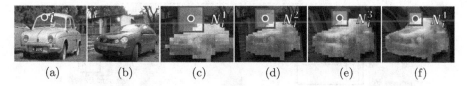

(a)   (b)   (c)   (d)   (e)   (f)

Fig. 3. Visualization of the constrained search window N_i^k: (a) source image and a reference pixel (blue colored). The matching costs are visualized as the heat maps for the reference pixel at (c) level 1, (d) level 2, (e) level 3, and (f) pixel-level. (color figure online)

computed using extracted features $\mathbf{F}^k$ and $\mathbf{F}'^{,k}$. Unlike conventional approaches that quantize search spaces for estimating depth [6], optical flow [7], or similarity transformations [17], quantizing the 6-D affine transformation defined over an infinite continuous solution space is computationally expensive and also degenerates the estimation accuracy. Instead, inspired by traditional robust geometry estimators such as RANSAC [39] or Hough voting [24], we first construct the cost volume computed with respect to translational motion only, and then determine the affine transformation for each block by passing it through subsequent convolutional layers to reliably prune incorrect matches.

Concretely, the matching costs between extracted features $\mathbf{F}^k$, $\mathbf{F}'^{,k}$ are computed within a search window as a rectified cosine similarity, such that

$$\mathbf{C}^k(i,j) = \max(0, \mathbf{F}'^{,k}(i) \cdot \mathbf{F}^k(j)), \quad \text{where} \quad j \in N_i^k. \tag{3}$$

A constrained search window N_i^k is centered at pixel i with the radius $r(k)$ as examplified in Fig. 3. In our pyramidal model, a relatively large radius is used at coarser levels to estimate a rough yet reliable affine transform as a guidance at subsequent finer levels. The radius becomes smaller as the level goes deeper where the regression network is likely to avoid local minima thanks to the guidance of affine transformation fields estimated on the previous level. Thus only reliable matching candidates are provided as an input to the following regression network where even fine-scaled geometric transformations can be estimated at deeper level. The constructed cost volume can be further utilized for generating the supervisions with correspondence consistency check as described in Sect. 3.3.

Grid-Level Regression. The constrained cost volume $\mathbf{C}^k$ is passed through successive CNNs and bilinear upsampling layer to estimate the affine transformation field such that $\mathbf{T}^k = \mathcal{F}(\mathbf{C}^k; \mathbf{W}_g^k)$, where $\mathbf{W}_g^k$ is the grid-level regression network parameter at the level k. Since each level in the pyramid has a simplified task (it only has to estimate residual transformation field), the regression networks can be simple to have 3–6 convolutional layers.

Within the hierarchy of the pyramidal model, our first starts to estimate the transformation from an entire image and then progressively increase the degree of freedom of the transformation by dividing each grid into four rectangular grids, yielding $2^{k-1} \times 2^{k-1}$ grid of affine fields at level k. However, the estimated coarse

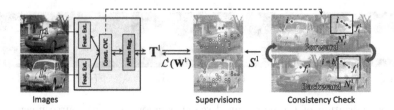

Fig. 4. Training the grid-level module at level 1. By using the correspondence consistency, tentative sparse correspondences are determined and used to train the network.

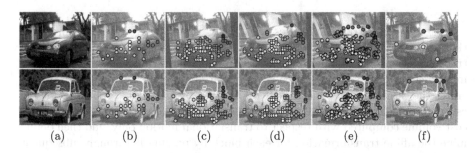

(a)   (b)   (c)   (d)   (e)   (f)

Fig. 5. Visualization of the generated supervisions at each level: (a) source and target images, (b) level 1, (c) level 2, (d) level 3, (e) pixel level, (f) GT keypoints. The tentative positive samples are color-coded. (Best viewed in color.)

affine field has the discontinuities between nearby affine fields occuring blocky artifacts around grid boundaries as shown in (d) and (f) of Fig. 6. To alleviate this, a bilinear upsampler [13] is applied at the end of successive CNNs, upsampling a coarse grid-wise affine field to the original resolution of the input image I. This simple strategy regularizes the affine field to be smooth, suppressing the artifacts considerably as examplified in Fig. 6.

Note that the composition of the estimated affine fields from level 1 to k can be computed as multiplications of augmented matrix in homogeneous coordinates such that

$$\mathbf{M}(\mathbf{T}_i^{[1,k]}) = \prod_{n \in \{1,\dots,k\}} \mathbf{M}(\mathbf{T}_i^n) \tag{4}$$

where $\mathbf{M}(\mathbf{T})$ represents $\mathbf{T}$ in homogeneous coordinates as $[\mathbf{T}; [0,0,1]]$.

Pixel-Level Regression. To improve the matching ability localizing fine-grained object boundaries, we additionally formulate a pixel-level module. Similar to the grid-level modules, it also consists of feature extraction, constrained cost volume construction, and regression network. The main difference is that an encoder-decoder architecture is employed for the regression network, which has been adopted in many pixel-level prediction tasks such as disparity estimation [40], optical flow [41], or semantic segmentation [42]. Taking a warped image I^{K+1} as an input, a constrained cost volume $\mathbf{C}^{K+1}$ is computed and the

---

Algorithm 1. Pyramidal Affine Regression Network

Input: images I, I'
Output: network parameters $\mathbf{W}_c$, $\mathbf{W}_g$, $\mathbf{W}_p$, affine fields $\mathbf{T}^*$
1 : Compute convolutional activations of target image I'
    for $k = 1 : K$ do
2 :   Compute image I^k by warping I^{k-1} with $\mathbf{T}^{k-1}$ when $k > 1$
3 :   [**Only when training**] : Initialize affine fields as $\mathbf{T}_i^k = [\mathbf{I}_{2\times2}, \mathbf{0}_{2\times1}]$
      /* *Feature Extraction* */
4 :   Compute convolutional activations of I^k and extract features $\mathbf{F}^k$, $\mathbf{F}'^{,k}$
      /* *Constrained Correlation Volume* */
5 :   Construct the constrained cost volume $\mathbf{C}^k$ with radius $r(k)$
6 :   [**Only when training**] : Generate supervisions S^k and train the network
      /* *Affine Transformation Field Regression* */
7 :   [**Only when testing**] : Estimate affine fields $\mathbf{T}^k = \mathcal{F}(\mathbf{C}^k; \mathbf{W}_g^k)$
    end for
8 : Estimate pixel-level affine fields $\mathbf{T}' = \mathcal{F}(\mathbf{C}^{K+1}; \mathbf{W}_p)$
9 : Compute final affine fields $\mathbf{M}(\mathbf{T}_i^*) = \prod_{n \in \{1,\dots,K\}} \mathbf{M}(\mathbf{T}^n) \cdot \mathbf{M}(\mathbf{T}_i')$

---

pixel-level affine field is regressed through the encoder-decoder network such that $\mathbf{T}' = \mathcal{F}(\mathbf{C}^{K+1}; \mathbf{W}_p)$, where $\mathbf{W}_p$ is the pixel-level regression network parameter. The final affine transformation field between source and target image can be computed as $\mathbf{M}(\mathbf{T}_i^*) = \mathbf{M}(\mathbf{T}_i^{[1,K]}) \cdot \mathbf{M}(\mathbf{T}'_i)$.

3.3 Training

Generating Progressive Supervisions. A major challenge of semantic correspondence with CNNs is the lack of ground-truth correspondence maps for training data. A possible approach is to synthetically generate a set of image pairs transformed by applying random transformation fields to make the pseudo ground-truth [11,12], but this approach cannot reflect the *realistic* appearance variations and geometric transformations well.

Instead of using synthetically deformed imagery, we propose to generate supervisions directly from the *semantically related* image pairs as shown in Fig. 4, where the correspondence consistency check [35, 48] is applied to the constructed cost volume of each level. Intuitively, the correspondence relation from a source image to a target image should be consistent with that from the target image to the source image. Given the constrained cost volume $\mathbf{C}^k$, the best match f_i^k is computed by searching the maximum score for each point i, $f_i^k = \text{argmax}_j \mathbf{C}^k(i,j)$. We also compute the backward best match b_i^k for f_i^k such that $b_i^k = \text{argmax}_m \mathbf{C}^k(m, f_i)$ to identify that the best match f_i^k is consistent or not. By running this consistency check along our pyramidal model, we actively collect the tentative positive samples at each level such that $S^k = \{i | i = b_i^k, i \in \Omega\}$. We found that the generated supervisions are qualitatively and quantitatively superior to the sparse ground-truth keypoints as examplified in Fig. 5.

For the accuracy of supervisions, we limit the correspondence candidate regions using object location priors such as bounding boxes or masks contain-

(a)   (b)   (c)   (d)   (e)   (f)   (g)   (h)

Fig. 6. Qualitative results of the PARN at each level: (a) source image, (b) target image, warping result at (c) level 1, (d) level 2 without upsampling layer, (e) level 2, (f) level 3 without upsampling layer, (g) level 3, and (h) pixel-level.

ing the target object to be matched, which are provided in most benchmarks [21,43,44]. Note that our approach is conceptually similar to [8], but we generate the supervisions from the constrained cost volume in a hierarchical manner so that the false positive samples are avoided which is critical to train the geometry regression network.

Loss Function. To train the module at level k, the loss function is defined as a distance between the flows at the positive samples and the flow fields computed by applying estimated affine transformation field such that

$$\mathcal{L}^k(\mathbf{W}^k) = \frac{1}{N} \sum_{i \in S^k} \|\mathbf{T}_i^k \mathbf{i} - (i - f_i^k)\|^2, \tag{5}$$

where $\mathbf{W}^k$ is the parameters of feature extraction network and regression network at level k and N is the number of training samples. Algorithm 1 provides an overall summary of PARN.

4   Experimental Results

4.1   Experimental Settings

For feature extraction networks in each regression module, we used the ImageNet pretrained VGGNet-16 [45] and ResNet-101 [38] with their network parameters. For the grid-level regressions, we used three grid-level modules ($K = 3$), followed by a single pixel-level module. For $M(k)$ in the feature extraction step, we sampled convolutional activations after intermediate pooling layers such as 'conv5-3', 'conv4-3', and 'conv3-3'. The radius of search space $r(k)$ is set to the ratio of the whole search space, and decreases as the level goes deeper such that $\{1/10, 1/10, 1/15, 1/15\}$.

In the following, we comprehensively evaluated PARN through comparisons to state-of-the-art dense semantic correspondences, including SIFT Flow [24], DSP [3], and OHG [22]. Furthermore, geometric-invariant methods including PF [30], SCNet [31], CNNGM [12], DCTM [10]. The performance was measured on Taniai benchmark [19], PF-PASCAL dataset [20], and Caltech-101 [21].

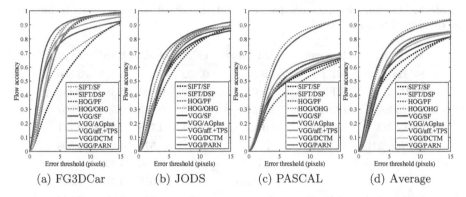

| (a) FG3DCar | (b) JODS | (c) PASCAL | (d) Average |

Fig. 7. Average matching accuracy with respect to endpoint error threshold on the Taniai benchmark [19]: (from left to right) FG3DCar, JODS, PASCAL, and average.

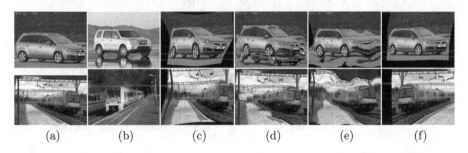

(a)   (b)   (c)   (d)   (e)   (f)

Fig. 8. Qualitative results on the Taniai benchmark [19]: (a) source image, (b) target image, (c) CNNGM-Aff.TPS [12], (d) SCNet-AG+ [31], (e) DCTM [10], (f) PARN. The source images were warped to the target images using correspondences.

4.2   Training Details

For training, we used the PF-PASCAL dataset [20] that consists of 1,351 image pairs selected from PASCAL-berkely keypoint annotations of 20 object classes. We did not use the ground-truth keypoints at all to learn the network, but we utilized the masks for the accuracy of generated supervisions. We used 800 pairs as a training data, and further divide the rest of PF-PASCAL data into 200 validation pairs and 350 testing pairs. Additionally, we synthetically augment the training pair 10 times by applying randomly generated geometric transformations including horizontal flipping [12]. To generate the most accurate supervisions in the first level, we additionally apply M-estimator SAmple and Consensus (MSAC) [46] to build the initial supervisions $\mathbf{T}^0$ and restrict the search space with the estimated transformation. We sequentially trained the regression modules for 120k iterations each with a batch size of 16 and further finetune all the regression networks in an end-to-end manner [14]. The more details of experimental settings and training are provided in the supplemental material.

Table 1. Matching accuracy compared to state-of-the-art correspondence techniques on the Taniai benchmark [19].

Methods	Descriptor	Matching	FG3D.	JODS	PASC.	Avg.
SF [2]	SIFT	SF	0.632	0.509	0.360	0.500
DSP [3]	SIFT	DSP	0.487	0.465	0.382	0.445
PF [30]	HOG	LOM	0.786	0.653	0.531	0.657
OHG [22]	HOG	OHG	0.875	0.708	**0.729**	0.771
SCNet [31]	VGG-16	A	0.774	0.574	0.476	0.608
		AG	0.764	0.600	0.463	0.609
		AGplus	0.776	0.608	0.474	0.619
CNNGM [12]	VGG-16	Aff.	0.771	0.662	0.501	0.644
		Aff.+TPS	0.835	0.656	0.527	0.672
DCTM [10]	VGG-16	DCTM	0.790	0.611	0.528	0.630
	Affine-FCSS		0.891	0.721	0.610	0.740
Baseline	VGG-16	SF	0.756	0.490	0.360	0.535
		PARN-Lv1	0.783	0.668	0.641	0.697
		PARN-Lv2	0.837	0.689	0.656	0.739
		PARN-Lv3	0.869	0.707	0.681	0.752
Proposed	VGG-16	PARN	0.876	0.716	0.688	0.760
	ResNet-101		**0.895**	**0.759**	0.712	**0.788**

4.3 Ablation Study

To validate the components within PARN, we additionally evaluated it at each level such as 'PARN-Lv1', 'PARN-Lv2', and 'PARN-Lv3' as shown in Fig. 6 and Table 1. For quantitative evaluations, we used the matching accuracy on the Taniai benchmark [19], which is described in details in the following section. As expected, even though the global transformation was estimated roughly well in the coarest level (i.e. level 1), the fine-grained matching details cannot be achieved reliably, thus showing the limited performance. However, as the levels go deeper, the localization ability has been improved while maintaining globally estimated transformations.

The performance of the backbone network was also evaluated with a standard SIFT flow optimization [2]. Note that the evaluation of the pixel-level module only in our networks is impracticable, since it requires a pixel-level supervision that does not exist in the current public datasets for semantic correspondence.

4.4 Results

See the supplemental material for more qualitative results.

(a)   (b)   (c)   (d)   (e)   (f)

Fig. 9. Qualitative results on the PF-PASCAL benchmark [20]: (a) source image, (b) target image, (c) CNNGM-Aff.+TPS [12], (d) SCNet-AG+ [31], (e) DCTM [10], (f) PARN. The source images were warped to the target images using correspondences.

Taniai Benchmark. We evaluated PARN compared to other state-of-the-art methods on the Taniai benchmark [19], which consists of 400 image pairs divided into three groups: FG3DCar, JODS, and PASCAL. Flow accuracy was measured by computing the proportion of foreground pixels with an absolute flow endpoint error that is smaller than a certain threshold T, after resizing images so that its larger dimension is 100 pixels. Figure 7 shows the flow accuracy with varying error threshold T. Our method outperforms especially when the error thershold is small. This clearly demonstrates the advantage of our hierarchical model in terms of both localization precision and appearance invariance.

Table 1 summarizes the matching accuracy for various dense semantic correspondence techniques at the fixed threshold ($T = 5$ pixels). The quantitative results of 'PARN-Lv1' and 'CNNGM-Aff' in Table 1 verify the benefits of our weakly supervised training scheme. Whereas 'CNNGM-Aff.' is also trained in weakly supervised manner, it relys only on the synthetically deformed image pairs while our method employs semantically sensitive supervisions. Note that we implemented our regression module at level 1 in the same architecture of 'CNNGM-Aff.'. From the qualitative results of Fig. 8, while DCTM is trapped in local minima unless an appropriate initial solution is given, our method progressively predicts locally-varying affine transformation fields and able to handle relatively large semantic variations including flip variations without handcrafted parameter tuning. The superiority of PARN can be seen by comparing to the correspondence techniques with the same 'VGG-16' descriptor in Table 1 and Fig. 7 and even outperforms the supervised learning based method of [31]. We also evaluated with ResNet-101 [38] as a backbone network to demonstrate the performance boosting of our method with more powerful features, where our method achieves the best performance on average.

PF-PASCAL Benchmark. We also evaluated PARN on the testing set of PF-PASCAL benchmark [30]. For the evaluation metric, we used the probability of

Table 2. Matching accuracy compared to state-of-the-art correspondence techniques on the PF-PASCAL benchmark [30] and Caltech-101 dataset [21].

Dataset	PF-PASCAL			Caltech-101		
Methods	PCK			LT-ACC	IoU	LOC-ERR
	$\alpha = 0.05$	$\alpha = 0.1$	$\alpha = 0.15$			
SF [2]	0.192	0.334	0.492	0.75	0.48	0.32
DSP [3]	0.198	0.372	0.414	0.77	0.47	0.35
PF [30]	0.235	0.453	0.621	0.78	0.50	0.25
OHG [22]	-	-	-	0.81	0.55	0.19
SCNet [31]	0.260	0.482	0.658	0.79	0.51	0.25
CNNGM [12]	0.254	0.461	0.641	0.80	0.56	0.25
DCTM [10]	0.257	0.477	0.648	0.84	0.53	**0.18**
PARN	**0.268**	**0.491**	**0.662**	**0.87**	**0.65**	0.21

correct keypoint (PCK) between flow-warped keypoints and the ground-truth. The warped keypoints are deemed to be correctly predicted if they lie within $\alpha \cdot \max(h, w)$ pixels of the ground-truth keypoints for $\alpha \in [0, 1]$, where h and w are the height and width of the object bounding box, respectively. Figure 9 shows qualitative results for dense flow estimation.

Without ground-truth annotations, our PARN has shown the outperforming performance compared to other methods in Table 2 where [31] is trained in fully supervised manner. The relatively modest gain may come from the limited evaluation only on the sparsely annotated keypoints of PF-PASCAL benchmark. However, the qualitative results of our method in Fig. 9 indicates that the performance can be significantly boosted when dense annotations are given for evaluation. Although [31] estimates the sparse correspondences in a geometrically plausible model, they compute the final dense semantic flow by linearly interpolating them which may not consider the semantic structures of target image. By contrast, our method leverages a pyramidal model where the smoothness constraint is naturally imposed among semantic scales within deep networks (Fig. 10).

Caltech-101 Dataset. Our evaluations also include the Caltech-101 dataset [21]. Following the experimental protocol in [21], we randomly selected 15 pairs of images for each object class, and evaluated matching accuracy with three metrics: label transfer accuracy (LT-ACC), the IoU metric, and the localization error (LOC-ERR) of corresponding pixel positions. Note that compared to other benchmarks described above, the Caltech-101 dataset provides image pairs from more diverse classes, enabling us to evaluate our method under more general correspondence settings. For the results, our PARN clearly outperforms the semantic correspondence techniques in terms of LT-ACC and IoU metrics. Table 2 summarizes the matching accuracy compared to state-of-the-art methods.

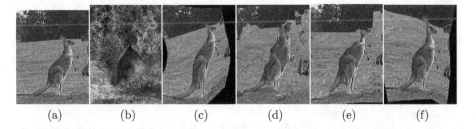

(a)   (b)   (c)   (d)   (e)   (f)

Fig. 10. Qualitative result on the Caltech-101 benchmark [21]: (a) source image, (b) target image, (c) CNNGM-Aff.+TPS [12], (d) SCNet-AG+ [31], (e) DCTM [10], (f) PARN. The source image was warped to the target images using correspondences.

5 Conclusion

We presented a novel CNN architecture, called PARN, which estimates locally-varying affine transformation fields across semantically similar images. Our method defined on pyramidal model first estimates a global affine transformation over an entire image and then progressively increases the transformation flexibility. In contrast to previous CNN based methods for geometric field estimations, our method yields locally-varying affine transformation fields that lie in the continuous solution space. Moreover, our network was trained in a weakly-supervised manner, using correspondence consistency within object bounding boxes in the training image pairs. We believe PARN can potentially benefit instance-level object detection and segmentation, thanks to its robustness to severe geometric variations.

Acknowledgement. This research was supported by Next-Generation Information Computing Development Program through the National Research Foundation of Korea(NRF) funded by the Ministry of Science, ICT (NRF-2017M3C4A7069370).

References

1. HaCohen, Y., Shechtman, E., Goldman, D.B., Lischinski, D.: Non-rigid dense correspondence with applications for image enhancement. ACM Trans. Graph. (TOG) **30**(4), 70 (2011)
2. Liu, C., Yuen, J., Torralba, A.: Sift flow: dense correspondence across scenes and its applications. IEEE Trans. PAMI **33**(5), 815–830 (2011)
3. Kim, J., Liu, C., Sha, F., Grauman, K.: Deformable spatial pyramid matching for fast dense correspondences. In: CVPR (2013)
4. Yang, H., Lin, W.Y., Lu, J.: Daisy filter flow: a generalized discrete approach to dense correspondences. In: CVPR (2014)
5. Zhou, T., Lee, Y.J., Yu, S.X., Efros, A.A.: Flowweb: joint image set alignment by weaving consistent, pixel-wise correspondences. In: CVPR (2015)
6. Scharstein, D., Szeliski, R.: A taxonomy and evaluation of dense two-frame stereo correspondence algorithms. IJCV **47**(1), 7–42 (2002)

7. Butler, D.J., Wulff, J., Stanley, G.B., Black, M.J.: A naturalistic open source movie for optical flow evaluation. In: Fitzgibbon, A., Lazebnik, S., Perona, P., Sato, Y., Schmid, C. (eds.) ECCV 2012. LNCS, vol. 7577, pp. 611–625. Springer, Heidelberg (2012). https://doi.org/10.1007/978-3-642-33783-3_44
8. Kim, S., Min, D., Ham, B., Jeon, S., Lin, S., Sohn, K.: FCSS: fully convolutional self-similarity for dense semantic correspondence. In: CVPR (2017)
9. Choy, C.B., Gwak, J., Savarese, S., Chandraker, M.: Universal correspondence network. In: NIPS (2016)
10. Kim, S., Min, D., Lin, S., Sohn, K.: DCTM: discrete-continuous transformation matching for semantic flow. In: ICCV (2017)
11. DeTone, D., Malisiewicz, T., Rabinovich, A.: Deep image homography estimation. arXiv preprint arXiv:1606.03798 (2016)
12. Rocco, I., Arandjelović, R., Sivic, J.: Convolutional neural network architecture for geometric matching. In: CVPR (2017)
13. Jaderberg, M., Simonyan, K., Zisserman, A., Kavukcuoglu, K.: Spatial transformer networks. In: NIPS (2015)
14. Lin, C.H., Lucey, S.: Inverse compositional spatial transformer networks. In: CVPR (2017)
15. Schneider, N., Piewak, F., Stiller, C., Franke, U.: RegNet: multimodal sensor registration using deep neural networks. In: IV (2017)
16. Dai, J., et al.: Deformable convolutional networks. In: ICCV (2017)
17. Hur, J., Lim, H., Park, C., Ahn, S.C.: Generalized deformable spatial pyramid: geometry-preserving dense correspondence estimation. In: CVPR (2015)
18. Tola, E., Lepetit, V., Fua, P.: Daisy: an efficient dense descriptor applied to wide-baseline stereo. IEEE Trans. PAMI **32**(5), 815–830 (2010)
19. Taniai, T., Sinha, S.N., Sato, Y.: Joint recovery of dense correspondence and cosegmentation in two images. In: CVPR (2016)
20. Ham, B., Cho, M., Schmid, C., Ponce, J.: Proposal flow: semantic correspondences from object proposals. IEEE Trans. PAMI **40**, 1711–1725 (2017)
21. Li, F.F., Fergus, R., Perona, P.: One-shot learning of object categories. IEEE Trans. PAMI **28**(4), 594–611 (2006)
22. Yang, F., Li, X., Cheng, H., Li, J., Chen, L.: Object-aware dense semantic correspondence. In: CVPR (2017)
23. Bristow, H., Valmadre, J., Lucey, S.: Dense semantic correspondence where every pixel is a classifier. In: ICCV (2015)
24. Lowe, D.: Distinctive image features from scale-invariant keypoints. IJCV **60**(2), 91–110 (2004)
25. Zhou, T., Krahenbuhl, P., Aubry, M., Huang, Q., Efros, A.A.: Learning dense correspondence via 3D-guided cycle consistency. In: CVPR (2016)
26. http://www.shapenet.org/
27. Novotny, D., Larlus, D., Vedaldi, A.: Anchornet: a weakly supervised network to learn geometry-sensitive features for semantic matching. In: CVPR (2017)
28. Hassner, T., Mayzels, V., Zelnik-Manor, L.: On sifts and their scales. In: CVPR (2012)
29. Qiu, W., Wang, X., Bai, X., Yuille, A., Tu, Z.: Scale-space sift flow. In: WACV (2014)
30. Ham, B., Cho, M., Schmid, C., Ponce, J.: Proposal flow. In: CVPR (2016)
31. Han, K., et al.: SCNet: learning semantic correspondence. In: ICCV (2017)
32. Li, Y., Min, D., Brown, M.S., Do, M.N., Lu, J.: SPM-BP: Sped-up patchmatch belief propagation for continuous MRFs. In: ICCV (2015)

33. Hosni, A., Rhemann, C., Bleyer, M., Rother, C., Gelautz, M.: Fast cost-volume filtering for visual correspondence and beyond. IEEE Trans. PAMI **35**(2), 504–511 (2013)

34. Lu, J., Yang, H., Min, D., Do, M.N.: Patchmatch filter: efficient edge-aware filtering meets randomized search for fast correspondence field estimation. In: CVPR (2013)

35. Revaud, J., Weinzaepfel, P., Harchaoui, Z., Schmid, C.: Deepmatcing: Hierarchical deformable dense matching. IJCV **120**, 300–323 (2015)

36. Ranjan, A., Black, M.J.: Optical flow estimation using a spatial pyramid network. In: CVPR (2017)

37. Krizhevsky, A., Sutskever, I., Hinton, G.E.: Imagenet classification with deep convolutional neural networks. In: NIPS (2012)

38. He, K., Zhang, X., Ren, S., Sun, J.: Deep residual learning for image recognition. In: CVPR (2016)

39. Fischler, M.A., Bolles, R.C.: Random sample consensus: a paradigm for model fitting with applications to image analysis and automated cartography. Commun. ACM **24**(6), 381–395 (1981)

40. Godard, C., Mac Aodha, O., Brostow, G.J.: Unsupervised monocular depth estimation with left-right consistency. In: CVPR (2017)

41. Fischer, P., et al.: FlowNet: learning optical flow with convolutional networks. In: ICCV (2015)

42. Noh, H., Hong, S., Han, B.: Learning deconvolution network for semantic segmentation. In: ICCV (2015)

43. Everingham, M., Van Gool, L., Williams, C.K.I., Winn, J., Zisseman, A.: The pascal visual object classes (VOC) challenge. IJCV **88**(2), 303–338 (2010)

44. Chen, X., Mottaghi, R., Liu, X., Fidler, S., Urtasum, R., Yuille, A.: Detect what you can: detecting and representing objects using holistic models and body parts. In: CVPR (2014)

45. Simonyan, K., Zisserman, A.: Very deep convolutional networks for large-scale image recognition. In: ICLR (2015)

46. Torr, P.H., Zisserman, A.: MLESAC: a new robust estimator with application to estimating image geometry. Comput. Vis. Image Underst. **78**(1), 138–156 (2000)

Start, Follow, Read: End-to-End Full-Page Handwriting Recognition

Curtis Wigington[1,2]($\boxtimes$), Chris Tensmeyer[1,2], Brian Davis[1], William Barrett[1],
Brian Price[2], and Scott Cohen[2]

[1] Brigham Young University, Provo, USA
[2] Adobe Research, San Jose, USA
wigingto@adobe.com
https://github.com/cwig/start_follow_read

Abstract. Despite decades of research, offline handwriting recognition (HWR) of degraded historical documents remains a challenging problem, which if solved could greatly improve the searchability of online cultural heritage archives. HWR models are often limited by the accuracy of the preceding steps of text detection and segmentation. Motivated by this, we present a deep learning model that jointly learns text detection, segmentation, and recognition using mostly images without detection or segmentation annotations. Our Start, Follow, Read (SFR) model is composed of a Region Proposal Network to find the start position of text lines, a novel line follower network that incrementally follows and preprocesses lines of (perhaps curved) text into dewarped images suitable for recognition by a CNN-LSTM network. SFR exceeds the performance of the winner of the ICDAR2017 handwriting recognition competition, even when not using the provided competition region annotations.

Keywords: Handwriting recognition · Document analysis
Historical document processing · Text detection
Text line segmentation

1 Introduction

In offline handwriting recognition (HWR), images of handwritten documents are converted into digital text. Though recognition accuracy on modern printed documents has reached acceptable performance for some languages [28], HWR for degraded historical documents remains a challenging problem due to large variations in handwriting appearance and various noise factors. Achieving accurate HWR in this domain would help promote and preserve cultural heritage by improving efforts to create publicly available transcriptions of historical documents. Such efforts are being performed by many national archives and other

Electronic supplementary material The online version of this chapter (https://doi.org/10.1007/978-3-030-01231-1_23) contains supplementary material, which is available to authorized users.

V. Ferrari et al. (Eds.): ECCV 2018, LNCS 11210, pp. 372–388, 2018.
https://doi.org/10.1007/978-3-030-01231-1_23

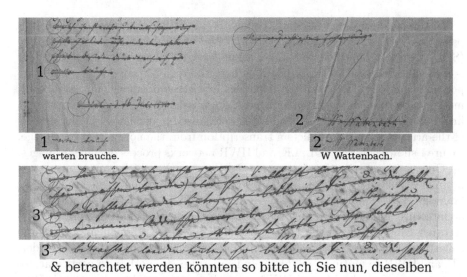

Fig. 1. Start, Follow, Read on two document snippets. Red circles and arrows show the Start-of-Line finder network's detected position, scale, and direction. Blue lines show the path taken by the Line Follower network to produce normalized text lines; three lines are shown with the HWR network's transcription. (Color figure online)

organizations around the world, but typically use manual transcriptions, which are costly and time-consuming to produce. While this work focuses discussion on one of the most difficult HWR domains, i.e. historical documents [9], our proposed methods are equally applicable to other HWR domains.

For most HWR models, text lines must be detected and segmented from the image before recognition can occur. This is challenging for historical documents because they may contain significant amounts of noise, such as stains, tears, uneven illumination, and ink fade, seepage, and bleed-through. Errors in the detection or segmentation of text propagate to the recognition stage, and as noted in [25], the majority of errors in complete HWR systems are due to incorrect line segmentation rather than incorrect character or word recognition. Despite this, line detection and segmentation are commonly performed by separate algorithms in an independent fashion and many HWR models are designed, trained, and evaluated only in the context of ground truth line segmentations [18,29].

A few works have attempted to combine detection, segmentation, and recognition. Bluche et al. proposed a recurrent model that detects and recognizes text lines using a soft-attention mechanism [3]. However, this method is slow because the model processes the whole image twice to transcribe each text line. Furthermore, the method does not allow for preprocessing detected lines of text (e.g. normalize text height), which is shown to improve HWR performance [11]. In contrast, our proposed model efficiently detects all text lines in a single pass and uses learned preprocessing before applying the HWR model on each line independently, allowing each line to be recognized in parallel.

In this work, we present Start, Follow, Read (SFR), a novel end-to-end full-page handwriting recognition model comprised of 3 sub-models: a Start-of-Line (SOL) finder, a Line Follower (LF), a line-level HWR model. The SOL finder is a Region Proposal Network (RPN) where the regions proposed are the start positions and orientations of the text lines in a given document image. The LF model starts at each predicted SOL position, incrementally steps along the text line, following curvature, and produces a normalized text image. Finally, a state-of-the-art HWR model predicts a transcription from the normalized line image. Figure 1 shows how the SOL, LF, and HWR networks process document images.

One main contribution is our novel LF network, which can segment and normalize curved text (e.g. Fig. 1 bottom) that cannot be segmented with a bounding box. Though [19] previously used a SOL network, we propose a new architecture and a new training scheme that optimizes recognition performance. Another contribution is the joint training of the three components on a large collection of images that have transcriptions only, which allows the SOL finder, LF, and HWR to mutually adapt to, and supervise, each other. In particular, we demonstrate that the LF and HWR networks can be used to derive and refine latent targets for the SOL network; this method only requires pre-training on a small number of images (e.g. 50) with additional segmentation labels.

We demonstrate state-of-the-art performance on the ICDAR2017 HWR competition dataset [25]. This competition represents a common scenario where a collection is manually transcribed, but segmentations are not annotated. While the best previous result is 71.5 BLEU score using the provided region annotations (57.3 BLEU without), SFR achieves 73.0 BLEU with region annotations, and performs only slightly worse with a 72.3 BLEU score without regions.

2   Related Work

Though segmentation and recognition are critical components of HWR, most prior works solve these problems independently: text lines are detected, segmented, and preprocessed into rectangular image snippets before being transcribed by a recognition model. Errors in the detection, segmentation, or preprocessing steps often lead to poor recognition. In contrast, SFR jointly performs detection, segmentation, preprocessing, and recognition in an end-to-end model.

Text Line Detection/Segmentation. Often, peaks in vertical projection profiles (summing pixels along rows) are used to detect transitions from dark text to lighter inter-line space [1,13,26]. However, these methods are sensitive to images with noise and curved handwriting (e.g. the image in Fig. 1). Additionally, such methods assume that distinct text lines cannot be horizontally adjacent, an assumption that is violated in practice. The recursive XY cut algorithm also considers the horizontal projection profile to make vertical image cuts along detected white space, but requires manually tuning of threshold values [14].

Seam carving [2] based methods improve on projection profile methods because seams can follow the curves of text lines. Boiangiu et al. use a pixel information measure for computing an energy map for seam carving [5], while

Saabni and El-Sana use a signed distance transform to compute the energy [24]. The winner of the ICDAR2017 handwriting recognition competition [25] corrected the output of a seam carving method by using a Convolutional Neural Network (CNN) to predict if lines were over-segmented or under-segmented.

Tian et al. [31] use a Region Proposal Network (RPN), similar to Faster-RCNN [23], to predict bounding boxes for text in the wild detection. However, unlike Faster-RCNN, their RPN predicts many small boxes along the text line in order to follow skewed or curved lines. These boxes must be clustered in a separate step, which may result in over- or under-segmentation.

Handwriting Recognition. Some early handwriting recognition models used machine learning models such as neural networks and Support Vector Machines (SVM) to learn whole word, character and stroke classifiers using handcrafted features [17,32]. However, such methods required further segmentation of text line images into primitives such as characters or strokes, which itself was error prone. Hidden Markov Model (HMM) approaches similar to those used in speech recognition then became popular because they were able to perform alignment to refine segmentation hypotheses [20]. These approaches are often combined with a Language Model (LM) or lexicon to refine predictions to more closely resemble valid natural language [6].

The introduction of the Connectionist Temporal Classification (CTC) loss [10] allowed recurrent neural network (RNN) character classifiers to perform alignment similar to HMMs, which led to the current dominance of RNN approaches for HWR. Long-Short Term Memory (LSTM) networks combined with convolutional networks, CTC, and LM decoding represent the current state-of-the-art in HWR [11]. Additional improvements, such as Multi-Dimensional LSTMs [12], neural network LMs [34], and warp based data augmentation [33] have also been proposed. Preprocessing text lines to deslant, increase contrast, normalize text height, and remove noise is also a critical component of many HWR systems [11].

Combined Segmentation and Recognition. Moysset et al. proposed predicting SOL positions with a RPN and then applying a HWR network to axis-aligned bounding boxes beginning at the SOL [19]. However, the two models are trained independently and bounding box segmentations cannot handle curved text. Recurrently computing an attention mask for recognition has been applied at the line-level [3] and the character level [4] and though these methods are computationally expensive, they have been shown to successfully follow slanted lines on clean datasets of modern handwriting with well-separated text lines. In contrast, we demonstrate our work on a more challenging dataset of noisy historical handwritten documents.

3   Proposed Model: Start, Follow, Read

In order to jointly learn text detection, segmentation, and recognition, we propose the SFR model with three components: the Start of Line (SOL) network, the Line Follower (LF) network, and the Handwriting Recognition (HWR) network.

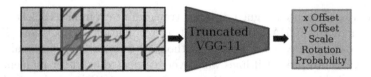

Fig. 2. The SOL network densely predicts x and y offsets, scale, rotation angle, and probability of occurrence for every 16×16 input patch. Contrary to left-right segmentation methods, this allows detection of horizontally adjacent text lines. (Color figure online)

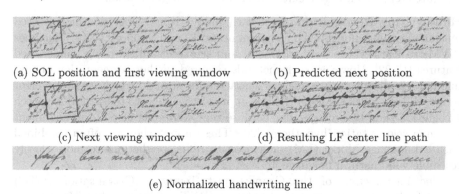

(a) SOL position and first viewing window   (b) Predicted next position

(c) Next viewing window   (d) Resulting LF center line path

(e) Normalized handwriting line

Fig. 3. The LF begins at a SOL (a) and regresses a new position indicated by the second blue dot in (b). The next input is a new viewing window (c). This process repeats until it reaches the image edge. The purple and green lines in (d) show the segmentation that produces the normalized handwriting line (e). (Color figure online)

After pre-training each network (Sect. 3.3) individually, we jointly train the models using only ground truth (GT) transcriptions (with line breaks) (Sect. 3.3).

3.1   Network Description

Start-of-Line Network. Our Start-of-Line (SOL) network is a RPN that detects the starting points of text lines. We formulate the SOL task similar to [19], but we use a truncated VGG-11 architecture [27] instead of an MDL-STM architecture to densely predict SOL positions (Fig. 2). For an image patch, we regress (x_0, y_0) coordinates, scale s_0, rotation θ_0, and probability of occurrence p_0. For image patches with a SOL (e.g. red box in Fig. 2), the network should predict $p_0 = 1$, otherwise 0. We remove the fully connected and final pooling layers of VGG-11 for a prediction stride of 16×16 and, similar to Faster R-CNN [23], predicted (x, y) coordinates are offsets relative to the patch center. The scale and rotation correspond to the size of handwriting and slant of the text line.

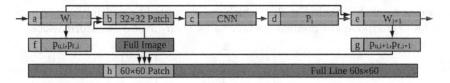

Fig. 4. Using the current transformation W_i (a), we resample a 32×32 patch (b) from the input image. A CNN regresses a transform change (d) used to compute the next transformation (e). Using the upper and lower points (f, g) of the LF path, we resample a 60×60 patch to be part of the normalized, segmented line.

Line Follower. After identifying the SOL position, our novel LF network follows the handwriting line in incremental steps and outputs a dewarped text line image suitable for HWR (see Fig. 3). Instead of segmenting text lines with a bounding box (e.g. [19]), the LF network segments polygonal regions and is capable of following and straightening arbitrarily curved text.

The LF is a recurrent network that given a current position and angle of rotation (x_i, y_i, θ_i), resamples a small viewing window (red box in Fig. 3a) that is fed to a CNN to regress $(x_{i+1}, y_{i+1}, \theta_{i+1})$ (Fig. 3b). This process is repeated until the image edge (Figs. 3c and d), and during training we use the HWR network to decide where the text line ends. The initial position and rotation is determined by a predicted SOL. The size of the viewing window is determined by the predicted SOL scale and remains fixed.

Resampling the input image to obtain the viewing window is done similarly to the Spatial Transform Network [15] using an affine transformation matrix that maps input image coordinates to viewing image coordinates (see Fig. 4). This allows LF errors to be backpropagated through viewing windows. The first viewing window matrix, $W_0 = AW_{SOL}$, is the composition of the mapping defined by a transformation SOL matrix W_{SOL} (defined by values of the SOL network prediction) and a look-ahead matrix A:

$$W_{SOL} = \begin{bmatrix} \frac{1}{s_0} & 0 & 0 \\ 0 & \frac{1}{s_0} & 0 \\ 0 & 0 & 1 \end{bmatrix} \begin{bmatrix} \cos(\theta_0) & -\sin(\theta_0) & 0 \\ \sin(\theta_0) & \cos(\theta_0) & 0 \\ 0 & 0 & 1 \end{bmatrix} \begin{bmatrix} 1 & 0 & -x_0 \\ 0 & 1 & -y_0 \\ 0 & 0 & 1 \end{bmatrix}, \quad A = \begin{bmatrix} 0.5 & 0 & -1 \\ 0 & 0.5 & 0 \\ 0 & 0 & 1 \end{bmatrix} \quad (1)$$

The look-ahead matrix gives the LF network enough context to correctly follow lines. For each step i, we extract a 32×32 viewing window patch by resampling according to W_i. When resampling, the (x, y) coordinates in the patch are normalized to the range $(-1, 1)$. Given the $(i-1)^{\text{th}}$ viewing window patch, the LF network regresses x_i, y_i and θ_i, which are used to form the prediction matrix P_i. We then compute $W_i = P_i W_{i-1}$ with

$$P_i = \begin{bmatrix} \cos(\theta_i) & -\sin(\theta_i) & 0 \\ \sin(\theta_i) & \cos(\theta_i) & 0 \\ 0 & 0 & 1 \end{bmatrix} \begin{bmatrix} 1 & 0 & -x_i \\ 0 & 1 & -y_i \\ 0 & 0 & 1 \end{bmatrix} \quad (2)$$

To obtain the output image for HWR, we first represent the normalized handwriting line path as a sequence of upper and lower coordinate pairs, $p_{u,i}$ and $p_{\ell,i}$

(green and purple lines in Fig. 3d), which are computed by multiplying the upper and lower midpoints of predicted windows by their inverse transformations:

$$p_{u,i}, p_{\ell,i} = \begin{bmatrix} x_{u,i} & x_{\ell,i} \\ y_{u,i} & y_{\ell,i} \\ 1 & 1 \end{bmatrix} = W_i^{-1} A \begin{bmatrix} 0 & 0 \\ -1 & 1 \\ 1 & 1 \end{bmatrix} \tag{3}$$

We extract the handwriting line by mapping each $p_{u,i}$, $p_{\ell,i}$, $p_{u,i+1}$, and $p_{\ell,i+1}$ to the corners of a 60×60 patch. We concatenate all such patches to form a full handwriting line of size $60s \times 60$ where s is the number of LF steps.

The architecture of the LF is a 7-layer CNN with 3×3 kernels and 64, 128, 256, 256, 512, and 512 feature maps on the 6 convolution layers. We apply Batch Normalization (BN) after layers 4 and 5 and 2×2 Max Pooling (MP) after layers 1, 2, 4, and 6. A fully connected layer is used to regress the X, Y, θ outputs with initial bias parameters for X initialized to 1 and biases for Y and θ initialized to 0. This initialization is a prior that lines are straight and read left-to-right.

Handwriting Recognition. After the LF network produces a normalized line image, it is fed to a CNN-LSTM network to produce a transcription. The CNN part of the HWR network learns high level features that are vertically collapsed to create a horizontal 1D sequence that is fed to a Bidirection LSTM model. In the BLSTM, learned context features propagate forward and backwards along the sequence before a character classifier is applied to each output time step.

The output sequence of character predictions is much longer than the GT transcriptions, but includes a blank character for use in the CTC decoding step [10]. Decoding is performed by first collapsing non-blank repeating characters and then removing the blanks, e.g. the output `--hh--e-lll-1----oo--` is decoded as `hello`. While the CTC loss does not explicitly enforce alignment between predicted characters and the input image, in practice, we are able to exploit this alignment to refine SOL predictions (see Sect. 3.3).

The architecture of our HWR network is on a CNN-LSTM HWR network [33] and is similar to our LF network. The input size is $W \times 60$, where W, can dynamically vary. There are 6 convolutional layers with 3×3 filters with 64, 128, 256, 256, 512, and 512 feature maps respectively. BN is applied after layers 4 and 5, and 2×2 MP (stride 2) is applied after layers 1, 2. To collapse features vertically we use 2×2 MP with a vertical stride of 2 and a horizontal stride of 1 after layers 4 and 6. Features are concatenated vertically to form a sequence of 1024-dimensional feature vectors that are fed to a 2-layer BLSTM with 512 hidden nodes and 0.5 probability of node dropout. A fully connected layer is applied at each time step to produce character classifications.

The HWR also serves an additional function. LF always runs to the edge of the page and in many cases intersects other columns or SOL positions. The HWR implicitly learns during training when to stop reading (similar to [19]) and as a result we do not need additional post processing to determine when the line ends.

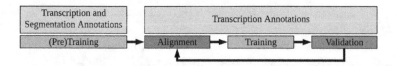

Fig. 5. Our network is first pre-trained on a small training set with segmentation and transcription annotations. The three phase training process is performed over a much larger training set that has only transcription annotations.

3.2 Post Processing

We introduce a novel non-maximal suppression method for the SOL and LF networks. Given any two LF path prediction we consider the first N steps (we used $N = 6$). We form a polygon by joining start and end points of the center lines. If the area of the resulting polygon is below a threshold proportional to its length, we suppress the line with the lowest SOL probability.

To correct recognitions errors we employ an HMM-based 10-g character-level language model (LM) that has been trained on the training set transcriptions using the Kaldi toolkit [21]. Character-level LMs typically correct out-of-vocabulary words better than word-level LMs [16].

3.3 Training

Figure 5 summarizes the full training process: (1) Networks are pretrained using a small number of images with GT SOL, segmentations, and line-level transcriptions (Sect. 3.3); (2) Alignment (Sect. 3.3) on a large number of training images with only GT transcriptions produces bootstrapped targets for the SOL and LF networks; (3) Individual networks are trained using SOL and LF targets from alignment and GT transcriptions for the HWR network; (4) Validation is performed over the entire validation set using the best individual weights of each network. Steps 2–4 are repeated until convergence.

Start-of-Line Network. We create the training set for our SOL network by resizing images to be 512 pixels wide and sampling 256×256 patches, with half the patches containing SOLs. Patches are allowed to extend outside the image by padding with each edge's average color. We use the loss function proposed for the multibox object detection model [8], which performs an alignment between the highest probability predicted SOL positions and the target positions.

$$L(l, p; t) = \sum_{n=0}^{N} \sum_{m=0}^{M} X_{nm}(\alpha \| l_n - t_m \|_2^2 - log(p_n)) - (1 - X_{nm})log(1 - p_n) \quad (4)$$

where t_m is a target position, p_n is the probability of SOL occurrence, and l_n is a transformation of the directly predicted $(x_n, y_n, s_n, \theta_n)$:

$$l_n = (-\sin(\theta_n)s_n + x_n, -\cos(\theta_n)s_n + y_n, \sin(\theta_n)s_n + x_n, \cos(\theta_n)s_n + y_n), \quad (5)$$

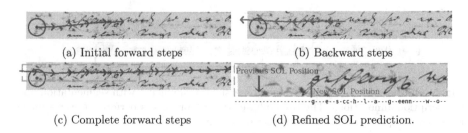

(a) Initial forward steps   (b) Backward steps

(c) Complete forward steps   (d) Refined SOL prediction.

Fig. 6. SOL refinement process. In (b), the LF does not backtrack to the initial (incorrect) SOL. The LF passes through the correct SOL in (c), which is identified using the alignment (d) induced by CTC decoding in the HWR network.

X_{nm} is a binary alignment matrix between the N predictions and M target positions, while α weights the relative importance of the positional loss and the confidence loss. In our experiments, $\alpha = 0.01$ and we compute the X_{nm} that minimizes L given (l, p, t) using bipartite graph matching as in [8].

Line Follower. While the LF outputs a normalized text line image, the defining image transformation is piece-wise affine and is parameterized by a sequence of upper and lower coordinate points. Thus, for supervision we construct pairs of target coordinate points that induce the desired piece-wise affine transformation and train the LF using a Mean-Square Error (MSE) loss.

$$loss = \sum_{i=0} \|p_{u,i} - t_{u,i}\|_2^2 + \|p_{\ell,i} - t_{\ell,i}\|_2^2 \qquad (6)$$

The LF starts at the first target points, $t_{u,0}$ and $t_{\ell,0}$, and every 4th step resets to the corresponding target points. This way, if the LF deviates from the handwriting it can recover without introducing large and uninformative errors into the training procedure. To help the LF be robust to incorrect previous predictions, after resetting to a target position we randomly perturb the LF position by a translation of $\Delta x, \Delta y \in [-2, 2]$ pixels and a rotation of $\Delta\theta \in [-0.1, 0.1]$ radians.

Handwriting Recognition. We train the HWR network on line images with the aligned GT transcription using CTC loss [10]. For data augmentation, we apply Random Warp Grid Distortions (RWGD) [33] to model variations in handwriting shape, contrast augmentation [30] to learn invariance to text/background contrast, and global hue perturbation to handle different colors of paper and ink.

Pre-training. Before joint training can be effective, each network needs to achieve a reasonable level of accuracy. Individual networks are pre-trained on a small number of images that have SOL, segmentation, and line-level transcription annotations. This follows the same procedure as described in the previous three subsections, but the actual GT is used for targets.

Alignment. After the networks are pre-trained, we perform an alignment between SFR predicted line transcriptions with GT line transcriptions for images with only transcription annotations, i.e. no corresponding spatial GT information. The main purpose of this alignment is to create bootstrapped training targets for the SOL and LF networks because the images lack GT for detection and segmentation. For each GT text line, we keep track of the best predicted SOL and segmentation points, where best is defined by the accuracy of the corresponding predicted line transcription produced by the HWR network.

Alignment and training are alternated (see Fig. 5) as better alignment improves network training and vice versa. To perform the alignment, we first run the SOL finder on the whole image and obtain dense SOL predictions. On predicted SOLs with probability above a threshold, we then apply the LF and HWR networks to obtain a predicted segmentation and transcription. For each GT line, we find the predicted transcription that minimizes the Character Error Rate (CER), which is equivalent to string edit distance. If the CER is lower than the best previous prediction for that GT line, we update that line's target SOL and segmentation points to be those predicted by the SOL and LF networks.

The final step in alignment is to refine the SOL position using spatial information extracted from the LF and HWR networks. To refine a SOL target, we run the LF forward $s = 5$ steps from the current best SOL (Fig. 6a), and then backwards for $s + 1$ steps (Fig. 6b). We then move the current best SOL up or down to align with the backwards path. This works because even if the LF does not start on the text line, it quickly finds the text line in the forward steps and then can follow it back to its start using backwards steps. Next, we run the LF and HWR from this new SOL and find the first non-blank predicted character before CTC decoding (Fig. 6d). We then shift the SOL left and right to align with the image location of this character.

To find the end of the handwriting line, we find the last non-blank character during CTC decoding. Once we have identified line ends, we no longer run the LF past the end of lines, which helps speed training.

End-to-End Training. Though our SFR model is end-to-end differentiable in that the CTC loss can backpropagate through the HWR and LF networks to the SOL network, in practice we observed no increase in performance when using end-to-end training on the dataset used in this work. End-to-end training is much slower, and the three networks take significantly different amounts of time to train, with the HWR network taking the most time by far. We have concluded that the majority of errors made by our SFR model are not likely to be fixed by end-to-end error backpropagation because (1) the transcription CTC loss cannot fix very bad segmentations and (2) our joint training provides adequate supervision when predicted SOL and segmentations are reasonably good.

4   Results

We evaluate our SFR model on the 2017 ICDAR HWR full page competition dataset [25] of 1800s German handwriting, which has two training sets. The

Table 1. ICDAR 2017 HWR Competition results [25] compared to our method.

Method	BLEU with ROIs	BLEU without ROIs
Start, Follow, Read (ours)	**73.0**	**72.3**
BYU	71.5	57.3
ParisTech	48.3	–
LITIS	37.2	–

Table 2. Line-level dataset results. *indicates non-standard train/test split.

Method	Page-level	RIMES		IAM	
		CER	WER	CER	WER
Start, Follow, Read (ours)	X	**2.1**	**9.3**	6.4	23.2
Bluche [3]	X	2.9	12.6	7.9	24.6
Puigcerver [34]		2.3	9.6	**5.8***	**18.4***

first set has 50 fully annotated images with line-level segmentations and transcriptions. The second set of 10,000 images has only transcriptions (containing line breaks). This dataset, to our knowledge, is the largest and most challenging public HWR benchmark with 206,161 handwriting lines and 1,769,195 words. The test data is not public, so we use the BLEU score metric reported by the public evaluation server[1]. The competition test data provides multiple regions of interest (ROIs) per image to facilitate text line segmentation, and the evaluation server protocol requires that all predicted text lines be assigned to a ROI. We also evaluate on the IAM and Rimes line-level datasets.

4.1 Quantitative Results

The fully annotated 50 images are used to pre-train the network (see Fig. 5). We then jointly train on 9,000 images (1,000 for validation) by alternating alignment, training, and validation steps. We then submitted two sets of predictions to the evaluation server: one set exploiting the ROI information and one set without. To exploit ROI information, we mask out all other parts of the image using the median image color before running SFR.

Though we also evaluate without ROIs, the evaluation server still requires each line to be assigned to a ROI. After running SFR on full pages (no masking), we simply assign each line prediction to the region in which it has the most overlap. Predictions mostly outside any ROI are discarded, though sometimes these are real unannotated text lines that are completely outside the given ROIs.

---

[1] https://scriptnet.iit.demokritos.gr/competitions/~icdar2017htr/.

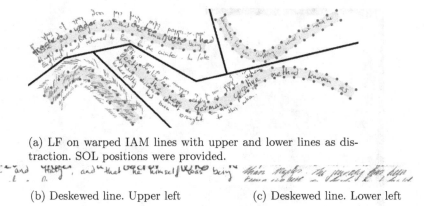

(a) LF on warped IAM lines with upper and lower lines as distraction. SOL positions were provided.

(b) Deskewed line. Upper left   (c) Deskewed line. Lower left

Fig. 7. Results from warped IAM dataset.

The competition systems made predictions over each ROI by first cropping to the ROI bounding box [25]. The BYU system was evaluated without ROIs using the same process as SFR except lines are only discarded if they intersect no ROI. This difference was necessary because their segmentations span the entire image and too many good text lines would have been discarded.

Table 1 compares SFR with the competition results. Our SFR model achieves the highest BLEU score at 73.0 using ROI annotations, but performance only degrades slightly to 72.3 without ROIs. This shows that the SOL and LF networks perform well and do not benefit much from a priori knowledge of text line location. In contrast, the winning competition system scores 71.5 using the ROIs, but its performance drops significantly to 57.3 without the ROIs.

Table 2 shows results for the IAM (English) and RIMES (French) line-level datasets. Like [3], we evaluated our page-level method on line-level datasets where we do not use the provided line segmentation annotations during training or evaluation, except for 10 pretraining images. We achieved state-of-the-art results on RIMES, outperforming [22] which uses the segmentation annotations for training and evaluation. On IAM, we outperformed the best previously proposed page-level model [3], and we note that [22] used a non-standard data split, so their results are not directly comparable. Results shown in Table 2 are without LM decoding, so that the raw recognition models can be fairly compared.

4.2   Qualitative Results

We produced a synthetic dataset to test the robustness of the LF on very curved lines. To generate the data we randomly warped real handwriting lines from the IAM dataset [18] and added distracting lines above and below. We provided the SOL position and did not employ the HWR. Figure 7 shows results from the

(a) Document written in the 1400s from the 2016 ICFHR HWR competition [29]

(b) English document from the ICDAR competition on baseline detection[7]

Fig. 8. Images from other collections applied to our trained model

validation set. Even when text lines are somewhat overlapping (Fig. 7b), the LF is able to stay on the correct line. Though the synthetic warping is exaggerated, this suggests the LF can learn to follow less extreme real-world curvature.

Figure 9 shows some results on our ICDAR2017 HWR dataset validation set. On clean images, SFR often produces a perfect transcription (Fig. 9a), and only minor errors on noisy handwriting (Fig. 9b). The LF performs well on complicated layouts, such as horizontally adjacent lines (Fig. 9c). However, some noisy lines cause the LF to jump between lines. (Fig. 9d).

We also applied the trained SFR model to other image datasets and found that the SOL and LF networks generalize even to documents in different languages. Figure 8a shows that SFR correctly segments a document written in Early Modern German and we see similar results on a English document (Fig. 8b). Of course, the HWR network would need to be retrained to handle other languages, though due to the modularity of SFR, the HWR network can be retrained while preserving the previous SOL and LF networks. Additional images can be viewed in the supplementary material.

dispositions que vous avez données à fin
que nos Ingenieurs pouissent avoir les
pièces necessaires pour accomplir leur

(a) No errors

eindringlichsten Zureden für jezige angesprochene
Hülfe, auch deutlich auf die Verpflichtung dessin's
hinzuweisen, die der Gotthardkomite schuldig.
Anerkennung für die so volle Aufnahme & Wohl

(b) Noisy lines, few transcription errors

die Versicherung meiner aufrichten Werthschätzung, mit der ich
die Ehre habe ich setze,
                Huerrn Wohlgebornen
                      gehorsamster Sinner
Luzern den 1 Juny 1857.   J. K. Truttmann, in oben
                      Grund No 471.

(c) Complex layout, few transcription errors

der mehrerwähnten Stelle Ihres Buches zu Haun-
de liegen, zukommen lassen zu wollen &
Wenn ich Sie im fernern ersuchen muß, die-
ser gefälligst mit möglichster Beförderung

(d) Noisy lines, LF error. HWR stopped reading after the error.

Fig. 9. Results from the ICDAR 2017 competition dataset. Colored lines represent different detected lines. Green, red, and purple characters represent insertion, substitution, and omission errors respectively. (Color figure online)

5   Conclusion

We have introduced a novel Start, Follow, Read model for full-page HWR and demonstrated state-of-the-art performance on a challenging dataset of historical handwriting, even when not exploiting given ROI information. We improved upon a previous SOL method and introduced a novel LF network that learns to segment and normalize handwriting lines for input to a HWR network. After initial pre-training, our novel training framework is able to jointly train the networks on documents using only line-level transcriptions. This is significant because when human annotators transcribe documents, they often do not annotate any segmentation or spatial information.

We believe that further improvements can be made by predicting the end-of-line (EOL), in addition of SOL, and applying the LF backwards. Then, the SOL and EOL results can mutually constrain each other and lead to improved segmentation. Also, we did not extensively explore network architectures, so performance could increase with improved architectures such as Residual Networks.

References

1. Antonacopoulos, A., Karatzas, D.: Document image analysis for World War II personal records. In: Workshop on Document Image Analysis for Libraries, pp. 336–341. IEEE (2004)
2. Avidan, S., Shamir, A.: Seam carving for content-aware image resizing. In: ACM SIGGRAPH 2007 Papers, SIGGRAPH 2007. ACM (2007). https://doi.org/10.1145/1275808.1276390
3. Bluche, T.: Joint line segmentation and transcription for end-to-end handwritten paragraph recognition. In: Advances in Neural Information Processing Systems (NIPS), pp. 838–846 (2016)
4. Bluche, T., Louradour, J., Messina, R.: Scan, attend and read: end-to-end handwritten paragraph recognition with MDLSTM attention, April 2016
5. Boiangiu, C.A., Tanase, M., Ioanitescu, R.: Handwritten documents text line segmentation based on information energy. Int. J. Comput. Commun. Control. (IJCCC) **9**, 8–15 (2014)
6. Bunke, H., Bengio, S., Vinciarelli, A.: Offline recognition of unconstrained handwritten texts using HMMs and statistical language models. IEEE Trans. Pattern Anal. Mach. Intell. (TPAMI) **26**(6), 709–720 (2004)
7. Diem, M., Kleber, F., Fiel, S., Grüning, T., Gatos, B.: cBAD: ICDAR2017 competition on baseline detection. In: 14th International Conference on Document Analysis and Recognition (ICDAR), pp. 1355–1360. IEEE (2017)
8. Erhan, D., Szegedy, C., Toshev, A., Anguelov, D.: Scalable object detection using deep neural networks. CoRR abs/1312.2249 (2013). http://arxiv.org/abs/1312.2249
9. Frinken, V., Fischer, A., Martínez-Hinarejos, C.D.: Handwriting recognition in historical documents using very large vocabularies. In: 2nd International Workshop on Historical Document Imaging and Processing (HIP), pp. 67–72. ACM (2013)
10. Graves, A., Fernández, S., Gomez, F., Schmidhuber, J.: Connectionist temporal classification: labelling unsegmented sequence data with recurrent neural networks. In: 23rd International Conference on Machine Learning, pp. 369–376. ACM (2006)

11. Graves, A., Liwicki, M., Fernández, S., Bertolami, R., Bunke, H., Schmidhuber, J.: A novel connectionist system for unconstrained handwriting recognition. IEEE Trans. Pattern Anal. Mach. Intell. (TPAMI) **31**(5), 855–868 (2009)
12. Graves, A., Schmidhuber, J.: Offline handwriting recognition with multidimensional recurrent neural networks. In: Advances in Neural Information Processing Systems (NIPS), pp. 545–552 (2009)
13. Ha, J., Haralick, R.M., Phillips, I.T.: Document page decomposition by the bounding-box project. In: 3rd International Conference on Document Analysis and Recognition (ICDAR), vol. 2, pp. 1119–1122. IEEE (1995). https://doi.org/10.1109/ICDAR.1995.602115
14. He, J., Downton, A.C.: User-assisted archive document image analysis for digital library construction. In: International Conference on Document Analysis and Recognition, pp. 498–502. IEEE (2003)
15. Jaderberg, M., Simonyan, K., Zisserman, A., Kavukcuoglu, K.: Spatial transformer networks. In: Advances in Neural Information Processing Systems (NIPS), pp. 2017–2025 (2015)
16. Kozielski, M., Rybach, D., Hahn, S., Schlüter, R., Ney, H.: Open vocabulary handwriting recognition using combined word-level and character-level language models. In: 2013 IEEE International Conference on Acoustics, Speech and Signal Processing, pp. 8257–8261, May 2013. https://doi.org/10.1109/ICASSP.2013.6639275
17. Lorigo, L.M., Govindaraju, V.: Offline arabic handwriting recognition: a survey. IEEE Trans. Pattern Anal. Mach. Intell. (TPAMI) **28**(5), 712–724 (2006)
18. Marti, U.V., Bunke, H.: The IAM-database: an English sentence database for offline handwriting recognition. Int. J. Doc. Anal. Recognit. **5**(1), 39–46 (2002)
19. Moysset, B., Kermorvant, C., Wolf, C.: Full-page text recognition: learning where to start and when to stop. In: 14th International Conference on Document Analysis and Recognition (ICDAR), pp. 871–876. IEEE (2017). https://doi.org/10.1109/ICDAR.2017.147
20. Plötz, T., Fink, G.A.: Markov models for offline handwriting recognition: a survey. Int. J. Doc. Anal. Recognit. (IJDAR) **12**(4), 269 (2009)
21. Povey, D., et al.: The Kaldi speech recognition toolkit. In: IEEE 2011 Workshop on Automatic Speech Recognition and Understanding. IEEE Signal Processing Society, December 2011. IEEE Catalog No. CFP11SRW-USB
22. Puigcerver, J.: Are multidimensional recurrent layers really necessary for handwritten text recognition? In: 14th International Conference on Document Analysis and Recognition (ICDAR), pp. 67–72. IEEE, November 2017. https://doi.org/10.1109/ICDAR.2017.20
23. Ren, S., He, K., Girshick, R., Sun, J.: Faster R-CNN: towards real-time object detection with region proposal networks. IEEE Trans. Pattern Anal. Mach. Intell. **39**(6), 1137–1149 (2017)
24. Saabni, R., El-Sana, J.: Language-independent text lines extraction using seam carving. In: 11th International Conference on Document Analysis and Recognition (ICDAR), pp. 563–568. IEEE (2011)
25. Sanchez, J.A., Romero, V., Toselli, A.H., Villegas, M., Vidal, E.: ICDAR2017 competition on handwritten text recognition on the READ dataset. In: 14th International Conference on Document Analysis and Recognition (ICDAR), pp. 1383–1388. IEEE, November 2017. http://doi.ieeecomputersociety.org/10.1109/ICDAR.2017.226
26. Shapiro, V., Gluhchev, G., Sgurev, V.: Handwritten document image segmentation and analysis. Pattern Recognit. Lett. **14**(1), 71–78 (1993)

27. Simonyan, K., Zisserman, A.: Very deep convolutional networks for large-scale image recognition. CoRR abs/1409.1556 (2014). http://arxiv.org/abs/1409.1556
28. Smith, R.: Tutorial: tesseract blends old and new OCR technology (2016)
29. Sanchez, J.A., Romero, V., Toselli, A.H., Vidal, E.: ICFHR2016 competition on handwritten text recognition on the READ dataset. In: 15th International Conference on Frontiers in Handwriting Recognition (ICFHR), pp. 630–635. IEEE, October 2016. https://doi.org/10.1109/ICFHR.2016.0120
30. Tensmeyer, C., Saunders, D., Martinez, T.: Convolutional neural networks for font classification. In: 14th International Conference on Document Analysis and Recognition (ICDAR), pp. 985–990. IEEE, November 2018. http://doi.ieeecomputersociety.org/10.1109/ICDAR.2017.164
31. Tian, Z., Huang, W., He, T., He, P., Qiao, Y.: Detecting text in natural image with connectionist text proposal network. CoRR abs/1609.03605 (2016). http://arxiv.org/abs/1609.03605
32. Vinciarelli, A.: A survey on off-line cursive word recognition. Pattern Recognit. 35(7), 1433–1446 (2002)
33. Wigington, C., Stewart, S., Davis, B., Barrett, W., Price, B., Cohen, S.: Data augmentation for recognition of handwritten words and lines using a CNN-LSTM network. In: 14th International Conference on Document Analysis and Recognition (ICDAR), pp. 639–645 (2017)
34. Zamora-Martinez, F., Frinken, V., España-Boquera, S., Castro-Bleda, M.J., Fischer, A., Bunke, H.: Neural network language models for off-line handwriting recognition. Pattern Recognit. 47(4), 1642–1652 (2014)

PM-GANs: Discriminative Representation Learning for Action Recognition Using Partial-Modalities

Lan Wang[1,2] , Chenqiang Gao[1,2]([✉]), Luyu Yang[3], Yue Zhao[1,2],
Wangmeng Zuo[4], and Deyu Meng[5]

[1] School of Communication and Information Engineering,
Chongqing University of Posts and Telecommunications, Chongqing 400065, China
gaocq@cqupt.edu.cn
[2] Chongqing Key Laboratory of Signal and Information Processing,
Chongqing 400065, China
[3] University of Maryland College Park, College Park, MD 20742, USA
[4] Harbin Institute of Technology, Harbin 150001, China
[5] Xi'an Jiaotong University, Xi'an 710049, China

Abstract. Data of different modalities generally convey complimentary but heterogeneous information, and a more discriminative representation is often preferred by combining multiple data modalities like the RGB and infrared features. However in reality, obtaining both data channels is challenging due to many limitations. For example, the RGB surveillance cameras are often restricted from private spaces, which is in conflict with the need of abnormal activity detection for personal security. As a result, using partial data channels to build a full representation of multi-modalities is clearly desired. In this paper, we propose a novel Partial-modal Generative Adversarial Networks (PM-GANs) that learns a full-modal representation using data from only partial modalities. The full representation is achieved by a generated representation in place of the missing data channel. Extensive experiments are conducted to verify the performance of our proposed method on action recognition, compared with four state-of-the-art methods. Meanwhile, a new Infrared-Visible Dataset for action recognition is introduced, and will be the first publicly available action dataset that contains paired infrared and visible spectrum. (The dataset will be available at http://www.escience.cn/people/gaochenqiang/Publications.html).

Keywords: Cross-modal representation
Generative adversarial networks · Infrared action recognition
Infrared dataset

1 Introduction

Human action recognition [11,31,48,51,55,59] aims to recognize the ongoing action from a video clip. As one of the most important tasks in computer vision,

© Springer Nature Switzerland AG 2018
V. Ferrari et al. (Eds.): ECCV 2018, LNCS 11210, pp. 389–406, 2018.
https://doi.org/10.1007/978-3-030-01231-1_24

action recognition plays a significant role in many useful applications like video surveillance [24,49], human-computer interaction [32,43] and content retrieval [2, 60], with great potentials in artificial intelligence. As a result, massive attention has been dedicated to this area which made large progress over the past decades. Most state-of-the-art methods have contributed to the tasks in visible imaging videos, and show saturated performances among the widely-used benchmark datasets including KTH [52] and UCF101 [14]. Generally speaking, the task of action recognition is quite well-addressed and has already been applied to real-world problems.

However, there are still many occasions where visible imaging is limited. First, the RGB cameras rely heavily on the light conditions, and perform poorly when light is insufficient or over-abundant. Action recognition from night-view RGB data remains a rather difficult task. Moreover, as an act to protect the fundamental human dignity–Privacy, RGB cameras are strictly restricted from most private areas including the personal residential area, public washroom where abnormal human activities are likely to threat personal security. Infrared cameras, that capture the heat radiation of objects, are excellent alternatives in these occasions [13]. The application of thermal imaging in military affairs and police surveillance has continued for years, and has more potentials beyond the government use. With many advantages over the RGB camera, it is predicted that infrared cameras will become more common in public spaces like hospitals, nursing centers for elderly and home security systems [35].

While infrared cameras can fill the limited spots of RGB cameras, many visible features are nevertheless lost in the infrared spectrum due to their similarity in temperature [58,62]. Visible features like color, texture are effective clues in activity representations. Since the two are complementary to each other, it is desired to utilize both visible and infrared features to benefit the task of action recognition. Furthermore, it will be more desired to utilize both feature domains when ONLY infrared data is available. In the previous cases when the demand of abnormal action recognition and the demand of privacy conflicted, it will be great if we can obtain both infrared and visible features, while use only the infrared data. The question is, how can one obtain visible features when the visible data is missing? The situation is not unique to the task of action recognition. In fact, data with different modalities of complementary benefits widely exists in multimedia such as systems with multiple sensors, product details with combined information of text description and images [39]. Here we are inspired by the intra-modal feature representations to make up for the missing data using adversarial learning with the available part of the data channel.

Recently, much attention has been given to cross-modal feature representations [6,10,16,23,57] dealing with unpaired data, which maps multiple feature spaces onto a common one, or generates a different representation via adversarial training. The basic model of generative adversarial networks (GANs) [8,15,41] consists of a generative model G and a discriminative model D. Many interesting image-to-image translations such as genre translation, face and pose transformation indicate the broader potentials of GANs to explore the hidden correlations in cross-modal representations [35,38]. Inspired by this, we therefore seek an algorithm that can translate from the infrared representation to the visible domain, which allows us to further exploit the benefits of both feature spaces with only part of the data modalities. More generally speaking, we aim at an architecture that learns a full representation for data of different modalities, using partial modalities. Different from the existing works of cross-modal which seeks a common representation from different data spaces, our goal is to exploit the transferable ability among different modalities, which is further utilized to construct a full-modal representation when only partial data modalities are available.

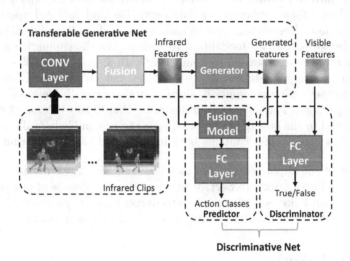

Fig. 1. The framework of the proposed Partial-modal Generative Adversarial Networks (PM-GANs). Infrared video clips are sent to the transferable generative net to produce fake feature representation of the visible spectrum. And the discriminator attempts to distinguish between the generated features and the real ones. The predictor construct a full representation using the generated features and infrared features to conduct classification

With a completely different target, in this paper we propose a novel Partial-modal Generative Adversarial Networks (PM-GANs), which aims to learn the transferable representation among data of heterogeneous modalities using cross-modal adversarial mechanism and build discriminative full-modal representation architecture using data of one/partial modalities. The main contributions are summarized as follows.

- **Partial-modal representation** is proposed to deal with missing data modalities. Specifically, the partial-modal representation aims to obtain the transferable representation among data with different modalities. And when only partial-modal representations are accessible, the model can still generate a comprehensive description, as if constructed with data of all modalities.

- **Partial-modal GANs architecture** is proposed that can exploit the complementary benefits of all data channels with heterogeneous features using only one/partial channels. The generative model learns to fit the transferable distribution that characterizes the feature representation in the specific data channels that are likely to be missing in practice. Meanwhile, the discriminative model learns to judge whether the translated distribution is representative enough for the full modalities. Extensive experiment results reveal the effectiveness of the PM-GANs architecture, which outperforms four state-of-the-art methods in the task of action recognition.
- **Partial-modal evaluation dataset** is newly introduced, which provides paired data of two different modalities–visible and infrared spectrum of human actions. Researchers can evaluate the transferable ability of the algorithms between the two modalities, as well as the discriminative ability of the generated representation by comparing with a series of baselines we provided in this paper. Meanwhile, the dataset can be used as a benchmark for bi-channel action recognition, since it is also carefully designed to serve for this purpose. The dataset contains more than 2,000 videos, 12 different actions, and to the best of our knowledge, is the first publicly available action recognition dataset that contains both infrared and visible spectrum.

The rest of the paper is organized as follows. In Sect. 2, we review the background and related works. In Sect. 3, we elaborate the details of our proposed method. Section 4 presents the newly-introduced dataset, its evaluations, and the experimental results on it. Finally, Sect. 5 draws the conclusion.

2   Related Work

Transfer Learning and Cross-Modal Representation: In the classical pattern recognition and machine learning tasks, sufficient training data that has variations in modality is clearly a desired but unrealistic goal [46,47], thus restricting the representative ability of the model. Among the studies to address this problem, transfer learning attempts to transfer the feature space from a source domain to a target domain, and to lessen the adaption conflicts via domain adaption [12,36,37,50]. The transferred knowledge type is not restricted to feature representation or instance, and it also contains modality-correlation. With different aims, cross-dataset and cross-modal feature representation fall into feature-representation transfer by adapting the representations from different domains to a single common latent space, where features of multiple modalities are jointly learned and combined. Among these algorithms, Canonical Correlation Analysis (CCA) [19,61] is a widely used one, which seeks to maximize the correlation between the projected vectors of two modalities. Another classical algorithm is Data Fusion Hashing (DFH) [3] that embeds the input data from two arbitrary spaces into a Hamming space in a supervised way. Differently, Cross-View Hashing (CVH) [27] maximizes the weighted cumulative correlation and can be viewed as the general representation of CCA.

In recent years, with the renaissance of neural networks, many deep learning based transfer learning and cross-modal representation methods have been proposed as well. Cross Modal Distillation (CMD) [16] learns representations for modalities with limited labeled data which are not able to be directly trained on deep networks. Bishifting Autoencoder Network [23] attempts to alleviate the discrepancy between the source and target datasets to the same space. To further take the feature alignment and auxiliary domain data into consideration, Aligned-to-generalized encoder (AGE) [35] is proposed to map the aligned feature representations to the same generalized feature space with low intra-class variation and high interclass variation. Since GANs have been proposed by Goodfellow *et al.* [15] in 2014, a series of GANs-based methods have arisen for a wide variety of problems. Recently, a Cross-modal Generative Adversarial Networks for Common Representation Learning (CM-GANs) [38] is proposed. CM-GANs seeks to unify the inconsistent distribution and representation of different modalities by filling the heterogeneity of knowledge types like image and text. In contrast, we have completely different goal, which aims to use only partial data modalities to obtain a full-modal representation. Our focus is beyond the jointly-learned representation of multiple feature spaces, and takes one step further to achieve a discriminative partial-modality representation, which corresponds to our original aim of handling the problem of insufficient training data and data types.

Infrared Action Recognition and Dataset: Most previous contributions [33,42] to the progress of action recognition have been made to the visible spectrum. Early approaches utilized the hand-crafted representation followed by classifiers, such as 3D Histogram of Gradient (HOG3D) [26], Histogram of Optical Flow (HOF) [29], Space Time Interest Points (STIP) [28] and Trajectories [53]. Wang et al. [54] proposed the Improved Dense Trajectories (iDT) representation, making breakthroughs among hand-crafted features. In hand-crafted representation scheme, encoding methods such as Bag of Words (BoW) [30], Fisher vector [44], VLAD [7] are applied to aggregate the descriptors into video-level representation. Benefiting from the success of Convolutional Neural Networks (CNNs) in image classification, several deep network architectures have been proposed for action recognition. Simonyan *et al.* [48] proposed a two-stream CNNs architecture which simultaneously captured appearance and motion information by spatial and temporal nets. Tran *et al.* [49] investigated 3D ConvNets [21,24] in large-scale supervised training datasets and effective deep architectures, achieving significant improvements. Wang *et al.* [56] proposed a temporal segment network to investigate long-term temporal information. Carreira *et al.* [5] designed a two-stream inflated 3D ConvNet, inflating filters and pooling kernels into 3D to learn seamless spatiotemporal feature extractors.

Recently, increasing efforts have been devoted to infrared action recognition [13]. Corresponding to the classical methods employed in visible spectrum, spatiotemporal representation for human action recognition is also used under thermal imaging scenarios [17]. The combination of both visible and thermal

imaging to improve human silhouette detection is also introduced by Han *et al.*
[18]. However, the scenario has not been studied where infrared data is available
while the RGB channel is missing. The scenario has great potential in real-world
of protecting privacy while benefiting the task of action recognition, and is meaningful to both the study of pattern recognition and the welfare of the community
at large. Therefore, we are motivated to dedicate to improving the situation by
constructing a robust and discriminative partial-modal representations, and to
specify action recognition as the case in this paper.

3 Proposed Approach

The overall pipeline of the proposed PM-GANs for action recognition is shown
in Fig. 1. Our goal is to generate a full-modal representation using only the
partial modalities. The framework learns the transferable representation among
different data channels based on conditional adversarial networks. Based on the
transferred representation, the framework builds a discriminative full-modal representation network using only part of the data channels.

3.1 Transferable Basis for Partial Modality

The transferable ability with the PM-GANs architecture is the basis for the
construction of full-modal representation with partial modality. We assume that
there exists a mapping from an observed distribution f_{Vis} and an input distribution f_{Inf}, producing an output representation which shares the feature of the
observed f_{Vis}. Therefore, we attempt to learn a generator G to generate the
feature distribution of the missing data channel f_{Vis} from the partially available
distribution denoted as f_{Inf}. Based on the scheme of conditional adversarial networks, the generator immediately transforms the partially available distribution
f_{Inf} and noise z to output the missing distribution via the following equation:

$$\min_{G} \max_{D} \mathcal{L}(G, D) = \mathbb{E}_{f_{Vis} \sim P_{data}(f_{Vis})}[\log D(f_{Vis})] + \\ \mathbb{E}_{f_{Inf} \sim P_{data}(f_{Inf}), z \sim P_{data}(z)}[\log(1 - D(G(f_{Inf}, z)))], \quad (1)$$

where $G(f_{Inf}, z)$ denotes the output distribution. The input distribution f_{Inf}
and observed distribution f_{Vis} denote the data of infrared and RGB channels
respectively in our action recognition task. The generator G is designed to minimize this objective to fake the generated distribution as well as possible, while
the real output feature discriminator D tries to maximize its accuracy of telling
the real from the fake one.

In this work, the discriminator is also designed for pattern recognition. Thus,
another prediction loss is explored:

$$\mathcal{L}_p(G, D_p) = \mathbb{E}_{f_{Inf} \sim P_{data}(f_{Inf}), z \sim P_{data}(z)}[L_{cls}(l, D_p(f_{Inf}, G(f_{Inf}, z)))], \quad (2)$$

where l denotes the correct label of partially available data samples, in the form
of one-hot vector, and L_{cls} is log loss over the predicted class confidences vector

and the ground truth label. For convenience, we denote the discriminator part and the predictor part of discriminative net as D_d and D_p respectively. Finally, the objective function can be formulated as:

$$\mathcal{L}_{PM-GANs}(G, D_d, D_p) = -\mathbb{E}_{f_{Vis} \sim P_{data}(f_{Vis})}[\log D_d(f_{Vis})]$$
$$- \mathbb{E}_{f_{Inf} \sim P_{data}(f_{Inf}), z \sim P_{data}(z)}[\log(1 - D_d(G(f_{Inf}, z)))]$$
$$+ \mathbb{E}_{f_{Inf} \sim P_{data}(f_{Inf}), z \sim P_{data}(z)}[L_{cls}(l, D_p(f_{Inf}, G(f_{Inf}, z)))].$$

$$(3)$$

3.2 Transferable Net

The transferable net simulates the target distribution from the convolutional feature map of the partially-available data distribution, which, as shown in Fig. 2, is made as an input of the generator to obtain feature maps of missing distribution. The input clips are denoted as $\{f_{Inf}^{(1)}, f_{Inf}^{(2)}, \ldots, f_{Inf}^{(T)}\}$, where $f_{Inf}^{(i)} \in \mathbb{R}^{H \times W \times D}$ and H, W, D denote the height, width and number of channels of feature maps. To incorporate all feature maps into a high-level representation, the sum fusion model in [9] is applied to compute the sum of T feature maps at the same spatial location i, j and feature channel d:

$$f_{Inf}^{sum}(i, j, d) = f_{Inf}^{(1)}(i, j, d) + f_{Inf}^{(2)}(i, j, d) + \cdots + f_{Inf}^{(T)}(i, j, d), \qquad (4)$$

where $1 \le i \le H$, $1 \le j \le W$, $1 \le d \le D$. The final feature map of the input distribution is computed as the average value of sum feature map f_{Inf}^{sum} in each

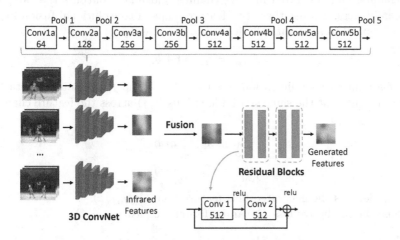

Fig. 2. The proposed transferable generative net is built upon the C3D network [49]. Video clips are sent to 3D ConvNet to obtain feature maps of each clip $f_{Inf}^{(i)}$ and all feature maps are fused as f_{Inf} to represent the whole action video. Then, residual blocks are added to this net to produce fake feature maps f_g similar to the visible spectrum

location, denoted as f_{Inf}. Then the generator takes the final input feature map and generates the fake target feature map, $G(f_{Inf}, z)$. The generator consists of two residual blocks [20] to produce feature map with the same size as infrared feature map. Thus, the generative loss L_G is expressed as:

$$L_G = -\log(D_d(G(f_{Inf}, z))).\tag{5}$$

3.3   Discriminative Net Using Partial Modality

To enable the generative net to produce full-modal representation which incorporates the complementary benefits among data of different modalities, a two-part discriminative net is designed, as shown in Fig. 1. The discriminative net contains a discriminator part and a predictor part. The discriminator part follows the scheme of conventional discriminator in GAN which is applied to distinguish between real and fake visible feature map in order to boost the quality of generated fake feature. Specifically, the discriminator part consists of a fully-connected layer followed by a sigmoid function, which produces an adversarial loss. Thus, the adversarial loss L_a is defined as:

$$L_a = -\log D_d(f_{Vis}) - \log(1 - D_d(G(f_{Inf,z}))),\tag{6}$$

where L_a encourages the discriminator network to distinguish the generated target feature representation from real one.

The predictor aims to boost the accuracy of assigning the right label to each feature distribution. It consists of a fully-connected layer followed by a softmax layer which takes the fusion of the feature map of both the partially-available data channel and generated missing channel and finally outputs the category-level confidences. To fuse these two feature maps, a convolutional fusion model in [9] is applied to automatically learn the fusion weights:

$$f_{conv} = f_{cat} * \mathbf{f} + b,\tag{7}$$

where $\mathbf{f}$ are filters with dimensions $1 \times 1 \times 2D \times D$, and f_{cat} denotes the stack of two feature maps at the same spatial locations (i, j) across the feature channels d:

$$\begin{aligned} f_{cat}^{(i,j,2d)} &= f_{Inf}^{(i,j,d)}, \\ f_{cat}^{(i,j,2d-1)} &= f_g^{(i,j,d)}, \end{aligned}\tag{8}$$

where f_g denotes the generated fake feature map $G(f_{Inf}, z)$.

Thus, the predictive loss L_p can be formulated as:

$$L_p = -\log l \cdot D_p(f_{Inf}, G(f_{Inf}, z)).\tag{9}$$

The final discriminative loss L_D can be defined as the weighted sum of adversarial loss and predictive loss:

$$L_D = w_1 \cdot L_a + w_2 \cdot L_p.\tag{10}$$

In the training process, the transferable net and the full-modal discriminative net are alternatively trained until the generated feature of missing channel becomes close to real and the discriminative net achieves precise recognition. In the testing process, we only need to send one/part of the data modality into the PM-GANs framework, and the generative net will automatically generate a transferred feature representation for the missing modality, and the predictor of discriminative net constructs a full-modal representation and predicts the label.

4   Experiments

In this section, we first introduce our new dataset for partial-modality infrared action recognition. In detail, the specifications and a complete evaluation of the dataset will be elaborated. For the experiment part, we introduce the configurations of the experiments and show the results and analyses corresponding to our method. Specifically our experiments are in three folds. First, we assess the effectiveness of the transferable net by comparing the generated feature representations with the real ones. Second, we evaluate the discriminative net ability using partial data modality. Finally, we compare our approach with four state-of-the-art methods to verify the effectiveness of the PM-GANs.

4.1   Cross-Modal Infrared-Visible Dataset for Action Recognition

We introduce a new action recognition dataset, which is constructed by paired videos of both RGB and infrared data channels. Each action class contains a singular action type, and each video sample contains one action class. In total there are 12 classes of both individual actions and person-person interactive actions. For individual actions: one hand wave (wave1), multiple hands wave (wave2), handclap, walk, jog, jump, skip, and interactive actions: handshake, hug, push, punch and fight. For each action class, there are 100 paired videos, with a frame rate of 25 fps. The frame resolutions are 256×293 for infrared channel and 480×720 for RGB channel. Each action is performed by around 50 different volunteers. A sample of the frames is illustrated in Fig. 3. The duration of videos varies from several seconds to more than 10 s.

In order to simulate the real-world variations, four scenario variables are considered: the background complexity, season, occlusion, and viewpoint.

Background Complexity: In our newly-introduced dataset, the background varies from relatively simple scenes (plain background) to complex ones (with moving objects). For simple background, there are only one or two people performing actions, as shown in Fig. 3(c). While for complex background, interrupting pedestrian activities concur with the objective action in different degrees, as shown in Fig. 3(d).

Season: The infrared channel is heavily effected by the seasons, because it reflects the heat radiation of objects. In winter, when ambient temperature is in a low value, the imaging of human body is salient and clear. However, in summer, the contrast between human and background is ambiguous. Thus, we divide the seasons into three categories: winter, spring/autumn, summer, as shown in Fig. 3(e)–(h). The video number proportions of these three seasons are 30%, 50%, and 20%, respectively. All actions were performed in these three seasons.

Occlusion: Specific videos with occlusions from 0% to over 50% are arranged in each action class to promote the diversity and complexity of dataset, as shown in Fig. 3(a)–(b).

(a) Slight occlusion   (b) Heavy occlusion

(c) Slight background cluster   (d) Heavy background cluster

(e) Winter-Center View   (f) Autumn-Left View

(g) Summer-Center View   (h) Summer-Left View

Fig. 3. Example paired frames for the action "wave2" in the newly introduced multi-modal dataset for action recognition. The left ones are in infrared channel and the right ones are in RGB channel

Viewpoint: The variation of different viewpoints is also an important factor considered. The video clips under the front-view, left-side-view, right-side-view are all included in the dataset, as shown in Fig. 3(e)–(h).

We split 75% of the paired video clip couples as the training set, and the rest as the testing set. To investigate the suitable representations for each spectrum and the most complimentary representation couples, we select several effective representations to test their discriminative ability on RGB channel, infrared channel, and the combined channels.

We feed the original video clips, the MHI image clips [1] and the optical flow clips [29], denoted as "Org", "MHI", and "Optical Flow", into the 3D-CNN [49] to obtain spatiotemporal features. The 3D-CNN takes a 16-frame clip as inputs and performs 3D convolution and 3D pooling, which calculates the appearance and motion information simultaneously. Specifically, we extract the output of the last fully connected layer and conduct a max pooling to all clip features of one video. In the case of two-modality fusion, we directly concatenate the features of infrared channel and RGB channel. After that, a linear SVM classifier is trained to obtain the final recognition results. The 3D-CNN is fine-tuned by the corresponding maps of our training set.

Table 1. The evaluation results of different features on different channels and their fusion on the proposed dataset

Method	Descriptor	Accuracy (%)
Infrared Channel	Org	55%
	Optical flow	69.67%
	MHI	61%
RGB Channel	Org	49%
	Optical flow	78.66%
	MHI	65.33%
Fusion	Org	55.33%
	Optical flow	80.67%
	MHI	68.67%

As shown in Table 1, the performances of different representations for both infrared and RGB channels and their combined results are listed. It is clearly observed that for both infrared and RGB channels, the 3D-CNN features after optical flows achieve the best performance. In two modalities fusion, the 3D-CNN features after optical flows in RGB channel can effectively boost the performance of using the infrared channel only. Thus, in the following experiments of transferable nets and discriminative nets [50], the optical flows are selected as input for representation learning via PM-GANs.

4.2   Implementation Details

For the input data, we compute optical flows using the toolbox of Liu [34]. The 3D ConvNet in transferable generative net is fine-tuned on the infrared optical flows of training set. And the adversarial visible feature maps are extracted from a 3D ConvNet fine-tuned on the visible optical flows of training set. The sampled numbers of clips T is set as 5, and each clip has a duration of 16 frames. The loss weights w_1 and w_2 are set as 0.1 and 0.9 respectively. We set the initial learning rate at 2×10^{-5}. The whole network is trained with ADAM optimization algorithm [25] with $\beta_1 = 0.5$ and $\beta_2 = 0.999$, batch size of 30 on a single NVIDIA GeForce GTX TITAN X GPU with 12 GB memory. The framework is implemented using TensorFlow library and accelerated by CUDA 8.0.

4.3   Transferable Net Evaluations

The PM-GANs model is evaluated on the proposed action recognition dataset. We present the results of five different modalities as shown in Table 2. For single modality, we utilize the 3D ConvNet part and the predictor part without fusion model for training and testing. And for the case of real infrared and RGB channel fusion, we directly input the real feature map of RGB channel to the fusion model instead of using generated ones. From Table 2, we can observe the generated RGB representations perform better than the original infrared ones, which shows that the PM-GANs have indeed discovered useful information through modality transfer. Moreover, the fusion of infrared and generated RGB representations achieves an Accuracy of 78%. Although it performs worse than the original RGB channels and the fusion of infrared and RGB channels, it only utilizes the information of infrared channel in the testing process.

Table 2. Evaluation results on the discriminative ability of transferable modality

Data modalities	Accuracy (%)
Infrared channel	71.67%
RGB channel	79.33%
Generated RGB	76.67%
Infrared + RGB channels	82.33%
Infrared channel + Generated RGB	78%

In order to analyze the intra-class performance, the confusion matrices are drawn in Fig. 4. As observed, the proposed method generally shows good performance in action classification: in most classes, the testing samples are assigned the correct label. However, we notice that the "punch", "skip" action samples are likely to be classified as "push" and "jump" respectively. One likely reason

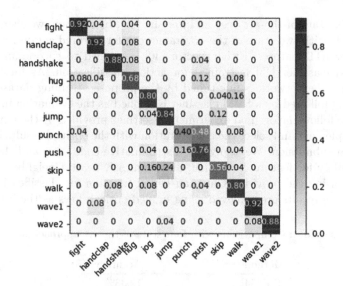

Fig. 4. The results illustrated in confusion matrices using the proposed method

is that two sets of actions are similar in both movement and process, sometimes even hard to distinguish for human eyes.

To get insight into how effective the transferable ability of PM-GANs are, we rearrange the training and testing splits. Specifically, we utilize the scenes of Spring/Autumn and Summer for training, and Winter for testing. We use this split to examine the generalization ability of the proposed model. As can be seen in Table 3, the generated fake RGB representations outperform the original infrared ones, which shows the robust transferability of PM-GANs.

Table 3. Evaluation of the models generalization ability using a separate dataset

Modalities of a separate dataset	Accuracy (%)
Infrared channel	74.17%
RGB channel	79.44%
Generated RGB	77.78%
Infrared + RGB channels	82.78%
Infrared channel + Generated RGB	80.28%

4.4 Comparisons with Other Methods

To evaluate the effectiveness of PM-GANs, we compare our method with four state-of-the-art methods, including the most effective handcrafted features iDT

[54], and the state-of-the-art deep architecture [49]. In addition, we also compare our methods with two state-of-the-art framework for infrared action recognition [13, 22]. For iDT features, Fisher Vector [40] is applied to encode and then a linear SVM classifier [45] is trained for action classification. As for the C3D architecture, the network is fine-tuned by the proposed training dataset. Then max pooling followed by a SVM classifier is applied as the evaluation in Table 1. For [13], we follow the original experimental settings provided by the author. For [22], we implement and select the configuration with the optimal results based on the original submission. We apply the discriminative code layer and the second fusion strategy for feature extraction, and train a K-nearest neighbor classifier (KNN) [4] using the provided Gaussian kernel function for classification. Note that all of the results are achieved using unified optical flows as the input.

Table 4. Comparisons with four state-of-the-art approaches

Method	Accuracy (%)
iDT [54]	72.33%
C3D [49]	69.67%
Two-stream CNN [13]	68%
Two-stream 3D-CNN [22]	74.67%
PM-GANs	78%

Table 4 presents the accuracy of the competing approaches. As observed, the handcrafted iDT method achieves comparable results with some high-level architecture. Methods using 3D-CNN outperform the method with 2D-CNN architecture. One reason to explain is that the 3D-CNN architecture is better in modeling temporal variations. The two-stream 3D-CNNs outperform the conventional iDT framework and robust C3D models, showing effective strength of the proposed discriminative code layer. Our proposed PM-GANs achieve the highest accuracy, which shows the effectiveness of the transferred feature representation and the robustness of our constructed model using only part of the data modalities.

5   Conclusions

In this paper, we proposed a novel Partial-modal Generative Adversarial Networks to construct a discriminative full-modal representation with only part of the data modalities being available. Our method learns the transferable representation among heterogeneous data modalities using adversarial learning, and build a discriminative net that represents all modalities. Our method is evaluated in the task of action recognition and outperforms four state-of-the-art methods on the newly-introduced dataset. The dataset, which contains paired videos in both infrared and visible spectrum, will be made as the first publicly available visible-infrared dataset for action recognition.

Acknowledgment. This work is supported by the National Natural Science Foundation of China (No. 61571071, 61661166011, 61721002), the Natural Science Foundation of Chongqing Science and Technology Commission (No. cstc2018jcyjAX0227) and the Research Innovation Program for Postgraduate of Chongqing (No. CYS17222).

References

1. Bobick, A.F., Davis, J.W.: The recognition of human movement using temporal templates. IEEE Trans. Pattern Anal. Mach. Intell. **23**(3), 257–267 (2001)
2. Bouwmans, T., Zahzah, E.H.: Robust PCA via principal component pursuit: a review for a comparative evaluation in video surveillance. Comput. Vis. Image Underst. **122**, 22–34 (2014)
3. Bronstein, M.M., Bronstein, A.M., Michel, F., Paragios, N.: Data fusion through cross-modality metric learning using similarity-sensitive hashing. In: 2010 IEEE Conference on Computer Vision and Pattern Recognition (CVPR), pp. 3594–3601. IEEE (2010)
4. Bui, D.T., Nguyen, Q.P., Hoang, N.D., Klempe, H.: A novel fuzzy k-nearest neighbor inference model with differential evolution for spatial prediction of rainfall-induced shallow landslides in a tropical hilly area using GIS. Landslides **14**(1), 1–17 (2017)
5. Carreira, J., Zisserman, A.: Quo vadis, action recognition? A new model and the kinetics dataset. In: 2017 IEEE Conference on Computer Vision and Pattern Recognition (CVPR), pp. 4724–4733. IEEE (2017)
6. Castrejon, L., Aytar, Y., Vondrick, C., Pirsiavash, H., Torralba, A.: Learning aligned cross-modal representations from weakly aligned data. In: 2016 IEEE Conference on Computer Vision and Pattern Recognition (CVPR), pp. 2940–2949. IEEE (2016)
7. Delhumeau, J., Gosselin, P.H., Jégou, H., Pérez, P.: Revisiting the VLAD image representation. In: Proceedings of the 21st ACM International Conference on Multimedia, pp. 653–656. ACM (2013)
8. Denton, E.L., Chintala, S., Fergus, R., et al.: Deep generative image models using a Laplacian pyramid of adversarial networks. In: Advances in Neural Information Processing Systems (NIPS), pp. 1486–1494. MIT Press (2015)
9. Feichtenhofer, C., Pinz, A., Zisserman, A.: Convolutional two-stream network fusion for video action recognition. In: 2016 IEEE Conference on Computer Vision and Pattern Recognition (CVPR), pp. 1933–1941. IEEE (2016)
10. Feng, F., Wang, X., Li, R.: Cross-modal retrieval with correspondence autoencoder. In: Proceedings of the 22nd ACM International Conference on Multimedia, pp. 7–16. ACM (2014)
11. Fernando, B., Gavves, E., Oramas, J., Ghodrati, A., Tuytelaars, T.: Rank pooling for action recognition. IEEE Trans. Pattern Anal. Mach. Intell. **39**(4), 773–787 (2017)
12. Ganin, Y., Lempitsky, V.: Unsupervised domain adaptation by backpropagation. In: International Conference on Machine Learning (ICML), pp. 1180–1189. ACM (2015)
13. Gao, C., et al.: Infar dataset: infrared action recognition at different times. Neurocomputing **212**, 36–47 (2016)
14. van Gemert, J.C., Jain, M., Gati, E., Snoek, C.G., et al.: Apt: Action localization proposals from dense trajectories. In: British Machine Vision Conference (BMVC), pp. 177.1–177.12. British Machine Vision Association (2015)

15. Goodfellow, I., et al.: Generative adversarial nets. In: Advances in Neural Information Processing Systems (NIPS), pp. 2672–2680. MIT Press (2014)
16. Gupta, S., Hoffman, J., Malik, J.: Cross modal distillation for supervision transfer. In: 2016 IEEE Conference on Computer Vision and Pattern Recognition (CVPR), pp. 2827–2836. IEEE (2016)
17. Han, J., Bhanu, B.: Human activity recognition in thermal infrared imagery. In: 2015 IEEE Conference on Computer Vision and Pattern Recognition (CVPR Workshops), p. 17. IEEE (2005)
18. Han, J., Bhanu, B.: Fusion of color and infrared video for moving human detection. Pattern Recogn. **40**(6), 1771–1784 (2007)
19. Hardoon, D.R., Szedmak, S., Shawe-Taylor, J.: Canonical correlation analysis: an overview with application to learning methods. Neural Comput. **16**(12), 2639–2664 (2004)
20. He, K., Zhang, X., Ren, S., Sun, J.: Deep residual learning for image recognition. In: 2016 IEEE Conference on Computer Vision and Pattern Recognition (CVPR), pp. 770–778. IEEE (2016)
21. Ji, S., Yang, M., Yu, K.: 3D convolutional neural networks for human action recognition. IEEE Trans. Pattern Anal. Mach. Intell. **35**(1), 221–231 (2012)
22. Jiang, Z., Rozgic, V., Adali, S.: Learning spatiotemporal features for infrared action recognition with 3D convolutional neural networks. In: 2017 IEEE Conference on Computer Vision and Pattern Recognition (CVPR Workshops). IEEE (2017)
23. Kang, C., Xiang, S., Liao, S., Xu, C., Pan, C.: Learning consistent feature representation for cross-modal multimedia retrieval. IEEE Trans. Multimed. **17**(3), 370–381 (2015)
24. Karpathy, A., Toderici, G., Shetty, S., Leung, T., Sukthankar, R., Fei-Fei, L.: Large-scale video classification with convolutional neural networks. In: 2014 IEEE Conference on Computer Vision and Pattern Recognition (CVPR), pp. 1725–1732. IEEE (2014)
25. Kingma, D.P., Ba, J.: Adam: a method for stochastic optimization. arXiv preprint arXiv:1412.6980 (2014)
26. Klaser, A., Marszałek, M., Schmid, C.: A spatio-temporal descriptor based on 3D-gradients. In: British Machine Vision Conference (BMVC), pp. 275-1–10. British Machine Vision Association (2008)
27. Kumar, S., Udupa, R.: Learning hash functions for cross-view similarity search. In: International Koint Conference on Artificial Intelligence (IJCAI), pp. 1360–1365. AAAI Press (2011)
28. Laptev, I.: On space-time interest points. Int. J. Comput. Vis. **64**(2–3), 107–123 (2005)
29. Laptev, I., Marszalek, M., Schmid, C., Rozenfeld, B.: Learning realistic human actions from movies. In: 2008 IEEE Conference on Computer Vision and Pattern Recognition (CVPR), pp. 1–8. IEEE (2008)
30. Li, T., Mei, T., Kweon, I.S., Hua, X.S.: Contextual bag-of-words for visual categorization. IEEE Trans. Circ. Syst. Video Technol. **21**(4), 381–392 (2011)
31. Li, Z., Gavrilyuk, K., Gavves, E., Jain, M., Snoek, C.G.: Videolstm convolves, attends and flows for action recognition. Comput. Vis. Image Underst. **166**, 41–50 (2018)
32. Lindtner, S., Hertz, G.D., Dourish, P.: Emerging sites of HCI innovation: hackerspaces, hardware startups & incubators. In: Proceedings of the SIGCHI Conference on Human Factors in Computing Systems, pp. 439–448. ACM (2014)

33. Liu, A.A., Xu, N., Nie, W.Z., Su, Y.T., Wong, Y., Kankanhalli, M.: Benchmarking a multimodal and multiview and interactive dataset for human action recognition. IEEE Trans. Cybern. **47**(7), 1781–1794 (2017)

34. Liu, C., et al.: Beyond pixels: exploring new representations and applications for motion analysis. Ph.D. thesis, Massachusetts Institute of Technology (2009)

35. Liu, Y., Lu, Z., Li, J., Yao, C., Deng, Y.: Transferable feature representation for visible-to-infrared cross-dataset human action recognition. Complexity **2018**, Article ID 5345241, 20 p. (2018)

36. Long, M., Cao, Y., Wang, J., Jordan, M.: Learning transferable features with deep adaptation networks. In: International Conference on Machine Learning (ICML), pp. 97–105. ACM (2015)

37. Patel, V.M., Gopalan, R., Li, R., Chellappa, R.: Visual domain adaptation: a survey of recent advances. IEEE Sig. Process. Mag. **32**(3), 53–69 (2015)

38. Peng, Y., Qi, J., Yuan, Y.: CM-GANs: cross-modal generative adversarial networks for common representation learning. arXiv preprint arXiv:1710.05106 (2017)

39. Pereira, J.C., et al.: On the role of correlation and abstraction in cross-modal multimedia retrieval. IEEE Trans. Pattern Anal. Mach. Intell. **36**(3), 521–535 (2014)

40. Perronnin, F., Sánchez, J., Mensink, T.: Improving the fisher kernel for large-scale image classification. In: Daniilidis, K., Maragos, P., Paragios, N. (eds.) ECCV 2010. LNCS, vol. 6314, pp. 143–156. Springer, Heidelberg (2010). https://doi.org/10.1007/978-3-642-15561-1_11

41. Radford, A., Metz, L., Chintala, S.: Unsupervised representation learning with deep convolutional generative adversarial networks. arXiv preprint arXiv:1511.06434 (2015)

42. Rahmani, H., Mian, A., Shah, M.: Learning a deep model for human action recognition from novel viewpoints. IEEE Trans. Pattern Anal. Mach. Intell. **40**(3), 667–681 (2018)

43. Rautaray, S.S., Agrawal, A.: Vision based hand gesture recognition for human computer interaction: a survey. Artif. Intell. Rev. **43**(1), 1–54 (2015)

44. Sánchez, J., Perronnin, F., Mensink, T., Verbeek, J.: Image classification with the fisher vector: theory and practice. Int. J. Comput. Vis. **105**(3), 222–245 (2013)

45. Schuldt, C., Laptev, I., Caputo, B.: Recognizing human actions: a local SVM approach. In: 2004 International Conference on Pattern Recognition, (ICPR), vol. 3, pp. 32–36. IEEE (2004)

46. Shao, L., Zhu, F., Li, X.: Transfer learning for visual categorization: a survey. IEEE Trans. Neural Netw. Learn. Syst. **26**(5), 1019–1034 (2015)

47. Shin, H.C., et al.: Deep convolutional neural networks for computer-aided detection: CNN architectures, dataset characteristics and transfer learning. IEEE Trans. Med. Imaging **35**(5), 1285–1298 (2016)

48. Simonyan, K., Zisserman, A.: Two-stream convolutional networks for action recognition in videos. In: Advances in Neural Information Processing Systems (NIPS), pp. 568–576. MIT Press (2014)

49. Tran, D., Bourdev, L., Fergus, R., Torresani, L., Paluri, M.: Learning spatiotemporal features with 3D convolutional networks. In: 2015 IEEE International Conference on Computer Vision (ICCV), pp. 4489–4497. IEEE (2015)

50. Tzeng, E., Hoffman, J., Saenko, K., Darrell, T.: Adversarial discriminative domain adaptation. In: 2017 IEEE Conference on Computer Vision and Pattern Recognition (CVPR), pp. 2962–2971. IEEE (2017)

51. Varol, G., Laptev, I., Schmid, C.: Long-term temporal convolutions for action recognition. IEEE Trans. Pattern Anal. Mach. Intell. **40**, 1510–1517 (2018)

52. Veeriah, V., Zhuang, N., Qi, G.J.: Differential recurrent neural networks for action recognition. In: 2015 IEEE International Conference on Computer Vision (ICCV), pp. 4041–4049. IEEE (2015)

53. Wang, H., Kläser, A., Schmid, C., Liu, C.L.: Dense trajectories and motion boundary descriptors for action recognition. Int. J. Comput. Vis. **103**(1), 60–79 (2013)

54. Wang, H., Oneata, D., Verbeek, J., Schmid, C.: A robust and efficient video representation for action recognition. Int. J. Comput. Vis. **119**(3), 219–238 (2016)

55. Wang, L., Qiao, Y., Tang, X.: Action recognition with trajectory-pooled deep-convolutional descriptors. In: 2015 IEEE Conference on Computer Vision and Pattern Recognition (CVPR), pp. 4305–4314. IEEE (2015)

56. Wang, L., et al.: Temporal segment networks: towards good practices for deep action recognition. In: Leibe, B., Matas, J., Sebe, N., Welling, M. (eds.) ECCV 2016. LNCS, vol. 9912, pp. 20–36. Springer, Cham (2016). https://doi.org/10.1007/978-3-319-46484-8_2

57. Wei, Y., et al.: Cross-modal retrieval with CNN visual features: a new baseline. IEEE Trans. Cybern. **47**(2), 449–460 (2017)

58. Wu, A., Zheng, W.S., Yu, H.X., Gong, S., Lai, J.: RGB-infrared cross-modality person re-identification. In: 2017 IEEE Conference on Computer Vision and Pattern Recognition (CVPR), pp. 5380–5389. IEEE (2017)

59. Yang, L., Gao, C., Meng, D., Jiang, L.: A novel group-sparsity-optimization-based feature selection model for complex interaction recognition. In: Cremers, D., Reid, I., Saito, H., Yang, M.-H. (eds.) ACCV 2014. LNCS, vol. 9007, pp. 508–521. Springer, Cham (2015). https://doi.org/10.1007/978-3-319-16814-2_33

60. Yang, Y., Zha, Z.J., Gao, Y., Zhu, X., Chua, T.S.: Exploiting web images for semantic video indexing via robust sample-specific loss. IEEE Trans. Multimed. **16**(6), 1677–1689 (2014)

61. Yeh, Y.R., Huang, C.H., Wang, Y.C.F.: Heterogeneous domain adaptation and classification by exploiting the correlation subspace. IEEE Trans. Image Process. **23**(5), 2009–2018 (2014)

62. Zollhöfer, M., et al.: Real-time non-rigid reconstruction using an RGB-D camera. ACM Trans. Graph. (TOG) **33**(4), 156 (2014)

WildDash - Creating Hazard-Aware Benchmarks

Oliver Zendel$^{(\boxtimes)}$, Katrin Honauer, Markus Murschitz, Daniel Steininger,
and Gustavo Fernández Domínguez

AIT, Austrian Institute of Technology, Giefinggasse 4, 1210 Vienna, Austria
{oliver.zendel,katrin.honauer.fl,markus.murschitz,daniel.steininger,
gustavo.fernandez}@ait.ac.at

Abstract. Test datasets should contain many different challenging
aspects so that the robustness and real-world applicability of algorithms
can be assessed. In this work, we present a new test dataset for semantic
and instance segmentation for the automotive domain. We have conducted a thorough risk analysis to identify situations and aspects that
can reduce the output performance for these tasks. Based on this analysis we have designed our new dataset. Meta-information is supplied to
mark which individual visual hazards are present in each test case. Furthermore, a new benchmark evaluation method is presented that uses
the meta-information to calculate the robustness of a given algorithm
with respect to the individual hazards. We show how this new approach
allows for a more expressive characterization of algorithm robustness by
comparing three baseline algorithms.

Keywords: Test data · Autonomous driving · Validation · Testing
Safety analysis · Semantic segmentation · Instance segmentation

1 Introduction

Recent advances in machine learning have transformed the way we approach
Computer Vision (CV) tasks. Focus has shifted from algorithm design towards
network architectures and data engineering. This refers in this context to the
creation and selection of suitable datasets for training, validation, and testing.

This work focuses on the creation of validation datasets and their accompanying benchmarks. Our goal is to establish meaningful metrics and evaluations that
reflect real-world robustness of the tested algorithms for the CV tasks of semantic
segmentation and instance segmentation, especially for autonomous driving (AD).
These tasks represent essential steps necessary for scene understanding and have
recently seen huge improvements thanks to deep learning approaches. At the same

Electronic supplementary material The online version of this chapter (https://
doi.org/10.1007/978-3-030-01231-1_25) contains supplementary material, which is
available to authorized users.

© Springer Nature Switzerland AG 2018
V. Ferrari et al. (Eds.): ECCV 2018, LNCS 11210, pp. 407–421, 2018.
https://doi.org/10.1007/978-3-030-01231-1_25

Fig. 1. Examples of hazards found in the *WildDash* dataset. See Table 1 for descriptions.

time, they are basic building blocks of vision-based advanced driver-assistance systems (ADAS) and are therefore employed in high-risk systems.

Demanding CV tasks are becoming increasingly important in safety-relevant ADAS applications. This requires solutions that are robust against many performance-reducing factors (e.g. illumination changes, reflections, distortions, image noise). These factors can be seen as hazards, influences potentially harmful to algorithm performance. Each hazard poses a potential risk and should be tested thoroughly to evaluate the robustness and safety of the accompanying system. Classic risk analysis applied to machine learning systems encompasses an inherent problem: Even if the learning process itself is well-understood, the relation between cause and effect, and the origin of erroneous behaviors are often hard to comprehend: if something goes wrong, it can be difficult to trace back the reason. Incorporating well-categorized test data promises to overcome this issue. Highly expressive meta-information (i.e. describing which aspects and hazards are present in a given test image) allows for reasoning based on empirical evaluations during the test phase: if a statistically significant amount of tests containing a specific hazard fails, it can be assumed that the system is not robust against this hazard. The underlying assumption of this work is: if we use machine-learning-based mechanisms in systems that represent potential risks to human life, a systematic approach comprehensible to humans for testing these components is essential. Only then, sufficient certainty can be obtained regarding the underlying risk and its propagation from one sub-system to others. Data, metrics, and methodologies presented in this work are designed based on this assumption.

Another influential factor regarding the quality of a test set is the inherent dataset bias (see [1]). Most of the publicly available datasets for semantic and instance segmentation in the ADAS context published in recent years still suffer from being too focused on a certain geographical region. These datasets have a strong bias towards Western countries, especially Central Europe. The dataset presented in this work aims to minimize this shortcoming. It embraces the global diversity of traffic situations by including test cases from all over the world. Furthermore, a great variety of different ego vehicles with varying camera setups extracted from dashcam video material is provided. This ultimately results in a vivid cross-section of traffic scenarios, hence the title *WildDash*.

Fig. 2. Example frames of existing datasets. From left to right: CamVid, Cityscapes, KITTI, Playing for Benchmarks, and Mapillary Vistas.

The main contribution of this work is a novel dataset for semantic and instance segmentation, that (i) allows for backtracking of failed tests to visual risk factors and therefore pinpointing weaknesses, (ii) adds negative test cases to avoid false positives, and (iii) has low regional bias and low camera setup bias due to its wide range of sources.

Section 2 gives a thorough overview of existing datasets for semantic and instance segmentation focused on ADAS applications. Section 3 summarizes our process of applying an established risk-analysis method to create a checklist of critical aspects that should be covered by test data to evaluate algorithm robustness. Section 4 explains how we applied the generated checklist and designed our new test dataset: *WildDash*. In Sect. 5, we demonstrate how the additional meta-information about included hazards can be used to create new hazard-aware metrics for performance evaluation. Section 6 describes the training setup of our baseline models and presents detailed segmentation results on specific aspects of *WildDash*. Section 7 gives a short outlook, followed by a summary in Sect. 8.

2   Related Work

2.1   Segmentation Datasets

Brostow et al. [2] introduced *CamVid*, one of the first datasets focusing on semantic segmentation for driving scenarios (see Fig. 2). It is composed of five video sequences captured in Cambridge consisting of 701 densely annotated images, distinguishing between 31 semantic classes. In 2013 the 6D Vision group [3] published the initial version of the *Daimler Urban Dataset* [4]. It contains 5000 coarsely labeled images (*ground, sky, building, vehicle, pedestrian*) extracted from two videos recorded in Germany.

The release of the *Cityscapes* Dataset [5] in 2015 marks a breakthrough in semantic scene understanding. Several video sequences were captured in cities across Germany and Switzerland and 25000 images labeled (5000 fine/20000 coarse) with 30 different classes. The corresponding benchmark is still the most commonly used reference, currently listing 106 algorithms for semantic segmentation and 29 algorithms for instance segmentation (July 2018). In the year 2017, the *Raincouver* dataset [6] contributed additional frames depicting road layouts and traffic participants under varying weather and lighting conditions. Published in the same year, *Mighty AI Sample Data* [7] is composed of dashcam images representing different driving scenarios in the metropolitan area of Seattle. The year 2018 marked two more major contributions in terms of quality and data variability, which represent a further step towards reducing dataset bias. One of them is *Mapillary Vistas Dataset* [8] which contains more than 25000 high-resolution images covering around 64 semantic classes, including varying lighting conditions, locations and camera setups. *Berkeley Deep Drive* [9], on the other hand, specializes more on challenging weather conditions and different times of the day. The *KITTI Vision Benchmark Suite*, first introduced by Geiger et al. [10] in 2012 and aimed at multiple tasks such as stereo, object detection, and tracking was updated in 2018 with ground truth for semantic segmentation [11].

In addition to annotations of real images, a number of synthetically generated datasets emerged in recent years. One of the first contributions to the area of Urban Scene Understanding was *Virtual KITTI* by Gaidon et al. [12] in 2016. It represents a virtual reconstruction of the original KITTI dataset, enhanced by a higher variety of weather conditions. Published in the same year, *SYNTHIA* [13] focuses on multiple scenarios (cities, motorways and green areas) in diverse illumination, weather conditions, and varying seasons. A recent update called *SYNTHIA-SF* [14] furthermore follows the Cityscapes labeling policy. In the following year, Richter et al. [15] introduced the synthetic benchmark suite *Playing for Benchmarks*. It covers multiple vision tasks such as semantic segmentation, optical flow, and object tracking. High-resolution image sequences for a driving distance of 184 Km are provided with corresponding ground-truth annotations.

2.2   Risk Analysis in Computer Vision

A number of publications regarding risk analysis in CV have been published during the last years, since the community seemingly gained awareness for the necessity to train and test for increasingly difficult conditions.

In 2015, Zendel et al. [16] introduced the concept of risk analysis for CV tasks. In contrast to high-level driving hazards (e.g. car crash, near-miss events as in the SHRP 2 NDS database [17]), this work focuses on visual hazards (e.g. blur, glare, and overexposure). They create a checklist of such hazards that can impair algorithm performance. The list has more than 1000 generic entries which can be used as seeds for creating specialized entries for individual CV tasks. Such were presented for stereo vision in 2017 in *Analyzing Computer Vision Data* [18] where they strongly emphasize on the underrated aspect of *negative test cases*. These are tests where algorithms are expected to fail. Since most of the data is highly focused on training, many works do not consider the negative test class, neither in the evaluation metric nor in the data itself. For a safe and robust system it is important that an algorithm does not 'overreact' and knows when it is not able to provide a reliable result. No indications have been found in any of the mentioned evaluation frameworks and benchmarks that true negative test cases are evaluated. Most common is the *don't-care*-approach (e.g. in Cityscapes), where all the regions that are annotated using a negative (=unknown/invalid) class are not evaluated. This means that an image containing only negative classes is not evaluated at all.

Both risk analysis publications [16] and [18] include interesting claims and tools for measuring and improving test data quality. However, the authors only apply their concepts to existing test datasets and do not create a new dataset themselves.

In this work we are trying to build upon their work and actually create a dataset allowing for hazard-aware evaluation of algorithms. In addition, *Wild-Dash* deliberately introduces negative test cases to close this crucial gap.

3 Risk Analysis

The process of collecting a comprehensive list of factors that pose risks to a system and the overall assessment of these risk factors is called risk analysis. For the course of the *WildDash* dataset, we started with the results from a publicly available generic CV risk analysis called CV-HAZOP [16]. The generic entries from this list are *concretized* to create a version specific to the current task at hand. The first step of conducting the risk analysis is the definition of the CV task itself that shall be evaluated.

We designed our dataset as an organic extension to existing datasets. Thus, we chose to use a task definition close to the one used in the popular Cityscapes [5] dataset. It provides a valuable tool solving important tasks for autonomous driving: navigation, scene understanding and collision avoidance. The task definition categorizes test cases: those which are in-scope as *positive* test cases vs. those lying outside the task definition as *negative* test cases.

3.1 Task Definition: Semantic Segmentation

The algorithm shall assign a single best fitting label to each pixel of a given color image. The specific labels and semantics for these labels can be found in Cordts et al. [5] and focus on scene understanding for autonomous driving.

In essence, the task focuses on assigning each pixel in an image to exactly one of these possible classes: *road, sidewalk, parking, rail track, person, rider, car, truck, bus, on rails, motorcycle, bicycle, caravan, building, wall, fence, guard rail, bridge, tunnel, pole, traffic sign, traffic light, vegetation, terrain, sky, ground, dynamic,* and *static.*

All scenes depict frontal vehicle views of traffic scenarios. The camera angle and orientation should be comparable to a human driver or co-driver. It can be positioned outside the vehicle or behind the windscreen.

Some of the labels do not affect the results because they are not part of the evaluation in the Cityscapes benchmark. Other labels cause varying annotations, as the corresponding concepts are hard to narrow down into a concrete task description for an annotator. To correct this, we deviate from the original work of Cordts et al. [5] as follows:

- The *trailer* label is not used. Trailers are labeled as the vehicle that is attached to it and parked trailers without an attached vehicle as *dynamic.*

- The label *pole group* is not used. These parts are labeled as *pole*.
- Areas within large gaps in an instance label are annotated by the content visible in that hole, in contrast to being filled with the enclosing label (original Cityscapes). Whenever content is clearly visible through the hole consisting of more than just a few pixels, it is annotated accordingly.

The original Cityscapes labels are focusing on German cities. We are refining and augmenting some of the definitions to clarify their meaning within a broader worldwide context:

- Construction work vehicles and agriculture vehicles are labeled as *truck*.
- Overhead bridges and their support pillars/beams are labeled as *bridge*. Roads/sidewalks/etc. on bridges still keep their respective labels.
- Two/Three/Four-wheeled muscle-powered vehicles are labeled as *bicycle*.
- Three-wheeled motorized vehicles are labeled as *motorcycle* (e.g. auto rickshaws, tuk-tuk, taxi rickshaws) with the exception of vehicles that are intended primarily for transport purposes which get the *truck* label.

3.2 Task Definition: Instance Segmentation

Instance segmentation starts with the same task description as semantic segmentation but enforces unique instance labels for individual objects (separate labels even for adjoint instances). To keep this benchmark compatible with Cityscapes, we also limit instance segmentation to these classes: *person, rider, car, truck, bus, on rails, motorcycle, bicycle, caravan*.

3.3 Concretization of the CV-HAZOP List

The concretization process as described in *Analyzing Computer Vision Data* [18] starts from the generic CV-HAZOP list. Using the task definitions (Sects. 3.1 and 3.2), the relevant hazards are filtered. In our case, we filtered out most temporal effects (as the task description requires a working algorithm from just one image without other sequence information). The remaining entries of the list were reviewed and each fitting entry was reformulated to clearly state the hazard for the given task definition.

3.4 Clustering of Hazards

Getting a specific evaluation for each identified hazard would be the ideal outcome of a hazard-aware dataset. However, real-world data sources do not always yield enough test cases to conclusively evaluate each risk by itself. Furthermore, the effects seen within an image often cannot be attributed to a single specific cause (e.g. blur could either be the result of motion or a defocused camera). Thus multiple risks with common effects on output quality were clustered into groups. The concretized entries have been clustered into these ten risk clusters: blur, coverage, distortion, hood, occlusion, overexposure, particles, underexposure, variations, and windscreen. See Table 1 for an explanation of each risk cluster and Fig. 1 for example images containing these hazards.

Table 1. Risk clusters for *WildDash*. Figure 1 contains examples in the same order

Risk cluster	Hazard examples
blur	Effects of motion blur, camera focus blur, and compression artifacts
coverage	Numerous types of road coverage and changes to road appearance
distortion	Lens distortion effects (e.g. wide angle)
hood	Ego-vehicle's engine cover (bonnet) is visible
occlusion	Occlusion by another object or the image border
overexposure	Overexposed areas, glare and halo effects
particles	Particles reducing visibility (e.g. mist, fog, rain, snow)
underexposure	Underexposed areas, twilight, night shots
variations	Intra-class variations, uncommon object representations
windscreen	Windscreen smudges, raindrops and reflections of the interior

4 WildDash Setup

4.1 Dataset Collection

Gathering a lot of challenging data without strong content bias is a hard task. Therefore, the input images of our dataset are collected from contributions of many 'YouTube' authors who either released their content under CC-BY license or individually agreed to let us extract sample frames from their videos. Potential online material is considered of interest with regard to the task descriptions (Sects. 3.1 and 3.2) if it met the following requirements: (i) data was recorded using a dashcam, (ii) front driving direction, (iii) at least one hazard situation arises, (iv) some frames before and after the hazard situation exist. This allows for a later expansion of our dataset towards semantic flow algorithms. All such videos are marked as a potential candidate for *WildDash*. From the set of candidate sequences, individual interesting frames were selected with the specific hazards in mind. Additionally, the content bias was reduced by trying to create a mixture of different countries, road geometries, driving situations, and seasons.

This selection resulted in a subset of about 1800 frames. A meta-analysis was conducted for each frame to select the final list of frames for the public validation and the private benchmarking dataset.

4.2 Meta-data Analysis

In order to calculate hazard-aware metrics the presence of hazards in each frame needs to be identified. Another design goal of *WildDash* is limited redundancy and maximal variability in domain-related aspects. Therefore, (i) domain-related and (ii) hazard-related meta-data is added to each frame. The following predefined values (denoted as set {.}) are possible:

- Domain-related: *environment* {'city', 'highway', 'off-road', 'overland', 'suburban', 'tunnel', 'other'} and *road-geometry* {'straight', 'curve', 'roundabout', 'intersection', 'other'}.

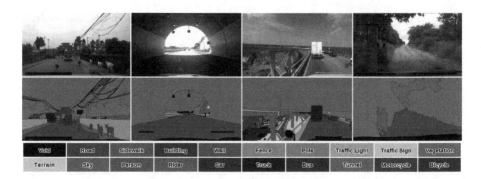

Fig. 3. Positive test cases from wd_val_01 (cn0000, si0005, us0006, and zm0001) together with a visualization of the respective semantic segmentation and color legend.

- Hazards-related: One severity value {'none', 'low', 'high'} for each of the ten risk clusters from Table 1.

The severity for a given risk is set to 'high' if large parts of the image are clearly affected or the appearance of humans/vehicles is affected. All other occurrences of the risk are represented by 'low' severity or if not present by 'none'.

4.3   Positive Test Cases

Based on the meta list, a diverse set of test frames covering each of the hazards has been selected and separated into a public validation set (wd_val_01, GT is published) of 70 test cases and a hidden benchmark set (wd_bench_01, GT is withheld) of 141 test cases. The GT has been generated using a dedicated annotation service and many additional hours by the authors to ensure consistent quality. Figure 3 shows a few examples taken from the WildDash public validation set.

4.4   Negative Test Cases

One of the central requirements presented by Zendel et al. [18] is the inclusion of negative test cases: tests that are expected to fail. The point of having these images in the dataset is to see how the system behaves when it is operating outside its specifications. A robust solution will recognize that it cannot operate in the given situation and reduce the confidence. Ideally, a perfect system flags truly unknown data as invalid. Table 2 lists test cases which increasingly divert from the region of operation of a regular assisted driving system while Fig. 4 shows some of the respective input images. With 141 positive and 15 negative test cases the WildDash benchmarking set wd_bench_01 contains a total of 156 test cases.

Table 2. Negative test cases from wd_bench_01.

Altered valid scenes		Abstract/Image noise	
wd0141	RGB/BGR channels switched	wd0142	White wall close-up
wd0143	Black-and-white image	wd0144	Digital image receive noise
wd0148	Upside-down version	wd0146	Analog image receive noise
wd0151	Color-inverted image	wd0147	Black image with error text
wd0155	Image cut and rearranged	wd0154	Black sensor noise
Out-of-scope images			
wd0145	Only sky with clouds		
wd0149	Macro-shot anthill		
wd0150	Indoor group photo		
wd0152	Aquarium		
wd0153	Abstract road scene with toys		

Fig. 4. Negative test cases wd0141, wd0142, wd0145, wd0146, and wd0152. See Table 2 for content descriptions

5   Hazard-Aware Evaluation Metrics

The meta-analysis of the dataset allows for the creation of subsets for each of the identified hazard clusters. For each group, all frames are divided by severity into three groups: none, low and high. Performance evaluation can be conducted for each severity-subset to obtain a coarse measure of the individual hazard's impact on an algorithm's performance. The Intersection over Union (IoU) measure [19] represents the 'de facto' established metric for assessing the quality of semantic segmentation algorithms. For each label the ratio of true positives (i.e. the intersection of predicted and annotated labels) over the union of true positives, false positives and false negatives is evaluated. The IoU scores per label class are averaged to calculate a single performance score per hazard subset called mean IoU (mIoU). The *impact* of the individual hazard reflects its negative effect on the algorithm's performance. It is calculated as: $r_{impact} = 1.0 - \frac{min(mIoU_{low}, mIoU_{none})}{max(mIoU_{low}, mIoU_{high})}$. Therefore, a value of 0.0 implies no impact, while a score of e.g. 0.5 corresponds to a hazard of reducing performance by 50%. The subset *low* represents border cases between influential and non-influential test cases and thus $mIoU_{low}$ is present at both numerator and denominator.

Occlusions are only relevant for foreground objects with instance annotations. To mitigate this, the risk cluster *occlusions* evaluates only labels with instance annotations (human and vehicle category) and ignores the single label with the largest area (as this is normally the fully visible occluder).

5.1 Evaluating Negative Test Cases

Evaluation of negative test cases might seem straight forward at first: per definition we expect an algorithm to fail for negative test cases in a graceful manner, i.e. mark the output as invalid. This creates a paradox situation: output marked as invalid is considered to be correct while any other output is counted as incorrect. This binary form of evaluation is not very appropriate, especially as the borderline between positive and negative test cases is ambiguous. Just because a specific situation/aspect is not clearly stated in the domain/task definition does not make it a clean negative test case (i.e. 'algorithm must fail here'). Often, a test case states a situation that is clearly not part of the system's task definition; for example, an upside down image of a street scene. It is still possible to assign unambiguous legitimate semantic labels for this test image. In these cases, we treat all algorithm output as correct, that is either equal to such legitimate label, or marked as invalid.

6   Evaluation

This section provides first valuable insights concerning opportunities and shortcomings of recently published datasets predominantly used in the research field of semantic segmentation. For this purpose, three baseline models (i.e. cityscapes, mapillary, mapillary+) varying with regard to the amount and source of training data, were trained from scratch and thoroughly evaluated on subsets of the *WildDash* dataset representing specific visual hazards.

6.1 Experimental Setup

This section describes the setup of the baseline models, which are based on the pytorch implementation of Dilated Residual Networks (drn) [20]. Employing dilated convolution for semantic segmentation facilitates an efficient aggregation of features at multiple scale levels without losses introduced by downsampling. To ensure comparability between all models, each experiment has been carried out with the same training configuration. The network architecture drn-d38 was selected due to the balance between labeling accuracy and training duration it provides. Moreover, the input batches consist of 8 pairs of input images and corresponding annotations each, and are randomly rescaled by a factor between 0.5 and 2 to improve scale invariance, randomly flipped in horizontal direction, and finally randomly cropped to a size of 896 × 896 pixels. As a pre-processing step, the *Mapillary Vistas* dataset has been rescaled and cropped to fit the resolution of Cityscapes (2048 × 1024 pixels). Since the *Cityscapes* dataset consists of 3475 pixel-level annotations, subdivided into 2975 training and 500 validation images, and therefore provides the least amount of training data, a subset of

Table 3. mIoU scores of the conducted experiments on varying target datasets

Baseline model/dataset	Cityscapes	Mapillary	WildDash (val/bench)	WildDash negative test cases
cityscapes	**63.79**	30.31	16.5/15.4	7.2
mapillary	44.81	50.24	29.3/27.4	12.9
mapillary+	46.34	**52.34**	**30.7/29.8**	**27.4**

Mapillary with a similar number of images has been used to train the comparable baseline method, further referred to as mapillary. During our experiments the 1525 *Cityscapes* and 5000 *Mapillary* test images are not included, since they are withheld for benchmarking purposes and thus not publicly available. The baseline method mapillary+ uses all publicly available *Mapillary* data of 18000 training and 2000 validation images. To cope with the increased amount of sampled input data a faster decay of the learning rate was achieved by lowering the step size from 100 to 17 epochs during the last experiment. Training input has been restricted to the labels evaluated in the *WildDash* benchmark without performing any further label aggregation.

6.2 Cross-Dataset Validation

To quantify shortcomings and the degree of variability inherent to semantic segmentation datasets, the learned models are validated on three target datasets. A detailed overview of the corresponding evaluation is given in Table 3.

As expected, the models perform best on the datasets they have been trained on. The highest mIoU of 63.79 is achieved by the cityscapes model. However, the validation set of the *Cityscapes* dataset consists of only three image sequences captured in Central European cities. The results of this model on datasets like *Mapillary* and *WildDash* show that training solely on *Cityscapes* images is insufficient to generalize for more challenging ADAS scenarios. The model cannot cope with visual hazards effectively. The highest score on *WildDash* is achieved by the mapillary+ experiment with mIoU scores of 30.7 on validation and 29.8 on the test set, based on more distinct scene diversity and global coverage present within the training data of Mapillary. Exemplary results of our baseline experiments on *WildDash* validation images are shown in Fig. 5. As long as input images bear a high resemblance to the training set of *Cityscapes*, as shown in the first row, no significant loss in labeling performance occures. However, models like mapillary and mapillary+ are clearly more robust to the challenging *WildDash* scenarios.

6.3 Testing Visual Hazards

Detailed results on varying subsets of the *WildDash* test dataset, representing a diverse range of visual hazards, are reported in Table 4[1]. As expected, the influence of the individual hazards is clearly reflected in the algorithm performance.

---

[1] See supplementary material for additional results including instance segmentations.

Fig. 5. Qualitative results of our baseline models on *WildDash* validation images (left to right: input image, corresponding ground truth, and the inferred labelings of our baseline models cityscapes, mapillary, and mapillary+)

Table 4. mIoU scores of the baseline model mapillary+ on hazard-related *WildDash* subsets, grouped by their severity of the respective hazard. The impact score, which is introduced in Sect. 5, quantifies the potential negative influence of a specific hazard on the labeling performance

hazard	blur	coverage	distortions	hood	occlusion	overexp	underexp	particles	windscreen	variations
none	29.0	31.0	**31.4**	**32.9**	26.4	**32.2**	**31.5**	30.2	**31.8**	29.0
low	**32.2**	28.6	28.2	27.8	**32.1**	23.5	31.0	29.3	28.5	**30.7**
high	26.6	**32.8**	26.8	22.4	30.4	17.0	20.8	29.3	27.8	27.9
impact	0.17	0.08	0.15	0.32	0.05	**0.47**	0.34	0.03	0.12	0.09

Evaluating hazards causing significant image degradations (e.g. blur, over- and underexposure) show an high impact, thus leading to lower algorithm performance. On the other hand, effects caused by lens distortions lead to a graceful decrease of labeling accuracy. Furthermore, mixing environmental effects such as fog and heavy rain with slight snowfall, leads to high variations in algorithm performance. This will be considered in the future, by partitioning the risk cluster *particles* as two disjunct subsets.

6.4   Testing Domain-Related Aspects

As already discussed, another important aspect of test data is a distinctive and comprehensive coverage of domain aspects, such as differences regarding environments and varying types of road layouts. The influence of these aspects is presented in Table 5. As the results show, labeling performance varies strongly with regard to the domain. Unsurprisingly, tunnel scenes tend to yield inferior accuracy due to a mixture of low light conditions and homogeneously textured regions, as well as their relatively rare occurrence within the training data. The algorithm performs robust in the city, sub-urban, and overland domain, which can be explained by the high number of learned urban scenes, constituting 90 percent of the *Mapillary* dataset and the low complexity of overland scenes. As

Table 5. mIoU scores of the baseline model mapillary+ on domain subsets of *WildDash*

domain	city	highway	offroad	overland	suburban	tunnel	curve	intersection	roundabout	straight
mIoU	31.3	24.5	**32.7**	29.3	31.6	19.6	28.7	31.7	**36.6**	28.0

for variations in road layouts, the best labeling scores are achieved in round-about scenes, followed by those containing intersections. This could be caused by the strong uniformity present within these subgroups and lower vehicle speeds leading to reduced motion blur.

6.5   Negative Test Cases

Labeling results of negative test cases show typical characteristics dependent on the specific subgroup. Representative qualitative results are shown in Fig. 6. If the system is confronted with upside-down images, the trained model partially relies on implicitly learned location priors, resulting in a clearly visible labeling conflict between road and sky in the top region. Labeling performance on abstract test cases, on the other hand, is strongly influenced by image noise and high-frequency texture features, leading to a drift towards properties resembling similar labels. The significantly lower confidence scores of altered and out-of-scope images may be used to suppress the labeling partially or completely, giving the system the ability to recognize cases where it is operating outside its specification.

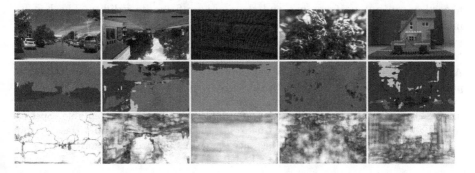

Fig. 6. Input images, semantic segmentation results and corresponding confidence of baseline model mapillary+ on *WildDash* test images (left to right: positive test case, altered valid image, abstract image and two out-of-scope images).

7   Outlook

The benchmark has now started its operation at the website wilddash.cc. It allows everyone to submit their algorithm results for evaluation. In the future, we want to increase the number of validation and benchmark images, as well as the number of test cases for each hazard cluster (especially for the high severity subsets). Also, the number of hazard clusters will most probably increase. All those improvements and extensions will be adapted according to the results of upcoming submissions. We are confident, that user feedback will help us to improve and advance *WildDash* and the concept of hazard-aware metrics in general.

8   Conclusions

In this paper we presented a new validation and benchmarking dataset for semantic and instance segmentation in autonomous driving: *WildDash*. After analyzing the current state-of-the-art and its shortcomings, we have created *WildDash* with the benefits of: (i) less dataset bias by having a large variety of road scenarios from different countries, roads layouts as well as weather and lighting conditions; (ii) more difficult scenarios with visual hazards and improved meta-information, clarifying for each test image which hazard is covered; (iii) inclusion of negative test cases where we expect the algorithm to fail.

The dataset allows for hazard-aware evaluation of algorithms: The influence of hazards such as blur, underexposure or lens distortion can directly be measured. This helps to pinpoint the best areas for improvements and can guide future algorithm development. Adding negative test cases to the benchmark further improves *WildDash*'s focus on robustness: we look even beyond difficult test cases and check algorithms outside their comfort zone. The evaluation of three baseline models using *WildDash* data shows strong influence of each separate hazard on output performance and therefore confirms its validity. The benchmark is now open and we invite all CV experts dealing with these tasks to evaluate their algorithms by visiting our new website: `wilddash.cc`.

Acknowledgement. The research was supported by ECSEL JU under the H2020 project grant agreement No. 737469 AutoDrive - Advancing fail-aware, fail-safe, and fail-operational electronic components, systems, and architectures for fully automated driving to make future mobility safer, affordable, and end-user acceptable. Special thanks go to all authors who allowed us to use their video material and Hassan Abu Alhaija from HCI for supplying the instance segmentation example algorithms.

References

1. Torralba, A., Efros, A.: Unbiased look at dataset bias. In: CVPR, pp. 1521–1528 (2011)
2. Brostow, G.J., Shotton, J., Fauqueur, J., Cipolla, R.: Segmentation and recognition using structure from motion point clouds. In: Forsyth, D., Torr, P., Zisserman, A. (eds.) ECCV 2008. LNCS, vol. 5302, pp. 44–57. Springer, Heidelberg (2008). https://doi.org/10.1007/978-3-540-88682-2_5
3. Franke, U., Gehrig, S., Rabe, C.: Daimler Böblingen, 6D-Vision. http://www.6d-vision.com. Accessed 15 Nov 2016

4. Scharwächter, T., Enzweiler, M., Franke, U., Roth, S.: Stixmantics: a medium-level model for real-time semantic scene understanding. In: Fleet, D., Pajdla, T., Schiele, B., Tuytelaars, T. (eds.) ECCV 2014. LNCS, vol. 8693, pp. 533–548. Springer, Cham (2014). https://doi.org/10.1007/978-3-319-10602-1_35

5. Cordts, M., et al.: The cityscapes dataset. In: CVPR Workshop on The Future of Datasets in Vision (2015)

6. Tung, F., Chen, J., Meng, L., Little, J.J.: The raincouver scene parsing benchmark for self-driving in adverse weather and at night. IEEE Robot. Autom. Lett. **2**(4), 2188–2193 (2017)

7. Mighty AI: Mighty AI Sample Data. https://info.mty.ai/semantic-segmentation-data. Accessed 07 Mar 2018

8. Mapillary Research: Mapillary Vistas Dataset. https://www.mapillary.com/dataset/vistas. Accessed 16 Feb 2018

9. University of California, Berkeley, U.: Berkeley deep drive. http://data-bdd.berkeley.edu/. Accessed 07 Mar 2018

10. Geiger, A., Lenz, P., Urtasun, R.: Are we ready for autonomous driving? the KITTI vision benchmark suite. In: CVPR (2012)

11. Geiger, A., Lenz, P., Stiller, C., Urtasun, R.: The KITTI Vision Benchmark Suite. http://www.cvlibs.net/datasets/kitti/eval_semantics.php. Accessed 16 Feb 2018

12. Gaidon, A., Wang, Q., Cabon, Y., Vig, E.: Virtual worlds as proxy for multi-object tracking analysis. In: CVPR (2016)

13. Ros, G., Sellart, L., Materzynska, J., Vazquez, D., Lopez, A.: The SYNTHIA dataset: a large collection of synthetic images for semantic segmentation of urban scenes. In: CVPR (2016)

14. Hernandez-Juarez, D., et al.: Slanted stixels: representing San Francisco steepest streets. In: BMVC (2017)

15. Richter, S.R., Hayder, Z., Koltun, V.: Playing for benchmarks. In: ICCV (2017)

16. Zendel, O., Murschitz, M., Humenberger, M., Herzner, W.: CV-HAZOP: introducing test data validation for computer vision. In: ICCV (2015)

17. Transportation Research Board of the National Academy of Sciences: The 2nd Strategic Highway Research Program Naturalistic Driving Study Dataset. Available from the SHRP 2 NDS InSight Data Dissemination web site (2013)

18. Zendel, O., Honauer, K., Murschitz, M., Humenberger, M., Dominguez, G.F.: Analyzing computer vision data - the good, the bad and the ugly. In: CVPR, pp. 6670–6680 (2017)

19. Everingham, M., Eslami, S.M.A., Van Gool, L., Williams, C.K.I., Winn, J., Zisserman, A.: The pascal visual object classes challenge: a retrospective. Int. J. Comput. Vis. **111**(1), 98–136 (2015)

20. Yu, F., Koltun, V., Funkhouser, T.: Dilated residual networks. In: CVPR (2017)

Generative Adversarial Network with Spatial Attention for Face Attribute Editing

Gang Zhang[1,2] , Meina Kan[1,3] , Shiguang Shan[1,3(✉)] , and Xilin Chen[1]

[1] Key Lab of Intelligent Information Processing of Chinese Academy of Sciences, Institute of Computing Technology, CAS, Beijing 100190, China
gang.zhang@vipl.ict.ac.cn, {kanmeina,sgshan,xlchen}@ict.ac.cn
[2] University of Chinese Academy of Sciences, Beijing 100049, China
[3] CAS Center for Excellence in Brain Science and Intelligence Technology, Shanghai, China

Abstract. Face attribute editing aims at editing the face image with the given attribute. Most existing works employ Generative Adversarial Network (GAN) to operate face attribute editing. However, these methods inevitably change the attribute-irrelevant regions, as shown in Fig. 1. Therefore, we introduce the spatial attention mechanism into GAN framework (referred to as SaGAN), to only alter the attribute-specific region and keep the rest unchanged. Our approach SaGAN consists of a generator and a discriminator. The generator contains an attribute manipulation network (AMN) to edit the face image, and a spatial attention network (SAN) to localize the attribute-specific region which restricts the alternation of AMN within this region. The discriminator endeavors to distinguish the generated images from the real ones, and classify the face attribute. Experiments demonstrate that our approach can achieve promising visual results, and keep those attribute-irrelevant regions unchanged. Besides, our approach can benefit the face recognition by data augmentation.

Keywords: Face attribute editing · GAN · Spatial attention
Data augmentation

1 Introduction

Face attribute editing is the task that alters the face image towards a given attribute. It has been widely used in facial animation, art, entertainment, and face expression recognition [1–4] and has drawn increasing attentions in recent years. The desired result of face attribute editing (e.g. expression editing or removing/wearing eyeglasses etc.) is that the attribute-specific region is altered to the given attribute while the rest irrelevant region keeps unchanged.

Electronic supplementary material The online version of this chapter (https:// doi.org/10.1007/978-3-030-01231-1_26) contains supplementary material, which is available to authorized users.

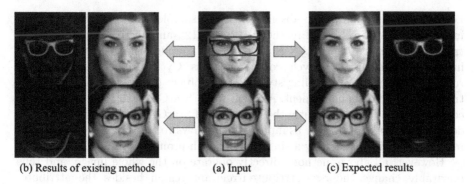

(b) Results of existing methods   (a) Input   (c) Expected results

Fig. 1. Illustration of Face attribute editing. (a) Shows the input face images, and the attributes to be edited are eyeglass and mouth close, with the corresponding attribute-specific region marked in red boxes respectively. (b) Shows the residual images and the attribute edited images from existing methods, where the whole image is altered although the attribute to be edited is local. (c) Shows the expected edited images and the expected residual images respectively, where only those attribute-specific region should be altered and the rest keep unchanged. The residual images are defined as the differences between the input face images and the edited face images. (color figure online)

In early years, face attribute editing is treated as a regression problem by using paired training samples, such as face frontalization or face eyeglasses removal. Zhu *et al.* [5] proposed a face frontalization method, which takes as input a face image to regress the desired frontal face image by minimizing the pixel-wise image reconstruction loss. To remove the eyeglasses from a face image, Zhang *et al.* [6] trained a model of multi-variable linear regression with training samples collected from face images with eyeglasses and their corresponding face images without eyeglasses. The performance of these methods heavily depends on the paired training datas, which are however quite difficult to acquire.

Recently, Generative Adversarial Network (GAN), proposed by Goodfellow *et al.* [7], has achieved great progress in image generation [8–10], image super resolution [11] and neural style transfer [12,13]. Face attribute editing also benefits a lot from GAN, which treats the face attribute editing as an unpaired image-to-image translation task. The conventional GAN framework consists of a generator and a discriminator. The discriminator learns to distinguish the generated images from the real ones, while the generator manages to fool the discriminator to produce photo-realistic images. The GAN approaches take the original face image as input and generate the edited face image with the given attribute. An extension for specific generation is conditional GANs (cGANs) [14], which allows to generate specific images given a conditional signal. Furthermore, IcGAN [15] introduces an encoder to the cGANs forming an invertible conditional GANs (IcGAN) for face attribute editing, which maps the input face image into a latent representation and an attribute vector. The face image with new attributes is generated with the altered attributes vector as the condition.

For better generation in the absence of paired samples, dual learning has been introduced into GAN-based methods [12]. In [12], an effective unpaired image translation method CycleGAN is proposed by coupling the generation and its inverse mapping under a cycle consistency loss. CycleGAN is used in a wide range of applications, including style transfer, object transfiguration, attributes transfer and photo enhancement. A recent work, StarGAN [16], also adopts cycle consistency loss, but differently the generator of StarGAN takes an image and a domain manipulation vector as input, which allows to translate images between multiple domains using only a single model with promising results.

However, all above methods directly operate on the whole image, and thus inevitably change the rest attribute-irrelevant region besides the attribute-specific region. To avoid change the whole images, Shen *et al.* [17] models the face attribute editing as learning a sparse residual image, which is defined as the difference between the input face image and the desired manipulated image. This method is referred to as ResGAN in this work for short. Compared with operating on the whole image, learning the residual image avoids changing the attribute-irrelevant region by restraining most regions of the residual image as zero. This work is quite insightful to enforce the manipulation mainly concentrate on local areas especially for those local attributes. However, the location and the appearance of target attributes are modeled in single sparse residual image which is actually hard for a favorable optimization than modeling them separately, and this can be seen from the Fig. 4 in [17], where the response of the residual image scattered the whole image although the strong response of the residual image mainly concentrate on the local areas, even for the eyeglass attribute.

Inspired by the ResGAN [17], in this work we introduce the spatial attention mechanism into GAN for more accurate face attribute editing. Spatial attention mechanism allows one to select those prior part and ignore the rest for further faster or more accurate processing, which has performed successfully in image classification [18–20], and semantic segmentation [21], etc. For face attribute editing, spatial attention mechanism can be used to restrict the manipulation only within the attribute-specific regions. The proposed GAN with spatial attention (referred to as SaGAN) consists of a generator and a discriminator. The generator aims at generating face images with target attribute for an input image. The generator is made up of two networks, an attribute manipulation network (AMN) to edit the face image with the given attribute and a spatial attention network (SAN) to localize the attribute-specific region which restricts the alternation of AMN within this region. As adversary of the generator, the discriminator distinguishes the generated images from the real ones, and classifies the face attribute. Compared with the ones operating on the whole image or learning a sparse residual image, the proposed SaGAN can precisely localize the attribute-specific region for editing by utilizing the spatial attention mechanism. Experiments demonstrate that the proposed SaGAN achieves promising visual results and further benefits the face recognition by data augmentation.

In brief, our contribution can be summarized in three-folds:

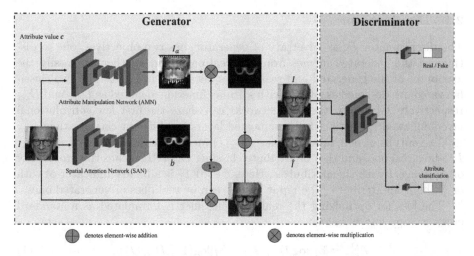

Fig. 2. An overview of our proposed SaGAN, consisting of a generator G and a discriminator D. G consists of an attribute manipulation network (AMN) to edit the face image with the given attribute, and a spatial attention network (SAN) to localize the attribute-specific region which restricts the alternation of AMN within this region. D learns to distinguish the generated images from the real ones, and classify the face attribute.

- The spatial attention is introduced to the GAN framework, forming an end -to-end generative model for face attribute editing (referred to as SaGAN), which can only alter those attribute-specific region and keep the rest irrelevant region remain the same.
- The proposed SaGAN adopts single generator with attribute as conditional signal rather than two dual ones for two inverse face attribute editing.
- The proposed SaGAN achieves quite promising results especially for those local attributes with the attribute-irrelevant details well preserved. Besides, our approach also benefits the face recognition by data augmentation.

2 Generative Adversarial Network with Spatial Attention

In this section, we will first describe the details of the generative adversarial network with spatial attention (SaGAN) method; and then give a detailed discussion about the difference from the existing methods.

An overview of SaGAN is shown in Fig. 2. For a given input image I and an attribute value c, the goal of face attribute editing is to translate I into an new image $\hat{I}$, which should be realistic, with attribute c and look the same as the input image excluding the attribute-specific region. The SaGAN consists of a generator G and a discriminator D in adversarial manner.

2.1   Discriminator

The discriminator D, as adversary of generator, has two objectives, one to distinguish the generated images from the real ones, and another to classify the attributes of the generated and real images, as shown in Fig. 2. The two classifiers are both designed as a CNN with softmax function, denoted as D_{src} and D_{cls} respectively. Generally, the two networks can share the first few convolutional layers followed by distinct fully-connected layers for different classifications.

The output of real/fake classifier $D_{src}(I)$ means the probability of an image I to be a real one, and that of attribute classifier $D_{cls}(c|I)$ means the probability of an image I with the attribute c. Here, $c \in \{0, 1\}$ is a binary indicator of with or without an attribute. The input images can be real ones or generated ones.

The loss for optimizing the real/fake classifier is formulated as a standard cross-entropy loss as below:

$$\mathcal{L}_{src}^{D} = \mathbb{E}_I[\log D_{src}(I)] + \mathbb{E}_{\hat{I}}[\log(1 - D_{src}(\hat{I}))], \tag{1}$$

where I is the real image and $\hat{I}$ is the generated image. Similarly, the loss for optimizing the attribute classifier is also formulated as a standard cross-entropy loss as below:

$$\mathcal{L}_{cls}^{D} = \mathbb{E}_{I,c^g}[-\log D_{cls}(c^g|I)], \tag{2}$$

where c^g is the ground truth attribute label of the real image I.

Finally, the overall loss function for discriminator D is formulated as follows:

$$\min_{D_{src},D_{cls}} \mathcal{L}_D = \mathcal{L}_{src}^{D} + \mathcal{L}_{cls}^{D}. \tag{3}$$

By minimizing Eq. (3), the obtained discriminator D can well separate the real images from those fake ones, and correctly predict the probability that an image I is with the attribute c.

2.2   Generator

The generator G endeavors to translate an input face image I into an edited face image $\hat{I}$ conditioned on an attribute value c, formulated as follows:

$$\hat{I} = G(I, c), \tag{4}$$

G contains two modules, an attribute manipulation network (AMN) denoted as F_m and a spatial attention network (SAN) denoted as F_a. AMN focuses on how to manipulate and SAN focuses on where to manipulate.

The attribute manipulation network takes a face image I and an attribute value c as input, and outputs an edited face image I_a, which is formulated as

$$I_a = F_m(I, c). \tag{5}$$

The spatial attention network takes the face image I as input, and predict a spatial attention mask b, which is used to restrict the alternation of AMN within this region, formulated as below:

$$b = F_a(I), \tag{6}$$

Ideally, the attribute-specific region of b should be 1, and the rest regions should be 0. In practice, the values may be any continuous number between 0 and 1 after the optimization. Therefore, those regions with non-zeros attention values are all regarded as attribute-specific region, and the rest with zero attention values are regarded as attribute-irrelevant region.

Guided by the attention mask, in the final edited face image $\hat{I}$, the attribute-specific regions are manipulated towards the target attribute while the rest regions remain the same, formulated as below:

$$\hat{I} = G(I, c) = I_a \cdot b + I \cdot (1 - b), \tag{7}$$

A favorable attribute edited image should be realistic, correctly with target attribute c, and also with modest manipulation, i.e. keep those attribute-irrelevant regions unchanged. So naturally, three kinds of losses are needed to ensure the achieving of these goals.

Firstly, to make the edited face image $\hat{I}$ photo-realistic, an adversarial loss is designed to confuse the real/fake classifier following most GAN-based methods:

$$\mathcal{L}_{src}^{G} = \mathbb{E}_{\hat{I}}[- \log D_{src}(\hat{I})]. \tag{8}$$

Secondly, to make $\hat{I}$ be correctly with target attribute c, an attribute classification loss is designed to enforce the attribute prediction of $\hat{I}$ from the attribute classifier approximates the target value c as below:

$$\mathcal{L}_{cls}^{G} = \mathbb{E}_{\hat{I}}[- \log D_{cls}(c|\hat{I})]. \tag{9}$$

Last but not least, to keep the attribute-irrelevant region unchanged, a reconstruction loss is employed similar as CycleGAN [12] and StarGAN [16], which is formulated as follows:

$$\mathcal{L}_{rec}^{G} = \lambda_1 \mathbb{E}_{I,c,c^g}[(\|I - G(G(I,c), c^g)\|_1] + \lambda_2 \mathbb{E}_{I,c^g}[(\|I - G(I, c^g)\|_1], \tag{10}$$

where c^g is the original attribute of input image I, λ_1 and λ_2 are two balance parameters. The first term is dual reconstruction loss. In this loss, when an attribute edited image $\hat{I} = G(I, c)$ is translated back to the image $G(G(I,c), c^g)$ with the original attribute c^g, it is expected to be the same as the original image I. The second term is identity reconstruction loss, which guarantees that an input image I is not modified when edited by its own attribute label c^g. Here, the L1 norm is adopted for more clear reconstruction.

Finally, the overall objective function to optimize G is achieved as below:

$$\min_{F_m, F_a} \mathcal{L}_G = \mathcal{L}_{adv}^{G} + \mathcal{L}_{cls}^{G} + \mathcal{L}_{rec}^{G}. \tag{11}$$

For the whole SaGAN network, the generator G and the discriminator D can be easily optimized in an adversarial way, following most existing GAN-based and CNN-based methods.

2.3 Discussions

Differences with CycleGAN [12]. In terms of loss function, CycleGAN and our SaGAN are similar as they both adopt the adversarial loss, the dual reconstruction loss and the identity reconstruction loss, but they differ in the way of generating the attribute editing images. The CycleGAN operates on the whole image to produce an edited image and couples the counter editing of an attribute as a cycle architecture. Differently, our SaGAN introduces spatial attention mechanism to enforce the attribute manipulation only within the attribute-specific regions for more precise attribute editing, and achieves two counter editing via single model but with different conditional signal.

Differences with StarGAN [16]. Again, the most significant difference between StarGAN and our SaGAN is that StarGAN operates on the whole image while our SaGAN only focuses on the attribute-specific region. An advantage of StarGAN is that it can edit multiple attributes with one model, while our SaGAN can only edit one attribute which will be our future work.

Differences with ResGAN [17]. ResGAN and our SaGAN are the only two methods that aims at manipulating modest region, i.e. attribute-specific region, while keeping the rest remain unchanged. They are different in how to achieve this goal. ResGAN models the manipulation of attribute-specific region as a sparse residual image, which determines the attribute-specific region via the sparsity constraint. The sparsity degree depends on a control parameter but not the attribute itself. Differently, our SaGAN determines the attribute-specific region via an attention mask predicted from the spatial attention network, which is adaptive to the attribute, and thus more accurate than that from the simple sparsity constraint. Besides, ResGAN employs two generators for the counter editing of one attribute, while our SaGAN adopts a single generator but with different conditional signal.

3 Implementation Details

Optimization. To optimize the adversarial real/fake classification more stably, in all experiments the objectives in Eqs. (1) and (8) is optimized by using WGAN-GP [22], reformulated as

$$\mathcal{L}_{src}^{D} = -\mathbb{E}_I[D_{src}(I)] + \mathbb{E}_{\hat{I}}[D_{src}(\hat{I})] + \lambda_{gp}\mathbb{E}_{\tilde{I}}[(\|\nabla_{\tilde{I}}D_{src}(\tilde{I})\|_2 - 1)^2], \quad (12)$$

$$\mathcal{L}_{src}^{G} = -\mathbb{E}_{\hat{I}}[D_{src}(\hat{I})], \quad (13)$$

while $\tilde{I}$ is sampled uniformly along a straight line between the edited images $\hat{I}$ and the real images I. λ_{gp} is the coefficient of the gradient penalty which is empirically set as $\lambda_{gp} = 10$.

Network Architecture. The detailed architectures of our SaGAN are shown in Tables 1 and 2. For the generator, the two networks of AMN and SAN share

Table 1. The network architecture of generator G. I, O, K, P, and S denote the number of input channel, the number of output channel, kernel size, padding size and stride size respectively, and IN denotes the instance normalization.

Layer	Attribute Manipulation Network (AMN)	Spatial Attention Network (SAN)
L1	Conv(I4, O32, K7, P3, S1), IN, ReLU	Conv(I3, O32, K7, P3, S1), IN, ReLU
L2	Conv(I32, O64, K4, P1, S2), IN, ReLU	Conv(I32, O64, K4, P1, S2), IN, ReLU
L3	Conv(I64, O128, K4, P1, S2), IN, ReLU	Conv(I64, O128, K4, P1, S2), IN, ReLU
L4	Conv(I128, O256, K4, P1, S2), IN, ReLU	Conv(I128, O256, K4, P1, S2), IN, ReLU
L5	Residual Block(I256, O256, K3, P1, S1)	Residual Block(I256, O256, K3, P1, S1)
L6	Residual Block(I256, O256, K3, P1, S1)	Residual Block(I256, O256, K3, P1, S1)
L7	Residual Block(I256, O256, K3, P1, S1)	Residual Block(I256, O256, K3, P1, S1)
L8	Residual Block(I256, O256, K3, P1, S1)	Residual Block(I256, O256, K3, P1, S1)
L9	Deconv(I256, O128, K4, P1, S2), IN, ReLU	Deconv(I256, O128, K4, P1, S2), IN, ReLU
L10	Deconv(I128, O64, K4, P1, S2), IN, ReLU	Deconv(I128, O64, K4, P1, S2), IN, ReLU
L11	Deconv(I64, O32, K4, P1, S2), IN, ReLU	Deconv(I64, O32, K4, P1, S2), IN, ReLU
L12	Conv(I32, O3, K7, P3, S1), Tanh	Conv(I32, O1, K7, P3, S1), Sigmoid

Table 2. The network architecture of discriminator D. I, O, K, P, and S denote the number of input channel, the number of output channel, kernel size, padding size and stride size respectively, and IN denotes the instance normalization.

Layer	Discriminator	
L1	Conv(I3, O32, K4, P1, S2), Leaky ReLU	
L2	Conv(I32, O64, K4, P1, S2), Leaky ReLU	
L3	Conv(I64, O128, K4, P1, S2), Leaky ReLU	
L4	Conv(I128, O256, K4, P1, S2), Leaky ReLU	
L5	Conv(I256, O512, K4, P1, S2), Leaky ReLU	
L6	Conv(I512, O1024, K4, P1, S2), Leaky ReLU	
L7	src: CONV(I2014, O1, K3, P1, S1)	cls: CONV(I1024, O1, K2, P0, S1), Sigmoid

the same network architecture except slight difference in the input and output: (1) AMN takes as input a four-channel tensor, consisting of an input image and a given attribute value, while SAN just takes as input the input image. (2) AMN outputs a three-channel RGB image, while SAN outputs a single channel attention mask image. (3) AMN uses $Tanh$ as the activation function for the output layer as the input image has been normalized to $[-1, 1]$ like most existing GAN methods, while SAN adopts $Sigmoid$ as the attention is within $[0, 1]$. For the discriminator, the same architecture as PatchGAN [12, 23] is used considering its promising performance.

Training Settings. The parameters of all models are randomly initialized according to the normal distribution with mean as 0 and standard deviation as 0.02. During optimization of SaGAN, Adam [24] with $\beta_1 = 0.5$, $\beta_2 = 0.999$ and learning rate $lr = 0.0002$ is adopted as the optimizer. For all of our experiments, We set $\lambda_1 = 20$ and $\lambda_2 = 100$ in Eq. (10). And the batch size is set to 16. The generator is updated once, while the discriminator is updated three times.

4 Experiments

In this section, we firstly illustrate the datasets used for experiments; and then compare our SaGAN against recent methods on face attribute editing in terms of visual performance; and finally demonstrate that our SaGAN can benefit the face recognition by data augmentation.

4.1 Datasets

The CelebA [25] dataset contains 202,599 face images of 10,177 celebrities. Each face image is annotated with 40 binary attributes. The official aligned and cropped version of CelebA are used, and all images are resized to 128 × 128. The 8,177 people with the most samples are used for training and the rest 2,000 people for testing. In summary, the training data contains 191,649 images, and the testing data contains 10,950 images for evaluation of both face attribute editing and face verification. Besides, LFW [26] dataset is also used for testing the generalization of the proposed SaGAN. Four attributes are used as exemplars for editing, including *eyeglasses*, *mouth_slightly_open*, *smiling* and *no_beard*.

4.2 Visual Comparison on Face Attribute Editing

We first investigate the results of attribute editing and the attention mask generated by SaGAN. Then, we compare the proposed SaGAN with the state-of-the-art methods including CycleGAN [12], StarGAN [16] and ResGAN [17] on face attribute editing. All these methods are trained with the same training data. They are tested on both CelebA and LFW.

Investigation of SAN. The spatial attention network (SAN), aiming at localizing the attribute-specific region which restricts the face attribute editing within this region, plays an important role in the proposed SaGAN. Therefore, we visualize the corresponding spatial attention masks to figure out how SAN contributes to the performance for face attribute editing. As can be seen in Fig. 3, the spatial attention masks mainly concentrate on the attribute-specific regions, and those attribute-irrelevant regions are successfully suppressed. This helps to keep the attribute-irrelevant regions unchanged. For local attribute such as eyeglass, the spatial attention mask only have response around the eyes, while for the attribute that may involve the movement of global face such as mouth open and smiling, the spatial attention have response on larger or even the whole face area. This illustrates that the spatial attention network can adaptively and effectively determine the attribute-specific regions according to the attribute to edit.

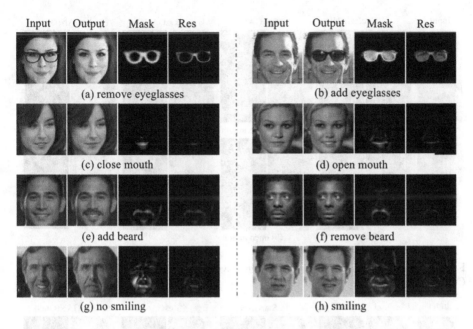

Fig. 3. Face attribute editing of our SaGAN on the CelebA dataset. "Mask" represents the spatial attention mask generated by SAN, while "Res" denotes the residual images.

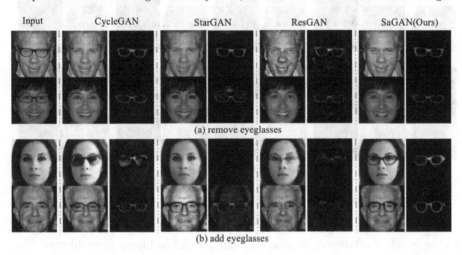

Fig. 4. Face attribute *eyeglasses* editing from different methods on the CelebA dataset.

Visual Results on CelebA. Figures 4 and 5 show the editing results on CelebA dataset for face attribute *eyeglasses* and *mouth_slightly_open* respectively. Compared with CycleGAN and StarGAN, ResGAN and our SaGAN preserves most attribute-irrelevant regions unchanged which is preferable. However, there are some artifacts on the attribute-specific regions from ResGAN especially

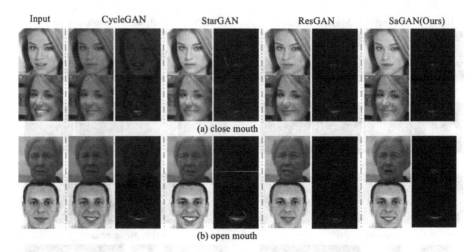

Fig. 5. Face attribute *mouth_slightly_open* editing from different methods on the CelebA dataset.

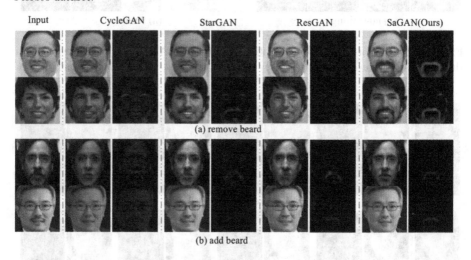

Fig. 6. Face attribute *no_beard* editing from different methods on the CelebA dataset.

on the eyeglass attribute. By contrast, our SaGAN achieves favorable manipulation on the attribute-specific region and preserve the rest irrelevant regions unchanged as well. The reason lies in that the generator of SaGAN contains a spatial attention module SAN for explicitly attribute-specific region detection, which makes the attribute manipulation network only concentrate on how to manipulate regardless of where to manipulate. Figure 6 shows the editing results of *no_beard*, and all methods inevitably change the gender of the input face as *no_beard* is correlated with gender (e.g. no woman has beards). Even so, SaGAN modifies the images modestly, e.g. preserves the most regions beyond cheek and

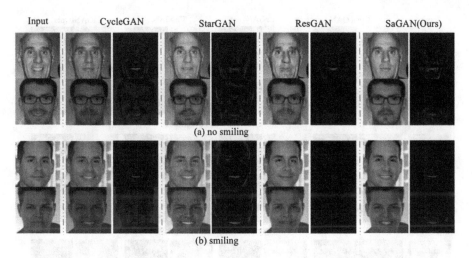

(a) no smiling

(b) smiling

Fig. 7. Face attribute *smile* editing from different methods on the CelebA dataset.

jaw. Figure 7 shows the results of global face attribute *smile*. Not surprisingly, SaGAN achieves better visual quality again demonstrating the effectiveness of the proposed method.

Visual Results on LFW. To investigate the generalization capability of SaGAN, the model trained on CelebA is further evaluated on the LFW dataset as shown in Fig. 9. As can be seen, all methods of CycleGAN, StarGAN and ResGAN degenerate on this dataset with those distorted results in Fig. 9, e.g. CycleGAN changes a male image to a female one after removing the beard. Surprisingly, SaGAN performs almost as good as on the CelebA, illustrating the robustness of our proposed method.

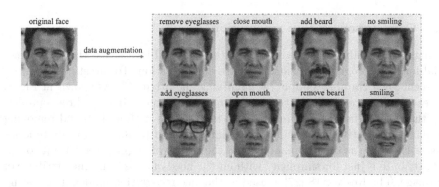

Fig. 8. Data augmentation on CelebA dataset.

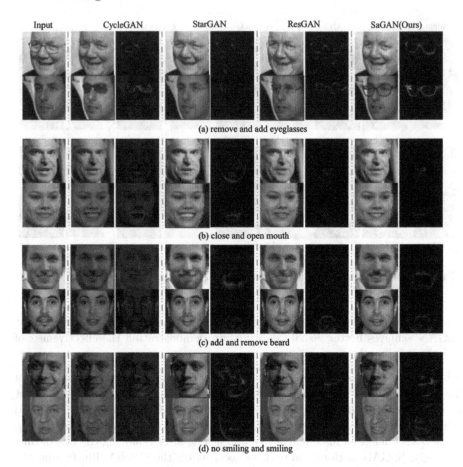

(a) remove and add eyeglasses

(b) close and open mouth

(c) add and remove beard

(d) no smiling and smiling

Fig. 9. Face attribute editing from different methods on the LFW dataset.

4.3   Comparison on face recognition

Seeing the favorable visual editing results, a natural idea is whether it is beneficial for face recognition by such as data augmentation. To investigate this, we augment each training sample by modifying the attribute. As shown in Fig. 8, for each attribute, a single training sample is augmented into three samples, e.g. the original face image and the two face images with adding and removing eyeglasses respectively. Actually, a face image edited by its own attribute looks almost the same as the original one, and the reason of augmenting with its original attribute is just for simplicity without the need of classifying the attribute of an image. The ResNet-18 [27] is used as the face recognition model. The testing is conducted on the test sets of CelebA and LFW which are the same as that for face attribute editing. On CelebA, one face image is randomly selected as target and the rest as query. On LFW, the standard protocol is employed. On both datasets, the performance is reported in terms of ROC curves.

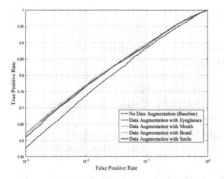 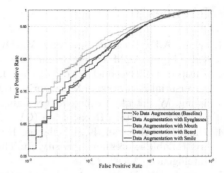

Fig. 10. Face verification on CelebA.   **Fig. 11.** Face verification on LFW.

Figure 10 shows the face verification results evaluated on CelebA. As can be observed, for each attribute, the model with data augmentation performs better than the baseline model without data augmentation, as the augmentation with accurately attribute editing images from our SaGAN enriches the variations of the training data leading to more robust model. The face verification results evaluated on LFW are shown in Fig. 11. As can be seen, the model with data augmentation with all face attributes expect *smile* are much better than the baseline model without data augmentation similar as that on the CelebA, demonstrating the benefits of our SaGAN for face verification. One possible reason for the slightly worse performance of augmentation with *smile* is that the smile faces in test data are few and the augmentation with *smile* makes the model biased to smile leading to performance degeneration.

5 Conclusions and Future Works

This work introduces the spatial attention mechanism into the GAN framework, forming a SaGAN method for more accurate face attribute editing. This kind of spatial attention mechanism ensures the manipulation of attributes only within the attribute-specific regions while keep the rest irrelevant regions unchanged. Experiments on CelebA and LFW, demonstrate that the proposed SaGAN performs better than the existing face attribute editing methods benefitted from the spatial attention mechanism. Besides, the proposed SaGAN can also benefit the face recognition through data augmentation. In the future, we will try to apply the proposed SaGAN to the general image editing tasks.

Acknowledgement. This work was partially supported by National Key Research and Development Program of China Grant 2017YFA0700804 Natural Science Foundation of China under contracts Nos. 61390511, 61772496 and 61532018.

References

1. Ichim, A.E., Bouaziz, S., Pauly, M.: Dynamic 3D avatar creation from hand-held video input. ACM Trans. Graph. (ToG) **34**(4), 45 (2015)
2. Antipov, G., Baccouche, M., Dugelay, J.L.: Face aging with conditional generative adversarial networks. arXiv preprint arXiv:1702.01983 (2017)
3. Wang, W., et al.: Recurrent face aging. In: The IEEE Conference on Computer Vision and Pattern Recognition (CVPR) (2016)
4. Ding, H., Sricharan, K., Chellappa, R.: ExprGAN: facial expression editing with controllable expression intensity. In: The Association for the Advance of Artificial Intelligence (AAAI) (2018)
5. Zhu, Z., Luo, P., Wang, X., Tang, X.: Recover canonical-view faces in the wild with deep neural networks. In: The IEEE Conference on Computer Vision and Pattern Recognition (CVPR) (2014)
6. Zhang, Z., Peng, Y.: Eyeglasses removal from facial image based on MVLR. The Era of Interactive Media. Springer, New York (2013). https://doi.org/10.1007/978-1-4614-3501-3_9
7. Goodfellow, I., et al.: Generative adversarial nets. In: Advances in Neural Information Processing Systems (NIPS) (2014)
8. Denton, E.L., Chintala, S., Fergus, R., et al.: Deep generative image models using a laplacian pyramid of adversarial networks. In: Advances in Neural Information Processing Systems (NIPS) (2015)
9. Salimans, T., Goodfellow, I., Zaremba, W., Cheung, V., Radford, A., Chen, X.: Improved techniques for training GANs. In: Advances in Neural Information Processing Systems (NIPS) (2016)
10. Berthelot, D., Schumm, T., Metz, L.: BEGAN: boundary equilibrium generative adversarial networks. arXiv preprint arXiv:1703.10717 (2017)
11. Ledig, C., et al.: Photo-realistic single image super-resolution using a generative adversarial network. arXiv preprint arXiv:1609.04802 (2016)
12. Zhu, J.Y., Park, T., Isola, P., Efros, A.A.: Unpaired image-to-image translation using cycle-consistent adversarial networks. In: The IEEE International Conference on Computer Vision (ICCV) (2017)
13. Zhang, X., Yu, F.X., Chang, S.F., Wang, S.: Deep transfer network: unsupervised domain adaptation. CoRR, abs/1503.00591 (2015)
14. Mirza, M., Osindero, S.: Conditional generative adversarial nets. arXiv preprint arXiv:1411.1784 (2014)
15. Perarnau, G., van de Weijer, J., Raducanu, B., Álvarez, J.M.: Invertible conditional GANs for image editing. arXiv preprint arXiv:1611.06355 (2016)
16. Choi, Y., Choi, M., Kim, M., Ha, J.W., Kim, S., Choo, J.: StarGAN: unified generative adversarial networks for multi-domain image-to-image translation. arXiv preprint arXiv:1711.09020 (2017)
17. Shen, W., Liu, R.: Learning residual images for face attribute manipulation. In: The IEEE Conference on Computer Vision and Pattern Recognition (CVPR) (2017)
18. Hu, J., Shen, L., Sun, G.: Squeeze-and-excitation networks. arXiv preprint arXiv:1709.01507 (2017)
19. Wang, F., et al.: Residual attention network for image classification. In: The IEEE Conference on Computer Vision and Pattern Recognition (CVPR) (2017)
20. Fu, J., Zheng, H., Mei, T.: Look closer to see better: Recurrent attention convolutional neural network for fine-grained image recognition. In: The IEEE Conference on Computer Vision and Pattern Recognition (CVPR) (2017)

21. Huang, Q., et al.: Semantic segmentation with reverse attention. In: British Machine Vision Conference (BMVC) (2017)
22. Gulrajani, I., Ahmed, F., Arjovsky, M., Dumoulin, V., Courville, A.C.: Improved training of Wasserstein GANs. In: Advances in Neural Information Processing Systems (NIPS) (2017)
23. Isola, P., Zhu, J.Y., Zhou, T., Efros, A.A.: Image-to-image translation with conditional adversarial networks. In: The IEEE Conference on Computer Vision and Pattern Recognition (CVPR) (2017)
24. Kingma, D.P., Ba, J.: Adam: a method for stochastic optimization. arXiv preprint arXiv:1412.6980 (2014)
25. Liu, Z., Luo, P., Wang, X., Tang, X.: Deep learning face attributes in the wild. In: The IEEE International Conference on Computer Vision (ICCV) (2015)
26. Huang, G.B., Ramesh, M., Berg, T., Learned-Miller, E.: Labeled faces in the wild: a database for studying face recognition in unconstrained environments. Technical report 07–49, University of Massachusetts, Amherst (2007)
27. He, K., Zhang, X., Ren, S., Sun, J.: Identity mappings in deep residual networks. In: Leibe, B., Matas, J., Sebe, N., Welling, M. (eds.) ECCV 2016. LNCS, vol. 9908, pp. 630–645. Springer, Cham (2016). https://doi.org/10.1007/978-3-319-46493-0_38

Realtime Time Synchronized Event-Based Stereo

Alex Zihao Zhu[(✉)], Yibo Chen, and Kostas Daniilidis

University of Pennsylvania, Philadelphia, PA 19104, USA
alexzhu@seas.upenn.edu

Abstract. In this work, we propose a novel event based stereo method which addresses the problem of motion blur for a moving event camera. Our method uses the velocity of the camera and a range of disparities to synchronize the positions of the events, as if they were captured at a single point in time. We represent these events using a pair of novel time synchronized event disparity volumes, which we show remove motion blur for pixels at the correct disparity in the volume, while further blurring pixels at the wrong disparity. We then apply a novel matching cost over these time synchronized event disparity volumes, which both rewards similarity between the volumes while penalizing blurriness. We show that our method outperforms more expensive, smoothing based event stereo methods, by evaluating on the Multi Vehicle Stereo Event Camera dataset.

Keywords: Event cameras · Stereo depth estimation 3D computer vision

1 Introduction

Event cameras are neuromorphically inspired asynchronous visual sensors that register changes in the log intensity of the image. When such a change is detected, the camera immediately returns an event, (x, y, t, p), to the host, consisting of the pixel position of the change, x, y, timestamp, t, accurate to microseconds, and polarity, $p \in \{-1, 1\}$, indicating whether the intensity decreased or increased. Over time, the output of the camera can be represented as a constant stream of events. The asynchronous nature of the cameras, combined with with extremely high temporal resolution, allow for high speed, low latency measurements, in situations where traditional cameras may fail. In addition, the cameras exhibit very high dynamic range (120 dB vs 60 dB for traditional cameras), allowing them to operate in a number of challenging lighting environments. Finally, the cameras also have much lower bandwidth and power consumption. One interesting use case for these cameras is stereo depth estimation, where they can provide high speed depth information for tasks such as obstacle avoidance and high speed 3D tracking.

Supplementary video: https://youtu.be/4oa7e4hsrYo.

© Springer Nature Switzerland AG 2018
V. Ferrari et al. (Eds.): ECCV 2018, LNCS 11210, pp. 438–452, 2018.
https://doi.org/10.1007/978-3-030-01231-1_27

However, a major problem facing general event-based methods is that of time synchronization. That is, events generated at different times may correspond to the same point in the image space, but will appear at different pixel positions due to the motion of the point. This problem manifests itself in two ways. Between cameras, this problem is analogous to having unsynchronized cameras for frame based stereo methods, where the epipolar constraint breaks down due to the motion between the images, and occurs when events are not generated at the same time between the two cameras. Within a single camera, this causes effects similar to the motion blur seen in frame based images. For the stereo matching problem, which is often solved using appearance based similarity metrics, this blurring is highly detrimental, as it often alters the appearance of each image differently. A number of event based stereo methods have approached these problem with asynchronous methods (e.g. [11,15,17]), which process each event independently. However, these methods must either forego the information provided by the spatial neighborhood around each event, or use fine tuned temporal windows to once again ensure time synchronization, as there are no guarantees that neighboring events were generated at a similar time.

In this work, we show that this problem can be resolved for stereo disparity matching if the velocity of the camera is known. In particular, we propose a novel event disparity volume for events from a stereo event camera pair, that uses the motion of the camera to temporally synchronize the events with temporal interpolation at each disparity. Our method takes inspiration from past works from Zhu et al. [19], Gallego et al. [5] and Rebecq et al. [13,14], which took advantage of the high temporal resolution of the events to remove motion blur from an event image using an estimate of the motion in the scene, such as optical flow or camera pose. To estimate optical flow, we use the motion field equation, given camera velocity and a set of disparities, and similarly interpolate the position of the events at each disparity to a single point in time, which we represent as a novel temporally synchronized event disparity volume. We show that, in addition to removing motion blur at the correct disparities (where the motion field equation is valid), this volume allows us to disambiguate otherwise challenging regions in the image by inducing additional motion blur.

We then define a novel matching cost over this event disparity volume, which rewards similarity between patches, while penalizing blurriness inside the patch. We show that this cost function is able to robustly distinguish the true disparity, while being extremely cheap to compute, using only bitwise comparison operations over a sliding window.

Our method, implemented in Tensorflow, runs in realtime at 40 ms on a laptop grade GPU, with significant further optimizations available. We evaluate our results on the Multi Vehicle Stereo Event Camera dataset[1] [20], and show significant improvements in disparity error over state of the art event based stereo methods, which rely on additional, more computationally expensive, smoothness regularizations.

The main contributions of this paper are summarized as:

---

[1] Dataset website: https://daniilidis-group.github.io/mvsec/.

- A novel method for using camera velocity to generate a time synchronized event disparity volume where regions at the correct disparity are in focus, while regions at the incorrect disparity are blurred.
- A novel block matching based cost function over an event disparity volume that jointly rewards similarity between left and right patches while penalizing blurriness in both patches.
- Evaluations on the Multi Vehicle Stereo Event Camera dataset, with comparisons against other state of the art methods, and evaluations of each component of the method.

2   Related Work

Early works in stereo depth estimation for event cameras, such as the works by Kogler et al. [7] and Rogister et al. [15], attempted to perform matching between individual events in a fully asynchronous fashion, using a combination of temporal and spatial constraints, which Kogler et al. showed to perform better than basic block matching between pairs of event images. However, these methods suffer from ambiguities in matching when single events are considered.

To address these ambiguities, Camuñas-Mesa et al. [2] use local spatial information in the form of local Gabor filters as features, while in [3], they track clusters of events to aid in tracking with occlusion. Zou et al. [22] use a novel local event context descriptor based on the distances between events in a window, which they extend in [23] to produce a dense disparity estimate. Similarly, Schraml et al. [16] use a cost based on the distance between events to generate panoramic depth maps.

In addition, several works have applied smoothing based regularizations to constrain ambiguous regions, which have seen great success in frame based stereo. Piatkowska et al. [11,12], have applied cooperative stereo methods [8] in an asynchronous fashion, while Xie et al. [17,18] have adapted belief propagation [1] and semiglobal matching [4], respectively, to similar effect. These regularizations have shown significant improvements over the prior state of the art.

These prior works have all shown promising results for event-based stereo matching, but do not explicitly handle the time synchronization problem without abandoning the rich spatial information around each pixel.

The problem of time synchronization has been approached in other problems, where it has been used to remove motion blur from event images. Zhu et al. [19] and Gallego et al. [5] use this synchronization as a cost function to estimate optical flow and angular velocity, respectively. Rebecq et al. [13] use the pose of a single camera from multiple views to generate a disparity space volume, in which the correct depth is similarly deblurred. Rebecq et al. [14] use a state estimator with pose and sparse depths to generate 'motion compensated' event images, on which they perform feature tracking. More recently, Mitrokhin et al. [9] use the synchronized images to perform object detection and tracking.

3   Method

The underlying problem of stereo disparity matching can be thought of as a data association problem. That is, to find correspondences between the points in the left and right images, at a given point in time. In this work, we assume that the cameras are calibrated and rectified, so that every epipolar line in both images is parallel to the x axis, and the correspondence problem is reduced to a 1D search along the x dimension. While some prior works such as [15] in the event based literature have tried to perform matching on an event by event basis, we use the spatial neighborhood around each pixel for a more detailed and robust matching, by making a locally constant depth assumption.

It is possible to perform matching on event images generated directly from the event positions. However, such an image generated from the raw events is very prone to motion blur, unless the time window is carefully selected, with a method such as the lifetime estimation in [10].

Motion blur is generated when events are captured at different points in time, such that events corresponding to the same point in the image may occur at different pixels due to the motion of that point. However, the works in [19], [5] and [14] show that motion blur can be removed from an event image if the optical flow for each pixel is known. In Sect. 3.1, we leverage this technique to both remove motion blur at the correct disparities, while further blurring the events at incorrect disparities. We then describe a novel event disparity volume representation of these time shifted events in Sect. 3.2, on which we apply a novel cost function that leverages this focus-defocus effect to allow us to discriminate the true disparity at each pixel, as described in Sect. 3.3. Finally, Sect. 3.4 discusses methods to then use the cost function to estimate the true disparity at each pixel.

An overview of the method can be found in Fig. 1

3.1   Time Synchronization Through Interpolation

For a given disparity, d, we can approximate optical flow using the motion field equation, with an assumption of known camera velocity. The motion field equation describes the relationship between the linear ($\mathbf{v}$) and angular ($\boldsymbol{\omega}$) velocity of a camera, depth Z of a point (x, y), which we treat here as a function of disparity, d, and the motion of the point in the image, which we approximate to be the optical flow $(\dot{x}_i, \dot{y}_i)$:

$$\begin{pmatrix} \dot{x}_i(d) \\ \dot{y}_i(d) \end{pmatrix} = \frac{1}{Z(d)} \begin{bmatrix} -1 & 0 & x_i \\ 0 & -1 & y_i \end{bmatrix} \mathbf{v} + \begin{bmatrix} x_i y_i & -(1 + x_i^2) & y_i \\ 1 + y_i^2 & -x_i y_i & -x_i \end{bmatrix} \boldsymbol{\omega} \tag{1}$$

$$Z(d) = \frac{fb}{d} \tag{2}$$

where f is the focal length of the camera and b is the baseline between the two cameras.

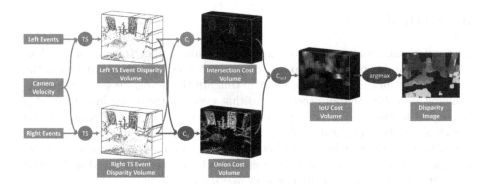

Fig. 1. Overview of our method. Given an input of left and right events and camera velocity, left and right time synchronized event disparity volumes are generated (Sects. 3.1 and 3.2). The intersection and union costs are calculated by combining the two disparity volumes, and the final IoU cost volume is computed (Sect. 3.3). Finally, the disparity is computed in a winner takes all scheme over the IoU cost volume (Sect. 3.4). Best viewed in color.

Assuming that the optical flow for each pixel is constant within each time window, we can then estimate the position of a point generating an event (x_i, y_i, t_i, p_i) at a constant time t' with linear interpolation:

$$\begin{pmatrix} x_i'(d) \\ y_i'(d) \end{pmatrix} = \begin{pmatrix} x_i \\ y_i \end{pmatrix} + \begin{pmatrix} \dot{x}_i(d) \\ \dot{y}_i(d) \end{pmatrix} (t' - t_i) \tag{3}$$

Assuming a static scene and accurate velocities and disparities, the set of time synchronized events, $\{ (x_i'(d)\ y_i'(d)\ t'\ p_i) \}$, is assumed to have no motion blur for all x_i and y_i with disparity d.

3.2   Time Synchronized Event Disparity Volume Generation

However, the true depth for each pixel is unknown for this problem. Instead, we select a range of disparities over which to search, and apply (3) to the set of events from the left camera for every disparity within the range.

At each disparity level, d, we generate an image based on the time shifted events, where a pixel with more positive events is set to 1, more negative events is set to –1, and no events is set to 0. Note that the time shifted event positions are rounded to the nearest integer to index into the image.

$$I_L(x, y, d) = \text{sign}\left(\sum_i p_i \right) \tag{4}$$

$$i \in \{i | (x_i'(d), y_i'(d)) = (x, y)\}$$

$$p_i \in \{-1, 1\}$$

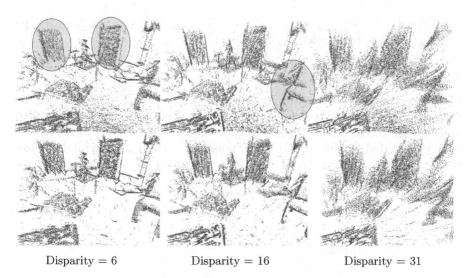

Disparity = 6   Disparity = 16   Disparity = 31

Fig. 2. Sample slices of the left (top) and right (bottom) time synchronized event disparity volumes at disparities 6 (left), 16 (middle) and 31 (right). Only positive pixels are shown for clarity. At disparity 6, the boards at the back are in focus, while at disparity 16, the chair in the front is in focus (both circled in yellow). The other features at the wrong depth are blurred. The right slices have been shifted horizontally by the disparity, as in (5), so that corresponding points should be at the same x position in both images. Best viewed in color.

This is similar to standard methods that generate images by summing events at each pixel, but the additional sign operator allows the image to be robust to the left or right camera generating more events at each pixel than the other.

The result is a 3D volume for the left camera, where each slice in the disparity dimension represents the images generated according to (4), using the disparity corresponding to that slice. That is, when the camera moves with some linear velocity, this flow would have a deblurring effect on points where the pixel position matches the disparity, and potentially apply further blurring on points where the disparity is incorrect. In the case when the camera's motion is pure rotation, the flow will produce unblurred images at each disparity slice.

We apply a similar operation to the events from the right camera, except that the x position of each shifted event is further shifted by the disparity at each level:

$$I_R(x, y, d) = \text{sign}\left(\sum_i p_i\right) \tag{5}$$

$$i \in \{i | (x'_i(d) + d, y'_i(d)) = (x, y)\}$$

$$p_i \in \{-1, 1\}$$

This generates a set of disparity volumes similar to traditional plane sweep volumes, where the potential matching right pixel corresponding to $I_L(x, y, d)$

is $I_R(x, y, d)$. We show some example slices of this volume in Fig. 2, where the blurring and deblurring effects can be clearly seen.

3.3 Matching Cost

Finally, we apply a novel sliding window matching cost that leverages both the deblurring and blurring effects of Sect. 3.1. First, it penalizes windows with many events, as this would indicate areas with an incorrect disparity due to the blurring incurred by the temporal interpolation. Given a local spatial window $W(x, y, d)$ around a pixel (x, y) at a given disparity d, we encode this using a union term, defined as:

$$C_U(x, y, d) = \sum_{x^*, y^* \in W(x, y, d)} I_L(x^*, y^*, d) \cup I_R(x^*, y^*, d) \tag{6}$$

$$a \cup b = \begin{cases} 1 & a \neq 0 \text{ or } b \neq 0 \\ 0 & \text{otherwise} \end{cases}$$

We carefully choose the union operator instead of addition, in order to not double penalize pixels with events in both volumes.

Second, the cost rewards windows that are similar. That is, we would like pixels between the two images to have events with the same polarity. We encode this using an intersection term, defined as:

$$C_I(x, y, d) = \sum_{x^*, y^* \in W(x, y, d)} I_L(x^*, y^*, d) \cap I_R(x^*, y^*, d) \tag{7}$$

$$a \cap b = \begin{cases} 1 & a = b \neq 0 \\ 0 & \text{otherwise} \end{cases}$$

This is similar to the tri-state logic error function presented in [7], except we explicitly do not reward pixels that are both 0 in the intersection term, as we only want to capture associations between events, and not between pixels without events.

The final cost, then, can be thought of as an analogy to the intersection over union cost:

$$C_{IoU}(x, y, d) = -\frac{C_I(x, y, d)}{C_U(x, y, d)} \tag{8}$$

Minimizing this final cost will implicitly maximize the similarity between the two windows, while minimizing the blurring in each. By computing this cost function at every pixel and disparity, we generate a cost volume, where each element (x, y, d) in the volume contains the cost of pixel (x, y) being at disparity d.

3.4 Disparity Estimation

Given the cost volume, the fastest way to obtain the estimate for the true disparity at each pixel is to compute the argmax across the disparity dimension of the cost volume, in a winner takes all fashion:

$$\hat{d}(x, y) = \arg \min_{d} \; C_{IoU}(x, y, d) \tag{9}$$

However, we can also apply any traditional optimization method for stereo disparity estimation over the cost volume, such as semi-global matching [4] or belief propagation [1].

3.5 Outlier Rejection

While the cost function in (8) was relatively robust in our experiments, there were still some regions of the image where it was unable to resolve the correct disparity, which we need to remove from the final output. In particular, we found that pixels with a low final IoU cost typically corresponded to pure noise in the image, where the number of intersection matches was low compared to the number of events in the window. Therefore, any disparities with C_{IoU} less than a parameter ϵ_c are considered outliers. In addition, windows with a low number of events do not provide enough support to find a meaningful match, and so we consider outliers any disparities with C_U less than $\epsilon_n \times \|W\|$, where ϵ_n is a parameter and $\|W\|$ is the number of pixels in the spatial neighborhood.

4   Implementation Details

In our experiments, unless otherwise stated, we use a disparity range ranging from 0 to 31 pixels, and a square window with side length of 24 pixels. For outlier rejection, ϵ_c and ϵ_n were both set to 0.1. At each time step, a constant number of events is passed to the algorithm. For our experiments, we used 15,000 events.

As every step of the algorithm is vectorizable with matrix notation, the algorithm was efficiently implemented on GPU in Tensorflow. In particular, (2) and (3) are implemented as a matrix operations, (4) and (5) are performed using scatter_nd, and the costs in (6) and (7) are computed by computing the costs for each pixel at each disparity, and applying two 1D depthwise convolutions with a kernel of ones of the same length as the window size (one along the rows, one along the columns).

With all operations fully vectorized, the algorithm takes 40 ms to run on a laptop NVIDIA 960M GPU, including transfer time to the GPU. With further optimizations and an implementation in raw CUDA or OpenCL, we expect this time to reduce further. This corresponds to a runtime of around 2.7 μs per event, compared to the 0.65–2 ms reported in [17]. However, it should be noted that the competing methods were implemented in MATLAB on CPU, and would almost certainly see speed improvements if ported to other languages/devices. In addition, our method is relatively insensitive to the number of events, as a large proportion of the run time (∼40%) is consumed in the sliding window cost. For example, processing a window of 30,000 events takes 46 ms to run, corresponding to a runtime of 1.53 μs per event.

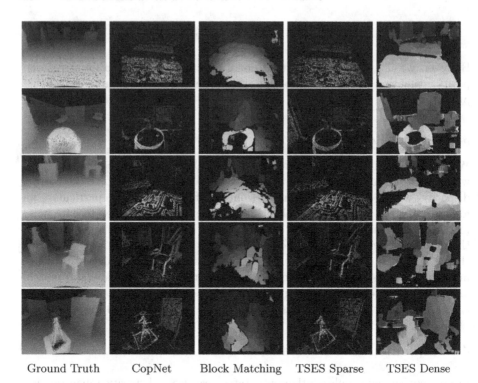

Ground Truth   CopNet   Block Matching   TSES Sparse   TSES Dense

Fig. 3. Sample outputs from TSES (our method), compared against CopNet and block matching, with ground truth from MVSEC. Pixels without disparities are dark blue. Note that the border of the CopNet and block matching results are empty due to the window size. Quantitative results were only computed over points with disparities. Best viewed in color.

5   Experiments

5.1   Data

We evaluated our algorithm on the Multi Vehicle Stereo Event Camera (MVSEC) dataset [20]. MVSEC provides data captured from a stereo event camera pair, along with grayscale images and ground truth depth and pose of the cameras. We tested our method on the indoor_flying sequences, and evaluated against the provided ground truth depth maps. These sequences were generated from a stereo event camera pair mounted on a hexacopter, and flown in an indoor environment, with ground truth generated from lidar measurements. In particular, we used the following depth map frames (zero index) from these indoor_ flying sequences for evaluation: indoor_flying1: 140–1200, indoor_flying2: 120–1420, indoor_flying3: 73–1616. These frames were selected to exclude the takeoff and landing frames where the ground is closer than our selected maximum disparity.

The driving sequences were not included as the majority of the points in those sequences were beyond the depth resolved by a disparity of 1, and so a sub-pixel

Table 1. Quantitative results from testing on the indoor_flying (IF) sequences of TSES (our method) and CopNet, along with ablation studies. Prefixes for the algorithm ablation are: IoU - Intersection over Union cost (8), I - Intersection cost (7), T - Time cost (10). Suffixes are with (S) and without (NS) time synchronization (3). Velocity noise was added to the linear and angular velocities separately, as zero mean Gaussian noise with variance equal to a percentage of the norm of each velocity.

	Mean disp. error (pix)			Mean depth error (m)			% Disp. err < 1		
	IF1	IF2	IF3	IF1	IF2	IF3	IF1	IF2	IF3
TSES	0.89	1.98	0.88	0.36	0.44	0.36	**82.3**	**70.1**	**82.3**
CopNet	1.03	1.54	1.01	0.61	1.00	0.64	70.4	52.8	70.6
BM	**0.73**	**1.02**	**0.82**	**0.23**	**0.21**	**0.27**	79.5	65.2	74.3
SGBM	1.96	3.06	1.86	0.38	0.38	0.41	69.9	56.8	66.7
Algorithm ablation									
T-S	1.30	2.54	1.39	0.50	0.58	0.57	77.3	64.9	76.7
I-S	1.71	3.59	1.99	0.67	0.99	0.77	74.2	60.7	72.5
IoU-NS	1.43	2.29	1.42	0.52	0.47	0.53	67.8	59.0	68.3
T-NS	1.85	2.78	1.84	0.76	0.66	0.78	64.2	55.6	64.0
I-NS	2.21	3.20	2.12	0.80	0.80	0.78	61.6	53.5	62.7
TSES w/outliers	1.87	2.83	1.73	1.28	1.18	1.15	74.3	64.3	75.2
Velocity noise ablation									
0%	**0.89**	1.98	**0.88**	**0.36**	**0.44**	**0.36**	**82.3**	70.1	82.3
5%	0.90	**1.97**	**0.88**	**0.36**	0.45	**0.36**	82.0	**70.5**	**82.4**
10%	0.91	1.98	**0.88**	0.37	0.45	**0.36**	81.6	70.1	82.3
20%	0.96	2.04	0.92	0.38	0.46	0.38	80.4	68.6	81.3
50%	1.21	2.44	1.23	0.47	0.58	0.51	74.5	61.5	74.5
100%	1.97	3.47	2.17	0.83	0.92	1.03	61.8	48.5	59.1
Window size ablation									
8 pix.	2.40	3.83	2.52	0.78	0.87	0.86	65.4	55.3	63.8
16 pix.	1.10	2.29	1.13	0.43	0.51	0.45	80.3	69.2	79.8
24 pix.	0.89	1.98	0.88	0.36	0.44	0.36	**82.3**	**70.1**	**82.3**
32 pix.	**0.86**	**1.97**	**0.84**	**0.34**	**0.43**	0.34	81.2	66.7	81.4
40 pix.	0.89	2.05	0.91	**0.34**	0.44	**0.33**	78.6	61.9	77.9

disparity estimator would be needed to achieve accurate results. In addition, we do not include results from indoor_flying4, as the majority of events are closer than the maximum disparity of 31, and are also generated by the low-texture floor, on which we could not generate reasonable results with any of the methods.

While our method generates disparity values whenever there are any events inside the spatial window, we report our results based on disparities on pixels where events appeared, in order to provide a fair comparison with other works.

We used the camera velocities provided in the dataset from [21], which were generated by linear interpolation of the lidar odometry poses provided from MVSEC, and are provided in addition to ground truth optical flow for the sequences in the dataset.

5.2   Comparisons

For comparison, we have implemented the CopNet method by Piatkowska et al. [12], and we include their results on the same dataset, using their provided parameters. For these experiments, we have used an α value of 1 (the scaling term in the matching cost, Eq. (3) in their paper), as the original paper stated a value of 0, which would result in a constant cost. In addition, we compare against block matching and semi-global block matching methods from OpenCV[2], applied to the grayscale frames from the DAVIS camera. Note that the grayscale frames are not time synchronized, and the time offset between the left and right frames is 4 ms, 14 ms and 14 ms for indoor_flying 1, 2 and 3, respectively. However, we were still able to achieve reasonable performance. The quantitative results of these comparisons can be found in Table 1.

In addition, we attempted an implementation of the belief propagation based work by Xie et al. [17], but were unable to obtain reasonable results over this dataset, which is significantly more complex than those evaluated in the original work, consisting of a few objects moving in the scene. We believe that this is because their matching cost ($D(d_p)$) attempts to match individual events, without using the spatial neighborhood around the event. In our experiments, this matching cost failed to identify the correct disparity over the majority of the image, which we believe led the belief propagation to output incorrect results.

5.3   Ablation Studies

In addition to the comparisons, we performed a number of ablation studies over the parameters of the algorithm. All results can be found in Table 1.

Algorithm Ablation. To test the effect of the time synchronized event disparity volumes, we performed additional experiments where the raw event positions were passed directly into (4) and (5) (i.e. by setting $(x'(d)_i, y'(d)_i) = (x_i, y_i)$). Experiments with and without time synchronization are denoted with the suffix -S and -NS, respectively.

To test the IoU cost, we tested with only the intersection cost (prefix I), as well as using the cost function from [12] (prefix T), which is defined as:

$$C_T(x, y, d) = \sum_{x^*, y^* \in W(x,y,d)} \frac{1}{(\alpha \cdot |I_L^t(x^*, y^*, d) - I_R^t(x^*, y^*, d)| + 1) \cdot C_U(x^*, y^*, d)}$$

(10)

---

[2] https://docs.opencv.org/3.4/d2/d6e/classcv_1_1StereoMatcher.html.

where α is set to 1, the event images I^t now represent the timestamp of the last event to arrive at each pixel and disparity:

$$I^t_L(x,y,d) = \max_{t_i} \{t_i | (x'_i(d), y'_i(d)) = (x,y)\} \tag{11}$$

$$I^t_R(x,y,d) = \max_{t_i} \{t_i | (x'_i(d) + d, y'_i(d)) = (x,y)\} \tag{12}$$

and we use our union cost in place of the number of events in the left window. We also tested with the inverse of the union cost, but this did not produce any reasonable results.

We also provide results of our full method, without the outlier rejection step.

Velocity Noise Ablation. In practice, it is difficult to estimate the cameras' velocity with the same accuracy as the ground truth. To test the effect of noise on the velocity estimate, we perform additional experiments where we add zero mean Gaussian noise to the linear and angular velocities. The variance of the noise is set to a given percentage of the norm of the linear and angular velocities, separately.

Window Size Ablation. We also tested the effects of the window size on the performance of our method over a range of window sizes.

5.4   Results and Discussion

Comparisons. We present some qualitative results in Fig. 3, comparing our method to CopNet, block matching and ground truth. While both sets of results look visually reasonable, we can see that our method suffers less from foreground fattening [6] (e.g. the chair in the fourth row). Our method does, however, tend to produce erroneous results on the edges of images in the dense disparity image, but these correspond to pixels without any events, and are thresholded away in the sparse disparity image.

In addition, we provide quantitative results in Table 1, where we can see that our full method outperforms CopNet across almost every measure, as well as the other methods in the ablation study. In particular, while the disparity errors are similar, CopNet performs significantly worse in depth overall. Upon examining the results. We found that this error from CopNet was largely due to the fact that the method had over-smoothed the disparity output. This was mostly due to the window size used, which is relatively large (39 × 39). This oversmoothing tends to pull far away points closer (overestimates disparities), which leads to higher depth errors, as they are higher at lower disparity levels. However, we observed that reducing the window sizes resulted in a further reduction in the overall matching accuracy due to increased ambiguity in the matching, as noted by the authors in the original paper [12], so there was no immediate solution for this problem.

The block matching method performed better in terms of mean errors across all three sequences, although the mean disparity errors for sequences 1 and 3 are both less than 1 pixel, which is within the range of the discretization error. In addition, our method has a higher percentage of points with disparity error <1 across all sequences.

We were unable to achieve comparable performance from semi-global block matching, which tended to over smooth incorrect regions in the image.

Algorithm Ablations. From the ablation study, we can see that removing each component of the method tends to result in a corresponding decrease in accuracy, with the time synchronization always resulting in better results. In addition, the addition of the union cost to the overall cost provides a significant improvement in accuracy over the intersection cost, which is a pure similarity measure.

Furthermore, we can see that our IoU cost outperforms the timestamp based cost in both situations, suggesting that it may be a better alternative for more complex methods, even without the time synchronization. When the proposed time synchronization is applied at the correct disparity, older timestamps are mapped to later timestamps from the same point in the image. As the time cost operates on an image that only keeps the latest timestamp, this results in images with timestamps that are very similar (all later events), which do not provide much discriminative power. Future work could consider all of the events that map to a pixel, but this requires a new cost function.

Finally, the results without outlier rejection have significantly higher mean disparity errors, suggesting that a large number of outliers were rejected by our method, while from the % disparity error < 1 results, we can see that only $<10\%$ of the points were rejected.

Velocity Noise Ablation. The velocity noise ablation results show stable errors up to noise with variance up to around 20% of the velocity norm. We believe that a conventional state estimation pipeline for event cameras should be able to reliably estimate the camera velocity within these error bounds.

Window Size Ablation. We found that window sizes between 24 and 40 pixels achieved the best results. However, larger window sizes increase the amount of foreground fattening, as well as the runtime of the algorithm. Therefore, we recommend a window size of 24 pixels for these test cases. In terms of run time, the algorithm took 33 ms, 40 ms and 50 ms to run for window sizes of 16, 24 and 32 pixels, respectively. Similarly, the runtime was 25 ms and 60 ms for disparity ranges of 16 and 48, with a window size of 24 pixels.

6   Conclusions

We have proposed a novel method for stereo event disparity matching which uses the motion of the camera to synchronize the event streams in time. We show that our method, consisting of a simple temporal interpolation of the events, along with a lightweight matching cost, is able to outperform state of the art methods which perform expensive regularizations on top of the disparity map. In addition, as our disparity results are at a single time, analogous to an image frame, they can be directly passed into any frame based architecture such as a state estimator, as compared to an asynchronous disparity stream. We envision that this method will be coupled with a method for estimating camera velocity, such as a visual odometry algorithm, for real time performance.

Acknowledgements. Thanks to Tobi Delbruck and the team at iniLabs for providing and supporting the DAVIS-346b cameras. We also gratefully appreciate support through the following grants: NSF-IIS-1703319, NSF-IIP-1439681 (I/UCRC), ARL RCTA W911NF-10-2-0016, and the DARPA FLA program.

References

1. Besse, F., Rother, C., Fitzgibbon, A., Kautz, J.: PMBP: patchmatch belief propagation for correspondence field estimation. Int. J. Comput. Vis. **110**(1), 2–13 (2014)
2. Camuñas-Mesa, L.A., Serrano-Gotarredona, T., Ieng, S.H., Benosman, R.B., Linares-Barranco, B.: On the use of orientation filters for 3D reconstruction in event-driven stereo vision. Front. Neurosci. **8**, 48 (2014)
3. Camuñas-Mesa, L.A., Serrano-Gotarredona, T., Ieng, S.H., Benosman, R., Linares-Barranco, B.: Event-driven stereo visual tracking algorithm to solve object occlusion. IEEE Trans. Neural Netw. Learn. Syst. **29**, 4223–4237 (2017)
4. Felzenszwalb, P.F., Huttenlocher, D.P.: Efficient belief propagation for early vision. Int. J. Comput. Vis. **70**(1), 41–54 (2006)
5. Gallego, G., Scaramuzza, D.: Accurate angular velocity estimation with an event camera. IEEE Robot. Autom. Lett. **2**(2), 632–639 (2017)
6. Geiger, A., Roser, M., Urtasun, R.: Efficient large-scale stereo matching. In: Kimmel, R., Klette, R., Sugimoto, A. (eds.) ACCV 2010. LNCS, vol. 6492, pp. 25–38. Springer, Heidelberg (2011). https://doi.org/10.1007/978-3-642-19315-6_3
7. Kogler, J., Humenberger, M., Sulzbachner, C.: Event-based stereo matching approaches for frameless address event stereo data. In: Bebis, G. (ed.) ISVC 2011. LNCS, vol. 6938, pp. 674–685. Springer, Heidelberg (2011). https://doi.org/10.1007/978-3-642-24028-7_62
8. Marr, D., Poggio, T.: Cooperative computation of stereo disparity. In: Vaina, L. (ed.) From the Retina to the Neocortex, pp. 239–243. Birkhäuser, Boston (1976). https://doi.org/10.1007/978-1-4684-6775-8_9
9. Mitrokhin, A., Fermuller, C., Parameshwara, C., Aloimonos, Y.: Event-based moving object detection and tracking. arXiv preprint arXiv:1803.04523 (2018)
10. Mueggler, E., Forster, C., Baumli, N., Gallego, G., Scaramuzza, D.: Lifetime estimation of events from dynamic vision sensors. In: 2015 IEEE International Conference on Robotics and Automation (ICRA), pp. 4874–4881. IEEE (2015)
11. Piatkowska, E., Belbachir, A.N., Gelautz, M.: Cooperative and asynchronous stereo vision for dynamic vision sensors. Meas. Sci. Technol. **25**(5), 055108 (2014)
12. Piatkowska, E., Kogler, J., Belbachir, N., Gelautz, M.: Improved cooperative stereo matching for dynamic vision sensors with ground truth evaluation. In: 2017 IEEE Conference on Computer Vision and Pattern Recognition Workshops (CVPRW), pp. 370–377. IEEE (2017)

13. Rebecq, H., Gallego, G., Mueggler, E., et al.: EMVS: event-based multi-view stereo—3D reconstruction with an event camera in real-time. Int. J. Comput. Vis. 1–21 (2017). https://doi.org/10.1007/s11263-017-1050-6

14. Rebecq, H., Horstschaefer, T., Scaramuzza, D.: Real-time visual-inertial odometry for event cameras using keyframe-based nonlinear optimization. In: British Machine Vision Conference (BMVC), vol. 3 (2017)

15. Rogister, P., Benosman, R., Ieng, S.H., Lichtsteiner, P., Delbruck, T.: Asynchronous event-based binocular stereo matching. IEEE Trans. Neural Netw. Learn. Syst. **23**(2), 347–353 (2012)

16. Schraml, S., Nabil Belbachir, A., Bischof, H.: Event-driven stereo matching for real-time 3D panoramic vision. In: Proceedings of the IEEE Conference on Computer Vision and Pattern Recognition, pp. 466–474 (2015)

17. Xie, Z., Chen, S., Orchard, G.: Event-based stereo depth estimation using belief propagation. Front. Neurosci. **11**, 535 (2017)

18. Xie, Z., Zhang, J., Wang, P.: Event-based stereo matching using semiglobal matching. Int. J. Adv. Robot. Syst. **15**(1) (2018). https://doi.org/10.1177/1729881417752759

19. Zhu, A.Z., Atanasov, N., Daniilidis, K.: Event-based feature tracking with probabilistic data association. In: 2017 IEEE International Conference on Robotics and Automation (ICRA), pp. 4465–4470. IEEE (2017)

20. Zhu, A.Z., Thakur, D., Ozaslan, T., Pfrommer, B., Kumar, V., Daniilidis, K.: The multi vehicle stereo event camera dataset: an event camera dataset for 3D perception. IEEE Robot. Autom. Lett. **3**, 2032–2039 (2018)

21. Zhu, A.Z., Yuan, L., Chaney, K., Daniilidis, K.: EV-FlowNet: self-supervised optical flow estimation for event-based cameras. arXiv preprint arXiv:1802.06898 (2018)

22. Zou, D., et al.: Context-aware event-driven stereo matching. In: 2016 IEEE International Conference on Image Processing (ICIP), pp. 1076–1080. IEEE (2016)

23. Zou, D., et al.: Robust dense depth map estimation from sparse DVS stereos. In: British Machine Vision Conference (BMVC), vol. 3 (2017)

OmniDepth: Dense Depth Estimation
for Indoors Spherical Panoramas

Nikolaos Zioulis$^{(\boxtimes)}$ ⓘ, Antonis Karakottas ⓘ, Dimitrios Zarpalas,
and Petros Daras

Centre for Research and Technology Hellas (CERTH) - Information Technologies
Institute (ITI) - Visual Computing Lab (VCL), Thessaloniki, Greece
{nzioulis,ankarako,zarpalas,daras}@iti.gr
http://vcl.iti.gr

Abstract. Recent work on depth estimation up to now has only focused
on projective images ignoring 360° content which is now increasingly and
more easily produced. We show that monocular depth estimation models trained on traditional images produce sub-optimal results on omnidirectional images, showcasing the need for training directly on 360°
datasets, which however, are hard to acquire. In this work, we circumvent the challenges associated with acquiring high quality 360° datasets
with ground truth depth annotations, by re-using recently released large
scale 3D datasets and re-purposing them to 360° via rendering. This
dataset, which is considerably larger than similar projective datasets, is
publicly offered to the community to enable future research in this direction. We use this dataset to learn in an end-to-end fashion the task of
depth estimation from 360° images. We show promising results in our
synthesized data as well as in unseen realistic images.

Keywords: Omnidirectional media · 360° · Spherical panorama
Scene understanding · Depth estimation · Synthetic dataset
Learning with virtual data

1 Introduction

One of the fundamental challenges in computer and 3D vision is the estimation
of a scene's depth. Depth estimation leads to a three-dimensional understanding
of the world which is very important to numerous applications. These vary from
creating 3D maps [1] and allowing navigation in real-world environments [2], to
enabling stereoscopic rendering [3], synthesizing novel views out of pre-captured
content [4] and even compositing 3D objects into it [5]. Depth information has
been shown to boost the effectiveness of many vision tasks related to scene
understanding when utilized jointly with color information [6,7].

N. Zioulis and A. Karakottas—Equal contribution.

Electronic supplementary material The online version of this chapter (https://
doi.org/10.1007/978-3-030-01231-1_28) contains supplementary material, which is
available to authorized users.

© Springer Nature Switzerland AG 2018
V. Ferrari et al. (Eds.): ECCV 2018, LNCS 11210, pp. 453–471, 2018.
https://doi.org/10.1007/978-3-030-01231-1_28

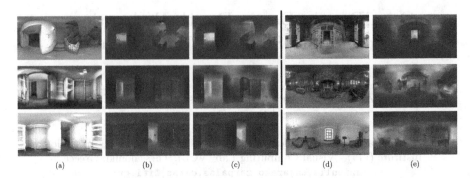

Fig. 1. We learn the task of predicting depth directly from omnidirectional indoor scene images. Results from our RectNet model are presented (left to right): (a) 360° image samples from our test set, (b) corresponding ground truth depth, (c) predicted depth maps of the test image samples, (d) 360° unseen image samples from the Sun360 dataset, (e) predicted depth maps of the Sun360 image samples.

Similar to how babies start to perceive depth from two viewpoints and then by ego-motion and observation of objects' motions, researchers have tackled the problem of estimating depth via methods built on multi-view consistency [8,9] and structure-from-motion (SfM) [10]. But humans are also driven by past experiences and contextual similarities and apply this collective knowledge when presented with new scenes. Likewise, with the advent of more effective machine learning techniques, recent research focuses on learning to predict depth and has led to impressive results even with completely unsupervised learning approaches.

However, learning based approaches have only focused on traditional 2D content captured by typical pinhole projection model based cameras. With the emergence of efficient spherical cameras and rigs, omnidirectional (360°) content is now more easily and consistently produced and is witnessing increased adoption in entertainment and marketing productions, robotics and vehicular applications as well as coverage of events and even journalism. Consumers can now experience 360° content in mobile phones, desktops and, more importantly, the new arising medium – Virtual Reality (VR) – headsets.

Depth and/or geometry extraction from omnidirectional content has been approached similar to traditional 2D content via omnidirectional stereo [11–14] and SfM [4] analytical solutions. There are inherent problems though to applying learning based methods to 360° content as a result of its acquisition process that inhibits the creation of high quality datasets. Coupling them with 360° LIDARs would produce low resolution depths and would also insert the depth sensor into the content itself, a drawback that also exists when aiming to acquire stereo datasets. One alternative would be to manually re-position the camera but that would be tedious and error prone as a consistent baseline would not be possible.

In this work, we train a CNN to learn to estimate a scene's depth given an omnidirectional (equirectangular) image as input[1] (Fig. 1). To circumvent the lack of available training data we resort to re-using existing 3D datasets and re-purposing them for use within a 360° context. This is accomplished by generating diverse 360° views via rendering. We use this dataset for learning to infer depth from omnidirectional content. In summary, our contributions are the following:

1. We present the first, to the authors' knowledge, learning based dense depth estimation method that was trained with and operates directly on omnidirectional content in the form of equirectangular images.
2. We offer a dataset consisting of 360° color images paired with ground truth 360° depth maps in equirectangular format. The dataset is available online[2].
3. We propose and validate, a CNN auto-encoder architecture specifically designed for estimating depth directly on equirectangular images.
4. We show how monocular depth estimation methods trained on traditional 2D images fall short or produce low quality results when applied to equirectangular inputs, highlighting the need for learning directly on the 360° domain.

2   Related Work

Since this work aims to learn the task of omnidirectional dense depth estimation, and given that - to the authors' knowledge - no other similar work exists, we first review non-learning based methods for geometric scene understanding based on 360° images. We then examine learning based approaches for spherical content and, finally, present recent monocular dense depth estimation methods.

2.1   Geometric Understanding on 360° Images

Similar to pinhole projection model cameras, the same multi-view geometry [8] principles apply to 360° images. By observing the scene from multiple view-points and establishing correspondences between them, the underlying geometrical structure can be estimated. For 360° cameras the conventional binocular or multi-view stereo [9] problem is reformulated to binocular or multi-view spherical stereo [11] respectively, by taking into account the different projection model and after defining the disparity as angular displacements. By estimating the disparity (i.e. depth), complete scenes can be 3D reconstructed from multiple [14,15] or even just two [12,13] spherical viewpoints. However, all these approaches require multiple 360° images to estimate the scene's geometry. Recently it was shown that 360° videos acquired with a moving camera can be used to 3D reconstruct a scene's geometry via SfM [4] and enable 6 DOF viewing in VR headsets.

There are also approaches that require only a single image to understand indoors scenes and estimate their layout. PanoContext [16], generates a 3D room

---

[1] We use the terms omnidirectional image, 360° image, spherical panorama and equirectangular image interchangeably in this document.

[2] http://vcl.iti.gr/360-dataset/.

layout hypothesis given an indoor 360° image in equirectangular format. With the estimations being bounding boxes, the inferred geometry is only a coarse approximation of the scene. Similar in spirit, the work of Yang et al. [17] generates complete room layouts from panoramic indoor images by combining superpixel information, vanishing points estimation and a geometric context prior under a Manhattan world assumption. However, focusing on room layout estimation, it is unable to recover finer details and structures of the scene. Another similar approach [18] addresses the problem of geometric scene understanding from another perspective. Under a maximum a posteriori estimation it unifies semantic, pose and location cues to generate CAD models of the observed scenes. Finally, in [19] a spherical stereo pair is used to estimate both the room layout but also object and material attributes. After retrieving the scene's depth by stereo matching and subsequently calculating the normals, the equirectangular image is projected to the faces of a cube that are then fed to a CNN whose object predictions are fused into the 360° image to finally reconstruct the 3D layout.

2.2   Learning for 360° Images

One of the first approaches to estimate distances purely from omnidirectional input [20] under a machine learning setting utilized Gaussian processes. Instead of estimating the distance of each pixel, a range value per image column was predicted to drive robotic navigation. Nowadays, with the establishment of CNNs, there are two straightforward ways to apply current CNN processing pipelines to spherical input. Either directly on a projected (typically equirectangular) image, or by projecting the spherical content to the faces of a cube (cubemap) and running the CNN predictions on them, which are then merged by back-projecting them to the spherical domain. The latter approach was selected by an artistic style transfer work [21], where each face was re-styled separately and then the cubemap was re-mapped back to the equirectangular domain. Likewise, in SalNet360 [22], saliency predictions on the cube's faces are refined using their spherical coordinates and then merged back to 360°. The former approach, applying a CNN directly to the equirectangular image, was opted for in [23] to increase the dynamic range of outdoor panoramas.

More recently, new techniques for applying CNNs to omnidirectional input were presented. Given the difficulty to model the projection's distortion directly in typical CNNs as well as achieve invariance to the viewpoint's rotation, the alternative pursued by [24] is based on graph-based deep learning. Specifically they model distortion directly into the graph's structure and apply it to a classification task. A novel approach taken in [25] is to learn appropriate convolution weights for equirectangular projected spherical images by transferring them from an existing network trained on traditional 2D images. This conversion from the 2D to the 360° domain is accomplished by enforcing consistency between the predictions of the 2D projected views and those in the 360° image. Moreover, recent work on convolutions [26,27] that in addition to learning their weights also learn their shape, are very well suited for learning the distortion model of spherical images, even though they have only been applied to fisheye lenses up to now [28]. Finally, very recently, Spherical CNNs were proposed in [29,30] that are based in a rotation-equivariant definition of spherical cross-correlation. However these were only demonstrated in classification and single variable regression problems. In addition, they are also applied in the spectral domain while we formulate our network design for the spatial image domain.

2.3 Monocular Depth Estimation

Depth estimation from monocular input has attracted lots of interest lately. While there are some impressive non learning based approaches [31–33], they come with their limitations, namely reliance on optical flow and relevance of the training dataset. Still, most recent research has focused on machine learning to address the ill-posed depth estimation problem. Initially, the work of Eigen et al. [34] trained a CNN in a coarse-to-fine scheme using direct depth supervision from RGB-D images. In a subsequent continuation of their work [6], they trained a multi-task network that among predicting semantic labels and normals, also estimated a scene's depth. Their results showed that jointly learning the tasks achieved higher performance due to their complementarity. In a recent similar work [35], a multi-task network that among other modalities also estimated depth, was trained using synthetic data and a domain adaptation loss based on adversarial learning, to increase its robustness when running on real scenes. Laina et al. [36] designed a directly supervised fully convolutional residual network (FCRN) with novel up-projection blocks that achieved impressive results for indoor scenes and was also used in a SLAM pipeline [1].

Another body of work focused on applying Conditional Random Fields (CRFs) to the depth estimation problem. Initially, the output of a deep network was refined using a hierarchical CRF [37], with Liu et al. [38] further exploring the interplay between CNNs and CRFs for depth estimation in their work. Recently, multi-scale CRFs were used and trained in an end-to-end manner along with the CNN [39]. Dense depth estimation has also been addressed as a classification problem. Since perfect regression is usually impossible, dense probabilities were estimated in [40] and then optimized to estimate the final depth map. Similarly, in [41] and [42] depth values were discretized in bins and densely classified, to be afterwards refined either via a hierarchical fusion scheme or through the use of a CRF respectively. Taking a step further, a regression-classification cascaded network was proposed in [43] where a low spatial resolution depth map was regressed and then refined by a classification branch.

The concurrent works of Garg et al. [44] and Godard et al. [45] showed that unsupervised learning of the depth estimation task is possible. This is accomplished by an intermediate task, view synthesis, and allowed training by only using stereo pair input with known baselines. In a similar fashion, using view synthesis as the main supervisory signal, learning to estimate depth was also achieved by training with pure video sequences in a completely unsupervised manner [46–50]. Another novel unsupervised depth estimation method relies on aperture supervision [51] by simply acquiring training data in various focus levels. Finally, in [52] it was shown that a CNN can be trained to estimate depth from monocular input with only relative depth annotations.

3   Synthesizing Data

End-to-end training of deep networks requires a large amount of annotated ground truth data. While for typical pinhole camera datasets this was partly addressed by using depth sensors [53] or laser scanners [54] such an approach is impractical for spherical images due to a larger diversity in resolution for 360° cameras and laser scanners, and because each 360° sensor would be visible from the other one. As much as approaches like the one employed in [55] could be used to in-paint the sensor regions, these would still be the result of an algorithmic process and not the acquisition process itself, potentially introducing errors and artifacts that would reduce the quality of the data. This also applies to unsupervised stereo approaches that require the simultaneous capture of the scene from two viewpoints. Although one could re-position the same sensor to acquire clean panoramas, a consistent baseline would not be possible. More recently, unsupervised approaches for inferring a scene's depth have emerged that are trained with video sequences. However, they assume a moving camera as they rely on view synthesis as the supervisory signal which is not a typical setting for indoors 360° captures, but for action camera like recordings.

360D Dataset: Instead, we rely on generating a dataset with ground truth depth by synthesizing both the color and the depth image via rendering. To accomplish that we leverage the latest efforts in creating publicly available textured 3D datasets of indoors scenes. Specifically, we use two computer generated (CG) datasets, SunCG [56] and SceneNet [57], and two realistic ones acquired by scanning indoor buildings, Stanford2D3D [58,59] and Matterport3D [60]. We use a path tracing renderer[3] to render our dataset by placing a spherical camera and a uniform point light at the same position $\mathbf{c} \in \mathbb{R}^3$ in the scene. We then acquire the rendered image $I(\mathbf{p}) \in \mathbb{R}, \mathbf{p} = (u, v) \in \mathbb{N}^2$, as well as the underlying z-buffer that was generated as a result of the graphics rendering process, that serves as the ground truth depth $D(\mathbf{p}) \in \mathbb{R}$. It should be noted that unlike pinhole camera model images, the z-buffer in this case does not contain the z coordinate value of the 3D point $\mathbf{v}(\mathbf{p}) \in \mathbb{R}^3$, corresponding to pixel $\mathbf{p}$, but instead the 3D point's radius $r = \|\mathbf{v} - \mathbf{c}\|$, in the camera's spherical coordinate system.

For the two CG indoors datasets we place the camera and the light at the center of each house, while for the two scanned indoors datasets we use the pose information available (estimated during the scanning process) and thus, for each building we generate multiple 360° data samples. Given that the latter two datasets were scanned, their geometries contain holes or inaccurate/coarse estimations, and also have lighting information baked into the models. On the other hand, the CG datasets contain perfect per pixel depth but lack the realism

---

[3] https://www.cycles-renderer.org.

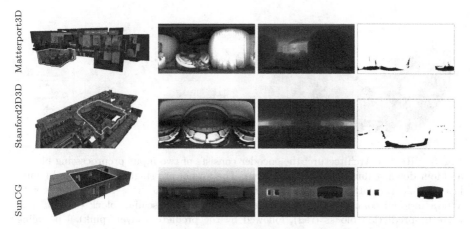

Matterport3D

Stanford2D3D

SunCG

Fig. 2. Example renders from our dataset, from left to right: the 3D building with a green highlight denoting the rendered scene, color output, corresponding depth map, and the binary mask depicting the missing regions in black. (Color figure online)

of the scanned datasets, creating a complementary mix. However, as no scanning poses are available, the centered poses may sometimes be placed within or on top of objects and we also observed missing information in some scenes (e.g. walls/ceilings) that, given SunCG's size, are impractical to manually correct.

For each pose, we augment the dataset by rotating the camera in 90° resulting in 4 distinct viewpoints per pose sample. Given the size of SunCG, we only utilize a subset of it and end up using **11118** houses, resulting in a 24.36% utilization. The remaining three datasets are completely rendered. This results in a total of **88384** renders and **22096** unique viewpoints. Our generated *360D* dataset contains a mix of synthetic and realistic 360° color I and depth D image data in a variety of indoors contexts (houses, offices, educational spaces, different room layouts) and is publicly available at http://vcl.iti.gr/360-dataset/.

4   Omnidirectional Depth Estimation

The majority of recent CNN architectures for dense estimation follow the autoencoder structure, in which an encoder encodes the input, by progressively decreasing its spatial dimensions, to a representation of much smaller size, and a decoder that regresses to the desired output by upscaling this representation.

We use two encoder-decoder network architectures that are structured differently. The first resembles those found in similar works in the literature [36,45], while the second is designed from scratch to be more suitable for learning with 360° images. Both networks are fully convolutional [61] and predict an equirectangular depth map with the only input being a 360° color image in equirectangular format. We use ELUs [62] as the activation function which also remove the need for batch normalization [63] and its added computational complexity.

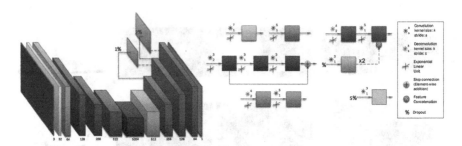

Fig. 3. UResNet Architecture: the encoder consists of two input preprocessing blocks, and four down-scaling blocks (dark green). The former are single convolutional (conv) layers while the latter consist of a strided conv and two more regular convs with a skip/residual connection. The decoder contains one upscaling block (orange) and three up-prediction blocks (red), followed by the prediction layer (pink). Up-scaling is achieved with a strided deconv followed by a conv, and similarly, up-predictions additionally branch out to estimate a depth prediction at the corresponding scale with an extra conv that is concatenated with the features of the next block's last layer. (Color figure online)

UResNet: In this unbalanced ResNet, the encoding and decoding parts are not symmetrical, with the decoder being shallower. The encoder is built with skip connections [64], a technique that helps when training deeper architectures by preventing gradient degradation, allowing for larger receptive fields. More detailed architectural information is presented in Fig. 3 where the network is decomposed into processing blocks.

RectNet: Omnidirectional images differ from traditional images in the sense that they capture global (full 360°) visual information and, when in equirectangular format, suffer from high distortions along their y (i.e. latitude) axis. Therefore, the second architecture's design aims to exploit and address these properties of spherical panoramas while keeping some of the desirable properties of UResNet like skip connections. Capturing the 360° image's global context is achieved by increasing the effective receptive field (RF) of each neuron by utilizing dilated convolutions [65]. Instead of progressive downscaling as in most depth estimation networks and similarly UResNet, we only drop the spatial dimensions by a factor of 4. Then, inspired by [66], we use progressively increasing dilations to increase the RF to about half the input's spatial dimensions and increase global scene understanding. In addition, within each dilation block we utilize 1×1 convolutions to reduce the spatial correlations of the feature maps.

   The distortion factor of spherical panoramas increases towards the sphere's poles and is therefore different for every image row. This means that information is scattered horizontally, as we vertically approach the two poles. In order to account for this varying distortion we alter our input blocks, as their features are closer to natural image ones (e.g. edges). Following [25], where 2D CNN filters are transfered into distorted (practically rectangular) row-wise versions to increase performance when applied to the 360° domain, we use rectangle filters

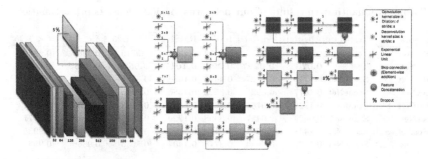

Fig. 4. RectNet Architecture: the encoder consists of two preprocessing blocks (yellow and blue) and a downscaling block (dark green), followed by two increasing dilation blocks (light green and black). The preprocessing blocks concatenate features produced by convolutions (convs) with different filter sizes, accounting for the equirectangular projection's varying distortion factor. The down-scaling block comprises a strided and two regular convs. (Color figure online)

along with traditional square filters and vary the resolution of the rectangle ones to account for different distortion levels. However, this variation is done while also preserving the area of the filter to be as close as possible to the original square filter's. The outputs of the rectangle and square filters are concatenated while preserving the overall output feature count. The detailed architecture is presented in Fig. 4.

Training Loss: Given that we synthesize perfect ground truth depth annotations D_{gt}, as presented in Sect. 3, we take a completely supervised approach. Even though most approaches using synthetic data fail to generalize to realistic input, our dataset contains an interesting mix of synthetic (CAD) renders as well as realistic ones. The scanned data are acquired from real environments and, as a result, their renders are very realistic. Following previous work, we predict depth D_{pred}^s against downscaled versions of the ground truth data D_{gt}^s at multiple scales (with s being the downscaling factor) and upsample these predictions using nearest neighbor interpolation to later concatenate them with the subsequent higher spatial dimension feature maps. We also use the dropout technique [67] in those layers used to produce each prediction. Further, we use L2 loss for regressing the dense depth output $E_{depth}(\mathbf{p}) = \|D_{gt}(\mathbf{p}) - D_{pred}(\mathbf{p})\|^2$ and additionally add a smoothness term $E_{smooth}(\mathbf{p}) = \|\nabla D(\mathbf{p})\|^2$ for the predicted depth map by minimizing its gradient.

Although our rendered depth maps are accurate in terms of depth, in practice there are missing regions in the rendered output. These are either because of missing information in the CAD models (e.g. walls/ceilings) or the imperfect process of large scale 3D scanning, with visual examples illustrated in Fig. 2. These missing regions/holes manifest as a specific color ("clear color"), selected during rendering, in the rendered image and as infinity ("far") values in the rendered depth map. As these outlier values will destabilize the training process,

Table 1. Quantitative results of our networks for 360° dense depth estimation.

Network	Tested on	Abs Rel ↓	Sq Rel ↓	RMS ↓	RMSlog ↓	$\delta < 1.25$ ↑	$\delta < 1.2^2$ ↑	$\delta < 1.25^3$ ↑
UResNet	Test set	0.0835	0.0416	0.3374	0.1204	0.9319	0.9889	0.9968
RectNet	Test set	**0.0702**	**0.0297**	**0.2911**	**0.1017**	**0.9574**	**0.9933**	**0.9979**
UResNet	SceneNet	0.1218	0.0727	0.4066	0.1538	0.8598	0.9815	0.9962
RectNet	SceneNet	0.1077	0.699	0.3572	0.1386	0.8965	0.9879	0.9971
UResNet -S2R	Stanford	0.1226	0.0768	0.489	0.1667	0.8593	0.9756	0.9942
RectNet -S2R	Stanford	0.0824	0.0457	0.3998	0.1229	0.928	0.9879	0.9971
UResNet -S2R	SceneNet	0.1448	0.0991	0.517	0.1792	0.7898	0.9761	0.9935
RectNet -S2R	SceneNet	0.1079	0.0644	0.3778	0.1404	0.8966	0.9866	0.996

we ignore them during backpropagation by using a per pixel $\mathbf{p}$ binary mask $M(\mathbf{p})$ that is zero in these missing regions. This allows us to train the network even with incomplete or slightly inaccurate/erroneous 3D models. Thus, our final loss function is:

$$E_{loss}(\mathbf{p}) = \sum_s \alpha_s M(\mathbf{p}) E_{depth}(\mathbf{p}) + \sum_s \beta_s M(\mathbf{p}) E_{smooth}(\mathbf{p}), \qquad (1)$$

where α_s, β_s are the weights for each scale of the depth and smoothing term.

5   Results

We evaluate the performance of our two 360° depth estimation networks by first conducting an intra assessment of the two models and then offering quantitative comparisons with other depth estimation methods. Finally, we present comparative qualitative results in unseen, realistic data of everyday scenes.

Training Details: Our networks are trained using Caffe [68] on a single NVIDIA Titan X. We use Xavier weight initialization [69] and ADAM [70] as the optimizer with its default parameters $[\beta_1, \beta_2, \epsilon] = [0.9, 0.999, 10^{-8}]$ and an initial learning rate of 0.0002. Our input dimensions are 512×256 and are given in equirectangular format, with our depth predictions being equal sized.

We split our dataset into corresponding train and tests sets as follows: (i) Initially we remove 1 complete area from Stanford2D3D, 3 complete buildings from Matterport3D and 3 CAD scenes from SunCG for our test set totaling 1,298 samples. (ii) We skip SceneNet entirely and use it as our validation set. (iii) Then, from the remaining SunCG, Stanford2D3D and Matterport3D samples we automatically remove scenes which contain regions with very large or small depth values (>5% of total image area above $20m$ or under $0.5m$). Finally, we are left with a train-set that consists of 34,679[4] RGB 360° images along with their corresponding ground truth depth map annotations. Our loss weights for UResNet are $[\alpha_1, \alpha_2, \alpha_4, \beta_1] = [0.445, 0.275, 0.13, 0.15]$, and for RectNet they are

---

[4] Only a subset of SunCG was used by prioritizing larger scenes given the length of the rendering process. However, a larger subset is publicly available.

Table 2. Quantitative results against other monocular depth estimation models.

Network		Abs Rel↓	Sq Rel ↓	RMS ↓	RMS(log) ↓	$\delta < 1.25$ ↑	$\delta < 1.25^2$ ↑	$\delta < 1.25^3$ ↑
UResNet		0.0835	0.0416	0.3374	0.1204	0.9319	0.9889	0.9968
RectNet		**0.0702**	**0.0297**	**0.2911**	**0.1017**	**0.9574**	**0.9933**	**0.9979**
Equirect.	Godard et al. [45]	0.4747	2.3783	7.2097	0.82	0.297	0.79	0.751
	Laina et al. [36]	0.3181	0.4469	0.941	0.376	0.4922	0.7792	0.915
	Liu et al. [38]	0.4202	0.7597	1.1596	0.44	0.3889	0.7044	0.8774
Cubemap	Godard et al. [45]	0.2552	0.9864	4.4524	0.5087	0.3096	0.5506	0.7202
	Laina et al. [36]	0.1423	0.2544	0.7751	02497	0.5198	0.8032	0.9175
	Liu et al. [38]	0.1869	0.4076	0.9243	0.2961	0.424	0.7148	0.8705

$[\alpha_1, \alpha_2, \beta_1, \beta_2] = [0.535, 0.272, 0.134, 0.068]$. For quantitative evaluation we use the same error metrics as previous works [6,34,36,38,45] (arrows next to each metric in the tables denote the direction of better performance).

Model Performance: Table 1 presents the results of our two models in our test set, and in the unseen synthetic SceneNet generated data, after training for 10 epochs in all of our train set. We observe that RectNet – which was designed with 360° input in mind – performs better than the standard UResNet even with far fewer parameters ($\sim 8.8M$ vs $\sim 51.2M$). In order to assess their efficacy and generalization capabilities we perform a leave-one-out evaluation. We train both networks initially only in the synthetic SunCG generated data for 10 epochs, and then finetune them in the realistic Matterport3D generated data for another 10 epochs. This train is suffixed with "-S2R". We then evaluate them in the entirety of the Stanford2D3D generated dataset, as well as in the SceneNet one. Comparable results to the previous train with all datasets are observed. Again, RectNet outperforms UResNet – albeit both perform slightly worse as expected due to being trained with less amount of data.

The increased performance of RectNet against UResNet in every error metric or accuracy, can be attributed to its larger RF, which for 360° images is very important as it allows the network to capture the global context more efficiently[5]. Despite the fact that UResNet is much deeper than RectNet and significantly drops the input's spatial dimensions, RectNet still achieves a larger receptive field. Specifically, UResNet has a 190×190 RF compared to that of RectNet which is 266×276. In addition, RectNet drops the input's spatial dimensions only by a factor of 4, maintaining denser information in the extracted features.

Comparison Against Other Methods: Given that there are no other methods to perform dense depth estimation for 360° images, we assess its performance against the state of the art in monocular depth estimation models. Since the predictions of these methods are defined in different scales, we scale the estimated depth maps by a scalar $\tilde{s}$, which matches their median with our ground truth like [46], i.e. $\tilde{s} = median(D_{gt})/median(D_{pred})$. Moreover, we evaluate the

---

[5] Varying RF experiments supporting this claim can be found in the supplement.

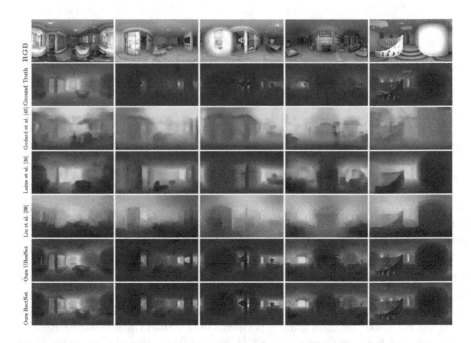

Fig. 5. Qualitative results on our test split.

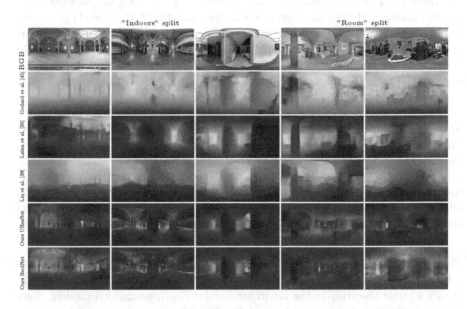

Fig. 6. Qualitative results on the "Room" and "Indoors" Sun360 splits.

Table 3. Per cube face quantitative results against other monocular models.

Network	AbsRel ↓	SqRel ↓	RMSE ↓	RMSElog ↓	$\delta < 1.25$ ↑	$\delta < 1.25^2$ ↑	$\delta N 1.25^3$ ↑
UResNet	0.0097	0.0062	0.1289	0.041	0.9245	0.9853	0.9955
RectNet	**0.008**	**0.0042**	**0.1113**	**0.03504**	**0.9497**	**0.9907**	**0.9969**
Godard et al. [45]	0.0453	0.1743	1.6559	0.1958	0.4524	0.7023	0.8315
Laina et al. [36]	0.03	0.0549	0.3152	0.1033	0.6353	0.8616	0.9412
Liu et al. [38]	0.0312	0.0532	0.3048	0.107	0.603	0.8412	0.9338

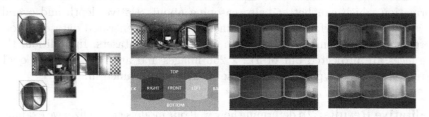

Fig. 7. Cubemap projection (left) and merged monocular predictions (right).

masked depth maps as mentioned in Sect. 3 in order to ignore the missing values. Table 2 presents the results of state-of-the-art methods when applied directly on our test split in the equirectangular domain (with a sample of qualitative results presented in Fig. 5). We offer results for the model of Laina et al. [36], trained with direct depth supervision in indoor scenes, Godard et al. [45], trained in an unsupervised manner in outdoor driving scenes using calibrated stereo pairs, and the method of Liu et al. [38], which combines learning with CRFs and is trained in indoor scenes. As observed by the results, the performance of all the methods directly on equirectangular images is poor, and our main models outperform them. However, inferior performance is expected as these were not trained directly in the equirectangular domain but in perspective images. Nonetheless, Laina et al. [36] and Liu et al. [38] achieve much better results than Godard et al. [45]. This is also expected as the latter is trained in an outdoor setting, with very different statistics than our indoor dataset.

For a more fair comparison we use a cubemap projection (Fig. 7 (left)) of all spherical images and then run each model on the projected cube faces which are typical perspective images. After acquiring the predictions, we merge all cube faces' depth maps by projecting them back to the equirectangular domain to be evaluated. However, since the top and bottom cube face projections will be mostly planar, we ignore them during evaluation of all metrics. While monocular performance is improved compared to when applied directly to equirectangular images, their quantitative performance is still inferior to our models. Further, the runtime performance is also worse as multiple inferences need to run, one for each face, incurring a much higher computational cost. Moreover, another apparent issue is the lack of consistency between the predictions of each face. This is shown in Fig. 7 (right) where it is clear that the depth scales of each face are different. This is in line with the observations in [21], but is more pronounced in the depth estimation case, than the style transfer one. Based on this observation, we evaluate each cube face separately against the ground truth values of that face alone which is also median scaled separately. The average values of the front, back, right and left faces for each monocular model against the obtained by our models on the same faces alone are presented in Table 3. Although the performance of the monocular models is further improved, our models still perform better. This can be attributed to various reasons besides training directly on equirectangular domain. One explanation is that 360° images capture global information which can better help reasoning about relative depth and overall increase inference performance. The other is that our generated dataset is considerably larger and more diverse than other indoor datasets. In addition, the cube faces are projected out of 512×256 images and are thus, of lower quality/resolution than typical images these models were trained in.

Qualitative Results: To determine how well our models generalize, we examine their performance on completely unseen data found in the Sun360 dataset [71], where no ground truth depth is available. The Sun360 dataset comprises realistic environment captures and has also been used in the work of Yang et al. [17] for room layout estimation. We offer some qualitative results on a data split from [17], referred to as "Room", as well as an additional split of indoor scenes that we select from the Sun360 dataset, referred to as "Indoors". These are presented in Fig. 6 for our two models as well as the monocular ones that were quantitatively evaluated. Our models are able to estimate the scenes' depth with the only monocular model to produce plausible results being the one of Laina et al. [36]. We also observe that UResNet offers smoother predictions than the better performing RectNet, unlike the results obtained on our test split. More qualitative results can be found in the supplementary material where comparison with the method of Yang et al. [17] is also offered.

6   Conclusions

We have presented a learning framework to estimate a scene's depth from a single 360° image. Our models were trained in a completely supervised manner with ground truth depth. To accomplish this, we overcame the dataset unavailability and difficulty in acquisition for paired 360° color and depth image pairs. This was achieved by re-using 3D datasets with both synthetic and real-world scanned indoors scenes and synthesizing a 360° dataset via rendering. 360° depth information can be useful for a variety of tasks, like in adding automation in the composition of 3D elements within spherical content [72].

Since our approach is the first work for dense 360° depth estimation, there are many challenges that still need to be overcome. Our datasets only cover indoor cases, limiting the networks' applicability to outdoor settings, and are generated with perfect camera vertical alignment with constant lighting and no stitching artifacts. This issue is further accentuated as the scanned datasets had lighting information baked into them during scanning. This can potentially hamper robustness when applied in real world conditions that also contain a much higher dynamic range of luminosity.

For future work, we want to explore unsupervised learning approaches that are based on view synthesis as the supervisory signal. Furthermore, robustness to real world scenes can be achieved, either by utilizing GANs as generators of realistic content, or by using a discriminator to identify plausible/real images.

Acknowledgements. This work was supported and received funding from the European Union Horizon H2020 Framework Programme funded project Hyper360, under Grant Agreement no. 761934 (http://www.hyper360.eu/). We are also grateful and acknowledge the support of NVIDIA for a hardware donation.

References

1. Tateno, K., Tombari, F., Laina, I., Navab, N.: CNN-SLAM: real-time dense monocular slam with learned depth prediction. In: 2017 IEEE Conference on Computer Vision and Pattern Recognition (CVPR). pp. 6565–6574, July 2017
2. Mo, K., Li, H., Lin, Z., Lee, J.Y.: The AdobeIndoorNav dataset: towards deep reinforcement learning based real-world indoor robot visual navigation (2018)
3. Hedman, P., Alsisan, S., Szeliski, R., Kopf, J.: Casual 3D photography. ACM Trans. Graph. (TOG) **36**(6), 234 (2017)
4. Huang, J., Chen, Z., Ceylan, D., Jin, H.: 6-DOF VR videos with a single 360-camera. In: 2017 IEEE Virtual Reality (VR), pp. 37–44. IEEE (2017)
5. Karsch, K.: Automatic scene inference for 3D object compositing. ACM Trans. Graph. (TOG) **33**(3), 32 (2014)
6. Eigen, D., Fergus, R.: Predicting depth, surface normals and semantic labels with a common multi-scale convolutional architecture. In: Proceedings of the IEEE International Conference on Computer Vision, pp. 2650–2658 (2015)
7. Ren, X., Bo, L., Fox, D.: RGB-(D) scene labeling: features and algorithms. In: 2012 IEEE Conference on Computer Vision and Pattern Recognition (CVPR), pp. 2759–2766. IEEE (2012)
8. Hartley, R., Zisserman, A.: Multiple View Geometry in Computer Vision, 2nd edn. Cambridge University Press, Cambridge (2000)
9. Furukawa, Y., Hernández, C., et al.: Multi-view stereo: a tutorial. Found. Trends® in Comput. Graph. Vis. **9**(1–2), 1–148 (2015)
10. Özyeşil, O., Voroninski, V., Basri, R., Singer, A.: A survey of structure from motion*. Acta Numerica **26**, 305–364 (2017)
11. Li, S.: Binocular spherical stereo. IEEE Trans. Intell. Transp. Syst. **9**(4), 589–600 (2008)
12. Ma, C., Shi, L., Huang, H., Yan, M.: 3D reconstruction from full-view fisheye camera. arXiv preprint arXiv:1506.06273 (2015)
13. Pathak, S., Moro, A., Yamashita, A., Asama, H.: Dense 3D reconstruction from two spherical images via optical flow-based equirectangular epipolar rectification. In: 2016 IEEE International Conference on Imaging Systems and Techniques (IST), pp. 140–145. IEEE (2016)
14. Li, S., Fukumori, K.: Spherical stereo for the construction of immersive VR environment. In: Proceedings of Virtual Reality, VR 2005, pp. 217–222. IEEE (2005)
15. Kim, H., Hilton, A.: 3D scene reconstruction from multiple spherical stereo pairs. Int. J. Comput. Vis. **104**(1), 94–116 (2013)

16. Zhang, Y., Song, S., Tan, P., Xiao, J.: PanoContext: a whole-room 3D context model for panoramic scene understanding. In: Fleet, D., Pajdla, T., Schiele, B., Tuytelaars, T. (eds.) ECCV 2014. LNCS, vol. 8694, pp. 668–686. Springer, Cham (2014). https://doi.org/10.1007/978-3-319-10599-4_43

17. Yang, H., Zhang, H.: Efficient 3D room shape recovery from a single panorama. In: Proceedings of the IEEE Conference on Computer Vision and Pattern Recognition, pp. 5422–5430 (2016)

18. Xu, J., Stenger, B., Kerola, T., Tung, T.: Pano2CAD: room layout from a single panorama image. In: 2017 IEEE Winter Conference on Applications of Computer Vision (WACV), pp. 354–362. IEEE (2017)

19. Kim, H., de Campos, T., Hilton, A.: Room layout estimation with object and material attributes information using a spherical camera. In: 2016 Fourth International Conference on 3D Vision (3DV), pp. 519–527. IEEE (2016)

20. Plagemann, C., Stachniss, C., Hess, J., Endres, F., Franklin, N.: A nonparametric learning approach to range sensing from omnidirectional vision. Robot. Auton. Syst. 58(6), 762–772 (2010)

21. Ruder, M., Dosovitskiy, A., Brox, T.: Artistic style transfer for videos and spherical images. Int. J. Comput. Vis. 126(11), 1199–1219 (2018)

22. Monroy, R., Lutz, S., Chalasani, T., Smolic, A.: SalNet360: saliency maps for omnidirectional images with CNN. arXiv preprint arXiv:1709.06505 (2017)

23. Zhang, J., Lalonde, J.F.: Learning high dynamic range from outdoor panoramas. In: Proceedings of the IEEE Conference on Computer Vision and Pattern Recognition, pp. 4519–4528 (2017)

24. Frossard, P., Khasanova, R.: Graph-based classification of omnidirectional images. In: 2017 IEEE International Conference on Computer Vision Workshop (ICCVW), pp. 860–869. IEEE (2017)

25. Su, Y.C., Grauman, K.: Learning spherical convolution for fast features from 360 imagery. In: Advances in Neural Information Processing Systems, pp. 529–539 (2017)

26. Jeon, Y., Kim, J.: Active convolution: learning the shape of convolution for image classification. In: 2017 IEEE Conference on Computer Vision and Pattern Recognition (CVPR), pp. 1846–1854. IEEE (2017)

27. Dai, J., et al.: Deformable convolutional networks. In: Proceedings of the IEEE Conference on Computer Vision and Pattern Recognition, pp. 764–773 (2017)

28. Deng, L., Yang, M., Li, H., Li, T., Hu, B., Wang, C.: Restricted deformable convolution based road scene semantic segmentation using surround view cameras. arXiv preprint arXiv:1801.00708 (2018)

29. Cohen, T., Geiger, M., Welling, M.: Convolutional networks for spherical signals. In: Principled Approaches to Deep Learning Workshop ICML 2017 (2017)

30. Cohen, T.S., Geiger, M., Köhler, J., Welling, M.: Spherical CNNs. In: International Conference on Learning Representations (ICLR) (2018)

31. Ranftl, R., Vineet, V., Chen, Q., Koltun, V.: Dense monocular depth estimation in complex dynamic scenes. In: Proceedings of the IEEE Conference on Computer Vision and Pattern Recognition, pp. 4058–4066 (2016)

32. Liu, M., Salzmann, M., He, X.: Discrete-continuous depth estimation from a single image. In: 2014 IEEE Conference on Computer Vision and Pattern Recognition (CVPR), pp. 716–723. IEEE (2014)

33. Karsch, K., Liu, C., Kang, S.B.: Depth transfer: depth extraction from videos using nonparametric sampling. In: Hassner, T., Liu, C. (eds.) Dense Image Correspondences for Computer Vision, pp. 173–205. Springer, Cham (2016). https://doi.org/10.1007/978-3-319-23048-1_9

34. Eigen, D., Puhrsch, C., Fergus, R.: Depth map prediction from a single image using a multi-scale deep network. In: Advances in Neural Information Processing Systems, pp. 2366–2374 (2014)
35. Ren, Z., Lee, Y.J.: Cross-domain self-supervised multi-task feature learning using synthetic imagery. In: IEEE Conference on Computer Vision and Pattern Recognition (CVPR) (2018)
36. Laina, I., Rupprecht, C., Belagiannis, V., Tombari, F., Navab, N.: Deeper depth prediction with fully convolutional residual networks. In: 2016 Fourth International Conference on 3D Vision (3DV), pp. 239–248. IEEE (2016)
37. Li, B., Shen, C., Dai, Y., van den Hengel, A., He, M.: Depth and surface normal estimation from monocular images using regression on deep features and hierarchical CRFs. In: Proceedings of the IEEE Conference on Computer Vision and Pattern Recognition, pp. 1119–1127 (2015)
38. Liu, F., Shen, C., Lin, G., Reid, I.: Learning depth from single monocular images using deep convolutional neural fields. IEEE Trans. Pattern Anal. Mach. Intell. **38**(10), 2024–2039 (2016)
39. Xu, D., Ricci, E., Ouyang, W., Wang, X., Sebe, N.: Multi-scale continuous CRFs as sequential deep networks for monocular depth estimation. In: Proceedings of CVPR (2017)
40. Chakrabarti, A., Shao, J., Shakhnarovich, G.: Depth from a single image by harmonizing overcomplete local network predictions. In: Advances in Neural Information Processing Systems, pp. 2658–2666 (2016)
41. Li, B., Dai, Y., He, M.: Monocular depth estimation with hierarchical fusion of dilated CNNs and soft-weighted-sum inference. Pattern Recogn. **83**, 328–339 (2018)
42. Cao, Y., Wu, Z., Shen, C.: Estimating depth from monocular images as classification using deep fully convolutional residual networks. IEEE Trans. Circ. Syst. Video Technol. (2017)
43. Fu, H., Gong, M., Wang, C., Tao, D.: A compromise principle in deep monocular depth estimation. arXiv preprint arXiv:1708.08267 (2017)
44. Garg, R., B.G., V.K., Carneiro, G., Reid, I.: Unsupervised CNN for single view depth estimation: geometry to the rescue. In: Leibe, B., Matas, J., Sebe, N., Welling, M. (eds.) ECCV 2016. LNCS, vol. 9912, pp. 740–756. Springer, Cham (2016). https://doi.org/10.1007/978-3-319-46484-8_45
45. Godard, C., Mac Aodha, O., Brostow, G.J.: Unsupervised monocular depth estimation with left-right consistency. In: CVPR (2017)
46. Zhou, T., Brown, M., Snavely, N., Lowe, D.G.: Unsupervised learning of depth and ego-motion from video. In: CVPR, vol. 2, p. 7 (2017)
47. Wang, C., Buenaposada, J.M., Zhu, R., Lucey, S.: Learning depth from monocular videos using direct methods. IEEE Conference on Computer Vision and Pattern Recognition (2018)
48. Mahjourian, R., Wicke, M., Angelova, A.: Unsupervised learning of depth and ego-motion from monocular video using 3D geometric constraints. In: Proceedings of the IEEE Conference on Computer Vision and Pattern Recognition (2018)
49. Yang, Z., Wang, P., Xu, W., Zhao, L., Nevatia, R.: Unsupervised learning of geometry with edge-aware depth-normal consistency. arXiv preprint arXiv:1711.03665 (2017)
50. Yin, Z., Shi, J.: GeoNet: unsupervised learning of dense depth, optical flow and camera pose. In: Proceedings of the IEEE Conference on Computer Vision and Pattern Recognition (2018)

51. Srinivasan, P.P., Garg, R., Wadhwa, N., Ng, R., Barron, J.T.: Aperture supervision for monocular depth estimation (2017)
52. Chen, W., Fu, Z., Yang, D., Deng, J.: Single-image depth perception in the wild. In: Advances in Neural Information Processing Systems, pp. 730–738 (2016)
53. Silberman, N., Hoiem, D., Kohli, P., Fergus, R.: Indoor segmentation and support inference from RGBD images. In: Fitzgibbon, A., Lazebnik, S., Perona, P., Sato, Y., Schmid, C. (eds.) ECCV 2012. LNCS, vol. 7576, pp. 746–760. Springer, Heidelberg (2012). https://doi.org/10.1007/978-3-642-33715-4_54
54. Saxena, A., Sun, M., Ng, A.Y.: Make3D: learning 3D scene structure from a single still image. IEEE Trans. Pattern Anal. Mach. Intell. 31(5), 824–840 (2009)
55. Matzen, K., Cohen, M.F., Evans, B., Kopf, J., Szeliski, R.: Low-cost 360 stereo photography and video capture. ACM Trans. Graph. (TOG) 36(4), 148 (2017)
56. Song, S., Yu, F., Zeng, A., Chang, A.X., Savva, M., Funkhouser, T.: Semantic scene completion from a single depth image. In: IEEE Conference on Computer Vision and Pattern Recognition (2017)
57. Handa, A., Pătrăucean, V., Stent, S., Cipolla, R.: SceneNet: an annotated model generator for indoor scene understanding. In: 2016 IEEE International Conference on Robotics and Automation (ICRA), pp. 5737–5743. IEEE (2016)
58. Armeni, I., Sax, S., Zamir, A.R., Savarese, S.: Joint 2D-3D-semantic data for indoor scene understanding. arXiv preprint arXiv:1702.01105 (2017)
59. Armeni, I., et al.: 3D semantic parsing of large-scale indoor spaces. In: Proceedings of the IEEE Conference on Computer Vision and Pattern Recognition, pp. 1534–1543 (2016)
60. Chang, A., et al.: Matterport3D: learning from RGB-D data in indoor environments. In: International Conference on 3D Vision (3DV) (2017)
61. Long, J., Shelhamer, E., Darrell, T.: Fully convolutional networks for semantic segmentation. In: Proceedings of the IEEE Conference on Computer Vision and Pattern Recognition, pp. 3431–3440 (2015)
62. Clevert, D.A., Unterthiner, T., Hochreiter, S.: Fast and accurate deep network learning by exponential linear units (ELUs). arXiv preprint arXiv:1511.07289 (2015)
63. Ioffe, S., Szegedy, C.: Batch normalization: accelerating deep network training by reducing internal covariate shift. In: International Conference on Machine Learning, pp. 448–456 (2015)
64. He, K., Zhang, X., Ren, S., Sun, J.: Deep residual learning for image recognition. In: Proceedings of the IEEE Conference on Computer Vision and Pattern Recognition, pp. 770–778 (2016)
65. Yu, F., Koltun, V., Funkhouser, T.: Dilated residual networks. In: Computer Vision and Pattern Recognition, vol. 1 (2017)
66. van Noord, N., Postma, E.O.: Light-weight pixel context encoders for image inpainting. CoRR abs/1801.05585 (2018)
67. Srivastava, N., Hinton, G., Krizhevsky, A., Sutskever, I., Salakhutdinov, R.: Dropout: a simple way to prevent neural networks from overfitting. J. Mach. Learn. Res. 15(1), 1929–1958 (2014)
68. Jia, Y., et al.: Caffe: convolutional architecture for fast feature embedding. In: Proceedings of the 22nd ACM International Conference on Multimedia, MM 2014, pp. 675–678. ACM, New York (2014)
69. Glorot, X., Bengio, Y.: Understanding the difficulty of training deep feedforward neural networks. In: Proceedings of the Thirteenth International Conference on Artificial Intelligence and Statistics, Proceedings of Machine Learning Research, vol. 9. PMLR, pp. 249–256, 13–15 May 2010

70. Kingma, D.P., Ba, J.: Adam: a method for stochastic optimization. arXiv preprint arXiv:1412.6980 (2014)
71. Xiao, J., Ehinger, K.A., Oliva, A., Torralba, A.: Recognizing scene viewpoint using panoramic place representation. In: 2012 IEEE Conference on Computer Vision and Pattern Recognition (CVPR), pp. 2695–2702. IEEE (2012)
72. Rhee, T., Petikam, L., Allen, B., Chalmers, A.: MR360: mixed reality rendering for 360 panoramic videos. IEEE Trans. Visual. Comput. Graph. **23**(4), 1379–1388 (2017)

Simple Baselines for Human Pose Estimation and Tracking

Bin Xiao[1(✉)], Haiping Wu[2], and Yichen Wei[1]

[1] Microsoft Research Asia, Beijing, China
{Bin.Xiao,yichenw}@microsoft.com
[2] University of Electronic Science and Technology of China, Chengdu, China
v-haipwu@microsoft.com

Abstract. There has been significant progress on pose estimation and increasing interests on pose tracking in recent years. At the same time, the overall algorithm and system complexity increases as well, making the algorithm analysis and comparison more difficult. This work provides simple and effective baseline methods. They are helpful for inspiring and evaluating new ideas for the field. State-of-the-art results are achieved on challenging benchmarks. The code will be available at https://github.com/leoxiaobin/pose.pytorch.

Keywords: Human pose estimation · Human pose tracking

1 Introduction

Similar as many vision tasks, the progress on human pose estimation problem is significantly advanced by deep learning. Since the pioneer work in [30,31], the performance on the MPII benchmark [3] has become saturated in three years, starting from about 80% PCKH@0.5 [30] to more than 90% [7,8,22,33]. The progress on the more recent and challenging COCO human pose benchmark [20] is even faster. The mAP metric is increased from 60.5 (COCO 2016 Challenge winner [5,9]) to 72.1 (COCO 2017 Challenge winner [6,9]) in one year. With the quick maturity of pose estimation, a more challenging task of "simultaneous pose detection and tracking in the wild" has been introduced recently [2].

At the same time, the network architecture and experiment practice have steadily become more complex. This makes the algorithm analysis and comparison more difficult. For example, the leading methods [7,8,22,33] on MPII benchmark [3] have considerable difference in many details but minor difference in accuracy. It is hard to tell which details are crucial. Also, the representative works [5,6,12,21,24] on COCO benchmark are also complex but differ significantly. Comparison between such works is mostly on system level and less

---

B. Xiao and H. Wu—Equal contribution.

H. Wu—This work is done when Haiping Wu is an intern at Microsoft Research Asia.

© Springer Nature Switzerland AG 2018
V. Ferrari et al. (Eds.): ECCV 2018, LNCS 11210, pp. 472–487, 2018.
https://doi.org/10.1007/978-3-030-01231-1_29

informative. About pose tracking, although there has not been much work [2], the system complexity can be expected to further increase due to the increased problem dimension and solution space.

This work aims to ease this problem by asking a question from the opposite direction, *how good could a simple method be?* To answer the question, this work provides baseline methods for both pose estimation and tracking. They are quite simple but surprisingly effective. Thus, they hopefully would help inspiring new ideas and simplifying their evaluation. The code, as well as pre-trained models, will be released to facilitate the research community.

Our pose estimation is based on a few deconvolutional layers added on a backbone network, ResNet [13] in this work. It is probably the simplest way to estimate heat maps from deep and low resolution feature maps. Our *single* model's best result achieves the state-of-the-art at mAP of 73.7 on COCO test-dev split, which has an improvement of 1.6% and 0.7% over the winner of COCO 2017 keypoint Challenge's single model and their ensembled model [6,9].

Our pose tracking follows a similar pipeline of the winner [11] of ICCV'17 PoseTrack Challenge [2]. The single person pose estimation uses our own method as above. The pose tracking uses the same greedy matching method as in [11]. *Our only modification is to use optical flow based pose propagation and similarity measurement.* Our best result achieves a mAP score of 74.6 and a MOTA score of 57.8, an absolute 15% and 6% improvement over 59.6 and 51.8 of the winner of ICCV'17 PoseTrack Challenge [11,26]. It is the new state-of-the-art.

This work is not based on any theoretic evidence. It is based on simple techniques and validated by comprehensive ablation experiments, at our best. Note that we do not claim any algorithmic superiority over previous methods, in spite of better results. We do not perform complete and fair comparison with previous methods, because this is difficult and not our intent. As stated, the contribution of this work are solid baselines for the field.

2   Pose Estimation Using a Deconvolution Head Network

ResNet [13] is the most common backbone network for image feature extraction. It is also used in [6,24] for pose estimation. Our method simply adds a few deconvolutional layers over the last convolution stage in the ResNet, called C_5. The whole network structure is illustrated in Fig. 1(c). We adopt this structure because it is arguably the simplest to generate heatmaps from deep and low resolution features and also adopted in the state-of-the-art Mask R-CNN [12].

By default, three deconvolutional layers with batch normalization [15] and ReLU activation [19] are used. Each layer has 256 filters with 4×4 kernel. The stride is 2. A 1×1 convolutional layer is added at last to generate predicted heatmaps $\{H_1 \ldots H_k\}$ for all k key points.

Same as in [22,30], Mean Squared Error (MSE) is used as the loss between the predicted heatmaps and targeted heatmaps. The targeted heatmap $\hat{H}_k$ for joint k is generated by applying a 2D gaussian centered on the kth joint's ground truth location.

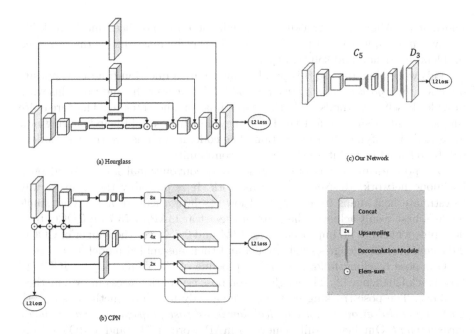

Fig. 1. Illustration of two state-of-the-art network architectures for pose estimation (a) one stage in Hourglass [22], (b) CPN [6], and our simple baseline (c).

Discussions. To understand the simplicity and rationality of our baseline, we discuss two state-of-the-art network architectures as references, namely, Hourglass [22] and CPN [6]. They are illustrated in Fig. 1.

Hourglass [22] is the dominant approach on MPII benchmark as it is the basis for all leading methods [7,8,33]. It features in a multi-stage architecture with repeated bottom-up, top-down processing and skip layer feature concatenation.

Cascaded pyramid network (CPN) [6] is the leading method on COCO 2017 keypoint challenge [9]. It also involves skip layer feature concatenation and an online hard keypoint mining step.

Comparing the three architectures in Fig. 1, it is clear that our method differs from [6,22] in *how high resolution feature maps are generated*. Both works [6,22] use upsampling to increase the feature map resolution and put convolutional parameters in other blocks. In contrary, our method combines the upsampling and convolutional parameters into deconvolutional layers in a much simpler way, without using skip layer connections.

A commonality of the three methods is that three upsampling steps and also three levels of non-linearity (from the deepest feature) are used to obtain high-resolution feature maps and heatmaps. Based on above observations and the good performance of our baseline, it seems that *obtaining high resolution feature maps is crucial, but no matter how*. Note that this discussion is only preliminary and heuristic. It is hard to conclude which architecture in Fig. 1 is better. This is not the intent of this work.

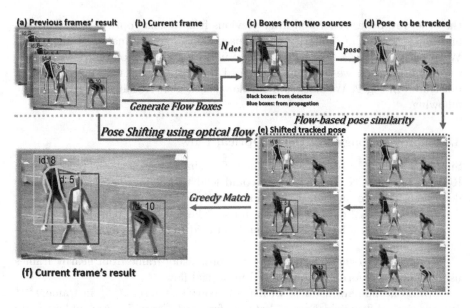

Fig. 2. The proposed flow-based pose tracking framework.

3 Pose Tracking Based on Optical Flow

Multi-person pose tracking in videos first estimates human poses in frames, and then tracks these human pose by assigning a unique identification number (id) to them across frames. We present human instance P with id as $P = (J, id)$, where $J = \{j_i\}_{1:N_J}$ is the coordinates set of N_J body joints and id indicates the tracking id. When processing the kth frame I^k, we have the already processed human instances set $\mathcal{P}^{k-1} = \{P_i^{k-1}\}_{1:N_{k-1}}$ in frame I^{k-1} and the instances set $\mathcal{P}^k = \{P_i^k\}_{1:N_k}$ in frame I^k whose id is to be assigned, where N_{k-1} and N_k are the instance number in frame I^{k-1} and I^k. If one instance P_j^k in current frame I^k is linked to the instance P_i^{k-1} in I^{k-1} frame, then id_i^{k-1} is propagated to id_j^k, otherwise a new id is assigned to P_j^k, indicating a new track.

The winner [11] of ICCV'17 PoseTrack Challenge [2] solves this multi-person pose tracking problem by first estimating human pose in frames using Mask R-CNN [12], and then performing online tracking using a greedy bipartite matching algorithm frame by frame.

The greedy matching algorithm is to first assign the id of P_i^{k-1} in frame I^{k-1} to P_j^k in frame I^k if the similarity between P_i^{k-1} and P_j^k is the highest, then remove these two instances from consideration, and repeat the id assigning process with the highest similarity. When an instance P_j^k in frame I^k has no existing P_i^{k-1} left to link, a new id number is assigned, which indicates a new instance comes up.

We mainly follow this pipeline in [11] with two differences. One is that we have two different kinds of human boxes, one is from a human detector and the other are boxes generated from previous frames using optical flow. The second difference is the similarity metric used by the greedy matching algorithm. We propose to use a flow-based pose similarity metric. Combined with these two modifications, we have our enhanced flow-based pose tracking algorithm, illustrated in Fig. 2. We elaborate our flow-based pose tracking algorithm in the following.

3.1 Joint Propagation Using Optical Flow

Simply applying a detector designed for single image level (e.g. Faster-RCNN [27], R-FCN [16]) to videos could lead to missing detections and false detections due to motion blur and occlusion introduced by video frames. As shown in Fig. 2(c), the detector misses the left black person due to fast motion. Temporal information is often leveraged to generate more robust detections [35,36].

We propose to generate boxes for the processing frame from nearby frames using temporal information expressed in optical flow.

Given one human instance with joints coordinates set J_i^{k-1} in frame I^{k-1} and the optical flow field $F_{k-1 \rightarrow k}$ between frame I^{k-1} and I^k, we could estimate the corresponding joints coordinates set $\hat{J}_i^k$ in frame I^k by propagating the joints coordinates set J_i^{k-1} according to $F_{k-1 \rightarrow k}$. More specifically, for each joint location (x, y) in J_i^{k-1}, the propagated joint location would be $(x + \delta x, y + \delta y)$, where $\delta x, \delta y$ are the flow field values at joint location (x, y). Then we compute a bounding of the propagated joints coordinates set $\hat{J}_i^k$, and expand that box by some extend (15% in experiments) as the candidates box for pose estimation.

When the processing frame is difficult for human detectors that could lead to missing detections due to motion blur or occlusion, we could have boxes propagated from previous frames where people have been detected correctly. As shown in Fig. 2(c), for the left black person in images, since we have the tracked result in previous frames in Fig. 2(a), the propagated boxes successfully contain this person.

3.2 Flow-Based Pose Similarity

Using bounding box IoU (Intersection-over-Union) as the similarity metric (S_{Bbox}) to link instances could be problematic when an instance moves fast thus the boxes do not overlap, and in crowed scenes where boxes may not have the corresponding relationship with instances. A more fine-grained metric could be a pose similarity (S_{Pose}) which calculates the body joints distance between two instances using Object Keypoint Similarity (OKS). The pose similarity could also be problematic when the pose of the same person is different across frames due to pose changing. We propose to use a flow-based pose similarity metric.

Given one instance J_i^k in frame I^k and one instance J_j^l in frame I^l, the flow-based pose similarity metric is represented as

$$S_{Flow}(J_i^k, J_j^l) = OKS(\hat{J}_i^l, J_j^l), \tag{1}$$

where OKS represents calculating the Object Keypoint Similarity (OKS) between two human pose, and $\hat{J}_i^l$ represents the propagated joints for J_i^k from frame I^k to I^l using optical flow field $F_{k\rightarrow l}$.

Due to occlusions with other people or objects, people often disappear and re-appear again. Considering consecutive two frames is not enough, thus we have the flow-based pose similarity considering multi frames, denoted as $S_{Multi-flow}$, meaning the propagated $\hat{J}_k$ comes from multi previous frames. In this way, we could relink instances even disappearing in middle frames.

3.3   Flow-Based Pose Tracking Algorithm

With the joint propagation using optical flow and the flow-based pose similarity, we propose the flow-based pose tracking algorithm combining these two, as presented in Algorithm 1. Table 1 summarizes the notations used in Algorithm 1.

Table 1. Notations in Algorithm 1.

I^k	k^{th} frame
Q	Tracked instances queue
L_Q	Max capacity of Q
$\mathcal{P}^k$	Instances set in k^{th} frame
$\mathcal{J}^k$	Instances set of body joints in k^{th} frame
P_i^k	i^{th} instance in k^{th} frame
J_i^k	Body joints set of ith instance in k^{th} frame
$F_{k\rightarrow l}$	Flow field from k^{th} frame to l^{th} frame
M_{sim}	Similarity matrix
B_{det}^k	Boxes from person detector in k^{th} frame
B_{flow}^k	Boxes generated by joint propagating in k^{th} frame
$B_{unified}^k$	Boxes unified by box NMS in k^{th} frame
$\mathcal{N}_{det}$	Person detection network
$\mathcal{N}_{pose}$	Human pose estimation network
$\mathcal{N}_{flow}$	Flow estimation network
$\mathcal{F}_{sim}$	Function for calculating similarity matrix
$\mathcal{F}_{NMS}$	Function for NMS operation
$\mathcal{F}_{FlowBoxGen}$	Function for generating boxes by joint propagating
$\mathcal{F}_{AssignID}$	Function for assigning instance id

First, we solve the pose estimation problem. For the processing frame in videos, the boxes from a human detector and boxes generated by propagating joints from previous frames using optical flow are unified using a bounding box

---

Algorithm 1. The flow-based inference algorithm for video human pose tracking

1: **input**: video frames $\{I^k\}$, $Q = []$, Q's max capacity L_Q.
2: $B_{\text{det}}^0 = \mathcal{N}_{\text{det}}(I^0)$
3: $\mathcal{J}^0 = \mathcal{N}_{\text{pose}}(I^0, B_{\text{det}}^0)$
4: $\mathcal{P}^0 = (\mathcal{J}^0, id)$ ▷ initialize the id for the first frame
5: $Q = [\mathcal{P}_0]$ ▷ append the instance set $\mathcal{P}_0$ to Q
6: **for** $k = 1$ **to** ∞ **do**
7:     $B_{\text{det}}^k = \mathcal{N}_{\text{det}}(I^k)$
8:     $B_{\text{flow}}^k = \mathcal{F}_{\text{FlowBoxGen}}(\mathcal{J}^{k-1}, F_{k-1 \to k})$
9:     $B_{\text{unified}}^k = \mathcal{F}_{\text{NMS}}(B_{\text{det}}^k, B_{\text{flow}}^k)$ ▷ unify detection boxes and flow boxes
10:    $\mathcal{J}^k = \mathcal{N}_{\text{pose}}(I^k, B_{\text{unified}}^k)$
11:    $M_{\text{sim}} = \mathcal{F}_{\text{sim}}(Q, \mathcal{J}^k)$
12:    $\mathcal{P}^k = \mathcal{F}_{\text{AssignID}}(M_{\text{sim}}, \mathcal{J}^k)$
13:    append $\mathcal{P}^k$ to Q ▷ update the Q
14: **end for**

Non-Maximum Suppression (NMS) operation. The boxes generated by propagating joints serve as the complement of missing detections of the detector (e.g. in Fig. 2(c)). Then we estimate human pose using the cropped and resized images by these boxes through our proposed pose estimation network in Sect. 2.

Second, we solve the tracking problem. We store the tracked instances in a double-ended queue (Deque) with fixed length L_Q, denoted as

$$Q = [\mathcal{P}_{k-1}, \mathcal{P}_{k-2}, \ldots, \mathcal{P}_{k-L_Q}] \tag{2}$$

where $\mathcal{P}_{k-i}$ means tracked instances set in previous frame I^{k-i} and the Q's length L_Q indicates how many previous frames considered when performing matching.

The Q could be used to capture previous multi frames' linking relationship, initialized in the first frame in a video. For the kth frame I^k, we calculate the flow-based pose similarity matrix M_{sim} between the untracked instances set of body joints $\mathcal{J}^k$ (id is none) and previous instances sets in Q. Then we assign id to each body joints instance J in $\mathcal{J}^k$ to get assigned instance set $\mathcal{P}^k$ by using greedy matching and M_{sim}. Finally we update our tracked instances Q by adding up k^{th} frame instances set $\mathcal{P}^k$.

4   Experiments

4.1   Pose Estimation on COCO

The COCO Keypoint Challenge [20] requires localization of multi-person keypoints in challenging uncontrolled conditions. The COCO train, validation, and test sets contain more than 200k images and 250k person instances labeled with keypoints. 150k instances of them are publicly available for training and validation. Our models are only trained on all COCO *train2017* dataset (includes 57K images and 150K person instances) no extra data involved, ablation are studied on the *val2017* set and finally we report the final results on *test-dev2017* set to make a fair comparison with the public state-of-the-art results [5,6,12,24].

The COCO evaluation defines the object keypoint similarity (OKS) and uses the mean average precision (AP) over 10 OKS thresholds as main competition metric [9]. The OKS plays the same role as the IoU in object detection. It is calculated from the distance between predicted points and ground truth points normalized by scale of the person.

Training. The ground truth human box is made to a fixed aspect ratio, e.g., *height:width* = 4:3 by extending the box in height or width. It is then cropped from the image and resized to a fixed resolution. The default resolution is 256:192. It is the same as the state-of-the-art method [6] for a fair comparison. Data augmentation includes scale ($\pm30\%$), rotation ($\pm40°$) and flip.

Our ResNet [13] backbone network is initialized by pre-training on ImageNet classification task [28]. In the training for pose estimation, the base learning rate is 1e−3. It drops to 1e−4 at 90 epochs and 1e−5 at 120 epochs. There are 140 epochs in total. Mini-batch size is 128. Adam [18] optimizer is used. Four GPUs on a GPU server is used.

ResNet of depth 50, 101 and 152 layers are experimented. ResNet-50 is used by default, unless otherwise noted.

Testing. A two-stage top-down paradigm is applied, similar as in [6,24]. For detection, by default we use a faster-RCNN [27] detector with detection AP 56.4 for the person category on COCO *val2017*. Following the common practice in [6,22], the joint location is predicted on the averaged heatmaps of the original and flipped image. A quarter offset in the direction from highest response to the second highest response is used to obtain the final location.

Table 2. Ablation study of our method on COCO val2017 dataset. Those settings used in comparison are in **bold**. For example, (a, e, f) compares backbones.

Method	Backbone	Input size	#Deconv. layers	Deconv. kernel size	*AP*
a	**ResNet-50**	**256 × 192**	3	**4**	70.4
b	ResNet-50	256 × 192	2	4	67.9
c	ResNet-50	256 × 192	3	**2**	70.1
d	ResNet-50	256 × 192	3	**3**	70.3
e	**ResNet-101**	256 × 192	3	4	71.4
f	**ResNet-152**	256 × 192	3	4	72.0
g	ResNet-50	**128 × 96**	3	4	60.6
h	ResNet-50	**384 × 288**	3	4	72.2

480   B. Xiao et al.

Ablation Study. Table 2 investigates various options in our baseline in Sect. 2.

1. *Heat map resolution.* Method (a) uses three deconvolutional layers to generate 64 × 48 heatmaps. Method (b) generates 32 × 24 heatmaps with two deconvolutional layers. (a) outperform (b) by 2.5 AP with only slightly increased model capacity. By default, three deconvolutional layers are used.
2. *Kernel size.* Methods (a, c, d) show that a smaller kernel size gives a marginally decrease in AP, which is 0.3 point decrease from kernel size 4 to 2. By default, deconvolution kernel size of 4 is used.
3. *Backbone.* As in most vision tasks, a deeper backbone model has better performance. Methods (a, e, f) show steady improvement by using deeper backbone models. AP increase is 1.0 from ResNet-50 to Resnet-101 and 1.6 from ResNet-50 to ResNet-152.
4. *Image size.* Methods (a, g, h) show that image size is critical for performance. From method (a) to (g), the image size is reduced by half and AP drops points. On the other hand, relative 75% computation is saved. Method (h) uses a large image size and increases 1.8 AP from method (a), at the cost of higher computational cost.

Table 3. Comparison with Hourglass [22] and CPN [6] on COCO val2017 dataset. Their results are cited from [6]. OHKM means Online Hard Keypoints Mining.

Method	Backbone	Input size	OHKM	AP
8-stage Hourglass	-	256 × 192	✗	66.9
8-stage Hourglass	-	256 × 256	✗	67.1
CPN	ResNet-50	256 × 192	✗	68.6
CPN	ResNet-50	384 × 288	✗	70.6
CPN	ResNet-50	256 × 192	✓	69.4
CPN	ResNet-50	384 × 288	✓	71.6
Ours	ResNet-50	256 × 192	✗	70.4
Ours	ResNet-50	384 × 288	✗	72.2

Comparison with Other Methods on COCO val2017. Table 3 compares our results with a 8-stage Hourglass [22] and CPN [6]. All the three methods use a similar top-down two-stage paradigm. For reference, the person detection AP of hourglass [22] and CPN [6] is 55.3 [6], which is comparable to ours 56.4.

Compared with Hourglass [6,22], our baseline has an improvement of 3.5 in AP. Both methods use an input size of 256 × 192 and no Online Hard Keypoints Mining (OHKM) involved.

CPN [6] and our baseline use the same backbone of ResNet-50. When OHKM is not used, our baseline outperforms CPN [6] by 1.8 AP for input size 256 × 192, and 1.6 AP for input size 384×288. When OHKM is used in CPN [6], our baseline is better by 0.6 AP for both input sizes.

Note that the results of Hourglass [22] and CPN [6] are cited from [6] and not implemented by us. Therefore, the performance difference could come from implementation difference. Nevertheless, we believe it is safe to conclude that our baseline has comparable results but is simpler.

Table 4. Comparisons on COCO test-dev dataset. Top: methods in the literature, trained only on COCO training dataset. Middle: results submitted to COCO test-dev leaderboard [9], which have either extra training data (*) or models ensamled ($^+$). Bottom: our single model results, trained only on COCO training dataset.

Method	Backbone	Input size	AP	AP_{50}	AP_{75}	AP_m	AP_l	AR
CMU-Pose [5]	-	-	61.8	84.9	67.5	57.1	68.2	66.5
Mask-RCNN [12]	ResNet-50-FPN	-	63.1	87.3	68.7	57.8	71.4	-
G-RMI [24]	ResNet-101	353 × 257	64.9	85.5	71.3	62.3	70.0	69.7
CPN [6]	ResNet-Inception	384 × 288	72.1	91.4	80.0	68.7	77.2	78.5
FAIR* [9]	ResNeXt-101-FPN	-	69.2	90.4	77.0	64.9	76.3	75.2
G-RMI* [9]	ResNet-152	353 × 257	71.0	87.9	77.7	69.0	75.2	75.8
oks* [9]	-	-	72.0	90.3	79.7	67.6	78.4	77.1
bangbangren*$^+$ [9]	ResNet-101	-	72.8	89.4	79.6	68.6	**80.0**	78.7
CPN$^+$ [6,9]	ResNet-Inception	384 × 288	73.0	**91.7**	80.9	69.5	78.1	**79.0**
Ours	ResNet-152	384 × 288	**73.7**	91.9	**81.1**	**70.3**	**80.0**	79.0

Comparisons on COCO test-dev Dataset. Table 4 summarizes the results of other state-of-the-art methods in the literature on COCO Keypoint Leaderboard [9] and COCO *test-dev* dataset. For our baseline here, a human detector with *person detection* AP of 60.9 on COCO *std-dev* split dataset is used. For reference, CPN [6] use a human detector with *person detection* AP of 62.9 on COCO *minival* split dataset.

Compared with CMU-Pose [5], which is a bottom-up approach for multi-person pose estimation, our method is significantly better. Both G-RMI [24] and CPN [6] have a similar top-down pipeline with ours. G-RMI also uses ResNet as backbone, as ours. Using the same backbone Resnet-101, our method outperforms G-RMI for both small (256 × 192) and large input size (384 × 288). CPN uses a stronger backbone of ResNet-Inception [29]. As evidence, the top-1 error rate on ImageNet validation set of Resnet-Inception and ResNet-152 are 18.7% and 21.4% respectively [29]. Yet, for the same input size 384 × 288, our result 73.7 outperforms both CPN's single model and their ensembled model, which have 72.1 and 73.0 respectively.

4.2 Pose Estimation and Tracking on PoseTrack

PoseTrack [2] dataset is a large-scale benchmark for multi-person pose estimation and tracking in videos. It requires not only pose estimation in single frames, but also temporal tracking across frames. It contains 514 videos including 66,374 frames in total, split into 300, 50 and 208 videos for training, validation and test set respectively. For training videos, 30 frames from the center are annotated. For validation and test videos, besides 30 frames from the center, every fourth frame is also annotated for evaluating long range articulated tracking. The annotations include 15 body keypoints location, a unique person id and a head bounding box for each person instance.

The dataset has three tasks. Task 1 evaluates single-frame pose estimation using mean average precision (mAP) metric as is done in [25]. Task 2 also evaluates pose estimation but allows usage of temporal information across frames. Task 3 evaluates tracking using multi-object tracking metrics [4]. As our tracking baseline uses temporal information, we report results on Task 2 and 3. Note that our pose estimation baseline also performs best on Task 1 but is not reported here for simplicity.

Training. Our pose estimation model is fine-tuned from those pre-trained on COCO in Sect. 4.1. As only key points are annotated, we obtain the ground truth box of a person instance by extending the bounding box of its all key points by 15% in length (7.5% on both sides). The same data augmentation as in Sect. 4.1 is used. During training, the base learning rate is 1e−4. It drops to 1e−5 at 10 epochs and 1e−6 at 15 epochs. There are 20 epochs in total. Other hyper parameters are the same as in Sect. 4.1.

Testing. Our flow based tracking baseline is closely related to the human detector's performance, as the propagated boxes could affect boxes from a detector. To investigate its effect, we experiment with two off-the-shelf detectors, a faster but less accurate R-FCN [16] and a slower but more accurate FPN-DCN [10]. Both use ResNet-101 backbone and are obtained from public implementation [1]. No additional fine tuning of detectors on PoseTrack dataset is performed.

Similar as in [11], we first drop low-confidence detections, which tends to decrease the mAP metric but increase the MOTA tracking metric. Also, since the tracking metric MOT penalizes false positives equally regardless of the scores, we drop low confidence joints first to generate the result as in [11]. We choose the boxes and joints drop threshold in a data-driven manner on validation set, 0.5 and 0.4 respectively.

For optical flow estimation, the fastest model FlowNet2S in FlowNet family [14] is used, as provided on [23]. We use the PoseTrack evaluation toolkit for results on validation set and report final results on test set from the evaluation server. Figure 3 illustrates some results of our approach on PoseTrack test dataset.

Our main ablation study is performed on ResNet-50 with input size 256×192, which is already strong when compared with state-of-the-art. Our best result is on ResNet-152 with input size 384×288.

Effect of Joint Propagation. Table 5 shows that using boxes from joint propagation introduces improvement on both mAP and MOTA metrics using different

Fig. 3. Some sample results on PoseTrack Challenge test set.

Table 5. Ablation study on PoseTrack Challenge validation dataset. Top: Results of ResNet-50 backbone using R-FCN detector. Middle: Results of ResNet-50 backbone using FPN-DCN detector. Bottom:Results of ResNet-152 backbone using FPN-DCN detector.

Method	Backbone	Detector	With joint propagation	Similarity metric	mAP total	MOTA total
a_1	ResNet-50	R-FCN	✗	S_{Bbox}	66.0	57.6
a_2	ResNet-50	R-FCN	✗	S_{Pose}	66.0	57.7
a_3	ResNet-50	R-FCN	✓	S_{Bbox}	70.3	61.4
a_4	ResNet-50	R-FCN	✓	S_{Pose}	70.3	61.8
a_5	ResNet-50	R-FCN	✓	S_{Flow}	70.3	61.8
a_6	ResNet-50	R-FCN	✓	$S_{Multi-Flow}$	**70.3**	**62.2**
b_1	ResNet-50	FPN-DCN	✗	S_{Bbox}	69.3	59.8
b_2	ResNet-50	FPN-DCN	✗	S_{Pose}	69.3	59.7
b_3	ResNet-50	FPN-DCN	✓	S_{Bbox}	72.4	62.1
b_4	ResNet-50	FPN-DCN	✓	S_{Pose}	72.4	61.8
b_5	ResNet-50	FPN-DCN	✓	S_{Flow}	72.4	62.4
b_6	ResNet-50	FPN-DCN	✓	$S_{Multi-Flow}$	**72.4**	**62.9**
c_1	ResNet-152	FPN-DCN	✗	S_{Bbox}	72.9	62.0
c_2	ResNet-152	FPN-DCN	✗	S_{Pose}	72.9	61.9
c_3	ResNet-152	FPN-DCN	✓	S_{Bbox}	76.7	64.8
c_4	ResNet-152	FPN-DCN	✓	S_{Pose}	76.7	64.9
c_5	ResNet-152	FPN-DCN	✓	S_{Flow}	76.7	65.1
c_6	ResNet-152	FPN-DCN	✓	$S_{Multi-Flow}$	**76.7**	**65.4**

Table 6. Multi-person pose estimation performance on PoseTrack Challenge dataset. "*" means models trained on train + validation set. Top: Results on PoseTrack validation set. Bottom: Results on PoseTrack test set

Method	Dataset	Head mAP	Sho. mAP	Elb. mAP	Wri. mAP	Hip mAP	Knee mAP	Ank. mAP	Total mAP
Girdhar et al. [11]	val	67.5	70.2	62.0	51.7	60.7	58.7	49.8	60.6
Xiu et al. [32]	val	66.7	73.3	68.3	61.1	67.5	67.0	61.3	66.5
Ours:ResNet-50	val	79.1	80.5	75.5	66.0	70.8	70.0	61.7	72.4
Ours:ResNet-152	val	81.7	83.4	80.0	72.4	75.3	74.8	67.1	**76.7**
Girdhar et al.* [11]	test	-	-	-	-	-	-	-	59.6
Xiu et al. [32]	test	64.9	67.5	65.0	59.0	62.5	62.8	57.9	63.0
Ours:ResNet-50	test	76.4	77.2	72.2	65.1	68.5	66.9	60.3	70.0
Ours:ResNet-152	test	79.5	79.7	76.4	70.7	71.6	71.3	64.9	**73.9**

backbones and detectors. With R-FCN detector, using boxes from joint propagation (method a_3 vs. a_1) introduces improvement of 4.3% mAP and 3.8% MOTA. With the better FPN-DCN detector, using boxes from joint propagation (method b_3 vs. b_1) introduces improvement of 3.1% mAP and 2.3% MOTA. With ResNet-152 as backbone (method c_3 vs. c_1), improvement is 3.8% mAP and 2.8% MOTA. Note that such improvement does not only come from more boxes. As noted in [11], simply keeping more boxes of a detector, e.g., by using a smaller threshold, would lead to an improvement in mAP, but a drop in MOTA since more false positives would be introduced. The joint propagation improves both mAP and MOTA metrics, indicating that it finds more persons that are missed by the detector, possibly due to motion blur or occlusion in video frames.

Another interesting observation is that the less accurate R-FCN detector benefits more from joint propagation. For example, the gap between using FPN-DCN and R-FCN detector in ResNet-50 is decreased from 3.3% mAP and 2.2% MOTA (from a_1 to b_1) to 2.1% mAP and 0.4% MOTA (from a_3 to b_3). Also, method a_3 outperforms method b_1 by 1.0% mAP and 1.6% MOTA, indicating that a weak detector R-FCN combined with joint propagation could perform better than a strong detector FPN-DCN along. While, the former is more efficient as joint propagation is fast.

Effect of Flow-Based Pose Similarity. Flow-based pose similarity is shown working better when compared with bounding box similarity and pose similarity in Table 5. For example, flow-based similarity using multi frames (method b_6) and single frame (method b_5) outperforms bounding box similarity (method b_3) by 0.8% MOTA and 0.3% MOTA.

Note that flow-based pose similarity is better than bounding box similarity when person moves fast and their boxes do not overlap. Method b_6 with flow-based pose similarity considers multi frames and have an 0.5% MOTA improvement when compared to method b_5, which considers only one previous frame. This improvement comes from the case when people are lost shortly due to occlusion and appear again.

Comparison with State-of-the-Art. We report our results on both Task 2 and Task 3 on PoseTrack dataset. As verified in Table 5, method b_6 and c_6 are the best settings and used here. Backbones are ResNet-50 and ResNet-152, respectively. The detector is FPN-DCN [10].

Table 6 reports the results on pose estimation (Task 2). Our small model (ResNet-50) outperforms the other methods already by a large margin. Our larger model (ResNet-152) further improves the state-of-the-art. On validation set it has an absolute 16.1% improvement in mAP over [11], which is the winner of ICCV'17 PoseTrack Challenge, and also has an 10.2% improvement over a recent work [32], which is the previous best.

Table 7 reports the results on pose tracking (Task 3). Compared with [11] on validation and test dataset, our larger model (ResNet-152) has an 10.2 and 5.8 improvement in MOTA over its 55.2 and 51.8 respectively. Compared with the recent work [32], our best model (ResNet-152) has 7.1% and 6.6% improvement on validation and test dataset respectively. Note that our smaller model (ResNet-50) also outperform the other methods [11,32].

Table 8 summarizes the results on PoseTrack's leaderboard. Our baseline outperforms all public entries by a large margin. Note that all methods differ significantly and this comparison is only on system level.

Table 7. Multi-person Pose Tracking Performance on PoseTrack Challenge dataset. "*" means models trained on train + validation set. Top: Results on PoseTrack validation set. Bottom: Results on PoseTrack test set

Method	Dataset	MOTA Head	MOTA Sho.	MOTA Elb.	MOTA Wri.	MOTA Hip	MOTA Knee	MOTA Ank.	MOTA Total	MOTP Total	Prec Total	Rec Total
Girdhar et al. [11]	val	61.7	65.5	57.3	45.7	54.3	53.1	45.7	55.2	61.5	66.4	88.1
Xiu et al. [32]	val	59.8	67.0	59.8	51.6	60.0	58.4	50.5	58.3	67.8	70.3	87.0
Ours:ResNet-50	val	72.1	74.0	61.2	53.4	62.4	61.6	50.7	62.9	84.5	86.3	76.0
Ours:ResNet-152	val	73.9	75.9	63.7	56.1	65.5	65.1	53.5	65.4	85.4	85.5	80.3
Girdhar et al.* [11]	test	-	-	-	-	-	-	-	51.8	-	-	-
Xiu et al. [32]	test	52.0	57.4	52.8	46.6	51.0	51.2	45.3	51.0	16.9	71.2	78.9
Ours:ResNet-50	test	65.9	67.0	51.5	48.0	56.2	54.6	46.9	56.4	45.5	81.0	75.7
Ours:ResNet-152	test	67.1	68.4	52.2	48.9	56.1	56.6	48.8	57.6	62.6	79.4	79.9

Table 8. Results of mulit-person pose tracking on PoseTrack challenge leaderboard. "*" means models trained on train + validation set.

Entry	Additional training dataset	mAP	MOTA
ProTracker [11]	COCO	59.6	51.8
PoseFlow [26]	COCO + MPII-Pose	63.0	51.0
MVIG [26]	COCO + MPII-Pose	63.2	50.7
BUTD2 [17]	COCO	59.2	50.6
SOPT-PT [26]	COCO + MPII-Pose	58.2	42.0
ML-LAB [34]	COCO + MPII-Pose	70.3	41.8
Ours:ResNet152*	COCO	**74.6**	**57.8**

5   Conclusions

We present simple and strong baselines for pose estimation and tracking. They achieve state-of-the-art results on challenging benchmarks. They are validated via comprehensive ablation studies. We hope such baselines would benefit the field by easing the idea development and evaluation.

References

1. Deformable-ConvNet. https://github.com/msracver/Deformable-ConvNets
2. Andriluka, M., et al.: PoseTrack: a benchmark for human pose estimation and tracking. In: Proceedings of the IEEE Conference on Computer Vision and Pattern Recognition, pp. 5167–5176 (2018)
3. Andriluka, M., Pishchulin, L., Gehler, P., Schiele, B.: 2D human pose estimation: new benchmark and state of the art analysis. In: IEEE Conference on Computer Vision and Pattern Recognition (CVPR), June 2014
4. Bernardin, K., Stiefelhagen, R.: Evaluating multiple object tracking performance: the CLEAR MOT metrics. J. Image Video Process. **2008**, 1 (2008)
5. Cao, Z., Simon, T., Wei, S.E., Sheikh, Y.: Realtime multi-person 2D pose estimation using part affinity fields. In: CVPR (2017)
6. Chen, Y., Wang, Z., Peng, Y., Zhang, Z., Yu, G., Sun, J.: Cascaded pyramid network for multi-person pose estimation. In: CVPR (2018)
7. Chen, Y., Shen, C., Wei, X.S., Liu, L., Yang, J.: Adversarial posenet: a structure-aware convolutional network for human pose estimation. In: IEEE International Conference on Computer Vision, pp. 1212–1221 (2017)
8. Chu, X., Yang, W., Ouyang, W., Ma, C., Yuille, A.L., Wang, X.: Multi-context attention for human pose estimation. In: Proceedings of the IEEE Conference on Computer Vision and Pattern Recognition, pp. 1831–1840 (2017)
9. COCO: COCO Leader Board. http://cocodataset.org
10. Dai, J., et al.: Deformable convolutional networks. In: Proceedings of the IEEE International Conference on Computer Vision, pp. 764–773 (2017)
11. Girdhar, R., Gkioxari, G., Torresani, L., Paluri, M., Tran, D.: Detect-and-track: efficient pose estimation in videos. In: Proceedings of the IEEE Conference on Computer Vision and Pattern Recognition, pp. 350–359 (2018)
12. He, K., Gkioxari, G., Dollár, P., Girshick, R.: Mask R-CNN. In: 2017 IEEE International Conference on Computer Vision (ICCV), pp. 2980–2988. IEEE (2017)
13. He, K., Zhang, X., Ren, S., Sun, J.: Deep residual learning for image recognition. In: Proceedings of the IEEE Conference on Computer Vision and Pattern Recognition, pp. 770–778 (2016)
14. Ilg, E., Mayer, N., Saikia, T., Keuper, M., Dosovitskiy, A., Brox, T.: FlowNet 2.0: evolution of optical flow estimation with deep networks. In: IEEE Conference on Computer Vision and Pattern Recognition (CVPR), vol. 2 (2017)
15. Ioffe, S., Szegedy, C.: Batch normalization: accelerating deep network training by reducing internal covariate shift. In: International Conference on Machine Learning, pp. 448–456 (2015)
16. Dai, J., Li, Y., He, K., Sun, J.: R-FCN: object detection via region-based fully convolutional networks. In: NIPS (2016)
17. Jin, S., et al.: Towards multi-person pose tracking: bottom-up and top-down methods. In: ICCV PoseTrack Workshop (2017)

18. Kingma, D.P., Ba, J.: Adam: a method for stochastic optimization. In: ICLR (2015)
19. Krizhevsky, A., Sutskever, I., Hinton, G.E.: Imagenet classification with deep convolutional neural networks. In: Advances in Neural Information Processing Systems, pp. 1097–1105 (2012)
20. Lin, T.-Y., et al.: Microsoft COCO: common objects in context. In: Fleet, D., Pajdla, T., Schiele, B., Tuytelaars, T. (eds.) ECCV 2014. LNCS, vol. 8693, pp. 740–755. Springer, Cham (2014). https://doi.org/10.1007/978-3-319-10602-1_48
21. Newell, A., Huang, Z., Deng, J.: Associative embedding: end-to-end learning for joint detection and grouping. In: Advances in Neural Information Processing Systems, pp. 2274–2284 (2017)
22. Newell, A., Yang, K., Deng, J.: Stacked hourglass networks for human pose estimation. In: Leibe, B., Matas, J., Sebe, N., Welling, M. (eds.) ECCV 2016. LNCS, vol. 9912, pp. 483–499. Springer, Cham (2016). https://doi.org/10.1007/978-3-319-46484-8_29
23. NVIDIA: flownet2-pytorch (2018). https://github.com/NVIDIA/flownet2-pytorch. Accessed March 2018
24. Papandreou, G., et al.: Towards accurate multi-person pose estimation in the wild. In: 2017 IEEE Conference on Computer Vision and Pattern Recognition (CVPR), pp. 3711–3719. IEEE (2017)
25. Pishchulin, L., et al.: DeepCut: joint subset partition and labeling for multi person pose estimation. In: Proceedings of the IEEE Conference on Computer Vision and Pattern Recognition, pp. 4929–4937 (2016)
26. PoseTrack: PoseTrack Leader Board. https://posetrack.net/leaderboard.php
27. Ren, S., He, K., Girshick, R., Sun, J.: Faster R-CNN: towards real-time object detection with region proposal networks. In: Advances in Neural Information Processing Systems, pp. 91–99 (2015)
28. Russakovsky, O., Deng, J., Su, H., Krause, J., Satheesh, S., Ma, S., Huang, Z., Karpathy, A., Khosla, A., Bernstein, M.: Imagenet large scale visual recognition challenge. Int. J. Comput. Vis. 115(3), 211–252 (2015)
29. Szegedy, C., Ioffe, S., Vanhoucke, V., Alemi, A.A.: Inception-v4, inception-resnet and the impact of residual connections on learning. In: AAAI, vol. 4, p. 12 (2017)
30. Tompson, J.J., Jain, A., LeCun, Y., Bregler, C.: Joint training of a convolutional network and a graphical model for human pose estimation. In: Advances in Neural Information Processing Systems, pp. 1799–1807 (2014)
31. Toshev, A., Szegedy, C.: DeepPose: human pose estimation via deep neural networks. In: Proceedings of the IEEE Conference on Computer Vision and Pattern Recognition, pp. 1653–1660 (2014)
32. Xiu, Y., Li, J., Wang, H., Fang, Y., Lu, C.: Pose Flow: efficient online pose tracking. arXiv preprint arXiv:1802.00977 (2018)
33. Yang, W., Li, S., Ouyang, W., Li, H., Wang, X.: Learning feature pyramids for human pose estimation. In: IEEE International Conference on Computer Vision (2017)
34. Zhu, X., Jiang, Y., Luo, Z.: Multi-person pose estimation for posetrack with enhanced part affinity fields. In: ICCV PoseTrack Workshop (2017)
35. Zhu, X., Wang, Y., Dai, J., Yuan, L., Wei, Y.: Flow-guided feature aggregation for video object detection. In: 2017 IEEE International Conference on Computer Vision (ICCV), pp. 408–417. IEEE (2017)
36. Zhu, X., Xiong, Y., Dai, J., Yuan, L., Wei, Y.: Deep feature flow for video recognition. In: Proceedings of the CVPR, vol. 2, p. 7 (2017)

Affine Correspondences Between Central Cameras for Rapid Relative Pose Estimation

Iván Eichhardt$^{(\boxtimes)}$ and Dmitry Chetverikov

MTA SZTAKI, Kende u. 13-17, Budapest 1111, Hungary
{ivan.eichhardt,dmitry.chetverikov}@sztaki.mta.hu

Abstract. This paper presents a novel algorithm to estimate the relative pose, *i.e.* the 3D rotation and translation of two cameras, from two affine correspondences (ACs) considering any central camera model. The solver is built on new epipolar constraints describing the relationship of an AC and any central views. We also show that the pinhole case is a specialization of the proposed approach. Benefiting from the low number of required correspondences, robust estimators like LO-RANSAC need fewer samples, and thus terminate earlier than using the five-point method. Tests on publicly available datasets containing pinhole, fisheye and catadioptric camera images confirmed that the method often leads to results superior to the state-of-the-art in terms of geometric accuracy.

Keywords: Relative pose · Affine correspondences · Central cameras

1 Introduction

Methods solving geometric computer vision problems using ACs typically use three times fewer correspondences [2] compared to point–based counterparts. This is also the case for this work, since with the proposed epipolar constraints, a total of three linear equations are yielded per correspondence.

A Local Affine Frame (LAF) is a pair $(\mathbf{x}, \mathbf{M})$ of a point $\mathbf{x} \in \mathbb{R}^2$ and a 2D affine transformation $\mathbf{M} \in \mathbb{R}^{2 \times 2}$ which describes the local shape and orientation of the region. Scale invariant features are often sufficient for establishing correct Point Correspondences (PCs), which can then be used for solving computer vision problems. However, there are cases when affine invariant feature/region detectors are preferable [26]. LAFs can be obtained using affine invariant feature extractors [12–14,16,28]. From a pair of corresponding LAFs, $(\mathbf{x}_1, \mathbf{M}_1)$ and $(\mathbf{x}_2, \mathbf{M}_2)$, an AC $(\mathbf{x}_1, \mathbf{x}_2, \mathbf{A})$ can be constructed, where $(\mathbf{x}_1, \mathbf{x}_2)$ is a PC and $\mathbf{A} = \mathbf{M}_2 \mathbf{M}_1^{-1}$ is the affinity. In the planar case for perspective views (*i.e.* the pinhole camera model is valid), $\mathbf{A}$ is the gradient of the underlying homography.

Electronic supplementary material The online version of this chapter (https:// doi.org/10.1007/978-3-030-01231-1_30) contains supplementary material, which is available to authorized users.

© Springer Nature Switzerland AG 2018
V. Ferrari et al. (Eds.): ECCV 2018, LNCS 11210, pp. 488–503, 2018.
https://doi.org/10.1007/978-3-030-01231-1_30

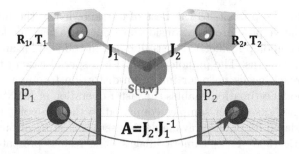

Fig. 1. Illustration of cameras represented by projection functions p_i and poses $\mathbf{R}_i$, $\mathbf{T}_i$, $i = 1, 2$. Parametric surface $S(u, v)$ has gradients $\mathbf{J}_i$ and the affinity $\mathbf{A}$.

Mainstream methods using PCs to solve computer vision problems completely disregard the information in $\mathbf{M}$. Hartley proposed the normalized eight–point algorithm [8] for determining the epipolar geometry between pinhole views. Nistér [17] developed a minimal, five–point solver for the relative pose problem. Minimal methods, *i.e.* minimal in the number of samples used for estimation, are useful when dealing with combinatorially intensive problems, often used with robust methods [7,10,25] enabling the removal of numerous outliers.

Methods using ACs to estimate geometry, using the extra information in $\mathbf{A}$, are a new kind of "minimal" solvers typically trisecting the number of minimum samples compared to PC–based counterparts. However, to solve computer vision problems these methods consider only the strictly pinhole case [2,9,18,20,21] ignoring real–world cameras with a distortion or wide Field–of–View (FoV). These works rely on the fact that $\mathbf{A}$ and $\mathbf{H}$ are related and deduce their results using components of $\mathbf{H}$ and known properties of the epipolar geometry. Based on this relation, Köser and Koch [9] describes a method for camera resection using a single AC. For the epipolar geometry estimation, Riggi *et al.* [22] and Perdoch *et al.* [18] used ACs to generate additional PCs for a PC–based solver. Bentolila *et al.* [2] demonstrated that *three* ACs are sufficient for fundamental matrix estimation. Raposo and Barreto [21] presented a method for relative pose estimation using two ACs, for pinhole views. They demonstrated its applicability in rather controlled conditions. Baráth *et al.* [1] proposed a method to estimates the focal length with the fundamental matrix for pinhole views using two ACs.

In contrast to the above mentioned works, few use ACs for geometric model estimation between non-pinhole views [5,15,19]. Molnár and Eichhardt [15] generalized epipolar geometry using ACs. They proposed non-linear equations that constrain the geometry without using the essential matrix. Since the essential matrix is central to the relative pose estimation problem, the current work proposes novel *linear* constraints on its elements, directly applicable to arbitrary central cameras (including wide–FoV or omnidirectional). A new method for the estimation of the relative pose is also presented.

Contribution. We present, to the best of our knowledge, the first algorithm to solve the relative pose problem considering general camera models and using two ACs. New epipolar geometric constraints are introduced for an AC between general central cameras. The pinhole case [21] is a special case of the proposed one. Our approach needs no prior image un-distortion to operate. Using only two ACs for model estimation enables the faster operation of RANSAC and LO-RANSAC as they take fewer samples compared to the five-point method. The method is validated on publicly available datasets consisting of pinhole, fisheye and catadioptric (360° FoV) camera images. The results presented are often superior to the state-of-the-art in terms of accuracy.

2   Mapping Between General Projective Views

Notations. 2D points are denoted as $\mathbf{x}$. Vectors are written in bold lower-case letters and matrices in bold capitals. Jacobians are denoted by the ∇ operator, i.e. $\nabla f(\mathbf{x}) = [\partial_1 f \ldots \partial_n f](\mathbf{x}) \in \mathbb{R}^{m \times n}$, where f is differentiable at $\mathbf{x} \in \mathbb{R}^n$. Hereafter "chain rule" stands for the chain rule for differentiation.

Local Approximation of Projection. Consider a continuously differentiable parametric surface $S(\mathbf{z}) \in \mathbb{R}^3$, $\mathbf{z} \in \mathbb{R}^2$ and some function $p_i : \mathbb{R}^3 \to \mathbb{R}^2$ (basically, the camera model) projecting the 3D points of S onto the image plane:

$$\mathbf{x}_i \doteq p_i(\mathbf{R}_i S(\mathbf{z}_0) + \mathbf{T}_i) \tag{1}$$

for a point $\mathbf{z}_0$ of the parameter space of S, where $\mathbf{R}_i$ and $\mathbf{T}_i$ are the global rotation and translation (the pose) of view i, respectively. Applying the chain rule, the Jacobian of Eq. (1) is

$$\mathbf{J}_i \doteq \nabla_{\mathbf{z}}[\mathbf{x}_i] = \nabla p_i(\mathbf{R}_i S(\mathbf{z}_0) + \mathbf{T}_i) \mathbf{R}_i \nabla S(\mathbf{z}_0). \tag{2}$$

$\mathbf{J}_i$ can be interpreted as a local relative affine transformation between infinitesimal environments of the surface S at the point $\mathbf{z}_1$ and its projection at the point $\mathbf{x}_i$. See Fig. 1 for an additional explanation.

The "Affinity". Let $f : \mathbb{R}^2 \to \mathbb{R}^2$ be a mapping between the views as follows:

$$f(\mathbf{x}_1) = \mathbf{x}_2. \tag{3}$$

Assume that for all $\mathbf{z} \in \mathrm{dom}(S)$

$$f(p_1(\mathbf{R}_1 S(\mathbf{z}) + \mathbf{T}_1)) = p_2(\mathbf{R}_2 S(\mathbf{z}) + \mathbf{T}_2), \tag{4}$$

with respective p_i, $i \in \{1, 2\}$ and poses as denoted before, thus f being compatible with the epipolar geometry of the two views. The Taylor expansion of Eq. (4) around $\mathbf{x}_1$ is $f(\mathbf{y}) \approx \mathbf{x}_2 + \mathbf{A}(\mathbf{y} - \mathbf{x}_1)$, where $\mathbf{A}$ is the Jacobian of f, an *affinity*, *i.e.* a mapping between the infinitesimal environments of $\mathbf{x}_1$ and $\mathbf{x}_2$. The affinity can be expressed using $\mathbf{J}_i$, $i = 1, 2$ and the chain rule:

$$\mathbf{A} = \mathbf{J}_2 \mathbf{J}_1^{-1}. \tag{5}$$

In practice, $\mathbf{J}_i$ are related to LAFs $(\mathbf{x}_i, \mathbf{M}_i)$. The components of the affinity $\mathbf{M}_i$ of a pair of corresponding LAFs are related to Jacobians $\mathbf{J}_i$ at $\mathbf{x}_i$ by a mutual transformation $\mathbf{B}$: $\mathbf{M}_i = \mathbf{J}_i \mathbf{B}$. Thus $\mathbf{A}$ can be expressed using corresponding LAFs: $\mathbf{M}_2 \mathbf{M}_1^{-1} = (\mathbf{J}_2 \mathbf{B})(\mathbf{J}_1 \mathbf{B})^{-1} = \mathbf{J}_2 \mathbf{B} \mathbf{B}^{-1} \mathbf{J}_1^{-1} = \mathbf{J}_2 \mathbf{J}_1^{-1} = \mathbf{A}$.

3 Epipolar Constraints Based on an AC

Now consider $q_i : \mathbb{R}^2 \to \mathbb{R}^3$, $p_i \circ q_i = \mathrm{Id}_{\mathbb{R}^2}$, image-to-camera projection functions. The well–known epipolar constraint can be formulated using the PC $(\mathbf{x}_1, \mathbf{x}_2)$ as

$$q_2(\mathbf{x}_2)^{\mathrm{T}} \mathbf{E} q_1(\mathbf{x}_1) = 0, \tag{6}$$

where $\mathbf{E} = \mathbf{R}[\mathbf{t}]_\times$ is the essential matrix. Using the bijection f and substituting $f(\mathbf{x}_1)$ for $\mathbf{x}_2$, the following equation for $\mathbf{x}_1$ is obtained:

$$q_2(f(\mathbf{x}_1))^{\mathrm{T}} \mathbf{E} q_1(\mathbf{x}_1) = 0. \tag{7}$$

New Epipolar Constraints. Applying the gradient operator $\nabla_{\mathbf{x}_1}$ to both sides and using the chain product rule results in the following two *new epipolar constraints* that now use the AC $(\mathbf{x}_1, \mathbf{x}_2, \mathbf{A})$:

$$\mathbf{A}^{\mathrm{T}} (\nabla q_2(\mathbf{x}_2))^{\mathrm{T}} \mathbf{E} q_1(\mathbf{x}_1) + (\nabla q_1(\mathbf{x}_1))^{\mathrm{T}} \mathbf{E}^{\mathrm{T}} q_2(\mathbf{x}_2) = \mathbf{0}, \tag{8}$$

since $\nabla_{\mathbf{x}_1} [q_2(f(\mathbf{x}_1))] = \nabla q_2(\mathbf{x}_2) \mathbf{A}$.

Since $\mathbf{x}_1$ has two components, the gradient provides two extra equations (one for each partial derivative) in addition to the epipolar constraint (6). This means that three constraints are given for each correspondence reducing from 8 to 3 the number of samples required to estimate the elements of $\mathbf{E}$.

4 Relative Pose Using Two ACs

The epipolar constraint (6) can also be written as

$$\widetilde{\mathbf{v}} \widetilde{\mathbf{E}} = 0, \tag{9}$$

where

$$\widetilde{\mathbf{v}} = \left[w_x \mathbf{v}^{\mathrm{T}}, \, w_y \mathbf{v}^{\mathrm{T}}, \, w_z \mathbf{v}^{\mathrm{T}} \right],$$

$$\widetilde{\mathbf{E}} = \left[e_{11}, \, e_{12}, \, e_{13}, \, e_{21}, \, e_{22}, \, e_{23}, \, e_{31}, \, e_{32}, \, e_{33} \right]^{\mathrm{T}}.$$

The line vector $\widetilde{\mathbf{v}}$ is constructed from the components of $\mathbf{v} = q_1(\mathbf{x}_1)$ and $\mathbf{w} = q_2(\mathbf{x}_2) = [w_x, w_y, w_z]^T$. $\widetilde{\mathbf{E}}$ is a vector containing the elements of $\mathbf{E}$:

$$\mathbf{E} = \begin{bmatrix} e_{11} & e_{12} & e_{13} \\ e_{21} & e_{22} & e_{23} \\ e_{31} & e_{32} & e_{33} \end{bmatrix}.$$

The two rows of Eq. (8) can be formulated in a similar manner as follows:

$$\widetilde{\mathbf{Q}}\widetilde{\mathbf{E}} = \mathbf{0}, \tag{10}$$

where

$$\widetilde{\mathbf{Q}} = [w_x\mathbf{V}, w_y\mathbf{V}, w_z\mathbf{V}] + \mathbf{A}^T [\mathbf{W}_1\mathbf{v}^T, \mathbf{W}_2\mathbf{v}^T, \mathbf{W}_3\mathbf{v}^T],$$
$$\mathbf{V} = (\nabla q_1(\mathbf{x}_1))^T,$$
$$\mathbf{W} = (\nabla q_2(\mathbf{x}_2))^T = [\mathbf{W}_1\ \mathbf{W}_2\ \mathbf{W}_3].$$

Now let us construct a matrix $\widetilde{\mathbf{B}} \in \mathbb{R}^{3\times 9}$ whose first row is $\widetilde{\mathbf{v}}^T$, while the second and the third rows are the two rows of $\widetilde{\mathbf{Q}}$, respectively. The compound system that describes the relation of the essential matrix to an AC is as follows:

$$\widetilde{\mathbf{B}}\widetilde{\mathbf{E}} = \mathbf{0}. \tag{11}$$

The matrices $\widetilde{\mathbf{B}}^{(j)}$, $j = 1, 2, 3$, can be constructed using three different ACs. The null–space of the compound system of these matrices is $\widetilde{\mathbf{E}}$, which provides the elements of the essential matrix $\mathbf{E}$ up to a scale.

With more correspondences, an over–determined system can also be constructed. Its solution is the singular vector with the smallest singular value.

4.1 "2AC" Solver – Essential Matrix from Two Correspondences

The essential matrix $\mathbf{E}$ has 5 degrees of freedom since one of its singular values is zero with its two non–zero ones being equal, which leads to the following cubic constraints [6, 17] on $\mathbf{E}$:

$$2\mathbf{E}\mathbf{E}^T\mathbf{E} - \mathrm{tr}\left(\mathbf{E}\mathbf{E}^T\right)\mathbf{E} = \mathbf{0}. \tag{12}$$

Also, since one of the singular values of $\mathbf{E}$ is zero

$$\det(\mathbf{E}) = 0. \tag{13}$$

The five–point solvers for essential matrix estimation [11, 17] use the null–space of a 5×9 matrix or the four singular vectors of an over–determined system, corresponding to the least four singular values, take their linear combination with coefficients $x, y, z, 1$ and substitute it into Eqs. (12) and (13) which give a polynomial system. The solutions of the polynomial system can then be back–substituted into the linear combination. The essential matrix can be decomposed into rotation and translation, after handling ambiguities [8, 11, 17].

Similarly to the five–point algorithm, one can construct a solution using only two ACs, hence the name of the solver is "2AC". The proposed solver *approximates* the four–dimensional nullspace using SVD. That is, (11) yields 3 equations per correspondence, the resulting 6×9 coefficient matrix would have a 3-dimensional nullspace. Instead, the four right singular vectors are used, corresponding to the least four singular values of the SVD decomposition.

4.2 Special Case: Pinhole Cameras

State of the art methods using LAFs to estimate epipolar geometry [2,3,21] rely on perspective views (*i.e.* pinhole camera). Our approach handles any central projection cameras (*e.g.* wide–FoV or panoramic ones) in a stereo configuration, allowing for a wider range of applications.

The pinhole camera case is a special case of the proposed one. From the relation of the homography and the affinity, Raposo and Barreto [21] derived a matrix equation yielding three equations for the epipolar constraint using an AC. Note that in this paper *no existence of a homography was assumed* between the views, f can be any, more general, or higher–order mapping. This work and their formulation shows that: (i) the first row in their work is the well–known epipolar constraint for a point correspondence, Eq. (9); (ii) and the second and third rows are equivalent to Eq. (10).

Let $\mathbf{v} = \begin{bmatrix} x_1 & x_2 & 1 \end{bmatrix}^{\mathrm{T}}$ and $\mathbf{w} = \begin{bmatrix} y_1 & y_2 & 1 \end{bmatrix}^{\mathrm{T}}$, thus, $\nabla q_i(\mathbf{x}_i)$ is also modified:

$$\nabla q_i(\mathbf{x}_i) = \begin{bmatrix} 1 & 0 & 0 \\ 0 & 1 & 0 \end{bmatrix}. \tag{14}$$

Substituting $\mathbf{v}$, $\mathbf{w}$ and $\nabla q_i(\mathbf{x}_i)$ into Eqs. (9) and (10) yields (15) and (16), respectively. Together, they form the 22nd equation of [21].

$$\begin{bmatrix} x_1 y_1 & x_1 y_2 & x_1 & x_2 y_1 & x_2 y_2 & x_2 & y_1 & y_2 & 1 \end{bmatrix} \widetilde{\mathbf{E}} = 0, \tag{15}$$

$$\begin{bmatrix} a_1 x_1 + y_1 & a_3 x_1 + y_2 & 1 & a_1 x_2 & a_3 x_2 & 0 & a_1 & a_3 & 0 \\ a_2 x_1 & a_4 x_1 & 0 & a_2 x_2 + y_1 & a_4 x_2 + y_2 & 1 & a_2 & a_4 & 0 \end{bmatrix} \widetilde{\mathbf{E}} = \mathbf{0}. \tag{16}$$

5 Handling Noise in ACs

A PC can be considered a "0th–order", an AC a "1st–order" information, which is more sensitive to noise. This section discusses how to cope with noisy ACs.

Extracting LAFs. The VLFeat library [27] is capable of extracting covariant features using different scale–space based detectors and the affine shape adaptation algorithm [12,14]. It is also capable of extracting dominant gradient directions from shape–adapted local frame of pixels. The number of iterations and the patch size used in these steps are sufficient for obtaining a robust descriptor, but the affine part of the resulting LAF is rather susceptible to noise. By tuning these parameters, one can enhance the applicability of LAFs for AC–based algorithms. Note that in the tests the default settings of VLFeat were used.

Photometric Refinement. After establishing correspondences, the affine part (**A**) of ACs can be further refined [21] minimizing the photometric discrepancy between the LAFs. The drawback of this approach is an extra time demand over feature extraction, although it can be massively parallelized. Note that in the tests, photometric refinement was primarily applied in the semi–synthetic and, partially, in the real–world evaluation. The rest of the real–world tests show that using Locally Optimized RANSAC (Sect. 5.1) has additional benefits, *e.g.* it is significantly less time–consuming, but still provides high accuracy.

5.1 Locally Optimized RANSAC

Sampling noisy ACs *without photometric refinement*, compared to PCs, might yield fewer robust hypotheses during traditional RANSAC iterations. However, there are two benefits of using ACs: *(a)* these hypotheses are still close to the true model; *(b)* combinatorially, sampling two elements is much better compared to samples of five elements: $\binom{N}{2} \ll \binom{N}{5}$. These benefits have the potential to boost LO-RANSAC [4,10] approach, enabling rapid runtime, with significantly fewer RANSAC-iterations and local optimization steps [10].

Hybrid LO-RANSAC. In this paper, a modified version of LO$^+$ [10] was applied as follows: First, (i) sample *minimal two-sets* of correspondences and use the proposed solver "2AC" for generating hypotheses; then (ii) apply the *local optimization step* to refine the support set of the most recently selected maximal hypothesis. See real–world tests (Sect. 6.4) for details of the performance of this LO-RANSAC approach.

6 Experimental Results

Since the essential matrix estimation for the pinhole case [21] is a special case of the proposed one, the evaluation will mainly focus on more general, central–projection models, such as (i) cameras with fisheye lens; (ii) catadioptric cameras; (iii) and other cameras with radial and tangential distortion.

Robustified versions of the five–point algorithm "5PT" [17] and variants of the proposed approach are compared using two and five correspondences denoted as "2AC" and "5AC". To obtain their robustified versions, MSAC [25] was applied. The minimum and maximum number of iterations were set to 10 and 2048, respectively, and failure probability of the estimator was set to 10^{-5}. The angular error metric $\sin^{-1}\left(\frac{q_2(\mathbf{x}_2)^\mathsf{T}\mathbf{E}q_1(\mathbf{x}_1)}{\|\mathbf{E}q_1(\mathbf{x}_1)\|}\right)$ was used with the MSAC whose threshold was normally set to $0.15°$ unless otherwise stated.

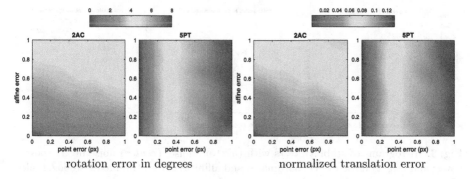

rotation error in degrees   normalized translation error

Fig. 2. Plots of sensitivity to noise in points (*axis x*) and affine (*axis y*) components.

6.1 Synthetic Tests

In the synthetic tests 2AC and 5PT are compared. The synthetic scene consisted of 5 oriented points uniformly sampled from the range $[-1, 1]^3$, with surface normals sampled on the unit sphere, viewed by two pinhole cameras having radial distortion. The distance of the camera centers from the origin varied from 2 to 3 units, the distance between the cameras from 0.1 to 1.0 units. The optical axes intersected in a point uniformly sampled from $[-1, 1]^3$.

To obtain PCs, oriented points were projected to the camera images. The affine parameters of ACs were calculated using the surface normals based on Eq. (2). Two uncorrelated sources of Gaussian noise, σ_p and σ_a, were added to the points in $\mathbb{R}^2$ and the affine parameters in $\mathbb{R}^{2\times2}$, respectively. For each level of noise σ_p and σ_a, the test was repeated 100 times building the synthetic scene, using 2AC and 5PT, and averaging rotation and translation errors. The results are shown on Fig. 2. For low levels of σ_a, 2AC always outperforms 5PT. However, stronger noise in affine parameters deteriorates the results of 2AC. 5PT is of course not affected by σ_a. Note that noise added to 2D positions is a realistic model of real–world conditions, while noise added to the affinity is a less realistic one.

6.2 Stability Tests

In this section the numerical stability of the proposed solver is compared to existing work and their behavior on different levels of synthetic noise is also investigated. It is important to note that these stability tests are all performed using a *pinhole camera with no distortion* since the solver of [21] is only designed for the pinhole camera model. The setup for these tests are similar to the one described in the previous section. The stability test shows the distribution of the matrix error $\min\left(\|\mathbf{E} - \mathbf{E}_{gt}\|, \|\mathbf{E} + \mathbf{E}_{gt}\|\right)$ from 30000 samples. All results can be seen in Fig. 3.

With no noise added, the pinhole camera based solver [21] shows a slightly better stability than the 5-point solver of Nistér [17] and 2AC. The proposed

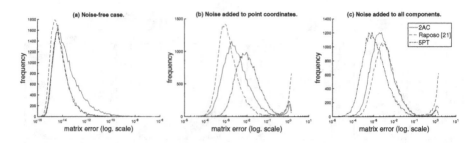

Fig. 3. Histograms of stability tests with (*left*) no noise; (*center*) noise in 2D coordinates; and (*right*) noise in 2D coordinates and affinities. Horizontal axes are log. scales of error exponents and vertical axes are their frequency.

solver here performs worse since 2AC uses an approximate nullspace acquired using SVD. All six linear equations are used that can be formed from two Affine Correspondences, to estimate a four–dimensional nullspace instead of their true, three–dimensional nullspace.

As the level of synthetic noise added to point coordinates increases, the 5-point solver becomes the worst among the three. 2AC and the pinhole-based method [21] show similar stability to the previous test. However, the solvers begin to produce larger errors to the right of the "10^0" on the horizontal logarithmic scale of the diagrams. These estimations failed. The largest number of failed cases are produced by the method in [21].

Adding synthetic noise to both point coordinates and affinity components results in the third diagram of Fig. 3. In this case solvers based on AC–s perform worse compared to the 5-point solver. The second best is 2AC and [21] is third.

6.3   Semi–Synthetic Tests

The semi–synthetic tests were based on the Multi–FoV dataset [29], with ray-traced views of scenes through perspective, fisheye and catadioptric [23] cameras. The dataset provides two scenes with the cameras traversing them, obtaining ground–truth poses, color images and depth maps. For the tests, the ground truth 3D points were sampled from the depth maps of the scene "vfr".

Similarly to the synthetic tests, PCs are established using the known spatial points. The affine transformation part (**A**) of each AC was initially set to the identity matrix, then refined using gradient–descent based photometric refinement on local areas of the color images, similarly as in the work of Raposo and Barreto [21]. The refinement used the symmetric cost function of summed squared differences between local patches of the color images. The patches were 20 × 20 pixel size windows centered on the points of a PC. The matrix **A** was refined maximizing photometric similarity. Outliers were uniformly sampled from the image space prior to photometric refinement.

In these tests, the robustified versions of 5PT and 2AC were compared. Using both methods, essential matrices and the corresponding sets of inliers were esti-

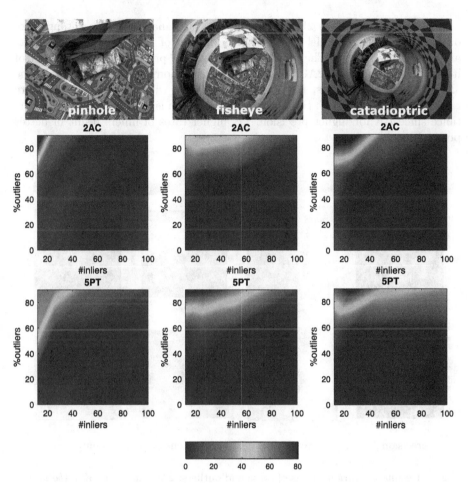

Fig. 4. Rotation errors versus number of inliers and percentage of outliers for 2AC (*2nd row*) and 5PT (*3rd row*). Frames (*1st row*) from the "vfr" scene [29]. Left to right: perspective, fisheye, Catadioptric views. Errors are measured after bundle adjustment.

mated. Essential matrices were then decomposed to relative rotation and translation, to be further refined using bundle adjustment (BA) on the inlier set. For different numbers of input inliers and outliers and levels of 2D noise, the performance of the methods were evaluated based on (i) mean and root mean square (RMS) errors of relative rotation and translation; (ii) runtime and number of iterations; and (iii) precision and recall.

Figure 4 shows rotation errors for the pinhole, fisheye and catadioptric cameras, comparing the effect of different levels of inliers and outliers in the sample set. The plots indicate that 5PT is the most sensitive to decreasing number of inliers and increasing number of outliers.

The effect of noise on 2D coordinates was also analyzed while adding more outliers. The fisheye model was used on a dataset of 100 matches. The results are presented in Fig. 5. The plots show the average precision, recall, number of iterations, and runtime. 2AC has the highest precision and the smallest runtime and number of iterations, but its recall decreases with increasing noise more rapidly compared to 5PT. However, higher precision is usually of greater importance since BA for higher precision, *i.e.* higher rates of inliers result in better pose estimation.

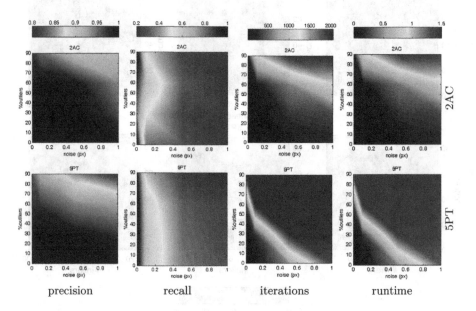

precision   recall   iterations   runtime

Fig. 5. Results for various levels of noise and outliers: 2AC (*top*) and 5PT (*bottom*).

6.4   Real–World Tests

There are two parts of this real–world evaluation: *(A)* extracted correspondences are further enhanced using simple photometric refinement (see Sect. 5), and in *(B)* the features are used without refinement, but locally optimized RANSAC (see Sect. 5.1) is used to provide high–quality results.

(A) with Photometric Refinement. In this section the proposed approach is compared to the five–point algorithm using image pairs from the Strecha Dense MVS dataset [24]. The input features were extracted using an affine–invariant version of the Difference of Gaussians (DoG) extractor [27] and photometrically refined as in the semi–synthetic tests. As before, the estimated relative pose was refined by performing BA on the inlier set obtained by the robust estimator.

Each test was repeated 100 times with the input features and matches unaltered. Table 1 shows the evaluation of the methods 2AC, 3AC, 5AC and 5PT on the Strecha Dense MVS dataset [24]. The table contains four columns for each scene and for each method: rotation RMSE in degrees, translation RMSE normalized to the ground truth, timing in seconds and number of RANSAC iterations. Regarding rotation and translation errors, 5AC performs best while 2AC and 3AC perform worse than 5PT. As for the runtime and number of RANSAC iterations, the estimators using two or three affine correspondences are the best, and for two scenes out of three, 5AC has lower runtime and number of iterations compared to 5PT. The Dense MVS dataset [24] contains scenes with rather diverse geometry and texture. The extracted affine correspondences can be less reliable compared to the ones in the semi–synthetic tests. In the real–world tests, 3AC outperforms 2AC. We believe that adding more correspondences to the otherwise minimal solver of 2AC, e.g. using 5AC, will increase the reliability of estimations resulting in a better inlier set facilitating the BA of relative pose.

Table 1. Evaluation of relative motion estimation on the Dense MVS dataset [24]. Top rows: three scenes of, brackets containing images pairs and numbers of correspondences extracted. Columns: solvers, (ρ) rotation and (τ) translation errors, (t) timing in seconds and (n) number of iterations for each scene and for each method. Errors are measured after bundle adjustment. Best results are highlighted.

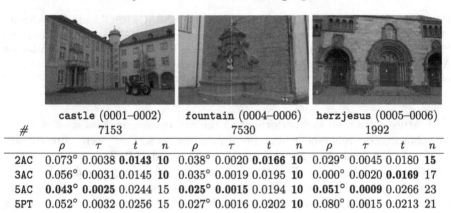

#	castle (0001–0002) 7153				fountain (0004–0006) 7530				herzjesus (0005–0006) 1992			
	ρ	τ	t	n	ρ	τ	t	n	ρ	τ	t	n
2AC	0.073°	0.0038	**0.0143**	10	0.038°	0.0020	**0.0166**	10	0.029°	0.0045	0.0180	15
3AC	0.056°	0.0031	0.0145	10	0.035°	0.0019	0.0195	10	0.000°	0.0020	**0.0169**	17
5AC	**0.043°**	**0.0025**	0.0244	15	**0.025°**	**0.0015**	0.0194	10	**0.051°**	**0.0009**	0.0266	23
5PT	0.052°	0.0032	0.0256	15	0.027°	0.0016	0.0202	10	0.080°	0.0015	0.0213	21

(B) Using Locally Optimized RANSAC. These tests, in contrast to above, were performed without using photometric refinement. RANSAC ("RSC") and a modified version of "LO$^+$" [10] performed robust estimation, using the five-point solver "5PT" and the proposed one "2AC". See Sect. 5.1 for more details on the proposed locally optimized approach. These different pairings are denoted as follows: 2AC-RSC, 2AC-LO$^+$, 5PT-RSC, 5PT-LO$^+$, undistort+[21]. Images of the test database are shown in Fig. 7. The images were taken by a Point Gray Blackfly camera with YV2.8x2.8SA-2 wide-FoV lens attached.

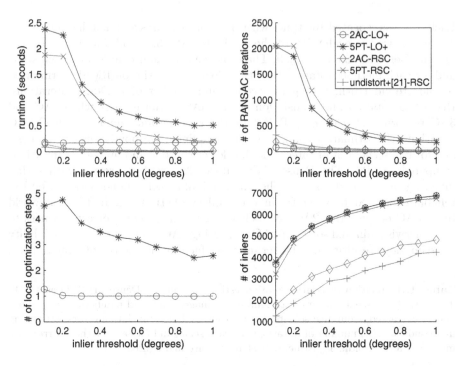

Fig. 6. Real-world ("Sarok" dataset) evaluation of RANSAC "RSC" and LO-RANSAC "LO$^+$" robust estimation using the proposed two-point "2AC" and the five-point "5PT" solvers. "undistort+[21]" denotes [21] using RANSAC applied to undistorted ACs (see d^{-1} in supplementary material). Diagrams compare (*top*) runtime and number of iterations; and (*bottom*) number of LO-steps and number of inliers.

Feature extraction was performed on the raw images, *without un-distortion*. No photometric refinement was performed on ACs, they were directly fed to the robust methods with the solvers "2AC" and "5PT". "undistort+[21]" denotes [21], applied to undistorted ACs (see Eq. (13) in supp. material).

Figure 6 shows the evaluation results on the first two images of Fig. 7. It is clear that 2AC-LO$^+$ outperforms all other variants in terms of speed (3 to 8 times better runtime), number of iterations (orders of magnitude fewer) and local optimization steps. The inlier sets returned by 2AC and 5PT using LO$^+$ are nigh-identical, but larger than the RANSAC-only variants. The overall performance of [21] is the worst. The supplementary contains further comparative evaluation using several real-world cases and feature extractors.

Fig. 7. Image of a scene "Sarok" used for real-world evaluation taken by a Point Gray Blackfly camera with YV2.8x2.8SA-2 wide-FoV lens attached.

7 Conclusion

In the paper a new method (2AC) was presented for relative pose estimation based on novel epipolar constraints using Affine Correspondences. The minimum number of correspondences needed for pose estimation is reduced to two. The method is applicable to arbitrary central–projection models including cameras [23] with wide fields of view (e.g. over 180° or omnidirectional). The pinhole–camera based approach [21] was shown to be a specialization of the proposed one. Stability tests showed that if the "affinity" is noisy, the pinhole based method [21] is outperformed. Additionally, 2AC needs no prior image un-distortion. Tests indicate that the five–point algorithm [17] is inferior in runtime and in the number of iterations when using MSAC [25] and LO$^+$ [10]. The quality of estimated pose is also worse after bundle adjustment. The proposed LO-RANSAC approach uses raw ACs to provide state-of-the-art quality in less time.

Based on the new epipolar constraints, other AC-based solvers can be constructed, e.g. to estimate additional camera parameters. With more constraints given per correspondence, fewer samples are needed for model estimation, thus robust estimation combined with such a solver will terminate earlier. The supplementary material contains additional evaluation and other material, e.g. Jacobians of projection functions.

References

1. Barath, D., Toth, T., Hajder, L.: A minimal solution for two-view focal-length estimation using two affine correspondences. In: Conference on Computer Vision and Pattern Recognition, July 2017
2. Bentolila, J., Francos, J.M.: Conic epipolar constraints from affine correspondences. Comput. Vis. Image Underst. **122**, 105–114 (2014)
3. Bentolila, J., Francos, J.M.: Homography and fundamental matrix estimation from region matches using an affine error metric. J. Math. Imaging Vis. **49**, 481–491 (2014)
4. Chum, O., Matas, J., Kittler, J.: Locally optimized RANSAC. In: Michaelis, B., Krell, G. (eds.) Pattern Recognition. LNCS, pp. 236–243. Springer, Heidelberg (2003). https://doi.org/10.1007/978-3-540-45243-0_31

5. Eichhardt, I., Hajder, L.: Computer vision meets geometric modeling: multi-view reconstruction of surface points and normals using affine correspondences. In: International Conference on Computer Vision Workshops, pp. 2427–2435, October 2017

6. Faugeras, O.: Three-Dimensional Computer Vision: A Geometric Viewpoint. M. I. T. Press, Cambridge (1993)

7. Fischler, M.A., Bolles, R.C.: Random sample consensus: a paradigm for model fitting with applications to image analysis and automated cartography. Commun. ACM **24**(6), 381–395 (1981)

8. Hartley, R.I.: In defense of the eight-point algorithm. IEEE Trans. Pattern Anal. Mach. Intell. **19**(6), 580–593 (1997)

9. Köser, K., Koch, R.: Differential spatial resection - pose estimation using a single local image feature. In: Forsyth, D., Torr, P., Zisserman, A. (eds.) ECCV 2008 Part IV. LNCS, vol. 5305, pp. 312–325. Springer, Heidelberg (2008). https://doi.org/10.1007/978-3-540-88693-8_23

10. Lebeda, K., Matas, J., Chum, O.: Fixing the locally optimized RANSAC-full experimental evaluation. In: Proceedings of British Machine Vision Conference, pp. 1–11. Citeseer (2012)

11. Li, H., Hartley, R.: Five-point motion estimation made easy. In: Proceedings of International Conference on Pattern Recognition, vol. 1, pp. 630–633. IEEE (2006)

12. Lindeberg, T., Gårding, J.: Shape-adapted smoothing in estimation of 3-D shape cues from affine deformations of local 2-D brightness structure. Image Vis. Comput. **15**(6), 415–434 (1997)

13. Matas, J., Chum, O., Urban, M., Pajdla, T.: Robust wide-baseline stereo from maximally stable extremal regions. Image Vis. Comput. **22**(10), 761–767 (2004)

14. Mikolajczyk, K., Schmid, C.: An affine invariant interest point detector. In: Heyden, A., Sparr, G., Nielsen, M., Johansen, P. (eds.) ECCV 2002 Part I. LNCS, vol. 2350, pp. 128–142. Springer, Heidelberg (2002). https://doi.org/10.1007/3-540-47969-4_9

15. Molnár, J., Eichhardt, I.: A differential geometry approach to camera-independent image correspondence. Comput. Vis. Image Underst. **169**, 90–107 (2018)

16. Morel, J.M., Yu, G.: ASIFT: a new framework for fully affine invariant image comparison. SIAM J. Imaging Sci. **2**(2), 438–469 (2009)

17. Nistér, D.: An efficient solution to the five-point relative pose problem. IEEE Trans. Pattern Anal. Mach. Intell. **26**(6), 756–770 (2004)

18. Perdoch, M., Matas, J., Chum, O.: Epipolar geometry from two correspondences. In: Proceedings of International Conference on Pattern Recognition, vol. 4, pp. 215–219. IEEE (2006)

19. Pritts, J., Kukelova, Z., Larsson, V., Chum, O.: Radially-distorted conjugate translations. In: Conference on Computer Vision and Pattern Recognition, June 2018

20. Raposo, C., Barreto, J.P.: πMatch: monocular vSLAM and piecewise planar reconstruction using fast plane correspondences. In: Leibe, B., Matas, J., Sebe, N., Welling, M. (eds.) ECCV 2016 Part VIII. LNCS, vol. 9912, pp. 380–395. Springer, Cham (2016). https://doi.org/10.1007/978-3-319-46484-8_23

21. Raposo, C., Barreto, J.P.: Theory and practice of structure-from-motion using affine correspondences. In: Conference on Computer Vision and Pattern Recognition, pp. 5470–5478 (2016)

22. Riggi, F., Toews, M., Arbel, T.: Fundamental matrix estimation via TIP-transfer of invariant parameters. In: Proceedings of International Conference on Pattern Recognition, vol. 2, pp. 21–24. IEEE (2006)

23. Scaramuzza, D., Martinelli, A., Siegwart, R.: A flexible technique for accurate omnidirectional camera calibration and structure from motion. In: Proceedings of IEEE Conference on Computer Vision Systems, pp. 45–45. IEEE (2006)
24. Strecha, C., Von Hansen, W., Van Gool, L., Fua, P., Thoennessen, U.: On benchmarking camera calibration and multi-view stereo for high resolution imagery. In: Conference on Computer Vision and Pattern Recognition, pp. 1–8. IEEE (2008)
25. Torr, P., Zisserman, A.: Robust computation and parametrization of multiple view relations. In: Conference on Computer Vision and Pattern Recognition, pp. 727–732. IEEE (1998)
26. Tuytelaars, T., Mikolajczyk, K.: Local invariant feature detectors: a survey. Found. Trends® Comput. Graph. Vis. 3(3), 177–280 (2008)
27. Vedaldi, A., Fulkerson, B.: VLFeat - an open and portable library of computer vision algorithms. In: Proceedings of ACM Conference on Multimedia (2010)
28. Xu, Y., Monasse, P., Géraud, T., Najman, L.: Tree-based morse regions: a topological approach to local feature detection. IEEE Trans. Image Process. 23(12), 5612–5625 (2014)
29. Zhang, Z., Rebecq, H., Forster, C., Scaramuzza, D.: Benefit of large field-of-view cameras for visual odometry. In: Proceedings of IEEE Conference on Robotics and Automation, pp. 801–808. IEEE (2016)

Convnets and Imagenet Beyond Accuracy: Understanding Mistakes and Uncovering Biases

Pierre Stock[(✉)] and Moustapha Cisse

Facebook AI Research, Paris, France
pstock@fb.com, moustaphacisse@google.com

Abstract. Convnets and Imagenet have driven the recent success of deep learning for image classification. However, the marked slowdown in performance improvement combined with the lack of robustness of neural networks to adversarial examples and their tendency to exhibit undesirable biases question the reliability of these methods. This work investigates these questions from the perspective of the end-user by using human subject studies and explanations. The contribution of this study is threefold. We first experimentally demonstrate that the accuracy and robustness of Convnets measured on Imagenet are vastly underestimated. Next, we show that explanations can mitigate the impact of misclassified adversarial examples from the perspective of the end-user. We finally introduce a novel tool for uncovering the undesirable biases learned by a model. These contributions also show that explanations are a valuable tool both for improving our understanding of Convnets' predictions and for designing more reliable models.

Keywords: Bias detection · Interpretability · Adversarial examples

1 Introduction

Convolutional neural networks [1,2] and Imagenet [3] (the dataset and the challenge) have been instrumental to the recent breakthroughs in computer vision. Imagenet has provided Convnets with the data they needed to demonstrate their superiority compared to the previously used handcrafted features such as Fisher Vectors [4]. In turn, this success has triggered a renewed interest in convolutional approaches. Consequently, novel architectures such as ResNets [5] and DenseNets [6] have been introduced to improve the state of the art performance on Imagenet. The impact of this virtuous circle has permeated all aspects of computer vision and deep learning at large. Indeed, the use of feature extractors pre-trained on Imagenet is now ubiquitous. For example, the state of the art image segmentation [7,8] or pose estimation models [9,10] heavily rely on pre-trained Imagenet features. Besides, convolutional architectures initially

---

M. Cisse—Now Google AI Ghana Lead.

© Springer Nature Switzerland AG 2018
V. Ferrari et al. (Eds.): ECCV 2018, LNCS 11210, pp. 504–519, 2018.
https://doi.org/10.1007/978-3-030-01231-1_31

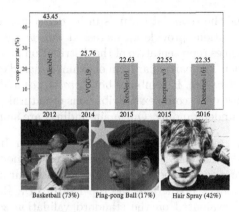

Fig. 1. Top: performance evolution of various CNN architectures on Imagenet. Bottom: some images sampled from the Internet and misclassified by a ResNet-101.

developed for image classification such as Residual Networks are now routinely used for machine translation [11] and speech recognition [12].

Since 2012, the top-1 error of state of the art (SOTA) models on Imagenet has been reduced from 43.45% to 22.35%. Recently, the evolution of the best performance seems to plateau (see Fig. 1) despite the efforts in designing novel architectures [5,6], introducing new data augmentation schemes [13] and optimization algorithms [14]. Concomitantly, several studies have demonstrated the lack of robustness of deep neural networks to adversarial examples [15–17] and raised questions about their tendency to exhibit (undesirable) biases [18]. Adversarial examples [15] are synthetic images designed to be indistinguishable from natural ones by a human, yet they are capable of fooling the best image classification systems. Undesirable biases are patterns or behaviors learned from the data, they are often highly influential in the decision of the model but are not aligned with the values of the society in which the model operates. Examples of such biases include *racial* and *gender biases* [19]. While accuracy has been the leading factor in the broad adoption of deep learning across the industries, its *sustained improvement* together with other desirable properties such as *robustness to adversarial examples* and *immunity to biases* will be critical in maintaining the trust in the technology. It is therefore essential to improve our understanding of these questions from the perspective of the end-user in the context of Imagenet classification.

In this work, we take a step in this direction by assessing the predictions of SOTA models on the validation set of Imagenet. We show that *human studies* and *explanations* can be valuable tools to perform this task. Human studies yield a new judgment of the quality of the model's predictions from the perspective of the end-user, in addition to the traditional ground truth used to evaluate the model. We also use both *feature-based* and *example-based* explanations. On the one hand, explaining the prediction of a black box classifier by a subset of the features of its input can yield valuable insights into the workings of the models and underline the essential features in its decision. On the other hand, example-based explanations provide an increased *interpretability* of the model by highlighting instances representative of the distribution of a given category as captured by the model. The particular form of example-based explanation we use is called *model criticism* [20]. It combines both *prototypes* and *criticisms* and is proven to better capture the complex distributions of natural images. Therefore, it facilitates human understanding. Our main findings are summarized below:

- The accuracy of convolutional networks evaluated on Imagenet is *vastly underestimated*. We find that when the mistakes of the model are assessed by human subjects and considered correct when at least four out of five humans agree with the model's prediction, the top-1 error of a ResNet-101 trained on Imagenet and evaluated on the standard validation set decreases from 22.69% to 9.47%. Similarly, the top-5 error decreases from 6.44% to 1.94%. This observation holds across models. It explains the marked slowndown in accuracy improvement and suggests that Imagenet is almost solved.
- The robustness of ConvNets to adversarial examples is also underestimated. In addition, we show that providing explanations helps to mitigate the mis-classification of adversarial examples from the perspective of the end-user.
- *Model Criticism* is a valuable tool for detecting the biases in the predictions of the models. Further, adversarial examples can be effectively used for model criticism.

Similar observations to our first point existed in prior work [21]. However, the scale, the conclusions and the implications of our study are different. Indeed we consider that if top-5 error is the measure of interest, Imagenet is (almost) solved. In the next section, we summarize the related work before presenting our experiments and results in details.

2   Related Work

Adversarial Examples. Deep neural networks can achieve high accuracy on previously unseen examples while being vulnerable to small adversarial perturbations of their inputs [15]. Such perturbed inputs, called adversarial examples, have recently aroused keen interest in the community [15,17,22,23]. Several studies have subsequently analyzed the phenomenon [24–26] and various approaches have been proposed to improve the robustness of neural networks [13,27–30]. More closely related to our work are the different proposals aiming at generating better adversarial examples [22,31]. Given an input (train or test) example (x, y), an adversarial example is a perturbed version of the original pattern $\tilde{x} = x + \delta_x$ where δ_x is small enough for $\tilde{x}$ to be undistinguishable from x by a human, but causes the network to predict an incorrect target. Given the network g_θ (where θ is the set of parameters) and a p-norm, the adversarial example is formally defined as:

$$\tilde{x} = \operatorname*{argmax}_{\tilde{x}:\|\tilde{x}-x\|_p \leq \epsilon} \ell\big(g_\theta(\tilde{x}), y\big) \tag{1}$$

where ϵ represents the strength of the adversary. Assuming the loss function $\ell(\cdot)$ is differentiable, [25] propose to take the first order taylor expansion of $x \mapsto \ell(g_\theta(x), y)$ to compute δ_x by solving the following simpler problem:

$$\tilde{x} = \underset{\tilde{x}: \|\tilde{x}-x\|_p \le \epsilon}{\operatorname{argmax}} \left(\nabla_x \ell(g_\theta(x), y)\right)^T (\tilde{x} - x). \qquad (2)$$

When $p = \infty$, then $\tilde{x} = x + \epsilon \cdot \operatorname{sign}(\nabla_x \ell(g_\theta(x), y))$ which corresponds to the *fast gradient sign method* [22]. If instead $p = 2$, we obtain $\tilde{x} = x + \epsilon \cdot \nabla_x \ell(g_\theta(x), y)$ where $\nabla_x \ell(g_\theta(x), y)$ is often normalized. Optionally, one can perform more iterations of these steps using a smaller step-size. This strategy has several variants [31,32]. In the rest of the paper, we refer to this method by *iterative fast gradient method* (IFGM) and will use it both to measure the robustness of a given model and to perform model criticism.

Model Criticism. Example-based explanations are a well-known tool in the realm of cognitive science for facilitating human understanding [33]. They have extensively been used in case-based reasoning (CBR) to improve the interpretability of the models [34–36]. In most cases, it consists in helping a human to understand a complex distribution (or the statistics captured by a model) by presenting her with a set of prototypical examples. However, when the distribution or the model for which one is seeking explanation is complex (as is often the case with real-world data), prototypes may not be enough. Recently, Kim et al. [20] have proposed to use, in addition to the prototypes, data points sampled from regions of the input space not well captured by the model or the prototypes. Such examples, called *criticism*, are known to improve the human's mental model of the distribution.

Kim et al. [20] introduced MMD-critic, an approach inspired by bayesian model criticism [37] to select the *prototypes* and the *critics* among a given set of examples. MMD-critic uses the maximum mean discrepancy [38] and large-scale submodular optimization [39]. Given a set of examples $\mathcal{D} = \{(x, y)\}_{i=1}^n$, let $S \subset \{1, \ldots, n\}$ such that $\mathcal{D}_S = \{x_i, i \in S\}$. Given a RKHS with kernel function $k(\cdot, \cdot)$, the prototypes of MMD-critic are selected by minimizing the maximum mean discrepancy between $\mathcal{D}$ and $\mathcal{D}_S$. This is formally written as:

$$\max_{S \in 2^{[n]}, |S| \le m} J_b(S) = \frac{2}{n|S|} \sum_{i \in [n], j \in S} k(x_i, x_j) - \frac{1}{|S|^2} \sum_{i,j \in S} k(x_i, x_j) \qquad (3)$$

Given a set of prototypes, the criticisms are similarly selected using MMD to maximize the deviation from the prototypes. The objective function in this case is regularized to promote diversity among the criticisms. A greedy algorithm can be used to select both prototypes and criticisms since the corresponding optimization problems are provably submodular and monotone under certain conditions [39]. In our experimental study, we will use MMD-critic as a baseline for example-based explanations.

Feature-Based Explanation. Machine learning and especially Deep Neural Networks (DNNs) lie at the core of more and more technological advances across various fields. However, those models are still widely considered as *black boxes*, leading end users to mistrust the predictions or even the underlying models. In order to promote the adoption of such algorithms and to foster their positive technological impact, recent studies have been focusing on understanding a model from the human perspective [40–43].

In particular, [44] propose to explain the predictions of any classifier g_θ (denoted as g) by approximating it locally with an interpretable model h. The role of h is to provide qualitative understanding between the input x and the classifier's output $g(x)$ for a given class. In the case where the input x is an image, h will act on vector $x' \in \{0,1\}^d$ denoting the presence or absence of the d super-pixels that partition the image x to *explain* the classifier's decision.

Finding the best explanation $\xi(x)$ among the candidates h can be formulated as:

$$\xi(x) = \operatorname*{argmin}_{h \in H} \mathcal{L}(g, h, \pi_x) + \Omega(h) \tag{4}$$

where the best explanation minimizes a local weighted loss $\mathcal{L}$ between g and h in the vicinity π_x of x, regularized by the complexity $\Omega(h)$ of such an explanation. The authors restrict $h \in H$ to be a linear model such that $h(z') = w_h z'$. They further define the vicinity of two samples using the exponential kernel

$$\pi_x(z) = e^{\frac{\|x-z\|^2}{\sigma^2}} \tag{5}$$

and define the local weighted loss $\mathcal{L}$ as:

$$\mathcal{L}(g, h, \pi_x) = \sum_{z,z' \in \mathcal{Z}} \pi_x(z) \left(g(z) - h(z')\right)^2 \tag{6}$$

where $\mathcal{Z}$ if the dataset of n perturbed samples obtained from x by randomly activating or deactivating some super-pixels in x. Note that z' denotes the one-hot encoding of the super-pixels whereas z is the actual image formed by those super-pixels. Finally, the interpretability of the representation is controlled by

$$\Omega(h) = \begin{cases} 0 & \text{if } \|w_h\|_0 < K \\ +\infty & \text{otherwise} \end{cases} \tag{7}$$

The authors solve this optimization problem by first selecting K features with Lasso and then learning the weights w_g *via* least squares. In the case of DNNs, an explanation generated by this algorithm called LIME allows the user to just highlight the super-pixels with positive weights towards a specific class (see Fig. 5). In what follows we set $\sigma = 0.25$, $n = 1000$ and keep K constant. In the following we refer to an image prompted solely with its top super-pixels as an image *with attention*.

3   Experiments

3.1   Human Subject Study of Classification Errors

We conduct a study of the misclassifications of various pre-trained architectures (*e.g.* ResNet-18, ResNet-101, DenseNet-121, DenseNet-161) with human subjects on Amazon Mechanical Turk (AMT). To this end, we use the center-cropped images of size 224×224 from the standard validation set of Imagenet. The same setting holds in all our experiments. For every architecture, we consider all the examples misclassified by the model. Each of these examples is presented to five (5) different turkers together with the class (C) predicted by the model. Each turker is then asked the following question *"Is class C relevant for this image."* The possible answers are *yes* and *no*. The former means that the turker agrees with the prediction of the network, while the latter means that the example is misclassified. We take the following measures to ensured high quality answers: (1) we only recruit *master turkers*, *i.e.* turkers who have demonstrated excellence across a wide range of tasks and are awarded the masters qualification by Amazon (2) we mitigate the effect of bad turkers by aggregating 5 independent answers for every question (3) we manually sample more than 500 questions and successfully cross-validated our own guesses with the answers from the turkers, finding that 4 or more positive answers over 5 leads to almost no false positives.

Figure 2 shows a breakdown of the misclassified images by a ResNet-101 (resp. a ResNet-18) according to the number of positive answers they receive from the turkers. Our first results show that for a ResNet-101 (resp. a ResNet-18), for 39.76% (resp. 27.14%) of the misclassified examples, all the turkers (5/5) agree with the prediction of the model. If we further consider the prediction of the model for a given image to be correct if at least four turkers out of five (4/5) agree with it, the rectified Top-1 error of the models are drastically reduced.

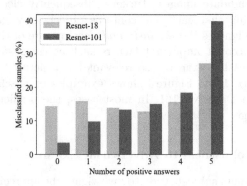

Fig. 2. Positive answers for misclassified samples. An image is prompted to 5 different subjects and a **positive** answer means the subject **agrees with the predicted class**

Table 1 shows the original Top-1 errors together with the rectified versions. For the ResNet-101 and the DenseNet-161, the rectified Top-1 error is respec-

Table 1. Standard and rectified Top-1 errors for various models. Rectified Top-1 errors are significantly lower.

Model	Top-1 error	Rectified Top-1 error
Resnet-18	31.39	17.93
Resnet-101	22.69	9.47
Densenet-121	25.53	14.37
Densenet-161	22.85	10.87

tively 9.47% and 10.87%. Similarly, the top-5 error of the ResNet-101 on a single crop is 6.44%. When we present the misclassified images to the turkers together with the top 5 predictions of the model, the rectified top-5 error drops to 1.94%. When instead of submitting to the turker the misclassified images (*i.e* top-1-misclassified images), we present them the pictures for which the ground truth is not in the top-5 predictions (*i.e.* top-5-misclassified images), the rectified top-5 error drops further to 1.37%. This shows that while the top-5 score is often used to mitigate the fact that many classes are present in the same image, it does not reflect the whole multi-label nature of those images. Moreover, the observation on top-5 is in line with the conclusions regarding top-1. If top-5 is the important measure, this experiment suggests that Imagenet is (almost) solved as far as accuracy is concerned, therefore explaining the marked slowdown in performance improvement observed recently on Imagenet.

The difference between the ground truth labeling of the images and the predictions of the models validated by the turkers can be traced back to the collection protocol of Imagenet. Indeed to create the dataset, Deng et al. [3] first queried several image search engines (using the synsets extracted from WordNet) to obtain good candidate images. Turkers subsequently cleaned the collected images by validating that each one contains objects of a given synset. This labeling procedure ignores the *intrinsic multilabel* nature of the images, neither does it take into account important factors such as *compositionality*. Indeed, it is natural that the label `wing` is also relevant for a picture displaying a plane and labelled as `airliner`. Figure 3 shows examples of misclassifications by a RestNet-101 and a DenseNet-161. In most cases, the predicted class is (also) present in the image.

3.2 Study of Robustness to Adversarial Examples

We conducted a human subject study to investigate the appreciation of adversarial perturbation by end-users. Similarly to the human subject study of misclassifications, we used the center-cropped images of the Imagenet validation set. Next, we consider a subset of 20 classes and generate an adversarial example from each legitimate image using the IFGSM attack on a pre-trained ResNet-101. We used a step size of $\epsilon = 0.001$ and a maximum number of iterations of $M = 10$. This attack deteriorated the accuracy of the network on the vali-

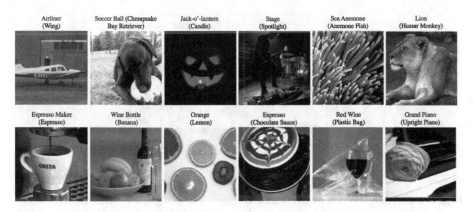

Fig. 3. Some test samples misclassified by a ResNet-101 (first row) and a Densenet-161 (second row). The predicted class is indicated in red, the ground truth in black and in parenthesis. All those examples gathered more than four (4 or 5) positive answers over 5 on AMT. Note that no adversarial noise has been added to the images. (Color figure online)

dation set from 77.31% down to 7.96%. Note that by definition, we only need to generate adversarial samples for the correctly predicted test images. We also only consider non-targeted attacks since targetted attacks often require larger distorsion from the adversary and are more challenging if the target categories are far from the ones predicted in case of non-targetted attacks.

We consider two settings in this experiment. In the first configuration, we present the turkers with the whole adversarial image together with the prediction of the network. We then ask each turker if the predicted label is relevant to the given picture. Again, the possible answers are *yes* and *no*. Each image is shown to five (5) different turkers. In the second configuration, we show each turker the interpretation image generated by LIME instead of the whole adversarial image using the top 8 most important features. The rest of the experimental setup is identical to the previous configuration where we showed the whole images to the turkers. If a turker participated in the second experiment with the interpretation images after participating in the first experiment where the whole images are displayed, his answers could be biased. To avoid this issue, we perform the two studies with three days intervals. Similarly to our previous experiments, we report the rectified Top-1 error on adversarial examples by considering the prediction of the model as correct if at least 4/5 turkers agree with it.

Table 2 shows the standard and the rectified Top-1 errors for the adversarial examples. Two observations can be made. First, the robustness of the models as measured by the Top-1 error on adversarial samples generated from the validation set of Imagenet is also underestimated. Indeed, when the whole images are displayed to them, the turkers agree with 22.01% of the predictions of the networks on adversarial examples. This suggests that often, the predicted label is easily identifiable in the picture by a human. Figure 5 shows an example (labeled

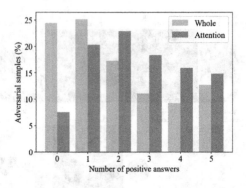

Fig. 4. Positive answers for adversarial samples. The images are either displayed as a whole (entire image) or with attention (explanation). Every image is prompted to 5 different subjects. A **positive** answer means the subject **agrees with the predicted adversarial class**.

Table 2. Standard and rectified Top-1 errors on adversarial examples for the whole images and the explanations.

Setting	Top-1 error	Rectified Top-1 error
Whole image	92.04	76.78
Explanation	92.04	70.68

jeep) with the explanations of the predictions for the legitimate and adversarial versions respectively. One can see that the adversarial perturbation exploits the ambiguity of the image by shifting the attention of the model towards regions supporting the adversarial prediction (*e.g.* the red cross).

The second substantial observation is that the percentage of agreement between the predictions of the model and the turkers increases from 22.01% to 30.80% when the explanation is shown instead of the whole image (see also Fig. 4). We further inspected the adversarial images on which the turkers agree with the model's prediction when the explanation is shown but mostly disagree when the whole image is shown. Figure 6 displays examples of such images. In most cases, even though the predicted label does not seem correct when looking at the whole image, the explanation has one of the two following effects. It either reveals the relevant object supporting the prediction (e.g., Tripod image) or creates an ambiguous context that renders the predicted label plausible (e.g., Torch or Honeycomb images). In all cases, providing explanations to the user mitigates the impact of misclassifications due to adversarial perturbations.

3.3   Adversarial Examples for Model Criticism

Example-based explanation methods such as model criticism aim at summarizing the statistics learned by a model by using a carefully selected subset of

Fig. 5. Left: an adversarial image of the true class `Jeep` predicted as `Ambulance` by the network. Center: the explanation of the clean image for its prediction (`Jeep`). Right: the explanation of the adversarial image for its prediction (`Ambulance`). (Color figure online)

Fig. 6. Adversarial samples, displayed as a whole (entire image, first row) or with explanation (only *k* top super-pixels, second row). The adversarial class is indicated in red, the true class in black and between parenthesis. In red is also displayed the percentage of positive answers for the displayed image (over 5 answers). In both cases, a **positive** answer means the subject **agrees with the predicted adversarial class**. (Color figure online)

examples. MMD-critic proposes an effective selection procedure combining prototypes and criticisms for improving interpretability. Though applicable to a pre-trained neural network by using the hidden representation of the examples, it only indirectly exploits the discriminative nature of the classifier. In this work, we argue that adversarial examples can be an accurate alternative to MMD-critic for model criticism. In particular, they offer a natural way of selecting prototypes and criticism based on the number of steps of FGSM necessary to change the decision of a classifier for a given example. Indeed, for a given class and a fixed number of maximum steps M of IFGSM, the examples that are still correctly classified after M steps can be considered as useful prototypes since they are very representative of what the classifier has learned from the data for this class. In contrast, the examples whose decision change after 1 or few steps of FGSM are more likely to be valid criticisms because they do not quite fit the model.

We conducted a human study to evaluate our hypothesis. At each round, we present a turker with six classes represented by six images each, as well a target

Table 3. Results of the Prototype and Criticism study. We report the average success rate of the task (assign a target image to one of the six groups) for the seven conditions. The adversarial selection procedures outperforms MMD-critic as well as the other baselines used in the study.

Condition	Mean (%)	Std (%)
Adv - Prototypes and Criticisms	**57.06**	3.22
MMD - Prototypes and Criticisms	50.64	3.25
Probs - Prototypes and Criticisms	49.36	3.26
Adv - Prototypes only	55.02	3.23
MMD - Prototypes only	53.18	3.24
Probs - Prototypes only	52.44	3.25
Random	49.80	3.25

sample randomly drawn from one of those six classes. We measure how well the subject can assign the target sample to the class it belongs. The assignment task requires a class to be well-explained by its six images. The challenge is, therefore, to select well those candidate images. The adversarial method selects as prototypes the examples not misclassified IFGSM after $M = 10$ steps, and as criticism the examples misclassified after one step. In addition to MMD-critic (using $\lambda = 10^{-5}$), we compare the adversarial approach to a simple baseline using the probabilities for selecting the prototypes (considerable confidence, e.g., >0.9) and the criticisms (little confidence, e.g., <0.1). We also compare with the baseline randomly sampling examples from a given class. For each method (except the random baseline), we experiment with showing six prototypes only vs. showing three prototypes and three criticisms instead.

To properly exploit the results, we discarded answers based on the time spent by the turkers on the question to only consider answers given in the range from 20 s to 3 min. This resulted in 1, 600 valid answers for which we report the results in Table 3. Two observations arise from those results. First, the prototypes and criticisms sampled using the adversarial method represent better the class distribution and achieve higher scores for the assignment task both when only prototypes are used (55.02%) and when prototypes are combined with criticisms (57.06%). Second, the use of criticisms additionally to the prototypes always helps to better grasp the class distribution.

More qualitatively, we display in Figs. 7a and b some prototypes and criticisms for the class **Banana** generated using respectively the MMD and the adversarial method for the test samples, that demonstrate the superiority of the adversarial method.

3.4   Uncovering Biases with Model Criticism

To uncover the undesirable biases learned by the model, we use our adversarial example approach to model criticism since it worked better than MMD-critic in

Fig. 7. (a) Prototypes (first row) and Criticisms (second row) for the Banana class when using the MMD-critic method. (b) Prototypes (first row) and Criticisms (second row), for the Banana class when using the adversarial selection.

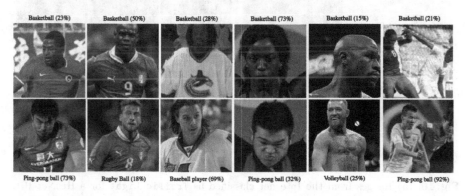

Fig. 8. Pairs of pictures (columns) sampled over the Internet along with their prediction by a ResNet-101. (Color figure online)

our previous experiments. We consider the class basketball (for which humans often appear in the images). We select and inspect a reduced subset of prototypes and criticisms from the category basketball. The percentage of basketball training images on which at least one white person appears is about 55%. Similarly, the percentage of images on which at least one black person appears is 53%. This relative balance contrasts with the statistics captured by the model. Indeed, on the one hand, we found that about 78% of the prototypes contain at least one black person and only 44% for prototypes contain one white person or more. On the other hand, for criticisms, 90% of the images contain at least one white person and only about 20% include one black person or more. This suggests that the model has learned a biased representation of the class basketball where images containing black persons are prototypical. To further validate this hypothesis, we sample pairs of similar pictures from the Internet.

Fig. 9. Prototypes (first row) and Criticisms (second row) for the test images of the `Basketball` class, adv method.

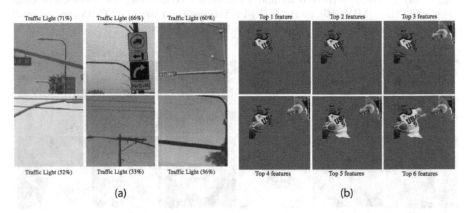

(a)   (b)

Fig. 10. (a) Images from the Internet classified as `Traffic Light` for a ResNet-101. (b) Explanation path of a ResNet-101 for a test sample of the `Basketball` class. Note that the first feature to appear includes the writing on the jersey and then the basket ball. (Color figure online)

The pairs are sampled such that the primary apparent difference between the two images is the skin color of the persons. We then fed images to the model and gathered the predictions. Figure 8 shows the results of the experiments. All images containing a black person are classified as basketball while similar photos with persons of different skin color are labeled differently. Figure 10b provides additional supporting evidence for this hypothesis. It shows the progressive feature based explanation path uncovering the super-pixels of an example (correctly classified as `basketball`) by their order of importance. The most importance super-pixels depict the jersey and the skin color of the player. The reasons why the model learns these biases are unclear. One hypothesis is that despite the balanced distribution of races in pictures labeled basketball, black persons are more represented in this class in comparison to the other classes. A similar phenomenon has also been noted in the context of textual data. [19,45]. We defer further investigations on this to future studies (Fig. 9).

Remark. We have focused on racial biases because a human can easily spot them. In fact, we have found similar biases where pictures displaying Asians dressed in red are very often classified as `ping-pong ball`. However, we hypothesize the biases of the model are numerous and diverse. For example, we also have found that the model often predicts the class `traffic light` for images of a blue sky with street lamps as depicted in Fig. 10a. In any case, model criticism has proven effective in uncovering the undesirable hidden biases learned by the model.

4   Conclusion

Through human studies and explanations, we have proven that the performance of SOTA models on Imagenet is underestimated. This leaves little room for improvement and calls for new large-scale benchmarks involving for example multi-label annotations. We have also improved our understanding of adversarial examples from the perspective of the end-user and positioned model criticism as a valuable tool for uncovering undesirable biases. These results open an exciting perspective on designing explanations and automating bias detection in vision models. Our study suggests that more research in these topics will be necessary to sustain the use of machine learning as a general purpose technology and to achieve new breakthroughs in image classification.

References

1. Lecun, Y., Bottou, L., Bengio, Y., Haffner, P.: Gradient-based learning applied to document recognition. In: Proceedings of the IEEE (1998)
2. Krizhevsky, A., Sutskever, I., Hinton, G.E.: Imagenet classification with deep convolutional neural networks. In: Proceedings of the 25th International Conference on Neural Information Processing Systems, vol. 1 (2012)
3. Deng, J., Dong, W., Socher, R., Li, L.J., Li, K., Fei-Fei, L.: ImageNet: a large-scale hierarchical image database. In: CVPR09 (2009)
4. Perronnin, F., Sánchez, J., Mensink, T.: Improving the fisher Kernel for large-scale image classification. In: Daniilidis, K., Maragos, P., Paragios, N. (eds.) ECCV 2010 Part IV. LNCS, vol. 6314, pp. 143–156. Springer, Heidelberg (2010). https://doi.org/10.1007/978-3-642-15561-1_11
5. He, K., Zhang, X., Ren, S., Sun, J.: Deep residual learning for image recognition. In: 2016 IEEE Conference on Computer Vision and Pattern Recognition (CVPR) (2016)
6. Huang, G., Liu, Z., Weinberger, K.Q.: Densely connected convolutional networks. CoRR (2016)
7. Girshick, R.: Fast R-CNN. In: Proceedings of the 2015 IEEE International Conference on Computer Vision (ICCV). ICCV 2015 (2015)
8. He, K., Gkioxari, G., Dollár, P., Girshick, R.B.: Mask R-CNN. CoRR abs/1703.06870 (2017)
9. Insafutdinov, E., Pishchulin, L., Andres, B., Andriluka, M., Schiele, B.: DeeperCut: a deeper, stronger, and faster multi-person pose estimation model. CoRR abs/1605.03170 (2016)

10. Bulat, A., Tzimiropoulos, G.: Human pose estimation via convolutional part heatmap regression. In: Leibe, B., Matas, J., Sebe, N., Welling, M. (eds.) ECCV 2016 Part VII. LNCS, vol. 9911, pp. 717–732. Springer, Cham (2016). https://doi.org/10.1007/978-3-319-46478-7_44

11. Gehring, J., Auli, M., Grangier, D., Yarats, D., Dauphin, Y.N.: Convolutional sequence to sequence learning. CoRR (2017)

12. Wang, Y., Deng, X., Pu, S., Huang, Z.: Residual convolutional CTC networks for automatic speech recognition. CoRR (2017)

13. Zhang, H., Cissé, M., Dauphin, Y.N., Lopez-Paz, D.: mixup: beyond empirical risk minimization. CoRR (2017)

14. Kingma, D.P., Ba, J.: Adam: a method for stochastic optimization. CoRR (2014)

15. Szegedy, C., et al.: Intriguing properties of neural networks. CoRR (2013)

16. Goodfellow, I.J., Shlens, J., Szegedy, C.: Explaining and harnessing adversarial examples (2014)

17. Cissé, M., Adi, Y., Neverova, N., Keshet, J.: Houdini: fooling deep structured visual and speech recognition models with adversarial examples. In: Advances in Neural Information Processing Systems 30: Annual Conference on Neural Information Processing Systems 2017, 4–9 December 2017, Long Beach, CA, USA (2017)

18. Ritter, S., Barrett, D.G.T., Santoro, A., Botvinick, M.M.: Cognitive psychology for deep neural networks: a shape bias case study. In: Proceedings of the 34th International Conference on Machine Learning. Proceedings of Machine Learning Research (2017)

19. Bolukbasi, T., Chang, K., Zou, J.Y., Saligrama, V., Kalai, A.: Man is to computer programmer as woman is to homemaker? Debiasing word embeddings. CoRR (2016)

20. Kim, B., Khanna, R., Koyejo, O.O.: Examples are not enough, learn to criticize! Criticism for interpretability. In: Advances in Neural Information Processing Systems 29 (2016)

21. Karpathy, A.: What i learned from competing against a convnet on imagenet. http://karpathy.github.io/2014/09/02/what-i-learned-from-competing-against-a-convnet-on-imagenet/

22. Goodfellow, I., Shlens, J., Szegedy, C.: Explaining and harnessing adversarial examples. In: International Conference on Learning Representations (2015)

23. Tabacof, P., Valle, E.: Exploring the space of adversarial images. CoRR (2015)

24. Fawzi, A., Fawzi, O., Frossard, P.: Analysis of classifiers' robustness to adversarial perturbations. CoRR (2015)

25. Shaham, U., Yamada, Y., Negahban, S.: Understanding adversarial training: increasing local stability of neural nets through robust optimization. CoRR (2015)

26. Fawzi, A., Moosavi-Dezfooli, S., Frossard, P.: Robustness of classifiers: from adversarial to random noise. CoRR (2016)

27. Papernot, N., McDaniel, P.D., Wu, X., Jha, S., Swami, A.: Distillation as a defense to adversarial perturbations against deep neural networks. In: 2016 IEEE Symposium on Security and Privacy (SP) (2016)

28. Cisse, M., Bojanowski, P., Grave, E., Dauphin, Y., Usunier, N.: Parseval networks: improving robustness to adversarial examples. In: Proceedings of the 34th International Conference on Machine Learning (2017)

29. Kurakin, A., Boneh, D., Tramr, F., Goodfellow, I., Papernot, N., McDaniel, P.: Ensemble adversarial training: attacks and defenses (2018)

30. Guo, C., Rana, M., Cissé, M., van der Maaten, L.: Countering adversarial images using input transformations. CoRR (2017)

31. Moosavi-Dezfooli, S., Fawzi, A., Frossard, P.: DeepFool: a simple and accurate method to fool deep neural networks. CoRR (2015)
32. Kurakin, A., Goodfellow, I.J., Bengio, S.: Adversarial examples in the physical world. CoRR (2016)
33. Simon, H.A., Newell, A.: Human problem solving: the state of the theory in 1970. Am. Psychol. **26**, 145 (1972)
34. Aamodt, A., Plaza, E.: Case-based reasoning; foundational issues, methodological variations, and system approaches. AI Commun. **7**, 39–59 (1994)
35. Bichindaritz, I., Marling, C.: Case-based reasoning in the health sciences: what's next? Artif. Intell. Med. **36**, 127–135 (2006)
36. Kim, B., Rudin, C., Shah, J.A.: The Bayesian case model: a generative approach for case-based reasoning and prototype classification. In: Advances in Neural Information Processing Systems 27 (2014)
37. Gelman, A.: Bayesian data analysis using R (2006)
38. Gretton, A., Borgwardt, K.M., Rasch, M., Schölkopf, B., Smola, A.J.: A kernel method for the two-sample-problem. In: Proceedings of the 19th International Conference on Neural Information Processing Systems, NIPS 2006 (2006)
39. Badanidiyuru, A., Mirzasoleiman, B., Karbasi, A., Krause, A.: Streaming submodular maximization: massive data summarization on the fly. In: Proceedings of the 20th ACM SIGKDD International Conference on Knowledge Discovery and Data Mining (2014)
40. Lipton, Z.C.: The mythos of model interpretability. CoRR (2016)
41. Samek, W., Wiegand, T., Muller, K.: Explainable artificial intelligence: understanding, visualizing and interpreting deep learning models. CoRR (2017)
42. Montavon, G., Samek, W., Muller, K.: Methods for interpreting and understanding deep neural networks. CoRR (2017)
43. Dong, Y., Su, H., Zhu, J., Bao, F.: Towards interpretable deep neural networks by leveraging adversarial examples. CoRR (2017)
44. Ribeiro, M.T., Singh, S., Guestrin, C.: "why should i trust you?": Explaining the predictions of any classifier. In: Proceedings of the 22Nd ACM SIGKDD International Conference on Knowledge Discovery and Data Mining (2016)
45. Paperno, D., Marelli, M., Tentori, K., Baroni, M.: Corpus-based estimates of word association predict biases in judgment of word co-occurrence likelihood. Cogn. Psychol. **74**, 66–83 (2014)

RESOUND: Towards Action Recognition Without Representation Bias

Yingwei Li, Yi Li$^{(\boxtimes)}$, and Nuno Vasconcelos

UC San Diego, San Diego, USA
{yil325,yil898,nvasconcelos}@ucsd.edu

Abstract. While large datasets have proven to be a key enabler for progress in computer vision, they can have biases that lead to erroneous conclusions. The notion of the representation bias of a dataset is proposed to combat this problem. It captures the fact that representations other than the ground-truth representation can achieve good performance on any given dataset. When this is the case, the dataset is said not to be well calibrated. Dataset calibration is shown to be a necessary condition for the standard state-of-the-art evaluation practice to converge to the ground-truth representation. A procedure, RESOUND, is proposed to quantify and minimize representation bias. Its application to the problem of action recognition shows that current datasets are biased towards static representations (objects, scenes and people). Two versions of RESOUND are studied. An Explicit RESOUND procedure is proposed to assemble new datasets by sampling existing datasets. An implicit RESOUND procedure is used to guide the creation of a new dataset, Diving48, of over 18,000 video clips of competitive diving actions, spanning 48 fine-grained dive classes. Experimental evaluation confirms the effectiveness of RESOUND to reduce the static biases of current datasets.

1 Introduction

In recent years, convolutional neural networks (CNNs) have achieved great success in image understanding problems, such as object recognition or semantic segmentation. A key enabling factor was the introduction of large scale image datasets such as ImageNet, MS COCO, and others. These have two main properties. First, they contain enough samples to constrain the millions of parameters of modern CNNs. Second, they cover a large enough variety of visual concepts to enable the learning of visual representations that generalize across many tasks. While similar efforts have been pursued for video, progress has been slower. One difficulty is that video classes can be discriminated over different time spans. This results on a hierarchy of representations for temporal discrimination.

Static representations, which span single video frames, lie at the bottom of this hierarchy. They suffice for video classification when static cues, such as objects, are discriminant for different video classes. For example, the classes in the "playing musical instrument" branch of ActivityNet [3] differ in the instrument being played. The next hierarchy level is that of short-term motion representations, typically based on optical flow, spanning a pair of frames. They

© Springer Nature Switzerland AG 2018
V. Ferrari et al. (Eds.): ECCV 2018, LNCS 11210, pp. 520–535, 2018.
https://doi.org/10.1007/978-3-030-01231-1_32

suffice when classes have identical static cues, but different short-term motion patterns. Finally, the top level of the hierarchy includes representations of video dynamics. These address video classes with identical static elements and short-term motion, but different in the temporal arrangement of these elements. They are needed for discrimination between classes such as "triple jump" and "long jump," in an Olympic sportscast, with identical backgrounds and short-term motions (running and jumping), only differing in the composition of the latter.

Clearly, more sophisticated temporal reasoning requires representations at higher levels of the hierarchy. What is less clear is how to evaluate the relative importance of the different levels for action recognition. Current video CNNs tend to use very simple temporal representations. For example, the prevalent two-stream CNN model [17] augments a static CNN with a stream that processes optical flow. There have been attempts to deploy networks with more sophisticated temporal representations, e.g. RNN [5,24] and 3D CNN [7,20], yet existing benchmarks have not produced strong evidence in favor of these models. It is unclear, at this point, if this is a limitation of the models or of the benchmarks.

One suspicious observation is that, on many of the existing datasets, static representations achieve reasonably good performance. This is because the datasets exhibit at least three types of static biases. The first is object bias. For example, "playing piano" is the only class depicting pianos, in both ActivitNet and UCF101. A piano detector is enough to pick out this class. The second is scene bias. For example, while the "basketball dunk" and "soccer juggling" classes have distinct temporal patterns, they can be discriminated by classifying the background into basketball court or soccer field. Finally, there is frequently a person bias. While classes like "brushing hair" contain mostly face close-ups, "military marching" videos usually contain long shots of groups in military uniforms.

It should be noted that there is nothing intrinsically wrong about biases. If a person detector is useful to recognize certain actions, action recognition systems should use person detectors. The problem is that, if care is not exercised during dataset assembly, these biases could undermine the evaluation of action recognition systems. For example, an action recognition dataset could be solvable by cobbling together enough object detectors. This would elicit the inference that "action recognition is simply object recognition." Such an inference would likely be met with skepticism by most vision researchers. The problem is compounded by the fact that biases do not even need to be obvious, since modern deep networks can easily identify and "overfit to" any biases due to a skewed data collection. Finally, to make matters worse, biases are cumulative, i.e. static biases combine with motion biases and dynamics biases to enable artificial discrimination. Hence, investigating the importance of representations at a certain level of hierarchy requires eliminating the biases of all levels below it.

These problems are frequently faced by social scientists, who spend substantial time introducing "controls" in their data: A study of whether exercise prevents heart attacks has to "control" factors such as age, wealth, or family history, so that subjects are chosen to avoid biases towards any of these factors. Similarly, vision researchers can only draw conclusions from their datasets if they are not biased towards certain representations.

In this work, we investigate the question of assembling datasets without such biases. Despite extensive recent efforts in dataset collection, this question has received surprisingly little attention. One reason is that, until recently, vision researchers were concerned about more fundamental forms of bias, such as dataset bias [19], which captures how algorithms trained on one dataset generalize to other datasets of the same task. Dataset bias can be analyzed with the classical statistical tools of bias and variance. It occurs because (1) learning algorithms are statistical estimators, and (2) estimates from too little data have high variance and generalize poorly. With the introduction of large datasets, such as ImageNet [4], dataset bias has been drastically reduced in the past few years. However, simply collecting larger datasets will not eliminate representation bias.

While dataset bias is a property of the algorithm (ameliorated by large datasets), representation bias is a property of the dataset. As in social science research, it can only be avoided by controlling biases during dataset collection. We formalize this concept with the notion of a *well calibrated dataset*, which only favors the ground-truth representation for the vision task at hand, i.e. has no significant biases for other representations. We then show that the standard vision practice of identifying the "state of the art" representation only converges to the ground-truth representation if datasets are well calibrated. This motivates a new measure of the representation bias of a dataset, which guides a new *RepreSentatiOn UNbiased Dataset* (RESOUND) collection framework.

RESOUND is a generic procedure, applicable to the assembly of datasets for many tasks. Its distinguishing features are that it (1) explicitly defines a set of representation classes, (2) quantifies the biases of a dataset with respect to them, and (3) enables the formulation of explicit optimization methods for assembling unbiased datasets. In this work, this is in two ways. First, by using RESOUND to guide the assembly of a new video dataset, Diving48, aimed for studies on the importance of different levels of the representation hierarchy for action recognition. This is a dataset of competitive diving, with few noticeable biases for static representations. RESOUND is used to quantify these biases, showing that they are much smaller than in previous action recognition datasets. Second, by formulating an optimization problem to sample new datasets, with minimal representation bias, from the existing ones.

Overall, the paper makes four main contributions. First, it formalizes the notion of representation bias and provides some theoretical justification for how to measure it. Second, it introduces a new dataset collection procedure, RESOUND, that (1) forces vision researchers to establish controls for vision tasks (the representation families against which bias is computed), and (2) objectively quantifies representation biases. Third, it demonstrates the effectiveness of RESOUND, by introducing a new action recognition dataset, Diving48, that is shown to drastically reduce several biases of previous datasets. Fourth, the RESOUND procedure is also used to sample existing datasets to reduce bias.

2   Related Work

Action recognition has many possible sources of bias. Early datasets (Weizmann [2], KTH [14]) were collected in controlled environments, minimizing static biases. Nevertheless, most classes were distinguishable at the short-term motion level. These datasets were also too small for training deep CNNs. Modern datasets, such as UCF101 [18], HMDB51 [10], ActivityNet [3] and Kinetics [8] are much larger in size and numbers of classes. However, they have strong static biases that enable static representations to perform surprisingly well. For example, the RGB stream of Temporal Segment Network [22] with 3 frames of input achieves 85.1% accuracy on UCF101.

The idea that biases of datasets can lead to erroneous conclusions on the merit of different representations is not new. It has motivated efforts in fine grained classification, where classes are defined within a narrow domain, e.g. birds [21], dogs [9], or shoes [23]. This eliminates many of the biases present in more general problems. Large scale generic object recognition datasets, such as ImageNet, account for this through a mix of breadth and depth, i.e. by including large numbers of classes but making subsets of them fine-grained. For action recognition, the effect of biases on the evaluation of different representations is more subtle. A general rule is that representations in the higher levels of the temporal discrimination hierarchy are needed for finer grained video recognition. However, it does not suffice to consider fine grained recognition problems. As illustrated by Weizmann and KTH, short-term motion biases could suffice for class discrimination, even when static biases are eliminated.

A popular fine-grained action recognition dataset is the MPII-Cooking Activities Dataset [13]. It has some controls for static and motion bias, by capturing all videos in the same kitchen, using a static camera, and focusing on the hands of food preparers. However, because it focuses on short-term activities, such as "putting on" vs "removing" a lid, or various forms of cutting food, it has strong short-term motion biases. Hence, it cannot be used to investigate the importance of representations at higher levels of the temporal discrimination hierarchy. Furthermore, because different actions classes (e.g. "cutting" vs. "opening/closing") are by definition associated with different objects it has a non-trivial amount of object bias. This is unlike the now proposed Diving48 dataset, where all classes have identical objects (divers) and similar forms of short-term motion.

Recently, [15] analyzed action recognition by considering multiple datasets and algorithms and pointed out future directions for algorithm design. In this work, we are more focused on the process of dataset assembly. This is a new idea, we are not aware of any dataset with explicit controls for representation bias. While it is expected that dataset authors would consider the issue and try to control for some biases, it is not known what these are, and the biases have not been quantified. In fact, we are not aware of any previous attempt to develop an objective and replicable procedure to quantify and minimize dataset bias, such as RESOUND, or a dataset that with objectively quantified biases, such as Diving48.

3 Representation Bias

In this section, we introduce the notion of representation bias and discuss how it can be avoided.

3.1 Dataset Bias

While many datasets have been assembled for computer vision, there has been limited progress in establishing an objective and quantitative characterization of them. Over the years, vision researchers have grown a healthy skepticism of "good dataset performance". It has long been known that an algorithm that performs well in a given dataset, does not necessarily perform well on others. This is denoted dataset bias [19]. In recent years, significant effort has been devoted to combating such bias, with significant success.

These advances have been guided by well known principles in statistics. This is because a CNN learned with cross-entropy loss is a maximum likelihood (ML) estimator $\hat{\theta}$ of ground-truth parameters θ. Consider in this discussion a simpler problem of estimating the head probability p in a coin toss. Given a dataset $\mathcal{D} = \{x_1, \ldots, x_n\}$ of samples from n independent Bernoulli random variables X_i of probability p, the ML estimator is well known to be the sample mean

$$\hat{p}_{\text{ML}} = \frac{1}{n} \sum_i x_i. \tag{1}$$

Over the years, statisticians have developed many measures of goodness of such algorithms. The most commonly used are bias and variance

$$\text{Bias}(\hat{p}_{\text{ML}}) = \mathbb{E}[\hat{p}_{\text{ML}}] - p \tag{2}$$

$$\text{Var}(\hat{p}_{\text{ML}}) = \mathbb{E}[(\hat{p}_{\text{ML}} - \mathbb{E}[\hat{p}_{\text{ML}}])^2]. \tag{3}$$

The algorithm of (1) is known to be unbiased and have variance that decreases as the dataset size n grows, according to $\text{Var}(\hat{p}_{\text{ML}}) = \frac{1}{n}p(1 - p)$. Similar but more complex formulas can be derived for many ML algorithms, including CNN learning. These results justify the common practice of evaluation on multiple datasets. If the algorithm is an unbiased estimate of the optimal algorithm it will, on average, produce optimal results. If is also has low variance, it produces close to optimal results when applied to any dataset. Hence, when evaluated over a few datasets, the algorithm is likely to beat other algorithms and become the state of the art.

Note that the common definition of "dataset bias" [19], i.e. that an algorithm performs well on dataset A but not on dataset B, simply means that the algorithm has large variance. Since variance decreases with dataset size n, it has always been known that, to avoid it, datasets should be "large enough". The extensive data collection efforts of the recent past have produced some more objective rules of thumb, e.g. "1,000 examples per class," that appear to suffice to control the variance of current CNN models.

3.2   Representation Bias

Unfortunately, dataset bias is not the only bias that affects vision. A second, and more subtle, type of bias is *representation bias*. To understand this, we return to the coin toss example. For most coins in the world, the probability of heads is $p = 0.5$. However, it is possible that a dataset researcher would only have access to biased coins, say with $p = 0.3$. By using the algorithm of (1) to estimate p, with a large enough n, the researcher would eventually conclude that $p = 0.3$. Furthermore, using (2)–(3), he would conclude that there is no dataset bias and announce to the world that $p = 0.3$. Note that there is nothing wrong with this practice, except the final conclusion that there is something universal about $p = 0.3$. On the contrary, because the scientist used a biased dataset, he obtained a biased response.

The important observation is that standard dataset collection practices, such as "make n larger," will not solve the problem. These practices address dataset bias, which is a property of the representation. On the other hand, representation bias is a property of the dataset. While evaluating the representation ϕ on multiple (or larger) datasets $\mathcal{D}_i$ is an effective way to detect dataset bias, representation bias can only be detected by comparing the performance of multiple representations ϕ_i on the dataset $\mathcal{D}$. More importantly, the two are unrelated, in the sense that a representation ϕ may be unbiased towards a dataset $\mathcal{D}$, even when $\mathcal{D}$ has a strong bias for ϕ. It follows that standard evaluation practices, which mostly measure dataset bias, fail to guarantee that their conclusions are not tainted by representation bias.

This problem is difficult to avoid in computer vision, where biases can be very subtle. For example, a single object in the background could give away the class of a video. It is certainly possible to assemble datasets of video classes that can be discriminated by the presence or absence of certain objects. This does not mean that object recognition is sufficient for video classification. Only that the datasets are biased towards object-based representations. To avoid this problem, the datasets must be well calibrated.

3.3   Calibrated Datasets

Representation is a mathematical characterization of some property of the visual world. For example, optical flow is a representation of motion. A representation ϕ can be used to design many algorithms γ_ϕ to accomplish any task of interest, e.g. different algorithms that use optical flow to classify video. A representation family $\mathcal{R}$ is a set of representations that share some property. For example, the family of static representations includes all representations for visual properties of single images, i.e. representations that do not account for motion.

Let $\mathcal{M}(\mathcal{D}, \gamma)$ be a measure of performance, e.g. classification accuracy, of algorithm γ on dataset $\mathcal{D}$. The performance of the representation ϕ is defined as

$$\mathcal{M}(\mathcal{D}, \phi) = \max_{\gamma_\phi} \mathcal{M}(\mathcal{D}, \gamma_\phi) \qquad (4)$$

where the max is taken over all algorithms based on the representation. Representation bias reflects the fact that a dataset $\mathcal{D}$ has a preference for some representation ϕ, i.e. $\mathcal{M}(\mathcal{D}, \phi)$ is high.

The fact that a dataset has a preference for ϕ is not necessarily good or bad. In fact, all datasets are expected to be biased for the *ground truth representation*, (GTR) ϕ_g, the representation that is truly needed to solve the vision problem. A dataset $\mathcal{D}$ is said to be *well calibrated* if this representation has the best performance

$$\phi_g = \arg\max_\phi \mathcal{M}(\mathcal{D}, \phi) \qquad (5)$$

and the maximum is *unique*, i.e.

$$\mathcal{M}(\mathcal{D}, \phi) < \mathcal{M}(\mathcal{D}, \phi_g) \quad \forall \phi \neq \phi_g. \qquad (6)$$

In general, the GTR is unknown. A commonly used proxy in vision is the *state-of-the-art* (SoA) representation

$$\phi_{soa} = \arg\max_{\phi \in \mathcal{S}} \mathcal{M}(\mathcal{D}, \phi) \qquad (7)$$

where $\mathcal{S}$ is a finite set of representations proposed in the literature. If the dataset $\mathcal{D}$ is well calibrated, ϕ_{soa} will converge to ϕ_g as $\mathcal{S}$ expands, i.e. as more representations are tested. This is not guaranteed when $\mathcal{D}$ is not well calibrated. Unfortunately, it is usually impossible to know if this is the case. An alternative is to measure of bias.

3.4   Measuring Representation Bias

While the best possible performance on a dataset, e.g. the Bayes error of a classification task, is usually impossible to determine, the contrary holds for the worst performance. For classification, this corresponds to the random assignment of examples to classes, or "chance level performance". This is denoted as

$$\mathcal{M}_{rnd} = \min_\phi \mathcal{M}(\mathcal{D}, \phi). \qquad (8)$$

The bias of a dataset $\mathcal{D}$ for a representation ϕ is defined as

$$\mathcal{B}(\mathcal{D}, \phi) = \log \frac{\mathcal{M}(\mathcal{D}, \phi)}{\mathcal{M}_{rnd}}. \qquad (9)$$

When bias is zero, the representation has chance level performance and the dataset is said to be unbiased for the representation.

A dataset for which (5) holds but (6) does not, since there is a family of representations $\mathcal{R}$ such that $\mathcal{M}(\mathcal{D}, \phi) = \mathcal{M}(\mathcal{D}, \phi_g) \, \forall \phi \in \mathcal{R}$, can be made well calibrated by addition of data $\mathcal{D}'$ that reduces the bias towards the representations in $\mathcal{R}$, i.e. $\mathcal{B}(\mathcal{D} \cup \mathcal{D}', \phi) < \mathcal{B}(\mathcal{D}, \phi) \, \forall \phi \in \mathcal{R}$, while guaranteeing that (5) still holds. Similarly, a dataset can be designed to be minimally biased towards a representation family $\mathcal{R}$. This consists of selecting the dataset

$$\mathcal{D}^* = \arg\min_{\mathcal{D} \in \mathcal{T}(\phi_g)} \max_{\phi \in \mathcal{R}} \mathcal{B}(\mathcal{D}, \phi) \qquad (10)$$

Algorithm 1: Representation biases.

Input : Dataset $\mathcal{D}$; representation families $\{\mathcal{R}_1, \ldots, \mathcal{R}_K\}$.
Output: Representation biases $\{b_1, \ldots, b_K\}$.

1 **for** $k = 1, \ldots, K$ **do**
2 $\quad$ R_k = number of representations in $\mathcal{R}_k$;
3 $\quad$ **for** $r = 1, \ldots, R_k$ **do**
4 $\quad\quad$ $M_{k,r}$ = number of algorithms based on representation $\phi_{k,r}$;
5 $\quad\quad$ **for** $m = 1, \ldots, M_{k,r}$ **do**
6 $\quad\quad\quad$ $\gamma_{\phi_{k,r}}^m$: m^{th} algorithm based on $\phi_{k,r}$; Measure $\mathcal{M}(\mathcal{D}, \gamma_{\phi_{k,r}}^m)$
7 $\quad\quad$ **end**
8 $\quad\quad$ Measure $\mathcal{M}(\mathcal{D}, \phi_{k,r})$ with (4);
9 $\quad\quad$ Measure bias $\mathcal{B}(\mathcal{D}, \phi_{k,r})$ with (9);
10 $\quad$ **end**
11 $\quad$ Compute $b_k = \max_r \mathcal{B}(\mathcal{D}, \phi_{k,r})$;
12 **end**

---

where $\mathcal{T}(\phi_g)$ is the set of datasets for which (5) holds.

Note that the constraint $\mathcal{D} \in \mathcal{T}(\phi_g)$ is somewhat redundant, since it has to hold for any valid dataset collection effort. It simply means that the dataset is an object recognition dataset or an action recognition dataset. Researchers assembling such datasets already need to make sure that they assign the highest score to the GTR for object recognition or action recognition, respectively. The main novelty of (10) is the notion that the datasets should also be minimally biased towards the family of representations $\mathcal{R}$.

3.5 Measuring Bias at the Class Level

Definition (9) can be extended to measure class-level bias. Consider a dataset of C classes. Rather than using a single classification problem to measure $\mathcal{M}(\mathcal{D}, \phi)$, C one-vs-all binary classifiers are defined. The bias for class c is then defined as

$$\mathcal{B}_c(\mathcal{D}, \phi) = \log \frac{\mathcal{M}_c(\mathcal{D}, \phi)}{\mathcal{M}_{rnd}}, \tag{11}$$

where $\mathcal{M}_c$ is the performance on the classification problem that opposes c to all other classes. To alleviate the effects of sample imbalance, performance is measured with average precision instead of classification accuracy.

4   RESOUND Dataset Collection

In general, it is impossible to guarantee that a dataset is minimally biased towards all representation families that do not contain ϕ_g. In fact, it is usually impossible to even list all such families. What is possible is to *define* a set of representation families $\mathcal{R}_i$ towards which the dataset aims to be unbiased, *measure* the bias of the dataset for at least one representation in each $\mathcal{R}_i$, and *show* that the biases are smaller than previous datasets in the literature. This is denoted *REpreSentatiOn UNbiased Dataset* (RESOUND) collection. The steps taken to measure the biases of the dataset are summarized in Algorithm 1.

Two strategies are possible to implement RESOUND in practice. The first is explicit optimization, where dataset $\mathcal{D}^*$ is produced by an algorithm. This could, for example, start from an existing dataset $\mathcal{D}$ and add or eliminate examples so as to optimize (10). The second is an implicit optimization, which identifies classes likely to be unbiased with respect to the representation family $\mathcal{R}$. For example, if $\mathcal{R}$ is the family of object representations, this requires defining classes without distinguishable objects in either foreground or background. We next illustrate this by applying RESOUND to the problem of action recognition.

4.1   Explicit RESOUND

One possible strategy to assemble a K-class dataset $\mathcal{D}^*$ of minimal bias is to select K classes from an existing dataset $\mathcal{D}$. Let $\mathcal{D}$ have $C > K$ classes, i.e. a set of class labels $\mathcal{D}_y = \{d_1, \ldots, d_C\}$, where d_i denoted the ith class of $\mathcal{D}$. The goal is to find the label set of $\mathcal{D}^*$ i.e. a set $\mathcal{D}_y^* = \{c_1, \ldots, c_K\}$, such that: (1) c_i are classes from $\mathcal{D}$, i.e. $c_i \in \mathcal{D}_y$; (2) c_i are mutually exclusive, $c_i \neq c_j, \forall i \neq j$; (3) $\mathcal{D}^*$ has minimal bias.

Using the class-level bias measurement of (11) then leads to the following optimization problem.

$$\mathcal{D}_y^* = \underset{c_1, \ldots, c_K \in \mathcal{D}_y}{\arg \min} \quad \sum_{k=1}^{K} \mathcal{B}_{c_k}(\mathcal{D}^*, \phi) \tag{12}$$

$$\text{subject to} \quad 1 \leq c_i \leq C; c_i \neq c_j, \quad \forall i \neq j \tag{13}$$

Since this is a combinatorial problem, a global optimum can only be achieved by exhaustive search. Furthermore, because the bias $\mathcal{B}_{c_k}(\mathcal{D}^*, \phi)$ of class c_k depends on other classes in $\mathcal{D}^*$, the biases have to be computed for each class configuration. For small values of K, the time complexity of this search is acceptable. The problem of how to scale up this process is left for future research.

4.2   Implicit RESOUND: The Diving48 Dataset

In this section, we describe the application of RESOUND in creating an action recognition dataset, Diving48. The goal of this data collection effort was to enable further study of the question "what is the right level of representation for action recognition?" The current evidence is that optical flow representations, such as the two-stream network of [17], are sufficient. However, current datasets exhibit biases that could lead to this conclusion, even if it is incorrect. By producing a dataset with no (or small) such biases, we expect to use it to investigate the importance of short-time motion vs long-term dynamics representations. Since we were not interested in the role of static cues, the dataset should be unbiased towards static representations. However, it would be too difficult to consider all static cues. To keep the problem manageable, it was decided to emphasize the most prevalent static biases of existing datasets: *objects*, *scenes*, and *people*. For this, we considered the domain of competitive diving.

Diving is an interesting domain for the study of action recognition, for various reasons. First, there is a finite set of action (dive) classes, which are unambiguously defined and standardized by FINA [1]. Second, the dives differ in subtle sub-components, known as *elements*, that the divers perform and are graded on. This generates a very rich set of fine-grained action classes. Since some of the dives defined in [1] are rarely performed by athletes (due to their difficulty), a subset of 48 dives were selected as classes of the Diving48 Dataset. Third, and perhaps most important, diving scenes give rise to much fewer biases than other scenes commonly used for action recognition. This is because there are many different divers per competition, there are no background objects that give away the dive class, the scenes tend to be quite similar (a board, a pool, and spectators in the background) in all dives, and the divers have more or less the same static visual attributes. In this way, the diving domain addressed all biases that we had set out to eliminate. This was verified by comparing the biases of Diving48 to those of previous datasets.

Because there are many diving videos on the web, it was relatively easy to find and download a sufficient number of videos of diving platform and springboard, shot in major diving competitions. However, these event videos are usually not segmented. They are usually long videos, including hundreds of diving instances, performed by different divers, and replayed from different camera views and at different playback speeds. To ease the labeling process, the videos were automatically segmented into clips approximately one-minute-long, which were then annotated on Amazon Mechanical Turk with two major tasks. The first was to transcribe the information board that appears in each clip before the start of the dive. This contains meta information such as the diving type and difficulty score, which is used to produce ground truth for the dataset. The second was to precisely segment each diving instance, by determining the start and end video frames of the dive, and labeling the playback view and speed. Each segmentation task was assigned to 3 Turkers and a majority vote based on IOU of temporal intervals was used to reduce labeling noise. This produced 18,404 segmented dive video clips, which were used to create Diving48. A random set of 16,067 clips was selected as train set and the remaining 2,337 as test set. To avoid biases for certain competitions, the train/test split guaranteed that not all clips from the same competition were assigned into the same split.

Figure 1 shows a prefix tree that summarizes the 48 dive classes in the dataset. Each class is defined by the path from the root node to a leaf node. For example, dive 32 is defined by the sequence "Backwards take-off → 1.5 Somersault → Half Twist, with a Free body position". Note that discrimination between many of the classes requires a fine-grained representation of dynamics. For example, dive 16 and dive 18 only differ in the number of somersaults; while dive 33 and dive 34 differ only in the flight position.

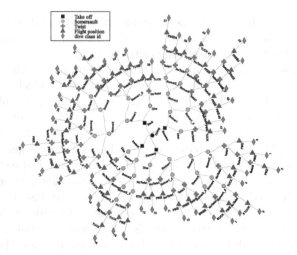

Fig. 1. Definitions of dive class in Diving48 as a prefix tree.

5   Experiments

Three sets of experiments were performed. The first was a RESOUND experiment, aimed to measure biases on existing and the proposed Diving48 dataset. The second was meant to confirm that RESOUND sampling of existing datasets can effectively produce datasets with minimal biases. The third aimed to investigate the original question of the importance of dynamic modeling for action recognition.

5.1   Datasets

The biases of Diving48 were compared to those of seven popular datasets, whose statistics are shown in Table 1. KTH [14], Hollywood2 [11] are small datasets introduced in the early history of video action recognition. They were collected in a more controlled fashion, with e.g. fixed background. HMDB51 [10] and UCF101 [18] are modern datasets with larger scale and less constrained videos. ActivityNet [3], Kinetics [8] and Charades [16] are three recent datasets, collected by crowd-sourcing. All experiments were used on the official train/test splits for each dataset. Dataset level bias is measured with (9), using accuracy as performance metric. For class level bias, average precision is used in (11).

5.2   RESOUND Experiments

A set of RESOUND experiments were performed to compare the representation biases of Diving48 and existing datasets. Three static biases were considered in Algorithm 1, using three representation families $\mathcal{R} = \{\mathcal{R}_{object}, \mathcal{R}_{scene}, \mathcal{R}_{people}\}$. For each family, we considered a single representation—CNN features, and a

Table 1. Statistics and biases of various video action recognition datasets.

Dataset	#samples	#classes	Avg. #frames	$\mathcal{B}(\mathcal{D}, \phi_{object})$	$\mathcal{B}(\mathcal{D}, \phi_{scene})$	$\mathcal{B}(\mathcal{D}, \phi_{people})$	$\mathcal{M}_{rnd}$
KTH	599	6	482.7	**1.47**	1.39	1.47	0.17
Hollywood2	823	10	345.2	1.69	1.61	1.64	0.10
HMDB51	6766	51	96.6	3.16	2.92	2.98	0.020
UCF101	13320	101	187.3	4.33	4.09	4.23	0.010
ActivityNet	28108	200	1365.5	3.69	3.37	3.49	0.0050
Kinetics	429256	400	279.1	4.51	3.96	4.31	0.0025
Charades	99618	157	310.0	2.12	2.01	2.04	0.0063
Diving48	18404	48	159.6	**1.48**	**1.26**	**1.44**	0.021

single algorithm—ResNet50 [6]. The networks varied on how they were trained: ϕ_{object} was trained on the 1,000 object classes of ImageNet [4], ϕ_{scene} on the 365 scene classes of the Places365 scene classification dataset [25], and ϕ_{people} on the 204 classes of people attributes of the COCO-attributes dataset [12].

These networks were used, without fine-tuning, to measure the representation bias of each dataset. A 2,048 dimensional feature vector was extracted at the penultimate layer, per video frame. A linear classifier was then trained with cross-entropy loss to perform action recognition, using the feature vectors extracted from each action class. It was then applied to 25 frames drawn uniformly from each test clip, and the prediction scores were averaged to obtain a clip-level score. Finally, the clips were assigned to the class of largest score. The resulting classification rates were used to compute the bias $\mathcal{B}(\mathcal{D}, \phi)$, according to (9).

The biases of all datasets are listed in Table 1. Note that bias is a logarithmic measure and small variations of bias can mean non-trivial differences in recognition accuracy. A few observations can be made from the table. First, all existing datasets have much larger biases than Diving48. This suggests that the latter is more suitable for studying the importance of dynamics in action recognition. Second, all datasets have stronger bias for objects, then people, and then scenes. Interestingly, the three biases are *similar* for each dataset. This suggests that there is interdependency between the biases of any dataset. Third, all biases vary significantly *across* datasets. Clearly, the amount of bias does not appear to be mitigated by dataset size: the largest dataset (Kinetics) is also the most biased. This shows that, while a good strategy to mitigate dataset bias, simply increasing dataset size is not a solution for the problem of representation bias. On the other hand, a small dataset does not guarantee low representation bias. For example, UCF101 is relatively small but has the second largest average bias, and is the dataset most strongly biased to scene representations. Fourth, bias appears to be positively correlated with the number of classes. This makes intuitive sense. Note, however, that this effect is dependent on how the dataset is assembled. For example, HMDB51 has a number of classes similar to Diving48, but much larger object bias. In fact, Diving48 has bias equivalent to that of the 6 class KTH dataset. Nevertheless, the positive correlation with number of classes suggests that representation bias *will become a more important problem*

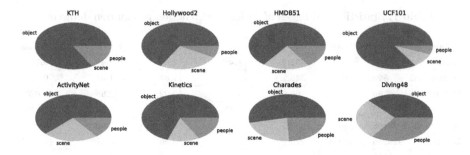

Fig. 2. Distribution of the dominant class bias ϕ_{r*}^c.

as datasets grow. Certainly, some of the most recent datasets, e.g. ActivityNet and Kinetics, have some of the largest amounts of representation bias.

5.3   Class-Level Dominant Bias

We next evaluate biases at the class level, using (11). For each class c, a **dominant bias** ϕ_{r*}^c is identified with

$$r^* = \arg\max_r \; \mathcal{B}_c(\mathcal{D}, \phi_r). \tag{14}$$

Figure 2 summarizes the distribution of this dominant bias on each dataset of Table 1. It is clear that most classes of all datasets are dominantly biased for object representation. However, different datasets have different bias properties. For example, KTH classes are more biased to people representation than scene representation, while this is reverse for Hollywood2. Diving48 has the most uniform distribution. These plots can be used to derive guidelines on how to mitigate the biases of the different datasets. For example, object bias can be decreased by augmenting all the classes where it is dominant with videos where the objects do not appear, have a larger diversity of appearance and/or motion, etc.

5.4   Explicit RESOUND

We have also investigated the possibility of creating unbiased datasets from existing biased datasets, using the explicit RESOUND procedure of (13). Due to the large computational complexity, we have so far only used $K = 3$. This is geared more to test the feasibility of the approach than a practical solution, which will require the development of special purpose optimization algorithms. To test the effectiveness of explicit RESOUND sampling, the biases of the resulting datasets were compared to those obtained by random sampling. Table 2 shows that in all cases, the datasets produced by explicit RESOUND have significantly smaller biases than those produced by random sampling. And the optimization results make intuitive sense, e.g. for ActivityNet, the selected classes are { "Hanging wallpaper", "Installing carpet", "Painting"}, which are all household actions.

Table 2. Explicit RESOUND $(\mathcal{D}_y^*)$ biases after sampling. Results of random sampling $(\mathcal{D}_{rand})$ were evaluated on 10 runs and are reported as mean $\pm$ std.

Dataset	$\phi = \phi_{object}$		$\phi = \phi_{scene}$		$\phi = \phi_{people}$	
	$\mathcal{B}(\mathcal{D}_y^*, \phi)$	$\mathcal{B}(\mathcal{D}_{rand}, \phi)$	$\mathcal{B}(\mathcal{D}_y^*, \phi)$	$\mathcal{B}(\mathcal{D}_{rand}, \phi)$	$\mathcal{B}(\mathcal{D}_y^*, \phi)$	$\mathcal{B}(\mathcal{D}_{rand}, \phi)$
KTH	0.39	0.99 ± 0.09	0.29	0.80 ± 0.17	0.44	0.86 ± 0.20
Hollywood2	0.44	0.86 ± 0.07	0.28	0.66 ± 0.13	0.33	0.68 ± 0.08
HMDB51	0.00	0.82 ± 0.54	0.00	0.99 ± 0.05	0.00	0.90 ± 0.13
UCF101	0.55	1.08 ± 0.02	0.65	1.02 ± 0.09	0.46	1.08 ± 0.02
ActivityNet	0.41	0.89 ± 0.10	0.14	0.79 ± 0.09	0.00	0.84 ± 0.11
Kinetics	0.41	1.00 ± 0.11	0.30	1.01 ± 0.08	0.33	0.94 ± 0.11
Charades	0.00	0.62 ± 0.20	0.00	0.67 ± 0.18	0.00	0.73 ± 0.14

Table 3. Recognition accuracy on Diving48.

TSN (RGB)	TSN (Flow)	TSN (RGB + Flow)	C3D (L = 8)	C3D (L = 16)	C3D(L = 32)	C3D(L = 64)
16.77	19.64	20.28	11.51	16.43	21.01	**27.60**

5.5   Classification with Dynamics

We finish by using Diving48 to investigate the importance of dynamics for action recognition. The goal was not to introduce new algorithms but to rely on off-the-shelf models of dynamics. Existing models for this evaluation include TSN [22] and the C3D [7]. For C3D, varying number of frames L is an objective measure of the extent of dynamics modeling. We set $L = 8, 16, 32$ and 64. The action recognition performance on Diving48 is shown in Table 3. First, the best performing C3D model with the largest extent of dynamics modeling achieves the best result, verifying that Diving48 is more than flow modeling. Second, the C3D results improve monotonically with L, showing that a moderate level of dynamics modeling is required to achieve good performance on this dataset. Nevertheless, the best overall performance (27.60%) is still fairly low. This shows that research is needed on more sophisticated representations of dynamics.

6   Conclusion

In this paper, we have introduced the concepts of well calibrated datasets and representation bias, and the RESOUND algorithm to objectively quantify the representation biases of a dataset. An instantiation of RESOUND in its explicit optimization form was used to sample existing datasets, so as to assemble new datasets with smaller biases. Another instantiation of RESOUND was used to compare the static representation bias of a new action recognition dataset, Diving48, to those in the literature. This showed that existing datasets have too much bias for static representations to meaningfully evaluate the role of dynamics in action recognition. Diving48, which was shown to have much smaller biases, is a better candidate for such studies. Preliminary classification results, with static representations and 3D CNNs, indicate that modeling of dynamics can indeed be important for action recognition. We hope that this work, and the proposed dataset, will inspire interest in action recognition tasks without static bias, as well as research in models of video dynamics. We also hope that procedures like RESOUND will become more prevalent in vision, enabling (1) more scientific approaches to dataset collection, and (2) control over factors that can undermine the conclusions derived from vision experiments.

References

1. Fédération internationale de natation. http://www.fina.org/
2. Bregonzio, M., Gong, S., Xiang, T.: Recognising action as clouds of space-time interest points. In: 2009 IEEE Conference on Computer Vision and Pattern Recognition, CVPR 2009, pp. 1948–1955. IEEE (2009)
3. Caba Heilbron, F., Escorcia, V., Ghanem, B., Carlos Niebles, J.: ActivityNet: a large-scale video benchmark for human activity understanding. In: Proceedings of the IEEE Conference on Computer Vision and Pattern Recognition, pp. 961–970 (2015)
4. Deng, J., Dong, W., Socher, R., Li, L.J., Li, K., Fei-Fei, L.: ImageNet: a large-scale hierarchical image database. In: 2009 IEEE Conference on Computer Vision and Pattern Recognition, CVPR 2009, pp. 248–255. IEEE (2009)
5. Donahue, J., et al.: Long-term recurrent convolutional networks for visual recognition and description. In: Proceedings of the IEEE Conference on Computer Vision and Pattern Recognition, pp. 2625–2634 (2015)
6. He, K., Zhang, X., Ren, S., Sun, J.: Deep residual learning for image recognition. In: Proceedings of the IEEE Conference on Computer Vision and Pattern Recognition, pp. 770–778 (2016)
7. Ji, S., Xu, W., Yang, M., Yu, K.: 3D convolutional neural networks for human action recognition. IEEE Trans. Pattern Anal. Mach. Intell. 35(1), 221–231 (2013)
8. Kay, W., et al.: The kinetics human action video dataset. arXiv preprint arXiv:1705.06950 (2017)
9. Khosla, A., Jayadevaprakash, N., Yao, B., Li, F.F.: Novel dataset for fine-grained image categorization: stanford dogs. In: Proceedings of CVPR Workshop on Fine-Grained Visual Categorization (FGVC), vol. 2, p. 1 (2011)
10. Kuehne, H., Jhuang, H., Stiefelhagen, R., Serre, T.: HMDB51: a large video database for human motion recognition. In: Nagel, W., Kroner, D., Resch, M. (eds.) High Performance Computing in Science and Engineering '12, pp. 571–582. Springer, Berlin (2013). https://doi.org/10.1007/978-3-642-33374-3_41
11. Marszałek, M., Laptev, I., Schmid, C.: Actions in context. In: IEEE Conference on Computer Vision and Pattern Recognition (2009)
12. Patterson, G., Hays, J.: COCO attributes: attributes for people, animals, and objects. In: Leibe, B., Matas, J., Sebe, N., Welling, M. (eds.) ECCV 2016. LNCS, vol. 9910, pp. 85–100. Springer, Cham (2016). https://doi.org/10.1007/978-3-319-46466-4_6
13. Rohrbach, M., Amin, S., Andriluka, M., Schiele, B.: A database for fine grained activity detection of cooking activities. In: 2012 IEEE Conference on Computer Vision and Pattern Recognition (CVPR), pp. 1194–1201. IEEE (2012)

14. Schuldt, C., Laptev, I., Caputo, B.: Recognizing human actions: a local SVM app-roach. In: 2004 Proceedings of the 17th International Conference on Pattern Recognition, ICPR 2004, vol. 3, pp. 32–36. IEEE (2004)

15. Sigurdsson, G.A., Russakovsky, O., Gupta, A.: What actions are needed for understanding human actions in videos? In: 2017 IEEE International Conference on Computer Vision (ICCV), pp. 2156–2165. IEEE (2017)

16. Sigurdsson, G.A., Varol, G., Wang, X., Farhadi, A., Laptev, I., Gupta, A.: Hollywood in homes: crowdsourcing data collection for activity understanding. In: Leibe, B., Matas, J., Sebe, N., Welling, M. (eds.) ECCV 2016. LNCS, vol. 9905, pp. 510–526. Springer, Cham (2016). https://doi.org/10.1007/978-3-319-46448-0_31

17. Simonyan, K., Zisserman, A.: Two-stream convolutional networks for action recognition in videos. In: Advances in Neural Information Processing Systems, pp. 568–576 (2014)

18. Soomro, K., Zamir, A.R., Shah, M.: UCF101: a dataset of 101 human actions classes from videos in the wild. arXiv preprint arXiv:1212.0402 (2012)

19. Torralba, A., Efros, A.A.: Unbiased look at dataset bias. In: 2011 IEEE Conference on Computer Vision and Pattern Recognition (CVPR), pp. 1521–1528. IEEE (2011)

20. Tran, D., Bourdev, L., Fergus, R., Torresani, L., Paluri, M.: Learning spatiotemporal features with 3D convolutional networks. In: Proceedings of the IEEE International Conference on Computer Vision, pp. 4489–4497 (2015)

21. Wah, C., Branson, S., Welinder, P., Perona, P., Belongie, S.: The Caltech-UCSD birds-200-2011 dataset. Technical report CNS-TR-2011-001, California Institute of Technology (2011)

22. Wang, L., et al.: Temporal segment networks: towards good practices for deep action recognition. In: Leibe, B., Matas, J., Sebe, N., Welling, M. (eds.) ECCV 2016. LNCS, vol. 9912, pp. 20–36. Springer, Cham (2016). https://doi.org/10.1007/978-3-319-46484-8_2

23. Yu, A., Grauman, K.: Fine-grained visual comparisons with local learning. In: Proceedings of the IEEE Conference on Computer Vision and Pattern Recognition, pp. 192–199 (2014)

24. Ng, J.Y.-H., Hausknecht, M., Vijayanarasimhan, S., Vinyals, O., Monga, R., Toderici, G.: Beyond short snippets: deep networks for video classification. In: Proceedings of the IEEE Conference on Computer Vision and Pattern Recognition, pp. 4694–4702 (2015)

25. Zhou, B., Lapedriza, A., Khosla, A., Oliva, A., Torralba, A.: Places: a 10 million image database for scene recognition. IEEE Trans. Pattern Anal. Mach. Intell. 40, 1452–1464 (2017)

Integral Human Pose Regression

Xiao Sun[1], Bin Xiao[1], Fangyin Wei[2], Shuang Liang[3(✉)], and Yichen Wei[1]

[1] Microsoft Research, Beijing, China
{xias,Bin.Xiao,yichenw}@microsoft.com
[2] Peking University, Beijing, China
weifangyin@pku.edu.cn
[3] Tongji University, Shanghai, China
shuangliang@tongji.edu.cn

Abstract. State-of-the-art human pose estimation methods are based on heat map representation. In spite of the good performance, the representation has a few issues in nature, such as non-differentiable post-processing and quantization error. This work shows that a simple *integral* operation relates and unifies the heat map representation and joint regression, thus avoiding the above issues. It is differentiable, efficient, and compatible with *any* heat map based methods. Its effectiveness is convincingly validated via comprehensive ablation experiments under various settings, specifically on 3D pose estimation, for the first time.

Keywords: Integral regression · Human pose estimation
Deep learning

1 Introduction

Human pose estimation has been extensively studied [3,24,28]. Recent years have seen significant progress on the problem, using deep convolutional neural networks (CNNs). Best performing methods on 2D pose estimation are all detection based [2]. They generate a likelihood heat map for each joint and locate the joint as the point with the maximum likelihood in the map. The heat maps are also extended for 3D pose estimation and shown promising [37].

Despite its good performance, a heat map representation bears a few drawbacks in nature. The "taking-maximum" operation is not differentiable and prevents training from being end-to-end. A heat map has lower resolution than that of input image due to the down sampling steps in a deep neural network. This causes inevitable quantization errors. Using image and heat map with higher resolution helps to increase accuracy but is computational and storage demanding, especially for 3D heat maps.

From another viewpoint, pose estimation is essentially a regression problem. A regression approach performs end-to-end learning and produces continuous output. It avoids the issues above. However, regression methods are not as effective as well as detection based methods for 2D human pose estimation.

© Springer Nature Switzerland AG 2018
V. Ferrari et al. (Eds.): ECCV 2018, LNCS 11210, pp. 536–553, 2018.
https://doi.org/10.1007/978-3-030-01231-1_33

Among the best-performing methods in the 2D pose benchmark [2], only one method [7] is regression based. A possible reason is that regression learning is more difficult than heat map learning, because the latter is supervised by dense pixel information. While regression methods are widely used for 3D pose estimation [14,21,30–32,35,42,43,55,56], its performance is still not satisfactory.

Existing works are either detection based or regression based. There is clear discrepancy between the two categories and there is little work studying their relation. This work shows that a simple operation would relate and unify the heat map representation and joint regression. It modifies the "taking-maximum" operation to "taking-expectation". The joint is estimated as the integration of all locations in the heat map, weighted by their probabilities (normalized from likelihoods). We call this approach *integral regression*. It shares the merits of both heat map representation and regression approaches, while avoiding their drawbacks. The integral function is differentiable and allows end-to-end training. It is simple and brings little overhead in computation and storage. Moreover, it can be easily combined with *any* heat map based methods.

The integral operation itself is not new. It has been known as *soft-argmax* and used in the previous works [27,45,52]. Specifically, two contemporary works [29, 34] also apply it for human pose estimation. Nevertheless, these works have limited ablation experiments. The effectiveness of integral regression is not fully evaluated. Specifically, they only perform experiments on MPII 2D benchmark, on which the performance is nearly saturated. It is yet unclear whether the approach is effective under other settings, such as 3D pose estimation. See Sect. 3 for more discussions.

Because the integral regression is parameter free and only transforms the pose representation from a heat map to a joint, it does not affect other algorithm design choices and can be combined with any of them, including different *tasks, heat map and joint losses, network architectures, image and heat map resolutions*. See Fig. 1 for a summarization. We conduct comprehensive experiments to investigate the performance of integral regression under all such settings and find consistent improvement. Such results verify the effectiveness of integral representation.

Our main contribution is applying integral regression under various experiment settings and verifying its effectiveness. Specifically, we firstly show that integral regression significantly improves the 3D pose estimation, enables the mixed usage of 3D and 2D data, and achieves state-of-the-art results on Human3.6M [24]. Our results on 2D pose benchmarks (MPII [3] and COCO [28]) is also competitive. Code[1] will be released to facilitate future work.

2 Integral Pose Regression

Given a learnt heat map $\mathbf{H}_k$ for k^{th} joint, each location in the map represents the probability of the location being the joint. The final joint location coordinate

---

[1] https://github.com/JimmySuen/integral-human-pose.

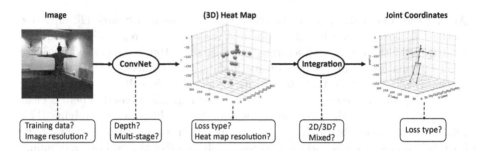

Fig. 1. Overview of pose estimation pipeline and all our ablation experiment settings.

$\mathbf{J}_k$ is obtained as the location $\mathbf{p}$ with the *maximum likelihood* as

$$\mathbf{J}_k = \arg\max_{\mathbf{p}} \mathbf{H}_k(\mathbf{p}). \tag{1}$$

This approach has two main drawbacks. First, Eq. (1) is *non-differentiable*, reducing itself to a post-processing step but not a component of learning. The training is not end-to-end. The supervision could only be imposed on the heat maps for learning.

Second, the heat map representation leads to *quantization error*. The heat map resolution is much lower than the input image resolution due to the down sampling steps in a deep neural network. The joint localization precision is thus limited by the quantization factor, which poses challenges for accurate joint localization. Using larger heat maps could alleviate this problem, but at the cost of extra storage and computation.

Regression methods have two clear advantages over heat map based methods. First, learning is *end-to-end* and driven by the goal of joint prediction, bridging the common gap between learning and inference. Second, the output is *continuous* and up to arbitrary localization accuracy, in principle. This is opposed to the quantization problem in heat maps.

We present a unified approach that transforms the heat map into joint location coordinate and fundamentally narrows down the gap between heat map and regression based method. It brings principled and practical benefits.

Our approach simply modifies the *max* operation in Eq. (1) to take expectation, as

$$\mathbf{J}_k = \int_{\mathbf{p}\in\Omega} \mathbf{p} \cdot \tilde{\mathbf{H}}_k(\mathbf{p}). \tag{2}$$

Here, $\tilde{\mathbf{H}}_k$ is the normalized heat map and Ω is its domain. The estimated joint is the integration of all locations $\mathbf{p}$ in the domain, weighted by their probabilities.

Normalization is to make all elements of $\tilde{\mathbf{H}}_k(\mathbf{p})$ non-negative and sum to one. [34] has already discussed it and we use softmax in this paper as

$$\tilde{\mathbf{H}}_k(\mathbf{p}) = \frac{e^{\mathbf{H}_k(\mathbf{p})}}{\int_{\mathbf{q}\in\Omega} e^{\mathbf{H}_k(\mathbf{q})}}. \tag{3}$$

The discrete form of Eq. (2) is

$$\mathbf{J}_k = \sum_{p_z=1}^{D} \sum_{p_y=1}^{H} \sum_{p_x=1}^{W} \mathbf{p} \cdot \tilde{\mathbf{H}}_k(\mathbf{p}), \tag{4}$$

By default, the heat map is 3D. Its resolution on depth, height, and width are denoted as $D, H,$ and W respectively. $D = 1$ for 2D heat maps.

In this way, any heat map based approach can be augmented for joint estimation by appending the integral function in Eq. (4) to the heat map $\mathbf{H}_k$ and adopting a regression loss for $\mathbf{J}_k$. We call this approach *integral pose regression.*

Integral pose regression shares all the merits of both heat map based and regression approaches. The integral function in Eq. (4) is differentiable and allows end-to-end training. It is simple, fast and non-parametric. It can be easily combined with any heat map based methods, while adding negligible overhead in computation and memory for either training or inference. Its underlying heat map representation makes it easy to train. It has continuous output and does not suffer from the quantization problem.

2.1   Joint 3D and 2D Training

A lack of diverse training data is a severe problem for 3D human pose estimation. Several efforts have been made to combine 3D and 2D training [31,41,43,51,55]. Since integral regression provides a unified setting for both 2D and 3D pose estimation, it is a simple and general solution to facilitate joint 3D and 2D training so as to address this data issue in 3D human pose estimation.

Recently, Sun et al. [42] introduce a simple yet effective way to mix 2D and 3D data for 3D human pose estimation and show tremendous improvement. The key is to separate the 2D part (xy) of the joint prediction $\mathbf{J}_k$ from the depth part (z) so that the xy part can be supervised by the abundant 2D data.

Integral regression can naturally adopt this mixed training technique, thanks to the *differentiability* of integral operation in Eq. (4). We also obtain enormous improvement from this technique in our experiments and this improvement is feasible due to the integral formulation.

However, the underlying 3D heat map still can not be supervised by the abundant 2D data. To address this problem, we further decompose the integral function Eq. (4) into a two-step version to generate separate x, y, z heat map target. For example, for the x target, we first integrate the 3D heat map into 1D x heat vectors Eq. (5)

$$\tilde{\mathbf{V}}_k^x = \sum_{p_z=1}^{D} \sum_{p_y=1}^{H} \tilde{\mathbf{H}}_k(\mathbf{p}), \tag{5}$$

and then, further integrate the 1D x heat vector into x joint coordinate Eq. (6)

$$\mathbf{J}_k^x = \sum_{p_x=1}^{W} \mathbf{p} \cdot \tilde{\mathbf{V}}_k(\mathbf{p}). \tag{6}$$

Corresponding y and z formulation should be easy to infer. In this way, the x, y, z targets are separated at the first step, allowing the 2D and 3D mixed data training strategy. We obtain significant improvements from both direct and two-step integral regression for 3D pose estimation.

3   Methodology for Comprehensive Experiment

The main contribution of this work is a comprehensive methodology for ablation experiments to evaluate the performance of the integral regression under various conditions. Figure 1 illustrates the overview of the framework and the decision choices at each stage.

The related works [29, 34] only experimented with 2D pose estimation on MPII benchmark [2]. They also have limited ablation experiments. Specifically, [29] provides only system-level comparison results without any ablation experiments. [34] studies the heat map normalization methods, heat map regularization and backbone networks, which is far less comprehensive than ours.

Tasks. Our approach is general and is ready for both 2D and 3D pose estimation tasks, indistinguishably. Consistent improvements are obtained from both tasks. Particularly, 2D and 3D data can be easily mixed simultaneously in the training. The 3D task benefits more from this technique and outperforms previous works by large margins.

Network Architecture. We use a simple network architecture that is widely adopted in other vision tasks such as object detection and segmentation [19, 20]. It consists of a deep convolutional *backbone* network to extract convolutional features from the input image, and a shallow *head* network to estimate the target output (heat maps or joints) from the features.

In the experiment, we show that our approach is a flexible component which can be easily embedded into various backbone networks and the result is less affected by the network capacity than the heat map. Specifically, *network designs* ResNet [20] and HourGlass [33], *network depth* ResNet18, 50, 101 [20], *multi-stage* design [7, 49] are investigated.

Heat Map Losses. In the literature, there are several choices of loss function for heat maps. The most widely adopted is mean squared error (or *L2* distance) between the predicted heat map and ground-truth heat map with a 2D Gaussian blob centered on the ground truth joint location [5, 6, 10, 12, 13, 33, 48, 49]. In this work, the Gaussian blob has standard deviation $\sigma = 1$ as in [33]. Our baseline with this loss is denoted as H1 (H for heat map).

The recent Mask RCNN work [19] uses a one-hot $m \times m$ ground truth mask where only a single location is labeled as joint. It uses the cross-entropy loss over an m^2-way softmax output. Our baseline with this loss is denoted as H2.

Another line of works [22, 36, 38] solve a per-pixel binary classification problem, thus using binary cross-entropy loss. Each location in each heat map is classified as a joint or not. Following [22, 38], the ground truth heat map for each joint is constructed by assigning a positive label 1 at each location within

15 pixels to the ground truth joint, and negative label 0 otherwise. Our baseline with this implementation is denoted as H3.

In the experiment, we show that our approach works well with any of these heat map losses. Though, these manually designed heat map losses might have different performances on different tasks and need careful network hyperparameter tuning individually, the integral version (I1, I2, I3) of them would get prominent improvement and produce consistent results.

Heat Map and Joint Loss Combination. For the joint coordinate loss, we experimented with both $L1$ and $L2$ distances between the predicted joints and ground truth joints as loss functions. We found that $L1$ loss works consistently better than $L2$ loss. We thus adopt $L1$ loss in all of our experiments.

Note that our integral regression can be trained with or without intermediate heat map losses. For the latter case, a variant of integral regression method is defined, denoted as I*. The network is the same, but the loss on heat maps is not used. The training supervision signal is only on joint, not on heat maps. In the experiment, we find that integral regression works well with or without heat map supervisions. The best performance depends on specific tasks. For example, for 2D task I1 obtains the best performance, while for 3D task I* obtains the best performance.

Image and Heat Map Resolutions. Due to the quantization error of heat map, high image and heat map resolutions are usually required for high localization accuracy. However, it is demanding for memory and computation especially for 3D heat map. In the experiment, we show that our approach is more robust to the image and heat map resolution variation. This makes it a better choice when the computational capabilities are restricted, in practical scenarios.

4 Datasets and Evaluation Metrics

Our approach is validated on three benchmark datasets.

Human3.6M [24] is the largest 3D human pose benchmark. The dataset is captured in controlled environment. It consists of 3.6 millions of video frames. 11 subjects (5 females and 6 males) are captured from 4 camera viewpoints, performing 15 activities. The image appearance of the subjects and the background is simple. Accurate 3D human joint locations are obtained from motion capture devices. For evaluation, many previous works [4,8,25,31,32,37, 41,44,46,51,53,54,56] use the mean per joint position error (*MPJPE*). Some works [4,8,32,41,51,54] firstly align the predicted 3D pose and ground truth 3D pose with a rigid transformation using *Procrustes Analysis* [18] and then compute MPJPE. We call this metric *PA MPJPE*.

MPII [3] is the benchmark dataset for single person 2D pose estimation. The images were collected from YouTube videos, covering daily human activities with complex poses and image appearances. There are about $25k$ images. In total, about $29k$ annotated poses are for training and another $7k$ are for testing. For evaluation, Percentage of Correct Keypoints (PCK) metric is used. An estimated keypoint is considered correct if its distance from ground truth keypoint is less than a fraction α of the head segment length. The metric is denoted as PCKh@α. Commonly, PCKh@0.5 metric is used for the benchmark [2]. In order to evaluate under high localization accuracy, which is also the strength of regression methods, we also use PCKh@0.1 and AUC (area under curve, the averaged PCKh when α varies from 0 to 0.5) metrics.

The *COCO* Keypoint Challenge [28] requires "in the wild" multi-person detection and pose estimation in challenging, uncontrolled conditions. The COCO train, validation, and test sets, containing more than 200k images and 250k person instances labeled with keypoints. 150k instances of them are publicly available for training and validation. The COCO evaluation defines the object keypoint similarity (OKS) and uses the mean average precision (AP) over 10 OKS thresholds as main competition metric [1]. The OKS plays the same role as the IoU in object detection. It is calculated from the distance between predicted points and ground truth points normalized by the scale of the person.

5   Experiments

Training. Our training and network architecture is similar for all the three datasets. ResNet [20] and HourGlass [33] (ResNet and HourGlass on Human3.6M and MPII, ResNet-101 on COCO) are adopted as the backbone network. ResNet is pre-trained on ImageNet classification dataset [16]. HourGlass is trained from scratch. Normal distribution with 1e$-$3 standard deviation is used to initialize the HourGlass and head network parameters.

The head network for heat map is fully convolutional. It firstly use deconvolution layers (4×4 kernel, stride 2) to upsample the feature map to the required resolution (64×64 by default). The number of output channels is fixed to 256 as in [19]. Then, a 1×1 conv layer is used to produce K heat maps. Both heat map baseline and our integral regression are based on this head network.

We also implement a most widely used regression head network as a regression baseline for comparison. Following [7,42,55,56], first an average pooling layer reduces the spatial dimensionality of the convolutional features. Then, a fully connected layer outputs $3K$ ($2K$) joint coordinates. We denote our regression baseline as R1 (R for regression).

We use a simple multi-stage implementation based on ResNet-50, the features from conv3 block are shared as input to all stages. Each stage then concatenates this feature with the heat maps from the previous stage, and passes through the conv4 and conv5 blocks to generate its own deep feature. The heat map head is then appended to output heat maps, supervised with the ground truth and losses. Depending on the loss function used on the heat map, this multi-stage baseline is denoted as MS-H1(2, 3).

MxNet [9] is used for implementation. Adam is used for optimization. The input image is normalized to 256×256. Data augmentation includes random translation ($\pm 2\%$ of the image size), scale ($\pm 25\%$), rotation ($\pm 30^{circ}$) and flip. In all experiments, the base learning rate is 1e$-$3. It drops to 1e$-$5 when the loss on the validation set saturates. Each method is trained with enough number of iterations until performance on validation set saturates. Mini-batch size is 128. Four GPUs are used. Batch-normalization [23] is used. Other training details are provided in individual experiments.

For integral regression methods (I1, I2, I3, and their multi-stage versions), the network is pre-trained only using heat map loss (thus their H versions) and then, only integral loss is used. We found this training strategy working slightly better than training from scratch using both losses.

5.1 Experiments on MPII

Since the annotation on MPII test set is not available, all our ablation studies are evaluated on an about $3k$ validation set which is separated out from the training set, following previous common practice [33]. Training is performed on the remaining training data.

Table 1. Comparison between methods using heat maps, direct regression, and integral regression on MPII validation set. Backbone network is ResNet-50. The performance gain is shown in the subscript

Metric	R1	H1	H2	H3	I*	I1	I2	I3
@0.5	84.6	86.8	86.4	83.0	$86.0_{\uparrow 1.4}$	$\mathbf{87.3}_{\uparrow 0.5}$	$86.9_{\uparrow 0.5}$	$86.6_{\uparrow 3.6}$
@0.1	25.0	17.2	17.6	12.6	$28.3_{\uparrow 3.3}$	$29.3_{\uparrow 12.1}$	$\mathbf{29.7}_{\uparrow 12.1}$	$29.1_{\uparrow 16.5}$
AUC	54.1	52.9	53.1	46.3	$56.6_{\uparrow 2.5}$	$\mathbf{58.3}_{\uparrow 5.4}$	$\mathbf{58.3}_{\uparrow 5.2}$	$57.7_{\uparrow 11.4}$

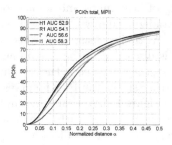

Fig. 2. Curves of PCKh@α of different methods while α varies from 0 to 0.5.

Effect of Integral Regression. Table 1 presents a comprehensive comparison. We first note that all integral regression methods (I1, I2, I3) clearly outperform their heat map based counterpart (H1, H2, H3). The improvement is especially significant on PCKh@0.1 with high localization accuracy requirement. For example, the improvement of I1 to H1 is +0.5 on PCKh@0.5, but +12.1 on PCKh@0.1. The overall improvement on AUC is significant (+5.4). Among the three heat map based methods, H3 performs the worst. After using integral regression (I3), it is greatly improved, eg., AUC from 46.3 to 57.7 (+11.4). Such results show that *joint training of heat maps and joint is effective.* The significant improvement on localization accuracy (PCKh@0.1 metric) is attributed to the joint regression representation.

Surprisingly, I* performs quite well. It is only slightly worse than I1/I2/I3 methods. It outperforms H1/H2/H3 on PCKh@0.1 and AUC, thanks to its regression representation. It outperforms R1, indicating that integral regression is better than direct regression, as both methods use exactly the same supervision and almost the same network (actually R1 has more parameters).

Ground Truth   R1   H1   I1   Ground Truth   R1   H1   I1

Fig. 3. Example results of regression baseline (R1), detection baseline (H1) and integral regression (I1).

From the above comparison, we can draw two conclusions. First, integral regression using an underlying heat map representation is effective ($I^* > H$, $I^* > R$). It works even without supervision on the heat map. Second, joint training of heat maps and joint coordinate prediction combines the benefits of two paradigms and works best ($I > H, R, I^*$).

As H3 is consistently worse than the other two and hard to implement for 3D, it is discarded in the remaining experiments. As H1 and I1 perform best in 2D pose, they are used in the remaining 2D (MPII and COCO) experiments. Figure 2 further shows the PCKh curves of H1, R1, I^* and I1 for better illustration.

Figure 3 shows some example results. Regression prediction (R1) is usually not well aligned with local image features like corners or edges. On the contrary, detection prediction (H1) is well aligned with image feature but hard to distinguish locally similar patches, getting trapped into local maximum easily. Integral regression (H1) shares the merits of both heat map representation and joint regression approaches. It effectively and consistently improves both baselines.

Effect of Resolution. Table 2 compares the results using two input image sizes and two output heat map sizes.

Not surprisingly, using large image size and heat map size obtains better accuracy, under all cases. However, integral regression (I1) is much less affected by the resolution than heat map based method (H1). It is thus a favorable choice when computational complexity is crucial and a small resolution is in demand.

For example, when heat map is downsized by half on image size 256 (a to b), 1.1 G FLOPs (relative 15%) is saved. I1 only drops 0.6 in AUC while H1 drops 4.8. This gap is more significant on image size 128 (c to d). 0.3G FLOPs (relative 17%) is saved. I1 only drops 3.5 in AUC while H1 drops 12.5.

When image is downsized by half (b to d), 4.7 G FLOPs is saved (relative 76%). I1 only drops 11.1 in AUC while H1 drops 18.8.

Thus, we conclude that *integral regression significantly alleviates the problems of quantization error or needs of large resolution in heat map based methods.*

Table 2. For two methods (H1/I1), two input image→feature map (**f**) resolutions, and two heat map sizes (using either 3 or 2 upsampling layers), the performance metric (mAP@0.5, map@0.1, AUC), the computation (in FLOPs) and the amount of network parameters. Note that setting (b) is used in all other experiments

Size	×2, ×2, ×2	×2, ×2	Size	×2, ×2, ×2	×2, ×2
256 → 8	(a) → 16 → 32 → 64	(b) → 16 → 32	128 → 4	(c) → 8 → 16 → 32	(d) → 8 → 16
H1	86.7/28.0/57.7	86.8/17.2/52.9		81.6/13.6/46.6	75.4/5.6 /34.1
I1	86.6/32.1/58.9	87.3/29.3/58.3		83.2/20.6/50.7	80.9/16.1/47.2
FLOPs	7.3G	6.2G		1.8G	1.5G
params	26M	26M		26M	26M

Effect of Network Capacity. Table 3 shows results using different backbones on two methods. While all methods are improved using a network with large capacity, integral regression I1 keeps outperforming heat map based method H1.

While a large network improves accuracy, a high complexity is also introduced. Integral regression I1 using ResNet-18 already achieves accuracy comparable with H1 using ResNet-101. This makes it a better choice when a small network is in favor, in practical scenarios.

Table 3. PCKh@0.5, PCKh@0.1 and AUC metrics (top) of three methods, and model complexity (bottom) of three backbone networks. Note that ResNet-50 is used in all other experiments

	ResNet-18	ResNet-50	ResNet-101
H1	85.5/15.7/50.8	86.8/17.2/52.9	87.3/17.3/53.3
I1	86.0/25.7/55.6	87.3/29.3/58.3	87.9/30.3/59.0
FLOPs	2.8G	6.2G	11.0G
params	12M	26M	45M

Table 4. PCKh@0.5, PCKh@0.1 and AUC metrics of a multi-stage network with and without integral regression

Stage	MS-H1	MS-I1
1	86.8/17.2/52.9	87.3/29.3/58.3
2	86.9/17.6/53.4	87.7/32.0/59.5
3	87.1/17.8/53.7	87.8/32.4/59.9
4	87.4/17.8/54.0	88.1/32.3/60.1

Effect in Multi-stage. Table 4 shows the results of our multi-stage implementation with or without using integral regression. There are two conclusions. First, integral regression can be effectively combined with a multi-stage architecture and performance improves as stage increases. Second, integral regression outperforms its heat map based counterpart on all stages. Specifically, MS-I1 stage-2 result 87.7 is already better than MS-H1 state-4 result 87.4.

Conclusions. From the above ablation studies, we can conclude that *effectiveness of integral regression is attributed to its representation.* It works under different heat map losses (H1, H2, H3), different training (joint or not), different resolution, and different network architectures (depth or multi-stage). Consistent yet even stronger conclusions can also be derived from COCO benchmark in Sect. 5.2 and 3D pose benchmarks in Sect. 5.3.

Table 5. Comparison to state-of-the-art works on MPII

Method (heat map based)	Tompson [47]	Raf [39]	Wei [49]	Bulat [5]	Newell [33]	Yang [50]	Ours		
							H1	MS-H1	HG-H1
Mean (PCKh@0.5)	82.0	86.3	88.5	89.7	90.9	92.0	89.4	89.8	90.4
Method (regression)	Carreira [7]		Sun [42]		R1 (Ours)		I1	MS-I1	HG-I1
Mean (PCKh@0.5)	81.3		86.4		87.0		90.0	90.7	91.0

Result on the MPII Test Benchmark. Table 5 summarizes the results of our methods, as well as state-of-the-art methods. In these experiments, our training is performed on all 29k training samples. We also adopt the flip test trick as used in [33]. Increasing the training data and using flip test would increase about 2.5 mAP@0.5 from validation dataset to test dataset.

We first note that our baselines have good performance, indicating they are valid and strong baselines. H1 and MS-H1 in the heat map based section has 89.4 and 89.8 PCKh, respectively, already comparable to many multi-stage methods that are usually much more complex. R1 in regression section is already the best performing regression method.

Our integral regression further improves both baselines (I1>H1, MS-I1>MS-H1, 4 stages used) and achieves results competitive with other methods. We also re-implement the HourGlass architecture [33], denoted as HG-H1. Consistent improvement is observed using integral regression HG-I1. While the accuracy of our approach is slightly below the state-of-the-art, we point out that the recent leading approaches [10,12,13,50] are all quite complex, making direct and fair comparison with these works difficult. Integral regression is simple, effective and can be combined with most other heat map based approaches, as validated in our baseline multi-stage and the HourGlass experiments. Combination with these approaches is left as future work.

Table 6. COCO **test-dev** results

	Backbone	AP^{kp}	AP^{kp}_{50}	AP^{kp}_{75}	AP^{kp}_{M}	AP^{kp}_{L}
CMU-Pose [6]		61.8	84.9	67.5	57.1	68.2
Mask R-CNN [19]	ResNet-50-FPN	63.1	87.3	68.7	57.8	71.4
G-RMI [36]	ResNet-101(353×257)	64.9	85.5	71.3	62.3	70.0
Ours: H1	ResNet-101(256×256)	66.3	**88.4**	74.6	62.9	72.1
Ours: I1	ResNet-101(256×256)	**67.8**	88.2	**74.8**	**63.9**	**74.0**

5.2   Experiments on COCO

Person Box Detection. We follow a two-stage top-down paradigm similar as in [36]. For human detection, we use Faster-RCNN [40] equipped with deformable convolution [15]. We uses Xception [11] as the backbone network. The box detection AP on COCO test-dev is 0.49. For reference, this number in [36] is 0.487. Thus, the person detection performance is similar.

Following [36], we use the keypoint-based Non-Maximum-Suppression (NMS) mechanism building directly on the OKS metric to avoid duplicate pose detections. We also use the pose rescoring technique [36] to compute a refined instance confidence estimation that takes the keypoint heat map score into account.

Pose Estimation. We experimented with heat map based method (H1) and our integral regression methods (I1). All settings are the same as experiments on MPII, except that we use ResNet-101 as our backbone and use 3 deconvolution layers (4×4 kernel, stride 2) to upsample the feature maps.

Results. Table 6 summarizes the results of our methods, as well as state-of-the-art on COCO test-dev dataset. Our experiments are performed on COCO training data, no extra data is added. The baseline model (H1) is a one-stage ResNet-101 architecture. Our baseline model H1 is already superior to the state of the art top-down method [36]. Our integral regression further increases AP^{kp} by 1.5 points and achieves the state-of-the-art result.

5.3   Experiments on Human3.6M

In the literature, there are two widely used evaluation protocols. They have different training and testing data split.

Protocol 1. Six subjects (S1, S5, S6, S7, S8, S9) are used in training. Evaluation is performed on every 64th frame of Subject 11. *PA MPJPE* is used for evaluation.

Protocol 2. Five subjects (S1, S5, S6, S7, S8) are used in training. Evaluation is performed on every 64th frame of subjects (S9, S11). *MPJPE* is used for evaluation.

Two training strategies are used on whether use extra 2D data or not. *Strategy 1* only use Human3.6M data for training. For integral regression, we use Eq. (4). *Strategy 2* mix Human3.6M and MPII data for training, each mini-batch consists of half 2D and half 3D samples, randomly sampled and shuffled. In this strategy, we use the two-step integral function Eqs. (5) and (6) so that we can add 2D data on both heat map and joint losses for training as explained in Sect. 2.1.

Effect of Integral Regression. Table 7 compares the integral regression (I*,I1,I2) with corresponding baselines (R1, H1,H2) under two training strategies. Protocol 2 is used. Backbone is ResNet50. We observe several conclusions.

First, integral regression significantly improves the baselines in both training strategies. Specifically, without using extra 2D data, the integral regression (I*, I1, I2) improves (R1, H1, H2) by 6.0%, 13.2%, 17.7% respectively. I2 outperforms

Table 7. Comparison between methods using heat maps, direct regression, and integral regression. Protocol 2 is used. Two training strategies are investigated. Backbone network is ResNet-50. The relative performance gain is shown in the subscript

Training data strategy	R1	H1	H2	I*	I1	I2
Strategy 1	106.6	99.5	80.4	$100.2_{\downarrow 6.0\%}$	$86.4_{\downarrow 13.2\%}$	$\mathbf{66.2}_{\downarrow 17.7\%}$
Strategy 2	56.2	63.6	59.3	$\mathbf{49.6}_{\downarrow 11.7\%}$	$52.7_{\downarrow 17.1\%}$	$52.4_{\downarrow 11.6\%}$

Table 8. Comparison with Coarse-to-Fine Volumetric Prediction [37] trained only on Human3.6M. Protocol 2 is used. Evaluation metric is MPJPE. d_i denotes the z-dimension resolution for the supervision provided at the i-th hourglass component. Our I1 wins at both stages

Network architecture (HourGlass [33])	Coarse-to-fine. [37]	Ours H1	Ours I1
One stage ($d = 64$)	85.8	85.5	**78.7**
Two stage ($d_1 = 1, d_2 = 64$)	69.8	68.0	**64.1**

all previous works in this setting. When using extra 2D data, the baselines have already achieved very competitive results. Integral regression further improves them by 11.7%, 17.1%, 11.6%, respectively. I* achieves the new state-of-the-art in this setting and outperforms previous works by large margins, see Table 10(B). Second, all methods are significantly improved after using MPII data. This is feasible because of integral formulation Eqs. (5) and (6) generates x, y, z predictions individually and keep differentiable.

Effect of Backbone Network. [37] is the only previous work using 3D heat map representation. They use a different backbone network, multi-stage Hour-Glass. In Table 8, we follow exactly the same practice as in [37] for a fair comparison using this backbone network. Only Human3.6M data is used for training and Protocol 2 is used for evaluation.

We have several observations. First, our baseline implementation H1 is strong enough that is already better than [37] at both stages. Therefore, it serves as a competitive reference. Second, our integral regression I1 further improves H1 at both stages by 6.8 mm (relative 8.0%) at stage 1 and 3.9 mm (relative 5.7%) at stage 2. We can conclude that the integral regression also works effectively with HourGlass and multi-stage backbone on the 3D pose problem and our two-stage I1 sets the new state-of-the-art in this setting, see Table 11.

Effect of Resolution. Table 9 investigates the effect of input image and heat map resolution on 3D problem. We can also have similar conclusions as in Table 2. Integral regression (I2) is much less affected by the resolution than heat map based method (H2). It is thus a favorable choice when computational complexity is crucial and a small resolution is in demand.

Table 9. For two methods (H2/I2), two input image → feature map (**f**) resolutions, and two heat map sizes (using either 3 or 2 upsampling layers). Strategy 2 and Protocol 2 are used. Backbone network is ResNet-50

Size	×2, ×2, ×2	×2, ×2	Size	×2, ×2, ×2	×2, ×2
256 → 8	(a) → 16 → 32 → 64	(b) → 16 → 32	128 → 4	(c) → 8 → 16 → 32	(d) → 8 → 16
H2	59.3	61.5		66.6	86.4
I2	52.4	51.7		57.1	60.9

Table 10. Comparison with previous work on Human3.6M. All methods used extra 2D training data. Ours use MPII data in the training. Methods in Group A and B use Protocol 1 and 2, respectively. Ours is the best single-image method under both scenarios. Methods with * exploit temporal information and are complementary to ours. We even outperform them in Protocol 2

Method (A, Pro. 1)	Hossain [21]*	Dabral [14]*	Yasin [51]	Rogez [41]	Chen [8]	Moreno [32]	Zhou [54]	Martinez [30]	Kanazawa [26]	Sun [42]	Fang [17]	Ours
PA MPJPE	42.0	36.3	108.3	88.1	82.7	76.5	55.3	47.7	56.8	48.3	45.7	**40.6**

Method (B, Pro. 2)	Hossain [21]*	Dabral [14]*	Chen [8]	Tome [46]	Moreno [32]	Zhou [54]	Jahangiri [25]	Mehta [31]	Martinez [30]	Kanazawa [26]	Fang [17]	Sun [42]	Ours
MPJPE	51.9	52.1	114.2	88.4	87.3	79.9	77.6	72.9	62.9	88.0	60.4	59.1	**49.6**

Table 11. Comparison with previous work on Human3.6M. Protocol 2 is used. No extra training data is used. Ours is the best

Method	Zhou [53]	Tekin [44]	Xingyi [56]	Sun [42]	Pavlakos [37]	Ours
MPJPE	113.0	125.0	107.3	92.4	71.9	**64.1**

For example, when heat map is downsized by half on image size 256 (a to b). I2 even gets slightly better while H2 drops 2.2 mm on MPJPE. This gap is more significant on image size 128 (c to d). I2 only drops 3.8 mm in MPJPE while H2 drops 19.8 mm. When image is downsized by half (b to d). I2 only drops in 9.2 mm on MPJPE while H2 drops 24.9 mm.

Consistent yet even stronger conclusions are derived on 3D task, compared with Table 2 on 2D task.

Comparison with the State of the Art. Previous works are abundant with different experiment settings and fall into three categories. They are compared to our method in Table 10(A), (B) and Table 11 respectively.

Our approach is the best single-image method that outperforms previous works by large margins. Specifically, it improves the state-of-the-art, by 5.1 mm (relative 11.2%) in Table 10(A), 9.5 mm (relative 16.1%) in Table 10(B), and

7.8 mm (relative 10.8%) in Table 11. Note that Dabral et al. [14] and Hossain et al. [21] exploit temporal information and are complementary to our approach. Nevertheless, ours is already very close to them in Table 10(A) and even better in Table 10(B).

6 Conclusions

We present a simple and effective integral regression approach that unifies the heat map representation and joint regression approaches, thus sharing the merits of both. Solid experiment results validate the efficacy of the approach. Strong performance is obtained using simple and cheap baseline networks, making our approach a favorable choice in practical scenarios. We apply the integral regression on both 3D and 2D human pose estimation tasks and push the very state-of-the-art on MPII, COCO and Human3.6M benchmarks.

References

1. COCO Leader Board. http://cocodataset.org
2. MPII Leader Board. http://human-pose.mpi-inf.mpg.de
3. Andriluka, M., Pishchulin, L., Gehler, P., Schiele, B.: 2D human pose estimation: new benchmark and state of the art analysis. In: Proceedings of the IEEE Conference on computer Vision and Pattern Recognition, pp. 3686–3693 (2014)
4. Bogo, F., Kanazawa, A., Lassner, C., Gehler, P., Romero, J., Black, M.J.: Keep it SMPL: automatic estimation of 3D human pose and shape from a single image. In: Leibe, B., Matas, J., Sebe, N., Welling, M. (eds.) ECCV 2016. LNCS, vol. 9909, pp. 561–578. Springer, Cham (2016). https://doi.org/10.1007/978-3-319-46454-1_34
5. Bulat, A., Tzimiropoulos, G.: Human pose estimation via convolutional part heatmap regression. In: Leibe, B., Matas, J., Sebe, N., Welling, M. (eds.) ECCV 2016. LNCS, vol. 9911, pp. 717–732. Springer, Cham (2016). https://doi.org/10.1007/978-3-319-46478-7_44
6. Cao, Z., Simon, T., Wei, S.E., Sheikh, Y.: Realtime multi-person 2D pose estimation using part affinity fields. arXiv preprint arXiv:1611.08050 (2016)
7. Carreira, J., Agrawal, P., Fragkiadaki, K., Malik, J.: Human pose estimation with iterative error feedback. In: Proceedings of the IEEE Conference on Computer Vision and Pattern Recognition, pp. 4733–4742 (2016)
8. Chen, C.H., Ramanan, D.: 3D human pose estimation = 2D pose estimation + matching. arXiv preprint arXiv:1612.06524 (2016)
9. Chen, T., et al.: MxNet: a flexible and efficient machine learning library for heterogeneous distributed systems. arXiv preprint arXiv:1512.01274 (2015)
10. Chen, Y., Shen, C., Wei, X.S., Liu, L., Yang, J.: Adversarial PoseNet: a structure-aware convolutional network for human pose estimation. arXiv preprint arXiv:1705.00389 (2017)
11. Chollet, F.: Xception: deep learning with depthwise separable convolutions. arXiv preprint arXiv:1610.02357 (2016)
12. Chou, C.J., Chien, J.T., Chen, H.T.: Self adversarial training for human pose estimation. arXiv preprint arXiv:1707.02439 (2017)
13. Chu, X., Yang, W., Ouyang, W., Ma, C., Yuille, A.L., Wang, X.: Multi-context attention for human pose estimation. arXiv preprint arXiv:1702.07432 (2017)

14. Dabral, R., Mundhada, A., Kusupati, U., Afaque, S., Jain, A.: Structure-aware and temporally coherent 3D human pose estimation. arXiv preprint arXiv:1711.09250 (2017)
15. Dai, J., et al.: Deformable convolutional networks. arXiv preprint arXiv:1703.06211 (2017)
16. Deng, J., Dong, W., Socher, R., Li, L.J., Li, K., Fei-Fei, L.: ImageNet: a large-scale hierarchical image database. In: IEEE Conference on Computer Vision and Pattern Recognition, CVPR 2009, pp. 248–255. IEEE (2009)
17. Fang, H.S., Xu, Y., Wang, W., Liu, X., Zhu, S.C.: Learning pose grammar to encode human body configuration for 3D pose estimation. In: AAAI (2018)
18. Gower, J.C.: Generalized procrustes analysis. Psychometrika 40(1), 33–51 (1975)
19. He, K., Gkioxari, G., Dollar, P., Girshick, R.: Mask R-CNN. In: International Conference on Computer Vision (2017)
20. He, K., Zhang, X., Ren, S., Sun, J.: Deep residual learning for image recognition. In: Proceedings of the IEEE Conference on Computer Vision and Pattern Recognition, pp. 770–778 (2016)
21. Hossain, M.R.I., Little, J.J.: Exploiting temporal information for 3D pose estimation. arXiv preprint arXiv:1711.08585 (2017)
22. Insafutdinov, E., Pishchulin, L., Andres, B., Andriluka, M., Schiele, B.: DeeperCut: a deeper, stronger, and faster multi-person pose estimation model. In: European Conference on Computer Vision. pp. 34–50. Springer (2016)
23. Ioffe, S., Szegedy, C.: Batch normalization: accelerating deep network training by reducing internal covariate shift. arXiv preprint arXiv:1502.03167 (2015)
24. Ionescu, C., Papava, D., Olaru, V., Sminchisescu, C.: Human3. 6m: large scale datasets and predictive methods for 3D human sensing in natural environments. IEEE Trans. Pattern Anal. Mach. Intell. 36(7), 1325–1339 (2014)
25. Jahangiri, E., Yuille, A.L.: Generating multiple hypotheses for human 3D pose consistent with 2D joint detections. arXiv preprint arXiv:1702.02258 (2017)
26. Kanazawa, A., Black, M.J., Jacobs, D.W., Malik, J.: End-to-end recovery of human shape and pose. arXiv preprint arXiv:1712.06584 (2017)
27. Levine, S., Finn, C., Darrell, T., Abbeel, P.: End-to-end training of deep visuomotor policies. J. Mach. Learn. Res. 17(1), 1334–1373 (2016)
28. Lin, T.-Y., et al.: Microsoft COCO: common objects in context. In: Fleet, D., Pajdla, T., Schiele, B., Tuytelaars, T. (eds.) ECCV 2014. LNCS, vol. 8693, pp. 740–755. Springer, Cham (2014). https://doi.org/10.1007/978-3-319-10602-1_48
29. Luvizon, D.C., Tabia, H., Picard, D.: Human pose regression by combining indirect part detection and contextual information. arXiv preprint arXiv:1710.02322 (2017)
30. Martinez, J., Hossain, R., Romero, J., Little, J.J.: A simple yet effective baseline for 3D human pose estimation. arXiv preprint arXiv:1705.03098 (2017)
31. Mehta, D., Rhodin, H., Casas, D., Sotnychenko, O., Xu, W., Theobalt, C.: Monocular 3D human pose estimation in the wild using improved CNN supervision. arXiv preprint arXiv:1611.09813 (2016)
32. Moreno-Noguer, F.: 3D human pose estimation from a single image via distance matrix regression. arXiv preprint arXiv:1611.09010 (2016)
33. Newell, A., Yang, K., Deng, J.: Stacked hourglass networks for human pose estimation. In: Leibe, B., Matas, J., Sebe, N., Welling, M. (eds.) ECCV 2016. LNCS, vol. 9912, pp. 483–499. Springer, Cham (2016). https://doi.org/10.1007/978-3-319-46484-8_29
34. Nibali, A., He, Z., Morgan, S., Prendergast, L.: Numerical coordinate regression with convolutional neural networks. arXiv preprint arXiv:1801.07372 (2018)

35. Nie, B.X., Wei, P., Zhu, S.C.: Monocular 3D human pose estimation by predicting depth on joints. In: Proceedings of IEEE International Conference on Computer Vision, pp. 3447–3455 (2017)
36. Papandreou, G., et al.: Towards accurate multi-person pose estimation in the wild. arXiv preprint arXiv:1701.01779 (2017)
37. Pavlakos, G., Zhou, X., Derpanis, K.G., Daniilidis, K.: Coarse-to-fine volumetric prediction for single-image 3D human pose. arXiv preprint arXiv:1611.07828 (2016)
38. Pishchulin, L., et al.: DeepCut: joint subset partition and labeling for multi person pose estimation. In: Proceedings of the IEEE Conference on Computer Vision and Pattern Recognition, pp. 4929–4937 (2016)
39. Rafi, U., Kostrikov, I., Gall, J., Leibe, B.: An efficient convolutional network for human pose estimation. In: BMVC, vol. 1, p. 2 (2016)
40. Ren, S., He, K., Girshick, R., Sun, J.: Faster R-CNN: towards real-time object detection with region proposal networks. In: Advances in Neural Information Processing Systems, pp. 91–99 (2015)
41. Rogez, G., Schmid, C.: MoCap-guided data augmentation for 3D pose estimation in the wild. In: Advances in Neural Information Processing Systems, pp. 3108–3116 (2016)
42. Sun, X., Shang, J., Liang, S., Wei, Y.: Compositional human pose regression. In: International Conference on Computer Vision (2017)
43. Tekin, B., Marquez Neila, P., Salzmann, M., Fua, P.: Learning to fuse 2D and 3D image cues for monocular body pose estimation. In: International Conference on Computer Vision (ICCV). No. EPFL-CONF-230311 (2017)
44. Tekin, B., Rozantsev, A., Lepetit, V., Fua, P.: Direct prediction of 3D body poses from motion compensated sequences. In: Proceedings of the IEEE Conference on Computer Vision and Pattern Recognition, pp. 991–1000 (2016)
45. Thewlis, J., Bilen, H., Vedaldi, A.: Unsupervised learning of object landmarks by factorized spatial embeddings. In: Proceedings of ICCV (2017)
46. Tome, D., Russell, C., Agapito, L.: Lifting from the deep: convolutional 3D pose estimation from a single image. arXiv preprint arXiv:1701.00295 (2017)
47. Tompson, J., Goroshin, R., Jain, A., LeCun, Y., Bregler, C.: Efficient object localization using convolutional networks. In: Proceedings of the IEEE Conference on Computer Vision and Pattern Recognition, pp. 648–656 (2015)
48. Tompson, J.J., Jain, A., LeCun, Y., Bregler, C.: Joint training of a convolutional network and a graphical model for human pose estimation. In: Advances in Neural Information Processing Systems, pp. 1799–1807 (2014)
49. Wei, S.E., Ramakrishna, V., Kanade, T., Sheikh, Y.: Convolutional pose machines. In: Proceedings of the IEEE Conference on Computer Vision and Pattern Recognition, pp. 4724–4732 (2016)
50. Yang, W., Li, S., Ouyang, W., Li, H., Wang, X.: Learning feature pyramids for human pose estimation. In: The IEEE International Conference on Computer Vision (ICCV), vol. 2 (2017)
51. Yasin, H., Iqbal, U., Kruger, B., Weber, A., Gall, J.: A dual-source approach for 3D pose estimation from a single image. In: Proceedings of the IEEE Conference on Computer Vision and Pattern Recognition, pp. 4948–4956 (2016)
52. Yi, K.M., Trulls, E., Lepetit, V., Fua, P.: LIFT: learned invariant feature transform. In: Leibe, B., Matas, J., Sebe, N., Welling, M. (eds.) ECCV 2016. LNCS, vol. 9910, pp. 467–483. Springer, Cham (2016). https://doi.org/10.1007/978-3-319-46466-4_28

53. Zhou, X., Zhu, M., Leonardos, S., Derpanis, K.G., Daniilidis, K.: Sparseness meets deepness: 3D human pose estimation from monocular video. In: Proceedings of the IEEE Conference on Computer Vision and Pattern Recognition, pp. 4966–4975 (2016)
54. Zhou, X., Zhu, M., Pavlakos, G., Leonardos, S., Derpanis, K.G., Daniilidis, K.: MonoCap: monocular human motion capture using a cnn coupled with a geometric prior. arXiv preprint arXiv:1701.02354 (2017)
55. Zhou, X., Huang, Q., Sun, X., Xue, X., Wei, Y.: Towards 3D human pose estimation in the wild: a weakly-supervised approach. In: International Conference on Computer Vision (2017)
56. Zhou, X., Sun, X., Zhang, W., Liang, S., Wei, Y.: Deep kinematic pose regression. In: Hua, G., Jégou, H. (eds.) ECCV 2016. LNCS, vol. 9915, pp. 186–201. Springer, Cham (2016). https://doi.org/10.1007/978-3-319-49409-8_17

Quadtree Convolutional Neural Networks

Pradeep Kumar Jayaraman$^{(\boxtimes)}$, Jianhan Mei, Jianfei Cai, and Jianmin Zheng

Nanyang Technological University, Singapore, Singapore
{pradeepkj,ASJFCai,ASJMZheng}@ntu.edu.sg, jianhan001@e.ntu.edu.sg

Abstract. This paper presents a Quadtree Convolutional Neural Network (QCNN) for efficiently learning from image datasets representing sparse data such as handwriting, pen strokes, freehand sketches, etc. Instead of storing the sparse sketches in regular dense tensors, our method decomposes and represents the image as a linear quadtree that is only refined in the non-empty portions of the image. The actual image data corresponding to non-zero pixels is stored in the finest nodes of the quadtree. Convolution and pooling operations are restricted to the sparse pixels, leading to better efficiency in computation time as well as memory usage. Specifically, the computational and memory costs in QCNN grow linearly in the number of non-zero pixels, as opposed to traditional CNNs where the costs are quadratic in the number of pixels. This enables QCNN to learn from sparse images much faster and process high resolution images without the memory constraints faced by traditional CNNs. We study QCNN on four sparse image datasets for sketch classification and simplification tasks. The results show that QCNN can obtain comparable accuracy with large reduction in computational and memory costs.

Keywords: Quadtree · Neural network · Sparse convolution

1 Introduction

Convolutional neural networks (CNNs) are a powerful and popular method for various tasks involving the analysis of images, videos and three-dimensional objects. Most of the real world image data such as natural photographs or volumetric meshes can be represented as dense tensors, and indeed, conventional CNNs were originally proposed to optimally learn features from such data by local weight connections and parameter sharing. On the other hand, it is observed that some datasets are sparse in nature. For example, images representing freeform 2D sketches and handwriting only consist of a set of one-dimensional lines occupying a sparse subset of the 2D image plane, while point clouds or triangle meshes are only defined in a small subset of the 3D space. Unfortunately, most of the traditional CNN architectures, particularly for images, are unable to exploit the sparsity of such data, and learning from such datasets is unnecessarily inefficient in both training time and memory consumption. This is particularly of concern with the rise of deep networks that are being increasingly employed to various high resolution sparse images in applications such as sketch simplification [1], as well as to resource-scarce mobile or embedded devices.

© Springer Nature Switzerland AG 2018
V. Ferrari et al. (Eds.): ECCV 2018, LNCS 11210, pp. 554–569, 2018.
https://doi.org/10.1007/978-3-030-01231-1_34

In the case of 3D data, convolutional neural networks were originally designed by voxelizing the mesh into dense 3D tensors [2]. Due to memory and computational constraints, however, this approach does not scale to high resolutions. To alleviate this, recent works such as OctNets [3], O-CNN [4], and OGN [5] decompose the 3D meshes hierarchically into octrees and adapt CNN operations to consider the special octree structure.

Inspired by such 3D works, we present in this paper a quadtree convolutional neural network (QCNN) for efficiently learning from sparse 2D image datasets. While those 3D networks were designed to deal with 3D shapes represented by meshes or point clouds, we target general sparse images which usually have more arbitrary structure or topology. This will enable the developed method to have wide applications, especially on mobile devices where the computing power and memory are limited. Our main idea is to decompose sparse images into quadtrees, store the non-zero image pixels in the finest nodes, and design special data representation that takes the features of CPU and GPU into consideration. The computation effort will be concentrated on the areas of interest, which avoids the storage of empty pixels that do not provide meaningful information and thus reduces the memory consumption. We start with the finest level of the quadtree and perform convolutions on these nodes to compute the features, followed by pooling which downsamples the features and propagates them to the next coarser quadtree level. This operation can be stacked multiple times before finally obtaining the network output with respect to some predefined target and loss function.

Our approach has several advantages in terms of efficiency. First, since we only store non-zero pixels of the image in the bottom most level of the sparse quadtree, the storage and computational requirements are linear in the number of non-zero pixels and completely independent of image resolution. Second, it is well known that modern CPUs and GPUs are highly efficient in processing data that are contiguous in memory. Hence we use a linear quadtree representation where each level of the quadtree is stored as a linear 1D array by indexing the quadtree nodes with space-filling z-order curves. Third, we adapt CNN operations in the quadtree by considering the special data representation. Convolution that requires neighborhood access for each quadtree node in the same depth is achieved via an efficient look-up table based scheme using the Moser-de Bruijn sequence, and pooling is as simple as assigning the maximum/average of every four children nodes to their parent nodes. We demonstrate the efficiency of QCNN in terms of computational effort on several sparse image datasets for classification and sketch simplification.

2   Related Work

2.1   Hierarchical Data Representation

The quadtree [6] and octree [7] are hierarchical representations of 2D and 3D spatial data, respectively, and generalizations of the binary tree. They have been extensively used in various graphics and image processing applications such as collision detection, ray tracing, and level-of-details [8–10]. It is common to implement quadtrees and octrees using pointers. However, for representing data hierarchically for CNN training purposes, this is infeasible since CPUs and GPUs are efficient in processing contiguous array data. Linear quadtrees or octrees [11], where 2D/3D node indices in each level of the tree are converted to 1D indices using space-filling curves, are more relevant to our application.

2.2 Sparse Convolutional Neural Networks

Using sparsity can result in higher resolution inputs to be processed efficiently. However, there are only a few network architectures that exploit sparsity. Initially, CNNs were employed to process 3D data by voxelizing the meshes into 3D dense volumetric tensors [2]. Since this representation has a high computation and memory cost, the input resolution had to be restricted to around 30^3. Graham proposed a sparse version of the CNN for 2D image [12] and 3D voxel [13] data that only performs convolutions on non-zero sites and their neighbors within the receptive field of the kernel. Nevertheless, the approach becomes inefficient when a large number of convolution layers are placed in between the pooling layers since the feature map dilates after each convolution. The feature dilation problem was recently handled by Graham and Maaten [14] by restricting convolutions only on the non-zero sites. Their works require additional book-keeping for indexing the non-zero pixels for each layer's output, as well as efficient hash table implementations.

Quadtree/octree structures on the other hand can be computed in one shot and clearly define the structure of the data beforehand, independently of the convolution or pooling parameters in the network. Additionally, they can be linearly represented as a simple contiguous array, thanks to their regular structure. Moreover, simply conforming the feature maps to the quadtree/octree structure is sufficient to significantly prevent feature dilation. To support high resolution 3D data, Riegler et al. [3] combined octree and a grid structure, and limited CNN operations to the interior volume of 3D shapes. While this is efficient compared to using dense voxels, storing the interior volume of 3D surface data is still wasteful. Wang et al. [4] only considered the surface voxels of the 3D data in the octree representation and drastically improved memory and computational costs in performing CNN operations. Similar to octrees, our work introduces the quadtree structure for efficiently learning from sparse image data.

3   Quadtree Convolution Neural Network

3.1   Motivation

Consider a general scenario where a dense n-dimensional tensor used to represent some input that is to be fed into a convolutional neural network. This tensor could represent grayscale images ($n = 2$), color images ($n = 3$), voxels from 3D points clouds or surfaces ($n = 3$), etc. Sparsity arises in an n-dimensional tensor whenever it is used to represent a lower-dimensional ($<$n) manifold. Examples include a set of freehand pen strokes that are 1-manifolds in 2D grayscale images and triangle meshes that are 2-manifolds stored in 3D volumes. Even if the object of interest only occupies a small portion of the space it resides in, the storage costs of a representing such objects with a dense tensor grows in the order of n with increasing resolution, as does the computational cost of applying convolutions to extract feature maps. For example, in this paper where we mainly consider sparse grayscale image data ($n = 2$), an $N \times N$ image requires a storage cost of N^2, and convolving $M \times M$ kernels to compute C feature maps requires $M^2 N^2 C$ multiply-accumulate (MACC) operations (assuming unit stride), both of which are of quadratic complexity in the total number of pixels.

By representing the image as a quadtree which is only subdivided when non-zero pixels exist in a quadrant, the non-zero pixels (without the loss of generality) in the input image correspond to the nodes in the finest quadtree level. Hence, the storage requirement of the image data is roughly N_{nz} denoting the number of non-zero pixels (where $N_{nz} \ll N^2$). If we restrict the convolutions to these non-zero pixels, then we need $M^2 N_{nz} C$ MACC operations. This process is of linear complexity in the number of pixels stored in the quadtree level and independent of the image resolution N.

There are several advantages of using a quadtree to hierarchically represent the image data for convolutional neural networks. First, the quadtree can be efficiently computed once for each image, and its structure then remains fixed throughout the forward and backward passes and requires no further bookkeeping. Its structure defines the locations of the non-zero pixels hierarchically and the nodes that are non-empty in each level. Convolutions are performed on the pixels that correspond to the nodes in the bottommost level of the quadtree, resulting in feature maps that fit in the same level. By simply restricting computations to the sparse quadtree nodes, we can ensure that feature maps do not dilate in the deeper layers of the network even when repeated convolution layers are stacked, hence retaining the sparse nature of the input. Second, since the quadtree structure is by definition hierarchical, downsampling and upsampling features can be performed easily and efficiently. Pooling downsamples the feature map such that it can be stored in the previous level of the quadtree, and is carried out by assigning the maximum or average of the children nodes at the current level into their parent node in the previous coarser level. Upsampling can be performed similarly by traversing the quadtree in the opposite direction.

3.2   Representing Images as Linear Quadtrees

We use a linear quadtree to decompose the input image, where nodes at each level are stored in a contiguous array for convenient and efficient processing in both CPU and GPU, as opposed to a pointer based quadtree. An image of dimension $2^\ell \times 2^\ell$ can be decomposed into an ℓ-level quadtree. Each of the nodes at level $l \in [1, \ldots, \ell]$ can be represented as a list of 1D indices. A common strategy to linearize indices is the interleaved bit representation. For example, given a 2D index, say ($x = 4, y = 5$) of a quadtree node from level 3, which is ($100_2, 101_2$) in binary, the linear quadtree index is given by interleaving each of the binary digits corresponding to y and x alternatively, yielding $110010_2 = 50$. This linearization has two advantages: First, it is locality preserving as opposed to row-column indexing and ensures higher cache hits when looking up neighbors during CNN operations since they are mapped to nearby locations in 1D. Second, this indexing maps every four quadtree nodes sequentially in 1D memory, which leads to easy and efficient implementations of downsampling/upsampling operations.

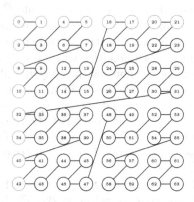

Fig. 1. Z-order indexing: 2D quadtree nodes (level $l = 3$ in this example) are linearized into a 1D array using Z-order curves as shown by the index values in circles. The 1D indices along the topmost row (colored red) are a Moser-de Bruijn sequence $(0, 4^0, 4^1, 4^0 + 4^1, \ldots)$, and those along the leftmost column are simply the same sequence scaled by 2. (Color figure online)

Note that the interleaved coordinate representation is a space filling z-order curve of order l which maps 2D coordinates to 1D indices. One can observe from the z-order curves that their path follows a regular sequence. The top row highlighted in red in Fig. 1, is a Moser-de Bruijn sequence in which each number is a sum of unique powers of 4. The left column is the same sequence scaled by 2. We generate a 1D lookup table for the sequence in the top row $t : \mathbb{Z}_{\geq} \to \mathbb{Z}_{\geq}$ defined as: $t(0) = 0$, and $t(i) = (t(i-1) + 0\text{xaaaaaaab})$ & $0\text{x}55555555$, assuming that the quadtree node indices are represented with 32-bit unsigned integers. From this, the z-order index can be obtained as $z(x, y) = t(x) | (t(y) <<1)$, where $|$ and $<<$ are the bitwise or and left shift operators, respectively. For example, $z(4, 2) = t(4) | (t(2) <<1) = 16 | (4 <<1) = 24$. This lookup table is always generated of size 2^ℓ, which denotes the width or height of the quadtree in the maximum depth, and reused for all the computations including those in the coarser levels.

3.3   Quadtree CNN Operations

Data Structure. To facilitate CNN operations such as convolution and pooling on the quadtree, we employ a custom data structure that is different from

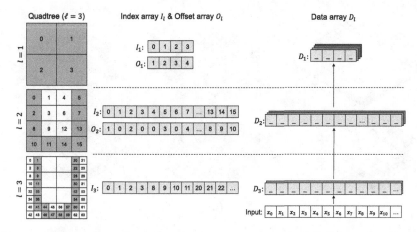

Fig. 2. Data structure for representing the image as a linear quadtree to support CNN operations. Left: quadtree generated for a U-shape image (numbers represent z-order indices), where gray nodes contain non-zero pixels in their bounds, while white nodes contain only zero pixels. Gray nodes are subdivided in the next level. Middle: Index array contains the corresponding z-order indices; offset array contains a monotonic sequence starting from 1 for gray nodes, white nodes are set to 0. Right: Data array holding the feature maps in each quadtree level.

commonly employed tensors in convolutional neural networks. This is necessary since unlike traditional grayscale images which store pixel data in a single 2D array, the linear quadtree stores quadtree node indices with non-zero pixels as a hierarchy of 1D arrays, and the pixel values themselves as a single 1D array corresponding to the deepest quadtree level. Moreover, since we only subdivide the non-empty quadtree nodes, we store an additional array, similar to O-CNN [4], to record the parent-child relationship (see Fig. 2):

Index array I: stores the z-order indices of all the nodes in the quadtree level-wise. We denote by $I_l[i]$ the index of a node i at level l. It is mainly used to lookup the indices of non-zero pixels and restrict convolutions on these nodes to extract features efficiently.

Offset array O: stores a monotonic sequence of integers starting from 1 to mark nodes that are to be subdivided (i.e., gray nodes in Fig. 2). If a node i is not subdivided (white nodes in Fig. 2), then its corresponding value is set to 0. The offset array is of same size as the index array, i.e., one value for each node, and we denote by $O_l[i]$ the offset of a node i at level l. We use O_l for pooling features from children nodes at level $l + 1$ to parent nodes at level l and upsampling features from parent nodes at level l to children nodes at level $l + 1$. For example, $O_2[5] = 3$ means that the 3rd set of quadruples (nodes 20–23 in I_3) in level 3, are the children of node 5 in I_2 in level 2. The index and offset arrays are generated once from the input image, and remain fixed afterwards throughout training/testing.

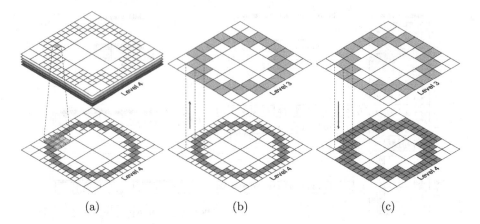

(a)   (b)   (c)

Fig. 3. Illustration of CNN operations on quadtrees. (a) Convolutions are restricted on the sparse quadtree nodes, and produce feature maps that fit in the same quadtree level. (b) Pooling downsamples the feature maps such that it fits in the previous quadtree level. (c) Upsampling resizes the feature map such that it fits in the next quadtree level.

Data array D: contains the feature maps at each level of the quadtree and is initially only available for the deepest quadtree level ℓ after performing convolution. It contains the values corresponding to the nodes indexed by I_ℓ in an array of dimensions $d \times e$ where d in the number of channels, and e is the number of stored quadtree nodes. The data array corresponding to other quadtree levels are eventually generated by the pooling operation which downsamples the feature maps.

Minibatch Representation. When using dense tensors, minibatches are created by concatenating a set of images along one of the axes; this operation requires all axes in the tensor which are smaller than the minibatch axis to agree in dimensions. Since quadtree structures vary among different images, we update the index arrays I_l of each of the B quadtrees in a minibatch by adding $4^l b$, where $b \in [0 .. B - 1]$. We then concatenate them together level-wise to form a single larger quadtree representing the entire batch. From this, individual quadtrees can be identified by computing $b = \lfloor (I_l[i] / 4^l) \rfloor$, while the local indices are given by $(I_l[i] \bmod 4^l)$. Similarly, the offset arrays O_l of each quadtree are updated to form a monotonic sequence throughout the batch and concatenated level-wise.

Having defined the data structure, we now discuss the adaptation of various CNN operations from images to quadtrees.

Convolution. The convolution is the most important and expensive operation in convolutional neural networks. We implement convolutions on the quadtree as a single matrix multiplication [15] which can be carried out by highly optimized matrix multiplication libraries on the CPU and GPU. The coefficients of the filters are arranged row-wise in a $c \times df^2$ matrix, and the pixels in the receptive field around each of the e quadtree nodes $D_l^{\text{in}}[\cdot, \cdot]$ in each input channel are arranged column-wise in a $df^2 \times e$ matrix, where d is the number of input channels, c is the number of output channels, f is the filter size, and e is the number of quadtree nodes in level l:

$$
D_l^{\text{out}} := \begin{bmatrix} w_0^0 & w_1^0 & w_2^0 & \cdots \\ w_0^1 & w_1^1 & w_2^1 & \cdots \\ \vdots & \vdots & \vdots & \vdots \\ w_0^{c-1} & w_1^{c-1} & w_2^{c-1} & \cdots \end{bmatrix} \begin{bmatrix} \vdots & \vdots & \cdots & \vdots \\ D_l^{\text{in}}[0,0] & D_l^{\text{in}}[0,1] & \cdots & D_l^{\text{in}}[d-1,0] \\ \vdots & \vdots & \vdots & \vdots \\ D_l^{\text{in}}[1,0] & D_l^{\text{in}}[1,1] & \cdots & D_l^{\text{in}}[d-1,1] \\ \vdots & \vdots & \vdots & \vdots \end{bmatrix}
$$

Here, the superscript in w_*^* runs from $[0 \mathrel{..} c-1]$ indexing the number of filters, while the subscript runs from $[0 \mathrel{..} df^2 - 1]$. This is different from traditional CNNs in two ways: first, only the non-zero quadtree nodes participate in convolutions, and second, the neighborhood lookup is different since the quadtree nodes are linearized into a 1D array in z-order. In detail, a node at index z in 1D can be deinterleaved once to obtain the 2D index (x, y). From this, it is straightforward to compute the neighbors using the lookup table $t(\cdot)$ proposed in Sect. 3.2 in constant time. If the neighbor index is present in the index array I_l, then its pixel value from D_l is assigned to the corresponding coefficient in the matrix above; otherwise it is set to 0 assuming a black background. Additionally, since the quadtree structure is fixed for each input sample, we can precompute the neighbors once and reuse them for convolutional operations throughout the network for even better efficiency.

We begin applying the convolution operation on the data D_ℓ stored in the finest quadtree nodes at level ℓ to obtain c output feature maps (see Fig. 3a) which fit in the same quadtree level if a unit stride is used. It is not possible to use arbitrary strides in QCNN since the output would then not conform to the quadtree structure. However, strides which are powers of 2 can be supported— for example, convolving the input data which resides at level l with a stride 2^s, where $s \in [0 \mathrel{..} l)$, will result in an output that will fit in level $l - s$. We only use unit stride in all our experiments and leave downsampling to the pooling layers.

Pooling. A common and important operation in convolutional neural networks is pooling, used to downsample the feature maps and aggregate information as we go deeper into the network. As demonstrated by Springenberg, et al. [16], pooling can be achieved by convolving with non-unit strides without any loss of accuracy. However, since the pooling operation is generally more efficient than convolutions, we implement it as follows. Pooling in QCNNs are particularly simple—we only need to assign the maximum (or average) of the 4 children nodes in level $l + 1$ to their corresponding parent node at level l, see Fig. 3b.

This is easy to implement since the quadtree nodes are linearized in z-order, and all 4 children nodes corresponding to a parent are stored in succession:

$$D_l[i] := \text{pool}(\{D_{l+1}[4(O_l[i] - 1) + j]\}), \ j \in [0 .. 3]$$

where the pool($\cdot$) function computes the maximum or average of the set.

Upsampling. Another common operation in convolutional neural networks is upsampling the feature maps, which can be used for visualization [17] or as part of autoencoder-like, or U-shaped network architectures [18] where features are concisely encoded using pooling and decoded using deconvolution, unpooling or upsampling. In this work, we implement upsampling by resizing the feature maps to a higher resolution, which is followed by a learnable convolution layer. Upsampling in QCNN is performed by traversing the quadtree in the opposite direction compared to pooling, i.e., we assign the value of the parent node in level $l - 1$ to all 4 children in level l:

$$D_l[4(O_{l-1}[i] - 1) + j] := D_{l-1}[i], \ j \in [0 .. 3]$$

which roughly corresponds to nearest neighbor interpolation, see Fig. 3c.

   With these fundamental operations defined on the quadtree, it is straightforward to compose them to design commonly used CNN architectures.

4   Experiments

We demonstrate the efficiency and versatility of our QCNN by conducting experiments on sparse image datasets for supervised classification and sketch simplification. We study the performance as well as training behavior of QCNNs compared to CNNs and show that QCNNs are well-behaved and converge to results achieved with traditional CNNs with much less computation time and memory. Our implementation is in C++ and CUDA (built upon the Caffe [19] framework), and runs on an NVIDIA GTX 1080 GPU with 8 GB memory.

   For brevity, in the following we denote a convolution unit by $C_l(c)$ which is composed of: (1) a quadtree convolutional layer with 3×3 filters that accepts data D_l^{in} from a quadtree of level l as input and outputs c feature maps D_l^{out} fitting in the same level, (2) a batch normalization layer that normalizes the minibatch using the mean and standard deviation computed from elements in D_l^{out}, and (3) a rectified linear unit activation function [20]: $\text{ReLU}(x) = \max(0, x)$. We denote by P_l a quadtree max pooling layer that downsamples the feature maps from level l to $l - 1$ and by U_l a quadtree upsampling layer that resizes feature maps from level l to $l + 1$.

   After completing all the quadtree convolutional and pooling operations in the network, we apply a quadtree padding operation denoted as "pad", to convert the sparse quadtree based feature maps into dense ones by zero padding the empty quadtree nodes and reshaping the quadtree minibatch of size B with d channels into a 4D dense tensor of dimensions $B \times d \times 2^l \times 2^l$. This is necessary to align the features computed for different images before feeding them to the fully-connected layers, since their quadtree structures are different.

4.1   Classification

We train traditional CNNs and our quadtree CNNs with similar network architectures on four sparse image datasets. Note that this experiment is mainly to study the behaviour of QCNN compared to traditional CNN and is not tuned to obtain the best accuracy.

MNIST is a popular dataset of numeric digits [0–9] consisting of grayscale images of size 28×28 that are split into $60,000$ training and $10,000$ test images. We zero pad each image to 32×32, and decompose them into quadtrees of level 5. The network structure is defined as:

$$\text{input} \rightarrow C_5(32) \rightarrow C_5(32) \rightarrow P_5 \rightarrow C_4(64) \rightarrow C_4(64) \rightarrow P_4 \rightarrow \text{pad} \rightarrow \text{FC}(1024)$$
$$\rightarrow \text{ReLU} \rightarrow \text{Dropout}(0.5) \rightarrow \text{FC}(K) \rightarrow \sigma,$$

where C_*, P_* are the quadtree based convolutional units and pooling operations, respectively, defined earlier, pad is the quadtree padding operation to align features from different inputs, Dropout [21] with a rate of 0.5 is used to prevent overfitting, $\text{FC}(n)$ is a fully-connected layer with an n-element vector as output, and σ is the softmax function that normalizes each element in its input into the range $[0, 1]$ such that the result is a discrete probability distribution, defined as $\sigma(x_j) = \frac{\exp x_j}{\sum_{k=1}^{n} \exp x_k}, j \in [1 \mathinner{\ldotp\ldotp} n]$, and K corresponds to the total number of classes in the dataset (10 in this case).

EMNIST Balanced [22] extends the classic MNIST dataset with more samples including alphabets, and contains $112,800$ training and $18,800$ test images of size 28×28. The 26 upper and lower case alphabets ([A–Z], [a–z]), and 10 digits ([0–9]) are combined into a total of $K = 47$ balanced classes. We zero pad the images as before and decompose them into quadtrees of level 5. We train them on a network that is defined exactly as in the previous case.

CASIA-HWDB1.1 [23] is a huge database of more than a million handwritten Chinese character sample images representing $3,866$ classes. We experiment with a 200-class subset of the dataset comprising $48,020$ training and $11,947$ test images. Since the images are of varying dimensions, we rescale them into 64×64, and decompose them into quadtrees of level 6. The network that we use for training is:

$$\text{input} \rightarrow C_6(64) \rightarrow P_6 \rightarrow C_5(128) \rightarrow P_5 \rightarrow C_4(256) \rightarrow P_4 \rightarrow C_3(512) \rightarrow P_3$$
$$\rightarrow \text{pad} \rightarrow \text{FC}(1024) \rightarrow \text{Dropout}(0.5) \rightarrow \text{FC}(200) \rightarrow \sigma.$$

TU-Berlin Sketch Dataset [24] contains $20,000$ images of freehand sketches drawn by non-experts, with 80 images in each of the $K = 250$ classes, in raster and vector formats. We split the dataset into $18,000$ training and 2000 test images, and resize each image into dimension 128×128. We then decompose the images into quadtrees of level 7. The network for training is defined as:

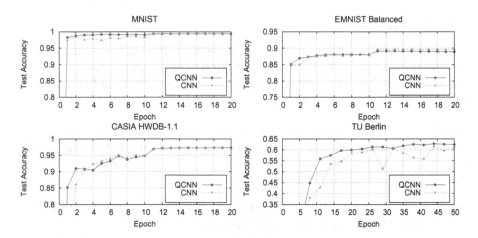

Fig. 4. Comparison of mean test accuracy (computed from 5 runs) of QCNN and traditional CNN classifiers progressively during training on various datasets.

$$\text{input} \to C_7(32) \to C_7(32) \to C_7(32) \to P_7 \to C_6(64) \to C_6(64) \to P_6$$
$$\to C_5(128) \to P_5 \to C_4(256) \to P_4 \to C_3(512) \to P_3 \to C_2(1024)$$
$$\to \text{pad} \to \text{Dropout}(0.5) \to \text{FC}(250) \to \sigma.$$

All these datasets are particularly suitable for our QCNN since the images are sparse in nature. We use the standard cross entropy loss for classification and use stochastic gradient descent for optimizing the first three networks with a learning rate 0.05, decayed by a factor of 10 after every 10 epochs, for 20 epochs, and ADADELTA optimization method [25] for the last network for 50 epochs (which provided better results compared to SGD). Weights are initialized using Glorot et al.'s technique [26], and regularized by a decay factor of 5×10^{-4}, while biases are initialized to zero. We do not perform any data augmentation for simplicity.

The computational statistics of the classification experiments are summarized in Table 1. We compare our QCNN results with those obtained by a traditional CNN with the same network architecture, initial weights, and hyperparameters. It can be seen that QCNNs are highly efficient in terms of computational effort (represented in column 3 as the number of multiply-accumulate operations in the convolutional layers) while yielding similar test accuracies (column 2). In practice, we observed that deeper networks train faster, for example, the TU-Berlin QCNN took one-third the training time compared to traditional CNN. To study the behaviour of QCNN throughout the training phase, we plot the learning curves in Fig. 4 comparing the test accuracy after each epoch of training. It is apparent that QCNNs closely follow CNNs in terms of accuracy on all the datasets throughout the training phase, while being computationally efficient.

Table 1. Computational statistics for classification comparing QCNNs and CNNs based on mean accuracy and standard deviation at the end of training from 5 runs, and average multiply-accumulate operations per sample (during forward pass) in the convolutional layers.

Dataset	Non-zero pixels (%)	Accuracy (%)		#MACC ($\times 10^6$)	
		CNN	QCNN	CNN	QCNN
MNIST	32.82	99.48($\pm$0.03)	99.39($\pm$0.02)	18.36	6.1
EMNIST Balanced	44.15	89.53($\pm$0.09)	88.89($\pm$0.18)	18.36	9.03
CASIA-HWDB1.1	19.06	97.44($\pm$0.12)	97.36($\pm$0.08)	229.34	136.7
TU-Berlin	4.53	61.13($\pm$2.04)	62.44($\pm$1.16)	837.53	257.07

4.2 Sketch Simplification

We next study QCNN for the task of sketch simplification [1]. This application is again suitable for our method since relatively high resolution sparse images are trained on deep convolutional neural networks.

We adapt the TU-Berlin sketch dataset for this experiment by synthesizing an inverse dataset consisting of sketchy rough line drawings. We utilize the SVG version of TU-Berlin dataset where each file represents a clean sketch drawing as a collection of paths in Bézier form. We duplicate each path 3 times and apply random affine transformations where the rotation angle and translation are drawn from Gaussian distributions with zero mean and standard deviations of 1.5° and 2, respectively. We repeat this for all SVG files in the dataset and rasterize them while setting the stroke width of the paths to 1px.

Next, we decompose all the rough sketches into quadtrees and represent the corresponding clean sketches using the same quadtree structure so that both are directly comparable during training. We define an encoding-decoding QCNN similar to Simo-Serra et al. [1]:

$$\text{sketchy} \to C_\ell(48) \to C_\ell(48) \to P_\ell \to C_{\ell-1}(128) \to C_{\ell-1}(128) \to P_{\ell-1}$$
$$\to C_{\ell-2}(256) \to C_{\ell-2}(256) \to C_{\ell-2}(256) \to P_{\ell-2} \to C_{\ell-3}(256)$$
$$\to C_{\ell-3}(512) \to C_{\ell-3}(1024) \to C_{\ell-3}(1024) \to C_{\ell-3}(1024) \to C_{\ell-3}(1024)$$
$$\to C_{\ell-3}(512) \to C_{\ell-3}(256) \to U_{\ell-3} \to C_{\ell-2}(256) \to C_{\ell-2}(256)$$
$$\to C_{\ell-2}(128) \to U_{\ell-2} \to C_{\ell-1}(128) \to C_{\ell-1}(128) \to C_{\ell-1}(48)$$
$$\to U_{\ell-1} \to C_\ell(48) \to C_\ell(24) \to \text{conv}(1) \to \text{sigmoid} \to \text{clean image}$$

We introduce skip connections between the input of each pooling layer to the output of each corresponding upsampling layer in the same level to speed up the convergence. Note that we did not tune the network architecture or dataset to obtain best results, but rather study the performance and training behaviour. We train the network for 20 epochs with the mean-squared error loss between the rough and clean sketch data stored in the quadtrees using the ADADELTA [25]

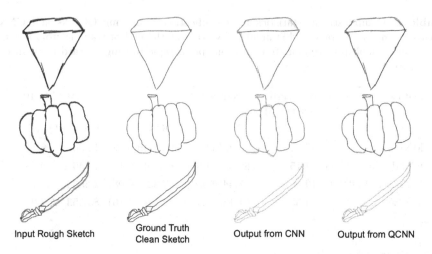

| Input Rough Sketch | Ground Truth Clean Sketch | Output from CNN | Output from QCNN |

Fig. 5. Sketch simplification results obtained with traditional CNN and QCNN trained using the same network architecture.

optimization method. As before, we also train a traditional CNN similarly for this task to compare the results as well as computational and memory usage. As shown in Fig. 5, QCNN can obtain comparable simplified sketches, while greatly reducing computation and memory use, see Table 2. Training QCNN in our setup took only around one-fourth the time compared to CNN. We used images of dimension 256×256 ($\ell = 8$) for this experiment. However, since sketch simplification typically involves high-resolution images leading to extended training time, we also compute and provide the computation and memory usage for higher resolutions to illustrate the drastically increasing complexity, see second and third rows in Table 2.

To study the learning behaviour of QCNN, we visualize the evolution of the learning process by retrieving the weights of the models throughout the training phase and visualizing the simplified results, as shown in Fig. 6. It is apparent that the learning behaviour of QCNN is stable and quite similar to traditional CNN for this task which involves a deep network, while being highly computation and memory efficient.

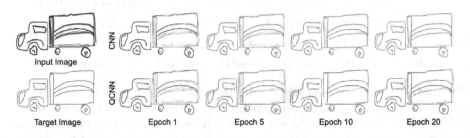

| Input Image | | Epoch 1 | Epoch 5 | Epoch 10 | Epoch 20 |
| Target Image | | | | | |

Fig. 6. Visualization of learning process for sketch simplification evolving throughout training.

Table 2. Computational statistics for sketch simplification comparing QCNNs and CNNs based on average multiply-accumulate operations and memory usage per sample (forward pass) in convolutional layers.

Resolution	#MACC ($\times 10^8$)		Memory (MB)	
	CNN	QCNN	CNN	QCNN
256×256	724.76	137.54	127.14	13.5
512×512	2899.05	349.28	508.56	35.35
1024×1024	11596.21	917.14	2034.24	97.9

5   Conclusion

We have presented a quadtree convolutional neural network (QCNN) that can efficiently learn from sparse image datasets. Thanks to the quadtree-based representation that decomposes the image only in the presence of non-zero pixels, storing and computing feature maps is of linear complexity in the number of non-zero pixels and independent of image resolution. QCNNs are applicable in a wide range of applications involving sparse images. Particularly, we have demonstrated the use of QCNNs on sparse image classification and sketch simplification, where similar classification and simplification results are obtained but with much lower computational complexity and memory cost, compared to traditional convolutional neural networks. This feature makes QCNN very suitable for applications on mobile devices whose computing power is limited.

In future, we wish to study QCNNs with other network architectures in more detail such as residual networks [27], to learn from extremely large datasets such as Google Quickdraw [28]. We are also interested in extending our approach to recurrent architectures to learn from sparse image sequences and improve the learning speed of adversarial networks for training on sketch-like datasets [29].

Acknowledgements. We thank the anonymous reviewers for their constructive comments. This research is supported by the National Research Foundation under Virtual Singapore Award No. NRF2015VSG-AA3DCM001-018, and the BeingTogether Centre, a collaboration between Nanyang Technological University (NTU) Singapore and University of North Carolina (UNC) at Chapel Hill. The BeingTogether Centre is supported by the National Research Foundation, Prime Ministers Office, Singapore under its International Research Centres in Singapore Funding Initiative. This research is also supported in part by Singapore MoE Tier-2 Grant (MOE2016-T2-2-065).

References

1. Simo-Serra, E., Iizuka, S., Sasaki, K., Ishikawa, H.: Learning to simplify: fully convolutional networks for rough sketch cleanup. ACM Trans. Graph. **35**(4), 121:1–121:11 (2016)
2. Wu, Z., et al.: 3D shapeNets: a deep representation for volumetric shapes. In: 2015 IEEE Conference on Computer Vision and Pattern Recognition (CVPR), pp. 1912–1920 (2015)

3. Riegler, G., Ulusoy, A.O., Geiger, A.: OctNet: learning deep 3D representations at high resolutions. In: 2017 IEEE Conference on Computer Vision and Pattern Recognition (CVPR), pp. 6620–6629 (2017)
4. Wang, P.S., Liu, Y., Guo, Y.X., Sun, C.Y., Tong, X.: O-CNN: octree-based convolutional neural networks for 3D shape analysis. ACM Trans. Graph. **36**(4), 72:1–72:11 (2017)
5. Tatarchenko, M., Dosovitskiy, A., Brox, T.: Octree generating networks: efficient convolutional architectures for high-resolution 3D outputs. CoRR abs/1703.09438 (2017)
6. Hunter, G.M., Steiglitz, K.: Operations on images using quad trees. IEEE Trans. Pattern Anal. Mach. Intell. **1**(2), 145–153 (1979)
7. Jackins, C.L., Tanimoto, S.L.: Oct-trees and their use in representing three-dimensional objects. Comput. Graph. Image Process. **14**(3), 249–270 (1980)
8. Gervautz, M., Purgathofer, W.: A simple method for color quantization: octree quantization. In: Magnenat-Thalmann, N., Thalmann, D. (eds.) New Trends in Computer Graphics, pp. 219–231. Springer, Heidelberg (1988). https://doi.org/10.1007/978-3-642-83492-9_20
9. Sullivan, G.J., Baker, R.L.: Efficient quadtree coding of images and video. IEEE Trans. Image Process. **3**(3), 327–331 (1994)
10. Agarwala, A.: Efficient gradient-domain compositing using quadtrees. ACM Trans. Graph. **26**(3), 94 (2007)
11. Gargantini, I.: An effective way to represent quadtrees. Commun. ACM **25**(12), 905–910 (1982)
12. Graham, B.: Spatially-sparse convolutional neural networks. CoRR abs/1409.6070 (2014)
13. Graham, B.: Sparse 3D convolutional neural networks. In: Xianghua Xie, M.W.J., Tam, G.K.L. (eds.) Proceedings of the British Machine Vision Conference (BMVC), pp. 150.1–150.9. BMVA Press (2015)
14. Graham, B., van der Maaten, L.: Submanifold sparse convolutional networks. CoRR abs/1706.01307 (2017)
15. Chellapilla, K., Puri, S., Simard, P.: High performance convolutional neural networks for document processing. In: Lorette, G. (ed.) Proceedings - Tenth International Workshop on Frontiers in Handwriting Recognition. Université de Rennes 1, Suvisoft (2006)
16. Springenberg, J.T., Dosovitskiy, A., Brox, T., Riedmiller, M.A.: Striving for simplicity: the all convolutional net. CoRR abs/1412.6806 (2014)
17. Zeiler, M.D., Fergus, R.: Visualizing and understanding convolutional networks. In: Fleet, D., Pajdla, T., Schiele, B., Tuytelaars, T. (eds.) Computer Vision - ECCV 2014. LNCS, pp. 818–833. Springer, Cham (2014). https://doi.org/10.1007/978-3-319-10590-1_53
18. Ronneberger, O., Fischer, P., Brox, T.: U-net: convolutional networks for biomedical image segmentation. In: Navab, N., Hornegger, J., Wells, W.M., Frangi, A.F. (eds.) Medical Image Computing and Computer-Assisted Intervention - MICCAI 2015. LNCS, pp. 234–241. Springer, Cham (2015). https://doi.org/10.1007/978-3-319-24574-4_28
19. Jia, Y., et al.: Caffe: convolutional architecture for fast feature embedding. arXiv preprint arXiv:1408.5093 (2014)
20. Nair, V., Hinton, G.E.: Rectified linear units improve restricted Boltzmann machines. In: Proceedings of the 27th International Conference on International Conference on Machine Learning ICML2010, USA, Omnipress, pp. 807–814 (2010)

21. Srivastava, N., Hinton, G., Krizhevsky, A., Sutskever, I., Salakhutdinov, R.: Dropout: a simple way to prevent neural networks from overfitting. J. Mach. Learn. Res. **15**, 1929–1958 (2014)
22. Cohen, G., Afshar, S., Tapson, J., van Schaik, A.: EMNIST: an extension of MNIST to handwritten letters. CoRR abs/1702.05373 (2017)
23. Liu, C.L., Yin, F., Wang, D.H., Wang, Q.F.: Online and offline handwritten chinese character recognition: benchmarking on new databases. Pattern Recogn. **46**(1), 155–162 (2013)
24. Eitz, M., Hays, J., Alexa, M.: How do humans sketch objects? ACM Trans. Graph. **31**(4), 44:1–44:10 (2012)
25. Zeiler, M.D.: ADADELTA: an adaptive learning rate method. CoRR abs/1212.5701 (2012)
26. Glorot, X., Bengio, Y.: Understanding the difficulty of training deep feedforward neural networks. In: Proceedings of the Thirteenth International Conference on Artificial Intelligence and Statistics. Proceedings of Machine Learning Research, PMLR, vol. 9, pp. 249–256 (2010)
27. He, K., Zhang, X., Ren, S., Sun, J.: Deep residual learning for image recognition. In: 2016 Proceedings of IEEE Conference on Computer Vision and Pattern Recognition (CVPR), pp. 770–778 (2016)
28. Ha, D., Eck, D.: A neural representation of sketch drawings. CoRR abs/1704.03477 (2017)
29. Simo-Serra, E., Iizuka, S., Ishikawa, H.: Mastering sketching: adversarial augmentation for structured prediction. CoRR abs/1703.08966 (2017)

Learning to Predict Crisp Boundaries

Ruoxi Deng[1], Chunhua Shen[2], Shengjun Liu[1(✉)], Huibing Wang[3],
and Xinru Liu[1]

[1] Central South University, Changsha, China
shjliu.cg@csu.edu.cn
[2] The University of Adelaide, Adelaide, Australia
[3] Dalian University of Technology, Dalian, China

Abstract. Recent methods for boundary or edge detection built on
Deep Convolutional Neural Networks (Cnns) typically suffer from the
issue of predicted edges being thick and need post-processing to obtain
crisp boundaries. Highly imbalanced categories of boundary versus background in training data is one of main reasons for the above problem.
In this work, the aim is to make CNNs produce sharp boundaries without post-processing. We introduce a novel loss for boundary detection,
which is very effective for classifying imbalanced data and allows CNNs
to produce crisp boundaries. Moreover, we propose an end-to-end network which adopts the bottom-up/top-down architecture to tackle the
task. The proposed network effectively leverages hierarchical features and
produces pixel-accurate boundary mask, which is critical to reconstruct
the edge map. Our experiments illustrate that directly making crisp prediction not only promotes the visual results of CNNs, but also achieves
better results against the state-of-the-art on the BSDS500 dataset (ODS
F-score of .815) and the NYU Depth dataset (ODS F-score of .762).

Keywords: Edge detection · Contour detection
Convolutional neural networks

1 Introduction

Edge detection is a long-standing task in computer vision [1,2]. In early years,
the objective is defined as to find sudden changes of discontinuities in intensity
images [3]. Nowadays, it is expected to localize semantically meaningful objects
boundaries, which play a fundamental and significant role in many computer
vision tasks such as image segmentation [4–7] and optical flow [8,9]. In the
past few years, deep convolutional neural networks (CNNs) have dominated the
research on edge detection. CNN based methods, such as DeepEdge [10], Deep-
Contour [11], HED [12] and RCF [13], take advantage of its remarkable ability
of hierarchical feature learning and have demonstrated state-of-the-art F-score
performance on the benchmarks such as BSDS500 [5] and NYUDv2 [14].

Part of this work was done when R. Deng and H. Wang were visiting The University
of Adelaide.

© Springer Nature Switzerland AG 2018
V. Ferrari et al. (Eds.): ECCV 2018, LNCS 11210, pp. 570–586, 2018.
https://doi.org/10.1007/978-3-030-01231-1_35

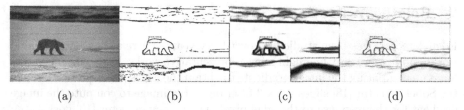

(a)   (b)   (c)   (d)

Fig. 1. (a) is an example image from the BSDS500 dataset [5]. (b) is the result of the Sobel detector [15]. Here (c) is the output of the HED detector [12]. (d) is the output of our proposed method. All the predictions do not apply post-processing.

Although CNN-based methods are good at producing semantically meaningful contours, we observe a common behavior that their prediction is much thicker than the result of classic methods. For example, in Fig. 1 we show two prediction examples from the Sobel detector [15] and the HED detector, respectively. The edge of the polar bear that we highlight in the dotted rectangle on the HED result is roughly 10 pixels wide, which is two times wider than the Sobel result (roughly 4 pixels). Note that, the behavior of thick prediction is not only on the result of HED but also can be found in many recent representative works such as RCF [13], Casenet [16] and CEDN [17].

Existing works in the literature seldom discuss this issue of predicted boundaries being overly thick. One possible reason is that edge detection methods typically apply edge thinning post-processing to obtain one-pixel wide results after generating an initial prediction. Therefore it seems no difference that how wide the initial prediction is. However, this behavior attracts our attention and we believe it is worth finding out the reason behind it which in turn improves the quality of prediction. The work in [45] addressed this problem by proposing a refinement architecture (encoder-decoder) for achieving crips edges. As we show in our experiments, it only slightly improves the result of HED. Instead of modifying the convolutional network for boundary detection, we address this problem by investigating the loss function.

In this work, we explore and solve the thickness issue of CNN-based boundary predictions. We present an end-to-end fully convolutional network which is accurate, fast and convenient to perform image-to-boundary prediction. Our method consists of two key components, which are a fully convolutional neural network of the bottom-up/top-town architecture and a simple yet effective loss function. The method can automatically learn rich hierarchical features, resolve ambiguity in prediction and predict crisp results without postprocessing. Figure 1 gives an example of the improvement of edge quality between our method and the HED detector. More examples can be found in Sect. 4. We demonstrate that tackling the issue of thickness is critical for CNNs performing crisp edge detection, which improves the visual result as well as promotes the performance in terms of boundary detection evaluation metrics. We achieve the state-of-the-art performance on the BSDS500 dataset with the ODS F-score of 0.815 and the fast version of our method achieves ODS F-score of 0.808 at the speed of 30 FPS.

2   Related Work

Edge detection has been studied for over forty years. There are plenty of related works and here we only highlight a few representative works. Early edge detectors focus on computing the image gradients to obtain the edges [18–21]. For example, the Sobel detector [18] slides a 3×3 filter on a gray image to compute the image gradient for the response to the edge pixel. The Canny detector [19] goes a step further by removing the noise on the output map and employing non-maximum suppression to extract one-pixel wide contour. These traditional methods are often used as one of the fundamental features in many computer vision applications [4,22,23]. Learning-based methods [5,24–26] often ensemble different low-level features and train a classifier to generate object-level contours. Although these methods achieved great performance compared to traditional methods, they rely on hand-crafted features which limit their room for improvement.

Recent state-of-the-art methods for edge detection [12,13,27] are built on deep convolutional neural networks [28,29]. DeepEdge [10] extracts multiple patches surrounding an edge candidate point (extracted by the Canny detector) and feeds these patches into a multi-scale CNN to decide if it is an edge pixel. DeepContour [11] is also a patch-based approach which first divides an image into many patches then put these patches into the network to detect if the patch has a contour. Differing from these works, the HED detector [12] is an end-to-end fully convolutional neural network which takes an image as input and directly outputs the prediction. It proposes a weighted cross entropy loss and takes the skip-layer structure to make independent predictions from each block of the pre-trained VGG model [30] and average the results. RCF [13] also utilizes the skip-layer structure and the similar loss with HED, yet it makes independent predictions from each convolutional layer of the VGG model. CEDN [17] employs an encoder-decoder network and train the network on the extra data of Pascal VOC dataset. CASENet [16] proposes a novel task which is to assign each edge pixel to one or more semantic classes and solve the task by utilizing an end-to-end system similar to HED.

Summarizing the development of deep learning based methods, we find that the HED detector is very popular and has enlightened many subsequent methods such as RCF, CASENet and the works mentioned in the paper [31]. However, we observe empirically that the weighted cross entropy loss employed by the HED detector may have contributed to the resulted edges being thick. We verify this in the next section.

Contributions. In this work, we develop an end-to-end edge detection method. Our main contributions are as follows. We aim to detect crisp boundaries in images using deep learning. We explore the issue of predicted edges being overly thick, which can be found in almost all recent CNNs based methods. We propose a method that manages to tackle the thickness issue. It allows CNN-based methods to predict crisp edge without resorting to post-processing. Furthermore, our experiments show that our method outperforms previous state-of-the-art methods on the BSDS500 and NYUDv2 datasets.

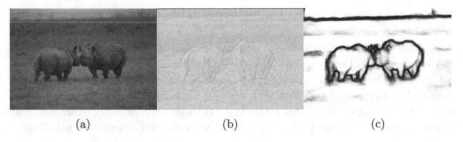

(a)   (b)   (c)

Fig. 2. A simple test on the class-balance weight β. From left to right: (a) is the original image from the BSDS500 dataset. (b) is the result of using the standard cross-entropy loss, i.e., $\beta = 0.5$. (c) is the result of using the weighted cross-entropy loss.

3 The Proposed Method

In this section, we describe the details of the proposed method. Loss function is the most important component in an end-to-end dense prediction system since the quality of prediction is most affected by its loss. Thus we first revisit the weighted cross entropy loss used in previous state-of-the-art methods. We then propose our edge detection system, including the loss based on image similarity and the network of bottom-up/top-down structure.

3.1 Revisiting the Weighted Cross-entropy Loss for Edge Detection

Previously fully convolutional networks (FCN) based edge-detection methods often employ the weighted cross entropy loss as adopted by the HED detector. It is well known that the cross-entropy loss is used to solve binary classification. However, the edge/non-edge pixels are of a highly imbalanced distribution (the majority of pixels are non-edge) thus the direct use of the cross-entropy loss would fail to train the network. To tackle the issue, HED uses the weighted cross entropy loss, which writes

$$\mathcal{L}(W, w) = -\beta \sum_{j \in Y_+} \log \Pr(y_j = 1 | X; W, w) - (1 - \beta) \sum_{j \in Y_-} \log \Pr(y_j = 0 | X; W, w),$$

(1)

where Y_+ and Y_- denotes the edge pixel set and non-edge pixel sets, respectively. $\beta = |Y_-|/|Y|$ and $1 - \beta = |Y_+|/|Y|$. X is the input image and $\Pr(y_j | X; W, w)$ is computed using softmax on the classification scores at pixel y_j.

The class-balance weights β and $1 - \beta$ are used to preserve and suppress the losses from the class of edge pixels and non-edge pixels, respectively. This simple solution helps CNN manage to better train the network. We perform a comparison test that uses the standard cross-entropy loss and the weighted loss on the same HED network structure, demonstrating the effectiveness of the weight β. The result of the test is shown in Fig. 2. As we can see, the standard loss fails to train the network since the result (Fig. 2b) is not an edge map but an 'embossed' image. However, if we carefully look at its details, we are able to find the contour of rhinoceros that has reasonable thickness and is thinner than the results of the weighted loss (Fig. 2c). It is likely to indicate that, although the class-balance weights β and $1 - \beta$ manage to make CNNs successfully trained, they cause the 'thickness' issue. This finding explains why recent methods such as RCF and Casenet tend to output overly thick edges. These two methods have employed the cross-entropy loss with the same strategy, i.e., setting weights on edge/non-edge pixels to balance the loss. To make the network trainable and output a crisp prediction at the same time, we will need alternative solutions.

3.2   The Proposed Loss Function for Edge Detection

We have shown that a distinct characteristic of edge map is that the data is highly biased because the vast majority of the pixels are non-edges. This highly biased issue would cause the learning to fail to find the crisp edges which are the 'rare events'.

Similar to our task, many applications such as fraud detection, medical image processing, and text classification are dealing with class imbalance data and there are corresponding solutions to these tasks [32–36]. Inspired by the work of [37] using the Dice coefficient [38] to solve the class-imbalance problem, we propose to use the Dice coefficient for edge detection.

Given an input image I and the ground-truth G, the activation map M is the input image I processed by a fully convolutional network F. Our objective is to obtain a prediction P. Our loss function L is given by

$$L(P, G) = Dist(P, G) = \frac{\sum_i^N p_i^2 + \sum_i^N g_i^2}{2 \sum_i^N p_i g_i}, \qquad (2)$$

where p_i, g_i denote the value of i-th pixel on the prediction map P and the ground-truth G, respectively. The prediction map P is computed from the activation map M by the sigmoid function. The loss function L is the reciprocal of the Dice coefficient. Since the Dice coefficient is a measure of similarity of two sets. Our loss is to compare the similarity of two sets P, G and minimizes their distance on the training data. We do not need to consider the issue of balancing the loss of edge/non-edge pixels by using the proposed loss and are able to achieve our objective—make the network trainable and predict crisp edges at the same time.

We should emphasize the way of computing our total loss in a mini-batch. Given a mini-batch of training samples and their corresponding ground-truth, our total loss is given by

$$L(MP, MG) = \sum_i^M Dist(MP_i, MG_i), \qquad (3)$$

where MP and MG denote a mini-batch of predictions and their ground-truth, respectively. M is the total number of training samples in the mini-batch. Since our loss function is based on the similarity of per image-ground-truth pair, our total loss of a mini-batch is the sum of the total distances over all pairs.

To achieve better performance, we propose to combine the cross-entropy loss and the proposed Dice loss. The Dice loss may be thought of as image-level that focuses on the similarity of two sets of image pixels. The cross-entropy loss concentrates on the pixel-level difference, since it is the sum of the distance of every corresponding pixel-pair between prediction and the ground-truth. Therefore the combined loss is able to hierarchically minimize the distance from image-level to pixel-level.

Our final loss function is given by:

$$L_{\text{final}}(P, G) = \alpha L(P, G) + \beta L_c(P, G), \tag{4}$$

where $L(P, G)$ is Eq. 2; $L_c(P, G)$ is the normal cross-entropy loss which is $L_c(P, G) = -\sum_j^N (g_j \log p_j + (1 - g_j)(1 - \log p_j))$. N is the total pixel number of an image. α and β are the parameters to control the influence of two losses. In experiments we set $\alpha = 1$ and $\beta = 0.001$. We also tried to use the weighted cross-entropy loss (Eq. 1) instead of L_c, and no improvement is observed. To compute the total loss in a mini-batch, we use Eq. 3 where $Dist(P, G)$ is replaced by $L_{\text{final}}(P, G)$. We emphasize that the proposed Dice loss $L(P, G)$ is the cornerstone for generating crisp edges. Using only the proposed Dice loss, we achieve an ODS F-score of .805 on the BSDS500 dataset.

The formulation (4) can be differentiated yielding the gradient

$$\frac{\partial L_{\text{final}}}{\partial p_k} = \alpha \frac{2p_k \sum_{i=1}^N p_i g_i - g_k(\sum_{i=1}^N p_i^2 + \sum_{i=1}^N g_i^2)}{2(\sum_{i=1}^N p_i g_i)^2} - \beta \frac{2g_k - 1}{p_k} \tag{5}$$

computed with respect to the k-th pixel of the prediction.

In the next subsection, we describe our network structure.

3.3 Network Architecture

We attempt to select the network structure which has multiple stages to efficiently capture hierarchical features and is able to fuse the features of different levels, so as to generate semantically meaningful contours. The success of HED shows the great importance of a carefully designed structure. In this paper, we look at another advanced structure, that is the bottom-up/top-down architecture [39] for inspiration to make better use of hierarchical features. The method of [39] achieves improved accuracy of object segmentation by proposing a novel top-down refinement approach. We hypothesize that this structure may also work for edge detection well since our task is related to object segmentation.

We follow the setting of the network [39] to apply the VGG-16 model [30] as the backbone and stack its 'refactored' structure of the refinement module to recover the resolution of features. However, we have the following modifications at the refinement module to make it suitable for edge detection: (i) to better extract side feature from each stage of VGG-16, we use the *ResNeXt* [40]

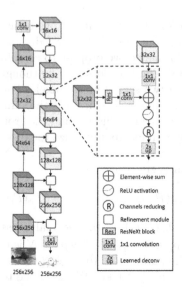

Fig. 3. Overview of the proposed network. Blue cubics indicate the features on the bottom-up path while yellow cubics indicate the mask-encoding on the top-down path. The backbone of our network is the VGG-16 model in which the last pooling layer and all the fully connected layers are removed. The mask-encoding from conv5_3 layer repeatedly goes through the proposed refinement module to recover its resolution. In a refinement module, the mask-encoding is fused with the side-output features and then reduces its channels by a factor of 2 and double its resolution to prepare for the fusion in the next refinement module. (Color figure online)

block to connect each side output layer, respectively conv1_2, conv2_2, conv3_3, conv4_3 and conv5_3. Thus, the feature from each side output first goes through a *ResNeXt* block then is fused with the mask-encoding from the top-down path; (ii) we use 1×1 *conv* layer to replace original 3×3 *conv* layers of the module. By doing so, we find the performance is improved with the decrease of model complexity; (iii) we use the learned *deconv* layer to double the resolution of fused features. Especially, the *deconv* layer is grouped. The group number equals to the channel number of the fused features. The grouped *deconv* layer allows our model to keep the performance with less model complexity. The modified refinement module is fully back-propable. We show the overall structure in Fig. 3 and our refinement module in the dotted rectangle.

Our network is simple yet very effective for edge detection. We highlight that it is vital for an edge-detection network to increase the ability of feature extraction with the decrease of model complexity. Compared to the original structure, our network has the advantage of using fewer parameters to achieve better performance. To be more specific, our network has 15.69M parameters and achieves an ODS of .808 on the BSDS500 dataset. Without the modifications described in (ii) and (iii), the parameter number increases to 22.64M but the performance decreases to ODS of .802.

The reason behind this phenomenon might be due to overfitting, as the dataset for edge detection has limited number of training samples (for example, the BSDS500 dataset only has only 200 training images). In experiments, we tried a few more sophisticated bottom-up/top-down networks such as Refinenet [41], but failed to achieve better performance possibly because of limited training data. Using the *ResNeXt* block is for the same reason. It groups the inside *conv* layers to decrease the model complexity. We also test the *ResNet* block [42] to extract the side features, which is used to compare the performance against the *ResNeXt* block. We find that they are both helpful to boost the performance while the *ResNeXT* block performs slightly better with roughly 50% complexity of the *ResNet* block.

4   Experiments

In this section, we first present the implementation details as well as a brief description of the datasets. Our experiments start with an ablation study of the proposed method. We then conduct a comparative study on HED to demonstrate the effectiveness of the proposed loss on the crispness of prediction. We further compare our method with the state-of-the-art edge detectors and demonstrate the advantages.

4.1   Implementation Details

We implement our method using Pytorch [43]. We evaluate edge detectors on Berkeley Segmentation Dataset (BSDS 500) and NYU depth dataset (NYUD), which are widely used in previous works [10–13,17]. The hyper-parameters of our model include: mini-batch size (36), input image resolution (480 × 320), weight-decay (1e−4), training epochs (30). We use the ADAM solver [44] for optimization.

Beside the hyper-parameters, the following several key issues are worth mentioning:

Data Augmentation. Data augmentation is an effective way to boost performance when the amount of training data is limited. We first randomly scale the image-label pairs (0.7 to 1.3). We then rotate the pairs to 16 different angles and crop the largest rectangle in the rotated angle. We finally flip the cropped images, which leads to an augmented training set from 200 images to more than 100k images.

Up-sampling Method. We employ learned deconvolution in the backward-refining pathway to progressively increase the resolution of feature maps. Although bilinear upsampling was demonstrated useful in HED, it is abandoned in our method. We observe in experiments that bilinear upsampling may make the prediction discontinuous at a number of locations and cause a slight decrease in performance.

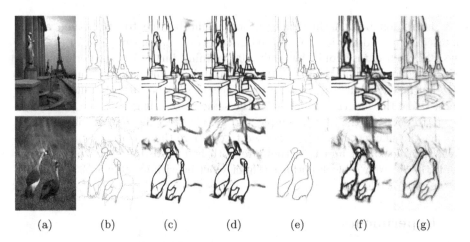

(a)	(b)	(c)	(d)	(e)	(f)	(g)

Fig. 4. Illustration of the qualitative results of the ablation study as well as applying the proposed loss with HED. From left to right: (a) input images in the BSDS500 dataset; (b) ground-truth; (c),(d),(e) are the predictions of the methods *Ours-w/o-rN-w/o-FL*, *Ours-w/o-FL* and *Ours* in the ablation study, respectively; (f), (g) are the predictions of the methods *HED-BL* and *HED-FL* in the comparative study, respectively. Our method, especially the proposed loss, shows a clear advantage in generating sharp boundaries.

Multi-scale Edge Detection. Inspired by the works [13,45], during testing we make use of multi-scale edge detection to further improve performance. We first resize an input image to three different resolutions (0.5×, 1.0× and 1.5× of the original size), which are fed into the network. We then resize the outputs back to the original size and average them to obtain the final prediction.

4.2 BSDS500 Dataset

Berkeley Segmentation Dataset (BSDS 500) [5] contains 200 training images, 100 validation images, and 200 testing images. Each image is annotated by multiple users. We use the train set (200 training images) for training and employ all the ground-truth labels to prepare the training data. That is, if an image has five annotations, we first create five copies of the image. Each copy is corresponding to one of the annotations, respectively. We then apply these five image-annotation pairs for data augmentation. This would introduce ambiguity in the ground-truth pairs because different annotators may disagree with each other for a small number of pixels. However, in this case, we are able to get more annotations for data augmentation. In the meantime, we observed that introducing certain ambiguity prevented the training from overfitting.

Ablation Study. We first conduct a series of ablation studies to evaluate the importance of each component in the proposed method. Our first experiment is

Table 1. Ablation studies of the proposed method on the BSDS500 dataset. NMS stands for non-maximum suppression. 'Ours-w/o-FL' refers to our method without the fusion loss. 'w/o-rN' refers to without all the ResNeXt blocks in the backward-refining path.

Method	ODS (after/before NMS)	OIS (after/before NMS)
Ours-w/o-rN-w/o-FL	.797/.671	.815/.678
Ours-w/o-FL	.798/.674	.815/.679
Ours	.800/.693	.816/.700

Table 2. Comparative studies of HED. HED-BL refers to HED trained by the balanced cross-entropy loss. HED-FL refers to HED trained via the proposed fusion loss.

Method	ODS (after/before NMS)	OIS (after/before NMS)
HED-BL	.781/.583	.798/.598
HED-FL	.783/.635	.802/.644

to examine the effectiveness of the basic encoder-decoder network (Ours-w/o-rN-w/o-FL) for the task. To this end, our baseline model is the proposed network removing all the ResNeXt blocks in the backward-refining path. We train this baseline using the balanced cross-entropy loss. Moreover, we trained two versions of the proposed network via the balanced cross-entropy loss (Ours-w/o-FL) and the proposed fusion loss (Ours), respectively.

The accuracy of prediction is evaluated via two standard measures: fixed contour threshold (ODS) and per-image best threshold (OIS).

Previous works tend to only examine the correctness of prediction since they apply a standard non-maximal suppression (NMS) to predicted edge maps before evaluation. While in this study and the following comparative study, we would like to evaluate each model twice (before and after NMS). By doing so, we can examine both the correctness and the sharpness since low-crispness prediction is prone to achieve low ODS scores, without the aid of NMS. We are aware that CED [45] and PMI [46] apply a different way to benchmark the crispness of predictions by varying a matching distance parameter. However, we consider that directly evaluating non-NMS results is simpler yet effective for the same purpose.

The quantitative results are listed in Table 1 and two qualitative examples are shown in Fig. 4(c)–(e). From the results, we observe three findings. Firstly, each component is able to improve performance; Secondly, a convolutional encoder-decoder network may be more competent for the task, compared to the network of HED. We can see that the baseline (Ours-w/o-rN-w/o-FL) achieves an ODS score .797, which significantly outperforms HED (.790 on the BSDS500 dataset). Lastly, both the quantitative and the qualitative results have demonstrated the effectiveness of the proposed fusion loss. By simply using the proposed fusion loss, the ODS f-score (before NMS) of our network is increased from .674 to .693 and the improvement of boundary sharpness can be also observed in Fig. 4(d) and (e).

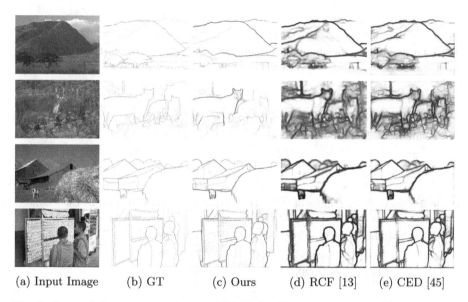

(a) Input Image   (b) GT   (c) Ours   (d) RCF [13]   (e) CED [45]

Fig. 5. State-of-the-art comparisons on BSDS500. From left to right: (a) the original images, (b) ground-truth, (c) the predictions of the proposed method, (d) the results of the RCF detector, (e) the results of the CED detector. Note that all the predictions are ent-to-end outputs and not postprocessed.

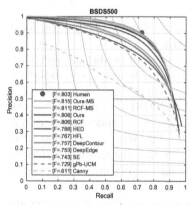

Fig. 6. Precision/recall curves on the BSDS500 dataset. Our method ahieves the best result (ODS = .815).

Table 3. Results on the BSDS500 dataset. MS refers to the multi-scale testing. VOC-aug refers to training with extra PASCAL VOC context data. † refers to GPU time.

Method	ODS	OIS	FPS
Canny [19]	.611	.676	28
GPb-UCM [5]	.729	.755	1/240
SE [26]	.743	.763	2.5
DeepContour [11]	.757	.776	1/30†
DeepEdge [10]	.753	.772	1/1000†
HFL [47]	.767	.788	5/6†
HED [12]	.788	.808	30†
CEDN [17]	.788	.804	10
MIL+G-DSN+MS+NCuts [27]	.813	.831	1
RCF-VOC-aug [13]	.806	.823	30†
RCF-MS-VOC-aug [13]	.811	.830	10†
CED [45]	.794	.811	30†
CED-MS [45]	.803	.820	10†
CED-MS-VOC-aug [45]	**.815**	.833	10†
Ours	.800	.816	30†
Ours-VOC-aug	.808	.824	30†
Ours-MS-VOC-aug	**.815**	**.834**	10†

Improving the Crispness of HED. As mentioned in Sect. 3.2, the proposed fusion loss plays a key role in our method in terms of generating sharp boundaries, which was demonstrated in the ablation study. One may ask a question: *Does the fusion loss only work on the convolutional encoder-decoder network? Could it also allow different methods such as HED to improve crispness?* To answer this question, we perform a comparative study on the HED edge detector. Similar to the ablation experiments, we evaluate two versions of HED: one is trained by means of the proposed fusion loss, the other is applying the balanced cross-entropy loss. Both methods are trained using deep supervision. Note that our training data of BSDS500 is generated in a different way, compared to HED [31], thus the performance of the re-implemented HED is slightly different from the original paper. We summarize the quantitative results in Table 2 and show two qualitative examples in Fig. 4(f) and (g).

The results are consistent with those of the ablation experiments. With the use of the proposed loss, *HED-FL* improves the non-NMS results over *HED-BL* by almost 9%, which is a significant increase at boundary crispness.

State-of-the-Art Comparisons. In this subsection, we further compare against the top performing edge detectors. The methods to be evaluated are composed of two classes: the first class is deep-learning based, which includes HED [12], RCF [13], DeepContour [11], DeepEdge [10], CED [45], HFL [47], CEDN [17], MIL+G-DSN+MS+NCuts [27] and our method; the second class contains SE [26], gPb-UCM [5] and the Canny detector [19]. We also follow the works of [13,17,27,45] to employ the extra training data from PASCAL VOC Context dataset [48]. The results are shown in Figs. 5, 6 and Table 3.

We first look at the qualitative result in Fig. 5. RCF and CED are the leading edge detectors at present. Especially, CED shares the same aim with our method, which is to solve the issue of boundary crispness. Comparing to the other methods, our approach shows a clear advantage in the quality of edge maps which are cleaner and sharper. Consider the 'cow' in the third example. Our method is able to precisely match its contour, whereas RCF and CED incur much more blurry and noisy edges. The qualitative comparisons suggest that our method generates sharper boundaries.

The quantitative results are summarized in Table 3. Figure 6 shows Precision-Recall curves of all methods. Note that, all the results have been post processed (using NMS) before evaluation. Without extra training data and the multi-scale testing, our method already outperforms most of the state-of-the-art edge detectors. By means of extra training data, our single-scale model achieves a significant improvement on ODS f-score from .800 to .808. With the multi-scale testing, our method achieves the same top performance with CED. However, CED adopted both the train and validation set for training while we only use the train set.

In addition to this, we evaluate the non-NMS results of CED (single-scale, without extra training data) and obtain the performance of ODS f-score of .655, OIS f-score of .662. The result is far behind our single-scale non-NMS performance (ODS f-score of .693). Another advantage of our method is that our detec-

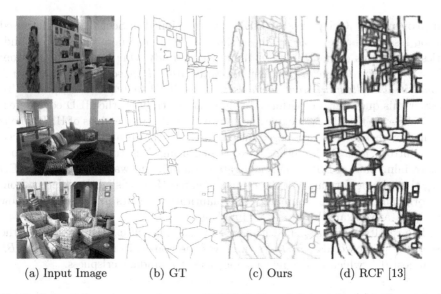

(a) Input Image　　　(b) GT　　　(c) Ours　　　(d) RCF [13]

Fig. 7. State-of-the-art comparisons on NYUDv2. From left to right: (a) is the original image, (b) is the groundtruth, (c) is the prediction of the proposed method, (d) is the result of the RCF detector. Note that the predictions of RCF and the proposed method are trained only on the RGB data. No postprocessing is applied.

tor is able to run in real time. The single scale detector can operate at 30FPS on a GTX980 GPU. Since our method is simple, effective and very fast, it is easy to be used along with high-level vision tasks such as image segmentation.

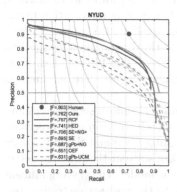

Fig. 8. Precision/recall curves on the NYUDv2 dataset. Our method trained on the RGB data and the HHA feature achieves the best result (ODS = .762).

Table 4. Results on the NYUDv2 dataset. † means GPU time.

Method	ODS	OIS	FPS
OEF [49]	.651	.667	1/2
gPb-UCM [5]	.631	.661	1/360
gPb+NG [50]	.687	.716	1/375
SE [26]	.695	.708	5
SE+NG+ [51]	.706	.734	1/15
HED-RGB [12]	.720	.734	20†
HED-HHA [12]	.682	.695	20†
HED-RGB-HHA [12]	.746	.761	10†
RCF-RGB [13]	.729	.742	20†
RCF-HHA [13]	.705	.715	20†
RCF-RGB-HHA [13]	.757	.771	10†
Ours-RGB	.739	.754	30†
Ours-HHA	.707	.719	30†
Ours-RGB-HHA	**.762**	**.778**	15†

4.3 NYUDv2 Dataset

The NYU depth dataset [14] is a large depth benchmark for indoor scenes, which is collected by a Microsoft Kinect sensor. It has a densely labeled dataset (every pixel has a depth annotation) which has 1449 pairs of aligned RGB and depth images. Gupta *et al.* [50] processed the data to generate edge annotation and split the dataset into 381 training images, 414 validation images, and 654 testing images. We follow their data-split setting and change several hyper-parameters of our method for training: mini-batch size (26), image resolution (480 × 480). The maximum tolerance allowed for correct matches of edge prediction in evaluation is increased from .0075 to .011, as used in [13,26,31]. We compare against the state-of-the-art methods which include OEF [49], gPb-UCM [5], gPb+NG [50], SE [26], SE+NG+ [51], HED [12] and RCF [13].

Motivated by the previous works [12,13], we leverage the depth information to improve performance. We employ the HHA feature [51] in which the depth information is encoded into three channels: horizontal disparity, height above ground, and angle with gravity. The way of employing the HHA feature is straightforward. We simply train two versions of the proposed network, one on the RGB data, another on HHA feature images. The final prediction is generated by directly averaging the output of the RGB model and HHA model.

We show the quantitative results in Table 4 and the precision-recall curve in Fig. 8. Our method achieves the best performance of ODS F-score .762. The qualitative results in Fig. 7 show consistent performance with those of the experiments on BSDS 500. Our prediction produces sharper boundaries against the leading competitor RCF, which demonstrates the effectiveness of our method.

5 Conclusions

In this work, we have presented a simple yet effective method for edge detection which achieves state-of-the-art results. We have shown that it is possible to achieve excellent boundary detection results using a carefully designed loss function and a simple convolutional encoder-decoder network.

In future work, we plan to extend the use of the edge detector to the tasks like object detection and optical flow which have the requirement of boundary sharpness and a fast processing speed.

Acknowledgement. This work is funded by the China Scholarship Council (Grant No. 201506370087), the National Natural Science Foundation of China (Grant No. 61572527, Grant No. 61628211, Grant No. 61602524).

References

1. Marr, D., Hildreth, E.: Theory of edge detection. Proc. Roy. Soc. Lond. B: Biol. Sci. **207**(1167), 187–217 (1980)
2. Gonzalez, R.C., Wood, R.E.: Digital Image Processing, 2nd edn. Prentice Hall, Upper Saddle. River (2014)

3. Torre, V., Poggio, T.A.: On edge detection. IEEE Trans. Pattern Anal. Mach. Intell. **2**, 147–163 (1986)
4. Senthilkumaran, N., Rajesh, R.: Edge detection techniques for image segmentation-a survey of soft computing approaches. Int. J. Recent Trends Eng. **1**(2), 250–254 (2009)
5. Arbelaez, P., Maire, M., Fowlkes, C., Malik, J.: Contour detection and hierarchical image segmentation. IEEE Trans. Pattern Anal. Mach. Intell. **33**(5), 898–916 (2011)
6. Chen, L.C., Barron, J.T., Papandreou, G., Murphy, K., Yuille, A.L.: Semantic image segmentation with task-specific edge detection using CNNs and a discriminatively trained domain transform. In: Proceedings of the IEEE Conference on Computer Vision and Pattern Recognition, pp. 4545–4554 (2016)
7. Bertasius, G., Shi, J., Torresani, L.: Semantic segmentation with boundary neural fields. In: Proceedings of the IEEE Conference on Computer Vision and Pattern Recognition, pp. 3602–3610 (2016)
8. Ren, X.: Local grouping for optical flow. In: IEEE Conference on Computer Vision and Pattern Recognition, CVPR 2008, pp. 1–8. IEEE (2008)
9. Revaud, J., Weinzaepfel, P., Harchaoui, Z., Schmid, C.: EpicFlow: edge-preserving interpolation of correspondences for optical flow. In: Proceedings of the IEEE Conference on Computer Vision and Pattern Recognition, pp. 1164–1172 (2015)
10. Bertasius, G., Shi, J., Torresani, L.: Deepedge: A multi-scale bifurcated deep network for top-down contour detection. In: Proceedings of the IEEE Conference on Computer Vision and Pattern Recognition, pp. 4380–4389 (2015)
11. Shen, W., Wang, X., Wang, Y., Bai, X., Zhang, Z.: Deepcontour: a deep convolutional feature learned by positive-sharing loss for contour detection. In: Proceedings of the IEEE Conference on Computer Vision and Pattern Recognition, pp. 3982–3991 (2015)
12. Xie, S., Tu, Z.: Holistically-nested edge detection. In: Proceedings of the IEEE International Conference on Computer Vision, pp. 1395–1403 (2015)
13. Liu, Y., Cheng, M.M., Hu, X., Wang, K., Bai, X.: Richer convolutional features for edge detection. arXiv preprint arXiv:1612.02103 (2016)
14. Silberman, N., Hoiem, D., Kohli, P., Fergus, R.: Indoor segmentation and support inference from RGBD images. In: Fitzgibbon, A., Lazebnik, S., Perona, P., Sato, Y., Schmid, C. (eds.) ECCV 2012. LNCS, vol. 7576, pp. 746–760. Springer, Heidelberg (2012). https://doi.org/10.1007/978-3-642-33715-4_54
15. Sobel, I.: Camera models and machine perception. Technical report, Department of Computer Science, Stanford University, California (1970)
16. Yu, Z., Feng, C., Liu, M.Y., Ramalingam, S.: Casenet: Deep category-aware semantic edge detection. arXiv e-Prints (2017)
17. Yang, J., Price, B., Cohen, S., Lee, H., Yang, M.H.: Object contour detection with a fully convolutional encoder-decoder network. In: Proceedings of the IEEE Conference on Computer Vision and Pattern Recognition, pp. 193–202 (2016)
18. Kittler, J.: On the accuracy of the sobel edge detector. Image Vis. Comput. **1**(1), 37–42 (1983)
19. Canny, J.: A computational approach to edge detection. IEEE Trans. Pattern Anal. Mach. Intell. **6**, 679–698 (1986)
20. Fram, J.R., Deutsch, E.S.: On the quantitative evaluation of edge detection schemes and their comparison with human performance. IEEE Trans. Comput. **C-24**(6), 616–628 (1975)
21. Perona, P., Malik, J.: Scale-space and edge detection using anisotropic diffusion. IEEE Trans. Pattern Anal. Mach. Intell. **12**(7), 629–639 (1990)

22. Lowe, D.G.: Distinctive image features from scale-invariant keypoints. Int. J. Comput. Vis. **60**(2), 91–110 (2004)
23. Siddiqui, M., Medioni, G.: Human pose estimation from a single view point, real-time range sensor. In: 2010 IEEE Computer Society Conference on Computer Vision and Pattern Recognition Workshops (CVPRW), pp. 1–8. IEEE (2010)
24. Martin, D.R., Fowlkes, C.C., Malik, J.: Learning to detect natural image boundaries using local brightness, color, and texture cues. IEEE Trans. Pattern Anal. Mach. Intell. **26**(5), 530–549 (2004)
25. Dollar, P., Tu, Z., Belongie, S.: Supervised learning of edges and object boundaries. In: 2006 IEEE Computer Society Conference on Computer Vision and Pattern Recognition, vol. 2, pp. 1964–1971. IEEE (2006)
26. Dollár, P., Zitnick, C.L.: Fast edge detection using structured forests. IEEE Trans. Pattern Anal. Mach. Intell. **37**(8), 1558–1570 (2015)
27. Kokkinos, I.: Pushing the boundaries of boundary detection using deep learning. arXiv preprint arXiv:1511.07386 (2015)
28. Krizhevsky, A., Sutskever, I., Hinton, G.E.: ImageNet classification with deep convolutional neural networks. In: Advances in Neural Information Processing Systems, pp. 1097–1105 (2012)
29. LeCun, Y., et al.: Handwritten digit recognition with a back-propagation network. In: Advances in Neural Information Processing Systems, pp. 396–404 (1990)
30. Simonyan, K., Zisserman, A.: Very deep convolutional networks for large-scale image recognition. arXiv preprint arXiv:1409.1556 (2014)
31. Xie, S., Tu, Z.: Holistically-nested edge detection. Int. J. Comput. Vis. **125**(1–3), 3–18 (2017)
32. Gu, J., Zhou, Y., Zuo, X.: Making class bias useful: a strategy of learning from imbalanced data. In: Yin, H., Tino, P., Corchado, E., Byrne, W., Yao, X. (eds.) IDEAL 2007. LNCS, vol. 4881, pp. 287–295. Springer, Heidelberg (2007). https://doi.org/10.1007/978-3-540-77226-2_30
33. Tang, L., Liu, H.: Bias analysis in text classification for highly skewed data. In: Fifth IEEE International Conference on Data Mining, 4-p. IEEE (2005)
34. Lusa, L., et al.: Class prediction for high-dimensional class-imbalanced data. BMC Bioinform. **11**(1), 523 (2010)
35. Haider, A.H., et al.: Unconscious race and class bias: its association with decision making by trauma and acute care surgeons. J. Trauma Acute Care Surg. **77**(3), 409–416 (2014)
36. Phillips, S.J., Dudík, M.: Generative and discriminative learning with unknown labeling bias. In: Advances in Neural information Processing Systems, pp. 401–408 (2009)
37. Milletari, F., Navab, N., Ahmadi, S.A.: V-net: Fully convolutional neural networks for volumetric medical image segmentation. In: 2016 Fourth International Conference on 3D Vision (3DV), pp. 565–571. IEEE (2016)
38. Dice, L.R.: Measures of the amount of ecologic association between species. Ecology **26**(3), 297–302 (1945)
39. Pinheiro, P.O., Lin, T.-Y., Collobert, R., Dollár, P.: Learning to refine object segments. In: Leibe, B., Matas, J., Sebe, N., Welling, M. (eds.) ECCV 2016. LNCS, vol. 9905, pp. 75–91. Springer, Cham (2016). https://doi.org/10.1007/978-3-319-46448-0_5
40. Xie, S., Girshick, R., Dollr, P., Tu, Z., He, K.: Aggregated residual transformations for deep neural networks (2016)

41. Lin, G., Milan, A., Shen, C., Reid, I.: RefineNet: Multi-path refinement networks for high-resolution semantic segmentation. In: IEEE Conference on Computer Vision and Pattern Recognition (CVPR) (2017)
42. He, K., Zhang, X., Ren, S., Sun, J.: Deep residual learning for image recognition. In: Proceedings of the IEEE Conference on Computer Vision and Pattern Recognition, pp. 770–778 (2016)
43. Adam Paszke, Sam Gross, S.C., Chanan, G.: PyTorch (2017)
44. Kingma, D.P., Ba, J.: Adam: a method for stochastic optimization. CoRR abs/1412.6980 (2014)
45. Wang, Y., Zhao, X., Huang, K.: Deep crisp boundaries. In: Proceedings of the IEEE Conference on Computer Vision and Pattern Recognition, pp. 3892–3900 (2017)
46. Isola, P., Zoran, D., Krishnan, D., Adelson, E.H.: Crisp boundary detection using pointwise mutual information. In: Fleet, D., Pajdla, T., Schiele, B., Tuytelaars, T. (eds.) ECCV 2014. LNCS, vol. 8691, pp. 799–814. Springer, Cham (2014). https://doi.org/10.1007/978-3-319-10578-9_52
47. Bertasius, G., Shi, J., Torresani, L.: High-for-low and low-for-high: efficient boundary detection from deep object features and its applications to high-level vision. In: Proceedings of the IEEE International Conference on Computer Vision, pp. 504–512 (2015)
48. Mottaghi, R., et al.: The role of context for object detection and semantic segmentation in the wild. In: Proceedings of the IEEE Conference on Computer Vision and Pattern Recognition, pp. 891–898 (2014)
49. Hallman, S., Fowlkes, C.C.: Oriented edge forests for boundary detection. In: Proceedings of the IEEE Conference on Computer Vision and Pattern Recognition, pp. 1732–1740 (2015)
50. Gupta, S., Arbelaez, P., Malik, J.: Perceptual organization and recognition of indoor scenes from RGB-D images. In: 2013 IEEE Conference on Computer Vision and Pattern Recognition (CVPR), pp. 564–571. IEEE (2013)
51. Gupta, S., Girshick, R., Arbeláez, P., Malik, J.: Learning rich features from RGB-D images for object detection and segmentation. In: Fleet, D., Pajdla, T., Schiele, B., Tuytelaars, T. (eds.) ECCV 2014. LNCS, vol. 8695, pp. 345–360. Springer, Cham (2014). https://doi.org/10.1007/978-3-319-10584-0_23

Image Manipulation with Perceptual Discriminators

Diana Sungatullina$^{(\boxtimes)}$, Egor Zakharov, Dmitry Ulyanov,
and Victor Lempitsky

Skolkovo Institute of Science and Technology, Moscow, Russia
{d.sungatullina,egor.zakharov,dmitry.ulyanov,lempitsky}@skoltech.ru

Abstract. Systems that perform image manipulation using deep convolutional networks have achieved remarkable realism. Perceptual losses and losses based on adversarial discriminators are the two main classes of learning objectives behind these advances. In this work, we show how these two ideas can be combined in a principled and non-additive manner for unaligned image translation tasks. This is accomplished through a special architecture of the discriminator network inside generative adversarial learning framework. The new architecture, that we call a *perceptual discriminator*, embeds the convolutional parts of a pre-trained deep classification network inside the discriminator network. The resulting architecture can be trained on unaligned image datasets, while benefiting from the robustness and efficiency of perceptual losses. We demonstrate the merits of the new architecture in a series of qualitative and quantitative comparisons with baseline approaches and state-of-the-art frameworks for unaligned image translation.

Keywords: Image translation · Image editing · Perceptual loss
Generative adversarial networks

1 Introduction

Generative convolutional neural networks have achieved remarkable success in image manipulation tasks both due to their ability to train on large amount of data [12,20,23] and due to natural image priors associated with such architectures [38]. Recently, the ability to train image manipulation ConvNets has been shown in the *unaligned* training scenario [5,42,43], where the training is based on sets of images annotated with the presence/absence of a certain attribute, rather than based on *aligned* datasets containing {input,output} image pairs. The ability to train from unaligned data provides considerable flexibility in dataset collection and in learning new manipulation effects, yet poses additional algorithmic challenges.

Generally, the realism of the deep image manipulation methods is known to depend strongly on the choice of the loss functions that are used to train

---

D. Sungatullina and E. Zakharov—Indicates equal contribution.

© Springer Nature Switzerland AG 2018
V. Ferrari et al. (Eds.): ECCV 2018, LNCS 11210, pp. 587–602, 2018.
https://doi.org/10.1007/978-3-030-01231-1_36

generative ConvNets. In particular, simplistic pixelwise losses (e.g. the squared distance loss) are known to limit the realism and are also non-trivial to apply in the unaligned training scenario. The rapid improvement of realism of deep image generation and processing is thus associated with two classes of loss functions that go beyond pixel-wise losses. The first group (so-called *perceptual losses*) are based on matching activations inside pre-trained deep convolutional networks (the VGG architecture trained for ILSVRC image classification is by far the most popular choice [35]). The second group consists of *adversarial losses*, where the loss function is defined implicitly using a separate *discriminator* network that is trained adversarially in parallel with the main generative network.

The two groups (perceptual losses and adversarial losses) are known to have largely complementary strengths and weaknesses. Thus, perceptual losses are easy to incorporate and are easy to scale to high-resolution images, however their use in unaligned training scenario is difficult, as these loss terms require a concrete target image to match the activations to. Adversarial losses have the potential to achieve higher realism and can be used naturally in the unaligned scenarios, yet adversarial training is known to be hard to set up properly, often suffer from mode collapse, and is hard to scale to high-resolution images. Combining perceptual and adversarial losses in an additive way has been popular [11,24,33,40]. Thus, a generative ConvNet can be trained by minimizing a linear combination of an adversarial and a perceptual (and potentially some other) losses. Yet such additive combination combines not only strengths but also weaknesses of the two approaches. In particular, the use of perceptual loss still incurs the use of aligned datasets for training.

In this work we present an architecture for realistic image manipulation, which combines perceptual and adversarial losses in a natural *non-additive* way. Importantly, the architecture keeps the ability of adversarial losses to train on unaligned datasets, while also benefiting from the stability of perceptual losses. Our idea is very simple and concerned with the particular design of the discriminator network for adversarial training. The design encapsulates the pretrained classification network as the initial part of the discriminator. During adversarial training, the generator network is effectively learned to match the activations inside several layers of this reference network, just like the perceptual losses do. We show that the incorporation of the pretrained network into the discriminator stabilizes the training and scales well to higher resolution images, as is common with perceptual losses. At the same time, the use of adversarial training allows to avoid the need for aligned training data.

Generally, we have found that the suggested architecture can be trained with little tuning to impose complex image manipulations, such as adding and removing smile to human faces, face ageing and rejuvenation, gender change, hair style change, etc. In the experiments, we show that our architecture can be used to perform complex manipulations at medium and high resolutions, and compare the proposed architecture with several adversarial learning-based baselines and recent methods for learning-based image manipulation.

2   Related Work

Generative ConvNets. Our approach is related to a rapidly growing body of works on ConvNets for image generation and editing. Some of the earlier important papers on ConvNet image generation [12] and image processing [10, 20, 23] used per-pixel loss functions and fully supervised setting, so that at test time the target image is known for each input. While this demonstrated the capability of ConvNets to generate realistic images, the proposed systems all had to be trained on aligned datasets and the amount of high-frequency details in the output images was limited due to defficiencies of pixel-wise loss functions.

Perceptual Losses. The work of Mahendran and Vedaldi [28] has demonstrated that the activations invoked by an image within a pre-trained convolutional network can be used to recover the original image. Gatys et al. [13] demonstrated that such activations can serve as content descriptors or texture descriptors of the input image, while Dosovitsky and Brox [11], Ulyanov et al. [37], Johnson et al. [21] have shown that the mismatches between the produced and the target activations can be used as so-called *perceptual losses* for a generative ConvNet. The recent work of [7] pushed the spatial resolution and the realism of images produced by a feed-forward ConvNet with perceptual losses to megapixel resolution. Generally, in all the above-mentioned works [7,11,21,37], the perceptual loss is applied in a fully supervised manner as for each training example the specific target deep activations (or the Gram matrix thereof) are given explicitly. Finally, [39] proposed a method that manipulates carefully aligned face images at high resolution by compositing desired activations of a deep pretrained network and finding an image that matches such activations using the non-feedforward optimization process similar to [13,28].

Adversarial Training. The most impressive results of generative ConvNets were obtained within generative adversarial networks (GANs) framework proposed originally by Goodfellow et al. [14]. The idea of adversarial training to implement the loss function as a separate trainable network (the *discriminator*), which is trained in parallel and in adversarial way with the generative ConvNet (the *generator*). Multiple follow-up works including [3,22,30,34] investigated the choice of convolutional architectures for the generator and for the discriminator. Achieving reliable and robust convergence of generator-discriminator pairs remains challenging [8,15,27], and in particular requires considerably more efforts than training with perceptual loss functions.

Unaligned Adversarial Training. While a lot of the original interest to GANs was associated with unconditional image generation, recently the emphasis has shifted to the conditional image synthesis. Most relevant to our work are adversarially-trained networks that perform image translation, i.e. generate output images conditioned on input images. While initial methods used aligned

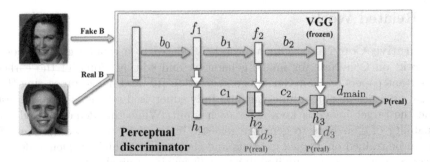

Fig. 1. The perceptual discriminator is composed of a pre-trained image classification network (such as VGG), split into blocks b_i. The parameters of those blocks are not changed during training, thus the discriminator retains access to so-called perceptual features. The outputs of these blocks are processed using learnable blocks of convolutional operations c_i and the outputs of those are used to predict the probability of an image being real or manipulated (the simpler version uses a single discriminator d_{main}, while additional path discriminators are used in the full version).

datasets for training [19,41], recently some impressive results have been obtained using unaligned training data, where only empirical distributions of the input and the output images are provided [5,42,43]. For face image manipulation, systems using adversarial training on unaligned data have been proposed in [6,9]. While we also make an emphasis on face manipulation, our contribution is orthogonal to [6,9] as perceptual discriminators can be introduced into their systems.

Combining Perceptual and Adversarial Losses. A growing number of works [11,24,40] use the combination of perceptual and adversarial loss functions to accomplish more stable training and to achieve convincing image manipulation at high resolution. Most recently, [33] showed that augmenting perceptual loss with the adversarial loss improves over the baseline system [7] (that has already achieved very impressive results) in the task of megapixel-sized conditional image synthesis. Invariably, the combination of perceptual and adversarial losses is performed in an additive manner, i.e. the two loss functions are weighted and added to each other (and potentially to some other terms). While such additive combination is simple and often very efficient, it limits learning to the aligned scenario, as perceptual terms still require to specify target activations for each training example. In this work, we propose a natural non-additive combination of perceptual losses and adversarial training that avoids the need for aligned data during training.

3   Perceptual Discriminators

3.1   Background and Motivation

Generative adversarial networks have shown impressive results in photorealistic image synthesis. The model includes a generative network G, that is trained to match the target distribution $p_{\text{target}}(\mathbf{y})$ in the data space $\mathcal{Y}$, and a discriminator network D that is trained to distinguish whether the input is real or generated by G. In the simplest form, the two networks optimize (play a zero-sum game) for the policy function $V(D, G)$:

$$\min_G \max_D V(D, G) = \mathbb{E}_{\mathbf{y} \sim p_{\text{target}}(\mathbf{y})} \log D(\mathbf{y}) + \mathbb{E}_{\mathbf{x} \sim p_{\text{source}}(\mathbf{x})} [\log(1 - D(G(\mathbf{x})))], \quad (1)$$

In (1), the source distribution $p_{\text{source}}(\mathbf{x})$ may correspond to a simple parametric distribution in a latent space such as the unit Gaussian, so that after training unconditional samples from the learned approximation to p_{target} can be drawn. Alternatively, $p_{\text{source}}(\mathbf{x})$ may correspond to another empirical distribution in the image space $\mathcal{X}$. In this case, the generator learns to *translate* images from $\mathcal{X}$ to $\mathcal{Y}$, or to *manipulate* images in the space $\mathcal{X}$ (when it coincides with $\mathcal{Y}$). Although our contribution (perceptual discriminators) is applicable to both unconditional synthesis and image manipulation/translation, we focus our evaluation on the latter scenario. For the low resolution datasets, we use the standard non-saturating GAN modification, where the generator maximizes the log-likelihood of the discriminator instead of minimizing the objective (1) [14]. For high-resolution images, following CycleGAN [42], we use the LSGAN formulation [29].

Converging to good equilibria for any of the proposed GAN games is known to be hard [8,15,27]. In general, the performance of the trained generator network crucially depends on the architecture of the discriminator network, that needs to learn to extract meaningful statistics, which are good for matching the target distribution p_{target}. The typical failure mode of GAN training is when the discriminator does not manage to learn such statistics before being "overpowered" by the generator.

3.2 Perceptual Discriminator Architecture

Multiple approaches have suggested to use activations invoked by an image $\mathbf{y}$ inside a deep pre-trained classification network $F(\mathbf{y})$ as statistics for such tasks as retrieval [4] or few-shot classification [31]. Mahendran and Vedaldi [28] have shown that activations computed after the convolutional part of such network retain most of the informations about the input $\mathbf{y}$, i.e. are essentially invertible. Subsequent works such as [11,13,21,37] all used such "perceptual" statistics to match low-level details such as texture content, certain image resolution, or particular artistic style.

Following this line of work, we suggest to base the GAN discriminator $D(\mathbf{y})$ on the perceptual statistics computed by the reference network F on the input image $\mathbf{y}$, which can be either real (coming from p_{target}) or fake (produced by the generator). Our motivation is that a discriminator that uses perceptual features has a better chance to learn good statistics than a discriminator initialized to a random network. For simplicity, we assume that the network F has a chain structure. E.g. F can be the VGGNet of [35].

Consider the subsequent blocks of the convolutional part of the reference network F, and denote them as $b_0, b_1, \ldots, b_{K-1}$. Each block may include one or more convolutional layers interleaved with non-linearities and pooling operations. Then, the perceptual statistics $\{f_1(\mathbf{y}), \ldots, f_K(\mathbf{y})\}$ are computed as:

$$f_1(\mathbf{y}) = b_0(\mathbf{y}) \tag{2}$$

$$f_i(\mathbf{y}) = b_{i-1}(f_{i-1}(\mathbf{y})), \quad i = 2, \ldots, K, \tag{3}$$

so that each $f_i(\mathbf{y})$ is a stack of convolutional maps of the spatial dimensions $W_i \times W_i$. The dimension W_i is determined by the preceeding size W_{i-1} as well as by the presence of strides and pooling operations inside b_i. In our experiments we use features from consecutive blocks, i.e. $W_i = W_{i-1}/2$.

The overall structure of our discriminator is shown in Fig. 1. The key novelty of our discriminator are the in-built perceptual statistics f_i (top of the image), which are known to be good at assessing image realism [13,21,39]. During the backpropagation, the gradients to the generator flow through the perceptual statistics extractors b_i, but the parameters of b_i are frozen and inherited from the network pretrained for large-scale classification. This stabilizes the training, and ensures that at each moment of time the discriminator has access to "good" features, and therefore cannot be overpowered by the generator easily.

In more detail, the proposed discriminator architecture combines together perceptual statistics using the following computations:

$$h_1(\mathbf{y}) = f_1(\mathbf{y}) \tag{4}$$

$$h_i(\mathbf{y}) = \texttt{stack}\left[c_{i-1}(h_{i-1}(\mathbf{y}), \phi_{i-1}), f_i(\mathbf{y})\right], \quad i = 2, \ldots, K, \tag{5}$$

where $\texttt{stack}$ denotes stacking operation, and the convolutional blocks c_j with learnable parameters ϕ_j (for $j = 1, \ldots, K - 1$) are composed of convolutions, leaky ReLU nonlinearities, and average pooling operations. Each of the c_j blocks thus transforms map stacks of the spatial size $W_j \times W_j$ to map stacks of the spatial size $W_{j+1} \times W_{j+1}$. Thus, the strides and pooling operations inside c_j match the strides and/or pooling operations inside b_j.

Using a series of convolutional and fully-connected layers with learnable parameters ψ_{main} applied to the representation $h_K(\mathbf{y})$, the discriminator outputs the probability d_{main} of the whole image $\mathbf{y}$ being real. For low- to medium-resolution images we perform experiments using only this probability. For high-resolution, we found that additional outputs from the discriminator resulted in better outcomes. Using the "patch discriminator" idea [19,42], to several feature representations h_j we apply a convolution+LeakyReLU block d_j with learnable parameters ψ_j that outputs probabilities $d_{j,p}$ at every spatial locations p. We then replace the regular log probability $\log D(\mathbf{y}) \equiv \log d_{\text{main}}$ of an image being real with:

$$\log D(\mathbf{y}) = \log d_{\text{main}}(\mathbf{y}) + \sum_j \sum_{p \in \text{Grid}(W_j \times W_j)} \log d_{j,p}(\mathbf{y}) \tag{6}$$

Note, that this makes our discriminator "multi-scale", since spatial resolution W_j varies for different j. The idea of multiple classifiers inside the discriminator have also been proposed recently in [18,40]. Unlike [18,40] where these classifiers are disjoint, in our architecture all such classifiers are different branches of the same network that has perceptual features underneath.

During training, the parameters of the c blocks inside the feature network F remain fixed, while the parameters ϕ_i of feature extractors c_i and the parameters ψ_i of the discriminators d_i are updated during the adversarial learning, which forces the "perceptual" alignment between the output of the generator and p_{target}. Thus, wrapping perceptual loss terms into additional layers c_i and d_i and putting them together into the adversarial discriminator allows us to use such perceptual terms in the unaligned training scenario. Such unaligned training was, in general, not possible with the "traditional" perceptual losses.

3.3   Architecture Details

Reference Network. Following multiple previous works [13,21,37], we consider the so-called *VGG network* from [35] trained on ILSVRC2012 [32] as the reference network F. In particular, we pick the VGG-19 variant, to which we simply refer to as VGG. While the perceptual features from VGG already work well, the original VGG architecture can be further improved. Radford et. al [30] reported that as far as leaky ReLU avoids sparse gradients, replacing ReLUs with leaky ReLUs [17] in the discriminator stabilizes the training process of GANs. For the same reasons, changing max pooling layers to average pooling removes unwanted sparseness in the backpropagated gradients. Following these observations, we construct the *VGG** network, which is particularly suitable for the adversarial game. We thus took the VGG-19 network pretrained on ILSVRC dataset, replaced all max pooling layers by average poolings, ReLU nonlinearities by leaky ReLUs with a negative slope 0.2 and then trained on the ILSVRC dataset for further two days. We compare the variants of our approach based on VGG and VGG* features below.

Generator Architecture. For the image manipulation experiments, we used transformer network proposed by Johnson et al. [21]. It consists of M convolutional layers with stride size 2, N residual blocks [16] and M upsampling layers, each one increases resolution by a factor of 2. We set M and N in a way that allows outputs of the last residual block to have large enough receptive field, but at the same time for generator and discriminator to have similar number of parameters. We provide detailed descriptions of architectures in [2].

Stabilizing the Generator. We have also used two additional methods to improve the generator learning and to prevent its collapse. First, we have added the *identity loss* [36,42] that ensures that the generator does not change the input, when it comes from the p_{target}. Thus, the following term is added to the maximization objective of the generator:

$$J_{\text{id}}^G = -\lambda_{\text{id}}\,\mathbb{E}_{\mathbf{y}\sim p_{\text{target}}}\lambda\big\|\mathbf{y} - G(\mathbf{y})\big\|_{L_1}, \tag{7}$$

where λ_{id} is a meta-parameter that controls the contribution of the weight, and $\| \cdot \|_{L_1}$ denotes pixel-wise L1-metric.

To achieve the best results for the hardest translation tasks, we have found the cycle idea from the CycleGAN [42] needed. We thus train two generators $G_{x \to y}$ and $G_{y \to x}$ operating in opposite directions in parallel (and jointly with two discriminators), while adding reciprocity terms ensuring that mappings $G_{x \to y} \circ G_{y \to x}$ and $G_{y \to x} \circ G_{x \to y}$ are close to identity mappings.

Moreover, we notice that usage of external features as inputs for the discriminator leads to fast convergence of the discriminator loss to zero. Even though this is expected, since our method essentially corresponds to pretraining of the discriminator, this behavior is one of the GAN failure cases [8] and on practice leads to bad results in harder tasks. Therefore we find pretraining of the generator to be required for increased stability. For image translation task we pretrain generator as autoencoder. Moreover, the necessity to pretrain the generator makes our approach fail to operate in DCGAN setting with unconditional generator.

After an additional stabilization through the pretraining and the identity and/or cycle losses, the generator becomes less prone to collapse. Overall, in the resulting approach it is neither easy for the discriminator to overpower the generator (this is prevented by the identity and/or cycle losses), nor is it easy for the generator to overpower the discriminator (as the latter always has access to perceptual features, which are good at judging the realism of the output).

4   Experiments

The goal of the experimental validation is two-fold. The primary goal is to validate the effect of perceptual discriminators as compared to baseline architectures which use traditional discriminators that do not have access to perceptual features. The secondary goal is to validate the ability of our full system based on perceptual discriminators to handle harder image translation/manipulation task with higher resolution and with less data. Extensive additional results are available on our project page [2]. We perform the bulk of our experiments on CelebA dataset [25], due to its large size, popularity and the availability of the attribute annotations (the dataset comprises over 200k of roughly-aligned images with 40 binary attributes; we use 160×160 central crops of the images). As harder image translation task, we use CelebA-HQ [22] dataset, which consists of high resolution versions of images from CelebA and is smaller in size. Lastly, we evaluate our model on problems with non-face datasets like apples to oranges and photo to Monet texture transfer tasks.

Experiments were carried out on NVIDIA DGX-2 server.

Qualitative Comparison on CelebA. Even though our contribution is orthogonal to a particular GAN-based image translation method, we chose one of them, provided modifications we proposed and compared it with the following important baselines in an attribute manipulation task:

| Input | DFI | DCGAN | VGG-GAN (ours) | VGG*-GAN (ours) | CycleGAN | FaceApp |

Fig. 2. Qualitative comparison of the proposed systems as well as baselines for neutral→smile image manipulation. As baselines, we show the results of DFI (perceptual features, no adversarial training) and DCGAN (same generator, no perceptual features in the discriminator). Systems with perceptual discriminators output more plausible manipulations.

- *DCGAN* [30]: in this baseline GAN system we used image translation model with generator and discriminator trained only with adversarial loss.
- *CycleGAN* [42]: this GAN-based method learns two reciprocal transforms in parallel with two discriminators in two domains. We have used the authors' code (PyTorch version).
- *DFI* [39]: to transform an image, this approach first determines target VGG feature representation by adding the feature vector corresponding to input image and the shift vector calculated using nearest neighbours in both domains. Then the resulting image is produced using optimization-based feature inversion as in [28]. We have used the authors' code.
- *FaceApp* [1]: is a very popular closed-source app that is known for the quality of its filters (transforms), although the exact algorithmic details are unknown.

Our model is represented by two basic variants.

- *VGG-GAN*: we use DCGAN as our base model. The discriminator has a single classifier and no generator pretraining or regularization is applied, other than identity loss mentioned in the previous section.
- *VGG*-GAN*: same as the previous model, but we use a finetuned VGG network variant with dense gradients.

The comparison with state-of-the-art image transformation systems is performed to verify the competitiveness of the proposed architecture (Fig. 2). In general, we observe that VGG*-GAN and VGG-GAN models consistently outperformed DCGAN variant, achieving higher effective resolution and obtaining

Table 1. Quantitative comparison: (a) Photorealism user study. We show the fraction of times each method has been chosen as "the best" among all in terms of photorealism and identity preservation (the higher the better). (b) C2ST results (cross-entropy, the higher the better). (c) Log-loss of classifier trained on real data for each class (the lower the better). See main text for details.

	(a) User study		(b) C2ST, $\times 10^{-2}$			(c) Classification loss		
	Smile	Age	Smile	Gender	Hair color	Smile	Gender	Hair color
DFI [39]	0.16	0.4	<0.1	<0.01	<0.01	1.3	0.5	1.14
FaceApp [1]	0.45	0.41	–	–	–	–	–	–
DCGAN [30]	–	–	0.6	0.03	0.06	0.6	1.5	2.33
CycleGAN [42]	0.03	0.04	5.3	0.35	0.49	1.2	0.8	2.41
VGG-GAN	–	–	8.6	0.21	0.96	0.4	0.1	1.3
VGG*-GAN	0.36	0.15	5.2	0.24	1.29	0.7	0.1	1.24
Real data	–	–	–	–	–	0.1	0.01	0.56

more plausible high-frequency details in the resulting images. While a more complex CycleGAN system is also capable of generating crisp images, we found that the synthesized smile often does not look plausible and does not match the face. DFI turns out to be successful in attribute manipulation, yet often produces undesirable artifacts, while FaceApp shows photorealistic results, but with low attribute diversity. Here we also evaluate the contribution of dense gradients idea for VGG encoder and find it providing minor quality improvements.

User Photorealism Study on CelebA. We have also performed an informal user study of the photorealism. The study enrolled 30 subjects unrelated to computer vision and evaluated the photorealism of VGG*-GAN, DFI, Cycle-GAN and FaceApp on smile and aging/rejuvenation transforms. To assess the photorealism, the subjects were presented quintuplets of photographs unseen during training. In each quintuplet the center photo was an image without the target attribute (e.g. real photo of neutral expression), while the other four pictures were manipulated by one of the methods and presented in random order. The subjects were then asked to pick one of the four manipulations that they found most plausible (both in terms of realism and identity preservation). While there was no hard time limit, the users were asked to make the pick as quickly as possible. Each subject was presented overall 30 quintuplets with 15 quantuplets allocated for each of the considered attribute. The results in Table 1a show that VGG*-GAN is competitive and in particular considerably better than the other feed-forward method in the comparison (CycleGAN), but FaceApp being the winner overall. This comes with the caveat that the training set of FaceApp is likely to be bigger than CelebA. We also speculate that the diversity of smiles in FaceApp seems to be lower (Fig. 2), which is the deficiency that is not reflected in this user study.

| Input | Blond hair | Black hair | Brown hair | Gender swap | Smile on/off |

Fig. 3. Results for VGG*-MS-CycleGAN attribute editing at 256 × 256 resolution on Celeba-HQ dataset. Networks have been trained to perform pairwise domain translation between the values of hair color, gender and smile attributes. Digital zoom-in recommended. See [2] for more manipulation examples.

Quantitative Results on CelebA. To get objective performance measure, we have used the classifier two-sample test (C2ST) [26] to quantitatively compare GANs with the proposed discriminators to other methods. For each method, we have thus learned a separate classifier to discriminate between hold-out set of real images from target distribution and synthesized images, produced by each of the methods. We split both hold-out set and the set of fake images into training and testing parts, fit the classifier to the training set and report the log-loss over the testing set in the Table 1b. The results comply with the qualitative observations: artifacts, produced by DCGAN and DFI are being easily detected by the classifier resulting in a very low log-loss. The proposed system stays on par with a more complex CycleGAN (better on two transforms out of three), proving that a perceptual discriminator can remove the need in two additional networks and cycle losses. Additionally, we evaluated attribute translation performance in a similar fashion to StarGAN [9]. We have trained a model for attribute classification on CelebA and measured average log-likelihood for the synthetic and real data to belong to the target class. Our method achieved lower log-loss than other methods on two out of three face attributes (see Table 1c).

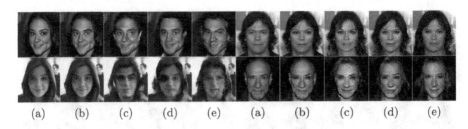

(a)   (b)   (c)   (d)   (e)   (a)   (b)   (c)   (d)   (e)

Fig. 4. We compare different architectures for the discriminator on CelebA-HQ 256 × 256 male ↔ female problem. We train all architectures in CycleGAN manner with LSGAN objective and compare different discriminator architectures. (a) Input, (b) VGG*-MS-CycleGAN: multi-scale perceptual discriminator with pretrained VGG* as a feature network F, (c) Rand-MS-CycleGAN: multi-scale perceptual discriminator with a feature network F having VGG* architecture with randomly-initialized weights, (d) MS-CycleGAN: multi-scale discriminator with the trunk shared across scales (as in our framework), where images serve as a direct input, (e) separate multi-scale discriminators similar to Wang et al. [40]. Digital zoom-in recommended.

Higher Resolution. We further evaluate our model on CelebA-HQ dataset. Here in order to obtain high quality results we use all proposed regularization methods. We refer to our best model as VGG*-MS-CycleGAN, which corresponds to the usage of VGG* network with dense gradients as an encoder, multi-scale perceptual discriminator based on VGG* network, CycleGAN regularization and pretraining of the generator. Following CycleGAN, we use LSGAN [29] as an adversarial objective for that model. We trained on 256 × 256 version of CelebA-HQ dataset and present attribute manipulation results in Fig. 3. As we can see, our model provides photorealistic samples while capturing differences between the attributes even for smaller amount of training samples (few thousands per domain) and higher resolution compared to our previous tests.

In order to ensure that each of our individual contributions affects the quality of these results, we consider three variations of our discriminator architecture and compare them to the alternative multi-scale discriminator proposed in Wang et al. [40]. While Wang et al. used multiple identical discriminators operating at different scales, we argue that this architecture has redundancy in terms of number of parameters and can be reduced to our architecture by combining these discriminators into a single network with shared trunk and separate multi-scale output branches (as is done in our method). Both variants are included into the comparison in Fig. 4. Also we consider *Rand-MS-CycleGAN* baseline that uses random weights in the feature extractor in order to tease apart the contribution of VGG* architecture as a feature network F and the effect of also having its weights pretrained on the success of the adversarial training. While the weights inside the VGG part were not frozen, so that adversarial training process could theoretically evolve good features in the discriminator, we were unable to make this baseline produce reasonable results. For high weight of the identity loss λ_{id} the resulting generator network produced near-identical results

Input   CycleGAN   VGG*-   Input   CycleGAN   VGG*-
                        CycleGAN   CycleGAN

Fig. 5. Comparison between CycleGAN and VGG*-MS-CycleGAN on painting↔photo translation task. It demonstrates the applicability of our approach beyond face image manipulation. See [2] for more examples.

to the inputs, while decreasing λ_{id} lead to severe generator collapse. We conclude that the architecture alone cannot explain the good performance of perceptual discriminators (which is validated below) and that having pretrained weights in the feature network is important.

Non-face Datasets. While the focus of our evaluation was on face attribute modification tasks, our contribution applies to other translation tasks, as we verify in this section by performing qualitative comparison with the Cycle-GAN and VGG*-MS-CycleGAN architectures on two non-face domains on which CycleGAN was originally evaluated: an artistic style transfer task (Monet-photographs) in Fig. 5 and an apple-orange conversion in Fig. 6 (the figures show representative results). To achieve fair comparison, we use the same amount of residual blocks and channels in the generator and the same number of down-sampling layers and initial amount of channels in discriminator both in our model and in the original CycleGAN. We used the authors' implementation of CycleGAN with default parameters. While the results on the style transfer task are inconclusive, for the harder apple-to-orange task we generally observe the performance of perceptual discriminators to be better.

Other Learning Formulations. Above, we have provided the evaluation of the perceptual discriminator idea to unaligned image translation tasks. In principle, perceptual discriminators can be used for other tasks, e.g. for unconditional generation and aligned image translation. In our preliminary experiments, we however were not able to achieve improvement over properly tuned baselines. In particular, for aligned image translation (including image superresolution) an additive combination of standard discriminator architectures and perceptual losses performs just as well as our method. This is not surprising, since the presence of alignment means that perceptual losses can be computed straight-

| Input | CycleGAN | VGG*-MS CycleGAN | Input | CycleGAN | VGG*-MS CycleGAN |

Fig. 6. Apple↔orange translation samples with CycleGAN and VGG*-MS-CycleGAN are shown. Zoom-in recommended. See [2] for more examples.

forwardly, while they also stabilize the GAN learning in this case. For unconditional image generation, a naive application of our idea leads to discriminators that quickly overpower generators in the initial stages of the game leading to learning collapse.

5   Summary

We have presented a new discriminator architecture for adversarial training that incorporates perceptual loss ideas with adversarial training. We have demonstrated its usefulness for unaligned image translation tasks, where the direct application of perceptual losses is infeasible. Our approach can be regarded as an instance of a more general idea of using transfer learning, so that easier discriminative learning formulations can be used to stabilize and improve GANs and other generative learning formulations.

Acknowledgements. This work has been supported by the Ministry of Education and Science of the Russian Federation (grant 14.756.31.0001).

References

1. Faceapp (2018). https://www.faceapp.com/
2. Project webpage (2018). http://egorzakharov.github.io/perceptual_gan
3. Arjovsky, M., Chintala, S., Bottou, L.: Wasserstein generative adversarial networks. In: Proceedings of ICML, pp. 214–223 (2017)
4. Babenko, A., Slesarev, A., Chigorin, A., Lempitsky, V.: Neural codes for image retrieval. In: Fleet, D., Pajdla, T., Schiele, B., Tuytelaars, T. (eds.) ECCV 2014. LNCS, vol. 8689, pp. 584–599. Springer, Cham (2014). https://doi.org/10.1007/978-3-319-10590-1_38
5. Benaim, S., Wolf, L.: One-sided unsupervised domain mapping. In: Proceedings of NIPS, pp. 752–762 (2017)

6. Brock, A., Lim, T., Ritchie, J.M., Weston, N.: Neural photo editing with introspective adversarial networks. CoRR abs/1609.07093 (2016)

7. Chen, Q., Koltun, V.: Photographic image synthesis with cascaded refinement networks. In: Proceedings of ICCV, pp. 1520–1529 (2017)

8. Chintala, S., Denton, E., Arjovsky, M., Mathieu, M.: How to train a GAN? Tips and tricks to make GANs work (2017). https://github.com/soumith/ganhacks

9. Choi, Y., Choi, M., Kim, M., Ha, J., Kim, S., Choo, J.: StarGAN: unified generative adversarial networks for multi-domain image-to-image translation. In: Proceedings of CVPR (2018)

10. Dong, C., Loy, C.C., He, K., Tang, X.: Learning a deep convolutional network for image super-resolution. In: Fleet, D., Pajdla, T., Schiele, B., Tuytelaars, T. (eds.) ECCV 2014. LNCS, vol. 8692, pp. 184–199. Springer, Cham (2014). https://doi.org/10.1007/978-3-319-10593-2_13

11. Dosovitskiy, A., Brox, T.: Generating images with perceptual similarity metrics based on deep networks. In: Proceedings of NIPS, pp. 658–666 (2016)

12. Dosovitskiy, A., Springenberg, J.T., Brox, T.: Learning to generate chairs with convolutional neural networks. In: Proceedings of CVPR, pp. 1538–1546 (2015)

13. Gatys, L.A., Ecker, A.S., Bethge, M.: Image style transfer using convolutional neural networks. In: Proceedings of CVPR, pp. 2414–2423 (2016)

14. Goodfellow, I., et al.: Generative adversarial nets. In: Proceedings of NIPS, pp. 2672–2680 (2014)

15. Goodfellow, I.J.: NIPS 2016 tutorial: Generative adversarial networks. CoRR abs/1701.00160 (2017)

16. He, K., Zhang, X., Ren, S., Sun, J.: Deep residual learning for image recognition. CoRR abs/1512.03385 (2015). http://arxiv.org/abs/1512.03385

17. He, K., Zhang, X., Ren, S., Sun, J.: Delving deep into rectifiers: surpassing human-level performance on imagenet classification. In: 2015 IEEE International Conference on Computer Vision, ICCV 2015, 7–13 December 2015, Santiago, Chile, pp. 1026–1034 (2015)

18. Iizuka, S., Simo-Serra, E., Ishikawa, H.: Globally and locally consistent image completion. ACM Trans. Graph. **36**(4), 107:1–107:14 (2017)

19. Isola, P., Zhu, J., Zhou, T., Efros, A.A.: Image-to-image translation with conditional adversarial networks. In: Proceedings of CVPR, pp. 5967–5976 (2017)

20. Jain, V., Seung, S.: Natural image denoising with convolutional networks. In: Proceedings of NIPS, pp. 769–776 (2009)

21. Johnson, J., Alahi, A., Fei-Fei, L.: Perceptual losses for real-time style transfer and super-resolution. In: Leibe, B., Matas, J., Sebe, N., Welling, M. (eds.) ECCV 2016. LNCS, vol. 9906, pp. 694–711. Springer, Cham (2016). https://doi.org/10.1007/978-3-319-46475-6_43

22. Karras, T., Aila, T., Laine, S., Lehtinen, J.: Progressive growing of GANs for improved quality, stability, and variation. CoRR abs/1710.10196 (2017)

23. Kim, J., Kwon Lee, J., Mu Lee, K.: Accurate image super-resolution using very deep convolutional networks. In: Proceedings of CVPR, pp. 1646–1654 (2016)

24. Ledig, C., et al.: Photo-realistic single image super-resolution using a generative adversarial network. In: Proceedings of CVPR (2017)

25. Liu, Z., Luo, P., Wang, X., Tang, X.: Deep learning face attributes in the wild. In: Proceedings of ICCV (2015)

26. Lopez-Paz, D., Oquab, M.: Revisiting classifier two-sample tests. arXiv preprint arXiv:1610.06545 (2016)

27. Lucic, M., Kurach, K., Michalski, M., Gelly, S., Bousquet, O.: Are GANs created equal? A large-scale study. CoRR abs/1711.10337 (2017)

28. Mahendran, A., Vedaldi, A.: Understanding deep image representations by inverting them. In: Proceedings of CVPR (2015)
29. Mao, X., Li, Q., Xie, H., Lau, R.Y.K., Wang, Z.: Multi-class generative adversarial networks with the L2 loss function. CoRR abs/1611.04076 (2016)
30. Radford, A., Metz, L., Chintala, S.: Unsupervised representation learning with deep convolutional generative adversarial networks. CoRR abs/1511.06434 (2015)
31. Razavian, A.S., Azizpour, H., Sullivan, J., Carlsson, S.: CNN features off-the-shelf: an astounding baseline for recognition. In: IEEE Conference on Computer Vision and Pattern Recognition, CVPR Workshops 2014, 23–28 June 2014, Columbus, OH, USA, pp. 512–519 (2014)
32. Russakovsky, O., et al.: Imagenet large scale visual recognition challenge. CoRR abs/1409.0575 (2014). http://arxiv.org/abs/1409.0575
33. Sajjadi, M.S.M., Scholkopf, B., Hirsch, M.: Enhancenet: single image super-resolution through automated texture synthesis. In: Proceedings of ICCV (2017)
34. Salimans, T., Goodfellow, I.J., Zaremba, W., Cheung, V., Radford, A., Chen, X.: Improved techniques for training GANs. In: Proceedings of NIPS, pp. 2226–2234 (2016)
35. Simonyan, K., Zisserman, A.: Very deep convolutional networks for large-scale image recognition. CoRR abs/1409.1556 (2014)
36. Taigman, Y., Polyak, A., Wolf, L.: Unsupervised cross-domain image generation. CoRR abs/1611.02200 (2016). http://arxiv.org/abs/1611.02200
37. Ulyanov, D., Lebedev, V., Vedaldi, A., Lempitsky, V.S.: Texture networks: feed-forward synthesis of textures and stylized images. In: Proceedings of ICML, pp. 1349–1357 (2016)
38. Ulyanov, D., Vedaldi, A., Lempitsky, V.S.: Deep image prior. In: Proceedings of CVPR (2018)
39. Upchurch, P., et al.: Deep feature interpolation for image content changes. In: Proceedings of CVPR, pp. 6090–6099 (2017)
40. Wang, T.C., Liu, M.Y., Zhu, J.Y., Tao, A., Kautz, J., Catanzaro, B.: High-resolution image synthesis and semantic manipulation with conditional GANs. arXiv preprint arXiv:1711.11585 (2017)
41. Zhang, H., et al.: Stackgan: Text to photo-realistic image synthesis with stacked generative adversarial networks. CoRR abs/1612.03242 (2016)
42. Zhu, J., Park, T., Isola, P., Efros, A.A.: Unpaired image-to-image translation using cycle-consistent adversarial networks. In: Proceedings of ICCV, pp. 2242–2251 (2017)
43. Zhu, J., et al.: Toward multimodal image-to-image translation. In: Proceedings of NIPS, pp. 465–476 (2017)

Structural Consistency and Controllability for Diverse Colorization

Safa Messaoud[(✉)], David Forsyth[(✉)], and Alexander G. Schwing[(✉)]

University of Illinois at Urbana-Champaign, Champaign, USA
{messaou2,aschwing,daf}@illinois.edu

Abstract. Colorizing a given gray-level image is an important task in the media and advertising industry. Due to the ambiguity inherent to colorization (many shades are often plausible), recent approaches started to explicitly model diversity. However, one of the most obvious artifacts, structural inconsistency, is rarely considered by existing methods which predict chrominance independently for every pixel. To address this issue, we develop a conditional random field based variational auto-encoder formulation which is able to achieve diversity while taking into account structural consistency. Moreover, we introduce a controllability mechanism that can incorporate external constraints from diverse sources including a user interface. Compared to existing baselines, we demonstrate that our method obtains more diverse and globally consistent colorizations on the LFW, LSUN-Church and ILSVRC-2015 datasets.

Keywords: Colorization · Gaussian-Conditional Random Field · VAE

1 Introduction

Colorization of images requires to predict the two missing channels of a provided gray-level input. Similar to other computer vision tasks like monocular depth-prediction or semantic segmentation, colorization is ill-posed. However, unlike the aforementioned tasks, colorization is also ambiguous, i.e., many different colorizations are perfectly plausible. For instance, differently colored shirts or cars are very reasonable, while there is certainly less diversity in shades of façades. Capturing these subtleties is a non-trivial problem.

Early work on colorization was therefore interactive, requiring some reference color image or scribbles [1–6]. To automate the process, classical methods formulated the task as a prediction problem [7,8], using datasets of limited sizes. More recent deep learning methods were shown to capture more intricate color properties on larger datasets [9–14]. However, all those methods have in common that they only produce a single colorization for a given gray-level image.

Electronic supplementary material The online version of this chapter (https://doi.org/10.1007/978-3-030-01231-1_37) contains supplementary material, which is available to authorized users.

© Springer Nature Switzerland AG 2018
V. Ferrari et al. (Eds.): ECCV 2018, LNCS 11210, pp. 603–619, 2018.
https://doi.org/10.1007/978-3-030-01231-1_37

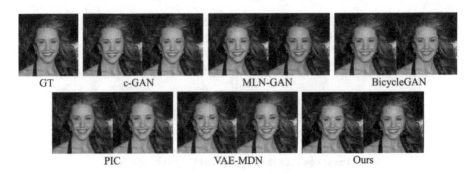

Fig. 1. Diverse colorizations of the ground truth (GT) generated by c-GAN [16], MLN-GAN [19], BicycleGAN [20], PIC [18], VAE-MDN [15] and our approach.

Hence, the ambiguity and multi-modality are often not modeled adequately. To this end, even more recently, diverse output space distributions for colorization were described using generative modeling techniques such as variational auto-encoders [15], generative adversarial nets [16], or auto-regressive models [17,18].

While approaches based on generative techniques can produce diverse colorizations by capturing a dataset distribution, they often lack structural consistency, e.g., parts of a shirt differ in color or the car is speckled. Inconsistencies are due to the fact that structural coherence is only encouraged implicitly when using deep net based generative methods. For example, in results obtained from [15,16,18–20] illustrated in Fig. 1, the color of the shoulder and neck differ as these models are sensitive to occlusion. In addition, existing diverse colorization techniques also often lack a form of controllability permitting to interfere while maintaining structural consistency.

To address both consistency and controllability, our developed method enhances the output space of variational auto-encoders [21] with a Gaussian Markov random field formulation. Our developed approach, which we train in an end-to-end manner, enables explicit modeling of the structural relationship between multiple pixels in an image. Beyond learning the structural consistency between pixels, we also develop a control mechanism which incorporates external constraints. This enables a user to interact with the generative process using color stokes. We illustrate visually appealing results on the Labelled Faces in the Wild (LFW) [22], LSUN-Church [23] and ILSVRC-2015 [24] datasets and assess the photo-realism aspect with a user study.

2   Related Work

As mentioned before, we develop a colorization technique which enhances variational auto-encoders with Gaussian Markov random fields. Before discussing the details, we review the three areas of colorization, Gaussian Markov random fields and variational auto-encoders subsequently.

Colorization: Early colorization methods rely on user-interaction in the form of a reference image or scribbles [1–6]. First attempts to automate the colorization process [7] rely on classifiers trained on datasets containing a few tens to a few thousands of images. Naturally, recent deep net based methods scaled to much larger datasets containing millions of images [9–14,25]. All these methods operate on a provided intensity field and produce a single color image which doesn't embrace the ambiguity of the task.

To address ambiguity, Royer *et al.* [18] use a PixelCNN [26] to learn a conditional model $p(x|g)$ of the color field x given the gray-level image g, and draw multiple samples from this distribution to obtain different colorizations. In addition to compelling results, failure modes are reported due to ignored complex long-range pixel interactions, e.g., if an object is split due to occlusion. Similarly, [17] uses PixelCNNs to learn multiple embeddings z of the gray-level image, before a convolutional refinement network is trained to obtain the final image. Note that in this case, instead of learning $p(x|g)$ directly, the color field x is represented by a low dimensional embedding z. Although, the aforementioned PixelCNN based approaches yield diverse colorization, they lack large scale spatial coherence and are prohibitively slow due to the auto-regressive, i.e., sequential, nature of the model.

Another conditional latent variable approach for diverse colorization was proposed by Deshpande *et al.* [15]. The authors train a variational auto-encoder to produce a low dimensional embedding of the color field. Then, a Mixture Density Network (MDN) [27] is used to learn a multi-modal distribution $p(z|g)$ over the latent codes. Latent samples are afterwards converted to multiple color fields using a decoder. This approach offers an efficient sampling mechanism. However, the output is often speckled because colors are sampled independently for each pixel.

Beyond the aforementioned probabilistic formulations, conditional generative adversarial networks [16] have been used to produce diverse colorizations. However, mode collapse, which results in the model producing one color version of the gray-level image, is a frequent concern in addition to consistency. This is mainly due to the generator learning to largely ignore the random noise vector when conditioned on a relevant context. [19] addresses the former issue by concatenating the input noise channel with several convolutional layers of the generator. A second solution is proposed by [20], where the connection between the output and latent code is encouraged to be invertible to avoid many to one mappings. These models show compelling results when tested on datasets with strong alignment between the samples, e.g., the LSUN bedroom dataset [23] in [19] and image-to-image translation datasets [16,28–31] in [20]. We will demonstrate in Sect. 4 that they lack global consistency on more complex datasets.

In contrast to the aforementioned formulations, we address both diversity and global structural consistency requirements while ensuring computational efficiency. To this end we formulate the colorization task by augmenting variational auto-encoder models with Gaussian Conditional Random Fields (G-CRFs). Using this approach, beyond modeling a structured output space distribution, controllability of the colorization process is natural.

Gaussian Conditional Markov Random Field: Markov random fields [32] and their conditional counter-part are a compelling tool to model correlations between variables. Theoretically, they are hence a good match for colorization tasks where we are interested in reasoning about color dependencies between different pixels. However, inference of the most likely configuration in classical Markov random fields defined over large output spaces is computationally demanding [33–36] and only tractable in a few special cases.

Gaussian Markov random fields [37] represent one of those cases which permit efficient and exact inference. They model the joint distribution of the data, e.g., the pixel values of the two color channels of an image as a multi-variate Gaussian density. Gaussian Markov random fields have been used in the past for different computer vision applications including semantic segmentation [38–40], human part segmentation and saliency estimation [39, 40], image labeling [41] and image denoising [42, 43]. A sparse Gaussian conditional random field trained with a LEARCH framework has been proposed for colorization in [8]. Different from this approach, we use a fully connected Gaussian conditional random field and learn its parameters end-to-end with a deep net. Beyond structural consistency, our goal is to jointly model the ambiguity which is an inherent part of the colorization task. To this end we make use of variational auto-encoders.

Variational Auto-Encoders: Variational auto-encoders (VAEs) [21] and conditional variants [44], i.e., conditional VAEs (CVAEs), have been used to model ambiguity in a variety of tasks [45, 46]. They are based on the manifold assumption stating that a high-dimensional data point x, such as a color image, can be modeled based on a low-dimensional embedding z and some auxiliary data g, such as a gray-level image. Formally, existence of a low-dimensional embedding space and a transformation via the conditional $p_\theta(x|z, g)$ is assumed. Given a dataset $\mathcal{D}$ containing pairs of conditioning information g and desired output x, i.e., given $\mathcal{D} = \{(g, x)\}$, CVAEs formulate maximization of the conditional log-likelihood $\ln p_\theta(x|g)$, parameterized by θ, by considering the following identity:

$$\ln p_\theta(x|g) - D_{\mathrm{KL}}(q_\phi(z|x, g), p_\theta(z|x, g)) = \tag{1}$$
$$-D_{\mathrm{KL}}(q_\phi(z|x, g), p(z|g)) + \mathbb{E}_{q_\phi(z|x,g)}[\ln p_\theta(x|g, z)].$$

Hereby, $D_{\mathrm{KL}}(\cdot, \cdot)$ denotes the Kullback-Leibler (KL) divergence between two distributions, and $q_\phi(z|x, g)$ is used to approximate the intractable posterior $p_\theta(z|x, g)$ of a deep net which models the conditional $p_\theta(x|g, z)$. The approximation of the posterior, i.e., $q_\phi(z|x, g)$, is referred to as the encoder, while the deep net used for reconstruction, i.e., for modeling the conditional $p_\theta(x|g, z)$, is typically called the decoder.

Since the KL-divergence is non-negative, we obtain a lower bound on the data log-likelihood $\ln p_\theta(x|g)$ when considering the right hand side of the identity given in Eq. 1. CVAEs minimize the negated version of this lower bound, i.e.,

$$\min_{\theta,\phi} D_{\mathrm{KL}}(q_\phi(z|x, g), p(z|g)) - \frac{1}{N}\sum_{i=1}^{N} \ln p_\theta(x|g, z^i), \tag{2}$$

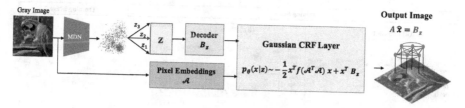

Fig. 2. A fully connected Gaussian Conditional Random Field (G-CRF) based VAE for diverse and globally coherent colorization. To generate diverse colorizations, we use a Mixture Density Network (MDN) to represent the multi-modal distribution of the color field embedding z given the gray-level image g. At test time, we sample multiple embeddings that are subsequently decoded to generate different colorizations. To ensure global consistency, we model the output space distribution of the decoder using a G-CRF.

where the expectation $\mathbb{E}_{q_\phi(z|x,g)}$ is approximated via N samples $z^i \sim q_\phi(z|x,g)$. For simplicity of the exposition, we ignored the summation over the samples in the dataset $\mathcal{D}$, and provide the objective for training of a single pair (x,g).

We next discuss how we combine those ingredients for diverse, controllable yet structurally coherent colorization.

3   Consistency and Controllability for Colorization

Our proposed colorization model has several appealing properties: (1) *diversity*, i.e., it generates diverse and realistic colorizations for a single gray-level image; (2) *global coherence*, enforced by explicitly modeling the output-space distribution of the generated color field using a fully connected Gaussian Conditional Random field (G-CRF); (3) *controllability*, i.e., our model can consider external constraints at run time efficiently. For example, the user can enforce a given object to have a specific color or two separated regions to have the same colorization.

3.1   Overview

We provide an overview of our approach in Fig. 2. Given a gray-level image g with P pixels, our goal is to produce different color fields $x \in \mathbb{R}^{2P}$ consisting of two channels $x_a \in \mathbb{R}^P$ and $x_b \in \mathbb{R}^P$ in the *Lab* color space. In addition, we enforce spatial coherence at a global scale and enable controllability using a Gaussian Markov random field which models the output space distribution.

To produce a diverse colorization, we want to learn a multi-modal conditional distribution $p(x|g)$ of the color field x given the gray-level image g. However, learning this conditional is challenging since the color field x and the intensity field g are high dimensional. Hence, training samples for learning $p(x|g)$ are sparsely scattered and the distribution is difficult to capture, even when using large datasets. Therefore, we assume the manifold hypothesis to hold, and we

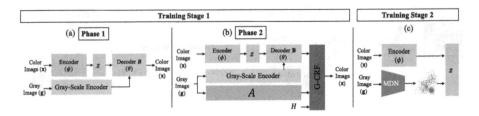

Fig. 3. Overview of the model architecture and the training procedure. In the first training stage, we learn a low dimensional embedding z of the *color field* x conditioned on the gray-level image g using a VAE. To disentangle color from structure, we first learn the unary term B in *phase 1*, then in *phase 2*, learn a precision matrix that encodes the *structure* of the image by imposing the constraint that pixels with similar intensities should have similar colorizations. To enable controllability, we use a training schedule specified in the matrix H to incrementally mask the decoded pixel colors in the unary term B and hence gradually rely on the A matrix to restore the colorization from the unary term. In the second training stage, we use an MDN to learn a multi-modal distribution of the latent embedding given the gray-level image.

choose to learn a conditional $p(x|z,g)$ based on low-dimensional embeddings z captured from x and g, by using a variational auto-encoder which approximates the intractable posterior $p(z|x,g)$ via an encoder. Deshpande *et al.* [15] demonstrated that sampling from the approximation of the posterior results in low variance of the generated images. Following [15], we opt for a multi-stage training procedure to directly sample from $p(z|g)$ as follows.

To capture the low-dimensional embedding, in a *first training stage*, we use a variational auto-encoder to learn a parametric uni-modal Gaussian encoder distribution $q_\phi(z|x,g) \sim \mathcal{N}(\mu_\phi, \sigma_\phi^2 I)$ of the color field embedding z given both the gray-level image g and the color image x (Fig. 3(a)). At the same time, we learn the parameters θ of the decoder $p_\theta(x|z,g)$.

Importantly, we note that the encoder $q_\phi(z|x,g)$ takes advantage of both the color image x and the gray-level intensities g when mapping to the latent representation z. Due to the use of the color image, we expect that this mapping can be captured to a reasonable degree using a uni-modal distribution, i.e., we use a Gaussian.

However, multiple colorizations can be obtained from a gray-scale image g during inference. Hence, following Deshpande *et al.* [15], we don't expect a uni-modal distribution $p(z|g)$ to be accurate during testing, when only conditioning on the gray-level image g.

To address this issue, in a *second training stage*, we train a Mixture Density Network (MDN) $p_\psi(z|g)$ to maximize the log-likelihood of embeddings z sampled from $q_\phi(z|x,g)$ (Fig. 3(b)). Intuitively, for a gray-level image, the MDN predicts the parameters of M Gaussian components each corresponding to a different colorization. The embedding z that was learned in the first stage is then tied to one of these components. The remaining components are optimized by close-by gray-level image embeddings.

At test time, N different embeddings $\{z\}_{k=1}^{N}$ are sampled from the MDN $p_\psi(z|g)$ and transformed by the decoder into diverse colorizations, as we show in Fig. 2.

To encourage globally coherent colorizations and to ensure controllability, we use a fully connected G-CRF layer to model the output space distribution. The negative log-posterior of the G-CRF has the form of a quadratic energy function:

$$E(x) = \frac{1}{2}x^T A_g x - B_{z,g} x. \tag{3}$$

It captures unary and higher order correlations (HOCs) between the pixels' colors for the a and b channels. Intuitively, the joint G-CRF enables the model to capture more global image statistics which turn out to yield more spatially coherent colorizations as we will show in Sect. 4. The unary term $B_{z,g}$ is obtained from the VAE decoder and encodes the color per pixel. The HOC term $A_g = f(A_g^T A_g)$ is responsible for encoding the structure of the input image. It is a function of the inner product of low rank pixel embeddings A_g, learned from the gray-level image and measuring the pairwise similarity between the pixels' intensities. The intuition is that pixels with similar intensities should have similar colorizations. The HOC term is shared between the different colorizations obtained at test time. Beyond global consistency, it also enables controllability by propagating user edits encoded in the unary term properly. Due to the symmetry of the HOC term, the quadratic energy function has a unique global minimum that can be obtained by solving the system of linear equations:

$$A_g x = B_{z,g}. \tag{4}$$

Subsequently, we drop the dependency of A and B on g and z for notational simplicity.

We now discuss how to perform inference in our model and how to learn the model parameters such that colorization and structure are disentangled and controllability is enabled by propagating user strokes.

3.2 Inference

In order to ensure a globally consistent colorization, we take advantage of the structure in the image. To this end, we encourage two pixels to have similar colors if their intensities are similar. Thus, we want to minimize the difference between the color field x for the a and b channels and the weighted average of the colors at similar pixels. More formally, we want to encourage the equalities $x_a = \hat{S}x_a$ and $x_b = \hat{S}x_b$, where $\hat{S} = \text{softmax}(A^T A)$ is a similarity matrix obtained from applying a softmax function to every row of the matrix resulting from $A^T A$. To simplify, we use the block-structured matrix $S = \text{diag}(\hat{S}, \hat{S})$.

In addition to capturing the structure, we obtain the color prior and controllability by encoding the user input in the computed unary term B. Hence, we add the constraint $Hx = \alpha$, where H is a diagonal matrix with 0 and 1 entries

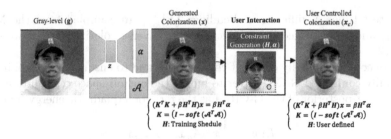

Fig. 4. Controllability: given a gray-level image, we learn to disentangle structure from colorization. The HOC term is used to propagate sparse user edits encoded in the H and α terms.

corresponding to whether the pixel's value isn't or is specified by the user, and α a vector encoding the color each pixel should be set to.

With the aforementioned intuition at hand we obtain the quadratic energy function to be minimized as:

$$E_{\theta,g,z}(x) = \frac{1}{2}\|(I - S)x\|^2 + \frac{1}{2}\beta\|Hx - \alpha\|^2,$$

with β being a hyper-parameter. This corresponds to a quadratic energy function of the form $\frac{1}{2}x^T A x + B x + C$, where $A = (S - I)^T(S - I) + \beta H^T H$, $B = -2\beta\alpha^T H$ and $C = \beta\alpha^T\alpha$. It's immediately apparent that the unary term only encodes color statistics while the HOC term is only responsible for structural consistency. Intuitively, the conditional $p_\theta(x|g, z)$ is interpreted as a Gaussian multi-variate density:

$$p_\theta(x|z, g) \propto \exp(-E_{\theta,g,z}(x)), \tag{5}$$

parametrized by the above defined energy function $E_{\theta,g,z}$. It can be easily checked that A is a positive definite full rank matrix. Hence, for a strictly positive definite matrix, inference is reduced to solving a linear system of equations:

$$((I - S)^T(I - S) + \beta H^T H)x = \beta H^T\alpha. \tag{6}$$

We solve the linear system above using the LU decomposition of the A matrix. How to learn the terms α and S will be explained in the following.

3.3 Learning

We now present the two training stages illustrated in Fig. 3 to ensure color and structure disentanglement and to produce diverse colorizations. We also discuss the modifications to the loss given in Eq. 2 during each stage.

Stage 1: Training a Structured Output Space Variational Auto-Encoder: During the first training stage, we use the variational auto-encoder formulation to learn a low-dimensional embedding for a given color field. This stage is divided into two phases to ensure color and structure disentanglement. In a first phase, we learn the unary term produced by the VAE decoder. In the second phase, we fix the weights of the VAE apart from the decoder's two top-most layers and learn a D-dimensional embedding matrix $\mathcal{A} \in \mathbb{R}^{D \times P}$ for the P pixels from the gray-level image. The matrix $\hat{S}$ obtained from applying a softmax to every row of $\mathcal{A}^T \mathcal{A}$ is used to encourage a smoothness prior $x = Sx$ for the a and b channels. In order to ensure that the S matrix learns the structure required for the controllability stage, where sparse user edits need to be propagated, we follow a training schedule where the unary terms are masked gradually using the H matrix. The input image is reconstructed from the sparse unary entries using the learned structure. When colorization from sparse user edits is desired, we solve the linear system from Eq. 6 for the learned HOC term and an H matrix and α term encoding the user edits, as illustrated in Fig. 4. We explain the details of the training schedule in the experimental section.

Given the new formulation of the G-CRF posterior, the program for the first training stage reads as follows:

$$\min_{\phi,\theta} D_{\mathrm{KL}}(\mathcal{N}(\boldsymbol{\mu}_\phi, \boldsymbol{\sigma}_\phi^2 \boldsymbol{I})), \mathcal{N}(0, \boldsymbol{I})) - \frac{1}{N} \sum_{i=1}^{N} \ln p_\theta(\boldsymbol{x}|\boldsymbol{z}^{(i)}, \boldsymbol{g}) \mathrm{s.t.} \boldsymbol{z}^{(i)} \sim \mathcal{N}(\boldsymbol{\mu}_\phi, \boldsymbol{\sigma}_\phi^2 \boldsymbol{I}). \quad (7)$$

Subsequently we use the term L to refer to the objective function of this program.

Stage 2: Training a Mixture Density Network (MDN): Since a color image x is not available during testing, in the second training stage, we capture the approximate posterior $q_\phi(z|x,g)$, a Gaussian which was learned in the first training stage, using a parametric distribution $p_\psi(z|g)$. Due to the dependence on the color image x we expect the approximate posterior $q_\phi(z|x,g)$ to be easier to model than $p_\psi(z|g)$. Therefore, we let $p_\psi(z|g)$ be a Gaussian Mixture Model (GMM) with M components. Its means, variances, and component weights are parameterized via a mixture density network (MDN) with parameters ψ. Intuitively, for a given gray-level image, we expect the M components to correspond to different colorizations. The colorfield embedding z learned from the first training stage is mapped to one of the components by minimizing the negative conditional log-likelihood, i.e., by minimizing:

$$- \ln p_\psi(z|g) = - \ln \sum_{i=1}^{M} \pi_{g,\psi}^{(i)} \mathcal{N}(z|\boldsymbol{\mu}_{g,\psi}^{(i)}, \sigma). \quad (8)$$

Hereby, $\pi_{g,\psi}^{(i)}$, $\boldsymbol{\mu}_{g,\psi}^{(i)}$ and σ refer to, respectively, the mixture coefficients, the means and a fixed co-variance of the GMM learned by an MDN network parametrized by ψ. However, minimizing $- \ln p_\psi(z|g)$ is hard as it involves the computation of the logarithm of a summation over the different exponential components. To avoid this, we explicitly assign the code z to that Gaussian component m, which

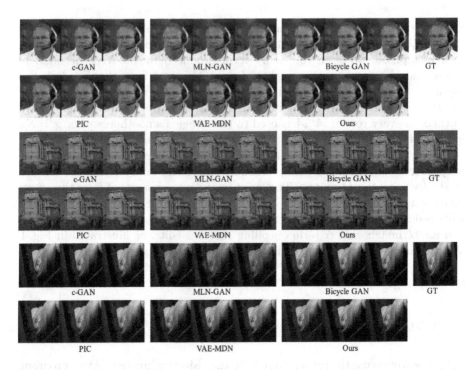

Fig. 5. Qualitative comparison of diverse colorizations obtained from c-GAN [16], MLN-GAN [19], BicycleGAN [20], PIC [18], VAE-MDN [15] and our approach.

has its mean closest to z, i.e., $m = \operatorname*{argmin}_i \|z - \boldsymbol{\mu}_{g,\psi}^{(i)}\|$. Hence, the negative log-likelihood loss $-\ln p_\psi(z|g)$ is reduced to solving the following program:

$$\min_\psi -\ln \pi_{g,\psi}^{(m)} + \frac{\|z - \boldsymbol{\mu}_{g,\psi}^{(m)}\|^2}{2\sigma^2} \quad \text{s.t.} \quad \begin{cases} z \sim q_\phi(z|\boldsymbol{x},\boldsymbol{g}) = \mathcal{N}(\boldsymbol{\mu}_\phi, \boldsymbol{\sigma}_\phi^2 \boldsymbol{I}) \\ m = \operatorname*{argmin}_{i \in \{1,\dots,M\}} \|z - \boldsymbol{\mu}_{g,\psi}^{(i)}\| \end{cases} . \quad (9)$$

Note that the latent samples z are obtained from the approximate posterior $q_\phi(z|\boldsymbol{x},\boldsymbol{g})$ learned in the first stage.

4   Results

Next, we present quantitative and qualitative results on three datasets of increasing color field complexity: (1) the Labelled Faces in the Wild dataset (LFW) [22], which consists of 13,233 face images aligned by deep funneling [47]; (2) the LSUN-Church dataset [23] containing 126,227 images and (3) the validation set of ILSVRC-2015 (ImageNet-Val) [24] with 50,000 images. We compare the diverse colorizations obtained by our model with three baselines representing three different generative models: (1) the Conditional Generative Adversarial

Table 1. Results of the user study (% of the model in **bold** winning).

	Ours vs *VAE-MDN*	*Ours* vs *PIC*	*VAE-MDN* vs *PIC*
LFW	61.12 %	59.04 %	57.17 %
LSUN-Church	66.89 %	71.61 %	54.46 %
ILSVRC-2015	54.79 %	66.98 %	62.88%

Table 2. Quantitaive comparison with baselines. We use the error-of-best per pixel (Eob.), the variance (Var.), the mean structural similarity SSIM across all pairs of colorizations generated for one image (SSIM.) and the training time (Train.) as performance metrics.

Method	LFW				LSUN-Church				ILSVRC-2015			
	eob.	Var.	SSIM.	Train.	eob.	Var.	SSIM.	Train.	eob.	Var.	SSIM.	Train.
c-GAN[16]	.047	$8.40e^{-6}$	.92	~4h	.048	$6.20e^{-6}$	.94	~39h	.048	$8.88e^{-6}$	.91	~18h
MLN-GAN[19]	.057	$2.83e^{-2}$	**.12**	~4h	.051	$2.48e^{-2}$	.34	~39h	.063	$1.73e^{-2}$	.38	~18h
BicycleGAN[20]	.045	$6.50e^{-3}$	.51	~4h	.048	$2.20e^{-2}$	.38	~39h	.042	$2.20e^{-2}$	**.15**	~18h
VAE-MDN[15]	.035	$1.81e^{-2}$	.49	~4h	.028	$1.05e^{-2}$	.77	~39h	.033	$7.17e^{-3}$	.48	~18h
PIC[18]	.043	$\mathbf{5.32e^{-2}}$	.36	~48h	.047	$7.40e^{-5}$	.91	~144h	.035	$\mathbf{6.74e^{-2}}$	.19	~96h
Ours	$\mathbf{11e^{-5}}$	$8.86e^{-3}$	.61	~4h	$\mathbf{93e^{-6}}$	$1.17e^{-2}$	.83	~39h	$\mathbf{12e^{-5}}$	$8.80e^{-3}$	.52	~18h

Network [16,19,20]; (2) the Variational Auto-encoder with MDN [15]; and (3) the Probabilistic Image Colorization model [18] based on PixelCNN. Note that [15] presents a comparison between VAE-MDN and a conditional VAE, demonstrating the benefits of the VAE-MDN approach.

4.1 Baselines

Conditional Generative Adversarial Network: We compare our approach with three GAN models: the c-GAN architecture proposed by Isola *et al.* [16], the GAN with multi-layer noise by Cao *et al.* [19] and the BicycleGAN by Zhu *et al.* [20].

Variational Auto-Encoder with Mixture Density Network (VAE-MDN): The architecture by Deshpande *et al.* [15] trains an MDN based auto-encoder to generate different colorizations. It is the basis for our method.

Probabilistic Image Colorization (PIC): The PIC model proposed by Royer *et al.* [18] uses a CNN network to learn an embedding of a gray-level images, which is then used as input for a PixelCNN network.

Comparison with Baselines: We qualitatively compare the diversity and global spatial consistency of the colorizations obtained by our models with the ones generated by the aforementioned baselines, in Figs. 1 and 5. We observe

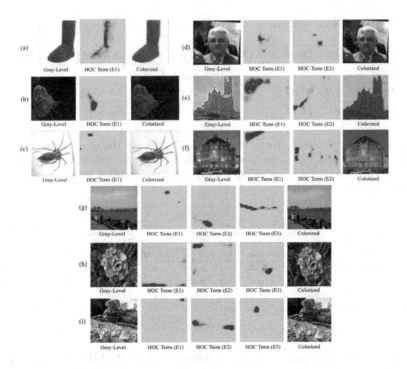

Fig. 6. Controllability: colorization from sparse user edits.

that our approach is the only one which generates a consistent colorization of the skin of the girl in Fig. 1. We are also able to uniformly color the ground, the snake, and the actor's coat in Fig. 5.

For global consistency evaluation, we perform a user study, presented in Table 1, where participants are asked to select the more realistic image from a pair of images at a time. We restrict the study to the three approaches with the overall lowest error-of-best (eob) per pixel reported in Table 2, namely VAE-MDN, PIC and our model. We use the clicking speed to filter out inattentive participants. Participants did neither know the paper content nor were the methods revealed to them. We gathered 5,374 votes from 271 unique users. The results show that users prefer results obtained with the proposed approach.

To evaluate diversity, we use two metrics: (1) the variance of diverse colorizations and (2) the mean structural similarity $SSIM$ [48] across all pairs of colorizations generated for one image. We report our results in Table 2.

Global Consistency: Our model noticeably outperforms all the baselines in producing spatially coherent results as demonstrated by the user study. PIC generates very diversified samples for the LFW and ILSVRC-2015 datasets but lacks long range spatial dependencies because of the auto-regressive nature of the model. For example, the snake in the second row of Fig. 5 has different colors

Table 3. Average PSNR (dB) (higher is better) vs. number of revealed points ($|H|$).

	Levin et al. [2]			Endo et al. [49]			Barron et al. [50]			Zhang et al. [14]			**Ours**		
$|H|$	10	50	100	10	50	100	10	50	100	10	50	100	10	50	100
PSNR	26.5	28.5	30	24.8	25.9	26	25.3	28	29	28	30.2	31.5	26.7	29.3	30.4

Fig. 7. Visualization of the unary term. The first row corresponds to the ground truth image. We visualize one possible colorization in the third row and its corresponding unary term in the second row.

for the head and the tail, and the woman's skin tone is inconsistent in Fig. 1. The VAE-MDN, BicycleGAN and MLN-GAN outputs are sometimes speckled and objects are not uniformly colored. For example, parts of the dome of the building in the second row of Fig. 5 are confused to be part of the sky and the shirt in the third row is speckled. In contrast, our model is capable of capturing complex long range dependencies. This is confirmed by the user study.

Diversity: Across all datasets, c-GAN suffers from mode collapse and is frequently unable to produce diverse colorizations. The PIC, MLN-GAN and BicycleGAN models yield the most diverse results at the expense of photo-realism. Our model produces diverse results while ensuring long range spatial consistency.

Controllability: For the controllably experiments, we set the β hyperparameter to 1 during training and to 5 during testing. We opt for the following training schedule, to force the model to encode the structure required to propagate sparse user inputs in the controllability experiments: We train the unary branch for 15 epochs (Stage1, Phase1), then train the HOC term for 15 epochs as well (Stage1, Phase2). We use the diagonal matrix H to randomly specify L pixels which colors are encoded by the unary branch α. We decrease L following a training schedule from 100% to 75%, 50%, 25% then 10% of the total number of pixels after respectively epochs 2, 4, 6, 8, 10 and 12. Note that additional stages could be added to the training schedule to accommodate for complex datasets where very sparse user input is desired. In Fig. 6, we show that with a single pixel as a user edit ($E1$), we are able to colorize a boot in pink, a sea coral in blue and the background behind the spider in yellow in respectively Fig. 6(a–c). With two edits ($E1$ and $E2$), we colorize a face in green (Zhang et al. [14] use 3 edits)

Fig. 8. Visualization of the HOC term. For every example, we show the ground truth image and three HOC terms corresponding to three different pixels marked in red.

in Fig. 6(d) and the sky and the building in different colors in Fig. 6(e,f). With three user edits ($E1$, $E2$ and $E3$), we show that we can colorize more complex images in Fig. 6(g–i). We show the edits E using red markers. We visualize the attention weights per pixel, corresponding to the pixel's row in the similarity matrix S, in blue, where darker shades correspond to stronger correlations.

Quantitatively, we report the average PSNR for 10, 50 and 100 edits on the ImageNet test set in Table 3, where edits (points) corresponding to randomly selected 7×7 patches are revealed to the algorithm. We observe that our method achieves slightly better results than the one proposed by Levin *et al.* [2] as our algorithms learns for every pixel color an 'attention mechanism' over all the pixels in the image while Levin *et al.* impose local smoothness.

Visualization of the HOC and Unary Terms: In order to obtain more insights into the model's dynamics, we visualize the unary terms, B, and the HOC terms, A, in respectively Figs. 7 and 8. As illustrated in Fig. 8, the HOC term has learned complex long range pixel affinities through end-to-end training. The results in Fig. 7 further suggest that the unary term outputs a colorization with possibly some noise or inconsistencies that the HOC term fixes to ensure global coherency. For example, for the picture in the second column in Fig. 7, the colors of the face, chest and shoulder predicted by the unary term are not consistent, and were fixed by the binary term which captured the long range correlation as it is shown in Fig. 8(c).

We notice different interesting strategies for encoding the long range correlations: On the LSUN-Church dataset, the model encourages local smoothness as every pixel seems to be strongly correlated to its neighbors. This is the case for the sky in Fig. 8(e). The model trained on the LFW dataset, however encoded long range correlation. To ensure consistency over a large area, it chooses some reference pixels and correlates every pixel in the area, as can be seen in Fig. 8(c).

We provide more results and details of the employed deep net architectures in the supplementary material.

5 Conclusion

We proposed a Gaussian conditional random field based variational auto-encoder formulation for colorization and illustrated its efficacy on a variety of benchmark datasets, outperforming existing methods. The developed approach goes beyond existing methods in that it doesn't only model the ambiguity which is inherent to the colorization task, but also takes into account structural consistency.

Acknowledgments. This material is based upon work supported in part by the National Science Foundation under Grant No. 1718221, Samsung, and 3M. We thank NVIDIA for providing the GPUs used for this research.

References

1. Welsh, T., Ashikhmin, M., Mueller, K.: Transferring color to greyscale images. In: SIGGRAPH (2002)
2. Levin, A., Lischinski, D., Weiss, Y.: Colorization using optimization. In: SIGGRAPH (2004)
3. Chia, A.Y.S., et al.: Semantic colorization with internet images. In: SIGGRAPH (2011)
4. Gupta, R.K., Chia, A.Y.S., Rajan, D., Ng, E.S., Zhiyong, H.: Image colorization using similar images. In: ACM Multimedia (2012)
5. Cohen-Or, D., Lischinski, D.: Colorization by example. In: Eurographics Symposium on Rendering (2005)
6. Morimoto, Y., Taguchi, Y., Naemura, T.: Automatic colorization of grayscale images using multiple images on the web. In: SIGGRAPH (2009)
7. Charpiat, G., Hofmann, M., Schölkopf, B.: Automatic image colorization via multimodal predictions. In: Forsyth, D., Torr, P., Zisserman, A. (eds.) ECCV 2008 Part III. LNCS, vol. 5304, pp. 126–139. Springer, Heidelberg (2008). https://doi.org/10.1007/978-3-540-88690-7_10
8. Deshpande, A., Rock, J., Forsyth, D.: Learning large-scale automatic image colorization. In: ICCV (2015)
9. Cheng, Z., Yang, Q., Sheng, B.: Deep colorization. In: ICCV (2015)
10. Iizuka, S., Simo-Serra, E., Ishikawa, H.: Let there be color!: Joint end-to-end learning of global and local image priors for automatic image colorization with simultaneous classification. In: SIGGRAPH (2016)
11. Larsson, G., Maire, M., Shakhnarovich, G.: Learning representations for automatic colorization. In: Leibe, B., Matas, J., Sebe, N., Welling, M. (eds.) ECCV 2016 Part IV. LNCS, vol. 9908, pp. 577–593. Springer, Cham (2016). https://doi.org/10.1007/978-3-319-46493-0_35
12. Zhang, R., Isola, P., Efros, A.A.: Colorful image colorization. In: Leibe, B., Matas, J., Sebe, N., Welling, M. (eds.) ECCV 2016 Part III. LNCS, vol. 9907, pp. 649–666. Springer, Cham (2016). https://doi.org/10.1007/978-3-319-46487-9_40

13. Varga, D., Szirányi, T.: Twin deep convolutional neural network for example-based image colorization. In: Felsberg, M., Heyden, A., Krüger, N. (eds.) CAIP 2017 Part I. LNCS, vol. 10424, pp. 184–195. Springer, Cham (2017). https://doi.org/10.1007/978-3-319-64689-3_15

14. Zhang, R., et al.: Real-time user-guided image colorization with learned deep priors. In: SIGGRAPH (2017)

15. Deshpande, A., Lu, J., Yeh, M.C., Forsyth, D.: Learning diverse image colorization. In: CVPR (2017)

16. Isola, P., Zhu, J.Y., Zhou, T., Efros, A.A.: Image-to-image translation with conditional adversarial networks. In: CVPR (2017)

17. Guadarrama, S., Dahl, R., Bieber, D., Norouzi, M., Shlens, J., Murphy, K.: PixColor: pixel recursive colorization. In: BMVC (2017)

18. Royer, A., Kolesnikov, A., Lampert, C.H.: Probabilistic image colorization. In: BMVC (2017)

19. Cao, Y., Zhou, Z., Zhang, W., Yu, Y.: Unsupervised diverse colorization via generative adversarial networks. arXiv preprint arXiv:1702.06674 (2017)

20. Zhu, J.Y., et al.: Toward multimodal image-to-image translation. In: NIPS (2017)

21. Kingma, D.P., Welling, M.: Auto-encoding variational bayes. In: ICLR (2014)

22. Learned-Miller, E., Huang, G.B., RoyChowdhury, A., Li, H., Hua, G.: Labeled faces in the wild: a survey. In: Kawulok, M., Celebi, M.E., Smolka, B. (eds.) Advances in Face Detection and Facial Image Analysis, pp. 189–248. Springer, Cham (2016). https://doi.org/10.1007/978-3-319-25958-1_8

23. Yu, F., Seff, A., Zhang, Y., Song, S., Funkhouser, T., Xiao, J.: LSUN: construction of a large-scale image dataset using deep learning with humans in the loop. CoRR, abs/1506.03365 (2015)

24. Russakovsky, O., et al.: Imagenet large scale visual recognition challenge. IJCV 115, 211–252 (2015)

25. Varga, D., Szirányi, T.: Twin deep convolutional neural network for example-based image colorization. In: Felsberg, M., Heyden, A., Krüger, N. (eds.) CAIP 2017 Part I. LNCS, vol. 10424, pp. 184–195. Springer, Cham (2017). https://doi.org/10.1007/978-3-319-64689-3_15

26. van den Oord, A., Kalchbrenner, N., Espeholt, L., Vinyals, O., Graves, A., et al.: Conditional image generation with PixelCNN decoders. In: NIPS (2016)

27. Bishop, C.M.: Mixture density networks. Aston University (1994)

28. Laffont, P.Y., Ren, Z., Tao, X., Qian, C., Hays, J.: Transient attributes for high-level understanding and editing of outdoor scenes. In: SIGGRAPH (2014)

29. Cordts, M., et al.: The cityscapes dataset for semantic urban scene understanding. In: CVPR (2016)

30. Yu, A., Grauman, K.: Fine-grained visual comparisons with local learning. In: CVPR (2014)

31. Zhu, J.-Y., Krähenbühl, P., Shechtman, E., Efros, A.A.: Generative visual manipulation on the natural image manifold. In: Leibe, B., Matas, J., Sebe, N., Welling, M. (eds.) ECCV 2016 Part V. LNCS, vol. 9909, pp. 597–613. Springer, Cham (2016). https://doi.org/10.1007/978-3-319-46454-1_36

32. Kindermann, R., Snell, J.L.: Markov Random Fields and Their Applications. American Mathematical Society, Providence (1980)

33. Schwing, A.G., Hazan, T., Pollefeys, M., Urtasun, R.: Distributed message passing for large scale graphical models. In: Proceedings of CVPR (2011)

34. Schwing, A.G., Hazan, T., Pollefeys, M., Urtasun, R.: Globally convergent dual MAP LP relaxation solvers using Fenchel-Young margins. In: Proceedings of NIPS (2012)

35. Schwing, A.G., Hazan, T., Pollefeys, M., Urtasun, R.: Globally convergent parallel MAP LP relaxation solver using the Frank-Wolfe algorithm. In: Proceedings of ICML (2014)

36. Meshi, O., Schwing, A.G.: Asynchronous parallel coordinate minimization for MAP inference. In: Proceedings of NIPS (2017)

37. Rue, H.: Gaussian Markov Random Fields: Theory and Applications. CRC Press, Boca Raton (2008)

38. Vemulapalli, R., Tuzel, O., Liu, M.Y., Chellapa, R.: Gaussian conditional random field network for semantic segmentation. In: CVPR (2016)

39. Chandra, S., Usunier, N., Kokkinos, I.: Dense and low-rank Gaussian CRFs using deep embeddings. In: ICCV (2017)

40. Chandra, S., Kokkinos, I.: Fast, exact and multi-scale inference for semantic image segmentation with deep Gaussian CRFs. In: Leibe, B., Matas, J., Sebe, N., Welling, M. (eds.) ECCV 2016 Part VII. LNCS, vol. 9911, pp. 402–418. Springer, Cham (2016). https://doi.org/10.1007/978-3-319-46478-7_25

41. Jancsary, J., Nowozin, S., Sharp, T., Rother, C.: Regression tree fieldsan efficient, non-parametric approach to image labeling problems. In: CVPR (2012)

42. Tappen, M.F., Liu, C., Adelson, E.H., Freeman, W.T.: Learning Gaussian conditional random fields for low-level vision. In: CVPR (2007)

43. Vemulapalli, R., Tuzel, O., Liu, M.Y.: Deep Gaussian conditional random field network: a model-based deep network for discriminative denoising. In: CVPR (2016)

44. Sohn, K., Lee, H., Yan, X.: Learning structured output representation using deep conditional generative models. In: NIPS (2015)

45. Wang, L., Schwing, A.G., Lazebnik, S.: Diverse and accurate image description using a variational auto-encoder with an additive Gaussian encoding space. In: NIPS (2017)

46. Jain*, U., Zhang*, Z., Schwing, A.G.: Creativity: senerating diverse questions using variational autoencoders. In: Proceedings of CVPR (2017). * Equal contribution

47. Huang, G., Mattar, M., Lee, H., Learned-Miller, E.G.: Learning to align from scratch. In: NIPS (2012)

48. Wang, Z., Bovik, A.C., Sheikh, H.R., Simoncelli, E.P.: Image quality assessment: from error visibility to structural similarity. In: IEEE TIP (2004)

49. Endo, Y., Iizuka, S., Kanamori, Y., Mitani, J.: DeepProp: extracting deep features from a single image for edit propagation. In: Eurographics (2016)

50. Barron, J.T., Poole, B.: The fast bilateral solver. In: Leibe, B., Matas, J., Sebe, N., Welling, M. (eds.) ECCV 2016 Part III. LNCS, vol. 9907, pp. 617–632. Springer, Cham (2016). https://doi.org/10.1007/978-3-319-46487-9_38

Open Set Learning with Counterfactual Images

Lawrence Neal[(✉)], Matthew Olson, Xiaoli Fern, Weng-Keen Wong,
and Fuxin Li

Collaborative Robotics and Intelligent Systems Institute, Oregon State University,
Corvallis, USA
nealla@oregonstate.edu

Abstract. In *open set recognition*, a classifier must label instances of known classes while detecting instances of unknown classes not encountered during training. To detect unknown classes while still generalizing to new instances of existing classes, we introduce a dataset augmentation technique that we call *counterfactual image generation*. Our approach, based on generative adversarial networks, generates examples that are close to training set examples yet do not belong to any training category. By augmenting training with examples generated by this optimization, we can reformulate open set recognition as classification with one additional class, which includes the set of novel and unknown examples. Our approach outperforms existing open set recognition algorithms on a selection of image classification tasks.

1 Introduction

In traditional image recognition tasks, all inputs are partitioned into a finite set of known classes, with equivalent training and testing distributions. However, many practical classification tasks may involve testing in the presence of *"unknown unknown"* classes not encountered during training [1]. We consider the problem of classifying known classes while simultaneously recognizing novel or unknown classes, a situation referred to as *open set recognition* [2].

A typical deep network trained for a closed-set image classification task uses the softmax function to generate for each input image the probability of classification for each known class. During training, all input examples are assumed to belong to one of K known classes. At test time, the model generates for each input x a probability $P(y_i|x)$ for each known class y_i. The highest-probability output class label y^* is selected as $y^* = \arg\max_{y_i} P(y_i|x)$ where $P(y|x)$ is a distribution among known classes such that $\sum_{i=1}^{K} P(y_i|x) = 1$.

In many practical applications, however, the set of known class labels is incomplete, so additional processing is required to distinguish between inputs belonging to the known classes and inputs belonging to the open set of classes not seen in training. The typical method for dealing with unknown classes involves

© Springer Nature Switzerland AG 2018
V. Ferrari et al. (Eds.): ECCV 2018, LNCS 11210, pp. 620–635, 2018.
https://doi.org/10.1007/978-3-030-01231-1_38

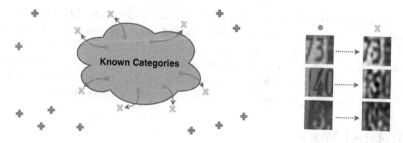

Fig. 1. Left: Given known examples (green dots) we generate counterfactual examples for the *unknown* class (red x). The decision boundary between known and counterfactual unknown examples extends to unknown examples (blue +), similar to the idea that one can train an SVM with only support vectors. Right: Example SVHN known examples and corresponding counterfactual unknown images. (Color figure online)

thresholding the output confidence scores of a closed-set classifier. Most commonly, a global threshold δ is applied to $P(y|x)$ to separate all positive-labeled examples from unknown examples:

$$y^* = \begin{cases} \arg\max_{y_i} P(y_i|x) & \text{if } \max_{y_i} P(y_i|x) > \delta \\ unknown & \text{else} \end{cases} \qquad (1)$$

However, this type of global thresholding assumes well calibrated probabilities, and breaks down in many real-world tasks. For example, convolutional network architectures can output incorrect high-confidence predictions when faced with test data from outside the training distribution, as evidenced by work in adversarial example generation [3]. Better methods are needed to facilitate the learning of a decision boundary between the known classes and the unknown open set classes.

A number of approaches exist to separate known from unknown data at test time. Some approaches involve learning a feature space through classification of training data, then detecting outliers in that feature space at test time [4,5]. Other approaches follow the anomaly detection paradigm– where the distribution of training data is modeled without classification, and inputs are compared to that model at test time [6]. Our approach follows another line of research, in which the set of unknown classes is modeled by synthetic data generated from a model trained on the known classes [7].

Figure 1 illustrates our procedure applied to the SVHN dataset, where digits 0 through 4 are known and 5 through 9 are unknown (ie. not included in the training data). We train a generative adversarial network on the set of known classes. Starting from the latent representation of a known example, we apply gradient descent in the latent space to produce a synthetic open set example. The set of synthetic open set examples provide a boundary between known and unknown classes.

Our contributions are the following: (1) We introduce the concept of *counterfactual image generation*, which aims to generate synthetic images that closely resemble a given real image, but satisfy certain properties, (2) we present a method for training a deep neural network for open set recognition using the output of a generative model, (3) we apply counterfactual image generation, in the latent space learned by a generative adversarial network, to generate synthetic images that resemble known classes images, but belong to the open set; and we show that they are useful for improving open set recognition.

2   Related Work

2.1   Open Set Recognition

A number of models and training procedures have been proposed to make image recognition models robust to the open set of unknown classes. Early work in this area primarily focused on SVM based approaches, such as 1-class SVM [8]. In [9], a novel training scheme is introduced to refine the linear decision boundaries learned by a 1-class or binary SVM to optimize both the empirical and the open set risk. In [4], based on the statistical Extreme Value Theory (EVT), a Weibull distribution is used to model the posterior probability of inclusion for each known class and an example is classified as open class if the probability is below a rejection threshold. In [2], W-SVM is introduced where Weibull distributions are further used to calibrate the scores produced by binary SVMs for open set recognition.

More recently, Bendale et al. explored a similar idea and introduced Weibull-based calibration to augment the softmax layer of a deep network, which they called "OpenMax" [5]. The last layer of the classifier, before the application of the softmax function, is termed the "activation vector". For each class, a mean activation vector is computed from the set of correctly-classified training examples. Distance to the corresponding mean activation vector is computed for each training example. For each class, a Weibull distribution is fit to the tail of largest distances from the mean activation vector. At test time, the cumulative distribution function of the Weibull distribution fit to distance from the mean is used to compute a probability that any input is an outlier for each class. In this way, a maximum radius is fit around each class in the activation vector feature space, and any activation vectors outside of this radius are detected as open set examples. The OpenMax approach is further developed in [7] and [10].

In [11], a network is trained to minimize the "II-loss", which encourages separation between classes in a learned representation space. The network can be applied to open set recognition tasks by detecting outliers in the learned feature space as unknown class examples.

2.2   Generative Adversarial Nets

The Generative Adversarial Network was initially developed as an adversarial minimax game in which two neural networks are simultaneously trained: a generator which maps random noise to "fake" generated examples and a discriminator which classifies between "fake" and "real" [12]. Variations of the GAN architecture condition the generator or discriminator on class labels [13], augment the generator with additional loss terms [14], or replace the discriminator's classification objective with a regression objective as in the Wasserstein critic [15]. The original and primary application of GAN models is the generation of images similar to a training set, and current state-of-the-art GAN models are capable of generating photo-realistic images at high resolution [16].

Generative adversarial nets have been applied to unsupervised representation learning, in which features learned on an unsupervised task transfer usefully to a supervised or semi-supervised task [17,18]. Architectures that combine generator networks with encoder networks, which invert the function learned by the generator, can be more stable during training and make it possible to distort or adjust real input examples while preserving their realism, which is useful for applications such as style transfer and single-image superresolution [19–22]. The use of generative adversarial networks for data augmentation has been explored in the context of image classification [23].

2.3 Generative Models for Open Set Recognition

Generative methods have the potential to directly estimate the distribution of observed examples, conditioned on class identity. This makes them potentially useful for open set recognition. A generative adversarial network is used in [6] to compute a measure of probability of inclusion in a known set at test time by mapping input images to points in the latent space of a generator.

Most closely related to our approach, the Generative OpenMax approach uses a conditional generative adversarial network to synthesize mixtures of known classes [7]. Through a rejection sampling process, synthesized images with low probability of inclusion in any known class are selected. These images are included in the training set as examples of the open set class. The Weibull-calibration of OpenMax is then applied to the final layer of a trained classifier. The Generative OpenMax (G-OpenMax) approach effectively detects new and unknown classes in monochrome digit datasets, but does not improve open set classification performance on natural images [7].

Different from G-OpenMax, our work uses an encoder-decoder GAN architecture to generate the synthetic open set examples. This allows the features learned from the known classes to be transfered to modeling new unknown classes. With this architecture, we further define a novel objective for generating synthetic open set examples, which starts from real images of known classes and morphs them based on the GAN model to generate "counterfactual" open set examples.

3   Counterfactual Image Generation

In logic, a conditional statement $p \rightarrow q$ is true if the antecedent statement p implies the consequent q. A counterfactual conditional, $p \,\square\!\!\rightarrow q$ is a conditional statement in which p is known to be false [24]. It can be interpreted as a *what-if* statement: if p were true, then q would be true as well. Lewis [24] suggests the following interpretation:

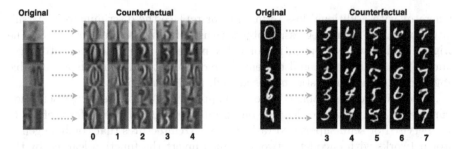

Fig. 2. Input examples and corresponding counterfactual images for known classes, generated by optimizing in latent space. Left: SVHN, Right: MNIST

"If kangaroos had no tails, they would topple over" seems to me to mean something like this: in any possible state of affairs in which kangaroos have no tails, and which resembles our actual state of affairs as much as kangaroos having no tails permits it to, the kangaroos topple over.

Motivated by this interpretation, we wish to model possible "states of affairs" and their relationships as vectors in the latent space of a generative adversarial neural network. Concretely, suppose:

- The *state of affairs* can be encoded as a vector $\mathbf{z} \in \mathbf{R}^n$
- The notion of *resemblance* between two states corresponds to a metric $||\mathbf{z_0} - \mathbf{z}^*||$
- There exists an indicator function $\mathbf{C_p(z)}$ that outputs 1 if p is true given z.

Given an actual state z_0 and logical statements p and q, finding the state of affairs in which p is true that resembles z_0 as much as possible can be posed as a numerical optimization problem:

$$\text{minimize} \quad ||z_0 - z^*||_2$$
$$\text{subject to} \quad C_p(z^*) = 1$$

We treat $C_p : \mathbf{R}^n \to \{0, 1\}$ as an indicator function with the value 1 if p is true. Given the optimal z^*, the truth value of the original counterfactual conditional can be determined:

$$p \,\square\!\!\to q \iff C_q(z^*) = 1$$

For a concrete example, let z be the latent representation of images of digits. Given an image of a random digit and its latent representation z_0, our formulation of counterfactual image generation can be used to answer the question "what would this image look like if this were a digit '3'?", where p is "being digit 3". In Fig. 2, we show images from the known set (left column), and the counterfactual images generated by optimizing them toward other known classes for the SVHN and MNIST datasets. We can see that by starting from different original images, the generated counterfactual images of the same class differ significantly from one another.

Optimization in the latent space is capable of producing examples that lie outside of the distribution of any known class, but nonetheless remain within a larger distribution within pixel space consisting of plausible images (see Fig. 3). The counterfactual image optimization connects to the concept of adversarial image generation explored in [25] and [26]. However, while optimization in pixel space produces adversarial examples, the counterfactual optimization is constrained to a manifold of realistic images learned by the generative model. The combination of diversity and realism makes generated images useful as training examples. In the following section, we show that training on counterfactual images can improve upon existing methods of open set classification.

4   Open Set Image Recognition

In this section, we will first provide an overview of our method for open set recognition, followed by a description of our generative model and the proposed approach for generating counterfactual open set images.

4.1   Overview of the Approach

We assume that a labeled training set X consists of labeled examples of K classes and a test set contains $M > K$ classes, including the known classes in addition to one or more unknown classes. We pose the open set recognition problem as a classification of $K + 1$ classes where all instances of the $M - K$ unknown classes must be assigned to the additional class.

We assume the open set classes and the known classes share the same latent space. The essence of our approach is to use the concept of counterfactual image generation to traverse in the latent space, generate synthetic open set examples that are just outside of the known class boundaries, and combine the original training examples of the known classes with the synthetic examples to train a standard classifier of $K + 1$ classes. Figure 3 provides a simple illustration of our high level idea.

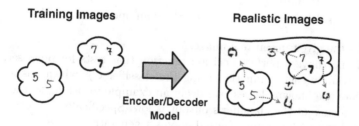

Fig. 3. Our model learns to encode training images into a latent space, and decode latent points into realistic images. The space of realistic images includes plausible but non-real examples which we use as training data for the open set of unknown classes.

4.2 The Generative Model

The standard DCGAN training objective penalizes the generation of any image outside of the training distribution, and generators normally suffer from some level of mode collapse.

Inspired by the use of reconstruction losses to regularize the training of generators to avoid mode collapsing in [27] and in [28], we use a training objective based on a combination of adversarial and reconstruction loss.

Our encoder-decoder GAN architecture consists of three components: an encoder network $E(x)$, which maps from images to a latent space, a generator network $G(z)$, which maps from latent space back to an image and a discriminator network D that discriminates fake (generated) images from real images.

The encoder and decoder networks are trained jointly as an autoencoder, with the objective to minimize the reconstruction error $||x - G(E(x))||_1$. Simultaneously, the discriminator network D is trained as a Wasserstein critic with gradient penalty. Training proceeds with alternating steps of optimization of the losses L_D and L_G, where:

$$\mathbf{L_D} = \sum_{x \in \mathbf{X}} D(G(E(x))) - D(x) + P(D) \tag{2}$$

$$\mathbf{L_G} = \sum_{x \in \mathbf{X}} ||x - G(E(x))||_1 - D(G(E(x))) \tag{3}$$

where $P(D) = \lambda(||\nabla_{\hat{x}} D(\hat{x})||_2 - 1)$ is the interpolated gradient penalty term of [29]. Finally, along with the generative model, we also train a simple K-class classifier C_K with cross-entropy loss on the labeled known classes.

4.3 Generating Counterfactual Open Set Examples

Our goal is to use counterfactual image generation to generate synthetic images that closely resemble real examples of known classes but lie on the other side of the true decision boundary between the known classes and the open set. This can be formulated as follows:

$$\text{minimize} \qquad ||E(x) - z^*||_2$$
$$\text{subject to} \qquad G(z^*) \text{ is an open set example}$$

where x is the given initial real image.

We do not have a perfect decision function that tests for open set, but we can approximate such a function using the classifier C_K which has learned to differentiate the known classes. We deem an example to belong to the open set if the confidence of the classifier's output is low. Specifically, we formulate the following objective for counterfactual open set generation:

$$z^* = \min_z ||z - E(x)||_2^2 + \log\left(1 + \sum_{i=1}^{K} \exp C_K(G(z))_i\right) \tag{4}$$

Here $C(G(z))_i$ are the logits of the classifier prediction for the counterfactual image $G(z)$ for class i. The second term of the objective is the negative log-likelihood of the unknown class, assuming the unknown class has a score of zero. By minimizing this term, we aim to simultaneously push the scores of all known classes to be low.

To generate a counterfactual image, we select an input seed image x at random from the training set. We encode the image to a latent point $z = E(x)$, then minimize Eq. (4) through gradient descent for a fixed number of steps to find z^*, then decode the latent point to generate the counterfactual image $G(z^*)$. Each counterfactual image $G(z^*)$ is augmented to the dataset with class label $K+1$, indicating the *unknown* class. After a sufficient number of open set examples have been synthesized, a new classifier C_{K+1} is trained on the augmented dataset.

4.4 Implementation Details

The architecture of our generative model broadly follows [14], with a few differences. Instead of the traditional GAN classification loss, our discriminator is trained as a Wasserstein critic with gradient penalty loss (see Eq. 3) as in [29]. The generator is trained jointly with an encoder E which maps from the input image space to the latent space of the generator, with an effect similar to [19]. The encoder architecture is equivalent to the discriminator, with adjustments to the final layer so that the output matches the dimensionality of the latent space, and no nonlinearity applied.

We additionally include a classifier, both for the baseline method and for our own method after training with generated open set examples. The classifier, both in the K-class and $K+1$ class training settings, has an equivalent architecture to the discriminator and encoder.

In order to easily transfer weights from the K-class to the $K+1$-class classifier, we follow the reparameterization trick from [14] by noting that a softmax layer with K input logits and K output probabilities is over-parameterized. The softmax function is invariant to the addition of any constant to all elements of its input: ie. $\mathrm{softmax}(x) = \mathrm{softmax}(x + C)$. Using this fact, the K-logit classifier can be recast as a $K+1$-class classifier simply by augmenting the K-dimensional vector of logits with an additional constant 0, then applying the softmax function resulting in a $K+1$-dimensional probability distribution.

Our generator network consists of blocks of transposed convolutional layers with stride 2, each block increasing the size of the output feature map by a factor of two. The discriminator, encoder, and classifier all consist of standard blocks of convolutional layers with strided convolutions reducing the size of the feature map after each block. The LeakyReLU nonlinearity is used in all layers, and batch normalization is applied between all internal layers. Dropout is applied at the end of each block in all networks except the generator. A full listing of layers, hyperparameters, and source code is available at https://github.com/lwneal/counterfactual-open-set.

5 Experiments

We evaluate the performance of the open set classifier C_{K+1} by partitioning the classes of labeled datasets into known and unknown sets. At training time, the only input to the network consists of the K known classes. At test time, the network must assign appropriate labels to examples of the known classes and label $K + 1$ to examples of the $M - K$ open set classes.

5.1 Datasets

We evaluate open set classification performance using the MNIST, SVHN, CIFAR-10, and Tiny-Imagenet datasets. The MNIST digit dataset consists of ten digit classes, each containing between 6313 and 7877 28×28 monochrome images in the training fold. We use the labeled subset of the Street View House Numbers dataset [30], consisting of ten digit classes each with between 9981 and 11379 32×32 color images. To test on a simple set of non-digit natural images, we apply our method to the CIFAR-10 dataset, consisting of 6000 32×32 color images of each of ten natural image categories. The Tiny-Imagenet dataset consists of 200 classes of 500 training and 100 test examples each, drawn from the Imagenet ILSVRC 2012 dataset and downsampled to 32×32.

Classes within each dataset are partitioned into separate **known** and **unknown** sets. Models are trained using examples drawn from the training fold of known classes, and tested using examples from the test fold of both known and unknown classes.

5.2 Metrics

Open set classification performance can be characterized by the overall accuracy or F-score for unknown class detection on a combination of known and unknown data. However, such combined metrics are sensitive not only to the effectiveness of the trained model, but also arbitrary calibration parameters. To disambiguate between model performance and calibration, we measure open set classification performance with two metrics.

Closed Set Accuracy. An open set classifier should remain capable of standard closed-set classification without unreasonably degrading accuracy. To ensure that the open set classifier is still effective when applied to the known subset of classes, we measure classification accuracy of the classifier applied only to the K known classes, with open set detection disabled.

Area Under the ROC Curve for Open Set Detection. In open set classification, it is not known at training time how rare or common examples from the unknown classes will be. For this reason, any approach to open set detection requires an arbitrary threshold or sensitivity to be set, either explicitly or within the training process. The Receiver Operating Characteristic (ROC) curve

Table 1. Open set classification: area under the ROC curve. Mean and standard deviation of the ROC AUC metric for selected datasets. Results averaged over 5 random partitions of known/open set classes. For all runs, $K = 6$ and $M = 10$.

Method	CIFAR-10	SVHN	MNIST
Softmax threshold	$.677 \pm .038$	$.886 \pm .014$	$.978 \pm .006$
OpenMax	$.695 \pm .044$	$.894 \pm .013$	$.981 \pm .005$
G-OpenMax*	$.675 \pm .044$	$.896 \pm .017$	$.984 \pm .005$
Ours	$\mathbf{.699 \pm .038}$	$\mathbf{.910 \pm .010}$	$\mathbf{.988 \pm .004}$

characterizes the performance of a detector as its sensitivity is varied from zero recall (in this case, no input is labeled as open set) to complete recall (all inputs labeled as open set).

Computing the area under the ROC curve (AUC) provides a calibration-free measure of detection performance, ranging from situations where open set classes are rare to situations in which the majority of input belong to unknown classes. To compute the ROC curve given a trained open set classifier, we vary a threshold $\theta \in [0, 1]$ which is compared to the predicted probability of the open set class $P(y_{K+1}|x) > \theta$ for each input image x.

5.3 Experiments

Open Set Classification. In the Open Set Classification experiment, each dataset is partitioned at random into 6 known and 4 unknown classes. We perform the open set classification experiment with the CIFAR, SVHN, and MNIST datasets, repeated over 5 runs with classes assigned at random to the known or unknown set.

Extended Open Set Classification. Following [9], we define the *openness* of a problem based on the number of training and test classes:

$$openness = 1 - \sqrt{\frac{K}{M}} \tag{5}$$

Table 2. Closed set accuracy. Classification accuracy among $K = 6$ known classes for the open set classifier trained on each dataset. Because softmax thresholding and OpenMax use the same network, classification results are identical.

Method	CIFAR-10	SVHN	MNIST
Softmax/OpenMax	$.801 \pm .032$	$.947 \pm .006$	$.995 \pm .002$
G-OpenMax*	$.816 \pm .035$	$.948 \pm .008$	$.996 \pm .001$
Ours	$\mathbf{.821 \pm .029}$	$\mathbf{.951 \pm .006}$	$.996 \pm .001$

The previous experiments test the effectiveness of the method where $K = 6$ and $M = 10$, so the openness score is fixed to $1 - \sqrt{\frac{6}{10}}$. To test the method in a range of greater openness scores, we perform additional experiments using the CIFAR10, CIFAR100, and TinyImagenet datasets.

We train on CIFAR10 as described previously with $K = 4$ known classes. At test time, in place of the remaining classes of CIFAR10 we draw 10 unknown classes at random from the more diverse CIFAR100 dataset. To avoid overlap between known and unknown classes, known classes are selected only from non-animal categories and unknown classes are selected from animal categories. The AUC metric for the resulting open set task is reported as **CIFAR+10**. This experiment is repeated drawing 50 classes from CIFAR100 (**CIFAR+50**). Finally for the larger **TinyImagenet** dataset we train with $K = 20$ known classes, and test on the full $M = 200$ set. Results reported for all methods are averaged among 5 separate samples of known/unknown classes.

5.4   Technical Details of Compared Approaches

Our Approach. We begin by training an ordinary K-class classifier C_K with cross-entropy loss on the labeled dataset. Simultaneously, we train the generative model consisting of encoder, generator, and discriminator on the labeled data, following the combined loss described in Sect. 4.

Once the classifier and generative model is fully trained, we apply the counterfactual image generation process. Beginning with encoded training set examples, the counterfactual image generation process finds points in the latent space of the generative model that decode to effective open set examples. For all experiments listed we generate 6400 example images. The original labeled dataset is augmented with the set of all generated images, and all generated images are labeled as open set examples. We initialize the new open-set classifier C_{K+1} with the weights of the baseline C_K classifier.

After training, we use the C_{K+1} classifier directly: unlike the OpenMax methods we do not perform additional outlier detection. For the open set detection task however, we further improve discrimination between known and unknown classes by including a measure of known class certainty. Given an output $P(y_i|x)$ for $i \in [1...K + 1]$ we recalibrate the probability of open set inclusion as

Table 3. Extended open set classification: area under the ROC curve. Known vs. unknown class detection for selected datasets. Results averaged over 5 random class partitions.

Method	CIFAR+10	CIFAR+50	TinyImagenet
Softmax threshold	.816	.805	.577
OpenMax	.817	.796	.576
G-OpenMax*	.827	.819	.580
Ours	**.838**	**.827**	**.586**

$$P^* = P(y_{K+1}|x) - \max_{i \le K} P(y_i|x) \qquad (6)$$

This modified value P^* is used for evaluation of the AUC metric (Table 3).

Softmax Threshold. We compare our open-set classification approach to a standard confidence-based method for the detection of unknown classes without dataset augmentation. In this method, a classifier network C_K is trained only on known classes and for each input x provides a class prediction $P(y|x)$ for the set of known classes y. For the purpose of open set detection, input images x such that $\max C_K(x) < \theta$ are detected as open set examples.

OpenMax. We implement the Weibull distribution fitting method from [5]. This approach augments the baseline classifier C_K with a new OpenMax layer replacing the softmax at the final layer of the network. First, the baseline network is applied to all inputs in the training set, and a mean activation vector is computed for each class based on the output of the penultimate network layer for all correctly classified examples. Given a mean activation vector for each class $j \in [1...K]$, a Weibull distribution with values $(\tau_j, \kappa_j, \lambda_j)$ is fit to the distance from the mean of the set of a number η of outlier examples of class j. We perform a grid search for values of η used in the FITHIGH function, and we find that $\eta = 20$ maximizes the AUC metric.

After fitting Weibull distributions for each class, we replace the softmax layer of the baseline classifier with the a new OpenMax layer. The output of the Open-Max layer is a distribution among $K+1$ classes, formed by recalibrating the input logits based on the cumulative distribution function of the Weibull distribution of distance from the mean of activation vectors, such that extreme outliers beyond a certain distance from any class mean are unlikely to be classified as that class.

We make one adjustment to the method as described in [5] to improve performance on the selected datasets. We find that in datasets with a small number of classes (fewer than 1000) the calibration of OpenMax scores using a selected number of top classes α is not required, and we can replace the $\frac{\alpha-i}{\alpha}$ term with a constant 1.

Generative OpenMax. The closest work to ours is the Generative OpenMax method from [7], which uses a conditional GAN that is no longer state-of-the-art. In order to provide a fair comparison with our method, we implemented a variant of Generative OpenMax using our encoder-decoder network instead of a conditional GAN.

Specifically, given the trained GAN and known-class classifier C_K, we select random pairs (x_1, x_2) of training examples and encode them into the latent space. We interpolate between the two examples in the latent space as in [7] and apply the generator to the resulting latent point to generate the image:

$$x_{\text{int}} = G(\theta E(x_1) + (1 - \theta)E(x_2))$$

where $\theta \in [0, 1]$ is drawn from a uniform distribution.

Once the images are generated, we then apply a sample selection process similar to that of [7] to identify a subset of the generated samples to include as open set examples. In particular, we use confidence thresholding – that is, generated examples for which C_K's prediction confidence is less than a fixed threshold $\max_i P(y_i|x_{\text{int}}) < \phi$ are selected for use as open set examples. In all experiments we set $\phi = 0.5$.

Once the requisite number of synthetic open set examples have been generated, a new C_{K+1} classifier is trained using the dataset augmented with the generated examples. For all experiments we generate 6,400 synthetic example images. At test time, the Weibull distributions of the OpenMax layer are fit to the penultimate layer activations of C_{K+1} and the OpenMax Weibull calibration process is performed. We report scores for this variant of Generative OpenMax as **G-OpenMax***.

5.5   Results

In Table 1, we present the open set detection performance of different approaches on three datasets as measured by the area under the ROC curves. The closed set accuracies are provided in Table 2. From the results we can see that classifiers trained using our method achieve better open set detection performance compared to the baselines and do not lose any accuracy when classifying among known classes.

It is interesting to note that all approaches perform most accurately on the MNIST digit dataset, followed closely by SVHN, with the natural image data of CIFAR and TinyImagenet trailing far behind, indicating that natural images are significantly more challenging for all approaches.

Note in Table 1, our version of the Generative OpenMax outperforms OpenMax on the more constrained digit datasets, but not in the CIFAR image dataset, which includes a wider range of natural image classes that may not be as easily separable as digits. This fits with the intuition given in [7] that generating latent space combinations of digit classes is likely to result in images close to real, but unknown digits. It is possible that combining the features of images of large deformable objects like animals is not as likely to result in realistic classes. However, using the counterfactual optimization, we find that we are able to generate examples that improve open set detection performance without hurting known class classification accuracy.

In Fig. 4, we plot the ROC curves for the SVHN and CIFAR datasets. We see that the curve of our method generally lies close to or above all other curves, suggesting a better performance across different sensitivity levels. In contrast, Generative OpenMax performed reasonably well for low false positive rate ranges, but became worse than the non-generative baselines when the false positive rates are high.

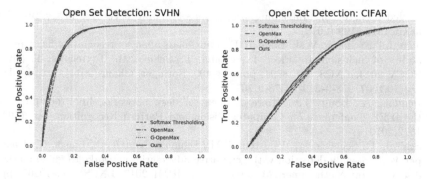

Fig. 4. Receiver operating curve plots for open set detection for the SVHN and CIFAR datasets, for $K = 6$.

6 Conclusions

In this paper we introduce a new method for open set recognition, which uses a generative model to synthesize examples that closely resemble images of known classes but likely belong to the open set.

Our work uses an encoder-decoder model trained with adversarial loss to learn a flexible latent space representation for images. We introduce counterfactual image generation, a technique which we apply to this latent space, which morphs any given real image into a synthetic one that is realistic looking but is classified as an alternative class. We apply counterfactual image generation to the trained GAN model to generate open set training examples, which are used to adapt a classifier to the open set recognition task. On low-resolution image datasets, our approach outperforms previous ones both in the task of detecting known vs. unknown classes and in classification among known classes.

For future work, we are interested in investigating how to best select initial seed examples for generating counterfactual open set images. We will also consider applying counterfactual image generation to data other than still images and increasing the size and resolution of the generative model.

Acknowledgments. This material is based upon work supported by the Defense Advanced Research Projects Agency (DARPA) under contract N66001-17-2-4030 and the National Science Foundation (NSF) grant 1356792. This material is also based upon work while Wong was serving at the NSF. Any opinion, findings, and conclusions or recommendations expressed in this material are those of the authors and do not necessarily reflect the views of NSF.

References

1. Dietterich, T.G.: Steps toward robust artificial intelligence. AI Mag. **38**(3), 3–24 (2017)
2. Scheirer, W.J., Jain, L.P., Boult, T.E.: Probability models for open set recognition. IEEE Trans. Pattern Anal. Mach. Intell. **36**(11), 2317–2324 (2014)

3. Szegedy, C., et al.: Intriguing properties of neural networks. arXiv preprint arXiv:1312.6199 (2013)
4. Jain, L.P., Scheirer, W.J., Boult, T.E.: Multi-class open set recognition using probability of inclusion. In: Fleet, D., Pajdla, T., Schiele, B., Tuytelaars, T. (eds.) ECCV 2014. LNCS, vol. 8691, pp. 393–409. Springer, Cham (2014). https://doi.org/10.1007/978-3-319-10578-9_26
5. Bendale, A., Boult, T.E.: Towards open set deep networks. In: Proceedings of the IEEE Conference on Computer Vision and Pattern Recognition, pp. 1563–1572(2016)
6. Schlegl, T., Seeböck, P., Waldstein, S.M., Schmidt-Erfurth, U., Langs, G.: Unsupervised anomaly detection with generative adversarial networks to guide marker discovery. In: Niethammer, M., et al. (eds.) IPMI 2017. LNCS, vol. 10265, pp. 146–157. Springer, Cham (2017). https://doi.org/10.1007/978-3-319-59050-9_12
7. Ge, Z., Demyanov, S., Chen, Z., Garnavi, R.: Generative openmax for multi-class open set classification. arXiv preprint arXiv:1707.07418 (2017)
8. Schölkopf, B., Williamson, R.C., Smola, A.J., Shawe-Taylor, J., Platt, J.C.: Support vector method for novelty detection. In: Advances in Neural Information Processing Systems, pp. 582–588 (2000)
9. Scheirer, W.J., de Rezende Rocha, A., Sapkota, A., Boult, T.E.: Toward open set recognition. IEEE Trans. Pattern Anal. Mach. Intell. **35**(7), 1757–1772 (2013)
10. Rozsa, A., Günther, M., Boult, T.E.: Adversarial robustness: softmax versus openmax. arXiv preprint arXiv:1708.01697 (2017)
11. Hassen, M., Chan, P.K.: Learning a neural-network-based representation for open set recognition. arXiv preprint arXiv:1802.04365 (2018)
12. Goodfellow, I., et al.: Generative adversarial nets. In: Advances in Neural Information Processing Systems, pp. 2672–2680 (2014)
13. Mirza, M., Osindero, S.: Conditional generative adversarial nets. arXiv preprint arXiv:1411.1784 (2014)
14. Salimans, T., Goodfellow, I., Zaremba, W., Cheung, V., Radford, A., Chen, X.: Improved techniques for training GANs. In: Advances in Neural Information Processing Systems, pp. 2234–2242 (2016)
15. Arjovsky, M., Chintala, S., Bottou, L.: Wasserstein GAN. arXiv preprint arXiv:1701.07875 (2017)
16. Karras, T., Aila, T., Laine, S., Lehtinen, J.: Progressive growing of GANs for improved quality, stability, and variation. arXiv preprint arXiv:1710.10196 (2017)
17. Springenberg, J.T.: Unsupervised and semi-supervised learning with categorical generative adversarial networks. arXiv preprint arXiv:1511.06390 (2015)
18. Dai, Z., Yang, Z., Yang, F., Cohen, W.W., Salakhutdinov, R.R.: Good semi-supervised learning that requires a bad GAN. In: Advances in Neural Information Processing Systems, pp. 6513–6523 (2017)
19. Nguyen, A., Yosinski, J., Bengio, Y., Dosovitskiy, A., Clune, J.: Plug & play generative networks: conditional iterative generation of images in latent space. arXiv preprint arXiv:1612.00005 (2016)
20. Ledig, C., et al.: Photo-realistic single image super-resolution using a generative adversarial network. arXiv preprint (2016)
21. Makhzani, A., Shlens, J., Jaitly, N., Goodfellow, I., Frey, B.: Adversarial autoencoders. arXiv preprint arXiv:1511.05644 (2015)
22. Dumoulin, V., et al.: Adversarially learned inference. arXiv preprint arXiv:1606.00704 (2016)
23. Sixt, L., Wild, B., Landgraf, T.: RenderGan: generating realistic labeled data. arXiv preprint arXiv:1611.01331 (2016)

24. Lewis, D.: Counterfactuals. Wiley, Hoboken (1973)
25. Goodfellow, I.J., Shlens, J., Szegedy, C.: Explaining and harnessing adversarial examples. arXiv preprint arXiv:1412.6572 (2014)
26. Moosavi Dezfooli, S.M., Fawzi, A., Frossard, P.: DeepFool: a simple and accurate method to fool deep neural networks. In: Proceedings of 2016 IEEE Conference on Computer Vision and Pattern Recognition (CVPR). Number EPFL-CONF-218057 (2016)
27. Berthelot, D., Schumm, T., Metz, L.: BEGAN: boundary equilibrium generative adversarial networks. arXiv preprint arXiv:1703.10717 (2017)
28. Zhu, J.Y., Park, T., Isola, P., Efros, A.A.: Unpaired image-to-image translation using cycle-consistent adversarial networks
29. Gulrajani, I., Ahmed, F., Arjovsky, M., Dumoulin, V., Courville, A.: Improved training of Wasserstein GANs. arXiv preprint arXiv:1704.00028 (2017)
30. Netzer, Y., Wang, T., Coates, A., Bissacco, A., Wu, B., Ng, A.Y.: Reading digits in natural images with unsupervised feature learning. In: NIPS Workshop on Deep Learning and Unsupervised Feature Learning, vol. 2011, p. 5 (2011)

Human Sensing

Audio-Visual Scene Analysis with Self-Supervised Multisensory Features

Andrew Owens[(✉)] and Alexei A. Efros

UC Berkeley, Berkeley, USA
owens@berkeley.edu

Abstract. The thud of a bouncing ball, the onset of speech as lips open—when visual and audio events occur together, it suggests that there might be a common, underlying event that produced both signals. In this paper, we argue that the visual and audio components of a video signal should be modeled jointly using a fused multisensory representation. We propose to learn such a representation in a self-supervised way, by training a neural network to predict whether video frames and audio are temporally aligned. We use this learned representation for three applications: (a) sound source localization, i.e. visualizing the source of sound in a video; (b) audio-visual action recognition; and (c) on/off-screen audio source separation, e.g. removing the off-screen translator's voice from a foreign official's speech. Code, models, and video results are available on our webpage: http://andrewowens.com/multisensory.

1 Introduction

As humans, we experience our world through a number of simultaneous sensory streams. When we bite into an apple, not only do we taste it, but—as Smith and Gasser [1] point out—we also hear it crunch, see its red skin, and feel the coolness of its core. The coincidence of sensations gives us strong evidence that they were generated by a common, underlying event [2], since it is unlikely that they co-occurred across multiple modalities merely by chance. These cross-modal, temporal co-occurrences therefore provide a useful learning signal: a model that is trained to detect them ought to discover multi-modal structures that are useful for other tasks. In much of traditional computer vision research, however, we have been avoiding the use of other, non-visual modalities, arguably making the perception problem harder, not easier.

In this paper, we learn a temporal, multisensory representation that fuses the visual and audio components of a video signal. We propose to train this model without using any manually labeled data. That is, rather than explicitly telling the model that, e.g., it should associate moving lips with speech or a thud with a bouncing ball, we have it discover these audio-visual associations through self-supervised training [3]. Specifically, we train a neural network on a "pretext" task of detecting misalignment between audio and visual streams in synthetically-shifted videos. The network observes raw audio and

© Springer Nature Switzerland AG 2018
V. Ferrari et al. (Eds.): ECCV 2018, LNCS 11210, pp. 639–658, 2018.
https://doi.org/10.1007/978-3-030-01231-1_39

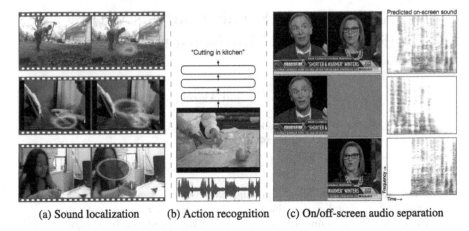

(a) Sound localization   (b) Action recognition   (c) On/off-screen audio separation

Fig. 1. Applications. We use self-supervision to learn an audio-visual representation that: (a) can be used to visualize the locations of sound sources in video; (b) is useful for visual and audio-visual action recognition; (c) can be applied to the task of separating on- and off-screen sounds. In (c), we demonstrate our source-separation model by visually masking each speaker and asking it to predict the on-screen audio. The predicted sound contains only the voice of the visible speaker. Please see our webpage for video results: http://andrewowens.com/multisensory.

video streams—some of which are aligned, and some that have been randomly shifted by a few seconds—and we task it with distinguishing between the two. This turns out to be a challenging training task that forces the network to fuse visual motion with audio information and, in the process, learn a useful audio-visual feature representation.

We demonstrate the usefulness of our multisensory representation in three audio-visual applications: (a) sound source localization, (b) audio-visual action recognition; and (c) on/off-screen sound source separation. Figure 1 shows examples of these applications. In Fig. 1(a), we visualize the sources of sound in a video using our network's learned attention map, i.e. the impact of an axe, the opening of a mouth, and moving hands of a musician. In Fig. 1(b), we show an application of our learned features to audio-visual action recognition, i.e. classifying a video of a chef chopping an onion. In Fig. 1(c), we demonstrate our novel on/off-screen sound source separation model's ability to separate the speakers' voices by visually masking them from the video.

The main contributions of this paper are: (1) learning a general video representation that fuses audio and visual information; (2) evaluating the usefulness of this representation qualitatively (by sound source visualization) and quantitatively (on an action recognition task); and (3) proposing a novel video-conditional source separation method that uses our representation to separate on- and off-screen sounds, and is the first method to work successfully on real-world video footage, e.g. television broadcasts. Our feature representation, as well as code and models for all applications are available online.

2 Related Work

Evidence from Psychophysics. While we often think of vision and hearing as being distinct systems, in humans they are closely intertwined [4] through a process known as *multisensory integration*. Perhaps the most compelling demonstration of this phenomenon is the McGurk effect [5], an illusion in which visual motion of a mouth changes one's interpretation of a spoken sound[1]. Hearing can also influence vision: the timing of a sound, for instance, affects whether we perceive two moving objects to be colliding or overlapping [2]. Moreover, psychologists have suggested that humans fuse audio and visual signals at a fairly early stage of processing [7,8], and that the two modalities are used jointly in perceptual grouping. For example, the McGurk effect is less effective when the viewer first watches a video where audio and visuals in a video are unrelated, as this causes the signals to become "unbound" (i.e. not grouped together) [9,10]. This multi-modal perceptual grouping process is often referred to as *audio-visual scene analysis* [7,10–12]. In this paper, we take inspiration from psychology and propose a self-supervised multisensory feature representation as a computational model of audio-visual scene analysis.

Self-supervised Learning. Self-supervised methods learn features by training a model to solve a task derived from the input data itself, without human labeling. Starting with the early work of de Sa [3], there have been many self-supervised methods that learn to find correlations between sight and sound [13–16]. These methods, however, have either learned the correspondence between static images and ambient sound [15,16], or have analyzed motion in very limited domains [13,14] (e.g. [14] only modeled drumstick impacts). Our learning task resembles Arandjelović and Zisserman [16], which predicts whether an image and an audio track are sampled from the same (or different) videos. Their task, however, is solvable from a single frame by recognizing semantics (e.g. indoor vs. outdoor scenes). Our inputs, by contrast, always come from the same video, and we predict whether they are aligned; hence our task requires motion analysis to solve. Time has also been used as supervisory signal, e.g. predicting the temporal ordering in a video [17–19]. In contrast, our network learns to analyze audio-visual actions, which are likely to correspond to salient physical processes.

Audio-Visual Alignment. While we study alignment for self-supervised learning, it has also been studied as an end in itself [20–22] e.g. in lip-reading applications [23]. Chung and Zisserman [22], the most closely related approach, train a two-stream network with an embedding loss. Since aligning speech videos is their end goal, they use a face detector (trained with labels) and a tracking system to crop the speaker's face. This allows them to address the problem with a 2D CNN that takes 5 channel-wise concatenated frames cropped around a mouth as input (they also propose using their image features for self-supervision; while promising, these results are very preliminary).

---

[1] For a particularly vivid demonstration, please see: https://www.youtube.com/watch?v=G-lN8vWm3m0 [6].

Sound Localization. The goal of visually locating the source of sounds in a video has a long history. The seminal work of Hershey et al. [24] localized sound sources by measuring mutual information between visual motion and audio using a Gaussian process model. Subsequent work also considered subspace methods [25], canonical correlations [26], and keypoints [27]. Our model learns to associate motions with sounds via self-supervision, without us having to explicitly model them.

Audio-Visual Source Separation. Blind source separation (BSS), i.e. separating the individual sound sources in an audio stream—also known as the *cocktail party* problem [28]—is a classic audio-understanding task [29]. Researchers have proposed many successful probabilistic approaches to this problem [30–33]. More recent deep learning approaches involve predicting an embedding that encodes the audio clustering [34,35], or optimizing a permutation invariant loss [36]. It is natural to also want to include the visual signal to solve this problem, often referred to as *Audio-Visual Source Separation*. For example, [25,37] masked frequencies based on their correlation with optical flow; [12] used graphical models; [27] used priors on harmonics; [38] used a sparsity-based factorization method; and [39] used a clustering method. Other methods use face detection and multi-microphone beamforming [40]. These methods make strong assumptions about the relationship between sound and motion, and have mostly been applied to lab-recorded video. Researchers have proposed learning-based methods that address these limitations, e.g. [41] use mixture models to predict separation masks. Recently, [42] proposed a convolutional network that isolates on-screen speech, although this model is relatively small-scale (tested on videos from one speaker). We do on/off-screen source separation on more challenging internet and broadcast videos by combining our representation with a u-net [43] regression model.

Concurrent Work. Concurrently and independently from us, a number of groups have proposed closely related methods for source separation and sound localization. Gabbay et al. [44,45] use a vision-to-sound method to separate speech, and propose a convolutional separation model. Unlike our work, they assume speaker identities are known. Ephrat et al. [46] and Afouras et al. [47] separate the speech of a user-chosen speaker from videos containing multiple speakers, using face detection and tracking systems to group the different speakers. Work by Zhao et al. [48] and Gao et al. [49] separate sound for multiple visible objects (e.g. musical instruments). This task involves associating objects with the sounds they typically make based on their appearance, while ours involves the "fine-grained" motion-analysis task of separating multiple speakers. There has also been recent work on localizing sound sources using a network's attention map [50–52]. These methods are similar to ours, but they largely localize objects and ambient sound in static images, while ours responds to actions in videos.

3   Learning a Self-supervised Multisensory Representation

We propose to learn a representation using self-supervision, by training a model to predict whether a video's audio and visual streams are temporally synchronized.

Aligning Sight with Sound. During training, we feed a neural network video clips. In half of them, the vision and sound streams are synchronized; in the others, we shift the audio by a few seconds. We train a network to distinguish between these examples. More specifically, we learn a model $p(y \mid I, A)$ that predicts whether the image stream I and audio stream A are synchronized, by maximizing the log-likelihood:

$$\mathcal{L}(\theta) = \frac{1}{2}\mathbb{E}_{I,A,t}[\log(p_\theta(y = 1 \mid I, A_0)) + \log(p_\theta(y = 0 \mid I, A_t))], \qquad (1)$$

where A_s is the audio track shifted by s secs., t is a random temporal shift, θ are the model parameters, and y is the event that the streams are synchronized. This learning problem is similar to noise-contrastive estimation [54], which trains a model to distinguish between real examples and noise; here, the noisy examples are misaligned videos.

Fused Audio-Visual Network Design. Solving this task requires the integration of low-level information across modalities. In order to detect misalignment in a video of human speech, for instance, the model must associate the subtle motion of lips with the timing of utterances in the sound. We hypothesize that early fusion of audio and visual streams is important for modeling actions that produce a signal in both modalities. We therefore propose to solve our task using a 3D multisensory convolutional network (CNN) with an early-fusion design (Fig. 2).

Before fusion, we apply a small number of 3D convolution and pooling operations to the video stream, reducing its temporal sampling rate by a factor of 4. We also apply a series of strided 1D convolutions to the input waveform, until its sampling rate matches that of the video network. We fuse the two subnetworks by concatenating their activations channel-wise, after spatially tiling the audio activations. The fused network then undergoes a series of 3D convolutions, followed by global average pooling [55]. We add residual connections between pairs of convolutions. We note that the network architecture resembles ResNet-18 [53] but with the extra audio subnetwork, and 3D convolutions instead of 2D ones (following work on inflated convolutions [56]).

Training. We train our model with 4.2-sec. videos, randomly shifting the audio by 2.0 to 5.8 seconds. We train our model on a dataset of approximately 750,000 videos randomly sampled from AudioSet [57]. We use full frame-rate videos (29.97 Hz), resulting in 125 frames per example. We select random 224×224 crops from resized 256×256 video frames, apply random left-right flipping, and use 21 kHz stereo sound. We sample these video clips from longer (10 sec.) videos. Optimization details can be found in the supplementary material.

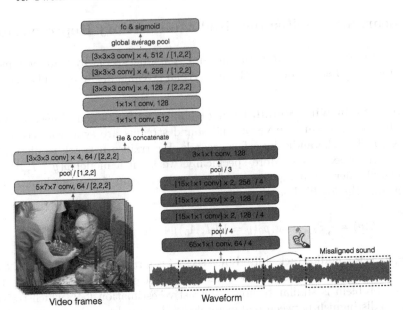

Fig. 2. Fused audio-visual network. We train an early-fusion, multisensory network to predict whether video frames and audio are temporally aligned. We include residual connections between pairs of convolutions [53]. We represent the input as a $T \times H \times W$ volume, and denote a stride by "/2". To generate misaligned samples, we synthetically shift the audio by a few seconds.

Task Performance. We found that the model obtained 59.9% accuracy on held-out videos for its alignment task (chance = 50%). While at first glance this may seem low, we note that in many videos the sounds occur off-screen [15]. Moreover, we found that this task is also challenging for humans. To get a better understanding of human ability, we showed 30 participants from Amazon Mechanical Turk 60 aligned/shifted video pairs, and asked them to identify the one with out-of-sync sound. We gave them 15 secs. of video (so they have significant temporal context) and used large, 5-sec. shifts. They solved the task with 66.6% ± 2.4% accuracy.

To help understand what actions the model can predict synchronization for, we also evaluated its accuracy on categories from the Kinetics dataset [58] (please see the supplementary material). It was most successful for classes involving human speech: e.g., *news anchoring, answering questions,* and *testifying*. Of course, the most important question is whether the learned audio-visual representation is useful for downstream tasks. We therefore turn out attention to applications.

Fig. 3. Visualizing sound sources. We show the video frames in held-out AudioSet videos with the strongest class activation map (CAM) response (we scale its range per image to compensate for the wide range of values).

Fig. 4. Examples with the weakest class activation map response (c.f. Fig. 3).

4   Visualizing the Locations of Sound Sources

One way of evaluating our representation is to visualize the audio-visual structures that it detects. A good audio-visual representation, we hypothesize, will pay special attention to *visual sound sources*—on-screen actions that make a sound, or whose motion is highly correlated with the onset of sound. We note that there is ambiguity in the notion of a sound source for in-the-wild videos. For example, a musician's lips, their larynx, and their tuba could all potentially be called the source of a sound. Hence we use this term to refer to motions that are correlated with production of a sound, and study it through network visualizations.

Fig. 5. Strongest CAM responses for classes in the Kinetics-Sounds dataset [16], after manually removing frames in which the activation was only to a face (which appear in almost all categories). We note that no labeled data was used for training. We do not rescale the heatmaps per image (i.e. the range used in this visualization is consistent across examples).

To do this, we apply the class activation map (CAM) method of Zhou et al. [59], which has been used for localizing ambient sounds [52]. Given a space-time video patch I_x, its corresponding audio A_x, and the features assigned to them by the last convolutional layer of our model, $f(I_x, A_x)$, we can estimate the probability of alignment with:

$$p(y \mid I_x, A_x) = \sigma(w^\top f(I_x, A_x)), \tag{2}$$

where y is the binary alignment label, σ the sigmoid function, and w is the model's final affine layer. We can therefore measure the information content of a patch—and, by our hypothesis, the likelihood that it is a sound source—by the magnitude of the prediction $|w^\top f(I_x, A_x)|$.

One might ask how this self-supervised approach to localization relates to generative approaches, such as classic mutual information methods [24,25]. To help understand this, we can view our audio-visual observations as having been produced by a generative process (using an analysis similar to [60]): we sample the label y, which determines the alignment, and then conditionally sample I_x and A_x. Rather than computing mutual information between the two modalities

Table 1. Action recognition on UCF-101 (split 1). We compared methods pretrained without labels (top), and with semantic labels (bottom). Our model, trained both with and without sound, significantly outperforms other self-supervised methods. Numbers annotated with "*" were obtained from their corresponding publications; we retrained/evaluated the other models.

Model	Acc.
Multisensory (full)	**82.1%**
Multisensory (spectrogram)	81.1%
Multisensory (random pairing [16])	78.7%
Multisensory (vision only)	77.6%
Multisensory (scratch)	68.1%
I3D-RGB (scratch) [56]	68.1%
O3N [19]*	60.3%
Purushwalkam et al. [61]*	55.4%
C3D [56,62]*	51.6%
Shuffle [17]*	50.9%
Wang et al. [61,63]*	41.5%
I3D-RGB + ImageNet [56]	84.2%
I3D-RGB + ImageNet + Kinetics [56]	**94.5%**

(which requires a generative model that self-supervised approaches do not have), we find the patch/sound that provides the most information about the latent variable y, based on our learned model $p(y \mid I_x, A_x)$.

Visualizations. What actions does our network respond to? First, we asked which space-time patches in our test set were most informative, according to Eq. 2. We show the top-ranked patches in Fig. 3, with the class activation map displayed as a heatmap and overlaid on its corresponding video frame. From this visualization, we can see that the network is selective to faces and moving mouths. The strongest responses that are not faces tend to be unusual but salient audio-visual stimuli (e.g. two top-ranking videos contain strobe lights and music). For comparison, we show the videos with the weakest response in Fig. 4; these contain relatively few faces.

Next, we asked how the model responds to videos that do not contain speech, and applied our method to the Kinetics-Sounds dataset [16]—a subset of Kinetics [58] classes that tend to contain a distinctive sound. We show the examples with the highest response for a variety of categories, after removing examples in which the response was solely to a face (which appear in almost every category). We show results in Fig. 5.

Finally, we asked how the model's attention varies with motion. To study this, we computed our CAM-based visualizations for videos, which we have included in the supplementary video (we also show some hand-chosen examples in Fig. 1(a)). These results qualitatively suggest that the model's attention varies with on-screen motion. This is in contrast to single-frame methods models [16,50,52], which largely attend to sound-making objects rather than actions.

5 Action Recognition

We have seen through visualizations that our representation conveys information about sound sources. We now ask whether it is useful for recognition tasks. To study this, we fine-tuned our model for action recognition using the UCF-101 dataset [64], initializing the weights with those learned from our alignment task. We provide the results in Table 1, and compare our model to other unsupervised learning and 3D CNN methods.

We train with 2.56-second subsequences, following [56], which we augment with random flipping and cropping, and small (up to one frame) audio shifts. At test time, we follow [65] and average the model's outputs over 25 clips from each video, and use a center 224×224 crop. See the supplementary material for optimization details.

Analysis. We see, first, that our model significantly outperforms self-supervised approaches that have previously been applied to this task, including Shuffle-and-Learn [17] (82.1% vs. 50.9% accuracy) and O3N [19] (60.3%). We suspect this is in part due to the fact that these methods either process a single frame or a short sequence, and they solve tasks that do not require extensive motion analysis. We then compared our model to methods that use supervised pretraining, focusing on the state-of-the-art I3D [56] model. While there is a large gap between our self-supervised model and a version of I3D that has been pretrained on the closely-related Kinetics dataset (94.5%), the performance of our model (with both sound and vision) is close to the (visual-only) I3D pretrained with ImageNet [66] (84.2%).

Next, we trained our multisensory network with the self-supervision task of [16] rather than our own, i.e. creating negative examples by randomly pairing the audio and visual streams from different videos, rather than by introducing misalignment. We found that this model performed significantly worse than ours (78.7%), perhaps due to the fact that its task can largely be solved without analyzing motion.

Finally, we asked how components of our model contribute to its performance. To test whether the model is obtaining its predictive power from audio, we trained a variation of the model in which the audio subnetwork was ablated (activations set to zero), finding that this results in a 5% drop in performance. This suggests both that sound is important for our results, and that our visual features are useful in isolation. We also tried training a variation of the model that operated on spectrograms, rather than raw waveforms, finding that this yielded similar performance (see supplementary material for details). To measure the importance of our self-supervised pretraining, we compared our model to a randomly initialized network (i.e. trained from scratch), finding that there was a significant (14%) drop in performance—similar in magnitude to removing ImageNet pretraining from I3D. These results suggest that the model has learned a representation that is useful both for vision-only and audio-visual action recognition.

6   On/Off-Screen Audio-Visual Source Separation

We now apply our representation to a classic audio-visual understanding task: separating on- and off-screen sound. To do this, we propose a source separation model that uses our learned features. Our formulation of the problem resembles recent audio-visual and audio-only separation work [34,36,42,67]. We create synthetic sound mixtures by summing an input video's ("on-screen") audio track with a randomly chosen ("off-screen") track from a random video. Our model is then tasked with separating these sounds.

Task. We consider models that take a spectrogram for the mixed audio as input and recover spectrogram for the two mixture components. Our simplest on/off-screen separation model learns to minimize:

$$\mathcal{L}_O(x_M, I) = \|x_F - f_F(x_M, I)\|_1 + \|x_B - f_B(x_M, I)\|_1, \qquad (3)$$

where x_M is the mixture sound, x_F and x_B are the spectrograms of the on- and off-screen sounds that comprise it (i.e. foreground and background), and f_F and f_B are our model's predictions of them conditional on the (audio-visual) video I.

We also consider models that segment the two sounds without regard for their on- or off-screen provenance, using the permutation invariant loss (PIT) of

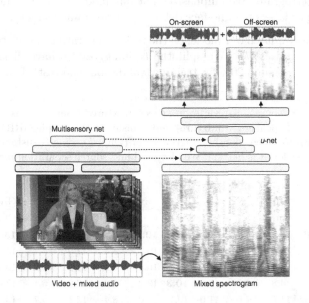

Fig. 6. Adapting our audio-visual network to a source separation task. Our model separates an input spectrogram into on- and off-screen audio streams. After each temporal downsampling layer, our multisensory features are concatenated with those of a u-net computed over spectrograms. We invert the spectrograms to obtain waveforms. The model operates on raw video, without any preprocessing (e.g. no face detection).

Yu et al. [36]. This loss is similar to Eq. 3, but it allows for the on- and off-screen sounds to be swapped without penalty:

$$\mathcal{L}_{\mathcal{P}}(x_F, x_B, \hat{x}_1, \hat{x}_2) = \min(L(\hat{x}_1, \hat{x}_2), L(\hat{x}_2, \hat{x}_1)), \tag{4}$$

where $L(x_i, x_j) = \|x_i - x_F\|_1 + \|x_j - x_B\|_1$ and $\hat{x}_1$ and $\hat{x}_2$ are the predictions.

6.1 Source Separation Model

We augment our audio-visual network with a u-net encoder-decoder [43,69,70] that maps the mixture sound to its on- and off-screen components (Fig. 6). To provide the u-net with video information, we include our multisensory network's features at three temporal scales: we concatenate the last layer of each temporal scale with the layer of the encoder that has the closest temporal sampling rate. Prior to concatenation, we use linear interpolation to make the video features match the audio sampling rate; we then mean-pool them spatially, and tile them over the frequency domain, thereby reshaping our 3D CNN's time/height/width shape to match the 2D encoder's time/frequency shape. We use parameters for u-net similar to [69], adding one pair of convolution layers to compensate for the large number of frequency channels in our spectrograms. We predict both the magnitude of the log-spectrogram and its phase (we scale the phase loss by 0.01 since it is less perceptually important). To obtain waveforms, we invert the predicted spectrogram. We emphasize that our model uses raw video, with no preprocessing or labels (e.g. no face detection or pretrained supervised features).

Training. We evaluated our model on the task of separating speech sounds using the VoxCeleb dataset [71]. We split the training/test to have disjoint speaker identities (72%, 8%, and 20% for training, validation, and test). During training,

Table 2. Source separation results on speech mixtures from the VoxCeleb (broken down by gender of speakers in mixture) and transfer to the simple GRID dataset. We evaluate the on/off-screen sound prediction error (On/off) using ℓ_1 distance to the true log-spectrograms (lower is better). We also use blind source separation metrics (higher is better) [68].

Method	All				Mixed sex		Same sex		GRID transfer	
	On/off	SDR	SIR	SAR	On/off	SDR	On/off	SDR	On/off	SDR
On/off + PIT	**11.2**	**7.6**	**12.1**	10.2	**10.6**	**8.8**	**11.8**	**6.5**	**13.0**	7.8
Full on/off	11.4	7.0	11.5	9.8	10.7	8.4	11.9	5.7	13.1	7.3
Mono	11.4	6.9	11.4	9.8	10.8	8.4	11.9	5.7	13.1	7.3
Single frame	14.8	5.0	7.8	**10.3**	13.2	7.2	16.2	3.1	17.8	5.7
No early fusion	11.6	7.0	11.0	10.1	11.0	8.4	12.1	5.7	13.5	6.9
Scratch	12.9	5.8	9.7	9.4	11.8	7.6	13.9	4.2	15.2	6.3
I3D + Kinetics	12.3	6.6	10.7	9.7	11.6	8.2	12.9	5.1	14.4	6.6
u-net PIT [36]	–	7.3	11.4	**10.3**	–	**8.8**	–	5.9	–	**8.1**
Deep Sep. [67]	–	1.3	3.0	8.7	–	1.9	–	0.8	–	2.2

Table 3. Comparison of audio-visual and audio-only separation methods on short (200 ms) videos. We compare SDR of the on-screen audio prediction (On-SDR) with audio resampled to 2 kHz.

VoxCeleb short videos (200ms)				
	On-SDR	SDR	SIR	SAR
Ours (on/off)	**7.6**	5.3	7.8	10.8
Hou et al. [42]	4.5	–	–	–
Gabbay et al. [44]	3.5	–	–	–
PIT-CNN [36]	–	**7.0**	10.1	**11.2**
u-net PIT [36]	–	**7.0**	**10.3**	11.0
Deep Sep. [67]	–	2.7	4.2	10.3

we sampled 2.1-sec. clips from longer 5-sec. clips, and normalized each waveform's mean squared amplitude to a constant value. We used spectrograms with a 64 ms frame length and a 16 ms step size, producing 128×1025 spectrograms. In each mini-batch of the optimization, we randomly paired video clips, making one the off-screen sound for the other. We jointly optimized our multisensory network and the u-net model, initializing the weights using our self-supervised representation (see supplementary material for details).

6.2 Evaluation

We compared our model to a variety of separation methods: (1) we replaced our self-supervised video representation with other features, (2) compared to audio-only methods using blind separation methods, (3) and compared to other audio-visual models.

Ablations. Since one of our main goals is to evaluate the quality of the learned features, we compared several variations of our model (Table 2). First, we replaced the multisensory features with the I3D network [56] pretrained on the Kinetics dataset—a 3D CNN-based representation that was very effective for action recognition (Sect. 5). This model performed significantly worse (11.4 vs. 12.3 spectrogram ℓ_1 loss for Eq. 3). One possible explanation is that our pretraining task requires extensive motion analysis, whereas even single-frame action recognition can still perform well [65,72].

We then asked how much of our representation's performance comes from motion features, rather than from recognizing properties of the speaker (e.g. gender). To test this, we trained the model with only a single frame (replicated temporally to make a video). We found a significant drop in performance (11.4 vs. 14.8 loss). The drop was particularly large for mixtures in which two speakers had the same gender—a case where lip motion is an important cue.

One might also ask whether early audio-visual fusion is helpful—the network, after all, fuses the modalities in the spectrogram encoder-decoder as well. To test

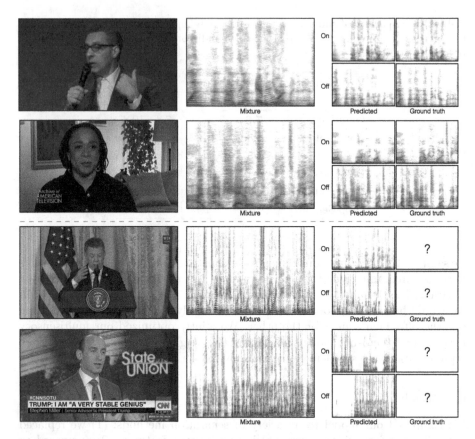

Fig. 7. Qualitative results from our on/off-screen separation model. We show an input frame and spectrogram for two synthetic mixtures from our test set, and two in-the-wild internet videos containing multiple speakers. The first (a male/male mixture) contains more artifacts than the second (a female/male mixture). The third video is a real-world mixture in which a female speaker (simultaneously) translates a male Spanish speaker into English. Finally, we separate the speech of two (male) speakers on a television news show. Although there is no ground truth for these real-world examples, the source separation method qualitatively separates the two voices. Please refer to our webpage (http://andrewowens.com/multisensory) for video source separation results.

this, we ablated the audio stream of our multisensory network and retrained the separation model. This model obtained worse performance, suggesting the fused audio is helpful even when it is available elsewhere. Finally, while the encoder-decoder uses only monaural audio, our representation uses stereo. To test whether it uses binaural cues, we converted all the audio to mono and re-evaluated it. We found that this did not significantly affect performance, which is perhaps due to the difficulty of using stereo cues in in-the-wild internet videos (e.g. 39% of the audio tracks were mono). Finally, we also transferred (without retraining) our learned models to the GRID dataset [73], a lab-recorded dataset in which people speak simple phrases in front of a plain background, finding a similar relative ordering of the methods.

Audio-Only Separation. To get a better understanding of our model's effectiveness, we compared it to audio-only separation methods. While these methods are not applicable to on/off-screen separation, we modified our model to have it separate audio using an extra permutation invariant loss (Eq. 4) and then compared the methods using blind separation metrics [68]: signal-to-distortion ratio (SDR), signal-to-interference ratio (SIR), and signal-to-artifacts ratio (SAR). For consistency across methods, we resampled predicted waveforms to 16 kHz (the minimum used by all methods), and used the mixture phase to invert our model's spectrogram, rather than the predicted phase (which none of the others predict).

We compared our model to PIT-CNN [36]. This model uses a VGG-style [74] CNN to predict two soft separation masks via a fully connected layer. These maps are multiplied by the input mixture to obtain the segmented streams. While this method worked well on short clips, we found it failed on longer inputs (e.g. obtaining 1.8 SDR in the experiment shown in Table 2). To create a stronger PIT baseline, we therefore created an audio-only version of our u-net model, optimizing the PIT loss instead of our on/off-screen loss, i.e. replacing the VGG-style network and masks with u-net. We confirmed that this model obtains similar performance on short sequences (Table 3), and found it successfully trained on longer videos. Finally, we compared with a pretrained separation model [67], which is based on recurrent networks and trained on the TSP dataset [75].

We found that our audio-visual model, when trained with a PIT loss, outperformed all of these methods, except for on the SAR metric, where the u-net PIT model was slightly better (which largely measures the presence of artifacts in the generated waveform). In particular, our model did significantly better than the audio-only methods when the genders of the two speakers in the mixture were the same (Table 2). Interestingly, we found that the audio-only methods still performed better on blind separation metrics when transferring to the lab-recorded GRID dataset, which we hypothesize is due to the significant domain shift.

Audio-Visual Separation. We compared to the audio-visual separation model of Hou et al. [42]. This model was designed for enhancing the speech of a previously known speaker, but we apply it to our task since it is the most closely related prior method. We also evaluated the network of Gabbay et al. [45] (a concurrent approach to ours). We trained these models using the same procedure as ours ([45] used speaker identities to create hard mixtures; we instead assumed speaker identities are unknown and mix randomly). Both models take very short (5-frame) video inputs. Therefore, following [45] we evaluated 200ms videos (Table 3). For these baselines, we cropped the video around the speaker's mouth using the Viola-Jones [76] lip detector of [45] (we do not use face detection for our own model). These methods use a small number of frequency bands in their (Mel-) STFT representations, which limits their quantitative performance. To address these limitations, we evaluated only the on-screen audio, and downsampled the audio to a low, common rate (2 kHz) before computing SDR. Our model significantly outperforms these methods. Qualitatively, we observed that [45] often smooths the input spectrogram, and we suspect its performance on source separation metrics may be affected by the relatively small number of frequency bands in its audio representation.

6.3   Qualitative Results

Our quantitative results suggest that our model can successfully separate on- and off-screen sounds. However, these metrics are limited in their ability to convey the quality of the predicted sound (and are sensitive to factors that may not be perceptually important, such as the frequency representation). Therefore, we also provide qualitative examples.

Real Mixtures. In Fig. 7, we show results for two synthetic mixtures from our test set, and two real-world mixtures: a simultaneous Spanish-to-English translation and a television interview with concurrent speech. We exploit the fact that our model is fully convolutional to apply it to these 8.3-sec. videos (4× longer than training videos). We include additional source separation examples in the videos on our webpage. This includes a random sample of (synthetically mixed) test videos, as well as results on in-the-wild videos that contain both on- and off-screen sound.

Multiple On-Screen Sound Sources. To demonstrate our model's ability to vary its prediction based on the speaker, we took a video in which two people are speaking on a TV debate show, visually masked one side of the screen (similar to [25]), and ran our source separation model. As shown in Fig. 1, when the speaker on the left is hidden, we hear the speaker on the right, and vice versa. Please see our video for results.

Large-Scale Training. We trained a larger variation of our model on significantly more data. For this, we combined the VoxCeleb and VoxCeleb2 [77] datasets (approx. 8× as manys videos), as in [47], and modeled ambient sounds by sampling background audio tracks from AudioSet approximately 8% of the time. To provide more temporal context, we trained with 4.1-sec. videos (approx. 256 STFT time samples). We also decreased the spectrogram frame length to 40 ms (513 frequency samples) and increased the weight of the phase loss to 0.2. Please see our video for results.

7   Discussion

In this paper, we presented a method for learning a temporal multisensory representation, and we showed through experiments that it was useful for three downstream tasks: (a) pretraining action recognition systems, (b) visualizing the locations of sound sources, and (c) on/off-screen source separation. We see this work as opening two potential directions for future research. The first is developing new methods for learning fused multisensory representations. We presented one method—detecting temporal misalignment—but one could also incorporate other learning signals, such as the information provided by ambient sound [15]. The other direction is to use our representation for additional audio-visual tasks. We presented several applications here, but there are other audio-understanding tasks could potentially benefit from visual information and, likewise, visual applications that could benefit from fused audio information.

Acknowledgements. This work was supported, in part, by DARPA grant FA8750-16-C-0166, U.C. Berkeley Center for Long-Term Cybersecurity, and Berkeley Deep-Drive. We thank Allan Jabri, David Fouhey, Andrew Liu, Morten Kolbæk, Xiaolong Wang, and Jitendra Malik for the helpful discussions.

References

1. Smith, L., Gasser, M.: The development of embodied cognition: six lessons from babies. Artif. Life **11**(1–2), 13–29 (2005)
2. Sekuler, R.: Sound alters visual motion perception. Nature **385**, 308 (1997)
3. de Sa, V.R.: Learning classification with unlabeled data. In: Advances in Neural Information Processing Systems (1994)
4. Shimojo, S., Shams, L.: Sensory modalities are not separate modalities: plasticity and interactions. Curr. Opin. Neurobiol. **11**, 505–509 (2001)
5. McGurk, H., MacDonald, J.: Hearing lips and seeing voices. Nature **264**, 746 (1976)
6. British Broadcasting Corporation: Is seeing believing? (2010)
7. Schwartz, J.L., Berthommier, F., Savariaux, C.: Audio-visual scene analysis: evidence for a "very-early" integration process in audio-visual speech perception. In: Seventh International Conference on Spoken Language Processing (2002)
8. Omata, K., Mogi, K.: Fusion and combination in audio-visual integration. In: Proceedings of the Royal Society of London A: Mathematical, Physical and Engineering Sciences (2008)
9. Nahorna, O., Berthommier, F., Schwartz, J.L.: Binding and unbinding the auditory and visual streams in the McGurk effect. J. Acoust. Soc. Am. **132**(2), 1061–1077 (2012)
10. Nahorna, O., Berthommier, F., Schwartz, J.L.: Audio-visual speech scene analysis: characterization of the dynamics of unbinding and rebinding the McGurk effect. J. Acoust. Soc. Am. **137**(1), 362–377 (2015)
11. Barker, J.P., Berthommier, F., Schwartz, J.L.: Is primitive AV coherence an aid to segment the scene? In: International Conference on Auditory-Visual Speech Processing, AVSP 1998 (1998)
12. Hershey, J., Attias, H., Jojic, N., Kristjansson, T.: Audio-visual graphical models for speech processing. In: Proceedings of IEEE International Conference on Acoustics, Speech, and Signal Processing, (ICASSP 2004), vol. 5, p. V-649. IEEE (2004)
13. Ngiam, J., Khosla, A., Kim, M., Nam, J., Lee, H., Ng, A.Y.: Multimodal deep learning. In: ICML (2011)
14. Owens, A., Isola, P., McDermott, J., Torralba, A., Adelson, E.H., Freeman, W.T.: Visually indicated sounds. In: CVPR (2016)
15. Owens, A., Wu, J., McDermott, J.H., Freeman, W.T., Torralba, A.: Ambient sound provides supervision for visual learning. In: Leibe, B., Matas, J., Sebe, N., Welling, M. (eds.) ECCV 2016. LNCS, vol. 9905, pp. 801–816. Springer, Cham (2016). https://doi.org/10.1007/978-3-319-46448-0_48

16. Arandjelović, R., Zisserman, A.: Look, listen and learn. In: ICCV (2017)
17. Misra, I., Zitnick, C.L., Hebert, M.: Shuffle and learn: unsupervised learning using temporal order verification. In: Leibe, B., Matas, J., Sebe, N., Welling, M. (eds.) ECCV 2016. LNCS, vol. 9905, pp. 527–544. Springer, Cham (2016). https://doi.org/10.1007/978-3-319-46448-0_32
18. Wei, D., Lim, J.J., Zisserman, A., Freeman, W.T.: Learning and using the arrow of time. In: CVPR (2018)
19. Fernando, B., Bilen, H., Gavves, E., Gould, S.: Self-supervised video representation learning with odd-one-out networks. In: 2017 IEEE Conference on Computer Vision and Pattern Recognition (CVPR), pp. 5729–5738. IEEE (2017)
20. McAllister, D.F., Rodman, R.D., Bitzer, D.L., Freeman, A.S.: Lip synchronization of speech. In: Audio-Visual Speech Processing: Computational & Cognitive Science Approaches (1997)
21. Marcheret, E., Potamianos, G., Vopicka, J., Goel, V.: Detecting audio-visual synchrony using deep neural networks. In: Sixteenth Annual Conference of the International Speech Communication Association (2015)
22. Chung, J.S., Zisserman, A.: Out of time: automated lip sync in the wild. In: Chen, C.-S., Lu, J., Ma, K.-K. (eds.) ACCV 2016. LNCS, vol. 10117, pp. 251–263. Springer, Cham (2017). https://doi.org/10.1007/978-3-319-54427-4_19
23. Chung, J.S., Senior, A., Vinyals, O., Zisserman, A.: Lip reading sentences in the wild. In: CVPR (2017)
24. Hershey, J.R., Movellan, J.R.: Audio vision: using audio-visual synchrony to locate sounds. In: NIPS (1999)
25. Fisher III, J.W., Darrell, T., Freeman, W.T., Viola, P.A.: Learning joint statistical models for audio-visual fusion and segregation. In: NIPS (2000)
26. Kidron, E., Schechner, Y.Y., Elad, M.: Pixels that sound. In: CVPR (2005)
27. Barzelay, Z., Schechner, Y.Y.: Harmony in motion. In: Conference on Computer Vision and Pattern Recognition, CVPR 2007 (2007)
28. Cherry, E.C.: Some experiments on the recognition of speech, with one and with two ears. J. Acoust. Soc. Am. 25, 975–979 (1953)
29. Bregman, A.S.: Auditory Scene Analysis: The Perceptual Organization of Sound. MIT Press, Cambridge (1994)
30. Ghahramani, Z., Jordan, M.I.: Factorial hidden Markov models. In: Advances in Neural Information Processing Systems, pp. 472–478 (1996)
31. Roweis, S.T.: One microphone source separation. In: Advances in Neural Information Processing Systems, pp. 793–799 (2001)
32. Cooke, M., Hershey, J.R., Rennie, S.J.: Monaural speech separation and recognition challenge. Comput. Speech Lang. 24(1), 1–15 (2010)
33. Virtanen, T.: Monaural sound source separation by nonnegative matrix factorization with temporal continuity and sparseness criteria. IEEE Trans. Audio Speech Lang. Process. 15(3), 1066–1074 (2007)
34. Hershey, J.R., Chen, Z., Le Roux, J., Watanabe, S.: Deep clustering: discriminative embeddings for segmentation and separation. In: 2016 IEEE International Conference on Acoustics, Speech and Signal Processing (ICASSP), pp. 31–35. IEEE (2016)
35. Chen, Z., Luo, Y., Mesgarani, N.: Deep attractor network for single-microphone speaker separation. In: 2017 IEEE International Conference on Acoustics, Speech and Signal Processing (ICASSP), pp. 246–250, March 2017
36. Yu, D., Kolbæk, M., Tan, Z.H., Jensen, J.: Permutation invariant training of deep models for speaker-independent multi-talker speech separation. In: Acoustics, Speech and Signal Processing (ICASSP) (2017)

37. Darrell, T., Fisher, J.W., Viola, P.: Audio-visual segmentation and "The Cocktail Party Effect". In: Tan, T., Shi, Y., Gao, W. (eds.) ICMI 2000. LNCS, vol. 1948, pp. 32–40. Springer, Heidelberg (2000). https://doi.org/10.1007/3-540-40063-X_5
38. Pu, J., et al.: Audio-visual object localization and separation using low-rank and sparsity. In: ICASSP (2017)
39. Casanovas, A.L., et al.: Blind audiovisual source separation based on sparse redundant representations. Trans. Multimedia 12, 358–371 (2010)
40. Rivet, B., et al.: Audiovisual speech source separation: an overview of key methodologies. IEEE Sig. Process. Mag. 31, 125–134 (2014)
41. Khan, F., Milner, B.: Speaker separation using visually-derived binary masks. In: Auditory-Visual Speech Processing (AVSP) (2013)
42. Hou, J.C., Wang, S.S., Lai, Y.H., Tsao, Y., Chang, H.W., Wang, H.M.: Audio-visual speech enhancement using multimodal deep convolutional neural networks (2017)
43. Ronneberger, O., Fischer, P., Brox, T.: U-Net: convolutional networks for biomedical image segmentation. In: Navab, N., Hornegger, J., Wells, W.M., Frangi, A.F. (eds.) MICCAI 2015. LNCS, vol. 9351, pp. 234–241. Springer, Cham (2015). https://doi.org/10.1007/978-3-319-24574-4_28
44. Gabbay, A., Ephrat, A., Halperin, T., Peleg, S.: Seeing through noise: Speaker separation and enhancement using visually-derived speech. arXiv preprint arXiv:1708.06767 (2017)
45. Gabbay, A., Shamir, A., Peleg, S.: Visual speech enhancement using noise-invariant training. arXiv preprint arXiv:1711.08789 (2017)
46. Ephrat, A., et al.: Looking to listen at the cocktail party: a speaker-independent audio-visual model for speech separation. In: SIGGRAPH (2018)
47. Afouras, T., Chung, J.S., Zisserman, A.: The conversation: Deep audio-visual speech enhancement. arXiv preprint arXiv:1804.04121 (2018)
48. Zhao, H., Gan, C., Rouditchenko, A., Vondrick, C., McDermott, J., Torralba, A.: The sound of pixels. arXiv preprint arXiv:1804.03160 (2018)
49. Gao, R., Feris, R., Grauman, K.: Learning to Separate Object Sounds by Watching Unlabeled Video. arXiv preprint arXiv:1804.01665 (2018)
50. Senocak, A., Oh, T.H., Kim, J., Yang, M.H., Kweon, I.S.: Learning to localize sound source in visual scenes. arXiv preprint arXiv:1803.03849 (2018)
51. Arandjelović, R., Zisserman, A.: Objects that sound. arXiv preprint arXiv:1712.06651 (2017)
52. Owens, A., Wu, J., McDermott, J.H., Freeman, W.T., Torralba, A.: Learning sight from sound: Ambient sound provides supervision for visual learning. arXiv preprint arXiv:1712.07271 (2017)
53. He, K., Zhang, X., Ren, S., Sun, J.: Deep residual learning for image recognition. In: CVPR (2016)
54. Gutmann, M., Hyvärinen, A.: Noise-contrastive estimation: a new estimation principle for unnormalized statistical models. In: Proceedings of the Thirteenth International Conference on Artificial Intelligence and Statistics (2010)
55. Lin, M., Chen, Q., Yan, S.: Network in network. arXiv preprint arXiv:1312.4400 (2013)
56. Carreira, J., Zisserman, A.: Quo vadis, action recognition? a new model and the kinetics dataset. arXiv preprint arXiv:1705.07750 (2017)
57. Gemmeke, J.F., et al.: Audio set: an ontology and human-labeled dataset for audio events. In: ICASSP (2017)
58. Kay, W., et al.: The kinetics human action video dataset. arXiv preprint arXiv:1705.06950 (2017)

59. Zhou, B., Khosla, A., Lapedriza, A., Oliva, A., Torralba, A.: Learning deep features for discriminative localization. In: Proceedings of the IEEE Conference on Computer Vision and Pattern Recognition, pp. 2921–2929 (2016)
60. Isola, P., Zoran, D., Krishnan, D., Adelson, E.H.: Learning visual groups from co-occurrences in space and time. arXiv preprint arXiv:1511.06811 (2015)
61. Purushwalkam, S., Gupta, A.: Pose from action: Unsupervised learning of pose features based on motion. arXiv preprint arXiv:1609.05420 (2016)
62. Tran, D., Bourdev, L., Fergus, R., Torresani, L., Paluri, M.: Learning spatiotemporal features with 3D convolutional networks. In: ICCV (2015)
63. Wang, X., Gupta, A.: Unsupervised learning of visual representations using videos. In: ICCV (2015)
64. Soomro, K., Zamir, A.R., Shah, M.: Ucf101: A dataset of 101 human actions classes from videos in the wild. arXiv preprint arXiv:1212.0402 (2012)
65. Simonyan, K., Zisserman, A.: Two-stream convolutional networks for action recognition in videos. In: Advances in Neural Information Processing Systems (2014)
66. Deng, J., Dong, W., Socher, R., Li, L.J., Li, K., Fei-Fei, L.: Imagenet: a large-scale hierarchical image database. In: CVPR (2009)
67. Huang, P.S., Kim, M., Hasegawa-Johnson, M., Smaragdis, P.: Joint optimization of masks and deep recurrent neural networks for monaural source separation. IEEE/ACM Trans. Audio Speech Lang. Process. 23(12), 2136–2147 (2015)
68. Vincent, E., Gribonval, R., Févotte, C.: Performance measurement in blind audio source separation. IEEE Trans. Audio Speech Lang. Process. 14, 1462–1469 (2006)
69. Isola, P., Zhu, J.Y., Zhou, T., Efros, A.A.: Image-to-image translation with conditional adversarial networks. arXiv preprint arXiv:1611.07004 (2016)
70. Michelsanti, D., Tan, Z.H.: Conditional generative adversarial networks for speech enhancement and noise-robust speaker verification. arXiv preprint arXiv:1709.01703 (2017)
71. Nagrani, A., Chung, J.S., Zisserman, A.: Voxceleb: a large-scale speaker identification dataset. arXiv preprint arXiv:1706.08612 (2017)
72. Karpathy, A., Toderici, G., Shetty, S., Leung, T., Sukthankar, R., Fei-Fei, L.: Large-scale video classification with convolutional neural networks. In: CVPR (2014)
73. Cooke, M., Barker, J., Cunningham, S., Shao, X.: An audio-visual corpus for speech perception and automatic speech recognition. J. Acoust. Soc. Am. 120, 2421–2424 (2006)
74. Simonyan, K., Zisserman, A.: Very deep convolutional networks for large-scale image recognition. arXiv preprint arXiv:1409.1556 (2014)
75. Kabal, P.: Tsp speech database. McGill University, Database Version (2002)
76. Viola, P., Jones, M.: Rapid object detection using a boosted cascade of simple features. In: Proceedings of the 2001 IEEE Computer Society Conference on Computer Vision and Pattern Recognition, CVPR 2001, vol. 1, p. I. IEEE (2001)
77. Chung, J.S., Nagrani, A., Zisserman, A.: Voxceleb2: Deep speaker recognition. arXiv preprint arXiv:1806.05622 (2018)

Jointly Discovering Visual Objects and Spoken Words from Raw Sensory Input

David Harwath[✉], Adrià Recasens, Dídac Surís, Galen Chuang, Antonio Torralba, and James Glass

Massachusetts Institute of Technology, Cambridge, USA
{dharwath,recasens,didac,torralba}@csail.mit.edu, glass@mit.edu

Abstract. In this paper, we explore neural network models that learn to associate segments of spoken audio captions with the semantically relevant portions of natural images that they refer to. We demonstrate that these audio-visual associative localizations emerge from network-internal representations learned as a by-product of training to perform an image-audio retrieval task. Our models operate directly on the image pixels and speech waveform, and do not rely on any conventional supervision in the form of labels, segmentations, or alignments between the modalities during training. We perform analysis using the Places 205 and ADE20k datasets demonstrating that our models implicitly learn semantically-coupled object and word detectors.

Keywords: Vision and language · Sound · Speech
Convolutional networks · Multimodal learning · Unsupervised learning

1 Introduction

Babies face an impressive learning challenge: they must learn to visually perceive the world around them, and to use language to communicate. They must discover the objects in the world and the words that refer to them. They must solve this problem when both inputs come in raw form: unsegmented, unaligned, and with enormous appearance variability both in the visual domain (due to pose, occlusion, illumination, etc.) and in the acoustic domain (due to the unique voice of every person, speaking rate, emotional state, background noise, accent, pronunciation, etc.). Babies learn to understand speech and recognize objects in an extremely weakly supervised fashion, aided not by ground-truth annotations, but by observation, repetition, multi-modal context, and environmental interaction [12,47]. In this paper, we do not attempt to model the cognitive development

Electronic supplementary material The online version of this chapter (https://doi.org/10.1007/978-3-030-01231-1_40) contains supplementary material, which is available to authorized users.

© Springer Nature Switzerland AG 2018
V. Ferrari et al. (Eds.): ECCV 2018, LNCS 11210, pp. 659–677, 2018.
https://doi.org/10.1007/978-3-030-01231-1_40

of humans, but instead ask whether a machine can jointly learn spoken language and visual perception when faced with similar constraints; that is, with inputs in the form of unaligned, unannotated raw speech audio and images (Fig. 1). To that end, we present models capable of jointly discovering words in raw speech audio, objects in raw images, and associating them with one another.

There has recently been a surge of interest in bridging the vision and natural language processing (NLP) communities, in large part thanks to the ability of deep neural networks to effectively model complex relationships within multi-modal data. Current work bringing together vision and language [2, 13, 14, 23, 28, 33, 34, 40, 41, 49, 50, 52] relies on written text. In this situation, the linguistic information is presented in a pre-processed form in which words have been segmented and clustered. The text word *car* has no variability between sentences (other than synonyms, capitalization, etc.), and it is already segmented apart from other words. This is dramatically different from how children learn language. The speech signal is continuous, noisy, unsegmented, and exhibits a wide number of non-lexical variabilities. The problem of segmenting and clustering the raw speech signal into discrete words is analogous to the problem of visual object discovery in images - the goal of this paper is to address both problems jointly.

Recent work has focused on cross modal learning between vision and sounds [3, 4, 36, 37]. This work has focused on using ambient sounds and video to discover sound generating objects in the world. In our work we will also use both vision and audio modalities except that the audio corresponds to speech. In this case, the problem is more challenging as the portions of the speech signal that refer to objects are shorter, creating a more

Fig. 1. The input to our models: images paired with waveforms of speech audio.

challenging temporal segmentation problem, and the number of categories is much larger. Using vision and speech was first studied in [19], but it was only used to relate full speech signals and images using a global embedding. Therefore the results focused on image and speech retrieval. Here we introduce a model able to segment both words in speech and objects in images without supervision.

The premise of this paper is as follows: given an image and a raw speech audio recording describing that image, we propose a neural model which can highlight the relevant regions of the image as they are being described in the speech. What makes our approach unique is the fact that we do not use any form of conventional speech recognition or transcription, nor do we use any conventional object detection or recognition models. In fact, both the speech and images are completely unsegmented, unaligned, and unannotated during training, aside from the assumption that we know which images and spoken captions belong together as illustrated in Fig. 1. We train our models to perform semantic retrieval at the whole-image and whole-caption level, and demonstrate that detection and localization of both visual objects and spoken words emerges as a by-product of this training.

2   Prior Work

Visual Object Recognition and Discovery. State of the art systems are trained using bounding box annotations for the training data [16,39], however other works investigate weakly-supervised or unsupervised object localization [5,7,9,56]. A large body of research has also focused on unsupervised visual object discovery, in which case there is no labeled training dataset available. One of the first works within this realm is [51], which utilized an iterative clustering and classification algorithm to discover object categories. Further works borrowed ideas from textual topic models [45], assuming that certain sets of objects generally appear together in the same image scene. More recently, CNNs have been adapted to this task [10,17], for example by learning to associate image patches which commonly appear adjacent to one another.

Unsupervised Speech Processing. Automatic speech recognition (ASR) systems have recently made great strides thanks to the revival of deep neural networks. Training a state-of-the-art ASR system requires thousands of hours of transcribed speech audio, along with expert-crafted pronunciation lexicons and text corpora covering millions, if not billions of words for language model training. The reliance on expensive, highly supervised training paradigms has restricted the application of ASR to the major languages of the world, accounting for a small fraction of the more than 7,000 human languages spoken worldwide [31]. Within the speech community, there is a continuing effort to develop algorithms less reliant on transcription and other forms of supervision. Generally, these take the form of segmentation and clustering algorithms whose goal is to divide a collection of spoken utterances at the boundaries of phones or words, and then group together segments which capture the same underlying unit. Popular approaches are based on dynamic time warping [21,22,38], or Bayesian generative models of the speech signal [25,30,35]. Neural networks have thus far been mostly utilized in this realm for learning frame-level acoustic features [24,42,48,54].

Fusion of Vision and Language. Joint modeling of images and natural language text has gained rapidly in popularity, encompassing tasks such as image captioning [13,23,28,49,52], visual question answering (VQA) [2,14,33,34,41], multimodal dialog [50], and text-to-image generation [40]. While most work has focused on representing natural language with text, there are a growing number of papers attempting to learn directly from the speech signal. A major early effort in this vein was the work of Roy [43,44], who learned correspondences between images of objects and the outputs of a supervised phoneme recognizer. Recently, it was demonstrated by Harwath et al. [19] that semantic correspondences could be learned between images and speech waveforms at the signal level, with subsequent works providing evidence that linguistic units approximating phonemes and words are implicitly learned by these models [1,8,11,18,26]. This paper follows in the same line of research, introducing the idea of "matchmap" networks which are capable of directly inferring semantic alignments between acoustic frames and image pixels.

Fusion of Vision and Sounds. A number of recent models have focused on integrating other acoustic signals to perform unsupervised discovery of objects and ambient sounds [3,4,36,37]. Our work concentrates on speech and word discovery. But combining both types of signals (speech and ambient sounds) opens a number of opportunities for future research beyond the scope of this paper.

3 Spoken Captions Dataset

For training our models, we use the Places Audio Caption dataset [18,19]. This dataset contains approximately 200,000 recordings collected via Amazon Mechanical Turk of people verbally describing the content of images from the Places 205 [58] image dataset. We augment this dataset by collecting an additional 200,000 captions, resulting in a grand total of 402,385 image/caption pairs for training and a held-out set of 1,000 additional pairs for validation. In order to perform a fine-grained analysis of our models ability to localize objects and words, we collected an additional set of captions for 9,895 images from the ADE20k dataset [59] whose underlying scene category was found in the Places 205 label set. The ADE20k data contains pixel-level object labels, and when combined with acoustic frame-level ASR hypotheses, we are able to determine which underlying words match which underlying objects. In all cases, we follow the original Places audio caption dataset and collect 1 caption per image. Aggregate statistics over the data are shown in Fig. 2. While we do not have exact ground truth transcriptions for the spoken captions, we use the Google ASR engine to derive hypotheses which we use for experimental analysis (but not training, except in the case of the text-based models). A vocabulary of 44,342 unique words were recognized within all 400k captions, which were spoken by 2,683 unique speakers. The distributions over both words and speakers follow a power law with a long tail (Fig. 2). We also note that the free-form nature of the spoken captions generally results in longer, more descriptive captions than exist in text captioning datasets. While MSCOCO [32] contains an average of just over 10 words per caption, the places audio captions are on average 20 words long, with an average duration of 10 s. The extended Places 205 audio caption corpus, the ADE20k caption data, and a PyTorch implementation of the model training code are available at http://groups.csail.mit.edu/sls/downloads/placesaudio/.

4 Models

Our model is similar to that of Harwath et al. [19], in which a pair of convolutional neural networks (CNN) [29] are used to independently encode a visual image and a spoken audio caption into a shared embedding space. What differentiates our models from prior work is the fact that instead of mapping entire images and spoken utterances to fixed points in an embedding space, we learn representations that are *distributed* both spatially and temporally, enabling our models to directly co-localize within both modalities. Our models are trained to optimize a ranking-based criterion [6,19,27], such that images and captions that belong together are more similar in the embedding space than mismatched image/caption pairs. Specifically, across a batch of B image/caption pairs (I_j, A_j) (where I_j represents the output of the image branch of the network for the jth image, and A_j the output of the audio branch for the jth caption) we compute the loss:

$$L = \sum_{j=1}^{B} \Big(\max(0, S(I_j, A_j^{imp}) - S(I_j, A_j) + \eta)$$

$$+ \max(0, S(I_j^{imp}, A_j) - S(I_j, A_j) + \eta) \Big), \tag{1}$$

where $S(I, A)$ represents the similarity score between an image I and audio caption A, I_j^{imp} represents the jth randomly chosen imposter image, A_j^{imp} the jth imposter caption, and η is a margin hyperparameter. We sample the imposter image and caption for each pair from the same minibatch, and fix η to 1 in our experiments. The choice of similarity function is flexible, which we explore in Sect. 4.3. This criterion directly enables semantic retrieval of images from captions and vice versa, but in this paper our focus is to explore how object and word *localization* naturally emerges as a by-product of this training scheme. An illustration of our two-branch matchmap networks is shown in Fig. 3. Next, we describe the modeling for each input mode.

4.1   Image Modeling

We follow [1, 8, 15, 18, 19, 26] by utilizing the architecture of the VGG16 network [46] to form the basis of the image branch. In all of these prior works, however, the weights of the VGG network were pre-trained on ImageNet, and thus had a significant amount of visual discriminative ability built-in to their models. We show that our models do not require this pre-training, and can be trained end-to-end in a completely unsupervised fashion. Additionally in these prior works, the entire VGG network below the classification layer was utilized to derive a single, global image embedding. One problem with this approach is that coupling the output of conv5 to fc1 involves a flattening operation, which makes it

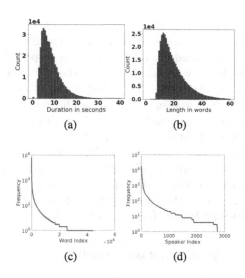

(a)

(b)

(c)

(d)

Fig. 2. Statistics of the 400k spoken captions. From left to right, the plots represent (a) the histogram over caption durations in seconds, (b) the histogram over caption lengths in words, (c) the estimated word frequencies across the captions, and (d) the number of captions per speaker.

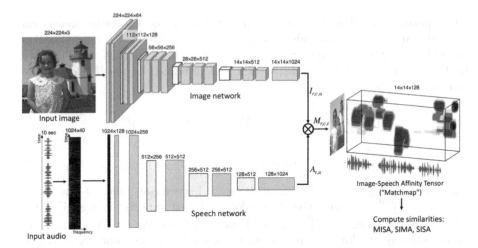

Fig. 3. The audio-visual matchmap model architecture (left), along with an example matchmap output (right), displaying a 3-D density of spatio-temporal similarity. Conv layers shown in blue, pooling layers shown in red, and BatchNorm layer shown in black. Each conv layer is followed by a ReLU. The first conv layer of the audio network uses filters that are 1 frame wide and span the entire frequency axis; subsequent layers of the audio network are hence 1-D convolutions with respective widths of 11, 17, 17, and 17. All maxpool operations in the audio network are 1-D along the time axis with a width of 3. An example spectrogram input of approx. 10 s (1024 frames) is shown to illustrate the pooling ratios. (Color figure online)

difficult to recover associations between any neuron above `conv5` and the spatially localized stimulus which was responsible for its output. We address this issue here by retaining only the convolutional banks up through `conv5` from the VGG network, and discarding `pool5` and everything above it. For a 224 by 224 pixel input image, the output of this portion of the network would be a 14 by 14 feature map across 512 channels, with each location within the map possessing a receptive field that can be related directly back to the input. In order to map an image into the shared embedding space, we apply a 3 by 3, 1024 channel, linear convolution (no nonlinearity) to the `conv5` feature map. Image pre-processing consists of resizing the smallest dimension to 256 pixels, taking a random 224 by 224 crop (the center crop is taken for validation), and normalizing the pixels according to a global mean and variance.

4.2 Audio Caption Modeling

To model the spoken audio captions, we use a model similar to that of [18], but modified to output a feature map across the audio during training, rather than a single embedding vector. The audio waveforms are represented as log Mel filter bank spectrograms. Computing these involves first removing the DC component of each recording via mean subtraction, followed by pre-emphasis filtering. The short-time Fourier transform is then computed using a 25 ms Hamming window with a 10 ms shift. We take the squared magnitude spectrum of each frame and compute the log energies within each of 40 Mel filter bands. We treat these final spectrograms as 1-channel images, and model them with the CNN displayed in Fig. 3. [19] utilized truncation and zero-padding of each spectrogram to a fixed length. While this enables batched inputs to the model, it introduces a degree of undesirable bias into the learned representations. Instead, we pad to a length long enough to fully capture the longest caption within a batch, and truncate the output feature map of each caption on an individual basis to remove the frames corresponding to zero-padding. Rather than manually normalizing the spectrograms, we employ a BatchNorm [20] layer at the front of the network. Next, we discuss methods for relating the visual and auditory feature maps to one another.

4.3 Joining the Image and Audio Branches

Zhou et al. [57] demonstrate that global average pooling applied to the conv5 layer of several popular CNN architectures not only provides good accuracy for image classification tasks, but also enables the recovery of spatial activation maps for a given target class at the conv5 layer, which can then be used for object localization. The idea that a pooled representation over an entire input used for training can then be unpooled for localized analysis is powerful because it does not require localized annotation of the training data, or even any explicit mechanism for localization in the objective function or network itself, beyond what already exists in the form of convolutional receptive fields. Although our models perform a ranking task and not classification, we can apply similar ideas to both the image and speech feature maps in order to compute their pairwise similarity, in the hopes to recover localizations of objects and words. Let I represent the output feature map output of the image network branch, A be the output feature map of the audio network branch, and I^p and A^p be their globally average-pooled counterparts. One straightforward choice of similarity function is the dot product between the pooled embeddings, $S(I, A) = I^{pT} A^p$. Notice that this is in fact equivalent to first computing a 3rd order tensor M such that $M_{r,c,t} = I^T_{r,c,:} A_{t,:}$, and then computing the average of all elements of M. Here we use the colon (:) to indicate selection of all elements across an indexing plane; in other words, $I_{r,c,:}$ is a 1024-dimensional vector representing the (r, c) coordinate of the image feature map, and $A_{t,:}$ is a 1024-dimensional vector representing the tth frame of the audio feature map. In this regard, the similarity between the global average pooled image and audio representations is simply the average similarity between *all* audio frames and *all* image regions. We call this similarity scoring function SISA (sum image, sum audio):

$$\text{SISA}(M) = \frac{1}{N_r N_c N_t} \sum_{r=1}^{N_r} \sum_{c=1}^{N_c} \sum_{t=1}^{N_t} M_{r,c,t} \tag{2}$$

Because M reflects the localized similarity between a small image region (possibly containing an object) and a small segment of audio (possibly containing a word), we dub M the "matchmap" tensor between and image and an audio caption. As it is not completely realistic to expect all words within a caption to simultaneously match all objects within an image, we consider computing the similarity between an image and an audio caption using several alternative functions of the matchmap density. By replacing the averaging summation over image patches with a simple maximum, MISA (max image, sum audio) effectively matches each frame of the caption with the most similar image patch, and then averages over the caption frames:

$$\text{MISA}(M) = \frac{1}{N_t} \sum_{t=1}^{N_t} \max_{r,c}(M_{r,c,t}) \tag{3}$$

By preserving the sum over image regions but taking the maximum across the audio caption, SIMA (sum image, max audio) matches each image region with only the audio frame with the highest similarity to that region:

$$\text{SIMA}(M) = \frac{1}{N_r N_c} \sum_{r=1}^{N_r} \sum_{c=1}^{N_c} \max_{t}(M_{r,c,t}) \tag{4}$$

In the next section, we explore the use of these similarities for learning semantic correspondences between objects within images and spoken words within their captions.

5   Experiments

5.1   Image and Caption Retrieval

All models were trained using the sampled margin ranking objective outlined in Eq. 1, using stochastic gradient descent with a batch size of 128. We used a fixed momentum of 0.9 and an initial learning rate of 0.001 that decayed by a factor of 10 every 70 epochs; generally our models converged in less than 150 epochs. We use a held-out set of 1,000 image/caption pairs from the Places audio caption dataset to validate the models on the image/caption retrieval task, similar to the one described in [1, 8, 18, 19]. This task serves to provide a single, high-level metric which captures how well the model has learned to semantically bridge the audio and visual modalities. While providing a good indication of a model's overall ability, it does not directly examine which specific aspects of language and visual perception are being captured. Table 1 displays the image/caption recall scores achieved when training a matchmap model using the SISA, MISA, and SIMA

Table 1. Recall scores on the held out set of 1,000 images/captions for the three matchmap similarity functions. We also show results for the baseline models which use automatic speech recognition-derived text captions. The (P) indicates the use of an image branch pre-trained on ImageNet

Model	Speech						ASR text					
	Caption to image			Image to caption			Caption to image			Image to caption		
	R@1	R@5	R@10	R@1	R@5	R@10	R@1	R@5	R@10	R@1	R@5	R@10
SISA	.063	.191	.274	.048	.166	.249	.136	.365	.503	.106	.309	.430
MISA	.079	.225	.314	.057	.191	.291	.162	.417	.547	.113	.309	.447
SIMA	.073	.213	.284	.065	.168	.255	.134	.389	.513	.145	.336	.459
SISA(P)	.165	.431	.559	.120	.363	.506	.230	.525	.665	.174	.462	.611
MISA(P)	.200	.469	.604	.127	.375	.528	.271	.567	.701	.183	.489	.622
SIMA(P)	.147	.375	.506	.139	.367	.483	.215	.518	.639	.220	.494	.599
[19](P)	.148	.403	.548	.121	.335	.463	-	-	-	-	-	-
[18](P)	.161	.404	.564	.130	.378	.542	-	-	-	-	-	-

similarity functions, both with a fully randomly initialized network as well as with an image branch pre-trained on ImageNet. In all cases, the MISA similarity measure is the best performing, although all three measures achieve respectable scores. Unsurprisingly, using a pre-trained image network significantly increases the recall scores. In Table 1, we compare our models against reimplementations of two previously published speech-to-image models (both of which utilized pre-trained VGG16 networks). We also compare against baselines that operate on automatic speech recognition (ASR) derived text transcriptions of the spoken captions. The text-based model we used is based on the architecture of the speech and image model, but replaces the speech audio branch with a CNN that operates on word sequences. The ASR text network uses a 200-dimensional word embedding layer, followed by a 512 channel, 1-dimensional convolution across windows of 3 words with a ReLU nonlinearity. A final convolution with a window size of 3 and no nonlinearity maps these activations into the 1024 multimodal embedding space. Both previously published baselines we compare to used the full VGG network, deriving an embedding for the entire image from the fc2 outputs. In the pre-trained case, our best recall scores for the MISA model outperform [19] overall as well as [18] on image recall; the caption recall score is slightly lower than that of [18]. This demonstrates that there is not much to be lost when doing away with the fully connected layers of VGG, and much to be gained in the form of the localization matchmaps.

5.2   Speech-Prompted Object Localization

To evaluate our models' ability to associate spoken words with visual objects in a more fine-grained sense, we use the spoken captions for the ADE20k [59] dataset. The ADE20k images contain pixel-level object masks and labels - in conjunction with a time-aligned transcription produced via ASR (we use the public Google

Fig. 4. Speech-prompted localization maps for several word/object pairs. From top to bottom and from left to right, the queries are instances of the spoken words "WOMAN," "BRIDGE,", "SKYLINE", "TRAIN", "CLOTHES" and "VEHICLES" extracted from each image's accompanying speech caption.

SpeechRecognition API for this purpose), we can associate each matchmap cell with a specific visual object label as well as a word label. These labels enable us to analyze which words are being associated with which objects. We do this by performing speech-prompted object localization. Given a word in the speech beginning at time t_1 and ending at time t_2, we derive a heatmap across the image by summing the matchmap between t_1 and t_2. We then normalize the heatmap to sit within the interval $[0, 1]$, threshold the heatmap, and evaluate the intersection over union (IoU) of the detection mask with the ADE20k label mask for whatever object was referenced by the word.

Because there are a very large number of different words appearing in the speech, and no one-to-one mapping between words and ADE20k objects exists, we manually define a set of 100 word-object pairings. We choose commonly occurring (at least 9 occurrences) pairs that are unambiguous, such as the word "building" and object "building," the word "man" and the "person" object, etc. For each word-object pair, we compute an average IoU score across all instances of the word-object pair appearing together in an ADE20k image and its associated caption. We then average these scores across all 100 word-object pairs and report results for each model type in Table 2. We also report the IoU scores for the ASR text-based baseline models described in Sect. 5.1. Figure 4 displays a sampling of localization heatmaps for several query words using the non-pretrained speech MISA network.

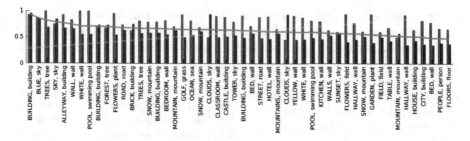

Fig. 5. Some clusters (speech and visual) found by our approach. Each cluster is jointly labeled with the most common word (capital letters) and object (lowercase letters). For each cluster we show the precision for both the word (blue) and object (red) labels, as well as their harmonic mean (magenta). The average cluster size across the top 50 clusters was 44. (Color figure online)

5.3 Clustering of Audio-Visual Patterns

The next experiment we consider is automatic discovery of audio-visual clusters from the ADE20k matchmaps using the fully random speech MISA network. Once a matchmap has been computed for an image and caption pair, we smooth it with an average or max pooling window of size 7 across the temporal dimension before binarizing it according to a threshold. In practice, we set this threshold on a matchmap-specific basis to be 1.5 standard deviations above the mean value of the smoothed matchmap. Next, we extract volumetric connected components and their associated masks over the image and audio. We average pool the image and audio feature maps within these masks, producing a pair of vectors for each component. Because we found the image and speech representations to exhibit different dynamic ranges, we first rescale them by the average L2 norms across all derived image vectors and speech vectors, respectively. We concatenate the image and speech vectors for each component, and finally perform Birch clustering [53] with 1000 target clusters for the first step, and an agglomerative final step that resulted in 135 clusters. To derive word labels for each cluster, we take the most frequent word label as overlapped by the components belonging to a cluster. To generate the object labels, we compute the number of pixels belonging to each ADE20k class assigned to a particular cluster, and take the most common label. We display the labels and their purities for the top 50 most pure clusters in Fig. 5.

5.4 Concept Discovery: Building an Image-Word Dictionary

Figure 5 shows the clusters learned by our model. Interestingly, the audio and image networks are able to agree to a common representation of knowledge, clustering similar concepts together. Since both representations are directly multiplied by a dot product, both networks have to agree on the meaning of these different dimensions. To further explore this phenomenon, we decided to visualize the concepts associated with each of these dimensions for both image and audio networks separately and then find a quantitative strategy to evaluate the agreement.

To visualize the concepts associated with each of the dimensions in the image path, we use the unit visualization technique introduced in [55]. A set of images is run through the image network and the ones that activate the most that particular dimension get selected. Then, we can visualize the spatial activations in the top activated images. The same procedure can be done for the audio network, where we get a set of descriptions that maximally activate that neuron. Finally, with the temporal map, we can find which part of the description has produced that activation. Some most activated words and images can be found in Fig. 6. We show four dimensions with their associated most activated word in the audio neuron, and the most activated images in the image neuron. Interestingly, these pairs of concepts have been found completely independently, as we did not use the final activation (after the dot product) to pick the images.

Table 2. Speech-prompted and ASR-prompted object localization IoU scores on ADE20K, averaged across the 100 word-object pairs. 'Rand.' indicates a randomly initialized model, while 'Pre.' indicates an image branch pre-trained on ImageNet. The full-frame baseline IoU was 0.16

Sim. func.	Speech		ASR text	
	Rand.	Pre.	Rand.	Pre.
SIMA	.1607	.1857	.1743	.1995
SISA	.1637	.1970	.1750	.2161
MISA	.1795	.2324	.2060	.2413

The pairs image-word allow us to explore multiple questions. First, can we build an image-word dictionary by only listening to descriptions of images? As we show in Fig. 6, we do. It is important to remember that these pairs are learned in a completely unsupervised fashion, without any concept previously learned by the network. Furthermore, in the scenario of a language without written representation, we could just have an image-audio dictionary using exactly the same technique.

Another important question is whether a better audio-visual dictionary is indicative of a better model architecture. We would expect that a better model should learn more total concepts. In this section we propose a metric to quantify this dictionary quality. This metric will help us to compute the quality of each individual neuron and of each particular model.

To quantify the quality of the dictionary, we need to find a common space between the written descriptions and the image activations. Again, this common space comes from a segmentation dataset. Using [59], we can rank the most detected objects by each of the neurons. We pass through the network approx. 10,000 images from the ADE20k dataset and check for each neuron which classes are most activated for that particular dimension. As a result, we have a set of

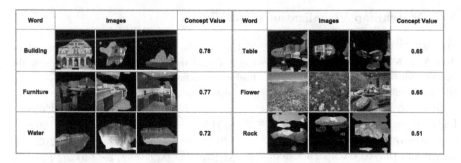

Word	Images	Concept Value	Word	Images	Concept Value
Building		0.78	Table		0.65
Furniture		0.77	Flower		0.65
Water		0.72	Rock		0.51

Fig. 6. Matching the most activated images in the image network and the activated words in the audio network we can establish pairs of image-word, as shown in the figure. We also define a concept value, which captures the agreement between both networks and ranges from 0 (no agreement) to 1 (full agreement).

object labels associated with the image neuron (coming from the segmentation classes), and a word associated with the audio neuron. Using the WordNet tree, we can compute the word distance between these concepts and define the following metric:

$$c = \sum_{i=1}^{|O^{\mathrm{im}}|} w_i Sim_{\mathrm{wup}}(o_i^{\mathrm{im}}, o^{\mathrm{au}}), \tag{5}$$

with $o_i^{\mathrm{im}} \in O^{\mathrm{im}}$, where O^{im} is the set of classes present in the TOP5 segmented images and $Sim_{\mathrm{wup}}(., .)$ is the Wu and Palmer WordNet-based similarity, with range $[0, 1]$ (higher is more similar). We weight the similarity with w_i, which is proportional to intersection over union of the pixels for that class into the masked region of the image. Using this metric, we can then assign one value per dimension, which measures how well both the audio network and the image network agree on that particular concept. The numerical values for six concept pairs are shown in Fig. 6. We see how neurons with higher value are cleaner and more related with its counterpart. The bottom right neuron shows an example of low concept value, where the audio word is "rock" but the neuron images show mountains in general. Anecdotally, we found $c > 0.6$ to be a good indicator that a concept has been learned.

Finally, we analyze the relation between the concepts learned and the architecture used in Table 3. Interestingly, the four maintain the same order in the three different cases, indicating that the architecture does influence the number of concepts learned.

5.5   Matchmap Visualizations and Videos

We can visualize the matchmaps in several ways. The 3-dimensional density shown in Fig. 3 is perhaps the simplest, although it can be difficult to read as a still image. Instead, we can treat it as a stack of masks overlayed on top of the image and played back as a video. We use the matchmap score to

Table 3. The number of concepts learned by the different networks with different losses. We find it is consistently highest for MISA.

Sim. func.	Speech		ASR text	
	Rand.	Pre.	Rand.	Pre.
SIMA	166	124	96	96
SISA	210	192	103	102
MISA	242	277	140	150

modulate the alpha channel of the image synchronously with the speech audio. The resulting video is able to highlight the salient regions of the images as the speaker is describing them.

We can also extract volumetric connected components from the density and project them down onto the image and spectrogram axes; visualizations of this are shown in Figs. 7 and 8. We apply a small amount of thresholding and smoothing to prevent the matchmaps from being too fragmented. We use a temporal max pooling window with a size of 7 frames, and normalize the scores to fall within the interval $[0, 1]$ and sum to 1. We zero out all the cells outside the top p percentage of the total mass within the matchmap. In practice, p values between 0.15 and 0.3 produced attractive results.

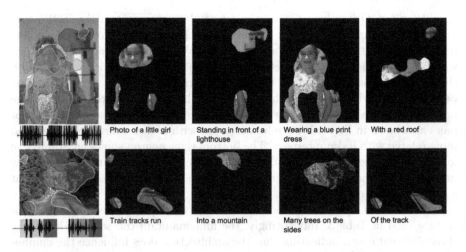

Fig. 7. On the left are shown two images and their speech signals. Each color corresponds to one connected component derived from two matchmaps from a fully random MISA network. The masks on the right display the segments that correspond to each speech segment. We show the caption words obtained from the ASR transcriptions below the masks. Note that those words were never used for learning, only for analysis.

Fig. 8. Additional examples of discovered image segments and speech fragments using the fully random MISA speech network.

6   Conclusions

In this paper, we introduced audio-visual "matchmap" neural networks which are capable of directly learning the semantic correspondences between speech frames and image pixels without the need for annotated training data in either modality. We applied these networks for semantic image/spoken caption search, speech-prompted object localization, audio-visual clustering and concept discovery, and real-time, speech-driven, semantic highlighting. We also introduced an extended version of the Places audio caption dataset [19], doubling the total number of captions. Additionally, we introduced nearly 10,000 captions for the ADE20k dataset. There are numerous avenues for future work, including expansion of the models to handle videos, environmental sounds, additional languages, etc. It may possible to directly generate images given a spoken description, or generate artificial speech describing a visual scene. More focused datasets that go beyond simple spoken descriptions and explicitly address relations between objects within the scene could be leveraged to learn richer linguistic representations. Finally, a crucial element of human language learning is the dialog feedback loop, and future work should investigate the addition of that mechanism to the models.

Acknowledgments. The authors would like to thank Toyota Research Institute, Inc. for supporting this work.

References

1. Alishahi, A., Barking, M., Chrupala, G.: Encoding of phonology in a recurrent neural model of grounded speech. In: CoNLL (2017)
2. Antol, S., et al.: VQA: visual question answering. In: Proceedings of the IEEE International Conference on Computer Vision (ICCV) (2015)
3. Arandjelovic, R., Zisserman, A.: Look, listen, and learn. In: ICCV (2017)
4. Aytar, Y., Vondrick, C., Torralba, A.: SoundNet: learning sound representations from unlabeled video. In: Advances in Neural Information Processing Systems, vol. 29, pp. 892–900 (2016)
5. Bergamo, A., Bazzani, L., Anguelov, D., Torresani, L.: Self-taught object localization with deep networks. CoRR abs/1409.3964 (2014). http://arxiv.org/abs/1409.3964
6. Bromley, J., Guyon, I., LeCun, Y., Säckinger, E., Shah, R.: Signature verification using a "siamese" time delay neural network. In: Cowan, J.D., Tesauro, G., Alspector, J. (eds.) Advances in Neural Information Processing Systems, vol. 6, pp. 737–744. Morgan-Kaufmann (1994)
7. Cho, M., Kwak, S., Schmid, C., Ponce, J.: Unsupervised object discovery and localization in the wild: part-based matching with bottom-up region proposals. In: Proceedings of the IEEE Conference on Computer Vision and Pattern Recognition (CVPR) (2015)
8. Chrupala, G., Gelderloos, L., Alishahi, A.: Representations of language in a model of visually grounded speech signal. In: ACL (2017)
9. Cinbis, R., Verbeek, J., Schmid, C.: Weakly supervised object localization with multi-fold multiple instance learning. IEEE Trans. Pattern Anal. Mach. Intell. (PAMI) 39(1), 189–203 (2016)
10. Doersch, C., Gupta, A., Efros, A.A.: Unsupervised visual representation learning by context prediction. CoRR abs/1505.05192 (2015). http://arxiv.org/abs/1505.05192
11. Drexler, J., Glass, J.: Analysis of audio-visual features for unsupervised speech recognition. In: Grounded Language Understanding Workshop (2017)
12. Dupoux, E.: Cognitive science in the era of artificial intelligence: a roadmap for reverse-engineering the infant language-learner. Cognition 173, 43–59 (2018)
13. Fang, H., et al.: From captions to visual concepts and back. In: Proceedings of the IEEE Conference on Computer Vision and Pattern Recognition (CVPR) (2015)
14. Gao, H., Mao, J., Zhou, J., Huang, Z., Yuille, A.: Are you talking to a machine? Dataset and methods for multilingual image question answering. In: NIPS (2015)
15. Gelderloos, L., Chrupała, G.: From phonemes to images: levels of representation in a recurrent neural model of visually-grounded language learning. arXiv:1610.03342 (2016)
16. Girshick, R., Donahue, J., Darrell, T., Malik, J.: Rich feature hierarchies for accurate object detection and semantic segmentation. In: Proceedings of the IEEE Conference on Computer Vision and Pattern Recognition (CVPR) (2013)
17. Guérin, J., Gibaru, O., Thiery, S., Nyiri, E.: CNN features are also great at unsupervised classification. CoRR abs/1707.01700 (2017). http://arxiv.org/abs/1707.01700
18. Harwath, D., Glass, J.: Learning word-like units from joint audio-visual analysis. In: Proceedings of the Annual Meeting of the Association for Computational Linguistics (ACL) (2017)

19. Harwath, D., Torralba, A., Glass, J.R.: Unsupervised learning of spoken language with visual context. In: Proceedings of the Neural Information Processing Systems (NIPS) (2016)
20. Ioffe, S., Szegedy, C.: Batch normalization: accelerating deep network training by reducing internal covariate shift. J. Mach. Learn. Res. (JMLR) (2015)
21. Jansen, A., Church, K., Hermansky, H.: Toward spoken term discovery at scale with zero resources. In: Proceedings of the Annual Conference of International Speech Communication Association (INTERSPEECH) (2010)
22. Jansen, A., Van Durme, B.: Efficient spoken term discovery using randomized algorithms. In: Proceedings of the IEEE Workshop on Automfatic Speech Recognition and Understanding (ASRU) (2011)
23. Johnson, J., Karpathy, A., Fei-Fei, L.: DenseCap: fully convolutional localization networks for dense captioning. In: Proceedings of the IEEE Conference on Computer Vision and Pattern Recognition (CVPR) (2016)
24. Kamper, H., Elsner, M., Jansen, A., Goldwater, S.: Unsupervised neural network based feature extraction using weak top-down constraints. In: Proceedings of the International Conference on Acoustics, Speech and Signal Processing (ICASSP) (2015)
25. Kamper, H., Jansen, A., Goldwater, S.: Unsupervised word segmentation and lexicon discovery using acoustic word embeddings. IEEE Trans. Audio Speech Lang. Process. 24(4), 669–679 (2016)
26. Kamper, H., Settle, S., Shakhnarovich, G., Livescu, K.: Visually grounded learning of keyword prediction from untranscribed speech. In: INTERSPEECH (2017)
27. Karpathy, A., Joulin, A., Fei-Fei, L.: Deep fragment embeddings for bidirectional image sentence mapping. In: Proceedings of the Neural Information Processing Systems (NIPS) (2014)
28. Karpathy, A., Li, F.F.: Deep visual-semantic alignments for generating image descriptions. In: Proceedings of the IEEE Conference on Computer Vision and Pattern Recognition (CVPR) (2015)
29. LeCun, Y., Bottou, L., Bengio, Y., Haffner, P.: Gradient-based learning applied to document recognition. Proc. IEEE 86(11), 2278–2324 (1998)
30. Lee, C., Glass, J.: A nonparametric Bayesian approach to acoustic model discovery. In: Proceedings of the Annual Meeting of the Association for Computational Linguistics (ACL) (2012)
31. Lewis, M.P., Simon, G.F., Fennig, C.D.: Ethnologue: Languages of the World, 9th edn. SIL International (2016). http://www.ethnologue.com
32. Lin, T., et al.: Microsoft COCO: common objects in context. arXiv:1405.0312 (2015)
33. Malinowski, M., Fritz, M.: A multi-world approach to question answering about real-world scenes based on uncertain input. In: NIPS (2014)
34. Malinowski, M., Rohrbach, M., Fritz, M.: Ask your neurons: a neural-based approach to answering questions about images. In: ICCV (2015)
35. Ondel, L., Burget, L., Cernocky, J.: Variational inference for acoustic unit discovery. In: 5th Workshop on Spoken Language Technology for Under-Resourced Language (2016)
36. Owens, A., Isola, P., McDermott, J.H., Torralba, A., Adelson, E.H., Freeman, W.T.: Visually indicated sounds. In: 2016 IEEE Conference on Computer Vision and Pattern Recognition, CVPR 2016, Las Vegas, NV, USA, 27–30 June 2016, pp. 2405–2413 (2016)

37. Owens, A., Wu, J., McDermott, J.H., Freeman, W.T., Torralba, A.: Ambient sound provides supervision for visual learning. In: Leibe, B., Matas, J., Sebe, N., Welling, M. (eds.) ECCV 2016. LNCS, vol. 9905, pp. 801–816. Springer, Cham (2016). https://doi.org/10.1007/978-3-319-46448-0_48

38. Park, A., Glass, J.: Unsupervised pattern discovery in speech. IEEE Trans. Audio Speech Lang. Process. **16**(1), 186–197 (2008)

39. Redmon, J., Divvala, S., Girshick, R., Farhadi, A.: You only look once: unified, real-time object detection. In: Proceedings of the IEEE Conference on Computer Vision and Pattern Recognition (CVPR) (2016)

40. Reed, S.E., Akata, Z., Yan, X., Logeswaran, L., Schiele, B., Lee, H.: Generative adversarial text to image synthesis. CoRR abs/1605.05396 (2016). http://arxiv.org/abs/1605.05396

41. Ren, M., Kiros, R., Zemel, R.: Exploring models and data for image question answering. In: NIPS (2015)

42. Renshaw, D., Kamper, H., Jansen, A., Goldwater, S.: A comparison of neural network methods for unsupervised representation learning on the zero resource speech challenge. In: Proceedings of the Annual Conference of International Speech Communication Association (INTERSPEECH) (2015)

43. Roy, D.: Grounded spoken language acquisition: experiments in word learning. IEEE Trans. Multimed. **5**(2), 197–209 (2003)

44. Roy, D., Pentland, A.: Learning words from sights and sounds: a computational model. Cogn. Sci. **26**, 113–146 (2002)

45. Russell, B., Efros, A., Sivic, J., Freeman, W., Zisserman, A.: Using multiple segmentations to discover objects and their extent in image collections. In: Proceedings of the IEEE Conference on Computer Vision and Pattern Recognition (CVPR) (2006)

46. Simonyan, K., Zisserman, A.: Very deep convolutional networks for large-scale image recognition. CoRR abs/1409.1556 (2014)

47. Spelke, E.S.: Principles of object perception. Cogn. Sci. **14**(1), 29–56 (1990). https://doi.org/10.1016/0364-0213(90)90025-R. http://www.sciencedirect.com/science/article/pii/036402139090025R

48. Thiolliere, R., Dunbar, E., Synnaeve, G., Versteegh, M., Dupoux, E.: A hybrid dynamic time warping-deep neural network architecture for unsupervised acoustic modeling. In: Proceedings of the Annual Conference of International Speech Communication Association (INTERSPEECH) (2015)

49. Vinyals, O., Toshev, A., Bengio, S., Erhan, D.: Show and tell: a neural image caption generator. In: Proceedings of the IEEE Conference on Computer Vision and Pattern Recognition (CVPR) (2015)

50. de Vries, H., Strub, F., Chandar, S., Pietquin, O., Larochelle, H., Courville, A.C.: GuessWhat?! Visual object discovery through multi-modal dialogue. In: Proceedings of the IEEE Conference on Computer Vision and Pattern Recognition (CVPR) (2017)

51. Weber, M., Welling, M., Perona, P.: Towards automatic discovery of object categories. In: Proceedings of the IEEE Conference on Computer Vision and Pattern Recognition (CVPR) (2010)

52. Xu, K., et al.: Show, attend and tell: neural image caption generation with visual attention. In: ICML (2015)

53. Zhang, T., Ramakrishnan, R., Livny, M.: BIRCH: an efficient data clustering method for very large databases. In: ACM SIGMOD International Conference on Management of Data, pp. 103–114 (1996)

54. Zhang, Y., Salakhutdinov, R., Chang, H.A., Glass, J.: Resource configurable spoken query detection using deep Boltzmann machines. In: Proceedings of the International Conference on Acoustics, Speech and Signal Processing (ICASSP) (2012)
55. Zhou, B., Khosla, A., Lapedriza, A., Oliva, A., Torralba, A.: Object detectors emerge in deep scene CNNs. arXiv preprint arXiv:1412.6856 (2014)
56. Zhou, B., Khosla, A., Lapedriza, A., Oliva, A., Torralba, A.: Object detectors emerge in deep scene CNNs. In: Proceedings of the International Conference on Learning Representations (ICLR) (2015)
57. Zhou, B., Khosla, A., Lapedriza, A., Oliva, A., Torralba, A.: Learning deep features for discriminative localization. In: Proceedings of the IEEE Conference on Computer Vision and Pattern Recognition (CVPR) (2016)
58. Zhou, B., Lapedriza, A., Xiao, J., Torralba, A., Oliva, A.: Learning deep features for scene recognition using places database. In: Proceedings of the Neural Information Processing Systems (NIPS) (2014)
59. Zhou, B., Zhao, H., Puig, X., Fidler, S., Barriuso, A., Torralba, A.: Scene parsing through ADE20K dataset. In: Proceedings of the IEEE Conference on Computer Vision and Pattern Recognition (CVPR) (2017)

Weakly-Supervised 3D Hand Pose Estimation from Monocular RGB Images

Yujun Cai[1]($\boxtimes$)(ID), Liuhao Ge[1], Jianfei Cai[2], and Junsong Yuan[3]

[1] Institute for Media Innovation, Interdisciplinary Graduate School,
Nanyang Technological University, Singapore, Singapore
{yujun001,ge0001ao}@e.ntu.edu.sg
[2] School of Computer Science and Engineering, Nanyang Technological University,
Singapore, Singapore
asjfcai@ntu.edu.sg
[3] Department of Computer Science and Engineering,
State University of New York at Buffalo, Buffalo, NY, USA
jsyuan@buffalo.edu

Abstract. Compared with depth-based 3D hand pose estimation, it is more challenging to infer 3D hand pose from monocular RGB images, due to substantial depth ambiguity and the difficulty of obtaining fully-annotated training data. Different from existing learning-based monocular RGB-input approaches that require accurate 3D annotations for training, we propose to leverage the depth images that can be easily obtained from commodity RGB-D cameras during training, while during testing we take only RGB inputs for 3D joint predictions. In this way, we alleviate the burden of the costly 3D annotations in real-world dataset. Particularly, we propose a weakly-supervised method, adapting from fully-annotated synthetic dataset to weakly-labeled real-world dataset with the aid of a depth regularizer, which generates depth maps from predicted 3D pose and serves as weak supervision for 3D pose regression. Extensive experiments on benchmark datasets validate the effectiveness of the proposed depth regularizer in both weakly-supervised and fully-supervised settings.

Keywords: 3D hand pose estimation · Weakly-supervised methods Depth regularizer

This research is supported by the BeingTogether Centre, a collaboration between Nanyang Technological University (NTU) Singapore and University of North Carolina (UNC) at Chapel Hill. The BeingTogether Centre is supported by the National Research Foundation, Prime Minister's Office, Singapore under its International Research Centres in Singapore Funding Initiative. This research is also supported in part by Singapore MoE Tier-2 Grant (MOE2016-T2-2-065) and start-up funds from University at Buffalo.

V. Ferrari et al. (Eds.): ECCV 2018, LNCS 11210, pp. 678–694, 2018.
https://doi.org/10.1007/978-3-030-01231-1_41

1 Introduction

Articulated hand pose estimation has aroused a long-standing study in the past decades [23,38,39], since it plays a significant role in numerous applications such as human-computer interaction and virtual reality. Although 3D hand pose estimation with depth cameras [6,7,13,26,41] has gained tremendous success in recent years, the advance in monocular RGB-based 3D hand pose estimation [15,18,27,46], however, still remains limited. Due to the availability of RGB cameras, the RGB-based solution for 3D hand pose estimation is more favored than depth-based solutions in many vision applications.

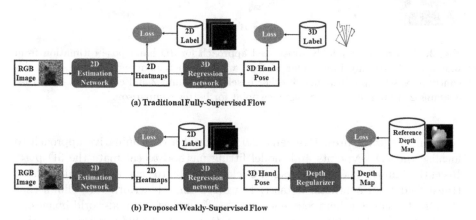

Fig. 1. Illustration of weakly supervised 3D hand pose estimation. Different from conventional fully-supervised methods (a) that use 3D labels to guide joint predictions, our proposed weakly-supervised method (b) leverages the reference depth map, which can be easily obtained by consumer-grade depth camera, to provide weak supervision. Note that we only need the reference depth map during training as a regularizer. During testing, the trained model can predict 3D hand pose from RGB-only input.

Compared with depth images, single-view RGB images exhibit inherent depth ambiguity, which makes 3D hand pose estimation from single RGB images a challenging problem. To overcome the ambiguity, recent work on RGB-based 3D hand pose estimation [46] rely on large amount of labeled data for training, while comprehensive real-world dataset with complete 3D annotations is often difficult to obtain, thus limiting the performance. Specifically, compared with 2D annotations, providing 3D annotations for real-world RGB images is typically more difficult since 2D locations can be directly defined in the RGB images while 3D locations cannot be easily labeled by human annotator. To address this problem, Zimmermann et al. [46] turned to render low-cost synthetic hands with 3D models, from which the ground truth of 3D joints can be easily obtained. Although achieving good performance on the synthetic dataset, this method, however, does not generalize well to real image dataset due to the domain shift

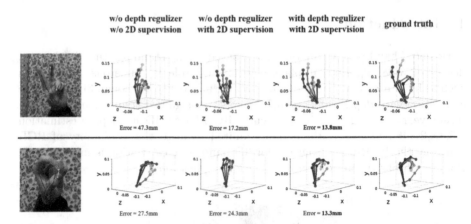

Fig. 2. We present a weakly-supervised approach for 3D hand pose estimation from monocular RGB-only input. Our method with depth regularizer (column 4) significantly boosts the performance of other baselines (column 2 and column 3). Note that columns 2–5 are shown in a novel viewpoint for better comparison.

between image features. Paschalis [22] employed a discriminative approach to localize the 2D keypoints and model fitting method to calculate the 3D pose. Recently, Muller *et al.* [18] leveraged CycleGANs [45] to generate a "real" dataset transferred from synthetic dataset. However, limited performance shows that there still exists gap between generated "real" images and real-world images.

Our proposed weakly-supervised adaptation method addresses this limitation in a novel perspective. We observe that most previous work [18,27,46] for hand pose estimation from real-world single-view RGB images focus on training with complete 3D annotations, which are expensive and time-consuming to obtain, while ignoring the depth images that can be easily captured by commodity RGB-D cameras. Moreover, it is indicated that such low-cost depth images contain rich cues for 3D hand pose labels, as depth-based methods show decent performance on 3D pose estimation. Based on these observations, we propose to leverage the easily captured depth images to compensate the scarcity of entire 3D annotations during training, while during testing we take only RGB inputs for 3D hand pose estimation. Figure 1 illustrates the concept of our proposed weakly supervised 3D hand pose estimation method, which alleviates the burden of the costly 3D annotations in real-world datasets.

In particular, similar to the previous work [1,32,37,42,44] in body pose estimation, we apply a cascaded network architecture including a 2D pose estimation network and a 3D regression network. We note that directly transferring the network trained on synthetic dataset to real-world dataset usually produces poor estimation accuracy, due to the domain gap between them. To address this problem, inspired by [4,19], we innovate the structure with a depth regularizer, which generates depth images from predicted 3D hand pose and regularizes the predicted 3D regression by supervising the rendered depth map, as shown in

Fig. 1(b). This network essentially learns the mapping from 3D pose to its corresponding depth map, which can be used for the knowledge transfer from the fully-annotated synthetic images to weakly-labeled real-world images without entire 3D annotations. Additionally, we apply the depth regularizer to the fully-supervised setting. The effectiveness of the depth regularizer is experimentally verified for both our weakly-supervised and fully-supervised methods on two benchmark datasets: RHD [46] and STB datasets [43].

To summarize, this work makes the following contributions:

- We innovatively introduce the weakly supervised problem of leveraging low-cost depth maps during training for 3D hand pose estimation from RGB images, which releases the burden of 3D joint labeling.
- We propose an end-to-end learning based 3D hand pose estimation model for weakly-supervised adaptation from fully-annotated synthetic images to weakly-labeled real-world images. Particularly, we introduce a depth regularizer supervised by the easily captured depth images, which considerably enhances the estimation accuracy compared with weakly-supervised baselines (see Fig. 2).
- We conduct experiments on the two benchmark datasets, which show that our weakly-supervised approach compares favorably with existing works and our proposed fully-supervised method outperforms all the state-of-the-art methods.

2 Related Work

3D hand pose estimation has been studied extensively for a long time, with vast theoretical innovations and important applications. Early works [17,23,28] on 3D hand pose estimation from monocular color input used complex model-fitting schemes which require strong prior knowledge on physics or dynamics and multiple hypotheses. These sophisticated methods, however, usually suffer from low estimation accuracy and restricted environments, which result in limited prospects in real-world applications. While multi-view approaches [21,35] alleviate the occlusion problem and provide decent accuracy, they require sophisticated mesh models and optimization strategies that prohibit them from real-time tasks.

The emergence of low-cost consumer-grade depth sensors in the last few years greatly promotes the research on depth-based 3D hand pose estimation, since the captured depth images provide richer context that significantly reduces depth ambiguity. With the prevailing of deep learning technology [10], learning-based 3D hand pose estimation from single depth images has also been introduced, which can achieve state-of-the-art 3D pose estimation performance in real time. In general, they can be classified into generative approaches [16,20,34], discriminative approaches [5–8,13,40] and hybrid approaches [25,30,31].

Inspired by the great improvement of CNN-based 3D hand pose estimation from depth images [24], deep learning has also been adopted in some recent works on monocular RGB-based applications [18,46]. In particular, Zimmermann et al.

[46] proposed a deep network that learns an implicit 3D articulation prior of joint locations in canonical coordinates, as well as constructs a synthetic dataset to tackle the problem of insufficient annotations. Muller *et al.* [18] embedded a "GANerated" network which transfers the synthetic images to "real" ones so as to reduce the domain shift between them. The performance gain achieved by these methods indicates a promising direction, although estimating 3D hand pose from single-view RGB images is far more challenging due to the absence of depth information. Our work, as a follow-up exploration, aims at alleviating the burden of 3D annotations in real-world dataset by bridging the gap between fully-annotated synthetic images and weakly-labeled real-world images.

Dibra *et al.* [4] is the closest work in spirit to our approach, which proposed an end-to-end network that enables the adaptation from synthetic dataset to unlabeled real-world dataset. However, we want to emphasize that our method is significantly different from [4] in several aspects. Firstly, our work is targeted at 3D hand pose estimation from single RGB input, whereas [4] focuses on depth-based predictions. Secondly, compared with [4] that leverages a rigged 3D hand model to synthesize depth images, we use a simple fully-convolutional network to infer the corresponding depth maps from the predicted 3D hand pose. To the best of our knowledge, our weakly-supervised adaptation is the first learning-based attempt that introduces a depth regularizer to monocular-RGB based 3D hand pose estimation. This presents an alternative solution for this problem and will enable further research of utilizing depth images in RGB-input applications.

3 Methodology

3.1 Overview

Our target is to infer 3D hand pose from a monocular RGB image, where the 3D hand pose is represented by a set of 3D joint coordinates $\mathbf{\Phi} = \{\phi_k\}_{k=1}^{K} \in \Lambda_{3D}$. Here Λ_{3D} is the $K \times 3$ dimensional hand joint space with $K = 21$ in our case. Figure 3 depicts the proposed network architecture, which utilizes a cascaded architecture inspired from [44]. It consists of a 2D pose estimation network (convolutional pose machines - CPM), a 3D regression network, and a depth regularizer. Given a cropped single RGB image containing human hand with certain gesture, we aim to get the 2D heatmap and the corresponding depth of each joint from the proposed end-to-end network. The 2D joint locations are denoted as $\mathbf{\Phi}_{2D} \in \Lambda_{2D}$, where $\Lambda_{2D} \in \mathcal{R}^{K \times 2}$ and the depth values are denoted as $\mathbf{\Phi}_z \in \Lambda_z$, where $\Lambda_z \in \mathcal{R}^{K \times 1}$. The final output 3D joint locations are represented in the camera coordinate system, where the first two coordinates are converted from the image plane coordinates using the camera intrinsic matrix, and the third coordinate is the joint depth. Note that our depth regularizer is only utilized during training. During testing, only 2D estimation network and regression network are used to predict joint locations.

The depth regularizer is the key part to facilitate the proposed weakly super-vised training, *i.e.*, relieve the painful joint depth annotations for real-world dataset by making use of the rough depth maps, which can be easily captured

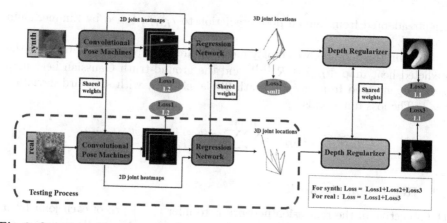

Fig. 3. Overview of our proposed weakly-supervised 3D hand pose regression network, which is trained in an end-to-end manner. During training, cropped images from both synthetic dataset and real image dataset are mixed in each single batch as the input to the network. To compensate the absence of ground truth annotations for joint depth in real data, we extend the network with a depth regularizer by leveraging the corresponding depth maps available in both synthetic and real datasets to provide a weak supervision. During testing, real images only go through the part of the network in the dashed line box. The obtained 2D heatmaps and joint depth are concatenated as the output of the network.

by consumer-grade depth cameras. In addition, our experiments show that the introduced depth regularizer can slightly improve 3D hand pose prediction of fully-supervised methods as well, since it serves as an additional constraint for the 3D hand pose space.

The entire network is trained with a Rendered Hand Pose Dataset (RHD) created by [46] and a real-world dataset from Stereo Hand Pose Tracking Benchmark [43]. For ease of representation, the synthesized dataset and the real-world dataset are denoted as I_{RHD} and I_{STB}, respectively. Note that for weakly-supervised learning, our model is pretrained on I_{RHD} and then adapted to I_{STB} by fusing the training of both datasets. For fully-supervised learning, the two datasets are used independently in the training and evaluation processes.

3.2 2D Pose Estimation Network

For 2D pose estimation, we adopt the encoder-decoder architecture similar to the Convolutional Pose Machines by Wei *et al.* [36] and [46], which is fully convolutional with successively refined heatmaps in resolution. The network outputs K low-resolution heatmaps. The intensity on each heat-map indicates the confidence of a joint locating in the 2D position. Here we predict each joint by applying the MMSE (Minimum mean square error given a posterior) estimator, which can be viewed as taking the integration of all locations weighed by their probabilities in the heat map, as proposed in [29]. We initialize the network with weights adapted from human pose prediction to I_{RHD}, tuned by Zimmermann et al. [46].

To train this module, we employ mean square error (or L2 loss) between the predicted heat map $\hat{\Phi}_{HM} \in \mathcal{R}^{H \times W}$ and the ground-truth Gaussian heat map $G(\Phi_{2D}^{gt})$ generated from ground truth 2D labels Φ_{2D}^{gt} with standard deviation $\sigma = 1$. The loss function is

$$L_{2D}(\hat{\Phi}_{HM}, \Phi_{2D}^{gt}) = \sum_h^H \sum_w^W (\hat{\Phi}_{HM}^{(h,w)} - G(\Phi_{2D}^{gt})^{(h,w)})^2. \tag{1}$$

3.3   Regression Network

The objective of the regression network is to infer the depth of each joint from the obtained 2D heatmap. Most previous work [2,32,46] in 3D human pose and hand pose estimation based on single image attempt to lift the set of 2D heatmaps into 3D space directly, while a key issue for this strategy is how to distinguish between the multiple 3D poses inferred from a single 2D skeleton. Inspired from [44], our method exploits contextual information to reduce the ambiguity of lifting 2D heatmaps to 3D locations, by extracting the intermediate image evidence in 2D pose estimation network concatenated with the predicted 2D heatmaps as the input to the regression network. We employ a simple yet effective depth regression network structure with only two convolutional layers and three fully-connected layers. Note that here we infer a scale-invariant and translation-invariant representation of joint depth, by subtracting each hand joint with the location of root keypoint and then normalizing it by the distance between a certain pair of keypoints, as done in [18,46].

For fully-supervised learning, we simply apply smooth L1 loss introduced in [9] between our predicted joint depth $\hat{\Phi}_z$ and the ground truth label Φ_z^{gt}. For weakly-supervised learning, no penalty is enforced because of the absence of 3D annotations. To address this issue, we introduce a novel depth regularizer as weak supervision for joint depth regression, which will be elaborated in Sect. 3.4.

Overall, the loss function of the regression network is defined as

$$L_z(\hat{\Phi}_z, \Phi_z^{gt}) = \begin{cases} smooth_{L1}(\hat{\Phi}_z, \Phi_z^{gt}) &, if \text{ full supervision} \\ 0 &, if \text{ weak supervision} \end{cases} \tag{2}$$

in which

$$smooth_{L1}(x) = \begin{cases} 0.5x^2, & if |x| < 1 \\ |x| - 0.5, & otherwise. \end{cases} \tag{3}$$

3.4   Depth Regularizer

The purpose of the depth regularizer is to take the easily-captured depth images as an implicit constraint of physical structures that can be applied to both weakly-supervised and fully-supervised situations. Figure 4 shows the architecture of the proposed depth regularizer, which is fully-convolutional with six layers, inspired by [3,19]. Each layer contains a transposed convolution followed by

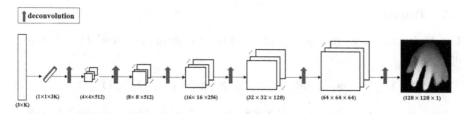

Fig. 4. Network architecture of our proposed depth regularizer. Given 3D hand joint locations as the input, the depth regularizer is able to render the corresponding depth map by gradually enlarging the intermediate feature maps and finally combining them into a single depth image.

a Relu, after which the feature map is expanded along both image dimensions. In the first five layers, batch normalization [12] and drop out [11] are introduced before Relu in order to reduce the dependency on the initialization and alleviate from overfitting the training data. The final layer combines all feature maps to generate the corresponding depth image from 3D hand pose.

Let $(\hat{\Phi}_{3D}, D)$ denote a training sample, where $\hat{\Phi}_{3D}$ is the input of the depth regularizer containing a set of 3D hand joint locations, and $\mathbf{D}$ is the corresponding depth image. We normalize $\mathbf{D}$ into $\mathbf{D}_n$:

$$\mathbf{D}_n = \sum_{i,j} \frac{d_{max} - d_{ij}}{d_{range}} \tag{4}$$

where d_{ij} is the depth value at the image location (i, j), and d_{max} and d_{range} represent the maximum depth value and the depth range, respectively. Note that the normalized depth value tends to be larger when located closer to the camera and background is set to 0 in this process.

The input of the network $\hat{\Phi}_{3D} = \{(\Phi_{2D}^{gt}, \mathbf{X}_z)\}$ contains two parts: the ground truth 2D labels Φ_{2D}^{gt} in the image coordinate system and the joint depth $\mathbf{X}_z$. Note that the reason we use ground truth 2D locations rather than our predicted 2D results is to simplify the training process since no back-propagation from the depth regularizer is fed back into the 2D pose estimation network. For the joint depth $\mathbf{X}_z$, we apply the same normalization:

$$\mathbf{X}_z = \frac{d_{max} - \hat{\Phi}_z \cdot L_{scale} - d_{root}}{d_{range}} \tag{5}$$

where $\hat{\Phi}_z$ denotes the predicted joint depth from the regression network, which is a set of root-relative and normalized values and can be recovered to global coordinates by multiplying with hand scale L_{scale} and shifting to root depth d_{root}.

To train the depth regularizer, we adopt L1 norm to minimize the difference between the generated depth image $\hat{\mathbf{D}}_n$ and the corresponding ground truth $\mathbf{D}_n$:

$$L_{dep}(\hat{\mathbf{D}}_n, \mathbf{D}_n) = |\hat{\mathbf{D}}_n - \mathbf{D}_n| \tag{6}$$

3.5 Training

Combining the losses in Eqs. (1), (2), and (6), we obtain the overall loss function as

$$L = \lambda_{2D} L_{2D}(\hat{\mathbf{\Phi}}_{HM}, \mathbf{\Phi}_{2D}^{gt}) + \lambda_z L_z(\hat{\mathbf{\Phi}}_z, \mathbf{\Phi}_z^{gt}) + \lambda_{dep} L_{dep}(\hat{\mathbf{D}}_n, \mathbf{D}_n). \qquad (7)$$

Adam optimization [14] is used for training. For weakly-supervised learning, similar to [44] and [33], we adopt fused training where each mini-batch contains both the synthetic and the real training examples (half-half), shuffled randomly during the training process. In our experiments, we adopt a three-stage training process, which is more effective in practice compared with direct end-to-end training. In particular, *Stage 1* initializes the regression network and fine-tunes the 2D pose estimation network with weights from Zimmermann *et al.* [46], which are adapted from the Convolutional Pose Machines [36]. *Stage 2* initializes the depth regularizer, as described in Sect. 3.4. *Stage 3* fine-tunes the whole network with all the training data, which is an end-to-end training.

4   Experiments

4.1   Implementation Details

Our method is implemented with Pytorch. For the first training stage described in Sect. 3.5, we take 60 epochs with an initial learning rate of 10^{-7}, a batch size of 8 and a regularization strength of 5×10^{-4}. For Stage 2 and Stage 3, we spend 40 and 20 epochs, respectively. During the fine-tunning process of the whole network, we set $\lambda_{2D} = 1$, $\lambda_z = 0.1$ and $\lambda_{dep} = 1$. All experiments are conducted on one GeForce GTX 1080 GPU with CUDA 8.0.

4.2   Datasets and Metrics

We evaluate our method on two publicly available datasets: Rendered Hand Pose Dataset (RHD) [46] and a real-world dataset from Stereo Hand Pose Tracking Benchmark (STB) [43].

RHD is a synthetic dataset of rendered hand images with a resolution of 320×320, which is built upon 20 different characters performing 39 actions and is composed of 41,258 images for training and 2,728 images for testing. All samples are annotated with 2D and 3D keypoint locations. For each RGB image, the corresponding depth image is also provided. This dataset is considerably challenging due to the large variations in viewpoints and hand shapes, as well as the large visual diversity induced by random noise and different illuminations. With all the labels provided, we train the entire proposed network, including the 2D pose estimation network, the regression network and the depth regularizer.

STB is a real world dataset containing two subsets with an image resolution of 640×480: the stereo subset STB-BB captured from a Point Grey Bumblebee2 stereo camera and the color-depth subset STB-SK captured from an

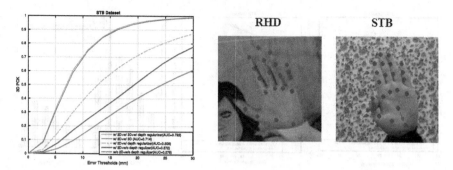

Fig. 5. Left: comparisons of 3D PCK results of different baselines with our method on STB [43]. Our proposed weakly-supervised method, w/ 2D + w/ depth regularizer, significantly outperforms other weakly-supervised baselines(Orange and Green curve). Right: Different annotation schemes on RHD [46] and STB [43] dataset. Note that we move the root joint location of STB dataset from palm to wrist keypoint to make the two datasets consistent with each other. (Color figure online)

active depth camera. Note that the two types of images are captured simultaneously with the same resolution, identical camera pose, and similar viewpoints. Both STB-BB and STB-SK provide 2D and 3D annotations of 21 keypoints. For weakly-supervised experiments, we use color-depth pairs in STB-SK with 2D annotations, as well as root depth (*i.e.*, wrist in the experiments) and hand scale (the distance between a certain pair of keypoints). For fully-supervised experiments, both color-depth pairs (STB-BB) and stereo pairs (STB-SK) with 2D and 3D annotations are utilized to train the whole network. Note that all experiments conducted on STB dataset follow the same training and evaluation protocol used in [18,46], which trains on 10 sequences and tests on the other two.

We evaluate the 3D hand pose estimation performance with two metrics. The first metric is the area under the curve (AUC) on the percentage of correct keypoints (PCK) score, which is a popular criterion to evaluate the pose estimation accuracy with different thresholds, as proposed in [18,46]. The second metric is the mean error distance in z-dimension over all testing frames, which is used to further analyse the impact of the proposed depth regularizer. Following the same condition used in [18,46], we assume that the global hand scale and the root depth are known in the experimental evaluations so that we can report PCK curve based on 3D hand joint locations in the global domain, which are computed from the output root-relative articulations.

4.3 Quantitative Results

Weak Supervision. We first evaluate the impact of weak label constraints on STB dataset compared with fully-supervised methods with complete 2D and 3D annotations. Specifically, we compare our proposed weakly-supervised approach (**w/ 2D + w/ depth regularizer**) with three baselines: (a) **w/o 2D + w/o**

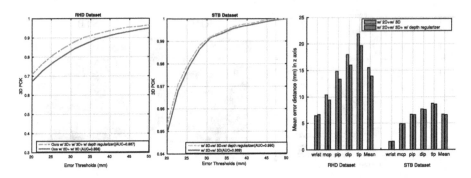

Fig. 6. The effect of the proposed depth regularizer in fully-supervised setting on RHD [46] and STB datasets [43]. Left: 3D PCK on RHD dataset. Middle: 3D PCK on STB dataset. Right: mean joint error distances in z-dimension on RHD and STB datasets.

depth regularizer: directly using pretrained model based on RHD dataset; (b) **w/ 2D + w/o depth regularizer**: tuning the pretrained network with 2D labels in STB dataset and (c) **w/ 2D + w/ 3D**: fully-supervised method with complete 2D and 3D annotations.

As illustrated in the left part of Fig. 5, the fully-supervised method achieves the best performance while directly transferring the model trained on synthetic data with no adaptation (baseline-a) yields the worst estimation results. This is not surprising, since the fully-supervised method provides the most effective constraint in the 3D hand pose estimation task and real-world images have considerable domain shift from synthetic ones. Note that these two baselines serve as upper bound and lower bound for our weakly-supervised method. Compared with baseline-a, by fine-tuning the pretrained model with the 2D labels of the real images, baseline-b significantly improves the AUC value from 0.667 to 0.807. Moreover, adding our proposed depth regularizer further increases AUC to 0.889, which demonstrates the effectiveness of the depth regularizer.

We note that STB and RHD datasets adopt different schemes for 2D and 3D annotations, as shown in the right part of Fig. 5. In particular, STB dataset annotates palm position as root joint, which is different from RHD dataset that uses wrist position as root keypoint. Thus, we move the palm joint in STB to wrist point so as to make the annotations consistent for fused training. To evaluate the introduced noise of moving root joint, we compare our results of fully-supervised method on STB dataset with palm-relative and wrist-relative representations. Original palm-relative representation performs slightly better, reducing the mean error by about 0.6 mm. Besides, it is also noted that MCP (Metacarpophalangeal joints) positions are closer to wrist joint in STB dataset and labels for STB dataset are relatively noisy compared with synthetic dataset RHD (*e.g.*, thumb dip is annotated in the background). Due to these differences, we argue that there exists a bias between our pose predictions and the ground truth provided by STB dataset, which might decrease the reported estimation

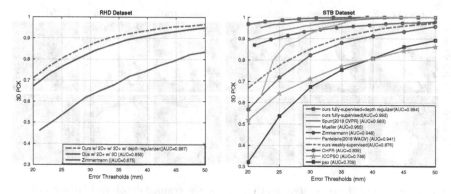

Fig. 7. Comparisons with state-of-the-art methods on RHD [46] and STB [43]. Left: 3D PCK on RHD dataset. Right: 3D PCK on STB dataset.

accuracy of our proposed weakly-supervised approach. Furthermore, these inconsistencies, on the other hand, suggest the necessity of the introduced depth regularizer, since it provides certain prior knowledge of hand pose and shapes.

Fully-Supervised 3D Hand Pose Estimation. We also evaluate the effectiveness of the depth regularizer in the fully-supervised setting on both RHD and STB datasets. Note that the two datasets are trained independently in this case. As presented in Fig. 6 (left) and (middle), our fully-supervised method with depth regularizer outperforms that without depth regularizer on both RHD and STB dataset, with improvement of 0.031 and 0.001 in AUC, respectively. Figure 6 (right) shows the mean joint error in z-dimension, indicating that adding depth regularizer is able to slightly improve the fully-supervised results in the joint depth estimation.

Comparisons with State-of-the-Arts. Figure 7 shows the comparisons with state-of-the-art methods [18,22,27,43,46] on both RHD and STB datasets. It can be seen that on RHD dataset, even without the depth regularizer, our fully-supervised method significantly outperforms the state-of-the-art method [46], improving the AUC value from 0.675 to 0.887. On STB dataset, our fully-supervised method achieves the best results compared with all existing methods. Note that our weakly-supervised method is also superior to some of the existing works, which demonstrates the potential values for the weakly-supervised exploration when complete 3D annotations are difficult to obtain in real-world dataset. It is also noted that the AUC values of our proposed methods in Fig. 7 are slightly different from their counterparts in Sect. 4.3. This is because here we test on the stereo pair subset STB-BB rather than the color-depth subset STB-SK.

4.4 Qualitative Results

Figure 9 shows some visual results of our proposed weakly-supervised approach and baselines. For a better comparison, we show the 3D skeleton reconstructions

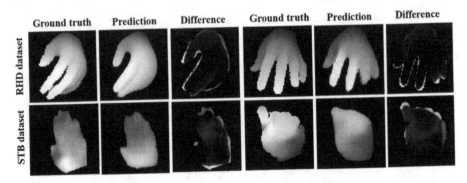

Fig. 8. Samples of the generated depth maps by the trained depth regularizer with the input of ground truth 3D hand joint locations. Our trained depth regularizer is able to render plausible and convincing depth maps. Note that the errors are mainly located around contours of the hand, where the reference depth images (e.g. captured by depth camera) are typically noisy.

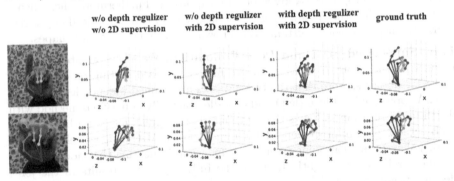

Fig. 9. Visual results of our proposed weakly-supervised approach (column 1, 4) and other baselines (column 2, 3), compared with ground truth (column 5). Note that columns 2–5 are shown at a novel viewpoint for easy comparison.

at a novel view and the skeleton reconstructions of our method at the original view are overlaid with the input images. It can be seen that, after additionally imposing the depth regularizer with the reference depth images, our weakly-supervised approach on real-world dataset yields considerably better estimation accuracy, especially in terms of global orientation, which is consistent with our aforementioned quantitative analysis.

Figure 10 shows some visual results of our fully-supervised methods on RHD and STB datasets. We exhibit samples captured from various viewpoints with serious self-occlusions. It can be seen that our fully-supervised approach with the depth regularizer is robust to various hand orientations and complicated pose articulations.

Although the depth regularizer is only used in training but not in testing, it is interesting to see whether it has learned a manifold of hand poses. Thus, we

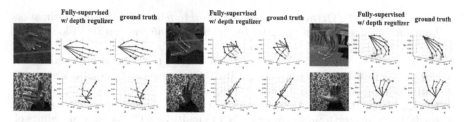

Fig. 10. Visual results of our fully-supervised method on RHD and STB datasets. First row: RHD dataset. Second row: STB dataset. Note that skeletons are shown at a novel viewpoint for easy comparison.

collect some samples of the depth images generated by our well trained depth regularizer, given ground truth 3D hand joint locations, as shown in Fig. 8. We can see that our depth regularizer is able to render smooth and convincing depth images for hand poses in large variations and self-occlusions.

5   Conclusions

Building a large real-world hand dataset with full 3D annotations is often one of the major bottlenecks for learning-based approaches in 3D hand pose estimation task. To address this problem, our approach presents one way to adapt weakly-labeled real-world dataset from fully-annotated synthetic dataset with the aid of low-cost depth images, which, to our knowledge, is the first exploration of leveraging depth maps to compensate the absence of entire 3D annotations. To be specific, we introduce a simple yet effective end-to-end architecture consisting of a 2D estimation network, a regression network and a novel depth regularizer. Quantitative and qualitative experimental results show that our weakly-supervised method compares favorably with the existing works and our fully-supervised approach considerably outperforms the state-of-the-art methods. We note that we only show one way for weakly-supervised 3D hand pose estimation. There is a large space for un-/weakly-supervised learning.

References

1. Bogo, F., Kanazawa, A., Lassner, C., Gehler, P., Romero, J., Black, M.J.: Keep it SMPL: automatic estimation of 3D human pose and shape from a single image. In: Leibe, B., Matas, J., Sebe, N., Welling, M. (eds.) ECCV 2016. LNCS, vol. 9909, pp. 561–578. Springer, Cham (2016). https://doi.org/10.1007/978-3-319-46454-1_34
2. Chen, C.H., Ramanan, D.: 3D human pose estimation = 2D pose estimation + matching. In: CVPR, vol. 2, p. 6 (2017)
3. Çiçek, Ö., Abdulkadir, A., Lienkamp, S.S., Brox, T., Ronneberger, O.: 3D U-Net: learning dense volumetric segmentation from sparse annotation. In: Ourselin, S., Joskowicz, L., Sabuncu, M.R., Unal, G., Wells, W. (eds.) MICCAI 2016. LNCS, vol. 9901, pp. 424–432. Springer, Cham (2016). https://doi.org/10.1007/978-3-319-46723-8_49

4. Dibra, E., Wolf, T., Oztireli, C., Gross, M.: How to refine 3D hand pose estimation from unlabelled depth data? In: 2017 International Conference on 3D Vision (3DV), pp. 135–144. IEEE (2017)

5. Ge, L., Cai, Y., Weng, J., Yuan, J.: Hand PointNet: 3D hand pose estimation using point sets. In: Proceedings of the IEEE Conference on Computer Vision and Pattern Recognition, pp. 8417–8426 (2018)

6. Ge, L., Liang, H., Yuan, J., Thalmann, D.: Robust 3D hand pose estimation in single depth images: from single-view CNN to multi-view CNNs. In: Proceedings of the IEEE Conference on Computer Vision and Pattern Recognition, pp. 3593–3601 (2016)

7. Ge, L., Liang, H., Yuan, J., Thalmann, D.: 3D convolutional neural networks for efficient and robust hand pose estimation from single depth images. In: Proceedings of the IEEE Conference on Computer Vision and Pattern Recognition, vol. 1, p. 5 (2017)

8. Ge, L., Ren, Z., Yuan, J.: Point-to-point regression PointNet for 3D hand pose estimation. In: Proceedings of European Conference on Computer Vision (2018)

9. Girshick, R.: Fast R-CNN. In: 2015 IEEE International Conference on Computer Vision (ICCV), pp. 1440–1448. IEEE (2015)

10. Gu, J., et al.: Recent advances in convolutional neural networks. Pattern Recognit. **77**, 354–377 (2017)

11. Hinton, G.E., Srivastava, N., Krizhevsky, A., Sutskever, I., Salakhutdinov, R.R.: Improving neural networks by preventing co-adaptation of feature detectors. arXiv preprint arXiv:1207.0580 (2012)

12. Ioffe, S., Szegedy, C.: Batch normalization: accelerating deep network training by reducing internal covariate shift. In: International Conference on Machine Learning, pp. 448–456 (2015)

13. Keskin, C., Kıraç, F., Kara, Y.E., Akarun, L.: Hand pose estimation and hand shape classification using multi-layered randomized decision forests. In: Fitzgibbon, A., Lazebnik, S., Perona, P., Sato, Y., Schmid, C. (eds.) ECCV 2012. LNCS, vol. 7577, pp. 852–863. Springer, Heidelberg (2012). https://doi.org/10.1007/978-3-642-33783-3_61

14. Kingma, D.P., Ba, J.: Adam: a method for stochastic optimization. arXiv preprint arXiv:1412.6980 (2014)

15. Liang, H., Yuan, J., Thalman, D.: Egocentric hand pose estimation and distance recovery in a single RGB image. In: 2015 IEEE International Conference on Multimedia and Expo (ICME), pp. 1–6. IEEE (2015)

16. Liang, H., Yuan, J., Thalmann, D., Zhang, Z.: Model-based hand pose estimation via spatial-temporal hand parsing and 3D fingertip localization. Vis. Comput. **29**(6–8), 837–848 (2013)

17. Lu, S., Metaxas, D., Samaras, D., Oliensis, J.: Using multiple cues for hand tracking and model refinement. In: 2003 IEEE Computer Society Conference on Computer Vision and Pattern Recognition, Proceedings, vol. 2, pp. II-443. IEEE (2003)

18. Mueller, F., et al.: GANerated hands for real-time 3D hand tracking from monocular RGB. In: Proceedings of Computer Vision and Pattern Recognition (CVPR), June 2018. https://handtracker.mpi-inf.mpg.de/projects/GANeratedHands/

19. Oberweger, M., Wohlhart, P., Lepetit, V.: Training a feedback loop for hand pose estimation. In: Proceedings of the IEEE International Conference on Computer Vision, pp. 3316–3324 (2015)

20. Oikonomidis, I., Kyriazis, N., Argyros, A.A.: Efficient model-based 3D tracking of hand articulations using Kinect. In: BmVC, vol. 1, p. 3 (2011)

21. Oikonomidis, I., Kyriazis, N., Argyros, A.A.: Full DOF tracking of a hand interacting with an object by modeling occlusions and physical constraints. In: 2011 IEEE International Conference on Computer Vision (ICCV), pp. 2088–2095. IEEE (2011)
22. Panteleris, P., Oikonomidis, I., Argyros, A.: Using a single RGB frame for real time 3D hand pose estimation in the wild. In: 2018 IEEE Winter Conference on Applications of Computer Vision (WACV), pp. 436–445. IEEE (2018)
23. Rehg, J.M., Kanade, T.: DigitEyes: vision-based hand tracking for human-computer interaction. In: Proceedings of the 1994 IEEE Workshop on Motion of Non-Rigid and Articulated Objects, pp. 16–22. IEEE (1994)
24. Ren, Z., Yuan, J., Meng, J., Zhang, Z.: Robust part-based hand gesture recognition using Kinect sensor. IEEE Trans. Multimed. **15**, 1110–1120 (2016)
25. Sharp, T., et al.: Accurate, robust, and flexible real-time hand tracking. In: Proceedings of the 33rd Annual ACM Conference on Human Factors in Computing Systems, pp. 3633–3642. ACM (2015)
26. Shotton, J., et al.: Efficient human pose estimation from single depth images. IEEE Trans. Pattern Anal. Mach. Intell. **35**(12), 2821–2840 (2013)
27. Spurr, A., Song, J., Park, S., Hilliges, O.: Cross-modal deep variational hand pose estimation. In: Proceedings of the IEEE Conference on Computer Vision and Pattern Recognition, pp. 89–98 (2018)
28. Stenger, B., Thayananthan, A., Torr, P.H., Cipolla, R.: Model-based hand tracking using a hierarchical Bayesian filter. IEEE Trans. Pattern Anal. Mach. Intell. **28**(9), 1372–1384 (2006)
29. Sun, X., Xiao, B., Liang, S., Wei, Y.: Integral human pose regression. arXiv preprint arXiv:1711.08229 (2017)
30. Tang, D., Taylor, J., Kohli, P., Keskin, C., Kim, T.K., Shotton, J.: Opening the black box: hierarchical sampling optimization for estimating human hand pose. In: Proceedings of the IEEE International Conference on Computer Vision, pp. 3325–3333 (2015)
31. Taylor, J., et al.: Efficient and precise interactive hand tracking through joint, continuous optimization of pose and correspondences. ACM Trans. Graph. (TOG) **35**(4), 143 (2016)
32. Tome, D., Russell, C., Agapito, L.: Lifting from the deep: convolutional 3D pose estimation from a single image. In: CVPR 2017 Proceedings, pp. 2500–2509 (2017)
33. Tzeng, E., Hoffman, J., Darrell, T., Saenko, K.: Simultaneous deep transfer across domains and tasks. In: 2015 IEEE International Conference on Computer Vision (ICCV), pp. 4068–4076. IEEE (2015)
34. Tzionas, D., Ballan, L., Srikantha, A., Aponte, P., Pollefeys, M., Gall, J.: Capturing hands in action using discriminative salient points and physics simulation. Int. J. Comput. Vis. **118**(2), 172–193 (2016)
35. Wang, R., Paris, S., Popović, J.: 6D hands: markerless hand-tracking for computer aided design. In: Proceedings of the 24th Annual ACM Symposium on User Interface Software and Technology, pp. 549–558. ACM (2011)
36. Wei, S.E., Ramakrishna, V., Kanade, T., Sheikh, Y.: Convolutional pose machines. In: Proceedings of the IEEE Conference on Computer Vision and Pattern Recognition, pp. 4724–4732 (2016)
37. Wu, J., et al.: Single image 3D interpreter network. In: Leibe, B., Matas, J., Sebe, N., Welling, M. (eds.) ECCV 2016. LNCS, vol. 9910, pp. 365–382. Springer, Cham (2016). https://doi.org/10.1007/978-3-319-46466-4_22
38. Wu, Y., Huang, T.S.: Capturing articulated human hand motion: a divide-and-conquer approach. In: The Proceedings of the Seventh IEEE International Conference on Computer Vision, vol. 1, pp. 606–611. IEEE (1999)

39. Wu, Y., Huang, T.S.: View-independent recognition of hand postures. In: CVPR, p. 2088. IEEE (2000)
40. Xu, C., Cheng, L.: Efficient hand pose estimation from a single depth image. In: 2013 IEEE International Conference on Computer Vision (ICCV), pp. 3456–3462. IEEE (2013)
41. Yang, Y., Ramanan, D.: Articulated pose estimation with flexible mixtures-of-parts. In: 2011 IEEE Conference on Computer Vision and Pattern Recognition (CVPR), pp. 1385–1392. IEEE (2011)
42. Yasin, H., Iqbal, U., Kruger, B., Weber, A., Gall, J.: A dual-source approach for 3D pose estimation from a single image. In: Proceedings of the IEEE Conference on Computer Vision and Pattern Recognition, pp. 4948–4956 (2016)
43. Zhang, J., Jiao, J., Chen, M., Qu, L., Xu, X., Yang, Q.: 3D hand pose tracking and estimation using stereo matching. arXiv preprint arXiv:1610.07214 (2016)
44. Zhou, X., Huang, Q., Sun, X., Xue, X., Wei, Y.: Towards 3D human pose estimation in the wild: a weakly-supervised approach. In: IEEE International Conference on Computer Vision (2017)
45. Zhu, J.Y., Park, T., Isola, P., Efros, A.A.: Unpaired image-to-image translation using cycle-consistent adversarial networks. In: 2017 IEEE International Conference on Computer Vision (ICCV), pp. 2242–2251. IEEE (2017)
46. Zimmermann, C., Brox, T.: Learning to estimate 3D hand pose from single RGB images. In: International Conference on Computer Vision (2017)

DeepIM: Deep Iterative Matching for 6D Pose Estimation

Yi Li[1](✉), Gu Wang[1], Xiangyang Ji[1], Yu Xiang[2], and Dieter Fox[2]

[1] Tsinghua University and BNRist, Beijing, China
yili.matrix@gmail.com, wangg16@mails.tsinghua.edu.cn,
xyji@tsinghua.edu.cn
[2] University of Washington and NVIDIA Research, Seattle, USA
{yux,dieterf}@nvidia.com

Abstract. Estimating the 6D pose of objects from images is an important problem in various applications such as robot manipulation and virtual reality. While direct regression of images to object poses has limited accuracy, matching rendered images of an object against the input image can produce accurate results. In this work, we propose a novel deep neural network for 6D pose matching named DeepIM. Given an initial pose estimation, our network is able to iteratively refine the pose by matching the rendered image against the observed image. The network is trained to predict a relative pose transformation using an untangled representation of 3D location and 3D orientation and an iterative training process. Experiments on two commonly used benchmarks for 6D pose estimation demonstrate that DeepIM achieves large improvements over state-of-the-art methods. We furthermore show that DeepIM is able to match previously unseen objects.

Keywords: 3D object recognition · 6D object pose estimation

1 Introduction

Localizing objects in 3D from images is important in many real world applications. For instance, in a robot manipulation task, the ability to recognize the 6D pose of objects, i.e., 3D location and 3D orientation of objects, provides useful information for grasp and motion planning. In a virtual reality application, 6D object pose estimation enables virtual interactions between humans and objects. While several recent techniques have used depth cameras for object pose estimation, such cameras have limitations with respect to frame rate, field of view, resolution, and depth range, making it very difficult to detect small, thin, transparent, or fast moving objects. Unfortunately, RGB-only 6D object

Electronic supplementary material The online version of this chapter (https://doi.org/10.1007/978-3-030-01231-1_42) contains supplementary material, which is available to authorized users.

ⓒ Springer Nature Switzerland AG 2018
V. Ferrari et al. (Eds.): ECCV 2018, LNCS 11210, pp. 695–711, 2018.
https://doi.org/10.1007/978-3-030-01231-1_42

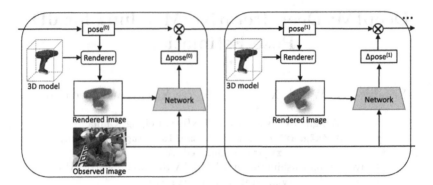

Fig. 1. We propose DeepIM, a deep iterative matching network for 6D object pose estimation. The network is trained to predict a relative SE(3) transformation that can be applied to an initial pose estimation for iterative pose refinement.

pose estimation is still a challenging problem, since the appearance of objects in the images changes according to a number of factors, such as lighting, pose variations, and occlusions between objects. Furthermore, a robust 6D pose estimation method needs to handle both textured and textureless objects.

Traditionally, the 6D pose estimation problem has been tackled by matching local features extracted from an image to features in a 3D model of the object [4, 16, 23]. By using the 2D-3D correspondences, the 6D pose of the object can be recovered. Unfortunately, such methods cannot handle textureless objects well since only few local features can be extracted for them. To handle textureless objects, two classes of approaches were proposed in the literature. Methods in the first class learn to estimate the 3D model coordinates of pixels or key points of the object in the input image. In this way, the 2D-3D correspondences are established for 6D pose estimation [1, 20, 26]. Methods in the second class convert the 6D pose estimation problem into a pose classification problem by discretizing the pose space [9] or into a pose regression problem [29]. These methods can deal with textureless objects, but they are not able to achieve highly accurate pose estimation, since small errors in the classification or regression stage directly lead to pose mismatches. A common way to improve the pose accuracy is pose refinement: Given an initial pose estimation, a synthetic RGB image can be rendered and used to match against the target input image. Then a new pose is computed to increase the matching score. Existing methods for pose refinement use either hand-crafted image features [27] or matching score functions [20].

In this work, we propose DeepIM, a new refinement technique based on a deep neural network for iterative 6D pose matching. Given an initial 6D pose estimation of an object in a test image, DeepIM predicts a relative SE(3) transformation that matches a rendered view of the object against the observed image. By iteratively re-rendering the object based on the improved pose estimates, the two input images to the network become more and more similar, thereby enabling the network to generate more and more accurate pose estimates. Figure 1 illustrates the iterative matching procedure of our network for pose refinement.

This work makes the following main contributions. (i) We introduce a deep network for iterative, image-based pose refinement that does not require any hand-crafted image features, automatically learning an internal refinement mechanism. (ii) We propose an untangled representation of the SE(3) transformation between object poses to achieve accurate pose estimates. This representation also enables our approach to refine pose estimates of unseen objects. (iii) We have conducted extensive experiments on the LINEMOD [9] and the Occlusion [1] datasets to evaluate the accuracy and various properties of DeepIM. These experiments show that our approach achieves large improvements over state-of-the-art RGB-only methods on both datasets. Furthermore, initial experiments demonstrate that DeepIM is able to accurately match poses for textureless objects (T-LESS [10]) and for unseen objects [28]. The rest of the paper is organized as follows. After reviewing related works in Sect. 2, we describe our approach for pose matching in Sect. 3. Experiments are presented in Sects. 4, and 5 concludes the paper.

2   Related Work

RGB-D Based 6D Pose Estimation: When depth information is available, it can be combined with RGB images to improve 6D pose estimation. A common strategy of using depth is to convert a depth image into a 3D point cloud, and then match the 3D model of an object against the 3D point cloud. For example, [9] render the 3D model of an object into templates of surface normals, and then match these templates against normals computed from the point cloud. [1,2,17] regress each pixel on the object in the input image to the 3D coordinate of that pixel on the 3D model. When depth images are available, the 3D coordinate regression establishes correspondences between 3D scene points and 3D model points, from which the 6D pose of the object can be computed by solving a least-squares problem. For pose refinement, the Iterative Closest Point (ICP) algorithm is widely used to refine an initial pose estimate [9,17,30]. However, ICP is sensitive to the initial estimate and may converge to local minima.

RGB Based 6D Pose Estimation: Traditionally, pose estimation using RGB images is tackled by matching local features [4,16,23]. However, these methods cannot handle textureless objects very well. Recent approaches apply machine learning, especially deep learning, for 6D pose estimation using RGB images only [1,13]. The state-of-the-art methods [11,20,26,29] augment deep learning based object detection or segmentation methods [8,14,15,21] for 6D pose estimation. However, the performance of these methods is still not comparable to RGB-D based methods. We believe that this performance gap is so large due to the lack of an effective pose refinement procedure using RGB images only. Our work is complementary to existing 6D pose estimation methods by providing a novel iterative pose matching network for pose refinement on RGB images.

The approaches most relevant to ours are the object pose refinement network in [20] and the iterative hand pose estimation approaches in [3,19]. Compared

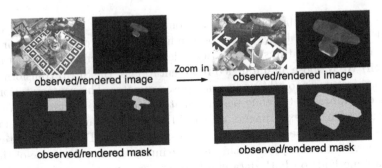

Fig. 2. DeepIM operates on a zoomed in, up-sampled input image, the rendered image, and the two object masks (480 × 640 in our case after zooming in).

to these techniques, our network is designed to directly regress to relative SE(3) transformations. We are able to do this due to our untangled representation of rotation and translation and the reference frame we used for rotation, which also allows our approach to match unseen objects. As shown in [18], the choice of reference frame is important to achieve good pose estimation results. Our work is also related to recent visual servoing methods based on deep neural networks [5,24] that estimate the relative camera pose between two image frames, while we focus on 6D pose refinement of objects.

3   DeepIM Framework

In this section, we describe our deep iterative matching network for 6D pose estimation. Given an observed image and an initial pose estimate of an object in the image, we design the network to directly output a relative SE(3) transformation that can be applied to the initial pose to improve the estimate. We first present our strategy of zooming in the observed image and the rendered image that are used as inputs of the network. Then we describe our network architecture for pose matching. After that, we introduce an untangled representation of the relative SE(3) transformation and a new loss function for pose regression. Finally, we describe our procedure for training and testing the network.

3.1   High-Resolution Zoom in

It can be difficult to extract useful features for matching if objects in the input image are very small. To obtain enough details for pose matching, we zoom in the observed image and the rendered image before feeding them into the network, as shown in Fig. 2. Specifically, in the i-th stage of the iterative matching, given a 6D pose estimate $\mathbf{p}^{(i-1)}$ from the previous step, we render a synthetic image using the 3D object model viewed according to $\mathbf{p}^{(i-1)}$. We additionally generate one foreground mask for the observed image and rendered image. The four images are cropped using an enlarged bounding box according to the observed mask and

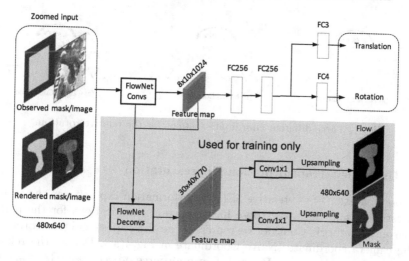

Fig. 3. DeepIM uses a FlowNetSimple backbone to predict a relative SE(3) transformation to match the observed and rendered image of an object.

the rendered mask, where we make sure the enlarged bounding box has the same aspect ratio as the input image and is centered at the 2D projection of the origin of the 3D object model. Finally, we zoom in and perform bilinear up-sampling to achieve the same size as the original image (480×640 in our experiments). Importantly, the aspect ratio of the object is not changed during this operation.

3.2   Network Structure

Figure 3 illustrates the network architecture of DeepIM. The observed image, the rendered image, and the two masks, are concatenated into an eight-channel tensor input to the network (3 channels for observed/rendered image, 1 channel for each mask). We use the FlowNetSimple architecture from [6] as the backbone network, which is trained to predict optical flow between two images. We tried using the VGG16 image classification network [25] as the backbone network, but the results were very poor, confirming the intuition that a representation related to optical flow is very useful for pose matching. The pose estimation branch takes the feature map after 11 convolution layers from FlowNetSimple as input. It contains two fully-connected layers each with dimension 256, followed by two additional fully-connected layers for predicting the quaternion of the 3D rotation and the 3D translation, respectively. During training, we also add two auxiliary branches to regularize the feature representation of the network and increase training stability. One branch is trained for predicting optical flow between the rendered image and the observed image, and the other branch for predicting the foreground mask of the object in the observed image.

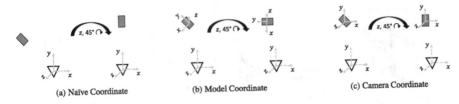

(a) Naïve Coordinate   (b) Model Coordinate   (c) Camera Coordinate

Fig. 4. Three different coordinate systems for the relative rotation.

3.3   Untangled Transformation Representation

The representation of the relative SE(3) transformation $\Delta\mathbf{p}$ between the current pose estimate and the target pose has important ramifications for the performance of the network. Consider we represent the object pose and transformation in the camera coordinate (Naive Coordinate in Fig. 4(a)). Denote the relative rotation and translation as $[\mathbf{R}_\Delta|\mathbf{t}_\Delta]$. Given a source object pose $[\mathbf{R}_{\text{src}}|\mathbf{t}_{\text{src}}]$, the transformed target pose would be as follows:

$$\mathbf{R}_{\text{tgt}} = \mathbf{R}_\Delta \mathbf{R}_{\text{src}}, \quad \mathbf{t}_{\text{tgt}} = \mathbf{R}_\Delta \mathbf{t}_{\text{src}} + \mathbf{t}_\Delta, \tag{1}$$

where $[\mathbf{R}_{\text{tgt}}|\mathbf{t}_{\text{tgt}}]$ denotes the target pose. The $\mathbf{R}_\Delta\mathbf{t}_{\text{src}}$ term indicates that a rotation will cause the object not only to rotate, but also translate in the image even if the translation vector $\mathbf{t}_\Delta$ equals to zero. Furthermore, the translation $\mathbf{t}_\Delta$ is in the metric of the 3D space (meter, for instance), which couples object size with distance in the metric space, thereby requiring the network to memorize the size of each object if it has to translate a mis-match in images to distance offset. It is obvious that such a representation is not appropriate. To eliminate such problems, we propose to decouple the estimation of $\mathbf{R}_\Delta$ and $\mathbf{t}_\Delta$. For rotation, we move the center of rotation from the origin of the camera to the center of the object in the camera frame, given by the current pose estimate. Then a rotation would not change the translation of the object in the camera frame. The remaining question is how to choose the axes of the coordinate frame for rotation. One way is to use the axes of the coordinate frame as specified in the 3D object model (Model Coordinate in Fig. 4(b)). However, such a representation would require the network to memorize the coordinate frames of each object, which makes the training more difficult and cannot be generalized to pose matching of unseen objects. Instead, we use axes parallel to the axes of the camera frame when computing the relative rotation (Camera Coordinate in Fig. 4(c)). By doing so, the network can be trained to estimate the relative rotation independently of the coordinate frame of the 3D object model.

To estimate the relative translation, let $\mathbf{t}_{\text{tgt}} = (x_{\text{tgt}}, y_{\text{tgt}}, z_{\text{tgt}})$ and $\mathbf{t}_{\text{src}} = (x_{\text{src}}, y_{\text{src}}, z_{\text{src}})$ be the target translation and the source translation. Then a straightforward way to represent it is $\mathbf{t}_\Delta = (\Delta_x, \Delta_y, \Delta_z) = \mathbf{t}_{\text{tgt}} - \mathbf{t}_{\text{src}}$. However, it is not easy for the network to estimate the relative translation in 3D space given only 2D images without depth information. The network has to recognize the size of the object, and map the translation in 2D space to 3D according to the object size. Such a representation is not only difficult for the network to learn, but also has problems when dealing with uknown objects or objects with similar appearance but different sizes. Instead of training the network to directly regress to the vector in the 3D space, we propose to regress to the object changes in the 2D image space. Specifically, we train the network to regress to the relative translation $\mathbf{t}_\Delta = (v_x, v_y, v_z)$, where v_x and v_y denote the number of pixels the object should move along the image x-axis and y-axis and v_z is the scale change of the object:

$$
\begin{aligned}
v_x &= f_x(x_{\mathrm{tgt}}/z_{\mathrm{tgt}} - x_{\mathrm{src}}/z_{\mathrm{src}}), \\
v_y &= f_y(y_{\mathrm{tgt}}/z_{\mathrm{tgt}} - y_{\mathrm{src}}/z_{\mathrm{src}}), \\
v_z &= \log(z_{\mathrm{src}}/z_{\mathrm{tgt}}),
\end{aligned}
\tag{2}
$$

where f_x and f_y denote the focal lengths of the camera. The scale change v_z is defined to be independent of the absolute object size or distance by using the ratio between the distances of the rendered and observed object. We use logarithm for v_z to make sure that value zero corresponds to no change in scale or distance. Considering the fact that f_x and f_y are constant for a specific dataset, we simply fix it to 1 in training and testing the network.

Our representation of the relative transformation has several advantages. First, rotation does not influence the estimation of translation, so that the translation no longer needs to offset the movement caused by rotation around the camera center. Second, the intermediate variables v_x, v_y, v_z represent simple translations and scale change in the image space. Third, this representation does not require any prior knowledge of the object. Using such a representation, the DeepIM network can operate independently of the actual size of the object and its internal model coordinate framework. It only has to learn to transform the rendered image such that it becomes more similar to the observed image.

3.4 Matching Loss

A straightforward way to train the pose estimation network is to use separate loss functions for rotation and translation. For example, we can use the angular distance between two rotations to measure the rotation error and use the L2 distance to measure the translation error. However, using two different loss functions for rotation and translation suffers from the difficulty of balancing the two losses. [12] proposed a geometric reprojection error as the loss function for pose regression that computes the average distance between the 2D projections of 3D points in the scene using the ground truth pose and the estimated pose. Considering the fact that we want to accurately predict the object pose in 3D, we introduce a modified version of the geometric reprojection loss in [12], and we call it the Point Matching Loss. Given the ground truth pose $\mathbf{p} = [\mathbf{R}|\mathbf{t}]$ and the estimated pose $\hat{\mathbf{p}} = [\hat{\mathbf{R}}|\hat{\mathbf{t}}]$, the point matching loss is computed as:

$$
L_{\mathrm{pose}}(\mathbf{p}, \hat{\mathbf{p}}) = \frac{1}{n} \sum_{i=1}^{n} L_1\big((\mathbf{R}\mathbf{x}_i + \mathbf{t}) - (\hat{\mathbf{R}}\mathbf{x}_i + \hat{\mathbf{t}})\big),
\tag{3}
$$

where $\mathbf{x}_i$ denotes a randomly selected 3D point on the object model and n is the total number of points (we choose 3,000 points in our experiments). The point matching loss computes the average L1 distance between 3D points transformed by the ground truth pose and the estimate pose. In this way, it measures how the transformed 3D models match against each other for pose estimation.

3.5 Training and Testing

In training, we assume that we have 3D object models and images annotated with ground truth 6D object poses. By adding noises to the ground truth poses as the initial poses, we can generate the required observed and rendered inputs to the network along with the pose target output that is the pose difference between the ground truth pose and the noisy pose. Then we can train the network to predict the relative transformation between the initial pose and the target pose.

During testing, we find that the iterative pose refinement can significantly improve the accuracy. To see, let $\mathbf{p}^{(i)}$ be the pose estimate after the i-th iteration of the network. If the initial pose estimate $\mathbf{p}^{(0)}$ is relatively far from the correct pose, the rendered image $\mathbf{x}_{\text{rend}}(\mathbf{p}^{(0)})$ may have only little viewpoint overlap with the observed image $\mathbf{x}_{\text{obs}}$. In such cases, it is very difficult to accurately estimate the relative pose transformation $\Delta\mathbf{p}^{(0)}$ directly. This task is even harder if the network has no priori knowledge about the object to be matched. In general, it is reasonable to assume that if the network improves the pose estimate $\mathbf{p}^{(i+1)}$ by updating $\mathbf{p}^{(i)}$ with $\Delta\mathbf{p}^{(i)}$ in the i-th iteration, then the image rendered according to this new estimate, $\mathbf{x}_{\text{rend}}(\mathbf{p}^{(i+1)})$ is also more similar to the observed image $\mathbf{x}_{\text{obs}}$ than $\mathbf{x}_{\text{rend}}(\mathbf{p}^{(i)})$ was in the previous iteration, thereby providing input that can be matched more accurately.

However, we found that, if we train the network to regress the relative pose in a single step, the estimates of the trained network do not improve over multiple iterations in testing. To generate a more realistic data distribution for training similar to testing, we perform multiple iterations during training as well. Specifically, for each training image and pose, we apply the transformation predicted from the network to the pose and use the transformed pose estimate as another training example for the network in the next iteration. By repeating this process multiple times, the training data better represents the test distribution and the trained network also achieves significantly better results during iterative testing (such an approach has also proven useful for iterative hand pose matching [19]).

4 Experiments

We conduct extensive experiments on the LINEMOD dataset [9] and the Occlusion LINEMOD dataset [2] to evaluate our DeepIM framework for 6D object pose estimation. We test different properties of DeepIM and show that it surpasses other RGB-only methods by a large margin. We also show that our network can be applied to pose matching of unseen objects during training.

4.1 Implementation Details

Training: We use the pre-trained FlowNetSimple [6] to initialize the weights in our network. Weights of the new layers are randomly initialized, except for the additional weights in the first conv layer that deals with the input masks and the fully-connected layer that predicts the translation, which are initialized with zeros. Other than predicting the pose transformation, the network also predicts the optical flow and the foreground mask. Although including the two additional losses in training does not increase the pose estimation performance, we found that they help to make the training more stable. Specifically, we use the optical flow loss L_{flow} as in FlowNet [6] and the sigmoid cross-entropy loss as the mask loss L_{mask}. Two deconvolutional blocks in FlowNet are inherited to produce the feature map used for the mask and the optical flow prediction, whose spatial scale is 0.0625. Two 1×1 convolutional layers with output channel 1 (mask prediction) and 2 (flow prediction) are appended after this feature map. The predictions are then bilinearly up-sampled to the original image size (480×640) to compute losses. The overall loss is $L = \alpha L_{pose} + \beta L_{flow} + \gamma L_{mask}$, where we use $\alpha = 0.1$, $\beta = 0.25$, $\gamma = 0.03$ throughout the experiments (except some of our ablation studies). Each training batch contains 16 images. We train the network with 4 GPUs where each GPU processes 4 images. We generate 4 items for each image as described in Sect. 3.1: two images and two masks. The observed mask is randomly dilated with no more than 10 pixels to avoid over-fitting.

Testing: The mask prediction branch and the optical flow branch are removed during testing. Since there is no ground truth segmentation of the object in testing, we use the tightest bounding box of the rendered mask m_{rend} instead, so the network searches the neighborhood near the estimated pose to find the target object to match. Unless specified, we use the pose estimates from PoseCNN [29] as the initial poses. Our DeepIM network runs at 12 fps per object using an NVIDIA 1080 Ti GPU with 2 iterations during testing.

4.2 Evaluation Metrics

We use the following three evaluation metrics for 6D object pose estimation. (i) The *5°, 5 cm* metric considers an estimated pose to be correct if its rotation error is within 5° and the translation error is below 5 cm. (ii) The *6D Pose* metric [9] computes the average distance between the 3D model points transformed using the estimated pose and the ground truth pose. For symmetric objects, we use the closet point distance in computing the average distance. An estimated pose is correct if the average distance is within 10% of the 3D model diameter. (iii) The *2D Projection* metric computes the average distance of the 3D model points projected onto the image using the estimated pose and the ground truth pose. An estimated pose is correct if the average distance is smaller than 5 pixels.

Table 1. Ablation study of the number of iterations during training and testing.

train iter	init	1			2			4		
test iter		1	2	4	1	2	4	1	2	4
5 cm 5°	19.4	57.4	58.8	54.6	76.3	86.2	86.7	70.2	83.7	85.2
6D Pose	62.7	77.9	79.0	76.1	83.1	88.7	89.1	80.9	87.6	88.6
Proj. 2D	70.2	92.4	92.6	89.7	96.1	97.8	97.6	94.6	97.4	97.5

4.3 Experiments on the LINEMOD Dataset

The LINEMOD dataset contains 15 objects. We train and test our method on 13 of them as other methods in the literature. We follow the procedure in [2] to split the dataset into the training and test sets, with around 200 images for each object in the training set and 1,000 images in the test set.

Training Strategy: For every image, we generate 10 random poses near the ground truth pose, resulting in 2,000 training samples for each object in the training set. Furthermore, we generate 10,000 synthetic images for each object where the pose distribution is similar to the real training set. For each synthetic image, we generate 1 random pose near its ground truth pose. Thus, we have a total of 12,000 training samples for each object in training. The background of a synthetic image is replaced with a randomly chosen indoor image from PASCAL VOC [7]. We train the networks for 8 epochs with initial learning rate 0.0001. The learning rate is divided by 10 after the 4th and 6th epoch, respectively.

Ablation Study on Iterative Training and Testing: Table 1 shows the results that use different numbers of iterations during training and testing. The networks with *train_iter* = 1 and *train_iter* = 2 are trained with 32 and 16 epochs respectively to keep the total number of updates the same as *train_iter* = 4. The table shows that without iterative training (*train_iter* = 1), multiple iteration testing does not improve, potentially even making the results worse (*test_iter* = 4). We believe that the reason is due to the fact that the network is not trained with enough rendered poses close to their ground truth poses. The table also shows that one more iteration during training and testing already improves the results by a large margin. The network trained with 2 iterations and tested with 2 iterations is slightly better than the one trained with 4 iterations and tested with 4 iterations. This may be because the LINEMOD dataset is not sufficiently difficult to generate further improvements by using 3 or 4 iterations. Since it is not straightforward to determine how many iterations to use in each dataset, we use 4 iterations during training and testing in all other experiments.

Ablation Study on the Zoom in Strategy, Network Structures, Transformation Representations, and Loss Functions: Table 2 summarizes the ablation studies on various aspects of DeepIM. The "zoom" column indicates whether the network uses full images as its input or zoomed in bounding boxes up-sampled to the original image size. Comparing rows 5 and 7 shows that the higher resolution achieved via zooming in provides very significant improvements.

Table 2. Ablation study on different design choices of the DeepIM network on the LINEMOD dataset.

Row	Methods					5 cm 5°	6D Pose	Proj. 2D
	Zoom	Regressor	Network	Coordinate	Loss			
1	✓	-	sep.	camera	PM	83.3	87.6	96.2
2	✓	sep.	shared	model	PM	79.2	87.5	95.4
3	✓	sep.	shared	camera	PM	86.6	89.5	96.7
4		shared	shared	naive	PM	16.6	44.3	62.5
5		shared	shared	camera	PM	38.3	65.2	80.8
6	✓	shared	shared	camera	Dist	86.5	79.2	96.2
7	✓	shared	shared	camera	PM	85.2	88.6	97.5

"Regressor": We train the DeepIM network jointly over all objects, generating a pose transformation independent of the specific input object (labeled "shared" in "regressor" column). Alternatively, we could train a different 6D pose regressor for each individual object by using a separate fully connected layer for each object after the final FC256 layer shown in Fig. 3. This setting is labeled as "sep." in Table 2. Comparing rows 3 and 7 shows that both approaches provide nearly indistinguishable results. But the shared network provides some efficiency gains.

"Network": Similarly, instead of training a single network over all objects, we could train separate networks, one for each object as in [20]. Comparing row 1 to 7 shows that a single, shared network provides better results than individual ones, which indicates that training on multiple objects can help the network learn a more general representation for matching.

"Coordinate": This column investigates the impact of our choice of coordinate frame to reason about object transformations, as described in Fig. 4. The row labeled "naive" provides results when choosing the camera frame of reference as the representation for the object pose, rows labeled "model" move the center of rotation to the object model and choose the object model coordinate frame to reason about rotations, and the "camera" rows provide our approach of moving the center into the object model while keeping the camera coordinate frame for rotations. Comparing rows 2 and 3 shows that reasoning in the camera rotation frame provides slight improvements. Furthermore, it should be noted that only our "camera" approach is able to operate on unseen objects. Comparing rows 4 and 5 shows the large improvements our representation achieves over the naive approach of reasoning fully in the camera frame of reference.

"Loss": The traditional loss for pose estimation is specified by the distance ("Dist") between the estimated and ground truth 6D pose coordinates, i.e., angular distance for rotation and euclidean distance for translation. Comparing rows

706 Y. Li et al.

6 and 7 indicates that our point matching loss ("PM") provides significantly better results especially on the 6D pose metric, which is the most important measure for reasoning in 3D space.

Application to Different Initial Pose Estimation Networks: Table 3 provides results when we initialize DeepIM with two different pose estimation networks. The first one is PoseCNN [29], and the second one is a simple 6D pose estimation method based on Faster R-CNN [22]. Specifically, we use the bounding box of the object from Faster R-CNN to estimate the 3D translation of the object. The center of the bounding box is treated as the center of the object. The distance of the object is estimated by maximizing the overlap of the projection of the 3D object model with the bounding box. To estimate the 3D rotation of the object, we add a rotation regression branch to Faster R-CNN as in PoseCNN. As we can see in Table 3, our network achieves very similar pose estimation accuracy even when initialized with the estimates from the extension of Faster R-CNN, which are not as accurate as those provided by PoseCNN [29].

Table 3. Ablation study on two different methods for generating initial poses on the LINEMOD dataset.

Method	PoseCNN	PoseCNN+OURS	Faster R-CNN	Faster R-CNN+OURS
5 cm 5°	19.4	85.2	11.9	83.4
6D Pose	62.7	88.6	33.1	86.9
Proj. 2D	70.2	97.5	20.9	95.7

Comparison with the State-of-the-Art 6D Pose Estimation Methods: Table 4 shows the comparison with the best color-only techniques on the LINEMOD dataset. DeepIM achieves very significant improvements over all prior methods, even those that also deploy refinement steps (BB8 [20] and SSD-6D [11]).

Table 4. Comparison with state-of-the-art methods on the LINEMOD dataset

Methods	[2]	BB8 w ref. [20]	SSD-6D w ref. [11]	Tekin et al. [26]	PoseCNN [29]	PoseCNN [29] +OURS
5 cm 5°	40.6	69.0	-	-	19.4	**85.2**
6D Pose	50.2	62.7	79	55.95	62.7	**88.6**
Proj. 2D	73.7	89.3	-	90.37	70.2	**97.5**

4.4 Experiments on the Occlusion LINEMOD Dataset

The Occlusion LINEMOD dataset proposed in [2] shares the same images used in LINEMOD [9], but annotated 8 objects in one video that are heavily occluded.

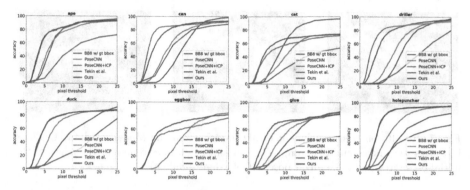

Fig. 5. Comparison with state-of-the-art methods on the Occlusion LINEMOD dataset [2]. Accuracies are measured via the Projection 2D metric.

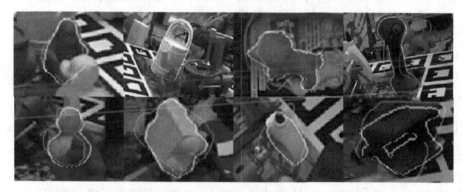

Fig. 6. Examples of refined poses on the Occlusion LILNEMOD dataset using the results from PoseCNN [29] as initial poses. The red and green lines represent the silhouettes of the initial estimates and our refined poses, respectively.

Training: For every real image, we generate 10 random poses as described in Sect. 4.3. Considering the fact that most of the training data lacks occlusions, we generated about 20,000 synthetic images with multiple objects in each image. By doing so, every object has around 12,000 images which are partially occluded, and a total of 22,000 images for each object in training. We perform the same background replacement and training procedure as in the LINEMOD dataset.

Comparison with the State-of-the-Art Methods: The comparison between our method and other RGB-only methods is shown in Fig. 5. We only show the plots with accuracies on the 2D Projection metric because these are the only results reported in [20] and [26] (results for eggbox and glue use a symmetric version of this accuracy). It can be seen that our method greatly improves the pose accuracy generated by PoseCNN and surpasses all other RGB-only methods by a large margin. It should be noted that BB8 [20] achieves the reported results only when using ground truth bounding boxes during testing. Our method is

Fig. 7. Results on pose refinement of 3D models from the ModelNet dataset. These instances were not seen in training. The red and green lines represent the edges of the initial estimates and our refined poses. (Color figure online)

even competitive with the results that use depth information and ICP to refine the estimates of PoseCNN. Figure 6 shows some pose refinement results from our method on the Occlusion LINEMOD dataset.

4.5 Application to Unseen Objects and Unseen Categories

As stated in Sect. 3.3, we designed the untangled pose representation such that it is independent of the coordinate frame and the size of a specific 3D object model. Therefore, the pose transformations correspond to operations in the image space. This opens the question whether DeepIM can refine the poses of objects that are not included in the training set. In this experiment, we use the 3D models of airplanes, cars and chairs from the ModelNet dataset [28]. For each of these categories, we train a network on no more than 200 3D models and test its performance on 70 unseen 3D models from the same category. For training, we generate 50 images for each model and train the network for 4 epochs. We found that our network can perform accurate refinement on these unseen models. See Fig. 7 for example results. We also tested our framework on refining the poses of unseen object categories, where the training categories and the test categories are completely different. Please see the supplementary material for more details.

5 Conclusion

In this work we introduce DeepIM, a novel framework for iterative pose matching using color images only. Given an initial 6D pose estimation of an object, we have designed a new deep neural network to directly output a *relative* pose transformation that improves the pose estimate. The network automatically learns to match object poses during training. We introduce an untangled pose representation that is also independent of the object size and the coordinate frame of the 3D object model. In this way, the network can even match poses of unseen objects, as shown in our experiments. Our method significantly outperforms state-of-the-art 6D pose estimation methods using color images only and provides performance close to methods that use depth images for pose refinement, such as using the iterative closest point algorithm. Example visualizations of our results on LINEMOD, ModelNet, and T-LESS can be found here: https://rse-lab.cs.washington.edu/projects/deepim.

This work opens up various directions for future research. For instance, we expect that a stereo version of DeepIM could further improve pose accuracy. Furthermore, DeepIM indicates that it is possible to produce accurate 6D pose estimates using color images only, enabling the use of cameras that capture high resolution images at high frame rates with a large field of view, providing estimates useful for applications such as robot manipulation.

Acknowledgments. This work was funded in part by a Siemens grant. We would also like to thank NVIDIA for generously providing the DGX station used for this research via the NVIDIA Robotics Lab and the UW NVIDIA AI Lab (NVAIL). This work was also Supported by National Key R&D Program of China 2017YFB1002202, NSFC Projects 61620106005, 61325003, Beijing Municipal Sci. & Tech. Commission Z181100008918014 and THU Initiative Scientific Research Program.

References

1. Brachmann, E., Krull, A., Michel, F., Gumhold, S., Shotton, J., Rother, C.: Learning 6D object pose estimation using 3D object coordinates. In: Fleet, D., Pajdla, T., Schiele, B., Tuytelaars, T. (eds.) ECCV 2014. LNCS, vol. 8690, pp. 536–551. Springer, Cham (2014). https://doi.org/10.1007/978-3-319-10605-2_35
2. Brachmann, E., Michel, F., Krull, A., Ying Yang, M., Gumhold, S., Rother, C.: Uncertainty-driven 6D pose estimation of objects and scenes from a single RGB image. In: IEEE Conference on Computer Vision and Pattern Recognition (CVPR), pp. 3364–3372 (2016)
3. Carreira, J., Agrawal, P., Fragkiadaki, K., Malik, J.: Human pose estimation with iterative error feedback. In: IEEE Conference on Computer Vision and Pattern Recognition (CVPR) (2016)
4. Collet, A., Martinez, M., Srinivasa, S.S.: The MOPED framework: object recognition and pose estimation for manipulation. Int. J. Robot. Res. (IJRR) 30(10), 1284–1306 (2011)
5. Costante, G., Ciarfuglia, T.A.: LS-VO: learning dense optical subspace for robust visual odometry estimation. IEEE Robot. Autom. Lett. 3(3), 1735–1742 (2018)
6. Dosovitskiy, A., et al.: FlowNet: learning optical flow with convolutional networks. In: IEEE International Conference on Computer Vision (ICCV), pp. 2758–2766 (2015)
7. Everingham, M., Van Gool, L., Williams, C.K., Winn, J., Zisserman, A.: The pascal visual object classes (VOC) challenge. Int. J. Comput. Vis. (ICCV) 88(2), 303–338 (2010)
8. Girshick, R.: Fast R-CNN. In: IEEE International Conference on Computer Vision (ICCV), pp. 1440–1448 (2015)
9. Hinterstoisser, S., et al.: Model based training, detection and pose estimation of texture-less 3D objects in heavily cluttered scenes. In: Lee, K.M., Matsushita, Y., Rehg, J.M., Hu, Z. (eds.) ACCV 2012. LNCS, vol. 7724, pp. 548–562. Springer, Heidelberg (2013). https://doi.org/10.1007/978-3-642-37331-2_42

10. Hodan, T., Haluza, P., Obdržálek, Š., Matas, J., Lourakis, M., Zabulis, X.: T-less: an RGB-D dataset for 6D pose estimation of texture-less objects. In: IEEE Winter Conference on Applications of Computer Vision (WACV), pp. 880–888. IEEE (2017)

11. Kehl, W., Manhardt, F., Tombari, F., Ilic, S., Navab, N.: SSD-6D: making RGB-based 3D detection and 6D pose estimation great again. In: IEEE Conference on Computer Vision and Pattern Recognition (CVPR), pp. 1521–1529 (2017)

12. Kendall, A., Cipolla, R.: Geometric loss functions for camera pose regression with deep learning. In: IEEE Conference on Computer Vision and Pattern Recognition (CVPR) (2017)

13. Krull, A., Brachmann, E., Michel, F., Ying Yang, M., Gumhold, S., Rother, C.: Learning analysis-by-synthesis for 6D pose estimation in RGB-D images. In: IEEE International Conference on Computer Vision (ICCV), pp. 954–962 (2015)

14. Liu, W., et al.: SSD: single shot multibox detector. In: Leibe, B., Matas, J., Sebe, N., Welling, M. (eds.) ECCV 2016. LNCS, vol. 9905, pp. 21–37. Springer, Cham (2016). https://doi.org/10.1007/978-3-319-46448-0_2

15. Long, J., Shelhamer, E., Darrell, T.: Fully convolutional networks for semantic segmentation. In: IEEE Conference on Computer Vision and Pattern Recognition (CVPR), pp. 3431–3440 (2015)

16. Lowe, D.G.: Object recognition from local scale-invariant features. In: IEEE International Conference on Computer Vision (ICCV), vol. 2, pp. 1150–1157 (1999)

17. Michel, F., et al.: Global hypothesis generation for 6D object pose estimation. In: IEEE Conference on Computer Vision and Pattern Recognition (CVPR) (2017)

18. Mousavian, A., Anguelov, D., Flynn, J., Košecká, J.: 3D bounding box estimation using deep learning and geometry. In: IEEE Conference on Computer Vision and Pattern Recognition (CVPR), pp. 5632–5640 (2017)

19. Oberweger, M., Wohlhart, P., Lepetit, V.: Training a feedback loop for hand pose estimation. In: IEEE International Conference on Computer Vision (ICCV) (2015)

20. Rad, M., Lepetit, V.: BB8: a scalable, accurate, robust to partial occlusion method for predicting the 3D poses of challenging objects without using depth. In: IEEE International Conference on Computer Vision (ICCV) (2017)

21. Redmon, J., Divvala, S., Girshick, R., Farhadi, A.: You only look once: unified, real-time object detection. In: IEEE Conference on Computer Vision and Pattern Recognition (CVPR), pp. 779–788 (2016)

22. Ren, S., He, K., Girshick, R., Sun, J.: Faster R-CNN: towards real-time object detection with region proposal networks. In: Advances in Neural Information Processing Systems (NIPS) (2015)

23. Rothganger, F., Lazebnik, S., Schmid, C., Ponce, J.: 3D object modeling and recognition using local affine-invariant image descriptors and multi-view spatial constraints. Int. J. Comput. Vis. (IJCV) 66(3), 231–259 (2006)

24. Saxena, A., Pandya, H., Kumar, G., Gaud, A., Krishna, K.M.: Exploring convolutional networks for end-to-end visual servoing. In: IEEE International Conference on Robotics and Automation (ICRA), pp. 3817–3823 (2017)

25. Simonyan, K., Zisserman, A.: Very deep convolutional networks for large-scale image recognition. arXiv preprint arXiv:1409.1556 (2014)

26. Tekin, B., Sinha, S.N., Fua, P.: Real-time seamless single shot 6D object pose prediction. arXiv preprint arXiv:1711.08848 (2017)

27. Tjaden, H., Schwanecke, U., Schömer, E.: Real-time monocular pose estimation of 3D objects using temporally consistent local color histograms. In: IEEE Conference on Computer Vision and Pattern Recognition (CVPR), pp. 124–132 (2017)

28. Wu, Z., et al.: 3D shapenets: a deep representation for volumetric shapes. In: IEEE conference on Computer Vision and Pattern Recognition (CVPR), pp. 1912–1920 (2015)
29. Xiang, Y., Schmidt, T., Narayanan, V., Fox, D.: PoseCNN: a convolutional neural network for 6D object pose estimation in cluttered scenes. arXiv preprint arXiv:1711.00199 (2017)
30. Zeng, A., et al.: Multi-view self-supervised deep learning for 6D pose estimation in the Amazon picking challenge. In: IEEE International Conference on Robotics and Automation (ICRA), pp. 1386–1383 (2017)

Implicit 3D Orientation Learning for 6D Object Detection from RGB Images

Martin Sundermeyer[1](✉)(iD), Zoltan-Csaba Marton[1](✉)(iD),
Maximilian Durner[1](✉)(iD), Manuel Brucker[1](✉)(iD), and Rudolph Triebel[1,2](✉)(iD)

[1] German Aerospace Center (DLR), 82234 Wessling, Germany
{martin.sundermeyer,zoltan.marton,maximilian.durner,
manuel.brucker,rudolph.triebel}@dlr.de
[2] Technical University of Munich, 80333 Munich, Germany

Abstract. We propose a real-time RGB-based pipeline for object detection and 6D pose estimation. Our novel 3D orientation estimation is based on a variant of the Denoising Autoencoder that is trained on simulated views of a 3D model using Domain Randomization.

This so-called Augmented Autoencoder has several advantages over existing methods: It does not require real, pose-annotated training data, generalizes to various test sensors and inherently handles object and view symmetries. Instead of learning an explicit mapping from input images to object poses, it provides an implicit representation of object orientations defined by samples in a latent space. Experiments on the T-LESS and LineMOD datasets show that our method outperforms similar model-based approaches and competes with state-of-the art approaches that require real pose-annotated images.

Keywords: 6D object detection · Pose estimation
Domain Randomization · Autoencoder · Synthetic data
Pose ambiguity · Symmetries

1 Introduction

One of the most important components of modern computer vision systems for applications such as mobile robotic manipulation and augmented reality is a reliable and fast 6D object detection module. Although, there are very encouraging recent results [12,15,17,38,40], a flexible, general, robust and fast solution is not available, yet. The reasons for this are manifold. First and foremost, current solutions are not robust enough against typical challenges such as object occlusions, different kinds of background clutter, and dynamic changes of the environment. Second, existing methods often require certain object properties

Electronic supplementary material The online version of this chapter (https://doi.org/10.1007/978-3-030-01231-1_43) contains supplementary material, which is available to authorized users.

V. Ferrari et al. (Eds.): ECCV 2018, LNCS 11210, pp. 712–729, 2018.
https://doi.org/10.1007/978-3-030-01231-1_43

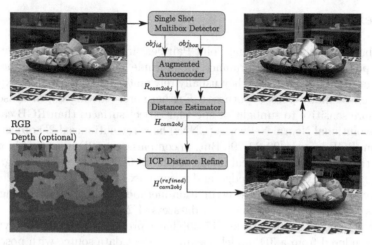

Fig. 1. Our 6D object detection pipeline with homogeneous transformation $H_{cam2obj} \in \mathcal{R}^{4x4}$ (top-right) and depth-refined result $H_{cam2obj}^{(refined)}$ (bottom-right)

such as enough textural surface structure or an asymmetric shape to avoid confusions. And finally, current systems are not efficient in terms of run-time and in the amount of annotated training data they require.

Therefore, we propose a novel approach that directly addresses these issues. Concretely, our method operates on single RGB images, which significantly increases the usability as no depth information is required. We note though that depth maps may be incorporated optionally to refine the estimation. As a first step, we apply a Single Shot Multibox Detector (SSD) [22] that provides object bounding boxes and identifiers. On the resulting scene crops, we employ our novel 3D orientation estimation algorithm, which is based on a previously trained deep network architecture. While deep networks are also used in existing approaches, our approach differs in that we do not explicitly learn from 3D pose annotations during training. Instead, we *implicitly* learn representations from rendered 3D model views. This is accomplished by training a generalized version of the Denoising Autoencoder [39], that we call *'Augmented Autoencoder (AAE)'*, using a novel Domain Randomization [36] strategy. Our approach has several advantages: First, since the training is independent from concrete representations of object orientations within $SO(3)$ (e.g. quaternions), we can handle ambiguous poses caused by symmetric views because we avoid one-to-many mappings from images to orientations. Second, we learn representations that specifically encode 3D orientations while achieving robustness against occlusion, cluttered backgrounds and generalizing to different environments and test sensors. Finally, the AAE does not require any real pose-annotated training data. Instead, it is trained to encode 3D model views in a self-supervised way, overcoming the need of a large pose-annotated dataset. A schematic overview of the approach is shown in Fig. 1.

2   Related Work

Depth-based methods (e.g. using Point Pair Features (PPF) [12,38]) have shown robust pose estimation performance on multiple datasets, winning the SIXD challenge 2017 [14]. However, they usually rely on the computationally expensive evaluation of many pose hypotheses. Furthermore, existing depth sensors are often more sensitive to sunlight or specular object surfaces than RGB cameras.

Convolutional Neural Networks (CNNs) have revolutionized 2D object detection from RGB images [20,22,29]. But, in comparison to 2D bounding box annotation, the effort of labeling real images with full 6D object poses is magnitudes higher, requires expert knowledge and a complex setup [15]. Nevertheless, the majority of learning-based pose estimation methods use real labeled images and are thus restricted to pose-annotated datasets [4,28,35,40].

In consequence, some works [17,40] have proposed to train on synthetic images rendered from a 3D model, yielding a great data source with pose labels free of charge. However, naive training on synthetic data does not typically generalize to real test images. Therefore, a main challenge is to bridge the domain gap that separates simulated views from real camera recordings.

2.1   Simulation to Reality Transfer

There exist three major strategies to generalize from synthetic to real data:

Photo-Realistic Rendering of object views and backgrounds has shown mixed generalization performance for tasks like object detection and viewpoint estimation [25,26,30,34]. It is suitable for simple environments and performs well if jointly trained with a relatively small amount of real annotated images. However, photo-realistic modeling is always imperfect and requires much effort.

Domain Adaptation (DA) [5] refers to leveraging training data from a source domain to a target domain of which a small portion of labeled data (supervised DA) or unlabeled data (unsupervised DA) is available. Generative Adversarial Networks (GANs) have been deployed for unsupervised DA by generating realistic from synthetic images to train classifiers [33], 3D pose estimators [3] and grasping algorithms [2]. While constituting a promising approach, GANs often yield fragile training results. Supervised DA can lower the need for real annotated data, but does not abstain from it.

Domain Randomization (DR) builds upon the hypothesis that by training a model on rendered views in a variety of semi-realistic settings (augmented with random lighting conditions, backgrounds, saturation, etc.), it will also generalize to real images. Tobin et al. [36] demonstrated the potential of the Domain Randomization (DR) paradigm for 3D shape detection using CNNs. Hinterstoisser et al. [13] showed that by training only the head network of FasterRCNN [29] with randomized synthetic views of a textured 3D model, it also generalizes well to real images. It must be noted, that their rendering is almost photo-realistic as the textured 3D models have very high quality. Recently, Kehl et al. [17] pioneered an end-to-end CNN, called 'SSD6D', for 6D object detection that uses a moderate DR strategy to utilize synthetic training data. The authors render views of textured 3D object reconstructions at random poses on top of MS COCO background images [21] while varying brightness and contrast. This lets the network generalize to real images and enables 6D detection at 10 Hz. Like us, for very accurate distance estimation they rely on Iterative Closest Point (ICP) post-processing using depth data. In contrast, we do not treat 3D orientation estimation as a classification task.

2.2 Learning Representations of 3D Orientations

We describe the difficulties of training with fixed SO(3) parameterizations which will motivate the learning of object-specific representations.

Regression. Since rotations live in a continuous space, it seems natural to directly regress a fixed SO(3) parameterizations like quaternions. However, representational constraints and pose ambiguities can introduce convergence issues [32]. In practice, direct regression approaches for full 3D object orientation estimation have not been very successful [23].

Classification of 3D object orientations requires a discretization of SO(3). Even rather coarse intervals of $\sim 5^o$ lead to over 50.000 possible classes. Since each class appears only sparsely in the training data, this hinders convergence. In SSD6D [17] the 3D orientation is learned by separately classifying a discretized viewpoint and in-plane rotation, thus reducing the complexity to $\mathcal{O}(n^2)$. However, for non-canonical views, e.g. if an object is seen from above, a change of viewpoint can be nearly equivalent to a change of in-plane rotation which yields ambiguous class combinations. In general, the relation between different orientations is ignored when performing one-hot classification.

Symmetries are a severe issue when relying on fixed representations of 3D orientations since they cause pose ambiguities (Fig. 2). If not manually addressed, identical training images can have different orientation labels assigned which can significantly disturb the learning process. In order to cope with ambiguous objects, most approaches in literature are manually adapted [9,17,28,40]. The strategies reach from ignoring one axis of rotation [9,40] over adapting the discretization according to the object [17] to the training of an extra CNN to predict symmetries [28]. These depict tedious, manual ways to filter out object symmetries (2a) in advance, but treating ambiguities due to self-occlusions (2b) and occlusions (2c) are harder to address. Symmetries do not only affect regression and classification methods, but any learning-based algorithm that discriminates object views solely by fixed SO(3) representations.

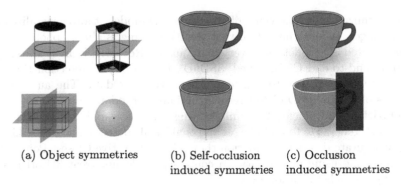

(a) Object symmetries   (b) Self-occlusion   (c) Occlusion
                          induced symmetries   induced symmetries

Fig. 2. Causes of pose ambiguities

Descriptor Learning can be used to learn a representation that relates object views in a low-dimensional space. Wohlhart et al. [40] introduced a CNN-based descriptor learning approach using a triplet loss that minimizes/maximizes the Euclidean distance between similar/dissimilar object orientations. Although mixing in synthetic data, the training also relies on pose-annotated sensor data. Furthermore, the approach is not immune against symmetries because the loss can be dominated by ambiguous object views that appear the same but have opposite orientations. Baltnas et al. [1] extended this work by enforcing proportionality between descriptor and pose distances. They acknowledge the problem of object symmetries by weighting the pose distance loss with the depth difference of the object at the considered poses. This heuristic increases the accuracy on symmetric objects with respect to [40]. Our work is also based on learning descriptors, but we train self-supervised Augmented Autoencoders (AAEs) such that the learning process itself is independent of any fixed SO(3) representation. This means that descriptors are learned solely based on the appearance of object views and thus symmetrical ambiguities are inherently regarded. Assigning 3D orientations to the descriptors only happens after the training. Furthermore, unlike [1,40] we can abstain from the use of real labeled data for training.

Kehl et al. [18] train an Autoencoder architecture on random RGB-D scene patches from the LineMOD dataset [10]. At test time, descriptors from scene and object patches are compared to find the 6D pose. Since the approach requires the evaluation of a lot of patches, it takes about 670ms per prediction. Furthermore, using local patches means to ignore holistic relations between object features which is crucial if few texture exists. Instead we train on holistic object views and explicitly learn domain invariance.

3   Method

In the following, we mainly focus on the novel 3D orientation estimation technique based on the Augmented Autoencoder (AAE).

1   Autoencoders

he original Autoencoder (AE), introduced by Hinton et al. [31], is a dimen-
onality reduction technique for high dimensional data such as images, audio or
pth. It consists of an Encoder Φ and a Decoder Ψ, both arbitrary learnable
nction approximators which are usually neural networks. The training objec-
ve is to reconstruct the input $x \in \mathcal{R}^D$ after passing through a low-dimensional
ottleneck, referred to as the latent representation $z \in \mathcal{R}^n$ with $n \ll D$:

$$\hat{x} = (\Psi \circ \Phi)(x) = \Psi(z) \tag{1}$$

he per-sample loss is simply a sum over the pixel-wise L2 distance

$$\ell_2 = \sum_{i \in \mathcal{D}} \parallel x_{(i)} - \hat{x}_{(i)} \parallel_2 \tag{2}$$

he resulting latent space can, for example, be used for unsupervised clustering.
enoising Autoencoders [39] have a modified training procedure. Here, artificial
ndom noise is applied to the input images $x \in \mathcal{R}^D$ while the reconstruction
rget stays clean. The trained model can be used to reconstruct denoised test
ages. But how is the latent representation affected?

ypothesis 1: *The Denoising AE produces latent representations which are
variant to noise because it facilitates the reconstruction of de-noised images.*
'e will demonstrate that this training strategy actually enforces invariance not
ly against noise but against a variety of different input augmentations. Finally,
allows us to bridge the domain gap between simulated and real data.

2   Augmented Autoencoder

he motivation behind the AAE is to control what the latent representation
icodes and which properties are ignored. We apply random augmentations
$augm(.)$ to the input images $x \in \mathcal{R}^D$ against which the encoding shall become
variant. The reconstruction target remains Eq. (2) but Eq. (1) becomes

$$\hat{x} = (\Psi \circ \Phi \circ f_{augm})(x) = (\Psi \circ \Phi)(x') = \Psi(z') \tag{3}$$

o make evident that **Hypothesis 1** holds for geometric transformations, we
arn latent representations of binary images depicting a 2D square at different
ales, in-plane translations and rotations. Our goal is to encode only the in-
ane rotations $r \in [0, 2\pi]$ in a two dimensional latent space $z \in \mathcal{R}^2$ independent
 scale or translation. Figure 3 depicts the results after training a CNN-based
E architecture similar to the model in Fig. 5. It can be observed that the AEs
ained on reconstructing squares at fixed scale and translation (1) or random
ale and translation (2) do not clearly encode rotation alone, but are also sen-
tive to other latent factors. Instead, the encoding of the AAE (3) becomes
variant to translation and scale such that all squares with coinciding orien-
ation are mapped to the same code. Furthermore, the latent representation is

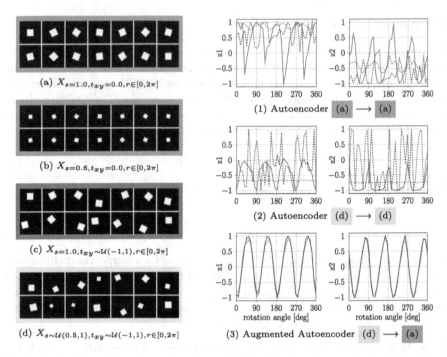

(a) $X_{s=1.0, t_{xy}=0.0, r \in [0, 2\pi]}$

(b) $X_{s=0.6, t_{xy}=0.0, r \in [0, 2\pi]}$

(c) $X_{s=1.0, t_{xy} \sim \mathcal{U}(-1,1), r \in [0, 2\pi]}$

(d) $X_{s \sim \mathcal{U}(0.5,1), t_{xy} \sim \mathcal{U}(-1,1), r \in [0, 2\pi]}$

(1) Autoencoder (a) $\longrightarrow$ (a)

(2) Autoencoder (d) $\longrightarrow$ (d)

(3) Augmented Autoencoder (d) $\longrightarrow$ (a)

Fig. 3. Left: 64×64 squares from four distributions (a, b, c and d) distinguished by scale (s) and translation (t_{xy}) that are used for training and testing [24]. Right: Normalized latent dimensions z_1 and z_2 for all rotations (r) of the distribution (a), (b) or (c) after training ordinary AEs (1), (2) and an AAE (3) to reconstruct squares of the same orientation.

much smoother and the latent dimensions imitate a shifted sine and cosine function with frequency $f = \frac{4}{2\pi}$ respectively. The reason is that the square has two perpendicular axes of symmetry, i.e. after rotating $\frac{\pi}{2}$ the square appears the same. This property of representing the orientation based on the appearance of an object rather than on a fixed parametrization is valuable to avoid ambiguities due to symmetries when teaching 3D object orientations.

3.3 Learning 3D Orientation from Synthetic Object Views

Our toy problem showed that we can explicitly learn representations of object in-plane rotations using a geometric augmentation technique. Applying the same geometric input augmentations we can encode the whole SO(3) space of views from a 3D object model (CAD or 3D reconstruction) while being robust against inaccurate object detections. However, the encoder would still be unable to relate image crops from real RGB sensors because (1) the 3D model and the real object differ, (2) simulated and real lighting conditions differ, (3) the network can't distinguish the object from background clutter and foreground occlusions. Instead of trying to imitate every detail of specific real sensor recordings in simulation we

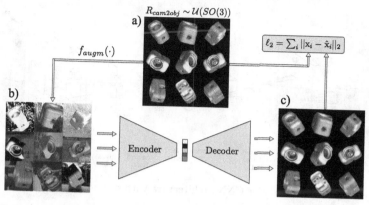

Fig. 4. Training process for the AAE; (a) reconstruction target batch x of uniformly sampled SO(3) object views; (b) geometric and color augmented input; (c) reconstruction $\hat{x}$ after 30000 iterations

propose a Domain Randomization (DR) technique within the AAE framework to make the encodings invariant to insignificant environment and sensor variations. The goal is that the trained encoder treats the differences to real camera images as just another irrelevant variation. Therefore, while keeping reconstruction targets clean, we randomly apply additional augmentations to the input training views: (1) rendering with random light positions and randomized diffuse and specular reflection (simple Phong model [27] in OpenGL), (2) inserting random background images from the Pascal VOC dataset [6], (3) varying image contrast, brightness, Gaussian blur and color distortions, (4) applying occlusions using random object masks or black squares. Figure 4 depicts an exemplary training process for synthetic views of object 5 from T-LESS [15].

3.4 Network Architecture and Training Details

The convolutional Autoencoder architecture that is used in our experiments is depicted in Fig. 5. We use a bootstrapped pixel-wise L2 loss which is only computed on the pixels with the largest errors (per image bootstrap factor $b = 4$). Thereby, finer details are reconstructed and the training does not converge to local minima. Using OpenGL, we render 20000 views of each object uniformly at random 3D orientations and constant distance along the camera axis (700 mm). The resulting images are quadratically cropped and resized to $128 \times 128 \times 3$ as shown in Fig. 4. All geometric and color input augmentations besides the rendering with random lighting are applied online during training at uniform random strength, parameters are found in the supplement. We use the Adam [19] optimizer with a learning rate of 2×10^{-4}, Xavier initialization [7], a batch size $= 64$ and 30000 iterations which takes $\sim$4 h on a single Nvidia Geforce GTX 1080.

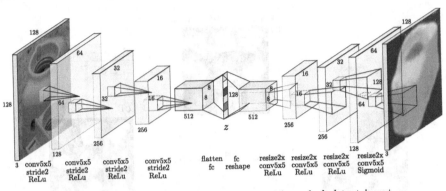

Fig. 5. Autoencoder CNN architecture with occluded test input

3.5 Codebook Creation and Test Procedure

After training, the AAE is able to extract a 3D object from real scene crops of many different camera sensors (Fig. 8). The clarity and orientation of the decoder reconstruction is an indicator of the encoding quality. To determine 3D object orientations from test scene crops we create a codebook (Fig. 6 (top)):

(1) Render clean, synthetic object views at equidistant viewpoints from a full view-sphere (based on a refined icosahedron [8])
(2) Rotate each view in-plane at fixed intervals to cover the whole SO(3)
(3) Create a codebook by generating latent codes $z \in \mathcal{R}^{128}$ for all resulting images and assigning their corresponding rotation $R_{cam2obj} \in \mathcal{R}^{3x3}$

At test time, the considered object(s) are first detected in an RGB scene. The area is quadratically cropped and resized to match the encoder input size. After encoding we compute the cosine similarity between the test code $z_{test} \in \mathcal{R}^{128}$ and all codes $z_i \in \mathcal{R}^{128}$ from the codebook:

$$cos_i = \frac{z_i \, z_{test}}{\|z_i\| \|z_{test}\|} \qquad (4)$$

The highest similarities are determined in a k-Nearest-Neighbor (kNN) search and the corresponding rotation matrices $\{R_{kNN}\}$ from the codebook are returned as estimates of the 3D object orientation. We use cosine similarity because (1) it can be very efficiently computed on a single GPU even for large codebooks. In our experiments we have 2562 equidistant viewpoints ×36 in-plane rotation = 92232 total entries. (2) We observed that, presumably due to the circular nature of rotations, scaling a latent test code does not change the object orientation of the decoder reconstruction (Fig. 7).

3.6 Extending to 6D Object Detection

Training the Object Detector. We finetune SSD with VGG16 base [22] using object recordings on black background from different viewpoints which

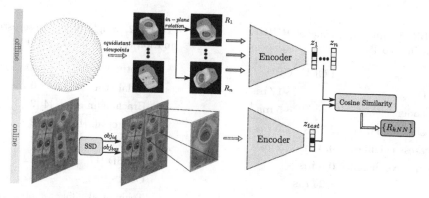

Fig. 6. Top: creating a codebook from the encodings of discrete synthetic object views; bottom: object detection and 3D orientation estimation using the nearest neighbor(s) with highest cosine similarity from the codebook

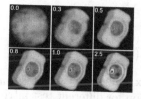

Fig. 7. AAE decoder reconstruction of a test code $z_{test} \in \mathcal{R}^{128}$ scaled by a factor $s \in [0, 2.5]$

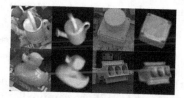

Fig. 8. AAE decoder reconstruction of LineMOD (left) and T-LESS (right) scene crops

are provided in the training datasets of LineMOD and T-LESS. We also train RetinaNet [20] with ResNet50 backbone which is slower but more accurate. Multiple objects are copied in a scene at random orientation, scale and translation. Bounding box annotations are adapted accordingly. As for the AAE, the black background is replaced with Pascal VOC images. During training with 60000 scenes, we apply various color and geometric augmentations.

Projective Distance Estimation. We estimate the full 3D translation t_{pred} from camera to object center, similar to [17]. Therefore, for each synthetic object view in the codebook, we save the diagonal length $l_{syn,i}$ of its 2D bounding box. At test time, we compute the ratio between the detected bounding box diagonal l_{test} and the corresponding codebook diagonal l_{syn,max_cos}, i.e. at similar orientation. The pinhole camera model yields the distance estimate $t_{pred,z}$

$$t_{pred,z} = t_{syn,z} \times \frac{l_{syn,max\_cos}}{l_{test}} \times \frac{f_{test}}{f_{syn}} \tag{5}$$

Table 1. Inference time of RGB pipeline blocks

	4 CPUs	GPU
SSD	-	~17 ms
Encoder	-	~5 ms
Cosine similarity	2.5 ms	1.3 ms
Nearest neighbor	0.3 ms	3.2 ms
Projective distance	0.4 ms	-
		~24 ms

Table 2. Single object pose estimation runtime w/o refinement

Method	fps
Vidal et al. [38]	0.2
Brachmann et al. [4]	2
Kehl et al. [18]	2
BB8 [28]	4
SSD6D [17]	12
OURS	42
Tekin et al. [35]	50

with synthetic rendering distance $t_{syn,z}$ and focal lengths f_{test}, f_{syn} of the test sensor and synthetic views. It follows that

$$\begin{pmatrix} t_{pred,x} \\ t_{pred,y} \end{pmatrix} = \frac{t_{pred,z}}{f_{test}} \begin{pmatrix} (bb_{cent,test,x} - p_{test,x}) - (bb_{cent,syn,x} - p_{syn,x}) \\ (bb_{cent,test,y} - p_{test,y}) - (bb_{cent,syn,y} - p_{syn,y}) \end{pmatrix} \quad (6)$$

with principal points p_{test}, p_{syn} and bounding box centers $bb_{cent,test}, bb_{cent,syn}$. In contrast to [17], we can predict the 3D translation for different test intrinsics.

ICP Refinement. Optionally, the estimate is refined on depth data using a standard ICP approach [41] taking ~200 ms on CPU. Details in supplement (Table 2).

Inference Time. SSD with VGG16 base and 31 classes plus the AAE (Fig. 5) with a codebook size of 92232 × 128 yield the average inference times depicted in Table 1. We conclude that the RGB-based pipeline is real-time capable at ~42 Hz on a Nvidia GTX 1080. This enables augmented reality and robotic applications and leaves room for tracking algorithms. Multiple encoders and corresponding codebooks fit into the GPU memory, making multi-object pose estimation feasible.

4 Evaluation

We evaluate the AAE and the whole 6D detection pipeline on the T-LESS [15] and LineMOD [10] datasets. Example sequences are found in the supplement.

4.1 Test Conditions

Few RGB-based pose estimation approaches (e.g. [17,37]) only rely on 3D model information. Most methods make use of real pose annotated data and often even

Table 3. Ablation study on color augmentations for different test sensors. Object 5, all scenes, T-LESS [15]. Standard deviation of three runs in brackets.

Train RGB	Test RGB	Dyn. light	Add	Contrast	Multiply	Invert	AUC_{vsd}
3D reconstruction	Primesense	✓					0.472 (± 0.013)
		✓	✓				0.611 (±0.030)
		✓	✓	✓			0.825 (±0.015)
		✓	✓	✓	✓		0.876 (±0.019)
		✓	✓	✓	✓	✓	**0.877** (±0.005)
		✓	✓	✓			0.861 (±0.014)
Primesense	Primesense	✓	✓	✓			0.890 (±0.003)
3D reconstruction	Kinect	✓					0.461 (±0.022)
		✓	✓				0.580 (±0.014)
		✓	✓	✓			0.701 (±0.046)
		✓	✓	✓	✓		0.855 (±0.016)
		✓	✓	✓	✓	✓	0.897 (±0.008)
		✓	✓	✓			**0.903** (±0.016)
Kinect	Kinect	✓	✓	✓			0.917 (±0.007)

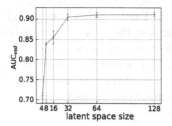

(a) Effect of latent space size, standard deviation in red

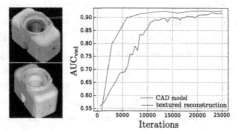

(b) Training on CAD model (bottom) vs. textured 3D reconstruction (top)

Fig. 9. Testing object 5 on all 504 Kinect RGB views of scene 2 in T-LESS

train and test on the same scenes (e.g. at slightly different viewpoints) [1,4,40]. It is common practice to ignore in-plane rotations or only consider object poses that appear in the dataset [28,40] which also limits applicability. Symmetric object views are often individually treated [1,28] or ignored [40]. The SIXD challenge [14] is an attempt to make fair comparisons between 6D localization algorithms by prohibiting the use of test scene pixels. We follow these strict evaluation guidelines, but treat the harder problem of 6D detection where it is unknown which of the considered objects are present in the scene. This is especially difficult in the T-LESS dataset since objects are very similar.

4.2   Metrics

The Visible Surface Discrepancy (err_{vsd}) [16] is an ambiguity-invariant pose error function that is determined by the distance between the estimated and ground truth visible object depth surfaces. As in the SIXD challenge, we report the recall of correct 6D object poses at $err_{vsd} < 0.3$ with tolerance $\tau = 20\,\mathrm{mm}$ and >10% object visibility. Although the Average Distance of Model Points (ADD) [11]) metric can't handle pose ambiguities, we also present it for the LineMOD dataset following the protocol in [11] $(k_m = 0.1)$. For objects with symmetric views (eggbox, glue), [11] computes the average distance to the *closest* model point. In our ablation studies we also report the AUC_{vsd}, which represents the area under the 'err_{vsd} vs. recall' curve: $AUC_{vsd} = \int_0^1 recall(err_{vsd})\,derr_{vsd}$

4.3   Ablation Studies

To assess the AAE alone, in this subsection we only predict the 3D orientation of Object 5 from the T-LESS dataset on Primesense and Kinect RGB scene crops. Table 3 shows the influence of different input augmentations. It can be seen that the effect of different color augmentations is cumulative. For texture-less objects, even the inversion of color channels seems to be beneficial since it prevents overfitting to synthetic color information. Furthermore, training with real object recordings provided in T-LESS with random Pascal VOC background and augmentations yields only slightly better performance than the training with synthetic data. Figure 9a depicts the effect of different latent space sizes on the 3D pose estimation accuracy. Performance starts to saturate at $dim = 64$. In Fig. 9b we demonstrate that our Domain Randomization strategy even allows the generalization from untextured CAD models.

4.4   6D Object Detection

First, we report RGB-only results consisting of 2D detection, 3D orientation estimation and projective distance estimation. Although these results are visually appealing, the distance estimation is refined using a simple cloud-based ICP to compete with state-of-the-art depth-based methods. Table 4 presents our 6D detection evaluation on all scenes of the T-LESS dataset, which contains a lot of pose ambiguities. Our refined results outperform the recent local patch descriptor approach from Kehl et al. [18] even though they only do 6D localization. The state-of-the-art (in terms of average accuracy in the SIXD challenge [14]) from Vidal et al. [38] performs a time consuming search through pose hypotheses (average of 4.9 s/object). Our approach yields comparable accuracy while being much more efficient. The right part of Table 4 shows results with ground truth bounding boxes yielding an upper limit on the pose estimation performance. The appendix shows some failure cases, mostly stemming from missed

Table 4. T-LESS: Object recall for $err_{vsd} < 0.3$ on all Primesense test scenes [a]

Object	6D Detection - SSD		6D Detection - retina		6D localization		w/GT 2D BBs	
	OURS RGB	OURS +Depth (ICP)	OURS RGB	OURS +Depth (ICP)	Kehl [18] RGB-D +ICP	Vidal [38] Depth +ICP	OURS RGB	OURS +Depth (ICP)
1	5.65	15.79	8.87	22.32	-	43	12.33	28.05
2	5.46	22.14	13.22	29.49	-	47	11.23	37.30
3	7.05	32.65	12.47	38.26	-	69	13.11	46.15
4	4.61	18.58	6.56	23.07	-	63	12.71	35.30
5	36.45	69.39	34.80	76.10	-	69	66.70	90.29
6	23.15	61.32	20.24	67.64	-	67	52.30	88.28
7	15.97	68.45	16.21	73.88	-	77	36.58	81.75
8	10.86	43.18	19.74	67.02	-	79	22.05	82.65
9	19.59	67.12	36.21	78.24	-	90	46.49	84.38
10	10.47	58.61	11.55	77.65	-	68	14.31	83.12
11	4.35	32.52	6.31	35.89	-	69	15.01	57.26
12	7.80	40.53	8.15	49.30	-	82	31.34	73.75
13	3.30	29.31	4.91	42.50	-	56	13.60	65.01
14	2.85	26.12	4.61	30.53	-	47	45.32	76.05
15	7.90	52.34	26.71	83.73	-	52	50.00	90.56
16	13.06	61.64	21.73	67.42	-	81	36.09	70.57
17	41.70	77.46	64.84	86.17	-	83	81.11	90.49
18	47.17	81.08	14.30	84.34	-	80	52.62	87.47
19	15.95	45.48	22.46	50.54	-	55	50.75	82.50
20	2.17	7.60	5.27	14.75	-	47	37.75	53.84
21	19.77	38.98	17.93	40.31	-	63	50.89	72.10
22	11.01	25.42	18.63	35.23	-	70	47.60	61.74
23	7.98	30.24	18.63	42.52	-	85	35.18	54.65
24	4.74	49.48	4.23	59.54	-	70	11.24	81.34
25	21.91	50.00	18.76	70.89	-	48	37.12	88.54
26	10.04	57.85	12.62	66.20	-	55	28.33	90.66
27	7.42	47.22	21.13	73.51	-	60	21.86	77.63
28	21.78	44.80	23.07	61.20	-	69	42.58	67.10
29	15.33	53.71	26.65	73.05	-	65	57.01	87.68
30	34.63	86.34	29.58	92.90	-	84	70.42	96.45
Mean	**14.67**	**46.51**	**18.35**	**57.14**	**35.9**	**66.3**	**36.79**	**72.76**

[a] Since the 3D reconstructions of the T-LESS plugs (Objects 19–23) are missing the pins, we instead use their untextured CAD models

detections or strong occlusions. In Table 5 we compare our method against the recently introduced SSD6D [17] and other methods on the LineMOD dataset. SSD6D also trains on synthetic views of 3D models, but their performance seems quite dependent on a sophisticated occlusion-aware, projective ICP refinement step. Our basic ICP sometimes converges to similarly shaped objects in the vicinity. In the RGB domain our method outperforms SSD6D.

Table 5. LineMOD: object recall (ADD [11] metric) using different training and test data, results taken from [35]

Test data	RGB					+Depth (ICP)	
Train data	RGB w/o real pose labels		RGB with real pose labels			+Depth	
Object	SSD6D [17]	OURS	Brachmann [4]	BB8 [28]	Tekin [35]	OURS	SSD6D [17]
Ape	0.00	3.96	-	27.9	21.62	20.55	65
Benchvise	0.18	20.92	-	62.0	81.80	64.25	80
Cam	0.41	30.47	-	40.1	36.57	63.20	78
Can	1.35	35.87	-	48.1	68.80	76.09	86
Cat	0.51	17.90	-	45.2	41.82	72.01	70
Driller	2.58	23.99	-	58.6	63.51	41.58	73
Duck	0.00	4.86	-	32.8	27.23	32.38	66
Eggbox	8.90	81.01	-	40.0	69.58	98.64	100
Glue	0.00	45.49	-	27.0	80.02	96.39	100
Holepuncher	0.30	17.60	-	42.4	42.63	49.88	49
Iron	8.86	32.03	-	67.0	74.97	63.11	78
Lamp	8.2	60.47	-	39.9	71.11	91.69	73
Phone	0.18	33.79	-	35.2	47.74	70.96	79
Mean	2.42	28.65	32.3	43.6	55.95	64.67	79

5   Conclusion

We have proposed a new self-supervised training strategy for Autoencoder architectures that enables robust 3D object orientation estimation on various RGB sensors while training only on synthetic views of a 3D model. By demanding the Autoencoder to revert geometric and color input augmentations, we learn representations that (1) specifically encode 3D object orientations, (2) are invariant to a significant domain gap between synthetic and real RGB images, (3) inherently regard pose ambiguities from symmetric object views. Around this approach, we created a real-time (42 fps), RGB-based pipeline for 6D object detection which is especially suitable when pose-annotated RGB sensor data is not available.

Acknowledgement. We would like to thank Dr. Ingo Kossyk, Dimitri Henkel and Max Denninger for helpful discussions. We also thank the reviewers for their useful comments.

References

1. Balntas, V., Doumanoglou, A., Sahin, C., Sock, J., Kouskouridas, R., Kim, T.K.: Pose guided RGBD feature learning for 3D object pose estimation. In: Proceedings of the IEEE Conference on Computer Vision and Pattern Recognition (CVPR), pp. 3856–3864 (2017)
2. Bousmalis, K., et al.: Using simulation and domain adaptation to improve efficiency of deep robotic grasping. arXiv preprint arXiv:1709.07857 (2017)
3. Bousmalis, K., Silberman, N., Dohan, D., Erhan, D., Krishnan, D.: Unsupervised pixel-level domain adaptation with generative adversarial networks. In: Proceedings of the IEEE Conference on Computer Vision and Pattern Recognition (CVPR), vol. 1, p. 7 (2017)

4. Brachmann, E., Michel, F., Krull, A., Ying Yang, M., Gumhold, S., Rother, C.: Uncertainty-driven 6D pose estimation of objects and scenes from a single RGB image. In: Proceedings of the IEEE Conference on Computer Vision and Pattern Recognition (CVPR), pp. 3364–3372 (2016)

5. Csurka, G.: Domain adaptation for visual applications: a comprehensive survey. arXiv preprint arXiv:1702.05374 (2017)

6. Everingham, M., Van Gool, L., Williams, C.K.I., Winn, J., Zisserman, A.: The PASCAL visual object classes challenge 2012 (VOC 2012) results. http://www.pascal-network.org/challenges/VOC/voc2012/workshop/index.html

7. Glorot, X., Bengio, Y.: Understanding the difficulty of training deep feedforward neural networks. In: Proceedings of the Thirteenth International Conference on Artificial Intelligence and Statistics (AISTATS), pp. 249–256 (2010)

8. Hinterstoisser, S., Benhimane, S., Lepetit, V., Fua, P., Navab, N.: Simultaneous recognition and homography extraction of local patches with a simple linear classifier. In: Proceedings of the British Machine Conference (BMVC), pp. 1–10 (2008)

9. Hinterstoisser, S., Cagniart, C., Ilic, S., Sturm, P., Navab, N., Fua, P., Lepetit, V.: Gradient response maps for real-time detection of textureless objects. IEEE Trans. Pattern Anal. Mach. Intell. 34(5), 876–888 (2012)

10. Hinterstoisser, S., et al.: Multimodal templates for real-time detection of texture-less objects in heavily cluttered scenes. In: Proceedings of the IEEE International Conference on Computer Vision (ICCV), pp. 858–865. IEEE (2011)

11. Hinterstoisser, S., et al.: Model based training, detection and pose estimation of texture-less 3D objects in heavily cluttered scenes. In: Lee, K.M., Matsushita, Y., Rehg, J.M., Hu, Z. (eds.) ACCV 2012. LNCS, vol. 7724, pp. 548–562. Springer, Heidelberg (2013). https://doi.org/10.1007/978-3-642-37331-2_42

12. Hinterstoisser, S., Lepetit, V., Rajkumar, N., Konolige, K.: Going further with point pair features. In: Leibe, B., Matas, J., Sebe, N., Welling, M. (eds.) ECCV 2016. LNCS, vol. 9907, pp. 834–848. Springer, Cham (2016). https://doi.org/10.1007/978-3-319-46487-9_51

13. Hinterstoisser, S., Lepetit, V., Wohlhart, P., Konolige, K.: On pre-trained image features and synthetic images for deep learning. arXiv preprint arXiv:1710.10710 (2017)

14. Hodan, T.: SIXD Challenge (2017). http://cmp.felk.cvut.cz/sixd/challenge_2017/

15. Hodaň, T., Haluza, P., Obdržálek, Š., Matas, J., Lourakis, M., Zabulis, X.: T-LESS: an RGB-D dataset for 6D pose estimation of texture-less objects. In: IEEE Winter Conference on Applications of Computer Vision (WACV) (2017)

16. Hodaň, T., Matas, J., Obdržálek, Š.: On evaluation of 6D object pose estimation. In: Hua, G., Jégou, H. (eds.) ECCV 2016. LNCS, vol. 9915, pp. 606–619. Springer, Cham (2016). https://doi.org/10.1007/978-3-319-49409-8_52

17. Kehl, W., Manhardt, F., Tombari, F., Ilic, S., Navab, N.: SSD-6D: making RGB-based 3D detection and 6D pose estimation great again. In: Proceedings of the IEEE Conference on Computer Vision and Pattern Recognition (CVPR), pp. 1521–1529 (2017)

18. Kehl, W., Milletari, F., Tombari, F., Ilic, S., Navab, N.: Deep learning of local RGB-D patches for 3D object detection and 6D pose estimation. In: Leibe, B., Matas, J., Sebe, N., Welling, M. (eds.) ECCV 2016. LNCS, vol. 9907, pp. 205–220. Springer, Cham (2016). https://doi.org/10.1007/978-3-319-46487-9_13

19. Kingma, D., Ba, J.: Adam: a method for stochastic optimization. arXiv preprint arXiv:1412.6980 (2014)

20. Lin, T.Y., Goyal, P., Girshick, R., He, K., Dollár, P.: Focal loss for dense object detection. arXiv preprint arXiv:1708.02002 (2017)

21. Lin, T.-Y., et al.: Microsoft COCO: common objects in context. In: Fleet, D., Pajdla, T., Schiele, B., Tuytelaars, T. (eds.) ECCV 2014. LNCS, vol. 8693, pp. 740–755. Springer, Cham (2014). https://doi.org/10.1007/978-3-319-10602-1_48

22. Liu, W., et al.: SSD: single shot multibox detector. In: Leibe, B., Matas, J., Sebe, N., Welling, M. (eds.) ECCV 2016. LNCS, vol. 9905, pp. 21–37. Springer, Cham (2016). https://doi.org/10.1007/978-3-319-46448-0_2

23. Mahendran, S., Ali, H., Vidal, R.: 3D pose regression using convolutional neural networks. arXiv preprint arXiv:1708.05628 (2017)

24. Matthey, L., Higgins, I., Hassabis, D., Lerchner, A.: dSprites: disentanglement testing sprites dataset (2017). https://github.com/deepmind/dsprites-dataset/

25. Mitash, C., Bekris, K.E., Boularias, A.: A self-supervised learning system for object detection using physics simulation and multi-view pose estimation. In: Proceedings of the IEEE/RSJ International Conference on Intelligent Robots and Systems (IROS), pp. 545–551. IEEE (2017)

26. Movshovitz-Attias, Y., Kanade, T., Sheikh, Y.: How useful is photo-realistic rendering for visual learning? In: Hua, G., Jégou, H. (eds.) ECCV 2016. LNCS, vol. 9915, pp. 202–217. Springer, Cham (2016). https://doi.org/10.1007/978-3-319-49409-8_18

27. Phong, B.T.: Illumination for computer generated pictures. Commun. ACM **18**(6), 311–317 (1975)

28. Rad, M., Lepetit, V.: BB8: a scalable, accurate, robust to partial occlusion method for predicting the 3D poses of challenging objects without using depth. In: Proceedings of the IEEE International Conference on Computer Vision (ICCV) (2017)

29. Ren, S., He, K., Girshick, R., Sun, J.: Faster R-CNN: towards real-time object detection with region proposal networks. In: Proceedings of the IEEE Transactions on Pattern Analysis and Machine Intelligence (TPAMI), pp. 91–99 (2015)

30. Richter, S.R., Vineet, V., Roth, S., Koltun, V.: Playing for data: ground truth from computer games. In: Leibe, B., Matas, J., Sebe, N., Welling, M. (eds.) ECCV 2016. LNCS, vol. 9906, pp. 102–118. Springer, Cham (2016). https://doi.org/10.1007/978-3-319-46475-6_7

31. Rumelhart, D.E., Hinton, G.E., Williams, R.J.: Learning internal representations by error propagation. Technical report, California University, Institute for Cognitive Science, San Diego, La Jolla (1985)

32. Saxena, A., Driemeyer, J., Ng, A.Y.: Learning 3D object orientation from images. In: Proceedings of the IEEE International Conference on Robotics and Automation (ICRA), pp. 794–800. IEEE (2009)

33. Shrivastava, A., Pfister, T., Tuzel, O., Susskind, J., Wang, W., Webb, R.: Learning from simulated and unsupervised images through adversarial training. In: Proceedings of the IEEE Conference on Computer Vision and Pattern Recognition (CVPR), pp. 2242–2251. IEEE (2017)

34. Su, H., Qi, C.R., Li, Y., Guibas, L.J.: Render for CNN: viewpoint estimation in images using CNNs trained with rendered 3D model views. In: Proceedings of the IEEE International Conference on Computer Vision (ICCV), pp. 2686–2694 (2015)

35. Tekin, B., Sinha, S.N., Fua, P.: Real-time seamless single shot 6D object pose prediction. arXiv preprint arXiv:1711.08848 (2017)

36. Tobin, J., Fong, R., Ray, A., Schneider, J., Zaremba, W., Abbeel, P.: Domain randomization for transferring deep neural networks from simulation to the real world. In: Proceedings of the IEEE/RSJ International Conference on Intelligent Robots and Systems (IROS), pp. 23–30. IEEE (2017)

37. Ulrich, M., Wiedemann, C., Steger, C.: CAD-based recognition of 3D objects in monocular images. In: Proceedings of the IEEE International Conference on Robotics and Automation (ICRA), vol. 9, pp. 1191–1198 (2009)
38. Vidal, J., Lin, C.Y., Martí, R.: 6D pose estimation using an improved method based on point pair features. arXiv preprint arXiv:1802.08516 (2018)
39. Vincent, P., Larochelle, H., Lajoie, I., Bengio, Y., Manzagol, P.A.: Stacked denoising autoencoders: learning useful representations in a deep network with a local denoising criterion. J. Mach. Learn. Res. **11**(Dec), 3371–3408 (2010)
40. Wohlhart, P., Lepetit, V.: Learning descriptors for object recognition and 3D pose estimation. In: Proceedings of the IEEE Conference on Computer Vision and Pattern Recognition (CVPR), pp. 3109–3118 (2015)
41. Zhang, Z.: Iterative point matching for registration of free-form curves and surfaces. Int. J. Comput. Vis. **13**(2), 119–152 (1994)

Author Index

Printed in the United States
By Bookmasters